The New York Botanical Garden Illustrated Encyclopedia of Horticulture

Thomas H. Everett

Volume 10
Ste-Zy

Garland Publishing, Inc.
New York & London

15 14 13 12 11 10 9 8 7 6 5 4 3 2 1

Library of Congress Cataloging in Publication Data

Everett, Thomas H
   The New York Botanical Garden illustrated encyclopedia of horticulture.

     1. Horticulture—Dictionaries. 2. Gardening—Dictionaries. 3. Plants, Ornamental—Dictionaries. 4. Plants, Cultivated—Dictionaries. I. New York (City). Botanical Garden. II. Title.
SB317.58.E94   635.9'03'21   80-65941
ISBN 0-8240-7240-5

PHOTO CREDITS

Black and White

Arnold Arboretum, Jamaica Plain, Massachusetts: *Zenobia pulverulenta*, p. 3587. Desert Botanical Garden: *Stetsonia coryne*, p. 3235; *Thelocactus bicolor tricolor*, p. 3324. Ferry-Morse Seed Company: Seedling tomatoes transplanted to a flat, p. 3361; Plant tomatoes outdoors after the weather is agreeably warm; take care not to damage the roots unduly, p. 3362; Watering with a slow stream from the end of a hose positioned on a piece of canvas, p. 3533. Manning, Selvage & Lee, Inc.: Dandelions develop long, deep taproots, p. 3541. Netherlands Flower Institute: *Veltheimia viridifolia* (flowers), p. 3476. The New York Botanical Garden: Potting rooted cuttings of *Thuja*, p. 3337; *Tilia euchlora*, p. 3347; *Tipularia discolor*, p. 3355; *Tithonia rotundifolia*, p. 3357; *Tithonia diversifolia*, p. 3357; *Tofieldia racemosa*, p. 3358; *Trientalis borealis*, p. 3399; A colony of *Trillium grandiflorum*, p. 3402; *Trillium viride*, p. 3403; Tulips planted informally with peonies and other plants in narrow borders flanking the Long Walk, Van Courtland Manor, Croton-on-Hudson, New York, p. 3422; A lavish informal planting of tulips with a foreground of forget-me-nots, p. 3423; A Lily Flowered tulip variety (left foreground) with irises of *Phlox divaricata* (right foreground), p. 3425; *Ulmus americana* (leaves), p. 3443; *Vaccinium angustifolium*, p. 3456; *Vaccinium macrocarpon*, p. 3456; *Valeriana officinalis*, p. 3459; *Vallisneria spiralis* in an aquarium, p. 3461; *Vanilla planifolia*, p. 3467; An undetermined species of *Verbascum* in bloom, p. 3479; Tall verbascums in bloom provide strong vertical lines in the landscape, p. 3481; *Verbena canadensis* (flowers), p. 3483; *Vitex agnus-castus* (flowers), p. 3514; *Vriesia carinata*, p. 3518; In their full glory at The New York Botanical Garden are water-lilies, arrowheads, lotuses, and other aquatics, p. 3528; *Watsonia aletroides*, p. 3536; *Woodwardia areolata*, p. 3563; *Zephyranthes grandiflora*, p. 3588. Premium Peat Moss: Installed irrigation systems (part a), p. 3532. Other photographs by Thomas H. Everett.

Color

Malak: Tulips forced into early bloom outdoors. The New York Botanical Garden: *Stenoglottis longifolia, Tellima grandiflora, Tofieldia glutinosa, Trientalis borealis, Trillium viride, Xerophyllum tenax.* Other photographs by Thomas H. Everett.

Garland Publishing acknowledges Kenneth H. Holcombe, Jr. for photographic enlargement production.

Published by Garland Publishing, Inc.
136 Madison Avenue, New York, New York 10016

Printed in the United States of America

This work is dedicated to the honored memory of the distinguished horticulturists and botanists who most profoundly influenced my professional career: Allan Falconer of Cheadle Royal Gardens, Cheshire, England; William Jackson Bean, William Dallimore, and John Coutts of the Royal Botanic Gardens, Kew, England; and Dr. Elmer D. Merrill and Dr. Henry A. Gleason of The New York Botanical Garden.

Foreword

According to Webster, an encyclopedia is a book or set of books giving information on all or many branches of knowledge generally in articles alphabetically arranged. To the horticulturist or grower of plants, such a work is indispensable and one to be kept close at hand for frequent reference.

The appearance of *The New York Botanical Garden Illustrated Encyclopedia of Horticulture* by Thomas H. Everett is therefore welcomed as an important addition to the library of horticultural literature. Since horticulture is a living, growing subject, these volumes contain an immense amount of information not heretofore readily available. In addition to detailed descriptions of many thousands of plants given under their generic names and brief description of the characteristics of the more important plant families, together with lists of their genera known to be in cultivation, this Encyclopedia is replete with well-founded advice on how to use plants effectively in gardens and, where appropriate, indoors. Thoroughly practical directions and suggestions for growing plants are given in considerable detail and in easily understood language. Recommendations about what to do in the garden for all months of the year and in different geographical regions will be helpful to beginners and will serve as reminders to others.

The useful category of special subject entries (as distinct from the taxonomic presentations) consists of a wide variety of topics. It is safe to predict that one of the most popular will be Rock and Alpine Gardens. In this entry the author deals helpfully and adequately with a phase of horticulture that appeals to a growing group of devotees, and in doing so presents a distinctly fresh point of view. Many other examples could be cited.

The author's many years as a horticulturist and teacher well qualify him for the task of preparing this Encyclopedia. Because he has, over a period of more than a dozen years, written the entire text (submitting certain critical sections to specialists for review and suggestions) instead of farming out sections to a score or more specialists to write, the result is remarkably homogeneous and cohesive. The Encyclopedia is fully cross referenced so that one may locate a plant by either its scientific or common name.

If, as has been said, an encyclopedia should be all things to all people, then the present volumes richly deserve that accolade. Among the many who call it "friend" will be not only horticulturists ("gardeners," as our author likes to refer to them), but growers, breeders, writers, lecturers, arborists, ecologists, and professional botanists who are frequently called upon to answer questions to which only such a work can provide answers. It seems safe to predict that it will be many years before lovers and growers of plants will have at their command another reference work as authoritative and comprehensive as T. H. Everett's Encyclopedia.

John M. Fogg, Jr.
Director Emeritus, Arboretum of the Barnes Foundation
Emeritus Professor of Botany, University of Pennsylvania

Preface

The primary objective of *The New York Botanical Garden Illustrated Encyclopedia of Horticulture* is a comprehensive description and evaluation of horticulture as it is known and practiced in the United States and Canada by amateurs and by professionals, including those responsible for botanical gardens, public parks, and industrial landscapes. Although large-scale commercial methods of cultivating plants are not stressed, much of the content of the Encyclopedia is as basic to such operations as it is to other horticultural enterprises. Similarly, although landscape design is not treated on a professional level, landscape architects will find in the Encyclopedia a great deal of importance and interest to them. Emphasis throughout is placed on the appropriate employment of plants both outdoors and indoors, and particular attention is given to explaining in considerable detail the how- and when-to-do-it aspects of plant growing.

It may be useful to assess the meanings of two words I have used. Horticulture is simply gardening. It derives from the Latin *hortus,* garden, and *cultura,* culture, and alludes to the intensive cultivation in gardens and nurseries of flowers, fruits, vegetables, shrubs, trees, and other plants. The term is not applicable to the extensive field practices that characterize agriculture and forestry. Amateur, as employed by me, retains its classic meaning of a lover from the Latin *amator*; it refers to those who garden for pleasure rather than for financial gain or professional status. It carries no implication of lack of knowledge or skills and is not to be equated with novice, tyro, or dabbler. In truth, amateurs provide the solid basis upon which American horticulture rests; without them the importance of professionals would diminish. Numbered in millions, amateur gardeners are devotees of the most widespread avocation in the United States. This avocation is serviced by a great complex of nurseries, garden centers, and other suppliers; by landscape architects and landscape contractors; and by garden writers, garden lecturers, Cooperative Extension Agents, librarians, and others who dispense horticultural information. Numerous horticultural societies, garden clubs, and botanical gardens inspire and promote interest in America's greatest hobby and stand ready to help its enthusiasts.

Horticulture as a vocation presents a wide range of opportunities which appeal equally to women and men. It is a field in which excellent prospects still exist for capable entrepreneurs. Opportunities at professional levels occur too in nurseries and greenhouses, in the management of landscaped grounds of many types, and in teaching horticulture.

Some people confuse horticulture with botany. They are not the same. The distinction becomes more apparent if the word gardening is substituted for horticulture. Botany is the science that encompasses all systematized factual knowledge about plants, both wild and cultivated. It is only one of the several disciplines upon which horticulture is based. To become a capable gardener or a knowledgeable plantsman or plantswoman (I like these designations for gardeners who have a wide, intimate, and discerning knowledge of plants in addition to skill in growing them) it is not necessary to study botany formally, although such study is likely to add greatly to one's pleasure. In the practice of gardening, many botanical truths are learned from experience. I have known highly competent gardeners without formal training in botany and able and indeed distinguished botanists possessed of minimal horticultural knowledge and skills.

Horticulture is primarily an art and a craft, based upon science, and at some levels perhaps justly regarded as a science in its own right. As an art it calls for an appreciation of beauty and form as expressed in three-dimensional spatial relationships and an ability to translate aesthetic concepts into reality. The chief materials used to create gardens are living plants, most of which change in size and form with the passing of time and often show differences in color and texture and in other ways from season to season. Thus it is important that designers of gardens have a wide familiarity with the sorts of plants that lend themselves to their purposes and with plants' adaptability to the regions and to the sites where it is proposed to plant them.

As a craft, horticulture involves special skills often derived from ancient practices passed from generation to generation by word of mouth and apprenticeship-like contacts. As a technology it relies on this backlog of empirical knowledge supplemented by that acquired by scientific experiment and investigation, the results of which often serve to explain rather than supplant old beliefs and practices, but sometimes point the way to more expeditious methods of attaining similar results. And from time to time new techniques are developed that add dimensions to horticultural practice; among such of fairly recent years that come to mind are the manipulation of blooming season by artificial daylength, the propagation of orchids and some other plants by meristem tissue culture, and the development of soilless growing mixes as substitutes for soil.

One of the most significant developments in American horticulture in recent decades is the tremendous increase in the number of different kinds of plants that are cultivated by many more people than formerly. This is particularly true of indoor plants or houseplants, the sorts grown in homes, offices, and other interiors, but is by no means confined to that group. The relative affluence of our society and the freedom and frequency of travel both at home and abroad has contributed to this expansion, a phenomenon that will surely continue as avid collectors of the unusual bring into cultivation new plants from the wild and promote wider interest in sorts presently rare. Our garden flora is also constantly and beneficially expanded as a result of the work of both amateur and professional plant breeders.

It is impracticable in even the most comprehensive encyclopedia to describe or even list all plants that somewhere within a territory as large as the United States and Canada are grown in gardens. In this Encyclopedia the majority of genera known to be in cultivation are described, and descriptions and often other pertinent information about a complete or substantial number of their species and lesser categories are given. Sorts likely to be found only in collections of botanical gardens or in those of specialists may be omitted.

The vexing matter of plant nomenclature inevitably presents itself when an encyclopedia of horticulture is contemplated. Conflicts arise chiefly between the very understandable desire of gardeners and others who deal with cultivated plants to retain long-familiar names and the need to reflect up-to-date botanical interpretations. These points of view are basically irreconcilable and so accommodations must be reached.

As has been well demonstrated in the past, it is unrealistic to attempt to standardize the horticultural usage of plant names by decree or edict. To do so would negate scientific progress. But it is just as impracticable to expect gardeners, nurserymen, arborists, seedsmen, dealers in bulbs, and other amateur and professional horticulturists to keep current with the interpretations and recommendations of plant taxonomists; particularly as these sometimes fail to gain the acceptance even of other botanists and it is not unusual for scientists of equal stature and competence to prefer different names for the same plant.

In practice time is the great leveler. Newly proposed plant names accepted in botanical literature are likely to filter gradually into horticultural usage and eventually gain currency value, but this sometimes takes several years. The complete up-to-dateness and niceties of botanical naming are less likely to bedevil horticulturists than uncertainties concerned with correct plant identification. This is of prime importance. Whether a tree is labeled *Pseudotsuga douglasii*, *P. taxifolia*, or *P. menziesii* is of less concern than that the specimen so identified is indeed a Douglas-fir and not some other conifer.

After reflection I decided that the most sensible course to follow in *The New York Botanical Garden Illustrated Encyclopedia of Horticulture* was to accept almost in its entirety the nomenclature adopted in *Hortus Third* published in 1976. By doing so, much of the confusion that would result from two major comprehensive horticultural works of the late twentieth century using different names for the same plant is avoided, and it is hoped that for a period of years a degree of stability will be attained. Always those deeply concerned with critical groups of plants can adopt the recommendations of the latest monographers. Exceptions to the parallelism in nomenclature in this Encyclopedia and *Hortus Third* are to be found in the CACTACEAE for which, with certain reservations but for practical purposes, as explained in the Encyclopedia entry Cactuses, the nomenclature of Curt Backeburg's *Die Cactaceae*, published in 1958–62, is followed; and the ferns, where I mostly accepted the guidance of Dr. John T. Mickel of The New York Botanical Garden. The common or colloquial names employed are those deemed to have general acceptance. Cross references and synonomy are freely provided.

The convention of indicating typographically whether or not plants of status lesser than species represent entities that propagate and persist in the wild or are sorts that persist only in cultivation is not followed. Instead, as explained in the Encyclopedia entry Plant Names, the word variety is employed for all entities below specific rank and if in Latin form the name is written in italic, if in English or other modern language, in Roman type, with initial capital letter, and enclosed in single quotation marks.

Thomas H. Everett
Senior Horticulture Specialist
The New York Botanical Garden

Acknowledgments

I am indebted to many people for help and support generously given over the period of more than twelve years it has taken to bring this Encyclopedia to fruition. Chief credit belongs to four ladies. They are Lillian M. Weber and Nancy Callaghan, who besides accepting responsibility for the formidable task of filing and retrieving information, typing manuscript, proofreading, and the management of a vast collection of photographs, provided much wise council; Elizabeth C. Hall, librarian extraordinary, whose superb knowledge of horticultural and botanical literature was freely at my disposal; and Ellen, my wife, who displayed a deep understanding of the demands on time called for by an undertaking of this magnitude, and with rare patience accepted inevitable inconvenience. I am also obliged to my sister, Hette Everett, for the valuable help she freely gave on many occasions.

Of the botanists I repeatedly called upon for opinions and advice and from whom I sought elucidation of many details of their science abstruse to me, the most heavily burdened have been my friends and colleagues at The New York Botanical Garden, Dr. Rupert C. Barneby, Dr. Arthur Cronquist, and Dr. John T. Mickel. Other botanists and horticulturists with whom I held discussions or corresponded about matters pertinent to my text include Dr. Theodore M. Barkley, Dr. Lyman Benson, Dr. Ben Blackburn, Professor Harold Davidson, Dr. Otto Degener, Harold Epstein, Dr. John M. Fogg, Jr., Dr. Alwyn H. Gentry, Dr. Alfred B. Graf, Brian Halliwell, Dr. David R. Hunt, Dr. John P. Jessop, Dr. Tetsuo Koyama, Dr. Bassett Maguire, Dr. Roy A. Mecklenberg, Everitt L. Miller, Dr. Harold N. Moldenke, Dr. Dan H. Nicolson, Dr. Pascal P. Pirone, Dr. Ghillean Prance, Don Richardson, Stanley J. Smith, Ralph L. Snodsmith, Marco Polo Stufano, Dr. Bernard Verdcourt, Dr. Edgar T. Wherry, Dr. Trevor Whiffin, Dr. Richard P. Wunderlin, Dr. John J. Wurdack, Yuji Yoshimura, and Rudolf Ziesenhenne.

Without either exception or stint these conferees and correspondents shared with me their knowledge, thoughts, and judgments. Much of the bounty so gleaned is reflected in the text of the Encyclopedia, but none other than I am responsible for interpretations and opinions that appear there. To all who have helped, my special thanks are due and are gratefully proferred.

I acknowledge with much pleasure the excellent cooperation I have received from the Garland Publishing Company and most particularly from its President, Gavin Borden. To Ruth Adams, Geoffrey Braine, Nancy Isaac, Carol Miller, and Melinda Wirkus, I say thank you for working so understandingly and effectively with me and for shepherding my raw typescript through the necessary stages.

How to Use This Encyclopedia

A vast amount of information about how to use, propagate, and care for plants both indoors and outdoors is contained in the thousands of entries that compose *The New York Botanical Garden Illustrated Encyclopedia of Horticulture*. Some understanding of the Encyclopedia's organization is necessary in order to find what you want to know.

Arrangement of the Entries

Genera

The entries are arranged in alphabetical order. Most numerous are those that deal with taxonomic groups of plants. Here belong approximately 3,500 items entered under the genus name, such as ABIES, DIEFFENBACHIA, and JUGLANS. If instead of referring to these names you consult their common name equivalents of FIR, DUMB CANE, and WALNUT, you will find cross references to the genus names.

Bigeneric Hybrids & Chimeras

Hybrids between genera that have names equivalent to genus names—most of these belonging in the orchid family—are accorded separate entries. The same is true for the few chimeras or graft hybrids with names of similar status. Because bigeneric hybrids frequently have characteristics similar to those of their parents and require similar care, the entries for them are often briefer than the regular genus entries.

Families

Plant families are described under their botanical names, with their common name equivalents also given. Each description is followed by a list of the genera accorded separate entries in this Encyclopedia.

Vegetables, Fruits, Herbs, & Ornamentals

Vegetables and fruits that are commonly cultivated, such as broccoli, cabbage, potato, tomato, apple, peach, and raspberry; most culinary herbs, including basil, chives, parsley, sage, and tarragon; and a few popular ornamentals, such as azaleas, carnations, pansies, and poinsettias, are treated under their familiar names, with cross references to their genera. Discussions of a few herbs and some lesser known vegetables and fruits are given under their Latin scientific names with cross references to the common names.

Other Entries

The remaining entries in the Encyclopedia are cross references, definitions, and more substantial discussions of many subjects of interest to gardeners and others concerned with plants. For example, a calendar of gardening activity, by geographical area, is given under the names of the months and a glossary of frequently applied species names (technically, specific epithets) is provided in the entry Plant Names. A list of these general topics, which may provide additional information about a particular plant, is provided at the beginning of each volume of the Encyclopedia.

Cross References & Definitions

The cross references are of two chief types: those that give specific information, which may be all you wish to know at the moment:
Boojam Tree is *Idria columnaris*.
Cobra plant is *Darlingtonia californica*.
and those that refer to entries where fuller explanations are to be found:
Adhatoda. See Justicia.
Clubmoss. See Lycopodium and Selaginella.

Additional information about entries of the former type can, of course, be found by looking up the genus to which the plant belongs—*Idria* in the case of the boojam tree and *Darlingtonia* for the cobra plant.

ORGANIZATION OF THE GENUS ENTRIES

Pronunciation

Each genus name is followed by its pronunciation in parentheses. The stressed syllable is indicated by the diacritical mark ´ if the vowel sound is short as in man, pet, pink, hot, and up; or by ` if the vowel sound is long as in mane, pete, pine, home, and fluke.

Genus Common Names
Family Common Names
General Characteristics

Following the pronunciation, there may be one or more common names applicable to the genus as a whole or to certain of its kinds. Other names may be introduced later with the descriptions of the species or kinds. Early in the entry you will find the common and botanical names of the plant family to which the genus belongs, the number of species the genus contains, its natural geographical distribution, and the derivation of its name. A description that stresses the general characteristics of the genus follows, and this may be supplemented by historical data, uses of some or all of its members, and other pertinent information.

Identification of Plants

Descriptions of species, hybrids, and varieties appear next. The identification of unrecognized plants is a fairly common objective of gardeners; accordingly, in this Encyclopedia various species have been grouped within entries in ways that make their identification easier. The groupings may bring into proximity sorts that can be adapted for similar landscape uses or that require the same cultural care, or they may emphasize geographical origins of species or such categories as evergreen and deciduous or tall and low members of the same genus. Where the description of a species occurs, its name is designated in ***bold italic***. Under this plan, the description of a particular species can be found by referring to the group to which it belongs, scanning the entry for the species name in bold italic, or referring to the opening sentences of paragraphs which have been designed to serve as lead-ins to descriptive groupings.

Gardening & Landscape Uses
Cultivation
Pests & Diseases

At the end of genus entries, subentries giving information on garden and landscape uses, cultivation, and pests or diseases or both are included, or else reference is made to other genera or groupings for which these are similar.

General Subject Listings

The lists below organize some of the Encyclopedia entries into topics which may be of particular interest to the reader. They are also an aid in finding information other than Latin or common names of plants.

PLANT ANATOMY AND TERMS USED IN PLANT DESCRIPTIONS

All-America Selections
Alternate
Annual Rings
Anther
Apex
Ascending
Awl-Shaped
Axil, Axillary
Berry
Bloom
Bracts
Bud
Bulb
Bulbils
Bulblet
Bur
Burl
Calyx
Cambium Layer
Capsule
Carpel
Catkin
Centrals
Ciliate
Climber
Corm
Cormel
Cotyledon
Crown
Deciduous
Disk or Disc
Double Flowers
Drupe
Florets
Flower
Follicle
Frond
Fruit
Glaucous
Gymnosperms
Head
Hips
Hose-in-Hose

Inflorescence
Lanceolate
Leader
Leaf
Leggy
Linear
Lobe
Midrib
Mycelium
Node
Nut and Nutlet
Oblanceolate
Oblong
Obovate
Offset
Ovate
Palmate
Panicle
Pedate
Peltate
Perianth
Petal
Pinnate
Pip
Pistil
Pit
Pod
Pollen
Pompon
Pseudobulb
Radials
Ray Floret
Rhizome
Runners
Samara
Scion or Cion
Seeds
Sepal
Set
Shoot
Spore
Sprigs
Spur
Stamen
Stigma
Stipule

Stolon
Stool
Style
Subshrub
Taproot
Tepal
Terminal
Whorl

GARDENING TERMS AND INFORMATION

Acid and Alkaline Soils
Adobe
Aeration of the Soil
Air and Air Pollution
Air Drainage
Air Layering
Alpine Greenhouse or Alpine House
Amateur Gardener
April, Gardening Reminders For
Aquarium
Arbor
Arboretum
Arch
Asexual or Vegetative Propagation
Atmosphere
August, Gardening Reminders For
Balled and Burlapped
Banks and Steep Slopes
Bare-Root
Bark Ringing
Baskets, Hanging
Bed
Bedding and Bedding Plants
Bell Jar
Bench, Greenhouse
Blanching
Bleeding
Bog
Bolting
Border
Bottom Heat
Break, Breaking
Broadcast
Budding
Bulbs or Bulb Plants

Gardening Terms and Information (Continued)

Bush Fruits
Cape Bulbs
Capillary Benches
Capillary Mats
Carpet Bedding
Catch Crop
Chlorine in Water
Clay Soil
Clean Cultivation
Climates and Microclimates
Climbing
Cold Frame
Cooperative Extension Agent
Cooperative Extension Service
Cordon
County Agricultural Agent
Cover Crops
Crocking
Crocks
Cultivation
Cultivators
Cuttings, Propagation By
Damping Down
December, Gardening Reminders For
Deeply Prepared
Dibber or Dibble
Digging
Dipping
Dirt Gardener
Disbudding
Drainage and Draining
Drill
Drip
Drying Off
Dusts and Dusting
Dutch Bulbs
Dutch Hoe
Dwarfing Stocks
Earthing Up
East Malling Stocks
Ecology and Gardens
Edgings, Nonliving
Endangered Species and Natural Plant
  Distribution
Espalier
Fall Planting
Fallow
February, Gardening Reminders For
Fences
Flag
Flats
Floriculture
Flower Beds and Borders
Flower Shows
Flowering
Fluorescent Light Gardening
Foliar Feeding
Forcing
Forcing Cut Branches
Forks, Garden
Foundation Planting
Friable Soil
Frosts and Freezes
Fruit Growing
Full Sun
Fumigation
Furrow

Garden
Garden Centers
Garden Clubs
Garden Frames
Garden Line
Garden Planning
Gates
Gazebo
Girdling or Ring Barking
Girdling Roots
Glass
Glasshouse
Grading
Graft Hybrids
Grafting
Grafting Wax
Green Manuring
Greens
Ground
Groundcovers
Grow Hard, To
Grow On, To
Growth Retardants
Habit or Habit of Growth
Hanging Baskets, Pots, and Planters
Hardening Off
Hardpan
Head Back or Head In
Heaving of the Soil
Heavy Soil
Hedges
Heel
Heeling In
Herbaceous Border
Hill
Hilling Up
Hoes and Hoeing
Horticulture
Host or Host Plant
Hotbeds
Hotcaps
Hothouse
Humidity
Hydroponics or Nutriculture
Inarching and Approach Grafting
Inbreeding
Indoor Light Gardening
Intercropping or Companion Cropping
Irrigation
January, Gardening Reminders For
July, Gardening Reminders For
June, Gardening Reminders For
Labels
Landscape Architecture
Landscape Gardener
Lath House
Lawn Maintenance
Lawns, Their Making and Renovation
Layering
Lifting
Light
Light Soil
Loam
March, Gardening Reminders For
Marl
Marsh
May, Gardening Reminders For
Meadow
Measures

Meristem Tissue Culture
Microclimates
Mist and Misting
Mist Propagation
Mulching and Mulches
Naturalized
Novelties
November, Gardening Reminders For
Nursery
October, Gardening Reminders For
Orchard
Organic Gardening
Organic Matter
Over-Potted
Own-Root
Pan
Pans
Paths, Garden
Patio and Terrace Plantings
Pea Sticks or Pea Brush
Pinching
Pit Frame and Pit Greenhouse
Planning Gardens and Home Grounds
Plant Breeding
Planters
Planting and Transplanting
Pleach
Plug
Plunge
Pollard
Pot Off
Pot On
Pots and Pans
Potting and Repotting
Potting Soils and Potting Mixes
Potting Stick
Pricking Off and Pricking Out
Propagation
Protection for Plants
Pruning
Puddling
Raft
Rakes and Raking
Reserve Border
Resting
Retarding
Reversion
Ribbon Beds
Roof and Terrace Gardening
Rootstock
Rotary Tillers
Rotation of Crops
Sash
Seeds, Propagation By
September, Gardening Reminders For
Shading
Set
Shears
Silt
Slip
Soil Erosion
Soils and Their Management
Soil Sterilization
Soil Tests and Analyses
Spading
Sprays and Spraying
Staking and Tying
Stand
Starter Solution

xviii

Gardening Terms and Information (Continued)

State Agricultural Experimental Stations
Stock or Understock
Straightedge
Strawberry Jars
Strike
Stunt
Succession Cropping
Sundials
Syringing
Thinning or Thinning Out
Tillage
Tilth
Tools
Top-Dressing
Topiary Work
Training Plants
Tree Surgery
Tree Wrapping
Trenching
Trowels
Tubs
Watering
Weeds and Their Control
Window Boxes

FERTILIZERS AND OTHER SUBSTANCES RELATED TO GARDENING

Algicide
Aluminum Sulfate
Ammonium Nitrate
Ammonium Sulfate
Antibiotics
Ashes
Auxins
Basic Slag
Blood Meal
Bonemeal
Bordeaux Mixture
Calcium Carbonate
Calcium Chloride
Calcium Metaphosphate
Calcium Nitrate
Calcium Sulfate
Carbon Disulfide
Chalk
Charcoal
Coal Cinders
Cork Bark
Complete Fertilizer
Compost and Composting
Cottonseed Meal
Creosote
DDT
Dormant Sprays
Dried Blood
Fermate or Ferbam
Fertilizers
Fishmeal
Formaldehyde
Fungicides
Gibberellic Acid
Green Manuring
Growth Retardants
Guano
Herbicides or Weed-Killers
Hoof and Horn Meal

Hormones
Humus
Insecticide
John Innes Composts
Lime and Liming
Liquid Fertilizer
Liquid Manure
Manures
Mulching and Mulches
Muriate of Potash
Nitrate of Ammonia
Nitrate of Lime
Nitrate of Potash
Nitrate of Soda
Nitrogen
Orchid Peat
Organic Matter
Osmunda Fiber or Osmundine
Oyster Shells
Peat
Peat Moss
Permanganate of Potash
Potassium
Potassium Chloride
Potassium-Magnesium Sulfate
Potassium Nitrate
Potassium Permanganate
Potassium Sulfate
Pyrethrum
Rock Phosphate
Rotenone
Salt Hay or Salt Marsh Hay
Sand
Sawdust
Sodium Chloride
Sprays and Spraying
Sulfate
Superphosphate
Trace Elements
Urea
Urea-Form Fertilizers
Vermiculite
Wood Ashes

TECHNICAL TERMS

Acre
Alternate Host
Annuals
Antidessicant or Antitranspirant
Biennals
Binomial
Botany
Chromosome
Climate
Clone
Composite
Conservation
Cross or Crossbred
Cross Fertilization
Cross Pollination
Cultivar
Decumbent
Dicotyledon
Division
Dormant
Endemic
Environment
Family

Fasciation
Fertility
Fertilization
Flocculate
Floriculture
Genus
Germinate
Habitat
Half-Hardy
Half-Ripe
Hardy Annual
Hardy Perennial
Heredity
Hybrid
Indigenous
Juvenile Forms
Juvenility
Legume
Monocotyledon
Monoecious
Mutant or Sport
Mycorrhiza or Mycorhiza
Nitrification
Perennials
pH
Plant Families
Photoperiodism
Photosynthesis
Pollination
Pubescent
Saprophyte
Self-Fertile
Self-Sterile
Species
Standard
Sterile
Strain
Terrestrial
Tetraploid
Transpiration
Variety

TYPES OF GARDENS AND GARDENING

Alpine Garden
Artificial Light Gardening
Backyard Gardens
Biodynamic Gardening
Bog Gardens
Botanic Gardens and Arboretums
Bottle Garden
City Gardening
Colonial Gardens
Conservatory
Container Gardening
Cutting Garden
Desert Gardens
Dish Gardens
Flower Garden
Fluorescent Light Gardening
Formal and Semiformal Gardens
Greenhouses and Conservatories
Heath or Heather Garden
Herb Gardens
Hydroponics or Nutriculture
Indoor Lighting Gardening
Japanese Gardens
Kitchen Garden
Knot Gardens

Types of Gardens and Gardening (Continued)

Miniature Gardens
Native Plant Gardens
Naturalistic Gardens
Nutriculture
Organic Gardening
Rock and Alpine Gardens
Roof and Terrace Gardening
Salads or Salad Plants
Seaside Gardens
Shady Gardens
Sink Gardening
Terrariums
Vegetable Gardens
Water and Waterside Gardens
Wild Gardens

PESTS, DISEASES, AND OTHER TROUBLES

Ants
Aphids
Armyworms
Bagworms
Bees
Beetles
Billbugs
Biological Control of Pests
Birds
Blight
Blindness
Blotch
Borers
Budworms and Bud Moths
Bugs
Butterflies
Canker
Cankerworms or Inchworms
Casebearers
Caterpillars
Cats
Centipede, Garden
Chinch Bugs
Chipmunks
Club Root
Corn Earworm
Crickets
Cutworms
Damping Off
Deer
Die Back
Diseases of Plants
Downy Mildew
Earthworms
Earwigs
Edema
Fairy Rings
Fire Blight
Flies
Fungi or Funguses
Galls
Gas Injury

Gophers
Grasshoppers
Grubs
Gummosis
Hedgehog
Hornworms
Inchworms
Insects
Iron Chelates
Iron Deficiency
Lace Bugs
Lantana Bug
Lantern-Flies
Larva
Leaf Blight
Leaf Blister
Leaf Blotch
Leaf Curl
Leaf Cutters
Leaf Hoppers
Leaf Miners
Leaf Mold
Leaf Rollers
Leaf Scorch
Leaf Skeletonizer
Leaf Spot Disease
Leaf Tiers
Lightening Injury
Maggots
Mantis or Mantid
Mealybugs
Mice
Midges
Milky Disease
Millipedes
Mites
Mold
Moles
Mosaic Diseases
Moths
Muskrats
Needle Cast
Nematodes or Nemas
Parasite
Pests of Plants
Plant Hoppers
Plant Lice
Praying Mantis
Psyllids
Rabbits
Red Spider Mite
Rootworms
Rots
Rust
Sawflies
Scab Diseases
Scale Insects
Scorch or Sunscorch
Scurf
Slugs and Snails
Smut and White Smut Diseases
Sowbugs or Pillbugs

Spanworms
Spittlebugs
Springtails
Squirrels
Stunt
Suckers
Sun Scald
Thrips
Tree Hoppers
Virus
Walking-Stick Insects
Wasps
Webworms
Weevils
Wilts
Witches' Brooms
Woodchucks

GROUPINGS OF PLANTS

Accent Plants
Aquatics
Aromatic Plants
Bedding and Bedding Plants
Berried Trees and Shrubs
Bible Plants
Broad-Leaved and Narrow-Leaved Trees
   and Shrubs
Bulbs or Bulb Plants
Bush Fruits
Carnivorous or Insectivorous Plants
Dried Flowers, Foliage, and Fruits
Edging Plants
Epiphyte or Air Plant
Evergreens
Everlastings
Fern Allies
Filmy Ferns
Florists' Flowers
Foliage Plants
Fragrant Plants and Flowers
Gift Plants
Graft Hybrids
Grasses, Ornamental
Hard-Wooded Plants
Houseplants or Indoor Plants
Japanese Dwarfed Trees
Medicinal or Drug Plants
Night-Blooming Plants
Ornamental-Fruited Plants
Pitcher Plants
Poisonous Plants
Shrubs
State Flowers
State Trees
Stone Fruits
Stone or Pebble Plants
Stove Plants
Succulents
Tender Plants
Trees
Windowed Plants

The New York
Botanical Garden
Illustrated Encyclopedia
of Horticulture

STEEPLEBUSH is *Spiraea tomentosa*.

STEER'S HEAD is *Dicentra uniflora*.

STEIRONEMA. See Lysimachia.

STELIS (Stél-is). Some 270 species of the orchid family ORCHIDACEAE compose tropical American and West Indian *Stelis*. The name was used by Theophrastus for an unidentified parasitic plant.

Tufted or creeping, and without pseudobulbs, stelises have one-leaved stems or branches, and tiny flowers in long terminal racemes. Each bloom has spreading, more or less united sepals, considerably shorter, broad petals, and, at the base of the column, a stalkless lip similar to the petals or narrower and sometimes three-lobed.

Tropical American *S. aprica*, 6 to 10 inches tall, has crowded erect stems and 2- to 4-inch-long, linear-oblong leaves. As long or longer than the leaves, the slender, arching racemes are crowded with 2-inch-wide flowers with a three-lobed lip. Native to Costa Rica, *S. tonduziana* (syn.

Stelis tonduziana

S. mirabilis), 6 to 10 inches tall, has crowded stems with somewhat arched, oblong-strap-shaped leaves about 4 inches long. The slender racemes are of many dull, light purple blooms a little over 2 inch across. They have a slightly three-lobed lip. An-

Stelis aemula

other Costa Rican, *S. aemula* forms crowded tufts of linear-oblong leaves 2 inches long or a little longer. Its tiny pale yellow flowers are in erect, narrow racemes 3 to 6 inches long.

Garden Uses and Cultivation. These orchids are interesting for inclusion in collections. The majority succeed under cool conditions and respond to treatment appropriate for *Pleurothallis*.

STELLARIA (Stel-lària) — Easter Bells or Stitchwort. The most familiar *Stellaria*, to many gardeners, is an unwanted annual one, the common chickweed (*S. media*). Of the remaining more than 100 species of annuals and herbaceous perennials, a few are of some slight worth to gardeners; most are not. Belonging in the pink family CARYOPHYLLACEAE, which flaunts carnations, *Lychnis*, and *Saponaria* among its members, *Stellaria* makes no comparable display, yet its better members have some decorative merit. The genus takes its name from the Latin *stella*, a star, in reference to the appearance of the flowers.

Stellarias have slender stems, usually swollen at the nodes, and opposite leaves. White and small, the flowers are in repeatedly forking clusters. Usually they have five, occasionally only four each sepals and petals, or sometimes the petals are absent. When present they are usually deeply-notched or -cleft. Generally there are ten stamens, sometimes fewer. There are three styles. The fruits are small capsules. The group is widely distributed throughout temperate regions, and at high elevations in the tropics.

Easter bells or greater stitchwort (*S. holostea*), a native of Europe and Asia, is

Stellaria holostea

naturalized in North America. A perennial with a creeping rootstock, in the wild it favors thickets and hedge bottoms. More or less prostrate at the base, then erect, and up to 2 feet long, the slender stems, brittle at the nodes, have rigid, lanceolate leaves 1 inch to 4 inches long. The flowers, from 5 to slightly over 1 inch in di-

ameter, have petals cleft halfway to their bases and twice as long as the sepals.

The lesser stitchwort (*S. graminea*), also perennial, resembles the last, but has flowers under ½ inch across in more often branched clusters. Their petals are scarcely, if at all, longer than the sepals. This kind inhabits grasslands, heathlands, and open woods throughout Europe and parts of Asia; it is naturalized in North America. Variety *S. g. aurea*, with pale golden-yellow foliage, is cultivated.

Native American species include *S. longipes*, which occurs in moist soils from Nova Scotia to Alaska, New York, Minnesota, Arizona, and California, as well as in Europe and Asia, and *S. pubera*, indigenous to woodlands from New Jersey to Indiana, Florida, and Alabama. Both are perennials. With slender rhizomes, *S. longipes* has angled stems 6 inches to 1 foot long and linear-lanceolate to linear leaves ½ to a little over 1 inch long. The flower clusters are of few blooms ½ inch wide, with the petals longer than the sepals. The erect stems of *S. pubera*, 6 inches to 1½ feet long, have elliptic to ovate or oblanceolate leaves 1 inch to 4 inches long. In leafy, loose clusters, the flowers have petals shorter than the ¼-inch-long sepals. This species blooms early and then produces vigorous, chiefly non-flowering shoots.

Garden Uses and Cultivation. Except for *S. graminea aurea*, which is used in flower beds and sometimes rock gardens chiefly for its colored foliage, these plants will, in the main, be relegated to unimportant spots in naturalistic landscapes. They grow satisfactorily in ordinary soil in part-day shade or sun and are increased by seed and by division.

STEMMADENIA (Stemma-dènia). The twenty species of *Stemmadenia*, of the dogbane family APOCYNACEAE, are shrubs or small, or more rarely medium-sized, trees indigenous from southern Mexico to northern South America and closely related to *Tabernaemontana*, but with larger flowers with calyx lobes not all of the same size. The name comes from the Greek *stemma*, a crown, and *aden*, a gland.

Stemmadenias have opposite, stalked, mostly ovate-oblong, rarely spatula-shaped or lanceolate leaves. The flower stalks have three inconspicuous bracts, the calyxes five unequal-sized lobes. Yellow or yellowish-white, the five-lobed corollas are funnel-shaped or have slender, cylindrical tubes and spreading lobes (petals). There are five stamens that do not protrude and a slender style. The fruits are leathery, podlike follicles that are arranged in pairs.

A shrub 3 to 10 feet tall, of Central America, *S. galeottiana* (syn. *S. bella*) is a handsome ornamental. Its short-stalked, broad-elliptic, hairless leaves are 4 or 5 inches long and up to 2 inches wide. The fragrant flowers are funnel-shaped, about

2 inches long, and have 1-inch-long petals. They are yellow, or white with bright yellow throats. Their petals spread. The orange fruits are egg-shaped and about 1 inch long. From the last, *S. glabra,* of Central America, differs in having obovate leaves 5 to 8 inches long and about 3 inches broad, yellow flowers, and fruits about 2 inches long.

Garden and Landscape Uses and Cultivation. In the tropics and warm subtropics, the species described succeed in ordinary soils and are useful ornamentals. They are propagated by seed.

STENANDRIUM (Sten-ándrium). Native to the warmer parts of the Americas, the thirty species of *Stenandrium,* of the acanthus family ACANTHACEAE, are little known to gardeners. The name, derived from the Greek *stenos,* narrow, and *aner,* man, alludes to its slender stamens. Only one species appears to be cultivated, and that one rarely.

Stenandriums are evergreen, mostly stemless, herbaceous perennials with undivided, toothless, basal leaves and small, asymmetrical flowers in spikes. The calyxes are of five sepals, the corollas are tubular and five-lobed. There are four stamens in two pairs and one slender style. The fruits are capsules.

A matting native of Peru that, in bloom, is only about 3 inches high, *S. lindenii* has

Stenandrium lindenii

smooth, elliptic-obovate, prominently yellow-veined, dark green leaves purplish on their undersides. Its ¾-inch-long yellow flowers are in the axils of the small, toothed bracts of erect spikes. The plant sometimes grown as *S. igneum* is *Xantheranthemum igneum.*

Garden Uses and Cultivation. A choice and charming carpeter for ground beds in tropical conservatories and for planting around pools and in rock gardens in the moist tropics, *S. lindenii* is also attractive when grown several plants together in pans (shallow pots) in humid greenhouses and terrariums where a minimum temperature of 60°F is maintained. It grows without special care in porous soil, well enriched

with leaf mold or peat moss, always kept fairly moist, but not constantly saturated. Repotting or replanting may be done almost any time, preferably in spring. Well-rooted specimens benefit from occasional applications of dilute liquid fertilizer. High humidity is favorable. Shade from strong sun is necessary. Propagation is by division, by cuttings, and by seed.

STENANTHIUM (Sten-ánthium)—Feather Fleece. About five species are recognized as constituting the genus *Stenanthium,* of the lily family LILIACEAE. The name makes reference to the slender corolla segments and is derived from the Greek *stenos,* narrow, and *anthos,* a flower. This genus differs from the closely related *Zygadenus* in not having glands at the bases of its sepals and petals.

Stenanthiums have bulblike rootstocks and erect stems that branch, if at all, only in the terminal flowering portions. The leaves are chiefly basal or from the lower parts of the stems, and are narrowly-linear. The flowers, whitish, greenish, or purple, often nodding, and in slender branchless racemes, few-branched loose panicles, or pyramidal panicles, are narrowly- or very broadly-bell-shaped. They have six petals (or, more correctly, tepals), six stamens, and one style. The fruits are ovoid-oblong capsules.

The feather fleece (*S. gramineum*), which blooms in late summer or fall, inhabits moist woods and meadows from Pennsylvania to Indiana, Missouri, Florida, and Arkansas. It has stems 3 to 5 feet tall. The leaves are 1 foot to 1¼ feet long and up to ¾ inch broad. The starlike, fragrant flowers are whitish or greenish and of variable size even on the same plant, the largest ¾ inch or slightly more in diameter. They are many together in loose, usually branched clusters, 8 inches to 1½ feet long, with the central stalk continued as a long wandlike raceme and the branches spreading or drooping. The seed capsules are deflexed and about ½ inch long. Variety *S. g. robustum* (syn. *S. robustum*) has erect seed capsules. It grows in swamps from Pennsylvania to Ohio, South Carolina, and Tennessee.

Markedly different in appearance (and by some botanists placed in the separate genus *Stenanthella*) is *S. occidentale,* native from British Columbia to Alberta and California and favoring moist soils in mountain forests. From an ovoid bulb under 1 inch long it develops a solitary, erect stem 1 foot to 2 feet tall and linear to narrow-elliptic leaves up to 1 foot long. The flower clusters, racemes or lax panicles, 4 to 8 inches long, are composed of rather widely-spaced, nodding, purplish-green, faintly fragrant blooms about ¾ inch long that have their petals (more precisely, tepals) joined in their lower parts to form a tube and recurved above so that the flowers re-

Stenanthium gramineum robustum

semble those of hyacinths. This kind blooms in July and August.

Garden Uses. Although not commonly cultivated, stenanthiums are worthwhile for adding variety and interest to gardens, particularly because they bloom well after the spring and early summer abundance of bulbous flowers. They are adapted for native plant gardens in regions of their spontaneous occurrence and for informal and semiformal plantings in moist soil that contains a fair amount of organic matter. The western American species responds well to a soil made neutral or slightly alkaline with lime, the easterner needs moist, acid soil. Both appreciate shade from the strong summer sun. It is not unusual for these plants to flower irregularly, rather than every year.

Cultivation. Provided the soil is to their liking, these plants are not difficult. Once established, it is better that they be left undisturbed as long as they are doing well. A mulch of rich compost, leaf mold, or other suitable organic material maintained about them is helpful. New plants are obtained from fresh seed sown in sandy, peaty soil kept moderately moist.

STENOCACTUS. See Echinofossulocactus.

STENOCARPUS (Steno-cárpus) — Firewheel Tree. New Caledonia is home to most of the twenty-two species that compose *Stenocarpus,* of the protea family PROTEACEAE. Only four occur elsewhere, in Australia, with two extending into New Guinea and the Aru Islands. The name, from the Greek *stenos*, narrow, and *karpos*, fruit, refers to the usually slender follicles.

These are evergreen trees with alternate, leathery, deeply-lobed or lobeless leaves. On young specimens the leaves may be two- or three-times-pinnately-divided into very narrow segments. The flowers, in umbels or short racemes, are on stalks from the upper leaf axils, or at the ends of short shoots. They have slightly asymmetrical, tubular perianths with tubes slit along their lower sides. The four nearly globular perianth lobes (petals) are recurved. There are four stamens and one slender style. The fruits are leathery follicles (podlike fruits).

The firewheel tree (*S. sinuatus*) is from

Stenocarpus sinuatus

35 feet to, sometimes in the wild, 100 feet tall. Native to Queensland, it has stalked, undivided, oblong-lanceolate leaves 5 to 9 inches long, or deeply-pinnately-lobed ones up to 1 foot long, with one to four lobes on each side of the midrib. The very showy, brilliant scarlet blooms, orange-yellow at their tips and bases, spread from the centers of the umbels like the spokes of a wheel. There are twelve to twenty in each umbel, and the umbels are in clusters or racemes of two or more at or near the ends of the branches. The fruits are boat-shaped. The wood of this species is esteemed for cabinetmaking and indoor finishing.

Very distinct from the firewheel tree and less showy, Australian *S. salignus* is a tree usually 20 to 25 feet tall, but sometimes three times this. It has willowy, lanceolate-elliptic to broad-elliptic, lobeless, toothless leaves 2 to 5 inches long, and white or greenish-white blooms, 1 inch in diameter, many together in stalked clusters. The fruits are 2 to 4 inches long. Very similar *S. cunninghamii*, of Australia, has hairless instead of pubescent ovaries. In gardens *S. salignus* is often misnamed *S. cunninghamii*.

Garden and Landscape Uses and Cultivation. Hardy only in lands free or practically free of frost, and preferring Mediterranean-type climates, such as that of California, stenocarpuses, especially the firewheel tree, are admirable ornamentals. In Florida, the firewheel tree grows well,

but usually does not bloom. Stenocarpuses are useful as lawn specimens and for displaying in groups alone or with other trees or shrubs. They are satisfied with ordinary garden soil and need sun. Propagation is by seed or by cuttings.

STENOCEREUS (Steno-cèreus). Two species of the cactus family CACTACEAE, segregated by those who split genera finely as *Stenocereus*, are included by conservative botanists in *Lemaireocereus*. They are natives of Mexico. The name, derived from the Greek *stenos*, narrow, and that of the related genus *Cereus*, alludes to the form of the plants.

Stenocereuses have erect, jointed stems, with notched ribs, that are abundantly furnished with clusters of strong, needle-like spines. The short-funnel-shaped flowers, which open at night, have perianth tubes and ovaries that, like the fruits, are furnished with scales and bristles.

From 3 to 10 feet tall and freely-branched from the base, less often above, *S. stellatus* (syn. *Lemaireocereus stellatus*) has bluish-

Stenocereus stellatus

green stems 2½ to 3½ inches wide with eight to ten ribs. The spine clusters are of eight to twelve whitish radials, about ½ inch long, and one to three, or sometimes more, flattened centrals, ¾ to 1 inch long and of the same color. The flowers, 2 inches long, are white with reddish sepals. From the last, *S. treleasii* (syn. *Lemaireocereus treleasii*), which is up to 20 feet tall, differs in its stems rarely branching and in having about twenty ribs with shorter, yellowish spines in clusters of seven to nine.

Garden and Landscape Uses and Cultivation. These are fast-growing, attractive cactuses for outdoor landscaping in warm desert and semidesert regions and for inclusion in greenhouse collections. They prosper in well-drained, reasonably fertile soil in full sun and are readily increased by cuttings and by seed. For more information see Cactuses.

STENOCHLAENA (Steno-chlaèna). About five species of large, vigorous ferns, somewhat questionably allotted to the blechnum family BLECHNACEAE, and by some authorities included in the polypody family POLYPODIACEAE, constitute *Stenochlaena*. The genus inhabits Africa and the Pacific region. The name is from the Greek *stenos*, narrow, and *chlaina*, a cloak, and alludes to the absence of coverings (indusia) over the clusters of spore cases.

Stenochlaenas have creeping or climbing rhizomes of indefinite length, and pinnate, leathery fronds (leaves) rather like those of *Blechnum*. There are both fertile (spore-producing) and sterile fronds. As young plants these ferns usually begin life in the ground, but after their stems have ascended trees the plants lose their connection with the soil and become epiphytes (tree-perchers).

Native to warm parts of Asia, Polynesia, and Australia, *S. palustris* has sprawling or high-climbing rhizomes, and lustrous, pinnate fronds 1 foot to 4½ feet long by up to 1 foot wide or wider. The lanceolate leaflets of the sterile fronds are up to 8 inches long by ¾ inch to 1½ inches wide, thick-margined, and toothed. The leaflets of spore-producing fronds are linear, 5 inches to 1 foot long, and not over about ⅛ inch wide.

South African *S. tenuifolia* has wide-

Stenochlaena tenuifolia

spreading or climbing rhizomes. Its sterile leaves, 3 to 5 feet long or longer by 1 foot to 1½ feet wide, are composed of strap-shaped leaflets 6 to 9 inches long by ¾ inch to 1½ inches wide, with pointed apexes and thickened, finely-toothed margins. The fertile fronds are twice-pinnate and so finely divided that they suggest ostrich feathers. Their primary divisions are long-stalked, the ultimate segments widely spaced and extremely slender (almost threadlike).

Garden and Landscape Uses and Cultivation. Suited only for shaded locations in the humid tropics and subtropics and for greenhouses, the species described are usually grown as epiphytes (a plant that perches on trees, but takes no nourishment from them) by allowing them to grow up the trunk of trees, or by attaching them to tree fern trunks or other agreeable surfaces. They may also be planted in pans (shallow pots) that are well drained and contain a loose mixture, such as suits epiphytic orchids and bromeliads, consisting largely of osmunda fiber, shredded fir bark, or similar material. The rooting medium must be kept moist, but not soggy. Although greenhouse winter night temperatures of 60°F with daytime increases of five to fifteen degrees are often recommended, these plants do very well in temperatures five to ten degrees lower. A humid atmosphere and shade from sun are needed. Increase is by division and by spores. Additional information is given under Ferns.

STENODRABA (Steno-dràba). Except for its larger, linear seed pods, *Stenodraba*, of the Andes of South America, scarcely differs from much better known *Draba*. It consists of six species of low herbaceous plants of the mustard family CRUCIFERAE. The name comes from the Greek *stenos*, narrow, and *Draba*, the name of the related genus, and refers to the slender seed pods.

Inhabiting moist places at high altitudes in Chile, *S. colchaguensis* is a 1- to 3-inch-tall, tufted, deep-rooted perennial with fleshy, elliptic to obovate leaves ¾ inch long and usually toothed at their apexes. Its white, sometimes faintly blue-spotted flowers, in compact racemes, are succeeded by ⅓-inch-long seed pods.

Garden Uses and Cultivation. Little experience has been had with growing this rare plant. It is to be expected that conditions suitable for high altitude alpines would be appropriate. Its cultivation is unlikely to be attempted by other than alpine garden enthusiasts. Propagation is by seed and by cuttings taken very carefully from the parent plant and inserted in sand, fine pumice, or fine perlite in a cold frame or cool greenhouse.

STENOGLOTTIS (Steno-glóttis). South African and warmer territories to the north are the homes of *Stenoglottis*, a genus of four species of the orchid family ORCHIDACEAE. Their name, from the Greek *stenos*, narrow, and *glotta*, a tongue, alludes to the lip of the flower.

Somewhat resembling *Orchis*, these plants are terrestrials. They grow in the ground instead of perched on trees. They have fleshy roots, loose basal rosettes or tufts of foliage, and erect, loose or dense, somewhat one-sided racemes of pink to rosy-red blooms that open in succession over a long period. The flowers have separate sepals and somewhat narrower petals. The three- to five-lobed lip is contin-

uous with the base of the short, thick column.

Decidedly attractive *S. longifolia* has up to six oblong-lanceolate, wavy-edged leaves up to about 7 inches long and sometimes lightly flecked with purple. The many-

Stenoglottis longifolia

Stenoglottis longifolia (flowers)

flowered racemes attain heights of 1 foot to 2 feet. Their flowers, about ½ inch across, are pink to rosy-red or rosy-lavender with purplish spots on the five- to seven-lobed lip. This is a native of South Africa. Much like the last, but less robust and its flowers with a three-lobed lip, is *S. fimbriata*, of South Africa. The leaves of this are sometimes, but not always conspicuously spotted with purple. The slender, purple stem may carry as many as seventy-five small, rosy-mauve blooms.

Garden Uses and Cultivation. Interesting plants for the orchid fancier, these may be grown in well-drained pots or pans (shallow pots) in a mixture of osmunda fiber, turfy loam, chopped sphagnum moss, and coarse sand, with a little crushed charcoal added. They succeed in cool and intermediate-temperature greenhouses, and

Stenoglottis fimbriata

may be grown outdoors in essentially frost-free, Mediterranean-type climates. Throughout their periods of active growth plenty of water is needed, but after they die down and enter their resting season, it should be withheld or greatly reduced, but not to the extent that the soil dries completely. Partial shade is necessary. During the growing season applications of dilute liquid fertilizer are of benefit. Repotting must be done before the rooting medium rots or becomes stale and impedes the free passage of air and water. For more information see Orchids.

STENOLOBIUM STANS is *Tecoma stans*.

STENOMESSON (Steno-mèsson). Native to the Andes, the genus *Stenomesson*, of the amaryllis family AMARYLLIDACEAE, comprises about twenty species. Its name comes from the Greek *stenos*, narrow, and *messon*, middle, in allusion to the corolla tube usually being narrowed near its center.

Stenomessons are bulb plants with all basal, linear to lanceolate leaves and solid or hollow, flowering stalks topped with an umbel of one, few, or several long-tubular, funnel-shaped blooms. Each flower has six short perianth lobes (petals), and six

Stenomesson incarnatum (flowers)

stamens with their bases united to form a cup or corona, often toothed along its margins. There is one style. The fruits are capsules containing small black seeds.

Sorts cultivated include these: *S. incarnatum,* of Ecuador and Peru, has slightly glaucous leaves about 1½ feet long by ⅞ inch wide. Longer than the leaves, the flowering stalk carries an umbel of usually six more or less nodding blooms, 4 to 4½ inches long by about 1 inch across the bell-shaped mouth. They are orange-red with a broad black-green stripe down the outside of each perianth lobe and a pale stripe bordered with green on the inside. *S. luteum,* of Peru, has linear leaves, 4 to 8 inches long, and usually two-flowered flowering stalks about as long. The yellow blooms point upward and are about 2 inches long. The staminal cup is not toothed. *S. variegatum,* of Ecuador, has leaves up to 1 inch broad and a flowering stalk about 2 feet long, with an umbel of two to four light red to bright red blooms. The curved perianth tube is up to 3 inches long. The perianth segments have a green keel and are about 1 inch long. The staminal cup is toothed.

Garden Uses and Cultivation. Stenomessons are interesting for greenhouses and for planting outdoors in climates where little or no frost is experienced. They respond to fertile, well-drained soil and sunny locations. Indoors a winter night temperature of 45 to 55°F with an increase of five to fifteen degrees by day is satisfactory. When in active growth water freely and fertilize well-rooted specimens at two- or three-week intervals, but during the season of dormancy omit fertilizer and give water only if there appears to be danger of the bulbs shriveling. Repot when necessary just before new growth begins and then, too, take off offset bulbs needed for propagation. Increase can also be achieved by seed and by bulb cuttings.

STENOSPERMATION (Steno-spermàtion). South American evergreen climbers, of the Andes, that attach themselves to trees and other supports by aerial roots, stenospermations belong in the arum family ARACEAE. There are about twenty-five species. The name is derived from the Greek *stenos,* narrow, and *spermation,* a little seed, and alludes to the seeds.

Stenospermations have oblong-elliptic to lanceolate leaves disposed on two ranks and with many nearly parallel side veins stemming from the mid-vein. The bases of their stalks sheathe the stems. As with most members of the arum family, what appears to be the flower is a collection of tiny blooms affixed to a stalk and called a spadix, from the base of which a bract called a spathe grows. Using the calla-lily as a typical example of the family, the central yellow column is the spadix, the white, petal-like trumpet part the spathe. In *Sten-*

ospermation the spathes are boat-shaped and white. The spadixes, also white, are composed of all bisexual flowers. The fruits are berries.

Native to Colombia and Ecuador, *S. popayanense* is a choice foliage plant that increases in size rather slowly. It has thickish, lanceolate, leathery leaves up to about 1 foot long by approximately one-quarter as broad. They are carried more or less horizontally instead of with their blades nearly vertical as are those of many of their arum family relatives. Their long stalks sheathe the stems. The spadix is about 2¼ inches long, the spathe approximately 4 inches long. Widely distributed as a native in tropical South America, *S. spruceanum* has medium- to long-stalked, thickish, pointed-elliptic leaves with blades up to 11 inches long by 2½ inches wide. On drooping or nodding stalks, the inflorescence (floral structure) has a spathe up to 3 inches long and a considerably longer spadix. The fruits are reddish-orange.

Stenospermation spruceanum

Garden and Landscape Uses and Cultivation. Only in the humid tropics and warm subtropics can these plants be grown successfully outdoors. Their most common employment is as greenhouse and indoor decorative pot plants. They also succeed in ground beds in greenhouses. For satisfactory growth they need fertile soil containing an abundance of organic matter kept evenly moist, but not constantly saturated. Reasonably humid to decidedly moist atmospheric conditions, with shade from bright sun, suit. A minimum winter night temperature of about 60°F is required with daytime temperatures generally ten to fifteen degrees higher. To keep specimens that have filled their pots with roots in good condition give them occasional applications of dilute liquid fertilizer. Propagation is easily accomplished by air layering and by cuttings made from terminal portions of the stem or from stem sections each containing a single node or leaf. Plants can also be raised from seed.

STENOTAPHRUM (Steno-táphrum) — St. Augustine Grass. Only one of the seven species of *Stenotaphrum* is important horticulturally. It is the St. Augustine grass, which is much used for lawns in the south and other warm parts. Native from South Carolina to Texas and tropical America, it belongs in the grass family GRAMINEAE. Its name is from the Greek *stenos,* narrow, and *taphros,* a trench, and was applied in allusion to depressions in the stalks of the racemes of flowers.

The genus includes both annuals and perennials and inhabits the tropics and subtropics, chiefly in coastal regions. Its species have erect or creeping, leafy stems and folded, linear to lanceolate leaf blades. The flower spikelets are partly embedded in depressions in the stalks and alternate in two rows along one side of the stalks to form slender spikes. The spikelets, which drop whole at maturity, are nearly or quite stalkless. They are two-flowered; the lower flower is male or barren.

St. Augustine grass (*S. secundatum*), a coarse, creeping species up to 1 foot tall, has flattened stems and hairless leaf blades up to 6 inches long by ⅓ inch broad. The racemes of flowers have one to three green to whitish spikelets about ⅕ inch long. In *S. s. variegatum* the leaves are pleasingly marked with longitudinal stripes of creamy-white.

Stenotaphrum secundatum variegatum

Garden Uses and Cultivation. In addition to the common employment of St. Augustine grass for lawns in warm regions, its variegated variety is used as an ornamental in greenhouses and elsewhere where such a trailer can be used to good advantage. A good basket plant, it is useful to mix with other plants in urns, planters, and similar containers. For such purposes it is propagated by cuttings. It is grateful for fertile, well-drained soil always kept moist. Indoors a winter minimum temperature of 40 to 50°F is satisfactory. The great Brazilian landscape architect Roberto Burle Marx has created stunning effects with lawns made of adjacent areas, with long, free-style, sinuous margins, of plain green-leaved St. Augustine grass and its variegated-leaved variety.

STEPHANANDRA (Stephán-andra). Native to eastern Asia, *Stephanandra* consists of four species of graceful, deciduous shrubs of the rose family ROSACEAE. The name, which alludes to the grouping of the stamens, comes from the Greek *stephanos*, a crown, and *aner*, man, and hence male.

Stephanandras are close allies of *Neillia* and *Spiraea*. From the former they differ in having blooms of little display value in smaller, terminal clusters or panicles, in their styles being lateral instead of terminal, and in the fruits containing one or rarely two, instead of usually five, glossy seeds. Conspicuous, persistent, leafy stipules (appendages at the bases of the leafstalks) distinguish *Stephanandra* from *Spiraea*, which does not have these. Stephanandras have slender, rounded or angled branches. Their alternate leaves, toothed and generally lobed, are in two ranks. Bisexual, the slender-stalked, white or whitish blooms are in terminal clusters or panicles. They have cup-shaped calyx tubes, five calyx lobes (sepals), five petals, and ten to twenty stamens. The fruits are small podlike follicles.

The hardiest species survives throughout much of New England, although there the ends of its branches are likely to suffer some winter killing. It is *S. incisa* (syn. *S. flexuosa*), a common native of Japan and

Stephanandra incisa

Stephanandra incisa (flowers)

also a native of Korea. At its maximum 7 to 8 feet tall, but often lower, it is a bush as broad or broader than it is tall. It suckers freely from its base and has numerous arching, wiry, zigzag, brown branches. The leaves are long-pointed, short-stalked, triangular-ovate to heart-shaped, and deeply- and sharply-lobed, their margins double-toothed. They are ¾ inch to 2 inches long, or on strong shoots larger, and hairy on the veins beneath. About ⅕ inch in diameter, the greenish-white flowers come in early summer in loose panicles at the ends of short shoots of the previous year's growth. The panicles are up to 2¼ inches long. The blooms have ten stamens. In fall the foliage turns purplish. Rarely exceeding 3 feet in height and often lower, *S. i. crispa* is a useful variety. It has somewhat smaller leaves than the species. Its branches root readily where they are in contact with the soil.

Not quite as elegant, **S. tanakae** is a

Stephanandra tanakae (foliage)

much rarer native of Japan than *S. incisa*. It is a stronger grower, but is slightly less hardy. Up to 6 feet tall, it has many slender branches. Its coarser, short-stalked leaves are 2 to 5 inches long and two-thirds to fully as broad. They are long-pointed and less deeply-lobed than the leaves of *S. incisa*, although the lowest pair of lobes are often quite large. The leaf margins are toothed. The veins on the undersides of the leaves are usually more or less hairy. About ⅕ inch across, the white flowers are in panicles 2 to 4 inches long. They come in summer and have fifteen to twenty stamens. In fall the foliage changes to yellow and orange.

Garden and Landscape Uses. Although inferior to many popular hardy shrubs in floral display, and with fruits of no ornamental merit, stephanandras, especially *S. incisa* and its variety, appeal to gardeners because of the general attractiveness of their forms and the somewhat fernlike effect of their foliage. They are useful for fronts of shrubberies and other locations where foliage of good quality that complements

rather than competes aggressively with that of other plants is needed. These shrubs shear well and are satisfactory for hedges. In addition, *S. i. crispa* is very useful for covering and holding banks and steep slopes. Ordinary garden soil, not too dry, and open, sunny locations are preferred by stephanandras.

Cultivation. Little attention is needed by these easily satisfied shrubs. If the ends of the branches are killed over winter, the dead parts should be cut off in spring as soon as new growth is evident on the live portions. Occasionally a little judicious thinning of older, crowded branches may be desirable. This should be done as soon as the flowers fade. Old, neglected specimens can be rejuvenated by cutting them to about ground level in late winter or spring and then fertilizing. Hedges of stephanandras may be sheared one or more times a season. Increase is very easy by division, summer cuttings 2 to 3 inches long set in a greenhouse or cold frame propagating bed, preferably with slight bottom heat, or under mist, and by seed.

STEPHANIA (Stephà-nia). The genus *Stephania*, of the moonseed family MENISPERMACEAE, is little known horticulturally. The derivation of its name is uncertain. It may honor Professor Frederick Stephan, of Moscow, who died in 1817, or it may come from the Greek *stephanos*, a crown or garland.

Stephanias, most sorts vines, are native to warm parts of Africa, Asia, and Australia. They have attractive foliage and clusters of small unisexual flowers from the leaf axils. The leaves are usually peltate, which means that their stalks are attached to the blades at some distance from their margins and that there is no opening from the leaf margin to the top of the leafstalk. Male flowers have six to ten sepals, three to five fleshy petals, and six anthers. Female flowers have three to five sepals, petals as in male flowers, and a three- to six-parted style. The fruits are drupes (fruits plumlike in structure).

Kinds occasionally cultivated in greenhouses and in warm climates outdoors are **S. glabra** (syn. *S. rotunda*), a vigorous

Stephania glabra (tuber)

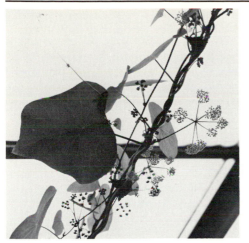

Stephania glabra in bloom

climber of tropical Asia, with a very large tuberous rootstock, glabrous, heart-shaped leaves, and loose clusters of small greenish flowers of little decorative significance; *S. glandulifera,* of Burma, which is similar; and *S. hernandifolia,* of India, the leaves of which are ovate to somewhat triangular.

Garden and Landscape Uses. In warm, dry, frost-free climates, these are interesting vines for clothing screens, porches, fences, and other supports. They grow well in greenhouses under conditions that suit many cactuses and succulents.

Stephania glandulifera (tuber)

Stephania glandulifera (foliage)

Cultivation. Stephanias thrive in sunny locations in any ordinary soil. In greenhouses they grow well where the minimum winter night temperature is 50 to 60°F and the day temperature a few degrees higher. They need very well-drained soil, full sun, and airy, not excessively humid conditions. From the time new growth begins in spring until stems and foliage die down in fall, they need moderate watering, enough to keep the soil evenly moist, but not saturated; during their period of winter dormancy water should be withheld entirely. Propagation is by seed sown in porous soil in a temperature of about 60°F.

STEPHANOCEREUS (Stephano-cèreus). Only one species of *Stephanocereus* is known and that, by conservative botanists, is included in *Cephalocereus.* Belonging to the cactus family CACTACEAE, and native to Brazil, this genus has a name derived from the Greek *stephanos,* a crown, and the name of the related genus *Cereus.* It alludes to the pseudocephalum.

The usually solitary, glaucous-green, branched or branchless stems of *S. leucostele* (syn. *Cephalocereus leucostele*), about 10 feet tall by 4 inches thick, have twelve to eighteen ribs. Their areoles produce many fine hairs, clusters of up to twenty whitish, needle-like radial spines, from very short to about ½ inch long, and one or two whitish to yellow centrals up to 1½ inches long. A beardlike crown (pseudocephalum) of white wool and long golden-yellow bristles tops the stem. As new growth is made, the stem grows through the mass of bristles and hairs, which remains as a persistent ring around the stem. In this, *Stephanocereus* resembles *Arrojadoa.* From the pseudocephalum, 3-inch-long, funnel-shaped, white flowers, which open at night, develop. Their perianth tubes and ovaries, like the fruits, are without scales or hairs.

Garden and Landscape Uses and Cultivation. These are as for *Cephalocereus.* For additional information see the Encyclopedia entry Cactuses.

STEPHANOMERIA (Stephano-mèria). A dozen or more species of annuals and herbaceous perennials of western North America constitute *Stephanomeria,* of the daisy family COMPOSITAE. The name, perhaps referring to the arrangement of the branches, is from the Greek *stephane,* a wreath, and *meros,* a division.

Stephanomerias have erect, branched or branchless stems and alternate, sometimes pinnately-lobed leaves that are linear to lanceolate or oblong. Usually the upper ones are much smaller than those below. Generally in panicles, the pink flower heads, of small to medium size, are composed of all strap-shaped florets and are remindful of the flower heads of chicory

(*Cichorium*). They expand only early in the day and close about noon or soon thereafter. The fruits are seedlike achenes.

Occasionally cultivated, *S. cichoriacea* is a perennial with a woody rootstock. Up to 5 feet tall, it has stems with or without wandlike branches, and pointed, oblong to oblong-lanceolate leaves that are woolly-hairy when young and nearly hairless later. They are stalkless, often distantly-toothed, and 2 to 8 inches long. The flower heads develop along naked branches on short stalks furnished with small bracts, or are stalkless. They are ¾ to nearly 1 inch in diameter. This summer-blooming species is native to California.

Garden Uses and Cultivation. This species is probably not hardy where winters are very severe, and its occasional cultivation is pretty much restricted to its home territory and places that provide similar mild winters and dryish summers. It is a sun-loving plant chiefly adapted for naturalistic landscaping and, where geographically appropriate, native plant gardens. It grows in ordinary, well-drained soil and is propagated by seed. Probably cuttings made from young shoots would also prove a satisfactory means of increase.

STEPHANOTIS (Stephan-òtis) — Madagascar-Jasmine. There are about fifteen species of *Stephanotis,* of the milkweed family ASCLEPIADACEAE. The generic name, from the Greek *stephanos,* a crown, and *otos,* an ear, refers to the five earlike appendages to the staminal crown at the center of the flower.

Native from Malaya to Malagasy (Madagascar), stephanotises are hairless shrubs or vines with opposite, undivided, leathery leaves. The flowers, in short-stalked, branched clusters from the leaf axils, have a leafy, five-parted calyx, and a tubular, five-lobed corolla that is either swollen near its base and funnel-shaped or has a narrow tube and wide-spreading lobes (petals). The fruits are podlike follicles.

Madagascar-jasmine (*S. floribunda*), native to Malagasy, is a woody, twining vine

Stephanotis floribunda

Stephanotis floribunda (seed pod)

with thick, evergreen, elliptic leaves 2 to 4 inches long, remindful of those of *Hoya*. The waxy-white flowers, 1 inch to 2 inches long, have spreading petals that form a five-pointed star when looked at full face. They are penetratingly and deliciously fragrant.

Garden Uses. In the Deep South, in Hawaii, and in other tropical and near-tropical climates, *S. floribunda* is a beautiful vine for outdoor cultivation; elsewhere it is suitable only for tropical greenhouses. Its flowers are much esteemed by florists for inclusion in bouquets and other decorative purposes.

Cultivation. This species will grow in a wide variety of soils, but gives best results in one porous enough for water to drain through fairly quickly and sufficiently fertile to encourage vigorous growth. A fairly high organic content is favorable. High temperatures and considerable humidity are important to success. In greenhouses, maintain a minimum winter night temperature of 55°F, 60 to 65°F is better. By day keep the greenhouse at least 65 to 70°F, and this may, with advantage, go up to 80°F or more in sunny weather during its season of active growth. Keep the soil evenly moist, but not constantly saturated, from spring through fall. In winter allow it to dry somewhat between applications, but never so much that it becomes absolutely dry. Dilute liquid fertilizer given to well-rooted specimens at two-week intervals from spring through late summer promotes health and vigor. Spray the foliage lightly with water in bright, sunny weather.

Stephanotises need good light to bloom well, but some shade from strong sun from spring to fall is essential. They do well in fairly restricted root spaces and can be accommodated excellently in large pots, tubs, or boxes. Repot or replant in early spring. Provide wires, a trellis, or other supports around which the long, slender shoots can twine. Because the blooms are produced on new shoots, attend to any pruning needed to restrain or thin out growth in late winter. Propagation may be by taking cuttings at any time, but most usually in

late winter or early spring. Make cuttings of firm young shoots and to speed rooting treat them with a hormone preparation. Plant them in sand, a mixture of sand or perlite and peat moss, or in vermiculite in a humid greenhouse propagating case, preferably where the rooting medium is maintained by bottom heat at a temperature about five degrees above that of the atmosphere. An alternative method of propagation is layering.

Pests. Stephanotises are much subject to infestations of mealybugs; scale insects are sometimes troublesome.

STEPS, GARDEN. Changing levels of terrain may offer the opportunity or even present the inevitability of introducing steps into gardens. When well designed, these not only facilitate perambulation but add charm. For the best effects they must be in scale with their surroundings and be constructed of appropriate materials. Quite obviously they should be safe and comfortable to use. To assure this last, the height of the risers (the vertical faces of the steps) and the distances between them (the level or nearly level treads) must be well proportioned. Commonly, steps less steep than indoor stairs are most practical in gardens. If the treads are 1 foot wide, the risers should not exceed 7 inches in height, and wider treads and lower risers are often preferable.

Steps can be strictly formal and architectural, with or without balustrades, parapets, or handrails, or they can be informal, even to the extent of rusticity so casual that they seem to be part of the natural landscape slightly adapted, perhaps, to the purpose they serve. Formal steps are usually of mortared masonry and make necessary well-drained, solid foundations extending well below the depth of winter freezing. The materials used may include field stone, dressed stone, flagstone, brick, or even concrete, although this last, unless very skillfully used, is apt to lack aesthetic appeal. Such materials can also be used in combination, but for the most harmonious results it is usually better not to employ more than two in the same flight of steps.

Less formal steps can be of uncemented cut stones or field stones that have at least two flat surfaces, one to serve as the riser and one as at least the front of the tread. Such free (not mortared) stones should always be laid on a bed of crushed stone, gravel, or sand to assure stability and free subsurface drainage. Wooden risers, and treads of some porous, loose material, such as gravel or tan bark, can be used as well. Satisfactory wooden risers are peeled locust logs treated with a wood preservative, and railroad ties that have been similarly treated under pressure. These may be held in place by lengths of metal pipe, steel pins, or stout pegs of locust driven

well into the ground near either end of each riser.

The relationship between the depth of the treads and the height of risers is designed to accommodate normal strides

Garden steps: (a) A severely formal, short flight in California

(b) A formal flight, leading down to a lawn, with curving stone risers, stone treads, and a mown grass landing

(c) A formal flight similar to the last, but with a short lowermost step leading to a path

(d) Formal steps of brick lead down from this terrace

(h) A rustic flight leading from a flagstone terrace

(e) Stone steps accommodate pleasingly to this change of grade

(i) These steps are of wooden railroad ties

(f) Steps (under construction) of rectangular blocks of stone without mortar

(j) Ramped steps with log risers and tan bark treads

(g) Casual steps of stone in a rock garden

to ninety, the former for long, narrow flights, the higher figures for short, wider flights. The treads may slope very slightly forward to the risers to assure free surface drainage. With flights of steps higher than 6 feet it is advantageous to relieve the climb or descent by having one or more flat landings to allow for pause or change of pace.

On slopes too steep for an uninterrupted path to afford comfortable walking, yet not steep enough to make necessary a flight of steps (ordinarily a twenty percent slope is the minimum to warrant steps), ramped steps often provide a satisfactory solution. These consist of risers 3 to 5 inches high, spaced 6 feet 3 inches to 8 feet apart (to allow for treads that slope at not more than ten or twelve percent and require three normal paces to traverse), or even longer intervals may separate the risers.

without necessitating shortening or lengthening them uncomfortably. With shallow risers the depths (from front to back) of the treads may be greater than with higher risers. Two formulae are used for determining this relationship. One is that the tread depth, in inches, added to twice the riser height should equal approximately twenty-six; the other is that the tread depth, again in inches, multiplied by the riser height should equal seventy-five

STERCULIA (Ster-cùlia) — Panama Tree. This is the type genus of the sterculia family STERCULIACEAE. Unflattering in its implication, the name *Sterculia* is a modification of that of the Roman mythological character Sterculius, which came from the Latin *stercus*, manure. So far as *Sterculia* is concerned, the allusion is to the foul odor of the blooms of some of its about 100 species, especially one in which added emphasis on this feature was placed by naming it *Sterculia foetida* (the word *foetida* means stinking).

Sterculias are deciduous or evergreen trees of the tropics and subtropics of the Americas and of the Old World, where they are especially abundant in Asia. They have alternate, often large leaves that may be lobeless, lobed, or divided into separate leaflets. Their flowers have no petals. They are unisexual or bisexual with either or both kinds on the same tree. Each has a five-cleft, often ornamental calyx, a column of ten to fifteen stamens, and five styles. The fruits consist of a few leathery or woody podlike follicles that radiate from their common stalk like the spokes of a wheel. Other plants previously named *Sterculia* include species of *Brachychiton* and *Firmiana simplex*.

The Panama tree (**S. apetala**) is the national tree of the Republic of Panama, the country being named after the tree. Native there and in other parts of tropical America, it is handsome and may attain a height of 130 feet. Deciduous, it has a broad, umbrella-shaped, heavy-foliaged crown, and attractive pleated, long-stalked leaves that are roundish in outline and usually have five deep lobes. Commonly 9 inches to 1 foot in diameter, they are sometimes wider. Their lower sides, at first densely-woolly with tiny star-shaped (stellate) hairs, become less so as they mature. Their upper sides are nearly hairless. In loose panicles about 8 inches long, the male and female flowers are interspersed. Clusters of blooms are borne from near the branch ends. The flowers are yellowish tinged or spotted with red or purple, ¾ to 1 inch in diameter, and hairy on their outsides. The hard, dark brown fruits consist of up to five pods, 2½ to 4 inches long, that open to release their two to five approximately 1-inch-long, black, edible seeds. The insides of the pods are clothed with needle-like hairs irritable to the skin.

From the tropics, chiefly coastal regions, of the Old World, comes *S. foetida.* It has a wide natural range, being represented in the floras of Africa, Asia, and Australia. It is deciduous to nearly evergreen, depending upon climate. Unlike those of *S. apetala*, its leaves are composed of five to eleven separate leaflets, and its red and yellow or purple flowers are foul-smelling. In the wild this kind is up to 100 feet tall, but in cultivation it is commonly lower. The leaves, congregated near the branch ends, are pinkish when young. Usually its branches are in tiers of four to eight. Its stout twigs, when young, are clothed with sticky hairs. From the tops of their long stalks the 5- to 7-inch-long lanceolate leaflets radiate. They are glossy above, dull on their undersurfaces. The downy flowers, ¾ inch to 1¼ inches in diameter, are in loose panicles up to 1 foot long. The two to five boat-shaped pods, 4 to 5 inches long, that form the starlike fruits, gape when ripe to release their ten to fifteen shining, purple-black seeds, each ¾ to 1 inch long and with a small yellow protuberance at one end. The seeds are edible raw or roasted, but uncooked have purgative properties. From them a useful oil is extracted.

Other sorts cultivated include *S. rubiginosa* and *S. villosa.* Native from India to Java, *S. rubiginosa* is a shrub or tree, up to about 20 feet tall, with undivided, pointed, obovate to lanceolate leaves 4 inches to 1 foot long, with starry hairs on their undersurfaces. The red-calyxed flowers, ½ to ¾ inch long, are in pendulous panicles. The fruits are of three- to six-seeded pods up to 4 inches long. A sparingly-branched, white-barked native of India, *S. villosa* is a tree with leaves up to 1½ feet long and with five or seven sometimes three-lobed lobes. Their undersides are velvety-hairy. In drooping panicles, the ½-inch-wide flowers have calyxes downy on their outsides, pink within.

Garden and Landscape Uses and Cultivation. For southern Florida, Hawaii, and places with similar warm climates, the species described are excellent for shade and ornament, with the reservation that, due to its ill-scented blooms, *S. foetida* should not be located near windows or elsewhere where the odor is likely to cause distress. The last-mentioned species is well adapted for locations close to the sea. Sterculias grow quite rapidly and in a variety of soils. They are propagated by seed.

STERCULIACEAE — Sterculia Family. Sixty genera accounting for 700 species of dicotyledonous trees, shrubs, and herbaceous plants, including a few vines, constitute the chiefly tropical family STERCULIACEAE. Its useful products include cocoa, from *Theobroma*, and the cola nut, from *Cola.* The leaves in this family are alternate or rarely nearly opposite. They are undivided, palmately-lobed, or divided into palmately-disposed leaflets and are toothed or toothless. The symmetrical, usually bisexual, sometimes unisexual flowers, in axillary or rarely terminal clusters or much less often solitary, have three to five, more or less partially united sepals and five, often small, contorted petals or are without petals. The five or more stamens are joined as a column with the anthers in a cluster at the top. The fruits are capsules or follicles that sometimes separate into leaflike carpels.

Genera cultivated include *Abroma, Brachychiton, Cola, Dombeya, Firmiana, Fremontodendron, Hermannia, Pterospermum, Pterygota, Sterculia, Theobroma, Thomasia,* and *Waltheria.*

STEREOSPERMUM (Stereo-spèrmum) — Pink-Jacaranda, Yellow Snake Tree. The common name of the species of *Stereospermum* most commonly cultivated in Florida alludes to a general likeness of its individual blooms to those of the more familiar *Jacaranda.* It is one of a genus of about two dozen species, natives of Africa and tropical Asia, belonging to the bignonia family BIGNONIACEAE. Its name, from the Greek *stereos*, hard, and *sperma*, seed, is of obvious application. The species sometimes called *S. sinicum* is *Radermachera sinica.*

From other members of its family, *Stereospermum* is distinguished by its scarcely-winged, almost bony seeds contained in cylindrical or quadrangular pods and attached to a corky axis. Stereospermums are trees with opposite, pinnate or twice-pinnate leaves. Their flowers, in big terminal or lateral panicles, are white, pink, lilac, or yellow. They have a two- to five-lobed calyx, a funnel-shaped to bell-shaped or tubular, slightly two-lipped corolla, and four stamens.

Pink-jacaranda (**S. kunthianum**) little resembles *Jacaranda* in foliage or general appearance. Handsome in bloom, it has been described as having more the aspect of a flowering peach than of *Jacaranda.* From 15 to rarely 40 feet tall, it is deciduous. The leaves are pinnate, up to 1 foot long, and have ovate leaflets about 5 inches long by one-half as broad. The fragrant flowers, borne in fall when the tree is leafless, and ranging on different trees from nearly white to pale pink, lilac, or deep pink, are produced in profusion in large, pendulous panicles. Trumpet-shaped, they are about 2 inches long and wide and have petals with crimped margins. The spirally-twisted

seed pods are 1½ to 2 inches long. As a wildling this is widely dispersed throughout Africa.

Yellow snake tree (*S. chelonoides*) is a deciduous native of India, southeastern Asia, and southern China. Its hairless leaves, 1 foot or so long, have seven to thirteen slender-pointed leaflets 4 to 6 inches long. The fragrant, deep buff-yellow blooms are lined with red. They are about 1¼ inches long by one-half as wide and have curled margins to the petals. The lower lip is three-lobed and hairy, the upper bends backward and is two-lobed. The slender, four-angled seed capsules are 1 foot to 2½ feet long and curved.

Garden and Landscape Uses and Cultivation. Pink-jacaranda and yellow snake tree are highly decorative and well suited for open locations and ordinary soils in the tropics and subtropics. In Florida pink-jacaranda has withstood temperatures of 24°F. Stereospermums are propagated by seed and by cuttings.

STERILE. As applied to plants, sterile means incapable of producing viable seeds or spores. Many hybrids and double-flowered varieties belong in this category. Some plants, notably certain varieties of pears, plums, and some other fruits, do not respond (are sterile) to their own pollen, but produce fruit if their flowers are pollinated by that of another (compatable) variety. Sterile also means free of living microorganisms, as in sterile soil.

STERIPHOMA (Steri-phòma). The tropical American genus *Steriphoma*, of the caper family CAPPARIDACEAE, consists of four species. Alluding to the stalks of the fruits being swollen at their apexes, the name is derived from the Greek *steriphoma*, a foundation.

Shrubs with alternate leaves with the stalk thickened at its apex, steriphomas have terminal racemes of showy, orange flowers with a two- or four-parted, irregularly-cleft calyx, four petals, and five to seven, but mostly six, protruding stamens. The fruits are long, narrow pods.

From 4 to 10 feet tall and a native of Guatemala and Venezuela, *S. paradoxum* has slender-pointed, oblong to oblong-lanceolate, evergreen leaves with blades 4 to 7 inches long and stalks of almost equal length. When young they are scurfy. In crowded racemes, the down-pointing, overlapping flowers have orange-yellow stalks 1 inch to 1½ inches long. They have a fuzzy, orange calyx split irregularly for one-half its length. The stamens and style are pale green.

Garden and Landscape Uses and Cultivation. A showy evergreen shrub for outdoors in the tropics and warm subtropics, the species described above is admirable for including in collections of tropical greenhouse plants. It prospers in well-

Steriphoma paradoxum

Sternbergia lutea

drained, fertile soil containing a fairly generous proportion of peat moss or leaf mold, and may be propagated by seed and by cuttings of young, firm shoots planted in a propagating bench with gentle bottom heat.

STERNBERGIA (Stern-bérgia). The botanically unobservant are likely to mistake these charming bulb plants for crocuses, but more sophisticated plantsmen and plantswomen will notice the six stamens, which preclude all possibility of their being members of the iris family IRIDACEAE, to which crocuses belong. Flowers of the iris family have only three stamens. Sternbergias belong to the amaryllis family AMARYLLIDACEAE, and thus, strange as it first appears, they are closer kin of daffodils, which they surely do not obviously resemble, than of crocuses. Named in honor of Count Kasper Moritz von Sternberg, botanist of Prague, Czechoslovakia, who died in 1838, Sternbergia comprises four species and a few varieties or, according to some authorities, eight species. It is native from the Mediterranean region to the Caucasus.

Unlike crocuses, which have solid bulblike organs called corms, sternbergias have true bulbs formed, like onions, with concentric layers. Their leaves are linear or narrowly-strap-shaped. Erect, usually solitary, funnel- to goblet-shaped, and yellow, the blooms have perianth tubes that broaden above into six lanceolate or obovate petals (more correctly, tepals). The slender style is tipped with an often trilobed stigma. The fruits are fleshy capsules. The bulbs of S. lutea, and probably of other kinds, are poisonous if eaten.

Autumn-flowering **S. lutea,** one of the most beautiful hardy bulb plants, is as easy to grow as it is lovely. Native to southern Europe and Asia Minor, in fall it sends up half a dozen or so dark green, slender, strap-shaped leaves 6 inches to 1 foot long. From the center of these, one or more rich golden chalices, 1½ to 2 inches long and perched on short stalks, are produced.

These blooms are of firm substance and remain decorative for a long time. The foliage stays all winter, dying in late spring. Varieties are S. l. angustifolia, with narrower leaves; S. l. graeca, the flowers of which are shorter-stalked and the leaves shorter; and S. l. sicula, in which the blooms are bigger and have narrower, more pointed petals than those of S. lutea. Fall-daffodil is a name sometimes applied to S. lutea.

Sternbergia lutea angustifolia

Other fall-bloomers are S. macrantha (syn. S. clusiana) and S. colchiciflora. Native to Asia Minor, **S. macrantha** differs from S. lutea in that its blooms come rather later and its glaucous leaves, ¾ inch wide, do not develop until spring. Earlier flowering than S. lutea, and with paler, very much more slender flowers that are without aboveground stalks, **S. colchiciflora,** of the Balkans, usually does not present its erect, twisted leaves until spring. They are very slender and about 4 inches long.

Early spring-blooming **S. fischerana,** except in its season of flowering, closely resembles S. lutea. It is a native of the Caucasus.

Garden and Landscape Uses. As embellishments for rock gardens, sternbergias

have much appeal. They can also, with good effect, be tucked into choice nooks at the fringes of shrubberies and fronts of flower borders where they can remain undisturbed. They are not suitable for sites where frequent spading or other uprooting influences are likely to occur. Newly planted bulbs commonly take two or three years to become established. It is a good plan to plant over them a shallow-rooted groundcover, such as creeping thyme, but not strong-rooting species that will seriously compete for moisture and nutrients.

Cultivation. Sternbergia bulbs should be planted in summer or as early in fall as they can be procured. If established specimens are to be transplanted, this is best done as soon as the foliage has died down or very shortly thereafter. Except for propagation, sternbergias should not be dug up or otherwise disturbed so long as they are doing well. The bulbs are planted at depths of 4 to 6 inches, after making sure that beneath them is a layer of earth several inches deep of a quality encouraging to roots. Sternbergias need sun or light, part-day shade and deep, nutritious soil that tends to be dryish rather than wet. All are probably hardy. Propagation is by offsets, bulb cuttings, and seed.

STETSONIA (Stet-sònia). The only species of Stetsonia is a massive cactus, one of the most striking features of hot desert regions in Argentina. It belongs to the cactus family CACTACEAE and was named to honor Francis Lynde Stetson, of New York, a lawyer, keen student of plants, and member of the Board of Managers of The New York Botanical Garden, who died in 1921.

In the wild from 15 to 25 feet tall, **S. coryne** has a very short trunk from which sprout numerous, up to 100 or more, upright and ascending, eight- or nine-ribbed,

Stetsonia coryne

stout branches that branch again above and form a broad head. The ribs are high, blunt, and more or less scalloped. Spaced along them are areoles (areas capable of producing spines and flowers), each with seven to nine spines of unequal length, the biggest up to 2 inches long. The flowers, solitary from the upper parts of the branches, have perianth tubes 4½ to 6 inches long and many white lobes (petals) that spread to form a bloom as wide as the length of the tube. There are numerous stamens. The fruits have not been botanically described.

Garden and Landscape Uses and Cultivation. Commonly known in cultivation only as young, small plants, *S. coryne* has by many cactus fanciers been found more difficult to grow than many other tree cactuses. In their young stages, seedlings seem to be particularly prone to rotting. Young stetsonias are very attractive. At first white, their spines gradually become black. For more information see Cactuses.

STEVENSONIA. See Phoenicophorium.

STEVIA (Stè-via). The plant commonly grown by florists and gardeners as *Stevia serrata* does not belong here; it is *Piqueria trinervia* and is quite different from the species to which the name *S. serrata* rightly belongs. The genus *Stevia* comprises 150 species of annuals, herbaceous perennials, and subshrubs of the daisy family COMPOSITAE. They are natives of the warmer parts of North America, Central America, and South America. Their name commemorates Dr. Peter James Esteve, a Spanish professor of botany, who died in 1566. One annual species, *S. rebaudiana* (syn. *Eupatorium rebaudianum*), the azucacaa of Paraguay, contains a glucoside one hundred and fifty times as sweet as sugar; its possibilities as a sweetening agent have been investigated.

Stevias have opposite or alternate, toothless, toothed, or sometimes three-lobed leaves, usually with three distinct veins, and clusters or panicles of white, pinkish, purplish, or purple, small flower heads of five or six tiny, tubular, five-toothed florets. Each flower head has a cylindrical, few-bracted involucre (collar of bracts). Until they are examined somewhat critically botanically, suffice it to say that the flower clusters look more like those of a *Gypsophila* or *Galium* than of a daisy relative. The flower heads are without ray florets. The fruits are seed-like achenes.

True *S. serrata* is indigenous from Texas to Arizona and Mexico. Erect, branched, and hairy, its stems have many, mostly alternate, often crowded, nearly hairless narrow leaves, 1 inch to 1½ inches long, generally irregularly-toothed and with their broadest parts above their middles. The white or pink flower heads are in loose clusters. This is a perennial about 1½ feet tall. Some 2 feet tall, perennial, and woody toward its base, *S. ivaefolia,* of Mexico, has diamond-lanceolate to spatula-shaped, toothed leaves about 1 inch long; the upper ones are stalkless and narrower than those below. The flowers are white to pink. Another perennial indigenous to Mexico, *S. purpurea,* about 1½ feet tall, has velvety-hairy stems and alternate leaves, those above lanceolate, the lower obovate, toothed at their apexes, and 1 inch to 1½ inches long. The flower heads are purple. Native to Arizona, New Mexico, and Mexico, *S. plummerae* is a perennial 1 foot to 1½ feet tall. Usually it has rather sparse foliage; its leaves are mostly opposite. They are elliptic to narrowly-oblong, up to 3½ inches long, and prominently toothed. The fragrant flowers are white or pink.

Garden and Landscape Uses and Cultivation. Stevias are of small horticultural importance. In regions of mild winters they may be used in informal areas and to a limited extent in flower borders. Within their natural range they are suitable for native plant gardens. They grow in ordinary soil in sunny locations and are increased by seed and by division.

STEWARTIA (Stewárt-ia). The seven species of *Stewartia* are deciduous trees or shrubs, native to the eastern United States and eastern Asia. Belonging in the tea family THEACEAE, they are relatives of camellias, *Gordonia,* and *Franklinia.* The generic name commemorates John Stuart, Earl of Bute, an eighteenth-century patron of botany. Sometimes the generic name is spelled *Stuartia,* but that was not its original form.

Stewartias are summer bloomers with handsome foliage and beautiful, white, cup-shaped or flattish flowers. Their trunks and major branches are covered with smooth, flaky, and often colorful bark. The leaves are alternate, undivided, short-stalked, and toothed. The flowers are solitary in the leaf axils or near the terminations of the shoots. They have a calyx of five or rarely six persistent sepals, with one or two conspicuous bracts just beneath, and five, rarely six or up to eight, obovate or nearly orbicular petals silky-hairy on their outsides and joined at their bases. The stamens are numerous, and there are five styles, joined or separate. The fruits, woody capsules, contain compressed and, except those of *S. ovata,* wingless seeds. From *Franklinia* this genus differs in its seed capsules splitting open only at their tops; from *Camellia* and *Gordonia* it differs in having deciduous foliage.

The American species, *S. ovata* and *S. malacodendron,* are more often tall shrubs than trees. Rarely exceeding 15 feet in height, *S. ovata* has hairless branchlets and ovate or elliptic leaves up to 5 inches long. Its flowers, 2½ to 3 inches across, have five

or six petals and white stamens with orange anthers. The styles are separate. The seeds are winged. Hardy as far north as southern New England, this is native from North Carolina and Tennessee to Florida. The magnificent variety *S. o. grandiflora* has flowers up to 4½ inches across with five

Stewartia ovata grandiflora

to eight petals and bright purple stamens. It is endemic to Georgia. Not hardy where winters are notably more severe than those of Washington, D.C., *S. malacodendron* is native from Virginia to Arkansas, Florida, and Louisiana. Sometimes 20 feet tall, but usually considerably lower and shrublike, it has pubescent young branchlets and elliptic to elliptic-oblong leaves that may be 4 inches long and have pubescent undersides and hair-fringed margins. The flowers, 3 to 4 inches across, have spreading petals, and united styles shorter than the stamens, which have purple stalks and bluish anthers.

Best known of Asian species and hardy in southern New England, *S. pseudocamellia* sometimes attains a height of 60 feet in its native Japan, in cultivation it is usually lower. Belonging to the group whose flowers have united styles, it differs from *S. malacodendron* in having smaller, more cup-shaped flowers, stamens with whitish

Stewartia pseudocamellia

Stewartia pseudocamellia (flowers)

Stewartia monadelpha

stalks and orange anthers, and fruits ovoid instead of depressed-globose. The branchlets are not zigzagged. The elliptic to obovate-elliptic leaves, about 3 inches long and distantly round-toothed, are hairless or have scattered hairs on their pale undersides. In fall they turn purplish. The flowers, their petals furry on their outsides, are 2 to 2½ inches wide. This tree has handsomely colored red bark that peels in large flakes. With almost as beautiful bark and larger flowers, Korean *S. koreana*, a rather rare, but very worthwhile

Stewartia koreana

ornamental tree, was first brought to America in 1917. Attaining heights up to 50 feet, this has mostly zigzagged, slightly flattened, hairless branchlets and elliptic to broad-ovate leaves up to 4 inches long that turn orange to orange-red in fall. The flattish flowers, borne in the axils of the lower leaves and about 3 inches in diameter, have five or six petals. The styles are united. This is hardy in southern New England. Tallest of stewartias, *S. monadelpha*, of Japan, there attains a height of 80 feet. It was introduced to America in 1917 and is hardy perhaps as far north as New York City. This has hairy branchlets, elliptic to obovate-elliptic, distantly-toothed leaves with pubescent undersides, and flowers 1 inch

to 1½ inches in diameter. The stamens have whitish stalks united at their bases and purple anthers. The styles are united. Chinese *S. sinensis*, a shrub or tree up to 30 or 35 feet high, has more or less elliptic leaves up to 4 inches long, sparingly-hairy or hairless below except on the midrib, and with round-toothed margins. The cup-shaped flowers are 2 inches wide. The whitish stalks of the stamens are joined in their lower thirds and are hairy below their middles. The styles are united. This species is hardy about as far north as New York City.

Garden and Landscape Uses. Stewartias are highly desirable ornamentals, attractive because of their fairly large, bright green leaves that assume interesting shades of orange, orange-red, and wine-red in fall and their beautiful flowers that provide a long season of display in high summer. In winter the beauty of their bark is displayed to advantage. They serve excellently as lawn specimens and can be used effectively near dwellings and other buildings if they are not crowded too closely against them. They grow best in deep, porous, fertile soils that are moderately moist, and need rather sheltered locations. A very little shade is desirable.

Cultivation. The cultivation of stewartias makes no special demands of the gardener. Once established they need minimum care; little or no pruning is necessary. They transplant without difficulty. Propagation is by seed, by layering, and by leafy cuttings in summer, preferably planted under mist.

STICK-TIGHT. See Bidens.

STICKWEED is *Hackelia*.

STICTOCARDIA (Sticto-càrdia). A dozen species of the morning glory family CONVOLVULACEAE constitute *Stictocardia*. Natives of the Old World and New World tropics, and most abundant in Malaysia, they are closely related to *Ipomoea*, differing most obviously in the way in which

their fruits open to disperse seed. The name, alluding to the gland-dotted undersides of the leaves, derives from the Greek *stiktos*, spotted, and *kardia*, a heart.

Stictocardias are woody or soft-stemmed twining vines or trailers with alternate, usually ovate leaves with heart-shaped bases, thickly besprinkled on their undersides with tiny black glands. The flowers, solitary or up to several together from the leaf axils, have a five-lobed calyx, a trumpet-shaped, red, purple, or white corolla, five stamens, and a style with a two-lobed stigma. The fruits, completely enclosed by the enlarged calyx, open by splitting in a highly irregular fashion.

African *S. beraviensis* (syn. *Ipomoea beraviensis*) has vigorous, woody stems and more or less hairy, ovate leaves 5 to 9 inches long. The bright red flowers are borne in clusters of few to several. Also African, *S. macalusoi* (syn. *Ipomoea macalusoi*) is a robust woody-stemmed climber or trailer with large, broadly-heart-shaped leaves and solitary or paired flowers, scarlet or scarlet and orange, with a paler perianth tube 2½ to 3 inches long.

Native to India and Malaysia, *S. campanulata* (syn. *Argyreia tiliaefolia*) is a vigorous species that somewhat resembles *Argyreia speciosa*, but is hairless or nearly so. It has ovate-heart-shaped leaves 2 to 4 inches long and trumpet-shaped violet, rose-purple, or white flowers about 2 inches across.

Garden and Landscape Uses and Cultivation. These are as for tropical species of *Argyreia* and *Ipomoea*.

STIFFTIA (Stíff-tia). This genus of seven species of the daisy family COMPOSITAE inhabits northern South America. Its name honors the Austrian court physician, Dr. A. J. von Stifft, who died in 1836.

Stifftias are shrubs, trees, and vines, with alternate, undivided, lobeless, toothless, leathery leaves. Their flower heads are yellowish, yellow, orange-yellow, or red. They are solitary and large, or smaller and in panicles. The florets that compose them are slender-tubular and have five narrow, recurved lobes. The fruits are long, thin achenes.

An evergreen shrub 6 to 9 feet tall, *Stifftia chrysantha*, of Brazil, is an unusual and

Stifftia chrysantha

effective ornamental. It has short-stalked, rigid, slender-pointed, lanceolate leaves. Its shaving-brush-like flower heads, solitary on short branchlets, are up to about 4 inches broad by 2 to 2½ inches tall and composed of orange-yellow florets and numerous long, pale pinkish-yellow hairs, technically the pappus. The florets have the lobes of their corollas rolled backward in tight coils. The two-branched styles protrude conspicuously.

Probably never introduced to cultivation in America or Europe, *S. uniflora* is a gorgeously flowered vine sometimes 60 feet tall. It has short-stalked, pointed-elliptic leaves up to 5 inches long by 2¼ inches broad and feathery panicles of flower heads up to 1 inch long, the showy parts of which are long tufts of protruding, raspberry-red hairs. The panicles are up to 7 inches long and broad.

Garden and Landscape Uses and Cultivation. Adapted for outdoor cultivation only in the humid tropics, *S. chrysantha* grows willingly in fertile, fairly moist soil in sun or part-day shade. It also thrives in greenhouses in pots or ground beds. Indoors, the temperature on winter nights should be 60 to 65°F and five to fifteen degrees higher by day. At other seasons more warmth is in order. At all times the atmosphere must be reasonably humid. Shade from strong summer sun is required. Cuttings planted in a propagating bench with mild bottom heat, and air layering are ready means of increase. Seed may also be used.

STIGMA. The portion, usually at the tip, of the female organ of a flower (the pistil) receptive to pollen is the stigma.

STIGMAPHYLLON (Stigmaphýl-lon) — Orchid Vine. The genus *Stigmaphyllon* includes sixty to seventy species of mostly twining, woody vines of tropical America and the West Indies, few of which are cultivated. It belongs in the malpighia family MALPIGHIACEAE. The name is derived from the Greek *stigma*, the female organ of a flower, and *phyllon*, a leaf. It refers to the leaflike appendages of the stigmas.

Stigmaphyllons have usually opposite, toothed or smooth-edged, rarely lobed leaves with two glands near the tops of their stalks. The yellow flowers, in axillary, umbel-like clusters, have a five-parted calyx, five clawed petals of unequal size, and ten unequal stamens, six of which are functional and four without anthers or deformed. The fruits are of one to three samaras.

The orchid vine (*S. ciliatum*) of the West Indies and northern South America, is most familiar. A slender evergreen twiner, which attains a height of 30 feet or sometimes more, it has smooth-surfaced, heart-shaped leaves, 1 inch to 3 inches long and almost as wide, fringed with hairs. The bright yellow flowers, about 1¼ inches across and

in stalked clusters of three to seven, have ruffled petals. They slightly resemble the blooms of oncidium orchids, hence the colloquial name. The three-parted fruits have a 1-inch-long wing to each part. Similar, but with thicker, ovate, smooth-edged or slightly-lobed, alternate and opposite leaves, gray-hairy beneath and 2 to 5 inches long, is Brazilian *S. littorale.* This has many more flowers in each cluster than *S. ciliatum*, and its flowers are about 1 inch in diameter. Both kinds bloom in spring and summer.

Other sorts that may be cultivated include these: *S. fulgens*, of tropical America, is a tall grower with broad-ovate leaves with silvery-hairy undersides. Its flower stalks are forked. *S. heterophyllum*, of Argentina, is a lofty vine with broad-ovate to nearly round or sometimes three-lobed leaves that are densely-silvery-hairy beneath. Its flowers are in long-stalked clusters. *S. humboldtianum*, of Mexico and Central America, has broad-ovate leaves with rounded or heart-shaped bases and hairy undersides. *S. jatrophaefolium*, of Uruguay, has light green, deeply-palmately-lobed, bristle-toothed leaves, and flowers many together in tight clusters.

Garden and Landscape Uses. The sorts described are hardy in parts of California where they have withstood temperatures as low as 22°F and are well adapted to tropical and subtropical climates. They succeed in any ordinary garden soil and respond favorably to some shade from the strongest sun. For training against supports fixed to buildings and for planting where their long slender stems can cascade and display their lovely blooms to fullest advantage, stigmaphyllons have much to recommend them. True, their individual flowers are frail and drop readily, but they are soon replaced by others. They are also excellent for growing on fences and garden walls. In greenhouses they succeed best when grown on pillars or along wires stretched a few inches beneath the glass of the roof.

Cultivation. These vines present no difficulties once they are well established, but often are slow to get started. Indeed, newly set-out plants may need a little coaxing to get them going. Good soil drainage and moderate rather than copious watering at that stage are needed. Pruning to keep the plants within bounds and to remove dead wood and untidy stems should be done in late winter or as soon as the blooming season is through. In greenhouses stigmaphyllons succeed best when planted in well-drained ground beds, but are not well adapted for pot cultivation. They thrive where the winter night temperature is about 55°F and the day temperature a few degrees higher. From spring to fall a minimum of 60°F at night should be maintained. Propagation is easily effected by cuttings taken in spring or early fall.

STILBOCARPA (Stilbo-cárpa). Belonging to the aralia family ARALIACEAE, the three species of *Stilbocarpa* are endemic to New Zealand and nearby islands. The name, from the Greek *stilbo*, to shine, and *karpos*, a fruit, refers to the glossy fruits.

Herbaceous perennials not hardy in the north, the sorts of this genus have undivided, round to kidney-shaped, toothed or slightly-lobed leaves with conspicuous veins. The tiny flowers, in umbels of smaller umbels with which are associated large leafy bracts, are unisexual or bisexual. They have generally five petals, the same number of stamens, and a three- or four-branched style. The fruits are berrylike drupes. Individual plants are predominantly unisexual.

Probably the only sort cultivated, *S. lyallii* (syn. *Kirkophytum lyallii*) has short stems and prostrate or arching stolons (runners) at the ends of which new plants develop. Its round to kidney-shaped leaves have hairy stalks and shallowly-lobed and toothed, prominently veined blades that may exceed 1 foot in diameter and are hairy beneath, but hairless or almost hairless on their upper surfaces. The umbels of reddish-purple flowers are congregated in heads up to 1 foot in diameter. This is endemic to Stewart Island and other islands off the coast of New Zealand.

Garden Uses and Cultivation. Because they are rare in cultivation little is known about the needs of these plants. Presumably they need porous soil not lacking in moisture and a comparatively cool, humid climate without extremes of heat or cold. Parts of the Pacific Northwest would seem to afford the most likely chances for success. Seed and careful division are means of increase.

STILLINGIA (Stil-língia)—Queen's Delight. Named in honor of Dr. Benjamin Stillingfleet, an English botanist, who died in 1771, the genus *Stillingia* consists of a few more than thirty species, of which thirty are natives of warm parts of the Americas, the remainder native to warm parts of the Old World. It belongs in the spurge family EUPHORBIACEAE.

Hairless, perennial herbaceous plants and shrubs, stillingias have alternate, undivided, toothed leaves and terminal spikes of small, petal-less, unisexual flowers with two- or three-lobed calyxes and one to three stamens. The styles are joined at their bases and spreading above. The fruits are three-seeded capsules. Male and female flowers are borne on the same plant, with the females located lower on the spikes than the males.

Queen's delight (*S. sylvatica*), a native of dry woodlands from Virginia to Florida, Texas, and Oklahoma, is a deep-rooted herbaceous perennial 1½ to 3 feet in height. It has ovate-lanceolate to oblanceolate leaves, 1½ to 3 inches long, with incurved glandular teeth. The stout, slender, erect spikes of tiny yellow blooms are 2 to 4 inches long.

Garden Uses and Cultivation. The species described here succeeds in any well-drained soil in part-shade. It is propagated by seed. Although not ornamental it may be cultivated in herb and medicinal gardens because of its uses in medicines.

STINK BELLS is *Fritillaria agrestis.*

STINKING BENJAMIN is *Trillium erectum.*

STIPA (Stì-pa) — Spear Grass, Feather Grass. The genus *Stipa* belongs in the grass family GRAMINEAE. It consists of about 100 species and has a wide natural distribution, especially in dry, warm-temperate regions, that includes North America. The name is derived from the Greek *stype,* tow or oakum, and alludes to the appearance of the flower heads of *S. pennata.* The esparto grass (*Stipa tenacissima*), a native of Spain and North Africa, is cultivated commercially for the strong fibers of its foliage, which are made into excellent paper, mats, ropes, and other products.

Stipas are more or less tufted, hardy and nonhardy perennials and annuals. Their leaves generally are tightly rolled and slender. The flower panicles, loose or compact, are usually slender and have one-flowered spikelets with often twisted, terminal awns (bristles). Those of some kinds are hydroscopic; they twist and untwist, shorten and lengthen, in response to the availability of moisture. The movement so induced enables the seed to work its way into the ground, to plant itself as it were. Unfortunately, it also makes it possible for those of some stipas, when caught in the wool or hair of animals, to bore their way into, and even through, the skin with the result that, if a vital part is reached, the creature dies.

One of the most ornamental and commonly grown stipas is the feather grass (*S. pennata*), a native of hot, dry places from central Europe to Siberia. Up to 3 feet in height, this perennial has numerous slender, arching stems terminating in dense, plumy flower heads with bristles up to 1 foot long, and feathered for most of their lengths from the tips downward with short hairs. Another perennial of decorative merit is *S. elegantissima,* an Australian species distinguished by the branches of its flower panicles being feathery-hairy. The bristles at the ends of the spikelets are 1¼ inches long. The leaves are erect, narrow, and rolled.

Garden and Landscape Uses and Cultivation. Stipas are attractive ornamentals for inclusion in flower borders and for the decoration of informal areas. Their flowers are useful for cutting and are effective fresh or dried. They are of easy cultivation in sunny locations in well-drained soils of moderate or better fertility. They are easily

raised from seed and, the perennial kinds, by division in spring or early fall. Their routine cultivation makes no special demands.

STIPULE. Appendages, usually small and generally in pairs, at the bases of leafstalks are called stipules. Often, as with roses, they are of leafy texture; sometimes they are glandlike.

STITCHWORT. See Stellaria.

STIZOLOBIUM. See Mucuna.

STOCK. The ten-week, intermediate or East Lothian, and Brampton stocks and the evening stock belong in *Matthiola,* the Virginian-stock and malcolm-stocks in *Malcolmia.*

STOCK or UNDERSTOCK. The terms stock and understock designate the rooted plant upon which the scion (bud or shoot) of another plant is or has been budded, grafted, or inarched.

STOKES'-ASTER is *Stokesia laevis.*

STOKESIA (Stok-èsia) — Stokes'-Aster. The native range of the only species of this excellent herbaceous perennial fails to indicate its hardiness. Confined in the wild from South Carolina to Louisiana, it can be grown outdoors in southern New England. A member of the daisy family COMPOSITAE that blooms in summer, fall, and, in parts of the Deep South, through much of the winter, *Stokesia* has a name that honors the English physician Jonathan Stokes, who died in 1831.

Stokes'-aster (*S. laevis* syn. *S. cyanea*) is so called because its flower heads bear considerable likeness to those of the China-aster (*Callistephus*). It is freely-branched and 1 foot to 2 feet tall. Its stems, frequently purplish, when young are sometimes hairy. The leaves are alternate and lanceolate. The lower ones, up to 8 inches long, are without lobes or teeth and taper below into flattened stalks. The upper leaves are

Stokesia laevis

Stokesia laevis (flowers)

smaller, shorter-stalked or stalkless, and have a few teeth toward their bases. Flattish or shallowly-cupped, the solitary flower heads terminate the branches. Typically they are lavender-blue to purplish and up to 3 to 4 inches wide in cultivation, often smaller in the wild. As is usual in the daisy family, the flower heads, commonly thought of as flowers, are composed of many florets, each technically a flower. In *Stokesia* the about fifteen, spreading, outer florets are petal-like, very much larger than the inner ones, and slashed in their upper parts into five narrow strips. The seedlike fruits are achenes.

Horticultural varieties of Stokes'-aster include a number with latinized names such as *S. l. alba,* with white; *S. l. lilacina,* with lilac; *S. l. caerulea,* with blue; *S. l. rosea,* with pink; and *S. l. lutea,* with pale yellow blooms. In addition, there are *S. l.* 'Silver Moon', with white blooms of greater purity than those of *S. l. alba,* and the blue-flowered selections *S. l.* 'Blue Danube' and *S. l.* 'Blue Star', the last with very large flowers.

Garden and Landscape Uses and Cultivation. Stokes'-aster is a good plant for the fronts of flower borders and similar locations and is remarkably free of pests and diseases. Its blooms are excellent for cutting. Dryish, fertile, well-drained soil and a location in full sun are necessary. Clayey earth and soil that remains wet for extended periods are fatal. In the north, plant in spring, in milder climates, in spring or fall. Allow 1 foot to 1¼ feet between plants. Once established, no special care is needed except that in cold climates winter protection in the form of a light covering of salt hay, branches of evergreens, or other material that allows free circulation of air to pass through it is desirable. This helps to minimize the harmful effects of alternate freezing and thawing, so damaging to this plant. An annual spring application of a complete garden fertilizer is beneficial. New plants are easily raised from seed sown in a cold frame or outdoor bed in spring. Improved horticultural varieties do not breed true from seed. To assure duplication they must be raised from divisions or root cuttings. Division is carried out in spring, but because of the nature of the plant, does not lead to rapid increase. Root cuttings 2 inches long are taken in February from plants in the ground or plants that were dug in fall and stored with their roots packed in soil in flats (shallow boxes) in a cold frame. The cuttings are started into growth in well-drained flats of porous, peaty soil in a cool greenhouse. When well started, the young plants are potted individually and later are planted in nursery beds outdoors.

STOLON. A stolon is a more or less horizontal shoot or stem at or below ground level that roots and develops new shoots from the nodes or apex. Essentially this is synonymous with runner.

STOMATIUM (Stom-àtium). Some forty species of low, very short-branched, perennial succulents related to *Mesembryanthemum* and belonging in the carpetweed family AIZOACEAE comprise *Stomatium*. The name derives from the Greek *stoma*, a mouth, and alludes to the appearance of the leaves. In the wild the genus is confined to the drier parts of South Africa. Some species included in it were previously segregated as *Agnirictus* on the basis that their corollas are not joined at their bases to the calyxes to form short tubes. The plant previously known as *S. musculinum* is *Chasmatophyllum musculinum*.

Stomatiums have crowded, very fleshy, opposite leaves, those of each pair joined at their bases and frequently unequal in

length. Alternate pairs are at right angles to each other. The leaves are triangular to more or less spoon-shaped or lanceolate, soft-skinned, dull, and finely-white-warted. At their margins are usually a few short, broad teeth. Opening at night and fragrant, the stalkless or short-stalked flowers are yellow or, rarely, white or pinkish. They have many linear petals and five or six short stigmas. The fruits are capsules.

Very compact and highly desirable, *S. suaveolens* has very fleshy, pale gray-green, finely-rough-surfaced leaves that assume a coppery hue in summer. They are up to ¾ inch long, erect or spreading, and somewhat recurved and becoming broader and thicker toward their tips. Their margins may or may not have a few teeth. The stalkless, yellow blooms come in summer or early fall. Larger than the last, *S. ermininum* blooms in summer. Its crowded, spreading leaves are light gray-green and roughened with fine translucent dots. Toward their apexes they have a few marginal teeth. Up to ¾ inch in length by about two-thirds as wide, they are flat on their upper sides, keeled beneath. The keel is without teeth. The short-stalked, yellow flowers are ¾ to 1 inch in diameter. Another summer-bloomer, *S. mustellinum* has prostrate branches and broad, spatula-shaped leaves, ½ to 1 inch long by one-half as broad, toothed at their edges. Grayish-green and roughened with largish translucent dots, they have flat upper surfaces and undersides keeled toward their apexes. The yellow blooms, about ¾ inch in diameter, are on stalks approximately as long.

Formerly segregated as *Agnirictus* and fairly commonly cultivated, *S. agninum* (syn. *Agnirictus agninus*) has soft, three-angled, oblongish, dull gray-green leaves about 2 inches in length by approximately ½ inch wide, with flat upper surfaces and warted with small green tubercles. They angle upward toward the tips of the stems and at their margins may or may not have a few short, blunt teeth. The pale yellow flowers are on stalks about ¾ inch long. The flower stalks distinguish this species from *S. lesliei* (syn. *Agnirictus lesliei*), which has stalkless yellow blooms at the ends of its shoots. Also, the tapering, three-angled leaves of the latter, up to 1¾ inches long by about ½ inch broad, finely-tubercled on their upper flat surfaces, and toothed at their edges, spread widely.

Other sorts cultivated include *S. fulleri*, which has gray-dotted, green leaves 1 inch to 1¼ inches long, by about ½ inch wide at the base. They have a flat upper surface and a rounded under one and are keeled toward the blunt, toothed apex. The ¾-inch-wide flowers are yellowish-white. White-dotted, gray-green, slightly-incurved, spreading leaves, up to 1¼ inches long, are typical of much-branched *S. murinum*. They thicken toward their tips and have a keel that like their margins is usually toothed. Solitary and up to 1 inch wide, the flowers are yellow.

Garden Uses and Cultivation. Stomatiums are delightful for inclusion in collections of choice, nonhardy succulents and are generally easy to cultivate. Most flower freely. They appreciate porous soil and the sunny, dryish conditions needed by all dwarf members of the *Mesembryanthemum* group. If kept too moist or too warm when days are short and light intensity is comparatively low, they grow out of character and become uninteresting. In winter they should be kept dry. At other seasons water them rather sparingly. Propagation is by seed and by cuttings. For additional information see Succulents.

STONE. This word forms parts of the common names of these plants: stone-cress (*Aethionema*), stone-mint (*Cunila origanoides*), and stone plant (*Gibbaeum*, *Imitaria*, *Lithops*, and *Pleiospilos*).

STONE FRUITS. This is a collective name for fruits (technically drupes) such as apricots, cherries, plums, and peaches, the usually solitary seeds of which are enclosed in a hard, lignified layer (the stone) surrounded by more or less soft flesh.

STONE OR PEBBLE PLANTS. Outstanding examples of plant mimicry, the stone or pebble plants or "living stones" as they are sometimes called, of South Africa, belong to a few genera of the *Mesembryanthemum* relationship of the family AIZOACEAE. So closely do they resemble the stones, pebbles, or angular pieces of rock that fre-

Stomatium, undetermined species

Stone or pebble plants: *Haworthia truncata* (left), *Argyroderma octophyllum* (center), and *Lithops lesliei* (right)

Seedling stone or pebble plants (*Argyroderma roseum*)

quently strew the ground of their native habitats that botanists and experienced plant collectors searching for them, unless they are in bloom, are apt to pass them by unnoticed. Their resemblance to small stones lies in their sizes, shapes, surface colorings, and textures. These likenesses are often accentuated by the plants being partly buried, so only their tops protrude above the ground. This amazingly close mimicry of their surroundings is considered to be effective as a safeguard against browsing animals, many of which fail to distinguish them from the rocks and stones among which they grow.

Stone or pebble plants are among the most intriguing and easiest of succulents to grow outdoors in warm, desert regions and in greenhouses and window gardens. Besides the fascination of their forms and colors, they attract with their usually improbably large, white, yellow, pink, or purple flowers, daisy-like in appearance, although not in structure.

Admirable effects can be had by planting several of any one sort in a well-drained pan (shallow flower pot) in very gritty, highly porous soil. Space the plants irregularly to simulate chance seedlings, rather than at even distances, then place among them, also casually and with some partly buried, small stones or pebbles that match

the plants as closely as possible in size and appearance.

For more information about these plants, which include some called windowed plants, and their cultural needs see the Encyclopedia entries Aloinopsis, Argyroderma, Cerochlamys, Cheiridopsis, Conophytum, Dinteranthus, Faucaria, Fenestraria, Frithia, Gibbaeum, Lithops, Mitrophyllum, Odontophorus, Ophthalmophyllum, Pleiospilos, Psammophora, Rhinephyllum, Stomatium, and Titanopsis. Also see the Encyclopedia entry Windowed Plants.

STONECROP. See Sedum.

STONEFACE. See Lithops.

STONEWORT. See Nitella.

STOOL. Compact root crowns or bases, of such plants as asters, chrysanthemums, and phloxes, that give rise to many new shoots that usually can be used for propagating are called stools.

STOPPING. See Pinching.

STORAX is *Styrax officinalis*.

STORKSBILL. See Pelargonium.

STOVE PLANTS. The name stove plants is an old-fashioned designation for plants grown in tropical greenhouses. Early examples of such greenhouses were called stoves or stove houses because of the primitive stovelike heating apparatus employed. Long after more effective equipment for heating came into use, stove houses and stove plants were commonly used terms, especially in the British Isles.

STRAIGHTEDGE. Useful in establishing grades on plots of ground of small to moderate size, a straightedge is a piece of wood, of any convenient size up to about 12 feet long, with one edge perfectly straight and the opposite edge or at least the center portion of it strictly parallel with it. In use, the straightedge is laid across the top of two pegs (short stakes) driven

A straightedge in use

into the ground and a level is placed along the center of the upper edge to check for levelness or inclination from the horizontal. Any adjustments needed to have the tops of the pegs or particular marks on them indicate the desired grade are then made by lowering or raising the pegs.

STRAIN. A strain is a population of plants within a variety that exhibits definite, usually attractive characteristics that are reproduced with considerable fidelity by its seedling offspring, but are not of sufficient morphological importance to warrant recognition of the group as a separate variety. Strains may be remarkable for their resistance to disease, better-than-average yields, tolerance of particular environments, and other qualities.

STRANVAESIA (Stran-vaèsia). This genus is composed of evergreen trees and shrubs of the rose family ROSACEAE. It inhabits continental Asia, Taiwan, and the Philippine Islands. There are ten species. From closely related *Photinia* they differ in that when the fruits are ripe the entire ovary is readily separable from the surrounding parts. The name commemorates William Fox-Strangways, an English botanist, who died in 1865.

Stranvaesias have alternate, undivided, toothed or toothless leaves and terminal, many-flowered clusters of small white blooms that have five-toothed calyxes, five usually obovate petals, about twenty stamens, and five styles joined in their lower parts. The small, berry-like, orange or red fruits are technically pomes (fruits structured like apples) resembling those of hawthorns.

A splendid ornamental from western China, *Stranvaesia davidiana* is justifiably popular in parts of California and other warm-temperate and subtropical places and is hardy at Washington, D.C. and perhaps in sheltered locations further north. Up to 25 feet in height, it has young shoots with silky hairs that soon drop and

Stranvaesia davidiana (fruits)

handsome oblong, oblong-lanceolate, or oblanceolate, pointed, toothless leaves 2¼ to 4½ inches long. They have short, often reddish, hairy stalks and are somewhat hairy on the midribs beneath. The short-lived flowers, ⅓ inch across, in loose, hairy-branched clusters 2 to 3½ inches wide, have red anthers. They come in early summer and are succeeded by red fruits, ⅓ inch across, that make their best display in early winter. Usually lower, and with wavy-margined, elliptic-oblong to oblong-lanceolate leaves up to 3 inches long, *S. d. undulata* (syn. *S. undulata*) has orange- or coral-red fruits, ¼ inch in diameter. In *S. d. salicifolia* (syn. *S. salicifolia*) the leaves have more veins than those of the typical species and are narrowly-lanceolate.

Stranvaesia davidiana undulata

Less well known, **S. nussia** (syn. *S. glaucescens*), a native of the Himalayas, is a tree up to 25 feet tall or somewhat taller, with young shoots covered with whitish hairs, and lanceolate to obovate, glossy, dark green, finely-toothed leaves up to 5 inches long. The flowers, about ½ inch in diameter, are in hairy-stalked clusters 2 to 4 inches wide. Pear-shaped, the light red fruits are about ¼ inch long. This is less hardy than *S. davidiana* and its varieties.

Garden and Landscape Uses and Cultivation. The kinds described above are useful ornamentals adaptable to various locations. They succeed in fertile soil but require ample space to show themselves to advantage. Stranvaesias are satisfactory in sun or part-day shade. No special care is needed. They appreciate being kept mulched, and being watered regularly during dry weather. Propagation is by cuttings and by seed. The latter germinate more readily if they are stratified for three months at 40°F before being sown.

STRATIFICATION. See Seeds, Propagation By.

STRATIOTES (Strati-òtes) — Water Soldier or Water-Aloe. One of the most interest-

ing aquatics, the water soldier is the only species of *Stratiotes*. A native of Europe and northern Asia, it belongs to the frog's bit family HYDROCHARITACEAE. Its name, derived from the Greek *stratiotes*, a soldier, alludes to its sharp, tough, sword-shaped leaves.

The water soldier (*S. aloides*) is a hardy

Stratiotes aloides

Stratiotes aloides, with *Lemna minor* covering the water surface

perennial that has the peculiarity of surfacing in spring and becoming partly emergent, and submerging before winter. After the plant sinks its leaves decay and only winter-hibernating buds persist. This remarkable plant has very short stems and stalkless, clustered leaves, triangular in section and saw-toothed. They are pointed-linear-lanceolate, fleshy, and ½ foot to 1¼ feet long by ¼ to 1 inch broad. The flowers, about 1½ inches wide, are unisexual and white. They arise from between a pair of bracts atop a short or elongated stem and have three sepals and three petals. The females are solitary, the males in twos or sometimes three or more together. The former have six pistils and rudimentary stamens, the latter about twelve stamens and sometimes a non-functional pistil. The water soldier produces runners that bear young plantlets.

Garden Uses and Cultivation. This plant is cultivated for its interesting habit rather than display. It may be accommodated in ponds and pools where the water is deep enough to allow it to sink to well below the level of freezing before the onset of winter. Propagation is by winter-resting buds and by shoots detached from floating plants.

STRAWBERRY. In addition to being the name of kinds of the genus *Fragaria*, treated in the next entry, strawberry forms parts of the common names of these plants: barren-strawberry (*Waldsteinia*), Indian- or mock-strawberry (*Duchesnea indica*), strawberry-begonia or strawberry-geranium (*Saxifraga stolonifera*), strawberry-blite (*Chenopodium capitatum*), strawberry bush (*Euonymus americana*), strawberry guava (*Psidium littorale*), and strawberry tree (*Arbutus unedo*).

STRAWBERRY. Probably the most esteemed of "berried" fruits, the strawberries of garden and marketplace are, compared with many other fruits, relative newcomers to cultivation. Identified botanically as *Fragaria ananassa*, the hybrid stocks now grown in numerous varieties have as ancestral parents *F. chiloensis*, the beach strawberry native from Alaska to California and in South America, and the wild strawberry of eastern North America, *F. virginiana*. In addition, alpine and hautbois strawberries, derivatives of European *Fragaria vesca* and *F. moschata*, are sometimes grown.

Although *F. chiloensis* had been cultivated by South American Indians earlier, it was not until about 1712 that Amedeé Francois Frezier brought plants to France. Of these, the first seen in Europe, only five survived and only one bore viable pollen, a fortunate circumstance because otherwise fruits would not have been produced. Later the French botanist Antoine Nicholas Duchesne, who was born in 1747 and died in 1827, planted *F. virginiana* along with *F. chiloensis* with the result that hybrids were produced that had the bisexual habit of *F. virginiana* and berries as large as those of *F. chiloensis*. Although the name was not applied until the twentieth century, these were the first of the group now identified as *F. ananassa*. Because of the pineapple fragrance of their fruits, they were called pine strawberries or fraisier-ananas. The first to approach modern varieties in size and quality of fruit, a variety named 'Keen's Seedling', raised in England in 1819, became the ancestor of modern varieties of Europe.

In America some garden planting of the native *F. virginiana* was done in the last two decades of the eighteenth century and limited commercial production of these started about 1800. Imported from England, 'Keen's Seedling' was popular from

1830 to 1840. The first hybrid to be raised artificially in America and the first great American variety, 'Hovey' was developed near Boston, Massachusetts, in 1834. Introduced twenty years later, 'Wilson', raised at Albany, New York, proved far more dependable as a market variety than 'Hovey' and made possible a remarkable and rapid expansion of the commercial growing of strawberries. From 1870 on, many new varieties were introduced. The first everbearing variety in America was discovered as a chance find in a planting in New York in 1898.

Adapted to a wider range of climate than any other temperate-region fruit, strawberries succeed practically throughout the continental United States, including Alaska. They need a sunny location, free circulation of air, and deep, fertile, well-drained, not excessively dry soil. Ground that lies wet throughout the winter will not do. Nor are very sandy or very clayey earths ideal, but by appropriate amelioration (deep spading, or its equivalent, and incorporating with them really generous amounts of compost or substitute decayed organic matter) these can be fitted for this crop. Although not very finicky about soil acidity or alkalinity, within reasonable bounds of course, strawberries are best suited for slightly acid ground. Soil capable of pro-

A strawberry plant in bloom

A strawberry plant in fruit

ducing good crops of most vegetables will grow strawberries.

Prepare the ground as suggested in the previous paragraph as well in advance of planting time as practicable, if it can be done, the previous fall for spring planting. If decayed manure is available, work that into the soil together with a dressing of superphosphate; if not, use a 5-10-5 or approximate equivalent fertilizer considered suitable for vegetables in your area.

Early spring is in most regions the best time to plant, but in areas of mild winters fall planting may be better. There are two chief systems, the hill method and the matted-row method, and two intermedi-

Strawberries planted in hills

ate ones. Because matted-rows produce a greater total weight of fruit from each acre and for each man-hour expended, commercial growers favor that plan or one of the intermediate methods. Hills, however, give more uniform crops of large fruits and better suit the needs of most home gardeners.

The hill system is effected by spacing plants 1 foot to 1½ feet apart in rows 2½ feet apart. Runners, except for a limited number that may be needed for propagation in anticipation of a new planting, are rigorously cut off as soon as they appear so that throughout the life of the bed the plants remain single, uncluttered individuals.

The matted-row system calls for setting plants 1½ to 2 feet apart in rows 3 to 4 feet from each other. Runners are left to grow undisturbed to form a mat or groundcover 1½ to 1¾ feet wide. Any that extend beyond this width are cut off when cultivating. Although this method is less demanding of labor than the hill system or the other systems now to be described, because of the strong competition between the plants an appreciable proportion of the berries are likely to be of less than first-class quality.

Intermediates between the hill and matted-row systems of planting are the hedgerow and spaced-bed methods. In the

first, plants are set 1¼ to 1½ feet apart in rows 2 to 2½ feet asunder. Each is permitted two runners. These are placed by hand so the young plants are in line with the mother plants. Alternatively, six runners are fanned out from the mother plant at angles of sixty degrees to the line of the row to create a wider row. All other runners are cut off. Spaced-beds are developed by setting plants 2 to 3 feet apart in rows 3½ to 4 feet apart and spacing the runners by hand to attain a uniform overall cover of plants about 8 inches apart over beds (strips) 1¼ to 2½ feet wide. Runners in excess of those needed to achieve this result are cut off promptly.

Set out only virus-free plants with an abundance of straw-colored or white, fibrous roots. Reject any with sparse, black roots. Good stock is obtainable from specialist nurseries or, if disease-free mother plants are available, easily raised at home. Immediately upon receipt from the nursery open the bundles and heel the plants in (plant them temporarily close together in a shallow trench) in a moist, shaded place. Should they be dry on arrival, soak them for an hour in water before heeling them in.

Plant with a trowel, or if two people are available, with a spade. One inserts the spade vertically into the ground and wiggles it back and forth to create a V-shaped opening into which the other spreads the roots. Correct depth is very important. Have the top of the crown of the plant exactly even with the finished level of the ground. As the spade is removed, use the foot to press the soil firmly against the roots so that not even a fairly strong tug will lift the plant from the ground.

A common mistake of impatient amateurs is to allow strawberries to fruit the first season. Except in Florida and other parts of the south where the crop is grown as an annual, it is very much better not to do this; instead, encourage them to become well established by relieving them of the added strain of producing fruits. To do this, remove all flowers as soon as they appear.

Weed control is of the highest importance. Throughout the existence of the planting never permit weeds to gain the upper hand. Frequent shallow surface cultivation supplemented with a little hand pulling close to the plants prevents this and at the same time encourages growth by preventing crusting of the soil and by admitting air and water. Except during the first season, cultivation is generally delayed until the main crop of berries is harvested, until then a mulch of straw, pine needles, or other suitable material that protects the berries from being splashed with soil serves to discourage weeds.

Watering during dry weather is essential for the best results. Strawberries, comparatively shallow rooted, soon suffer if the soil lacks moisture. Inadequate supplies during the developing and ripening period of the berries can easily reduce the crop by up to fifty percent or more. The equivalent of 1 inch of rain a week is an approximation of the water needs of this crop.

Harvesting strawberries, surely one of the most pleasant of gardening tasks, must be done with care. The fruits bruise easily and, improperly managed, soon deteriorate. As soon as possible after picking into small baskets, put them in a cellar or other cool, shaded place. During the season, a short one for regular varieties, more prolonged for everbearers, pick every other day or even every day. If at all possible avoid picking when the plants are wet.

After harvesting, refurbish sufficiently vigorous beds to be kept another year by cutting off old foliage, clearing away any weeds and small or unthrifty plants that crowd others, and, if gaps occur, positioning young runners to fill them.

Fertilizing established plantings should be delayed until after harvest. Earlier applications encourage the development of soft fruits, especially liable to rot, and are likely to decrease yields. Nitrogen in moderate amounts is the only element likely to be needed by soils properly prepared before planting, but no harm results and it may be more convenient for home gardeners to apply a complete fertilizer of a type used in vegetable gardens.

Winter protection is needed except in really mild climates. If neglected in regions of cold winters, the plants will be severely injured, as evidenced by reddened foliage, poor spring growth, and later wilting, and will ultimately die. This is the result of low temperatures and of the roots being damaged by alternate freezing and thawing.

Suitable winter mulches are wheat straw, pine needles, and salt hay. Rye and oat straws are also satisfactory, and if other materials are not available, newly fallen leaves, crushed corncobs, buckwheat hulls, or sawdust may be employed. Use enough to give, after the material has settled down, a layer 2 to 3 inches thick. Put the mulch on after the first two or three hard frosts and before the temperature drops to 20°F.

In spring, thin the mulch by raking some of it into the alleys between the beds, but leave enough to prevent the berries from being splashed, by rain or by watering, with soil, to conserve moisture and, to some extent at least, to discourage weeds.

Everbearing strawberries need somewhat different management. They are less robust and produce lighter crops and fewer runners than regular one-crop varieties. For them very fertile soil containing a high percentage of manure or rich compost is required. Plant in early spring in hills 1 foot to 1¼ feet apart.

Mulch with straw, sawdust, crushed corncobs, or buckwheat hulls, and keep all runners, except any needed after midsummer for propagation, cut off. To encourage the highest yield of late fruits pick off all flowers that develop before early July. If the plants are kept well watered in dry weather, harvesting will continue from early to mid-August until frost. Best results are had by treating everbearing varieties as annuals, setting out new plants each spring and discarding them when the harvest is completed.

Novelty methods of growing strawberries in home gardens include planting in barrels, decorative strawberry jars, and in pyramids, all of which can produce satisfactory results. For the first, obtain a strong wooden barrel. Bore holes, 2½ inches in diameter and spaced about 1 foot apart in a staggered pattern with the lowest ones a foot from the bottom, in the sides of the barrel, and a few holes for drainage in its bottom.

Stand the barrel on a few bricks to raise it 3 inches or so above the ground or, if you prefer, on a stout wooden platform fitted with castors so that it can be turned weekly to give the plants equal exposure to sun.

Assure drainage by placing 3 or 4 inches of broken bricks, gravel, crushed stone, or similar material in the bottom of the barrel and over that a layer of straw or leaves to prevent soil clogging the drainage. Then, to assure interior drainage, in the center of the barrel stand vertically a cylinder made of hardware cloth (heavy wire screening), 4 to 6 inches in diameter and long enough to reach to within 7 to 8 inches of the barrel's rim. Fill this with gravel, broken brick or suchlike material. Then around the cylinder fill the rest of the barrel with porous soil fortified with rich compost or rotted manure, and, at the rate of 6 ounces to each bushel, bonemeal. As this work proceeds, position the plants by pushing them through the holes and pack the soil firmly about their roots. Cover the top of the drainage core with a slate or hardware cloth and over that fill in with soil to within 2 inches of the rim. Then set a few plants to furnish the entire top of the barrel.

Decorative earthenware strawberry jars have planting pockets fashioned in their sides. Prepare them for planting in the same way as barrels and set one plant in each pocket and enough on the top surface of the soil to assure a covering.

Pyramids are made of three or four rings (short cylinders about 9 inches deep) of aluminum, zinc, or other suitable material, the largest 6 to 8 feet in diameter, the others decreased successively by 2 feet. The biggest is placed on the ground and filled with fertile soil. The next smallest is placed on top of the platform of soil so formed and itself is filled with soil. This procedure

is repeated until the smallest ring, 3 feet in diameter, forms the top tier. Set strawberry plants about 1 foot apart in the circular terraces of soil and to cover the top of the smallest circle. Ready-to-assemble kits to form pyramids are sold by dealers in horticultural supplies. These come with a hose connection that serves a centrally installed spray for watering and can be fitted with a net to afford protection from birds.

Varieties of strawberries are numerous, and new ones are frequently introduced. Because of this, and because varieties best suited for particular gardens differ according to region, none are listed here. Consult local experts, such as Cooperative Extension Agents, or follow the recommendations of your State Agricultural Experiment Station.

Alpine strawberries (*Fragaria vesca sempervirens*) and hautbois strawberries or frais de bois (*F. moschata*) are sometimes grown as novelties. Natives of Europe, these bear small, fragrant, exquisitely flavored fruits over a long season, but if the ground becomes dry, berry production is likely to be interrupted. These sorts respond to the same general cultivation as garden strawberries. There are a few varieties, some of which produce runners, others not. Of the former, 'Cresta' is one of the best. Runnerless 'Baron Solemacher' is popular. White fruits are borne by 'Bush White' on plants without runners. Runnerless sorts are propagated by seed.

Pests and diseases of strawberries are fairly numerous, but not all are probable in any one garden. When confronted with such troubles the best plan is to consult regional authorities, such as State Agricultural Experiment Stations and Cooperative Extension Agents. Birds can be troublesome, damaging the ripening fruits. The only effective means of checking this is to cover the beds with netting. Grubs of a number of insects, including the Japanese beetle, feed on strawberry roots. The strawberry weevil partially bites off the stalks of the flowers and lays eggs in the buds. The larvae of the strawberry crown borer feed on the crowns and roots of the plants. Other pests include aphids, mites, and nematodes.

The most serious disease is red stele, which causes marked stunting and dying. Roots of affected plants have red cores. Other diseases include botrytis or gray mold, which causes the fruits to rot, strawberry leaf spot, verticillium wilt, and virus diseases.

STRAWBERRY JARS. These are round, large-mouthed containers, usually of unglazed or glazed pottery, suitable for ornamenting steps, terraces, and other places. Taller than flower pots, with tops of the same diameter, they have bellied sides with several pocket-like openings.

A strawberry jar

Streblus brunoniana pendula

Strelitzia reginae

After the jars are filled with soil, strawberries or such low ornamentals as sedums are planted in the pockets and across their tops.

STRAWBERRY-RASPBERRY is *Rubus illecebrosus.*

STRAWBERRY-TOMATO. See the Encyclopedia entry Husk-Tomato, Strawberry-Tomato, and Ground-Cherry.

STRAWFLOWER is *Helichrysum bracteatum.*

STREBLUS (Stréb-lus) The genus *Streblus,* of the mulberry family MORACEAE, consists of twenty-two species and inhabits southwest Asia, Indo-Malaysia, and Malagasy (Madagascar). The name, from the Greek *streblos,* twisted, alludes to the distorted branches of some kinds.

The sorts of *Streblus* are alternate-leaved trees and shrubs containing milky sap. The flowers are unisexual with the sexes on the same or separate plants, the females solitary or in groups of up to four, the males in heads or spikes. They have four sepals, the males, four stamens, and the females a style with long branches. The fruits are berries.

An evergreen bush or tree up to 45 feet tall, *S. asper* has nearly stalkless, elliptic to obovate, slightly-toothed, rough-surfaced leaves 1 inch to 5 inches long. Fragrant, white or greenish flowers are borne, males and females on the same plant. The females have long stalks, the males are in small, solitary or paired, globular heads. The yellow or orange fruits, about ⅓ inch in diameter, contain one seed and sweet, edible pulp. In parts of the Orient the leaves of this species are used like sandpaper for polishing ivory and wood; paper is made from the bark. Less commonly cultivated, *S. brunoniana pendula* (syn. *Pseudomorus brunoniana pendula*), as known in gardens, is a quite handsome evergreen shrub with leathery, dark green, broad-

lanceolate leaves from 3 to 5 inches in length. Male specimens bear drooping, slender, tail-like spikes, up to 1¼ feet long, of tiny creamy flowers. It is a native of Norfolk Island.

Garden and Landscape Uses and Cultivation. These are attractive general-purpose furnishings for gardens in the tropics and warm subtropics and for growing in ground beds and containers in large greenhouses and conservatories. They thrive in well-drained, fertile soil kept moderately moist and respond to moderate fertilization. They are propagated by cuttings and by seed.

STREET TREES. See Trees.

STRELITZIA (Strel-ítzia)—Bird-of-Paradise. By some botanists this group of five species of South African plants is placed in the strelitzia family STRELITZIACEAE, by others it is included in the banana family MUSACEAE. Its most familiar member, the common bird-of-paradise (*Strelitzia reginae*), is much admired as a warm-climate, outdoor plant and for growing in greenhouses. An entirely unrelated plant, *Caesalpinia pulcherrima,* is also called bird-of-paradise. The name *Strelitzia* honors King George III of England's Queen Charlotte Sophia, Duchess of Mecklenburg-Strelitz.

Strelitzias are evergreen, herbaceous or woody-trunked perennials with fans of two-ranked, often slightly glaucous, bluish-green leaves that have undivided blades or, in one variety, are often bladeless. Their flowers are grouped in unusual-structured heads of striking appearance. These are often called flowers, but actually each consists of several blooms that open in succession from the top of a large, stiff, pointed, boat-shaped spathe consisting of one or two bracts. The blooms are bisexual and very asymmetrical. They have three long-pointed, conspicuously-displayed, narrowly-lanceolate, separate sepals, and three petals,

two of which are joined to form an arrow-shaped tongue and one of which is smaller. The five stamens and three-branched style lie in a groove of the tongue. The fruits are many-seeded capsules.

The common bird-of-paradise (*S. reginae* syn. *S. parvifolia*) is trunkless. Its

paddle-shaped leaves, with blades 9 inches to 1½ feet long by 4 to 6 inches wide, rise from the rhizomes to a height of 2½ to 4 feet or sometimes more. They are equaled by the stiff flower stalks, each topped by a head of blooms that suggests some large and gaily-colored tropical bird. Beak and head are represented by the often red-edged, green spathe, from the top of which sprout, like the crest of a glorious cockatoo, brilliant orange-yellow sepals and rich purple-blue petals, both about 3 inches long. The entire structure is 6 to 8 inches long. This species is somewhat variable and several varieties have been named, including *S. r. humilis,* which is dwarfer than the typical kind. Of unusual appearance, *S. r. juncea* (syns. *S. parvifolia juncea, S. juncea*) is remarkable because its leaves either have very small, narrowly-lanceolate or spatula-shaped blades or none. In the latter case the plant consists of a cluster of rigid, erect,

Strelitzia reginae juncea

Strelitzia reginae juncea (head of flowers)

sharply-pointed, reedlike leafstalks, and flowering stalks. From 3 to 4 feet in height, this has yellow-and-purple flowers.

White-and-blue or white flowers characterize the other cultivated strelitzias. Noblest in size is **S. nicolai,** which has a trunk up to 25 feet tall with 6-foot-long leaves fanned from its upper part and reaching still higher. The bases of its leaf blades are rounded. The blue-and-white flowers arise from big reddish chestnut spathes. The flower heads are short-stalked and nestle in the axils of the upper leaves.

Strelitzia nicolai

Strelitzia nicolai (head of flowers)

Similar, but with a trunk not over 18 feet high, with leaves with heart-shaped bases, and with all-white blooms, is **S. alba** (syn. *S. augusta*). Hybrid **S. kewensis,** intermediate between its parents *S. alba* and *S. reginae,* may have a trunk up to 5 feet high. Its flowers have pale yellow sepals and petals with lilac-pink markings.

Garden and Landscape Uses. These extraordinary plants, handsome in flower and foliage, provide strong elements in the landscape and lend a distinctly tropical appearance to it. This is especially true of giant *S. nicolai* and *S. alba,* which possess something of the aspect of the traveler's tree (*Ravenala*) or of bananas (*Musa*). The lower-growing, yellow-and-blue flowered kinds have the most showy blooms and, unlike the others, are sources of long-lasting and very beautiful cut flowers.

Strelitzias can be grown permanently outdoors only in warm climates where little or no frost is experienced. They can also be displayed to good effect in greenhouses. The larger ones are especially effective in large conservatories and look and grow well when associated with succulents and, under more humid conditions, with lusher tropical and subtropical plants. In greenhouses strelitzias succeed in ground beds and in large pots or tubs. They are often tried as houseplants, but unless conditions favor the production of strong growth and the plants can be accommodated in big containers, they are unlikely to prove especially good for that purpose. Specimens not sufficiently vigorous to bloom may linger for years.

Cultivation. For their best growth, strelitzias require deep, loamy, well-drained, fertile soil that does not lack for moisture, but is not wet, and full sunlight. They are gross feeders. Well-rooted specimens respond to generous applications of dilute liquid fertilizer, especially when making new leaf growth.

In greenhouses night temperatures in winter of 50 to 55°F are adequate. At other seasons they may be higher, and at all times day temperatures may exceed night ones by five to fifteen degrees. Repotting of large plants is needed at intervals of several years only. Young specimens are likely to need more frequent attention. Potting is best done in spring. Then, too, is the time to secure increase by the removal of rooted suckers or by division. Seeds give satisfactory results, but it takes several years for seedlings to attain blooming size. In nature these plants are pollinated by birds. If seeds are needed from cultivated plants it is necessary to hand pollinate the flowers. The seeds are often beautifully colored.

STREPTANTHERA (Strept-ánthera). The only two species of *Streptanthera,* of the iris family IRIDACEAE, are natives of South Africa. By some botanists they are included

in related *Sparaxis.* The name, alluding to the characteristically twisted anthers, is derived from the Greek *streptos,* twisted, and *anthera,* an anther.

Streptantheras have corms (bulblike organs similar to those of crocuses and gladioluses) and fans of all-basal, two-ranked leaves. The flowers, in spikes of five or less, have short-tubed, broadly-funnel-shaped perianths of three petal-like sepals and three petals. There are three stamens with spirally-twisted anthers and a three-branched style. The fruits are capsules.

From 8 inches to 1 foot tall, **S. cuprea** has fans of five to nine leaves 3 to 6 inches

Streptanthera cuprea

long by up to ¼ inch wide or a little wider. Branchless, the flowering stalks have four or fewer 2-inch-wide flowers, coppery-pink, sometimes paling to pink as they age, cross-banded with black, and with a purple throat. The dark purple anthers are not longer than the style. Variety *S. c. coccinea* has bright orange blooms with a blackish-purple center. From the last species and its variety, **S. elegans** differs in its stems, often forked near the base, slightly overtopping the leaves. Its flowers, one or two to a stalk, are nearly or quite white with a yellow throat cross-banded with purple.

Garden and Landscape Uses and Cultivation. These are as for *Ixia.*

STREPTHANTHUS. See Caulanthus.

STREPTOCALYX (Strepto-cályx). Closely related to *Aechmea,* the genus *Streptocalyx,* of the bromeliad family BROMELIACEAE, consists of some fourteen species, natives of tropical South America. Its name, alluding to a feature of the flowers, comes from the Greek *streptos,* twisted, and *kalyx,* a calyx.

Streptocalyxes are epiphytes (tree-perchers), sometimes very large, that in the wild commonly occupy the higher branches of trees in torrid, humid forests. Typically they form crowded rosettes of more or less strap-shaped, spiny-margined leaves. The violet to blue-violet flowers, accompanied by bright rose-pink to red bracts, are in erect, usually short-stalked or stalkless spikes or panicles. The fruits are berries.

Sorts cultivated include these: *S. furstenbergii* has a crowded rosette of thirty to forty dull green, channeled leaves margined with small, curved spines and 2 to 2½ feet long by about 3 inches wide toward the base. The sturdy, pink-bracted flower spike, 1 foot to 1½ feet long, does not fully emerge from the center of the rosette. *S. longifolius* has somewhat the aspect of the last, but its usually more numerous leaves are up to about 4 feet in length and scarcely exceed 1 inch in width. Also, the flower spike is shorter, generally not over 6 inches long. It has rusty-red bracts and white flowers. *S. poeppigii* has a rosette of very spiny green leaves, 1½ to 2 feet long by 1½ inches wide, penciled with gray lines on their undersides. The showy, somewhat loose flower spike, 1 foot to 1½ feet long, may show a tendency to droop. The white fruits remain attractive for a very long period. *S. poitaei* is not unlike *S. poeppigii*. It has a rosette of well-armed leaves up to 3 feet long and 1½ inches wide and a very showy flower spike with rose-red bracts and blue flowers. *S. williamsii* develops a rosette 3 to 4 feet in diameter of glossy, bright green leaves margined with small, sharp spines. In stout, conical spikes up to nearly 1½ feet tall, the blue-petaled flowers are accompanied by long-lasting, bright rose-pink, overlapping bracts.

Garden and Landscape Uses and Cultivation. These are as for *Vriesea*.

STREPTOCARPUS (Strepto-cárpus)—Cape-Primrose. As is true of many genera of the gesneria family GESNERIACEAE, the genus *Streptocarpus* attracted greatly increased attention from gardeners from the middle of the twentieth century on. Largely fostered by the American Gloxinia and Gesneriad Society, this popularity resulted in a number of species formerly not cultivated being made available. In addition, there are many hybrids. Predominantly natives of East Africa, South Africa, West Africa, and Malagasy (Madagascar), the more than 130 species include four native in Asia, none of which is cultivated, or discussed here. The name alludes to the manner in which the mature seed capsules rupture and twist into tight spirals. It derives from the Greek *streptos*, twisted, and *karpos*, fruit. The vernacular name Cape-primrose, rarely used except in literature, is not very appropriate. Except perhaps for the foliage of a few kinds, streptocarpuses have no likeness to primroses.

Streptocarpuses are nonhardy, stemmed or stemless herbaceous perennials or, more rarely, subshrubs or annuals. The leaves of the stemmed kinds are nearly always opposite. The stemless kinds have several leaves in tufts or rosettes or, some kinds, only one leaf. The flowers, one to many on leafless stalks from among the basal leaves or from the axils of stem leaves, have small calyxes of five linear lobes (sepals) and a long, cylindrical-tubed corolla ending in a two-lipped face of five more or less unequal, rounded lobes (petals). There are two fertile stamens and sometimes two or three staminodes (non-functional stamens). The fruits are slender, linear capsules.

The first recorded blooming of a streptocarpus in cultivation was that of *S. rexii*, at the Royal Botanic Gardens, Kew, England, in 1827. Almost thirty years passed before another species was brought to Europe and somewhat longer before the first hybrid, between *S. gardenii* and *S. polyanthus*, was raised. The ancestry of modern hybrids, however, does not stem back that far. It begins with crosses made at Kew after 1886, when *S. dunnii* first flowered there. This, mated with *S. rexii*, *S. parviflorus*, *S. wendlandii*, and other species, and back-crossed on *S. rexii* at Kew and elsewhere in England, gave rise to the complex group of hybrids now designated *S. hybridus* and culminating in 'Merton Giant', 'Constant Nymph', and varieties raised from the last. Except among fanciers of

Streptocarpus hybridus variety

Streptocarpus hybridus 'Constant Nymph'

gesneriads (plants of the gesneria family) variants of *S. hybridus* are the only streptocarpuses much cultivated. But gesneriad enthusiasts are numerous in America, and it is recorded that in 1972 about fifty species were being grown by them. The most important are described here.

Tufts or rosettes of essentially all-basal leaves are characteristic of the following species, natives of Africa: *S. candidus* has a brief vertical rhizome and many round-toothed leaves up to 2 feet long by 8 inches wide, their veins beneath often reddish. The 1½-inch-long, honey-scented flowers, up to twenty-five on a stalk, many open at one time, are white or bluish-white with a yellow stripe, streaked and spotted with violet on the bottom of the corolla tube, and with two violet-colored chevrons at the bottom of the lower lip. *S. cyanandrus* has tufts of leaves up to 6 inches long by 2 inches wide. The flowers, magenta-pink to blue, are 1 inch to 1½ inches long. *S. cyaneus*, allied to *S. rexii*, has a horizontal rhizome and round-toothed leaves up to 1¼ feet long by one-quarter as broad. One or two or sometimes up to six or more on each flowering stalk, the funnel-shaped blooms have 1-inch-long corolla tubes. They are white to purple or pink, with a yellow streak in the throat usually flanked by streaks of violet or reddish-violet that extend into the petals. *S. fanniniae* has creeping, rooting stemlike parts that, in the wild, may extend for hundreds of feet along the ground or cascade down cliffs. The round-toothed, oblongish leaves are up to 3 feet long by 9 inches wide. The flowering stalks, erect and up to 3 feet in height, have many honey-scented blooms open at one time. In color from nearly pure white to blue, with the upper parts of the blooms darker colored than the lower, the flowers are 1 inch to 1½ inches long. They have two longitudinal ridges along the floor of the corolla tube. These, often yellow, are spotted, streaked, or striped with violet. *S. gardenii* has a brief, erect rhizome and a rosette of strap-shaped, round-toothed leaves, up to 1 foot long by 3 inches broad and sometimes reddish beneath. Usually carrying one or two or sometimes up to six blooms, the flowering stalks are up to 6 inches tall. The flowers, more definitely two-lipped than those of its close ally *S. rexii*, with greenish corolla tubes with their mouths compressed downward, are predominantly lilac to pale violet with darker center lines on the upper lip and broken ones on the lower. *S. johannis* has a horizontal rhizome, and many leaves, up to almost 1¼ feet long by 4 inches broad, clothed with short hairs. The flowering stalks, 6 inches to 1 foot tall and mostly two- to six-flowered, are sometimes more prolific. The lavender-violet blooms, 1¼ to 1½ inches long, are whitish to pale lavender-violet, in their throats white or yellowish, the petals with darker violet mid-veins. The stigma has two lateral lobes. *S. kentaniensis* has many narrowly-strap-shaped to lanceolate leaves up to 8 inches long. They have very prominent mid-veins

Streptocarpus kentaniensis

and toothed margins. The flower stalks are two- to five-flowered. Approximately 1 inch long, the flowers are pale violet or lavender, with purple in the throat. *S. montanus* develops creeping, rooting rhizomes prominently marked with corky old leaf scars. Its blunt-elliptic leaves, up to 1 foot long by somewhat over one-half as wide but generally much smaller, are in tufts at the rhizome ends. The slender flowering stalks, up to 1 foot in height, bear loose clusters of pale to medium pink-violet blooms approximately ½ inch long, glandular-pubescent on their outsides, and with seven to nine violet stripes along the floor of the corolla. *S. montigena,* intermediate in characteristics between *S. rexii* and *S. meyeri,* may be a natural hybrid between those species. It has a short, erect rhizome and quite flat rosettes of glandular-hairy, round-toothed leaves up to 1 foot long by one-third as broad. The two- to twelve-bloomed flowering stalks, up to 8 inches long, carry violet, cream-colored, and yellow, funnel-shaped blooms, hairy on their outsides and 1½ to 2 inches long. *S. parviflorus* is the smallest flowered of the kinds closely allied to *S. rexii.* Like that species it has horizontal rhizomes, rosettes of long, strap-shaped leaves, and funnel-shaped blooms with three to seven purple lines along the floor of the corolla. The leaves, up to 1½ feet long by 3½ inches broad, are round-toothed. As many as twenty blooms may be borne on each flowering stalk, many open together. About 1 inch long, they are white, sometimes tinged violet, with a basal bar of yellow in the throat and the purple streaks previously mentioned. *S. primulifolius* is related to *S. rexii.* It has a stout horizontal rhizome and rosettes of hairy leaves up to 1½ feet long by 4½ inches wide. The one-, two-, or rarely up to four-bloomed flow-

ering stalks are nearly 1 foot long. The blooms, 2½ to 4 inches long, are pale bluish-violet marked with deep violet and with fine reddish-purple lines. The flowers of *S. p. formosus* (syn. *S. insignis*) have the corolla tube spotted with violet-purple and on the inside a yellow zone that laps onto the lower lip, which has purple-spotted veins. The corolla lobes are whitish, margined with violet. *S. prolixus* (syn. *S. gracilis*) has tufts of two or three round-toothed leaves up to 9 inches long by 6 inches wide. The flower stalks, stouter than those of related *S. polyanthus,* about 8 inches

Streptocarpus primulifolius formosus

Streptocarpus prolixus

tall, carry blooms a little over 1 inch long, that are medium violet to nearly white, with usually yellow in the throat. *S. rexii,* without or almost without rhizomes, has many strap-shaped, round-toothed, blunt leaves, up to 1 foot long by 2½ inches wide, with short hairs on both surfaces. The blooms, 1½ to 3 inches long, whitish to pale violet outside and whitish with seven longitudinal violet stripes inside, are usually one or two or sometimes up to six on flowering stalks up to 8 inches in length. *S. silvaticus* has two to five round-toothed leaves up to 4½ inches long by about 2½ inches wide. The flower stalks, about 6 inches long, have about ten 1½-inch-long pale violet blooms patterned with impressed lines, and a yellow-green throat.

Kinds with obvious stems bearing opposite leaves, without basal rosettes or tufts of foliage include the following: *S. caulescens,* 6 inches to 2 feet tall, has hairy, fleshy stems swollen at the nodes, and short-stalked, elliptic to ovate leaves, quite densely hairy on both surfaces, 1½ to 3 inches long by approximately one-half as broad. Profusely produced, its violet-purple blooms are in sprays, often branched, from the upper leaf axils. The blooms are ½ to ¾ inch long. *S. c. pallescens* has paler flowers. *S. glandulosissimus* (syn. *S. ruwenzoriensis*) has weak, straggling stems, hairy at first, hairless except at the swollen nodes later. The shortish-stalked, elliptic leaves of each pair are unequal in size. They have blades 1¼ to 4½ inches long by 1 inch to 2 inches wide. The rich violet to violet-blue flowers are 1 inch long or slightly longer. *S. hilsenbergii,* 6 inches to 2 feet in height and endemic to Malagasy (Madagascar), has somewhat woody-based, usually densely-hairy stems. Its ovate to elliptic, rarely elliptic-lanceolate, toothed, more or less hairy leaves have blades ¾ inch to 2¼ inches long. On stalks from the leaf axils, each with one to several blooms, the flowers range from light violet to bright red marked with darker patches and sometimes white. They are 1 inch to 2 inches long. *S. h. angustifolius* has narrow-elliptic leaves. *S. holstii,* of East African rain forests, has erect, branching stems up to 1½ feet tall. From *S. caulescens,* to which it is

Streptocarpus rexii

Streptocarpus holstii

Streptocarpus holstii (flowers)

allied, it differs in its more slender stems with thicker nodes, its much more sparsely-hairy foliage, and its larger, 1-inch-long, white-throated, bright blue flowers. **S. kirkii,** a native of East Africa, has slender, erect to straggling stems 6 inches to over 1 foot long and broad-ovate to nearly round leaves 1 inch to 2 inches long. The pale lilac, sometimes darker-spotted, pendulous blooms from the upper leaf axils, are ½ inch long or slightly longer. Up to ten together on stalks 3 to 4 inches in length, they are glandular-hairy outside. **S. saxorum,** an East African, has sprawling, few-

Streptocarpus kirkii

Streptocarpus saxorum

branched stems up to 2 feet long, when young hairy, especially at the nodes, with fleshy, elliptic to ovate leaves ¾ inch to 1¼ inches long, hairy above, less conspicuously so below, and crowded near their tips. The flowers are solitary or in pairs on 3-inch-long stalks from the leaf axils. They have ½-inch-long corolla tubes, chalk-white outside, white in the throat. The petals are pale violet. **S. stomandrus,** of East Africa, with rather straggly stems about 1 foot long, is well suited for hanging baskets. Its leaves are opposite, short-stalked, elliptic, and round-toothed. Those of each pair are of slightly different size. The attractive lavender-pink flowers are paired at the branch ends of loose sprays that come from the leaf axils. They are about 1¼ inches long.

Plants mostly with one leaf that die after they flower once, usually taking a year to a year and one-half from seed sowing to blooming, but sometimes longer, include species now to be considered. Where any vary from this pattern, mention is made of the fact. **S. confusus** has a leaf up to 1 foot long by approximately one-half as broad, usually reddish-purple beneath and with round-toothed margins. The about 1-foot-long flower stalks carry up to thirty-six flowers up to 1 inch long, pale to medium violet with white or pale yellow throats. The blooms of *S. c. lebomboensis* are up to 2 inches long. **S. cooksonii** differs from other species in that the lower petals of its flowers are white margined with deep purple, the upper ones purple. There is no yellow in the throat. Its leaf, up to 1¼ feet long and nearly one-half as wide, has round-toothed margins. The very stout flower stalks, 4 to 5 inches long, carry

Streptocarpus cooksonii

Streptocarpus cooksonii (flowers)

crowded blooms 1 inch to 1½ inches long. **S. cooperi,** closely related to *S. grandis,* has a leaf up to over 2 feet long and as wide as long. The flower stalks may be 2 feet long. They carry narrowly-trumpet-shaped, violet flowers, 2 to 2½ inches in length, marked with white on the bottom of the corolla tube and lip. **S. daviesii** is a perennial producing one leaf each year. The leaf is 10 inches long by 7 inches wide, its margins round-toothed. The flower stalks, about 4 inches long, carry pale to medium violet or rarely pink or white blooms with yellow-blotched, white throats. They are nearly 2 inches long. **S. dunnii** is of historic significance because of the part it has played in the parentage of many hybrids. Sometimes perennial and with multiple leaves, when single-leaved the leaf is occasionally up to 3 feet long by 7 inches wide, but usually considerably smaller. It

Streptocarpus dunnii

has coarsely-round-toothed margins. There are many blooms open at once. The flower stalks, up to 8 inches tall, bear pink to brick-red or crimson, funnel-shaped blooms about 1½ inches long. *S. erubescens* has a leaf often much smaller than its maximum of about 6 inches long by somewhat less wide. The two or three flower stalks, up to about 4 inches tall, bear few pink-flushed, white blooms approximately 1½ inches long. *S. eylesii* usually has one ir-regularly-toothed leaf up to 1 foot long by two-thirds as broad. Occasionally it has more than one leaf and is perennial. Car-ried to heights of up to 1 foot, the violet-purple blooms are 1½ to 2¼ inches long. They have sometimes a pale yellow patch in their white throats. *S. galpinii* is some-times perennial and has one to several leaves. They range from 1 inch to 6 inches long by one-half to nearly as wide. The funnel-shaped flowers, which vary con-siderably in color, but most often mauve with white throats, are ½ to 1 inch long by up to 1½ inches across their faces. *S. grandis* has a heart-shaped leaf up to 1¼ feet long by approximately 1 foot wide. Its flowers are carried on many stems to heights of 1¼ feet. They are 1 inch to 2 inches long, of variable color from pure white to medium violet or sometimes pinkish, and have cylindrical corolla tubes scarcely flared upward. There is usually a yellow or white stripe on the bottom of the corolla tube. *S. haygarthii,* closely related to *S. confusus,* is very variable. It has a wavy-edged, round-toothed, ovate leaf up to 1¼ feet long by somewhat less wide and often purplish on its underside. The up to nearly forty blooms are on flower stalks that may exceed 1 foot in length. From ¾ inch to nearly 2 inches long, the flowers are co-balt-violet to white. *S. michelmorei* has a more or less heart-shaped leaf up to a little over 1 foot long by almost as wide. The flowers, 1¼ to 2 inches long, are medium violet with a deep violet patch in the throat and a band of yellow behind it. Many blooms are open at once. *S. micranthus* has a wavy-margined, round-toothed leaf 2 to 6 inches long by approximately three-quarters as broad and often purplish be-neath. Slender and up to 6 inches long, the flower stalks carry many ¼-inch-long, cupped, white blooms. *S. molweniensis* has a leaf up to about 2 feet long by over one-half as wide. The flower stalks, up to about 6 inches tall, have few blooms open at one time. The flowers, white suffused with pale violet, are 1¼ to over 2 inches long. *S. po-lyanthus,* which sometimes has two or three leaves, is sometimes perennial. Its light green to gray-green leaves are up to 10 inches in length by about 6 inches in width. Their edges are round-toothed. Usually much shorter than their maximum of 10 inches, the flower stalks have blooms from a little over ½ inch to 1¾ inches long. They are pale violet, with a whitish, chalky

Streptocarpus polyanthus

underlay, to greenish-white. *S. pusillus* has a toothed, ruffled leaf, up to 9 inches in length by 6 inches wide, and often one or two leaves on the stalk just beneath the flower stalk. The numerous blooms, on

Streptocarpus pusillus

stalks up to 4½ inches high, are white and slightly over ½ inch long. *S. rimicola* much resembles the last. Its leaf is up to 2½ inches long by up to 2 inches wide. It has slightly smaller flowers that differ from those of *S. pusillus* in technical details only. *S. saundersii* is a handsome kind with a round-toothed leaf, often rich purple-red on its underside, up to 1½ feet long by 10 inches wide. The flower stalks, up to 1 foot tall, bear violet to pale violet or white blooms about 1½ inches long with, in their throats, a yellow stripe and two violet blotches. *S. solenanthus* belongs in the *S. cooperi* relationship. It has an ovate or ob-long leaf usually not over 6 inches long by 5 inches wide and often smaller, but oc-casionally more than twice as long and up to 6 inches wide. The 1- to 1½-inch-long blooms are violet to white and on stalks up to 6 inches long. *S. vandeleurii* has a nearly heart-shaped, round-toothed, quilted leaf up to 1 foot long and broad. Many of its wide-mouthed, strongly down-curved flowers, on stout stalks about 1 foot tall,

open at one time. A little over 2 inches long by about 1½ inches wide, they are creamy-white with a greenish-yellow blotch at the bottom of the lower lip. *S. wendlandii* has been much used in hybridizing. It has a

Streptocarpus wendlandii

leaf up to nearly 2 feet long by three-quar-ters as wide, its lower surface rich purple-red. The flowers, somewhat resembling those of *S. saundersii,* have narrower co-rolla tubes up to 2 inches long. Many are open at one time on stalks approximately 1 foot tall. They are of a medium violet hue with two darker blotches in the throat bordering a white stripe along the bottom of the corolla tubes. *S. wilmsii* is usually single-leaved and sometimes perennial. Round-toothed, the leaf is up to 10 inches long by 7 inches wide. The undersurface is paler than the light green upper one. Many of the about twenty-five blooms on each flower stalk are open at one time. They are fragrant, 1 inch to 1½ inches long, and white sometimes tinged with blue-vi-olet with a yellow stripe and purple spots and streaks in the throat.

Garden Uses. Streptocarpuses are pri-marily indoor plants grown in green-houses and sometimes in terrariums and elsewhere indoors with or without the use of artificial lights. The better ones are de-lightfully decorative and all appeal to the many modern gardeners who are espe-cially interested in gesneriads (plants of the gesneria family GESNERIACEAE). As a group streptocarpuses are not difficult to man-age. They need conditions akin to those that satisfy African-violets.

Cultivation. Propagation is easy by seed and, the perennials, by division and leaf cuttings. The seeds must be carefully sown in sandy, peaty soil. Because they are very small they need only a very light cover-ing of soil. A temperature of 60 to 70°F is suitable for germination. Streptocarpuses appreciate rather loose, fertile soil that contains a generous amount of leaf mold, peat moss, or other agreeable decayed or-ganic material. It must be kept evenly

Streptocarpus 'Constant Nymph'

Stenoglottis longifolia

Streptosolen jamesonii

Stewartia pseudocamellia (trunk)

Stifftia chrysantha

Streptocarpus hybrid

Stylophorum diphyllum

Steriphoma paradoxum

moist, but not saturated for long periods. A fairly humid, but not dank atmosphere suits. Some shade from strong sun is necessary, but not more than is required to prevent the foliage from scorching. It is very helpful to keep the pots containing streptocarpuses standing on a bed of cinders, sand, gravel, or other such material that can be kept moist. The moisture rising from such a stratum greatly benefits the plants. In winter a night temperature of 55°F is favorable. This should increase during the day, in proportion to the brightness of the weather, by from five to fifteen degrees. Summer temperatures may be higher. From babyhood streptocarpuses are transferred to successively bigger pots. Take care not to place them in containers too large. Most kinds are satisfactory when bloomed in 4- or 5-inch or at most 6-inch pots. Those that make large single leaves may be given bigger ones. When the final pots, the ones in which the plants are to bloom, become fairly well filled with roots, applications of dilute liquid fertilizer made at seven- to ten-day intervals will be of benefit.

The most common pests are red spider mites, mealybugs, and whiteflies.

STREPTOPUS (Strép-topus)—Twisted-Stalk. Both the common and botanical names of *Streptopus* refer to the twisted flower stalks of some kinds. The latter is from the Greek *streptos*, twisted, and *pous*, a foot. There are ten species, natives of North America, Europe, and Asia. They belong to the lily family LILIACEAE.

Streptopuses are hardy herbaceous perennials with horizontal rootstocks and erect, forking stems. They have alternate, stalkless or stem-clasping, pointed, elliptic to ovate, thin leaves with many parallel, longitudinal veins. The little bell- or wheel-shaped blooms, solitary or in pairs from the leaf axils, have six nearly similar perianth segments (petals or, more correctly, tepals), six stamens with short, flat stalks, and a slender, sometimes forked style. The fruits are berries.

Inhabiting rich, moist woodlands over much of North America, and occurring in Greenland, Europe, and Asia, *S. amplexifolius* is variable, and by some botanists several varieties are recognized. From 1½ to 3½ feet tall, it has hairless stems and ovate-oblong to ovate-lanceolate, stem-clasping leaves 2½ to 4½ inches long by up to 2½ inches wide and finely-toothed or toothless. The jointed flower stalks bear one or sometimes two nodding, ½-inch-long, greenish-white, bell-shaped blooms with reflexed petals. The usually ellipsoid berries are red and about ½ inch long.

With rose-pink or purplish flowers, and native from Labrador to Minnesota, North Carolina, and Michigan, and in western Canada, *S. roseus* is 1 foot to 2½ feet tall. It has branched or branchless stems that are finely-hairy, especially at the nodes. The stalkless, but not stem-clasping leaves are lanceolate to ovate-lanceolate, finely-hairy at their edges, and 2 to 4 inches long by up to 1½ inches wide. The flowers, nodding and solitary on jointed stalks nearly ½ inch long, are narrowly-bell-shaped with spreading petals. Nearly spherical, the red fruits are slightly under ½ inch long.

Quite distinct, *S. streptopoides* is indigenous to western North America, Japan, and eastern Siberia. From the kinds described above it differs in having wheel-shaped, pink or red flowers, with extremely short styles, on stalks that are not jointed. This has branchless or few-branched stems 6 inches to 1 foot tall and ovate-oblong leaves 1¾ to 3½ inches long that are stalkless, but not stem-clasping. The solitary, ¼-inch-wide flowers are pendulous. The berries are spherical and red. Variety *S. s. japonicus* is more robust. In *S. s. atrocarpus* the fruits are black.

Garden and Landscape Uses and Cultivation. Twisted-stalks are for moistish, woodland soils and lightly shaded locations. They are seen to best advantage in naturalistic surroundings, and, although their displays are modest, they have certain elegance and are worth planting for variety. In locations adapted to them they give little or no trouble. They are very easily increased by division, and by seed removed from ripe berries and sown immediately in a cold frame or protected, shaded place where they will not be disturbed outdoors. The seed soil must be kept evenly moist.

STREPTOSOLEN (Streptosò-len). The only member of *Streptosolen*, of the nightshade family SOLANACEAE, is a very handsome evergreen flowering shrub of Colombia and Ecuador. Once included in *Browallia*, it differs from that genus in having a twisted corolla tube that widens at the throat. The name, referring to this characteristic, is from the Greek *streptos*, twisted, and *solen*, a tube.

A somewhat clambering, rough-hairy shrub up to 6 feet tall or taller, *S. jamesonii* has slender branches and conspicuously veined and stalked, ovate leaves up to 1½ inches long. The flowers are in large showy clusters at the branch ends. They have corollas with yellow to orange-yellow tubes, 1 inch to 1¼ inches long, and five spreading lobes (petals) of a deeper, bright orange hue. There are four stamens, two of which are longer than the others. The fruits are somewhat leathery capsules.

Garden and Landscape Uses. This shrub may be grown permanently outdoors in California and in regions with similar frost-free or nearly frost-free climates where the humidity is not excessively high. It is also excellent in greenhouses and for outdoor

Streptosolen jamesonii

summer beds in regions where it is not hardy. When trained to a wall or other support, it may be carried to a height of 10 feet or more, or it may be kept as a shrub 4 to 6 feet tall. It is effective as a loose hedge. Specimens in pots, urns, or hanging baskets are very lovely, and the plant lends itself to training as a standard (to tree-form) for planting in summer beds and for decorating terraces, patios, steps, and other architectural features.

Cultivation. This plant is a sun-lover, at its best in warm, dryish atmospheric conditions. It grows in any ordinary well-drained garden soil, but will not stand stagnant moisture about its roots. Although fairly drought-resistant, it grows best when afforded reasonable supplies of water during the period of its chief vegetative growth; somewhat drier conditions later tend to induce prolific blooming. Containers in which it is cultivated must be well drained and the soil used to fill them, porous and fertile. Pruning, which consists of cutting back shoots of the previous season's growth, should be done in late winter or early spring. At the same time, all very weak shoots should be removed and then, too, container-grown specimens should be repotted or top-dressed. Propagation is easily achieved by cuttings at almost any time, but late summer and early fall are appropriate for rooting cuttings to give plants to bloom the following summer. Indoors a winter night temperature of 50°F with a few degrees increase during the day permitted is satisfactory. Following pruning and repotting or top-dressing, these temperatures can with advantage be increased by five or ten degrees. The chief pests are aphids, red spider mites, and whiteflies.

STRIKE. Chiefly British, strike is used both as a verb and noun. To strike cuttings means to root cuttings. A good strike of cuttings refers to a batch that has rooted satisfactorily.

STRING-OF-BEADS is *Senecio rowleyanus*.

STRING-OF-HEARTS is *Ceropegia woodii.*

STRIPED-SQUILL is *Puschkinia scilloides.*

STROBILANTHES (Strobil-ánthes). Numbering 250 species, *Strobilanthes,* of the acanthus family ACANTHACEAE, inhabits mostly warm parts of Asia and Malagasy (Madagascar), often forming forest undergrowth practically to the exclusion of other plants. Its name, from the Greek *strobilos,* a cone, and *anthos,* a flower, alludes to the clusters of flowers. The genus consists of herbaceous plants, subshrubs, and shrubs.

Strobiantheses are opposite-leaved and have blue-purple, white, or rarely yellow flowers, usually in clusters or spikes from the leaf axils or terminal. Each bloom has a deeply-five-lobed to almost five-parted calyx and a tubular, more or less funnel-shaped corolla that broadens above and has five spreading lobes (petals), two or four stamens, and a sensitive stigma that moves downward when touched. The fruits are capsules.

One of the loveliest foliage plants, *S. dyeranus,* of Burma, is popular as an out-

Strobilanthes dyeranus

door decorative in the humid tropics and as a specimen in tropical greenhouses. An erect, branching shrub or subshrub 2 or 3 feet tall, it has hairy stems and stalkless, elliptic, toothed leaves up to 8 inches long by 3 inches wide, purplish-red on their undersides, and green or silvery above, abundantly variegated with rich, rosy purple. Although the flowers, each 1 inch to 1½ inches long by almost as broad and in compact upright spikes about 1½ inches long, cannot compete with the foliage for beauty, they make quite a pretty display. Unfortunately, at blooming time the foliage is less intensely colored than when active vegetative growth is being made.

More recently brought into cultivation is *S.* 'Exotica'. This has the appearance of a very narrow-leaved *S. dyeranus* and is believed to be native to New Guinea. Another recent introduction to American horticulture, *S. lactatus* probably comes

Strobilanthes 'Exotica'

Strobilanthes lactatus

from Indonesia. This freely-branched subshrub is about 1 foot tall. It has short-stalked, pointed-ovate leaves scarcely or not toothed. They are purplish on their undersides and rich green, clearly and beautifully variegated with white, above. The flowers are pale purple.

Two rather similar nonhardy, winter- and spring-blooming species, admired for their flowers rather than their foliage, are *S. isophyllus* and *S. anisophyllus.* These much-branched subshrubs are 1 foot to 2 feet tall or sometimes a little taller. They have slender, somewhat zigzagged branches slightly swollen at the nodes (joints) and, in season, decorated for much of their lengths with short-stalked clusters of flowers from the leaf axils. The blooms are pinkish-lavender variegated with white and are about 1 inch long. The individuals of each pair of willow-like, narrow-lanceolate leaves are, in *S. isophyllus,* almost or quite equal in size, but in *S. anisophyllus,* one of each pair is much smaller than the other and is frequently so aborted that at first glance it seems that the stems carry alternate leaves. They are lustrous dark green above and paler on their undersides. Both species are natives of the Himalayan region.

Quite different from those described above, *S. atropurpureus,* of northern India and Kashmir, is a herbaceous perennial with stems that die to the ground each fall. At The New York Botanical Garden it has

Strobilanthes isophyllus

Strobilanthes isophyllus (flowers)

Strobilanthes atropurpureus

proved hardy outdoors. It forms clumps of vigorous stems, up to 6 feet tall, and broad-ovate, coarsely-toothed leaves. The rich purple flowers, in large, loose, terminal clusters, are borne freely in late summer. They are 1¼ to 1½ inches long and nearly as broad across their faces.

Garden and Landscape Uses and Cultivation. Except for *S. atropurpureus,* which grows without special care if accorded treatment that satisfies phloxes, asters, helianthuses, and other familiar hardy herbaceous perennials, the strobilantheses described here are not frost-hardy and can be grown permanently outdoors only in the tropics and subtropics. In addition, *S. dyeranus* and *S.* 'Exotica' can be used with good effect to add color to outdoor summer beds, but before fall frost they must be taken up, or better still cuttings taken from them and rooted, for wintering in a greenhouse. Indoors these and *S. lactatus* need high humidity and a minimum night temperature of 60 to 70°F, increased by five to fifteen degrees by day. Only when making fast growth, as they do under warm, humid conditions, does their foliage develop its finest coloring. Rich soil kept evenly moist, but not soggy, and shade from strong light are needed. Pinching out the tips of the shoots of young specimens is done to encourage branching, but too many pinches results in weak shoots with undersized leaves. Specimens that have filled their pots with roots respond to regular and generous applications of dilute liquid fertilizer. Young, vigorous plants are more beautiful than old ones, which have a tendency to become straggly. New stocks should be raised frequently from cuttings.

Not as tropical in their requirements as the colored foliage kinds, *S. isophyllus* and *S. anisophyllus* prosper under conditions that suit many begonias. In frostless regions they can be grown permanently outdoors under less humid conditions than are best for *S. dyeranus*. As greenhouse plants they are propagated by cuttings in late winter or spring, and during the period of the year when temperatures can be so controlled, are kept where the night temperature is 55 to 58°F and that by day a few degrees warmer. They need more light than the foliage kinds, slight shade from the strongest sun only being necessary. Fertile, loamy soil in well-drained containers is to their liking. It should be kept moderately moist, and after it is permeated with roots, watered at about weekly intervals with dilute liquid fertilizer. During the early part of the growing season, the tips of the shoots are pinched out two or three times to encourage branching. Neat staking is required. After flowering, the plants are cut back lightly and the soil is kept somewhat drier until it is time to start them into growth again to produce the next batch of cuttings. Instead of keeping the plants in a greenhouse all summer, after the weather warms they may be buried to the rims of their pots in a bed of sand or other suitable material in a sunny place outdoors, to be brought inside before frost. Although not commonly available, seeds of strobilantheses may be employed as sources of new plants.

STROMANTHE (Strom-ánthe). This genus of the maranta family MARANTACEAE comprises about a dozen species of *Calathea*-like, evergreen, herbaceous perennials of tropical South America. Its name derives from the Greek *stroma*, a bed or couch, and *anthos*, a flower, and alludes to the arrangement of the blooms, which are in terminal heads, racemes, or panicles. From closely related *Ctenanthe*, the genus *Stromanthe* differs in having deciduous and colored, instead of persistent and green, floral bracts and the outer circle of staminodes of its flowers consisting of two very small ones or none.

Stromanthes have horizontal rhizomes and leafy, usually branched stems. Their short-stalked leaves are paddle-shaped. The bisexual, asymmetrical blooms are usually rather loosely arranged in terminal heads or raceme-like clusters. They have three sepals, three narrower petals, and one fertile stamen. The fruits are subspherical capsules.

Most often cultivated, **S. porteana,** of Brazil, has thick rootstocks, hairy stems up to 6 feet in height, and short-stalked, oblong-paddle-shaped to broad-lanceolate, lustrous leaves up to 1½ feet in length. The leaves are slightly corrugated, and feathered with dark green, alternating with silvery-gray or silvery-white bands that curve outward and upward from midrib to margins. The leaf undersides are grayish-purple. The flowers are in the axils of blood-red bracts. Having thicker leaves than the last, **S. sanguinea,** also of Brazil,

Stromanthe sanguinea

is up to 5 feet tall. Its lustrous, dark olive-green, lanceolate leaves, with blades up to 1½ feet long, have blood-red undersides. The lower leaves have long stalks, the upper shorter ones. The flowers are in the axils of red bracts. Brazilian **S. amabilis** is a lower plant with broad, oblong-elliptic leaves ending in a short point. Their upper sides are bluish-green clearly marked with gray bands that curve outward and upward from the mid-vein. Beneath they are gray-green.

Garden and Landscape Uses and Cultivation. Only in the humid tropics and in greenhouses where similar environments are maintained are these plants serviceable decoratives. They are excellent for shaded sites where the soil is rich and moderately moist. In greenhouses high humidity and a minimum winter night temperature of 60°F must be maintained. On winter days, and both day and night at other seasons, considerably higher temperatures are advantageous. Propagation is mainly by division, but also by seed.

STROMBOCACTUS (Strombo-cáctus). The only species of *Strombocactus*, of the cactus family CACTACEAE, is, by those who favor reducing the number of genera in that perplexing group, included in *Ariocarpus*. Its name, in allusion to the form of the plants, is derived from the Greek *strombos*, a spinning top, and cactus. Sorts of *Turbinicarpus* are sometimes listed as *Strombocactus*.

An endemic of Mexico, **S. disciformis** (syn. *Ariocarpus disciformis*) has grayish-green, semispherical, top-shaped, low plant bodies with flattened apexes. They attain a maximum diameter of about 7 inches, but usually are not over about 2½ inches across. Their spirally-arranged, closely-set, scale-like tubercles when young have one to four sharp, light gray spines ½ inch long or a little longer but these soon drop. About 1 inch in diameter, the white or yellowish blooms, which come from the centers of the plants, have stigmas with purple lobes. The corolla tubes, ovaries, and fruits, naked of scales and bristles, contain minute seeds.

Garden Uses and Cultivation. These are as for *Ariocarpus*. For additional information see Cactuses.

STRONGYLODON (Strongy-lòdon) — Jade Vine. Consisting of twenty species, natives from Malagasy (Madagascar) to Ceylon, Australia, and islands of the Pacific, including Hawaii, *Strongylodon* belongs in the pea family LEGUMINOSAE. Its name derives from the Greek *strongylos*, round, and *odoys*, a tooth, and alludes to the teeth of the calyx.

Strongylodons are twining, woody vines, shrubs, and subshrubs, with leaves each with three leaflets. The showy, pea-like flowers, in long-stalked racemes or clusters, have a recurved standard or banner petal with appendages above the claw (narrowed basal portion) and a keel almost as long as the standard. There are ten stamens, nine of which are united and one separate. The fruits are stalked, ovate-oblong, cylindrical pods.

The jade vine (**S. macrobotrys**) is endemic to the Philippine Islands where it inhabits ravines in humid forests. It climbs, by means of twining, ropelike stems, to considerable heights, ever seeking the sunlight necessary for it to bloom. It has lustrous leaves with short-pointed, ovate-

Strongylodon macrobotrys festooning a tree in Durban, South Africa

oblong leaflets up to 6 inches long. Unusual and compellingly attractive, its great pendulous racemes, up to 3 feet long or longer are of surprisingly blue-green blooms. These are the reason for the name jade vine. Their hue is rare among flowers. Nor are the fruits without beauty. They are nearly cylindrical green pods, about 5 inches in length, containing six to twelve seeds. The individual blooms, 2½ to 3½ inches long, have strongly upturned beaks. The native Hawaiian *S. lucidus* has ovate, short-pointed leaves, up to about 5 inches long, and slender racemes of usually red, 1-inch-long flowers in drooping racemes, followed by flattened seed pods, 4 inches long by one-half as wide, containing one or two seeds. A form of this species, with 2-inch-long pink flowers, is reported growing in Samoa.

Garden and Landscape Uses and Cultivation. Adapted only for warm, humid climates, the jade vine and its Hawaiian relative succeed in any fairly good soil. They are propagated by seeds that, because they retain their germinating powers for a brief time only, should be sown soon after they ripen. Plants begin blooming in their third year. In Hawaii the jade vine is much appreciated for its flowers, which are used in leis and other decorations.

STROPHANTHUS (Stroph-ánthus). Trees, shrubs, and vines of the dogbane family APOCYNACEAE, numbering sixty species, compose *Strophanthus*. They are natives of Africa and tropical and subtropical Asia. The name, derived from the Greek *stroph-*

os, a twisted cord, and *anthos*, a flower, alludes to the long, slender, spiraled tails to the corolla lobes of many kinds. The group has received much attention as a source of cortisone and other drugs. Several of its members are used as native fish poisons. A few are cultivated as ornamentals.

Strophanthuses have evergreen or deciduous, hairless or hairy leaves, opposite or rarely in whorls (circles) of three or four. Their dense or loose, often showy flower clusters are at the branch ends or are terminal on short branchlets. They are of few to many blooms. Rarely the flowers are solitary. The calyx is five-parted. The tubular, funnel- to shallowly-bell-shaped corolla, with usually in its throat five pairs of projecting, clawlike appendages, has five lobes (petals), in many species prolonged into drooping, twisted, slender tails. The anthers of the five stamens join to form a cone. The often large fruits are podlike follicles, in divergent pairs, containing spindle-shaped seeds with tufts of hair at their apexes.

South African *S. speciosus* (syn. *S. capensis*) is a rambling or vining evergreen

Strophanthus speciosus

shrub. It has oblong-lanceolate leaves, 1½ to 3½ inches long, in whorls (circles) of three. The flowers, in clusters of up to six at the branch ends, have wide-mouthed, deep yellowish corollas, their petals with long, drooping, spirally-twisted tails. Each petal usually has a large red spot at its base near the wide throat of the bloom.

Other species are cultivated in tropical gardens. Native from Burma to Java, *S. caudatus* (syn. *S. dichotomus*) is an erect or sometimes tall-climbing shrub with opposite, short-stalked, ovate-elliptic, leathery, hairless leaves 3 to 8 inches long. Clustered at the branch ends, the white or yellowish, purple-stained flowers have corollas with tubes about 1 inch long, and petals, funnel-shaped in their lowest parts and above continued as twisted tails, 3 to 10 inches long. Another native of tropical Asia, *S. divaricatus,* a loose shrub about 4 feet tall, has elliptic-oblong leaves 1 inch

to 3 inches in length. Its greenish-yellow flowers, striped red in their throats, have petals with tails 1½ to 3 inches long.

Ornamental *S. preussii,* of West Africa, is a rather sprawling shrub with hairless, elliptic to oblong leaves 2 to 5 inches long. Its clustered flowers, at first white, change to yellow as they age. They have reddish-brown to purple stripes in their throats. Their very slender, dangling, purplish to reddish tails to the petals are from 4 inches to sometimes 1 foot or more in length. Another beautiful West African is *S. sarmentosus,* a clambering shrub with somewhat leathery, elliptic, hairless leaves and many clusters of large, creamy-yellow blooms frequently stained with purple and lined internally with rich purple. The petals have 2- to 3-inch-long, twisted yellow tails.

Two handsome rambling shrubs or climbers with large, funnel-shaped, big-nonia-like blooms without tails are *S. gratus* (syn. *Roupellia grata*) and *S. courmontii.* Both come from tropical Africa. Both have been used as arrow poisons. In the wild, *S. gratus* sometimes ascends tall trees. Its rose-scented, clustered flowers, 2½ to 3 inches across and pink with red centers, expand from crimson buds. They have thick, slightly recurved petals. The short-stalked, oblong-elliptic, hairless, leathery leaves are 3 inches to nearly 1 foot long. The fragrant blooms of *S. courmontii,* white or yellowish, richly stained with purple outside and striped with the same color inside their throats, are 2 to 3 inches wide or wider. This species has hairless, broadly-oblong to elliptic leaves up to 3 inches long.

Garden and Landscape Uses and Cultivation. Of the species described here, *S. speciosus* succeeds in the subtropics where little or no frost is experienced, the others generally need more tropical environments. All are sufficiently attractive to warrant planting as vines to screen walls, pillars, and other supports and as free-standing shrubs in open places. They succeed in ordinary soil in part-shade or sun and need little care other than trimming to shape or to size. This is best done as soon as flowering is through. The climbing kinds often can be induced to assume a shrub-like form by repeated pruning. Propagation is simply accomplished by seed and by cuttings. In greenhouses, strophanthuses succeed under conditions that suit *Allamanda.*

STROPHOCACTUS (Stròpho-cactus). The only species of *Strophocactus,* of the cactus family CACTACEAE, is uncommon in cultivation. Its name, from the Greek *strophos,* a twisted band, and cactus, alludes to its manner of growth.

Tree-climbing *S. wittii,* of the Amazon jungles, is a partial epiphyte with flat, leaf-like stems that spiral around and cling tightly to trunks and branches by aerial roots from their midribs. Their edges are eyelashed with tufts of wool, bristles, and fine spines. Night-opening and about 10 inches long, the reddish flowers have slender, sparsely-hairy, perianth tubes and spreading petals. The spiny, ovoid fruits are 1 inch to 1½ inches long.

Garden Uses and Cultivation. Not a great deal is reported about the needs and care of this reputedly rather difficult-to-grow species. It may be expected that environments appropriate for epiphyllums, rhipsalises, and other epiphytic cactuses will prove most suitable. It has been grown successfully at the Huntington Botanic Garden, San Marino, California. For additional information see Cactuses.

STROPHOSTYLES (Stropho-stỳles)—Wild-Bean. Three quite similar annual or perennial, twining or trailing, herbaceous plants of North America constitute *Strophostyles*, of the pea family LEGUMINOSAE. They are of minor horticultural importance, but are sometimes cultivated in wild gardens. The name, from the Greek *strophe*, turning, and *stylos*, a style, refers to the curved style.

Typical of the genus, **S. umbellata** occurs in dryish woods and fields from New York to Indiana, Missouri, Oklahoma, Florida, and Texas. It has slender twining stems and leaves of three leaflets. Its small pink, pea-like flowers are few to several on stalks much longer than the leaves. The leaflets, 1 inch to 2 inches long, are not lobed. Like those of the other kinds its seeds are pubescent.

The trailing wild-bean (**S. helvola**) has lobed leaflets, shorter flower stalks than *S. umbellata*, and pink flowers that turn green as they age. It occurs in dry soils from Quebec to Minnesota, South Dakota, Florida, and Texas. The third species, **S. leiosperma**, has lobeless leaflets. It differs from the others in having densely-hairy calyxes and seed pods densely- rather than sparsely-pubescent. It grows in dry or moist woods and on dunes and shores from Ohio to Wisconsin, South Dakota, Alabama, and Tennessee.

Garden Uses and Cultivation. Except in collections of native plants *Strophostyles* is not likely to be much cultivated. Its species are easy to grow under conditions approximating those they know in the wild and are propagated by seed.

STRUTHIOPTERIS. See Blechnum.

STRYCHNINE is *Strychnos nux-vomica*.

STRYCHNOS (Strých-nos) — Strychnine, Clearing Nut, Natal-Orange, Curare. The genus *Strychnos* belongs in the logania family LOGANIACEAE or, according to some botanists, in a separate family, the STRYCHNACEAE. Its name is that used by Theophrastus for some quite different plant. There are about 200 species, widely dispersed as natives of the tropics and subtropics.

Chief interest in this genus is not horticultural, but rests in its being the source of two of the most potent poisons known, both deadly, but properly used, of immense medicinal potential. Strychnine is obtained chiefly from the seeds of *Strychnos nux-vomica*, and also from those of *S. ignatii*, both natives of tropical Asia. Curare is a product of *S. toxifera* and other South American tall vining species probably not in cultivation in North America. These were sources of a deadly Indian arrow poison long before the great explorer–botanist Richard Schomburgk identified *S. toxifera* as such in the early 1830s. It is interesting to note that the effects of strychnine and curare are completely different. The first induces very violent muscular contractions, the latter relaxes muscles and brings on a limp paralysis that precedes death. Another matter of interest is that species of the quite unrelated South American genus of vines *Chonodendron*, of the moonseed family MENISPERMACEAE, are also important sources of curare. In addition to the kinds of *Strychnos* that are sources of strychnine and curare, one species is cultivated for its edible fruits, and seeds of another kind are used in Asia to precipitate sediment from drinking water.

The sorts of *Strychnos* are evergreen trees, shrubs, and vines of the tropics. They have opposite leaves, and usually white flowers with four or five each calyx parts and petals, five stamens, one style, and berry-like, but often hard-shelled, fruits.

Strychnine (**S. nux-vomica**) is a tree, nearly evergreen and about 40 feet tall, with ovate, five-veined leaves up to 3½ inches long by 2 inches wide, and many-flowered, terminal clusters, 1 inch to 2 inches across, of greenish flowers. The spherical, orange-like fruits are about 3 inches in diameter. This species is native to India. The clearing nut (**S. potatorum**), of India and Ceylon, is about 40 feet tall. It has elliptic, three-veined leaves about 2½ inches long by 1 inch broad, and nearly stalkless, axillary, 1-inch-wide clusters of flowers. The fruits, ½ to ⅔ inch in diameter, contain seeds that, when rubbed on the inside of a vessel in which water is stored, clear it of suspended mud. The edible-fruited Natal-orange (**S. spinosa**) inhabits Central Africa, South Africa, and Malagasy (Madagascar). It is a tall shrub or low tree with sharp spines about ¾ inch long. Its roundish leaves, up to 2 inches long, have five principal veins and are hairy. The flowers are small, greenish, and in clusters at the shoot ends. They give rise to spherical fruits, at first green and later brown, that have large seeds embedded in their fragrant, sweet pulp.

Although the fruits are edible, the leaves and roots are reported to be poisonous when eaten.

Garden and Landscape Uses and Cultivation. In frost-free, warm regions the Natal-orange is sometimes planted for interest and ornament; it succeeds in climates such as those of southern Florida and southern California. The other species discussed are not likely to be much cultivated except in tropical greenhouses of botanical gardens and to some extent outdoors in the humid tropics. All thrive in ordinary well-drained soil and are increased by seed and by cuttings.

STULTITIA (Stultít-ia). This South African genus of succulents is closely allied to *Stapelia*, from which it is segregated on the basis that the outer of the two crowns or coronas attached to the tube formed by the stamens is not lobed to its base. The possession of a raised ring or annulus around the mouth of the corolla separates *Stultitia* from *Caralluma*. There are six species of *Stultitia*, which belongs in the milkweed family ASCLEPIADACEAE. Its name, which means carelessness, commemorates a mistake made by its whimsical author, who first applied to it the name *Stapeliopsis*, overlooking the fact that this already belonged to a different plant.

With trailing, sprawling, or arching, four-angled stems that branch freely and root at intervals, **S. conjuncta** and **S. hardyi** differ markedly in growth habit from other kinds. Their stems, toothed at the angles, are green or grayish-green with purple markings. They are approximately ⅓ inch in diameter. Those of *S. conjuncta* are up to 6 inches in length, those of *S. hardyi* may exceed twice that. The flowers are solitary or clustered at the branch ends. Cup- or bell-shaped, with broad mouths and facing upward, they have usually five spreading lobes (petals). The flowers of *S. conjuncta* are light maroon inside the cup, cream-colored marked with red on their outsides; the lobes are cream-colored. The blooms of *S. hardyi* are predominantly liver-colored. They differ from those of *S. conjuncta* in the length of the corolla tube, in the shape of the corona, and in their longer petals.

Upright, four-angled stems, with conical, fleshy teeth, each having two tiny lateral projections at their bases, characterize *S. cooperi* (syn. *Stapelia cooperi*) and *S. tapscottii*. From 1½ to 2 inches tall, **S. cooperi** has pointed teeth on its stems about ¼ inch in length. The stems of **S. tapscottii** rise to a height of 4½ inches and have teeth ¾ inch long. The flowers of these kinds are starfish-shaped. Those of *S. cooperi* are in clusters of up to ten and are about 1½ inches wide. They have light purple upper surfaces roughened with yellowish warty tubercles with fine purple lines. On their outsides they are green with purple-brown stripes. The lower halves of the petal margins are fringed with hairs. The blooms of *S. tapscottii*, about 2 inches wide and in groups of three or four, are reddish with raised white markings and have a few hairs.

Garden Uses and Cultivation. These are collectors' items that need the same conditions and care as *Stapelia*.

STUNT. Stunted, unnaturally dwarf, and sometimes contorted growth may reflect a number of causes including such unfavorable environmental conditions as infertility of the soil, inadequate supply of water, too low temperature, and exposure to more or less constant wind. Loss of vitality resulting from infestations of insects, aphids, for example, may also result in stunting. Correction or elimination of the causal agents prevents or brings relief from stunting of these types.

More serious is stunting caused by virus infections. Examples include aster yellows, dahlia mosaic, and strawberry stunt diseases. Prompt elimination of affected plants and propagation exclusively from virus-free stock are the only effective procedures.

STURT'S DESERT-PEA is *Clianthus formosus*.

STYLE. The part of the female organ (the pistil) of a flower between the ovary and stigma is the style.

STYLIDIACEAE — Stylidium Family. This family, in the wild restricted to the southern hemisphere, contains 150 species of dicotyledons representing five genera of small herbaceous plants and subshrubs. They have more or less grasslike, undivided leaves, often in basal rosettes or in clusters on the stems. Bisexual or unisexual, the usually asymmetrical, often sticky-glandular flowers are in racemes or clusters. They have a calyx with five to seven lobes or sepals, a corolla of five petals, one of which is commonly markedly different from the others, two or rarely three stamens usually united with the style to form a single structure, and a style divided at its apex. The fruits are capsules containing many to few minute seeds. Species cultivated are *Forstera* and *Stylidium*.

STYLIDIUM (Styl-ídium) — Trigger Plant. In Australia, where the vast majority of the more than 130 species of *Stylidium* are native, they are called trigger plants. The allusion is to the manner in which the organ formed of the stamens and style is flicked with great rapidity in an arc across the face of the flower if its base is touched by an insect or other agent. After a time the column relaxes to its former "cocked" position. This rapid triggering reaction may be excited several times until the bloom is successfully fertilized by pollen. Trigger

plants belong to the stylidium family STYLIDIACEAE. The name, from the Greek *stylos*, a column, refers to the stamens and style, which are joined.

Stylidiums are small annuals, herbaceous perennials, and subshrubs with crowded, linear leaves in rosettes, or alternate. The perennials may have basal rosettes that increase in size yearly, or a short stem may grow from the rootstock with at its apex a rosette from which the following year arises another short stem terminated by a rosette, this process being repeated for several successive years. The white, pink, or red asymmetrical flowers are in racemes, branched clusters, or panicles. They have five persistent sepals forming

Stylidium, undetermined species

two lips, and a more or less two-lipped corolla of five lobes (petals), one of which is markedly smaller than the others. The column formed by the joining of the two stamens and style is long, protrudes to one side of the bloom, and is curved or bent so that its apex is below the petals. The fruits are capsules. Stylidiums occur wild in New Zealand and southeast Asia, as well as in Australia.

Australian *S. graminifolium* is up to about 2 feet tall. Its numerous stiff, narrow-linear, sometimes toothed leaves, 2 to 10 inches long, are in basal rosettes. The pink, glandular flowers, the individuals nearly stalkless and hairy on their outsides, form narrow racemes or interrupted spikes with stalks 1 foot to 1½ feet tall.

Its stems 2 inches to 1 foot long and furnished with closely set, linear leaves ½ inch to 1½ inches long, those at the apex in a rosette-like arrangement, *S. adnatum* is Australian. Its little pale pink flowers are in crowded spikelike racemes or panicles, sometimes 6 to 10 inches long, but often not over 2 to 3 inches long.

Garden and Landscape Uses and Cultivation. Occasionally cultivated in greenhouses and in California-type climates outdoors, stylidiums are chiefly interesting because of the peculiar irritability of

their stamens and style columns. They grow satisfactorily from seed, less readily from cuttings, and succeed in sunny locations in well-drained, sandy, peaty soil kept moderately moist. In greenhouses a winter night temperature of about 50°F, with an increase of five to fifteen degrees by day, suits.

STYLOMECON (Stylo-mècon) — Flaming-Poppy or Wind-Poppy. The beautiful, brilliant-flowered, poppy relative *Stylomecon* consists of one species of the poppy family PAPAVERACEAE, an endemic of North America. Its name, from the Greek *stylos*, a style, and *mekon*, a poppy, refers to the pistils of its flowers having styles. This distinguishes the wind-poppy from true poppies (*Papaver*), the flowers of which are without styles and which have several radiating stigmas joined to form a more or less flattened disk in the center of the bloom.

An erect, branched or branchless, hairless or sparsely pubescent annual 1 foot to 2 feet tall, the flaming-poppy or wind-poppy (*S. heterophylla*) has yellowish sap and alternate, irregularly-pinnately-lobed or twice-lobed, somewhat succulent, gray-green leaves. Its solitary flowers, 2 inches in diameter and plentifully produced, arise from the leaf axils on slender stalks. They have two early deciduous sepals and four orange-red petals, each with a purplish spot above its narrowed, greenish base. There are many stamens. The pistil has a slender, persistent style ending in a knoblike stigma. The fruits are top-shaped (obovoid) capsules, up to ½ inch long or slightly longer. They contain many dark seeds.

Garden Uses. The flaming-poppy is desirable for summer flower gardens. Its gaily colored blooms produce a cheerful effect in beds and borders, but, unfortunately, do not last well when cut and put in water. Within its natural range the flaming-poppy is splendid for native plant gardens.

Cultivation. Some gardeners sow seeds of this plant indoors and transplant the seedlings. This courts failure or at least poor results. The flaming-poppy greatly resents root disturbance. By far the best plan is to sow outdoors in early spring or, in mild climates, in fall. The seedlings are thinned, very carefully so that those left are not disturbed, to 6 inches apart, and are allowed to grow and bloom where they were sown. Porous, well-drained soil and light shade provide suitable growing conditions. Early removal of faded blooms prolongs the blooming season. No special care is needed.

STYLOPHORUM (Stylóph-orum)—Celandine-Poppy. Of the six or fewer species of *Stylophorum*, of the poppy family PAPAVERACEAE, one inhabits rich moist woods in eastern North America, the others eastern Asia. Only the first is known to be cultivated. The group consists of deciduous, herbaceous, rhizomatous perennials and is remarkably similar in general appearance to the greater celandine (*Chelidonium majus*), but differs in its flowers possessing well-developed, persistent, elongate styles, a characteristic responsible for the botanical name, derived from the Greek *stylos*, style, and *phoros*, a bearer.

Stylophorums have yellow sap, pinnately-lobed leaves, and flowers with two early deciduous sepals, four yellow or reddish-yellow petals, and numerous slender stamens. The flowers are few together in terminal clusters or sometimes solitary. In *Stylophorum*, the seed pods are ellipsoid, in *Chelidonium*, they are slender-cylindrical.

The celandine-poppy (*S. diphyllum*) has

Stylophorum diphyllum

branched stems 1 foot to 2 feet tall, several basal leaves, and a pair of leaves on the stem. The basal leaves, thin, long-stalked, and broadly-oblong to obovate in outline, are pinnately-cleft almost to their midribs into five or seven, lobed or toothed segments. The stem leaves are similar, but smaller. The terminal division is three-lobed. The deep yellow, saucer-shaped flowers, about 2 inches in diameter, are nodding in bud, upturned when expanded. The ellipsoid or spindle-shaped seed pods are pubescent. This sort is endemic to North America.

Garden Uses and Cultivation. The celandine-poppy is attractive and easy to grow; it blooms for a long period in summer and fall. It is suitable for informal areas, wild gardens, native plant gardens, and the fronts of flower borders. It needs some shade. Although it will grow in full sun, its foliage under such conditions is often damaged by "burning." This plant is best suited to fertile, moist, loose soil, but it is adaptable and may be expected to prosper in any ordinary garden earth. Propagation is by seed or by carefully di-

viding plants in early spring. Seeds may be sown as soon as they are ripe or in spring, in a cold frame or in a bed protected from animals and from other disturbances. The seedlings are transferred to shaded nursery beds in soil containing an abundance of leaf mold, humus, or peat moss, and in about a year, will be big enough to set in their flowering locations where they should be spaced about 1 foot apart. Unlike many members of the poppy family, this species transplants without difficulty.

STYLOPHYLLUM. See Dudleya.

STYPANDRA (Sty-pándra). Four Australian species of the lily family LILIACEAE constitute *Stypandra*. They are nonhardy, herbaceous perennials very much resembling *Dianella*, but differing in having egg-shaped, three-angled capsules instead of berries as fruits. The name, from the Greek *stype*, tow, and *andros*, male, alludes to the downy stamens.

Stypandras have thick rhizomes and long, narrow, stem-clasping or all-basal leaves. Their starry, blue flowers, in loose terminal clusters, have six perianth lobes, commonly called petals (more properly, tepals), six stamens with bearded stalks, and anthers that recurve after the pollen is shed. The black seeds are contained in three-angled capsules.

Sometimes cultivated, *S. glauca* is a robust species with linear to lancolate, gray-green leaves 4 inches long or longer and, on slender stalks up to 3 feet tall, clusters of ½-inch-wide blue flowers with yellow stamens. Forming clumps of leaves about 1 foot in length, *S. caespitosa*, an inhabitant of dampish soils, is about 1 foot tall and has bright blue flowers carried well above the foliage.

Garden and Landscape Uses and Cultivation. The uses and cultivation of these plants are the same as for *Dianella*.

STYRACACEAE — Storax Family. This family of 180 species of dicotyledonous trees and shrubs accommodated in six genera is native in the southeastern United States, from Mexico to South America, in eastern Asia, and, one species of *Styrax*, in the Mediterranean region. Its sorts have alternate, undivided, lobeless and generally toothless, often leathery leaves. The commonly bisexual flowers in terminal or axillary racemes or clusters or rarely solitary have a bell-shaped or tubular, five- or four-lobed calyx, a five- or four-lobed corolla, twice as many or less often just as many stamens as petals, united at their bases, and one style topped by a rounded or two- to five-lobed stigma. The fruits, drupes or capsules, are sometimes winged.

Genera cultivated include *Alniphyllum*, *Halesia*, *Pterostyrax*, *Rehderodendron*, *Sinojackia*, and *Styrax*.

STYRAX (Stỳ-rax) — Snowbell, Storax. Few of the about 100 species of *Styrax*, of the storax family STYRACACEAE, are familiar to gardeners. Those cultivated deserve to be more widely known. The genus is native in warm-temperate to tropical regions of the northern hemisphere. The name is the ancient Greek one of one species. From related *Halesia*, these plants differ in their flowers not having obviously inferior ovaries and their fruits being without wings.

Storaxes are deciduous and evergreen shrubs and small trees with alternate, short-stalked, lobeless leaves that have smooth or toothed margins and are more or less pubescent with branched, starlike (stellate) hairs. The blooms are in branched or branchless racemes at the ends of the short branchlets or occasionally are solitary and axillary. They have a slightly lobed calyx and a deeply-five- or rarely up to ten-lobed, more or less bell-shaped, white corolla. There are twice as many stamens as corolla lobes (commonly called petals) and a slender style. The fruits, egg-shaped to spherical, are dry or fleshy. They contain one or two large seeds.

Exploited to some extent for a gum-resin called storax, *S. officinalis*, of Europe and Asia Minor, a deciduous shrub or tree up to 20 feet tall, is not hardy in the north. It has ovate to broad-ovate, toothless leaves that, when young, like its young shoots and flower stalks, are clothed with whitish down. The pure white, orange-blossom-like, fragrant flowers have corollas ¾ inch long by about 1¼ inches wide. They have five to eight downy petals, stamens joined briefly at their bases, and are in few-flowered clusters. They are borne in late spring. Variety *S. o. californicus*, as its name indicates, is an inhabitant of California. A shrub, 5 to 8 feet tall with the corollas of its flowers four- to ten-lobed and about 1 inch long, it differs from the European type in having its stamens joined for one-third of their length from their bases.

Native American species of merit are *S. americanus* and *S. grandifolius*, both deciduous. The former, indigenous from Virginia to Missouri, Arkansas, Florida, and Louisiana, is hardy in southern New England. The other, which ranges wild from Virginia to Florida, is hardy about as far north as Philadelphia. A spring-flowering shrub 3 to 9 feet in height, *S. americanus* has elliptic to oblong, short-stalked leaves 1¼ to 3½ inches long, toothed or toothless, sparingly-hairy, and bright green. Its nodding flowers, solitary or in clusters of up to four, on short-hairy stalks ¼ to ½ inch long, have five spreading petals about ½ inch long. They are borne in early summer. The egg-shaped fruits are ⅓ inch in length. Variety *S. a. pulverulentus* is more densely-hairy and apparently less hardy than *S. americanus*. Differing in having many-flowered racemes and elliptic to obovate leaves 2¼ to 7 inches long, *S. grandifolius* is a shrub 4 to 12 feet tall. Its young shoots are clothed with yellowish hairs, the undersides of its leaves with grayish hairs. The fragrant flowers, up to 1 inch across, are in slender, pubescent racemes 2 to 4½ inches long. They are borne in May and are succeeded by subglobose fruits about ⅛ inch in diameter.

One of the hardiest and handsomest storaxes, *S. obassia,* of Japan, a deciduous tree up to 30 feet tall, neatly pyramidal, and with up-angled branches, thrives as far north as southern New England. In May it has many slender, horizontal or slightly drooping racemes of fragrant blooms. The racemes, 6 to 8 inches long, are unfortunately partly hidden beneath the dense foliage, but are displayed enough to attract attention. The leaves are handsome. They are short-stalked, broad-elliptic or broad-obovate to nearly round, and abruptly pointed. They are 4 to 8 inches long, distantly toothed except toward their bases, and without hairs. Dark green above, they have densely-pubescent undersides. The intensely white flowers have slightly spreading petals about ¾ inch long. The velvety fruits are pointed-egg-shaped and ¾ inch in diameter. About as hardy as *S. obassia,* Japanese *S. shiraiana* is a large shrub rare in its native land. It has broadly-

Styrax obassia (racemes of flowers)

rhombic to rhombic-obovate leaves irregularly-coarsely-toothed above their middles, hairy only when young. The short-stalked, ½- to ¾-inch-long, white flowers are in few-flowered racemes up to about 2½ inches long.

Slightly hardier than *S. obassia* and *S. shiraiana,* very decorative Japanese *S. japonicus* is a slender-branched, wide-spreading shrub or small tree up to 30 feet tall. Like *S. americanus,* it has, in clusters of few, waxy-white, five-petaled blooms, which, although appearing after the leaves develop, are displayed advantageously.

Styrax obassia

Styrax japonicus

Styrax obassia in bloom

Unlike those of *S. americanus,* their stalks are hairless and ¾ inch to 1¼ inches long. The leaves of this storax are broad-elliptic to elliptic-lanceolate, crenately-toothed, and 1 inch to 3 inches long. Hairy at first, they very soon become smooth. The flowers, in clusters of three to six, are nodding and have corollas about ½ inch long. Their petals spread slightly. The egg-shaped fruits are about ½ inch long.

Two attractive Chinese species, rare in cultivation and not reliably hardy in climates colder than that of Washington, D.C., are *S. hemsleyana* and *S. wilsonii.* A tree up to 30 feet tall, *S. hemsleyana* has pointed, lopsided-ovate to obovate leaves up to 5 inches or a little more long, hair-

less on their upper surfaces and sparingly-hairy beneath. About 1 inch in diameter, the flowers are in racemes up to 6 inches long. Except for its denser growth and smaller leaves, *S. wilsonii* much resembles *S. americanus.* An interesting characteristic is its tendency to flower when only a few inches high.

Garden and Landscape Uses. Storaxes, choice subjects for landscape planting, are of dimensions that make them appropriate for small as well as large properties. They combine well with other trees and shrubs and are suitable for use as single specimens or in mixed borders. They offer no brightly hued floral display and are less showy than flowering dogwoods, apples, and cherries, but they are refined and graceful in appearance and have much beauty and interest. These plants are best suited to sandy, porous soils enriched before planting with compost, peat moss, or other organic amendment, but they prosper in any ordinary garden soil that is neither excessively wet nor too dry. They need full sun or sun for at least most of the day.

Cultivation. The best method of raising storaxes is by seeds sown in sandy, peaty soil. When seeds are not available, leafy summer cuttings inserted in a propagating bed in a greenhouse or cold frame, if possible under mist, may be tried, but they are not usually easy to root. Alternatively, grafting onto seedlings of other species of *Styrax* or *Halesia* may be done, or the slower, but relatively sure method of layering may be employed. In their early years, storaxes are often slow to become established, but once settled in a favorable location, they usually grow with vigor and without trouble. Their routine needs are absolutely minimal. No regular systematic pruning is required.

SUAEDA (Suàe-da). Chiefly plants of saline soils along seashores and inland, the more than 100 species of this cosmopolitan genus of shrubs and herbaceous plants of the goosefoot family CHENOPODIACEAE are of little horticultural interest. The name *Suaeda* derives from the Arabian name, *suidah,* of one species.

A much-branched semievergreen shrub of heathlike aspect, *S. fruticosa* is about 3 feet tall. It has alternate, closely-set, semicylindrical, grayish-green, fleshy leaves from about ¼ to slightly over ½ inch long. The small greenish flowers, solitary or in terminal spikes, are not ornamental. The ellipsoid, glossy black fruits are a little over ½ inch long. This, a widely dispersed native of the Old World, is also indigenous to the western United States. It is hardy about as far north as southern New York.

Garden Uses and Cultivation. The species described here possesses some virtue for use in brackish soils and locations subjected to sea spray. It prospers in full sun and can be propagated by seed and by cuttings.

SUBMATUCANA (Sub-matucàna). Conservative botanists include *Submatucana*, of the cactus family CACTACEAE, in scarcely distinguishable *Matucana*. There are five species. The name *Submatucana* is contrived from that of its sister genus and the prefix *sub*, under.

Submatucanas are small cactuses with subglobular, solitary or clustered stems or plant bodies with notched ribs and clusters of needle-like spines. The funnel-shaped flowers, open by day, have a cylindrical perianth tube and spreading or reflexed petals. The face or lip of the bloom is oblique. The perianth tubes, ovaries, and fruits, in contrast to what is usual in *Matucana*, are more or less hairy, sometimes densely so. These plants are natives of Peru.

Lustrous green **S. aurantiaca** (syn. *Borzicactus aurantiacus*) has stems with sixteen ribs. In clusters of about twenty-five, the reddish-brown spines are 1 inch to 1½ inches long. The bright orange-yellow flowers are 3 inches long. Orange-purple blooms and clusters of up to thirty-five spines are borne by **S. calvescens**, which by some botanists is also included in *Borzicactus aurantiacus*. Its flowers red, **S. paucicostata** has chalky-whitish-green, prominently eight- to ten-ribbed stems and twisted spines, when young black, later gray.

Garden Uses and Cultivation. These are collectors' plants that need conditions satisfactory for most small desert cactuses. Propagation is by seed. For further information see Cactuses.

SUBSHRUB. Plants with stems with woody, shrublike, persistent lower parts and more or less perennial, herbaceous upper parts are called subshrubs. Examples include some sorts of artemisias, candytufts (*Iberis*), pachysandras, rock-roses (*Helianthemum*), and thymes (*Thymus*). Some authorities equate subshrub with undershrub, but it seems better to reserve the latter for low true shrubs that are likely to grow naturally beneath other shrubs or trees, as does, for instance, the Canadian yew (*Taxus canadensis*).

SUBSOIL. See Soils and Their Management.

SUCCESSION CROPPING. This is the practice, employed chiefly with vegetables and annuals for cutting, of maximizing productivity by sowing or planting during the same growing season a second crop to succeed one just harvested.

SUCCISA (Suc-cìsa)—Devil's-Bit-Scabious. Some botanists include this genus in closely

related *Scabiosa*. It belongs in the teasel family DIPSACEAE and comprises three or four Old World species. The name, from the Greek *succise*, cut off, alludes to the roots, which appear to be cut off at their lower ends.

Succisas are herbaceous plants that differ from *Scabiosa* in having soft, scalelike parts interspersed with the florets of the flower heads, and in other technical details. They have long-ovate, lobeless, hairless or nearly hairless leaves and lilac-purple, pinkish, yellowish, or whitish flower heads with the outer florets differing but slightly from the inner ones. The corolla of each floret has four more or less equal lobes. The seedlike fruits are achenes.

Devil's-bit-scabious (**Succisa pratensis** syn. *Scabiosa succisa*), a native of Europe and North Africa, is naturalized in North America. Up to 3 feet in height, but often much lower, and with stems that branch above, it is a hardy perennial that blooms in summer and fall. Its slender-stalked, opposite, oblanceolate to elliptic leaves are mostly confined to the lower parts of the stems. They diminish in size from below upward; the lower ones are long stalked, the upper stalkless. The spherical, blue or more rarely pinkish or white flower heads are long-stalked and ¾ inch to 1½ inches in diameter.

Garden Uses and Cultivation. Only rarely is the species described cultivated. It succeeds in sun or part-shade in dampish soils and is propagated by seed and by division.

SUCCORY is *Cichorium intybus*.

SUCCULENTS. The terms succulent and cactus are confused in the minds of a great many people. There is a strong tendency to label any fat, juicy plant with thick, fleshy stems or leaves a cactus. This is not accurate. Only plants that belong in the cactus family CACTACEAE are cactuses. True, all cactuses are succulents, but by no means are all succulents cactuses.

Succulents at Huntington Botanical Gardens, San Marino, California

This collection of succulents consists of all cactuses

Only the tallest specimen in this collection of succulents is a cactus

Succulence occurs in many plant families and, not infrequently, in many plants, notably some euphorbias of the spurge family EUPHORBIACEAE, that in outward form strongly resemble cactuses. The chief determiners of whether or not a plant is a cactus are the structure and form of its flowers and fruits, and the appearance of certain stem features. Succulent is a group name for a wide variety of plants belonging to many families and genera characterized by having stems or leaves or both consisting largely of fleshy (succulent), water-storing tissue.

Succulence provides a means of conserving water. It enables plants to live in deserts and other places where supplies are always scarce and to survive long seasonal dry periods, such as are typical of Mediterranean-type climates. The reason for succulence is not always immediately apparent until it is remembered that even in humid climates epiphytic (tree-perching) and cliff-inhabiting species may find only scanty supplies of water or may be called upon to survive dry conditions for extended periods. Seashore plants, often subjected to so much wind that, unless fleshy (or in some other way adapted to reduce water loss by transpiration), they would become desiccated and die, are often succulent. Some plants that grow in salty, brackish, or alkaline wetlands and bogs are succulent as well. The water supply there contains salts in such concentrations that the roots' ability to take up water is severely restricted; despite the obviously moist environment, the plant is in effect living under physiologically dry conditions. The majority of succulent plants are natives of warm regions, but some, notable among those cultivated are sedums and sempervivums, inhabit temperate or cold lands.

Horticulturally, succulents are in great favor. They are admired for their prevailingly odd, often charming, occasionally grotesque forms, for the hues of their stems or foliage or both, and for their often brightly colored and otherwise attractive flowers, those of some sorts, especially cactuses, often large.

Besides the obvious interest they hold for fanciers of this group of plants, succulents serve admirably as major elements in outdoor landscapes in warm dry regions and, some few, notably hardy sedums and sempervivums, in damper and colder climates.

Collections of succulents are grown by enthusiasts outdoors in suitable climates, in greenhouses, in window gardens, and in other appropriate indoor sites. Where winters are too cold or too wet for them to remain outdoors permanently, nonhardy succulents can be wintered indoors in a greenhouse or other suitable accommodation. They can be plunged (sunk) to the rims of their pots in beds outdoors for summer display, or be used to ornament patios, terraces, and similar places. Because mature succulents range from no bigger than a chestnut to trees of considerable size (the big ones, however, are usually attractive in small sizes), selections can be made to fit any accommodation. They are well suited for featuring in rock gardens devoted to desert plants.

Generally easy to grow, succulents have needs that vary to some extent among their numerous kinds. In this Encyclopedia these are detailed under the respective genera to which they belong, but it may not be inappropriate to here emphasize certain ground rules that are essential to success in the cultivation of all of this group of plants. First is the absolute need for sharp drainage and, in most instances, a dry or relatively dry atmosphere. This last, however, is by no means a universal need. There are kinds, such as sedums, sempervivums, and some crassulas, kalanchoes, and rocheas, as well as epiphytal cactuses, that are natives of climates constantly or intermittantly humid that do better in fairly moist than in arid atmospheres.

Although the majority of sorts require or endure exposure to full sun, some do better if afforded light shade from the most intense illumination of summer. This is especially true of specimens in green-houses or windows. A paling and possible eventual scorching of the most exposed parts of the foliage or stems indicates this need for shading.

Recognition of and respect for the resting, dormant, or semidormant seasons of many sorts of succulent plants is important to success. Most kinds rest in winter, some in summer. While in this state, water the plants only if there is danger of the roots becoming damagingly desiccated or of the tops shriveling to a harmful degree. Depending upon the kind of plant, this may involve an occasional soaking at long intervals or a complete withholding of water.

During their season of active growth, water fairly generously, but always allow the soil to become nearly dry between applications, then saturate it. Fertilize with caution. An excess of nitrogen is likely to induce lush, out-of-character growth and perhaps reduce disease resistance. On the other hand, starved specimens grow poorly and, especially such kinds as aeoniums, cotyledons, and echeverias, are likely to be miserable representatives of what they are capable of achieving.

For outdoor landscaping in warm, dry regions, succulents have much charm, but to achieve satisfactory effects it is necessary to employ them with understanding and restraint. Mixing them willy-nilly with plants that do not belong in desert or semidesert regions is not only incongruous to the extent of being distasteful, but is troublesome, often impossible, to the degree in which the two plant types require different amounts of water. Group succulents with other dry region plants in areas where they blend with each other and the adjacent landscape. If enough space is available, a desert garden of only such plants can be beautiful, interesting, appropriate, and less demanding of care than other more conventional developments.

Soil for most succulents should contain considerably less organic material than is desirable for most other plants. To ensure its porosity, a considerable content of such mineral matter as coarse sand, grit, perlite, or crushed brick is desirable, but enough loamy or even clayey topsoil should be included to assure stability, reasonable retention of moisture, and adequate nutrition.

Families notable for the succulent plants they contain include those now given. Some typical genera are listed in parentheses. AIZOACEAE (*Mesembryanthemum* and its many allied genera), AMARYLLIDACEAE (*Agave* and *Furcraea*), ASCLEPIADACEAE (*Caralluma*, *Ceropegia*, *Duvalia*, *Hoodia*, *Huernia*, *Stapelia*, and others), CACTACEAE (all genera, see the Encyclopedia entry Cactaceae), COMPOSITAE (*Othonna*, *Pachystegia*, and *Senecio*), CRASSULACEAE (*Cotyledon*, *Crassula*, *Echeveria*, *Kalanchoe*, *Sedum*, *Sempervivum*, and many other genera), EUPHORBIACEAE (*Euphorbia*, *Pedilanthus*, and *Synadenium*), GERANIACEAE (*Pelargonium* and *Sarcocaulon*), LILIACEAE (*Aloe*, *Gasteria*, *Haworthia*, and *Yucca*), and PORTULACACEAE (*Anacampseros*, *Portulacaria*, and *Talinum*).

SUCKERS. Shoots that develop from underground stems or from at or near the bases of trees and shrubs are called suckers. Some plants, red raspberries and *Cornus stolonifera*, for example, spread rapidly by these. Suckers are often produced abundantly by lilacs. In garden practice it is often necessary to remove all suckers or

Pruning away suckers from the base of a *Prunus*

to severely restrict the number allowed to develop. Any that sprout from below the graft-unions or bud-unions of grafted and budded plants reproduce characteristics of the understock and should be promptly removed. Similar secondary shoots that originate higher on trunks or branches are sometimes called suckers, but more commonly are called water sprouts.

Suckers detached with roots attached afford the usual method of propagating raspberries and can be conveniently employed to increase some other shrubs.

SUGANDA is *Coleus amboinicus*.

SUGAR. This word appears as parts of the common names of these plants: horse sugar (*Symplocos tinctoria*), sugar-apple (*Annona squamosa*), sugar bush (*Rhus ovata*), sugar cane (*Saccharum officinarum*), sugar gum (*Eucalyptus cladocalyx*), sugar palm (*Arenga pinnata*), and sugar scoop (*Tiarella unifoliata*).

SUGARBERRY is *Celtis laevigata*.

SUKSDORFIA (Suks-dórfia). Two Pacific North American plants constitute this genus of the saxifrage family SAXIFRAGACEAE. They are low, leafy-stemmed, herbaceous perennials with bulblike rootstocks and more or less kidney-shaped, crenated or three-times-lobed or divided leaves. The flowers, in loose panicles, have five sepals, the same number of petals and stamens, and two stigmas. The fruits are capsules. The genus is named after Wilhelm Nikolaus Suksdorf, botanist, of Washington, who died in 1932.

Native from California to British Columbia and the Rocky Mountains, *Suksdorfia ranunculifolia* (syn. *Hemieva ranunculifolia*), up to 1 foot tall or taller, has slender stems, and leaves divided to their bases into three leaflets up to ¾ inch long. Each leaflet is three- to four-lobed. Above, the leaves are smaller than those lower on the plant. The white petals are up to ¼ inch long. This kind inhabits wet rocks in mountain regions. A frailer species with fewer but larger, lavender or pinkish flowers, *S. violacea* occurs on wet cliffs and rocks from Montana to Washington and Oregon. It is up to 1 foot tall and has five- to seven-lobed, kidney-shaped leaves, the lower of which are stalked, the upper stalkless.

Garden Uses and Cultivation. Suksdorfias are appropriate for rock gardens. Little data regarding their cultivation are available. The obvious course for intending cultivators is to provide conditions as close as possible to those in which they grow naturally. They are unlikely to withstand very hot summers.

SULFATE. For sulfate of aluminum see Aluminum Sulfate. For sulfate of ammonia see Ammonium Sulfate. For sulfate of potash see Potassium Sulfate.

SULTANA is *Impatiens wallerana*.

SUMAC. See Rhus.

SUMMER. The word summer forms parts of the common names of these plants: summer-cypress (*Kochia scoparia culta*), summer-fir (*Artemisia gmelinii viridis*), summer-holly (*Comarostaphylis diversifolia*), summer-hyacinth (*Galtonia candicans*), summer snowflake (*Leucojum aestivum*), and summer sweet (*Clethra alnifolia*).

SUMMERHOUSES. Less commonly featured in gardens than formerly, summerhouses, here understood to include structures called gazebos and garden pavilions, can be useful and aesthetic. They afford opportunity to rest and read or otherwise spend pleasant hours in the garden, shaded from the sun and more or less protected from intrusion. Often, installed to satisfy need for an architectural feature to enhance the garden, they may terminate a vista, occupy a corner formed by the meeting of walls, or overlook an especially lovely view. Always, their style and size should be in keeping with their surroundings.

Summerhouses: (a) A well-placed hexagonal summerhouse with open sides

(b) An octagonal summerhouse with sides and roof of openwork lath

(c) Rustic in aspect, this summerhouse has a thatched roof

(d) This summerhouse terminates a short pier jutting into a lake

(e) A Japanese influence is clearly evident here

SUNN-HEMP is *Crotalaria juncea.*

SUN-ROSE. See Helianthemum.

SUN SCALD. Damage to plant tissues caused by too intense light is called sun scald. Not infrequently, it affects the trunks, chiefly on the south side, of young trees transplanted to open, exposed locations from nursery rows where they have been shaded by neighboring trees. To prevent such injury, wrap the trunks up to the lowest branches or beyond with strips of special wrapping paper or burlap and leave this in place for at least a year.

Trunks and branches of such older thin-barked trees as apples and beeches that have been shaded may also suffer if the shade is removed, as when a nearby tree is taken down or as a result of drastic pruning. Protect against the first by wrapping newly exposed trunks and limbs, as with newly transplanted young trees, or by covering them with a coat of limewash. If drastic pruning is needed, if possible attend to it gradually over a period of two or three years.

Boxwoods and other evergreens that have been heavily shaded by burlap or other winter covering sometimes suffer from sun scald when the protection is removed. Precautionary measures include removing the cover in two stages a couple of weeks apart and, so far as practicable, choosing the beginning of a spell of cloudy weather to do the work.

Unripe fruits of tomatoes exhibit whitish or yellowish surface patches or blisters and sustain damage to underlying tissues as a result of exposure to strong sun, particularly in hot, dry weather. To minimize this danger, avoid leaf loss as a result of disease, excessive watering, or excessive leaf removal when training plants to single stems. Other fruits, including apples and plums, may also suffer from sun scald.

In greenhouses and windows, parts of plants exposed to too-strong sun are susceptible to damage by scald. It shows first as a yellowing or whitening; on arching leaves, such as those of aspidistras, clivias, and some orchids, it is usually exhibited at the highest parts of the curves they make. Gradually, affected parts become brown and may eventually die. The need for adequate shade to prevent this from happening is obviously indicated.

Leaves of *Clivia* damaged by sun scald

SUN SCORCH. Akin to sun scald and not always clearly differentiable from it, sun scorch affects the foliage of deciduous trees, especially horsechestnuts and Japanese maples, and young growth of hemlocks, hydrangeas, wisterias, and some others. Manifested as a withering, browning, and dying of parts exposed to direct sun, it most commonly happens when shade temperatures exceed 90°F, particularly on dry, windy days. A combination of strong light, high temperature, and rapid loss of water by transpiration is the usual cause. Probability of damage can be reduced by maintaining mulches around susceptible trees, watering them adequately in dry weather, and spraying, before the damage occurs, with an antidesiccant (antitranspirant).

SUNBERRY or ORANGE SUNBERRY is *Solanum burbankii.*

SUNDEW. See Drosera. Portuguese-sundew is *Drosophyllum lusitanicum.*

SUNDIALS. No longer important as tellers of time, sundials can be attractive garden ornaments. They come in many interesting designs and serve excellently as focal points, especially in formal surroundings such as are typical of many rose and herb gardens.

To indicate time with reasonable accuracy, a sundial must be designed for the exact longitude and latitude it occupies and even then it will be precise only four days each year. Furthermore, in North America, only along the 75th, 90th, 105th, and 120th lines of longitude will the reading of a sundial correspond with North American standard time. East or west of those meridians, the time indicated will be faster or slower. Daylight saving time (summer time) adds a further complication.

Sundials: (a) A simple one atop a stone pedestal

(b) A metal worm pulled from the ground by a metal bird is the gnomon of this amusing sundial

(c) An armillary sphere sundial, with the gnomon an arrow

To position a horizontal sundial for the best accuracy, on April 16, June 15, September 1, or December 25, place it on top of its support, which must be perfectly level, and when the shadow cast by its gnomon points due north, turn the dial until noon is recorded by the shadow. Then fix the dial in that position.

SUNDROP or SUNDROPS. See Oenothera.

SUNFLOWER. See Helianthus.

SUPERPHOSPHATE. One of the most widely used phosphatic fertilizers, superphosphate is prepared by treating rock phosphate with sulfuric acid. See Fertilizers.

SUPPLE JACK is *Berchemia scandens.* Mountain supple jack is *Serjania exarta.*

SURINAM-CHERRY is *Eugenia uniflora.*

SUTERA (Sù-tera). Belonging in the figwort family SCROPHULARIACEAE, the about 140 species of *Sutera* are natives of Africa, chiefly the southern part. They include annuals, herbaceous perennials, and subshrubs. This genus is named in honor of the Swiss botanist Johann Rudolph Suter, who died in 1827.

Suteras have mostly opposite, generally toothed leaves, in some species with short shoots in their axils. Their flowers come from the leaf axils or are in terminal racemes or less often panicles. White, lavender-blue, yellow, orange, or reddish, they have five-toothed calyxes, and tubular corollas with five lobes (petals). There are one or two pairs of stamens and a club-shaped style ending in a blunt stigma. The fruits are capsules.

The showiest kind, which in bloom has much the aspect of a tall phlox, is subshrubby *S. grandiflora* (syn. *Chaenostoma grandiflorum*). This is 2 to 4 feet tall and

Sutera grandiflora

has mostly opposite, short-stalked, roundish-toothed, elliptic-oblong, hairy leaves up to little over 1 inch long. Its erect, rather loose, terminal racemes of lavender-blue flowers are up to 1 foot in length. They are of many blooms, ¾ inch to 1¼ inches long and wide, with spreading petals.

From 1 foot to 2 feet tall, *S. hispida* (syn. *Chaenostoma hispidum*), subshrubby and freely-branched, has erect, spreading, or prostrate branches. Its broad-elliptic to ovate, coarsely-toothed leaves are ½ inch to 1¼ inches long. The phlox-like blooms, white to mauve with orange-yellow centers, solitary from the leaf axils, and approximately ⅓ inch long and wide, are plentiful and make a pretty display.

Other sorts cultivated may include these: *S. caerulea* is a sticky annual, 1 foot to 1½ feet tall, with linear to oblong, toothed or toothless leaves up to 1½ inches long and racemes of yellow-throated, blue or mauve flowers. *S. fastigiata* (syn. *Chaenostoma fastigiatum*), a subshrub up to 1 foot tall, is densely-branched with oblong leaves up to ½ inch long, toothed near their apexes. The ½-inch-long flowers are in headlike racemes. *S. microphylla* (syn. *Chaenostoma microphyllum*) with glandular-hairy stems and branches, is up to 1 foot tall. Its lanceolate leaves, in four ranks and overlap-

ping, or clustered, are under ¼ inch long. The about ½-inch-long purple flowers come from the leaf axils. *S. phlogiflora* (syn. *Chaenostoma phlogiflorum*) is a glandular-hairy, spreading to suberect subshrub up to 2 feet tall. It has ovate to oblong or obovate, pinnately-lobed or toothed, clustered leaves up to ½ inch long and loose racemes of ½-inch-long purple to white flowers. *S. stenophylla*, a subshrub, is usually not over 1 foot tall with stems that branch in their upper parts. It has thick, narrow to linear, lobeless, toothless leaves ¾ inch to 1¼ inches long and flowers about ⅜ inch long in clustered racemes.

Garden and Landscape Uses and Cultivation. Suteras are not hardy in the north. The ones discussed above are suitable for outdoor gardens in California and other mild-climate regions and may be grown in greenhouses. The taller ones are excellent for adding a long season of summer color to flower beds and borders and for supplying cut flowers. The others, which also bloom for long periods, make good edgings to flower beds and paths.

Cultivation. These plants succeed in any ordinary, well-drained garden soil in sunny locations. They are easily raised from seed and from cuttings. For best results plant *C. grandiflorum* 1 foot to 1½ feet apart in groups of three or more. Single plants are too sparsely branched to give a satisfactory effect. Space plants of lower sorts 10 inches to 1 foot apart. After their first flush of bloom is over, shear them back to encourage new growth and a second blooming. During summer, water these plants liberally. Drier conditions are in order in winter.

In greenhouses suteras are easy to handle and are worthwhile pot plants. They grow well in environments that suit chrysanthemums and other sun-loving plants that need cool, airy conditions. In summer they may be plunged (buried to the rims of their pots) in sand, peat moss, or soil outdoors. During their early stages, pinch the tips out of the shoots of *S. grandiflora* to encourage branching. Fertile, well-drained soil is needed. Winter night temperatures of about 50°F are agreeable, with increases of five to fifteen degrees, depending on the brightness of the weather, permitted by day.

SUTHERLANDIA (Suther-lándia). Variously interpreted as consisting of up to as many as six species and of only one variable kind, *Sutherlandia* is a South African member of the pea family LEGUMINOSAE. The differences upon which the splits are based are chiefly foliage characteristics. The name commemorates James Sutherland, Scottish horticulturist and author, who died in 1719.

Sutherlandias are tender evergreen shrubs with pinnate leaves, and axillary

racemes of pea-shaped flowers succeeded by large pods, inflated like those of *Colutea*. The flowers have ten stamens, nine of which are joined and the other separate.

The kind commonly cultivated, *S. frutescens*, 5 to 15 feet in height, has graydowny young shoots, and leaves 2½ to 3½ inches long with thirteen to twenty-one lanceolate to oblong, somewhat hairy leaflets ¼ to ¾ inch long. The blooms are six to ten together on stalks with stiff hairs. They are bright red and about 1¼ inches

Sutherlandia frutescens in bloom

Sutherlandia frutescens with fruits

long. The bell-shaped calyx is five-lobed. The bloated, papery seed pods are up to 2 inches long by somewhat more than one-half as wide. Variety *S. f. microphylla* is distinguished by its leaves having smaller leaflets, hairless on their upper surfaces, and fewer flowers. In *S. f. tomentosa*, the leaflets, densely covered on both surfaces with silvery-white hairs, are obovate to roundish and ¼ inch long.

Garden and Landscape Uses. In nearly frost-free climates, especially those that are dryish, *S. frutescens* is attractive for planting outdoors as a general purpose shrub. It thrives in well-drained soil in full sun. It is also interesting as a cool greenhouse plant and as an annual for inclusion in outdoor summer flower beds. Treated as an annual, it can be used effectively intermixed with other plants in summer bedding.

Cultivation. Seeds germinate readily and afford an easy means of propagating sutherlandias. Cuttings of firm, but not hard, shoots root with fair facility in a greenhouse propagating bench. Sutherlandias prosper in any ordinary soil that assures sharp drainage and is not kept excessively wet. They enjoy full sun. In greenhouses a winter night temperature of 50°F, with a daytime increase of five to ten degrees, is satisfactory. Prune to shape and repot established specimens in spring. To have plants for temporary summer beds, propagation is usually accomplished the previous summer and the young plants carried through the winter in a cool greenhouse, or seed or cuttings may be started in a greenhouse in January or February.

SUTTONIA (Sut-tònia). Endemic to New Zealand, *Suttonia*, of the myrsine family MYRSINACEAE, comprises approximately fifteen species of evergreen shrubs and small trees. By some authorities it is included in very closely related *Myrsine*. The name commemorates the Reverend Charles Sutton, a clergyman of Norwich, England, and an amateur botanist of note, who died in 1812.

Suttonias have undivided leaves, alternate or clustered on short branchlets. The small flowers, in clusters from the leaf axils, have a deeply-five-toothed calyx, four or five petals, four or five stamens, and a short style. The fruits are one-seeded, drupelike berries.

A tree up to 30 feet tall, **S. australis** (syn. *Myrsine australis*) has dark bark, on younger branches red. Its blunt, usually wavy-edged, leathery leaves, hairy along their mid-veins, are obovate-oblong to broad-elliptic, 1½ to 2½ inches long by ½ to 1 inch wide. The little, whitish, unisexual flowers are in crowded clusters. They have four each sepals, petals, and stamens, or the sepals wanting, and an almost stalkless stigma. The tiny fruits are dark brown to black. A shrub up to 12 feet tall, **S. divaricata** (syn. *Myrsine divaricata*) has many spreading, rigid branches with usually drooping branchlets and obovate to reverse-heart-shaped leaves up to ½ inch long or sometimes a little longer. The minute flowers are in clusters of four or sometimes are solitary. The tiny fruits are purplish.

Garden and Landscape Uses and Cultivation. These shrubs, best adapted for mild, humid climates, are likely to do well in parts of California and the Pacific Northwest. They succeed in ordinary soils and may be propagated by seed and by cuttings.

SWAINSONA (Swain-sòna)—Darling-River-Pea. More than sixty species of *Swainsona*, sometimes spelled *Swainsonia*, inhabit Australia and one, an endemic, inhabits New Zealand. Few are known in cultivation. They are annual and perennial, herbaceous and subshrubby plants of the pea family LEGUMINOSAE. Their name honors the English horticulturist Isaac Swainson, who died in 1812.

Swainsonas have pinnate leaves with an odd number of toothless leaflets, and axillary, often stalked, racemes of pea-like, blue-violet, purple, red, white, or more rarely orange or yellow flowers. The calyxes, pubescent on their insides, have five lobes of nearly equal size. The upper or standard petal is large and rounded or kidney-shaped. The lateral ones are much smaller. The keel is broad and incurved. There are ten stamens, of which one is free and the others joined, and a bearded style. The fruits are inflated pods with sharply-pointed apexes. They contain several seeds. In Australia some species are troublesome cattle poisons.

Very ornamental, **S. galegifolia** is a hairless, somewhat straggling or semiclimbing, evergreen, herbaceous perennial or subshrub, native to eastern Australia. From 2 to 4 feet tall or taller, it has leaves with usually eleven to twenty-one oblong leaflets under ¾ inch in length. As known in cultivation the flowers are violet, pink, or white, but yellowish, brownish-red, and orange-red blooms reportedly appear in the wild. The blooms, in stalked racemes, are longer than the leaves and generally similar to those of the hardy everlasting pea (*Lathyrus latifolius*). The pods are 1 inch to 2 inches long. To the tips of their keels the flowers are about ½ inch long. Their calyxes are usually hairless. A white-flowered variety is *S. g. albiflora*.

The Darling-River-pea (**S. greyana**) is an evergreen, subshrubby or herbaceous perennial, 2 to 3 feet tall, with erect branches, and leaves with eleven to twenty-three oblong leaflets ¾ inch to 1½ inches long. Its pink flowers, in long, stalked racemes, have densely-white-hairy calyxes and are about ¾ inch long to the tips of their keels, with a standard petal ¾ inch wide or even wider. The pods are 1½ to 2 inches long.

Swainsona galegifolia

Garden and Landscape Uses. Swainsonas are not hardy in the north. They are grown in greenhouses and, in California and other mild-climate regions, outdoors. The white-flowered variety is most popular and is much esteemed as a cut flower and garden decoration. The blooms, which have much the appearance of sweet peas, but lack their fragrance, are borne over a long summer period. They last well as cut flowers.

Cultivation. Swainsonas respond to well-drained, moderately fertile soil and full sun. If the earth is excessively rich, they tend to make plenty of stem and foliage growth, but tend not to bloom well. In greenhouses a minimum winter night temperature of 40 to 50°F is adequate, and daytime temperatures at that season should not be more than five or ten degrees above the night ones. On all favorable occasions the greenhouse should be ventilated freely.

Because swainsonas bloom most abundantly when their roots are contained, it is usually better in greenhouses to grow them in pots, tubs, or boxes than in ground beds of any considerable extent. Plants may be kept permanently, but often the most satisfactory results are had from specimens under two years old. Cuttings are easy to root and are the common method of propagation. Seeds afford an alternative means of increase. Before sowing, the seeds should be soaked in tepid water for twenty-four hours or be abraded by rubbing with sandpaper wrapped around a brick or a piece of board. Good results are had from cuttings made from softwood terminal shoots taken in February or March and planted in a propagating bench with mild bottom heat. As soon as they are rooted, the cuttings are potted individually into 2½-inch pots, and before these are crowded with roots, into pots 4 inches in diameter. Transfer to larger containers is done as growth necessitates. The shoots are pinched occasionally to promote branching and are kept tied to stakes or other supports. The second spring the plants are given their final pinch and the plants are repotted. Treated in this way they bloom profusely during the summer. If old plants are retained they are cut back and repotted or top-dressed in early spring. Swainsonas in greenhouses need coarse, porous soil watered rather sparingly in winter and moderately during other seasons, but never excessively. When their final containers are well filled with roots, summer applications of dilute liquid fertilizer are of benefit.

SWAMP. The word swamp forms parts of the common names of these plants: swamp azalea or swamp-honeysuckle (*Rhododendron viscosum*—see Encyclopedia entry Azaleas), swamp-bay (*Persea palustris*), swamp-cypress (*Taxodium*), swamp-locust (*Gleditsia aquatica*), swamp-loose-strife (*De-*

codon verticillatus), swamp-mahogany (*Eucalyptus robusta*), swamp-pink (*Helonias bullata*), swamp-privet (*Forestiera acuminata*) swamp red-bay (*Persea palustris*), and swamp thistle (*Cirsium muticum*).

SWAN FLOWER. See Aristolochia.

SWAN ORCHID. See Cycnoches.

SWAN RIVER. This appears as parts of the common names of these plants: Swan-River-daisy (*Brachycome iberidifolia*), Swan River everlasting (*Helipterum manglesii*), Swan-River-myrtle (*Hypocalymma robustum*), and Swan-River-pea (*Brachysema lanceolatum*).

SWEATING WEED is *Hibiscus militaris*.

SWEET. This word forms parts of the vernacular names of these plants: sweet-alyssum (*Lobularia maritima*), sweet bay (*Laurus nobilis*), sweet-bay (*Magnolia virginiana* and *Persea palustris*), sweet brier (*Rosa eglanteria*), sweet cicely (*Myrrhis odorata* and *Osmorhiza odorata*), sweet-clover (*Melilotus*), sweet-coltsfoot (*Petasites fragrans*), sweet-fern (*Comptonia peregrina*), sweet flag (*Acorus calamus*), sweet gale (*Myrica gale*), sweet gum (*Liquidamber*), sweet-olive (*Osmanthus fragrans*), sweet-pepperbush (*Clethra alnifolia*), sweet rocket (*Hesperis matronalis*), sweet-sage (*Eurotia lanata*), sweet shrub (*Calycanthus*), sweet spire (*Itea virginica*), sweet sultan (*Centaurea moschata*), sweet-verbena-myrtle (*Backhousia citriodora*), and sweet woodruff (*Galium odoratum*).

SWEET PEAS. Among the most beloved of garden flowers, sweet peas are unsurpassed among annuals for grace and pleasing fragrance, for their wide variety of flower colors, for their usefulness as cut blooms, and for garden enjoyment. Derived from *Lathyrus odoratus*, an undistinguished, rather weedy native of Italy, modern varieties range from tall-growing vines to sorts not over 1 foot in height. Triumphs of plant breeders' skills, all are prolific bloomers that so long as the weather remains relatively cool produce from early summer until well into fall. Where hot summers prevail, they quit with the onset of really high temperatures.

The history of sweet peas in cultivation can be traced to the early years of the eighteenth century when Father Fransico Cupani of Palermo, Italy, sent seeds of the wild species to Dr. Uvedale, an English "curious collector of rare exotiks, plants and flowers." At first the newcomer, with its comparatively small blue-and-purple flowers, attracted little attention. A few decades later the notable variety 'Painted Lady', its blooms with blush-pink wing petals and a rose-pink standard, appeared and was popular for well over 100 years.

Sweet peas

Sweet peas blooming bounteously in a suburban garden

By the end of the eighteenth century, seedsmen were offering sweet peas with flowers of white, scarlet, and "black," the last probably very dark purple, as well as 'Painted Lady'. An improved form of the latter, raised in America about 1889, was named 'Blanche Ferry'. By 1900 no fewer than 264 varieties had been developed, a great many of the finest by the distinguished English plant breeder Henry Eckford, who began his remarkable work with sweet peas in about 1876. About ten years later American breeders became active and in the United States enthusiasm for growing and exhibiting sweet peas surpassed that in England. Beginning in 1893, dwarf or cupid sweet peas, varieties mostly not over 1 foot high, appeared spontaneously in California and in England, France, and Germany at about the same time, a remarkable example of simultaneous variation. Later, varieties especially adapted for blooming in greenhouses in winter were developed in America. Their availability resulted in extensive commercial production of cut blooms.

A remarkable advance came in 1901. The gardener to the Earl of Spencer exhibited in England a variety so different from earlier sweet peas that it became the standard against which all others were judged and the progenitor of a new class called Spencer sweet peas. The newcomer 'Countess Spencer' had lovely pink blooms much larger than those of the 'grandiflora' varieties and distinguished by their petals being beautifully waved or frilled.

To grow fine sweet peas, sound soil preparation and good care are needed. A degree of success can be had with no more effort than it requires to grow annuals, the seeds of which can be sown directly outdoors, but for superior results rather more is required.

A sunny location and free circulation of air are of paramount importance. The soil must be well drained, deep, fertile, and reasonably retentive of moisture. A neutral (pH 7) or near neutral reaction is best. Markedly acid soils will not do for sweet peas, but soils of limestone derivation give good results.

Preparation of the ground need not differ from that necessary to produce good crops of vegetables of rich-soil-loving kinds, such as cabbage, onions, potatoes, and peas. Spade, rotary till, or plow to a depth of 8 to 9 inches and incorporate with the soil generous amounts of good compost, half-rotted manure, or other soil-building organic matter. Further fortify it with an application of a complete garden fertilizer or, instead, if you have been fortunate enough to have been able to use manure freely, of superphosphate. Should the soil be acid (test pH 6 or lower), fork into the upper few inches a dressing of agricultural lime or ground limestone. If at all practicable complete this soil preparation in fall. If that cannot be done, attend to it as early as possible in spring.

On sandy and gravelly soils that drain rapidly and tend to warm up early, a surer way of courting success is to dig a trench 9 inches to 1 foot wide and at least 1 foot deep. Improve the under soil by forking into it as deeply as possible a considerable amount of compost or other suitable organic material and a dressing of superphosphate. Should the subsoil be utterly bad, remove some of it and increase the amount of organic additive, or replace it with a better grade.

Sow very early in spring, as soon as ground and weather permit, to assure the longest possible period of growth before, in regions of hot summers, high temperatures bring an end to flowering, or to steal an early start, sow four or five weeks earlier in 4-inch pots (five or six seeds to each) and grow your plants in a sunny greenhouse or similar accommodation where the night temperature is 50°F and that by day five to fifteen degrees higher. In climates mild enough for growth to take place through the winter, or at least for the plants to survive, sow in fall.

The best procedure with other than dwarf varieties for sweet peas grown for cut flowers is to distribute the seeds 2 to 3 inches apart over the full width of a 9-inch-wide, 3-inch-deep trench (a flat-bottomed depression the width of the blade of a spade). Or draw two parallel drills 6 to 8 inches apart and 2 to 3 inches deep and sow the seeds along them. Cover the seeds with 1 inch of soil. The advantage of the trench is that after the seeds are covered a shallow depression is left that is helpful when watering becomes necessary. Support must be provided. A fence of chicken wire or a row of stakes of twiggy brushwood, sharpened at their bottoms and pushed firmly into the ground, supplies this. Install the fence or row of stakes along the middle of the trench or between the two drills. Dwarf varieties intended to supply blooms for cutting may be sown in beds 3 to 4 feet wide with paths about 1½ feet wide between the beds. No supports are needed.

For garden display in mixed flower beds, tall varieties can be displayed to good effect by sowing them in a circle around a "tepee" of brushwood stakes that have their bases pushed into the ground and their tops leaned against each other, or around other supports the tendrils of the plants can grasp. Dwarf varieties are effective in patches toward the fronts of mixed beds. They need little or no support.

The finest exhibition-quality sweet peas are attainable by the cordon system of training. This depends upon allowing each plant generous space and restraining it to a single stem. Very thorough soil preparation, including liberal fertilizing, is basic to success and best done in fall.

Plants for cordon training are usually started early in a cool greenhouse or cold frame to be planted out from pots as early in spring as weather permits, when they are a few inches high. It is important that they be grown at all times in full sun and cool, airy conditions. The night temperature should be 40 to 50°F and that by day not more than five to ten degrees higher.

Sow the seeds, using an ordinary seed soil, 1½ to 2 inches apart in 4- or 5-inch pots, or 1 inch apart in rows 2½ to 3 inches apart in flats, and cover with ½ inch of sand. They should germinate in ten to twelve days. As soon as the seedlings have their first true leaves well formed, transplant them individually into 2½- or 3-inch pots. When separating them take great care not to break the roots. When the seedlings are about 3 inches high, pinch the tip of the stem out of each seedling to encourage the development of stronger shoots from the base of the plant.

In four to five weeks the plants will be ready for another move, this time into 4-inch pots. Enrich the soil for this potting by adding a quart of dried sheep manure and one-half a teacupful of superphosphate to each bushel of the mix. By now the weather is likely to be agreeable enough to permit putting the plants in a sunny cold frame without danger of them freezing. Keep the sash on the frames at night and on very cold days, but open them partway or completely remove them whenever the temperature is above 40°F. When the plants are well rooted in the new pots, cut off all except the two strongest shoots, or with orange-pink or orange-scarlet blooming varieties, which are notoriously weaker growers, all except one shoot.

Plant outdoors as early as can be done without danger of the plants being subjected to hard freezing. Before this is done they must be hardened by keeping the sash completely off the frame during the day for a period of at least a week. If this is done they will not be harmed by a light frost after planting.

In preparation for planting, erect sturdy, deeply-set end posts and, if necessary, intermediates, and stretch tightly between, at a height of 2 feet and 5 feet from the ground, two horizontal wires. Tie securely to these, vertically and 6 to 8 inches apart, 6- to 7-foot-long, ¾-inch-diameter bamboo canes. Remember, ultimately, when clothed with vines, these must withstand great pressures in strong winds. One cannot overemphasize the absolute need for strong posts driven deeply into the ground.

Plant, without disturbing the root balls, one plant at each cane. Do not, at this time, cut or prune the tops, but stick short pieces of brushwood into the ground near each plant to supply first support and direct the shoots to the canes. For the first two or three weeks, as the plants adjust to their new environment, growth will be slow. Once they have done this, more rapid development will take place and systematic training can begin.

Now cut away all except the strongest shoot from each plant and tie this rather loosely to its cane. From now on throughout the season look over the plants every three or four days to keep the stem (the cordon) tied to the cane and to pinch out promptly all side shoots and tendrils that develop. Also, until the plants attain a height of 4 to 5 feet, pinch out all flower buds, but after that allow them to develop. Then harvest the blooms promptly. Do not allow any to fade on the plants.

Other routine care consists of drenching the ground deeply with water whenever there is danger of the plants suffering from inadequate supplies, but not so often that the soil remains really wet for long periods. Throughout the early part of the season, keep the surface soil shallowly cultivated to destroy young weeds and admit air. When settled warm weather arrives, substitute for this attention a 3- or 4-inch mulch of loose compost, strawy litter, salt hay, crushed corncobs, peat moss, or other suitable material.

Newly planted sweet peas to be trained as cordons

Cordon-trained sweet peas in vigorous growth

Where summers are torrid, blooming will taper off; as with garden peas, the plants will fail when really hot weather arrives. This will usually be before they reach the tops of 8-foot canes. But in cooler climates they will continue to grow until fall frosts arrive. Where this happens, when they reach the tops of the canes very carefully untie them, lay the cordons on the ground along the row, and start each up another cane that is within reach of the terminal few inches of the stem. As a result, each plant will now have its lower 5 or 6 feet horizontal, the remainder growing vertically.

For winter and spring blooming in greenhouses, sweet peas are satisfactory and productive. Flowers may be had from Christmas until well into spring from August sowings. The plants may be accommodated in ground beds, boxes about 1 foot wide and deep and of any convenient length, or in 8- to 10-inch pots or tubs. They are less suited for growing in raised benches. Provide good drainage and porous, fertile soil to which, if its acidity tests lower than pH 6.5, a corrective application of ground limestone or lime has been made.

For early bloom choose early-flowering varieties. Others will not flower until late winter and spring. Tall-growing sorts are generally best for cut blooms, but dwarf, bush types make excellent decorative pot plants. Sow the seeds 1 inch deep in the beds or boxes where the plants are to remain or singly in 3-inch pots to give plants for transplanting to beds, boxes, or larger pots or tubs when they are 3 or 4 inches high. A temperature of 55 to 60°F encourages germination, but once the young plants are well up and throughout the remainder of their growing season, whenever outside temperatures permit, keep the night level at 40 to 50°F and that by day not more than five to ten degrees higher until the plants start flowering, then increase the night temperature to 50°F and the day temperatures correspondingly. On all favorable occasions ventilate the greenhouse freely.

For cut flowers, best results are had by training the plants in cordon fashion by spacing them 6 to 8 inches apart and limiting each to a single stem. Alternatively, they may be spaced about 4 inches apart and allowed to grow naturally up strings provided for that purpose. In large pots or tubs, stagger them about 4 inches apart and supply stakes of brushwood or other suitable supports to which they can cling.

Support for cordon-trained plants can be had by stretching a wire tightly along the row at the surface of the soil and nailing it firmly to each end of the bed or box. Then, between metal or wooden frameworks or rigid stakes erected at each end, stretch at a height of about 6 feet and directly overhead another wire. Now between the wires install veritical strings, one for each plant. Tie each securely to the bottom wire, stretch it tautly, and tie it to the top wire. As the plants grow, twine their stems around the strings. Tying is not necessary. When the tops of the strings are reached, cut the strings and lay the vines on the ground along the rows. Then restring the wires and start each plant up a new string 4 to 5 feet from its original one. Under the cordon system all side shoots and tendrils are picked off as soon as they appear, but this is not done with sweet peas allowed to grow naturally.

Routine care involves watering, in the early stages of growth with great care not to keep the soil too wet, and after the soil is well permeated by roots and spring approaches, applications of dilute liquid fertilizer. Keep flowers picked regularly so that seed pods never form. If they do, the length of the flowering season will be shortened.

SWEET-POTATO. Botanically quite distinct from the common white or "Irish" potato, the sweet-potato (*Ipomoea batatas*) belongs to the same genus as the morning glory. Believed to be of tropical American origin, but now widely dispersed in many tropical lands, it is primarily a crop for regions of long, hot summers. A minimum of four months of uninterrupted warm weather is needed for satisfactory results. Certain varieties of sweet-potatoes are known in North America as yams, which is confusing because they are entirely different from true yams, which are species of the unrelated genus *Dioscorea*.

Sweet-potatoes are most dependable from New Jersey southward, on the West Coast in central and southern California, and in parts of Arizona, New Mexico, and Texas. But in favorable localities home garden crops can be had somewhat further north, even on Long Island, New York. For best success, a decidedly sandy soil with a rather low nitrogen content is needed. Mucks and clayey ground are unsatisfactory.

Sweet-potatoes

Unlike common potatoes, sweet-potatoes are not propagated by cutting mature tubers into pieces and planting them. Instead, rooted sprouts or "draws" are used. These are obtained by setting medium-sized tubers in hotbeds in spring with about ½ inch of space between them, covering them with an inch or two of sand or sandy soil, and drenching with water. In a constant temperature of 75 to 85°F, growth soon begins and in four or five weeks many shoots 5 to 6 inches high will have developed from each tuber. The beds are then broken down and the rooted shoots separated. If the timing is right, the outside ground will by that time be adequately warm and there will be no danger of late frost. Specialist growers produce draws for sale and it is usually much more convenient to purchase them than to raise them at home.

Prepare the ground by spading, rotary tilling, or plowing. Be cautious of overfertilizing. An excess of nitrogen results in rank growth of vine at the expense of tuber production. If the ground has been heavily fertilized for the previous crop, fertil-izer may be unnecessary, but if the soil is of low fertility, a dressing of one low in nitrogen, say a 2-8-10 formula, at the rate of one-half pound to each 10 feet of row will be helpful. Should the ground be quite poor, a second application at the same rate may be made as a side dressing a month later.

Considerable room is needed for sweet-potatoes. In the south, space them 1½ to 2 feet apart in rows 4 to 5 feet from each other. In the north, 1¼ feet apart with 2½ to 3 feet between rows is satisfactory. Plant the draws in a ridge of soil 6 to 8 inches high and 1 foot wide at its base. Set them so that only the top leaf or two is above the surface. After growth is well begun, additional soil may be drawn up to the ridge. Subsequent care consists of keeping weeds down by shallow surface cultivation until the vines cover the ground densely enough to prevent further weed growth.

Harvest on a dry, bright day before frost blackens the foliage. Do this by cutting off the vines, then digging the tubers and separating them from the stems. Take great care not to bruise or cut them. Spread the tubers out in the sun for an hour or two and then take them indoors.

A period of "curing" is now needed; its length depends to some extent on the variety and the weather conditions that have prevailed. To cure, spread the tubers on slat trays or frames in a shed or other building where a constant temperature of 80 to 90°F is maintained and where ventilation is adequate to draw away humidity that the sweet-potatoes generate. Growers experienced in this procedure can judge by the appearance of the tubers when it has proceeded far enough; ordinarily it will be at the end of ten days to two weeks. Others may be guided by the development of new shoots on tubers in the warmest part of the storage area. The appearance of these gives reason to terminate curing, which is done by lowering the temperature gradually to 55°F. Temperatures lower than 50°F, if maintained for more than a few hours, harm the tubers. If only a few bushels are involved, the home gardener may be able to cure the tubers in crates or bushel baskets placed near the house furnace. Uncured sweet-potatoes keep in usable condition for only a short while.

Varieties with soft flesh include 'Centennial', 'Georgia Red', and 'Puerto Rico'. Sorts with drier flesh, generally better adapted to northern gardens, are 'Nemagold' and 'Yellow Jersey'.

Pests and a considerable variety of diseases may cause trouble, particularly nematodes and a stunting disease called yellow dwarf. If you suspect any of these consult your Cooperative Extension Agent or your State Agricultural Experiment Station.

A sweet-potato, rested in the neck of a jar partly filled with water, starting into growth

A sweet-potato growing vigorously in water in a container

A sweet-potato with three toothpicks stuck into it, suspended in the neck of a container partly filled with water, starting into growth

As houseplants, young sweet-potato vines are attractive and easy to raise. A favorite method is to stick three toothpicks or comparable slivers of wood into a tuber in a circle around its middle or a little nearer to its base and then to stand it with the toothpicks resting on the edge of a glass containing enough water to reach the bottom of the sweet potato. It helps if a few pieces of charcoal are put in the water to keep it fresh. Whenever needed, add water to keep the bottom of the sweet potato always wet. Put the glass in a sunny window in a warm room. The vining shoots may be trained to stakes or a trellis or allowed to hang. An alternative method that gives equally good results is to plant the tuber vertically, with its upper half ex-posed, in a well-drained pot of soil kept evenly moist.

SWEET SHRUB or SWEET-SCENTED SHRUB. See Calycanthus.

SWEET WILLIAM. This is the common name of *Dianthus barbatus*, an easily grown native of Europe and temperate Asia of which there are horticultural varieties in a wide range of attractive flower colors and combinations. Although perennial in mild climates, it is usual to treat sweet williams as biennials by raising them from seeds each year and discarding the plants after they are through blooming. There is an annual strain that flowers the first year from seeds, but this is distinctly inferior to the biennial sorts. The plant called wild sweet william is *Phlox divaricata*.

Blooming a little later than English daisies, forget-me-nots, polyanthus primroses, tulips, and most other spring bed-ding plants, sweet williams are admirable for planting alone in beds and as groups in mixed beds and borders. They can also be used advantageously to fill gaps at the fronts of shrub plantings and in similar locations. They furnish excellent cut flowers and, potted and gently forced in a cool greenhouse, delightful pot plants.

Sweet williams are bushy, 4 inches to 2 feet high, and well furnished with attractive, opposite, broad-lanceolate, glossy leaves 2 to 4 inches long. Each erect stem terminates in a wide, compact cluster of wheel-shaped, fragrant flowers, 1 inch or so in diameter, that range in color according to variety from creamy-white to deep maroon-red, with intermediates of many shades of pink and red. Sorts with flowers with a center eye of a different color than the remainder of the corolla are common. Single-flowered kinds are most popular, but double-flowered sorts are also grown. Seeds of these last give plants of which about sixty percent have double or semidouble blooms. They may be had true to type only by raising them from cuttings.

Sow seeds of sweet williams in May or June outdoors in a cold frame, or propagate double-flowered varieties by making cuttings of non-flowering shoots and planting them in a propagating bed in sand or perlite in a cold frame or greenhouse. As soon as the seedlings' second pair of leaves are well developed, transplant them to fertile, but not excessively rich soil in a sunny nursery bed, spacing them 6 inches apart in rows 1 foot to 1¼ feet apart, or in regions too cold for them to survive winters outdoors, to cold frames, spacing them 6 to 8 inches each way. Summer care consists of controlling weeds and, in dry weather, watering.

Transplanting to the locations where they are to bloom may, where they are winter-hardy, be done in early fall or early the following spring. It is very important to lift

Sweet williams (*Dianthus barbatus*)

Transplanting sweet williams to their flowering stations in spring

the plants with substantial balls of soil about their roots and not to break these through careless handling. Set them 9 inches to 1¼ feet apart. In severe climates leave them in the cold frame until spring, and during the winter cover the glass with mats on cold nights or by other appropriate means to afford protection from extremely low temperatures. Be sure to ventilate the frames freely on mild winter days. It is important that the plants be held in a state of dormancy and not be encouraged to start into new growth prematurely.

To have sweet williams bloom in a greenhouse in April and May, pot plants, lifted in September with good balls of earth from an outdoor nursery bed or cold frame, in containers just big enough to hold the roots comfortably. Water them thoroughly and return them to a cold frame buried to the rims of their pots in peat moss, sawdust, or some similar material. Ventilate the frame freely whenever the outdoor temperature is above 30°F. Cover the frames with mats if there is danger of the temperature dropping below 20°F. In January or February bring the plants into a sunny greenhouse where the night temperature is 45 to 50°F and that by day not more than five to ten degrees higher. Water to keep the soil evenly moist and, after growth is well started, give biweekly or weekly applications of dilute liquid fertilizer.

SWEETARA. This is the name of orchid hybrids the parents of which include *Paraphalaenopsis, Rhynchostylis,* and *Vanda*.

SWEETBELLS is *Leucothoe racemosa*.

SWEETLEAF. See Symplocos.

SWEETSHADE is *Hymenosporum flavum*.

SWEETSOP or SUGAR-APPLE is *Annona squamosa*.

SWERTIA (Swért-ia). If maintained separately from closely related *Frasera*, as is done in this Encyclopedia, *Swertia* consists of fifty or more species mostly native to Europe and temperate Asia, but also represented in the flora of North America. Plants presented in this Encyclopedia under *Frasera* are by some botanists included in *Swertia*. This genus belongs in the gentian family GENTIANACEAE. The name commemorates the sixteenth-century Dutch gardener and author Emanuel Sweert.

Swertias include annuals, biennials, and herbaceous perennials, usually with taproots. They have undivided, chiefly opposite or whorled (in circles of more than two), usually thickish leaves. Their flowers have four- or five-parted calyxes with the lobes deeply-cleft, deeply-four- or five-lobed, wheel-shaped corollas, each lobe (petal) with one or two glands, as many stamens as corolla lobes, a slender style, and a two-lobed stigma. The fruits are capsules.

Native in moist soils from the Rocky Mountains to California and Alaska and in Europe and Asia, *S. perennis* is a hardy perennial 9 inches to 1½ feet tall. It has long-stalked, ovate-oblong basal leaves, with blades up to 6 inches long, and a few chiefly opposite stem leaves, the upper ones smaller than those below. The bluish-purple flowers are more or less spotted with green or white or sometimes are all white. They are ¾ to over 1 inch in diameter.

Native to alpine meadows in the Himalayas, *S. perfoliata* is a hairless perennial 2 to 4 feet tall with hollow stems and opposite, seven-veined leaves. The basal ones are long-stalked, elliptic-lanceolate, and up to 8 inches long. Those on the stems are smaller. The blue-blotched, white flowers, in narrow spirelike panicles, are about 1½ inches in diameter. Also a native of the Himalayas, *S. petiolata* resembles the last, but has leaves with only five veins. From 3 to 8 inches tall, *S. multicaulis,* of high altitudes in the Himalayas, branches freely and has narrow, oblongish-spatula-shaped leaves 1½ to 2 inches long. Its flowers, about 1 inch in diameter, have five corolla lobes.

Garden and Landscape Uses and Cultivation. Swertias do best where summers are not excessively hot. The American species described is suitable for native plant gardens and other naturalistic plantings. It is easily raised from seed and succeeds in moist soil of ordinary garden or woodland quality in sun or light shade. The Himalayan sorts have similar needs and are propagated in the same manner. Charming *S. multicaulis* is choice for rock gardens.

SWIETENIA (Swiet-ènia)—Mahogony. The genus *Swietenia* consists of perhaps seven or eight species and belongs in the mahogany family MELIACEAE. It is native to tropical parts of North America, Central America, the West Indies, and South America. The name commemorates Ger-

ard von Swieten, a Dutch botanist, who died in 1772. The word mahogany is of aboriginal American origin.

Swietenias are large, evergreen or sometimes deciduous trees with alternate, hairless, pinnate, glossy leaves without a terminal leaflet, and small flowers in axillary and terminal panicles. Each flower has a five- or less often four-lobed calyx, five spreading petals, and ten stamens united to form a tube. The fruits are large woody capsules.

Mahogany, among the most prized and most beautiful of cabinet woods, is obtained from *S. macrophylla* and *S. mahagoni*. The wood of the former is known variously as Honduras, Central American, Venezuelan, Brazilian, and Peruvian mahogany, according to its source. Although the most abundant and commercially most important kind, this species' wood is not considered to be as good as that of *S. mahagoni*. Both are prized for furniture, musical instruments, interior finish, and shipbuilding, and are much used for veneer. They take a beautiful polish. Mahogany was greatly esteemed by the English eighteenth-century cabinetmakers Sheraton and Chippendale. The wood called Hawaiian mahogany is from a quite different and unrelated tree, *Acacia koa*, of the pea family LEGUMINOSAE.

West Indian mahogany (*S. mahagoni*), native to southernmost Florida, including the Keys, and some West Indian islands, is up to 75 feet tall with a swollen or buttressed trunk and a much-branched, often spreading head. Its leaves are up to 7 inches long. They commonly have four to ten short-stalked, pointed-ovate, toothless, glossy leaflets, 1 inch to 2½ inches long and divided by a reddish-brown midrib into two markedly unequal parts. The greenish-yellow to whitish flowers are in lateral panicles up to 6 inches in length. They have minute sepals and spreading petals, the latter about ⅛ inch long. The distinctive, woody, long-stalked, dark

Swietenia mahagoni

brown, erect fruits are football- to pear-shaped capsules up to 5 inches long. They open by splitting into five segments from the base upward. Each contains many winged seeds 2 inches long or longer by about ½ inch wide.

Honduran, Central American, Venezuelan, Brazilian, or Peruvian mahogany (*S. macrophylla*), a native of tropical America, ordinarily has a denser crown and much larger leaves, fruits, and flowers than the West Indian species. Attaining a height of about 60 feet, its leaves, 8 inches to 1¼ feet long, are composed of six to twelve short-stalked, asymmetrically ovate leaflets 2½ to 6 inches long. The fragrant, greenish-yellow blooms, almost ½ inch in diameter, are in panicles, sometimes more than 6 inches long, borne from the shoots near the bases of the young leaves. The flowers usually have five, but sometimes only four petals. The fruits are erect, egg- or pear-shaped, and 4½ to 7 inches long. A natural hybrid between the West Indian and Honduras mahogany is believed to occur on the island of St. Croix and is known locally as medium mahogany. This sort exhibits intermediate characteristics and the exceptional vigor often characteristic of hybrids. It grows with extraordinary rapidity. In quality its wood equals that of the West Indian mahogany.

Garden and Landscape Uses and Cultivation. Mahoganies are handsome street and shade trees for tropical and essentially tropical humid climates. They cast light, pleasing shade. The sort most commonly used for these purposes in southern Florida and Hawaii is *S. mahagoni*, but *S. macrophylla* is also planted. Both grow well near the sea and withstand some salt spray. They are at their best in deep fertile soil that does not lack for moisture. Propagation is usually by seed. Cuttings root with fair ease in a very humid atmosphere.

SWINGLEA (Swing-lèa)—Tabog. The only species of this genus of the rue family RUTACEAE is endemic to the Philippine Islands. Its name commemorates the American botanist, Walter T. Swingle, who died in 1952.

An orange relative, the tabog (*Swinglea glutinosa* syn. *Chaetospermum glutinosum*) is an evergreen, sharp-spined shrub or small tree. Its leaves, which are alternate, have narrowly-winged stalks and three oblong to oblong-ovate leaflets, the middle one much the largest and 1½ to 3½ inches long by ¾ to 2 inches wide. Solitary or in clusters of several from the leaf axils, the ¾-inch-wide flowers have five-lobed calyxes, five white petals, and ten stamens not united. The well-developed style ends in a thick, rounded stigma. The fruits are oblongish, longitudinally ribbed, and 2 to 3 inches long. They have a thick, hard, leathery rind and many hairy seeds.

Garden and Landscape Uses and Cultivation. As a shrub or tree for interest and ornament, this species is sometimes planted in warm, essentially frostless climates. It has been used as an understock for grafting citrus fruits. It succeeds under conditions that suit oranges and other citrus fruits and is propagated by seed and by cuttings.

SWISS CHARD. See Chard or Swiss Chard.

SWISS CHEESE PLANT is *Monstera deliciosa*.

SWITCH CANE is *Arundinaria gigantea tecta*.

SYAGRUS (Syág-rus). Fifty tropical American pinnate-leaved palms related to the coconut (*Cocos*) constitute *Syagrus*, of the palm family PALMAE. Its name is from the Latin *syagrus*, the name of a type of date palm referred to by Pliny.

Many species of this genus are low and some are entirely without trunks. They are of elegant appearance with leaves in a terminal crown and flower clusters with double spathes. The fruits have a hard shell covered with a fibrous outer layer. The lower parts of the leafstalk are often spiny.

Native to Brazil, *S. coronata* has a prominently-ringed trunk up to 30 feet in height. Its erect-spreading leaves, 6 to 9 feet long, have about one hundred narrow leaflets each side of the midrib. Their persistent bases remain attached to the trunk for a long time after the leaves have fallen. Its flower clusters have no more than sixty branches. Also Brazilian, *S. campestris* has a trunk 8 to 10 feet tall, swollen at its base. Its recurved, spreading leaves, 3 to 6 feet long, have thirty to forty narrow leaflets on each side of the midrib and a few spines on their stalks. The flower clusters, up to 24 feet long, are pendulous in fruit. Brazilian *S. flexuosa* (syn. *Cocos flexuosa*) is slender-trunked and attains a height of 9 to 12 feet. Its trunk is clothed with the bases of old leaves. The leaves are 3 to 6 feet in length with seventy or more slender leaflets on each side of the midrib. They are lax. The flower clusters are loose and long. The plant formerly called *S. weddelliana* (syn. *Cocos weddelliana*) is *Microcoelum weddellianum*.

Garden and Landscape Uses and Cultivation. Syagruses are attractive outdoors as single specimens and in groups. They are easily grown in containers and are well adapted for greenhouse cultivation. They prosper in any ordinary garden soil not excessively dry and thrive in humid, tropical conditions in sun or light shade. At least one, *S. campestris*, and perhaps others stand light frost. Their indoor culture is that recommended for *Arecastrum*. For additional information see Palms.

SYCAMORE. In North America this is a common name for *Platanus*. In the British Isles it is the common name of *Acer pseudoplatanus*, known in North America as the sycamore maple. The sycamore fig is *Ficus sycomorus*.

SYCOMORE. This is the biblical name of the sycamore fig (*Ficus sycomorus*).

SYCOPSIS (Sycóp-sis). The genus *Sycopsis*, of the witch hazel family HAMAMELIDACEAE, contains six species. It is native from China to the Himalayas and in the Philippine Islands. The name, alluding to some sorts having somewhat the aspect of certain species of *Ficus*, comes from the Greek *sykos*, fig, and *opsis*, resembling.

Evergreen shrubs and trees, the kinds of this genus have alternate, undivided, toothed or toothless leaves and, in heads surrounded by bracts, rather undistinguished unisexual flowers, both sexes on the same plant. The blooms, without petals, have a calyx with minute lobes. The males have eight stamens and a rudimentary, nonfunctional ovary, the females have an ovary contained in the calyx. The fruits are two-seeded, hairy capsules.

A bushy shrub or tree up to 20 feet tall, *S. sinensis*, of China, is hardy in sheltered places as far north as Boston, Massachusetts. It has strongly-veined, glossy, rather leathery, slightly-toothed or toothless, ovate to ovate-lanceolate leaves 2 to 44 inches long and one-third to one-half as broad. The flower heads, not over 1 inch long, have long-protruding stamens tipped with red anthers.

Sycopsis sinensis

Garden and Landscape Uses and Cultivation. The species described will chiefly appeal to gardeners interested in unusual shrubs. Thriving in ordinary soil in sun or part-shade, it may be propagated by seed and by cuttings of semimature shoots planted in a greenhouse propagating bench supplied with mild bottom heat.

SYMPHORICARPOS (Symphori-cárpos)—Snowberry or Waxberry, Wolfberry, Indian-Currant or Coralberry. To the honeysuckle family CAPRIFOLIACEAE, belongs this group of deciduous shrubs, several of which are well-known, easy-to-grow ornamentals especially admired for their colorful fruits. They have pleasant habits of growth and unobtrusive foliage that melds with that of other plants, but they make no significant show of bloom. Except for one native of central China, all eighteen species of *Symphoricarpos* are endemic to North America. The name, alluding to the closely clustered fruits, comes from the Greek *symphorein*, to bear together, and *karpos*, fruit. In the west, cattle and other animals browse on some species.

Symphoricarposes have opposite, short-stalked, undivided, toothless, sinuously-toothed or, on robust shoots, sometimes lobed leaves. Their small flowers, generally in terminal or axillary clusters or spikes, more rarely are solitary. They have four- or five-lobed calyxes, and four- or five-lobed, tubular corollas, bell-shaped or with slender tubes and wide-spreading lobes (petals). There are as many stamens as corolla lobes, and a slender style. Each berry-like fruit contains two seedlike nutlets. The species are often difficult to distinguish from one another.

Snowberry or waxberry (**S. albus** syn. *S. racemosus*) occurs as a native in dry and rocky soil from Quebec to Michigan, Minnesota, Pennsylvania, and West Virginia. Usually about 3 feet tall, but sometimes lower, this has short-stalked, blunt, elliptic-oblong to broad-elliptic leaves ¾ to a little over 1 inch long, pubescent on their undersides, and often with sinuous margins. Its bell-shaped, ⅓-inch-long, pinkish flowers are in pairs in short, interrupted spikes. Their corolla lobes are only one-half as long as the corolla tube. Neither stamens nor style, the latter only one-half the length of the corolla, protrude. The dead white to slightly creamy-white fruits, ¼ to ½ inch long and in largish clusters, make fine fall displays and persist through the winter, but in some sections soon become discolored as a result of being infected with anthracnose disease. This is unfortunately also true of **S. rivularis** (syn. *S. albus laevigatus*), also called snowberry and waxberry, a shrub 3 to 10 feet tall with larger leaves and berries than *S. albus*, but otherwise very similar. Native from Alaska to Montana and California, this is generally superior as an ornamental to *S. albus*.

Wolfberry (**S. occidentalis**) is another white-fruited species that, in the wild, favors dry, rocky soils. Native from Wisconsin to British Columbia, Missouri, and New Mexico, this 3-foot-tall shrub is extremely hardy. Its younger parts are pubescent. Its short-stalked, oblong to ovate-oblong, often coarsely-toothed leaves are up to a little over 2 inches long. The stalkless, funnel-shaped flowers, ¼ to ⅓ inch long, are few to many in short spikes in the axils of the

Symphoricarpos albus (fruits)

Symphoricarpos occidentalis (fruits)

Symphoricarpos rivularis (fruits)

Symphoricarpos chenaultii (fruits)

upper leaves or are at the branch ends. They differ from those of snowberry in having corollas lobed to one-half their lengths and in the style being as long as the corolla.

Indian-currant or coralberry (**S. orbiculatus**) has showy purplish-red fruits strung in angular clusters for long distances along slender, arching branches. Usually about 3 feet tall, but sometimes as tall as 5 feet, this spreads freely by suckers. Its blunt, broad-elliptic to ovate leaves, pubescent on their undersides, are ¾ inch to 1½ inches long. The tiny flowers are densely clustered. This very hardy species grows in dry rocky places, often at the fringes of woodlands, from Connecticut to Michigan, Colorado, North Carolina, and Louisiana. Variety *S. o. variegatus* has yellow-variegated foliage. The fruits of *S. o. leucocarpus* are white.

Hybrid **S. chenaultii**, which is hardy well into New England, has as parents *S. orbiculatus* and Mexican *S. microphyllus*. Because its fruits are slightly larger and a paler, clearer pink (with the sides away from the sun whitish) than those of *S. orbiculatus*, this 3-foot-tall shrub is an even better ornamental. A distinct variety, *S. c.* 'Hancock', does not exceed 2 feet in height and develops long prostrate shoots so that a single specimen may be 12 feet in diam-

eter. More complex hybrids, the results of crossing *S. chenaultii* and *S. rivularis*, are grouped as **S. doorenbosii.** These are hardy in southern New England. Several selections have been given varietal names. The best of these is *S. d.* 'Mother of Pearl', which has pale pink fruits.

Dark blue fruits distinguish Chinese **S. sinensis** from all other members of its genus. Up to 4½ feet tall and hairless, this slender-branched shrub has elliptic to rhombic-ovate leaves up to 1 inch long. Its tiny flowers are few together in stalked terminal spikes. It is hardy in southern New England.

Other kinds include these: **S. microphyllus**, of Mexico, erect and up to 10 feet tall, has ovate, bluish-green leaves, pubescent on their undersides and up to 2½ inches long, and white fruits. This is not hardy in the north. **S. mollis**, a variable native of western North America, is up to 1½ feet tall and has trailing stems 3 to 9 feet long. Its more or less hairy, mostly toothless leaves are elliptic to broad-ovate and not over 1½ inches long. The fruits are white. **S. oreophilus**, of western North America, is 4 to 5 feet tall and has hairy or hairless, elliptic to elliptic-ovate leaves mostly up to 2 inches long. Its berries are white to pinkish. *S. o. utahensis* (syn. *S. utahensis*) has shorter flowers. **S. vacci-**

Symphoricarpos microphyllus (fruits)

nioides, up to 4½ feet tall, spreads by underground runners. It has broad-elliptic leaves up to ¾ inch long. The pink flowers are solitary or in pairs, the fruits white. It is a native of western North America.

Garden and Landscape Uses. Snowberries and coralberries are perhaps not of primary horticultural importance, yet they are useful for particular locations. Were they rarer and more difficult to grow, they would undoubtedly receive more acclaim from gardeners. Except where subject to anthracnose disease, the most commonly grown snowberry (*S. rivularis*) presents over a long fall and winter season a remarkable show of handsome berries. These are displayed to excellent advantage in front of evergreens and where the branches that bear them can arch down a bank or over the top of a retaining wall. Although their fruits are of less unusual colors, the coralberry and its hybrid *S. chenaultii* are no less useful. Because of its suckering habit coralberry is suitable for planting on banks and slopes, a purpose also well served by *S. chenaultii* 'Hancock'. Symphoricarposes have the merits of enduring partial shade and city and seaside environments. They prosper in ordinary, even dryish soils, but are seen to best advantage where reasonable moisture is available.

Cultivation. Symphoricarposes make few demands on gardeners' time or skills. To have them at their best, crowded, weak, and dead shoots should be pruned out every year or two in winter or early spring. A mulch of compost, leaves, or other organic material is helpful, but not essential. Increase is by division, hardwood cuttings in fall, leafy cuttings in summer in a cold frame or greenhouse propagating bed or under mist, and seed.

SYMPHYANDRA (Symphy-ándra). Even the least botanically instructed have little difficulty in recognizing similarities between symphyandras and campanulas or bellflowers. They are kissing cousins, as it were, in the bellflower family CAMPANU-LACEAE. For differences between them we look at the anthers. In *Campanula* they are separate, in *Symphyandra* they are united into a tube surrounding the style. This gives reason for the name, from the Greek *symphio*, to grow together, and *andros*, an anther. The group is native from the eastern Mediterranean to the Caucasus with an extension into Korea. There are ten species.

Symphyandras are perennial herbaceous plants with broad, often heart-shaped, toothed leaves most of which are basal and usually long-stalked. The few stem leaves are alternate and mostly stalkless or nearly so. The usually nodding blooms, in loose panicles or racemes, are generally violet-blue, purple, or white. In one kind they are yellowish. They have five-parted calyxes, five-lobed, bell-shaped corollas, five stamens, and a single style with three stigmas. The fruits are pendent capsules that open at their bases.

As garden plants symphyandras are less well known than campanulas, although there is no good reason why this should be. True, they are less magnificent than the showiest bellflowers, such as canterbury bells, but they rival in display value many kinds that gardeners cherish.

Two of the most frequently cultivated species are *S. hoffmanii* and *S. wanneri*, the former a native of Yugoslavia, the latter of the eastern European Alps. From 1 foot to 1½ feet tall, *S. hoffmannii* is softly-hairy and has erect stems and lanceolate to oblanceolate, irregularly-toothed leaves. Its pendulous white flowers, 1 inch to 1½ inches long, are produced for a month or more in summer. Up to 1 foot tall, often not even over 6 inches tall, *S. wanneri* is rough-hairy. It has oblong-lanceolate, irregularly-sharp-toothed leaves, the basal ones with short, winged stalks, the stem ones stalkless. The nodding, narrowly-bell-shaped, blue-violet flowers, solitary on axillary and terminal stalks, are arranged on the branching stems in ample, panicle-like spires. They are about 1¼ inches in length.

Inhabiting rock crevices in the Caucasus mountains, *S. armena* has arching or somewhat flopping, branching stems up to 1 foot in length. The leaves are toothed and heart-shaped, the basal ones with long stalks, the upper ones very much smaller and nearly stalkless. Narrowly-bell-shaped and velvety-pubescent, the nodding, blue-violet flowers, about ¾ inch long, are in threes or fours on slender stalks. An erect native of Crete and Greece and 1- to 1½-feet-tall, *S. cretica* has heart-shaped-ovate, round-toothed leaves, the lower ones with blades up to 3 to 4 inches long and stalks about equal to them in length. The upper stem leaves are smaller and stalkless. The rather few 1-inch-long, pendulous, blue or white flowers are in one-sided terminal racemes.

Creamy-white flowers in racemes distinguish *S. pendula.* This is one of the most beautiful symphyandras. Its lax stems, 1 foot to 2 feet in length, have many bell-shaped blooms that are narrowed markedly toward their bases and have recurving corolla lobes. They are about 12 inches long. The numerous heart-shaped, coarsely-toothed basal leaves are long-stalked and bright green. This species is a native of the Caucasus.

Garden Uses and Cultivation. Because of their comparative rarity, symphyandras are most often accommodated in rock gardens and perennial beds and borders that are given a little special care. Not that they are difficult to grow, quite the contrary, but they make most appeal to keenly interested gardeners who like to watch their plants closely. Those with lax stems are seen to best advantage when planted a foot or two above eye level. The kinds discussed here are apparently hardy, but some, such as *S. cretica,* may not be where winters are severe. They succeed in sun or part-day shade, the latter being especially desirable for *S. hoffmannii.* They seem to find any ordinary, well-drained, reasonably moist, garden soil agreeable. Often they behave as biennials and die after flowering, but this seems not to be a well-de-

Symphyandra wanneri

Symphyandra pendula

fined characteristic, but rather the result of exhaustion following heavy seed production. If all or most of the blooms are removed promptly as they fade, so that the amount of seeds they are allowed to develop does not approach that of their fullest capability, they are likely to live after blooming. Even so, most are short-lived perennials and it is well to keep young plants coming along to ensure succession. Seeds germinate readily and afford the most reliable means of multiplication. They should be sown as soon as ripe or in spring. Under fair conditions the plants bloom the following year. Seedlings from self-sown seeds of *S. hoffmannii* often volunteer. Other methods of propagation are by division, and by cuttings of young shoots taken in spring.

SYMPHYLAN. See Centipede, Garden.

SYMPHYTUM (Sym-phỳtum) — Comfrey. The group of rather coarse, perennial herbaceous plants called comfreys, of the borage family BORAGINACEAE, consists of twenty-five species, natives of Europe and temperate Asia. A few are naturalized in North America. The name *Symphytum*, an ancient Greek one for the common comfrey, derives from *symphio*, to grow together. It refers to the joining or growing together of the base of the leaf and the stem upon which the leaf is borne.

This feature was recognized under the ancient and once widely accepted doctrine of signatures as clearly indicating the value of the plant for healing or causing to grow together broken bones. The doctrine of signatures held that the Creator in His infinite wisdom had marked each kind of plant useful for relieving pain or curing human ills with an indication or signature of its virtues. The common comfrey was also used for treating sprains, bruises, and suchlike afflictions. Certainly until very recent times, and perhaps still in the British Isles and other parts of northern Europe, it was employed for these purposes. Russian comfrey has been used for fodder and is highly regarded as a food for pigs and poultry. Its dry herbage is reported to contain about twenty-four percent protein. Prickly comfrey is also sometimes cultivated as fodder for goats, hogs, and rabbits.

Comfreys are more or less hairy plants with thick, fleshy, sometimes tuberous roots and alternate to nearly opposite stem leaves and larger basal ones. The leaves are not lobed. Blue, purplish, or yellowish, the nodding flowers are in one-sided, coiled racemes or forked clusters so characteristic of members of the borage family. They have a five-lobed calyx, a corolla with a tube widening in its upper part, and five spreading lobes. There are five non-protruding stamens and one style. The fruits are technically nutlets. The blooms of

Symphytum officinale

Symphytum officinale variegatum

Symphytum bear a general resemblance to those of *Mertensia*, but differ in having five conspicuous, long, tapering scales in their throats. From borages (*Borago*), comfreys may be distinguished by the stamens of their tubular flowers not being longer than the corolla tube.

Common comfrey (**S. officinale**), of Europe and Asia, has erect, branched stems 1½ to 3 feet tall, and lanceolate to ovate-lanceolate leaves that at their bases join the stem to form two wings or, in the basal leaves, are narrowed to winged leafstalks. The lower leaves are up to 8 inches long. Those above become progressively smaller. The dull blue, dull yellow, or whitish flowers are about ½ inch long. *S. o. variegatum* has leaves edged with white.

Prickly comfrey (**S. asperum**), native from Russia to Iran, closely approximates the common comfrey in size and aspect, but its leaves are not continued as wings down the stems and its stems are beset with stout, flattened, recurved prickles. Its attractive blue flowers are normally bigger than those of *S. officinale*.

Russian comfrey (**S. uplandicum**), a hybrid between *S. officinale* and *S. asperum*, is intermediate between its parents, but generally more closely resembles *S. asperum*. Up to 6 feet in height and of coarse

Symphytum uplandicum variegatum

Symphytum uplandicum variegatum (flowers)

Symphytum caucasicum

growth, its stems are branched and its flowers, pink in bud, are purple when open. The leaf bases either do not continue down the stems as wings or do so only for a short distance. Variety *S. u. variegatum* has leaves beautifully margined with creamy-white.

Other sorts sometimes cultivated include these: **S. caucasicum,** a much-branched, softly-hairy, clear-blue-flowered native of the Caucasus, is up to 2 feet tall. In bud its flowers are reddish-purple. They have calyxes not lobed to beneath their middles. *S. grandiflorum*, sometimes misidentified as *Pulmonaria lutea*, has branchless, prostrate or semiprostrate, rooting stems and yellow blooms. It is a native of the Caucasus. *S. orientale*, a whitish-flowered native of Asia Minor, has branched stems and calyxes not lobed to below their middles. *S. tauricum*, native from central Europe to Russia, is generally similar to *S. orientale*, but its whitish flowers have calyxes cleft to below their middles and its leaves have wavy margins and wrinkled upper surfaces. *S. tuberosum*, of Europe, has tuberous roots and branched or branchless stems up to 1½ feet tall. Its more or less rough-hairy leaves, the lower ones with winged stalks, those above stalkless, are pointed-ovate-lanceolate and more or less rough-hairy. The ¾-inch-long flowers are yellowish-white.

Garden Uses. Because of its ancient and long-continued uses, the common comfrey obviously merits a place in herb and medicinal gardens, but it and its tall kin are too coarse to be lightly admitted to other refined garden areas. They can be employed effectively, as much for their bold forms and foliage as for their floral effects, in semiwild and informal areas. The variegated-leaved varieties of common and Russian comfreys are excellent foliage

Symphytum orientale

Symphytum tuberosum

Symphytum tuberosum (flowers)

plants. The lower kinds, such as *S. grandiflorum* and *S. caucasicum*, may be admitted to large rock gardens, but not close to treasured plants of weaker growth.

Cultivation. Following their initial planting, comfreys need little or no care. They are very adaptable and, in any soil and location at all to their liking, are well able to take care of themselves. They thrive in part-shade or sun and are best accommodated in moistish soil of moderate fertility; excessive nitrogen may result in undesirable lushness. These plants are very easy to propagate by seed, division, and root-cuttings. So effective is the last-named method that scraps of root inadvertently left in the ground when old plants are taken up are likely to give rise to a crop of young ones.

SYMPLOCACEAE—Symplocos Family. Two genera accommodating approximately 500 species of shrubs and trees constitute this family of dicotyledons, which, except in Africa, is widely native in the tropics and subtropics. It is closely related to the tea family THEACEAE, the most consistent difference being that the flowers of the SYMPLOCACEAE are in racemes. The leaves are alternate, undivided, and often leathery. The flowers have a five-lobed calyx, a corolla with five or ten lobes (petals), five or some multiple of five stamens, and one style topped with a rounded or three-lobed stigma. The fruits are drupes.

The only genus ordinarily cultivated is *Symplocos*.

SYMPLOCARPUS (Symplo-cárpus)—Skunk-Cabbage. The derogatory colloquial name of this plant refers to the pervasive ill odor of all its parts, but this is apparent only when they are bruised. A common native of swampy grounds, especially in woodlands, from Nova Scotia and Quebec to Minnesota, Iowa, South Carolina, and North Carolina, the skunk-cabbage often occupies large tracts; it is also native in eastern Asia. The only species, *Symplocarpus foetidus* belongs in the arum family ARACEAE. Its name derives from the Greek *symploke*, a connection, and *karpos*, a fruit, and refers to its compound fruits. For

other plants called skunk-cabbage see Lysichitum.

In its range, the skunk-cabbage is just about the earliest wild flower to bloom. Long before the last snow has disappeared, and in favored places not long after the winter solstice, the curious, pointed, obese and hooded, fleshy spathes, open on one side and sheltering a short, stout spadix (spike) of small bisexual flowers, emerge and remain sitting on the ground. Close examination reveals beauty. Their lines are pleasing and their colors attractive, but not brilliant. The spathes, which remain in good condition for several weeks, are 3 to 6 inches long and spotted, blotched, and marbled with green and purple-brown. The short stalks that connect them with the thick underground rhizomes remain buried. The fruits, 3½ to 5 inches in diameter, are conglomerates of seeds, about ⅓ inch in diameter, embedded in the spongy spadix. Coming long after the flowers, the leaves finally are large and lush. They are basal, heart-shaped, and up to 3 feet long by 1 foot wide and have stalks up to 1 foot long.

Garden Uses. Because of its commonness in the wild and its aggressive takeover propensities, the skunk-cabbage is not likely to receive much consideration as a garden plant in regions where it is native. Elsewhere it may well be grown as a curiosity and for the decorative value of its immense leaves. Because its roots strike deeply and it spreads vigorously in wet soil, care should be taken in placing it; it is less easy to get rid of than to establish. Its blooms lend themselves for use in interesting winter and early spring flower arrangements. Planting may be done in

Symplocarpus foetidus (inflorescences and young leaves)

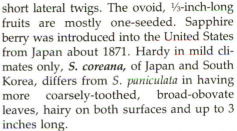

Symplocarpus foetidus with, at left, the spathe partly cut away to show the spadix

Young foliage of *Symplocarpus foetidus* growing vigorously

spring or early fall in moist or wet, somewhat acid soil, preferably deep and abundantly supplied with organic matter. It grows in shade or sun. Propagation is by division, or by seed sown in wet soil in late summer as soon as it is ripe.

SYMPLOCOS (Sym-plòcos) — Sapphire Berry, Sweetleaf. To gardeners only familiar with kinds in cultivation, it may come as a surprise that *Symplocos*, of the symplocos family SYMPLOCACEAE, contains 350 species and has a natural range that includes North America, Asia, Australia, and Polynesia. Most of its members are tropical and subtropical. The name, from the Greek *symplokos*, connected, refers to the stamens being united at their bases.

These are deciduous and evergreen shrubs and trees with alternate, undivided leaves and usually bisexual flowers in axillary clusters or panicles. The blooms have a five-lobed calyx. The corolla is five- or ten-lobed, the stamens numerous, and the style slender. The fruits are berry-like drupes.

The sapphire berry or Asian sweetleaf (*S. paniculata*) is most attractive. Native from Japan to Taiwan, China, and the Himalayas, and hardy in New England, this is deciduous. Under favorable conditions it may be 40 feet tall, but usually is considerably lower and often shrublike. Sapphire berry is so named because of its lovely intensely blue fruits, a color all too rare among berried trees and shrubs. The sadness is that the display lasts for such a short time. Birds are inordinately fond of the fleshy fruits and often strip the plants as they ripen. Sapphire berry has other attractions though. Its foliage is neat and its flowers are deliciously fragrant. The short-stalked leaves, which vary from oval to obovate, are up to 3½ inches long by about one-half as wide. They are somewhat hairy above, more conspicuously so on the veins beneath. The blooms, about ⅓ inch across in clusters 1½ to 2 inches long, have five petals and about thirty stamens, the latter responsible for the fluffy appearance of the flower clusters. This species blooms in early summer after its leaves have developed. The flower clusters are terminal and on

short lateral twigs. The ovoid, ⅓-inch-long fruits are mostly one-seeded. Sapphire berry was introduced into the United States from Japan about 1871. Hardy in mild climates only, **S. coreana**, of Japan and South Korea, differs from *S. paniculata* in having more coarsely-toothed, broad-obovate leaves, hairy on both surfaces and up to 3 inches long.

An evergreen small tree hardy in mild climates only, **S. lucida**, of Japan, has leathery, short-stalked, elliptic to oblong leaves up to 2¾ inches in length and with the midrib slightly raised on both surfaces. The pale yellow, stalkless flowers, about ⅝ inch in diameter and in crowded heads from the leaf axils, are succeeded by oblongish, black fruits about ½ inch long.

The only native American species, the sweetleaf or horse sugar (**S. tinctoria**) is a semievergreen native from Delaware to Florida and Louisiana not hardy much north of its natural range. It attains a height of 30 feet and has oval, slightly-toothed leaves up to 6 inches long. The fragrant, yellowish flowers, under ½ inch across and in dense clusters, are succeeded by orange or brown berries. The names horse sugar and sweetleaf refer to the sweet-flavored foliage, which affords favorite browsing for cattle and horses. Extracts of the bitter, aromatic bark of the stems and roots have been used medicinally. The leaves and fruits yield a yellow dye.

Garden and Landscape Uses and Cultivation. Symplocoses, especially *S. paniculata*, are useful additions to shrub borders and are effective as single specimens. They thrive in ordinary, well-drained garden soil of reasonable fertility. They need full sun. The only pruning called for is any necessary to keep them within appropriate bounds or to curb an occasional unruly branch. Propagation is by seeds sown as soon as they are ripe in a cold frame or outdoors in a bed protected from rodents. The seeds usually do not germinate until the second spring after sowing. Cuttings can be rooted in summer in a greenhouse propagating bench or under mist.

Symplocos paniculata

Symplocos paniculata (flowers)

SYNADENIUM (Synadèn-ium) — African Milk Bush. The genus *Synadenium*, of the spurge family EUPHORBIACEAE, contains fifteen species of succulent shrubs and small trees of Africa, Malagasy (Madagascar), and the Mascarene Islands. In appearance its sorts resemble shrubby euphorbias, to which they are closely related. The group differs from *Euphorbia* in its involucres having two glands united into a ring instead of being separate. The name reflects this, being derived from the Greek *syn*, united, and *aden*, a gland.

The African milk bush (*S. grantii*), of East Africa, is most common in cultivation.

Synadenium grantii (foliage)

Much-branched and up to 12 feet tall, it has thick, dark green, erect branches furnished with succulent, oblanceolate to obovate or spoon-shaped leaves 3 to 7 inches long by one-half as wide. Rich green above and with paler undersides, the leaves have reddish midribs. The small red flowers appear in late summer or fall in much-branched clusters from the leaf axils. The leaves of *S. g. rubra* have wine-red upper surfaces and are bright red-purple beneath. Sometimes called Sheba Valley death tree, *S. cupulare*, of South Africa, is an extremely poisonous shrub up to 5 feet in height. This has succulent green branches that become woody with age and ovate-wedge-shaped leaves up to 4 inches long by less than one-half as wide. Its small, greenish-yellow flowers are in branched clusters.

Garden and Landscape Uses. The African milk bush is a good ornamental for warm, frost-free climates and where space permits for inclusion in greenhouse collections of succulents. It is esteemed for its attractive habit of growth and foliage rather than its blooms. It forms an effective screen, associates well with buildings and other architectural features, and provides an attractive background for smaller plants. It thrives in sunny locations.

Cultivation. No special troubles attend the cultivation of synadeniums. Good drainage is essential; in wet soils the roots soon rot. Indoors, these plants are content with a winter night temperature of 45 to 50°F, with day temperatures a few degrees higher than those that prevail at night. Container-grown specimens of good size need repotting or retubbing at intervals of several years only, but if they have filled their containers with roots they benefit from occasional applications of dilute liquid fertilizer from spring through fall. Then, too, the soil should be kept moderately moist, but allowed to become nearly dry between waterings. In winter, much less frequent watering is needed and the soil may remain fairly dry for longer periods. Sharp drainage in pots, tubs, and greenhouse beds can be promoted by mixing with the soil liberal amounts of crushed brick, crocks, or coarse sand or perlite. Propagation is by cuttings. After making these, allow them to lie in an airy place out of direct sun for a few days before planting them in sand or perlite. This permits the cut surfaces to dry and their healing to begin.

SYNANDROSPADIX (Synandro-spàdix). One native of Argentina is the only species of *Synandrospadix*, of the arum family ARACEAE. Its name, derived from the Greek *syn*, together, *andros*, male, and *spadix*, a spadix, alludes to the male flowers being crowded on the spadix.

A nonhardy, deciduous, herbaceous perennial, *S. vermitoxicus* has a tuber from which sprout two or three somewhat fleshy leaves with ovate to spearhead-shaped blades up to about 1 foot long by 10 inches wide, and thick, channeled stalks about as long. The inflorescence, by the nonbotanical usually called the flower, has a shortish, stout stalk and a purple spathe (the petal-like part usual in the arum family and represented in the familiar calla-lily as a white or yellow trumpet) up to 9 inches long. Its lower part surrounds the spadix, its opening faces to one side. Spikelike, the purple spadix is 3 to 4 inches long. Its upper part is clothed with small male flowers below which is a zone of female flowers. The fruits are berries.

Synandrospadix vermitoxicus

Garden Uses and Cultivation. This unusual plant, grown as something of a curiosity, succeeds in humid tropical environments in light shade. It needs a fairly loose, porous soil containing an abundance of organic matter, kept evenly moist during its period of active growth and dry when it is dormant. Propagation is by offsets and by seed.

SYNCARPIA (Syn-cárpia)—Turpentine Tree. Confined in the wild to eastern Australia, *Syncarpia* comprises five species of which one is planted in the south and in Hawaii. It belongs in the myrtle family MYRTACEAE. Its name, from the Greek *syn*, together, and *karpos*, a fruit, alludes to the joined capsules.

The group consists of evergreen, opposite-leaved trees with globose heads of white flowers and fruits consisting of united capsules.

The turpentine tree (*S. glomulifera* syn. *S. laurifolia*) is called in its homeland red turpentine. The vernacular names allude to a kind of turpentine yielded by its bark. Its wood is highly resistant to fire and to termites and marine borers; it is the outstanding Australian lumber for salt water piling. In Australia the turpentine tree attains heights of 130 to 150 feet and sometimes considerably more. Straight-trunked and slender, it, like many Australian trees, has at different stages of its development two distinct types of foliage. Its juvenile leaves are opposite and very shortly stalked. Up to 1 inch long and two-thirds as broad, they are elliptic, and finely-hairy on their undersides. The thick, stiff, adult-type leaves are also opposite, but grouped so that they appear to be in whorls (circles of more than two). They are longer-stalked than the juvenile leaves, broadly-elliptic to ovate, and from ¾ inch to 1½ inches long by up to a little over ½ inch wide. Their upper surfaces are lustrous dark green; beneath they are clothed with matted, fine white or light brown hairs. Their margins tend to curl under. Mostly seven, but from six to ten in each head, the white flowers terminate stout 1- to 2-inch-long stalks that come from the bases of the new shoots. They have united calyxes with four or five short lobes about ¹⁄₁₆ inch long, and the same number of petals of similar size. There are many usually separate stamens and a single slender style. The hard, woody mass of fused seed capsules that forms the fruit is ½ to 1 inch broad.

Garden and Landscape Uses and Cultivation. Preferring deep, fertile soils, the turpentine tree is adaptable to less favorable ones. It has merit as a shade tree and is propagated by seed. It is not hardy in the north.

SYNECHANTHUS (Synechán-thus). Depending upon the authority consulted, two to six species of pinnately-leaved palms related to *Chamaedorea* constitute *Synechanthus*, of the palm family PALMACEAE. Although ornamental, they are not widely cultivated. The genus has a natural range from Mexico to Colombia. Its name, derived from the Greek *synechos*, continuous, and *anthos*, a flower, alludes to the arrangement of the blooms in the flower clusters, which, unlike those of *Chamaedorea*, contain flowers of both sexes.

Synechanthuses have solitary or clustered stems and pinnate leaves, with each leaflet with one or more chief veins, or much less frequently they have undivided leaves. The very small, yellowish to purplish, unisexual flowers, both sexes on the same plant, are in long-stalked panicles. The one-seeded fruits are yellow to reddish-yellow.

A graceful native of Central America, *S. fibrosus* has solitary, slender, strongly-ringed stems up to 18 feet tall, each terminating in a crown of spreading or ascending long-stalked leaves with blades up to 4 feet long and with thirty to forty drooping leaflets 1 foot to 1½ feet long. The slender-branched flower clusters are about one-third as long as the leaves. The fruits are about ¾ inch long. Very similar, but stemless, Mexican *S. mexicanus* has leaves up to 6 feet long and globose, orange fruits about ½ inch wide. Attaining a height of up to 20 feet, *S. panamensis* has yellow, pear-shaped fruits about ½ inch in length. Its stems usually clustered, rarely solitary, *S. warscewiczianus* (syn. *S. angustifolius*), of Central America, is up to 18 feet high and has long-stalked leaves with usually pinnate, but sometimes undivided blades that may be 5 feet long. The fruits are ⅝ inch to a little over 1 inch long.

Garden and Landscape Uses and Cultivation. These palms grow as natives in forests and woodlands. In cultivation they need shade from strong sun, moderately moist soil that contains an abundance of such organic matter as leaf mold or peat moss, and a fairly humid atmosphere. They may be used outdoors in such warm frost-free regions as Hawaii and southern Florida and as greenhouse specimens and houseplants. They require the same conditions and treatment as *Chamaedorea*. For additional information see the Encyclopedia entry Palms.

SYNGONIUM (Syn-gònium). Vining evergreens of the arum family ARACEAE compose *Syngonium*. In the wild they are usually epiphytes, that is, they grow on trees without being attached to the ground and without taking nourishment from their hosts. Confined in the wild to tropical America including the West Indies, this genus of about twenty species has a name that comes from the Greek *syn*, together, and *gone*, a seed, in allusion to the ovaries being united.

Syngoniums usually have rather widely-spaced leaves along stems that root from the nodes (joints). The foliage of young plants differs from that of mature ones. Juvenile leaves are ovate, adult ones longer-stalked and with three or more leaflets. At intermediate stages, arrow-shaped leaves are produced. As is common in the arum family, what are usually called flowers are technically inflorescences. They are clusters of blooms crowded in spikes, with, from the base of each spike, a petal-like bract or spathe, comparable to the white part of the familiar calla-lily. The true flowers are tiny, unisexual, and without petals. The lower portion of the spike is of female blooms, the upper part of males. In *Syngonium* the inflorescences generally are in clusters that terminate stalks that recurve or droop after the fruits form. The pale green to purplish spathes often change to bright red at fruiting time. The berry-like fruits are united to form ovoid composite fruits.

At maturity a slender-stemmed, tall vine or trailer, but very commonly seen in cultivation (often misnamed *Nephthytis*) in its more compact juvenile form, *S. podophyllum* is a native of humid forests and drier,

Syngonium podophyllum (juvenile)

exposed places from southern Mexico to Panama. The blades of juvenile leaves are arrow-shaped and up to 6 inches long. Adult foliage consists of leaves with stalks approximately 1½ feet long and blades cleft into five to eleven segments, the middle one about 8 inches long by approximately one-third as wide, the others progressively shorter and narrower outward. Rarely seen in cultivation, the spathes, after fruits have formed, are bright red. Horticulturists recognize many varieties as presumably belonging to this species. Most are juvenile forms, many with conspicuously variegated foliage. Arrow-shaped or lobed green leaves with ashy-colored or cream bands along the veins distinguish *S. p. albovirens*. Of compact habit, *S. p.* 'Emerald Gem' has glossy green, arrow-shaped leaves. Also compact, *S. p.* 'Imperial White'

Syngonium podophyllum albovirens

Syngonium podophyllum 'Trileaf Wonder'

has narrowly-green-bordered, pale greenish-white leaves. Slender, arrow-shaped to three-lobed leaves, dark green with paler green and ivory-white variegation, are typical of *S. p. tricolor*. Its adult-type deeply-lobed leaves produced early, *S. p.* 'Trileaf Wonder' has green leaves with grayish markings chiefly along the veins. Probably correctly identified as *S. p. xanthophyllum*, variety 'Green Gold' has arrow-shaped leaves preponderantly marbled and suffused with yellowish-green.

Much like *S. podophyllum*, but its adult-type leaves with generally narrower segments, the center one the largest and generally elliptic, *S. angustatum* (syn. *S. oerstedianum*) has three- to five-parted juvenile leaves. Variety *S. a. albolineatum* has its early leaves heart-shaped and broadly-silvery-centered or with silvery midribs and side veins. Its later leaves, of three to five segments, have white midribs. More conspicuously variegated varieties that are probably forms of this are *S.* 'Dot Mae' and *S.* 'Ruth Fraser'.

Native to Jamaica, *S. auritum* is a vine with dull or lustrous foliage. Its rather fleshy leaves have three or five lobes, the center one, the largest, up to 10 inches long. Variety *S. a.* 'Fantasy' has the blades and stalks of its leaves variegated with silver, cream, and white. Central Ameri-

Syngonium auritum (leaf and inflorescence)

can *S. hoffmannii* is a trailer or vine. Its arrow-shaped young leaves are grayish-green with their middles and veins silvery-white. The adult foliage of *S. macrophyllum* gives reason for its name, which means large-leaved. This native from Mexico to Panama has heart-shaped, velvety young leaves. Adult-phase leaves are lobed or divided. A dainty trailer or vine of Costa Rica, *S. wendlandii* has very distinctly white-veined juvenile leaves of velvety appearance with three leaflets or lobes. Its adult leaves are larger, and without white veins.

Syngonium macrophyllum

Kinds more recently brought into cultivation are *S. erythrophyllum*, *S. mauroanum*, and *S. standleyanum*, all natives of Central America. In its juvenile stages *S. erythrophyllum* has oblongish leaves, slightly arrow-shaped at their bases and, like the deeply-three-lobed adult leaves, often, but not always purplish-red on the undersides. The adult leaves have their middle lobe much bigger than the side ones, and up to 8 inches long. Juvenile and adult leaves of *S. mauroanum* are similar to each other except that the first have narrow silvery bands along the midribs of the three leaflets. The central leaflet is about 5 inches long, the lateral ones nearly as long. The latter are divided by their midribs into two

markedly-different-sized parts, the outer "half" being very much wider than the "half" nearer the central leaflet. The dull green leaves of *S. standleyanum* have many deeply sunken side veins angling from the midribs. In the juvenile state they are undivided and asymmetrically elliptic, sometimes with a pair of short lobes at the tapering to heart-shaped base. Adult leaves have three oblong-elliptic leaflets, the middle one up to 1 foot long by almost one-half as wide. The side leaflets are rather smaller.

Garden and Landscape Uses and Cultivation. As houseplants, syngoniums last well and are in favor for growing in pots, hanging baskets, and other containers. As very small plants they are used in dish gardens. In the tropics and warm subtropics they can be used effectively as climbers and groundcovers in quite heavily shaded as well as in fairly exposed locations. They succeed in ordinary soils, preferring those with a reasonably high content of organic matter that are moderately moist. Propagation is rapid by terminal and sectional stem cuttings, hammer cuttings, and division. Seeds may also be used, but not to perpetuate horticultural varieties. As houseplants and in greenhouses, syngoniums are most luxuriant where the atmosphere is humid, but they tolerate drier conditions remarkably well. Light shade from strong sun and a minimum temperature of 60°F are needed. Porous, fertile soil well supplied with organic matter suits best. Keep it moist, but not constantly wet. Allow it to dry somewhat between soakings. Too much water is detrimental. Specimens that have filled their containers with roots benefit from regular applications of dilute liquid fertilizer. Branching can be induced by pinching out the tips of the shoots. Repotting may be done during any season, but spring is preferred.

SYNNOTIA (Syn-nòtia). The genus *Synnotia*, of the iris family IRIDACEAE, in the wild is confined to South Africa. It bears a name commemorating W. Synnot, who collected plants there early in the nineteenth century. Related to *Sparaxis* and *Gladiolus*, it contains five species.

Synnotias have bulblike organs called corms that differ from true bulbs in not consisting of concentric layers like onions, or of overlapping scales like lily bulbs, but in being solid throughout. They have simple or forked stems, and linear to sword-shaped leaves in basal, fanlike rosettes. Several blooms are borne on each stem. Unlike those of *Sparaxis*, but resembling those of *Gladiolus*, they are markedly asymmetrical. Each is solitary in the axil of a deeply-lacerated spathe valve or bract (in *Gladiolus* the spathe valves are not dissected). The perianths of the flowers have tubes longer than the segments (petals, or

more properly, tepals). The upper petal is erect, the other five narrower and reflexed. There are three slender-stalked stamens, and a slender style with three very short branches. The fruits are membranous capsules.

From 9 inches to 1½ feet tall and with about six sword-shaped leaves about 6 inches long, *S. villosa* (syn. *S. bicolor*) has open, sometimes branched spikes of up to six violet and yellow blooms that have petals about 1 inch long. Not as tall, *S. metelerkampiae* develops six or seven broadly-linear leaves, 3 to 4 inches in length, and slender-tubed, dark violet blooms in loose, branched spikes of nine to twelve. The petals are ½ inch long, the upper one is broadly-ovate, the others narrower and with wavy margins.

Synnotia metelerkampiae

Garden and Landscape Uses and Cultivation. Less frequently cultivated than babianas, freesias, ixias, and some other South African bulb plants of the iris family, synnotias respond to the same conditions and care. They are suitable for growing in flower beds and rock gardens in mild climates, and in greenhouses. They bloom in late winter and spring. Increase is by natural multiplication of the corms and by seed.

SYNTHYRIS (Syń-thyris). Containing species of much charm, *Synthyris* is endemic to the mountains of western North America. It includes fifteen or fewer species of the figwort family SCROPHULARIACEAE. The name derives from the Greek *syn*, together, and *thyris*, a little door. It alludes to the valves of the seed capsules.

Synthyrises are low, hardy, herbaceous perennials. Their leaves, all basal, are long-stalked and have broad blades, toothed or more or less pinnately-lobed. Usually light to dark blue, more rarely pink or white, the flowers are in few-bracted racemes. They have calyxes of four sepals united at their bases, and bell-shaped to more wheel-shaped corollas of four usually very unequal petals, the lower parts of which are usually joined. The two stamens protrude. The fruits are capsules.

Most familiar to gardeners, **S. reniformis** has bell-shaped flowers, ¼ to ⅓ inch long, with corollas with tubes slightly longer than their lobes (petals). The latter are much more of nearly equal size than those of other species. Normally the blooms are light to dark blue, more rarely pink or white. They are in racemes 4 to 9 inches tall. The leaves of this synthyris, which in its home territory is called spring queen, are evergreen and nearly circular to somewhat kidney-shaped, with heart-shaped bases and round-toothed margins. Sparsely-hairy above and sometimes on their undersides, they are 2 to 3 inches in diameter. In *S. r. cordata* the leaves are proportionately much longer than wide. Plants cultivated as *S. rotundifolia sweetseri* belong here. The flowers of *S. r. alba* are white.

Another pleasing kind, **S. missurica** differs from the last in having shallower flowers with petals that spread more and that are considerably longer than the corolla tube. They are in erect racemes, 4 to 8 inches tall, with small bracts on the stalks below the blooms. The thick, lustrous, evergreen leaves, which suggest those of *Galax aphylla*, are 2 to 3 inches in diameter and round to somewhat kidney-shaped, with heart-shaped bases and double-toothed margins. They are hairless and, when young, often purplish. A rather common variant with leaves up to 6 inches broad is *S. m. major*. The blooms of *S. missurica* and its variety are most commonly a bold blue or purple-blue, but pink- and white-flowered departures are known. Although not even remotely related to *Muscari*, to which the name is ordinarily applied, in some parts of their native territories these synthyrises are called grape-hyacinths.

Less amenable to cultivation and offering more challenge to growers of alpine plants are *S. schizantha* and *S. platycarpa*. Its leaves thin and deciduous, **S. schizantha** displays its bright purple flowers in spring before its up to 6-inch-wide basal leaves appear. The flowering stems carry two leaflike bracts. The blooms of this species and *S. platycarpa* have their petals slashed at their margins into deep fringes. The foliage of *S. platycarpa* is evergreen. Its toothed leaves are more or less hairy on their undersides. The flowers are blue-purple.

Lobed or cleft leaves are featured by *S. canbyi*, *S. pinnatifida*, and *S. laciniata*, all small, high altitude, blue-flowered alpines. Similar to *S. laciniata*, *S. canbyi* has more deeply-cleft, hairless leaves. They are broadly-ovate to heart shaped and cut to about one-half their depth into toothed lobes. Variable **S. pinnatifida** has leaves deeply-pinnately-cleft to the extent that they sometimes look almost like small carrot leaves. They are hairless to densely-white-hairy.

Leaves twice-pinnately cleft (bipinnate) characterize *S. cymopteroides*, *S. hendersonii*, and *S. paysonii*, all choice alpines. Up to 6 inches tall, **S. cymopteroides** has finely-divided leaves up to 2 inches long by nearly as wide, white-hairy when young, but later losing much of their hair. The violet-blue flowers are about ¼ inch long. Also with stems and foliage white-hairy when young, and less so later, **S. hendersonii** has coarsely-divided leaves up to 2 inches long by scarcely over ½ inch wide, and ¼-inch-long, sky-blue flowers. This sort ordinarily is not over 3 inches high. Up to 8 inches tall, white-hairy in its younger parts, and less hairy later, **S. paysonii** has leaves up to 5½ inches long and stout racemes of ⅜-inch-long, violet-blue flowers.

Garden Uses and Cultivation. Rock gardens suitable for alpine plants, and alpine greenhouses afford the best environments for growing most species from high altitudes, but *S. reniformis*, *S. missurica*, and their varieties do well in less exclusive surroundings. These are satisfied with woodland-type soil, gritty enough to assure sharp drainage, yet always moderately moist. They need light shade. Even under good conditions the high alpine species are difficult to manage and often do not bloom freely. They are best in wet scree or moraine conditions or in alpine greenhouses. Propagation is by seed and by careful division after the plants are finished blooming.

SYRINGA (Sy-rínga) — Lilac. The genus *Syringa*, which belongs to the olive family OLEACEAE, consists of about thirty species of deciduous shrubs or occasionally small trees native to Europe and temperate Asia. Most gardeners and many others in temperate regions who know lilacs become a little confused when they are called by their botanical name *Syringa*, this because totally unrelated mock-oranges (*Philadelphus*) are sometimes known colloquially as syringas. The name, alluding to the hollow shoots, is derived from the Greek *syrinx*, a pipe. For clarity it is best to limit use of this word to lilacs. To most people lilacs mean fragrance, and indeed the flowers of the most popular kinds are deliciously perfumed, but there are others with little or no fragrance and an unfortunate few as ill-scented as the blooms of some of their close relatives the privets (*Ligustrum*). Nevertheless there are several sorts other than the common lilac and its varieties well worth growing.

Syringas have opposite leaves, usually undivided, rarely pinnate. The small flowers, in panicles at the ends of branches or lateral shoots, have a persistent, four-toothed, bell-shaped calyx, a narrowly-funnel-shaped to cylindrical corolla with four spreading or erect lobes (petals), two protruding or non-protruding stamens, and one style. The fruits, which clearly distinguish lilacs from privets (the fruits of which are berries) are dry capsules containing two-winged seeds.

The common lilac (*S. vulgaris*), that favorite of grandmother's garden and a native of southeastern Europe, often maintains itself in an apparently wild state for long periods around abandoned habitations. One of the earliest plants to reach North America from Europe, this species is hardy throughout New England. An erect-branched shrub or tree up to about 20 feet tall, it has shoots that at the completion of the season's growth are terminated by a pair of buds. Its hairless leaves, glaucous-green and pointed-ovate to heart-shaped, are 2 to 5 inches long and narrower than their lengths. The pale to deep lilac-colored, very fragrant blooms come after the foliage in spring. Individual flowers, about ⅓ inch long, are many together in panicles 6 to 10 inches long. Their stamens do not protrude. In *S. v. alba* the flowers are white.

Horticultural varieties of common lilac, exceedingly numerous and many very similar, are the most familiar and popular

Syringa vulgaris variety

Syringa vulgaris (flowers)

sorts. They are sometimes called French lilacs because the earliest produced, many still among the finest, were developed in the late nineteenth and early twentieth centuries in the nursery of the famous French plant breeders Victor Lemoine and his son Emile. The Lemoine introductions have been supplemented by others raised elsewhere, notably in Holland and the United States. Very fine collections are maintained at Highland Park, Rochester, New York, and the Arnold Arboretum, Jamaica Plain, Massachusetts. Dr. Donald Wyman, former horticulturist of the latter institution, recommends the following as generally most satisfactory:

Single white: 'Vestale', 'Mont Blanc', 'Jan Van Tol', 'Marie Finon'
Double white: 'Edith Cavell', 'Ellen Willmott'
Single violet: 'De Miribel', 'Cavour'
Double violet: 'Marechal Lannes', 'Violetta'
Single blue and bluish: 'President Lincoln', 'Decaisne', 'Maurice Barres'
Double blue and bluish: 'Olivier de Serres', 'Emile Gentil', 'Duc de Massa'
Single lilac: 'Marengo', 'Jacques Callot'
Double lilac: 'President Fallieres', 'Henri Martin', 'Victor Lemoine', 'Leon Gambetta'
Single pink and pinkish: 'Lucie Baltet', *S. v. macrostachya*
Double pink and pinkish: 'Mme Antoine Buchner', 'Katherine Havemeyer', 'Montaigne'
Single magenta: 'Marechal Foch', 'Mme F. Morel', 'Capitaine Baltet'
Double magenta: 'Paul Thirion', 'Paul Deschanel', 'Mrs. Edward Harding'
Single purple (or deep purple): 'Monge', 'Mrs. W. E. Marshall', 'Ludwig Spaeth'

From the common lilac, *S. oblata*, of China, differs in its nearly circular to kidney-shaped, hairless leaves, 2 to 4 inches long, being as wide or wider than their lengths. Their apexes are abruptly pointed, their bases heart-shaped. Up to 12 feet tall, this kind has densely-flowered lateral panicles 2 to 5 inches long. The ½-inch-long flowers are pinkish-lilac. The stamens do not protrude. The long-pointed leaves of *S. o. dilatata* are about 5 inches long. This species and its variety, the earliest to bloom of all lilacs, display their flowers before their leaves expand. They are unique in the genus in that their foliage often assumes attractive orange-red, reddish, to deep wine-red coloring in fall. These are hardy throughout New England. Later blooming than the common lilac, attractive *S. tomentella*, of China, 10 to 12 feet tall, has pointed, broad-elliptic to ovate leaves, 2 to 6 inches long by one-half as wide, with more or less wedge-shaped bases and downy undersides. The erect panicles of fragrant, light lilac-pink, ½-inch-long flowers are up to 8 inches long by 5 inches wide.

Hungarian lilac (*S. josikaea*), native to Hungary and extremely hardy, is up to 12 feet tall and has distinctly glossy, broadly-elliptic to oblongish leaves, 2 to 5 inches long, with rounded or broadly-wedge-shaped bases. Their undersides are glaucous and sparingly-hairy. The ½-inch-long, slightly fragrant, lilac-violet flowers, their petals not spreading widely, with funnel-shaped corolla tubes, are in panicles 4 to 7 inches long. This sort stands shearing well and is useful for hedges. Rather more handsome, but lacking the glossiness of foliage of the Hungarian lilac, Chinese *S. villosa*, when not in bloom, is sometimes confused with it. Equally as hardy, it is a shrub up to 10 feet tall with stout, upright branches. Its pointed, broadly-elliptic to oblong leaves, hairy on the veins of their undersides and finely-hairy along their edges, are 2 to 7 inches long. The panicles of scarcely fragrant, rosy-lilac to white flowers, often in threes from the shoot ends, are 4 to 7 inches long. Individual blooms, ½ inch long, have cylindrical corolla tubes and spreading petals. Like the Hungarian lilac, allied *S. wolfii*, of Korea and Manchuria, has fragrant flowers with funnel-shaped corolla tubes. Lilac-colored, they are in panicles 8 inches to 1 foot long. Also, the leaves of *S. wolfii*, bigger than those of *S. josikaea*, are 4 to 6 inches long and grayish-green on their undersides, where the veins, like the leaf edges, are somewhat hairy. The stalks of the flower panicles are also hairy. In the wild attaining heights of 20 feet, *S. wolfii* is hardy throughout most of New England.

Himalayan lilac (*S. emodii*), closely related to *S. villosa*, is much less hardy. Native to the Himalayan region and 15 feet tall or sometimes taller, this has hairless, elliptic to oblong leaves up to 6 inches long or longer, whitish on their undersides and, unlike those of the Hungarian lilac and *S. villosa*, covered with minute nipple-like projections. The unpleasantly-scented, pale mauve to whitish flowers with petals that eventually bend backward, are in wide,

dense panicles 4 to 6 inches long. The foliage of *S. e. aureo-variegata* is variegated with yellow. Less ornamental than the Himalayan lilac, but hardy in southern New England, the Yunnan lilac (*S. yunnanensis*), loosely branched, is about 10 feet tall. It differs from *S. emodii* in having pinkish flowers with nonprotruding anthers and petals not bending backward as the blooms age.

Akin to *S. villosa*, but with smaller, thinner leaves and more-slender-tubed flowers with nonprotruding anthers, *S. sweginzowii* is a Chinese of much merit. Up to about 15 feet in height, it has ovate-lanceolate to elliptic-lanceolate leaves 2 to 4 inches long by about one-half as wide, hairy on the main veins of their undersides. The fragrant, light rosy-lilac flowers, with the faces of the petals paler, are in erect panicles 6 to 8 inches long.

Pleasing pinkish flowers are borne early in the season by graceful *S. potaninii*, a 9-foot-tall native of western China hardy in southern New England. This has short-stalked, abruptly-pointed, elliptic-ovate to ovate, hairy leaves, 1½ to a little more than 2 inches long. Its flowers are in panicles up to 4 inches long. Allied to the last and also from western China, *S. julianae* is a graceful, spreading shrub, 5 to 6 feet in height, with persistently downy shoots and fragrant, lilac-purple blooms. Its short-stalked, elliptic-ovate leaves have pointed apexes and wedge-shaped bases. They are 1 inch to 2¼ inches long and hairy, densely so on their undersides. The stalks of the usually paired, 2- to 4-inch-long flower panicles are also pubescent.

Pendulous panicles of scentless flowers are characteristic of distinctive *S. reflexa* and *S. komarowii*, both natives of China and hardy in southern New England. Those of *S. reflexa*, the handsomer, in the bud stage are red, but later are predominantly white. About 12 feet tall, it has oblong to oblong-lanceolate, pointed leaves, hairless above, but hairy, especially along the veins, on their undersides. The flowers are in narrow, cylindrical panicles 4 to

Syringa yunnanensis

Syringa sweginzowii

10 inches long by up to 2 inches wide. Their petals, red on their outsides and white on their faces, spread only slightly. A variety with pure white flowers is *S. r. alba*. From *S. reflexa*, quite handsome *S. komarowii* (syn. *S. sargentiana*), up to about 15 feet tall, differs in having purple-pink flowers, paler on their outsides than within, in compact, cylindrical panicles 2 to 6 inches long.

Low shrub lilacs, species rarely exceeding 6 feet in height and better suited for some locations than taller ones, include notable **S. microphylla.** This, hardy in southern New England, has the additional merit of having small, neat leaves. A native of China, this is unique in being much broader than tall. Its leaves, ½ inch to 1½ inches long, are broad-ovate to ovate with rounded or wedge-shaped bases, and hairy at least along the veins on their undersides. In loose, pubescent-stalked, lateral panicles 2 to 2¾ inches long, the pale lilac-colored flowers are ⅓ inch long. Variety *S. m. superba* has deep pink blooms. Introduced from a Chinese garden in 1908 and unknown in the wild, *S. meyeri* is another attractive ornamental hardy in southern New England. Compact, and blooming while young and quite small, this grows slowly. It has broad-elliptic to obovate leaves, up to 2 inches long, and 4-inch-long, crowded panicles of ½-inch-long, violet-purple flowers.

Pinnately-divided or deeply-pinnately-lobed leaves are characteristic of *S. laciniata* and *S. pinnatifolia*. Native to China, *S. laciniata* is hardy in southern New England. About 6 feet tall, it has shoots up to 3 feet long with, along their lengths, a profusion of small panicles of pale lilac-colored flowers. An upright shrub some 10 feet in height and native to western China, *S. pinnatifolia* has leaves 1½ to 3½ inches long of seven or nine ovate to ovate-lanceolate leaflets up to 2¼ inches long. Rather disappointing in bloom, this has lilac-tinged, white flowers in panicles 1½ to 3 inches long. Native from Afghanistan to Tibet, *S. afghanica* is a low shrub with dainty, linear-lanceolate to ovate-lanceolate, pinnately-cleft leaves up to 3 inches long, and lilac flowers in slender panicles about 1½ inches long.

The late-flowering tree lilacs, *S. reticulata*, *S. r. mandschurica*, and *S. pekinensis*, differ from all others discussed here in their flowers having corolla tubes at most scarcely longer than their calyxes, and in their long-protruding stamens. Creamy-white and odorless or nearly so, they are displayed in June in panicles that except for their giant sizes suggest those of privets. These sorts constitute the botanical subgenus *Ligustrina*, which means privet-like. If restricted to a single trunk they become small trees; without such restriction they may develop as tall shrubs. They flower considerably later than most lilacs, in June. Japanese **S. reticulata** (syns. *S. amurensis japonica, S. japonica*), up to 30 feet high, is hardy through most of New England. Its leaves, 2 to 5 inches long and broad-ovate to heart-shaped, are, at least when young, hairy on their undersides. The creamy-white flowers in loose panicles up to 1 foot in length have an odor like those of privet. Native to northern China and Manchuria, *S. r. mandschurica* (syn. *S. amurensis*) is from 10 to 15 feet high and as hardy as the species. It has hairless, pointed, ovate to broad-ovate leaves, 2 to 5 inches long, with rounded or somewhat heart-shaped bases. The broad, usually paired panicles, 4 to 6 inches long, of nearly odorless, creamy-white flowers, up to ¼ inch long, come in June after most lilacs are through blooming. Because of its larger panicles of bloom, it surpasses typical *S. reticulata* as an ornamental. A native of northern China where it sometimes becomes 20 feet tall, *S. pekinensis* is usually lower in cultivation. From *S. reticulata* and *S. r. mandschurica* it differs in being less coarse and in having much more slender branches and leaves 2 to 4 inches long,

Syringa julianae

Syringa reflexa alba

Syringa microphylla

Syringa laciniata

Syringa reticulata

Syringa reticulata (flowers)

Syringa reticulata mandschurica

Syringa reticulata mandschurica (flowers)

ovate to ovate-lanceolate with tapered to rounded bases and hairless on both surfaces. The dense flower panicles, in pairs, are 3 to 5 inches long.

Hybrid lilacs resulting from the successful crossing of two species are fairly abundant. Not a true hybrid, very interesting **S. correlata** (syn. *S. chinensis alba*) is, in fact, a chimera or graft-hybrid. The inner tissues of its parts, consisting of cells of the hybrid *S. chinensis*, are clothed with an outer layer of cells of *S. vulgaris alba*. Most of its erect panicles are of very delicate lilac-colored flowers, but occasional ones of typical *S. chinensis* blooms are produced.

The first hybrid of which there is record, the Persian lilac (**S. persica**), believed to have been introduced to cultivation about 1614 and said to have been grown in England as early as 1640, has as parents *S. afghanica* and *S. laciniata*. Up to 6 or 7 feet tall, this elegant, rounded, slender-stemmed bush, as broad as it is high, has lanceolate leaves sometimes more or less pinnately-lobed and 1 inch to 2 inches or slightly more in length. Its fragrant, light lilac-colored blooms are in pendulous panicles 2 to 3½ inches long. Variety *S. p. laciniata*, which has more consistently pinnately-lobed leaves, is often confused with the species *S. laciniata*.

The Roven lilac (**S. chinensis** syn. *S. rothomagensis*), a hybrid between *S. persica* and *S. vulgaris* and raised at Roven, France, about 1777, is intermediate between its parents. It has large, rather loose, drooping panicles of fragrant, purple-lilac blooms. The flowers of *S. c. metensis* are pale lilac-pink, those of *S. c. saugeana*, lilac-red. *S. c. duplex* has double, purplish-lilac blooms. *S. c. nana* is of dwarf stature.

Preston hybrids (**S. prestoniae**) are extremely hardy. The initial cross, repeated since by other breeders, was made in Canada by Isabella Preston before 1925; the parents were *S. villosa* and *S. reflexa*. Unfortunately, far too many similar siblings were named. The best, highly esteemed, bloom some two weeks later than common lilac. Their leaves are as big as those of *S. villosa*. This hybrid has large, erect or drooping panicles of predominantly red-purple blooms. Recommended varieties are 'Audrey', 'Donald Wyman', 'Elinor', 'Handel', and 'Isabella'.

Other hybrids, generally intermediate between their parents, are these: **S. diversifolia,** offspring of *S. oblata giraldii* and *S. pinnatifolia* and raised at the Arnold Arboretum, Jamaica Plain, Massachusetts, in 1929, is a medium-sized to tall shrub with three- to five-lobed and lobeless leaves and usually paired flower panicles up to 4½ inches long. *S. d.* 'William Judd' has white flowers. **S. henryi,** raised in 1896 in France by crossing *S. josikaea* and *S. villosa*, is variable. Its best known variety *S. h.* 'Lutece' much resembles *S. villosa*, but has looser panicles of deeper pink flowers; those of *S. h. alba* are white. **S. hyacinthiflora** varieties, first raised in France in 1876 between *S. oblata* and *S. vulgaris*, and in the twentieth century in California using *S. oblata giraldii* as one parent, are attractive, variable early-bloomers. Among the best are 'Alice Eastwood', with double magenta flowers; 'Blue Hyacinth', its blooms single and mauve to light blue; 'Buffon', with single pale pink blooms; 'Clarke's Giant', which has single blooms rosy-mauve in bud, later lilac-blue; 'Ester Staley', with single blooms red in the bud stage, then pink; 'Lamartine', which has large panicles of lilac-blue flowers; *S. h. plena*, with delicate-violet blooms, in bud bright purple; and 'Purple Heart', with panicles of large deep purple flowers. **S. josiflexa** is the name of a pretty group of hybrids raised in the twentieth century in Canada by Isabella Preston. Their parents are *S. josikaea* and *S. reflexa*. These are medium to large-sized shrubs with loose panicles of fragrant pink blooms. The premier variety 'Bellicent' has immense panicles of rose-pink flowers. **S. nanceiana,** a variable hybrid between *S. henryi* and *S. sweginzowii* which originated in France in 1925, is a graceful, loose shrub. Its variety 'Floreal' has panicles of fragrant, lavender-mauve flowers. **S. swegiflexa** is a hybrid raised in Germany, around 1934, between *S. reflexa* and *S. sweginzowii*. A vigorous sort with large, crowded, cylindrical panicles of flowers, it is usually red in bud, pink when expanded.

Garden and Landscape Uses. Lilacs have a firm place in the affections of gardeners and other flower lovers, are used to good purpose by flower arrangers, and have inspired artists and poets. "Come to Kew in lilac time" one sang of Britain's national botanic garden. On lilac Sunday, Bostonians troupe in great numbers to admire the lilacs at the Arnold Arboretum. About the same time other thousands do so in Highland Park, Rochester, New York, and other favored places in the United States.

Are lilacs, then, plants for every garden where they can be successfully grown? The answer is not an unqualified yes. When appraised without sentimentality, it becomes clear these plants suffer from severe limitations as compared with some other deciduous shrubs and small trees. Granted they are lovely in bloom and the flowers of some, but by no means all, are deliciously fragrant, but this is about all they offer. When without foliage, most present uninteresting, rather awkward-looking skeletons of branches. With one minor exception they make no fall color display. Their fruits lack decorative appeal and indeed detract from tidiness desirable in gardens. And in late summer and fall the foliage of varieties of common lilac, *S. chinensis, S. persica,* and sometimes *S. oblata* is frequently whitened and made unsightly by mildew disease. Older branches are subject to invasions by borers. Infestations of scale insects, unless controlled by spraying, are likely to be troublesome.

Yet lilacs will and should continue to be planted, but only after careful appraisal of sites. Make sure they receive full sun. Avoid enclosed areas, interior corners of buildings, and other places where free air circulation is lacking or dampness may prevail. Such conditions favor mildew. Be sure the ground is well drained. Stagnant

Lilacs are popular cut flowers

Tabebuia impetiginosa

Syringa vulgaris variety

Swiss chard

Tagetes erecta, a tall and a short variety

Sweet william (*Dianthus barbatus*)

A well-located bush of a variety of *Syringa vulgaris*

Subcorbutia glomeriseta

Synandrospadix vermitoxicus

Tagetes patula, single-flowered

moisture, with consequent lack of air in the soil, is anathema to these shrubs. As to type of soil, lilacs are not overly particular. They prefer medium-heavy loams to sandy or gravelly earths and appreciate neutral or alkaline conditions and reasonable fertility. Poor soil and excessive dryness bring sad results, sparse, dried, and marred foliage, and weak growth that does not flower well.

All in all, the best locations for lilacs are at some distance from dwellings where they can be enjoyed during their blooming seasons, but are not too prominent at other

Lilacs located near dwellings are lovely when in bloom, but are of little interest at other seasons

A border of tall lilacs forms an effective screen from spring to fall

times. They may be used as informal screens and hedges, and taller sorts are seen to especially good advantage overhanging a wall or board fence that hides their lower parts and permits their heads to be displayed as immense and beautiful bouquets of bloom.

When purchasing, obtain "own root" plants, that is, plants raised from cuttings or, if only grafted plants are available, those worked on privet understocks. The reprehensible practice of grafting choice varieties on understocks of common lilac, now fortunately rarely practiced, is responsible for choice varieties "changing to

the old common purple-flowered kind." What actually happens is that vigorous suckers come from the understock and, because their foliage resembles that of the superior variety, pass unnoticed and eventually outgrow the variety, which in time may die. If suckers develop from privet understock, they are readily recognizable and can be quickly removed, but plants on such understock, unless they root from above the graft union, grow less satisfactorily and are shorter-lived than "own root" lilacs.

Cultivation. Lilacs transplant easily. Fall and early spring are the best seasons to move them. Care of established plants is not onerous, but for fine results certain attentions are needed. These include deep watering at approximately weekly intervals during long periods of dryness and, if the soil tends to be poor, fertilizing each year or alternate year. Too much nitrogen results in coarse, lush growth and fewer blooms. If the soil is naturally dryish, maintaining a mulch of compost or other organic material is beneficial.

Quantity and quality of bloom are greatly improved, particularly with young and middle-aged as distinct from really old specimens, if faded trusses of flowers are removed promptly. Do this by taking them between finger and thumb and snapping them sharply to one side without damaging the growth buds immediately below them. Contrary to the rather commonly expressed opinion, it is not seed pods that should be taken off, but the recently faded blooms. Formation of seeds drains the plants of energy that otherwise would stimulate growth and development of flower buds for the next season's display. It is that loss that the removal of faded flowers prevents.

Pruning is much misunderstood. As a routine attention, little is needed, but following flowering look the bushes over and, to whatever extent seems necessary to avoid overcrowding and admit a reasonable amount of light and air, cut out thin, weak, and ill-placed shoots and branches. An occasional shortening of a branch may be desirable, but those cut-back branches usually will not produce shoots that will flower the following season. This is to be remembered when cutting blooms for arrangements. Above all, do not shear or snip back all the shoots for the purpose of formal shaping.

Pruning old, rangy, overgrown lilacs calls for a different procedure. A bold approach, sacrificing all or a sizable proportion of bloom for a season, is called for. The best is to saw all trunks and branches 6 inches to 1 foot above ground level off before new growth begins in spring, then to fertilize and make sure during dry periods in summer to thoroughly soak the roots with water at about weekly intervals. An alternative, by some authorities a

preferred method and certainly one for those too weak-hearted to so boldly assault a prized lilac, is to cut about one-third of the stems down in this fashion one year and the others in succeeding springs.

Forcing lilacs into early bloom in greenhouses is less practiced than formerly, but is easy to do. Select young vigorous specimens well set with flower buds and in early fall plant them in pots or tubs just big enough to contain their root balls. Set them outdoors, in harsh climates with their containers plunged to their rims in leaves, compost, peat moss, or similar insulating material, and keep them well watered. From January on, bring successive batches into the greenhouse. Best results are had if the temperature at first is 40 to 50°F at night and a few degrees more by day, and is then raised about ten degrees after growth is well started. Spray the branches lightly several times daily with water to soften the buds and encourage growth. After flowering is through, gradually harden off the plants. Then, after danger of frost has passed, plant them in an agreeable location outdoors.

Propagation of lilac species can be by seed and by vegetative methods suitable for other kinds. Chief of these last are summer cuttings rooted under mist. Hardwood cuttings taken in fall with a heel of old wood attached to their bases are also successful. A simple and sure way is to remove and replant sucker growths that appear around old plants, but this is only satisfactory so far as perpetuating the variety grown if the mother plant is on its own roots, not grafted. If lilacs are grafted onto privet, and this is a very simple procedure, it is important when setting the young plants in nursery rows to plant them deeply with the graft union 3 or 4 inches beneath the surface. This encourages roots to develop from the tissues of the lilac itself and then the privet understock may be cut off and the lilac replanted as an "own root" specimen. If this is not done and if the privet understock remains, years later a graft blight is likely to develop and cause the sudden death of branches or even the entire bush.

SYRINGING. Less often used than formerly, the greenhouse gardeners' term syringing refers to forcefully spraying plants with a stream of water broken into small droplets to dislodge mealybugs, red spider mites, and some other pests, to wash away grime and dust, and incidentally to increase humidity. The word stems from the practice, chiefly European, but at one time employed to some extent in North America, of using for the operation a hand pump called a syringe. More commonly in America a hose, fitted with a special nozzle or its stream skillfully controlled by holding thumb or fingers across its end, was and is used for syringing.

Syringing is most practicable with plants that have firm, smooth, more or less leathery leaves, such as aspidistras, codiaeums, and philodendrons. Hairy-leaved sorts, such as African-violets, should not be syringed. Done with judgment on bright rather than dull days and always early enough that the foliage dries before nightfall, it is decidedly beneficial. It is unwise to syringe plants infested with foliar nematodes or infected with bacterial diseases as these are apt to be spread by the water.

When syringing, it is important to direct upward and manipulate the spray so that all the undersides of the leaves and the stems are reached. Take care not to use so much water that, unless this is desirable for other reasons, the soil is saturated. Houseplants of appropriate kinds benefit greatly from being syringed occasionally. This may be done most conveniently by standing them in a sink or bathtub or taking them outside, perhaps laying them horizontally if this is more convenient.

SYZYGIUM (Syzý-gium)—Australian Brush-Cherry, Rose-Apple or Jambos, Jambolan or Java-Plum, Clove Tree. Although some authorities include this genus in related *Eugenia,* most keep it separate. This they do on the technical difference that the embryo is divided. Also, the flowers are without staminal disks, often have their petals united, and usually have smooth-edged rather than lobed calyxes. So accepted, *Syzygium* contains between 400 and 500 species of evergreen trees and shrubs of the Old World tropics. They belong in the myrtle family MYRTACEAE. The name, from the Greek *syzygos,* united, alludes to the petals of some kinds being joined.

Syzygiums are nonhardy trees and shrubs. They have opposite, short-stalked, undivided, feather-veined leaves that, unlike those of eugenias, which are predominantly pubescent, are nearly always hairless. The flowers, solitary or in clusters or panicles, are usually at the ends of the shoots. They have a turban-shaped calyx sometimes with four or five lobes (sepals), four petals, many stamens, and one branchless style. The fruits are berries containing rough-surfaced seeds.

Australian brush-cherry (**S. paniculatum** syns. *Eugenia paniculata, E. myrtifolia*) is a tree up to 40 feet tall or taller. Its hairless leaves, 1½ to 3 inches long and pointed-oblong-lanceolate, when young are bronzy-colored or tinged with red. In branched panicles from the leaf axils or at the ends of short branchlets, the slightly fragrant, white flowers are ½ inch across. The egg-shaped, rosy-purple fruits, about ¾ inch long, are used for making jelly. Variety *S. p. australis* is smaller. Its flowers, unlike those of the typical species, do not stand well out from the foliage. Variety *S. p.* 'Antone Dwarf' is similar to if not identical with the last. Variety *S. p. compacta* is more compact than the typical species.

Syzygium paniculatum

Syzygium paniculatum australis (foliage and flowers)

The rose-apple or jambos (**S. jambos** syns. *Eugenia jambos, Jambos vulgaris*), a native of the East Indies, is a broad-headed, densely-foliaged tree up to about 30 feet tall. It has glossy, oblanceolate leaves up to 8 inches long. When very young they are wine-colored. The pompon-like white flowers are 2½ to 3 inches in diameter. From 1½ to 2 inches across, the hollow fruits are delicate yellow or pinkish-ivory-white. Their thin, crisp flesh is quite separate from the three or fewer large, brown seeds occupying the central cavity. The fruits may be eaten out of hand, candied, or made into jellies. They are fragrant and have a flavor of the scent of roses. Similar to the last, the Malay-apple, jambos, or large-fruited rose-apple (**S. malaccense** syn. *Eugenia malaccensis*) has pointed, oblong to elliptic leaves 5 to 10 inches long by about one-fifth as wide. The bright rose-red flowers, in clusters or panicles from the branches, have petals not united and numerous stamens. They are succeeded by pear-shaped, pink or white, rose-scented fruits about 2 inches long. Although rather insipid, they may be eaten raw, but are more frequently cooked or made into jellies.

The jambolan, jambolan-plum, or Java-plum (**S. cumini**) is a whitish-branched tree of compact habit commonly up to 40, exceptionally 80 feet tall. It has glossy, leathery, broad-elliptic to oblong leaves 3 to 8 inches long, dark green above, paler on their undersides, and when young reddish. They have conspicuous midribs. The ¼-inch-wide, white flowers are in branched clusters from leafless older parts of the shoots. They are succeeded by deep-maroon or purple fruits, ½ to 1 inch long, generally cylindrical-ovate, but sometimes curved. The fruits of individual trees vary considerably in eating quality. They range

Syzygium paniculatum (fruits)

Syzygium paniculatum 'Antone Dwarf'

from pleasantly mildly acid to tart and even mouth-puckering. They make good jelly.

The clove tree (**S. aromaticum** syns. *Eugenia aromatica, Caryophyllus aromaticus*), native to the Molucca Islands, is a medium-sized tree with elliptic-lanceolate leaves 3 to 5 inches long by 1 inch to 2 inches wide, tapered to both ends. In 1-inch-long, terminal panicles, the flowers are yellow. Picked in the bud stage and dried, they are the spice cloves.

Other sorts in cultivation include these: **S. aqueum** (syn. *Eugenia aquea*), called the water-rose-apple and believed to be a native of southern India, is 15 to 30 feet tall and has short-stalked leaves sometimes more than 6 inches long and heart-shaped at their bases. The 1-inch-wide, white, light purple, or red flowers, in clusters of seven or fewer in the leaf axils or at the shoot ends, are succeeded by edible, red or white, top-shaped fruits, ¾ inch to 1½ inches wide. **S. coolminianum,** because its fruits resemble those of the lilly-pilly (*Acmena smithii*), is called blue-lilly-pilly. Australian and white-barked, this shrub or tree up to 20 feet tall has elliptic-lanceolate leaves up to 4 inches long and glandular-dotted. In loose, few-flowered panicles, its blooms are creamy-white. About ½ inch in diameter, the fruits are violet. **S. grande** (syn. *Eugenia grandis*), the sea-apple, a tree up to 100 feet tall, is a native of tropical Asia. It has obovate to subcircular, glossy leaves 4 to 9 inches long, with a down-turned tip, and, in terminal and axillary compact panicles, fragrant, white flowers 1 inch to 1½ inches across. The spherical to pear-shaped, dryish, edible fruits, about 1 inch long, have green, leathery skin. **S. pycnanthum,** the wild-rose-apple, of Malaya, Sumatra, and Java, is an ornamental shrub or small tree with glossy, ovate-oblong to lanceolate leaves up to 1 foot in length. In clusters of two or three, the white or pinkish flowers are 1½ to 2 inches wide. Nearly spherical and about ½ inch in diameter,

Syzygium malaccense (fruits)

the fruits are deep red-purple. **S. samarangense,** of the Malay Archipelago, is called the Java-apple. From 20 to 30 feet in height, this has briefly-stalked, blunt, elliptic-oblong leaves up to 7 inches long and, in many-flowered clusters, white blooms 1½ inches wide. The pear-shaped, white or red fruits are 1 inch to 1½ inches long.

Garden and Landscape Uses and Cultivation. Of the kinds discussed above, the most frequently cultivated in the continental United States is the Australian brush-cherry. This is satisfactory in California and other warm-temperate and subtropical regions. Excellent for general-purpose landscaping, it is also attractive in containers. It stands shearing well and is a good hedge plant. The rose-apple succeeds in climates that suit the last. Admired for its handsome foliage and showy blooms, it also pleases with its fragrant fruits. The jambolan is planted in some warm countries as a windbreak. The other kinds we have discussed need more tropical, humid environments. They are often included in botanical collections of plants useful to man. All of these prosper in ordinary, reasonably fertile soils in sun or part-day shade. They may be pruned to shape at the beginning of a new growth period. Propagation is easy by seed and by cuttings.

Syzygium cumini (fruits)

T

TABEBUIA (Ta-be-bùia) — Trumpet Tree. The name *Tabebuia* is a modification of *tacyba bebuya*, a South American Indian name for trees of this genus of the big-nonia family BIGNONIACEAE. The genus consists of about 100 species of evergreen and deciduous trees and shrubs of tropical America and the West Indies. A few are greatly esteemed in warm regions, includ-ing Florida and Hawaii, as showy-flow-ered ornamentals. The tree sometimes named *T. donnell-smithii* is *Cybistax donnell-smithii*.

Tabebuias have mostly opposite, long-stalked leaves, undivided or composed of stalked, toothed or toothless leaflets that spread in finger-like fashion from the tips of the leafstalks. The flowers, commonly but not always, are in evidence when the trees are leafless. Clustered in terminal ra-cemes or panicles, they have irregularly three- or five-lobed, tubular or bell-shaped calyxes, and tubular, funnel-shaped, slightly two-lipped corollas, more or less pubescent on their insides, with five spreading lobes (petals). The four sta-mens, in two pairs, do not protrude be-yond the mouth of the corolla. There is a small staminode (nonfunctional stamen) and a slender style tipped with a two-lobed stigma. The fruits are usually long, slim, drooping capsules containing many winged seeds. Water-dispersed species have short, thick capsules with wingless seeds. The botany of *Tabebuia* is confusing and plants in cultivation are frequently misnamed.

Yellow-flowered, the beautiful silver trumpet tree, **T. argentea** (syn. *T. caraiba*), 25 to 40 feet tall, is justly a favorite. This frequently has a leaning or crooked trunk and a narrow head. Its leaves are of five or seven long-stalked, silvery-gray, nar-rowly-blunt-oblong leaflets, the largest about 6 inches long. Displayed in abun-dance in spring, with or without the foli-age, the flowers are 2 to 3½ inches long. They are succeeded by woody seed pods 3 to 6 inches long by about ¾ inch thick. Called yellow trumpet tree, yellow-te-coma, or yellow poui, **T. serratifolia** is often misidentified as *T. longiflora*, which name properly belongs to another species, a na-tive of Cuba. Except for its yellow blooms, *T. serratifolia* somewhat resembles *T. pal-lida*. Native to South America and Trini-dad and up to 30 feet tall or taller, this broad-headed, deciduous kind has leaves with five to seven unequal-sized, stalked leaflets, usually toothed at their apexes, the largest about 6 inches long. Very lovely **T. ochracea** (syn. *T. heterotricha*), of Central America and South America, usually is in leaf at blooming time. Up to 45 feet in height, it has leaves of five oblanceolate to nearly oblong leaflets round-tipped or ending in short points. The young shoots, leafstalks, and undersides of the leaves are densely-velvety-hairy. In dense clusters at the branch ends, the yellow flowers have conspicuously fuzzy calyxes, and corollas 1½ to 2 inches in length. The kind for-merly called *T. neochrysantha* is *T. ochracea neochrysantha*. A native of northern South America, this has golden-yellow flowers with yellow calyxes that, like the under-surfaces of the leaves, are thickly clothed with hairs.

Other yellow-flowered tabebuias are cultivated. Native in both moist and dry areas from Mexico to Venezuela, variable **T. chrysantha** (syns. *T. glomerata*, *T. rufes-cens*) ranges from a small tree to one up to 100 feet in height. It has a rounded or flat-tened crown. Its yellowish-red, short-haired flower buds, many together in rather crowded clusters at the branchlet ends, expand in succession into sweetly fra-grant, golden trumpets 1 inch to 3 inches long. The usually opposite leaves have five obovate to broad-elliptic leaflets up to about 7 inches in length, their undersides, and to a lesser extent their upper sides, more or less furnished with stellate (star-shaped) hairs. Yellow-flowered **T. guayacan**, in-digenous to rain forests from Mexico to Panama, in the wild attains heights up to 150 feet. Its leaves have five to seven lan-ceolate to narrowly-ovate leaflets, hairy beneath only in the axils of the veins. In

Tabebuia chrysantha

large, loose clusters at the branch tips, the handsome blooms, 2 to 2½ inches long, are displayed while the tree is leafless, all of each panicle being open at the same time. Yet another yellow-flowered kind possibly cultivated, Brazilian **T. umbellata** is a tree up to about 60 feet tall. It has hairless or slightly hairy leaves of seven pointed-el-liptic leaflets, and umbel-like clusters of nearly 3-inch-long flowers. The blooms are borne either while the tree is leafless or while it is in foliage.

Pink trumpet tree or pink-tecoma (**T. ro-sea**) is frequently misidentified as *T. pen-taphylla*. It is a variable evergreen or decid-uous species widely distributed from Mexico to tropical South America. From 60 to 90 feet tall, but in cultivation usually considerably lower, it has opposite, long-stalked leaves generally of five pointed, elliptic-oblong to elliptic-ovate, hairless, toothless leaflets up to 6 inches long. From 2 to 4 inches in length, the flowers, usu-ally paired in the panicles, are pale pink to rose-pink or lavender-pink, or are white with a yellow throat, the throat later be-coming white. The seed pods are 8 inches to over 1 foot long by ½ to 1 inch wide. In the wild favoring dryish regions, **T. impetiginosa** (syns. *T. avellanedae, T. palmeri*) is 15 to 50 feet in height. It has opposite leaves with five to seven ovate to elliptic leaflets 2 to 7 inches long by up to 3½ inches wide, hairy on their undersides in the axils of the lateral veins or less commonly over the whole surface. The flowers, in threes in rather crowded panicles, usually are displayed while the tree is leafless. Pink to purple, they have yellow throats that turn purple with age. They are narrowly-bell-shaped and 1½ to 3 inches long. This is native from Mexico to Argentina. The kind sometimes segregated as **T. ipe** is so closely similar to *T. impetiginosa* that it can scarcely be more than a variety of that species.

Tabebuia impetiginosa

Also pink-flowered, **T. pallida** (syn. *T. heterophylla*) is a variable kind of which at least two varieties are cultivated. One, which has leaves with narrowly-obcordate leaflets with an iridescent sheen, bears its pink blooms in one flush while quite bare of foliage. The other retains its foliage throughout the year and has leaves with three or five broad-elliptic to obovate, stalked leaflets with blades 2 to 6 inches long by nearly or quite one-half as broad. The pink blooms, which in Florida appear sporadically throughout the year, are 1½ to 2 inches long and wide.

Garden and Landscape Uses and Cultivation. In tropical and warm subtropical climates, tabebuias are among the most splendid flowering trees for use as lawn specimens and in other decorative plantings. They grow best in deep, fertile soils in sunny locations. Increase is by seed, cuttings, and air layering.

TABERNAEMONTANA (Tabernae-montàna)—Crape-Jasmine or Clavel de la India, Fleur d'Amour. About 150 species constitute *Tabernaemontana*, of the dogbane family APOCYNACEAE. Trees and shrubs of the Old World and the New World tropics, some are planted in warm regions for ornament. The name commemorates Ja-

kob Theodor von Bergzabern, physician and herbalist of Heidelberg, Germany, who Latinized Bergzabern as *Tabernaemontanus.* He died in 1590.

Tabernaemontanas are evergreens with milky sap, that of some sorts containing rubber, and opposite, usually hairless, pinnate-veined leaves. Their white or yellow blooms are in terminal, forked or little-branched clusters. They have mostly small, five-parted or five-lobed calyxes and corollas with five spreading, twisted lobes (petals). There are five stamens and one style. The fruits are paired, leathery, pod-like follicles containing rows of seeds coated with scarlet pulp.

In the Orient the pulp surrounding the seeds of the crape-jasmine is employed to some extent as a red dye, and the wood is reported to be used in perfumery and for incense. The roots, which play a part in Oriental medicine, are said to be poisonous.

The crape-jasmine or clavel de la India (**T. divaricata** syns. *T. coronaria, Ervatamia coronaria*) is sometimes called paper-gar-

Tabernaemontana divaricata

denia. Native to India, and cultivated and naturalized in many warm countries, it is a popular ornamental in the southern United States. An evergreen, much-branched shrub up to 8 feet tall or taller, it has stalked, thinnish, pointed, elliptic to elliptic-lanceolate, hairless leaves, lustrous above, paler on their undersurfaces, and with wavy margins. From 3 to 6 inches long, they have stalks with stem-clasping bases. The small clusters of flowers develop from the forks of the young branches and at their ends. Pure white, waxy, and with small yellow centers, the slender-tubed blooms are 1 inch to 2 inches across. Their petals have crimped or ruffled margins. The seed pods, in pairs, are red on their insides, recurved, and 1 inch to 2 inches long. Each two spread like a pair of horns. Often, cultivated plants do not bear seed pods freely. Double-flowered **T. d. flore-pleno,** the fleur

Tabernaemontana divaricata flore-pleno

d'amour, is especially lovely and has blooms that much resemble those of gardenias.

Other species sometimes cultivated are these: **T. citrifolia,** of the West Indies, Mexico, Central America, and South America, is a hairless shrub or tree 6 to 30 feet tall. It has oblong-elliptic to obovate-elliptic, short-stalked leaves 2 to 8 inches long and much-branched clusters of white, sweet-scented blooms 1 inch or somewhat more in diameter. **T. holstii,** of East Africa, is a shrub or tree up to 20 feet tall or sometimes taller, with pointed, broad-elliptic leaves 6 inches to 1 foot long or on occasion larger. The yellow-throated white flowers are about 1¼ inches long and slightly more across the face. They are very fragrant. The spherical fruits are up to 4 inches in diameter. **T. orientalis,** of Australia, has fragrant flowers about ½ inch in diameter succeeded by orange, egg-shaped fruits about ½ inch long. From the typical species, *T. o. angustisepala* differs in having narrower leaves, and fruits 1 inch to 1¼ inches long.

Garden and Landscape Uses. Tabernaemontanas can be used with good effect in borders and foundation plantings and as attractive informal hedges and boundaries. They may be used as backgrounds for smaller plants, as well. The attractive flowers are borne in succession and continuously over a very long period. They contrast beautifully with the foliage and are useful for cutting. The double ones are delightful for corsages. The crape-jasmine is a good greenhouse plant, blooming when quite small and easier to grow than gardenias. When accommodated in large pots or tubs, it is effective for decorating patios, terraces, and similar areas.

Cultivation. The crape-jasmine and other sorts described here flourish even in fairly poor soils, but will repay, by superior vigor and bloom, more kindly treatment. Fertile, well-drained soil that does not lack for moisture is best. Although they stand part-shade, they prosper better in sun. Once established, tabernaemontanas need minimum care. Any pruning needed to keep them shapely or restrict their size is done just before a new season of growth. Keeping the soil mulched is good practice. Propagation is easy by cuttings and layering, and the single-flowered kinds come readily from seed. The crape-jasmine is harmed by temperatures of 25°F and lower. If, however, the roots are not killed, it will send up new shoots in spring that will bloom the first year. Where winter damage is likely to occur, some gardeners dig up and pot smallish specimens in fall, and winter them in a light place indoors where they are not subject to freezing.

In greenhouses the crape-jasmine flourishes in any ordinary well-drained potting soil kept moderately moist, but not saturated. A night temperature in winter of 50 to 55°F is satisfactory (it gets along under even cooler conditions). By day the temperature may be five to ten degrees higher than that kept at night. A moderately moist atmosphere and full sun are desirable. In summer the plants may with advantage be stood outdoors. Needed pruning to shape and control size is done in late winter or early spring. Plants that have filled their containers with roots are helped by regular applications of dilute liquid fertilizers from spring through fall.

Pests and Diseases. Mealybugs, scales, and aphids are the chief insect pests. Whitefly and nematodes, so bothersome with gardenias, do not seem to be partial to crape-jasmine. A sooty mold fungus lives on the honeydew excreted by aphids and scales and mars the appearance of the foliage.

TABOG. See Swinglea.

TACAMAHAC is *Populus balsamifera*.

TACCA (Tác-ca) — Devil Flower or Bat Flower. The strange tacca family TACCA-CEAE consists of only *Tacca*, a genus of about ten species, most numerous as to sorts in tropical Asia, islands of the Pacific, and Australia, but represented also in tropical Africa and tropical America. The name *Tacca* is believed to derive from a native one used in Amboina. A starchy foodstuff called East Indian arrowroot is prepared from the rhizomes of *T. leontopetaloides* and some other species.

Taccas are hairless plants with stringy roots. Their all-basal leaves are stalked, and are without lobes or teeth or may be deeply-once or more times cleft, pinnately or palmately (like the spreading fingers of a hand), into many lobes. The few to numerous flowers, greenish, yellowish, purplish, or dark brown, are in dense clusters atop long leafless stalks and are accompanied by conspicuous bracts and many long, whisker-like processes that are thought to represent sterile flower stalks.

Tacca chantrieri

The flowers have perianths with tubes joined to the ovaries, and six spreading lobes (petals). The six stamens have wide filaments (stalks). There is a short, stout style topped by a star-shaped stigma. The fruits are berries.

The devil flower or bat flower (*T. chantrieri*), native to Malaya, is most frequent in cultivation. Its long-stalked leaves have undivided, broad-elliptic, lustrous, corrugated, olive-green blades up to 1½ feet long by 10 inches broad. The curious clusters of dark purple-brown blooms, each flower about 1⅓ inches wide, are framed by broad, blackish-maroon bracts that suggest a bat's wings and are accompanied by a beard of long, drooping filaments. Also called bat flower, *T. integrifolia* (syn. *T. cristata*), of southeast Asia, is similar to *T. chantrieri*, but somewhat smaller. Its flower clusters have bracts with a spread of about 1½ inches.

Native to Canton province, China, *T. plantaginea* (syn. *Schizocapsa plantaginea*) has stalked, smooth-edged, broadly-lanceolate, prominently-veined leaves 8 to 9 inches long, which, unlike those of similar *T. integrifolia*, have blades that extend as wings down the leafstalk. The umbels are of up to twenty blooms interspersed with threadlike filaments. The cup-shaped, greenish and brown flowers have short stalks and are succeeded by ⅜-inch-long fruits, much smaller than those of *T. integrifolia*.

Distinctive *T. leontopetaloides* (syn. *T. pinnatifida*) has leaves with stalks 1 foot to 3 feet long and blades 1 foot to 4 feet across with three pinnately-cleft lobes. The leaf blades are reminiscent of those of papaya (*Carica*). The greenish-purplish flowers, about 1½ inches in diameter and more numerous in the clusters than those of *T. chantrieri*, top long stalks. The clusters, backed by six to twelve large bracts, are accompanied by many drooping and spreading, whisker-like filaments 4 to 9 inches long. This species is widely distributed through the Old World tropics, including islands of the Pacific. Undoubtedly its wide range is partly the result of it having been transported as a food crop by primitive peoples. It exhibits slight variation in different areas. The Hawaiian phase is sometimes distinguished as *T. hawaiiensis*.

Garden and Landscape Uses and Cultivation. In the humid tropics, taccas are admirable for planting in shaded places in fertile, fairly moist soil that contains reasonable stores of organic matter. They make useful undercover beneath trees. Elsewhere they may be grown, either in

Tacca leontopetaloides

ground beds or pots, in greenhouses where the minimum night temperature in winter is 55 to 60°F and that by day five to fifteen degrees higher. At other seasons they appreciate even more warmth. A humid atmosphere should be maintained and watering done to keep the soil always moist without being for long periods soggy. To guard against excessive wetness the containers should be well drained. Taccas in greenhouses need coarse, rich, loamy soil that contains a fair amount of humus. They need shade except in winter. Established specimens respond to weekly applications of dilute liquid fertilizer from spring to fall. Repot every two or three years in spring, and, if increase is desired, divide the plants at that time. Propagation of some kinds can also be achieved by taking off tubers, and of all kinds, by seed sown in sandy, peaty soil in a temperature of 70 to 80°F.

TACCACEAE—Tacca Family. The characteristics of this family of monocotyledons are those of its only genus, *Tacca*.

TACCARUM (Tac-càrum). There are four species, close relatives of *Amorphophallus*, in the tropical American genus *Taccarum*, of the arum family ARACEAE. The name is derived from those of the related genera *Tacca* and *Arum*.

Taccarums are nonhardy, deciduous, tuberous, herbaceous perennials with solitary, long-stalked leaves that have blades of three divisions, the center one larger than the others, and all two- or three-times-pinnately-lobed. As is usual in the arum family, what is often thought to be a flower is an inflorescence. In *Taccarum* it tops a stalk much shorter than the stalk of the leaf and has a broad, more or less petallike bract called a spathe and a spikelike column or spadix upon which are, loosely arranged, many small unisexual flowers, the female ones on the basal portion, those above male.

Of unusual and appealing aspect, *T. weddellianum*, of Brazil, Bolivia, and Paraguay, has a large tuber from which develops a leaf with an erect stalk 1½ to 3 feet long and a nearly horizontal blade up to 1¼ feet in length, wider than long, and three-times-dissected into many small ultimate segments. The inflorescence, which appears with the leaf, has a 2- to 6-inch-long stalk, a boat-shaped spathe 4½ to 6 inches long, and a spadix 9 inches to 1¼ feet long. The spathe is yellowish-gray-green with conspicuous longitudinal veins. Because the pale yellow male flowers are on individual stalks about ¾ inch long that hold them out from the column upon which they are borne, at its height of bloom, the spadix has a distinctly torch-like appearance.

Garden and Landscape Uses and Cultivation. These are as for the genus *Amorphophallus*.

Taccarum weddellianum

Taccarum weddellianum (leaf)

Taccarum weddellianum (inflorescence)

TACINGA (Tacíng-a). This prickly-pear (*Opuntia*) relative consists of one species of the cactus family CACTACEAE and is native to Brazil. Its name is an anagram of Catinga, the name of a desert in Brazil. From prickly-pears, *Tacinga* differs in its clambering or vinelike habit of growth, in its flowers having green or violet-red petals, and in its long-protruding stamens that are not sensitive to being touched.

When young, erect and bushy, but later becoming a vine with somewhat branching, slender stems 3 to 40 feet long, *T. funalis* has flowers that open at night. They have few narrow, greenish, 1½-inch-long petals that bend or coil backward. The long-protruding stamens form a tube that surrounds the cream-colored style, which extends just beyond them and is tipped with a green, five-lobed stigma. Between the petals and stamens is a conspicuous circle of hairs. The long-egg-shaped fruits, up to 2 inches in length, contain a few white seeds. When young, the stems are soft and slightly-ribbed and bear vestigial leaves; from the areoles (specialized locations on the stems of cactuses from which are produced spines, hairs, flowers, etc.) sprout two or three spines and more numerous white glochids (minute barbed spines). The leaves and glochids soon shed and the stems, as they age, become more or less woody.

Garden and Landscape Uses and Cultivation. These are as for *Opuntia*. For more information see Cactuses.

TACITUS (Tac-itus). The only species of *Tacitus*, of the crassula family CRASSULACEAE, differs from allied *Echeveria* and *Graptopetalum* in floral details. The meaning of the name is apparently unexplained.

Endemic to Mexico, *T. bellus* is a nonhardy, evergreen perennial with one or more stemless, compact rosettes, 1 inch to 3 inches wide, of twenty-five to fifty hairless, obovate leaves with more or less pointed apexes and tapered to wedge-shaped bases. The flowering stalks, arising laterally from the rosette, bear few to several stalked blooms with five reflexed sepals, five or sometimes four deep pink, spreading petals, ten stamens, and five erect pistils, each with a long style.

Garden Uses and Cultivation. These are as for *Echeveria*.

TACSONIA. See Passiflora.

TAENIDIA (Taen-ídia). The only species of this genus inhabits rocky hillsides and dry woodlands from Quebec to Minnesota, Georgia, and Louisiana. A herbaceous perennial of the carrot family UMBELLIFERAE, it has a name that refers to the low ribs of its fruits, derived from the Greek *tainidion*, a little band.

A branching plant 1¼ to 2½ feet in height, *Taenidia integerrima* is hairless, with somewhat glaucous stems and mostly thrice-divided leaves. Only the upper ones are twice- or once-divided. The stalks of the lower leaves are long; those of the upper ones are shorter and completely sheathe the stems. The leaflets are ovate to elliptic, usually not toothed, and up to 1 inch long. The tiny, yellow, five-petaled flowers are in umbels of much smaller, long-stalked umbels. The inner flowers of the latter are short-stalked males, the bisexual outer ones have longer stalks. The flattened, wingless fruits are longitudinally ribbed and about ⅙ inch long.

Garden Uses and Cultivation. Suitable for native plant gardens and semiwild plantings, *T. integerrima* succeeds in ordinary soil in sun or part-day shade. It is increased by seed.

TAGETES (Tagèt-es) — African Marigold, French Marigold. The name marigold is applied to more than one kind of plant, frequently with an adjectival qualifier. Examples include marsh-marigold (*Caltha*), pot marigold (*Calendula*), Cape-marigold (*Dimorphotheca*), and African and French marigolds (*Tagetes*). Used alone, the name marigold historically belongs most properly to *Calendula*, the Mary's gold of the ancient herbalists, but in America marigold used by itself almost always refers to *Tagetes*. Certain kinds are called African marigolds and others French marigolds, but they are neither African nor French, but are derivatives of species native to the New World. In recent years something of a campaign has been conducted by a prominent American seed firm to popularize American marigold as a name for what we have called African marigold, but there is little virtue in such invented "common" names.

The genus *Tagetes* contains about thirty species of mostly annuals, but includes a few tender, herbaceous perennials, of the daisy family COMPOSITAE. Its name possibly honors Tages, an Etruscan god, but its derivation is not well established. The genus is indigenous from the southwestern United States to Argentina.

Species of *Tagetes* have strongly-scented foliage, but varieties without this have been bred. All are branching, erect or diffuse plants, with usually opposite and most commonly pinnately-dissected, ferny leaves. Those of a few species are only toothed. The flower heads, which vary considerably in size, are solitary or clustered. They have both disk and ray florets. There are many garden varieties, most of which have double flowers. The seedlike fruits are achenes.

The African marigold (*T. erecta*) as a native ranges from Mexico to Central America. A stout annual, it attains a height of 3 feet and has pinnate leaves and solitary, yellow to orange flower heads, 2 to 5 inches in diameter, that in cultivated varieties have

Tagetes erecta

many ray florets, but in wild specimens few.

The French marigold (*T. patula*), native to Mexico and Guatemala, is much branched, 6 inches to 1½ feet tall, and has finely-divided, ferny leaves and solitary flower heads about 1 inch across and yellow with reddish or brown markings.

The sweet-scented marigold (*T. lucida*), of Mexico and Guatemala, is distinct among cultivated kinds in that its leaves are finely-toothed, but not dissected, and its flower heads are in dense, terminal clusters. Each head, about ½ inch across, has only two or three ray florets. The flowers are yellow to orange-yellow. Although a perennial this is grown as an annual. It attains a height of 1½ to 2½ feet.

Popular **T. tenuifolia** (syn. *T. signata*), up to 2 feet tall, has very-finely-dissected, ferny leaves (much more finely cut than those of the French marigold) and solitary, few-rayed, yellow flower heads. More commonly cultivated than the species, its

variety, *T. t. pumila,* is 6 inches to 1 foot in height and forms a broad, compact plant thickly covered with starry blooms. Occasionally cultivated for seasoning and use in home medicines, **T. minuta** is a South American annual naturalized in parts of the United States. Up to 3 feet tall, it has pinnate leaves and flower heads under ½ inch wide, with usually three ray florets. African and French marigolds are offered in a tremendous range of varieties, differing in height, size, and type of bloom, flower color, and other characteristics. The flowers of African marigolds range in color from cream through lemon-yellow to golden-yellow and orange, those of French marigolds from clear yellow to orange and chestnut brown and various variegated patterns of these and similar colors. Descriptions of up-to-date varieties will be found in seedsmen's catalogs.

Garden Uses. Few annuals are more popular or easier to grow in most American gardens than the various kinds of marigolds. They are highly ornamental in flower beds and borders and may be used effectively in window and porch boxes. The dwarf French marigolds and *T. tenuifolia pumila* are admirable plants for low edgings. The brilliant flowers of the African marigolds and taller varieties of French marigolds are excellent for cutting, and plants of these kinds are well worth growing in greenhouses for the production of cut flowers in late winter and spring and as pot plants for display in conservatories and greenhouses. Most French marigolds do not bloom in extremely hot weather. In many parts of the United States they cease producing flowers through July and most of August, but make magnificent displays from then until frost.

A horticultural variety of *Tagetes erecta*

Horticultural varieties of French marigolds: (a) Single-flowered

Planting French marigolds: (a) Marking off the bed before spading it

(d) Setting out young plants from pots or flats

(b) Double-flowered

(b) Raking the soil level

(e) Watering immediately after planting

(c) The bed, ready for planting

(f) In full bloom a few weeks later

Cultivation. Tagetes can be raised from seed sown outdoors in early spring, and the seedlings either thinned out to the required distance between plants or transplanted. The latter method is preferable and, since they transplant with great ease and are big enough to handle easily, can be done expeditiously. If possible, transplanting should be done during cloudy, moist weather. A more usual method, which has the advantage of providing plants that flower earlier in the season than those from outdoor sowings, is to sow the seeds early indoors, transplant the seedlings 2 inches apart in flats, and plant them out in the garden from these at about the time it is safe to set out tomatoes. In their early stages, these plants grow quickly and seed sowing need not be done until six or seven weeks before the young plants are to be transferred to the garden. The seed germinates satisfactorily in a temperature of 60 to 65°F, and the young plants may be grown in a night temperature of 50°F, with a daytime rise of five or ten degrees permitted. At all times they need full sun.

In the garden, too, tagetes must be given a sunny location and a porous soil not excessively rich in nitrogen. African marigolds respond to more fertile soil than is desirable for other kinds, but even they should not be put in earth that is too rich.

The availability of too much nitrogen causes lush stem and leaf growth at the expense of bloom and can make the plants more susceptible to disease. These conditions can also result from excessive watering. A dressing of superphosphate worked into the soil before planting is helpful. African marigold plants should be spaced 1 foot to 1½ feet apart, French marigolds 8 inches to 1 foot, and *T. lucida* and *T. tenuifolia* about 1 foot. About 8 inches is satisfactory

spacing between plants of the popular *T. tenuifolia pumila*. Even tall varieties stand well and need little staking. Routine care consists chiefly of picking off faded blooms and, in the early stages, keeping down weeds. After the plants are half grown, their foliage usually is so dense and the ground beneath them so permeated with roots that weeds have scarcely a chance of getting started or of establishing themselves.

For late winter and spring blooming in greenhouses, seeds of African and tall French marigolds are sown from September to January in a temperature of about 60°F. The seedlings are transferred individually to small pots or are set 2 inches apart in flats, and later are potted on until they finally occupy containers 6 to 8 inches in diameter or, alternately, they are planted in ground beds or soil benches, spaced 4 inches to 1 foot apart depending upon the vigor of the variety and, in the case of the African kinds, the number of branches that individuals are allowed to

A French marigold as a flowering pot plant

develop. To obtain large flowers, the number of stems should be restricted to from one to several and all side shoots should be removed when quite small for some distance down from the top of the flowering stems. To have blooms before April, it is necessary to increase the day length by the use of artificial lights. Temperatures suitable for these plants are 50°F at night and 55 to 60°F during the day. At all times full exposure to sun is needed and the greenhouse should be well ventilated during favorable weather so that the atmosphere never becomes oppressively humid. These plants need generous amounts of water once their roots have taken possession of the available soil. Less is needed before then. Plants that have filled their containers with healthy roots are benefited by weekly applications of dilute liquid fertilizer.

Diseases and Pests. These plants are subject to several diseases including wilts and stem rots, root rots, botrytis blight, rust, and leaf spots. They are also susceptible to aster yellows virus disease. The chief pests are Japanese beetle, caterpillars, mites, nematodes, tarnished plant bug, leafhoppers, leaf tiers, and slugs.

TAHITIAN BRIDAL VEIL is *Gibasis geniculata.*

TAHITIAN-SPINACH is *Xanthosoma brasiliense.*

TAIL FLOWER. See Anthurium.

TAIL-GRAPE. See Artabotrys.

TAINIA. The plants sometimes cultivated under this name belong in the genus *Ascotainia.*

TAIWANIA (Taiwàn-ia). As understood by conservative botanists, *Taiwania* consists of one species, a native of Taiwan, China, and northern Burma. Some authorities treat the continental phases as distinct species, but there are insufficient consistent differences to warrant this. A conifer of the taxodium family TAXODIACEAE, the genus we are considering bears a name alluding to Taiwan, where it is native. In its botanical relationship it belongs nearest to the China-fir (*Cunninghamia*), differing chiefly in having two seeds to each fertile scale of its cones, instead of three, and two distinct types of leaves.

As its specific designation indicates, in appearance *T. cryptomerioides* resembles *Cryptomeria.* One of the tallest of Old World conifers, specimens in the wild occasionally reach heights in excess of 200 feet and have trunks 8 feet or more in diameter. Because this species was not discovered until 1904 and living material was not brought to America and Europe until about 1920, there are no mature trees in those regions.

As described from wild specimens, adult trees have straight trunks bare of branches for about one-half their heights and are topped with broad, dense heads of branches and foliage. When young, taiwanias form shapely pyramids. Their branches swing outward and upward and the branchlets hang gracefully from them. Young trees have juvenile-type foliage. Their spreading, sharp-pointed leaves, ⅓ to ⅔ inch long, are spirally arranged and triangular-sickle-shaped with their bases clasping the shoots. Adult leaves of older trees, less than ¼ inch long, are triangular and overlapping and hug the shoots for about one-half their lengths. Their tips are incurved. The male catkin-like cones are clustered at the tips of short branchlets. Female cones, which terminate the branches, are globose to ovoid-oblong and, at maturity, about ½ inch long.

Garden and Landscape Uses and Cultivation. This lovely conifer, unfortunately, is not hardy in regions of cold winters, but it should prove satisfactory in parts of the south and in California and in mild parts of the Pacific Northwest. Wherever it thrives it will prove to be a welcome addition to the list of evergreen trees of ornamental value and horticultural and botanical interest. It requires the same culture

as *Cryptomeria* and is propagated in the same manner. For more information see Conifers.

TALAUMA (Tal-aùma). Occurring in tropical Asia and from Mexico to tropical America and the West Indies, *Talauma* contains about fifty species of evergreen shrubs and trees. Related to *Magnolia* and *Liriodendron*, it belongs to the magnolia family MAGNOLIACEAE. Its name derives from a colloquial one of South America.

Talaumas differ from magnolias in the technical characteristics of their fruits, but otherwise are very similar. Their leaves are alternate, undivided, and without teeth. The magnolia-like blooms have three sepals, six or more petals, numerous stamens, and heads or spikes of many carpels. The compound fruits are up to 6 inches long.

From 50 to 60 feet in height, *T. hodgsonii* inhabits warm parts of the Himalayas. Its leathery, hairless, obovate-oblong leaves are up to 1½ feet long or a little longer by as much as 9 inches broad. The solitary, terminal, cup-shaped flowers are about 6 inches wide. They are spicily fragrant and have three purplish sepals and, generally, six ivory-white, fleshy petals. The egg-shaped fruits are 4 to 6 inches long.

Garden and Landscape Uses and Cultivation. These attractive trees and shrubs are suitable ornamentals for the tropics and subtropics. Good specimens may be seen in southern California, where they are at their best in very light shade. At 25°F they may suffer from frost damage; at temperatures over 100°F, when the atmosphere is dry, from sun scorch. Talaumas are propagated by seed and by approach grafting onto young plants of *Magnolia grandiflora.*

TALBOTIA. See Vellozia.

TALINUM (Ta-lìnum). Comprising about fifty species, *Talinum*, of the purslane family PORTULACACEAE, is represented in the floras of the Americas, Africa, and Asia, mostly in the warmer parts of those continents. The name is aboriginal, presumably African, and of unknown meaning.

Talinums are fleshy, hairless, herbaceous plants with flat or cylindrical, all-basal or alternate leaves. Their usually clustered, less often solitary flowers have two sepals, which in most sorts soon drop, five short-lived petals, five to numerous stamens, and one three-parted style. The fruits are capsules. In the tropics *T. triangulare* is sometimes cooked and eaten as a vegetable.

A hardy, herbaceous perennial, *T. teretifolium* prospers outdoors in the vicinity of New York City and perhaps further north. Native from Pennsylvania to Georgia and Texas, this sort has thick, fleshy roots and, in bloom, is 4 inches to 1 foot tall. Clustered on its short, tufted stems, its slender, cylindrical leaves are 1 inch to 2 inches long. In loose panicles on slender, leafless stalks, the pink flowers are ½ inch or slightly more in diameter. They have broad-ovate, persistent sepals and twelve to twenty stamens as long or a little longer than the style. Similar and probably as hardy, **T. mengesii,** wild from Tennessee to Georgia and Alabama, is somewhat bigger than *T. teretifolium* and has blooms up to 1 inch across with forty to 100 stamens and a much longer style. Native from Arkansas to Mexico, **T. calycinum** has much the aspect of *T. teretifolium,* but its 1-inch-wide, pink flowers have thirty or more stamens. This, too, may be as hardy or nearly as hardy as *T. teretifolium.*

Probably as cold-resistant as the kinds described above, but intolerant of humid climates, *T. okanoganense* (syn. *T. wayae*) and *T. spinescens* are exquisite natives of the state of Washington. Its numerous much-branched stems forming cushions rarely more than 2 inches across, **T. okanoganense** has nearly cylindrical, slender, gray leaves, ¼ to ½ inch long, that are deciduous, excepting the basal portions of their midribs that dry, harden, and are retained as usually curved, bristly appendages under ⅓ inch long. The white or less commonly yellowish or pinkish blooms, about ½ inch in diameter, are in flat-topped clusters. From the last, **T. spinescens** differs in forming dense clusters up to 6 inches wide and in having green leaves up to 1 inch long, the persistant midribs of which harden into straight, spinelike appendages ¼ to ½ inch long and stouter than those of *T. okanoganense.* The light red to deep crimson-magenta flowers have petals approximately ¾ inch wide.

Nonhardy, subshrubby sorts with tuberous roots include *T. paniculatum* (syn. *T. patens*), called fame flower and jewels-of-Ophir, and *T. triangulare,* both of South America and the West Indies and naturalized in the southern United States. The erect, branchless or nearly branchless stems, 9 inches to 5 feet tall, of **T. paniculatum** are pinkish in their younger parts, becoming slightly woody as they age. Mostly apparently opposite, the 2- to 4-inch-long, short-stalked or stalkless leaves, lanceolate to ovate or obovate, have tapered bases. In tall, airy, slender-stalked, leafless panicles, the carmine-red blooms, up to ½ inch wide, have fifteen to twenty stamens. Foliage attractively variegated with creamy-white and pink is characteristic of *T. p. variegatum.* The stems of **T. triangulare** are more woody than those of *T. paniculatum.* From 2 to 5 feet in height, this sort has alternate leaves on branchless stems. Spatula-shaped to narrow-elliptic,

Talinum paniculatum variegatum

they are 2 to 4 inches long and have tapered bases. In terminal clusters with triangular stalks, the purple, pink, or yellow flowers, about ¾ inch wide, have about thirty stamens.

Garden and Landscape Uses and Cultivation. The hardy and near hardy sorts are delightful plants for rock gardens, wall gardens, and similar places. The nonhardy sorts are useful in warm, frost-free regions for similar purposes and for cultivation in greenhouses and as window plants. They are especially well suited for inclusion in collections of succulent plants.

Cultivation. If the soil is excellently drained and dryish and if they are exposed to full sun, no difficulties are experienced in growing talinums. Indoors they succeed in temperatures from 45 to 60°F at night in winter, with increases of five to ten degrees or so by day. They withstand arid atmospheres well. Soil lean in nutrients suits better than richer soil. Allow it to become nearly dry between soakings. Propagation is very easy by seed and by cuttings.

TALISIA (Tal-ísia). Restricted in the wild to tropical Central America and South America, *Talisia,* of the soapberry family SAPINDACEAE, consists of fifty species of evergreen trees and shrubs. Its name is derived from a native South American one.

Talisias have alternate, pinnate, leathery leaves, with toothless leaflets in pairs without a terminal one. The small flowers, in branched panicles, have four or five sepals, four or five greenish or yellowish petals, and five to seven, commonly eight, stamens.

With leaves of one or two pairs of broad-elliptic leaflets, 2 to 4 inches long, and fruits similar to those of the Spanish-lime (*Melicoccus bijugatus*) to which it is related, South American **T. olivaeformis** in the wild is up to 60 feet tall. In southern Florida it is considerably lower. Its olive-like fruits

are edible, but, each containing a large stone and lacking much flesh, have little appeal.

Garden Uses and Cultivation. The species described has merit for ornament and shade. It seemingly adapts to ordinary soil and needs no special care. Two trees raised from seed at the Fairchild Tropical Garden, Miami, Florida, fruited when about ten years old. Since both specimens bore, it clearly is not necessary, as it is with the Spanish-lime, to have trees of different sexes growing in proximity to have fruit.

TALLOW NUT or TALLOW WOOD is *Ximenia americana.*

TAMARACK is *Larix laricina.*

TAMARICACEAE—Tamarisk Family. Mostly natives of subtropical and temperate-region deserts, semideserts, steppes, and seashores, the about 120 species of this family of dicotyledons are allotted among four genera. Chiefly northern hemisphere shrubs and trees with slender branches, they have alternate, undivided, heathlike or scalelike leaves. Their tiny, symmetrical, usually bisexual flowers are solitary or in slender racemes or panicles. They have four or five sepals, as many petals, which generally remain on the plants after they have withered, five to ten stamens sometimes joined at their bases, and three to five separate or united styles. The fruits are capsules containing hairy or sometimes winged seeds. Genera cultivated are *Myricaria* and *Tamarix.*

TAMARIND is *Tamarindus indica;* Manila-tamarind, *Pithecellobium dulce;* and wild-tamarind, *Lysiloma bahamensis.*

TAMARINDUS (Tam-aríndus)—Tamarind. One of the best-known trees of the tropics, and the only one of its genus, the tamarind belongs in the vast pea family LEGUMINOSAE. It is a native of tropical Africa and possibly southern Asia. Its generic name is derived from the Arabic *tamar-Hindi,* or Indian-date.

The tamarind (**Tamarindus indica**) is grown successfully in the warmest parts of Florida, indeed it is naturalized on the Keys, and commonly in Hawaii, where it also occurs spontaneously, but in neither place does it reach the huge size it attains in India, Malaya, and some other parts of the tropics. At its best, this magnificent species exceeds 80 feet in height and may have a trunk diameter of 25 feet. It has an open, wide-spreading head and graceful, feathery, evergreen foliage consisting of alternate, pinnate leaves with an even number, twenty to forty, of oblong, opposite leaflets up to ¾ inch long. The 1-inch-wide or somewhat larger, asym-

Tamarindus indica (foliage and flowers)

Tamarix ramosissima

metrical blooms are few together in lax racemes at the branch ends; their pale yellow petals are veined with red. The three upper are sizable and conspicuous, the two lower are represented by bristles hidden at the bottom of the column of stamens. The calyx is of four petal-like parts; there are three functional curved stamens and one slender style. The fruits of the tamarind are plump, slightly curved, velvety, cinnamon-brown pods, 3 to 8 inches long, with thin, brittle skins and up to twelve shiny, flattish seeds about ½ inch in diameter. The pods are slightly constricted between the seeds, which are embedded in soft, brownish pulp with fibers separating the individuals. The pods hang on the trees for several months.

The fruits of the tamarind are highly regarded in the tropics. Their nutritious pulp has a high sugar and tartaric acid content and is used in curries, chutneys, India relish, Worcestershire sauce, and in some foods as well as in cooling beverages; it is slightly laxative. In India and elsewhere, both the seeds and flowers are used as food, and the leaves and bark medicinally. The wood of this tree is used for furniture, charcoal, and fuel.

Since ancient times the tamarind has been important in the lives of the peoples of tropical Asia. It is a favorite village shade tree and Hindus sometimes perform a formal ceremony of "marrying" a tamarind tree to a mango tree before they eat the fruits of the latter.

Garden and Landscape Uses. Where space permits its adequate development, the tamarind is an imposing and beautiful shade and avenue tree, but it is too large for small properties. It is slow-growing, wind-resistant, and very adaptable as to soil, thriving in comparatively poor ones as well as those of greater fertility. Although distinctly tropical, well-established older trees will stand mild freezes, but young specimens are extremely sensitive to cold and are easily injured by low temperatures. The most common method of raising tamarinds is from seed, which germinates quickly in a temperature of 70°F

or above. They may also be air-layered, and grafting and inarching onto seedling understocks is sometimes resorted to for the propagation of especially desirable trees.

TAMARISK. See Tamarix. For false-tamarisk see Myricaria.

TAMARIX (Tá-marix) — Tamarisk. More than fifty species of shrubs and small trees of the Old World constitute *Tamarix*, of the tamarisk family TAMARICACEAE. Several are naturalized in North America. The name is an ancient Latin one.

Undetermined species of *Tamarix* naturalized in the Mojave Desert

Tamarisks are graceful plants with slender, feathery branches and branchlets and numerous tiny scalelike leaves something like those of heaths. Their small pink or white flowers, crowded in narrow cylindrical racemes, are often grouped into large, showy, plumelike panicles. They have four or five each sepals and petals, usually the same number of stamens, less often twice as many, and three or four styles. The fruits are capsules.

Hardy in southern Canada, *T. chinensis* (syn. *T. amurensis*), *T. ramosissima* (syns. *T. pentandra*, *T. odessana*), and *T. parviflora* are naturalized in the southwestern United States. Hybrids between them possibly exist. The Chinese tamarisk (*T. chinensis*), a native of China, Japan, and Mongolia, is a shrub up to 15 feet in height with more or less drooping branches and branchlets. It has bluish-green foliage and typically pink, five-petaled flowers in terminal panicles in summer. A variant of more erect growth that blooms in spring from branches of the previous year's growth is known in gardens as *T. juniperina.* Very much like the summer-blooming form of *T. chinensis* and differing chiefly in botanical details of its flowers of no significant interest to gardeners, *T. ramosissima* ranges in the wild from China, Korea, and the Soviet Union to Iraq and Iran. Native to the Balkans, Greece, Crete, and Turkey, *T. parviflora*

differs from *T. chinensis* and *T. ramosissima* in its flowers having only four petals. Plants grown as *T. tetrandra* belong here, the species correctly known by that name does not appear to be in cultivation. Up to 15 feet tall and with arching branches, *T. parviflora* in spring bears pale pink blooms in short lateral racemes along its branches.

Tamarix parviflora

Less hardy than any of the sorts discussed above, the French tamarisk (*T. gallica*) in gardens is sometimes called *T. algeriensis*. A native of southern Europe, this is up to 30 feet in height, but often considerably lower. It has five-petaled, white or pinkish flowers in summer. Their sepals are little or not at all toothed. This is hardy in southern New England. The Athel tamarisk (*T. aphylla*), native from North Africa to Afghanistan and up to 30 feet tall, has jointed branches and minute sheathing leaves that resemble those of the Australian-pine (*Casuarina*) and that give to the tree the appearance of being evergreen. Its five-petaled, pink blooms, in terminal panicles, are borne in summer. This tamarisk is hardy in regions of mild winters only. Native from North Africa and the Canary Islands to western Europe, *T. africana*, up to 10 feet tall or perhaps sometimes taller, has almost stalkless leaves. It displays its five-petaled, white or pale pink

Tamarix gallica

Tamarix gallica (flowers)

Tamarix aphylla in California

flowers in spring. Indigenous to the Mediterranean region, **T. canariensis** differs from *T. gallica* in having sepals much incised or toothed. It produces its five-petaled flowers in summer.

Garden and Landscape Uses. Tamarisks are ornamental, both in foliage and flower, and provide delicate elements in the landscape that contrast well with plants of bolder and more massive appearance. Several, valued for their late season of bloom, supply floral displays well after most shrubs have finished theirs.

Not the least of their attractive qualities is that they withstand dry conditions well and are excellent seaside plants, prospering even where they are subjected to salt spray. They are good plants for alkaline and saline soils, but may be grown without difficulty in neutral, slightly acid, and nonsaline ones. Old specimens do not transplant readily.

Cultivation. Good soil drainage is a first requirement of this group of shrubs. Also, they need full sun. It is not necessary that the soil be especially fertile, in fact they often do best in rather poor ground. Pruning must be regulated according to the time of flowering. Those kinds that bloom in spring, such as the spring-blooming form of *T. chinensis*, *T. parviflora*, and *T. africana*, are cut back as soon as blooming is through, thus allowing time for the development of new shoots that will flower the following spring. Summer-blooming tamarisks, such as the typical *T. chinensis*, *T. ramosissima*, and *T. gallica*, are pruned in late winter or early spring before new growth begins. Pruning consists of removing all weak, spindly, and crowded shoots and of shortening others partway or, if it is wished to severely restrict the plants to size, almost to the base of the shoots of those that last bloomed. Tamarisks are among the easiest of shrubs to propagate. They may be grown from seed sown in well-drained pots of sandy soil and covered but lightly with soil, or by cuttings. Cuttings made in fall from shoots of the current season's growth and planted in sandy soil outdoors in a sheltered place or in a cold frame root readily. The cuttings should be about 8 inches long and planted vertically with only their tips peeping out of the soil.

TAMPALA. Cultivated for its leaves or young shoots, which are cooked and eaten as a substitute for spinach or used raw in salads, tampala is a green-leaved form of *Amaranthus tricolor*, a species well known for its brightly-colored-leaved varieties grown for ornament.

Because it withstands high temperatures, tampala succeeds where summers are too hot for spinach. For the tenderest produce, make a succession of sowings at two- to three-week intervals, beginning at about the time it is safe to plant tomatoes outdoors. Sow in rows 1 foot apart and harvest the plants in their entirety when they are 5 to 6 inches high. Alternatively, sow in rows 2 feet apart and allow the plants to grow to near maturity. Then harvest by picking, over a long period, 4- to 5-inch-long shoot tips. If not too many are taken at one time, others soon sprout to provide for later pickings.

TAMUS (Tà-mus) — Black Bryony. Five species constitute this genus of the yam family DIOSCOREACEAE. Native to western

Europe, including the British Isles and the Mediterranean region, it is also represented in the native floras of the Canary Islands and Madeira. The name is based on the Latin *tamnus*, applied to some climbing plant, quite probably *Tamus communis*.

The sorts of *Tamus* are herbaceous, twining vines. They have tuberous roots and glossy, alternate, heart-shaped or three-lobed, long-pointed leaves. The small, greenish flowers, the sexes on separate plants, are in axillary racemes. They have six perianth parts (commonly referred to as petals) and, the males, six stamens. The fruits are red berries.

Black bryony (*T. communis*) is quite attractive and attains a height of several feet. It has black tubers and slightly bell-shaped flowers. Its foliage turns purplish and bright yellow in fall. The somewhat egg-shaped, juicy berries change, as they ripen, from soft emerald-green to translucent crimson. Like the tubers, they are dangerously poisonous if eaten. In Europe, the young shoots, which after cooking are apparently harmless, are sometimes cooked and eaten like asparagus. In times past black bryony was used medicinally.

Tamus communis with heart-shaped leaves (note the tiny flowers)

Tamus communis with lobed leaves

Garden Uses and Cultivation. Because of the possible attraction of its poisonous fruits to children, it is well to limit the cultivation of this species to male plants. The sexes cannot be segregated until the plants bloom, but batches of seedlings ordinarily produce twice as many males as females. Black bryony is a decorative climber for trellises and other supports around which its stems can twine and is appropriate for including in herb gardens and collections of plants of historic medicinal interest. It thrives in moistish, fertile soil in sun or part-shade, and is easily raised from seed and by division of the roots.

TAN BARK. Bark, such as that of hemlocks, certain oaks, and some other trees, that because of its high tannin content is used for tanning hides is called tan bark. In preparation for that use it is milled to a fairly uniform small size. Spent tan bark, tan bark that has served its purpose and has no further use in tanning, is excellent for surfacing garden paths, especially in woodland areas. It has the great advantages of being pleasing to the eye, springing to the tread, and inhospitable to weeds.

TANACETUM (Tana-cètum)—Tansy. Some fifty or sixty species of *Tanacetum* are acknowledged by botanists; few are cultivated. Confined to the wild in the northern hemisphere, including North America, they belong to the daisy family COMPOSITAE. Botanically closely related to *Chrysanthemum*, and by some botanists included in that genus, they are quite unlike the familiar chrysanthemums of gardens. The derivation of their name is not surely known.

Tanacetums are strongly-scented annuals, herbaceous perennials, and subshrubs. One, common tansy, was formerly highly regarded as a medicinal herb, especially as a vermifuge, and was used as an insecticide and for flavoring and garnishing. Tanacetums have alternate, uncut or dissected leaves and flat, yellow flower heads, of small to medium size, composed of all disk florets (the kind that form the central eyes of daisy flower heads) or of disk and small ray florets (ray florets are those that in daisies surround the central eye and look like petals). Usually the flower heads are in clusters, less commonly they are solitary. The involucres (collars) of bracts at their backs are in several rows. The seedlike fruits are achenes.

Common tansy (*T. vulgare* syn. *Chrysanthemum vulgare*) is an erect, vigorous perennial 2 to 3 feet tall. It has longitudinally-grooved stems and oblongish, hairless or nearly hairless, ferny leaves, 6 to 10 inches long, divided pinnately into about a dozen oblong or lanceolate segments, themselves pinnately-lobed or sharply-toothed. The lower leaves have stalks, the

Tanacetum vulgare

upper are stalkless. The button-like flower heads, ⅓ to ½ inch across and without ray florets, are many together in large, flattish-topped clusters. They are bright yellow. Variety *T. v. crispum* has attractively curled foliage. Common tansy, a native of Europe, is naturalized in North America.

An attractive native of limestone rocks and screes in Turkey, *T. densum* is a more or less erect subshrub, 3 inches to 1 foot tall, with white-hairy stems and foliage. Its ovate to broad-elliptic leaves are pinnate with the lobes pinnately-lobed. They are up to 1 inch long. The flower heads, in groups of few or sometimes solitary, are yellow. Variety *T. d. amani* differs from the typical species in technical details only.

Tanacetum vulgare crispum

Native from Maine to Oregon and Alaska, the Huron tansy (*T. huronense*) differs from common tansy in its stems and foliage being hairy and its flower heads, up to ¾ inch across, being in clusters of not more than fifteen and commonly having both disk and ray florets. About 2½ feet tall, this species has two- or three-times-pinnately-cut leaves up to 8 inches

Tanacetum densum amani

or more long. The flower heads are golden-yellow. Their ray florets may be inconspicuous or up to ⅙ inch long.

Inhabiting the San Francisco Bay area, of California, sturdy *T. camphoratum*, 1 foot to 2½ feet tall, has stems and foliage covered with a web of fine whitish hairs. The blunt-elliptic leaves, 4 to 8 inches long, have narrow-oblong leaflets with many short, sometimes toothed lobes. The ½- to ¾-inch-wide flower heads, in congested clusters of usually twelve or fewer, are without evident ray florets. Similar, but less hairy

Tanacetum huronense

and its flower heads with more or less obvious ray florets, **T. douglasii** is a native of coastal regions from California to British Columbia.

Low, subshrubby species from western North America include a few, rarely cultivated, that would surely be meritorious rock garden plants. They are natives of dry, frequently alkaline soils at usually considerable altitudes. One of the most notable, **T. nuttallii,** cushion-like and 4 to 8 inches in height, is densely-clothed with silvery-white hairs. Its chief leaves are wedge-shaped and have three- or five-toothed apexes, those of the flowering stems are narrower and not toothed. The few flower heads, ¼ inch broad, have tiny, four-lobed ray florets and are carried well above the foliage. Similar, but making an even denser cushion of stems and foliage and with leaves more deeply cut, is **T. capitatum.** Another worthwhile kind, **T. potentilloides,** is up to 1 foot tall and has silky-hairy leaves, up to 4 inches long, finely two- or three-times-pinnately-dissected into linear divisions. Its leaves are less silky-hairy than the smaller kinds mentioned above.

Garden and Landscape Uses and Cultivation. The taller tansies are easy to grow and well adapted for naturalistic areas, flower borders, and herb gardens. They prosper with minimum care in any ordinary soil not excessively wet. They need full sun. Division in spring or early fall is a simple and reliable means of increase. They can also be raised from seed. The dwarf species from high altitudes are likely to be more choosy. A very gritty, dryish soil containing crushed limestone and a sunny location in a rock garden are likely to afford the best chances of success, but even then, where summers are hot and humid, they may fail. They tempt rock garden enthusiasts. Increase is by seed and by cuttings.

TANAKAEA (Tanak-aèa). A near relative of the American genus *Leptarrhena,* the only species of *Tanakaea,* of the saxifrage family SAXIFRAGACEAE, is endemic to Japan and China. Its name honors the Japanese botanist Yoshio Tanaka.

A rare evergreen herbaceous perennial that in the wild favors wet rocks in shade, **T. radicans** has creeping rhizomes somewhat like the runners of a strawberry, and basal tufts of thickish, long-stalked, oblong to ovate-lanceolate, coarsely-irregularly-toothed leaves, green above and paler on their undersides. They are 1 inch to 3½ inches long by up to 2 inches wide. The hairy, leafless flower stalks, 4 inches to 1 foot long, terminate in feathery *Astilbe*-like panicles of tiny, whitish, petal-less flowers, solitary in the axils of bracts. They have a calyx with a short tube and usually five lobes (sepals), but sometimes only four and occasionally as many as seven. There are

ten stamens. The styles are short. The fruits are capsules.

Garden Uses and Cultivation. A hardy species suitable for rock and woodland gardens in porous, peaty soil in part-shade, *T. radicans* is propagated by seed and by division. It requires no special attention.

TANBARK-OAK is *Lithocarpus densiflorus.*

TANEKAHA is *Phyllocladus trichomanoides.*

TANGELO is *Citrus tangelo.*

TANGERINE is *Citrus reticulata.*

TANGLEBERRY is *Gaylussacia frondosa.*

TANIER. See Xanthosoma.

TANKAGE. See Fertilizers.

TANSY. See Tanacetum.

TAPE-GRASS. See Vallisneria.

TAPEINOCHEILOS (Tapeinochei-los). Some twenty species of the ginger family ZINGIBERACEAE constitute *Tapeinocheilos,* a genus native to the Moluccas, New Guinea, Bismarck Archipelago, and Australia. The name, alluding to the short lips of the flowers, derives from the Greek *tapeinos,* low, and *cheilos,* a lip.

These plants have leafy, canelike stems. Their flowers, surrounded by conspicuous bracts, are in dense, pineapple-like spikes without leafy crowns.

Native to the Molucca Islands, **T. ananassae** is 6 to 8 feet tall. From its base arise erect stems bearing scattered, narrow-

Tapeinocheilos ananassae (flowers)

obovate leaves about 5 to 6 inches long. The leafless flowering stalks, 1 foot to 3 feet long, arising directly from the root-stock, are covered with brownish bracts and terminate in ovoid spikes, 6 to 8 inches long by one-half as wide, of bright crimson or orange-red, recurved bracts and shorter, yellow flowers. The spikes remain attractive for many weeks.

Garden and Landscape Uses and Cultivation. These are as for hedychiums and zingibers.

TAPEWORM PLANT is *Senecio pendulus.*

TAPIOCA PLANT is *Manihot esculenta.*

TAPROOT. Many plants, such as carrots, dandelions, and hickories, have a main central root that grows directly downward, penetrates deeply, and provides excellent anchorage. Such roots are called taproots. Plants that develop them are

Tapeinocheilos ananassae

commonly more difficult to transplant successfully than those without taproots. To minimize the shock of transplanting and increase chances of success, it is generally helpful to root prune taprooted trees a year or two before transplanting them.

TAR FLOWER is *Befaria racemosa*.

TARA VINE is *Actinidia arguta*.

TARATA is *Pittosporum eugenioides*.

TARAXACUM (Taráx-acum) — Dandelion. The common dandelion, almost too well known to warrant description and universally abhorred as an invader of lawns, but appreciated as a supplier of "greens" and as a basis of a pleasant wine, belongs to a botanically monstrously complicated genus of the daisy family COMPOSITAE. More or less in despair, botanists have named more than a thousand species of *Taraxacum*, but those of conservative outlook recognize fewer than sixty. The whole mess is complicated by hybridization and by the ability of some kinds to produce fertile seeds without pollination and thus perpetuate themselves and establish uniform populations by a sort of live-bearing process, as well as by other factors. The name is believed to refer to medicinal uses of the plant and may come from the Greek *taraxo*, I have caused, and *achos*, pain, or from *taraxos*, disorder, and *akos*, remedy. The common name dandelion, in allusion to the toothed leaves, derives from the French *dent de lion* (tooth of a lion).

Fortunately, because the cultivation of the genus is practically limited to growing the common dandelion for greens, gardeners do not have to worry much about the nomenclatural problems presented by *Taraxacum*. Yet one cannot help but wonder if this might not be different if dandelions were less common, less prone to establish themselves where not wanted. Many a rare primrose and other recipients of assiduous attentions of gardeners have less to offer in beauty and brilliance than the humble, despised dandelion. Most gardeners know only dandelions with golden-yellow flowers, yet in Japan there are native kinds with white flower heads with yellow centers (a most attractive combination) and pale yellow flower heads. These may be worth the attentions of venturesome gardeners. Other sorts with pink or purplish flowers are known. One species of the genus, the Russian *T. kok-saghyz*, contains rubber and before the development of the synthetic product was, under pressure of World War II, exploited to some extent by the Russians.

The genus *Taraxacum*, of the daisy family COMPOSITAE, is native to temperate and cold regions, chiefly in the northern hemisphere. It consists of tap-rooted, milky-juiced, hardy, herbaceous perennials with their usually pinnately-lobed or jagged-

toothed, but sometimes smooth-edged leaves in basal rosettes. The solitary flower heads are atop hollow stalks. The seed heads, those of the common dandelion best known, are globular with the familiar feathery hair attachments that serve as parachutes to the seedlike fruits (achenes) facing outward.

Common dandelion (*T. officinale* syn. *T. dens-leonis*) has oblanceolate, jagged-toothed

Taraxacum officinale (seed head)

leaves 2 inches to over 1 foot long, slightly fleshy, and mostly hairless except for a few hairs beneath and on the mid-veins. The flower heads, on stalks 2 inches to 1½ feet tall, are usually 1½ to 2 inches in diameter and bright golden-yellow. The fragile, globular seed heads consist of narrow seeds with feathery "parachutes" attached. They are ideally constructed for distribution by wind and are carried long distances by that agency. For cultivation as greens see Dandelion.

TARES. Weeds of the genus *Vicia* are known as tares. As used in the Bible, the word probably refers to darnel grass (*Lolium temulentum*), a native of Europe common as a weed in North America, that contains a poison harmful to grazing animals and humans.

TARO. See Dasheen or Taro. For taro vine see Epipremnum, Monstera, and Raphidophora.

TARRAGON. Botanically *Artemisia dracunculus*, of the daisy family COMPOSITAE, tarragon is esteemed for its leaves and young shoots, which are used in salads, in the

preparation of tarragon vinegar, and fresh or dried for seasoning.

From 2 to 3 feet tall and bushy, this hardy perennial is appropriate in herb gardens, or you may tuck a few plants in a corner of a vegetable garden or plant them in boxes or other large containers. Two varieties, French tarragon, which has very smooth leaves, and Russian tarragon, with rougher leaves, are cultivated. The

Tarragon

French variety is usually considered superior. Ordinary well-drained, preferably neutral or slightly alkaline, not-too-rich soil and a sunny or slightly shaded location suit tarragon best. Set out young plants 1 foot to 1½ feet apart in early spring. Where winter cold is severe, protect the plants by mounding peat moss, sawdust, or sand over them. Remove this in spring. Because cultivated varieties of tarragon rarely if ever set seed, they must be propagated by division or by root cuttings in spring or by leafy stem cuttings, which root readily if made in summer and are planted in sand or perlite, in a shaded cold frame.

Harvest tarragon for storage by cutting the shoots as soon as the flower buds begin to form. Tie cut shoots in small bundles and suspend them in a shaded, dry, airy place. When they are thoroughly dry, strip the leaves off and pack them in tightly stoppered bottles or other containers.

To have fresh tarragon in winter, dig plants from the garden in late summer or early fall, cut them back to a height of 6 inches, and pot them in containers just big enough to hold their roots without undue crowding. Water the newly potted plants well and stand them in a cold frame or outdoors until late fall. Then bring them into a greenhouse or other sunny location indoors where the night temperature is 50 to 55°F and that by day not more than ten degrees higher.

TARTARIAN LAMB is *Cibotium barometz*.

TARTOGO is *Jatropha podagrica*.

TARWEED. See Madia.

TASMANIAN. As parts of vernacular names, Tasmanian occurs in Tasmanian-cedar (*Athrotaxis*), Tasmanian cypress-pine (*Callitris oblonga*), and Tasmanian waratah (*Telopea truncata*).

TASSEL. The word tassel forms parts of the common names of these plants: tassel flower (*Amaranthus caudatus* and *Emilia*), tassel-hyacinth (*Muscari comosum*), and silk tassel bush (*Garrya*).

TATTELE is *Pterygota alata*.

TAVARESIA (Tavar-èsia). The genus *Tavaresia* is composed of leafless succulents sometimes identified as *Decabelone*. Belonging to the *Stapelia* relationship of the milkweed family ASCLEPIADACEAE, it is widely distributed in tropical Africa and South Africa. It comprises three or four species. Its name commemorates a nineteenth-century Portuguese amateur botanist, Jose Tavares de Macedo.

Tavaresias have erect or ascending, cylindrical, six- to twelve-angled, knobby ridged stems, with each knob furnished with three bristles. The large blooms, several together from the bottoms of the young shoots, have calyxes of five sepals, and large, tubular, funnel- to bell-shaped, five-lobed corollas. Arising from the column of stamens in the center of the flower is a double corona or crown. The outer part is of ten slender, knob-tipped segments, the inner of five narrow lobes. The fruits are paired, spindle-shaped, somewhat diverging, podlike follicles.

So similar are the species that the suggestion has been made that they be accepted as subspecies of one kind. Particularly close are *T. grandiflora* (syn. *Dacabelone grandiflora*) and *T. barklyi* (syn. *Decabelone barklyi*). The chief difference being that the blooms of the former are typically about 4 inches long, those of the latter less than one-half as big. Both have stems with ten or more angles, which distinguishes them from *T. angolensis* (syn. *Decabelone elegans*), with more prominently six- or eight-angled stems. The flowers of the last are 1½ to 3 inches long.

The blooms of **T. grandiflora** have pale green outsides spotted with purple-red. Within they are purple-red at their bases and pale yellow speckled with yellow above. They are 4 to 4½ inches in diameter. Those of **T. barklyi** are generally similar in color, but only about 2 inches wide. In *T. grandiflora* the stems are deep green and 4 to 8 inches long, those of *T. barklyi* are under 4 inches long and bluish-green. The blooms of **T. angolensis**, in clusters of few, are 2 to 3½ inches wide. Inside and out they are pale yellow, spotted with purple-red, and uniformly of this color at the bases inside. The stems are 2½ to 5 inches long.

Garden Uses and Cultivation. These collectors' items need a carefully regulated environment and watchful attention. Perfectly drained, fertile soil is necessary, and they seem to succeed better in pans (shallow pots) than in deeper containers. A sunny greenhouse with a dry atmosphere, lightly shaded in the summer, and where the temperature on winter nights is 55 to 60°F, and that by day five or ten degrees higher, affords comfortable conditions. Watering must never be excessive. In winter the soil is kept nearly dry, somewhat moister, but not constantly wet at other times. Propagation is easy by seed. The seeds germinate in a few hours, but the young plants are very apt to rot. To circumvent this, some growers graft them onto seedling stapelias or *Ceropegia woodii*. For more information see Succulents.

TAWHIWHI is *Pittosporum tenuifolium*.

TAXACEAE—Yew Family. This group of gymnosperms consists of five genera of freely-branched trees and shrubs with narrow-linear or needle-like, alternate or rarely opposite, evergreen leaves often arranged in two ranks. The family is represented in the native floras of the northern hemisphere southward to Mexico and in the southern hemisphere in the Celebes Islands and New Caledonia. The primitive flowers, borne in the axils of the leaves, are unisexual, with the females solitary on short shoots and the males in catkin-like cones. The berry-like fruits contain one bony-shelled seed. Genera cultivated are *Taxus* and *Torreya*.

TAXODIACEAE — Taxodium Family. Ten genera of evergreen and deciduous gymnosperms, natives of North America, eastern Asia, and Tasmania constitute this family. Medium-sized to tall trees, they have spirally-arranged, sometimes apparently two-ranked, needle-like or awl-shaped leaves. The primitive flowers are in cones. The fruits are woody cones that differ from those of closely related PINACEAE in that each scale bears two to six seeds. Genera cultivated are *Athrotaxis*, *Cryptomeria*, *Cunninghamia*, *Glyptostrobus*, *Metasequoia*, *Sciadopitys*, *Sequoia*, *Sequoiadendron*, *Taiwania*, and *Taxodium*.

TAXODIUM (Taxò-dium) — Bald-Cypress, Swamp-Cypress, Pond-Cypress, Montezuma-Cypress. This genus, as now understood, consists of three species and is confined as a native to the southeastern United States and Mexico. Earlier, Chinese *Glyptostrobus* was included. Fossil records show that in prehistoric times, in the Tertiary period, it was abundant over large areas of North America, Asia, and Europe. Unique among conifers in that it includes both deciduous and evergreen species, *Taxodium* has a name derived from that of *Taxus*, the yew, and the Greek *eidos*, simi-

lar to, but its application is not especially apt. This genus is closely related to the dawn-redwood (*Metasequoia*) from which it is easily distinguished by its deciduous branchlets being alternate on the branches rather than in opposite pairs. It belongs in the taxodium family TAXODIACEAE.

Taxodiums are handsome and, as their vernacular name implies, partial to wet soils including those periodically inundated. As an adaptation to these environments, they send from their roots at varying distances from their trunks curious upright, vertical, conical, developments called "knees." These commonly rise to a height of 3 or 4 feet above the soil or water level, but sometimes they are as tall as 10 feet. They are of soft woody tissue covered with spongy bark and when old are often hollow. It is thought that the "knees" serve as means for air to reach the roots, but there is no absolute agreement about this, despite the fact that their function has long intrigued botanists. Specimens in soil not waterlogged do not ordinarily develop "knees."

Taxodium distichum with an abundance of "knees," Longwood Gardens, Kennett Square, Pennsylvania

The relationship of the "knees" to the main root system is of interest. Swamp- and pond-cypresses develop a system of stout, horizontal, shallow roots that radiate from the buttresses of the trunks. From the undersides of these, at intervals, stout perpendicular roots reach down to great depths. This combination of horizontal and vertical roots provides great stability in soft, wet soil and enables the trees to better withstand hurricanes, not uncommon where these trees are native. It has been observed that the "knees" are most usually located directly above the vertical anchor roots.

Like *Metasequoia* and *Glyptostrobus*, taxodiums have two distinct kinds of shoots, permanent, terminal or leading ones with leaves arranged spirally and with buds in the leaf axils, and lateral, deciduous shoots, without buds in the axils of their leaves, that drop with the leaves attached, in fall in the case of deciduous kinds, irregularly with others. The leaves of the deciduous shoots are linear and in two opposite rows.

During youth and middle age, taxodiums are characteristically narrow, but later they are likely to develop broad, round heads of branches that spread widely. Their soft foliage, very fine for the size of the trees, gives a light, feathery effect and that of deciduous kinds assumes warm, golden-brown tones before it is shed in fall. Male and female flowers are on the same tree, the former in terminal, pendulous clusters, the latter, in what later develop into fruiting cones, irregularly along the shoots. The cones are short-stalked and spherical or slightly ovoid. Their thick, woody scales are round-shield-shaped and each fertile one produces two seeds. The cones mature at the end of their first season.

As sources of lumber, these trees are of considerable importance. This is especially true of *T. distichum* and to a lesser extent of *T. d. nutans.* Their woods are similar and are commonly called cypress. The trees that produce them are, of course, quite distinct from the true cypresses (*Cupressus*). This cypress wood is particularly esteemed for its ability to resist decay when exposed to moisture or submerged. It is a favorite wood for greenhouse construction and, because of its attractive grain, is used for interior trim, paneling, and other decorative purposes. The kind known as pecky cypress is obtained from older trees infected with a fungus that results in narrow tunnels forming in the wood that, in turn, are responsible for attractive decorative patterns on the surfaces of the sawn wood. Pecky cypress is not as strong as wood unaffected by the fungus, but since the fungus dies when the tree is felled no further deterioration takes place. The wood of *T. mucronatum* is inferior to that of *T. distichum* and *T. d. nutans,* but is used locally in Mexico and Guatemala.

The bald-cypress (*T. distichum*), up to 150 feet in height, may have a trunk with a diameter, above its basal flaring part, of 6 to 12 feet. The buttressing at the base of the trunk is usually prominent on trees that grow in wet locations. Those in drier places (and under cultivation swamp-cypresses succeed in nonswampy ground) usually do not have greatly enlarged boles. On older trees the fibrous bark is reddish-brown and peels in long strips. The deciduous branchlets are horizontal and their leaves ½ to ¾ inch long, light green, and narrow-linear. Those on permanent shoots are smaller and scalelike. The purplish cones, up to 1¼ inches in diameter, are on stalks about ⅛ inch long. This species is native from Delaware to Illinois, Missouri, Arkansas, Louisiana, and Florida. A variety, *T. d. pendens,* has drooping branchlets. The pond-cypress (*T. d. nutans* syn. *T. ascen-*

Taxodium distichum, The Royal Botanic Gardens, Kew, England

Taxodium distichum (leaves and cones)

dens), native from Virginia to Florida and Alabama, at its maximum is only about one-half as tall as the tallest examples of *T. distichum* and has a narrower, thinner head of spreading branches with erect or sometimes drooping branchlets. Also, its leaves lie closer to the twigs than those of *T. distichum* and are smaller, up to ½ inch in length.

The Mexican swamp-cypress or Montezuma-cypress (*T. mucronatum*) inhabits the high tableland of Mexico and Guatemala and is usually evergreen, but may lose its leaves annually when planted near its northern limit of survival. Much tenderer than other kinds, it will grow in parts of California and in other regions of mild climates. Its leaves are shorter than those of *T. distichum,* its cones larger. Its deciduous branchlets are normally shed in their second year.

The famous Cypress-of-Tule is a magnificent specimen of this species. Called "El Gigante," it grows in the churchyard of Santa Maria de Tule in the village of Tule, Oaxaca, Mexico, and is one of the most massive of all living things. Its height of 140 feet is exceeded by many trees, but not the diameter of its huge, buttressed trunk, which averages 25 feet and, measured in one direction, exceeds 50 feet

Taxodium distichum nutans, The Royal Botanic Gardens, Kew, England

Taxodium mucronatum, Huntington Botanical Gardens, San Marino, California

from side to opposite side. If the convolutions of the buttresses are followed, the circumference of the trunk is 150 feet at its base and 108 feet at 5 feet above the ground. This specimen has a large rounded head. Uninformed guesses have placed the age of the giant at 4,000 to 5,000 years, but the distinguished Mexican botanist Dr. Cassiano Conzatti, after much study, gave the much more reliable figure of 2,000, and possibly 1,500 years, as the true age of this tree. It is now in a comparatively dry location, but there is clear evidence that the course of a nearby river has changed since the youth of the specimen and even now ample water is found at a depth of about 5 feet.

Garden and Landscape Uses. The only sorts of *Taxodium* in cultivation in the United States are native ones. The handsomest of these, because it has a fuller head, is *T. distichum*, however *T. d. nutans*, perhaps slightly less hardy, may be preferred where a narrower tree is more appropriate. The first is hardy at least as far north as Boston, Massachusetts. Neither spread widely enough as young or middle-aged specimens to provide good shade and so must be regarded as purely decorative elements in the landscape. As such they have much to recommend them. They are, of course, especially useful for planting in wet soils, but they also grow perfectly well in any well-drained garden earth that is dampish or at least never really dry, and indeed in the north are better accommodated in such than in swampy locations. They thrive and are displayed to good advantage when set on the shores of a pond, lake, or stream where some of their roots can reach down to the water and others explore the higher ground of a sloping bank. Because of their comparatively narrow heads taxodiums can be used to good purpose as screens, but always remember that the native kinds of the United States are deciduous and hide little in winter. Because of their preference for humid soils they are better adapted for screen plantings on level sites or along depressions than for high ground or ridges.

These trees are particularly interesting because, unlike most conifers, being deciduous they change in appearance with the changing seasons, a virtue they share with larches, golden-larches, and dawn-redwoods among commonly cultivated conifers. They leaf out very late in spring and are delightful when their fresh foliage forms a mist of pale green that gradually hides trunks and branches and then deepens to the slightly darker green of summer. With the approach of fall, a yellowing of the leaves is suffused slowly with warmer tints of russet and brown. Finally, the leaves drop to reveal a stark pattern of trunk and branches against late fall and winter skies.

The evergreen Montezuma-cypress (*T. mucronatum*) does not exhibit the marked seasonal changes of the others except when planted in climates where winters are cool enough to cause it to lose leaves in fall. Even then it is likely to be partially evergreen. Nor is it nearly as hardy as the other kinds. Its planting should be restricted to climates such as that of California.

Cultivation. These beautiful conifers make no special demands of the cultivator and are generally free of insects and diseases. They transplant without undue difficulty as young trees, but because of their wide-ranging, deep root systems, moving large specimens is likely to be hazardous to their survival. Seeds, sown as soon as possible after they are ripe in moist, sandy, peaty soil, are the most satisfactory means of increase, but taxodiums can also be raised from summer cuttings planted under mist or in a propagating bench in a very humid greenhouse or cold frame. Varieties are propagated by grafting them onto seedling understocks in late winter or spring in a greenhouse.

Diseases. A nonimportant twig-blight affects trees weakened through such other causes as sun-scald, low temperatures, or drought. Wood decay fungi may infect the trunks. Avoid injuring the trunks, and as a means of controlling both diseases, promote vigor by fertilizing if growth is poor and by watering in dry weather.

TAXUS (Táx-us)—Yew. The name *Taxus* is the ancient Latin one for yews. Ten closely related species of the northern hemisphere constitute the genus. So similar are they botanically that there is little doubt that, were they not as wildlings segregated geographically, they would be accepted as subspecies or varieties of one species. Horticulturally, especially with reference to hardiness, they exhibit important differences. The group consists of evergreen trees and shrubs of the yew family TAXACEAE.

Yews have leaves that originate spirally on the branches, but the stalks of most kinds are twisted so that the blades spread in two comblike ranks more or less in one plane. They are linear, flat, and often slightly sickle-shaped with their undersides marked with two broad, yellowish to grayish-green, lengthwise stripes. The flowers are of no ornamental significance. Males and females are on separate trees (very rarely a plant of one sex will develop a branch bearing flowers of the opposite sex). Male flower buds are globose. They originate from the leaf axils and are clustered along the undersides of the shoots. Females, similarly located, are smaller and decidedly pointed. The bright red, fleshy, berry-like fruits each contain a single hard seed cupped and almost completely enclosed in soft mucilaginous flesh of almost sickly sweetness; they are quite decorative. The flesh is edible, but the seeds are poisonous if chewed. Swallowed unbroken, they normally pass through the digestive system without harm and are excreted in viable condition. Natural dissemination of yews is commonly by seeds that birds have swallowed when eating the fruits and that are later excreted.

Most famous of yews is the English yew (**T. baccata**), a kind that occurs as a native from Europe to North Africa and the Himalayas. At its best it attains a height of 50 to 75 feet, spreads widely, and may have a trunk girth of 30 feet or more at 3 or 4 feet above the ground. Specimens of such dimensions are rare even in the British

Taxus baccata, an old specimen in Scotland

Isles, where this evergreen thrives. There are none in America for the quite sufficient reason that several hundred years are required for this slow-growing European to reach maximum size. Nevertheless, in Williamsburg, Virginia, there is an English yew well over 200 years old under which, it is said, George Washington proposed to Martha Custis. Yew trees well over 1,000 years old exist in the British Isles and some may be twice that age. The majority of these old-timers grow in ancient churchyards, where they have been protected for centuries.

Taxus baccata, Berlin, West Germany

Yew trees were sacred to the Druids and it is probable that their later association with Christian churches was because early missionaries established their places of worship on sites that had long been of religious significance to the heathen Britons, rather than that they planted yews near their new churches. In any case, the English yew has been of significance in both the spiritual and temporal affairs of Europeans since time immemorial. The ancient Egyptians employed it as a mourning symbol and so did the Greeks and Romans, who constructed funeral pyres with its wood. Throughout the ages, branches of yew have been used to decorate churches for Christmas and, especially, for Palm Sunday. For this latter occasion they were commonly employed together with sprays of goat willow (*Salix caprea*) bearing its bright yellow catkins. Because of this, both willow and yew came to be called palm and are still so known in some country places in Great Britain and in Ireland. It later became the practice to plant yews in churchyards and burial grounds, undoubtedly because of their sacred association and their use as convenient sources of church decorations for appropriate occasions, and also, it is thought, as assurance of a future supply of wood for making bows. Wood of the yew was esteemed beyond all others for this purpose. The famous English long bows were fashioned from it and so were many of the crossbows of continental Europe.

The reason for favoring churchyards as planting sites could be that they were inaccessible to grazing animals, for horses and cattle can sicken or die as the result of eating the foliage of yews. The foliage seems to be especially deadly if it has wilted before it is ingested, but the effects seem to be capricious, for at times both horses and cattle eat yew foliage without apparent harm. Perhaps the condition of the animal's stomach, whether or not it is empty at the time of ingestion, has a bearing on the results. Certainly deer eat yew foliage without harm. It is one of their favorite winter foods. With the exception of variety *T. b. repandens*, English yews cannot be regarded as reliable north of Washington, D.C., although occasional specimens prosper in the vicinities of Philadelphia and New York City.

The Irish yew (*T. b. stricta* syn. *T. b. fastigiata*) is a distinct and handsome variety of English yew. Unfortunately it is less hardy than the typical *T. baccata*. Its history is interesting. Two plants of it were found about 1780, in the mountains of Fermanagh, by a farmer named Willis who dug them up and planted one in his own garden and one in the gardens of Florence Court, the home of his landlord. The for-

Taxus baccata stricta in Ireland

Taxus baccata stricta in Scotland

mer lived for about a century and then died, but the latter continued to thrive and became the ancestor of all existing Irish yews. The Irish yew is female. It has almost black-green foliage and differs from English yew in that it has several to many strictly erect, spirelike main branches, and leaves that are not in flat sprays, but are distributed evenly around the shoots.

Dovaston yew (*T. b. dovastoniana*) is an extremely handsome variety of English yew easy to recognize because of its markedly pendulous branchlets. About as hardy as typical English yew, this, a male with widespreading, horizontal branches and dark green leaves, has been cultivated since about 1800.

Taxus baccata dovastoniana (foliage)

The hardiest variety of English yew is *T. b. repandens*, a nearly prostrate sort with horizontal branches that arch downward and dark blue-green leaves. Never exceeding about 3 feet in height, it is often lower. A variant with branchlets with golden-yellow leaves is known as *T. b. r. aurea*.

Other varieties of English yew are these: *T. b. adpressa*, a shrubby female of bushy habit, lacks a central leader and has much shorter leaves than those of the typical species that spread in all directions around the shoots. *T. b. aurea*, somewhat hardier

Taxus baccata repandens

than the type, is a female with foliage, golden-yellow at its tips and edges, that turns green in its second year. *T. b. elegantissima* forms a wide-spreading bush with more or less horizontal branches. It has leaves with light yellow stripes that later become whitish. *T. b. epacrioides* is a dwarf with slender branches and small, pointed, very narrow leaves. *T. b. erecta*, the Fulham yew, is bushy and has slender, erect branches and smaller, narrower leaves than the species. *T. b. glauca* is a strong grower with dark bluish-green leaves, glaucous-bluish on their undersides. *T. b. lutea* has very dark foliage and bright yellow fruits. *T. b. procumbens* has wide-spreading, prostrate branches with secondary branches at right angles to them. *T. b. semperaurea*, male and bushy, has erect branches and foliage that retains its yellow color through the second year. It is one of the best of the golden-leaved yews. *T. b. variegata*, with leaves margined with yellowish-white, is less vigorous and less hardy than the green-leaved English yew. *T. b. washingtonii* is a vigorous loose-growing variety up to 15 feet tall and about as broad as high, with leaves more or less tinted golden-yellow.

Japanese yew (**T. cuspidata**) is decidedly hardier than English yew and much more adaptable to most of the northeastern and northcentral United States. It survives in northern New England and in parts of southern Canada. A native of Japan, Korea, and Manchuria, it has been in cultivation in North America only from the middle of the nineteenth century, but since then has produced many varieties; crossed with *T. baccata* and *T. canadensis*, it is the parent of a series of hybrids. In its typical form, Japanese yew is an upright tree that in its native lands attains a height of 50 feet or more. It is pyramidal and closely furnished with ascending or somewhat spreading branches. From English yew it differs in having the scales of its winter buds pointed and keeled. Those of English yew are blunt and without keels. The undersides of its leaves are

Taxus cuspidata

Taxus cuspidata (fruits)

yellower than those of the English yew. In American nurseries the name *T. cuspidata capitata* is commonly and incorrectly applied to this typical form, the right name of which is *T. cuspidata*. To confuse matters further, a variety with wide-spreading, ascending branches that develops as a broad shrub with an open V-shaped center is misnamed *T. cuspidata*. It more properly should be labeled *T. c. expansa*. An exceedingly fine variety is *T. c. nana*, which, to add still more to nomenclatural confusion, is often offered in nurseries as

Taxus cuspidata nana

T. brevifolia, a name which belongs to an entirely different species, native to western North America. A wide-spreading shrub rarely more than 6 feet tall, *T. cuspidata nana* has branches with closely set, short side branches along their lengths. The short, dark green leaves are not in two distinct ranks.

Other varieties of Japanese yew are these: *T. c. aurescens*, less hardy than *T. cuspidata*, is a low variety with its young foliage tinged with yellow through most of the year. *T. c. columnaris* is a dwarf, columnar plant with medium to dark green foliage. *T. c. densa* is low, compact, and broader than high. Fifty-year-old specimens 20 feet across are not more than 4 feet tall. *T. c. luteo-baccata* has yellow fruits. *T. c. minima* is usually not more than 8 inches tall. *T. c. thayerae* is a female with light green foliage. It forms wide-spreading, low specimens whose centers are well filled with leafy branches.

Hybrids between English yew and Japanese yew known by the collective name **T. media** are hardy throughout much of New England. The first was raised about 1900 at the well-known Hunnewell Estate, Wellesley, Massachusetts, by its superintendent, Mr. T. Hatfield. The hybrids combine the hardiness of Japanese yew with the splendid ornamental qualities of English yew. The largest, up to 40 feet tall, are densely-branched and vary from being broad- to narrow-pyramidal in outline. With crowded, rather short leaves, *T. m. brownii* is a compact, broad-columnar male not over about 8 feet tall. Hick's yew (*T. m. hicksii*), somewhat like the Irish yew in

Taxus media hicksii

that it has many erect main branches and is columnar, is one of the most distinct *T. media* varieties. As it ages, its branches tend to spread outward under the weight of snow and other climatic influences. Then, its tidy, columnar habit often can be preserved only by wiring the branches together. Excellent *T. m. hatfieldii*, compact and conical, has ascending branches with leaves spreading all around them. *T. m.*

kelseyi is an erect, compact female that fruits abundantly. It attains a height of 12 feet or more and a spread of about 9 feet. *T. m. nigra* has exceptionally dark green foliage.

Chinese yew (**T. chinensis**), native to China, is a less well-known hardy species that in its native country attains a height of 50 feet. Its rather distantly spaced leaves, in two distinct ranks, are usually somewhat sickle-shaped.

Native American yews include the Western yew, Canada yew, and Florida yew. The first, **T. brevifolia**, native from British Columbia to California and Montana, and not to be confused with *T. cuspidata nana*, which often passes as *T. brevifolia* in nurseries and gardens, sometimes is 75 feet tall, though more often it does not exceed 40 feet in height. It has horizontal branches and somewhat drooping branchlets. Its leaves, two-ranked and in flat sprays, are narrower than those of the Japanese yew. It is not hardy in the north. Canada yew or ground-hemlock (**T. canadensis**) is a low and usually straggling shrub of woodlands. The least handsome of the genus, it is also the hardiest, being indigenous as far north as Newfoundland, Iowa, and Manitoba. With yellowish-green foliage, it does not exceed 6 feet in height and is often lower. Foliage slightly variegated with yellow is characteristic of *T. c. aurea*. A dense habit of growth distinguishes *T. c. compacta*. Varieties *T. c. fastigiata* and *T. c. stricta* are dwarf sorts with erect branches. A hybrid between *T. canadensis* and *T. cuspidata*, **T. hunnewelliana** is much like the latter, but is more slender and becomes reddish in winter. Scarcely known in cultivation, **T. floridana** is a nonhardy species up to 25 feet tall. It has slender, dark green leaves up to 1 inch long and is native to a very limited area on the eastern bank of the Apalachicola River in Florida.

Garden and Landscape Uses. Yews are among our finest evergreens for landscape work. Available in numerous varietal forms, they stand repeated pruning and shearing so well that they can be used as hedges, backgrounds, screens, and topiary as well as specimen plants allowed to grow naturally. Their dark green leaves produce a fine-textured effect that does not compete for attention objectionably with flowers or other plants near them. Female trees in fruit are especially attractive, their brightly colored "berries" contrast well with the somber green of the foliage. The fruits can, however, be a nuisance; in windy weather they may be blown for several feet from the tree and will adhere with surprising tenacity to any surface upon which they alight, be it a lady's dress or an automobile.

As landscape subjects, golden-leaved and color forms other than green are not generally recommended. Unless they are used

Taxus baccata sheared to formal shape

Taxus cuspidata trained to cover a chain link fence surrounding a tennis court: (a) The lower part sheared as a formal hedge with branches at the rear retained to screen the upper portion of the fence

Taxus baccata stricta flanking a stone archway in Scotland

Taxus cuspidata as a short hedge

(b) A few years later, the finished result

Taxus cuspidata espaliered against a wall

with restraint and carefully located they are apt to prove disturbing and tiresome elements in the landscape picture. The Canada yew can be employed to good effect as an undercover in fairly open woodlands. In such places it serves well to hold steep banks.

Cultivation. Yews are tolerant of quite a wide range of soil conditions, but will not survive in waterlogged ground nor prosper in wet, sticky, clay soils. Most favorable is a moderately moist, fertile, sandy loam. They stand shade well and flourish in full sun. They may be sheared repeatedly, one or more times a year if desired. Ordinarily the best time for shearing is just before new growth begins in spring. Because they have the ability to "break" (produce new shoots) from old wood, they may be pruned back to any degree deemed necessary or desirable. If the cutting back is extremely severe, it is well to fertilize immediately afterward and to make sure that the plants do not suffer for lack of moisture during the succeeding summer.

The best time to undertake massive pruning is late winter or early spring.

Yews have compact root systems and transplant well even when large. Quite small plants can be cut back and moved with bare roots, but larger plants should be taken with a ball of soil. That the possibility of moving large yews is not new is attested to by a report in the *Gardener's Chronicle*, of England, for 1880. In March of that year, a specimen of English yew near Dover, England, estimated to be more than 1,000 years old and with a trunk girth of 22 feet, was successfully transplanted. With it was taken a ball of soil 16 feet 5 inches by 11 feet 8 inches and 3 feet 6½ inches in depth. Tree and soil ball were estimated to weigh about fifty-six tons. This operation was no small achievement in the days before power tools and power-driven appliances.

Propagation of yews is easy by cuttings made in late summer or early fall set in a

A cold frame filled with rooted cuttings of *Taxus*

greenhouse propagating bench, a cold frame, or, in mild climates, directly in a shaded place outdoors. They also root readily under mist. Cuttings from lateral branches of tree types usually develop into spreading, bushy specimens. Only those made from tips of erect leading shoots are likely to produce tree-type specimens. Seeds afford a ready means of reproduction, but collected from hybrids or from horticultural varieties they often produce a variable swarm of seedlings. The seeds, freed from their surrounding pulp, may be sown in a cold frame in fall or mixed with slightly moist peat moss or sand, stored over winter at 30 or 40°F, and sown in spring. Yews can also be increased by layering and grafting.

Diseases and Pests. Fungus twig blight and leaf blight are the chief diseases of yews. They may be attacked by the black vine weevil, the strawberry root weevil, mealybugs, and scale insects.

TCHIHATCHEWIA (Tchiha-tchèwia). The only species of *Tchihatchewia*, of the mustard family CRUCIFERAE, is native to Armenia. Its name commemorates the famous Russian traveler and author, Count Pierre A. de Tchhatchef, who died in 1890.

An interesting herbaceous perennial 6 to 9 inches tall, conspicuously hairy *T. isatidea* has a stout, erect stem and spreading, recurved leaves 1½ to 2½ inches long and gradually increasing in size from the base of the stem upward. The vanilla-scented flowers are in erect panicles. They have four sepals, four spreading, bright rose-red petals, and six stamens, two of which are shorter than the others. The fruits are podlike.

Tchihatchewia isatidea

Garden Uses and Cultivation. This interesting plant is appropriate for rock gardens and alpine greenhouses. It succeeds in sunny locations in well-drained soil and is propagated by seed.

TEA. The source of the well-known beverage tea is *Camellia sinensis*. Other plants with common names containing the word tea are these: Appalachian-tea (*Viburnum cassinoides*), Labrador-tea (*Ledum groenlandicum*), Mexican-tea (*Chenopodium ambrosioides* and *Ephedra*), Morman-tea-bush (*Ephedra*), New Jersey-tea (*Ceanothus americanus*), Oswego-tea (*Monarda didyma*), pauper's-tea (*Sageretia thea*), Philippine-tea (*Ehretia microphylla*), tea-berry (*Viburnum cassinoides*), tea crab apple (*Malus hupehensis*), tea-plant (*Viburnum lentago*), tea rose (*Rosa odorata*), and tea tree (*Leptospermum*).

TEAK is *Tectona grandis*. Bastard-teak is *Butea monosperma*.

TEASEL. See Dipsacus. The teasel gourd is *Cucumis dipsaceus*.

TECOMA (Téc-oma) — Trumpet Bush or Yellow Bells or Yellow-Elder or Roble Amarillo. One of sixteen species of the bignonia family BIGNONIACEAE, *Tecoma stans* is a favorite shrub or small tree in the Deep

South, southern California, and other subtropical and tropical places; it is the official flower of Puerto Rico. The genus *Tecoma*, the name of which is derived from its Mexican name *tecomaxochitl*, ranges in the wild from southern Florida to Mexico, the West Indies, and Argentina.

Tecomas are shrubs and small trees with opposite, usually pinnate leaves with an odd number of toothed leaflets, but sometimes with undivided leaves. The yellow to orange blooms, in terminal panicles or racemes, have bell-shaped calyxes and funnel- to bell-shaped corollas. The latter are narrowed at their bases and are hairy on their insides near their bottoms. The four curved stamens, in two pairs of different lengths, do not protrude. There is one style with a two-lobed stigma. The winged seeds are in slender, podlike capsules.

Trumpet bush, yellow bells, yellow-elder, or roble amarillo (**T. stans** syn. *Stenolobium stans*), a native from southern

Tecoma stans

Florida and the West Indies to South America, is up to 25 feet tall. Its leaves, minutely-hairy or hairless, have five to thirteen stalkless or short-stalked, ovate-oblong to lanceolate leaflets 2 to 4 inches long. Bright yellow, slightly fragrant, 1½ to 2 inches long, and about 1¼ inches wide across their faces, the blooms have corolla tubes that narrow abruptly toward their bases and spreading, wavy corolla lobes (petals). The less-than-pencil-thick seed pods are up to 8 inches long. Variety *T. s. angustata* has narrower, more deeply-toothed leaves. A native of Arizona, Texas, and Mexico, it is more cold-resistant than the typical species. In *T. s. velutina* the undersides of the leaves are pubescent. Much like *T. stans*, but more treelike, **T. castanifolia** (syn. *T. gaudichaudii*), of Ecuador, has light green, coarse-toothed, pinnate leaves. Its brilliant yellow flowers, in ample clusters at the shoot ends, are displayed several times a year in the state of Florida.

A less common kind is **T. alata** (syn. *T. smithii*), of Peru, which was long believed to be a hybrid between *T. stans velutina* and *Tecomaria capensis*. A small tree or shrub, it has large, broad panicles of yellow and orange blooms. Its corolla tubes narrow gradually to their bases and the rounded lobes (petals) bend backward. The leaves are of eleven to thirteen oblong-elliptic leaflets that are up to 2 inches in length.

A native of Argentina, **T. garrocha** is a shrub 6 feet or so tall with leaves of seven to eleven short-stalked leaflets up to 2 inches in length and pointed-ovate. The blooms are in panicles of slender racemes up to 6 inches long. Their red corolla tubes narrow gradually toward their bases. The corolla lobes are yellow or salmon. The blooms are about 2 inches long by ¾ to 1 inch wide, the seed pods up to 4 inches long.

Garden and Landscape Uses. Tecomas are among the gayest and most handsome small trees and shrubs for warm climates. The native *T. stans* is very much esteemed in Florida and is one of the fall glories of that state. It and other kinds are admirable for many locations where their beauty can be fully displayed. They are suitable as single specimens and for group plantings. The yellow bells forms an excellent screen.

Cultivation. Tecomas prosper in fertile, well-drained soil in sunny locations. The yellow bells thrives especially well and grows rapidly in Florida on sandy, high, pine land. Its blooms attract many pollinating insects and hummingbirds.

For greenhouses *T. alata* is well suited. It behaves well in pots, preferring fertile, loamy, well-drained soil watered adequately to keep it always fairly moist, but not waterlogged. Regular applications of dilute liquid fertilizer from spring through fall are helpful. Best conditions are provided by a humid atmosphere and a minimum night temperature in winter of 55°F, with a daytime rise of five to ten degrees, or a little more on sunny days, permitted. At other seasons temperatures will naturally be higher. A little shade from strong summer sun is desirable. Fairly hard pruning is done in spring, and at that time repotting receives attention. Tecomas are easily raised from seed (in warm climates, plants from those self-sown are likely to spring up in some abundance). Cuttings root with ease.

TECOMANTHE (Tecomán-the). The seventeen species of *Tecomanthe*, of the bignonia family BIGNONIACEAE, are closely related to *Campsis*, but unlike the sorts of that genus, do not attach themselves to supports by stem rootlets. The name, formed from that of the allied genus *Tecoma*, and the Greek *anthos*, a flower, alludes to a resemblance.

Tecomanthes are tall, less frequently low, woody vines with opposite leaves of one to five leaflets sometimes toothed toward their apexes. The flowers are in racemes or rarely panicle-like arrangements from the leaf axils or, on older branches, from leaf scars. They have a usually bell-shaped, five-lobed calyx, a red, reddish, or rarely orange, tubular-bell-shaped corolla with five usually unequal lobes (petals). There are four stamens in pairs of different lengths and one style. The fruits are capsules.

Flowered for the first time in the United States at Longwood Gardens, Kennett Square, Pennsylvania, in 1960, **T. venusta,** of Australia and New Guinea, is a tall vine with leaves of five pointed-elliptic, toothless leaflets 3 to 4 inches in length. Its umbel-like clusters of up to sixteen pendulous blooms are produced on the stems, chiefly the older ones, even to the ground. Each flower is about 3½ inches long by 2 inches across its face. Light magenta-rose-pink on the outsides of their trumpet-shaped corollas, these flowers have paler pink and creamy-yellow interiors, red-lined in their throats. The seed pods are 10 inches long.

A tall, woody vine, **T. dendrophila,** of New Guinea, has 7-inch-long leaves of fine pointed-oblong leaflets. Borne on old wood, the flowers have a small, dark purple calyx and a narrowly-bell-shaped, slightly-two-lipped, deep rose-pink corolla about 4 inches long, with blunt lobes.

Garden and Landscape Uses and Cultivation. These handsome vines are suitable for outdoors in southern Florida, Hawaii, and other regions of reasonably humid, warm subtropical and tropical climates, and in large tropical greenhouses. They thrive in ordinary garden soil and withstand some shade. Propagation is by cuttings, layering, and seed.

TECOMARIA (Tecomàr-ia)—Cape-Honey-suckle. One of the three species of *Tecomaria* is commonly cultivated in the warmer parts of North America. This African genus belongs to the bignonia family BIGNONIACEAE. Its name, a variation of that of the New World genus *Tecoma*, reflects a close botanical relationship.

Tropical and subtropical, tecomarias are more or less climbing evergreen shrubs with opposite, pinnate leaves with an odd number of toothed leaflets. They bloom in late summer and fall. Their funnel-shaped flowers, in large, compact, terminal clusters, have slightly-curved corolla tubes and four flaring lobes, the upper one cleft at the apex, the two lateral lobes pointing backward at maturity. The stamens protrude and the style is slender and long-exerted. The fruits are capsules.

Cape-honeysuckle (**T. capensis**), of South Africa, is a rambling shrub 5 to 7 feet or so tall. It has leaves up to 6 inches long

Tecomaria capensis

with five to nine elliptic to broad-ovate leaflets, essentially hairless except sometimes for tufts in the leaf axils near the base of the underside. Its orange-red to scarlet flowers are about 2 inches long. Variety *T. c. aurea* has yellow flowers. Perhaps not

Tecomaria capensis aurea

distinct from it, *T. c. lutea*, introduced to the United States from South Africa by a Californian physician in 1954 or a little earlier, has clear yellow flowers. This shows some variation in flower color when raised from seed; for the most satisfactory results, it should be propagated vegetatively. Another recent introduction is a reputed hybrid between *T. capensis* and *T. shirensis,* very similar to *T. capensis,* but with minute hairs on the upper leaf surface and tufts of whitish hairs in the leaf axils beneath. Its rich brownish-red flowers, about 2 inches in length, have yellowish throats lined with dark brown.

East African **T. nyassae** (syn. *Tecoma nyassae*) is a shrub about 6 to 10 feet tall with leaves, 4 to 8 inches long, each of five to eleven pointed-elliptic leaflets 1½ to 2½ inches long. The flowers, 1 inch to 2½ inches long, have usually red-striped, orange corollas, more rarely cream-colored ones. Another native of East Africa, **T.**

A reputed hybrid between *Tecomaria capensis* and *T. shirensis*

shirensis (syn. *Tecoma shirensis*), up to 10 feet in height, has leaves 7 to 9 inches long with nine to thirteen ovate leaflets up to 3 inches long and tufts of hairs in the vein axils on their undersides. From 1½ to 2 inches in length, the orange flowers have red-striped corolla lobes (petals).

Garden and Landscape Uses and Cultivation. Cape-honeysuckle thrives outdoors in southern California, Florida, and Hawaii and along the Gulf Coast. It may be trained as a vine or grown as a shrub or hedge. It thrives in any fairly good garden soil and needs a warm, sunny location. Pruning, which should be done in spring, must be moderate if the plant is trained to climb, but if a shrub form is preferred, more severe cutting is in order. In large pots or tubs this plant is attractive for decorating terraces, patios, and similar places. In the north, such containers may be wintered in a light place indoors where a temperature of 40 to 50°F is maintained. During the early part of the growing season, they need more warmth and a sunny location. In summer they may be stood outdoors. Container-grown tecomarias need rich, well-drained soil. Water them freely from spring through fall, less freely in the winter. Throughout summer give them regular and frequent applications of dilute liquid fertilizer. Attend to top dressing, and repotting when needed, at the time of the spring pruning. For the most satisfactory result, *T. nyassae* and *T. shirensis* need a little more warmth in winter than *T. capensis*, but the hybrid between this last and *T. shirensis* gives satisfaction as an indoor plant when grown as recommended for container-grown Cape-honeysuckles. Tecomarias are easily raised from cuttings, root cuttings, and seed, and by layering. Pests that may need controlling are mealybugs, whiteflies, and scale insects.

TECOMELLA (Tecom-élla). The bignonia family BIGNONIACEAE is rich in handsome, mostly warm-country, flowering shrubs, trees, and vines. Well known among them

are jacarandas, trumpet vines, and African-tulip trees. Less familiar is the only species of *Tecomella*, a native of dryish parts of Arabia and southwest Asia. Its name is a diminutive of that of the related genus *Tecoma*, which it resembles except that its leaves are undivided rather than pinnate.

An evergreen or nearly evergreen shrub or small round-headed tree, *T. undulata* (syn. *Bignonia undulata*) on occasion is 30 to 40 feet tall, but is often smaller. Of rigid habit, it has spreading branches that droop at their ends. Varying considerably in size and shape, its undivided, gray-glaucous, thickish, bluntish leaves, mostly 6 to 7 inches long, are narrowly-oblong and have 1-inch-long stalks. In Florida the flowers open in spring. They are in clusters of five to ten at the ends of short branchlets and are reddish-orange, cup-shaped, and about 2 inches in diameter and in depth. The fruits are capsules.

Garden and Landscape Uses and Cultivation. Experience with this species in the United States is rather limited. It grows in southern Florida and undoubtedly would do well in other regions where not more than an occasional light frost occurs. It is resistant to both drought and brush fires and flourishes in sun in any reasonably good garden soil. Propagation is by seed and by cuttings.

TECOPHILAEA (Teco-philaèa) — Chilean-Crocus. Two species are the only representatives of *Tecophilaea*. They belong in the amaryllis family AMARYLLIDACEAE or, according to some authorities, in the tecophilaea family TECOPHILAEACEAE. They inhabit semiarid regions in Chile and perhaps Peru, at altitudes of up to nearly 10,000 feet. The name honors Tecofila Billiotti, a painter of flowers and a daughter of the early nineteenth-century Professor Colla, of Turin, Italy.

Tecophilaeas have small corms (bulblike organs that are solid instead of consisting of a series of layers as are true bulbs such as onions and lilies) and few linear to narrowly-lanceolate leaves. Their short, leafless flower stalks, which appear in spring, are partly enveloped by the sheathing leaf bases; they carry one to three blooms having much the aspect of blue or violet crocuses. Broadly-bell-shaped, they have six perianth parts (petals, or more correctly, tepals) that spread at maturity, three fertile and three nonfunctional stamens, the latter correctly called staminodes. The fruits are capsules.

The only species cultivated, *T. cyanocrocus* is 4 to 6 inches tall and typically has three leaves 3 to 5 inches long, usually wavy at their margins, and one to three rich blue blooms, 1 inch to 1½ inches long, with white veinings in their throats and outer petals sometimes margined with

white. The petals are obovate. Variety *T. c. elegans* (syn. *T. c. regelii*) has rather narrower leaves and petals. In *T. c. violacea* the flowers are violet-blue. The other species, *T. violaeflora* is believed not to be in cultivation.

Garden Uses and Cultivation. Highly regarded in the British Isles by fanciers of choice rock garden and alpine greenhouse plants, the Chilean-crocus is known to few in America, but is a challenge to serious growers of alpine plants. Because it starts into growth very early, its outdoor culture presents problems in regions where late frosts are prevalent. Little is known of its ability to survive hot summers. In all probability, success with it is most likely in the Pacific Northwest and regions where winters are mild and summers are not intensely hot. Planting is done in fall, setting the bulbs 2 to 2½ inches deep in well-drained, fertile, sandy, peaty soil. If the bulbs are planted in pots, afterward they are put in a cold frame or other cool, frost-free place and are brought into an alpine greenhouse when the shoots show aboveground. Propagation is by cormlets (tiny offset corms) and by seed.

TECTARIA (Tec-tària) — Button Fern. This very considerable genus of tropical and subtropical ferns of the aspidium family ASPIDIACEAE is less well represented in cultivation than might be expected. The button fern is the only species of the more than 200 recognized that is at all frequent. In the wild, the group is widespread in warm parts of both the Old World and the New World, with the greatest concentration of kinds in Asia. Its name, derived from the Latin *tectum*, a roof, alludes to the little coverings of the groups of spore cases.

A somewhat diverse genus, *Tectaria* includes a few species with undivided fronds (leaves) and a much greater number in which they are one- or more-times-pinnate or pinnately-lobed. They are never finely-dissected. These ferns have stout, short-creeping or erect, scaly rootstocks, and fronds in clusters. The leafstalks are often blackish, the blades prevailingly triangular. Usually only the main stalks of the fronds are hairy. The clusters of spore capsules are typically round and at the ends of veins.

Button fern (*T. cicutaria*) is so called because of the little button-like buds or bulbils that develop on its fronds. Native to the West Indies, this sort has thin, soft, fresh green, triangular fronds with stalks scaly at their bases or throughout their lengths and blades once- or twice-pinnate, with the final segments pinnately-lobed. Overall, the fronds may be 3½ feet or so long, with the stalks accounting for approximately one-third of their lengths. The rounded clusters of spore capsules are on

Tectaria cicutaria

Tectaria macrodonta

Tectaria heracleifolia

Tectaria subtriphylla

TECTONA (Téc-tona) — Teak. There are three species of the Indo-Malaysian genus *Tectona*, of the vervain family VERBENACEAE. The name is a modification of the southern Indian name *teka* of *T. grandis*.

Tectonas are tall, deciduous trees with undivided, opposite or whorled (in circles of three or more) leaves. In terminal panicles, the small white or bluish flowers have a five- to seven-lobed calyx, a tubular corolla with five to seven spreading lobes, five or six stamens, and one style. The fruits are drupes (fruits structured like plums).

Very different from the humble annuals and herbaceous perennials cultivated in flower gardens that belong in the same family, teak (**T. grandis**) is a mighty forest

Tectona grandis

Tectona grandis in Panama

the undersides of the leaves, well in from the margins. Less commonly cultivated, *T. incisa* is native from the West Indies to Mexico and Brazil. It is much like the last, but has fronds of seven or more, typically lobeless leaflets. The variety most usually grown, *T. i. pilosa,* has hairy fronds with wavy margins. Native from Florida and Texas to the American tropics, **T. heracleifolia** has triangular fronds 2 to 3 feet long, coarsely-divided into three or five broad, irregularly-toothed leaflets, the basal ones with a long-pointed lower lobe and the terminal one the largest.

A native of Malaysia, the Philippine Islands, the Solomon Islands, and Fiji, **T. macrodonta** has horizontal rhizomes up to 1 foot or more long and fronds 2 to 3 feet long by about one-half as wide. Their upper portions are deeply-pinnately-lobed; below there are many lanceolate leaflets up to 1 foot long by 6 to 8 inches wide. The small clusters of spore capsules are near the chief veins. Handsome **T. subtriphylla,** of India and Taiwan, has creeping rhizomes and arching, pinnate fronds, triangular in outline and 1 foot to 2 feet long by 8 inches to 1 foot wide. The terminal leaflet is deeply-three- to five-lobed. The comparatively large clusters of spore capsules are scattered.

Garden and Landscape Uses. In southern California, Florida, and other quite warm parts of the United States, the button fern and *T. incisa* and its variety can be grown outdoors in sheltered, shady places. They provide good foliage foils for smaller plants and are themselves quite lovely. They and other kinds are also attractive for cultivating in pots, tubs, and ground beds in greenhouses and conservatories.

Cultivation. Except where conditions are so cold and wet that fungus infections are encouraged, tectarias give little trouble to gardeners. They grow with vigor in deep soil that contains an abundance of compost, leaf mold, peat moss, or other agreeable organic material and that, although not lacking for moisture, is not wet. Shade and a location where strong winds do not create problems is needed.

In greenhouses tectarias succeed where the winter night temperature is about 55°F and that by day five to fifteen degrees higher. At other seasons more warmth is appropriate. The atmosphere should be humid. Propagation is by spores, division, and, with the button fern, by "buttons" that form on the fronds and root readily when they are removed or when they drop. For more information see Ferns.

tree up to 150 feet in height. Indigenous to India, Java, Burma, Thailand, and parts of the Indian Archipelago, it is extensively planted in tropical Asia for its lumber, which is one of the most important of tropical woods. Very hard and extraordinarily durable, this is used for ships' decks, flooring, railroad cars, piles, interior trim, paneling, carvings, fine furniture, and garden furniture and in greenhouse construction. Even when exposed to the weather unprotected by paint or other preservative, it is strongly resistant to decay. It weathers to a beautiful silvery-gray. This species has an open crown of spreading branches and comparatively few stalkless or nearly stalkless, leathery, rough-surfaced, elliptic or obovate leaves 1 foot to 3 feet long. They are opposite or in threes and, like the quadrangular young stems and the flower clusters, are covered with fine gray-green, stellate (star-shaped) hairs. The young foliage is bronzy. The tiny flowers, many together, are in terminal panicles. They are finely-pubescent. Each has a six-lobed, grayish calyx and a funnel-shaped corolla with six spreading, whitish lobes (petals), six stamens, and a slender style tipped with a hooked stigma. The spherical and finely-pubescent fruits, about ½ inch in diameter, are enclosed in inflated egg-shaped calyxes about 1 inch long. Each contains up to four small seeds.

Garden and Landscape Uses and Cultivation. In the West Indies, Central America, South America, and southern Florida, teak is sometimes planted as a shade and ornamental tree. In those places it does not ordinarily achieve the extreme heights it sometimes does in its homelands. In Puerto Rico, trees attain a height of 60 feet in twenty years. Its foliage is bold and handsome and its flower clusters have some decorative appeal. It thrives best in deep, fertile soils at low elevations. Propagation is by seed and by sucker shoots. The latter develop more rapidly in their early years than seedlings.

TEFF is *Eragrostis tef.*

TELEGRAPH PLANT is *Desmodium motorium.*

TELEKIA (Tel-èkia). Formerly included in *Buphthalmum,* from which it differs in the anthers of its flowers being bearded at their bases, *Telekia,* of the daisy family COMPOSITAE, consists of two species. The name *Telekia* honors the nineteenth-century Hungarian nobleman and patron of botany Samuel Teleki de Szek.

These plants are showy, hardy herbaceous perennials with alternate, undivided, toothed or toothless leaves, and quite large flower heads with four- or five-lobed disk florets (the kind that compose the eye of a daisy) and a single row of ray florets (petal-like ones that surround the eye). Both are yellow. The bracts of the involucre (collar behind the flower head) overlap. The seedlike fruits are achenes.

Handsome, of bold aspect, and 2 to 6 feet tall, *T. speciosa* (syn. *Buphthalmum speciosum*) ranges in the wild from southern Europe to adjacent Asia. Hairy and

Telekia speciosa

strongly scented, it has stems that branch in their upper parts and very large, coarsely-double-toothed, heart-shaped basal leaves and smaller stalkless, ovate, upper ones with coarsely-toothed margins. The flower heads, 2½ to 4 inches across and usually in groups of two to eight, rarely are solitary. From the last, *T. speciosissimum,* a native of limestone soils in northern Italy, differs in usually not exceeding 2 feet in height and having branchless stems terminating in a solitary flower head 1½ to 2½ inches in diameter.

Garden and Landscape Uses. Although somewhat coarse, telekias are useful garden plants. Of the easiest cultivation, they can be employed effectively in flower borders, naturalistic areas, and by watersides. For the last purpose *T. speciosa* is especially well adapted. They respond to moderately fertile soil, doing well in those of limestone derivation and in sunny locations.

Cultivation. Seed and division in spring or early fall provide ready methods of propagation. Plants raised from seeds sown early indoors and later planted in the garden are likely to bloom the first year. Established specimens benefit from a spring application of a complete garden fertilizer. If there is danger of wind breaking them, staking may be done, but usually this is not needed. When the plants begin to show signs of decreased vigor they should be dug up, divided, and replanted in soil deeply-spaded and conditioned by mixing in compost or other decayed organic material and fertilizer.

TELEPHIUM (Telèph-ium)—Orpine. Of the five Mediterranean-region and one Madagascan species of *Telephium,* of the pink family CARYOPHYLLACEAE, one is rarely cultivated. The name is a modification of the ancient Greek *telephion,* applied to a different plant.

Telephiums are woody-based perennials or subshrubs with alternate leaves (unusual for the family). Their flowers, in terminal clusters, have five each sepals, petals, and stamens and three, or more rarely

four, styles. The fruits are capsules and usually three-angled.

Native to western Europe from Switzerland southward, *T. imperati* is a hairless subshrub with thick rhizomes, and usually procumbent, branchless stems up to 1¼ feet long and woody toward their bases. Its glaucous, obovate to nearly spatula-shaped, blunt, somewhat fleshy leaves may be ½ inch long or slightly longer. The short-stalked blooms are generally in clusters of up to twenty, but sometimes the clusters contain forty or more blooms. The flowers have white petals, ⅓ inch long, and slightly shorter sepals. The seed capsules are beaked at their apexes. Variety *T. i. orientale,* a native of Greece and Crete, is smaller and slenderer and has narrower leaves and fewer-flowered clusters of blooms.

Garden Uses and Cultivation. Scarcely ornamental enough to be of interest to other than collectors, the species described may be used on sunny slopes and other unimportant places where the soil is thoroughly well drained. It propagates easily from seed and cuttings. Its hardiness is not precisely determined, but it probably will not survive very severe winters.

TELESONIX (Tel-ésonix). The only species of *Telesonix* belongs in the saxifrage family SAXIFRAGACEAE. Previously included in *Boykinia,* it is set apart on the basis of its blooms having ten instead of five stamens and other botanical details. The derivation of its name is uncertain.

Attractive and showy, bright carmine-pink flowers are borne few together in short panicles in summer on *T. jamesii* (syns. *T.*

Telesonix jamesii

heucheriformis, Boykinia jamesii). A hardy herbaceous perennial, endemic from South Dakota to Alberta, Colorado, and Nevada, this mountain species inhabits moist limestone cliffs and rocky slopes. It has short, thick rootstocks; hairy stems 2 to 6 or rarely 8 inches tall, often reddish toward their tops; and kidney-shaped to round, shallowly-lobed or double-round-toothed, glandular-pubescent leaves with blades 1 inch to 2 inches across. Each stem has one or two leaves and above them an often one-sided panicle of five to twenty-five blooms. The flowers have a five-lobed calyx and five spreading petals approximately ¼ inch long. The face of the bloom is about ¾ inch across.

Garden Uses and Cultivation. This beautiful American alpine is little cultivated. Where it can be grown successfully, it is lovely for rock gardens and alpine greenhouses, but for all practical purposes it is impossible to reestablish specimens collected from the wild. Gardeners wishing to try this challenging species should raise it from seed and grow it in pots until it is planted outdoors or continue it in pots in a cold frame or cool greenhouse. It needs very well-drained, gritty soil that does not dry excessively and good light, with shade during the hottest part of the day. Propagation is by seed and by cuttings.

TELLIMA (Tellìm-a) — Fringe Cups. The name of this genus is an anagram of *Mitella*, a sister genus, of the saxifrage family SAXIFRAGACEAE, that *Tellima* so closely resembles that it may in fact be regarded as the western American representative of the eastern American bishop's cap (*Mitella*). From *Mitella* the western plant differs chiefly in having seed capsules with two beaks. Those of the bishop's cap are without these appendages.

The only species, hardy perennial *T. grandiflora* occurs in moist woods and rocky places from California to Alaska. It has horizontal rootstocks, numerous basal and a few stem leaves, and erect, branchless, flowering stems 1 foot to 2½ feet tall. The leaves are more or less hairy, roundish or roundish-kidney-shaped with heart-shaped bases, shallowly-five- or seven-lobed, and toothed. The basal ones are 2 to 4 inches broad, the stem leaves are smaller. They have long stalks. The short-stalked flowers, urn- to bell-shaped, are in glandular-pubescent racemes. Each has an inflated five-toothed calyx; five fringed, reflexed petals about ¼ inch long, at first whitish, later reddish; and ten stamens. They are produced in late spring. For other plants previously named *Tellima* see Lithophragma.

Garden Uses and Cultivation. A plant for shaded, moist places where the soil contains liberal amounts of organic matter, this species, which has the general aspect of a *Heuchera*, is suitable for borders, woodland gardens, rock gardens, and informal areas. Although not showy, its blooms have a certain quaint charm and its foliage is attractive. It associates pleasingly with other woodlanders and is useful as a groundcover. No special care is needed. Planting may be done in spring

or fall, spacing the plants 1 foot to 1½ feet apart. Established specimens benefit from mulching with compost, leaf mold, or peat moss and from watering in dry weather. So long as they are doing well, they may be left undisturbed for years. Propagation by division in spring or early fall is simple to accomplish; seed sown in humusy, sandy soil also gives good results.

TELOPEA (Tel-òpea) — Waratah. This entirely Australian genus of the protea family PROTEACEAE includes among its four species the waratah, one of the most magnificent flowering shrubs in the world. The name comes from the Greek *telopas*, seen at a distance, and alludes, presumably, to the showy heads of bloom.

The sorts of *Telopea* are evergreen shrubs with alternate, toothed or toothless, leathery leaves. The bisexual flowers are crowded in dense, ovoid to globular heads at the branch ends. They have a long perianth tube with four petal-like segments that separate above. There are no true petals. There are four stamens and an undivided style. The fruits are follicles containing winged seeds.

The waratah (*T. speciosissima*), 6 to 8

Telopea speciosissima

feet tall and with erect, rigid branches, has oblongish leaves, rounded and usually coarsely-toothed at their apexes and narrowing markedly to their bases. They are 6 to 9 inches long. Tightly packed in cone-like, ovoid heads 3 to 4 inches wide and long, and ringed with a basal collar of large, bright red, petal-like bracts, the flowers are red. The flower heads vaguely resemble large-flowered chrysanthemums.

The Tasmanian waratah (*T. truncata*), 5 to 15 feet tall, has narrow, obovate to linear, pointed leaves 2 to 4 inches long with usually toothless, recurved margins. The red flowers are in dense, flattish heads 2 to 2½ inches in diameter. In variety *T. t.* 'Essie' the blooms are rich yellow.

Garden and Landscape Uses and Cultivation. Like many shrubs of the protea family, telopeas are difficult and usually

unpredictable in cultivation. Success is ample reason for special satisfaction. It is probable that the greatest danger of loss occurs during the seedling stages and that the care and management that has brought success to a few growers of proteas in California would be equally successful with *Telopea*. Investigations in Australia indicate that, for the successful cultivation of the waratah, soil with an extremely low phosphorus content is necessary. Propagation is by seed.

TEMPLE TREE. See Plumeria.

TEMPLETONIA (Temple-tònia). John Templeton, an Irish botanist who died in 1825, is commemorated by the name of this exclusively Australian genus of seven species of the pea family LEGUMINOSAE.

Templetonias consist of hairless, in some cases leafless, shrubs. When leaves are present they are alternate, undivided, and without lobes or teeth. Solitary or paired blooms come from the leaf axils or from joints on the stems where leaves would normally originate. They are pea-like, with a four- or five-lobed calyx, a recurved, ovate to nearly circular, standard or banner petal, narrow wing petals, and a narrow keel. There are five longer and five shorter stamens united into a tube, and a branchless, incurved, hairless style. The fruits are flattish pods containing seeds with fleshy appendages.

From 3 to 10 feet in height, *Templetonia retusa*, of southern and western Australia, has short-stalked, leathery, glaucous, elliptic to obovate leaves, ¾ inch to 1½ inches long and ½ to 1 inch broad, with the mid-veins prominent on the undersides. The flowers have calyxes with four short lobes. Their corollas are red, rarely yellow, and up to 1¼ inches long. The leathery seed pods are 2 inches long or shorter. This is a handsome flowering evergreen shrub.

Garden and Landscape Uses and Cultivation. Outdoor planting of templetonias is practicable only in regions with warm, dry, frost-free or essentially frost-free climates. They prosper where Australian acacias do well. The kind discussed above is a useful general-purpose flowering shrub. It needs full sun and well-drained, reasonably fertile ground. It blooms in spring. If pruning is deemed desirable to shape or restrict the bush, it should be done as soon as the blooms fade. Propagation is by seed, and by cuttings of firm shoots in summer. Until they are large enough to plant in their permanent locations, it is best to grow the young plants in cans or pots. In greenhouses this shrub responds to conditions and care appropriate for acacias.

TENDER PLANTS. The useful, but imprecise designation of tender is applied to plants of perennial duration that are not sufficiently hardy to survive winters outdoors and sometimes also to annuals and plants grown as annuals that are likely to be harmed by even light frosts. Therefore, whether a particular kind of plant is classed as tender will depend on geographical location and other environmental factors. See the Encyclopedia entries Hardy and Hardiness, and Protection For Plants.

TENT CATERPILLAR. See Caterpillars.

TEPAL. The outer organs of most flowers are of two kinds, the outermost the sepals, which form the calyx, inside them the petals, which form the corolla. Either or both may be wanting. Usually calyx and corolla are clearly differentiated, but sometimes sepals and petals are similar in size, shape, texture, and other characteristics. Then the calyx and corolla is referred to collectively as the perianth and their parts as tepals. If the tepals are all petal-like, as they are for instance in hyacinths, lilies, and tulips, it is usual, but somewhat inaccurate to call them all petals.

TEPHROCACTUS (Tephro-cáctus). Although most cultivators of cactuses follow botanists who favor splitting genera of the cactus family CACTACEAE finely and use the name *Tephrocactus* for a group of about sixty small South American species, there is no doubt, as conservative botanists proclaim, that these could well be included in nearly related *Opuntia*. They differ only in obscure technical details from the cylindrical-stemmed members of that genus. The name, derived from the Greek *tephros*, ash-colored, and cactus, alludes to the color of some sorts.

Tephrocactuses vary considerably in size according to species and range from low, flat, clumping sorts to low bushes. Their stems consist of loosely connected, nearly spherical to egg-shaped segments that may be smooth or lumpy (tubercled), but never ribbed. Their areoles, which may or may not be woolly, like those of opuntias bear glochids (minute, barbed, easily-detachable spines) and usually larger, more obvious spines and sometimes long hairs. The more or less wheel- to bell-shaped, day-opening blooms come from the segment ends. The fruits are spherical to egg-shaped. The flowers and fruits of some sorts described here have not been observed.

These are cultivated: **T. articulatus** (syn. *Opuntia articulata*) is the typical form of a group of varieties, most of which have conspicuous, broad, flattened spines, absent from the type itself. Upright and bushy, this sort has nearly spherical, up-to-2-inch-long, slightly-warted, spineless segments with long, red-brown glochids. Its flowers are white fading to pink. *T. a.*

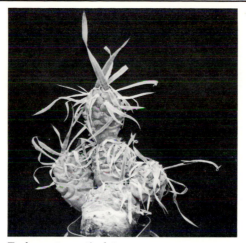
Tephrocactus articulatus

diadematus has yellowish blooms and spines 1 inch to 1½ inches long. *T. a. inermis* (syn. *T. a. strobiliformis*) has elongated, spineless segments that look like pine cones. *T. a. papyracanthus* has soft, broad, flat, papery spines 2 to 3 inches long. *T. a. polyacanthus* has twisted, angular spines up to 4 inches long and in clusters of five. *T. a. syringacanthus* has solitary or paired, flexible spines sometimes more than 2 inches long. *T. corotilla* (syns. *T. ignotus, Opuntia corotilla, O. ignota*) is spreading, freely-branched, and about 6 inches high. The stem segments, ellipsoid and up to 2¼ inches long by ¾ inch thick, have woolly areoles with usually one to seven needle-like spines about 1½ inches long. Sometimes they are spineless. About 1½ inches long, the flowers, at first creamy-white, later become pink. *T. floccosus* (syn. *Opuntia floccosa*), one of the most beautiful, sprawls to form clumps, several feet in diameter, of prominently-warted segments 2 to 4 inches long by

Tephrocactus articulatus syringacanthus

nearly or quite 1½ inches wide, densely clothed with curly, pure white, soft, woolly hairs. The slender yellow spines, in threes, twos, or solitary, are up to 1¼ inches long. The yellow to orange, 1½-inch-wide blooms are succeeded by warty, spherical fruits. *T. glomeratus* (syn. *Opuntia glomerata*, which name has also been applied to *T. articulatus*) is a low plant 2 to 6 inches across with egg-shaped segments mostly under 1¼ inches long that have areoles with yellow glochids and solitary, dark-tipped, light brown spines sharply bent near their bases and 1½ inches long. The flowers and fruits are not known. *T. mandragora* has a long, thick root. Longish-ovoid, its stem segments are about ¾ inch long. The small spines, in threes, twos, or solitary, spread sideways. *T. molinensis* (syn. *Opuntia guerkei*), spreading and densely-branched, has stems with spineless, ellipsoid to ovoid segments, 1 inch to 1½ inches long by ¾ to 1 inch thick, with brushlike clusters of yellow glochids. *T. ovatus* (syn. *Opuntia ovata*) forms clumps 3 to 5 inches high of small egg-shaped segments with, chiefly from their upper parts, clusters of usually five

Tephrocactus articulatus diadematus

to nine white-tipped, yellow, awl-shaped spines up to ½ inch long, the areoles of which sprout tufts of brown glochids. The fruits are described as dirty yellow and spiny. **T. pentlandii** (syn. *Opuntia pentlan-*

Tephrocactus pentlandii

dii) much resembles *T. glomeratus*, but has long spines that spread less widely. It forms close clumps 4 to 6 inches high and up to 3 feet wide. Its shallowly-warted or nearly smooth stem segments are ovoid to ellipsoid and mostly about 2 inches long by ¾ inch to 1½ inches wide. Their areoles have yellow glochids and, often only the upper ones, two to ten whitish to brownish spines up to 2½ inches in length. The blooms, yellow to reddish-yellow, are about 1½ inches wide. **T. rauhii** (syn. *Opuntia rauhii*) forms wide mats. Its cylindrical stems, up to about 1 foot high by 3 inches wide, are furnished with white hairs. **T. subterraneus** (syn. *Opuntia subterranea*) is small and has a very long, carrot-like taproot. Its few stem segments are ovoid, warty, and about 1½ inches in length. From each whitish areole sprout tufts of dark-colored glochids and one to seven flat, leathery, whitish spines, somewhat under ½ inch long.

Garden Uses and Cultivation. The cultivated tephrocactuses are among the most attractive of the *Opuntia* relationship of the cactus family. They have great appeal for collectors and are suitable for greenhouses and, in desert and semidesert regions, for outdoor rock gardens and similar places.

Most sorts are more finicky about the conditions under which they are grown than are most robust opuntias. Likely, this is related to their coming from high altitudes and having some of the requirements of subalpine plants. Be that as it may, they need a cool, dry environment and decidedly dry conditions at the roots during winter; at all times they need full sun. In greenhouses winter temperatures of 45 to 50°F at night, with a five to ten or, perhaps on sunny days, fifteen degree rise by day, are adequate. The soil must be very porous and kept moderately moist, but allowed to nearly dry between waterings, from spring to fall. Propagation is easy by cuttings and by seed. For further information see Cactuses.

TEPHROSIA (Teph-ròsia). Most abundant as to kinds in Africa and Australia, *Tephrosia*, of the pea family LEGUMINOSAE, is native to the eastern and western hemispheres, chiefly, but not exclusively, to the tropics and subtropics. It consists of herbaceous plants, subshrubs, and a few shrubs, and has a name derived from the Greek *tephros*, ashy, that alludes to the grayish foliage of many kinds. Some of its 300 species have been used as native fish poisons.

Tephrosias have pinnate leaves, generally silky-hairy at least on their undersides, with an uneven number, usually many, but sometimes only three or one, leaflets which, except for the terminal one, are opposite. Their pea-shaped flowers are in racemes that are terminal or are opposite the leaves, or are solitary or in pairs from the upper leaf axils. The blooms have five-toothed or five-lobed calyxes, sometimes with the two upper teeth or lobes united. The pink, red, purple, or white petals are clawed, that is, markedly narrowed toward their bases. The standard or banner one has a broad to nearly circular blade. The keel is incurved. Each bloom has ten stamens, nine of which are joined, and one separate or partly so. The fruits are pods.

Tephrosia, undetermined species (leaves and seed pods)

A quite lovely herbaceous species, **T. virginiana** (syn. *Cracca virginiana*) is wild, usually in sandy fields and similar places, from Massachusetts to Minnesota, Florida, and Texas. It forms clumps of more or less erect stems, 1 foot to 2 feet tall, and so resembles goat's-rue (*Galega officinalis*) that in many parts of its natural range it is known by that name. From 2½ to 4 inches long, its leaves have nine to twenty-nine oblong leaflets from ¾ to 1 inch long. The flowers are in erect, terminal, usually solitary, compact racemes, 2 to 3½ inches long. They have a pale yellow, standard or banner petal, pink or pale purple side ones, and a pink keel. The banners are ½ to ¾ inch long. This species is very variable as to hairiness, sometimes having its stems, foliage, and bracts of the racemes densely, conspicuously, and beautifully pubescent or sometimes clothed with only short hairs.

A rigid evergreen shrub 2 to 3 feet tall, South African **T. grandiflora** has leaves usually of eleven to fifteen leaflets, 1-inch-wide, reddish-mauve flowers in clustered racemes, and pods 2 to 2½ inches long. Another evergreen shrub of South Africa, **T. glomeruliflora**, about 7 feet in height, has bright pink blooms. Its white-hairy leaves are of 1¾-inch-long oblong leaflets. With white or reddish flowers and up to 10 feet tall, **T. candida**, of India, is naturalized in the West Indies. In some parts of the tropics it is used as a windbreak and as green manure. This has leaves 6 to 8 inches in length, with 2-inch-long leaflets, silky on their undersides, and flowers 1 inch in length in terminal racemes 6 to 9 inches long or longer. Its pods are 4 inches long.

Garden and Landscape Uses and Cultivation. The hardy species first discussed is useful for flower borders and for naturalizing in less formal areas. It succeeds in well-drained, somewhat acid soil and prefers full sun. Easily raised from seed, it can also be increased by dividing its woody rootstocks in spring. Shrubby evergreen tephrosias are hardy only in fairly mild climates. Nevertheless, the African species discussed here will stand considerable cold and, even if damaged by frost, so long as their roots are not killed, will renew themselves by sprouts from below. The shrubby kinds grow well in sandy soil, preferring those not excessively dry in summer. They require full sun. Propagation is by seed and by cuttings.

TEREBINTH TREE is *Pistacia terebinthus*.

TERMINAL. As said of shoots, buds, leaflets, and other plant parts, terminal has its usual meaning of being at or forming the end of something. A terminal shoot ends a trunk or branch; a terminal bud, a shoot; and a terminal leaflet, a pinnate leaf. These organs contrast with lateral or side shoots, buds, and leaflets.

TERMINALIA (Termin-àlia) — Tropical-Almond or Indian-Almond or Myrobalan. One of the approximately 250 species of *Terminalia*, of the combretum family COMBRETACEAE, is widely planted in the tropics as an ornamental, others are less commonly cultivated. The name, derived from the Latin *terminus*, an end, alludes to the leaves being concentrated toward the tips of the branchlets.

Terminalias are mostly large trees, chiefly natives of tropical Asia, but also represented in the native floras of other parts of the tropics of both the eastern and western hemispheres. They have usually alternate, or more rarely opposite, undivided, lobeless leaves, generally crowded toward the ends of the branches and branchlets. The petal-less flowers, small and bisexual or unisexual, in spikes or racemes, have a four- or five-parted calyx, tubular below and bell-shaped in its upper part. There are ten protruding stamens and one style. The fruits, typically one-seeded, are two- to five-angled or winged. From the bark, nuts, and roots of some kinds, tannin, dyes, and inks are made. Some species produce useful lumber.

The tropical- or Indian-almond or myrobalan (*T. catappa*) of Malaya, the East Indies, and Malagasy (Madagascar), succeeds in southern Florida and Hawaii and is much esteemed as a shade tree and ornamental. It produces edible seeds, generally referred to as nuts, from which a usable oil is expressed, and lumber used for construction and boat building. In Florida the squirrels are so fond of the nuts that few are available for human use. The tropical-almond is of distinguished appearance. Attaining a maximum height of some 80 feet, but often much lower in cultivation, it is deciduous or evergreen depending upon climate. It has a stout, often leaning trunk, tiers of wide-spreading horizontal branches, and handsome, lustrous, alternate leaves that are blunt or short-pointed, broadly-obovate, and short-stalked. From 6 inches to 1 foot long, they

Terminalia catappa (foliage and fruits)

are clustered almost in rosettes toward the branchlet ends; before they fall they turn red or reddish. The small greenish-white, slightly-scented flowers are in slender spikes up to 7 inches long. They are mostly males with usually a few bisexual flowers near the bases of the spikes. The fruits, 1 inch to 2 inches in length, flattened and broadly-ovate, have one or two winged edges. They are green, yellowish, or reddish and contain an oblong-elliptic stone surrounded by a thin rind. The stone encloses a delicately flavored seed about 1¼ inches long.

Other species sometimes cultivated include *T. arjuna*, a native of India that attains a height of 80 feet. It has oblong leaves, up to 6 inches long, and short spikes or panicles of bisexual greenish or white flowers. Its dark brown fruits have five wings. Also Indian, *T. tomentosa*,

sometimes 100 feet tall, has nearly opposite, elliptic leaves up to 8 inches in length, flowers in spikes, and five-winged, 2-inch-long fruits. Another native of India, and also of Burma, *T. myriocarpa* may become 100 feet tall. It has pointed-oblong, short-stalked, tapering leaves, up to 8 inches long, with toothed edges. The changeable, pink to white flowers are succeeded by yellow, winged fruits ⅛ inch long. From the island of Guam comes *T. saffordii*, characterized by thick, glossy, broadly-obovate leaves up to about 5 inches long, branchless flower spikes, and oblong fruits about ¾ inch long.

Small trees are *T. australis*, of southern Brazil, and *T. muelleri*, of Queensland. About 10 feet in height, *T. australis* has very short-stalked, lanceolate-ovate to ovate, smooth-edged leaves, 2 inches long or longer, and few-flowered spikes of greenish blooms about as long as the leaves. The Australian *T. muelleri* is a handsome species with leathery, blunt or short-pointed leaves up to 4 inches in length and somewhat narrowly-ovate. Its attractive tiny flowers, in axillary spikes, are followed by bluish fruits about ¾ inch long.

Garden and Landscape Uses. The chief ornamental use of the tropical-almond is as a shade and street tree. Other, less well-known species are generally represented only in the collections of specialists. The tropical-almond is salt-tolerant and is a

Terminalia catappa as a shade tree in Puerto Rico

good seaside tree, although it has the disadvantage of not being very resistant to hurricanes. It thrives on sandy seashores and grows rapidly, especially when young. It is a clean-looking tree of distinctive appearance and handsome aspect. In southern Florida and other warm regions where fall leaf color is not common, it is appreciated for its autumn foliage.

Cultivation. No special difficulty attends the cultivation of the tropical-almond in warm climates where it is sub-

Terminalia catappa, Santos, Brazil

jected to little or no frost. It prospers in any well-drained soil, even in extremely sandy ones, and is easily propagated by seed. In some regions thrips infest the foliage causing it to turn yellow and to fall prematurely. These can be controlled by spraying with an insecticide.

TERMITES. Although sometimes called white ants, termites are not closely related to ants. They belong to an entirely different order of insects. Termites are most easily distinguished from ants by their lack of a distinct "waist." Like ants, they live in large colonies whose members constitute various "castes," each of which assumes particular specialized tasks. Termites are of two distinct types, those that live entirely aboveground, and subterranean species that live in the ground from where, if opportunity affords, they sally to feed on dry wood aboveground. In North America subterranean termites are the most damaging to the wooden parts of buildings, fences, and other structures and to some extent to garden plants. Especially in warm regions, they sometimes injure trees and shrubs as well as various other plants including begonias, corn, chrysanthemums, geraniums, sweet-potatoes, and poinsettias.

To limit the likelihood of trouble, keep the garden free of all woody debris and never bury any in the soil. For posts and stakes use only redwood, which is resistant to termites, or a wood that has been impregnated with zinc chloride, mercuric chloride, or, if plants are not to be set near them, creosote. Ask your local Cooperative Extension Agent or your State Agricultural Experiment Station for recommendations of drenches that are available for treating plants and soil infested with termites.

TERNSTROEMIA (Tern-stroèmia). One handsome evergreen shrub or tree seems to be the only cultivated representative of this genus of about 100 species. Native to warm and warm-temperate parts of the Old World and the New World, *Ternstroemia* belongs in the tea family THEACEAE and is thus closely related to *Camellia*. Its name honors the Swedish naturalist, Christopher Ternstroem, who died in 1745.

Ternstroemias have hairless, undivided, toothless or nearly toothless leaves and solitary, axillary, bisexual flowers with five or rarely six sepals and petals. The many stamens are usually in two circles and have their stalks joined. There is a single style. The fruits are capsules. From nearly related *Cleyera* and *Eurya*, the genus *Ternstroemia* may be distinguished by the arrangement of its leaves, which are not distinctly alternate as in those genera, but clustered in tight spirals or whorls (circles of three or more) near the branch ends.

Sometimes confused in gardens with

Ternstroemia gymnanthera

Cleyera japonica, which has black fruits that do not split, red-fruited *T. gymnanthera*, native to Japan, China, Taiwan, India, and other parts of eastern Asia, is an excellent ornamental. In its native habitat a tall tree, in cultivation it is often a shrub. It has red-stalked, ovate leaves, shining-green above, paler beneath, and 1¾ to 2¾ inches long. The flowers, white and slightly over ½ inch in diameter, come in early summer. About the size of holly berries, the pendent, bright red fruits open to show two red seeds at maturity. This species is hardy as far north as Washington, D.C.

Garden and Landscape Uses. In mild climates this is an admirable outdoor evergreen. Its foliage is its chief and most dependable attraction. It succeeds in sun or part-shade. In sun it is more compact than in shade, and, being slow growing, may not for many years exceed 4 or 5 feet in height, becoming perhaps twice as wide as tall. Sometimes the small, fragrant flowers are succeeded by a crop of fruits that make quite a handsome display. In addition to being grown as a free-standing shrub, this *Ternstroemia* can be satisfactorily espaliered against walls and grown in containers.

Cultivation. Conditions that please azaleas, camellias, and daphnes are agreeable to this plant. The soil should be fertile, well-drained, and never excessively dry. It should be acid and contain an abundance of organic matter. Mulching with an organic material such as peat moss is decidedly beneficial. In their early stages, pinching out the ends of the shoots encourages branching and compact growth. The only other pruning needed is any deemed necessary to shape the plant or to contain it to size. It may be done just before new growth begins. Specimens in containers must be watered regularly and plentifully. Those that have filled their receptacles with roots respond to regular applications of dilute liquid fertilizer. Repotting may be needed at intervals of a few years. This is best done in late winter or spring. Propagation is by seed and by cuttings.

TERRARIUMS. Sometimes described as little greenhouses, terrariums are light-admitting boxes or other containers in which plants are grown. Often displayed as decorative features in homes, offices, and other indoor areas, they can also be used effectively as propagating units in which to raise plants from cuttings, seed, and in other ways and as "hospitals" in which to nurse back to health specimens that, from exposure to faulty environments, excessive damage to roots, or other causes, are in poor condition.

The greatest benefits terrariums provide result from the maintenance of a highly humid atmosphere within, from the protection they afford from drafts, and from their moderating effect on rapid temperature changes. Of these, the first is of greatest importance. Historically, terrariums derive from the Wardian cases that became popular in the nineteenth century following experiments carried out by Dr. Nathaniel Ward, a physician of London, England.

Wishing to observe the emergence of a sphinx moth, Dr. Ward in 1829 planted a chrysalis in moist soil in a wide-mouthed glass bottle and covered it with a lid. Watching the bottle from day to day, the doctor noticed and recorded that "the moisture which during the heat of the day arose from the mould, became condensed on the internal surface of the glass and returned whence it came, thus keeping the mould always in the same degree of humidity." To his immense surprise, "about a week prior to the final change of the insect, a seedling fern and a grass made their appearance on the surface of the mold."

This so intrigued the doctor that he placed the bottle outside the north-facing window of his study, where, to his amazement, the plants flourished without any attention for nearly four years. They perished because during his absence some rain water gained admission through the rusted lid.

By then and subsequently, Dr. Ward had under way other experiments with plants in bottles and in closed containers he called cases. In one he called the "alpine case," he cultivated a variety of mountain plants, including primulas, soldanellas, and eriophorums. In his "drawing-room case," he accommodated palms, ferns, and, suspended from a perforated bronze bar affixed beneath the roof of the case, cactuses and aloes. He grew various bulb plants and other spring flowers in one case, and in another, fairy roses.

In an interesting little book titled *On The Growth of Plant in Closely Glazed Cases*, published in 1842, Dr. Ward described his experiments and experiences and presented his conclusions. Besides advocating the cases as room decorations, Ward suggested another use for them that was to be of the utmost practical importance—their employment as containers for shipping growing plants on long journeys by sea.

From shortly after their invention to the middle of the twentieth century, when the availability of air transport made their use unnecessary, specially constructed Wardian cases provided the surest way of keeping delicate plants alive on long journeys. Thousands of kinds were in this way brought for the first time from distant lands to Europe and America. The vast rubber-growing industry of Malaya and Borneo began with small specimens of South America *Hevea brasiliensis* raised from seed at the Royal Botanic Garden, Kew, England, being sent to the Orient in such cases.

Wardian cases used for long-distance shipping were much less elegant than the often elaborate ones displayed in Victorian parlors and living rooms. They were stout wooden boxes with sides usually 6 to 8 inches deep, sufficient to accommodate the pots in which the plants were growing or their root balls. The ends were tall enough to allow space for the tops of the plants, and, above the level of the sides, were gabled.

The roof consisted of two glazed frames that were protected from breakage by wooden slats, with sufficient space between the slats to admit light, nailed horizontally across them. These were laid from gable to gable with their top edges meeting to form a ridge, and were screwed into place. To afford a little ventilation, a circular hole, an inch or two in diameter and covered with perforated zinc, was provided in each gable end.

Readying a Wardian case for shipment involved removing one or both roof lights. The plants, in or removed from their pots, were packed in moss or coconut fiber and secured firmly by strips of wood fixed across them and nailed to the sides of the case. Careful instructions as to where on the ship they were to be stored were provided. The location had to provide light, be shaded from direct sun, and be protected so there would be no danger of the plants freezing.

A simple, small terrarium

A small terrarium with cover removed

Modern terrariums (this name has practically replaced Wardian cases, except to identify the kind once employed for long-distance shipping) may be of any convenient size. They have one or more sides and a cover of clear, not colored, glass or transparent plastic, such as Lucite. The lid or the front should be adjustable to give ready access when necessary and to permit ventilation. This is not needed to "change the air" inside, but to reduce excessive humidity.

Most terrariums are boxlike or tanklike. Indeed fish tanks (aquariums) can serve the purpose very well. Large bottles and carboys are also used, but because their narrow necks afford only limited access, special planting techniques are necessary. About these, see the Encyclopedia entry Bottle Garden.

Although it is not essential that there be drainage holes in the bottoms of terrariums, their presence greatly reduces the likelihood of harm from overwatering. It is usually advisable to keep a metal or plastic tray under those with drain holes.

Plants in terrariums may be, and for decorative effects usually are, planted in a bed of soil or other rooting mix of a type suitable for houseplants or may be kept in pots. The last is usually most satisfactory if the unit is used for propagation and hospitalization, and for orchids, bromeliads, and other epiphytes.

Best effects in planted terrariums are usually had by "landscaping" the planting bed so that some parts are higher than others. Even a simple slope from back to front or side to side is likely to be preferable to a flat bed. Additional interest may be had by the judicious introduction of fragments of rock, pieces of dead branches, and other materials suggestive of natural environments. Less admirable is the use of mirrors to simulate water, figurines, and other trivia.

When choosing plants for a terrarium, select compatible kinds that prosper under identical conditions of temperature, humidity, and light. In most American homes, sorts of tropical and subtropical

provenance are likely to give the best results, but for a cool sun porch or other area where temperatures in winter remain in approximately the 35 to 55°F range, terrariums can be planted charmingly with dwarf native woodlanders and other cool-climate plants.

The growth of most terrarium plants is favored by bright daylight, but they should not be exposed to direct sun. Even cactuses and other succulents in terrariums are usually better off without that. If the location is dimly lighted the plants must either be limited to ferns and other sorts known to get along under such conditions or additional illumination must be provided; interesting effects may be obtained by lighting the terrarium for up to sixteen hours each day with fluorescent lights. (It is of interest to note that Dr. Ward experimented, not too successfully, however, by keeping one of his cases completely covered with a thick, dark cloth during daylight hours and exposing it for five or six hours out of each twenty-four to the light of a gas lamp. Clearly this did not provide adequate illumination, but it further reveals the inquiring mind of a good doctor.)

Except for cactuses and succulents, practically all terrarium plants benefit from considerably higher humidity than that of the outside air. Nevertheless, droplets of water accumulating on the inside of the glass signal too much humidity. If these appear, adjust the ventilation to allow the escape of moisture vapor and the admittance of air. Terrariums planted with cactuses and other succulents should be ventilated at all times.

Whether the terrarium has drain holes or not, and whether it is to be planted or used for pot plants, spread an inch or two of gravel, stone chips, small pieces of charcoal, or similar coarse material over its bottom to stand the pots on or to serve as a base for the planting mix, which should be a sterilized one. Before introducing the latter, cover the coarse material with moss or a layer or two of old nylon stocking to prevent it from becoming clogged by washings from the mix. Then add the mix, slightly damp, and contour it appropriately. Water the plants well an hour or two before planting.

Arranging the plants is a matter for individual preference and taste. Take care not to crowd them unduly or to have them pressing against the glass. Reasonable room is needed for growth. Arrange tall and low ones and those of various forms, colors, and leaf patterns to their best advantage and to complement each other. Keep scale in mind, so that the finished result convincingly suggests a natural landscape or a satisfying small portion of one.

Begin with the taller and background plants first and, as each is placed, carefully cover its roots with planting mix pressed moderately firm. Then fill in with smaller plants and groundcovers. Complete the job by watering gently with a fine spray so that the whole body of the mix is moistened, but no free water collects in the bottom of the terrarium.

Maintenance of an established terrarium is minimal. If temperatures and light are adequate, the most likely cause of trouble is improper watering. Theoretically, and indeed in fact, if a terrarium is kept, like Dr. Ward's original cases, tightly sealed, after the initial wetting following planting no further attention of this kind will ever be needed. The moisture inside is recycled to the atmosphere from the surface of the rooting mix and as transpiration from the plants, and, by condensing and running down the sides of the terrarium, back to the rooting mix again. A perfect, closed, endlessly repeated cycle is established.

But most plants thrive much better in an atmosphere less heavily charged with moisture than that of a constantly tightly sealed terrarium; such high humidity encourages the growth of harmful molds and rots, as well. To assure the most favorable growing conditions, it is advisable to provide at least a little ventilation by propping up the cover of the terrarium or ventilating it in some other convenient way. This is especially important if drops of water collect on the inside, but even if that does not occur, without ventilation the inside atmosphere is likely to be excessively humid. Ventilation of course reduces humidity by permitting the loss of moisture in the form of vapor. In time this loss dries the rooting mix to the extent that watering is needed. When that stage is reached, *but not before*, moisten the mix with a fine spray without giving enough water that there is danger of it collecting in a pool at the bottom of the terrarium.

Grooming to keep the container and its contents sparklingly clean and attractive needs periodic attention. Promptly pick any dead leaves and faded flowers. Wipe the inside of the glass with a moist cloth to free it of any suspicion of a scum of green algae that may develop and, as need for such attention develops, pinch back or prune plants that are growing out of scale. There may be occasional need to loosen the surface of the planting mix a little by pricking it over with a fork and perhaps to add a little more mix.

Fertilizing, because it is likely to induce excessive growth, is rarely advisable. If it is done, use a houseplant fertilizer very sparingly, not more than three or four times a year. By the time the rooting mix has become so lacking in nutrients that it can no longer support the plants adequately, it is usually better to take them out, install fresh mix, and replant the whole terrarium than to attempt to improve it by fertilizing.

Pests should give little or no trouble if a sterilized planting mix was used and if the plants were clean at the time of their installation. If these conditions are not met, problems difficult to solve are likely to develop. Correction is likely to necessitate removing infested plants, cleaning them thoroughly by washing in an insecticide or by other ways, and perhaps growing them out of the terrarium for a period to make sure they are quite free of pests before replanting them.

Plants suitable for humid terrariums in which the temperature range is approximately 60 to 75°F include some or all sorts of these kinds: aglaonemas, alternantheras, small-leaved begonias, bertolonias, small bromeliads, calatheas, chamaeranthemums, codiaeums (crotons), coleuses, corydylines, dracaenas, episcias, *Exacum affine*, small ferns, *Ficus pumila*, fittonias, gynuras, *Hemigraphis alternata*, *Hypoestes phyllostachys*, iresines, jacobinias, marantas, *Oxalis hedysaroides rubra*, *O. corymbosa aureoreticulata*, small palms, pellionias, peperomias, pileas, polysciases, saintpaulias (African-violets), small sansevierias, *Saxifraga stolonifera tricolor*, selaginellas, sinningias, streptocarpuses, and syngoniums.

Plants suitable for humid terrariums in which temperatures in winter do not exceed 60°F, and at night are usually about ten degrees lower, include these: *Acorus gramineus*, aucubas, *Buxus sempervirens* (boxwood), *Coprosma repens*, *Cymbalaria muralis* (Kenilworth-ivy), *Euonymus japonica*, fatshederas, hardy ferns, small-leaved varieties of *Hedera helix* (English ivy), *Lysimachia nummularia* (moneywort), *Malpighia coccigera*, *Mitchella repens* (partridge-berry), pachysandras, pittosporums, pyrolas, *Rosmarinus officinalis* (rosemary), *Saxifraga stolonifera*, and *Serissa foetida*.

Plants suitable for terrariums kept relatively dry and ventilated more freely than humid terrariums and in which the temperature on winter nights ranges from 50 to 60°F include all cactuses of appropriate sizes and a wide variety of such other small succulents as agaves, aloes, cotyledons, crassulas, echeverias, euphorbias, faucarias, gasterias, haworthias, kalanchoes, lithops, sedums, and stapelias.

TERRESTRIAL. Applied to certain sorts of bromeliads, orchids, and some other groups of plants, certain kinds of which grow on trees as epiphytes, terrestrial means growing in the ground.

TESTUDINARIA. See Dioscorea.

TETRACENTRON (Tetra-céntron). The only species of this genus is a deciduous tree native to China and Burma. Once included in the magnolia family MAGNOLIACEAE, and by some authorities in the trochodendron family TROCHODENDRACEAE, it is now considered as deserving separate status and constitutes the only genus of the tetracentron family TETRACENTRACEAE. The name comes from the Greek *tetra*, four, and *ken-*

tron, a spur, and makes reference to the four projections on the fruits.

In aspect, *Tetracentron* very much resembles the katsura tree (*Cercidiphyllum*), but is easily distinguished by its alternate leaves. It is hardy about as far north as New York City, and in sheltered locations in southern New England.

From 60 to 90 feet in height, *T. sinense* has round-toothed, broad-ovate to heart-shaped, pointed leaves, 3 to 5 inches long by up to 3½ inches wide, with five or seven veins curving upward and outward from the base. The bisexual, stalkless, yellowish flowers, in slender, pendulous spikes 4 to 6 inches long, are minute. They come in summer on short, spurlike branchlets, each with a solitary leaf. The blooms make no effective display. Petalless, they have four sepals, four stamens, and four carpels. The fruits are brown, deeply-four-lobed capsules about ⅙ inch long.

Garden and Landscape Uses and Cultivation. Its decorative appeal limited to its form and foliage, *T. sinense* is little grown except in arboretums and other special collections. Good looking, it is worth planting for variety. It succeeds in ordinary soils and is propagated by seed, by summer cuttings under mist or in a greenhouse propagating bench, and by layering. No regular pruning is needed.

TETRACLINIS (Tetraclì-nis). This genus, of a single species, is closely related to *Callitris* and *Widdringtonia*, but differs in having its leaves in four ranks in the manner of arbor-vitae (*Thuja*) and from *Callitris* in its cones having only four scales. It is an evergreen conifer belonging in the cypress family CUPRESSACEAE. Its name is from the Greek *tetra*, four, and *clinis*, valved, in allusion to the cones.

Commercially, *Tetraclinis* is exploited for its fragrant wood, which is often beautifully grained and is esteemed for fine cabinet work, and for a resin called sandarac, which is exuded from the trunk and is employed in manufacturing varnishes. The Romans used the wood of this tree, which is believed to have been known to them as "citrus," for roofing their temples and for furniture.

Native to North Africa, Malta, and southern Spain, *T. articulata* is a tree up to 40 or 50 feet in height with a compact head of ascending branches and flattened, jointed branchlets in sprays. The scalelike leaves are in fours with the lateral pair larger than the facial ones. Their bases are attached to the shoots, their pointed tips are free. The cones, globose, glaucous, and up to ½ inch in diameter, are at the tips of the shoots.

Garden and Landscape Uses and Cultivation. Little information is available regarding the use or cultivation of this rare conifer in North America. Judging from experience abroad, it prospers best in a dry

"Mediterranean" climate and should be worth trying in the southwest in sunny, dryish locations. For more information see Conifers.

TETRACOCCUS (Tetra-cóccus). Belonging to the spurge family EUPHORBIACEAE and endemic to the southwestern United States and Mexico, *Tetracoccus* has a name derived from the Greek *tetra*, four, and *kokkos*, a berry.

Five species of arid-region shrubs with small, alternate, undivided, stalked leaves, opposite or in whorls (circles) of three, these plants have tiny unisexual flowers with the sexes on separate plants. The flowers have six or seven sepals, no petals, and, depending upon sex, as many stamens as sepals or four protruding styles. The fruits are capsules.

Native to southern California, and Baja California, *T. dioicus*, up to 6 feet tall, is much-branched and hairless. Its mostly opposite, oblong to lanceolate or linear leaves are up to 1 inch long. The female flowers are solitary, the males in racemes up to 1 inch long.

Garden Uses and Cultivation. The species described succeeds in semidesert and desert regions and in some such places is used to some extent for landscaping. It is propagated by seed.

TETRAGONIA (Tetra-gònia) — New-Zealand-Spinach. Except for New-Zealand-spinach, grown as a potherb and vegetable, *Tetragonia* is practically unknown horticulturally. It comprises fifty to sixty species of herbaceous plants and subshrubs of temperate South America, Australia, New Zealand, eastern Asia, and Africa of the carpetweed family AIZOACEAE or, according to some botanists, with one other genus it constitutes the family TETRAGONIACEAE. The name, from the Greek *tetra*, four, and *gonia*, an angle, refers to the fruits.

Tetragonias are herbaceous plants, subshrubs, or small shrubs with prostrate or more or less trailing stems and alternate, undivided, sometimes fleshy leaves. The inconspicuous petal-less flowers, solitary or few together in the leaf axils, have a three- to seven-lobed calyx, one or more stamens, and three to eight stigmas. The fruits are nutlike or drupelike.

Native to New Zealand, Australia, Pacific islands, Japan, and South America, the New-Zealand-spinach (*T. tetragonioides* syn. *T. expansa*) is a vigorous, prostrate annual with somewhat fleshy stems and foliage. Its ovate, triangular-ovate, or more or less arrow-shaped, stalked leaves are up to 5 inches long on cultivated plants, smaller in the wild. The tiny flowers, solitary or sometimes paired, have four or five yellowish-green sepals, ten to twenty stamens, and three to eight styles. The fruits, which contain six to eight seeds, have two to four large, hornlike tubercles at their

Tetragonia tetragonioides

tops. For cultivation see New-Zealand-Spinach.

TETRAGONOLOBUS. See Lotus.

TETRANEMA (Tetra-nèma) — Mexican-Foxglove or Mexican-Violet. Botanists have conserved *Tetranema* as the accepted generic name for the plants often cultivated as *Allophyton*. It applies to a genus of three Mexican species of the figwort family SCROPHULARIACEAE and is derived from the Greek *tetra*, four, and *nema*, a thread, in allusion to the four stamens.

Tetranemas are low herbaceous perennials with opposite, hairless, undivided, slightly-toothed, obovate to oblongish leaves and small, two-lipped, tubular flowers. The upper lip of the corolla is two-lobed, the lower has four lobes. The fruits are somewhat compressed capsules.

A dainty plant of easy culture, the Mexican-foxglove or Mexican-violet (*T. roseum* syns. *T. mexicanum*, *Allophytum mexicanum*) somewhat resembles certain smaller gesneriads. It has fibrous roots and a very short stem ending in a rosette of crowded, narrowly-obovate, leathery, stalkless leaves, the largest up to 6 inches long. They are glaucous on their undersides. The dainty, ½-inch-long, nodding, trumpet-shaped blooms are borne in clusters over a long period, most plentifully in summer. They are on purplish stalks 4 to 8 inches long

Tetranema roseum

and are predominantly rosy-violet with their lower lips whitish.

Garden Uses and Cultivation. Only in frost-free regions is *T. roseum* hardy outdoors. In such places it is charming for rock gardens. More often it is grown in pots and planters in greenhouses and window gardens. Given porous soil of ordinary quality, watered moderately, but not excessively, it flourishes with abandon; in greenhouses, volunteer plants are likely to spring up beneath and on benches from self-sown seed. A night temperature of about 55°F in winter, with an increase of five to fifteen degrees by day, is satisfactory. In summer more warmth is appropriate. Humidity should be moderate. Good light with some shade from strongest sun is needed. Specimens that have filled their containers with roots benefit from applications of dilute liquid fertilizer. Repotting is best done in spring. Then, too, multiplication by division may be undertaken. Seed is a ready, alternate means of increase.

TETRANEURIS. See Hymenoxys.

TETRAPANAX (Tetrá-panax) — Rice Paper Plant. Only one species, a native of southern China and Taiwan, belongs in *Tetrapanax*, of the aralia family ARALIACEAE. Its generic name, from the Greek *tetra*, four, and *Panax*, a related genus, refers to its calyx lobes, petals, and stamens being in fours instead of in fives as in *Panax*. This also distinguishes it from the closely related *Fatsia*, which the rice paper plant otherwise resembles. The designation rice paper plant refers to the fact that it is from the thick pith of the stems of this species that Chinese rice paper is prepared, a fact not discovered by Europeans until many years after the product was known to them. Among other uses, rice paper is employed for making artificial flowers.

The rice paper plant (*T. papyriferus*) is an evergreen, spineless shrub, 6 to 8 feet in height, that spreads rapidly by sucker shoots. It develops many stout, erect stems and has long-stalked leaves up to 1 foot across, somewhat like those of the castor bean (*Ricinus*). In outline broadly-heart-shaped, they are divided halfway or less to their bases; their margins are toothed. Parts of stems and foliage are densely covered with a felt of stellate (star-shaped) hairs, which tends to disappear as the parts mature; the upper surfaces of older leaves are nearly hairless although their undersides remain white-felty. The small whitish to yellowish flowers are in spherical umbels, which in turn compose large panicles about 1½ feet in diameter. They are attractive to bees. All parts of the flower clusters are woolly-hairy. The fruits are small spherical berries.

Garden and Landscape Uses. This is a handsome shrub for places where its invasive habit presents no problems or can

Tetrapanax papyriferus

Tetrapanax papyriferus (flowers)

be controlled, but under no circumstances should it be located near choice, less vigorous plants. Its roots spread relentlessly and new shoots arise as much as 20 or 30 feet from the parent. One method of overcoming this is to confine this species to planters or other containers. When so accommodated it is excellent for decorating terraces, steps, patios, and similar places; its bold foliage associates splendidly with architecture. The lush foliage of the Chinese rice paper plant makes a pleasing and distinctive pattern in the landscape, contrasting well with that of finer texture and providing a splendid screen. In winter or very early spring, the huge panicles of bloom give much character to the plant.

This species is hardy only where little or no frost occurs. It is grown outdoors in California and Florida. In the northern part of the latter state, it is often killed to the ground in winter, but its roots survive and with the coming of warm weather soon develop new stems. This plant is sometimes grown in pots in greenhouse collections of plants useful to man.

Cultivation. In mild climates the Chinese rice paper plant thrives in any ordinary soil, the only attention needed being that necessary to prevent it from spreading too exuberantly. This may be done by regularly and ruthlessly digging out offending por-

tions. Propagation is easy by seed. Transplanted suckers may also be used, but often they are rather difficult to establish. This plant is simple to grow in planters, large pots, or tubs of porous fertile soil. Specimens grown in this way in regions where they will not winter outdoors may be kept through that season in a garage or outbuilding that is nearly or quite frostproof and that admits light. When grown in greenhouses, a winter minimum night temperature of 45 to 50°F is satisfactory. Plants in containers need abundant water from spring through fall, rather less in winter. During the spring-to-fall season, they benefit from weekly or biweekly applications of dilute liquid fertilizer.

TETRAPATHAEA (Tetra-pathaèa) — New-Zealand-Passion-Flower. This rather rare genus of almost subtropical habitats in New Zealand is the only native there belonging to the passion flower family PASSIFLORACEAE. It consists of one endemic species, a slender woody vine with rather insignificant flowers, but attractive fruits. The significance of the name is unexplained.

New-Zealand-passion-flower (*Tetrapathaea tetrandra* syn. *Passiflora tetrandra*) has alternate, oblong or ovate-lanceolate, toothless, glossy leaves, 1½ to 4 inches long, and slender, long tendrils. Its unisexual flowers, ½ to 1 inch across, have a central crown of white or yellowish filaments and usually four or occasionally five, greenish petals. Sometimes the petals are lacking. There are four, or rarely five, stamens. The blooms are clustered in the leaf axils and the females are succeeded by handsome bright orange fruits, 1 inch to 1½ inches in diameter containing many black seeds.

Garden Uses and Cultivation. These are the same as for subtropical kinds of passion flower (*Passiflora*).

TETRAPLASANDRA (Tetra-plasándra). The genus Tetraplasandra, of the aralia family ARALIACEAE, is represented by twenty species native to Hawaii, two to New Guinea and the Solomon Islands, and one each to the Celebes and the Philippine Islands. Its name comes from the Greek *tetraplasios*, fourfold, and *andra*, a stamen, and alludes to the flowers of the first species that was described as having four times as many stamens as petals.

Tetraplasandras are evergreen trees or shrubs with large, alternate, pinnate leaves that have an uneven number of leaflets. The small flowers are in terminal panicles or in umbels composed of smaller umbels. Bisexual, they have seven or eight petals, many thick-stalked stamens, and stalkless stigmas. The fruits are dry and capsule-like.

Called 'ohe'ohe by Hawaiians, Hawaiian **T. kauaiensis,** often cultivated as *T.*

meiandra, is grown in California and elsewhere in warm climates as an ornamental. Although sometimes 80 feet high in the wild, it is generally much lower in cultivation. It has stout branches and soft, leathery, coppery-stalked leaves of seven asymmetrical, ovate leaflets, paler on their undersides than above.

Garden and Landscape Uses and Cultivation. In regions of warm, frost-free climates, this attractive species is useful for planting outdoors in ordinary soils. It stands considerable shade and needs little care. It is also adaptable for growing in containers as a patio and room plant. It gets along with moderate light and in air somewhat too dry for many plants. It is at its best, however, under decidedly humid conditions. Indoors, temperatures in the 60 to 70°F range are satisfactory. Good loamy, well-drained, fertile soil is needed. Water to keep it moderately, but not excessively moist. Well-rooted, container-grown specimens are helped by occasionally soaking the soil with dilute liquid fertilizer. Propagation is by seed, by cuttings, and by air layering.

TETRAPLOID. The number of chromosomes (which carry the genes that determine hereditary factors) in each cell is normally constant for any particular species of plant or animal. One of each kind of chromosome the organism possesses is present in each gamete (sexual reproductive cell) and two (a pair) in each body cell. The total for the gamete is called the haploid number, that for a body cell the diploid number.

But variations sometimes occur naturally or may be induced artificially by the use of colchicine. Plants with three or more sets of chromosomes in their body cells are called polyploids. If they have three sets they are designated triploids, four sets tetraploids, five sets pentaploids, and so on up to octoploid for plants with eight sets of chromosomes. Very rarely is this number exceeded.

Tetraploids, the most common of polyploids, are fairly common among garden plants. Generally they are bigger and more vigorous than the diploid plants from which they are derived, and, not infrequently, are less capable of producing fertile seeds, although this is not always true.

TETRASTIGMA (Tetra-stígma) — Ayo. These grape vine relatives number ninety species of woody, tendril-bearing vines that in the wild occur in southeast Asia, Indonesia, and Australia. They belong in the grape family VITACEAE and have a name derived from the Greek *tetra*, four, and *stigma*, in reference to their stigmas being four-parted or four-lobed.

Tetrastigmas have alternate leaves that sometimes are deeply-palmately-lobed, but more often are divided into leaflets that spread in handlike fashion. Rarely are the leaflets reduced to one. The tiny bisexual or bisexual and unisexual blooms, in axillary umbels or clusters, are succeeded by two- to four-seeded berries. The flowers have four each sepals and petals, four stamens, and a stalkless stigma, which readily distinguishes *Tetrastigma* from related *Cissus* and *Parthenocissus*. The last differs also in having five-parted flowers.

Tall, slender, and with branchless, coiled tendrils, the ayo (*T. harmandii*) is a handsome native of the Philippine Islands. Its glossy leaves have three to seven, mostly five, elliptic to oblanceolate, stalked, toothed leaflets up to 3 inches long by about one-half as wide. Usually there is a center leaflet and on each side of it two others, sharing a common stalk. The numerous pale green flowers are in short-stalked clusters. The russet-brown, grape-like fruits contain colorless or cream-colored, juicy, edible flesh.

Of noble aspect, *T. voinieranum* (syn. *Vitis voinierana*) is a native of Indochina. Extremely vigorous, it has young shoots clothed, like the undersides of its leaves, with abundant rust-colored hairs. Its tendrils are long and branchless. The impressively large, fleshy leaves, of three or five stalked, coarsely-toothed, lustrous, broadly-obovate, wavy-edged leaflets up to 10 inches in length, are paler beneath than on their upper sides. The many little flowers are crowded in much-branched, rounded clusters about 1¾ inches across. The fruits are acid.

Tetrastigma voinieranum

Garden and Landscape Uses and Cultivation. Only in the tropics and subtropics are tetrastigmas suitable for outdoors. They are also satisfactory in warm, humid greenhouses. Their chief landscape values are to drape porches, trellises, pillars, and other supports that afford holds to their tendrils, with curtains of beautiful evergreen foliage. At their best in shaded locations in fertile soil that does not lack for moisture, but is not wet, these vines grow with great vigor. They need little care

other than occasional pruning to keep them in bounds. This is best done at the beginning of a new season of growth and consists of thinning out crowded stems and shortening older ones. In greenhouses, minimum winter night temperatures of 55 to 60°F are desirable. Day temperatures should be five to fifteen degrees higher than those at night, and at times of the year other than winter, all temperatures may be higher. The atmosphere must be humid. Increase is easy by cuttings, by layering, and by seed.

TETRATHECA (Tetra-thèca). The twenty species that constitute *Tetratheca* belong in the entirely Australian tremandra family TREMANDRACEAE. The name, from the Greek *tetra*, four, and *theke*, a cell, refers to the anthers.

Tetrathecas are low, heathlike shrubs or subshrubs. Their leaves are either in whorls (circles of three or more), in pairs, solitary, or sometimes represented by scales. The flowers, borne singly in the upper leaf axils, resemble those of *Boronia*. On slender stalks, they are up to 1 inch in diameter and have four or five small sepals and as many white, pink, or purplish-red petals. Eight oblong anthers nestle close to the base of the pistil. The fruits are small, flattened, two-seeded capsules.

One foot to 2 feet in height, *T. ericifolia* is usually rather bristly-hairy. It has narrow-linear leaves, up to ½ inch long and with recurved margins, in circles of four to six. Its nodding, rosy-pink flowers, ½ inch wide or a little wider and on stalks ¼ inch long, have purplish-brown stamens. They appear in spring. The leaves of *T. thymifolia* are ovate-lanceolate, ¼ to ½ inch long, and in threes or fours. Like the shoots they are hairy. The nodding blooms, ½ to ¾ inch in diameter and deep rose-pink with purple anthers, have stalks ¼ to ½ inch long. From the above, *T. hirsuta* differs in having leaves ½ to 1 inch long, most often alternate and, like the shoots, downy or hairy. From 1 foot to 2 feet tall, it has ¾-inch-wide blooms on stalks up to 1¼ inches long. Except in the bud stage they face upward.

Garden and Landscape Uses and Cultivation. In climates favorable to their growth, these very pretty low shrubs lend themselves for use in mass plantings in the same ways that heaths (*Erica*) and heather (*Calluna*) are commonly employed. They are also appropriate as single specimens and in groups in rock gardens. They need acid, sandy, peaty soil that is never excessively dry or wet and open sunny locations. As greenhouse pot plants they are considered rather difficult to grow. Like many fine-rooted, heathlike plants they are very sensitive to moisture. Excessive wetness as well as too dry soil can quickly result in disaster. Once their foliage shrivels or drops the plants rarely recover. The indoor treat-

ment and care that suits tender heaths (*Erica*) is considered appropriate for tetrathecas. To encourage branching, the shoots may be cut back immediately after they bloom and the tips of new ones pinched out later, but not after June. Propagation is easy by seed sown in sandy, peaty soil and by cuttings taken in late spring or early summer.

TEUCRIUM (Teù-crium)—Germander, Cat-Thyme. An adaptation of the ancient Greek name *teukrion* for some species, the name *Teucrium* honors Teucer, first king of Troy, who was believed to have first used the plants in medicine. The genus it designates belongs to the mint family LABIATAE and consists of aromatic annuals, herbaceous plants, subshrubs, and shrubs. Widely distributed in the wild in temperate and warm-temperate parts of the world, they are especially abundant in the Mediterranean region. There are 300 species.

Teucriums have opposite, lobed, toothed, or plain-edged leaves with those among the flowers reduced to bracts or similar to the lower ones. The blooms, from the leaf axils, are in whorls (circles or tiers) of few to many arranged in heads or spikes. They have five-toothed, tubular or bell-shaped calyxes, asymmetrical corollas with a prominent lower lip and a very much smaller, deeply-cleft upper one, four protruding stamens, and one style with two stigmas. The fruits are four seedlike nutlets.

American germander (*T. canadense*) is a variable inhabitant of wet soils throughout the United States and southern Canada. A herbaceous perennial, 1 foot to 3 feet tall, it has long rhizomes, erect, rarely branched, hairy stems, and toothed, more or less pointed, short-stalked, ovate-lanceolate to oblong leaves 2 to 4½ inches long. The flower spikes, 4 to 9 inches long, are of pinkish-purple blooms, ½ to ¾ inch long, in clusters of several from the axils of linear-lanceolate to linear bracts. Two commonly cultivated kinds, sometimes confused with each other in gardens, are the evergreen shrublets *T. chamaedrys* and *T. lucidum*. From 6 inches to 2 feet in height, *T. chamaedrys* has stems usually more or less prostrate below and sometimes rooting, then ascending or erect, and with recurved or matted hairs. The short-stalked, somewhat leathery leaves, up to ¾ inch long and more or less deeply-toothed, are ovate to oblong, those of the upper, flowering parts of the stems smaller than the ones below. The ¾-inch-long flowers are generally in whorls (circles of six or more). They are purplish-pink to reddish-purple dotted with white. From the last, *T. lucidum* differs in its more erect habit and its shinier foliage. Also, the hairs on its stems are neither recurved nor matted, but straight, and its blooms are mostly in

Teucrium chamaedrys

whorls of four or fewer. Both species are native of Europe.

Distinctive *T. fruticans*, a native of Europe, is an upright, evergreen shrub, 2 to 3 feet or more in height, with branches spreading at nearly right angles to the stems. Its younger shoots and undersides of its ovate to lanceolate, ¾- to 1¼-inch-long leaves are clothed with soft, whitish, yellowish, or brownish hairs. Blue or lilac-colored flowers, ¾ to 1 inch long and with much-protruding stamens, are borne from the leaf axils.

Teucrium fruticans

Teucrium fruticans (flowers)

Cat-thyme (*T. marum*) has a fascination for cats equal to that of catmint (*Nepeta cataria*). A subshrub 9 inches to nearly 2 feet tall, it has white-woolly stems, and broad-elliptic to elliptic-lanceolate, toothless leaves with rolled-under margins, green on their upper sides, white-hairy beneath, and up to ⅓ inch long. The purple flowers, a little over ¼ inch long, are crowded in one-sided racemes 1 to 2 inches long. Cat-thyme is native to dry soils in the Mediterranean region. Variety *T. m. roseum* has pink flowers, and very short-stalked, blunt-ovate leaves, with in-rolled margins, that are shining green above and ¾ to 1¼ inches long. The light blue or lavender flowers are in leafy spikes of few at the ends of the stems and branches. Another native of the Mediterranean region, *T. flavum* is a softly-hairy subshrub often inhabiting limestone

Teucrium flavum

soils. Freely-branched and 8 inches to 1½ feet tall, it has obovate, coarsely-round-toothed leaves with blades 1 to 2 inches long. In loose, spikelike arrangements 2 to 8 inches long, the about 1-inch-long yellow flowers have hairy calyxes half as long as the corollas.

A mountain species of Europe, *T. montanum*, sometimes called mountain germander and mountain-pennyroyal, is a dense, woody-based shrublet of dry, rocky places. Its main stems hug the ground and form a dense mat. From them come flower-bearing branches 2 to 10 inches tall. The linear-lanceolate, toothless leaves, up to ¾ inch long, have white-felted undersides. The ½-inch-long, pale yellow or cream-colored flowers are in flat or roundish heads. From the last, *T. pyrenaicum*, of the mountains of Spain where it occurs chiefly in dryish, limestone soils, differs in having larger, rounded, toothed, woolly heads of hooded, lavender and cream-colored blooms. This has trailing stems 4 to 8 inches long. It is not invasive.

Garden and Landscape Uses. With few exceptions, germanders make little appeal to gardeners. Hardy in southern New England, *T. chamaedrys* and *T. lucidum* are

Teucrium pyrenaicum

A low hedge of *Teucrium lucidum*

worthy of places in rock gardens and herb gardens. The latter lends itself to shearing as a miniature hedge. Other hardy kinds discussed above are *T. montanum*, *T. pyrenaicum*, and *T. canadense*, the first two suitable for rock gardens, the other, a damp soil plant, for inclusion in native plant gardens. All are appropriate in herb gardens. The other sorts described are not hardy in the north. In mild climates they may be used agreeably at the fronts of flower and shrub borders, in herb gardens, and in other more informal ways. They thrive in sunny places and adapt well to dryish soils. Occasionally they are grown in pots in greenhouses and sunny windows.

Cultivation. Teucriums are very easy to grow. Shrubby ones need pruning or shearing to shape from time to time. This is best done in spring. Light winter protection is advisable in cold climates for those on the borderline of hardiness. Increase is by seed, by cuttings, and, of some kinds, by division.

TEVE or DAGA is *Amorphophallus campanulatus*.

TEXAS and TEXAN. The words Texas or Texan occur in the vernacular names of these plants: glory-of-Texas (*Thelocactus bicolor schottii*), star-of-Texas (*Xanthisma texana*), Texan bluebells (*Eustoma grandiflorum*), Texan jujube (*Ziziphus obtusifolia*), Texas bluebonnet (*Lupinus subcarnosus*), Texas buckeye (*Aesculus arguta*), Texas-buckeye (*Ungnadia speciosa*), Texas-ebony (*Pithecellobium flexicaule*), Texas-mallow (*Malvaviscus arboreus drummondii*), Texas-mountain-laurel (*Sophora secundiflora*), and Texas umbrella tree (*Melia azedarach umbraculiformis*).

THALIA (Thà-lia). There are eleven species of *Thalia*, of the maranta family MARAN-TACEAE. In the wild, with the exception of one that is a native as far north as Missouri, they are confined to the tropics and subtropics of the Americas and Africa and chiefly inhabit swampy forests. The name commemorates the sixteenth-century German physician and naturalist Johann Thal.

Thalias are herbaceous perennials with long-stalked, calathea- or canna-like, all-basal leaves, the stalks of which enfold each other toward their bases to produce false stems. The flower panicles are of spikes, each with two vertical rows of bracts, which fall before the fruits mature. There is a pair of purplish, violet, or blue blooms in the axil of each bract. The blooms have three minute sepals and three petals. There is a circle of two staminodes (nonfunctional stamens) and one half-fertile stamen, and a solitary, outer, petal-like staminode, longer than the petals. The stigma is two-lipped. The fruits are capsules.

A native of swampy woods from South Carolina to Missouri, Florida, and Texas, ***T. dealbata*** is attractively coated with white powder. Its leaves have stalks 1 foot to 2 feet long, and paddle-shaped to lanceolate-elliptic blades from 8 inches to 1½ feet long or somewhat longer. Rising well above the foliage, sometimes to a height of 10 feet, but often lower, the flower stalks carry narrow panicles of erect or ascending spikes of purple blooms with petals ⅓ inch long and the largest staminode exceeding ½ inch in length.

Native from Florida to the West Indies and Argentina, ***T. geniculata*** differs from the last in not being white-powdery and in having looser, pendulous flower panicles with markedly zigzagged stalks.

Garden and Landscape Uses and Cultivation. Thalias are useful as graceful summer-flowering decoratives for boggy places and shallow ponds and pools. They serve well as accents among lower plants and are easy to grow. Lightly shaded or sunny locations suit them; they do well in fertile soil that contains generous supplies of organic material. They can be accommodated in large tubs or other containers or can be planted directly in soil bottoms. The soil surface should be covered by up to 2 or 3 feet of water or be at water level. If the roots do not freeze, *T. dealbata* will live through the winter even in the north, but *T. geniculata* needs warmer conditions to survive. Both are easily carried over in pools in greenhouses. Propagation is by division in early spring and by seed.

THALICTRUM (Thal-íctrum) — Meadow-Rue. Gardeners untutored in botany would be unlikely to suspect relationship between feathery-bloomed meadow-rues, golden buttercups, and large-flowered clematises, yet all belong to the buttercup family RAN-UNCULACEAE. In *Thalictrum*, meadow-rues possess a name that is a modification of *thaliktron*, used by the ancient Greeks for a plant, perhaps one of this group. The genus comprises some 150 species, chiefly natives of north temperate regions, but represented also in South America, tropical Africa, and South Africa.

Meadow-rues are small to tall herbaceous perennials, those in cultivation hardy in the north. The leaves of most sorts are two- or three-times-divided in threes (ternately) or pinnately-divided into comparatively small, angled, notched, or scalloped leaflets. Often they have a decidedly lacy or fernlike effect. In a few sorts the leaves are divided only once and in one, *T. rotundifolium*, they consist of a single leaflet. Most of the foliage is basal or low on the stems, which are erect and bear panicles or racemes of small, more or less tassel-like blooms. The flowers, without petals, have four or five usually early-deciduous, sometimes petal-like sepals and many stamens. The female element of the bloom consists of a few pistils that ripen into a small cluster of achenes that are the fruits. Most species have bisexual blooms, but in some they are unisexual with either the sexes on separate plants, one sex intermingled with bisexual blooms on the same plant, or male, female, and bisexual blooms on the same plant.

Thalictrum, undetermined species (flowers)

Elegantly-foliaged, but with flowers of insignificant display value, variable ***T. minus***, of Europe and northern Asia, is common in cultivation. Grown under various names, not infrequently as *T. adiantifolium*, it is 1½ to 3 feet tall and spreads by stolons or may form tight tufts. Hairless or somewhat glandular-hairy, it has furrowed stems and triangular leaves three- or four-times-pinnately-divided into many small, usually three-lobed, green or glaucous leaflets. The numerous little, greenish-yellow, bisexual flowers are in loose panicles branched above their middles. Their pendulous stamens have threadlike stalks.

Thalia dealbata

Commonly cultivated *T. aquilegifolium,* a native of Europe and northern Asia, is 2 to 5 feet tall, hairless, and more or less glaucous. It has hollow stems, and leaves two- or three-times-divided into three- or six-lobed leaflets, mostly as wide as long and toothed at their wide apexes. The small umbels of bisexual or occasionally unisexual, erect flowers are assembled in large much-branched panicles. They have tiny greenish to white sepals that soon fall and showy stamens almost ½ inch long that thicken in their upper parts and most commonly are lavender to purple. The achenes, pendent and long-stalked, have three wings. In *T. a. album* the flowers are white, in *T. a. atropurpureum* dark purple, in *T. a. roseum* pinkish-lilac.

The soft yellow, bisexual flowers of *T. flavum* also owe their display value to stamens rather than sepals. The latter, small and yellow, soon drop. Native to Europe, this is 2½ to 5 feet tall and has leaves two- or three-times-divided into mostly ovate leaflets three-toothed at their apexes and not conspicuously veined on their undersides. The stems, grooved lengthwise, are stout and not glaucous. They branch above to form compact panicles, the branches of which are terminated by roundish, rather dense assemblies of fuzzy blooms with yellow threadlike stamens not thickened above and under ⅓ inch long. The achenes, without stalks, are rounded at their apexes. From the last, *T. speciosissimum* (syn. *T. glaucum*), of Portugal, Spain, and northwest Africa, is distinguishable by its stems and foliage being glaucous and its leaflets being prominently veined on their undersides. Its bisexual or unisexual flowers have pale yellow sepals and bright yellow stamens. The achenes have pointed apexes.

Flowers with petal-like sepals that do not drop early and are largely responsible for the showiness of the blooms are borne by graceful *T. delavayi,* which is commonly cultivated as *T. dipterocarpum.* Native to western China, from 2 to 4 feet tall, and slender-stemmed, this has airy, hairless foliage of two- or three-times-divided leaves with toothed or toothless leaflets as long or longer than broad. From ½ to 1 inch in diameter, nodding, and in loose panicles of many, the beautiful mauve or less often white, bisexual flowers have spreading sepals and shorter, drooping, threadlike stamens. The achenes are long-stalked, scarcely or not winged. The very beautiful double-flowered meadow-rue 'Hewitt's Double' is seemingly a variety of *T. delavayi* and not of *T. dipterocarpum,* to which it is often attributed. This last, also native to western China and in general resembling *T. delavayi,* which in gardens commonly passes under its name, differs in its

Thalictrum 'Hewitt's Double'

flowers being somewhat smaller, scarcely over ½ inch wide, and in its achenes having two distinct, narrow wings.

Native American *T. polygamum* and *T. dasycarpum* are tall summer-blooming inhabitants of wet meadows and stream banks. The first, up to 6 feet tall, ranges from Canada to Ohio, Illinois, Missouri, and Colorado, the other, about 3 feet tall, from eastern Canada to North Carolina, Tennessee, and Indiana. Both have leaves divided into three-lobed leaflets mostly over ½ inch long and minutely-hairy on their undersides. Their not especially showy whitish flowers, mostly or all unisexual, are in panicles 1 foot long or longer. Technical differences in the flowers and fruits distinguish these species from each other.

Blooming in earliest spring, *T. dioicum* inhabits moist woodlands from Quebec to Manitoba, South Carolina, Georgia, Alabama, and Missouri. From 1 foot to 2½ feet high, this has long-stalked leaves mostly of three-toothed lobes. Male and female flowers, on separate plants, are yellow to greenish-yellow.

Dwarf *T. alpinum,* of wet and damp soils through much of northern Europe and Asia and from Greenland to Newfoundland, Alaska, Quebec, New Mexico, and California, is rarely 1 foot tall, more often under 6 inches tall. Its few leaves mostly under 2 inches long are all basal and nearly hairless. The rounded to obovate leaflets are toothed at their apexes. The bisexual flowers in branchless racemes have greenish sepals, and stamens that are not dilated. Loveliest of low kinds, Japanese *T. kiusianum,* which spreads slowly by underground rhizomes, is 2 to 5 inches high and without hairs. It has basal and stem foliage. The purplish leaves of three or nine broad-ovate, toothed leaflets are 1 inch to 2 inches long, those of the stems smaller than the basal ones. The tiny flowers have lavender-pink to purple sepals, and dilated stamens.

Garden and Landscape Uses. Meadow-rues are elegant garden plants, admired for

Thalictrum speciosissimum

Thalictrum kiusianum

the grace and beauty of their foliage as well as for their blooms. The taller ones are admirable for flower beds and borders and as sources of flowers for cutting, the dwarfs as adornments for rock gardens. American sorts are useful in wild and native plant gardens. A location in light shade or at least shaded from middle-of-the-day sun is needed. With regard to soil, meadow-rues are not fussy so long as it is not excessively dry. Moderately moist, well-drained, fertile earth not of a clayey character suits best.

Cultivation. Except for 'Hewitt's Double', which can only be increased by division, and sorts with rhizomes, such as *T. kiusianum*, seeds afford the best and most convenient means of increasing meadow-rues. Sow these in a nicely prepared seed bed in a cold frame in a lightly shaded place outdoors in May, or earlier in a greenhouse. Transplant the seedlings to nursery beds in rows 1 foot apart with 4 to 6 inches between individuals to make their first season's growth. In early fall or the following spring, set them in their permanent locations, spacing the taller growers about 1½ feet apart. The alternative to seed sowing as a means of increase is to divide established plants carefully. The preferred time to do this is early spring just as new growth begins.

Routine care is minimal. Be careful when hoeing or cultivating near meadow-rues in spring because most sorts do not break ground until quite late and there is danger of damaging the plants before this occurs. A spring dressing of a general purpose fertilizer is beneficial. Good results come from keeping the ground covered with compost, leaf mold, peat moss, or other organic mulch. In dry weather, deep waterings at about weekly intervals are desirable.

THAMNOCALAMUS (Thamno-cálamus). This genus consists of five Himalayan species of bamboos of the grass family GRAMINEAE. The name is from the Greek *thamnos*, a shrub, and *kalamos*, a reed, and refers to the appearance of the plants. From closely related *Arundinaria*, the genus *Thamnocalamus* differs in technical characteristics of its flower clusters and in the comparatively poorly developed tessellation of its leaves.

A compact clump-forming native of high altitudes in Sikkim and Bhutan, where it blooms annually, although this characteristic is not maintained by plants in cultivation, *T. aristatus* (syn. *Arundinaria aristata*) has brownish-green canes up to 15 feet tall or taller, with many reddish branches and branchlets. The leaf sheaths are not persistent. Up to 5 inches long by ½ inch broad, the leaves taper to points that are curiously twisted at their ends. Bright green above and gray-green on their undersurfaces, they are moderately tessellated. Their

margins are fringed with fine bristles. This bamboo is probably not hardy north of Washington, D.C. It is a handsome plant and is very satisfactory when grown as a tub specimen. A native of northern India, *T. falconeri* (syns. *Arundinaria falconeri*, *A. nobilis*) forms compact clumps of canes that under highly favorable conditions attain a height of 60 feet, but often do not exceed 30 feet. The peripheral canes of the clumps arch gracefully outward. The canes, at first green with brownish-purple marks at the nodes, are dull yellow with brownish-purple joints when mature. The leaf sheaths are soon deciduous. The leaves are mostly about 4 inches long by ½ inch broad, but terminal ones may be considerably larger. They show no tessellation and are bright green on their upper surfaces, paler green beneath. This species is most satisfactory when planted in partial shade and is hardy about as far north as Washington, D.C. It is a good tub plant. About 15 feet tall, *T. spathiflorus*, of Bhutan, Nepal, and Sikkim, forms compact clumps of slightly zigzagged canes that at first are green with a bluish-white waxy bloom, but later become pinkish-purple on the sides toward the sun. The branches, also pinkish-purple, are in twos or threes from each node. The leaf sheaths soon drop. Up to 6 inches long by ½ inch broad and with their margins bristly all around, the papery-thin leaves are pale green above, gray-green beneath, and finely tessellated. This bamboo is of delicate appearance and is very beautiful. It is probably slightly less hardy than those discussed above. For its satisfactory growth it needs partial shade. It is very satisfactory as a tub specimen.

Garden and Landscape Uses and Cultivation. For information on these subjects see Bamboos.

THAMNOSMA (Thamnós-ma) — Turpentine-Broom. The strong scent of this genus is acknowledged in its common and botanical names, the latter derived from the Greek *thamnos*, a shrub, and *osme*, an odor. Belonging in the rue family RUTACEAE it is a native of western North America, Arabia, Socotra, and Africa. There are eight or nine species. From *Cneoridium* they differ in having alternate leaves and two-compartmented, leathery, few-seeded fruit capsules, opening at their apexes.

Thamnosmas are glandular shrubs with early-deciduous foliage. Their bisexual flowers, about ⅓ inch long, are in raceme-like clusters and have persistent, four-lobed calyxes, four erect petals, eight stamens, and a slender style.

A desert native of rocky soils from California to Baja California, Utah, and New Mexico, *Cytisus*-like *T. montana* is yellowish-green, freely branched, and 1 foot to 2 feet tall. Its narrow-oblanceolate to linear leaves are ¼ to slightly over ½ inch long. Its blackish-purple flowers come in

spring. They have tiny calyxes and scarcely spreading petals. Four of the stamens are longer than the others, and the style extends slightly beyond the petals. The heart-shaped capsules contain one to three seeds.

Garden and Landscape Uses and Cultivation. The sort described is planted in its native region as low shrubbery and in gardens of native plants, but is little known elsewhere. It may be expected to prosper only under conditions that approach those of its native range. Propagation is by seed, and plants should be grown in containers until they are set in their permanent locations.

THEA. See Camellia.

THEACEAE—Tea Family. The sixteen genera of this Old World and New World family of dicotyledons, of tropical, subtropical, and warm temperate regions, consist of evergreen and deciduous, trees and shrubs with undivided leaves. The mostly solitary, bisexual and symmetrical flowers have a calyx of five to seven persistent sepals and a corolla of most often five, but sometimes fewer or more petals. The usually numerous stamens may be separate, in bundles, or united to form a tube. There are three to five, separate or united styles. The fruits are capsules or drupes. Cultivated genera include *Camellia*, *Cleyera*, *Eurya*, *Franklinia*, *Gordonia*, *Schima*, *Stewartia*, and *Ternstroemia*.

THELESPERMA (Theles-pérma). To *Thelesperma* belong twelve species of annuals, herbaceous perennials, and subshrubs of the daisy family COMPOSITAE, natives of the drier parts of North America, Argentina, and Uruguay. They are very closely related to *Coreopsis*, differing chiefly in that the inner bracts of the involucre (the collar of leafy organs below the flower head) are joined for at least one-third of their lengths instead of being completely or nearly separated. The name comes from the Greek *thele*, a nipple, and *sperma*, a seed, and refers to the shape of the fruits, which are seedlike achenes.

Thelespermas usually have daisy-type flower heads with both disk and ray florets, but sometimes the latter are lacking. Their leaves are opposite, the upper ones sometimes alternate, and are divided or not according to kind.

Most commonly cultivated, Texan *T. burridgeanum* (syns. *T. hybridum*, *Cosmidium burridgeanum*) has slender stems about 1½ feet tall that bear finely-divided leaves. Its flower heads, 1½ inches across, have purple disk florets and yellow-edged, deep orange ray florets. It was once mistakenly believed that this attractive species was a hybrid between *T. trifidum* and *Coreopsis tinctoria*. Another sort sometimes cultivated, *T. trifidum* (syn. *T. filifolium*) inhabits Texas and adjacent Mexico. Freely-branched and 1 foot to 2 feet tall, this has finely-dissected leaves and purple-centered, bright yellow flower heads about 1½ inches across.

Garden Uses and Cultivation. These fine flower garden annuals are useful both for ornamenting outdoor beds and borders and for cutting. They bloom freely throughout the summer and are best in sunny locations and fertile, porous soils of a somewhat sandy character. Their cultivation presents no difficulties. Seeds are sown in early spring, or in mild climates in fall, where the plants are to bloom, and the seedlings are thinned to about 6 inches apart. In exposed locations some support in the form of twiggy brushwood or other appropriate stakes is necessary. Routine care calls for keeping down weeds, removing faded flower heads, and watering in dry weather.

THELOCACTUS (Thelo-cáctus)—Glory-of-Texas. Seventeen species of *Thelocactus*, of the cactus family CACTACEAE, are accepted by radical "splitters" of cactus genera, others recognize fewer species or combine the group with *Echinocactus*, to which it is closely related. Most thelocactuses are natives of Mexico, one or more of the southwestern United States. The name, from the Greek *thele*, a nipple, and cactus, alludes to the prominent tubercles.

Thelocactuses have small to medium-sized, spherical to somewhat flattened-spherical stems or plant bodies with evident to obscure ribs cleft into prominences (tubercles) more or less grooved along their upper surfaces and spiny, often densely and even viciously so. Originating from the areoles of young tubercles at the tops of the plant bodies, the upturned, bell-shaped flowers, open by day, have scaly perianth tubes. The dry fruits open at their bases to release big black seeds.

Glory of Texas (*T. bicolor schottii*), as its well deserved vernacular name indicates, is attractive. It is a variety occurring in Texas and Mexico of a species the typical phase of which is endemic to Mexico. From that, the variety differs in its much longer spines, not, as has been asserted, in its having a greater number of radials. Egg-shaped to conical or nearly cylindrical, the eight-ribbed stems of **T. bicolor**, usually solitary, are sometimes branched from their bases and up to 10 inches tall by 5 inches wide, but mostly smaller. They have square-based tubercles each with a cluster of twelve to eighteen needle-like radials and three or four centrals. In the typical species the former vary in length from ¼ to ¾ inch, in the others from ¾ to very slightly over 1 inch. In *T. b. schottii* the radials are ½ inch to 2¼ inches, the centrals 1 inch to 3½ inches long. Flowers of both species and variety, 3 to 4 inches wide, have recurved, glossy, intensely fuchsia-pink petals with

scarlet bases. The fruits are up to ½ inch long. The blooms expand only in the afternoons of brilliant sunny days when temperatures are extremely high. Three or four hours later, when light begins to wane, they close forever. Endemic to a small region in Texas, *T. b. flavidispinus* (syns. *T. flavidispinus, Echinocactus flavidispinus*) has hemispherical to columnar stems, sometimes branched from their bases, up to 4 inches tall by 3 inches in diameter. They have thirteen ribs of conical tubercles. The spine clusters are of fourteen to twenty radials, ¼ to 1 inch long, yellow at first, but later bright red with yellow tips. Young specimens are without centrals, older ones develop one to three or more; they are yellow or yellow with bright red center parts, the biggest ½ inch to 1½ inches long. The flowers, 3 to 4 inches in diameter, are bright rose-pink to fuchsia-pink with scarlet bases. Other variants of *T. bicolor* sometimes recognized are *T. b. bolansis*, the spines of which are white, *T. b. pottsii*, which has spine clusters of about ten radials and longer, very stout centrals, and *T. b. tricolor*, with brilliant red spines. The last is sometimes, like *T. b. schottii*, called glory-of-Texas.

Thelocactus bicolor tricolor

Other kinds in cultivation include these: **T. bueckii** has solitary, indistinctly ribbed stems with pronounced, angled, pointed tubercles and clusters of four to seven needle-like, curved spines of unequal lengths, ½ inch to 2½ inches long, some curving outward. The 1-inch-wide blooms are dark red. **T. hastifer** (syn. *Echinocactus hastifer*) has cylindrical to club-shaped stems up to 6 inches tall and 2½ inches wide, with usually eighteen to twenty, sometimes fewer, spiraled, notched ribs. The spine clusters are of twenty to thirty

glassy-white, needle-like radials about ½ inch long and of about four centrals ¾ inch to 1¼ inches long, at first pale brown, later white. The violet-pink flowers are about 1½ inches in diameter. **T. heterochromus** (syn. *Echinocactus heterochromus*) has solitary, spherical or flattened-spherical stems with nine indistinct ribs of rounded tubercles. From woolly areoles sprout spine clusters of seven to ten strong, awl-shaped radials up to about 1 inch long and of one curved yellow central mottled with red. The fuchsia-pink to violet-red blooms are 2½ to 3 inches wide. **T. hexaedrophorus** (syn. *Echinocactus hexaedrophorus*) has solitary, very flattened to spherical stems 4 to 6 inches wide, with mostly thirteen obscure ribs of angled tubercles. The strong, awl-shaped spines are in clusters of six to nine, ½-inch-long, grayish-pink radials. The 3-inch-wide blooms are silvery-white. Variety *T. h. fossulatus* (syns. *T. fossulatus, Echinocactus fossulatus*) has spines in clusters of four or five, 1- to 1½-inch-long radials and usually a solitary 2-inch-long central. **T. leucacanthus** (syns. *T. leucanthus, Echinocactus leucacanthus*), very variable, typically has solitary or clustered, egg-shaped to short-cylindrical stems with eight to thirteen strongly evident spiraled ribs of conical tubercles. Up to 6 inches tall by about 3½ inches wide, they have woolly areoles. The spine clusters are of seven to twenty spreading radials, up to 1¼ inches long, and a solitary, strong, straight central 1½ to 2 inches long. The light yellow blooms are 1½ to 2 inches long. **T. lophothele** (syn. *Echinocactus lophothele*) has solitary or clustered, spherical to short-cylindrical stems up to 10 inches tall and 5 inches in diameter, with fifteen to twenty indefinite spiraling ribs with long tubercles. The spine clusters are of three to six, brown to black, bulbous-based radials, ½ inch to 1½ inches long, and sometimes a solitary, slightly longer central. The flowers have light yellow to greenish-yellow petals with reddish to red mid-veins or are pink to rose-red. They are 2 inches in diameter. **T. nidulans** (syn. *Echinocactus nidulans*) has solitary, nearly semispherical,

Thelocactus nidulans

bluish-gray-green stems, up to 8 inches in diameter, with about twenty ribs with pointed tubercles. The thick, rigid, slender-awl-shaped spines, at first brown to horn-yellow, becoming gray with age, are in clusters of about fifteen. About 1½ inches across, the flowers are yellowish-white. A variant with purplish blooms is reported. *T. rinconensis* (syn. *Echinocactus rinconensis*) has solitary, bluish- or grayish-green, distinctly thirteen-ribbed, grayish stems up to 3½ inches high by 5 inches wide. They are closely packed with long, pointed, pyramidal tubercles with clusters of four awl-shaped, ½-inch-long radial spines. The white blooms are 1½ inches in diameter. *T. schwarzii* has thirteen-ribbed stems approximately 2½ inches tall and wide. The spine clusters are of fourteen yellowish radials, the upper one of which is flattened, 1 inch long, and points outward. About 3½ inches in diameter, the purplish flowers have scarlet throats. *T. tulensis* (syn. *Echinocactus tulensis*) has spherical to short-cylindrical stems, up to 5 inches tall, that branch as they age and have more or less spiraled ribs with conical tubercles. The spines are in clusters of six to eight spreading, brown radials, from slightly under to a little over ½ inch long, and sometimes one or two thicker centrals approximately 1¼ inches long. The 1-inch-long blooms have pink petals with darker midribs. *T. wagnerianus* (syn. *Echinocactus wagnerianus*) has cylindrical stems branching from their bases and 6 to 8 inches tall by 2 to 2½ inches in diameter. They have thirteen ribs with pointed tubercles and spine clusters of twenty ½-inch-long, spreading, reddish-yellow radials and one to four bulbous-based centrals, when young bright red or yellow and red. Details of the blooms do not seem to be recorded in botanical literature.

Garden and Landscape Uses and Cultivation. Among the most attractive of small cactuses, the sorts of this genus are suitable for rock gardens and similar places in warm desert climates and for growing in beds or pots in greenhouses devoted to succulents. Most take kindly to domestication, but some, including the glory-of-Texas, can be recalcitrant. As with all desert cactuses, extremely well-drained soil is needed; most thelocactuses seem to appreciate one of a limestone character. Exposure to full sun and high temperatures in summer are favorable. Winter temperatures of 55°F at night and five to fifteen degrees higher by day are agreeable. Water, with good judgement, so that the soil becomes dryish between applications, and do so much more sparingly in winter than in other seasons. For more information see Cactuses.

THELYPODIUM (Thely-pòdium). Very closely allied to *Caulanthus*, from which it

differs most obviously in the calyxes of its flowers being more expanded rather than urn-shaped and narrowed at their tops, *Thelypodium* belongs to the mustard family CRUCIFERAE. There are possibly forty-five species, endemics to the western United States and Mexico, but some authorities transfer most of these to other genera. The name comes from the Greek *thelys*, female, and *pous*, a foot. It alludes to the ovary being stalked.

In a broad interpretation, this genus includes annuals, biennials, and perennials, with usually erect stems, and undivided leaves of varied shapes, the lower ones usually fiddle-shaped and lobed, those above without lobes. The flowers are white. They have four each sepals and spreading petals, six stamens, of which two are shorter than the others, and one style. The fruits are slender, erect, spreading, or deflexed pods.

In bloom, because its long, slender seed pods spread outward below the flower in the manner of those of the spider flower (*Cleome*), annual or biennial *T. wrightii* (syn. *Stanleyella wrightii*) is a conspicuous and attractive inhabitant of river bottoms in mountain regions. From 2 to 5 feet tall, it has white or purplish blooms, the expanded ones clustered at the tops of the stems. Its pinnately-cleft lower leaves have a large terminal lobe, the upper ones are more or less toothed. None is definitely stalked, but they narrow at their bases. Biennial *T. laciniatum*, from 1 foot to 6 feet tall, has often hollow stems, branched in their upper parts. Its glaucous, triangular-lanceolate leaves are mostly deeply-irregularly-cleft, but the upper ones are more shallowly-lobed or toothed. The white flowers in crowded, spikelike racemes are succeeded by slender, spreading seed pods somewhat like those of the spider flower (*Cleome*).

Garden and Landscape Uses and Cultivation. The species described are sometimes grown in native plant gardens and for ornament in regions where they are native, occasionally elsewhere. They are easily raised from seed sown where the plants are to remain in well-drained soil in sunny locations.

THELYPTERIS (Thelýp-teris). Formerly included in *Dryopteris*, this group of about 1,000 mostly medium-sized ferns of the aspidium family ASPIDIACEAE is now segregated as a separate genus. The name *Thelypteris* is from the Greek *thelys*, female, and *pteris*, fern. The species are native in many parts of the world, being most numerous in subtropical and temperate Asia.

These ferns have slender rhizomes, often with scales fringed with hairs; thin membranous leaves with veins that extend to their margins; and leafstalks containing two strap-shaped conducting bundles, as opposed to five to nine round ones in *Dryop-*

teris, and needle-like whitish hairs on the leaves, at least on the main veins of their upper surfaces. None of these characteristics apply to *Dryopteris*. The clusters of spore capsules are round and are on the veins on the undersides of the fronds (leaves). They usually have a small, kidney-shaped cover (indusium).

Hardy kinds of *Thelypteris* likely to be cultivated include the broad beech fern, northern beech fern, New York fern, Massachusetts fern, and marsh fern, all of which spread by running rhizomes. The two beech ferns have broadly-triangular, pinnate leaves with pinnately-lobed leaflets, and stalks longer than the leaf blades. Those of the broad beech fern (*T. hexagonoptera*), a native in moist woodlands from Quebec to Ontario, Minnesota, Florida, and Texas, are deciduous and not more than 1¾ feet long. The final divisions of each leaflet extend as wings along the midrib. This is not true of the northern beech fern (*T. phegopteris*), a deciduous native of moist woods and cliffs throughout the northern hemisphere, in North America extending from Labrador to Alaska, Oregon, Iowa, and North Carolina. This species has leaves up to 2¾ feet long. The New York fern (*T. noveboracensis*), the Massachusetts fern (*T. simulata*), and the marsh fern (*T. palustris*) have

Thelypteris noveboracensis

Thelypteris palustris

deciduous, narrowly-lanceolate, pinnate leaves that taper toward their bases, those of the New York fern sharply and markedly so that the lowermost leaflets are rudimentary, those of the others less noticeably. Their leaflets are pinnately-lobed. The New York fern is native to woods and margins of swamps from Newfoundland to Ontario, Minnesota, Georgia, Mississippi, and Arkansas. Its fronds are up to 3 feet long. The Massachusetts fern, a native of acid-soil swamps and moist woodlands from Nova Scotia to Virginia, has sterile fronds up to 9 inches long and fertile ones up to 1¼ feet in length. The veins of the divisions of the leaflets of both its sterile and fertile leaves are without branches. In contrast, the veins of the divisions of the sterile leaves of the marsh fern are forked, as are some of those of its fertile leaves. The marsh fern occurs in marshes and at the margins of bogs throughout the northern hemisphere and in South Africa. In the New World it is indigenous from Newfoundland to Manitoba, Florida, and Texas, and in Bermuda and Cuba. This species has sterile leaves up to about 1¼ feet long and fertile ones up to 2½ feet long.

Native from Nevada to California and British Columbia, the Sierra water fern (*T. nevadensis*) has running rhizomes and lanceolate, pinnate leaves, 1½ to 3 feet long, with the leaflets pinnately-lobed. Like those of the New York fern, the leaves taper sharply to their bases until the lowermost leaflets are very small. The leafstalks are straw-colored.

Tender species not hardy outdoors in the north, but grown in the open in California and other regions of mild climates as well as in greenhouses, include a number of decorative kinds. The tropical American *T. torresiana* (syn. *T. setigera*) has erect rhizomes and is distinct from others dealt with here in its broad-triangular leaves being thrice-pinnately-divided and in having white-waxy stalks. They are up to 4 feet in length and semievergreen. A deciduous native of Japan, Taiwan, and China, *T. de-cursive-pinnata* has erect rhizomes, and leaves about 3 feet long, narrowed to both ends and with their midribs winged except sometimes between a few of their lower leaflets. The wings are extensions of the lowermost divisions of the leaflets. Three rather similar species are *T. acuminata,* of Japan, Taiwan, and China, *T. dentata,* of the Old World and New World tropics, and *T. parasitica,* a native of the Old World tropics. All have fronds with a maximum length of about 3 feet. This group has the lowest veins of each leaflet segment joined to those of adjacent segments. From the others, *T. acuminata* can be recognized by its far-running rhizomes and its leaves, hairless except on the veins. Short-creeping rhizomes, and fronds that narrow toward their bases distinguish *T. opulenta* (syn. *T. extensa*) from the downy-leaved *T. dentata*, which has almost erect rhizomes.

A few other tender species, mostly difficult to identify with botanical certainty, are grown. A native of Florida, the West Indies, Mexico, and Central America, *T. augescens* has running rhizomes and stiff, usually erect, deciduous leaves up to 4 feet long. Lanceolate in outline and twice-pinnately-lobed, they narrow abruptly into a pinnately-lobed apex. Their leaf margins are not toothed. This is true, too, of the leaf margins of *T. normalis,* a similar species, native to the southeastern United States, Bermuda, and the West Indies, which has somewhat arching leaves, 2 to 3 feet long, that narrow gradually to a pinnately-lobed apex. From it, *T. puberula* differs in its more or less toothed leaf margins. A rare native of southern California and Baja California, this species has leaves up to 3 feet long. Easily confused with the last three is *T. patens,* of tropical America. It differs from them, however, in having erect rhizomes and the scales at the base of its leafstalks not being fringed with hairs. It is represented in cultivation by the variety *T. p.* 'Lepida', which has twice-pinnately-lobed, skeletonized leaves, with very slender leaflets with narrow lobes. The leaves are about 2 feet in length. Native to the Himalayan region, *T. ovata* has creeping rhizomes and delicately-divided fronds with wiry stalks up to about 8 inches long, and ovate, pinnate blades, 6 inches to 1 foot long, with slender, spreading, toothed leaflets. Tropical American *T. quadrangularis,* decidedly more heavily-foliaged than the last, has suberect rhizomes and arching, dark green, ovate, pinnate, somewhat hairy leaves with toothed leaflets.

Garden Uses and Cultivation. These ferns are of interest for grouping and mass planting and provide lacy foliage effects.

Thelypteris dentata

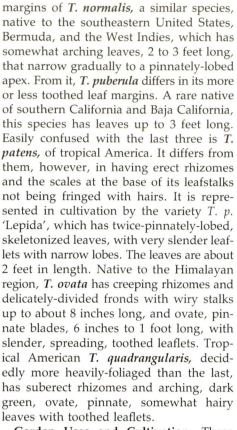

Thelypteris ovata

Thelypteris torresiana

Thelypteris opulenta

Thelypteris quadrangularis

Those with running or creeping rhizomes spread rapidly. They grow without difficulty in somewhat acid to neutral soil, well provided with organic matter, and in shade or part-shade. Most appreciate fairly moist conditions. This is especially true of *T. palustris*, but *T. acuminata* and *T. augescens* withstand dryish conditions quite well. They are propagated by division and by spores. For further information see the Encyclopedia entry Ferns.

THENARDIA (Then-árdia). Half a dozen Mexican and Central American species of milky-juiced, twining, woody vines compose *Thenardia*, of the dogbane family APOCYNACEAE. Their name commemorates the French biochemist Louis Jacques Thenard, who died in 1857.

The leaves of thenardias are opposite and stalked. The flowers, in umbel-like clusters from the leaf axils, have five-parted calyxes, and short-tubed, more or less wheel-shaped corollas with wide-spreading, twisted lobes (petals). The five stamens protrude. Their anthers form a cone. The fruits are pairs of long, podlike follicles.

Slender-stemmed and hairless, *T. floribunda*, of Mexico, is a handsome vine 10 feet tall or taller. Its short-pointed, elliptic leaves are 3 to 6 inches long by nearly one-half as wide. The somewhat cupped, slender-stalked, greenish-white to pink or purplish blooms, ¾ to 1 inch in diameter, are many together in loose clusters 3 to 4½ inches across.

Garden and Landscape Uses and Cultivation. In California and places with similar warm climates, the species described is useful as a climbing vine and as a groundcover. It is satisfied with ordinary garden soil and a place in sun or part-day shade. Increase is by cuttings and by layering.

THEOBROMA (Theo-bròma)—Cacao. The chief source of chocolate and cocoa, as well as of a fat, derived from its seeds and used in pharmaceutical and cosmetic preparations, *Theobroma cacao* is one of about thirty species of the sterculia family STERCULIACEAE. The genus consists of small trees indigenous to tropical Central America and South America. Its name is derived from the Greek *theos*, god, and *broma*, food, in allusion to the products of the cacao tree.

Theobromas have opposite, stalked, lobeless, toothless leaves and, from the trunks and branches or in the leaf axils, small flowers, clustered or solitary and succeeded by often large, woody seed pods. The blooms have calyxes of five lobes or separate sepals, five hooded petals narrowed to their bases, five petal-like staminodes (aborted stamens), and a slender style.

The cacao (*T. cacao*) is evergreen, 20 to 40 feet tall, and broad-headed. It has downy young shoots, and short-stalked, pointed-oblong leaves 6 inches to 1 foot in length. Its fragrant, creamy or yellowish, small flowers with pinkish calyxes are in clusters from the trunk and main branches. Football-shaped and longitudinally ribbed, the fruits, at first green, later reddish-brown, purplish, or yellowish, are 6 inches to 1 foot long and contain up to fifty or more 1-inch-wide seeds encased in whitish, mucilaginous pulp. The seeds contain the mild stimulant theobromine and from them are derived chocolate, cocoa, and cocoa butter. Chocolate is obtained by grinding the roasted seeds and retaining most of the fat. Cocoa results when most of the fat (cocoa butter) is removed from the pulverized roasted seeds. The Aztecs prepared a beverage of cacao seeds. These seeds were also used as money, the basis of their financial sys-

Theobroma cacao (fruits)

tem. In addition to *T. cacao*, some other species are exploited locally in their native countries for similar purposes.

Garden and Landscape Uses. Cacao is a quite ornamental small tree, suitable for planting in the humid tropics, and is cultivated among collections of plants useful to man in warm greenhouses. Its main attraction is its handsome foliage, which is especially beautiful at the beginnings of new flushes of growth when the young, limp, coppery leaves hang from the branch ends like tassels of damp seaweed. Soon they stiffen, straighten, and turn green. The flowers are not of much decorative merit, but the melon-like fruits borne directly on the trunk and large branches are curious and interesting and remain for many weeks.

Cultivation. As tropical garden plants, theobromas prefer rich, moistish soil, some shade, and shelter from strong wind. In greenhouses they need a humid atmosphere, a minimum winter temperature of 60°F, shade from summer sun, and generous watering. The soil should be coarse, fertile, and thoroughly drained. Repotting, needed by large specimens at intervals of several years only, is done in late winter or spring. Well-established specimens are favorably stimulated by regular applications of dilute liquid fertilizer from spring through fall. Propagation is by seed and by air layering.

THEOPHRASTA (Theo-phrásta). The genus *Theophrasta*, of the theophrasta family THEOPHRASTACEAE, consists of two species endemic to Hispaniola. Its name honors the great Greek philosopher Theophrastus, who died 285 B.C.

The sorts of this genus are hairless evergreen shrubs with branchless, erect, spiny stems with, crowded at their tops in rosettes, short-stalked, undivided, strongly-

Theobroma cacao (leaves and flowers)

spiny-toothed, net-veined, leathery leaves. In racemes of many, the flowers have a five-parted calyx, a cylindrical-bell-shaped, five-lobed corolla, five each stamens and staminodes (nonfunctional stamens), and a short style. The spherical fruits are many-seeded drupes.

From 1 foot to 3 feet tall, *T. americana* (syn. *T. fusca*) has linear-lanceolate to oblanceolate leaves up to 1½ feet long by about 2 inches wide. Dull brown at first, the urn-shaped flowers, in rusty-hairy racemes, become nearly black with age. The yellow to orange-yellow fruits are about 1½ inches in diameter. From the last, *T. jussieui* (syn. *T. densiflora*) differs in having oblanceolate leaves up to 1½ feet long by 2 to 4 inches wide and short racemes of white to pale yellow flowers, nearly 1 inch long, with spreading corolla lobes (petals). Its leaves are up to 1½ feet long by 2 to 4 inches wide. A handsome foliage plant sometimes cultivated under the name of this last species is obviously wrongly identified. Most probably it is a species of the related genus *Clavija*. True *Theophrasta* may not be in cultivation. The misidentified sort has stout, erect stems and firm, obovate, coarsely-toothed leaves 1 foot or more long.

Garden and Landscape Uses and Cultivation. As ornamentals theophrastas would make striking additions to gardens in the humid tropics and to plant collections in tropical greenhouses. Practically no information is available about their cultural needs, but they may be expected to respond to conditions and care appropriate for clavijas.

THEOPHRASTACEAE — Theophrasta Family. This typical South American and Hawaiian family of dicotyledons consists of four genera of evergreen trees and shrubs. Their undivided, sometimes spine-tipped leaves are alternate, opposite, or in whorls (circles of more than two). Bisexual or unisexual with the sexes on different plants, the symmetrical flowers have a calyx of five sepals, a five-lobed corolla with five stamens attached to it, and one style. The fruits are fleshy or leathery berries or drupes. Genera cultivated are *Clavija, Jacquinia,* and *Theophrasta*.

THERMOPSIS (Therm-ópsis). Natives of North America and temperate Asia, the thirty species of *Thermopsis* belong in the pea family LEGUMINOSAE. They are herbaceous perennials of lupine-like appearance, a fact that gives reason for their name, derived from the Greek *thermos*, a lupine, and *opsis*, resembling.

Thermopsises have woody rootstocks and erect, annual stems. Their alternate leaves have three leaflets that spread in finger-fashion from the top of the leaf-stalk. At the base of each is a pair of leaf-like appendages (stipules). Pea-shaped, the

usually yellow flowers are in erect, spire-like racemes, terminal or arising from the stem opposite the leaves. They have a narrowly-bell-shaped, two-lipped calyx, five petals, ten separate stamens, and one style. The fruits are many-seeded, flat, usually linear pods, stalkless or with short stalks. Except for the flat pods this genus scarcely differs from *Baptisia*.

One of the most attractive species, *T. montana*, native from the Rocky Mountains to Washington, has thick, somewhat branched stems up to 3 feet tall. Its leaves are of obovate to linear-lanceolate leaflets, 1 inch to 3 inches long, slightly hairy on their undersides. The flowers are loosely arranged in racemes 6 to 8 inches long. Densely-hairy, the 2- to 3-inch-long seed pods are held close against the stem on which they are borne. Taller, up to 5 feet high, *T. caroliniana* differs chiefly in its

Thermopsis caroliniana

blooms being in denser racemes, and its leaves, pubescent and glaucous on their undersides, having ovate to obovate leaflets 2 to 3 inches long by about one-half as wide. This sort is endemic from North Carolina to Georgia. Softly-hairy, much-branched, and 2 to 3 feet tall, *T. mollis* differs from those described above in having seed pods that spread widely instead of hugging the stalk that bears them. The leaves are of elliptic leaflets up to 1 inch long by ½ to ¾ inch wide. This is native from Virginia to Georgia. From 6 inches to 1¼ feet tall, *T. rhombifolia* is native chiefly east of the Rocky Mountains from Alberta to North Dakota, Nebraska, and Colorado. It has mostly branchless stems and ovate-lozenge-shaped leaflets ¾ inch to 1¼ inches long. In crowded terminal or axil-

lary racemes up to 4 inches long, the ten to thirty yellow flowers are approximately ¾ inch long. The seed pods, up to 2½ inches in length and generally silky-hairy, are spreading or recurved.

Native to Kamchatka and the Kurile Islands, *T. fabacea* is up to 3 feet tall. It has leaves with elliptic to broad-ovate to obovate leaflets, 1½ to 2½ inches long, with finely-hairy undersides. In terminal, erect racemes, the 1- to 1¼-inch-long flowers are yellow. The flat seed pods are up to 3 inches long or sometimes longer.

Thermopsis fabacea

Garden and Landscape Uses and Cultivation. These are excellent for perennial beds and are useful cut blooms. Hardy *T. caroliniana* survives outdoors at least as far north as southern New England. The others, except *T. fabacea*, are more tender. They succeed with little care in sunny locations, preferring deep, well-drained soils and enduring dry ones better than most popular perennials. Once established, they should not be transplanted unless it is quite necessary. Moving involves breaking their deep taproots. They recover slowly. It is possible to propagate by careful division in early spring, but seed affords a surer and more satisfactory means of increase. Sow the seed in a cold frame in fall or in a greenhouse in a temperature of about 60°F in late winter or early spring. Grow the young plants in pots until they are planted in their final locations. Routine care is minimal, although neat staking is likely to be needed. In cold areas a loose winter covering of branches of evergreens, salt hay, or other suitable material is advisable.

THEROPOGON (Thero-pògon). Not unlike the better known genus *Ophiopogon*, the only species of *Theropogon*, belonging to the lily family LILIACEAE, is indigenous to the Himalayas. Its name, alluding to its season of bloom and tufts of foliage, is from the Greek *theros*, summer, and *pogon*, a beard.

Not hardy in the north, yet capable of withstanding some frost, **T. pallidus** has tufts of evergreen, longitudinally-ribbed, grasslike leaves up to 1 foot long by up to ¼ inch wide. Its lily-of-the-valley-like flowers, white, pink, or tinged with red, are bell-shaped and ⅓ inch long. They are in gracefully arched, terminal racemes of ten to twenty, shorter than the leaves. They have six petals, six very short stamens, and a style with a minute stigma. They come in spring or early summer. The fruits are pea-sized, few-seeded berries.

Theropogon pallidus

Garden and Landscape Uses and Cultivation. This pretty herbaceous perennial is charming for rock gardens and as a groundcover. It may also be grown in pots or pans (shallow pots) in greenhouses. It succeeds in sun or light shade in nourishing sandy, peaty soil that is well drained, but does not become excessively dry. Propagation is by division as soon as flowering is through, and by seed. A greenhouse temperature of 45 to 50°F on winter nights is satisfactory. Slightly warmer conditions by day are appropriate.

THESPESIA (Thes-pèsia)—Portia Tree. Natives of the tropics of Asia, Africa, and islands of the Pacific, the fifteen species of trees, shrubs, and tall herbaceous plants that comprise *Thespesia* belong in the mallow family MALVACEAE. The name is derived from the Greek *thespesios*, divine, but the application is not clear; it may allude to the frequency with which it is planted near temples in the eastern tropics. Thespesias are closely related to the West Indian *Montezuma*, differing chiefly in their smaller flowers with persistent calyxes, and in having pubescent seeds. Only one species is commonly cultivated. The united styles distinguish both *Thespesia* and *Montezuma* from *Hibiscus*.

The portia tree (**T. populnea**) is up to 50 feet tall. It forms a dense head of spreading branches and has long-stalked, pointed-heart-shaped, evergreen leaves with blades 2 to 7 inches long. As its specific name suggests, its leaves somewhat resemble those of poplars. The mallow-like flowers, from the leaf axils, are 2 to 3 inches across and yellow with a maroon eye. They change to pink and dull purple as they age and remain on the plant for several days after they have faded. This tree blooms more or less throughout the year. The fruits, rounded and broader than long, are about 1½ inches wide. The portia tree is abundant along seacoasts throughout the range of the genus. Its flowers are chiefly pollinated by nectar-seeking birds. The inner bark of the portia tree is the source of a useful fiber and its hard, durable wood is used for furniture, gunstocks, wheel spokes, carts, and boats.

Garden and Landscape Uses and Cultivation. The portia tree is distinctly ornamental. In the humid tropics and in southern Florida and southern California this species is a useful shade and ornamental tree. It grows quickly and is especially suited for planting by the sea. It prospers in any average soil and is readily propagated from seed. It can also be increased by cuttings.

THEVETIA (Thev-ètia) — Yellow-Oleander or Be-Still Tree or Lucky Nut. One of the about ten species of *Thevetia*, of the dogbane family APOCYNACEAE, is a popular outdoor shrub in the Deep South and other warm-climate regions and is cultivated as a greenhouse and conservatory ornamental. Its name was given to commemorate the sixteenth-century French monk André Thevet, who traveled in Brazil.

Thevetias are hairless, milky-juiced shrubs and small trees, natives of tropical America and the West Indies. All parts of these plants are very poisonous if eaten. The sorts of *Thevetia* are readily distinguished from oleanders by their alternate leaves; those of oleanders are in twos, threes, or fours. From the closely related frangipani (*Plumeria*), they differ in their fleshy fruits, broader than long, which enclose a stone containing a solitary seed. The leaves of *Thevetia* are more or less leathery and have a prominent mid-vein and many parallel side veins. The yellow, funnel-shaped blooms, with five twisted corolla lobes, are in terminal, stalked clusters. The lobes do not spread widely. There are five stamens and a slender style ending in a two-lobed stigma.

The yellow-oleander, be-still tree, or lucky nut (**T. peruviana**, syn. *T. neriifolia*) is a bushy, leafy, rounded shrub or small tree up to 30 feet tall, but often lower. Its slender-linear leaves, narrowed at both ends, lustrous above, 3 to 6 inches long, and almost stalkless, are somewhat like those of oleander, but not as broad. Their margins are somewhat rolled-under. The mildly fragrant blooms, 2 to 3 inches long, are followed by somewhat triangular, thinly-fleshed fruits, at first red, but ripening black. They contain a seed about 1 inch in diameter. These, known as lucky nuts, are carried as charms or talismans in the West Indies. A variety of *T. peruviana* with deeper orange-yellow flowers is sometimes cultivated. Another species, **T. thevetioides,** native to Mexico, is similar, but its leaves have more conspicuous lateral veins and are pubescent beneath.

Garden and Landscape Uses. Because it blooms more or less continuously and is of good appearance and moderate size, the yellow-oleander is a useful garden plant. It is appropriate mixed with other shrubs or may be used alone or in groups. Locate it where its pleasing fragrance can be enjoyed. It is handsome when grown in containers to ornament patios, terraces, and similar places. In placing it, the fact that its parts are dangerously poisonous if swallowed should be borne in mind. It is hardy only in southern Florida, southern California, and regions with climates as warm or warmer. It thrives in full sun in well-drained sandy soils.

Cultivation. Seed or cuttings may be used to secure increase. No special care is needed beyond the occasional removal of overcrowded shoots and any cutting that may be required to keep the plant shapely or limit its size. When grown in greenhouses it requires the same care as oleanders. See Nerium.

THIMBLEBERRY is *Rubus parviflorus*.

THINNING or THINNING OUT. Thinning or thinning out are terms for operations that reduce the number of plants or plant parts with the objective of having those left develop to best advantage.

Seeds are commonly sown more closely together than would be satisfactory if all germinated and all the young plants were permitted to remain. To prevent overcrowding, seedlings may be thinned by pulling out and discarding the excess or, if they are ammenable, by transplanting them. It is important to thin seedlings be-

Thinning out seedlings

fore they attain such sizes at which, from lack of space and adequate light, they become weak and spindly. It is often advantageous to do the work in two steps, a first thinning that reduces immediate competition and a second one that, when they again begin to crowd, establishes final spacing. With carrots, lettuce, radishes, spinach, and some other crops, thinnings, especially second thinnings, provide produce useful for eating.

Thinning out as a pruning practice contrasts with heading back, the latter alluding to the severe shortening of main branches so that the shrub or head of a tree is considerably reduced in size. No such marked diminuation results from thinning out, which consists of the removal, down to their points of origin, of branches deemed least worthy of retention, having in mind the needs of others for light, air circulation, and space to develop, as well as the shapeliness of the shrub or tree.

Thinning out branches of a gooseberry to relieve overcrowding

Thinning out plums

Thinning fruits of many kinds, including apples, apricots, peaches, pears, and plums, is practiced. Besides resulting in improved size and quality of the fruits left to ripen, it may help to reduce a tendency of some sorts to crop heavily and spar-

ingly in alternate years. It also minimizes the likelihood of breakage of limbs caused by extra-heavy crops. Commercially, fruit thinning is often accomplished by the use of sprays, but in home gardens hand thinning is more practicable. It is done either about three weeks after full bloom or, depending upon the kind of fruit and the preference of the grower, after the "June drop," when many fruit trees make a final natural shedding of some of their immature fruits.

THISTLE. This is the common name of *Carduus* (also called plumeless thistle), *Cirsium* (called plumed thistle and including the bull thistle, Canada thistle, fishbone thistle, and swamp thistle), and *Onopordum*, the Scotch thistle. Plants with common names containing the word thistle that belong in other genera are these: blessed-thistle or our-Lady's-thistle (*Cnicus benedictus* and *Silybum marianum*), bluesow-thistle (*Lactuca alpina*), globe-thistle (*Echinops*), holy-thistle (*Cnicus benedictus* and *Silybum marianum*), milk-thistle or St.-Mary's-thistle (*Silybum marianum*), sage thistle (*Salvia carduacea*), and sow-thistle (*Sonchus*).

THLADIANTHA (Thladi-ántha). Fifteen species of tuberous-rooted, herbaceous perennial vines, of China and Indo-Malaysia, constitute *Thladiantha*, of the gourd family CUCURBITACEAE. The name, from the Greek *thladias*, a eunuch, and *anthos*, a flower, was given because the specimen originally examined by the botanist who applied it was without anthers (the effective male parts).

Thladianthas cling to suitable supports by branchless tendrils. They have heart-shaped leaves, fairly large, yellow, unisexual blooms with bell-shaped, five-lobed calyxes, and corollas, also bell-shaped, with five recurving lobes (petals). Male flowers have five stamens and may be solitary, but most commonly are in racemes. Females are similar, but are solitary and usually have five linear staminodes (nonfunctional stamens) in addition to a deeply-three-branched style and kidney-shaped stigmas. The fleshy, oblong fruits, with their many seeds horizontal, are green.

The hardiest species, *T. dubia*, of northern China, is naturalized from Quebec and New Hampshire to Manitoba. It has stems up to 5 feet long, and broadly-ovate, pointed, toothed, harshly-hairy, somewhat squashlike leaves 2 to 4 inches long. Usually in rather crowded racemes 2 to 3 inches long, the male flowers have petals ¾ to 1 inch long. The stalks of their stamens are downy. The female blooms, on more or less hairy stalks 2 to 3 inches long, have very hairy ovaries. Up to 2 inches long by one-half as wide, but usually smaller, the hairless fruits have ten shallow, longitudinal grooves.

Thladiantha dubia

More robust than the last, less hardy, and not hairy, *T. oliveri*, of central China, may have stems 30 feet long and leaves, similar in shape to those of *T. dubia*, but up to 8 inches long. Also, the flowers are more numerous. The males are in panicles, the females solitary. A hybrid between the species described here is reported, but seemingly is unnamed.

Garden and Landscape Uses. These vigorous vines of pleasing appearance are suitable for covering fences, porches, arbors, and other surfaces that provide holds for tendrils, and for planting on banks. They are of very easy cultivation in well-drained soil in sunny places. Because *T. dubia* spreads by its roots it is well to plant it only where it will not interfere with other plants. Propagation is by division and by seed.

THLASPI (Thlás-pi) — Penny-Cress. This group of about sixty species bears a name used by the ancient Greeks for some cresslike plant. It belongs in the mustard family CRUCIFERAE and is most abundant, as to species, in Europe and temperate Asia. A few kinds of *Thlaspi* are native to North America, a few to South America.

Thlaspis are low annuals and herbaceous perennials. Few have horticultural merit. They commonly have rosettes of basal foliage and more or less clasping stem leaves. They are hairless or may have branchless hairs. White, pink or purplish, the flowers are in racemes. Each has four sepals, four petals that spread to form a cross, six stamens, two of which are shorter than the others, and a short style. The flattened, keeled, or winged seed pods are circular to obovate, and in some kinds are notched at their apexes.

Dwarf perennial kinds sometimes cultivated include *T. bellidifolium*, a compact, densely-tufted native of the Balkans, 1 inch to 2 inches tall, with spatula-shaped, toothed basal leaves, and all of the stem leaves alternate. The dark purple flowers have yellow anthers. Differing in having running stems (stolens) up to 8 inches long, *T. rotundifolium*, of the mountains of southern Europe, is a somewhat variable kind 2 to 4 inches tall. Its leaves are broadly-ovate to nearly round, the lower stem ones opposite. The flowers are rosy-lilac to purple, rarely white, and fragrant. Distinguished by having smaller leaves not in definite rosettes and by its numerous stem leaves being crowded is *T. r. cepiifolium*. The plant sometimes called *T. limosellifolium* is *T. rotundifolium*.

Garden Uses and Cultivation. The kinds described are suitable for rock gardens. They succeed best in moraines, in extremely gritty soils that offer little fertility, are very well drained, and are underlain by a moist layer into which the roots can reach. Full sun, or full sun with a little shade during the heat of the day, are desirable. These plants should be divided every year or two. Division and seed afford easy means of increase.

THOMASIA (Thomás-ia). Two eighteenth-century collectors of Swiss plants, Peter and Abraham Thomas, are commemorated by *Thomasia*, a genus of twenty-five species of Australian shrubs or occasionally small trees of the sterculia family STERCULIACEAE. Thomasias are adaptable to cultivation only in climates that approximate the mildness they know in the wild; this confines their outdoor use in North America to southern California and similar favored regions.

Evergreen, and with shoots and foliage commonly with stellate (starlike) hairs, thomasias have alternate, usually lobed leaves. The white or purple flowers, petal-less or with petals so minute and scalelike that they are scarcely recognizable as such, have five-cleft, more or less petal-like calyxes, five stamens, and generally, alternating with them, five staminodes (nonfunctional stamens). The fruits are capsules.

A shrub 2 to 3 feet tall, *T. rugosa* has broad, wrinkled, heart-shaped to ovate leaves, 1 inch to 3 inches long, with their upper sides stellate-hairy and with depressed veins and their undersides densely-clothed with starry hairs. The few-flowered, slender-stalked racemes are up to 2½ inches long. The blooms are purple and ½ inch or slightly more in diameter. Loosely-branched and up to about 5 feet tall, *T. pauciflora,* of Western Australia, has stems and foliage clothed with stellate hairs. Its short-stalked, narrow-linear to narrow-triangular leaves, often with two short basal lobes, have blades 1½ to 2 inches long. The pink to lavender-pink flowers are ½ to ¾ inch wide. Slender-stemmed *T. purpurea,* 1 foot to 2 feet in height, has gray-downy shoots, and linear-oblong leaves ½ inch to 1½ inches long by approximately one-third as wide. Its racemes of a dozen or fewer blooms come from the leaf axils. They are 1 inch to 2 inches long. The flowers have calyxes about ¼ inch across that are light purple and petal-like. The petals are lacking or

Thomasia pauciflora

minute. The stamens have dark purple anthers. Native to Western Australia, *T. solanacea* is a shrub or small tree. It has ovate-heart-shaped leaves, 1½ to 3 inches long, with coarsely-sinuately-lobed margins and, especially when young, with undersides densely-clothed with stellate (star-shaped) hairs. At the base of each leafstalk are a pair of conspicuous, rounded stipules up to ½ inch wide. In racemes up to 2 inches long and sometimes branched, the ½-inch-wide, petal-less flowers are white with a pink center stripe down each calyx lobe.

Thomasia solanacea

Garden and Landscape Uses and Cultivation. Thomasias are suitable for planting at the fronts of shrub borders and in similar places; *T. purpurea* is suitable as a groundcover. They need sun and well-drained soil. Propagation is by seed, and by cuttings of short side shoots, rooted in a greenhouse or cold frame propagating bed, or under mist.

THOMPSONELLA (Thompson-élla). There are some differences of opinion as to whether the two species that compose the Mexican genus *Thompsonella*, of the orpine family CRASSULACEAE, should be included in *Echeveria* or maintained as a separate

entity. The latter view seems to prevail and is followed here. The name honors Charles Henry Thompson of the Missouri Botanical Garden. The flowers of *Thompsonella* differ from those of *Echeveria* in having thin petals that spread outward from their middles, as opposed to erect, usually thick petals, and in less obvious technical characters.

Thompsonellas are more or less glaucous and have fleshy, elliptic to oblanceolate leaves, commonly deeply-channeled above and often with wavy margins, in solitary, flattish, stemless or very short-stemmed rosettes. The starry flowers are crowded in erect, narrow, spikelike panicles or spikes that arise from the leaf axils. Each flower has a five-lobed calyx, five petals, ten stamens, and five carpels, each with a single style. The fruits are follicles.

The roots of *T. minutiflora* are carrot-like and its leaves are often marked with purple. The latter are 1 inch to 4 inches long by ⅓ to 1 inch broad and normally die completely at the beginning of the dormant season. The stalks that bear the flowers are 2 inches to 2 feet long or a little longer. Their lower parts are furnished with small leaves. The flowers are a little under to a little over ⅓ inch wide. They are yellow in the throats and have red corolla lobes marked with darker red. There are ten stamens. From the last, *T. platyphylla* differs in being slightly larger and in having smaller flowers. Its roots are not much thickened, and it normally retains some of its basal foliage through the winter.

Garden Uses and Cultivation. These are primarily plants for collectors of succulents. Their needs are as for *Echeveria*. For more information see Succulents.

THOMSONIA (Thomsòn-ia). Rare in cultivation, the only species of this genus, sometimes spelled *Thompsonia*, inhabits warm parts of the Himalayan region. It belongs in the arum family ARACEAE and has a name commemorating Anthony Todd Thomson, an English professor of materia medica, who died in 1849. It is a tuberous perennial.

From *Amorphophallus*, to which it is closely related, *Thomsonia napalensis* differs in having the top of its spadix covered with cone-shaped protuberances. It has a flattened-spherical tuber, some 4 to 5 inches in diameter, from which develops a solitary leaf, with a stalk 2 to 2½ feet long, and a blade with three main pinnately-lobed divisions, the final segments ovate to oblong-lanceolate, pointed, and up to 5 inches long. The leafstalk is green, irregularly spotted with brownish-green, and at its base brownish. Characteristic of the arum family, the feature usually called the flower is not a single bloom, but consists of a spadix with tiny flowers crowded along a spikelike axis, from the base of which comes a leaflike bract. This inflorescence (cluster of blooms and attendant parts) is structured like that of a calla-lily, in which the central yellow column is the spadix and the petal-like, trumpet-shaped, white part is the spathe. In *Thomsonia* the inflorescence tops a stalk 1½ to 3 feet long, spotted like the leafstalks. It develops when the plant is leafless. The stout, green spadix, up to 10 inches long, is thickly covered with little unisexual flowers, the functioning males with one to three stamens and purplish-yellow, the sterile males above them yellow, and, occupying the bottom of the spadix, the female flowers green. The boat-shaped, leathery, green spathe, 8 inches to 1½ feet in length, soon falls.

Garden Uses and Cultivation. This may be grown as a curiosity, outdoors in the tropics, and in greenhouses. It responds to the conditions and care needed by *Amorphophallus.*

THORN. Botanically, a thorn is a rigid, sharp-pointed outgrowth from the wood of a stem, that usually morphologically represents a modified branch. Similar, but smaller, weaker outgrowths that originate in the bark are called prickles. In common, nontechnical usage the two terms are more or less interchangeable.

THORN. This is the common name of *Crataegus,* which includes such well-known sorts as the cockspur thorn, Glastonbury thorn, and Washington thorn. Other plants with common names that include the word thorn are as follows: Christ-thorn (*Paliurus spina-christi*), hedge-thorn (*Carissa bispinosa*), Jerusalem-thorn (*Paliurus spina-christi* and *Parkinsonia aculeata*), kangaroo-thorn (*Acacia armata*), lily-thorn (*Catesbaea spinosa*), thorn-apple (*Datura stromonium*), and three-thorned-acacia (*Gleditsia triacanthos*).

THOROUGHWAX is *Bupleurum rotundifolium.*

THOROUGHWORT. See Eupatorium.

THRIFT. See Armeria. Prickly-thrift is *Acantholimon.*

THRINAX (Thrì-nax) — Peaberry Palm or Thatch Palm. Ten or fewer species, native to the Caribbean and adjacent regions, constitute *Thrinax,* of the palm family PALMAE. The name comes from the Greek *thrinax,* a trident, and alludes to the forked tips of the leaf segments.

These palms have solitary, erect, often slender trunks sometimes clothed with persistent leaf bases, topped by a compact, orbicular crown of rounded, fan-shaped leaves. Their small, bisexual flowers are in clusters that originate among and often extend beyond the foliage. Each has five to fifteen stamens. The blooms are succeeded by short,

dense, hanging clusters of spherical, one-seeded, pea-sized fruits. At maturity, these are generally ivory-white, but those of some kinds are gray, brownish, or purplish. Nearly related *Coccothrinax* has usually purple or black fruits.

Two species are most common in cultivation, *T. morrisii* (syns. *T. microcarpa, T. keyensis*) and *T. radiata* (syn. *T. floridana*). A stout, stocky tree up to 30 feet or more high and native to southern Florida and the West Indies, *T. morrisii* has leaves with nearly circular blades, up to 3½ feet across, split into about thirty segments and silvery-white on their undersides. The flowers and fruits are stalkless or nearly so. Indigenous to Florida, the West Indies, the Bahamas, and Belize, *T. radiata* attains heights of up to almost 40 feet and has leaves with 3-foot long stalks, and blades with fifty-one to sixty-three segments with clearly evident, scattered scales on their undersides. Its white flowers have five to ten stamens. The fruits, on stalks ⅜ inch long, are about ¼ inch in diameter. In cultivation this palm is often misidentified as *T. parviflora* and *T. excelsa.*

Native to Jamaica, *T. parviflora* is up to 30 feet tall with a trunk diameter of 6 inches. Its leafstalks are up to 4½ feet long. The leaf blades, in thirty-seven to fifty-seven segments up to 3 feet long, are devoid of visible scales on their undersides. The ivory-white to yellowish flowers have five to fifteen stamens and are in clusters up to 5 feet long or longer. The fruits, a little over ¼ inch in diameter, are shorter-stalked than those of *T. radiata.* Also Jamaican, *T. excelsa* (syn. *T. rex*), about 30

Thrinax parviflora, Jamaica, West Indies

feet in height, has a trunk up to 6 inches in diameter, leaves with a stalk up to 6 feet in length, and fifty-five to sixty-five broad, drooping segments, whitish on their undersides and up to 5 feet long. Its pink to purplish flowers and its fruits, the latter

Thrinax parviflora, a young specimen

about ⅜ inches in diameter, are short-stalked.

Garden and Landscape Uses. Peaberry palms are attractive garden and landscape trees that withstand seaside environments well. This is especially true of *T. radiata*, which is quite resistant to salt spray. They prosper in limestone soils and in full sun. Because they grow rather slowly and do not need a great deal of room, they are well suited for small properties and are admirable for growing in large pots and tubs. The hardiest appears to be *T. morrisii*, which at Daytona Beach, Florida, is reported to have withstood temperatures of 25°F without harm when nearby plants of *T. parviflora* were severely damaged.

Cultivation. These plants thrive in ordinary garden soil that is well drained and not excessively dry. They are propagated by seed sown in sandy, peaty soil in a temperature of 75 to 85°F. Under greenhouse cultivation, they need well-drained containers, coarse, porous, fertile soil, a humid atmosphere, and a minimum winter night temperature of 55 to 60°F, with higher temperatures by day and at other seasons. Some shade from strong summer sun is needed indoors. The soil should be always fairly moist, but not constantly saturated. Well-rooted specimens respond favorably to biweekly applications of dilute liquid fertilizer from spring through fall. For additional information see Palms.

THRIPS. Of the approximately 2,500 known species of thrips, the majority live on flowers and other plant parts including the foliage, bulbs, and corms, but a few are scavengers that feed on dead vegetation and yet others prey on mites, aphids, and similar small creatures, including other thrips. Several sorts are very serious pests of beans, chrysanthemums, citruses, ferns, gladioluses, onions, pears, peas, privets, and a wide variety of other plants outdoors and in greenhouses.

These are tiny insects, those prevalent in North America from about ⅟₂₅ to ⅟₁₀ inch long when fully grown. Some tropical species are bigger. At maturity, most kinds have two pairs of long, narrow wings conspicuously fringed with hairs, but there are wingless species and the young of all are without wings. The mouth parts of thrips are designed for piercing and rasping; with them, these pests damage plants by taking their juices and, in so doing, scarring and marring the surface tissues of leaves, petals, and fruits. Foliage affected often becomes streaked or mottled with silvery markings, in appearance not unlike those caused by red spider mites, but without the characteristic rusty look they often cause. Petals and other soft parts may be distorted as a result of feeding thrips. Not infrequently these insects compound their damage by spreading disease-causing bacteria and funguses.

In color, thrips vary from yellow through brown to black. Although discernible to the naked eye, they are more readily seeable with a hand lens. They move fairly rapidly, often with a slight wiggly motion.

Thrips multiply most rapidly in dry, hot environments. Most do so by laying eggs; some sorts produce fertile eggs without the intervention of males, which may be rare or absent. Individuals are sometimes bisexual. Females of some species bear young live. From birth, young thrips are much like wingless adults. Maturity is gradually attained through a series of molts involving partial metamorphosis. There is no pupating stage. For control of these pests, gardeners rely chiefly on contact insecticides including rotenone and pyrethrum.

THRIXANTHOCEREUS (Thrixantho-cèreus). Botanists with conservative outlooks include *Thrixanthocereus*, of the cactus family CACTACEAE, in *Espostoa*. When treated separately it comprises one species, native to Peru. The name, from the Greek *thrix*, hair, *anthos*, a flower, and the name of the related genus *Cereus*, makes reference to its blooms coming from a mass of hairs called a pseudocephalium.

A beautiful, erect, columnar, branchless or few-branched plant up to about 10 feet tall, *T. blossfeldiorum* (syn. *Espostoa blossfeldiorum*) has stems, 1½ to 3 inches thick, with eighteen to twenty-five low ribs. The spine clusters are of twenty to twenty-five slender, grayish-white radials, about ¼ inch long, and one blackish central, 1 inch or a little more in length. The creamy-white flowers, greenish on their outsides, come from an elongated pseudocephalium streaking downward from the top of the stem.

Garden and Landscape Uses and Cultivation. This is a beautiful, easy-to-grow species for outdoor landscaping in warm dry climates and for inclusion in greenhouse collections. It appreciates fertile, well-drained soil, full sun, and moderate watering. For more information see Cactuses.

THRIXSPERMUM (Thríx-spermum). Belonging to the orchid family ORCHIDACEAE, the genus *Thrixspermum* comprises possibly 100 species of mostly tree-perchers (epiphytes), natives of tropical Asia, Taiwan, Indonesia, Australia, and Polynesia. The name, derived from the Greek *thrix*, hair, and *sperma*, seed, alludes to the seeds being hair-shaped.

Thrixspermums have short to long stems clothed with the persistent bases of old leaves or with their lower parts leafless. The leaves are flat and often sickle-shaped, linear, or in some species absent. The short-lived flowers are in racemes with the blooms in two ranks or facing in all directions, according to kind. Those of some sorts have long, slender sepals and petals that give a spidery aspect to the blooms, in other sorts they are much broader and the flowers look much like those of dendrobiums. Although desirable for collections of orchid fanciers, few sorts are in cultivation.

Native to Malaya, Sumatra, and Borneo, *T. calceolus* has creeping or vining stems up to 4 feet or more in length. In two ranks, its oblongish, fleshy leaves are up to 4 inches long by 1¼ inches wide and notched at their apexes. The 2-inch-wide flowers, in racemes of few from the leaf axils, are pure white except for the comparatively large three-lobed lip, which is orange-yellow tipped with white. Malayan *T. lilacinum* has stems up to 6 feet tall furnished with ovate, clasping leaves up to about 1 inch long. In few-flowered racemes, up to 1 foot in length, the 1-inch-wide, white to light lilac-colored blooms have ovate sepals and petals and a lip with a conical center lobe and markedly curved side lobes.

Garden Uses and Cultivation. These are as for vandas. For more information see Orchids.

THROATWORT. See Trachelium.

THROWWAX is *Bupleurum rotundifolium*.

THRYALLIS. See Galphimia.

THUJA (Thù-ja)—Arbor-Vitae. There are only five species of *Thuja*, but the horticultural varieties of some kinds are so numerous that their precise identification is often a matter of extraordinary difficulty. The genus, the name of which is an adaptation of *thuja*, used by Theophrastus for a kind of juniper, belongs in the cypress family CUPRESSACEAE and is represented in the native floras of North America, China, and Japan. The common name arbor-vitae means tree of life. The tree formerly named *T. orientalis* is *Platycladus orientalis*.

Arbor-vitaes are pyramidal and densely-branched and -foliaged when young. Later they develop as tall pyramidal or columnar trees or remain bushy according to kind. Many horticultural varieties are low or dwarf and many have brightly colored foliage. The branches of arbor-vitaes are erect or spreading, and the branchlets, flattened in a horizontal plane, thin, flexible, and strong. Those of adult-type foliage are frondlike sprays of many finer branchlets, which remain for several seasons and then are shed. The tiny, scalelike leaves are in opposite pairs disposed in four ranks. Thujas are bisexual with male and female cones on different branchlets, the males at the bases of the shoots, the females from small terminal branchlets. The fruiting cones are ⅓ to ⅔ inch long and have three to ten pairs of scales with thickened ridges at their apexes. Each scale of two or three of the pairs is fertile and bears two or three seeds. The cones mature at the end of their first season. Arborvitaes much resemble false-cypresses (*Chamaecyparis*), the technical differences being that the cones of the former are ovoid and have scales that overlap like shingles on a roof, while the cones of the latter are globose or almost so and their scales are attached to their stalks inside their margins.

As producers of lumber, arbor-vitaes are of considerable importance. The wood of the giant arbor-vitae, called Western red-cedar, is very resistant to moisture and decay and is in demand for greenhouse benches, shingles and siding, closet linings, and general carpentry, as well as for poles and fences. Long before the white man came to North America, the Indians of the northwest employed planks of it to build their huts and carved totem poles from its trunks. The chief uses of the lumber of American arbor-vitae is for poles, posts, fences, shingles, railroad ties, and canoes. In the Orient, the woods of the native kinds are used for construction, interior finishing, and other purposes.

When arbor-vitaes are raised from seeds they, like some other conifers, at first have juvenile foliage altogether different from the adult foliage of more mature specimens. The juvenile leaves, in pairs, are needle-like and spreading, instead of scalelike and stem-hugging, and the shoots that bear them are not arranged in flat, frondlike sprays. In appearance, juvenile plants resemble certain junipers more than they do adults of their own kind, but they differ from junipers in having much softer foliage and in the leaves usually having whitish or grayish lines on their undersurfaces. Normally the juvenile stage lasts for a limited time, after which successive new leaves more and more resemble adult ones and finally are completely adult. The change from juvenile to adult foliage is characteristic of other members of the cypress family CUPRESSACEAE, but in *Thuja* and *Chamaecyparis* the situation is complicated by the fact that horticulturists have practiced methods of prolonging juvenility more or less indefinitely and of developing plants that retain their juvenile characters even though they continue to live for many years and attain their full size. This has been accomplished by propagating from juvenile shoots and repropagating from plants so produced, and repeating this through many generations. As a result of this, the curious situation arises in which there are two or more entities of very different appearance that are genetically and technically the same, but for horticultural purposes quite distinct. When these perpetual juvenile forms of *Thuja* and *Chamaecyparis* were first brought from the Orient to the attention of Western bota-

nists their true status was not apparent and they were thought to represent a separate genus to which the name *Retinospora* was applied. This name is still sometimes used in gardens, but it is without botanical sanction. Here they are treated as a matter of convenience as varieties of the species to which they belong.

The American arbor-vitae (**T. occidentalis**), an extremely hardy, narrowly-pyramidal or columnar tree up to 60 feet tall,

Thuja occidentalis: (a) A young specimen

(b) Older pyramidal specimens

(c) A group of older columnar specimens

Thuja occidentalis (adult-type leaves and female cones)

is native from Nova Scotia to Manitoba to Illinois, Tennessee, and North Carolina. Its trunk is usually prominently buttressed at its base and often forks low down. Its branches are short and spreading and have upturned ends. From spring to fall its leaves are bright green on their upper sides and yellowish or bluish-green beneath, but in winter they mostly assume an unpleasant yellowish-brown or brownish-green. They usually have conspicuous glands, and the leading shoots are noticeably compressed. The cones, about ½ inch in length, are pendulous when they mature. They have eight to ten scales, of which usually four bear seeds.

Many more than one hundred varieties of American arbor-vitae have been named, some so similar that it is impossible to de-

Thuja occidentalis variety

scribe them in such a way that they are identifiable. This is especially true because many of them change in appearance with age. A large proportion of the described variants are unavailable from trade sources and some probably are no longer in existence. In gardens and nurseries confusion exists regarding the identification and naming of kinds that are available. The only sure way for prospective planters to acquire what they want is to visit nurseries or other sources of supply and select the actual plants. A selection of the best-known varieties include these: *T. o. alba* (syn. *T. o.* 'Queen Victoria'), with white tips to its young branchlets; *T. o.* 'Columbia', a columnar form with the ends of its young branchlets white, perhaps the best silver-variegated variety; *T. o. compacta*, a slow-growing, dense and compact, slender kind; *T. o. douglasii pyramidalis*, an especially attractive variety with a dense, columnar form, rich green foliage, and its frondlike branches often crested at their ends; *T. o. douglasii aurea*, a good yellow-foliaged kind; *T. o. ellwangerana*, a broadly-rounded shrub that becomes quite brownish in winter, has some branches bearing juvenile and others adult foliage, and, unless sheared occasionally, tends to become a loose, open bush; *T. o. ellwangerana aurea*, similar but with yellowish leaves and slower growing; *T. o. ericoides*, low, dense, pyramidal, and with only juvenile leaves that are bright green in summer, purplish in winter; *T. o. fastigiata*, very dark green, slender, and

curved; *T. o. umbraculifera*, dwarf, umbrella-shaped, and dark green; *T. o. wareana* (syn. *T. o. robusta*), broadly-pyramidal, compact, and with dark green foliage, the sprays of branchlets, sometimes in vertical planes, retaining their green color with little change in winter; and *T. o. woodwardii*, dense, spherical, and with its dark green color not changing as markedly as most in winter.

The giant arbor-vitae (*T. plicata*) or, as it is sometimes called, the Western red-

Thuja plicata, Long Island, New York

Thuja plicata atrovirens, The New York Botanical Garden

and distinctly marked with white. The cones each have eight or ten scales, of which the three center pairs usually produce seeds. They are ½ inch long. Variety *T. p. atrovirens* has darker green leaves

than the typical species and grows more slowly. Variety *T. p. aureovariegata* is a vigorous, decorative kind with foliage marked with bands of yellow. The kind named *T. p. fastigiata* is very narrow and columnar. Slender, pendulous branches characterize *T. p. pendula*.

The Japanese arbor-vitae (*T. standishii*) somewhat resembles the giant arbor-vitae (*T. plicata*), but is considerably smaller. A

Thuja occidentalis fastigiata, Powerscourt, County Wicklow, Ireland

Thuja plicata, National Botanic Garden, Dublin, Ireland

Thuja standishii

columnar, a good hedge or accent plant; *T. o. globosa*, up to 4 feet tall, broader than high, of formal appearance, and with its fans of branchlets in vertical planes, resembling *T. o. compacta*, but not as tall; *T. o. pumila* (syn. *T. o.* 'Little Gem'), a dwarf, compact, broadly-rounded, wide-spreading bush; *T. o. lutea* (syn. *T. o.* 'George Peabody'), with bright yellow ends to its shoots, the best of the golden varieties; *T. o. recurva nana*, dwarf, round-topped, and the tips of its branchlets twisted or re-

cedar is indigenous from Alaska to northern California and eastward to Montana. Well deserving its common name, it towers, a majestic column or narrow spire of greenery, up to 200 feet in height. Its massive trunk, covered with cinnamon-red bark and sometimes 12 feet in diameter, is heavily buttressed. Its branches are short, horizontal, and often pendulous at their ends. The upper sides of the scale-like leaves are rich, lustrous green, their undersides without conspicuous glands

handsome native of Japan hardy in southern New England, it attains a maximum height of about 60 feet, but usually is not over 30 feet tall. Broader and rather more loosely-branched than other species, this grows more slowly. Distinguishing features are the triangular white marks on the undersides of its glandless, bright green or slightly yellow-green leaves and the absence of any strong aromatic fragrance when the leaves are crushed. The cones are ovoid, dark brown, and ½ inch long. The Japanese arbor-vitae is not as commonly cultivated as the American and Oriental arbor-vitaes.

Korean *T. koraiensis* is usually a low, spreading or even prostrate shrub or sometimes a narrow-pyramidal tree closely related to the Japanese arbor-vitae. From that species it differs in having glandular leaves glaucous over the whole of their undersides. Its sprays of branchlets are very much flattened. The cones have eight scales, two pairs of which are fertile. Rare in cultivation, this arbor-vitae is hardy in southern New England.

Garden and Landscape Uses. The American arbor-vitae and its varieties are among the hardiest of all evergreens, surviving winters well into northern Canada. Specimens of the Western arbor-vitae that are descendants of trees native near the easternmost natural limits of the range of the species are hardy in southern New England. Specimens that trace their ancestry to trees native to the Pacific Coast are less winter-hardy. The Japanese arbor-vitae is about as cold-resistant as the Western arbor-vitae.

Arbor-vitaes are among the most useful of evergreens for landscape purposes, although it must be confessed that the many variants of American arbor-vitae are frequently planted where other evergreens would be more appropriate and are too frequently set so closely together or are crowded by other trees or shrubs that they are soon ruined and never have the opportunity to develop their full beauty. Many, when young, are such symmetrical, brightly colored plants, and look so "cute," that they tempt inexperienced gardeners to purchase them and install them in foundation plantings and other shrubberies without much thought to the future; prospective planters are wise if they look around until they locate old-established plants of the kinds they propose to plant, which are likely to be in the gardens of older houses, public parks, cemeteries, and botanical gardens, before making final plans for their own plantings. This at least apprises them of the amount of space each plant will need

Young thujas in a nursery sales yard

and is likely to reveal that some of the brightly colored young plants in nurseries are likely to become less attractive in later years. Certainly the planting of golden-leaved varieties and others with unusual colored foliage has been much overdone. In general, those kinds with leaves of normal green meld better with the landscape and are easier to live with through the years. Like jewels, kinds with strikingly colored foliage or other conspicuous aberrant qualities should be used as occasional accents to emphasize the beauty of their settings rather than to compete with each other or to provide the complete evergreen adornment of the area.

Upright arbor-vitaes are excellent for screens, narrow hedges, backgrounds to flower borders, and as accent plants; those of broader, bushier habit can be used in many places where evergreen shrubbery is desirable; and the dwarfs and compact, low-growing varieties are appropriate for rock gardens, the fronts of borders, and as accent plants in small-scale gardens. All need full sun and a free circulation of air around them; without it, they soon become thin and straggly and lose foliage on their sides that are against other plants. Often this is not noticed until so much harm has been done that it is too late to do anything about it short of removing and discarding the plants and replacing them. Arbor-vitaes must have at least a moderately humid atmosphere. They do not prosper in dry, exposed locations, under the overhangs of roofs, or where heat is reflected from nearby walls. This is especially true of the American arbor-vitae and its varieties. All thrive best in a reasonably deep, moderately fertile, well-drained soil that is on the moist side, rather than excessively dry; it is useless to plant them in a thin soil overlying bedrock or on some equally impossible site and expect them to flourish. Under such unfavorable conditions they are particularly subject to infestations of red spider mites. For use in larger landscapes, they are as a rule too slender, stiff, or formal to be set out as solitary specimens, but they are effective in groups and are especially appropriate close to water, along the banks of lakes, streams, or ponds where the ground is high enough not to be waterlogged.

Cultivation. Dissatisfaction with arbor-vitaes is almost invariably the result of faulty placement rather than improper culture. When sited suitably, these plants need surprisingly little care; even when large they transplant without difficulty. They need no regular pruning, although a few loose-growing varieties benefit from an occasional shearing and all may be restricted in size by performing this operation annually. The shearing should neither remove more than most of the last season's growth nor extend back into older

wood. Late winter or early spring, before new growth begins, is an appropriate time for shearing. Keeping the soil about the plants mulched with compost, peat moss, or other organic mulch is beneficial; plants that have exhausted most of the nourishment from the soil through which their roots ramify, or plants in poorish soil to begin with, are improved by the application of a complete garden fertilizer each

A tall hedge of *Thuja occidentalis*

A screen of *Thuja occidentalis* fronted with *Kalmia latifolia*

A closely-sheared formal hedge planting of *Thuja occidentalis*

Thujopsis dolabrata

Topiary-trained specimens of *Thuja occidentalis*, Long Island, New York

spring. In dry periods, arbor-vitaes are helped by being watered deeply at regular intervals. Such applications are of special importance to specimens in foundation plantings where the drying of the soil is apt to be more severe than in more open locations. Toward the end of summer or in fall, the older branchlets and leaves, those a little way back from the tips, turn brown and eventually shed. This is natural and no cause for worry, but if the tips of the branchlets themselves shrivel or die it is an indication of trouble—excessive dryness, severe infestation with red spider mites, or other unfavorable circumstance. Propagation of the natural species is by seed sown in sandy, peaty soil in a protected bed outdoors, in a cold frame in fall or spring, or in a cool greenhouse in winter. Varieties, especially those of American arbor-vitae, root readily from cuttings taken in late summer and planted under mist or in a humid cold frame or cool greenhouse

Potting rooted cuttings of *Thuja*

propagating bench. They may also be increased by veneer grafting onto seedling understocks in a greenhouse in late winter or spring.

Diseases and Pests. Arbor-vitaes are affected by a leaf-blight and a tip-blight that cause affected parts to appear as though scorched by fire. They are controlled by spraying with copper fungicides. The insects that at times are troublesome are aphids, bagworms, borers, leaf-miners, mealybugs, red spider mites, and scales. For more information see Conifers.

THUJOPSIS (Thujóp-sis) — Hiba-Arbor-Vitae or False-Arbor-Vitae. The Japanese genus *Thujopsis* consists of a single species closely related to arbor-vitae (*Thuja*), from which it differs in its more globose cones having three to five seeds on each fertile scale instead of two or three and in its broader, very much flattened branchlets. The botanical differences are small, and some botanists consider the two genera one, accepting our present subject as a subgenus of *Thuja*. Be that as it may, in appearance the Hiba-arbor-vitae is distinct. It belongs in the cypress family CU-PRESSACEAE. Its name derives from the botanical name of arbor-vitae, *Thuja*, and the Greek *opsis*, like or similar to.

The Hiba-arbor-vitae or false-arbor-vitae (**T. dolabrata**) is a very beautiful evergreen tree that attains a height of about 50 feet, but is sometimes only shrubby. It is pyramidal and has spreading or drooping branches and flat branchlets in frond-like fans held in horizontal planes. The small scalelike leaves, in opposite pairs and forming four rows along the shoots, are dark glossy-green above and have conspicuous white patches on their under-

sides. The broad-ovoid cones of six to eight flat, woody scales are ½ inch long. The scales are thickened into a distinct and often hooked boss at their tips on their outsides. Attaining a height of 100 feet, *T. d. hondae*, native to northern Japan, has branchlets closer together and leaves smaller than those of the typical species. Also, its cones are more spherical and their scales are not conspicuously thickened at their ends. The variety *T. d. nana* has bright green foliage and is compact and dwarf. This kind grows very slowly. The variegated *T. d. variegata* has the tips of its branches, and often patches of leaves elsewhere, variegated with white. One of the important forest trees of Japan, the Hiba-arbor-vitae has fragrant wood that is used for construction, building, railroad ties, and other purposes.

Garden and Landscape Uses and Cultivation. Appropriate uses for this evergreen tree in ornamental landscapes are precisely the same as those suggested for arbor-vitaes (*Thuja*). Its cultural needs and methods of propagation are also the same, but because it shows much variation when raised from seed, it is most often increased by cuttings; even Japanese foresters follow this method to obtain uniform stock for planting. The Hiba-arbor-vitae grows slowly and, for its best development, requires a humid atmosphere. A fertile, moist, well-drained soil is best to its liking. For additional information see Conifers.

THUNBERGIA (Thun-bérgia)—Clock Vine, Black-Eyed-Susan-Vine. The distinguished Swedish botanist and traveler Karl Pehr Thunberg, who died in 1822, is honored by the name of this genus of the acanthus family ACANTHACEAE. Consisting of annuals and evergreen perennials, *Thunbergia* includes many twining vines and some shrubs. It inhabits Africa and the warmer parts of Asia and comprises well over 100 species.

Thunbergias have opposite, undivided leaves, commonly with basal lobes, and blooms solitary in the leaf axils, or in terminal, often pendent racemes. Flower colors are white, yellow, orange, red, blue, or purple. At the base of each bloom are two prominent, more or less leafy bracts that conceal the minute calyx and often part of the corolla tube. The calyx may be without lobes or teeth or have ten to fifteen. The funnel- to more or less bell-shaped corolla has a straight or curved tube swollen at one side and a nearly symmetrical to asymmetrical face composed of four or five lobes (petals) that in the bud stage are twisted to the left. There are four stamens. The fruits are beaked, leathery capsules containing four spherical seeds.

A bushy shrub, **T. erecta** (syn. *Mayenia erecta*) is native to tropical Africa. Of up-

Thunbergia erecta

right growth, this beautiful species is 3 to 6 feet tall. Its short-stalked, hairless, almost toothless, ovate leaves are 1 inch to 3 inches long. Solitary from the leaf axils, the stalked flowers have corollas with orange-yellow throats, curved, yellowish-white tubes 1½ to 2¾ inches long, and five spreading, rich blue-purple petals. The face of the flower is 1¼ to 1¾ inches across. The calyxes are seven- to ten-toothed. Variety *T. e. alba* has yellow-tubed, white flowers.

Another shrubby tropical African kind, **T. affinis** differs from the last in having a distinct tendency to climb, eventually becoming 12 feet tall, and in having noticeably toothed leaves and flowers about twice as big as those of *T. erecta*. From other shrubby kinds discussed here, **T. vogeliana,** of West Africa, differs in the bracts near the flowers being thick and rust-red. This species, 8 to 15 feet tall, has toothed or toothless, pointed-elliptic to oblongish leaves 3 to 6 inches in length by approximately one-half as wide. The flowers, about 1 inch long, have lobed or toothed calyxes, corollas with yellow tubes and throats, and violet petals.

Perennial, blue-flowered, woody vines rather alike in appearance are *T. grandiflora* and *T. laurifolia* (syn. *T. harrisii*). Both are natives of tropical Asia. Vigorous **T.**

Thunbergia grandiflora

grandiflora has thick, ovate, broad-ovate, or nearly round leaves, 5 to 8 inches long, with short, rough hairs on both surfaces and usually more or less heart-shaped bases from which radiate five to seven veins. Their margins are generally angularly-lobed or coarsely-toothed. The beautiful, asymmetrical flowers, with five corolla lobes, sometimes are solitary, but more often are crowded in drooping racemes of eight to ten. Sky-blue or darker, they have yellow throats, are about 3 inches in diameter, and have corolla tubes about 2½ inches long. In variety *T. g. alba* the blooms are white and larger than those of the blue-flowered species. The leaves of **T. laurifolia** differ from those of *T. grandiflora* in being narrower, not having heart-shaped bases, and usually being much less prominently toothed. Three to five veins radiate from their bases. They are 3 to 7 inches long, lanceolate to lanceolate-ovate, and not rough-hairy, although often slightly pubescent on their lower sides. The blooms, more symmetrical than those of *T. grandiflora*, are of similar size. They are in drooping racemes and are light blue with yellowish or whitish throats. This kind is also a vigorous grower.

White-flowered **T. fragrans** is a slender-stemmed, somewhat woody, perennial vine, native to India and naturalized in parts of the United States. It has thin-stalked, pointed-lanceolate to triangular-ovate leaves with, at the base on each side, one or two angular teeth. The leaves are 2 to 3 inches long. The solitary blooms are about 1¼ inches long by 1½ to 2 inches in diameter. Their calyxes are toothed. The five petals have notched apexes. Although described as having fragrant flowers, *T. fragrans,* as commonly cultivated, is scentless. It is probable that plants grown in gardens are *T. f. vestita,* a more hairy variety with nonfragrant flowers.

Red flowers with orange throats are borne by **T. coccinea,** of India. This nearly hairless, perennial, woody vine attains heights of 20 to 30 feet and has blunt, ovate

to oblongish, toothed, thick leaves, 5 to 7 inches long, with three or five veins spreading from their bases. The 1-inch-long flowers have toothless calyxes, and corollas with five petals that bend backward and are notched at their ends. They are crowded in drooping racemes up to 1½ feet long.

A handsome perennial, **T. mysorensis,** a woody vine of India, is about 15 feet tall.

Thunbergia mysorensis (racemes of flowers)

Thunbergia mysorensis (leaves and an individual flower)

It has scarcely-hairy, rather long-stalked, elliptic to oblong-lanceolate, toothed or toothless leaves, 4 to 6 inches long, with three veins spreading from their bases. The markedly asymmetrical flowers, 1½ to 2 inches long by 2 inches wide, are in drooping racemes from the ends of short branches. They have toothless calyxes, purplish corolla tubes with yellow throats, and four yellow, orange, or maroon-red petals, three of which bend backward. The stamens and style are shorter than the upper petal and occupy a groove in it.

Brilliant orange flowers are borne by perennial **T. gregorii** (syn. *T. gibsonii*), a na-

Thunbergia gregorii

tive of tropical Africa. A vigorous vine, this has ovate to broadly-triangular leaves with stalks 1 inch to 2½ inches long and blades 2 to 3 inches long. Five or seven veins radiate from the base of the leaf. The blooms have lobed calyxes and are 1½ to 1¾ inches long and wide.

Black-eyed-Susan-vine (**T. alata**), commonly grown as an annual, but where not

Thunbergia alata

killed by frost, a perennial, is popular. It attains heights of 5 to 8 feet and has hairy stems and foliage. Its ovate to almost triangular leaves have toothed blades, heart- to nearly arrow-shaped at their bases, 1 inch to 3 inches long, and with winged stalks about as long. The solitary, nearly symmetrical, long-stalked blooms vary in color from nearly white to cream, buff-yellow, or rich orange. Typically they have very dark purple centers. The corolla tubes are about 1½ inches long. Across their faces the five-petaled flowers measure 1¼ to 1¾ inches. Several color variations of this African species have been accorded recognition. These include *T. a. bakeri*, with pure white flowers; *T. a. alba*, with white flowers with dark centers; *T. a. lutea*, with yel-

Thunbergia natalensis

low flowers without dark centers; and *T. a. aurantiaca*, with intensely orange blooms with very dark eyes.

An erect herbaceous plant or subshrub of bushy growth, **T. natalensis** has quadrangular, glaucous stems abundantly furnished with stalkless, pointed-ovate, more or less hairy, toothless leaves up to 3 inches long and 1½ to 2 inches broad. The solitary blooms, pale blue with yellow throats, are on erect stalks. They have curved corolla tubes, 1 inch to 2 inches long, and five petals that spread to give the blooms faces 1¼ to 2 inches across. This species is a native of South Africa.

Garden and Landscape Uses. Thunbergias are among the most decorative and useful flowering shrubs and vines for the tropics and subtropics and for greenhouses. In addition, black-eyed-Susan-vine, as well as *T. gregorii* and *T. fragrans*, can be grown as outdoor annuals even in the north. The black-eyed-Susan-vine is attractive in hanging baskets and pots as well as in gardens. The hardiest thunbergia appears to be *T. natalensis*. This withstands some frost, but not hard freezing. In southern England it persists in beds along the outsides of greenhouse walls and in similarly protected locations.

Shrubby *T. erecta* is popular in southern Florida, Hawaii, and most tropical and subtropical places, and also is excellent in warm greenhouses. It associates pleasingly with *Allamanda neriifolia* and can be used to good effect as a general purpose shrub and for hedges.

The vining kinds are lovely and indeed magnificent for draping arbors, pergolas, porches, and other supports that afford holds for their twining stems. In greenhouses, the more vigorous growers are better in ground beds than in containers, although good results can be had in large pots or tubs if there is adequate room for the tops to develop without need for excessive pruning and if generous fertilizing is practiced. The vigorous growers are not suitable for small greenhouses; the cutting back necessary to limit them in size severely reduces flower production.

Cultivation. Black-eyed-Susan-vine is most commonly raised from seed, and other thunbergias can be. Cuttings of all kinds root with reasonable facility in humid conditions in a greenhouse propagating bench where the temperature is 70°F. Another easy method of increase is by layering. As a group thunbergias are sun-lovers, but most stand part-day shade. In greenhouses light shade from strong summer sun is needed. Not fussy about soil, thunbergias are satisfied with any that is well drained and of moderate fertility. No more pruning is needed than is necessary to keep the plants tidy and shapely. Late winter or spring, before new growth begins, is the best time of the year to attend to this.

As greenhouse plants, most thunbergias need night temperatures in winter of 60°F, with a daytime increase of five to fifteen degrees. At other seasons temperatures should be higher. A decidedly moist atmosphere is desirable for most kinds, but black-eyed-Susan-vine and *T. gregorii* need less humid conditions. All are watered freely from spring to fall, less generously in winter. Then, the soil is permitted to become dryish between applications, and the atmosphere is kept drier than at other seasons. Container specimens that are well rooted benefit from regular applications from spring to fall of dilute liquid fertilizer.

THUNIA (Thù-nia). Half a dozen much-alike species of the orchid family ORCHIDACEAE compose *Thunia*. Natives of southeastern Asia and India, they bear a name that commemorates the distinguished orchid fancier Count Thun-Tetschen, of Bohemia, who died in 1873.

Deciduous and without pseudobulbs, thunias have clusters of erect, leafy stems, vaguely suggesting those of bamboos, and terminal, nodding racemes of showy blooms. The position of the flowers at the stem ends distinguishes *Thunia* from *Phaius*, with which it was once united. The stems bear flowers in their first season, then lose their leaves, but remain as reservoirs of foodstuffs and as supports for the new shoots of the following season. They do not again produce foliage. The alternate, stalkless leaves are in two ranks, with those near the bases of the stems smaller than those above. The flowers, each with a large bract at its base, have spreading, similar sepals and petals and a short-spurred, slightly three-lobed, flaring lip decorated with five to seven crests of fleshy hairs, its lower part surrounding the column.

Beautiful **T. alba**, of northern India, Burma, and Thailand, usually does not exceed 2 feet, but sometimes attains 3½ feet in height. Its largest leaves are ordinarily not over 9 inches long. Often the white sepals and petals of its up to 3-inch-wide

Thunia alba marshalliana

blooms, which are in racemes of five to ten, do not spread widely. The purple-marked, bell-shaped lip is commonly veined with yellow. The blooms of *T. a. nivalis* have a pure white lip. Variety *T. a. marshalliana* (syn. *T. marshalliana*) is taller and more robust than the species. Its showy flowers, except for the yellow, orange-red-veined lip, which has five orange crests, are pure white and come from the axils of white bracts. Fragrant and up to 4 or even 5 inches across, the blooms are in racemes of three to twelve.

Garden Uses and Cultivation. Among the easiest of tropical orchids to grow and handsome both in foliage and bloom, thunias succeed in intermediate- and warm-temperature greenhouses. After their leaves fall, they are rested by keeping them in a temperature of 50 to 55°F where the atmosphere is less humid than before and by watering them no oftener than necessary to keep the stems from shriveling. Annual repotting is done when new growth begins in February or March. Osmunda or tree fern fiber, mixed with an equal amount of turfy loam, half as much each dried cow manure and gritty sand, and some chopped charcoal suits. As much of the old compost as possible is removed from the roots before the new compost is packed around them. The newly potted specimens are put where the air is humid and temperatures of 60 to 70°F are maintained. At first water is given sparingly, more freely as stem and leaf growth increases, and liberally after the foliage is fully developed until, after flowering is through, the leaves begin to turn yellow. Then, water is gradually withheld and the resting season begins. While they are in active growth thunias prosper under conditions suitable for cattleyas. They can be propagated by sectional stem cuttings as well as by division. For more information see Orchids.

THURBERIA. See Gossypium.

THYME. See Thymus. Cat-thyme is *Teucrium marum*. Spanish-thyme is *Coleus amboinicus*.

THYMELAEACEAE—Mezereum Family. Especially abundant in Africa, the fifty genera of this tropical-, widely distributed subtropical-, and temperate-region family of dicotyledons are prevailingly trees, shrubs, and woody vines. A few are herbaceous perennials. Commonly, they have a tough, fibrous bark. Their usually small alternate or opposite leaves are undivided and without lobes or teeth. The symmetrical or very slightly asymmetrical flowers are generally bisexual, less often unisexual and then usually with the sexes on separate plants. Mostly they are in terminal or axillary heads, spikes, or racemes, rarely are they solitary. Each has a tubular calyx with four or five often petal-like lobes, the same number or two or no scalelike petals, as many, twice as many, or numerous stamens, and one style. The fruits are achenes, berries, drupes, or rarely capsules.

Genera cultivated include *Dais, Daphne, Dirca, Edgeworthia, Gnidia, Peddiea,* and *Pimelia*.

THYMOPHYLLA. See Dyssodia.

THYMUS (Thỳ-mus) — Thyme. Thymes include hardy and nonhardy, aromatic, small shrubs, subshrubs, and nearly herbaceous perennials, upright, spreading, or trailing, of the mint family LABIATAE. They are enjoyed for their neat habits, fragrance, and flowers, and some as flavorings. Common thyme is a staple kitchen herb. The genus *Thymus* comprises between 100 and 400 species depending upon the interpretations of different botanists. Admittedly difficult to classify and identify as to species and varieties, in the wild the group is endemic to temperate parts of the Old World, especially the Mediterranean region. Some kinds are naturalized in North America. The name comes from *thymos,* an ancient Greek name for a species of *Thymus* or *Satureja*.

The leaves of thymes are small, opposite, undivided, and toothless. The upper ones associated with the flowers are, in a few species, large and showy. The small white, pink, purplish, or red blooms are in few-flowered whorls (tiers) disposed in axillary or terminal clusters, sometimes of the interrupted type, that is, with short lengths of stem visible between successive whorls. The blooms have tubular, ten- to thirteen-veined calyxes with the upper of two lips three- or more rarely five-lobed and the lower cleft into two slender lobes usually fringed with bristly hairs. The corollas, also two-lipped, have the upper lip notched and the lower with a comparatively large lobe flanked on each side by a smaller one. There are four usually protruding stamens and a solitary style with two stigmas. The fruits are of four tiny, seedlike nutlets.

Common thyme (**T. vulgaris**), a native of southern Europe, is a more or less upright shrub 6 to 8 inches tall. It has erect, wiry, minutely-hairy, woody stems, and stalkless or nearly stalkless, oblong-lanceolate to linear leaves from ¼ to a little over ½ inch long and more or less clustered. They have rolled-under, but not hair-fringed edges and gray-hairy undersides. The short, interrupted clusters of lilac-colored to purplish-pink flowers terminate the stems and branchlets. Individual blooms are under ¼ inch long. Varieties are *T. v. argenteus,* with white-variegated foliage; *T. v. aureus,* with leaves variegated with yellow; and *T. v. roseus,* with pink flowers. Closely related **T. hyemalis,** of Spain, differs from common thyme in blooming from fall to spring rather than in summer and in having shorter leaves with their margins fringed with hairs at their bases. Its blooms are rosy-purple.

Thymus vulgaris argenteus

Thymus vulgaris aureus

Lemon thyme or wild thyme (**T. serpyllum**), of northwestern Europe, is rarely cultivated, but its common and botanical names are often misapplied to other sorts, among them *T. pannonicus, T. praecox,* and *T. pulegioides.* The true plant forms mats of prostrate, rooting stems, woody toward their bases, from which sprout erect flowering branches 2 to 4 inches tall and hairy on four sides. Almost stalkless, the linear to elliptic, or somewhat spatula-shaped leaves are ¼ to ³⁄₁₆ inch long. The purple flowers are in headlike assemblages. Not to be confused with the last, a lemon-scented hybrid between *T. vulgaris* and *T. pulegioides,* named **T. citriodorus,** is commonly grown and is often called lemon thyme. This is a variable low shrub with erect, hairy stems, and generally hairless, slender, ovate to lanceolate, short-stalked leaves up to a little over ½ inch long and with usually rolled-under margins. The tiny pale lilac-colored blooms are in narrow, cylindrical clusters.

Highly variable **T. pulegioides** has a wide distribution in Europe including the British Isles. The names *T. chamaedrys, T. effusus, T. glaber, T. montanus,* and *T. pulchellus* have been applied to some of its variants, but are no longer tenable. Characteristically, *T. pulegioides* is a spreading subshrub from a few inches to 1 foot tall, with stems with four sides, two opposite ones of which are hairy and the others hairless, or with hairs only along the angles. The leaves are lanceolate, elliptic, or ovate, stalked, and commonly about ⅓ inch long. The usually lilac-mauve, but sometimes white or red, tiny blooms are in cylindrical, generally interrupted clusters ⅓ inch wide. The blooms of *T. p. alba* are white, those of *T. p. coccineus* and *T. p. kermesinus* are red.

Showy bracts associated with the flower clusters are a feature of one of the most ornamental thymes, **T. cephalotus,** native to Portugal, a freely-branched bush up to 7 inches in height. It has upright, hairy stems, and clustered, linear to linear-oblanceolate, stalkless leaves slightly over ½ inch long or shorter. They have turned-under, hair-fringed margins and hairless upper sides and may or may not be minutely-hairy beneath. The compact flower clusters, ¾ inch to 1¼ inches long by ½ inch wide, are of pale violet blooms somewhat over ½ inch long and enhanced by showy, conspicuously veined, purple-violet, toothless bracts, hairy on their undersides and along their edges. Another kind with showy ornamental floral bracts is **T. membranaceus,** a bushlet rarely over 8 inches tall. This has twiggy, wiry, minutely-hairy, erect shoots and stiff, grayish-green, hairy, linear to lanceolate leaves with rolled-under margins. They are a little under to a little over ½ inch long. The ½-inch-long white flowers, in egg-shaped, terminal clusters, are about ¾ inch in length and decorated with showy greenish-white or pinkish, conspicuously veined, toothless, ovate bracts that are finely-hairy on their undersides. This is a native of Spain.

Erect, bushy, and from 6 inches to 1 foot tall, **T. broussonetii,** of Morocco, has four-angled, hairy stems, and short-stalked, elliptic to narrowly-ovate leaves that are smooth except for a few hairs near the bases of their not-turned-under margins. The rounded flower clusters, up to 1½ inches long by one-half as wide, are composed of reddish, ¾-inch-long blooms associated with conspicuous, broadly-ovate, toothless, prominently veined, purplish-red bracts, up to a little over ½ inch long, fringed with hairs.

Very distinct **T. carnosus,** a native of Portugal, in gardens is not infrequently misnamed *T. nitidus.* An altogether charming, tight shrublet, stiffly erect and up to 9 inches tall, it has crowded, upright, almost parallel, minutely-hairy stems, and thick, narrowly-elliptic, slightly hairy leaves, under ⅕ inch long, that have strongly rolled-under margins and are clustered in obviously separated tiers. The ¼-inch-long, pale lilac to pink or white blooms are in rounded clusters about ⅓ inch wide.

Caraway-scented herba barona is **T. herba-barona.** A native of Corsica and Sicily, it is an upright to procumbent subshrub up to 6 inches tall. Usually minutely-hairy, but sometimes smooth, its stems bear short-stalked, ovate to lanceolate, pointed leaves, about ⅓ inch long, that are hairless or minutely-hairy and have their lower margins hair-fringed. The interrupted, loose, spherical or oblongish clusters of ¼-inch-long, deep pink flowers are not quite ½ inch in length.

Widespread in the wild from the Balkan Peninsula to southern Russia and the Caucasus, variable **T. pannonicus** (syn. *T. marschallianus*) forms from a woody base rather spreading clumps of hairy, erect stems up to 8 inches tall. Its lanceolate, short-stalked or stalkless leaves, ½ to ¾ inch long, are without hairs, except toward their bases along the edges. The cy-

lindrical, usually interrupted heads of pink flowers, each ¼ inch long, are about ½ inch in diameter. Remarkable because of its very broad, ovate leaves up to ¾ inch in length and short-stalked, **T. nummularius,** an indigene of Asia Minor and the Caucasus, is bushy and has erect, four-angled stems up to 6 inches or occasionally 1 foot tall. They are hairy on two of their four sides. The ⅓-inch-long, lilac-pink flowers are in rounded heads up to 1 inch wide.

Mother of thyme (**T. praecox-arcticus** syns. *T. britannicus, T. drucei*), native to western Europe including the British Isles,

Thymus praecox-arcticus

is a low, creeping, mat-forming species quite frequently misnamed *T. serpyllum.* From true *T. serpyllum,* a Scandinavian species perhaps not in cultivation, it differs in having many more chromosomes and, more obviously, in its stems just below the flower clusters being hairy on only two opposite sides instead of evenly all around. Mother of thyme has long, slender, prostrate stems from which arise, to heights of 1 inch to 3 inches, the four-angled flowering shoots. Its elliptic to obovate leaves, hairless or nearly hairless except along their edges, are about ⅓ inch long. The small white to crimson flowers are in rounded clusters ½ to ¾ inch across. Among garden selections are *T. p. a. albus,* with white flowers; *T. p. a. coccineus,* with crimson blooms; and *T. p. a. splendens,* with red ones.

Other mat-forming thymes that have been confused with *T. praecox* varieties are **T. pseudolanuginosus** and **T. lanuginosus.** The first and the more common is in gardens frequently misnamed *T. serpyllum lanuginosus* and *T. lanuginosus.* From *T. lanuginosus* proper, a native of northern France and, except for its hairiness, similar to *T. serpyllum, T. pseudolanuginosus* differs in its stems being hairy on only two sides instead of evenly all around. Both *T. lanuginosus* and *T. pseudolanuginosus* have elliptic leaves densely-hairy on both sides. The origin of *T. pseudolanuginosus* is unknown. Its light pink flowers, not in headlike clusters, come from the leaf axils.

Thymus hirsutus

A Balkan Peninsula native cultivated as *T. lanicaulis* is perhaps more properly named **T. longidens lanicaulis.** Mat-forming, from slender, creeping stems, it develops densely-hairy, erect shoots 3 to 5 inches tall. Its narrow-elliptic leaves are short-stalked and about ½ inch long. Except sometimes for the mid-veins on their undersides and for the bases of their edges, they are hairless. Under ½ inch in diameter, the half-round flower clusters are of very tiny pink blooms. Another variable matting kind from the Balkans, also from the Crimea, is **T. hirsutus.** Not exceeding 3 inches in height, it has erect, hairy flower stems, and stalkless, linear, hairy leaves, under ½ inch in length, with rolled-under, hair-fringed margins. Up to a little over ½ inch across, the flower clusters are of tiny lilac-colored blooms. Closely similar **T. boissieri** differs in its leaves having hairs only along their edges.

Mat-forming **T. caespititius** (syns. *T. azoricus*, *T. micans*, *T. serpyllum micans*) is a native of the Iberian Peninsula, the Azores, and Madeira. It has slender, prostrate, leafy stems, and hairy branches 1 inch to 2½ inches tall. The linear to oblanceolate leaves, about ⅓ inch long, are hairless except along their margins. The loose, few-flowered clusters of pale lilac blooms are about ½ inch wide. Another kind with prostrate stems, **T. pallasianus** (syn. *T. odoratissimus*) is common in cultivation. Its flower stems, up to 4 inches tall, are hairy and its stalkless leaves, linear to lanceolate, are up to ½ inch in length. The tiny reddish-purple flowers are in hemispherical clusters about ½ inch in diameter. This is native to southern Russia.

Garden and Landscape Uses. Thymes are admirable for herb gardens, rock gardens, and dry walls, and the creeping ones are also excellent for chinks and crevices between paving and for forming lawnlike carpets through which such small bulb plants as scillas, grape-hyacinths, and crocuses can push their way without leaving, after they die down, ugly, unclothed spaces. The bushy thymes are not as hardy as gardeners in the north might wish. In cold climates it is necessary, or at least prudent, to winter stock plants in cool greenhouses or well-protected cold frames.

A path of random paving stones through a carpet of *Thymus praecox-arcticus*

Thymus praecox-arcticus in chinks between flagstones

The creeping, matting thymes are for the most part much hardier and rarely need any special protection. They are more likely to be harmed by excess wetness resulting from poor soil drainage than from cold, although some, notably the white-flowered varieties, seem less tolerant of low temperatures than others. All need full sun and warm dryish conditions. They are impatient of dankness. Porous soil lean in nutrients is best to their liking. Too rich a diet spells disaster or at least results in unseemly vigor that encourages susceptibility to disease and winter-killing.

Cultivation. Directions for growing culinary thymes are given under Thymus. Of the ornamentals, the more vigorous are among the easiest of plants to manage, but some of the choice minatures, such as *T. carnosus*, *T. herba-barona,* and *T. membranaceus*, do best when afforded the protection of an alpine greenhouse or a cold frame. They are very easily propagated by cuttings, and many kinds by division. Seeds grow readily, but those of horticultural varieties are not likely to give progeny identical to the parent plants, and because thymes hybridize freely, seeds obtained from specimens growing near other kinds often prove to be of mixed parentage.

THYSANOLAENA (Thysano-laèna). The only species of this perennial, bamboo-like, leafy grass is widely spread as a native through the Indo-Malaysian region. It belongs in the grass family GRAMINEAE and was named, in allusion to the hairs on the bracts from the axils of which the fertile

A lawnlike carpet of *Thymus praecox-arcticus albus* in a rock garden

flowers spring, from the Greek *thysanos*, a tassel, and *laina*, cloak.

Forming clumps of erect, solid stems up to 12 feet in height and woody in their lower parts, **Thysanolaena maxima** has broad, flat, leathery, hairless, narrowly- to oblong-lanceolate leaf blades up to 2 feet long or longer and sometimes exceeding 2½ inches in width. Its much-branched, loose to more or less compact, light green, yellowish, or pale brown flower panicles, up to 2 feet or more in length by about one-half as broad, in late summer are decidedly decorative. They have numerous small, two- or three-flowered spikelets, without awns (bristles). When mature, the spikelets drop intact. Only the second flower of each spikelet is fertile. In Asia the flower panicles are used for making brooms.

Garden and Landscape Uses and Cultivation. This grass is not hardy in the north, but in regions where little or no frost occurs it is a useful ornamental and is quite attractive as a screen or fence. It thrives in sun in any ordinary soil and is increased by division and by seed.

THYSANOTUS (Thysan-òtus). In Australia often called fringed-lilies, the approximately twenty-two species of *Thysanotus* are restricted in the wild to that continent, except for one that occurs in the Philippine Islands and southern China. The group belongs to the lily family LILIACEAE. Derived from the Greek *thysanotos*, fringed, the name alludes to a characteristic of the margins of the three inner perianth segments.

These are perennials, not hardy in the north. Some kinds have tuberous roots. The leaves are basal and grasslike, the stems erect or twining. Usually in umbels, the flowers have six separate perianth parts or petals. The outer three are narrower than the inner three. The latter are conspicuously fringed and become more or less spirally twisted when they fade. There are six, more rarely three, stamens, and an undivided slender style. The fruits are spherical capsules.

Without tubers and with short leaves that soon wither, **T. dichotomus** has intricately-branched, slender stems, 1 foot to 2 feet tall, forking from their lower parts. The attractive purple flowers come in summer. They are in umbels of one to four at the ends of the branches or branchlets and are about ½ inch long.

Garden Uses and Cultivation. The species described is grown in California and elsewhere where climates are similarly salubrious. It is a pleasant plant for rock gardens and the fronts of flower borders and succeeds in well-drained, fertile, sandy soil. Propagation is by division and by seed.

TI PLANT is *Cordyline terminalis*.

TIARELLA (Tiar-èlla)—Foam Flower, False-Mitrewort, Sugar Scoop. About half a dozen species, all North American, except one native of the Orient, constitute *Tiarella*, of the saxifrage family SAXIFRAGACEAE. The name, a Latinized diminutive of the Greek *tiara*, a kind of headdress, alludes to the shape of the fruits.

Tiarellas are inhabitants of damp woodlands and stream banks. They are herbaceous perennials, probably mostly hardy, although not all have been widely tested, but some may not survive in climate markedly dissimilar to those of their native ranges. Rhizome-forming, tiarellas have mostly basal foliage. Their long-stalked leaves are of three leaflets, or more commonly are undivided and palmately- (in handlike fashion) lobed. The flowers are small, in panicles or racemes, on stems that bear one to few small leaves. The blooms have five green, petal-like, sepals, usually the same number of petals, although these may be absent, ten long protruded stamens, and two carpels with beaklike styles. The fruits are few-seeded, paired capsules or follicles, with one of each pair usually smaller than the other.

Foam flower (**T. cordifolia**) is a beautiful, elegant native of cool, rich woodlands

Tiarella cordifolia

from Nova Scotia to Ontario, Michigan, and Alabama. It produces stolons (long, slender, aboveground, rooting runners) freely, by which the plants spread. Its basal leaves, very much like those of the familiar piggy-back plant (*Tolmiea menziesii*), are broad-ovate to nearly round, shallowly three- to five-lobed, round-toothed, and sparingly hairy. They grow in tufts or clusters and are up to 4 inches wide. They may be marbled with bronzy-red. The slender flower stalks, up to 1 foot tall and glandular-short-hairy, have a loose, branchless feathery raceme of white flowers, about ¼ inch across, that in masses give the cloud-like, foamy effect responsible for the common name. The oblong petals are longer than the petal-like sepals. Variants with

maroon as well as salmon-pink to wine-red flowers are known.

As lovely as the last, which it much resembles, but differing in not having stolons and in generally being more compact, **T. wherryi** is a native of the southern Ap-

Tiarella wherryi

palachian Mountains. Its sharply-three-lobed, ovate to heart-shaped leaves, up to 3½ inches wide, are blotched near their bases and turn red in fall. The starry, ¼-inch-wide, white to delicate pink blooms are in often dense, branchless racemes carried to heights of 6 inches to a little over twice that height.

Its foliage much like that of the foam flower, **T. unifoliata**, sometimes called sugar scoop, differs from that eastern species in its flowers, on stems up to 2 feet tall, being in panicles and in having threadlike, inconspicuous petals, and stamens of two markedly different lengths. The leaves have hairy stalks, and lobes that vary considerably in depth. This is indigenous from Montana to Alaska and California. The slight variant (its leafstalks are hairless, except at their tips, instead of hairy throughout) previously segregated as *T. californica* is included in *T. unifoliata*.

Leaves divided palmately (in hand-fashion) into three lobed and toothed leaflets are characteristic of **T. laciniata** and very similar **T. trifoliata**. The former is native to Vancouver, its offshore islands, and Washington, the other ranges from the Rocky Mountains to Alaska, the Aleutian Islands, and Oregon. They differ chiefly in the leaves of *T. trifoliata* being up to 4 inches wide and having leaflets cleft to no more than one-half their length. The slender-stalked, basal leaves of *T. laciniata* are somewhat hairy and generally glandular. They are up to 2½ inches wide. Their lateral leaflets are deeply-cleft into two unequal, toothed lobes, their center leaflet less deeply and symmetrically into three toothed segments. The flower stems of both are glandular-hairy and up to 1 foot tall or a little taller. The white flowers, in narrow panicles, have inconspicuous petals.

The only Oriental species, *T. polyphylla* is native to Japan, China, and the Himalayas. It has broadly-ovate, three-lobed, toothed, hairy-stalked leaves up to 2¾ inches wide and flower stems, 9 inches to 2 feet tall, with minute, white to reddish blooms in branchless racemes that have inconspicuous threadlike petals, or sometimes none.

Garden and Landscape Uses and Cultivation. For woodland gardens and other shaded places where moist soil is available, tiarellas are admirable and easily grown. One of the most beautiful is the foam flower. All kinds revel in earth with a goodly organic content. Once established they need little care and do not become weedy. Like good neighbors, they respect the territory of others. Seed sown in moist, peaty soil is an easy means of propagation, but division is so simple that it is the more usual method. Spring and early fall are the best seasons to attend to this.

TIBOUCHINA (Tibouchì-na)—Glory Bush. Although many are highly decorative, few of the approximately 350 species of *Tibouchina*, a tropical American genus of the melastoma family MELASTOMATACEAE, are cultivated. The name is an adaptation of a native South American one.

Small trees, shrubs, subshrubs, and a few herbaceous perennials constitute *Tibouchina*. They have opposite, undivided, elliptic, ovate or oblong, stalked leaves with three to nine prominent longitudinal veins. The flowers, solitary or in loose-branched clusters at the shoot ends, are often large and showy. They have five or rarely four sepals and petals and usually ten stamens. The fruits are capsules containing seeds that look like tiny spiraled shells.

The commonest kind in cultivation (*T. urvilleana*) has been misidentified since at least the beginning of the twentieth century as *T. semidecandra* and has also been known as *Lasiandra macrantha* and *Pleroma macrantha*. The name *T. semidecandra* is properly that of another species, apparently not cultivated. Native to Brazil, *T. urvilleana* is naturalized in Costa Rica and the Hawaiian Islands. A hairy shrub, 10 to 20 feet in height, of rather straggly habit and with brittle, four-angled stems, it has ovate to oblong-ovate, velvety-hairy leaves up to 6 inches long and with three to seven longitudinal veins. Its gorgeous, rich royal-purple flowers about 3 inches in diameter and solitary or three together, are held in a vertical plane like the blooms of pansies. Each has five large rounded petals, a narrow, pubescent calyx, and two bracts just beneath the flower. The curiously curved anthers and the stalks to which they are attached suggest the legs of a large spider, for which reason this plant is sometimes called Brazilian spider

Tibouchina urvilleana

flower. The rose-red flower buds contrast pleasingly with the expanded blooms. A sort that has been cultivated as *T. semidecandra floribunda* is *T. organensis,* a native of the Organ Mountains of Brazil. From *T. urvilleana* this differs in having flowers 4 inches or more in diameter, each with four floral bracts.

Other sorts, mostly natives of Brazil, include these: *T. bicolor,* of Bolivia, is a shrub with velvety-hairy shoots and hairy, five-veined oblong-lanceolate leaves 1½ to 3 inches long. Its 1½-inch-wide flowers have red and orange petals. *T. elegans,* up to 6 feet tall, has three-veined, stiffish leaves and purple flowers 2 inches or slightly more in diameter. *T. fothergillae* attains a height of 6 to 10 feet and has leaves with five main veins, and violet-colored flowers 2 inches or slightly more in diameter. *T. grandifolia* is a shrub up to 10 feet tall with bluntly-four-angled stems and oblong-ovate leaves 5 to 9 inches long, densely-hairy on their undersides. The 1-inch-wide, violet-colored flowers are in panicles up to 1½ feet long. *T. granulosa* is a tree up to 40 feet tall with four-winged branchlets, sparsely-hairy, firm leaves, and many-flowered clusters of rose-purple to purple-violet flowers, each about 2 inches across. *T. multiflora* has broader leaves and smaller blooms than any other kind listed here. Up to 6 feet tall, it has flower clusters with many violet-purple blooms, each about ¾ inch in width. *T. mutabilis* is a handsome tree, up to 20 feet tall, with stiff, five-veined leaves and many flowers about 3 inches in diameter that are at first white, but soon change to rosy-lavender and finally red-

dish-violet. *T. pilosa* in general appearance closely resembles *T. fothergillae* and may hybridize with it. It is a native of coastal rain forests. *T. regnellii* has leaves with five main veins and purple-violet flowers 3 inches or somewhat less in diameter.

Tibouchina granulosa in Brazil

Tibouchina granulosa (flowers)

Garden and Landscape Uses and Cultivation. In warm, essentially frost-free climates, tibouchinas can be grown permanently outdoors. Where cold winters prevail, they may be set outside during the summer and be housed indoors from fall to late spring. When this is done they should be kept in their pots or tubs, although these may be buried to their rims in the soil if the effect of plants growing in place is desired. When used in this way they bear a succession of handsome blooms over a long summer season. Tibouchinas thrive in fertile, reasonably moist soils in sun or with a little shade.

As permanent greenhouse plants, T. urvilleana and T. organensis are highly satisfactory in ground beds and in pots, in well-drained, coarse, fertile soil that contains an abundance of organic matter and is always moderately moist, but not constantly saturated. The first is at its best when trained as a vine or semivine up pillars or along wires stretched a few inches beneath the glass of the roof, but it can also be grown as a bush. Naturally more shrubby, T. organensis is not adaptable for training as a vine. It is better for growing as a bushy specimen in a container.

To secure attractive bush specimens in pots, take cuttings in early spring. As soon as they have rooted, pot them individually in 3-inch pots. When well rooted in these, pinch out their tips to cause them to branch; a week or ten days later transfer them to 5-inch pots; and about midsummer repot them in pots 6 or 7 inches in size. The ends of the shoots that develop as a result of the first pinch are pinched after they have developed two or three pairs of leaves. No further pinching is required the first season, the shoots that develop from the second pinch will bloom the following summer.

To train a plant as a vine, give it only one pinch and tie three or four of the resulting branches to a stake or other support. Allow these to grow as leaders, without further pinching their tips, until the height to which the plant is to grow is reached. This may take two, three, or more years. All side shoots that develop should be removed promptly if they are lower on the stems than branches are wanted. Others are allowed to grow, but are shortened at the late winter or early spring pruning.

Pruning plants more than a year old is done each late winter or spring. It consists of cutting out all very weak, crowded, and poorly placed shoots, shortening others, and cutting back all lateral branches to within a few buds of their bases.

Repotting specimens that need this attention is done at pruning time. Those that do not need repotting are top-dressed by removing an inch or two of surface soil and replacing it with new rich earth.

Minimum temperatures in the greenhouse in winter should be 50 to 55°F at night and five to ten degrees higher by day. After pruning, these temperatures may, with advantage, be raised five or ten degrees and not lowered until fall. The plants need a fairly humid atmosphere and light shade from strong sun. Well-rooted specimens respond favorably to weekly or biweekly applications of dilute liquid fertilizer throughout the growing season, but these should be omitted in winter.

Propagation is usually by cuttings made of short, firm shoots trimmed of their lower leaves and sliced cleanly across just beneath a node. These root readily in a mixture of coarse sand and peat moss, in sand alone, or in vermiculite or perlite, in a greenhouse propagating case or under a bell jar where the atmosphere is humid and shade from direct sun is provided. Tibouchinas are easily grown from seed sown in sandy, peaty soil in a temperature of about 70°F. They are remarkably free from diseases and pests. Rarely they are infected by scale insects and mealybugs, more often by red spider mites.

TICK-CLOVER or TICK-TREFOIL. See Desmodium.

TICKSEED. See Bidens, and Coreopsis.

TIDY TIPS is *Layia platyglossa*.

TIGER. The word tiger forms parts of the common names of these plants: tiger flower (*Tigridia*), tiger nuts (*Cyperus esculentus sativus*), and tiger's jaw (*Faucaria tigrina*).

TIGRIDIA (Ti-grídia) — Tiger Flower or Mexican Shell Flower. Among the most spectacular of easy-to-grow summer ornamentals, tiger flowers rate highly. Those commonly cultivated are all forms of very variable *Tigridia pavonia*, indigenous to Mexico and Guatemala. There are a dozen species represented in the wild from Mexico to Chile. The genus belongs in the iris family IRIDACEAE and is named, in allusion to the markings of its flowers, from the Latin *tigris*, a tiger.

Tigridias, like gladioluses, have bulblike parts technically called corms (which are solid rather than composed of concentric or overlapping scales as are true bulbs), but commonly referred to as bulbs. Their stems may or may not branch and are up to 2½ feet in height. There are a few longitudinally corrugated or pleated, narrow basal leaves, fewer, smaller stem ones, and, issuing from the axils of large leafy bracts called spathes, one or more up-facing blooms. These have six petals (more correctly, tepals) not joined, but coming together at their bases to form a large deep saucer or shallow cup from which the upper parts of the petals flare outward. The

three outer petals are largest. At the center of the flower the three stamens form a long protruding tube around the longer style, which is three-armed and has two branches to each arm. Individual blooms are short-lived. The fruits are capsules. Tigridias are deciduous and are dormant in winter.

Tigridia pavonia

The common tiger flower or Mexican shell flower (**T. pavonia**) is from 1½ to 2½ feet in height. It has usually branchless stems, several sword-shaped, long-pointed leaves, and flowers 3 to 6 inches in diameter, each lasting but a day, but developing in succession over a long period of time. They come in a wide variety of colors and handsome markings, in shades of cream, yellow, orange, pink, and red, as well as white. Their three outer petals have large, obovate, horizontally spreading blades. About one-half as long, the three inner petals are fiddle-shaped and have smaller pointed-ovate blades. Varieties are T. p. alba, with red-spotted white flowers; T. p. canariensis, with pale yellow blooms; T. p. carminea, the flowers of which are salmon-red with darker spots; T. p. conchiflora, which has bright yellow flowers; T. p. grandiflora, distinguished by its large multicolored blooms; T. p. lutea-immaculata (syn. T. p. aurea), which has clear yellow blooms; T. p. speciosa, the flowers of

Tigridia pavonia canariensis

which are deep red; and *T. p. watkinsonii*, with blooms of orange-red marked with scarlet, a hybrid between *T. pavonia* and *T. p. conchiflora*.

Garden Uses. Tiger flowers are magnificent for grouping at the fronts of flower borders and for tucking into little bays between shrubs in foundation plantings. Full sun is a must, sharp drainage essential. They need shelter from strong wind and revel in warm locations. Although fleeting, the blooms can be used attractively in arrangements. Tiger flowers are not hardy where their bulbs are frozen.

Cultivation. Tigridias are grown in the same way as gladioluses. Fertile, well-drained, ordinary garden soil, of not too clayey character, is to their liking. The bulbs are planted 5 to 6 inches apart, in the north not until all danger of frost has passed and the ground has warmed somewhat. In sandy soils, a planting depth of 4 or 5 inches is satisfactory for large bulbs; 3 inches is better in heavier earths. Small bulbs are set more shallowly. The quality of the soil beneath the bulbs is of even greater importance than that of the covering layer. Therefore, in preparing for tigridias it is very important to spade deeply and if the soil is of poor quality or at all clayey to improve its porosity by mixing very thoroughly with it generous amounts of grit or coarse sand, and, most important, compost, peat moss, leaf mold, or other suitable organic amendment; a dressing of a complete garden fertilizer is also in order at this time. If the bulbs are set more than 2 or 3 inches deep, it is better not to fill over them to soil level at planting time, but to cover them with only an inch or two of soil then and fill more in after they have sprouted and are well above ground level. Deep planting makes staking less necessary. In dry weather periodic watering is very helpful. Little other care is needed. After the foliage has died naturally, or after frost, the bulbs are dug up, dried off, freed of stems and foliage, and stored over winter in a temperature of about 50°F. Tigridias are propagated by offsets and by seed. Those raised from seed bloom when two or three years old. They flourish in greenhouses in well-drained pots containing porous, fertile soil and are attractive for summer display. Three bulbs planted in a 6-inch container are satisfactory, or they may be grown singly in 4- or 5-inch pots. They are planted in spring and placed in a temperature of about 60°F, watered sparingly at first, more copiously later. When their containers are well filled with roots, regular applications of dilute liquid fertilizer are given. From the time when the shoots show aboveground, the plants must be grown in full sun. After the flowers fade and the foliage dies naturally, water is withheld and the bulbs are stored dry until the following spring, when they are re-potted in fresh soil and started on a new cycle of growth.

TILIA (Tíl-ia)—Linden or Lime Tree, Basswood, Whitewood. Thirty species of deciduous trees with mucilaginous sap and plump, prominent winter buds constitute *Tilia*. They inhabit temperate regions of the northern hemisphere, in the mountains as far south as Mexico and Indochina. The genus is one of about fifty that constitute the linden family TILIACEAE, most members of which, with the notable exception of *Tilia*, are entirely tropical. The name is the classical Latin one.

The best lindens are handsome, fairly fast growers esteemed for shade and ornament. All have alternate, usually heart-shaped leaves, serrated at the margins and with stipules that fall early. They have asymmetrical bases and are in two opposite rows. The fragrant, yellow or yellowish-white flowers, ½ to ¾ inch in diameter, are borne in summer in usually pendulous, long-stalked clusters with the stalk attached for about one-half its length to a conspicuous pale green, strap-shaped bract. Each flower has five sepals, five petals, and often five petaloid staminodes (abortive stamens) that have the appearance of small petals. The presence or absence of staminodes is useful for identification. The numerous stamens have stalks forked at the tips. There is one style. The nutlike fruits, ovoid or globose and about the size of peas, usually contain one, but sometimes two or three seeds. The identification of lindens is complicated by the small differences between certain species, by the considerable variation that exists within some species, and by the occurrence of many natural and man-made hybrids.

Lindens, the name perhaps derived from the Anglo-Saxon *linde*, have been held in high regard for many centuries. Theophrastus, Pliny, and other early writers made frequent reference to them. Their flowers are a prolific source of honey, a product of great importance to the ancients and Western peoples everywhere before the introduction of cane and beet sugars; however, the blooms of some sorts may stupefy or poison bees. The strong, fibrous inner bark or bast, from whence comes our name basswood for lindens, is used for cordage, mats, sandals, and fishing nets. Early inhabitants of America, Europe, and Asia discovered its adaptability for these purposes and put it to good use, as do peoples of Russia and northern China today. The pale wood of lindens, soft, light, strong, straight-grained, and easily worked, is esteemed for utensils, carving, basket-making, venetian blinds, excelsior, food containers, piano keys, and interior trim. From the flowers of lindens an oil used in perfumery is distilled; one almost as useful as olive oil is contained in their seeds.

In the British Isles, lindens are called lime trees. The name of the Father of Modern Botany, Linnaeus (originally Linné), means linden.

Buddhist monks of northeastern Asia centuries ago chose the linden as a substitute symbol for the bo or bodhi tree (*Ficus religiosa*) in their religious symbolism. Because the sacred and tropical *Ficus*, under which the Buddha in India received enlightenment, is not hardy in northern China, the colloquial name of the *Ficus* was transferred to the linden and to this day Chinese Buddhists call it p'u t'i shu or bodhi tree. A somewhat parallel situation exists in northern Europe where palms are not hardy. There on Palm Sunday, branches of yew and willow are used as substitute religious symbols and are called "palms." In Europe, since toward the end of the seventeenth century when they became favorites of the great French landscape gardeners and were planted freely by them, lindens have been extremely popular for avenues and for pruning to formal shapes, as well as free-growing park trees. *Unter den Linden* in Berlin is one of numerous thoroughfares in Europe lined with lindens. In America, too, lindens have been much favored for city streets and as shade trees. As ornamentals, the European species and some hybrids of them are generally superior to the native American kinds and, unusual among hardy trees, sorts native to eastern Asia are less adaptable to American conditions than are natives of Europe and adjacent western Asia. The reverse is true of most genera.

The small-leaved European linden (*T. cordata*), the latest to bloom and one of the neatest in foliage, is perhaps the finest ornamental. A densely-pyramidal tree, up to 100 feet in height, but in cultivation in America considerably smaller, it has a compact, dense crown that gives good shade. Its 2- to 5-inch-long leaves, somewhat lustrous above and slightly glaucous beneath, are hairless except for conspicu-

Tilia cordata

Thunbergia mysorensis

Taxus cuspidata (fruits)

Telekia speciosa

Tellima grandiflora

Tetranema roseum

Tiarella cordifolia

Tibouchina granulosa

Telopea speciosissima

Tibouchina urvilleana

Thunbergia erecta

ous tufts of brown hairs in the vein axils on their undersides. The leaf margins are serrated with short-pointed teeth. The flowers have no staminodes. This, the common species of northern Europe, hardy in New England and adjacent Canada, is a rather slow grower. Variety *T. c. pyramidalis* is narrow-pyramidal. Other varieties are *T. c.* 'Greenspire', which, because of its straight trunk and well-disposed branches, is especially esteemed as a street tree; *T. c.* 'Handsworth', the year old, pale yellow-green twigs of which are decidedly attractive in winter; and *T. c.* 'Swedish Upright', a slow-growing, small, very slender tree. A sixty-year-old specimen at the Arnold Arboretum near Boston, Massachusetts, was recorded as being 35 feet tall and about 12 feet in diameter.

The Crimean linden (**T. euchlora**), another splendid shade tree, is a natural hybrid between *T. cordata* and *T. dasystyla*. Of graceful habit and with somewhat drooping branches, this sort is much planted in Europe. It has glossy, bright green leaves, 2 to 4 inches long, paler beneath than above and margined with long-pointed teeth. Tufts of brown hairs are in the vein axils beneath. The flowers are without staminodes. The Crimean linden grows faster than the small-leaved linden, has a densely-foliaged crown, and attains a height of about 60 feet. It is less hardy than the small-leaved linden, but can be relied upon in southern New England. Variety *T. e.* 'Redmond' is of tight pyramidal form.

The large-leaved linden (**T. platyphyllos**) has the widest natural distribution and is one of the biggest-leaved of European species. Although not the handsomest, for centuries it has been a favorite for planting in Europe and was probably brought to America in Colonial days. Pyramidal or round-topped and up to 120 feet in height, this has sharp-toothed leaves, 2½ to 5 inches long, that are pubescent, usually densely so, beneath and often on the distinctly yellowish upper surfaces. The yellowish-white flowers, usually in threes and without staminodes, are the earliest to open of all lindens. The large-leaved linden is more sensitive to dry conditions than most kinds. Varieties are *T. p. rubra*, with red branchlets; *T. p. laciniata*, with deeply irregularly-lobed leaves; *T. p. fastigiata*, a narrow-pyramidal tree; and *T. p. vitifolia*, with slightly three-lobed leaves.

The white or silver linden (**T. tomentosa**), of Europe and Asia Minor, grows to about 90 feet tall and has a broad, dense, pyramidal crown of very regular outline. Its branches are erect, and its leaves, 2 to 4 inches long, are green above and conspicuously white-pubescent beneath. They have stalks shorter than one-half the length of their blades and are sharp-toothed, double-toothed, or some-

Tilia euchlora

Tilia platyphyllos

times slightly lobed. The young branches are hairy. The flowers, which have staminodes, are reported to be narcotic or poisonous to bees. Hardy in most of New England, this stands high temperatures and drought better than other kinds.

Closely similar to the white or silver linden, Chinese *T. oliveri* differs from that species most noticeably in its young shoots being without hairs. An elegant tree up to 50 feet tall, *T. oliveri* was first introduced to European and American gardens in 1900.

The weeping or pendent silver linden (*T. petiolaris*) is often considered even lovelier than the silver linden because of its pendent branches. Except for this habit, it is very similar to *T. tomentosa*, but the stalks of its leaves are normally longer than one-half the length of the blade and its broad fruits are distinctly five-grooved, whereas those of *T. tomentosa* are egg-shaped, minutely-warty, but not grooved. The flowers of the weeping silver linden have staminodes. The tree attains a height of 80 feet and spreads widely. It has not been reported as being found in the wild, but it is surely a native of southeastern Europe or western Asia. The flowers contain some

substance that is poisonous or at least narcotic to bees, which often are found in large numbers lying stupefied beneath weeping silver lindens. This species is hardy in southern New England.

The American linden (*T. americana*), of the northern states and southern Canada, is large-leaved and has been planted freely as an ornamental. It becomes 120 feet tall and has green young branchlets without hairs. The leaves are broad-ovate, 4 to 6 inches long, and have coarse, long-pointed teeth. Dark green above, they have paler, glossy undersides with, except at their bases, tufts of hairs in the vein axils. In fall they change to yellow before they drop. When growing in cities the foliage of this species is often discolored by infestations of red spider mites. Variety *T. a. dentata* has coarsely-irregular-toothed leaves. Variety *T. a. fastigiata*, narrow-pyramidal, has erect branches. The leaves of *T. a. macrophylla* are 6 to 8 inches long.

Other sorts include these: **T. dasystyla**, of southeastern Europe and western Asia, up to 100 feet in height, has leaves up to 6 inches long with whitish hairs in the leaf axils beneath and bristle-toothed margins. Its flowers are without staminodes. This

is hardy in southern New England. **T. europaea** (syns. *T. intermedia, T. vulgaris*), a hybrid between *T. cordata* and *T. platyphyllos* and hardy in New England, has the disadvantages of producing abundant sucker growths from its base and being very subject to infestation by aphids. Densely-round-headed, up to 120 feet tall, and hardy in New England and southern Canada, this kind has comparatively thin, sharp-toothed leaves, up to 4 inches long, with dull green upper surfaces and bright green lower ones with tufts of hair in the axils of the veins. **T. henryana,** of China, 50 feet tall, has leaves 4 inches long or longer, brownish-hairy on their undersides and with bristly teeth. The flowers have staminodes. This is hardy in southern New England. **T. heterophylla** is closely related to *T. americana*. Attaining a height of 60 feet, it has fine-bristle-toothed leaves, up to 7 inches long, with lustrous upper surfaces and white-hairy lower ones. This is indigenous from Indiana to Florida. **T. japonica,** of Japan and hardy in southern New England, has fine-toothed leaves up to 3 inches long, when young bluish-green and hairy on the veins beneath, but hairless at maturity. Its flowers

Tilia tomentosa

Tilia petiolaris

Tilia oliveri, Hillier's Nursery, Winchester, England

Tilia tomentosa in winter (lowest branches self-layered and rooted into the ground)

Tilia petiolaris (leaves and fruits)

Tilia americana

Tilia americana (leaves and fruits)

Tilia europaea

have staminodes. **T. mandshurica,** of northeastern Asia, is up to 60 feet in height. Hardy in New England, it has leaves up to 6 inches long, devoid of tufts of hairs in the vein axils, but white-hairy beneath. Their margins have long-pointed, coarse teeth. The flowers have staminodes. **T. moltkei** is a hybrid between *T. americana* and *T. petiolaris*. Its leaves, gray-hairy beneath and up to 7 inches in length, are similar to those of *T. americana*. The tree grows vigorously and has somewhat drooping branches. Its flowers have staminodes. **T. mongolica,** of China and Mongolia, 30 to 35 feet tall, has nearly circular to ovate, often three-lobed, coarsely-toothed, slightly glaucous leaves up to nearly 3 inches long. Their undersides, except sometimes for tufts in the vein axils, are hairless. The flowers have staminodes. This is hardy in New England. **T. neglecta,** native from eastern Canada to Ohio, Georgia, and Texas, occasionally exceeds 100 feet in height. It has red twigs and leaves up to 8 inches long, lustrous and smooth above and hairy beneath, which have forward-pointing teeth. Its flowers have staminodes.

Garden and Landscape Uses. Lindens are handsome ornamentals and excellent for shade. They are among the most satisfactory of street trees if they receive reasonable attention in the matter of spraying for pest control. They stand repeated pruning better than most trees and so are well adapted for locations where space is restricted. They are excellent for pleaching. An attractive feature is the honey fragrance of their flowers, which perfumes the air in early and high summer. Most lindens make moderately fast growth, but they are not trees for dry climates or dry locations.

Cultivation. Lindens thrive in any fertile, well-drained soil that is not excessively dry. They transplant with ease and stand pruning well. They are propagated by seeds, which should be sown as soon as they are ripe or stratified then and sown in spring. If they are stored dry until

Tilia dasystyla, Arnold Arboretum, Jamaica Plain, Massachusetts

Tilia moltkei, Royal Botanic Gardens, Kew, England

Tilia cordata sheared formally, Long Island, New York

spring, they very likely will take two years to germinate. Lindens may also be increased by layering, grafting, and budding. Layering is best accomplished by the "mound" method. A young tree is cut off close to the ground and sandy soil is heaped in a mound among and around the shoots that spring from the stump. This is kept moist and after several months, when

the shoots have rooted into it, they are removed and planted in nursery rows as young individual trees. Grafted and budded specimens of lindens often take a long time before they develop distinct central leading shoots and frequently develop into poorly shaped trees.

Diseases and Pests. The chief diseases are leaf blight, leaf spots, canker, powdery

Tilias as street trees in Belgium, pruned severely back every two or three years

Tilias in Belgium, trained as espaliers

mildew, and sometimes anthracnose. Pests include aphids, red spider mites, borers, various beetles and other leaf chewing insects, lacebugs, caterpillars, and leaf miners.

TILIACEAE — Linden Family. The trees, shrubs, and comparatively few herbaceous species that compose this family of fifty genera of dicotyledons inhabit tropical, subtropical, and temperate regions throughout the world, with the greatest concentrations of kinds in southeastern Asia and Brazil. They have alternate or rarely opposite, frequently asymmetrical, undivided, often lobed or toothed leaves. The flowers, in terminal or axillary clusters or panicles, are usually bisexual, seldom unisexual, with the sexes on different plants. They have a calyx with five or much less often three or four sepals or lobes, five or fewer petals or none, numerous stamens sometimes united at their bases into five or ten bundles and sometimes represented by staminodes (nonfunctioning stamens), and one style with a headlike or lobed stigma. The fruits are capsules, drupes, or berries or are nutlike.

Genera cultivated include *Clappertonia, Corchoropsis, Corchorus, Entelea, Grewia, Luehea, Sparmannia,* and *Tilia.*

TILLAGE. Tillage embraces all operations designed to loosen the soil and provide opportunity to incorporate organic materials and other additives in preparation for seed sowing and planting. The chief tools and implements employed are spades, spading forks, rotary tillers, plows, and harrows. See Soils and Their Management.

TILLANDSIA (Till-ándsia) — Spanish-Moss or Graybeard, Ball-Moss or Bunch-Moss. By different authorities estimated to contain from somewhat less than 400 to 500 species, *Tillandsia,* the largest genus of the pineapple family BROMELIACEAE, is rich in ornamentals. Endemic to tropical, subtropical, and warm-temperate parts of the Americas, including the West Indies, it bears a name that commemorates the Swedish botanist and professor of medicine Elias Til-Landz, who died in 1693. One of the best-known species, Spanish-moss, is collected from the wild and used as packing material and, processed, as a horsehair-like material for stuffing upholstery.

Tillandsias are nonhardy, evergreen herbaceous perennials of great diversity of sizes and forms. A very few are ground-dwellers. The vast majority perch on trees or shrubs, some even on cactuses, as epiphytes, or cling to cliffs, rocks, and sometimes such artificial habitats as telephone wires. Most have rather scanty root systems and a few are rootless. Some have creeping stolons, some evident stems, and some are stemless or essentially so. Usually chiefly basal, often in rosettes and commonly more or less besprinkled with tiny scales, the leaves are often much widened at their bases. The flowers, usually borne singly in the axils of the bracts of spikes, panicles, or heads, less often solitary, have three each sepals and petals, which in the bud stage are twisted and rolled, six stamens, and a slender style. The fruits are capsules containing hairy seeds or seeds with a hairy tail. From closely related *Vriesia* the sorts of *Tillandsia* are distinguishable by the absence of scales (ligules) on the insides of the bases of the petals. The descriptions that follow are those of a representative selection of kinds. Others are grown by specialists.

Spanish-moss or Graybeard (*T. usneoides*), native from Florida to Texas and Argentina, is an atypical species, without roots, that does not form rosettes. Its strands, often many feet in length, of hoary-gray, very slender stems and foliage hang from and festoon trees and sometimes shrubs, producing a beautiful, but somewhat weird effect. The scattered, narrow-linear leaves are 1 inch to 3 inches long. Small and without display value, the yellowish flowers are solitary in the leaf axils.

Kinds with leaves not in rosettes, but distributed along definite stems, include

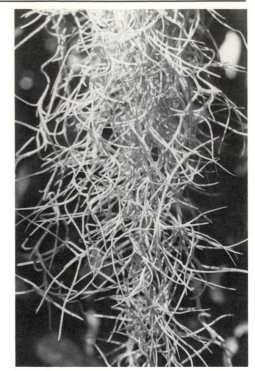

Tillandsia usneoides

Tillandsia usneoides draping live oaks (*Quercus virginiana*)

Swamp-cypress (*Taxodium*) heavily draped with *Tillandsia usneoides*

these: **T. albida,** of Mexico, has stems up to 1 foot long with rigid, spreading, silvery-white-scurfy leaves 4 to 5½ inches long. Each stem terminates in a long, zigzagged flowering stalk with bright red bracts and greenish-white flowers. **T. andreana,** of Colombia and Venezuela, forms dense clumps of erect stems about 6 inches long, thickly clothed with erect, slender, triangular leaves 1 inch to 1½ inches long and, except for the upper ones which are brick-red, gray-green. The solitary, stalkless flowers have scarlet petals. **T. araujei,** of Brazil, has spreading, branching stems up to 5 feet long with spiraled along most of their lengths slender, pointed green leaves 1 inch to 1½ inches long. In short terminal spikes of few, the flowers have pink and white petals. **T. crocata,** of Brazil, Bolivia, Uruguay, and Argentina, has slender, branched or branchless stems, up to 1 foot long, furnished with two rows of spreading or recurved, pointed-linear, extremely slender leaves, 3 to 6 inches long or longer. The slender, branchless flowering stalk ends in a lanceolate to elliptic spike, up to 1½ inches long, with overlapping bracts and one to six flowers with saffron-yellow to orange petals. **T. duratii** (syn. *T. decomposita*) is a rootless, densely-silvery-scaled Brazilian with twisted stems and curled leaves, from 6 inches to nearly 1 foot long, that provide anchorage by winding around suitable supports. Flowering stalks from 6 inches to 2 feet long terminate the stems and end in a spike or narrow panicle of fragrant blooms with lavender petals. **T. gilliesii,** of Peru, Argentina, and Bolivia, forms clumps of branchless or few-branched stems, up to about 9 inches long, with two rows of densely-gray-scaly, deeply-channeled, recurved leaves, ¾ inch to 2 inches or sometimes more in length and with overlapping bases. The one to three yellow-petaled flowers are borne in a short, silvery-bracted spike atop a slender stalk 3 to 5 inches long. **T. recurvata,** because it forms compact, ball-like masses of stems and foliage, is called ball-moss and bunch-

Tillandsia recurvata on a small tree in Baja California

A closer view of *Tillandsia recurvata* on a tree in Baja California

Tillandsia recurvata on a cactus in Baja California

Tillandsia recurvata on telephone wires, Tegucigalpa, Honduras

moss. It ranges from the southern United States to Argentina. It has slender, branched, often entwined stems, and in two ranks, almost threadlike, recurved leaves, ¾ inch to 2 inches long, clothed with gray or reddish scales. Solitary or few

together in little spikes atop stalks 2 to 5 inches long, the flowers have greenish-white or violet petals. **T. schiedeana** ranges from Mexico and the West Indies to northern South America. It has branched or branchless stems and slender, gray leaves up to 1¼ feet long. The branchless, pink flowering stalk, shorter or as long as the leaves, ends in a spike with rose-pink to red bracts and yellow-petaled flowers. **T. tenuifolia** (syn. *T. pulchella*) ranges from the West Indies to Argentina. It forms clumps of usually branched stems, up to 10 inches long, and rigid, narrow-triangular, channeled, gray-green leaves 2 to 4 inches long. The slender, short, pink flowering stalk carries in more than two rows blooms with blue, pink, or white petals. **T. tricholepis,** ranging from Brazil to Argentina, has much the aspect of a moss. It has densely-clustered, sometimes much-branched stems up to 10 inches tall, but usually much lower, clothed with many rows of up-pointing, awl-shaped leaves up to ⅜ inch long. The yellow- or green-petaled flowers are in reddish-bracted spikes atop slender stalks.

Much swollen, bulbous, egg- or spindle-shaped pseudobulbs consisting of a short stem covered by the broad, overlapping bases of leaves, the upper portions of which are much narrower, are characteristic of these tillandsias: **T. balbisiana,** native from Florida to northern South America, has pseudobulbs 4 to 5 inches long, and gray-green, often purple-edged, tapered-linear leaves with recurved-twisted tips. The branchless or pinnately-branched flowering stalk has usually red bracts and violet flowers. **T. bulbosa,** indigenous from Mexico to South America and the West Indies, has usually clusters of stemless rosettes of gray-scaly leaves with wide, often purple-margined bases that overlap to form a prominent pseudobulb. Above their broad bases they are 4 to 6 inches long, contorted, twisted, and tightly rolled. The short, red flowering stalk has one or more spikes with green or red bracts and up to eight flowers with blue or violet petals and protruding stamens. **T. butzii,** of Mexico and Central America, usually has clusters of rosettes with leaves, up to 1¾ feet long, that have much-expanded bases overlapped to form an egg-shaped pseudobulb. Above their bases they are slender, tightly rolled, and haphazardly twisted. They are green or purplish-green spotted with purplish-brown. From 8 inches to about 1 foot tall, the erect flowering stalk has one or more spikes, 1½ to 3½ inches long, of greenish to pink bracts and lilac- or violet-petaled flowers with protruding stamens. **T. caput-medusae,** of Central America, has clustered pseudobulbs from which squirm in all directions narrow, twisted, pointed, gray-scaly, channeled leaves 6 inches to 1 foot in length. The flowering stalk, up to about 6 inches long, has four or fewer short spikes with red bracts and flowers with light blue petals. **T. circinnata**, native from Florida to the West Indies, Mexico, and Colombia, is 4 inches to usually not over 8 inches tall. It has rosettes of rather few gray-scurfy leaves, the broad bases of which form a narrow-egg-shaped pseudobulb from which curve the slender leaf blades. From 2 to 4 inches long, the arching or recurved, pink flowering stalk has pale scales, and blooms with lavender petals. **T. disticha**, of Peru, has a distinct pseudobulb and leaves with wide bases and very slender, almost threadlike blades up to 1 foot long. The flowering stalk bears bracts similar to, but smaller than the lower leaves. At its apex it carries several 1- to 1½-inch-long narrow spikes with overlapping, triangular bracts and yellow-petaled flowers. **T. flexuosa** (syn. *T. aloifolia*), native from Florida to South America, has an ellipsoid pseudobulb and ten to twenty wide-based, narrowly-triangular, gray-green leaves 6 inches to 1½ feet long, often with indistinct silvery cross-bands. The wiry, branchless or few branched, sinuous flowering stalk, up to 3 feet long, has short, distantly spaced spikes with bright red bracts and white, pink, or purple flowers with protruding stamens. **T. paraensis**, of Brazil, has clustered, ovoid pseudobulbs and minutely-scaly, dull green, wide-based, narrow-triangular leaves up to 1¼ feet long. Its magenta-red-petaled flowers are in stalked, branchless, rather loose, narrow spikes, 5 to 10 inches long, clothed with erect, densely-scaly greenish, yellowish, purplish, or red bracts. **T. pruinosa**, wild from Mexico and the West Indies to Brazil, up to 6 inches tall, has elongated pseudobulbs and very slender, contorted leaves frosted with a scurf of gray or reddish scales and about as long as the pseudobulbs. The flowering stalk carries one or more flattened 2- to 3-inch-long spikes with two rows of overlapping, densely-scaly, pink bracts and flowers with violet-based, white petals. **T. selerana**, of Mexico and Guatemala, is densely covered with silvery-gray scales. It has an ovoid pseudobulb, up to 4½ inches long, and pointed, contorted, triangular-linear leaves. The flowering stem has six or fewer flattened, bracted spikes up to 4 inches long and with violet flowers. **T. streptophylla**, of the West Indies, Mexico, and Central America, has a pseudobulb up to about 3 inches thick and many narrow-triangular leaves from 6 inches to a foot long and up to a little over ½ inch wide that grasp suitable supports with their twisted, coiled ends. The bright red flowering stalk has up to twenty erect, 3- to 6-inch-long, pink-bracted branches arranged pinnately and bearing flowers with blue-violet to purple petals.

Sorts with rosettes of foliage and flowers displayed along the two edges of stalked, branchless, much-flattened, elliptic to broad-ovate spikes that have two rows of pinnately-arranged, neatly overlapping bracts and resemble the flower spikes of certain vriesias include these: *T. anceps*, which ranges from Central America to Trinidad and Brazil, has a rosette of many narrow, recurved leaves, 6 inches to 1 foot long, broadened and streaked with reddish-brown at their bases. The short-stalked flower spike, 4 to 5 inches long by up to 2 inches wide, has green or greenish-margined, pink bracts and flowers with blue and white or white petals. **T. cyanea**, of Ecuador, has a rosette of forty to fifty

Tillandsia cyanea

or more semi-erect and recurved leaves, 1 foot to 1¼ feet long by ⅝ inch wide, striped lengthwise on their backs at their bases with brown. The ovate flower spike, its base not lifted above the foliage, has rose-pink to red bracts and up to twenty flowers with spreading, 1-inch-long, violet-blue petals. **T. lampropoda**, of Mexico and Central America, has a narrow rosette of nearly erect leaves, wide at their bases, tapered to long points, and 9 inches to 1¼ feet long. The flowering stalk, clothed with erect, overlapping bracts, is topped by spikes about 6 inches to 1 foot long or longer with yellow, red, or green bracts and yellow-petaled flowers. **T. lindenii**, of Ecuador and Peru, resembles *T. cyanea*, but differs in its 4- to 6-inch-long flower spike having a longer stalk that lifts it above the foliage and in its white-eyed, deep blue flowers being bigger. Its rosette is of spreading-recurved leaves 8 inches to 1¼ feet long by about ½ inch wide. The flowers of *T. l. caeca* lack white centers. A handsome intermediate hybrid between this last and *T. cyanea* is named *T. 'Emilie'*. **T. multicaulis**, of Mexico to Panama, forms a dense rosette of pointed, strap-shaped leaves 9 inches to 1¼ feet long by 1 to 1½ inches wide, with broader bases. Each produces from the leaf axils one to several, short-stalked, elliptic flower spikes 5 to 6 inches long and with closely overlapping bright red bracts. The flowers have blue petals.

Tillandsia lindenii

Tillandsia 'Emilie'

Absence of distinct leafy stems and pseudobulbs, foliage in rosettes, and flowers in various arrangements other than broad, two-edged, elliptic or ovate spikes atop branchless flowering stems are characteristic of these sorts: **T. achyrostachys**, of Mexico, has a rosette of recurved, narrow, light green leaves markedly widened toward their bases and 6 to 10 inches long. The yellowish-green-petaled flowers, with protruding stamens, are in a flat, narrow spike that juts above the foliage and has overlapping rose-pink bracts. **T. andrieuxii** (syn. *T. benthamiana andrieuxii*), of Mexico and Costa Rica, has spiraled, black-based, narrow-triangular, gray-scaly recurved leaves 4 to 6 inches long. The branchless flowering stalk, 3 to 6 inches long, bears a spike 2 to 3 inches long with rose-pink bracts and up to eight violet-petaled flowers. **T. argentea**, of Mexico, Central America, and the West Indies, is a delightful miniature. It forms dense rosettes of many very slender, almost hairlike, pale gray leaves 2 to 3½ inches long. The wiry flowering stalk, 6 inches to 1 foot long, ends in a loose raceme of six or fewer flowers with red or purple petals and protruding stamens. **T. bandensis,** of South America, is a miniature with compact clusters of rosettes of slender, gray-green-scaly leaves, 1 inch to 2 inches long. The slender flowering stalk carries to a height of 2 or 3 inches a spike of four or fewer, blue- or violet-petaled flowers. **T. benthamiana,** of Central America, has often clustered rosettes with many recurved, broad-based, slender, tapering, gray-scaly, channeled leaves 4 to 8 inches long. The short, stout, usually branchless flowering stalk terminates in a 3-inch-long spike with large dusty-pink bracts. The flowers have violet to bright pink or yellowish petals and conspicuously protruding stamens. **T. brachycaulos,** of Mexico and Central America, has a rosette of many recurved, tapering, channeled leaves, 6 to 9 inches long, that at flowering time turn red. The short-branched or apparently branchless flowering stalk terminates in a head of leafy bracts and flowers with blue-violet petals. **T. cacticola,** of Peru, grows on cactuses. It has a rosette of whitish-gray leaves, 1 foot to 1¼ feet long, tapered from 1-inch-wide bases to pointed apexes. The 1- to 1½-foot-long flowering stalk has lavender-pink bracts and fragrant flowers with blue-tipped, ivory-white petals. **T. capitata,** of Mexico, has a rosette of triangular, channeled leaves, 6 inches to 1 foot long, from the center of which sprouts a flowering stalk with a large head with tapered bracts and blue-purple flowers with protruding stamens. In some forms the foliage becomes bright red at flowering time, in others the inner leaves turn greenish-yellow and brown. **T. chaetophylla,** of Mexico, has clustered rosettes of very slender, gray leaves 9 inches to 1 foot long. Approximately as long, the branchless pink flowering stalk, clothed with overlapping bracts that end in slender points, terminates in a flattened spike, 2½ to 3½ inches long, with in two ranks pink bracts and flowers with violet petals. **T. complanata,** of the West Indies, Central America, and South America, is a variable kind with a rosette of leaves 9 inches to 1½ feet long, usually suffused and streaked with purple especially toward their bases and often purple beneath. The several slender, erect, arching, or drooping flowering stalks that sprout from the leaf axils terminate in 1- to 2-inch-long spikes with green or red bracts and flowers with light blue petals. **T. deppeana,** a variable, handsome native from Mexico and the West Indies to Bolivia, Colombia, and Ecuador, has symmetrical rosettes of many soft, green leaves 1 foot to 3 feet long, the outer ones spreading or recurved, the inner ones erect. Furnished with rose-pink to bright red bracts, its erect flowering stalk with many spreading, flattened branches 4 inches to 1 foot long rises to a height of 3 to 6 feet.

The flowers have violet-blue petals. **T. exserta,** of Mexico, forms often rootless rosettes of densely-white-scaly, strongly recurved and coiled, slender, narrow-triangular leaves, up to about 9 inches long, with short, broad bases. The branched or branchless pinkish flowering stalk carries spikes with pink or red bracts and flowers with narrow, violet petals. **T. fasciculata,** the wild-pineapple of Florida, the West Indies, and Central America, is very variable. It has a many-leaved rosette of gray- or bluish-green, narrow, broad-based, scurfy leaves that angle upward and that are 6 inches to 1½ feet long. The erect flowering stalk, up to 3 feet tall, ends in a large, few- to many-branched panicle with whitish, creamy-yellow, green, or red bracts and flowers with violet petals. Several variants have been named as varieties. **T. festucoides,** of Florida, the West Indies, Mexico, and Central America, has clustered rosettes of many very slender-linear, erect, finely-scurfy leaves 9 inches to 1 foot long or somewhat longer. The flowering stalk bears erect bracts with tails resembling the leaves, but smaller. It terminates in a panicle that tops the foliage and has reddish bracts and flowers with blue-violet petals. **T. flabellata,** of Mexico and Central America, has a crowded rosette of green or red, arching, narrow-triangular leaves, 6 inches to 1¼ feet long. From the top of a very short stalk sprout several long, narrow spikes clothed with erect, overlapping, red bracts with, in the axils of the upper ones, flowers with violet petals. **T. geminiflora,** native from Brazil to Argentina, has a rosette of thirty to forty narrow-triangular, erect to recurved leaves thickly covered with gray or pinkish-gray scales and 3 to 7 inches long. The rather short flowering stalk terminates in a short-pyramidal, moderately crowded panicle, 2 to 3 inches long, with purplish-pink or pink bracts and flowers with bright pink to purplish-pink petals. **T. grandis,** of Mexico and Central America, has an imposing water-holding rosette of strap-shaped, often purplish-tinged leaves, 2 to 5 feet long and from 1½ to 6 inches wide. From 8 to 12 feet tall or taller, the candelabrum-branched flowering stalk bears greenish-white-petaled flowers that open only at night and have long-protruding stamens. A smaller, unnamed variant, previously called T. viridiflora, has a branchless or few-branched flowering stalk. **T. imperialis,** of Mexico, has rosettes of pointed-strap-shaped leaves, 1 inch to 2 inches wide and with broader bases. They are 1 foot to 1½ feet long. Atop a short, branchless stalk, the massive, conical, 6- to 8-inch-long flower spike has brilliant red bracts and purple-petaled flowers. **T. ionantha,** a delightful mite from Mexico and Central America, forms tufts of rosettes of densely-silvery-scaled, pointed-linear, channeled leaves, 1½ to 2½ inches long, that at

Tillandsia ionantha

Tillandsia ionantha growing on a slab of tree fern trunk

flowering time turn rosy-red. The very brief flowering stalk is hidden so that the heads of few bright purple flowers nestle at the centers of the rosettes. Variety *T. i. scaposa* differs in having a visible flowering stalk that lifts the blooms above the foliage. **T. ixioides,** of Bolivia, Paraguay, Uruguay, and Argentina, forms clumps of rosettes of erect, pointed, narrow-lanceolate, channeled, densely-white-scaly leaves 3 to 6 inches long. Ten or fewer bright-yellow-petaled flowers are borne in a spike that terminates an about 3-inch-long stalk. **T. juncea** ranges from Florida to northern South America. It has a rosette of many, erect, slender, rushlike, coppery-tinged, olive-green leaves, 1 foot to 1¼ feet long and with silvery-scaled undersides. About as long, the erect flowering stalk, covered with overlapping, slender-pointed bracts, terminates in an ovoid head, 2 to 3 inches long, with bright red bracts and purple-petaled flowers. *T. karwinskyana*, of Mexico, has clustered rosettes of linear, silvery-scaly, broad-based leaves 6 inches to 1 foot long. Topping the foliage, the branchless, wiry, flowering stalk bears a slender spike, 3 to 4 inches in length, with in two ranks flowers with lilac-colored petals. *T. lieboldiana*, of Mexico and Central America, has a rosette of erect to slightly arching, pointed, strap-shaped leaves 6 inches to 1½ feet long and, above their broader, sometimes dark bases, about 1 inch wide. They are often spotted or tinged purple. In a long, erect, red-bracted panicle carried well above the foliage, the purple-petaled flowers are in short, somewhat distantly spaced spikes. *T. lorentziana*, of South America, has rosettes of recurved, tapered, densely-silvery-scaled, channeled leaves 6 inches to 1 foot long by up to ¾ inch wide at their bases. The white flowers, usually striped with blue or purple, are in open, long-stalked, pink-bracted panicles with branches 1½ to 3½ inches long. *T. magnusiana*, of Mexico and Central America, has much the aspect of *T. plumosa*. Its silvery-scaled, 4- to 5-inch-long leaves form spherical rosettes. The violet-petaled flowers are in pairs on a stalk so short that they nestle close to the center of the rosette. *T. monodelpha*, of Central America, northern South America, and Trinidad, has a rosette of linear-triangular, mostly recurved leaves, 5 inches to 1 foot long, with light purple to maroon undersides. The slender, erect, branchless flowering stalk terminates in a spike with two ranks of rather distantly spaced green and red bracts from the axils of which sprout fragrant, white- or yellow-petaled flowers. *T. plumosa*, of Mexico and Central America, has a dense spherical rosette of numerous very slender, almost threadlike leaves, 2 to 3½ inches long and densely clothed with silvery-gray, hairlike scales. The violet flowers, in stalked or nearly stalkless heads, are scarcely higher than the foliage. *T. polystachya*, native to Florida and the West Indies and from Mexico to Brazil and Bolivia, is slate-gray to dark gray-green. It has narrow, recurved, channeled, sometimes red-tinged, scaly leaves that taper to long points. The leafy flowering stalk has usually few rigid, erect, slender, flattened branches, with bright red or yellow-tinged, overlapping bracts, and flowers with violet petals. *T. prodigiosa*, of Mexico and Guatemala, has rosettes of broad, soft, purplish-spotted, green or grayish-green leaves 1½ to 2 feet long. Its pendulous flowering stalk, 3 to 6 feet long, has numerous flat spikes, 3 to 4 inches long, with showy yellow to bright red bracts and flowers with violet petals. *T. punctulata*, native from Mexico to Panama, has stolons and rosettes of thirty to forty leaves

6 inches to 1 foot long. From broad, dark chocolate-brown bases, they narrow quickly to spreading, recurved, tapering blades. The bright-red-bracted flowering stalk, up to 1 foot long or longer, terminates in one to three conical spikes of flowers with white-tipped, black-purple petals. *T. stricta* is a variable species of wide distribution in South America and Trinidad. Most typically it has rosettes of slender, more or less recurved, silvery-scaled leaves 3 to 6 inches long. The short, erect or arching flowering stalk has red bracts and several spikes of flowers with petals at first violet-blue, later becoming deep red. *T. tricolor*, of Mexico and Central America, has branching rhizomes and crowded tufts of rosettes of many narrow, purple-based, dark green, scaly leaves, 9 inches to 1 foot long and tapered from a ½-inch-wide base to a sharp point. A little longer than the leaves, the red flowering stalks terminate in a flat, 3-inch-long spike of green, yellow, and bright red bracts. The flowers are violet. Variety *T. t. melanocrater* has smaller rosettes of leaves with black bases and silvery dots on their undersides. The flowering stalk is branched and scarcely, if at all, longer than the leaves. *T. unco* (syn. *T. argentina*), of Argentina, is a little species with clustered rosettes of narrow, dark gray leaves, 1 inch to 2½ inches long, in a branchless yellow-bracted spike as long or scarcely longer than the foliage. The flowers have rose-pink petals. *T. utriculata*, of Florida, the West Indies, and northeastern South America, has a rosette of narrow, recurved leaves, about 2 feet long, that taper from a short, broad base to a slender, pointed apex. Erect and up to 6 feet long, the loose-branched panicle of flowers has red-margined, green bracts and erect, greenish-white flowers. This rarely produces offsets. *T. valenzuelana*, of Florida to northern South America, has a water-holding rosette of many narrow-triangular, silvery-scaled leaves 8 inches to 1½ feet long. The slender, pinnately-branched or branchless, arching or pendent flowering stalk, up to 2 feet long, has pink to red bracts and flowers with lilac or violet petals. *T. violacea*, of Mexico, has a rosette of pointed-triangular leaves 1 foot to 2 feet long and, at their bases, 1½ to 2 inches wide. The pendulous flowering stalk bears large bracts similar to, but smaller than the rosette leaves. It terminates in a crowded panicle, up to 1½ feet long, of 1½- to 2½-inch-long spikes with pink or reddish-tipped overlapping bracts and flowers with violet petals.

Garden and Landscape Uses. Tillandsias greatly interest collectors of bromeliads and a great many are sufficiently decorative to deserve the attention of others. In the humid tropics and subtropics, and some species in drier, warm regions, epiphytic kinds can be established on

rough-barked trees, including palms, and in the crotches of trees, whereas ground-dwellers can be naturalized in well-drained beds of coarse rooting mixes of generous organic content. They may also be accommodated in pots or other containers, and some sorts prosper and can be displayed to advantage attached to slabs of tree fern trunk or cork bark.

In greenhouses and other favorable indoor environments, such as window gardens and terrariums, many sorts behave well in containers or attached to tree fern or cork bark. They are also suitable for planting on artificial "trees" formed by attaching pieces of cork bark to a metal pipe framework or to a dead branched section of a tree in such a way that pockets are created to hold the mix in which bromeliads, orchids, and other epiphytes are planted.

Cultivation. This is as for *Vriesia*.

TILTH. The physical condition of land relative to its suitability for seed sowing and planting is referred to as its tilth. Thus, ground in good tilth is well-drained, porous, and friable (crumbly).

TINANTIA (Tin-ántia). Annuals or herbaceous perennials numbering eight species compose *Tinantia*, of the spiderwort family COMMELINACEAE. The name of the genus, which in the wild ranges through warm parts of the Americas including the West Indies, honors Francois A. Tinant, of Luxemburg, who died in 1858. The plant previously named *T. anomala* is *Commelinantia anomala*.

Tinantias are medium-sized to fairly large and bear a general resemblance to *Tradescantia*. They have ascending or erect stems, and alternate, largish leaves with bases sheathing the stems. The flowers, few to many in terminal, stalked clusters, are medium-sized and violet, blue, pink, or white. They have three conspicuous, leafy sepals, three petals that vary greatly in size and often in color, and six fertile stamens, the upper three with bearded stalks, the lower three hairless. The fruits are capsules.

Native from Mexico to Venezuela, *T. erecta* (syn. *T. fugax*) has stems up to 1½ feet tall, hairy or hairless, and often rooting from their lower nodes. The pointed or blunt, ovate to obovate-elliptic leaves, 3½ to 10 inches long, are sparsely-hairy. The flowers, few to many in clusters with densely-hairy stalks, are pink, purple, or blue, and about ½ inch long.

Garden and Landscape Uses and Cultivation. The species described above may be planted permanently outdoors in warm, frost-free climates, and elsewhere can be wintered in greenhouses and planted out in summer. It succeeds in ordinary soil in sun and is easily increased by seed, cuttings, and division. Seeds may be sown directly outdoors in spring and the seedlings thinned sufficiently to prevent overcrowding, or they may be started early indoors.

TINNEA (Tín-nea). Few white women, or men for that matter, penetrated the wilds of central Africa in the mid-nineteenth century. The name of this genus, which belongs to the mint family LABIATAE, commemorates three Dutch women who did. The first introduction into cultivation of *Tinnea aethiopica* resulted from seeds sent to her brother in Liverpool, England, by Alexandrine Tinne, who with her mother, Henriette Tinne, and her aunt journeyed from 1856 to 1858 in the heart of what was then called the dark continent. True, *Tinnea* had been found earlier, but no living material had been collected. The genus contains thirty species.

Tinneas are more or less hairy herbaceous perennials and subshrubs, mostly natives of tropical Africa, but also present in the southern part of the continent. They have undivided leaves, the uppermost reduced in size and bractlike, and fragrant vinous-black-purple to smoky-purple or mauve, short-tubular flowers with two-lipped, laterally-flattened calyxes, and two-lipped corollas, the spreading lower lips of which are conspicuously longer than the two-lobed upper ones. There are four stamens. The seeds are small. The blooms, in terminal racemes, are in whorls (tiers) of two or three.

The kind cultivated, **T. aethiopica**, a subshrub 4 to 6 feet in height, blooms satisfactorily when much smaller. Of hoary appearance, it is freely-branched and twiggy and has ovate, toothless leaves narrowing to slender stalks. The livid, maroon-purple corollas of the flowers contrast pleasingly with the pale green, broad, tubular calyxes, which are shorter than the corolla tubes. Variety *T. a. dentata* has elliptic, slightly to conspicuously toothed leaves. Its flowers are sometimes, if not always, pale mauve; their corolla tubes are completely enclosed by the calyx.

Garden Uses and Cultivation. Tropical, fairly humid conditions are needed for the successful cultivation of this plant. Afforded these, it grows with ease. It appreciates porous, fertile soil kept evenly moist, but not constantly saturated, and light shade from powerful sun. It may be expected to thrive in southern Florida and Hawaii. In greenhouses it may be accommodated where the minimum winter night temperature is 60°F. By day this may be exceeded by five to fifteen degrees; at other seasons higher temperatures are favorable. A rather airy, buoyant atmosphere is more to the liking of *T. aethiopica* than one that is dank and oppressively humid. Well-rooted specimens respond to occasional applications of dilute liquid fertilizer from

spring to fall. Pruning to shape and repotting are done in late winter. In the plants' early stages, frequent pinching out of the shoot tips is necessary to induce a desirable bushy habit. Propagation is easy by cuttings. Plants can also be raised from seed.

TIPA OR TIPU TREE is *Tipuana tipu.*

TIPUANA (Tipu-àna)—Tipu or Tipa Tree. Some botanists admit only the tipu or tipa tree in *Tipuana*, others accept ten species. Be that as it may, in the wild the genus is restricted to tropical South America and consists of trees of the pea family LEGUMINOSAE. Its name is believed to be a modified version of its Brazilian one.

Tipuanas have pinnate leaves with alternate leaflets and a terminal one, and showy, loosely-branched, terminal panicles of yellow or light purplish, pea-shaped flowers. The stamens are joined. The fruits are few-seeded, winged pods.

The tipu tree (**T. tipu**, syns. *T. speciosa, Machaerium tipu*) in cultivation is 30 feet tall

Tipuana tipu (fruits)

or taller; in the wild it sometimes attains a height of 100 feet and develops buttresses at the base of its trunk. Its leaves have eleven to twenty-five leaflets, notched at their tips and about 1½ inches long. The bright yellow blooms, about ¾ inch long, appear with the new leaves. The fruits, which remain on the tree for many months, resemble one-half of a maple "key" and are 2 to 3 inches long. They have a long wing that extends along one side of the small ellipsoid pod and for more than twice the length of the pod beyond its apex. This species is native to Argentina and Bolivia. In its homelands its wood, which takes a high polish, is greatly esteemed for cabinetwork and other uses, its bark is employed locally for dyeing and tanning, and its leaves are used in veterinary medicine.

Garden and Landscape Uses and Cultivation. The tipu tree is much planted in parts of South America and other warm-

climate regions as an ornamental shade and street tree. It is showy in bloom and grows well under ordinary conditions of soil and sun. It is propagated by seed.

TIPULARIA (Tipu-lària) — Crane-Fly Orchid. In recognition of a fanciful resemblance of its flowers to the insect, *Tipularia* is named from the Latin *tipula*, the crane-fly. It consists of one American and two Asian species of the orchid family ORCHIDACEAE and is rather closely related to *Aplectrum*, but differs in having spurred blooms.

Tipularias are deciduous and grow in the ground, not like many tropical orchids that perch on trees. They have tubers in strings connected by short rhizomes. The leaves are basal and solitary. The flower stalks are leafless, with a few small bracts, and end in loose, bractless racemes. The blooms have separate, similar, narrowly-oblong or oblanceolate sepals and petals, and a lip with a long middle lobe and two very much smaller basal ones flanking it. To the rear the lip extends as a long, slender spur.

Inhabiting rich, humid woodlands from Massachusetts to Indiana, Florida, and Louisiana, the crane-fly orchid (**T. discolor**) produces long-stalked, often pur-

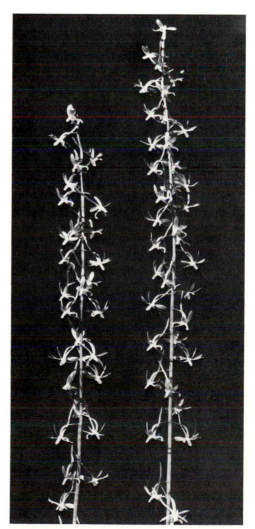

Tipularia discolor

ple-blotched, broad-elliptic to heart-shaped leaves, 2 to 4 inches long, in fall. The slender flower stalks, with their racemes of bloom 4 inches to over 1 foot tall, appear in summer. The nodding flowers have yellowish to bronzy, often purple-veined sepals, petals up to about ⅓ inch long, and a light purple lip with the expanded part approximately the same length and with a spur up to 1 inch long.

Garden Uses and Cultivation. Likely to appeal only to those with an enthusiastic interest in native plants, the crane-fly orchid can be accommodated in both woodlands and rock gardens in acid soil containing an abundance of organic matter. The conditions should duplicate as nearly as possible the environments it favors in the wild. Increase is by natural multiplication. For further details see Orchids.

TISCHLERIA (Tisch-lèria). Technical details of the fruits (capsules) distinguish the one species of this genus of the carpetweed family AIZOACEAE from very closely related *Carruanthus*. Both are close kin of *Bergeranthus* and belong in the *Mesembryanthemum* section of their family. The name honors a German, Dr. Georg Tischler.

Native to South Africa and hardy only in warm climates, *Tischleria peersii* has dull

Tischleria peersii

yellowish-green, shorter leaves with more and larger teeth than those of *Carruanthus ringens*. They are opposite, with alternate pairs set at right angles to each other, and are about 1½ inches long by ½ inch wide or a little wider. Three-angled, more or less club-shaped, and without dots, they have chinlike ends. The flowers, on stalks about ¾ inch long and with four small bracts, develop in summer and open in the evenings. They are yellow and ¾ to 1 inch in diameter.

Garden Uses and Cultivation. These are the same as for *Bergeranthus*. See also Succulents.

TITANOPSIS (Titan-ópsis). Among the choicest South African *Mesembryanthemum* relatives, the eight species of *Titanopsis* belong in the carpetweed family AIZOACEAE. The name, alluding to the flowers, comes from that of the sun god Titan and the Greek *opsis*, resembling.

Very succulent, these small plants form clusters of rosettes of four to eight or more, blunt, spatula-shaped, four-ranked leaves with broad, more or less triangular ends. They are commonly bluish-green, gray-green, yellowish, or reddish, and markedly warted, especially near their apexes. The short-stalked to nearly stalkless yellow to orange flowers expand in summer. They have a deeply-six-lobed calyx, numerous petals in one or two circles, many stamens, and five or six stigmas. The fruits are capsules.

Beautifully lime-encrusted in appearance, *T. calcarea* is most commonly culti-

Titanopsis calcarea

vated. Its rosettes of usually two or three pairs of rugged-surfaced, broadly-spatula-shaped leaves, 1 inch or so long by ½ to ¾ inch wide and with rounded triangular ends, are bluish-green with grayish-white, sometimes reddish-tinted warts. In the wild the exposed parts of the leaves so closely match the color and texture of the surrounding limestone detritus that this little plant must be accounted one of the most remarkable examples of plant mimicry. Its nearly stalkless pale yellow to nearly orange blooms are ¾ to 1 inch in diameter. Quite similar *T. fulleri* has rosettes of mostly five or six pairs of leaves. Its blooms are deep yellow and ¾ inch in diameter. Another intriguing kind, *T. schwantesii* has rosettes of leaves up to 1¼ inches long that gradually broaden upward from the base and then suddenly widen into rounded triangular apexes nearly ½ inch across. They are pale glaucous-gray, densely-blistered with yellow-brown. From ½ to ¾ inch across, the blooms are pale yellow. Similar to the last, but with very blunt leaf ends so that the leaves are nearly perfect triangles, *T. hugo-schlechteri* has dull-green to

grayish, more or less red-tinged leaves up to slightly over ½ inch long. Their upper parts are conspicuously furnished with light gray to reddish, flat warts. The plant previously known as *T. setifera* is *Aloinopsis setifera*.

Garden Uses and Cultivation. These extraordinary desert plants are gems for inclusion in collections of choice succulents. Grown outdoors only in warm, desert climates, more commonly they are cultivated in greenhouses. They need full sun and respond to care that suits *Lithops*. In the main, they are not difficult. Of the kinds described above *T. hugo-schlechteri* is most finicky. Well-drained, sandy soil with generous amounts of crushed limestone or lime plaster mixed in is to their liking. It should be watered moderately from spring through fall, more sparingly or not at all in winter. It is better that water be given by immersing the containers and allowing the moisture to seep from below than by pouring it on the soil surface. Water lying in the rosettes for extended periods causes them to rot. Although in their natural homes titanopsises often grow with only their leaf tips showing aboveground, this will not do for plants in cultivation. They must be planted with the entire plant body, except the roots, above the soil surface. Propagation may be by division in spring, but plants come so readily from seed that seed sowing is usually the preferred method.

TITHONIA (Ti-thònia). Sunflower relatives, tithonias belong to the daisy family COMPOSITAE. Their name is derived from that of Tithonus, consort of Aurora, the dawn goddess. The ten species of *Tithonia* are natives of Mexico, Central America, and the West Indies.

Mostly annuals, often more or less woody toward their bases, tithonias more rarely are perennial and shrublike. None is winter hardy in the north. From sunflowers (*Helianthus*) they are most conveniently distinguished by the very considerable thickening or swelling upward, in clublike fashion, of the stems beneath the flower heads. Also, when present, the pappus (scalelike appendages accompanying the flowers and fruits) is persistent in *Tithonia*, not in *Helianthus*. Tithonias have mostly alternate, occasionally opposite, lobed or lobeless, stalked leaves with three chief veins. Their medium-sized to large, yellow, orange, or red, sunflower-like flower heads are carried on long stalks that come from the leaf axils. Those of cultivated kinds are displayed to fine advantage. The disk florets that compose the centers of the flower heads are bisexual, the showy, petal-like ray florets are sterile. The bracts of the involucre (collar) at the back of each flower head are in two to five rows and are graduated or nearly equal in size. The seedlike fruits (achenes) are four-angled.

A bushy annual of vigorous growth and up to 6 feet tall or thereabouts, **T. rotundifolia** (syn. *T. speciosa*) has cylindrical stems, and alternate, usually lobeless, but sometimes three-lobed, toothed, triangular-ovate leaves that narrow at their bases

Tithonia rotundifolia

into winged stalks. They are 3 inches to almost 1 foot long by about three-fourths as wide and are hairy on their undersides, at least along the veins. The flower heads, terminating stalks up to 1 foot long, are about 3 inches in diameter and bright orange or orange-scarlet. The bracts of the involucre are in two rows, those of the inner row with sharp tips. Selected horticultural varieties are more compact and have large, brightly colored flower heads.

Perennial **T. diversifolia,** 9 to 20 feet tall, has four-angled stems, and alternate, obovate or obovate-oblong, usually three- to five-lobed, toothed leaves, ovate to tri-

Tithonia diversifolia

angular-ovate and 3 to 8 inches long, that narrow below into winged stalks. The yellow to orange flower heads, 2½ to 6 inches in diameter, have involucres of four or five rows of round-ended bracts. This species is naturalized in many warm countries.

Garden and Landscape Uses. Somewhat coarse and leafy, tithonias serve usefully where space is adequate to display them effectively, but are not well adapted for small, intimate areas. They are useful for beds and borders and as temporary fillers in gaps at the fronts of shrub plantings. Their flowers are excellent for cutting. These plants revel in warmth and sunshine and prosper in well-drained soil of medium to rather low fertility. Too rich a diet encourages exuberant development of stems and foliage without corresponding increases in the number or quality of the blooms.

Cultivation. Tithonias are best treated as annuals. When so grown they are satisfactory in the north and flower well in late summer and fall. Seeds may be sown outdoors, either where the plants are to remain or in a seed bed from which they are transplanted to their flowering stations. Alternatively, they can be started indoors early and the young plants planted outdoors about the time it is safe to set out tomatoes. Indoor sowing is done in a temperature of about 60°F six to eight weeks before the plants are to be set in the garden. Spacing of 2½ to 3½ feet between individual plants is needed. Routine care consists of staking to prevent wind and storm damage, watering periodically during spells of dry weather, and prompt removal of faded flower heads.

TITI is *Cliftonia monophylla.*

TITOKI is *Alectryon excelsum.*

TOAD-LILY. See Tricyrtis.

TOADFLAX. See Linaria.

TOADSHADE is *Trillium sessile.*

TOATOA is *Phyllocladus glaucus.*

TOBACCO. See Nicotiana. Indian-tobacco is *Lobelia inflata.* Ladies'-tobacco is *Antennaria plantaginifolia.*

TOBACCO BUDWORM. See Corn Earworm.

TOCOCA (Tocò-ca). Native to Central America and northern South America, *Tococa,* of the melastoma family MELASTOMATACEAE, consists of fifty species of shrubs. Although little known in cultivation, several have attractive foliage and blooms and are suitable for gardens in the tropics and warm subtropics and for greenhouses. The name is a slight modification of the native name of one species.

Tococas have large, usually thin, toothed or toothless leaves with three to seven prominent longitudinal veins from their bases and, some sorts, a two-lobed bladder at the bottom of the blade or on the leafstalk. The showy, white or pink flowers, in panicles, are often associated with large bracts. They have five- or four-lobed calyxes, the same number of obovate or oblong, blunt or notched petals, twice as many stamens as petals, and one style. The fruits are berries.

Rather difficult to grow well, **T. platyphylla** (syns. *T. latifolia, Sphaerogyne latifolia*) has short, bristly, sprawling stems, and broadly-ovate to nearly round, minutely-toothed leaves, up to 1 foot long, with bristly stalks, but without bladders. The blooms are rose-pink to red.

Garden and Landscape Uses and Cultivation. As components of shrub and flower beds, tococas have merit in tropical gardens and for ornamenting large tropical greenhouses. They succeed in ordinary soils that contain fairly generous amounts of leaf mold, peat moss, or other decayed organic matter. Increase is had by seed, and from hammer cuttings consisting of a section of a stem including one node with a leaf attached, planted in a warm propagating bed, preferably one with bottom heat, early in the year. Greenhouse environments should be warm, humid, and with shade from strong sun. A minimum winter night temperature of 60°F, with higher temperatures during the day and at other seasons, are needed. Water to keep the soil always moderately moist. Well-rooted specimens benefit from regular applications of dilute liquid fertilizer.

TODEA (To-dèa). As here presented, *Todea,* of the osmunda family OSMUNDACEAE, consists of a single species of evergreen fern native to Australia, New Zealand, and South Africa. Other species sometimes included are discussed under *Leptopteris.* The name *Todea* commemorates the mycologist Henry Julius Tode, of Mecklenburg, Germany, who died in 1797.

The most obvious difference between *Todea* and *Leptopteris* is the very much firmer, more leathery fronds (leaves) of the former as compared with the soft, flimsy ones of the latter. Because of this, *Todea* is much more tolerant of dryish atmospheric conditions and lends itself for exploitation as an ornamental where *Leptopteris* would not prosper.

A small tree fern with a trunk up to 4 feet tall, **T. barbara** (syn. *T. africana*) has twice-pinnate leaves with stalks up to 2 feet long and blades that are 3 to 4 feet long and 8 inches to well over 1 foot broad. The primary divisions of the leaves are 4 to 8 inches in length; their divisions, linear-lanceolate, bluntly-toothed, and ¾ to 2 inches long, are numerous and close together. The clusters of spore-bearing organs are crowded along the minor veins of

Todea barbara

the ultimate leaf divisions and at maturity may cover the whole underside of each frond.

Garden and Landscape Uses. Very resistant to rather difficult environments, *T. barbara* is a handsome ornament for shaded places outdoors and in lath houses in warm climates, and is quite superb for conservatories and greenhouses. It may also be used with considerable success as a room plant.

Cultivation. Fertile, sandy, peaty soil that does not lack for moisture, yet is well drained and never waterlogged, is to the liking of todeas. In greenhouses a winter night temperature of 45 to 50°F is satisfactory, but more rapid growth is had at temperatures five to ten degrees higher. Day temperatures should range, according to the brightness of the day, from five to fifteen degrees above those maintained at night. A moderately to highly humid atmosphere and shade from strong sun are needed. Well-rooted specimens are helped by regular applications of dilute liquid fertilizer. Propagation is by spores. Sporelings grow slowly, but may be encouraged to develop faster by keeping them in higher temperatures than those recommended for mature plants. See Ferns for additional information.

TOFIELDIA (To-fièldia) — False-Asphodel, White Featherling. About twenty species of herbaceous perennials of the lily family LILIACEAE constitute *Tofieldia*. They inhabit north temperate regions and the Andes. The name commemorates the English botanist Thomas Tofield, who died in 1779.

Tofieldias have slender rootstocks and several basal or near-basal, linear leaves in two ranks. The flowering stalk, which usually bears one to three small leaves, terminates in a dense raceme of small, greenish or brownish blooms in groups of two to four or singly and with six spreading or erect petals (more correctly, tepals), six stamens with flattened stalks, and three short styles. The fruits are capsules with

the persistent perianth parts (petals or, more correctly, tepals) attached.

Native to wet, acid soils from New Jersey to Virginia, Florida, and Texas, *T. racemosa* has erect basal leaves 8 inches to

Tofieldia racemosa

over 1 foot long and up to ⅕ inch wide. The stems, 1 foot to 2 feet tall, and minutely-hairy in their flowering parts, have cream-colored flowers mostly in clusters of two, three, or four. Under ½ inch wide, they are in racemes 2 to 6 inches in length. Closely similar *T. glutinosa* has mostly a more northerly range that extends from Newfoundland to Alaska and California, although it also occurs in the mountains of North Carolina. A chief difference is that its seed capsules are about twice as long as the perianth instead of only about equaling it in length. The white featherling (*T. glabra*), native to North Carolina and Georgia, is 1 foot to 2 feet tall. Its white flowers, under ¼ inch long, come singly rather than in groups along the stalk.

Three natives of Japan are cultivated. From 3 to 5 inches tall, *T. coccinea* (syn. *T. nutans*) has slender-linear, laterally-flattened, rough-edged leaves 1 inch to 2 inches long. Its white to brownish, nodding flowers, about ⅛ inch long, have yellow anthers. More robust *T. japonica*, 1 foot to 1½ feet tall or a little taller, has rough-edged, laterally-flattened linear leaves, the basal ones up to 1¼ feet long and ⅓ inch wide, the one or two on the stem much shorter. Sticky-glandular in their upper parts, the flowering stalks carry racemes up to 3 inches long of about ¼-inch-long white flowers with dark purple anthers. Rarely over 4½ inches tall, but sometimes attaining nearly twice that height, *T. nuda* has smooth-edged, linear, laterally-flattened leaves, the basal ones up to 4½

inches or occasionally over 1 foot long, the stem leaves much shorter. The flowers, about ⅙ inch long, are white with dark purple anthers.

Garden and Landscape Uses and Cultivation. Of minor horticultural importance, tofieldias may be used in native plant gardens and for colonizing semiwild areas. They are suitable for moist and wet soils and are propagated by division and by seed.

TOLMIEA (Tolm-ièa)—Pick-a-Back or Piggy Back Plant. The only species of this genus of the saxifrage family SAXIFRAGACEAE is very popular as a houseplant and is useful for shady, outdoor gardens. It is hardy at least as far north as southern New England. Native to moist woodlands in the Pacific Northwest and California, *Tolmiea menziesii* was named to honor a surgeon of the Hudson's Bay Company, Dr. William Tolmie, who died in 1886. From closely related *Tiarella* it differs in its flowers having three instead of ten stamens.

The pick-a-back or piggy back plant (*T. menziesii*) is a low, evergreen, herbaceous perennial of tufted habit. Hairy throughout, it has thin, long-stalked, shallowly five- or seven-lobed, toothed leaves, with ovate-heart-shaped blades up to 4 inches broad by almost as long. The upper leaves are smaller than those below. An unusual feature, responsible for the common name, is the plentiful development of pert plantlets at the bases of the leaf blades. Of small decorative interest, the asymmetrical, greenish to chocolate-brown nodding flowers, about ⅓ inch long, are in airy racemes. They have calyxes with three larger and two smaller lobes, four petals, three stamens, and two styles. The fruits are capsules.

Garden and Landscape Uses and Cultivation. This grateful species is content with minimum care. It makes an attractive and interesting window plant, as well as a nice adornment for woodlands, rock gardens, and other outdoor areas where there is enough shade to preclude its foliage being scorched and the soil is moistish. It does well, as it often occurs in the wild, at watersides. For its best comfort the soil should be reasonably loose and contain a fairly high proportion of leaf mold, compost, peat moss, or other decayed organic matter, but not too much, otherwise too soft, gross foliage may result. The pick-a-back plant makes nice specimens in pots and pans (shallow pots) 4 or 5 inches in diameter. Well-rooted specimens should be given dilute liquid fertilizer regularly. It is important that the plants receive as much light as they will stand without their foliage becoming bleached or scorched. Too much shade results in weak, floppy leaves. Indoors, the best results are had in cool places. Ideally a night temperature in winter of 45 to 50°F with a five to fifteen de-

Tolmiea menziesii showing plantlets on its leaves

Tolmiea menziesii as a groundcover

Tolmiea menziesii as a pot plant

Tolmiea menziesii in a hanging basket

Tolpis barbata

milky sap. They have one to many usually branched stems and smooth-edged, lobed or toothed leaves. The flower heads are of all petal-like florets. There is no central disk as in a daisy. The fruits are achenes.

Annual **T. barbata,** which looks somewhat like a hawkweed (*Hieracium*) and has, in fact, been offered in seedsmen's catalogs as "golden yellow hawkweed," is a native of southern Europe. From 8 inches to 1 foot in height and slender, this has basal tufts of lanceolate, remotely-toothed leaves and thin, erect, branched stems, terminating with flower heads composed of strap-shaped florets (petal-like parts) and 1½ to 2 inches in width. The flower heads are yellow with maroon centers. Beneath the heads of flowers and extending down the stems for some little distance are threadlike bracts.

Garden Uses and Cultivation. Although by no means the showiest of annuals, this species is useful for adding variety to flower gardens and can be used to supply summer color in rock gardens. It blooms from midsummer to frost. No difficulty attends its cultivation. Sow seeds in early spring where the plants are to bloom and rake them into the surface soil. When the young plants have their second pair of leaves, thin them out to about 6 inches apart. Summer care consists of controlling weeds, removing faded blooms, and watering during dry weather.

TOLU BALSAM TREE is *Myroxylon balsamum.*

TOMATILLO is *Physalis ixocarpa.*

TOMATO. Besides being the name of the familiar vegetable garden fruit, dealt with in the next entry, the word tomato appears in the common names of these plants: husk-tomato or strawberry-tomato (*Physalis pruinosa* and *P. pubescens*) and tree-tomato (*Cyphomandra betacea*).

gree increase by day serves, but higher temperatures are tolerated if the light is good and the atmosphere is not too arid. The soil must be always moderately moist. Increase is easy by division, which may be done at any time, and by removing the leaves bearing plantlets and planting them in sandy, peaty soil. The soil must be kept moist, as must the surrounding atmosphere, until the young plants are well established. This can be assured by keeping them in a terrarium, or covered with a glass jar or bag or tent of transparent polyethylene plastic film.

TOLPIS (Tól-pis). The Mediterranean region, the Canary Islands, the Azores, and Ethiopia are homes to the twenty species of *Tolpis*, of the daisy family COMPOSITAE. The derivation of the generic name is unknown.

These dandelion relatives are annuals and herbaceous perennials containing

TOMATO. In addition to its immense commerical importance, the tomato is one of the most esteemed and universally cultivated home garden crops. It accommodates to a wide variety of locations and soils and is raised successfully by city gardeners in yards and on roofs, terraces, and even window sills, as well as by practically all suburban and country gardeners who grow vegetables. Modern varieties are chiefly derivatives of *Lycopersicon lycopersicum*, the small-fruited cherry types of *L. pimpinellifolium*, of the nightshade family

Solanaceae. Their pleasantly flavored fruits, much esteemed for salads, cooking, and juice, are rich sources of vitamins A, B_1, and C. A particular advantage is that they develop and ripen in succession so that a harvest over a period of many weeks is obtained from the same plants.

Great variability among varieties exists. Plants range from dwarf to tall, and fruits from those of sometimes a pound or more in weight to others not much bigger than a currant. They may be spherical or plum- or pear-shaped. Red-fruited sorts are most popular, but others have yellow, orange-

yellow, and creamy-white fruits, and in some the skins are fuzzy in the manner of peaches.

Brought from its native South America to Europe as long ago as 1596, the tomato was known to the Western world for nearly two centuries before it was recognized and finally accepted as a food plant. Until then it was grown only as a curiosity and ornamental. Called love-apple, it was thought to be, like several of its close relatives, poisonous.

In North America the possibilities of tomatoes as edibles seems to have been first suggested in 1781. About then they were being grown by Thomas Jefferson. Some seven years later a Frenchman tried, unsuccessfully, to persuade Philadelphians of their healthful qualities. The first record of the crop being regularly marketed was in 1812 in New Orleans, Louisiana. By 1835 tomatoes were being quoted at the Quincy Hall market in Boston, Massachusetts, but it was about the middle of the century before they became at all well known and much later before they achieved real popularity.

Prime needs for success are warm weather and full exposure to sun. Almost any well-drained soil suits or can easily be made suitable. It should be decidedly fertile, but with nutrients balanced so that there is no great excess of nitrogen. If there is, stem and foliage growth will be stimulated at the expense of the fruits.

Prepare the soil by spading, rotary tilling, or plowing and, if low in organic content, by incorporating compost, rotted manure, peat moss, commercial humus, or other suitable material. In addition, a dressing of fertilizer with a relatively high content of phosphorus and potassium is likely to be beneficial. Superphosphate or bonemeal may be used to provide the phosphorus, and unleached wood ashes or sulfate of potash to provide the potassium, if the ground is so rich that no nitrogen is needed; otherwise a commerical formulation, such as a 5-10-5 suitable for vegetables, may be used.

New plants from seeds are raised each year. This is so because, although tomatoes are really nonhardy perennials, they are almost invariably grown as annuals to be discarded at the end of their first cropping season. It is worth noting, however, that, although very seldom done, it is quite easy to propagate them from cuttings, and plants raised in this way in late summer can be continued in a greenhouse to crop in winter or spring.

Because wide spacing is needed between individuals and because transplanting allows them to be set deeper in the ground with the advantage that the first fruits will be lower, seeds are sown in pots, other containers, or in special seed beds rather than where the plants are to remain. In parts of the south and elsewhere

Types of tomato fruits: (a) The familiar large, spherical tomato

(c) The plum-shaped tomato

(b) The pear-shaped tomato

(d) The small, cherry-like tomato

where the growing season is long and warm and early cropping is not of first importance, seeding may be done outdoors. However, where the growing season is shorter, or if an early harvest is desired even where it is long, indoor sowing is the rule.

To raise plants in a greenhouse or perhaps in a sunny window in which a greenhouse environment can be approximated, sow about six weeks in advance of the expected date of planting outdoors. Pots, pans (shallow pots), or flats are suitable containers. Have them clean and place a layer of crocks sufficient to assure sharp drainage over their bottoms. Cover this with leaves, straw, or even an old nylon stocking to prevent the drainage from becoming clogged, then fill with soil. Let this be a porous mix of good topsoil, peat moss or leaf mold, and coarse sand or perlite in about equal proportions, passed through a ¾-inch screen. No fertilizer is needed.

Firm the soil with your fingers and level it. Then scatter the seeds over its surface so they are spaced about ½ inch apart, or, if you prefer, make shallow drills (grooves) 2 to 3 inches apart in flats and sprinkle the seeds more thickly along these. In either case press the seeds gently into the surface, cover with ¼ inch of the soil mix, and again press lightly with a flat piece of board. Water with a fine spray, taking care not to flood or disturb the soil, and then cover with a sheet of glass or polyethelene plastic raised an inch or so above the soil, followed by heavy paper to give shade.

Put the containers of newly sown seeds where the temperature is 70 to 75°F. After the first few days inspect them daily. Keep the soil evenly damp, but not constantly saturated, and at the very first sign of germination remove the shade and tilt the glass or punch some holes in the plastic to admit air. For the first two or three days, shade them from strong sun with cheesecloth or similar material, and then, as soon as the young shoots have completely emerged, expose them fully. Common mistakes made by amateurs include failing to remove the shade early enough and growing the young plants without sufficient light, both of which result in thin, weak, drawn (unduly tall) seedlings. In difficult environments the use of artificial light as a supplement to natural light can be advantageous, but usually plants grown under such conditions are less sturdy than those raised with all-day exposure to sun.

Transplant the seedlings as soon as they have grown their second pair of leaves (the first pair of regular tomato leaf shape) to flats, spacing them 3 to 4 inches apart, or individually to pots. Use a fairly coarse mix of topsoil, peat moss or humus, and coarse sand or perlite, to which has been added a pound of bonemeal or one-half that amount of a 5-10-5 fertilizer, or its approx-

Seedling tomatoes transplanted to a flat

imate equivalent, to each bushel. Set the plants so that their seed leaves (the first pair produced) rest on the soil surface. Keep them growing in a temperature of 60 to 65°F at night, five to fifteen degrees higher, depending upon the brightness of the weather, by day. About two weeks prior to transplanting them outdoors, harden the plants by standing them in a cold frame or sheltered, sunny spot outdoors.

Spacing in the garden should relate to the type and vigor of the variety and to the method of cultivation adopted. Most varieties, especially those favored by home gardeners, have stems that unless pruned or broken off continue to lengthen and produce a succession of flowers and fruits throughout the season. These are known as indeterminate varieties. The stems of determinate varieties, after a period of growth, produce at their apex a cluster of flowers and then cease to lengthen. Determinate varieties are more compact than indeterminate ones and ripen a large proportion of their fruits at approximately the same time. For this and other reasons they are often favored by commercial growers who employ mechanical harvesters.

Commercial growers commonly set the plants about 4 feet apart in rows 6 feet asunder and allow them to sprawl without staking. Because of the large amount of land this requires and because spoilage of fruits in contact with the soil occurs, this is not an attractive procedure for home gardeners.

Tomatoes supported by stakes, trellises, or other means that permit closer spacing produce heavier crops from smaller areas of ground and with less wastage than unsup-

ported plants, although individuals of the latter may bear more heavily. Unless you use vertical cylinders of wire mesh (positioned after the plants are set out), have the supports in place before planting.

A single stake for each plant is excellent. Have it stout enough to support a mature, full-foliaged, heavily-fruited plant, and of such a length that when driven a foot or two into the ground it protrudes to a height of 5 or 6 feet. Wooden stakes 1½ to 2 inches square are satisfactory. If the plants are trained to one stem, the preferred method, they may be spaced 2 feet apart in rows 3½ to 4 feet asunder. If each is permitted two or three main stems, somewhat wider spacing between individuals in the rows will be beneficial.

Tomatoes supported by one stake to each plant: (a) Shortly after planting

(b) Tying the stems to the stakes with soft string

Tomatoes supported by an A frame: (a) Tying the stems of young plants to the frame

Take care, when removing the plants from pots, flats, or beds, and in subsequent handling, not to damage the roots more than is unavoidable and not to expose them to sun or wind. For each plant make a hole, with a trowel, big enough to accommodate the roots without crowding. Set the plant with the top of its root ball about 2 inches below the surface, push soil around the roots, and press it moderately firmly. Finish the job by leveling the soil and soaking that around the plant with water.

With young plants that are excessively tall and leggy, instead of compact and with leaves close together, make the planting hole of normal depth to accommodate the ball, but about 1 foot long and with its bottom gradually sloped upward to the end close to the stake. Set the root ball on its

(c) The first fruits

(b) Later, the plants in full growth

Delay planting until the weather is warm and settled. Newly set tomatoes are likely to be severely checked by temperatures below 50°F. If the soil in which the plants are growing is dryish, water it thoroughly at least an hour in advance of planting.

When setting out 'leggy" (excessively tall and thin) tomato plants: (a) Scoop out a long hole rather than circular one

Other systems of support are employed. One such is to erect an A-shaped framework of any desired length and 4 to 5 feet tall of lathlike strips of wood. Have the sides inclined at an angle of forty-five to sixty degrees to meet in a peak like that of a roof. Set tomato plants 3 to 4 feet apart along both sides of this structure and train their stems to it, thinning out the branches sufficiently to avoid too much crowding.

A more recent plan employs cylinders, some 5 feet high and 1½ feet in diameter, formed of stout wire mesh with 6-inch squares such as is used for reinforcing concrete. Such mesh permits easy harvesting. Have the plants 3 to 4 feet apart in rows 5 to 6 feet asunder and place one of these wire "corsets" over each, anchoring it, if need be, by tying it to a stake driven into the ground. As the plants grow they will lean outward, the wire will afford support.

Plant tomatoes outdoors after the weather is agreeably warm; take care not to damage the roots unduly

(b) Lay the plant in it with its stem angling slightly upward and only its upper part above ground level

(c) Taking care not to break the stem, fill soil over its lower part

(d) Press the soil lightly

(e) Water with a fine spray

side at the deep end of the hole and lay the stem of the plant along the bottom with its leafy top protruding. Do this carefully so that the stem does not break, then cover its length in the hole with soil. Soon, new

roots will develop from the buried stem and the top will grow and bear its first flowers and fruits much closer to the ground than if the plant were set out in the normal way.

Subsequent care is not arduous, but staked tomatoes need regular, frequent attention in the matters of tying to their supports and removing the many surplus side shoots that develop throughout the season. If these are not pinched out before they are 2 or 3 inches long, they appropriate to themselves too great a share of the moisture and nutrients available to the plant and soon develop into a choking tangle. Once a week is not too often to check for needed tying and shoot removal.

Surplus sideshoots: (a) Such as the one shown here in the leaf axil

(b) Should be pinched out while they are quite small

Keep the soil fairly moist throughout the early part of the season by watering deeply when necessary, but be more cautious about this after the fruits begin to ripen. Excess moisture from then on can cause the fruits to crack, particularly if it is applied following a period during which the soil has been excessively dry.

Mulching around and between the plants with organic material, such as coarse compost, straw, salt hay, or with black plastic mulch greatly reduces the need for watering and also checks weed growth. If mulching is not practiced, weeds are most easily held in check by shallow surface cultivation with a scuffle hoe or other appropriate tool.

Harvest tomatoes promptly as they ripen. In hot, humid weather the fruits will be firmer and crisper if picked just before they are dead ripe and allowed to complete the ripening process indoors at room temperature. If they are to be stored, keep them in a cool, dry place.

At the end of the season, before hard frost, harvest all remaining fruits. Spread out those that are beginning to turn color in shallow boxes or trays and put them in a cool, frostproof cellar, attic, garage, or similar place, where they will ripen over a period of several weeks. Tomatoes finished in this way may lack something of the wonderful flavor of fruits allowed to ripen or almost ripen on the vines, but they are superior to store-purchased tomatoes picked while immature and then shipped long distances. An alternative end-of-season treatment is to pull up the entire vines and hang them from the ceiling of the storage room. Fruits that are ''showing color'' will then ripen before they are actually removed from the vines.

As container plants outdoors in summer, tomatoes are very satisfactory producers of fruit and can serve decoratively on patios, terraces, window sills, and similar places. They do well as single plants in pots, tubs, or boxes 8 inches to 1 foot in diameter and depth, and the miniature varieties with even less root room. In long, troughlike planters, space them 1 foot to 1¼ feet apart.

Make sure the containers are well drained. Use a loamy, porous soil mix approximating in character the soil of a good vegetable garden. The mix suggested later for greenhouse tomatoes is satisfactory. Raise the young plants as advised for outdoor planting and plant them in the containers in which they are to fruit when it is time to plant tomatoes in the garden.

Restrict each plant to a single stem and keep it tied to a stake or other support. Water often enough to keep the foliage from wilting, but do not keep the soil constantly wet. After the containers are filled with roots and the first fruits have formed, apply dilute liquid fertilizer at weekly intervals.

In greenhouses, welcome harvests can be had, with little trouble from early fall until the next summer's outdoor crop begins to ripen, from tomatoes in ground beds, benches, planters, large pots, or tubs. For satisfactory results, exposure to full sun is necessary and the temperature should be 55 to 60°F at night, five to ten or, in

Miniature tomato 'Tiny Tim' in a 6-inch pot

A greenhouse-grown tomato with well-placed trusses of flowers that promise a good crop of fruits

very bright weather, up to fifteen degrees higher by day. Whenever weather permits, ventilate the greenhouse to prevent the buildup of excessive humidity and to assure a buoyant, airy atmosphere.

To provide for harvesting over a long season, make two sowings of seeds, the first in July for a crop that will ripen fruits in fall and early winter, the second in September or October to give ripe fruits in winter and spring. Choose, if possible, varieties recommended for greenhouse cultivation, but if none are available success can be achieved with any early-maturing variety.

Transplant the seedlings individually to small pots and, when these become filled with roots, to the 4-inch size. Keep the plants in full sun and take care not to crowd them so they shade each other. The next move will be to successively bigger pots or tubs until each plant occupies one 8 to 10 inches in diameter, or are spaced 1 foot to 1¼ feet apart in planters, benches, or ground beds. Use a porous, loamy, rather coarse soil made moderately fertile by the addition of a complete fertilizer, but not overly rich in organic matter. Unless the fertilizer used has a high phosphate content, the addition to the mix of superphosphate at the rate of ⅛ pint to each bushel will bring added benefit.

Limit each plant to a single stem by pinching out, while quite small, all side shoots that develop. Support the stem with a stake, by tying it to a wire, or, if the plants are in beds or benches, by twining them, as they grow, around vertical strings pulled tautly and tied to horizontal wires stretched at ground level and others parallel to them some 6 feet higher.

Stimulate the production of fruits by applying to the expanded flowers one of the hormone fruit-setting sprays sold for the purpose or by shaking the plants gently at about daily intervals.

Varieties of tomatoes are numerous and new ones are introduced with fair frequency. The characteristics that differentiate them are well described in seed catalogs. The differences include, besides height, vigor, and often whether their growth is indeterminate or determinate, the color, size, and shape of the fruits and, often of considerable importance, their disease-resistant qualities.

Pests and Diseases. These are somewhat numerous, but generally are fairly easily controlled. For the best current information consult the local Cooperative Extension Agent or the publications of your State Agricultural Experiment Stations. Common pests include aphids, cutworms, flea beetles, and red spider mites. Additionally, there is a large caterpillar, called the tomato hornworm, which eats the foliage, and the tomato fruitworm (identical with the corn earworm), which eats the fruits. Hand-picking is effective against these caterpillars.

Important diseases are fusarium and verticillium wilts, best combated by planting resistant varieties. Other diseases include anthracnose, early blight, late blight, and mosaic disease. A condition called blossom-end rot, manifested, as the name suggests, by a blackening and rotting of the fruits at the end opposite the stalk, is caused by too-acid soil and uneven supplies of water. Correcting the soil to a pH of 6 to 6.5 by liming and paying proper attention to watering forestalls this. Excessive transpiration in hot, sunny weather is often responsible for the older leaves of tomatoes, especially those staked and grown to single stems, curling in a rather distressing fashion. Only temporary light shading will alleviate this.

TOMATO FRUITWORM. See Corn Earworm.

TONELLA (Tonél-la). Two western North American species constitute *Tonella*, of the figwort family SCROPHULARIACEAE. The meaning of the name is not known. Closely related to *Collinsia*, this genus differs chiefly in some of its stem leaves being three-lobed or thrice-divided and in its flowers having the lower lips of the corolla with three lobes instead of two.

Tonellas are slender, branching annuals with opposite leaves and small flowers with a five-cleft calyx, a short-tubed, five-lobed corolla, four stamens, and one style. The fruits are capsules.

Inhabiting mostly shaded slopes at moderate altitudes in the mountains from California to Washington, *T. tenella* (syn. *T. collinsioides*), 6 inches to 1 foot in height, has stems sometimes finely-pubescent above the nodes, and leaves with blades up to ½ inch in length and pubescent on their upper surfaces. The lower ones are stalked, roundish to ovate, and may or may not be notched on each side. The upper ones are divided into three lanceolate to ovate segments. The tiny white or pale blue blooms, sometimes dotted with purple, have corollas that are scarcely longer than the calyxes.

Garden Uses and Cultivation. The species described is attractive for patches or drifts in rock gardens, as edgings, and for the fronts of flower borders. It prefers a porous, well-drained soil and sunny location and is best adapted for climates where summers are not excessively hot. Seeds are sown in spring where the plants are to bloom and raked lightly into the soil surface. If the seedlings come up too thickly they are thinned to 3 inches apart.

TOOG is *Bischofia javanica*.

TOOLS. The basic tools for gardening are not many, and the ease with which tasks may be accomplished and the pleasures of working in the garden will be greatly enhanced if they are well chosen and properly cared for.

Of first importance is to select sizes suitable to the physical capabilities of the user. It is folly to expect smallish women or youngsters to cope with spades, spading forks, or hedge shears designed for a large man. Next, consider quality, which in turn is generally reflected in price. Although cheap tools may be adequate for occasional, casual use, more often they are not good enough for the serious gardener. The materials of which they are made, their construction, and most importantly their handling qualities and balance are likely to be inferior.

Unless lost or unwisely lent, garden tools last for many years, sometimes a lifetime or longer. Because of this, and because the number of "musts" among them are few, the initial cost of assembling a kit of tools need not be great. Certainly this is true so far as hand tools are concerned. Only if one embarks on acquiring a longish list of gadget tools and expensive power-driven equipment is the cost likely to increase significantly.

A fairly adequate furnishment includes a spade, spading fork, shovel, trowel, two or three types of rakes, two or three types of hoes and cultivators, pruning shears, lopping shears, grass edging shears, pruning saw, wheelbarrow, lawn mower, sprayer (and perhaps a duster), hose, sprinkler, watering can, and broom. To these may be added dibbles, measuring

Some basic garden tools: Leaning against a wheelbarrow containing a hose and sprinkler are a trowel, scuffle hoe, draw hoe, rake, spade, and, to one side of the last, a spading fork

After each use clean the metal parts of all tools, such as this spade, by: (a) Removing all soil or other adherent material

(b) And wiping all rustable metal parts with a slightly oily rag

rods, potting sticks, and a garden line, all of which are easily fashioned at home, and one or more sharp knives for pruning, making cuttings, grafting, and budding.

Care of tools consists of cleaning and returning them to their storage place promptly after each use. Do not leave them outdoors. Some, including spades, spading forks, rakes, and trowels, can be had with metal parts of stainless steel. These are more expensive than those of ordinary steel, but have the advantage of not rusting.

To clean tools, wipe them free of all soil and debris, then, except the knives, rub their metal parts (unless of stainless steel) with an oily rag. Keep the moving parts of

such implements as lawn mowers and sprayers oiled regularly, and the blades of shears sharp. After each use, wash out sprayers thoroughly and leave their covers open to allow their tanks to dry. Coil hoses and hang them on pegs.

TOOTHACHE TREE is *Zanthoxylum americanum*.

TOOTHWORT. See Dentaria.

TOP-DRESSING. As the term suggests, to top-dress is to apply a dressing of something to the soil surface. It differs from mulching chiefly in its primary purpose being to supply nutrients, rather than to suppress weeds or conserve moisture. Top-

To top-dress an amaryllis (*Hippeastrum*):
(a) Prick away old surface soil

(b) Remove any small offset bulbs

(c) Firm newly added soil

(d) Pot the offset bulb

To top-dress a standard-trained
(tree-form) azalea: (a) Remove unwanted
sprouts from the "trunk"

(b) Scratch loose some of the surface soil

dressings may be fertilizers, fertilizers mixed with screened soil, compost, commercial humus, or peat moss, or any of these materials or manure used alone.

Both plants in the ground and those in pots, tubs, and other planters may often be top-dressed with advantage. Lawns and rock gardens are especially likely to respond to this treatment. When it is not desirable or practicable to repot plants that have filled their containers with roots, it is usually helpful to top-dress them at the time that repotting would otherwise receive attention.

When top-dressing, take care not to unduly disturb roots. Usually it is beneficial to loosen the soil to which the dressing is to be applied by scratching it lightly with a cultivator or similar tool or to take a pointed stick or hand fork and prick away a little of the surface soil of container plants.

(c) Remove the loosened soil

(d) Replace it with a fertile mixture

(e) Water thoroughly with a fine spray

This loosening and roughening allows the top-dressing to mix more surely with the old soil.

TOPATO. See Potomato.

TOPIARY WORK. The training of shrubs and small trees to formal shapes and their maintenance by repeated shearing is called

Top-dressing is an important spring procedure in rock gardens

topiary work or topiary. The art of producing them is an ancient one, certainly practiced by the Romans and perhaps by earlier peoples. Well conceived, adequately maintained, and displayed in appropriate surroundings, topiary is congruous and aesthetically satisfying, but ill-designed or improperly cared for, or in landscapes in which it does not blend, it can be an absurdity or abomination.

In effect, topiary is living sculpture. Examples may be of geometrical shapes, real, whimsical, or fantastic animals or birds or human figures may be simulated, and letters, crowns, and other devices may be represented. Formal surroundings, particularly near old buildings, afford perhaps the best opportunities for displaying topiary work advantageously, but topiary can also be used effectively, especially in its simpler forms, in more modern landscapes. One of the best known and oldest topiary gardens, open to the public, is at Levens Hall, Cumbria, England. Topiary is also featured at Williamsburg, Virginia, at Longwood Gardens, Kennett Square, Pennsylvania, and at the Hunnewell Estate, Wellesley, Massachusetts.

Favorite subjects for this art include boxwood (*Buxus*), yew (*Taxus*), holly (*Ilex*), cypress (*Cupressus*), privet (*Ligustrum*), myrtle (*Myrtus*), rosemary (*Rosmarinus*), and *Eugenia*. For best results, one should start with fairly young specimens planted in deep, fertile soil. Training, which may necessitate bracing some stems by tying them to others (in such a way that the ties will not cut into the bark as the stems thicken), may be necessary, and surely shearing two, three, or more times a year will be called for, for a few to many years, depending

Topiary featuring birds

upon the size and character of the example to be developed and the type of shrub or tree. And always, adequate fertilizing, watering during dry weather, and necessary pest and disease control must be given attention.

TOPINAMBOUR. See Calathea.

Ancient specimens of topiary at Levens Hall, Cumbria, England

Ancient specimens of topiary at Levens Hall, Cumbria, England

Topiary at Colonial Williamsburg, Virginia

Specimens of topiary at Longwood Gardens, Kennett Square, Pennsylvania

In the Hunnewell Estate Topiary Garden, Wellesley, Massachusetts

TORCH-GINGER is *Nicolaia elatior*.

TORCH-LILY. See Kniphofia.

TORENIA (Tor-ènia). One species of *Torenia* is widely cultivated in North America, a few others less commonly. Belonging to the figwort family SCROPHULARIA-CEAE, the genus, named after the Reverend Olaf Toren, of the Swedish East India Company, who died in 1752, comprises

A splendid specimen of topiary in yew (*Taxus baccata*) in Scotland

about fifty species, natives of warm parts of Africa and Asia.

Torenias are annuals and herbaceous perennials with *Mimulus*-like blooms and opposite, usually toothed, undivided leaves. They are mostly freely-branched. Some are trailers. The flowers are solitary from the leaf axils or terminal in short, few-flowered racemes. They have tubular three- to five-toothed or two-lipped calyxes, pleated or with three to five prominent wings. The tubular corollas are often expanded toward their mouths and two-lipped, with the lower lip three-lobed, and the upper two-lobed or merely notched. There are four stamens, two of which are longer than the others. The fruits are oblong capsules.

The wishbone flower (**T. fournieri**), of Indochina, is a much-branched, hairless annual about 1 foot tall. It has ovate to ovate-heart-shaped, toothed leaves, 1½ to 2 inches long, with stalks about one-half as long as the blades. The pretty blooms have somewhat inflated, often purplish, broadly-five-winged calyxes, and corollas with a pale violet and yellow tube, about 1 inch long, and spreading lobes. The upper lip is light blue or lavender, the lower lobe is rich, deep, velvety violet, and the center lobe is marked with a blotch of yellow. A horticultural variety with white

Torenia fournieri

flowers blotched with yellow on the lower lip is grown, as are others more compact than the typical species.

Yellow-flowered **T. baillonii** has been confused in gardens with *T. flava*. The latter has small, short-stalked, yellow blooms of no garden merit. Native to Indochina, *T. baillonii* is an erect or sprawling annual or perhaps sometimes a perennial. It has stalked, ovate, toothed leaves, up to a little over 2 inches long, and flowers with

Torenia baillonii

small, wingless calyxes, and long-stalked corollas, with the upper parts of their ¾- to 1-inch-long tubes and their throats brownish-purple and their spreading lobes bright yellow. They measure nearly 1 inch in diameter.

A beautiful trailing perennial that shows to advantage in hanging baskets, *T. asiatica,* of India, has stalked, triangular-ovate leaves, with blades mostly under 1 inch in length, and approximately 1-inch-long, violet-purple flowers with white lower lips. Very similar *T. concolor* (syn. *T. asiatica concolor*) differs in its blooms being nearly uniformly purple-blue and in its having narrowly-ovate leaves, generally somewhat larger than those of *T. asiatica*. This is native to southern China and Taiwan.

Torenia concolor

Annual *T. violacea* (syn. *T. peduncularis*), of India, and up to 1 foot in height, has sprawling stems and ovate-triangular leaves 1½ to 2½ inches long. Its flowers have corollas with yellow tubes and pale blue petals that are blotched with yellow and purple.

Garden and Landscape Uses. Among the most reliable of garden annuals, *T. fournieri* and its varieties are splendid for blooming in summer in outdoor beds and window and porch boxes; in the south they are much used as substitutes for pansies in winter and spring displays. They are also pleasing in pots in greenhouses and window gardens. The trailing kinds are effective in hanging baskets. All stand full sun, but are grateful for some relief from its greatest intensity, and are among the few annuals that can be depended upon to make a display in partial shade. Fertile soil, well drained and fairly moist, is to their best liking, but they get along under less favorable circumstances. It is not unusual for self-sown seedlings to spring up in abundance where plants have been the previous year.

Cultivation. Seeds provide a ready means of raising torenias, but perennial kinds are commonly, and annual kinds can be, increased by cuttings. Seeds may be sown directly outdoors where the plants are to remain, but in the north it is better to start them indoors in a temperature of 60 to 65°F some eight or nine weeks before it is safe to transfer the plants to garden beds. This should not be done until the weather is settled and fairly warm and it is safe to set out tomatoes, begonias, and other tender plants.

TORNILLO is *Prosopis pubescens*.

TOROTE is *Bursera microphylla*.

TORREYA (Torrèy-a) — California-Nutmeg, Stinking-Cedar. The name *Torreya* commemorates the distinguished American botanist Dr. John Torrey, who died in 1875. The genus it identifies consists of six species of evergreen trees or shrubs of the yew family TAXACEAE, natives of North America and eastern Asia. They differ from yews (*Taxus*) in having seeds completely enclosed in a fleshy covering in the manner of an olive or a plum and from the plum-yew (*Cephalotaxus*) in technical characteristics of the female flowers and, more obviously, in the two glaucous or brownish longitudinal lines on the undersides of the leaves being narrower than the green that margins them, whereas in the plum-yew the glaucous bands are broader than the bordering green. Also, the branches of plum-yew are strictly in opposite pairs; those of *Torreya* are only approximately so.

Torreyas have branches in whorls (tiers) and stiff, linear, bristle-tipped, sharp-pointed leaves arranged spirally, but dis-

Torreya, undetermined species

posed to give the impression of being in two ranks. The leaves, lustrous and slightly convex above, on their undersides are marked on either side of the raised midrib with a narrow, whitish or brownish line sunk into the leaf surface. Male and female flowers may be on the same or different trees. When both are on the same plant, generally they are on separate branches. Male cones develop singly in the leaf axils of current season's shoots, females arise near the bases of current year's shoots. The olive-like fruits ripen in their second season.

The best-known American species, the California-nutmeg (*T. californica*), earns its common name from the appearance of its seeds, which somewhat resemble nutmegs. This native of California is a handsome species, usually up to 70 feet and sometimes well over 100 feet in height. Its branches are spreading and slightly pendulous, its branchlets drooping. It has thin, smooth bark, that of two-year-old branches is reddish-brown. Strongly aromatic when bruised, its linear leaves are 1½ to 3 inches long and ⅛ inch broad. The fruits are 1 inch to 1¾ inches long and light green streaked with purple. This tree is not hardy in the north, but is a worthwhile species for milder sections and is reliably hardy in climates not more severe than that of Washington, D.C.

The stinking-cedar (*T. taxifolia*), of Florida, has foliage that when crushed emits a noxious odor. In this it differs from its West Coast relative, as it does also in its two-year-old branches being yellowish-green or yellowish-brown and in its leaves being up to 1½ inches long. The stinking-cedar is a rather open-headed tree rarely 50 feet tall, possibly hardy in favored locations as far north as Virginia, but the best results are had with it in regions of milder winters.

The hardiest sort, Japanese torreya (*T. nucifera*) lives outdoors in sheltered locations in southern New England, but there it never attains its maximum height of 80 feet recorded in its native Japan. In cultivation it is ordinarily up to 40 feet tall and toward the northern limits of where it may be grown is usually only a tall shrub. It is pyramidal and open-headed with slightly drooping branches. The two-year-old branchlets, like those of the California-nutmeg, are reddish-brown and, as with that species, its foliage is strongly aromatic when crushed. This sort differs from the California-nutmeg in having linear-lanceolate leaves up to 1¼ inches long. Its fruits, about 1 inch long, are green, lightly tinged with purple. The seeds are edible and in Japan an oil is obtained from them. The wood of this is esteemed in Japan for cabinet work. Variety *T. n. radicans* grows from a tufted base and has prostrate branches up to 8 feet long.

The Chinese torreya (*T. grandis*), a native of eastern China, not hardy in the north, is suited only for regions of moderately mild winters. It is slightly more resistant to cold than the California-nutmeg. From the Japanese torreya it is distinguishable by the yellowish-green color of its two-year-old branches, from the stinking-cedar, which has its second-season branches of the same color, by its yellowish-green foliage, which is scarcely ill-scented when bruised, and by its leaves being up to 1 inch long. In its native habitat this species is sometimes 80 feet tall, but mostly is lower and often is shrubby. It is not common in cultivation. Two other Chinese species, *T. fargesii*, related to *T. nucifera*, but with darker foliage and differing in botanical details, and *T. jackii*, which is somewhat like the California-nutmeg, but with longer, sickle-shaped leaves, are perhaps not in cultivation.

Garden and Landscape Uses. As garden ornamentals, torreyas have about the same values as yews, which they closely resemble. Under cultivation they generally develop as tall shrubs or small trees rather than the big specimens they sometimes are in their native haunts. They form good screens and useful backgrounds to flower borders and may be used with good effect as single specimens, in groups, or mixed with other trees and shrubs in beds and borders. Torreyas find any ordinary, reasonably fertile and well-drained soil that is on the moist side agreeable. Unlike many evergreens, they do not object to limestone soils. They appreciate partial shade.

Cultivation. No special difficulties attend the cultivation of torreyas. They transplant readily and may be pruned to any extent necessary to keep them shapely. Should they become overgrown through neglect or other cause, it is safe to cut them back severely just before the beginning of a new growing season. If this is done, they should be fertilized and mulched afterward and watered freely in dry weather during the summer following the operation. Propagation is by seeds sown in sandy, peaty soil or by veneer grafting in winter or early spring onto understocks of

the plum-yew (*Cephalotaxus*). Only erect terminal shoots should be employed as grafting scions, laterals develop into asymmetrical plants without definite leaders. Torreyas can also be rooted from cuttings taken in summer or early fall and planted under mist or in a propagating bench in a very humid greenhouse or cold frame, but plants from cuttings grow very slowly for which reason the other means of increase are generally preferred. For more general information see Conifers.

TORU is *Persoonia toru*.

TORUS. The botanical term torus, the equivalent of receptacle, designates the end of a stem or stalk, usually enlarged or elongated, upon which some or all parts of a flower or flowers are borne. Such a feature is usually well developed in the flower heads of plants of the daisy family COMPOSITAE, as well as in the flowers of some other families.

TOTARA is *Podocarpus totara*.

TOTEM POLE. This name is sometimes used for *Euphorbia ingens monstrosa*. The totem pole cactus is *Lophocereus schottii monstrosus*.

TOUCH-ME-NOT. This common name of European *Impatiens noli-tangere* is sometimes applied to North American *I. capensis* and other species of the genus. The touch-me-not tree is *Laportea gigas*.

TOUMEYA. See Pediocactus.

TOURRETTIA (Tour-rèttia). Sometimes spelled *Tourretia*, the genus *Tourrettia*, of the bignonia family BIGNONIACEAE, consists of one species, native from Mexico to Peru. Its name commemorates Marc Antoine L. C. de Latourrette, a French botanist, who died in 1793.

A vining herbaceous plant or subshrub, *T. lappacea* (syn. *T. volubilis*), attaining heights of 6 feet or so, has bright green, opposite, stalked leaves that are twice- or thrice-divided into thin, coarsely-toothed, pointed-elliptic to ovate, stalked leaflets, with blades 1 inch to 2 inches long and with usually a slender, branched tendril with each leaf. The brilliant red to purple-violet flowers, carried in long, terminal, spikelike racemes, are slender-tubular and about ¾ inch long. They have two-lipped calyxes, and a corolla with one arched lip or with one such and a small tooth representing another. There are four stamens and a style, shorter than the corolla, with a three-branched stigma. The fruits, egg-shaped to conical, burrlike capsules covered with long, recurved prickles, are 1 inch to 2 inches long.

Garden Uses and Cultivation. This curious vine is best treated as an annual either

by, in the Deep South and other places that have long growing seasons, sowing directly outdoors in spring or by sowing earlier indoors and raising the young plants in pots in a greenhouse until warm weather arrives, and then planting them outdoors. They need a sunny location and ordinary fertile soil. A trellis or other suitable support to which their tendrils can attach themselves is requisite.

TOWER-OF-JEWELS is *Echium pininana*.

TOWNSENDIA (Townsénd-ia). Twenty-one species of quite lovely western North American *Townsendia*, of the daisy family COMPOSITAE, are recognized. A few are cultivated, chiefly by rock gardeners and, in appropriate regions, by devotees of native plant gardening. Otherwise the group is not of great horticultural importance. It consists mostly of hardy herbaceous perennials, a few biennials, and annuals. Its name commemorates David Townsend, an American amateur botanist, who died in 1858.

Townsendias are most closely related to *Aster*, *Erigeron*, and *Boltonia*, among familiar cultivated plants. These differ from it and each other chiefly in details of the hairs attached to the ovaries, the pappus. Townsendias are mostly low, tap-rooted plants with alternate, linear to spoon-shaped, undivided leaves lacking marginal teeth. Their usually solitary flower heads resemble those of *Aster*, they have yellow central disks and white, purplish pink, or violet-blue ray florets.

Perennial species worth considering include *T. exscapa* (syns. *T. sericea*, *T. wilcoxiana*), which has the widest natural dis-

Townsendia exscapa

tribution of any and is the most commonly cultivated. A native of the Great Plains from Alberta to Arizona, it is low and is tufted with narrow leaves, up to 2 inches long, and white or pink flower heads, as much in diameter, that scarcely rise above the foliage. Very similar *T. hookeri* has a natural range from Colorado to Canada. It forms a cushion of grayish, narrowly-linear leaves and bears solitary, usually stalkless heads with white rays, often tinged purplish on their undersides, 1¼ to 1¾ inches in diameter. One of the handsomest is **T. rothrockii**, endemic to high altitudes in Colorado. It has violet-rayed, solitary flower heads, about 1¾ inches across, carried on short stems to just above the tuft of green, spoon-shaped leaves. A taller species is **T. formosa.** Each of its branchless stems rises to a height of 1 foot to 2 feet and is topped by a solitary flower head, 2 inches in diameter, with rays white above and purplish on their undersides.

For one season of bloom the biennials are satisfactory. They flower in their second year and then die. These include *T. grandiflora, T. parryi,* and *T. florifera.* With branched stems up to 9 inches high and flower heads, 2 inches in diameter, with white rays marked beneath with a stripe of pink, **T. grandiflora** is native from South Dakota to New Mexico. Having solitary flower heads, almost 2½ inches across and with violet-blue rays, atop stems 2 inches to over 1 foot tall, **T. parryi** is one of the most attractive species. It is native from Wyoming and Idaho to Canada. The last-mentioned biennial, **T. florifera** is indigenous from Utah and Nevada to Oregon, and in Washington. The stalks of its white- or pink-rayed flower heads, each 1½ inches across, are usually about 4 inches tall and branchless, but may be up to 10 inches and branched.

Garden Uses and Cultivation. The chief garden uses are indicated in the opening paragraph of this treatment. As to cultivation, townsendias give no great trouble provided the soil is extremely well drained; these more or less desert plants will not survive wetness for long periods. Because of their deep taproots they are better left undisturbed once they are well established, but as seedlings and small plants they may be moved without difficulty. Both the perennials and biennials are easily raised from seeds sown in sandy, porous soil around the month of May, or the perennials may be started earlier indoors. The seedlings are transplanted to nursery beds or cold frames in rows 6 to 8 inches apart, with 4 inches between the plants in the rows. They are moved to their flowering quarters in fall or the following spring. In their final locations spacing of 4 to 6 inches is usually adequate.

TOYON is *Heteromeles arbutifolia.*

TRACE ELEMENTS. For long it was believed that plants needed only nitrogen, phosphorus, potassium, and possibly calcium from the soil. Research has proved that other elements are necessary, notably magnesium and sulfur, in appreciable amounts, several others in minute quantities. The last, called trace elements, include boron, copper, iron, manganese, molybdenum, and zinc. Not essential, but beneficial, are chlorine and sodium. Some twenty other elements absorbed in minute quantities are nonessential and possibly without benefit.

Most garden soils are not lacking in trace elements, but in certain regions, one or more are in short supply or absent and, for satisfactory results, it is necessary to remedy the deficiencies. Cooperative Extension Agents can advise about local needs. Do not waste money and effort on trace elements unless they are needed.

The trace element iron, necessary for the production of chlorophyll and the photosynthesis of sugars, even though present in adequate amounts, is sometimes tied with other elements in insoluble compounds so that it is unavailable to the plant. This results in the foliage becoming chlorotic (yellow except usually along the veins), a condition more common in alkaline soils than in acid soils, although it may occur in the latter. It can be corrected by acidifying the soil or by applying iron chelates or ferrous sulfate to the soil or as foliage sprays.

TRACHELIUM (Trachèl-ium)—Throatwort. Ten or fewer species, natives of the Mediterranean region, compose *Trachelium,* a genus of the bellflower family CAMPANULACEAE, that in aspect differs markedly from most of its relatives. Both its botanical and common names allude to supposed virtues for alleviating diseases of the throat. The botanical name is derived from the Greek *trachelos,* a neck.

Throatworts are herbaceous perennials and, with the possible exception of *T. rumelianum,* not hardy in the north. They have usually erect stems and alternate, undivided leaves. The numerous small, purplish, blue, or white, tubular, but not bell-shaped flowers are in terminal clusters. Each has a five-lobed calyx, a five-lobed corolla, five stamens, and one long-protruding style. The fruits are capsules.

The most familiar kind, **T. caeruleum** is 3 to 4 feet tall, leafy, and essentially hairless. Its leaves, up to 3 inches long, are stalked, pointed-ovate to pointed-elliptic, and have bluntly-double-toothed margins. Toward their tops the reddish stems branch freely and widely and the branch ends terminate in flattish clusters of numerous upturned, blue or lavender-mauve, slightly fragrant, starry flowers, each about ¼ inch long. The flowers of *T. c. album* are not a very good white, being less pleasing than the color of the typical species. An endemic of Sicily, *T. c. lanceolatum* has leaves narrower than those of the species and winged stalks.

Native to limestone soils in Greece and the Balkan Peninsula, **T. rumelianum** (syns. *T. jacquinii rumelianum, Diosphaera rumelianum*), not over 6 inches tall, has sharp-toothed, oblong to ovate leaves. Borne in late summer in flattish, fuzzy-looking, branched clusters, the minute flowers of **T. asperuloides** are blue-purple or white. Native to southern Greece, this charming kind is 2 inches tall and forms a compact mound several inches across. Its subspherical to ovate-spatula-shaped leaves are up to ¼ inch across. The pink flowers, one to five from the axils of the upper leaves, are about ¼ inch across.

Trachelium rumelianum

Trachelium caeruleum

Trachelium asperuloides

Garden Uses. The taller throatworts described are admirable for flower gardens and for pots in greenhouses. Their flowers are useful for cutting. In not-too-cold climates, *T. rumelianum* and *T. asperuloides* are suitable for rock gardens and dry walls.

Cultivation. Best results are had by treating *T. caeruleum* as a biennial or annual. To cultivate it as a biennial, sow seeds in sandy soil in June or July and transplant the seedlings to small pots. Keep them growing in a cool, lightly shaded greenhouse or cold frame, or plunged to the rims of their pots in a bed of sand or ashes outdoors. When the young plants are about 3 inches high, pinch out their tips to encourage branching and, when the branches attain a length of 3 inches, pinch out the tips of the branches. As soon as the roots fill the pots, transplant to containers an inch or two wider until 5- or 6-inch pots are attained. Use porous, fertile soil. If it is acid, add a little lime. Except in regions where little or no frost occurs, the plants must be wintered in a cool greenhouse or a cold frame where they will not freeze. Winter night temperatures of 40 to 45°F are adequate, but in spring they may be increased by five degrees. Day temperatures may be five to ten degrees above those maintained at night. In spring, after danger of cold weather has past, the plants may be set about 1 foot apart in the garden or be repotted into 6- or 7-inch pots and kept in the greenhouse.

Tracheliums need adequate supplies of water at all times. Moist soil that is porous and well drained encourages thrifty growth. When their final pots are filled with roots, the plants benefit from regular applications of dilute liquid fertilizer from late spring to fall. If they are kept in a greenhouse in summer it should be ventilated freely and, to preserve the color of the flowers and extend the blooming season, lightly shaded. Seeds are usually preferred for propagation, but cuttings can also be used.

When grown as an annual, *T. caeruleum* is raised from seeds sown in a greenhouse in a temperature of 55 to 60°F from January to March. As soon as the young plants are big enough to handle, transplant them singly to 2½-inch pots and later to those of a 4- or 5-inch size. Pinch them once or leave them unpinched to develop a single, taller stem. Whichever is done, plants from spring-sown seeds will be shorter than those raised as biennials. Grow the young plants in 55°F at night and five or ten degrees warmer by day until they are planted outdoors. Before planting outdoors, harden them in a cold frame or sheltered place outdoors for a week or two. Alternatively, they may be kept in pots and bloomed in the greenhouse.

In rock gardens and in pans in alpine greenhouses, *T. asperuloides* and *T. rumelianum* succeed in well-drained, gritty, limestone soil. Light shade from strong sun is desirable. Propagation is by seed and by division.

TRACHELOSPERMUM (Trachelo-spérmum) —Star-Jasmine or Confederate-Jasmine, Climbing-Dogbane. Belonging to the dogbane family APOCYNACEAE, the genus *Trachelospermum* has a rather unusual natural distribution. Comprising ten or more species, it occurs from Japan to India and is represented in North America by one native kind. Its name is from the Greek *trachelos*, a neck, and *sperma*, a seed. It alludes to the form of the seeds.

Trachelospermums are milky-juiced vines or shrubs with opposite, short-stalked, more or less leathery, undivided leaves, the veins of which are pinnately-arranged. In terminal or axillary, sometimes umbel-like panicles, the flowers are white, yellowish, or rarely reddish. They have a small, five-parted calyx with, at its base on the inside, five or ten scales or glands; a slender, straight-tubed corolla with five spreading, overlapping lobes (petals); and five stamens, their tips sometimes protruding from the throat of the bloom, their anthers joined to the stigma that ends the slender style. The fruits are paired, elongated, podlike follicles, the tips of each pair sometimes united.

Star-jasmine or Confederate-jasmine (*T. jasminoides* syn. *Rhynchospermum jasminoides*) is a slender-stemmed evergreen vine native to southern China. Its short-pointed, toothless, elliptic to obovate leaves, 2 to 4 inches long, are hairless, or sometimes hairy on their undersides. Delightfully fragrant, the starry, short-tubed, white flowers, in axillary clusters or sprays with stalks longer than the leaves, have leafy calyxes with reflexed lobes. Their anthers do not protrude from the throat of the flower. Variety *T. j. japonicum* has white-veined leaves that turn bronze in fall. The sometimes red-tinged leaves of *T. j. variegatum* are edged and blotched with white.

Much like *T. jasminoides*, but with broader leaves and distinctly yellowish-white blooms, the anthers of which protrude somewhat from their throats, *T. asiaticum* (syn. *T. divaricatum*) is a native of Japan and Korea. Native to northeastern India, *T. lucidum* (syn. *T. fragrans*) differs from the star-jasmine in its calyx being neither leafy nor conspicuously hairy. Also, its lobes are triangular rather than spatula-shaped. Its leaves, elliptic to obovate-elliptic, are up to 5 inches long. In both terminal and lateral groups, the short-stalked flower clusters are of white or cream-colored blooms; their anthers do not protrude from the throat. The plant commonly cultivated as *T. fragrans* is *Chonemorpha fragrans*.

American *T. difforme*, called climbing-dogbane, a high-climbing vine native in swamps and wet woodlands from Delaware to Illinois, Oklahoma, Florida, and Texas, has lanceolate or sometimes reverse-lanceolate leaves and ½-inch-wide,

Trachelospermum jasminoides

short-tubed, pale yellow blooms clustered on short branches from the leaf axils.

Garden and Landscape Uses. The native American species is occasionally cultivated in botanical collections and, in the south, in gardens of native plants under conditions approximating those under which it grows in the wild. The others are popular outdoors in the south, in California, and other warm regions and as greenhouse and sometimes window garden plants. They may be used as vines or, with appropriate tip pruning or shearing, as shrubs or groundcovers, 1½ to 2 feet tall.

A groundcover of *Trachelospermum jasminoides*

Trachelospermum asiaticum as a groundcover

Cultivation. Trachelospermums are not fussy. They prosper in ordinary soils, preferring somewhat acid ones, containing a fair organic content, that do not dry unduly. A little shade from bright sun is beneficial. Indoors, they may be accommodated in pots or tubs. As young plants they grow rather slowly if kept cool. For them, a winter night temperature of 55°F, with a daytime rise of five to fifteen degrees depending upon the brightness of the weather, is suitable. Larger plants are satisfied with temperatures five degrees lower. In summer they may be put outside in a

lightly shaded place. Watering should be fairly generous from spring to fall, less so in winter. Large specimens need potting only at intervals of a few years. In intervening springs top-dress with rich soil. Summer applications of mild liquid fertilizers benefit well-rooted specimens. The stems may be trained and tied to stakes or wires or other supports. As a groundcover set plants 1½ to 3 feet apart and shear back shoots that grow erectly. Propagation is by cuttings, layers, and seed. The chief pests are mealybugs, red spider mites, and scale insects.

TRACHYCARPUS (Trachycárpus). In this genus of the palm family PALMAE belong eight Himalayan and eastern Asian fan-leaved species, of which one is probably the hardiest of all palms. It is the windmill palm, which lives outdoors in sheltered locations at Victoria, British Columbia, Hampton, Virginia, and Edinburgh, Scotland. The name *Trachycarpus* derives from the Greek *trachys*, rough, and *karpos*, fruit. It refers to the irregular appearance of the fruits.

This genus consists of small to medium-sized trees with solitary or clustered, usually shaggy or fiber-covered trunks and rounded or somewhat kidney-shaped leaves cut into many narrow segments. The branched flower spikes arise among the leaves and bear bisexual or unisexual, small, yellow blooms. Individual trees are often unisexual. The bluish fruits are three-lobed or irregular and as large or slightly larger than peas.

The commonest sort, the windmill palm (*T. fortunei*), a native of China widely planted in Japan, has a solitary slender trunk up to about 30 feet tall and covered with black hairlike fibers. The leaf segments of mature specimens usually droop. A lower kind with stiff leaf segments that do not droop, *T. wagnerianus*, is also a native of China that is planted in Japan. It is

Trachycarpus fortunei, a young specimen, Chelsea Physic Garden, London, England

Trachycarpus fortunei, an old specimen in Ireland

Trachycarpus fortunei (crown of foliage)

less hardy than the windmill palm, but survives from Georgia southward and in California. Differing in having more than one trunk, *T. caespitosus* is about as hardy as the last and is probably a native of eastern Asia. Up to 15 feet in height, it has leaves with stiff, outstanding segments and sharply saw-toothed stalks. Unlike any of the above in having trunks not covered with fibrous sheaths is *T. martianus*, of the Himalayan region. This is probably less hardy than those mentioned above.

Garden and Landscape Uses. The windmill palm is handsome and well suited for planting as solitary specimens and for grouping. It can be used in avenues and to provide accent points in formal gardens. One of its chief values is to give a tropical or subtropical flavor to gardens in regions where it is too cold for other palms to survive. The other species have similar uses, but are less hardy.

Cultivation. No difficulties attend the cultivation of members of this genus. They succeed in any fairly good, well-drained soil in sun or light shade. It is better that they be sheltered from strong winds as these are apt to tear the foliage. Toward the northern limits of where they can be expected to survive, sites for them should be chosen that assure shelter from cold winds; low spots likely to be frost pockets because of poor air drainage should be avoided as well. Large pots or tubs in which they are grown should be adequately drained and the soil used should be coarse, fertile, and porous. They may be grown throughout the year in a cool greenhouse, minimum winter night temperature 40 to 50°F, or stood outside in summer and wintered in a greenhouse, cellar, garage, or some similar, light, frost-proof place. Watering should be generous from spring through fall, more sparing in winter. Well-established plants benefit from biweekly applications of dilute liquid fertilizer from spring through fall. Greenhouses in which these palms are kept through the summer should be lightly shaded at that season. Propagation is by fresh seed sown in sandy, peaty soil in a temperature of about 70°F. For further information see Palms.

TRACHYMENE (Trachýmen-e) — Blue Lace Flower. The most popular of the two cultivated species of *Trachymene* is better known to gardeners by its now obsolete name of *Didiscus coerulea*. The genus comprises in excess of a dozen species of annual and perennial herbaceous plants, natives of Australia, Fiji, Borneo, the Philippine Islands, and Malaysia, and is a member of the carrot family UMBELLI-FERAE. The generic name derives from the Greek *trachys*, rough, and *hymen*, a membrane, and alludes to a characteristic of the fruits of some species. The fruits are dry and flattened.

The blue lace flower (*T. coerulea*), of Australia, the most commonly cultivated kind, is a slender-stemmed, branching, erect annual, 1½ to 2½ feet tall, with twice- or thrice-divided leaves, the segments of which are narrow and three-lobed. The foliage is chiefly on the stems and is rather scanty. The small flowers are in flat heads, 2 to 3 inches wide, carried on slender stiff stems closely resembling those of the wild carrot or Queen Anne's lace, but of a pretty pale blue or lavender hue. The other cultivated kind, *T. pilosa,* also Australian, about 6 inches in height, has leaves divided into linear lobes and small, blue flowers in short-stalked heads.

Trachymene coerulea

Garden Uses. The trachymenes described here are attractive annuals for outdoor display, and the blue lace flower for cutting for indoor arrangements. For this purpose it may be grown in greenhouses for winter bloom as well as outdoors in summer. The other species is useful for the fronts of flower beds and borders and as an edging plant, and is attractive in rock gardens.

Cultivation. Porous, well-drained soil of medium fertility suits these plants best. They do not prosper in clayey earth. The seeds are rather slow to germinate. Those of the blue lace flower, in a temperature of 60 to 65°F, take about twenty days before the seedlings break the soil surface. Sow outdoors at a depth of about ¼ inch in early spring where the plants are to bloom; for cut flowers, sow in rows 1 foot to 1½ feet apart and thin the seedlings to about 4 inches apart. To have decorative patches in a flower bed, broadcast the seeds thinly, rake them into the surface, and thin out the resulting seedlings to allow 6 to 8 inches between individuals. Sow seeds of *T. pilosa* broadcast or, when the plant is grown as an edging, in rows 6 to 8 inches apart. Thin out the young plants to 3 or 4 inches apart.

For early bloom, plants of both species, raised from seeds sown indoors about ten weeks before planting-out time, can be set in the garden about the time it is safe to plant tomatoes. The young plants may be grown in flats, but better results are usually achieved by growing them singly in small pots. These are sun-loving plants that should not be expected to prosper in shady places.

In greenhouses the blue lace flower can be bloomed from fall until late spring. It responds well to supplemental lighting; to assure blooms for cutting during the depth of winter it is essential to lengthen the day by this means. This plant needs a minimum temperature of 55 to 60°F at night with a rise of five to ten degrees during the day. The soil must be porous and the beds or benches thoroughly drained. Care must be exercised in watering because an excessively wet soil, especially in winter or before the roots have taken full possession of it, can easily bring failure. It is very helpful to keep the surface of the soil stirred shallowly. This admits air, dries the surface layer, and reduces the risk of loss from rotting of the lower stems. The blue lace flower needs full sun except that in late spring and early summer when the light is extremely strong and temperatures in the greenhouse rise unduly; a very light shade over the glass improves the color of the flowers and reduces the danger of quick spoilage. When grown in beds or benches, young plants from 2½- or 3-inch pots are planted about 8 inches apart. The blue lace flower requires rather a long season of growth and produces flowers for cutting over an extended period. For winter bloom, sow seeds in August. The blue lace flower is also satisfactory in pots. For this purpose it is best to grow three or four plants in containers 5 or 6 inches in diameter.

TRACHYPHRYNIUM. See Hybophrynium.

TRACHYSTEMON (Trachy-stèmon). Very much like borage (*Borago*), but having flowers with linear corolla lobes (petals), and anthers much shorter than the stalks on which they are borne and without appendages, *Trachystemon* consists of two species, natives of the eastern Mediterranean region. It belongs in the borage family BORAGINACEAE and has a name derived from the Greek *trachys*, rough, and *stemon*, a stamen, in allusion to the rough-stalked stamens of one species.

Trachystemons are erect, branched, herbaceous perennials with bristly-hairy stems and foliage. Their flowers, in rather loose, branched panicles, are stalked and have five-cleft calyxes, and corollas with cylindrical tubes and five spreading, or eventually back-turned, narrow lobes. There are five stamens. The fruits consist of four small nutlets.

Sometimes called Eastern-borage, **T. orientalis** has thick, creeping rhizomes. It attains a height of 1 foot to 2 feet. Its long-stalked lower leaves are heart-shaped and up to 1 foot long. Those above are ovate-lanceolate. The flowering parts of the stems are branched and almost leafless. Bluish-purple, the numerous flowers are ½ inch wide or slightly wider. Their stamens form a cone that projects forward. The petals spread widely or they are slightly reflexed.

Garden Uses and Cultivation. Although less decorative than borage and with flowers of less clear hues, *T. orientalis* (syn. *Borago orientalis*) is worth planting for variety. It is best suited for lightly shaded places in naturalistic landscapes, such as at the fringes of woodlands, and is quite hardy, but just how much cold it will stand is uncertain. It thrives in ordinary garden soils, is easily grown from seed, and may be increased by division and root cuttings.

TRADESCANTIA (Trades-cántia) — Spiderwort, Wandering Jew. One of the most remarkable horticulturists of the seventeenth century, John Tradescant, gardener to Charles I of England, is commemorated by the name of this familiar genus. Tradescant, who died in 1638, established collections of living plants, natural history specimens, artifacts, and curiosities at South Lambeth near London, which were added to significantly by his son, also named John, who died in 1662. Father and son traveled widely, the son to Virginia. Their collections became the basis of the Ashmolean Museum at Oxford.

The genus *Tradescantia* is confined in the wild to the Americas. It comprises about sixty species of the spiderwort family COMMELINACEAE and includes hardy and nonhardy sorts. In gardens *Zebrina pendula* and some kinds of *Commelina* are frequently mistakenly named *Tradescantia*, as are sometimes species of *Callisia, Cuthbertia, Dichorisandra, Gibasis, Hadrodemas,* and *Setcreasea.*

In habit of growth tradescantias differ considerably. Some are trailers, some erect, some deciduous, and some evergreen. Their flowers are more constant. Occasionally solitary, much more commonly they are in clusters of few to many arising from a nest of one to three leaflike bracts. More or less stalked, each bloom has three concave sepals, three obovate to nearly circular petals that are not united at their bases into a tube, six stamens generally all fertile, and one style. The fruits are capsules.

The finest hardy herbaceous kinds, commonly cultivated as varieties of *T. virginiana*, are hybrids of that species, *T. ohiensis*, and *T. subaspera*. The correct group name for these very beautiful hybrids is **T. andersoniana.** They prevailingly are somewhat lower plants with stouter, erect stems and larger, more brilliantly colored flowers, up to 1 inch or more across, than *T. virginiana*. Varieties belonging here include *T. a. alba*, flowers white; *T. a. caerulea*, flowers blue; *T. a. carnea*, flowers pinkish; *T. a. coccinea*, flowers reddish; *T. a. hutchinsonii*, flowers light blue; *T. a. lilacina*, flowers pale lilac; *T. a. major*, flowers double; *T. a. nana*, dwarf; *T. a. purpurea*, flowers purple; *T. a. rubra*, flowers purplish-red; and *T. a. violacea*, flowers violet. Among fine sorts that bear 'fancy' rather than Latinized names are 'Osprey', white; 'Iris Pritchard', white, tinged violet;

'Isis', deep blue; 'James Stratton', deep blue; 'James C. Weguelin', porcelain-blue; 'Pauline', orchid-mauve; and 'Purple Dome', brilliant purple.

Common spiderwort (**T. virginiana**) is native in moist woodlands and prairies from Maine to Michigan, Minnesota, Georgia, Tennessee, and Missouri. Essentially hairless or minutely-hairy, it is a deciduous herbaceous perennial 1 foot to 2 feet tall. It has few to many erect stems with usually two to four linear leaves up to over ½ inch wide and often smaller and narrower than the bracts from which the usually solitary terminal cluster of flowers comes. The blooms, 1 inch to 1¼ inches wide, have hairy or hairless, but not glandular, leafy sepals and blue to purple petals. Much like the last and of similar size, **T. bracteata,** native from Minnesota to Iowa, Texas, and Arizona, differs chiefly in the stalks of its individual flowers and their sepals being densely clothed with a mixture of glandular and nonglandular hairs. This has pink to blue flowers. Those of *T. b. rosea* are rose-pink.

Native from southern New England to Minnesota, Florida, and Texas, hairless and glaucous **T. ohiensis** (syns. *T. canaliculata, T. reflexa*), up to 3 feet tall, has leaves up to 1½ feet long by 1¾ inches wide. Its blue, rose-pink, or rarely white flowers are ¾ inch to 1½ inches across. Endemic to the Ozark region of Missouri, Arkansas, and Oklahoma, **T. ozarkana** is a pretty species with stems 6 inches to 1½ feet tall. It has fleshy, ovate to linear-lanceolate, pointed leaves 4 to about 10 inches long and, in clusters of several, pale rose-pink to purple or white flowers, 1 inch to 1½ inches across, with broad-ovate petals. Native from Pennsylvania to Missouri and Florida, **T. subaspera,** 1½ to 3 feet tall, has rather stout hairless or sparingly-hairy

Tradescantia andersoniana variety

Tradescantia virginiana

Tradescantia ozarkana

Tradescantia fluminensis

Tradescantia fluminensis variegata

stems and leaves, the latter lanceolate, mostly from 4 to 8 inches long, and up to 1½ inches wide. The pale to deep blue or rarely white flowers are about 1 inch in diameter.

Wandering Jew (*T. fluminensis*) shares its vernacular name with *T. albiflora* and *Zebrina pendula*. The last differs from the tradescantias in the petals of its flowers being joined at their bases to form a short corolla tube. Native to Brazil, Uruguay, and Paraguay, *T. fluminensis* has trailing, succulent stems that root from the nodes and alternate, ovate-oblong to oblong, lustrous, fleshy leaves, about 1½ inches long by one-half as wide, that especially when grown in sun are usually stained purplered on their undersides. The stalkless flower clusters, cosseted in a pair of broad-lanceolate bracts of unequal size, are of many stalked, white flowers, about ½ inch wide, with hairy-stalked stamens. The

leaves of *T. f. variegata* are attractively banded lengthwise with creamy-white and pale yellow. Also called wandering Jew, *T. albiflora* has much in common with *T. fluminensis*. The most obvious differences are that its leaves are only one-quarter to one-third as wide as they are long and have plain green undersurfaces. The small, white blooms are sparsely produced. Vigorous *T. a. albovittata* has bluish-green leaves striped and edged with white. Very succulent *T. a. laekenensis* 'Rainbow' has pale green, ovate leaves with lengthwise, purplish-tinted, white stripes. Trailing or creeping *T. blossfeldiana* is an evergreen native of Brazil and perhaps Argentina. It has thick, fleshy, sparingly-hairy, purple stems and narrow, oblong to elliptic, stalkless leaves, up to 4 inches long by 1¼ inches wide, with olive-green upper surfaces and pur-

plish undersides thickly clothed with long white hairs. In compact clusters freely borne, the small blooms have purple-tipped, white petals. The leaves of *T. b. variegata* are striped lengthwise with creamy-white, pale green, and yellow. They have a purple midrib. Native to Brazil, *T. crassula* has erect, branched stems, 1½ to 2 feet tall, and lanceolate to oblong-lanceolate, fleshy, green leaves up to 4 inches long and hairless except for a fringe along the margin. The white flowers, ¼ to ½ inch wide, are in mostly terminal umbels. Peruvian *T. navicularis* is a creeper with sparsely-branched stems with two ranks of bronzy-green, pointed-ovate, ¾-inch-long, fleshy leaves mottled with purple on their undersides and with hair-fringed margins. The small, stalked flowers are bright rose-purple. Mexican *T. sillamontana* is a trailer with fleshy stems and leaves, the latter ovate and stem-clasping, loosely clothed with long, fluffy, white hairs. The upper surfaces of the leaves are dark green, whereas the undersides, like the stems, are purplish. The flowers are orchid-pink.

Garden and Landscape Uses. Native species of spiderwort are appropriate for native plant gardens, informal and semiformal places, and *T. virginiana* may be acceptable in more formal beds, but generally varieties of the hybrid *T. andersoniana* are the most desirable hardy sorts. They succeed with little attention in ordinary soil, in light shade or sun, and seem to give the best results if the ground is on the dryish side, rather than as moist as their parent species favor in the wild.

Nonhardy tradescantias in the tropics and warm subtropics are excellent outdoor plants, the trailing sorts as groundcovers.

Tradescantia albiflora albovittata

Tradescantia blossfeldiana (flowers)

Tradescantia blossfeldiana variegata

Tradescantia blossfeldiana

Tradescantia crassula

They are highly regarded as easy-to-grow greenhouse and window plants, the trailers suitable for hanging baskets as well as pots. Among these last, *T. albiflora* and *T. fluminensis* and their varieties are best known, being almost ubiquitous under benches and in other out-of-the-way places in many greenhouses.

Indoors these plants succeed with various amounts of warmth from that of the coolest frost-free greenhouses to those where tropical conditions prevail. They generally readily adapt to a variety of conditions. Ordinary soil suits.

Cultivation. Division, the commonest means of multiplying hardy tradescantias, may also be used with nonhardy ones. For the latter, however, cuttings, which root with the greatest ease imaginable, are more often used. Keep the soil moderately moist, somewhat drier for those with very thick stems and foliage and for those that are

Tillandsia ionantha

Tofieldia glutinosa

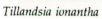
Trientalis borealis

Tithonia rotundifolia

Tigridia pavonia

Trichoglottis breviracema

Trillium grandiflorum, double-flowered

Trollius europaeus

Trillium viride

Tradescantia sillamontana

decidedly hairy. Also, do not splash water on the foliage of such kinds and keep the atmosphere somewhat drier than for non-succulent, hairless sorts. Collectors of succulents often include *T. navicularis* among their desert-type plants.

TRAGOPOGON (Trago-pògon) — Goat's Beard, Salsify or Vegetable-Oyster. None of the perhaps fifty species of this genus of the daisy family COMPOSITAE receives serious attention as an ornamental, but one is occasionally cultivated as a vegetable. It and a few others are naturalized in North America. The genus is native in Europe, Asia, and North Africa. Its name comes from the Greek *tragos*, a goat, and *pogon*, a beard. It alludes to the appearance of the seed heads. The kind commonly called goat's beard (*T. pratensis*) is an introduced weed in North America.

Tragopogons have yellow or purple flower heads with the florets all strap-shaped (like those of a dandelion rather than like the disk florets of daisies' centers). They are biennial or perennial, herbaceous, tap-rooted plants with milky sap. Their alternate, usually more or less grass-like, linear leaves clasp the stems with their bases. They are neither lobed nor toothed. The flower heads, solitary at the branch ends, have involucres (collars) of a single row of equal-sized, erect bracts. The long, slender seeds have a cluster of feathery hairs at one end.

Salsify or vegetable-oyster (*T. porrifolius*) is a hardy, hairless biennial, 1¼ to 4 feet in height, with leaves up to 1 foot long by ¾ inch broad. Immediately beneath the flower heads, which have involucres of usually eight, rarely fewer or more, pointed bracts 1 inch to 1½ inches long, the stems conspicuously thicken. The florets, shorter than the involucres, are purple. A plume of feathery hairs is attached to each seed by a long slender stalk. For cultivation as a vegetable see the Encyclopedia entry titled Salsify, Oyster Plant, or Vegetable Oyster.

TRAILING-ARBUTUS is *Epigaea repens*.

TRAINING PLANTS. Training consists of those attentions given plants, especially during their early, formative stages, for the purposes of encouraging or causing them to assume forms different from those they would establish without such controls. Most frequently, trained plants are more or less formalized.

Familiar examples of plants that have been subjected to training are trees with branches evenly spaced to admit light and air to all parts, street trees with their lowest branches high enough not to interfere with traffic, such ornamentals as bay trees, chrysanthemums, fuchsias, heliotropes, geraniums, and lantanas that are grown as standards (with a single branchless trunk topped with a moplike head of branches, foliage, and flowers), hedges formed and made dense and compact by repeated shearing, espaliered trees and shrubs, vines restricted to trellises, pillars, posts, wires, and other supports, topiary work, and bonsai.

The chief operations of training are pruning (which includes pinching and shearing) to eliminate unwanted shoots or branches, to encourage the growth of new, advantageously located shoots and branches, and to restrict specimens to size, and positioning trunks, branches, and shoots, usually by tying or in other ways attaching them to supports or, with bonsai, by wiring.

Supports may include stakes, posts, trellises, wires, walls, and frameworks of wire or chicken wire. Positioning of the shoots and branches on the supports is usually done in such fashion that the space available is covered uniformly and all parts of the plant receive adequate light. For more details see the Encyclopedia entries Pruning, Espalier, Hedges, and Bonsai.

TRANSPIRATION. An understanding of this basic physiological process is important to gardeners. Transpiration is the loss of water in the form of vapor, chiefly from leaves through stomata (tiny pores), to a lesser extent through similar openings in stems called lenticels, and from other plant parts. The loss, under favorable conditions promptly replaced by water absorbed by the roots, takes place whenever the relative humidity of the atmosphere is appreciably below 100 percent.

Tradescantia sillamontana (foliage and flowers)

Tradescantia sillamontana as a pot plant

If loss of moisture by transpiration exceeds replacement for any appreciable time, soft tissues wilt and die and firmer tissues dry and die. If wilting has not proceeded too far, the leaves of many plants recover when water is made available to the roots, but even so, harm may come from interruption of photosynthesis (the food elaborating process). Commonly this is not fully restored until several hours after the wilted foliage becomes turgid.

The rate of loss increases with low humidity, exposure to wind or other air currents, higher temperatures up to an optimum for each sort of plant, and increased light. In short, weather that favors the drying of laundry and other types of evaporation also promotes transpiration.

Reducing water loss by transpiration is often desirable and sometimes essential to the success of garden procedures. Quite obviously cuttings, leafy shoots severed from the roots that previously supplied them with water and now severely limited as to the amounts they can absorb, soon wilt and die if measures are not taken to control loss of moisture from their leaves. The same is true, although often to a lesser degree, of plants that have lost a significant proportion of their roots as a result of transplanting. Precautions against excessive transpiration is also occasioned when plants that need comparatively high humidity are grown in greenhouses and other environments where, unless special measures are taken, they transpire more water than their roots can replace. Death or serious winter damage to trees and shrubs, particularly evergreens, can result from their tops transpiring more water than their roots can absorb when the ground is frozen.

Methods of reducing transpiration include raising the humidity in greenhouses by wetting down (damping down) interior surfaces and by spraying or misting the plants with water. Comparatively high humidity is maintained in propagating cases and terrariums by keeping them closed or nearly closed to conserve the moisture within. Temporary shade and shelter from wind are frequently employed to reduce the transpiration of newly transplanted and repotted plants. In regions of harsh winters, similar measures are often used and antidesiccant sprays are employed to reduce the likelihood of winter killing among trees and shrubs. For more information see the Encyclopedia entry Protection for Plants.

TRANSPLANTING. See Planting and Transplanting.

TRAPA (Trà-pa)—Water-Chestnut or Water Caltrop or Jesuits' Nut, Water Nut, Singhara Nut. This genus consists of one very variable or, according to some authorities, up to thirty more finely separated species.

It must not be confused with another plant called water-chestnut, which belongs in the genus *Eleocharis*. The name, alluding to the fruits, is derived from *calcitrappa*, the Latin name of the caltrop, an instrument of war with four sharp iron points, so designed that when thrown on the ground one point always pointed upward and, therefore, presented a serious danger to cavalry.

Native to warmer parts of the eastern hemisphere, with one sort naturalized in North America, *Trapa* is closely related to *Oenothera*, of the evening-primrose family ONAGRACEAE, but by most modern botanists it is accorded a family of its own, the water nut family TRAPACEAE. The chief differences between these families are that the water nut family has flowers with a semi-inferior instead of a fully inferior ovary and four instead of the usual eight stamens of ONAGRACEAE.

Trapas are floating aquatics with two kinds of leaves. The underwater ones are opposite, the floating ones spread in rosette fashion. The latter have inflated leafstalks that provide buoyancy and are toothed. The flowers, solitary, small, and short-stalked, are borne in the leaf axils. They have a four-parted calyx, four corolla segments (petals), four stamens, and one style. The curious large, woody or bony, more or less top-shaped fruits contain within a thin wall an edible nut with sculptured surfaces and two or four prominent horns.

The water-chestnut, water caltrop, or Jesuits' nut (*T. natans*) is sparingly naturalized in North America. It has linear, soon deciduous, submersed leaves and an open rosette of mottled floating leaves that are hairless except on their veins beneath. In addition, the stems below water bear green organs that look like deeply-pinnately-lobed leaves. Botanists consider these to be specialized roots. The floating leaves have stalks markedly swollen near their middles and up to 6 inches long, those of successive leaves becoming progressively shorter above, which permits them to be disposed over the water surface without interfering with each other. The leaf blades are rhomboidal, and sharply-toothed above their middles. The white flowers are about ⅔ inch across. The curious four-horned, bony fruits are 2 to 3 inches from tip to tip of the most distantly spaced horns. This species is hardy. Closely related to *T. natans* is *T. verbanensis*, a native of Lake Maggiore in Italy. It has three-angled fruits, with only two horns, and triangular leaves.

The singhara nut (*T. bispinosa*) has smaller fruits than the water-chestnut. They measure about ¾ inch across the body and usually have only two horns. Also, the undersides of the leaves and leafstalks are very hairy. The leaf blades are 2½ to 3½ inches in diameter. Most curious of all in

the appearance of its fruits is *T. bicornis*, a Chinese species. Its fruits strongly suggest the head of a bull; they have two stout, long, downturned horns and a wrinkled body that represents the face of the animal.

Garden Uses. The water-chestnut is a dainty, attractive, and interesting addition to pools and is easy to grow. The other species are less hardy and are not likely to be cultivated except by specialists in water plants. All are at their best in full sun in slightly acid water where they have opportunity to root into nourishing mud. They provide shelter for fish.

Cultivation. For their satisfactory growth *T. bicornis* and *T. bispinosa* need tropical or subtropical conditions, but *T. natans* and *T. verbanensis* succeed in colder water. All may be grown as annuals. Seeds that have dried will not germinate; from gathering until they are sown they must be kept in water or wet moss. They are planted in spring in pots of soil covered with ½ inch of sand and submerged 2 or 3 inches beneath the water surface. The young plants are transferred, as soon as they are big enough to handle easily, to large pots or tubs of rich soil or to fertile mud beneath 1 foot to 2 feet of water. The fruits of these plants are edible and are eaten raw or cooked.

TRAPACEAE—Water-Chestnut Family. The characteristics of this family are those of its only genus, *Trapa*.

TRAUTVETTERIA (Traut-vettèria). The genus *Trautvetteria*, which inhabits North America and Japan, has been variously interpreted by botanists as consisting of one, two, or three species. The former view seems to prevail and is accepted here. Belonging in the buttercup family RANUNCULACEAE, and related to *Thalictrum* and *Cimicifuga*, the plant was named in honor of the Russian botanist Ernst Rudolf von Trautvetter, who died in 1889.

A stout herbaceous perennial 2 to 3 feet tall, *T. carolinensis* has hairless or nearly hairless leaves, broadly-kidney-shaped in outline, and deeply-palmately (in hand-fashion), five- to eleven-lobed, with the lobes pointed and irregularly-sharply-toothed. The basal leaves have long stalks, and blades up to 1 foot across. The stem leaves are smaller, much shorter, and stalked or stalkless. Branching above, the slender stems terminate in clusters of small white flowers with many conspicuous, club-shaped stamens that become ⅓ inch long or slightly longer; they produce a fluffy effect. There are three to five small sepals, but no petals. The fruits are one-seeded small pods (follicles) with the persistent styles attached. The western American form of this species is sometimes distinguished as *T. grandis*, the Japanese form as *T. japonica*. Both are very similar to *T.*

carolinensis as it grows in the wild from Pennsylvania to Illinois, Indiana, Georgia, Kentucky, and Missouri.

Garden and Landscape Uses and Cultivation. Suitable for borders, informal areas, and native plant gardens, this plant thrives without trouble. It does best in moderately moist, fertile soil and is readily propagated by division in spring or early fall, and by seed.

TRAVELER'S JOY is *Clematis vitalba*.

TRAVELERS'-PALM or TRAVELERS' TREE is *Ravenala madagascariensis*.

TREBIZONDE-DATE is *Elaeagnus angustifolia*.

TREE. As parts of the common names of plants the word tree occurs in these: tree-alfalfa (*Medicago arborea*), tree-anemone (*Carpenteria californica*), tree-aster (*Olearia*), tree-celandine (*Macleaya*), tree fern (*Cibotium, Cyathea, Dicksonia*), tree-heliotrope (*Messerschmidia argentea*), tree-mallow (*Lavatera arborea*), tree-of-heaven (*Ailanthus altissima*), tree-of-sadness (*Nyctanthes arbor-tristis*), tree-poppy (*Dendromecon*), tree-tomato (*Cyphomandra betacea*), and wild-tree-tobacco (*Acnistus*).

TREE SURGERY. This term minimally covers all maintenance and repair operations that involve major cutting or boring into the trunks, branches, or main roots of comparatively large trees. But modern tree surgeons do much more. They engage in fertilizing trees, spraying to control pests

To repair the loss of a large limb by storm damage: (a) Smooth the wood that the tearing of the bark has exposed by cutting away irregularities

(b) Smooth the edges of firmly adherent bark with a chisel

(c) Cover the exposed surfaces with tree wound paint

and diseases, alleviating problems resulting from grade changes, and, when the occasion demands, installing lightning rods. They also take down and remove dead or unwanted trees.

It is decidedly unwise for untrained amateurs to undertake procedures other than minor tree surgery. It is especially hazardous for them to climb into trees or to operate from ladders. Unstable footholds, branches that break treacherously and unexpectedly, the use of dangerous tools in unfamiliar surroundings, and per-

haps electric power lines are some of the dangers they face. When substantial tree surgery is needed, engage a professional, but before doing so check his reputation and reliability and make sure he is adequately insured.

Preventive surgery includes pruning to limit the size of the head of a tree or to reduce the strain on a weak crotch. It also includes strengthening such crotches by linking together the branches that form them, some distance above the axil of the crotch, with steel screw bolts, screw rods, or steel cables, all of which, made specially for the purpose, are commercially available. Screw bolts may also be used to hold together the edges of splits in trunks caused by lightning, or by wind storms causing twisting.

Cavities in trunks, crotches, and branches need early attention. Contrary to a widely held belief, treatment of these is rarely effective in ending the decay of heartwood. This, because the hyphae (strands) of the fungus, although invisible to the eye, penetrate apparently sound wood for consid-

To repair damage to a young tree caused by careless use of construction machinery: (a) Cleanly pare the margins of the wound with a sharp knife

(b) Round the bottom of the wound

(c) Cover the exposed surfaces with tree wound paint

A pipe drain inserted in a tree trunk and directed downward from the base of a cavity

may be desirable to add strength and stability by installing across it and through its opposite sides metal screw rods.

Next, protect the newly cut bark, sapwood, and especially the cambium by painting the edges of the opening with shellac, and sterilize exposed heartwood by painting it with copper sulfate dissolved in water in a nonmetallic container at the rate of ¼ ounce to 1 gallon of water, or with creosote. Take particular care that the latter does not come in contact with the cambium. Finally, finish with a coat of tree wound paint.

Experts differ in their opinions about the advisability of leaving treated cavities open and repainting them every year or so or of filling them with one of several solid materials employed for the purpose. Such materials include cement, others are based on rubber. Preponderance of modern thought seems to favor the first procedure, but in some cases, at least, filling may have a persuasive cosmetic appeal.

erable distances, sometimes several feet, beyond the rotted tissue, and its complete renewal is usually impracticable and may indeed do more harm than good by weakening the structure of the tree. Treatment of cavities can, however, prevent further impairment of the cambium and other living tissues, encourage healing growth, and do much to improve the health and prolong the life of trees.

Begin treatment by removing all decayed, discolored, water-soaked, and in-

sect-riddled tissues down to apparently sound wood. Then shape the opening to eliminate, if possible, any water-holding pockets and give it a more or less pointed-elliptic outline with the long axis of the ellipse lined in the direction of the flow of sap. With deep cavities, it may be necessary to install a pipe drain opening to the outside to allow the escape of water, although this is less satisfactory than, when possible, shaping the cavity to prevent accumulations. If the cavity is a long one it

Girdling roots, those that, instead of radiating from the trunk, wrap around its base at or just below ground level, can cause much harm by interfering with the upward and downward flow of sap. They commonly result from planting out of containers young trees with one or more chief roots already established in encircling fashion, or from carelessly crowding the

After surgery consisting of shaping the wound, paring its edges, and painting exposed surfaces, this tree trunk is making a vigorous new growth of callus that will eventually close the wound

The trunk of this ancient apple tree, which through rot lost all of its heartwood, lived for several decades after being strengthened by metal screw rods

Tree wrapping with a strip of burlap: (a) Wind the strip spirally around the trunk

After a few years, rot invaded the wood behind this filling, causing further damage; many tree surgeons prefer to retain open cavities and paint their surfaces periodically

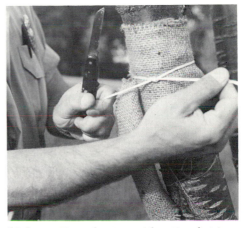

(b) Secure it at the top with a tie of string

Roots that girdle the bases of the trunks of trees, unless severed, can cause severe damage by restricting water conduction

roots of a young tree in a hole not big enough to allow them to spread out.

If a girdling root is suspected, carefully remove the upper few inches of soil from around the trunk and with a chisel or saw cut a 2-inch section out of the offending root. If you merely cut through without removing a piece of the root, the two ends may grow together again.

TREE WRAPPING. The barks of newly transplanted trees, especially those taken from nursery rows or other places where they were close enough together for their trunks to be shaded, may suffer severely from sun scald, this partly as a result of the root system's reduced ability to supply water. Another hazard is infestation by borers to which many kinds of woody plants are especially liable following transplanting. Tree wrapping circumvents these troubles. It is done with long strips of 4- or 6-inch burlap or strong paper manufactured for the purpose. Begin at the first branch by tying the end of the strip to the trunk. Then wind the wrap in tight spirals, like a surgical bandage, downward. Let each spiral overlap the previous one by one-half its width so that a double thickness of wrap covers the trunk. When the bottom of the trunk is reached, tie securely. Or, alternatively, begin at the base of the trunk and spiral the wrap upward. Then secure the wrap in position with binder twine or other strong string wound around the trunk in spirals in an opposite direction to those of the wrap. Keep the trunks wrapped for two years. It is advisable at the end of the first year to take off the original wrap, inspect the trunk to make sure that no borers have gained access, and rewrap.

TREEHOPPERS. Close relatives of leafhoppers and plant hoppers, treehoppers are jumping insects, mostly about ½ inch long and those that occur in North America generally green or brown, that are of almost ludicrous appearance. They infest beans, tomatoes, watermelons, and some other garden crops, as well as trees, shrubs, grasses, and weeds. From leafhoppers and plant hoppers they are distinguished by having in place of a thorax a much enlarged, knobby, horned, or otherwise grotesquely-shaped development called a pronotum.

Treehoppers tend to collect in groups or flocks of the mature and young. When approached or when danger threatens, they scuttle to the opposite side of branch or twig or, if more obviously disturbed, hop or fly some little distance away.

Much of the harm done by treehoppers results from the manner in which females deposit their eggs. This is accomplished by cutting deeply into plant tissues and placing the eggs in the incisions, a procedure that frequently causes stunting, distortion, and death of twigs and branches.

Control measures include spraying with a contact insecticide and good sanitation to destroy weeds and, when practicable, plants of the pea family, such as sweet-clover and alfalfa, which frequently harbor the immature insects.

TREES. In forested regions, the dominant flora, in other extensive areas sharing their prominence with different types of vegetation, and absent from some native floras, trees are a mighty asset to the world and have had and continue to have a tremendous influence on mankind.

Besides their importance as sources of useful products including lumbers, paper pulp, tars, turpentine, cork, tying and tanning materials, rubber, fruits, nuts, spices, beverages, maple sugar, and drugs, they preserve and improve the environment by checking soil erosion, conserving rainfall, purifying the atmosphere, and providing homes and often sustenance for myriads of wild creatures and epiphytic plants.

Here our concern is with the horticultural significance of trees, their management, and their cultivation in gardens, parks, and other landscaped areas, as well as along streets and boulevards, and their selection for particular purposes.

Although the concept of what constitutes a tree is fairly well understood, it is impossible to provide a simple, unchallengable definition of what is meant by the word. This is true because in height, form, and other important features trees as a group merge imperceptibly into shrubs and woody vines, and because, in harsh environments, individuals of some species that in favored areas are unquestionably trees of substantial size develop as bushes sometimes not over a few inches high. This may occur at the northern limits of distribution, at high altitudes, and along seashores or other windswept habitats. Despite this, an attempt at explaining what the word tree commonly implies must be made.

First, a tree is a perennial with a definite trunk or chief axis. Usually this is without branches for some sensible distance above the ground, but sometimes the main trunk divides quite low, even at ground level into more than one trunk of approximately equal importance; most palms and tree ferns are without branches. Besides the presence of a dominant trunk or trunks, height is often an element taken rather arbitrarily into consideration in deciding whether or not a particular specimen warrants the designation tree. Not uncommonly, this is set at 15 or 20 feet, but as long as there is an obvious trunk or trunks, gardeners not infrequently include lower plants in their tree category, even such sorts as the artificially produced bonsai or Japanese miniature trees.

Trees occur in the major divisions of the plant kingdom called pteridophytes, gymnosperms, and angiosperms and are represented in many families. There are de-

ciduous and evergreen kinds and a few, such as casuarinas and certain cactuses and euphorbias, that except for tiny scalelike organs are essentially leafless.

The tallest known trees are redwoods (*Sequoia sempervirens*), one or more of which in California exceed 350 feet in height. Their nearest rival is an Australian-mountain-ash (*Eucalyptus regnans*), in Victoria, Australia. Record for the greatest bulk of wood in a single tree belongs with the giant sequoia (*Sequoiadendron giganteum*), an endemic of California, and, for greatest girth, depending upon how this is measured, to the African baobab (*Adansonia digitata*) or a specimen of Montezuma-cypress (*Taxodium mucronatum*) known as "El Gigante" at Tule, Oaxaca, Mexico. The first develops a barrel-shaped trunk that may have a circumference over 85 feet at a few feet above the ground; "El Gigante," of exceptional size for its species, has a flanged or buttressed trunk that, if all the ins and outs are accounted for, has a circumference at its base of approximately 160 feet.

The age of the vast majority of trees can be determined or very closely approximated by counting annual rings. Not uncommonly, especially in humid regions, people unfamiliar with the comparatively rapid growth of many kinds until they approach their maximum sizes, greatly overestimate the ages of large specimens as well as of those contorted by exposure to wind or other adverse circumstances. Once near maximum size is attained, growth slows markedly and a tree that has

lived twice as long may appear no older to those unfamiliar with this aspect than a specimen that is about the same size. Still, some trees do attain remarkable ages.

Believed to be the oldest living organisms, specimens of bristle-cone pines (*Pinus aristata*), a species that rarely exceeds 40 feet in height, have been in the mountains of California and Nevada for almost 4,600 years. The oldest big trees (*Sequoiadendron*) do not live over 4,000 years, but these are exceptional. The great majority of conifers live for not more than 100 to 200 years. Many kinds of deciduous trees have longer life spans.

Aesthetically, trees are of very great importance. Commonly they are the most conspicuous and enduring living elements in the landscape. The retention of favorably sited specimens and the placement of new ones deserves the most careful consideration, as does the maintenance of their health and vigor. Ornamentals include evergreens and deciduous kinds, some of which provide a wealth of bloom and, some others, decorative fruits. There are trees with brightly colored or otherwise attractive barks and many with foliage that assumes rich autumn hues.

On home grounds, trees can serve significantly to complement the house, afford shade and shelter, screen undesirable views, and enhance privacy; some kinds, of course, are grown for their edible fruits. Many of the same purposes are served by trees employed in landscaping industrial and commercial sites, such as shopping centers and amusement parks. In public

Trees in home landscapes: (a) Oaks provide a handsome setting for this home

(b) A flowering cherry enhances this Californian home

(c) Tall deciduous trees cast welcome shade on this inviting terrace in Englewood, New Jersey

(d) A live oak (*Quercus virginiana*) located advantageously in Williamsburg, Virginia

(e) Deciduous trees provide a substantial background for this perennial border in California

(f) Coconut palms (*Cocos nucifera*) in front gardens, Key West, Florida

parks and along parkways, as well as in city, town, and suburban streets, trees can be pleasant amenities that afford shade and visual satisfaction by making more agreeable otherwise relatively bleak prospects, helping to blanket noise, and assisting in minimizing air pollution. Other special-purpose employments of trees include their uses in shelter belts and for stabilizing soils. Which kinds to choose depends upon the geographical region, the particular purpose or purposes the trees are to serve, the space available, the type of soil, the exposure, and other environmental de-

Trees in public landscapes: (a) A free-standing Norway maple (*Acer platanoides*) at Wave Hill Gardens, the Bronx, New York City

(b) A picturesque Scots pine, Cambridge Botanic Garden, England

(c) Pin oaks (*Quercus palustris*) as street trees, Mount Vernon, New York

(e) *Magnolia grandiflora* in a sheltered location at The New York Botanical Garden

(f) A square in Pasadena, California, attractively planted with trees

(d) An imposing avenue of deciduous trees, Versailles, France

tails. Freedom from or resistance to pests, diseases, storm damage, and other possible troubles must also be considered. The lists now to be presented are of genera that include sorts appropriate for home grounds. Not all, of course, are hardy in all parts of North America, nor will all prosper everywhere they survive. Before making final selections, study the sorts that are thriving locally and consult arboretums, State Agricultural Experiment Stations, reliable nurseries, or other authoritative sources about other possibilities.

Evergreens assume particular importance where privacy or screening are needed. For those purposes it is often desirable to plant them in groups or belts. Some kinds make good hedges. But well-placed single specimens and free-standing small groups on lawns and other areas can also be very effective.

The chief kinds of narrow-leaved (coniferous) evergreens include arbor-vitaes (*Thuja*), araucarias, cedars (*Cedrus*), cryptomerias, cunninghamias, cypresses (*Cupressus*), Douglas-firs (*Pseudotsuga*), false-cypresses (*Chamaecyparis*), firs (*Abies*), hemlocks (*Tsuga*), incense-cedar (*Calocedrus*), junipers (*Juniperus*), Montezuma-cypress (*Taxodium*), pines (*Pinus*), redwoods (*Sequoia*), spruces (*Picea*), umbrella-pine (*Sciadopitys*), and yews (*Taxus*).

Broad-leaved evergreen trees, many of which make brave displays of bloom, include acacias, African-tulip-tree (*Spathodea*), bottle brushes (*Callistemon* and *Melaleuca*), boxwoods (*Buxus*), bull-bay (*Magnolia grandiflora*), California-laurel (*Umbellularia*), camellias, camphor (*Cinnamomum*), carob (*Ceratonia*), cassias, citruses, eucalyptuses, eugenias, figs (*Ficus*), giant chinquapin (*Castanopsis*), hollies (*Ilex*), lagunaria, laurel (*Laurus*), leptospermums, lignum-vitae (*Guaiacum*), live oaks (*Quer-cus*), loquat (*Eriobotrya*), macadamias, madrone and strawberry tree (*Arbutus*), mahogany (*Swietenia*), mayten (*Maytenus*), oleanders (*Nerium*), olive (*Olea*), palms (many kinds), photinias, pittosporums, privets (*Ligustrum*), and Queensland umbrella tree (*Brassaia*).

Deciduous trees in great variety can be grown in regions of ample rainfall. In drier areas, such as parts of the Great Plains, the Southwest, and the West, the choice is more limited, especially if irrigation is not available. Belonging in this category are shade trees, mostly large, some of imposing ultimate stature, a few of which provide handsome displays of bloom. There are also smaller trees, many remarkable for their attractive flowers, fruits, or sometimes both.

Large deciduous trees showy in bloom include black locust (*Robinia*), catalpas, empress tree (*Paulownia*), horse-chestnuts and buckeyes (*Aesculus*), jacarandas, royal poinciana (*Delonix regia*), sophoras, tulip tree (*Liriodendron*), and yellow-wood (*Cladrastis*).

Large deciduous trees not remarkable for their bloom include alders (*Alnus*), ashes (*Fraxinus*), bald-cypress (*Taxodium*), beeches (*Fagus*), birches (*Betula*), cedrela, chinaberry (*Melia*), cork trees (*Phellodendron*), dawn-redwood (*Metasequoia*), golden-larch (*Pseudolarix*), grevilleas, hackberries (*Celtis*), hazels (*Corylus*), hickories (*Carya*), honey-locusts (*Gleditsia*), hop-hornbeams

(*Ostrya*), hornbeams (*Carpinus*), katsura tree (*Cercidiphyllum*), Kentucky coffee tree (*Gymnocladus*), larch (*Larix*), lindens (*Tilia*), maidenhair tree (*Ginkgo*), maples (*Acer*), mulberries (*Morus*), oaks (*Quercus*), parrotia, pistacias, planes (*Platanus*), poplars (*Populus*), Russian-olive (*Elaeagnus*), sassafras, sour gum (*Nyssa*), sweet gum (*Liquidamber*), walnuts (*Juglans*), willows (*Salix*), wingnuts (*Pterocarya*), and zelkovas.

Smaller deciduous trees with attractive displays of flowers, fruits, or both include bauhinias, buckthorns (*Rhamnus*), cassias, chaste tree (*Vitex*), crab apples (*Malus*), crape-myrtle (*Lagerstroemia*), dogwoods (*Cornus*), dove tree (*Davidia*), epaulette tree (*Pterostyrax*), euonymuses, evodias, flowering apricots (*Prunus*), flowering cherries (*Prunus*), flowering peaches (*Prunus*), flowering pears (*Pyrus*), flowering plums (*Prunus*), Franklin tree (*Franklinia*), fringe tree (*Chionanthus*), golden chain (*Laburnum*), golden-rain trees (*Koelreuteria*), hawthorns (*Crataegus*), Jerusalem-thorn (*Parkinsonia*), lilacs (*Syringa*), maackias, magnolias, mountain-ashes (*Sorbus*), photinias, pussy willows (*Salix*), redbuds (*Cercis*), rose-of-Sharon (*Hibiscus*), shadblows (*Amelanchier*), silk tree (*Albizia*), silverbell (*Halesia*), smoke tree (*Cotinus*), sorrel tree (*Oxydendrum*), stewartias, styraxes, tabebuias, trifoliate-orange (*Poncirus*), and xanthoceras.

The choice of street trees and attention to their planting and maintenance requires special care. The selection must obviously be adapted to the geographical area. It would be unrealistic to expect sorts that prosper in southern California to give satisfaction in New England or kinds adapted there to flourish in Louisiana. Fortunately there are kinds for all regions.

Poor judgment of kinds to plant has brought in the past, and if exercised in the future will bring, problems and regrets. Forest giants likely to outgrow available space are to be avoided and so are such trees as the silver maple (*Acer saccharinum*), which has brittle wood and is much subject to storm damage. Horse-chestnuts, some maples, and certain other sorts of trees can be hazardous to automobile traffic because their fallen leaves, when wet, may cause skidding. The fallen fruits of some trees, crab apples, flowering cherries, hawthorns, horse-chestnuts, and mulberries, for example, are also objectionable. Other sorts to be avoided are those, such as poplars and willows, that have roots especially likely to clog drains or raise sidewalks. High on the list of factors to be appraised is resistance to pests and diseases.

In mid-city and other heavily built-up areas there are often other problems that further restrict wise choices. Trouble may come from heat reflected from nearby buildings or from underground steam conduits, and frequently from the very limited volume of often unsuitable soil, which results in poor root development. Inadequate aeration of the soil caused by paving too near the trunks is a frequent cause of trouble. Ideally, a minimum of 8 feet in all directions from the trunk should be uncovered or at most covered with an open metal grating. Smog, smoke, fumes from automobiles, and the attentions of dogs can further complicate matters.

State Agricultural Experiment Stations can usually supply recommended lists of street trees suitable for their regions, and these make a good starting point. The lists that follow may be used as guides, but other kinds are also worthy of consideration. Weigh carefully the virtues and possible disadvantages of all before making final choices.

For wide streets, trees may be selected from the following: green or red ash (*Fraxinus pennsylvanica*), velvet ash (*F. velutina*), white ash (*F. americana*), black-olive (*Bucida buceras*), bull-bay (*Magnolia grandiflora*), camphor tree (*Cinnamomum camphora*), cedars (*Cedrus,* all species), dawn-redwood (*Metasequoia glyptostroboides*), diamond-leaf pittosporum (*Pittosporum rhombifolium*), eucalyptuses (several species), flame tree (*Brachychiton acerifolius*), honey-locust (*Gleditsia triacanthos*), thornless varieties, horsetail tree (*Casuarina equisetifolia*), *Kalopanax pictus*, katsura tree (*Cercidiphyllum japonicum*), maidenhair tree (*Ginkgo biloba*), sugar maple (*Acer saccharum*), sycamore maple (*A. pseudoplatanus*), Monterey cypress (*Cupressus macrocarpa*), burr oak (*Quercus macrocarpa*), California live oak (*Q. agrifolia*), live oak (*Q. virginiana*), red oak (*Q. rubra*), willow oak (*Q. phellos*), plane trees (*Platanus acerifolia, P. racemosa*), Queensland pyramid tree (*Lagunaria patersonii*), royal palm (*Roystonea regia*), silk-oak (*Grevillea robusta*), sugarberry (*Celtis laevigata*), tulip tree (*Liriodendron tulipifera*), white pine (*Pinus strobus*), white poplar (*Populus alba*), and *Zelkova serrata.*

For streets of medium width, suitable trees may be chosen from this list: cajeput tree (*Melaleuca leucadendron*), Chinaberry (*Melia azedarach*), hop-hornbeam (*Ostrya virginiana*), mayten (*Maytenus boaria*), mulberry, fruitless (*Morus alba* 'Kingan'), Norway maple (*Acer platanoides*), cork oak (*Quercus suber*), laurel oak (*Q. laurifolia*), scarlet oak (*Q. coccinea*), silverbell (*Halesia monticola*), sorrel tree (*Oxydendrum arboreum*), sweet gum (*Liquidambar styraciflua*), Victorian-box (*Pittosporum undulatum*), and wax-leaf privet (*Ligustrum lucidum*).

For suburban streets, a list of small trees suggested by Dr. Donald Wyman, Horticulturist Emeritus of the Arnold Arboretum, Jamaica Plain, Massachusetts, includes the following: Cornelian-cherries (*Cornus mas* and *C. officinalis*), *Evodia danielii,* flowering cherries (*Prunus serrulata* varieties and *P. sargentii columnaris*), flowering dogwoods (*Cornus florida* and *C.* *kousa*), fringe tree (*Chionanthus virginicus*), golden-rain tree (*Koelreuteria paniculata*), hawthorns (*Crataegus arnoldiana, C. coccinioides, C. crus-galli, C. lavallei, C. mollis, C. monogyna, C. m. stricta, C. nitida, C. phaenopyrum, C. p. fastigiata, C. pinnatifida major, C. pruinosa, C. punctata, C. succulenta,* and *C. viridis*), hornbeams (*Carpinus japonica, C. caroliniana,* and *C. betulus fastigiata*), lilac (*Syringa reticulata*), linden (*Tilia platyphyllos fastigiata*), Amur maple (*Acer ginnala*), hedge maple (*A. campestre*), mountain maple (*A. spicatum*), paperbark maple (*A. griseum*), Tartarian maple (*A. tataricum*), vine maple (*A. circinatum*), mayten (*Maytenus boaria*), silverbell (*Halesia carolina*), snowbells (*Styrax japonicus* and *S. obassia*), sweetleaf (*Symplocos paniculata*), viburnums (*Viburnum prunifolium*), *V. rufidulum* and *V. sieboldii*), and wax-leaf privet (*Ligustrum lucidum*).

Maintenance of trees should be considered in two phases, that needed during the first one to three years following planting and the subsequent care of established specimens. Techniques of planting, including the initial pruning, the provision of support, and watering, are explained in the Encyclopedia entries Planting and Transplanting, Pruning, and Staking and Tying.

The first-year's after-planting care includes keeping the soil moist enough to supply the needs of the tree and to encourage vigorous root growth. Yet water must not be supplied at such frequent intervals that air in the soil is displaced for such long periods that roots suffer from lack of oxygen and funguses that rot roots are encouraged. Deciduous trees planted in fall in most regions will not require watering after the initial soaking until the following late spring or summer. Evergreens, because they are usually planted earlier and because they do not reduce the water loss of transpiration by dropping their foliage, are more sensitive to shortage of soil moisture. If the fall is dry, be sure to water them then as often as may be necessary and, in dry regions, on through the winter.

Whether planted in fall or spring, trees benefit immensely from watering during the first and often the second spring and summer following. Without this, they may not survive. Spring watering of deciduous kinds will not normally be needed until they sprout new foliage. When water is given, it is imperative that enough be supplied to saturate the entire body of soil occupied by the roots, as well as some of the adjacent ground. Relate the frequency of application to the amount of rainfall and to the type of soil and the time it takes to dry. To forestall the possibility of the water running down the sides of the root ball without penetrating it, it is sometimes desirable to pierce the ball in a few places with a crowbar or soil auger.

Other care to be given during the first

two or three years following planting includes any pruning needed to "raise the head" (to establish a clean trunk of desired height), to prevent the development of undesirable crotches, and to encourage shapeliness. Also, at intervals, inspect stakes and guy wires to make sure they are functioning satisfactorily and pay particular attention to ties, loosening or replacing them as often as it becomes necessary before they cut into the bark as the trunk or branches thicken.

Maintenance of established trees calls for an awareness of and alertness to their needs. Under favorable circumstances individuals of many kinds prosper for many years, sometimes indefinitely, with little or no attention, others may need more regular care, especially with reference to disease and pest control. Pruning, as explained in the Encyclopedia entry Pruning, may require some attention from time to time.

Treatment of wounds resulting from storm breakage, damage by automobile collisions, or other causes is important. As with wounds to the human body, the objectives are to encourage the formation of healing tissue that may eventually close the opening and to prevent admission and proliferation of organisms that cause disease and decay. Prompt attention is obviously advantageous. If necessary, prune damaged branches back to suitable lengths, and shape and smooth with a chisel or sharp knife exposed under-tissues. The preferred shape, the one that encourages rapid healing, is an ellipse with round-pointed ends, its long axis parallel with the normal flow of sap. Paint the edges of the shaped cut (the cambium region) with shellac and then the entire area with tree wound paint. Renew the paint at least once a year until the wound has healed over completely.

Cavities caused by the destruction of underlying tissues, including heartwood, by wood-rotting funguses and insects, result when wounds that fail to heal naturally are neglected. Eventually they may reach such sizes that they weaken the tree structurally and breakage results. Prompt treatment of cavities is of great importance. Other procedures that special circumstances may require are the provision of additional support for heavy limbs and weak or split crotches. For information concerning the treatment of cavities and the provision of support see the Encyclopedia entry Tree Surgery.

Fertilizing benefits trees that lack vigor because the soil in which they grow is more or less deficient in nutrients. In gardens and other landscape plantings this is not uncommon because leaves and other debris that under forest conditions accumulate, decay, and return nutrients to the ground, are generally collected and taken away, or perhaps they blow away. Furthermore, many such trees in landscaped areas are surrounded by lawn or groundcovers that first utilize most fertilizing materials applied to the surface. Although fertilizing is often desirable, it should not be overdone. Excessive applications of nitrogen can cause overly vigorous, sappy growth that is much more frequently subject to diseases, such as fire blight, and pests.

Tree fertilizers are usually formulated to have a higher relative nitrogen content than vegetable and general garden fertilizers. Analyses such as 10-6-4 and 10-8-6 are commonly recommended. Apply from 2 to 5 pounds of one of these for each inch of trunk diameter at 4 to 5 feet above ground level (breast height). Be more sparing in amounts applied to evergreens than in amounts applied to deciduous trees. For acid-soil sorts, use only fertilizers that have an acid reaction.

Distribution of the fertilizer for small trees growing in ground free of other vegetation can be done by spreading it over the chief area occupied by the roots and hoeing or forking it lightly into the surface, but for larger trees and specimens in lawns or ground carpeted with groundcovers it is better to fill the fertilizer into holes about 1½ feet deep made with a crowbar or soil auger and spaced about 2 feet apart in a circle encompassing the outer two-thirds of the spread of the branches and about one-third beyond, that is, in the area most often containing the most feeding roots. After the fertilizer is apportioned equally among the holes, the latter are filled with good topsoil or peat moss tamped moderately firm.

An alternative method of fertilizing trees, but one not always practicable, is to maintain around them at all times, extending to some little distance beyond the spread of the branches, a 3- or 4-inch-thick mulch of good compost, well-rotted manure, or other decayed organic material. Such mulches are especially helpful to many evergreens.

Damage by insects, mites, and other small creatures, and diseases mostly caused by funguses and bacteria and some by viruses, may occur with most trees. A few sorts, such as cryptomerias and ginkgoes, are remarkably free from such troubles and a few others are so susceptible that serious consideration should be given to the risks involved and the care they will need before they are chosen for planting.

Notable examples of disease-prone trees are chestnuts and elms, some of all kinds of which in many regions are subject to uncontrollable infections that nearly always result in death. Diseases statistically less deadly, but which weaken and disfigure and, if neglected under some circumstances, may kill, are more common. Examples of these include fire blight, which is a serious threat to apples and pears and a rather lesser one to some ornamentals, especially hawthorns, mountain-ashes, and certain other members of the rose family ROSACEAE. Many members of that family and some other families are also prone to crown gall, which causes tumerous swellings on the roots, at the base of the tree, and sometimes on aboveground parts. Gradual loss of vigor and dying back of branches over a period of years is often the result of the roots being parasitized by shoestring root rot fungus. Another root-invading fungus causes verticillium wilt, which affects a wide selection of trees, causing sudden wilting of the foliage on one or more branches. Less likely to result in death than the diseases referred to above are anthracnose, various cankers (although some of these, such as the one that attacks lombardy poplars, can be deadly), many leaf spots, mildews, rusts, scab diseases, and twig blights.

Insects and other small creatures, such as mites, that infest trees are fairly numerous and often are more prevalent in particular regions than in others. Some confine their activities to one or only a few kinds of trees, while others are less particular. The chief culprits include aphids, beetles, borers, caterpillars of many kinds, lace bugs, leafhoppers, leaf miners, mealybugs, mites, scale insects, treehoppers, and whiteflies.

Because of the relative high cost of spraying tall trees, infections and infestations for which that is the effective treatment, if not too distressing, are frequently allowed to run their natural courses without treatment, and trees in reasonable health usually survive with little or no permanent damage from a fairly wide spectrum of troubles including mildews, leaf spots, aphids, leafhoppers, a variety of caterpillars, and many others. But it must be remembered that not all diseases and pests that attack trees are so relatively benign. If at all in doubt, seek expert advice, always remembering that commercial tree spraying service concerns may tend to be a little overenthusiastic about the dangers of failing to spray.

TREFOIL. See Trifolium. Bird's-foot-trefoil is *Lotus corniculatus*. Moon-trefoil is *Medicago arborea*. Tick-trefoil is *Desmodium*.

TREMA (Trè-ma). Consisting of evergreen trees and shrubs, *Trema* belongs to the elm family ULMACEAE. There are thirty species, inhabitants of the tropics and subtropics of the Old World and the New World. The name, from the Greek *trema*, a hole, refers to the tiny pits in the stones of the fruits. From the bark of *T. cannabina*, fiber for native fish nets is obtained. This species is also a source of local medicines.

Tremas have short-stalked, often two-ranked, toothed leaves with veins feathering pinnately from the midrib or with three chief ones radiating from their bases. The small, petal-less flowers, in nearly stalkless clusters in the leaf axils, are unisexual with the sexes on the same or different plants, or more rarely bisexual. They have five or rarely four sepals and four or five stamens. The style is divided into two branches. The fruits are drupes (fruits structured like plums).

Native to South Africa and Arabia, *T. bracteolata* is much-branched and up to 20 feet tall or perhaps sometimes taller. Its leaves, 2 to 4 inches long by nearly one-half as broad, change to bright orange before they drop. They are ovate-oblong to ovate-lanceolate, pointed, and have round-toothed margins. Three main veins spread from their bases. The black fruits are about ⅙ inch in diameter. Tropical African *T. guineensis*, up to 15 feet tall, has pointed-ovate, more or less hairy leaves up to 6 inches long and spherical black fruits ⅓ inch in diameter.

Possibly indigenous to Hawaii, as well as to a region extending from India to southern China and Samoa, *T. cannabina* (syn. *T. amboinensis*) is a shrub or tree up to about 20 feet tall. Its two-ranked, slender-tipped, leaves are long-ovate and 3 to 6 inches in length. From their bases three prominent veins diverge. The undersides of the leaves are more or less softly-hairy, their upper sides rough-hairy. The leaf margins are fine-toothed. The tiny white or pale yellow flowers are in clusters almost 1 inch long. The fruits are black, hairy, and about ⅛ inch long.

Similar to the last, *T. orientalis* is a tree 25 to 60 feet tall with finely-toothed, oblong-ovate leaves 3 to 6 inches in length and almost or quite one-half as broad. They are densely-silky-hairy on both sides and often rough-hairy above. The greenish fruits are up to ⅒ inch in diameter. This species is a native of China, southeastern Asia, and Malaysia.

Garden and Landscape Uses and Cultivation. Tremas are planted, to some extent, for ornament in Hawaii, southern Florida, and other warm regions. They prefer deep, well-drained, fertile soil that does not dry excessively, and sun or part-day shade. Attractive as a young specimen, *T. orientalis* often becomes less so as it ages. Propagation is by seed and by cuttings.

TREMANDRACEAE — Tremandra Family. Endemic to Australia and Tasmania, this family of dicotyledons consists of three genera of small, slender shrubs or subshrubs of heathlike aspect. Their small, undivided, sometimes toothed, often narrow and glandular leaves are alternate, opposite, or in whorls (circles of three or more). The solitary, bisexual, symmetrical flowers come from the leaf axils. They have four, five, or seldom three sepals, the same number of petals as sepals, and twice as

many stamens. There is one slender style. The fruits are capsules containing often hairy seeds. The only genus at all commonly cultivated is *Tetratheca*.

TRENCHING. Because of the great amount of labor it requires, trenching is no longer practiced. Often referred to in older garden books, this method of preparing ground for planting involves turning it over with a spade to a depth of 2½ to 3 feet. Bastard trenching, double digging, or double spading is a similar procedure in which the soil is moved to a depth of 1½ to 2 feet. See Spading.

Bastard trenching or double digging in progress

TREVESIA (Trev-èsia). Tropical and subtropical, prickly, hairy or hairless trees and shrubs with large, alternate leaves lobed like the fingers of a wide-spread hand (palmately) constitute *Trevesia*, of the aralia family ARALIACEAE. Natives of Asia and Indonesia, there are ten species. The name commemorates a family of nineteenth-century Italian patrons of botany named Treves de Bonfigli.

Trevesias have small blooms in racemes or panicles of umbels. The calyxes are scarcely-toothed. There are seven to twelve petals, as many stamens as petals, and a grooved pillar formed of the five or six united styles. The fruits are nearly spherical to egg-shaped berries.

Of striking and unusual appearance, *T. palmata* is very decorative. An evergreen tree, 15 to 20 feet tall, with a thorny, often branchless trunk, it has chiefly near the top of the trunk, long-stalked, lustrous, prominently-veined leaves, round in outline and 1 foot to 2 feet in diameter. The center portion of the leaf is solid. From it radiate usually seven or nine, more rarely five, more or less stalked, pointed, ovate-oblong, toothed lobes. The 1-inch-wide, yellowish flowers are in erect panicles that, when young, have stalks clothed with reddish-brown, woolly hairs. From the typical species, the snowflake plant or snowflake tree (*T. p. micholitzii*) differs in having silvery-dotted leaves shaped like

Trevesia palmata

Trevesia palmata micholitzii

Trevesia sundaica

formalized depictions of snowflakes. From the solid center of the leaf radiate in palmate fashion seven to nine conspicuously stalked, deeply-pinnately-cleft lobes.

With leaves shaped similarly to those of the snowflake plant, but plain green, *T. burckii* (syn. *T. sanderi*) is a native of Bor-

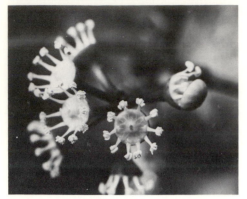

Trevesia sundaica (flowers)

neo and Sumatra. A prickly-stemmed shrub 4 to 5 feet tall, this has leaves up to 2 feet across. Its little flowers are in racemes with reddish-hairy stalks. Sumatra and Java are the home territories of *T. sundaica,* a shrub or tree, up to 25 feet in height, that by some authorities is considered to be a variety of *T. palmata.* From that sort it differs in the lobes of its leaves being narrower.

Garden and Landscape Uses. Trevesias are adapted for outdoor cultivation in the humid tropics. There, they are admirable for beds, borders, and less formal groupings of plants admired for their foliage. They do well in light to moderate shade and respond to deep, fertile, reasonably moist soil. No special care is needed. They are also splendid pot and tub plants, for outdoors in warm climates, and for conservatories and large greenhouses.

Cultivation. Indoors, a minimum winter night temperature of 60°F suits. By day in winter, and night and day at other seasons, considerably more warmth is advantageous. The atmosphere must be humid. Shade from strong sun is needed. Fertile, well-drained, loamy soil encourages good growth. Specimens that have filled their containers with healthy roots are much benefited by monthly or twice monthly applications of dilute liquid fertilizer. Propagation is by seed and by air layering.

TREVOA (Tre-vòa). This South American genus of six species of spiny shrubs and small trees of the buckthorn family RHAMNACEAE is not much known in cultivation. Its name commemorates a Spanish botanist, Señor Trevo. Trevoas have opposite, three-veined leaves. The little flowers, with four- or five-parted calyxes and corollas, in clusters in the leaf axils, have peculiarly hooded petals, each protecting a stamen. The fruits are small berries.

Native to Chile and not hardy in the north, *Trevoa trinervis* is a wide-spreading bush or small tree, 10 feet or so tall, with branches armed with pairs of sharp, stout spines, ½ to 1 inch long, the alternate pairs at right angles to those above and below them. Obovate to broad-elliptic or oblong, with margins finely-toothed or

toothless, the short-stalked leaves are ½ to 1 inch in length. The tiny flowers, with yellowish calyxes and white corollas, are freely produced in clusters of two to four from the leaf axils.

Garden and Landscape Uses and Cultivation. In frost-free and nearly frost-free climates, the species described is sometimes planted as an ornamental. It grows in ordinary soil in sun or part-day shade and is propagated by seed and cuttings.

TRIADENUM (Tri-adènum) — Marsh-St.-John's-Wort. Belonging in the St.-John's-wort family HYPERICACEAE, this North American and eastern Asian genus takes its name from the Greek *treis,* three, and *aden,* a gland. It alludes to three glands that alternate with the group of stamens. There are six to ten species, four of which are natives of North America. From *Hypericum* they differ in technical characteristics and, the American sorts at least, in having pink or greenish instead of yellow flowers.

Triadenums are hardy, perennial, herbaceous, marsh plants with erect stems, leaves opposite or in threes, and axillary and terminal panicles of small, five-sepaled and five-petaled flowers. There are nine stamens in groups of three and as many styles as carpels. The fruits are many-seeded capsules.

Inhabiting bogs, marshes, and wet soils from Nova Scotia to Florida and Mississippi, *T. virginicum* (syn. *Hypericum virginicum*), 1 foot to 3 feet tall, has stalkless, blunt, ovate-oblong to elliptic leaves up to slightly over 2 inches long by about one-third as wide. They are bespattered with translucent dots clearly visible when the leaf is held to the light. The flowers, about ¾ inch across, have rounded, spreading petals and are borne freely at the ends of the stems and short leafy axillary branches.

Garden and Landscape Uses and Cultivation. Of modest horticultural interest as a plant for bog gardens and wet places, especially in native plant collections, this species may be grown without difficulty in sunny locations. Propagation is by seed.

TRICALYSIA. See Kraussia.

TRICHANTHA. See Columnea.

TRICHILIA (Tric-hília). Except for a few natives of Africa and Malagasy (Madagascar), the about 300 species of *Trichilia,* of the mahogany family MELIACEAE, are inhabitants of the tropics of the New World. The name, alluding to the usually three-celled ovary, comes from the greek *tricha,* in three parts.

Trichilias are trees and shrubs. They have alternate, pinnate leaves with an uneven number of opposite or alternate leaflets, or are of three leaflets. Many together in panicles terminal or from the leaf axils, the small greenish, yellowish, or white blooms

have a calyx with four or five teeth or lobes, the same number of overlapping petals, and four to ten stamens more or less united as a tube. The fruits are leathery capsules that split open, much like those of *Euonymus,* to display the usually three seeds, each with either a red or yellow covering.

From 12 to 45 feet tall, *T. hirta,* of tropical America, has hairy young parts and leaves of usually nine to twenty-one, sometimes fewer, pointed, oblong-lanceolate to ovate-lanceolate leaflets 1½ to 5 inches long. The flowers, in long-stalked panicles, have usually five-lobed calyxes. West Indian *T. pallida* is a shrub or small tree up to 15 feet tall, hairy on its younger parts, and with leaves of three to seven oblong-elliptic to obovate leaflets, the terminal one, the largest, up to 7 or 8 inches long. In stalkless or nearly stalkless panicles, the white flowers have a usually four-lobed calyx. Tropical American and West Indian *T. spondioides* is a shrub or tree up to 20 feet tall. It has pinnate leaves up to about 1 foot long, with three to ten rather distantly-spaced pairs of pointed, ovate-oblong, hairless leaflets 1½ to 3½ inches long. The tiny greenish-yellow flowers are in narrow, long-stalked panicles few to several inches long. The capsules are hairy and about ½ inch in diameter. West African *T. zenkeri* is a tree with hairless or slightly hairy young parts and leaves with seven to eleven oblongish leaflets up to 9 inches long. Its very fragrant yellow or yellowish-green flowers are in panicles one-half as long as the leaves.

Garden and Landscape Uses and Cultivation. The sorts described are suitable for planting in southern Florida and other near tropical and tropical places for ornament. Prospering in ordinary soil in sunny locations, they are increased by seed.

TRICHINIUM. See Ptilotus.

TRICHOCAULON (Tricho-caùlon). Restricted in the wild to tropical and southern Africa, *Trichocaulon,* of the milkweed family ASCLEPIADACEAE, is a *Stapelia* relative comprising twenty-five species. Its name, referring to a characteristic of some kinds, comes from the Greek *trichinos,* hairy, and *kaulon,* a stem.

Trichocaulons are attractive, low, leafless succulents with broadly-cylindrical to long egg-shaped stems either beset with vertical rows of conical projections or tubercles, each ending in a stiff bristle or spine; covered with irregularly disposed, rounded tubercles without bristles or spines; or having eight or more strongly-toothed longitudinal angles. The flowers are solitary or in groups, the individuals of each group opening in succession. They originate from between the tubercles, either over considerable lengths of the stems or only from their tips, and are small compared with the blooms of many kinds of stapelias. The calyxes are five-lobed. The corollas, short-tubed or almost tubeless, have five spreading lobes (petals). The corona or crown is double, with the five outer segments notched or cleft, or it may consist of what is apparently one circle or five briefly three-lobed segments. The stamen column is short. The fruits are spindle-shaped follicles (pods). All the kinds discussed below are natives of southern Africa.

Bristly with conspicuous purple-brown spines, **T. delaetianum** forms clusters of stems, up to 2 inches thick by 4 to 8 inches tall, with numerous rows of tubercles. The shallowly-bell-shaped blooms, in groups of three or four, are under ½ inch wide. They are brownish-yellow inside and reddish-brown outside. The inner corona is cherry-red. Branching from their bases, the dull green, cylindrical to slightly club-shaped stems of **T. piliferum** are 6 to 8 inches tall and 1½ to 2 inches in diameter. They are thickly covered with twenty-five or more vertical rows of tubercles, each ending in a stiff, brown bristle up to ¼ inch long. The dark purple-brown flowers, ½ inch or slightly more across, are solitary or two or three together. They have broad-triangular petals and a slightly raised rim (annulus) around the shallow central cup. From the last, **T. annulatum** is distinguished by the very prominent raised annulus at the center of its darker colored, ¾-inch-wide, purple blooms. This attains heights of 6 inches to 1½ feet.

Stem tubercles without spines or bristles characterize the species now to be described. Decidedly knobby, dull green stems, a little more than 2 inches tall or shorter, and solitary or in clusters of up to six, are produced by **T. dinteri**. They are about 1½ inches in diameter. Their tubercles are markedly four- to six-sided and have deep, thin grooves between them. When young they bear minute, scalelike leaves. The approximately ⅓-inch-wide

Trichocaulon dinteri

flowers, in clusters of five or fewer, are bell-shaped. Their ground color is buff, but because of the great number of red-brown dots, red-brown predominates. The segments of the outer corona lobes are cleft into three teeth. From the last, **T. simile** differs in having blooms that have two-toothed outer segments to their coronas and are predominantly cream-colored, with some red spots.

Solitary or in clusters of two or three, the stems of **T. meloforme** are 2 to 3 inches tall and nearly as wide. They are covered with very slightly raised, mostly four-sided, flat, grayish-green tubercles. Singly or in

Trichocaulon meloforme

twos or threes, the blooms come only from the tops of the stems. They have shallowly-cupped centers, up to ⅓ inch wide, and are yellow, freely sprinkled with dark maroon-red. Their outsides are dark red. Much taller and branching freely from the bottoms of its up-to-7-inch-high, club-shaped stems, covered with scarcely raised, flat, more or less five-sided tubercles and 2 to 3½ inches thick, **T. engleri** has flowers in clusters of eight to fourteen. Broadly-bell-shaped and about ½ inch wide, they are yellow-green to cream-colored, with abundant very dark brown or red-brown dots. Another tall species, **T. keetman-shoopense** has stems in clusters of up to six, 6 inches in height, and under 1½ inches thick. Their raised, rounded, gray tubercles are tinged with violet or yellowish-brown. When young they are tipped with minute leaves. Five or fewer together, the approximately ½-inch-wide, shallowly-bell-shaped blooms are whitish-green to greenish-yellow, with red-brown spots of various sizes.

Garden Uses and Cultivation. Tricho-caulons are greatly admired components of choice collections of succulents. Their needs are those of stapelias.

TRICHOCENTRUM (Tricho-céntrum). Approximately thirty species constitute *Trichocentrum*, of the orchid family ORCHIDA-

CEAE. Derived from the Greek *trichos*, a hair, and *kentron*, a spur, the name alludes to the long, slender spur of the lip of the flower.

Natives of tropical America, trichocentrums are low epiphytes (tree-perchers) with stems that thicken into small pseudobulbs and terminate in one or sometimes two leathery, oblong to elliptic-oblong leaves. Stalks bearing one to few blooms originate from the bases of the pseudobulbs. The flowers have approximately similar, more or less spreading, separate sepals and petals. The lobed or lobeless lip is joined to the base of the short column and is prolonged into a spur.

Kinds cultivated include these: **T. albo-purpureum**, of northern South America, has ovoid pseudobulbs, 3 to 4 inches long, each with a fleshy, elliptic leaf up to 4½ inches long. Its solitary, somewhat variable flowers have red-tinged, brown, oblong sepals and petals smaller than the lip. The latter, about 1 inch long, is two-lobed at its apex and purple or white with, at its base, a pair of large purple blotches. **T. candidum**, of Guatemala, practically stemless, has broad-elliptic leaves 3 inches or so long and dropping stalks, with usually two ¾-inch-long, cream-colored or white-tinged-with-yellow flowers that have a small projection from the oblong lip representing a spur. **T. maculatum**, of Panama, is a low plant with thick, fleshy, sometimes red-spotted, linear-oblong to obovate leaves, 2

Trichocentrum candidum

Trichocentrum maculatum

to 3 inches long and about ¾ inch wide, with a markedly impressed mid-vein. The flowers, in racemes of few, are about 1½ inches long by up to 1 inch wide. They are white with a rosy-violet spot on the large, wavy lip and a broad, brown band on each petal. *T. pfavii*, of Central America, is almost stemless. Its wedge- to strap-shaped leaves are 3 to 5 inches long. Usually two on each short stalk, the 1¼-inch-wide flowers have spatula-shaped sepals and petals that are white, marked with brown at their bases, and a narrow, two-lobed, fan-shaped white lip with a reddish patch at its base and a very short, blunt spur. *T. tigrinum*, of Costa Rica and Ecuador, stemless, has oblong, red-dotted, dull green leaves 2½ to 3½ inches long. The solitary or less often paired flowers, 2 to 3 inches across, have linear sepals and petals that are yellowish or greenish-yellow spotted with red. Larger than the sepals and petals and two-lobed at its apex, the lip is white with a rose-red base. It has a disk with three yellow keels and a very short spur.

Garden Uses and Cultivation. Generally easy to grow, these orchids need a warm, humid environment with shade from strong sun. They are suited for growing on slabs of tree fern trunk and in pans or pots in bark chips or osmunda fiber. Their roots need very free drainage and are quickly damaged by stagnant water. For more information see Orchids.

TRICHOCEREUS (Tricho-cèreus). Consisting of about forty species, *Trichocereus*, which belongs in the cactus family CACTACEAE, is endemic to South America. Its name, from the Greek *thrix*, hair, and the name of related *Cereus*, alludes to the hairiness of the flowering parts.

Members of this genus range from columnar and treelike to low and prostrate. Characteristically, they have stout stems and branches with well-defined ribs and stout to bristly spines or none. The large funnel-shaped flowers open at night. Usually white, they have hairy corolla tubes and ovaries. The fruits are hairy. Plants treated in this Encyclopedia as *Haageocereus* and *Helianthocereus* are included by some authorities in *Trichocereus*.

Often treelike species mostly 10 feet tall or taller include the following: *T. bridgesii*, up to 15 feet tall, has four- to eight-ribbed, slightly glaucous, light green stems, the few branches 4 to 6 inches thick. Yellowish and 2 to 4 inches long, the spines are in clusters of six or fewer. The white flowers are about 6 to 7 inches in length. *T. chalaensis* has eight-ribbed stems, up to 6 inches in diameter, with clusters of six to ten radial spines under ½ inch long and two or three centrals up to 2 inches long. The flowers are white, about 7 inches long by 4 inches wide. *T. chilensis* (syn. *T. chiloensis*), up to 25 feet

tall, has stems erect, usually branched from near the base, with ten to seventeen lumpy ribs with spine clusters of eight to twelve radials, light yellow tipped with brown when young, later gray, from ½ to 1¼ inches long; a single central is 1½ to 4 inches in length. The flowers, white tinged with brown, are 5 inches long or longer. *T. pachanoi*, up to 20 feet tall, has erect, branched stems with six to eight ribs without spines or with a few about ½ inch long in clusters of three to seven. The 9-inch-long flowers are white. *T. peruvianus*, 6 to 12 feet tall and freely-branched, has stems about 8 inches in diameter, glaucous when young, and with six to eight ribs. The strong spines, in clusters of ten, are up to 1½ inches long. The flowers are large and white. *T. santiaguensis*, which resembles *T. spachianus*, is up to 22 feet tall and has main stems 2 feet thick, the branches about one-half as wide. They have about fourteen ribs and spine clusters of a dozen orange radials and one or two centrals. The 8-inch-wide blooms are white. *T. terscheckii*, attaining heights of up to 40 feet, has branches 6 to 8 inches in diameter. Its eight- to fourteen-ribbed stems have awl-shaped, yellow spines, 2 to 3 inches long, in clusters of eight to fifteen. The flowers are white and about 8 inches long and 5 inches in diameter. *T. werdermannianus*, up to 16 feet in height, has stems with ten to fourteen ribs. The main trunk may be 2 feet in diameter, the branches up to 6 inches thick. The spine clusters are of eight radials and one or two centrals about 3 inches long. The white flowers are about 8 inches long.

Kinds approximately 5 to 7 feet tall include these: *T. huascha* (syn. *Lobivia huascha*), of Argentina, forms clumps of 2½-inch-thick stems up to 5 feet tall with twelve to eighteen low, rounded ribs. In clusters of eight to ten, about ¼-inch-long radials, and one longer central, the spines are needle-like. The yellow to red flowers are 3 to 4 inches long. *T. macrogonus* has rather slender, bluish-green stems, mostly with seven ribs and clusters of brownish, strong, needle-like spines 1 inch to 2 inches long. The flowers are white, about 7 inches in length. *T. neolamprochlorus* has glossy, yellowish-green stems, about 3 inches in diameter, with about ten ribs and clusters of ten or more red-based yellow spines ½ to ¾ inch long. About 9 inches long and 7 inches across, the flowers are white. *T. spachianus* branches freely from the base; its erect stems are 2 to 3½ inches thick, with ten to fifteen ribs, and spines usually in clusters of eight 2-inch-long radials and two longer, stouter centrals. The flowers are white, fragrant, and about 8 inches in length by 6 inches in diameter.

Sorts not ordinarily over 3 feet tall include these: *T. candicans*, which forms

clumps several feet in diameter, has erect or somewhat sprawling, yellowish-green stems, with eight to ten ribs and clusters of fourteen to sixteen light brown, strong spines 1½ to 3 inches long. The 8-inch-long flowers are white. *T. courantii* (syn. *T. candicans courantii*) has clusters of stout, shiny, light green stems 1 foot long or somewhat longer with ten rounded ribs and clusters of ten to twenty light brown, awl-shaped spines, ½ inch to 1½ inches long, each cluster with one to four centrals. The flowers are 9 inches long. *T. litoralis* has stems usually prostrate, up to 3 feet in length, with twenty-one low, rounded, lumpy ribs. In clusters of ten to thirty, the spines are needle-like and ½ to ¾ inch long, are at first light brown, later gray. The flowers, white and about 5 inches long, by 4 inches in diameter, have corolla tubes clothed with black hairs. *T. purpureopilosus* has twelve-ribbed, columnar to club-shaped stems mostly 1 foot or little more long by 2½ to 3 inches thick. They have clusters of about twenty radial spines, ¼ inch in length, and about four longer, stouter centrals. The pinkish-white blooms are 8½ inches long by 5½ inches wide. *T. schickendantzii* forms clumps of dark green stems about 1 foot tall by 2½ inches in diameter. They have fourteen to eighteen ribs and groups of nine radial spines, ¼ inch long or a little longer, and two to eight centrals. Yellowish, the slender, short, needle-like spines are in clusters of ten to twenty. The white flowers are about 9 inches long. *T. shaferi* has clusters of cylindrical stems up to 2 feet long by about 5 inches in diameter. They have about fourteen ribs. The yellow spines, about ½ inch long, are slender and in clusters of about ten. The flowers are white and 6 to 7 inches long. *T. strigosus* forms clumps of very spiny stems up to 2 feet long by 2 inches or slightly more in diameter. They have fifteen to eighteen ribs and white, yellow, pink, brown, or black, needle-like spines ½ inch to 2 inches long in clusters of fifteen to twenty-five. The white flowers are 8 inches long. *T. s. longispinus* has

Trichocereus thelegonus

spines, red when young, longer than those of the typical species. *T. thelegonus* has dark green prostrate stems up to about 3 feet long, sometimes with erect branches. From 2 to 3 inches in diameter, they have about twelve ribs notched into six-sided tubercles. The spine clusters are of six to eight radials, up to ¾ inch long, with brown tips, later becoming gray, and one central, ¾ inch to 1½ inches in length. The white blooms are about 8 inches long. *T. trichosus* has gray-green to blue-green stems about 3 feet high, with nine ribs. The spines are in clusters of four to six radials, ½ inch to 1¼ inches long, and one central, about 3 inches long. About 10 inches long, the flowers are white.

Garden and Landscape Uses and Cultivation. Handsome cactuses, many of impressive size, the sorts of *Trichocereus* can be used with excellent effects for outdoor landscaping in warm, desert regions and are fine additions to indoor collections. Most are quite fast growers, bloom freely, and call for no special care. Reveling in sun, they are best satisfied with well-drained, fertile, somewhat acid soil and, except during their season of rest, respond to rather generous watering. They are less adversely affected by high temperatures than many cactuses that come from high altitudes. Some sorts, notably, *T. macrogonus*, *T. pachanoi*, *T. schickendantzii*, and *T. spachianus*, make good understocks upon which to graft other cactuses. For more information see Cactuses.

TRICHOCEROS (Tricho-cèros). The name of this genus of four South American species of the orchid family ORCHIDACEAE is sometimes spelled *Trichoceras*. It derives from the Greek *trichos*, hair, and *keras*, a horn, and alludes to a pair of hairy, horn-like protrusions from the column of the flower.

Rare in cultivation, these tree-perchers (epiphytes) have usually long, clambering rhizomes and small pseudobulbs topped by two rows of fleshy or leathery leaves. The flowers, in racemes at the tops of long, slender stalks, have spreading sepals and petals of about equal size or the petals somewhat smaller, and a spreading lip with narrow side lobes.

Native to Ecuador, Peru, and Bolivia, *Trichoceros parviflorus* has tiny, rather distantly-spaced pseudobulbs each topped with a few pointed, elliptic to ovate leaves 1¼ to 2½ inches long. In racemes of three to twenty that top slender, erect stems up to 1 foot tall, the nearly 1-inch-wide flowers have brown-lined, greenish to tan sepals and petals. The center of the bloom and the column and its horns are black-maroon. Similar in growth habit, *T. antennifer*, of Ecuador, has flowers with sepals that are green on their outsides and, like the petals and lip, spotted with violet on their insides.

Garden Uses and Cultivation. Of interest to collectors, these orchids respond to environments that suit cattleyas. To support their clambering, rooting rhizomes, at potting time a totem-pole-like piece of tree fern trunk may be positioned firmly in the pot or the plants may be attached to suspended slabs of tree fern trunks. The rooting medium must be kept moderately moist at all times. For more information see Orchids.

Trichoceros antennifer

Trichodiadema, undetermined species

Trichoceros antennifer (flower)

TRICHODIADEMA (Tricho-diadèma). An obvious and charming feature of most kinds, the starlike or tufted crown of stiff, spreading or erect bristles that tips each fleshy leaf, accounts for the name, derived from the Greek *trichos*, a hair, and *diadema*, a diadem, of this genus. The group consists of about thirty species, formerly included in *Mesembryanthemum,* belonging to the carpetweed family AIZOACEAE. It is native from South Africa to Ethiopia.

Trichodiademas are miniature succulent shrubs with more or less cylindrical leaves covered with tiny glistening pustules. Their solitary blooms are daisy-like in aspect, but in structure are very different; each is an individual flower, not a head of numerous florets (themselves really little flowers) as in the daisy family. The blooms of *Trichodiadema* are small to medium-sized. They have five to eight stigmas. In most kinds the flowers are pink to magenta, but the flowers of *T. decorum* have golden-yellow petals with ruby-red undersides. Some trichodiademas have large tuberous roots that are deep in the soil or are visible at the surface.

One of the best known, **T. densum** (syn. *Mesembryanthemum densum*), forms flattish, crowded mounds, up to about 3 inches in height, that suggest those of certain species of the cactus genus *Mammillaria,* although the two are not related. The ¾-inch-long leaves of *T. densum* terminate in bristly stars of twenty to twenty-five slender white hairs. The flowers, which open only in sun, are 1¼ to 2 inches across and magenta-carmine. They appear in fall or winter, an unusual blooming season for plants of the *Mesembryanthemum* relationship. Also winter-blooming, and similar to the last although not quite as lovely, is **T. stellatum.** From 2 to 4 inches tall and gray-green, this has leaves crowned with stars of twelve to fifteen white hairs. The flowers, 1¼ inches across, are light violet-red.

Crowns of eight to ten black bristles at the leaf tips characterize **T. barbatum,** which has turnip-like roots, is up to 4 inches tall, and has prostrate branches with rather distantly-spaced, gray-green leaves ⅓ to ½ inch long. Its bright red blooms, which come in summer, are ¾ inch across. Also with tuberous roots, but with leaves up to ⅓ inch long, and tipped with diadems of eight to twelve white bristles, **T. bulbosum** is up to 8 inches tall. This sort has dark red blooms ¾ inch across.

Shrubby and intricately-branched, **T. stelligerum** has lustrous, bright green leaves, up to ½ inch long, with crowns of five to ten, white or brownish hairs. Its bright purple-red blooms are 1¼ to 2 inches across. Erect, brown bristles at the leaf tips are featured by **T. intonsum** and **T. mirabile.** The former has rather distantly-spaced leaves, approximately ½ inch long, with eight to ten bristles at their ends. Its flowers are white to pink and ¾ inch across. The stems of bushy *T. mirabile* are clothed with white, bristly hairs, each with a spur at its base. From ½ to ¾ inch long, the green leaves end in eight to fourteen bristles. The flowers are pure white.

Trichodiadema densum showing stars of bristly hairs at the ends of the leaves

Trichodiadema densum in bloom

Prostrate stems up to 1 foot long or longer are characteristic of **T. setuliferum.** Its distantly-spaced leaves, 1 inch to 1½ inches long, end in a group of seven to sixteen spreading white hairs. The flowers are violet-red.

Garden Uses and Cultivation. Among the loveliest of dwarf succulents, trichodiademas appeal particularly to connoisseurs of such distinctive plants. Most commonly, they are accommodated in greenhouses, but they can be grown in rock gardens and similar sites in warm, desert areas. It is by no means impossible to have them flourish in sunny windows in cool rooms. For their best comfort indoors, night temperatures in winter should be about 50°F, with daytime ones not more than five to ten degrees higher. At other seasons, considerably warmer conditions are appropriate, but the atmosphere must never be excessively humid. Like most succulents these need very porous soil, which should be watered moderately during the season of growth, but kept nearly dry during their short period of winter dormancy. Propagation is easy by seed, and may be accomplished by cuttings, but this is a slower and less certain process than with many of the *Mesembryanthemum* clan. For additional information see Succulents.

TRICHOGLOTTIS (Tricho-glóttis). Some sixty species of tree-perching (epiphytic) orchids widely dispersed through tropical Asia, the Malay Archipelago, and the Philippine Islands constitute *Trichoglottis*, of the orchid family ORCHIDACEAE. The name, from the Greek *trichos,* hair, and *glottis,* a tongue, alludes to the fine hairs on the lip.

These plants, without pseudobulbs, have long drooping or climbing stems and oblong to strap-shaped, leathery leaves. Their flowers, most frequently yellowish with reddish-brown markings, vary considerably in size according to species.

Native to the Philippine Islands, *T. luzonensis* (syn. *Staurochilus luzonensis*) has erect stems up to about 2 feet long or rarely longer, and rather widely-spaced, leathery leaves 6 to 8 inches long. Its 1¼- to 1½-inch-wide, reddish-brown-spotted, dull yellow flowers are in freely-branched panicles 1½ to 3 feet long. Also an inhabitant of the Philippine Islands, *T. philippinensis* (syn. *Staurochilus philippinensis*) has erect or drooping stems, up to about 2 feet in length, and two ranks of fairly closely-set, oblong-elliptic leaves, 1½ to 2½ inches long. The fragrant flowers, about 1½ inches wide, are usually in pairs. The sepals and petals range from buff-yellow to reddish-brown, with yellow to whitish margins. The lip is patterned in the same colors. Variety *T. p. brachiata* (syn. *T. brachiata*) differs in its leaves being closer together and in its flowers being larger, up to nearly 2 inches wide, and almost always solitary. Some variation in flower color occurs. Most often the sepals and petals are deep crimson-purple to very dark brown, with a cream-colored edging, and the lip is white. Quite different *T. rosea* (syn. *T. flexuosa*), of the Philippine Islands, has slender, pendulous stems up to 1½ feet long and linear-lanceolate leaves about 3 inches long and nearly ½ inch wide. Solitary or in clusters of up to six, its flowers, in very short racemes, have yellowish-brown sepals and petals up to ¼ inch long, and a small white lip with a heart-shaped center lobe and two small side lobes. Variety *T. r. breviracemosa* (syn. *T. breviracemosa*), of Taiwan, differs in having somewhat larger flowers with white sepals and petals. Another Philippine Island native, *T. ionosma* has erect stems and spreading, strap-shaped leaves 6 to 10 inches long by 1 inch to 2 inches broad. The violet-scented flow-

Trichoglottis rosea breviracemosa

ers, fairly close together in often branched racemes from the leaf axils, have yellow sepals and petals heavily mottled with brown and a broadly-triangular, whitish lip lightly spotted with red.

Garden Uses and Cultivation. These are of interest to orchid collectors. They respond to conditions and care that suit tropical vandas.

TRICHOLAENA. For plants cultivated under this name see Rhynchelytrum.

TRICHOPETALUM (Tricho-pètalum). One fleshy-tuberous-rooted herbaceous perennial of Chile is the only species of *Trichopetalum*, of the lily family LILIACEAE. Its name, from the Greek *thrix,* a hair, and *petalon,* a petal, makes allusion to its fringed petals.

Related to *Anthericum,* from which it differs in its stamens being without hairs, its inner petals being long-fringed, and its style short and straight, *T. plumosum* (syns. *T. gracile, Bottionea thysanoloides*) is 9 inches to 3 feet tall. Its hairless, glaucous-green, deeply-channeled, narrowly-linear leaves, 4 inches to 1 foot in length, are mostly basal, with a few alternate on the stems. Terminating the usually branchless, but sometimes forked stems are two- to six-flowered racemes of greenish to white blooms, each ¾ inch wide. There are six perianth segments (petals or, more correctly, tepals), the outer three larger than the inner, which are conspicuously fringed with white hairs, six stamens, and a short, three-branched style. The fruits are many-seeded, oblong to almost linear capsules.

Garden and Landscape Uses and Cultivation. Not able to survive much frost, this is adapted for outdoor cultivation only where winters are decidedly mild. It may be accommodated in flower beds and less formal plantings, and prospers with minimal care in porous, reasonably fertile,

moderately moist soil in sun or part-day shade. Propagation is by seed and by division.

TRICHOPILIA (Tricho-pília). The genus *Trichopilia* belongs in the orchid family ORCHIDACEAE. Containing some thirty species, it is endemic from Mexico to South America. The name, from the Greek *trichos,* a hair, and *pilion,* a cap, alludes to the anther of the flower being hidden beneath a cap decorated with three tufts of hair.

Trichopilias include attractive sorts with beautiful, long-lasting, freely-produced blooms. Mostly they are tree-perchers (epiphytes). Sometimes they grow on cliffs, less commonly in the ground. They have short rhizomes and densely-crowded, often elongate, flattened, one-leaved pseudobulbs. Their flowers, which according to kind come in a wide range of colors, superficially resemble those of cattleyas and are long-lasting and often delightfully scented. Generally large, solitary or in racemes of few, they come from the bottoms of the pseudobulbs and have three spreading sepals, two spreading petals, and a trumpet-shaped or tubular lip.

Native to Central America and northern South America, *T. marginata* has markedly flattened pseudobulbs each with a leathery lanceolate to elliptic-lanceolate leaf

Trichopilia marginata

5 inches to 1 foot long by up to 2 inches wide. Very variable in color and somewhat fragrant, the 4- to 5-inch-wide blooms have similar, usually wavy-edged, reddish sepals and petals paling at their edges and a white lip with a rose-red tube and crested or wavy margins. They are in arching to pendulous racemes of two or three.

Indigenous to Costa Rica, Panama, and Colombia, *T. suavis* has flattened, crowded, oblong-ovoid to nearly spherical pseudo-

Trichopilia suavis

bulbs, 2½ to 3 inches long, each with an elliptic-lanceolate leaf 4½ to 10 inches long by up to 2 inches wide. The short, arching or pendulous racemes are of two or three 4-inch-wide blooms with a delicate hawthorn-like fragrance, variable in color, but most commonly with white to creamy-white sepals and petals, sometimes spotted with pink or red, and a similarly colored big frilled lip with orange markings in its throat.

Indigenous from Mexico to Honduras, *T. tortilis* has clusters of flattened, ovoid to stubby-cylindrical pseudobulbs 1½ to 4½ inches long. Their elliptic-lanceolate to elliptic-oblanceolate leaves are 3½ to 8 inches long by up to 1½ inches wide. Usually drooping, the slender flower stalks, up to 4 inches long, carry one or two fragrant blooms that, if spread out, may be 6 inches across. They have much-twisted, narrow, brownish-purple to light lavender sepals and petals irregularly edged with yellowish or greenish bands. Large and white to yellowish, the wavy-margined lip has a brown- or crimson-spotted, yellow throat. This blooms over a long period. Closely related to *T. tortilis* and perhaps only a variety of it, *T. turialvae* has fragrant 2½-inch-wide flowers, pure white except for some light orange-yellow streaks in the throat of the lip. This is a native of Costa Rica and Panama.

Very fragrant-flowered *T. fragrans* is a native of the West Indies and from Venezuela to Peru. This has narrow pseudobulbs, 4 to 5 inches long, and glossy, pointed, oblong-elliptic leaves up to 1 foot long by 2 inches wide. In erect to drooping racemes, the 3½- to 4½-inch-wide flowers have greenish-white, wavy-edged sepals and petals and a three-lobed, white lip with a yellow blotch. Also with fragrant flowers, *T. maculata,* of Panama, has clustered pseudobulbs up to 2 inches long encased in spotted, papery bracts and with an elliptic-lanceolate leaf 3 to 5 inches long. Solitary on arching or pendulous stalks, the 2- to 2½-inch-wide flowers have light yellow to greenish-yellow sepals and petals and a three-lobed white lip with a yellow blotch.

Garden Uses and Cultivation. Choice orchids for collectors, trichopilias are not difficult to grow. Their blooms are useful for corsages and similar purposes. Environmental conditions that suit cattleyas are generally satisfactory. These plants succeed in well-drained pots in osmunda or tree fern fiber packed fairly tightly, with its surface mounded to its center, and in bark chips. They can also be grown on rafts or slabs of tree fern trunk suspended from greenhouse roofs. When the plants are in active growth, plentiful supplies of water are needed, but as the season's growth matures they should be rested by withholding water for a few weeks. Most growers recommend dividing and repotting trichopilias every two or three years rather than allowing them to grow into very big specimens. For more information see Orchids.

TRICHOSANTHES (Trichosán-thes). The genus *Trichosanthes*, of the gourd family CUCURBITACEAE, comprises at least forty Asian, Polynesian, and Australian species of annual and perennial, nonwoody vines, a few of which are cultivated for their curious ornamental fruits. The name is derived from the Greek *trichos,* a hair, and *anthos,* a flower, and refers to the fringed edges of the blooms.

These plants, some species of which have tuberous roots, have alternate, lobed or lobeless, toothed or toothless leaves and usually branched tendrils. Their white, unisexual flowers, the sexes on the same or separate plants, are wheel- to cup-shaped. They have a five-lobed calyx and a conspicuously fringed corolla with five lobes or five petals. The female flowers, which are usually solitary, are succeeded by short to extraordinarily long, cucumber-type fruits that are technically pepos. The male flowers are in racemes and have three stamens.

The serpent, snake, or club gourd (*T. anguina*) is best known. A native of India, this annual species has very long trailing or climbing stems, broadly-ovate to triangular-ovate, sometimes shallowly-three-lobed leaves, and frail flowers with deeply-fringed petals. Its male blooms are on stalks 4 to 10 inches long. The very slender fruits resemble thin cucumbers. They are 1 foot to 6 feet long and, unless they hang from a support as they develop, usually twist and coil in the often fantastic manner that has earned for them the common names of snake and serpent gourds. When immature they are bright green, but they ripen to bright orange. In India, the fruits

Trichosanthes cucumeroides (fruit)

when young are used in curries and are eaten as a vegetable, when ripe they are fibrous, bitter, and inedible.

Less well-known kinds, both natives of Japan, are *T. cucumeroides* and *T. japonica*. A tuberous-rooted perennial, **T. cucumeroides** has short-hairy stems and usually lobed, ovate leaves, toothed or wavy at their margins and hairy on their undersides. Male and female flowers of this kind, unlike those of *T. anguina*, are on separate plants. The fruits, egg-shaped and cinnabar-red, are 2 to 3 inches long. They are sometimes dried and used as a substitute for soap. From the last, **T. japonica** differs in being essentially hairless. It has thick roots and ovate, shallowly-lobed, toothed or smooth-margined leaves and yellowish-green, broad-spindle-shaped fruits about 3 inches long.

Garden and Landscape Uses and Cultivation. The snake gourd and other kinds of *Trichosanthes* are cultivated chiefly as curiosities. They may be trained to cover fences and other supports to form temporary screens. Their cultivation is similar to that of cucumbers and squashes and the same as for *Lagenaria*. Even the perennial kinds can be grown successfully as annuals. For additional information see the entry Gourds, Ornamental.

TRICHOSPORUM. See Aeschynanthus.

TRICHOSTEMA (Tricho-stèma)—Blue Curls. Annual and perennial herbaceous plants and subshrubs constitute *Trichostema*, a genus of North American natives of the mint family LABIATAE. There are about sixteen species. They are strongly scented and have opposite, undivided leaves, and flowers in racemes or spikelike panicles. The name, from the Greek *trichos*, a hair, and *stemon*, a stamen, alludes to the slender stamen stalks.

These plants are related to *Teucrium*, but differ in the five lobes of their corollas being of nearly equal size. Trichostemas have flowers with five-lobed calyxes, and blue, pinkish, or white corollas, the tubes of which usually are longer than the calyxes. There are four stamens and a two-cleft, single style. The fruits consist of four one-seeded nutlets, usually called seeds, included in a persistent calyx.

Annual *T. dichotomum* inhabits usually dryish soils from Maine to Florida and Texas. It has much-branched, minutely-sticky-pubescent stems, up to 2½ feet tall, and more or less sticky, oblong-lanceolate to linear leaves, up to 3 inches long. Its blue, pink, or white blooms, about ¾ inch in length, are in spikelike panicles, not densely-woolly. The perennial *T. lanatum* is 2 to 6 feet in height. It is an attractive native of southern California where it inhabits dry slopes and chaparral. Much-branched, it is a rounded subshrub with linear-lanceolate leaves 1½ to 3 inches long

Trichostema lanatum

and woolly-hairy on their undersides. The flowers, densely-clothed with blue-purple woolly hairs, are about ½ inch long and occur in small groups in interrupted, woolly spikes.

Garden and Landscape Uses and Cultivation. Although not showy enough to compete with more popular annuals for the esteem of gardeners, *T. dichotomum* is sometimes grown to provide variety. Best suited for native plant and naturalistic gardens, it is raised from seeds sown in spring where the plants are to remain. The other species described is a handsome ornamental hardy only in a mild climate, such as that of southern California. It may be included in perennial borders and other plantings. It is usually raised from seed. Trichostemas need full sun and moderately fertile, freely-drained soil.

TRICHOSTIGMA (Tricho-stígma). The genus *Trichostigma*, of the pokeweed family PHYTOLACCACEAE, consists of four species native to tropical South America. Its name comes from the Greek *trichos*, a hair, and *stigma*, a stigma, and refers to that organ being hairy.

Trichostigmas are erect or semiclimbing shrubs with alternate, stalked, lobeless, toothless leaves, and racemes of small, petal-less flowers that have four sepals, eight to twenty-five petals, and a short style. The spherical fruits are small and berry-like.

Cultivated primarily for its attractive foliage, *T. peruvianum* is a semiclimbing shrub about 6 feet tall. It has pointed-elliptic, glossy, conspicuously-veined, metallic-green leaves with rich violet-red un-

Trichostigma peruvianum

dersides and unequal-sided bases. In long racemes, at first erect, but drooping as they age, the little whitish flowers are borne on reddish stems.

Garden Uses and Cultivation. No particular trouble is experienced in growing this plant outdoors in the humid tropics and subtropics, and in tropical greenhouses. It thrives in any ordinary fertile soil. In greenhouses it must be shaded lightly in summer and watered moderately from spring through fall, more sparingly in winter. Repotting and pruning specimens that have become leggy is done in late winter. Young plants should have the tips of their stems pinched out to encourage branching. Propagation is easy by cuttings and leaf cuttings. Seeds are also a satisfactory means of increase.

TRICUSPIDARIA. See Crinodendron.

TRICYRTIS (Tri-cýrtis) — Toad-Lily. This eastern Asian and Himalayan genus of the lily family LILIACEAE is not as well known to American gardeners as its merits deserve. Although its members are less gorgeous than lilies and some others of its relationship, they possess quiet beauty and are interesting and unusual. There are ten species. The name, from the Greek *treis*, three, and *kyrtos*, convex, alludes to the nectar sacs of the three outer petals.

Toad-lilies are deciduous, herbaceous perennials. They have short rhizomes, and usually branchless, erect or arching stems, with alternate, nearly stalkless or stem-clasping, ovate to oblongish leaves. The terminal or axillary blooms are mostly shallowly-bell-shaped. The perianth is of six petals (more correctly, tepals), not joined, and generally spotted on their insides. The bases of the outer three petals

Tricyrtis hirta

Tricyrtis hirta, a white-flowered variant

to 7 inches in length, the upper ones stem-clasping. Also with whitish flowers sprinkled with dark purple spots, **T. macropoda** differs from the two described above in its erect flowers, when more than one from a leaf axil or stem end, having a distinct peduncle (common stalk) to which the stalks of the individual blooms are attached, so that in effect the flowers are in loose panicles. The stems are hairy to hairless, the leaves ovate to oblong and up to 5 inches long by a little over 2 inches wide. The petals, up to ¾ inch long, flare outward in their upper halves. Native to China as well as Japan, **T. latifolia** is up to 2½ feet tall and, except near the flowers, is hairless or nearly so. It has ovate to obovate leaves 3½ to 6 inches long, short-pointed at their apexes and with heart-shaped bases that clasp the stems. In terminal, short-stalked clusters or from the upper leaf axils, the about-1-inch-long, up-facing, yellow flowers are spotted with purple on their insides.

Tricyrtis latifolia

Erect, yellow flowers, solitary or in pairs, and spotless or nearly so, their narrowly-obovate petals, 1 inch to 1½ inches long, are borne by **T. ohsumiensis.** This sort has nearly hairless stems 8 inches to 1½ feet tall and hairless, oblong-lanceolate to elliptic leaves up to 8 inches long by a little over 2 inches wide. Erect, the blooms of **T. flava,** one or two to a stem, are yellow, freely spotted with purple. Their petals are up to 1¼ inches long. This species has purplish hairy stems 1 foot to 1½ feet tall. Its leaves, broad-elliptic to oblanceolate, are up to 6 inches long. Dwarf **T. nana** has hairy stems up to 6 inches tall. The few leaves, up to 4½ inches long by 1½ inches wide, are pointed. The erect flowers, solitary or in pairs, have yellow petals ¾ inch long. They are spotted with brown-purple.

Nodding instead of up-facing flowers are characteristic of *T. macranthopsis* and two

closely allied species, *T. macrantha* and *T. ishiiana.* With arching to pendulous stems 1¼ to 2½ feet long, **T. macranthopsis** has oblong-ovate to ovate leaves, hairless above, slightly hairy on their undersides, with, at their bases, ears on both sides. They are up to 7 inches long by 2 inches wide. The solitary or few bell-shaped flowers are terminal or from the upper leaf axils. They are clear yellow with brownish spots inside. Beautiful **T. macrantha** differs in its stems having coarse, pale brown hairs and in its smaller leaves being more shallowly-heart-shaped at their bases and having ears on only one side of the stem. Flowers in terminal clusters distinguish **T. ishiiana** from the other two kinds. It has shorter stems than *T. macranthopsis* and smaller, nearly hairless leaves with two basal ears.

Tricyrtis macrantha

Garden and Landscape Uses and Cultivation. Toad-lilies are charming for woodland areas, shaded rock gardens, and similar places. Their hardiness is imperfectly known. In the vicinity of New York City and perhaps further north, *T. hirta* and *T. macrantha* are hardy, but some others seem to be less cold resistant. All find agreeable well-drained soil that never becomes excessively dry and that contains a generous admixture of leaf mold, peat moss, rich compost, or other decayed organic matter. Once they are established, except to propagate, it is better not to disturb them if they are doing well. Early spring is the best season to divide and transplant them. A mulch of decayed organic material is beneficial.

Increase is by division, and by fresh seed sown in a cold frame, in a protected, shady place outdoors, or, after being mixed with slightly damp peat moss in a polyethylene bag and stored for approximately three months at 40°F, in a cool greenhouse.

TRIDAX (Tri-dax). One or two annual species of this group of twenty-six tropical and

are hollowed or pouched. There are six stamens and three two-branched styles. The fruits are many-seeded capsules. All the kinds discussed below are Japanese.

Japanese toad-lily (**Tricyrtis hirta**) is commonest in cultivation. From 1 foot to 3 feet tall, it has velvety-hairy stems and foliage. The stem-clasping leaves are oblong-ovate and 4 to 6 inches long. Few to several, the erect blooms come from the leaf axils and furnish the stems, often for considerable lengths. They have whitish petals 1 inch long or slightly longer, erect except for a short portion near their apexes, which spread and are freely decorated with purplish to nearly black spots. From the last, **T. affinis** differs in its ¾-inch-long, purple-spotted, whitish petals spreading from their bases. This 1- to 2-foot-tall species is hairy or hairless. It has narrowly-oblong to broadly-oblanceolate leaves, up

subtropical American small annuals and herbaceous perennials are occasionally cultivated. The generic name is one used by Theophrastus for lettuce.

The genus *Tridax*, of the daisy family COMPOSITAE, has opposite, pinnately-divided or toothed leaves and long-stalked, solitary, daisy-type flower heads with yellow centers and white, pink, or yellow ray florets. The fruits are seedlike achenes.

A native of Mexico, *T. trilobata* (syn. *Galinsoga trilobata*), up to 1 foot in height, has erect stems that bear three-lobed or toothed leaves, variously cut, and bright yellow flower heads about 1 inch in di-

Tridax trilobata

ameter. The ray florets are five-toothed. As its synonym indicates, it was once included in the genus to which the ubiquitous immigrant weed called gallant soldiers (*Galinsoga parviflora*) belongs, and to this it is botanically closely related, but horticulturally much superior. Differing in having pink ray florets, Mexican *T. bicolor rosea*, 1 foot tall or slightly taller, has triangular leaves and flower heads 1½ to 2 inches across. The centers of the flower heads are yellow.

Garden Uses and Cultivation. These plants are meritorious for the fronts of flower garden beds and borders and for rock gardens and semiformal places. Their blooms are useful as cut flowers. Tridaxes are easily raised from seed, which may be sown in early spring outdoors where the plants are to remain or may be started early indoors. If the former plan is adopted, thin the seedlings to about 4 inches apart. Sow indoors in a temperature of 60 to 65°F about eight weeks before the young plants are to

be set in the garden, which may be done about the time it is safe to plant tomatoes. Transplant the seedlings 2 inches apart in flats and grow them in a sunny greenhouse or similar accommodation where the night temperature is about 50°F and is five or ten degrees below temperatures maintained during the day. When the plants are transplanted to the garden, allow about 4 inches between them. Sandy soil and sunny location suit these annuals. Routine care calls for no special effort. Weeds must be kept down and in dry weather watering may be needed.

TRIENTALIS (Trient-àlis) — Star Flower, Chickweed-Wintergreen. Four species of temperate and colder parts of the northern hemisphere constitute *Trientalis*, of the primrose family PRIMULACEAE. The name, from the Latin *triens*, one-third, is thought to allude to the individual flower stalks frequently being about one-third of the height of the plant, or possibly it refers to a common height of these plants, one-third of a foot.

Trientalises are low deciduous herbaceous perennials with slender rhizomes and branchless erect stems topped by a whorl (circle) of thin, well-developed leaves. Those leaves lower on the stems are often minute and scalelike. The few chickweed-like, starry, white or pink blooms on threadlike stalks from the leaf axils have a persistent calyx of five to seven sepals and a corolla cleft almost to the base into usually seven spreading, linear-lanceolate lobes. The base of the corolla forms a very short tube. The five to seven stamens are joined at their bases by a short membranous ring. The fruits are capsules containing few to many round seeds.

Eastern American *T. borealis* inhabits rich woods and bogs from Labrador and

Trientalis borealis

Newfoundland to Hudson Bay, Alberta, Virginia, Indiana, Illinois, and Minnesota. Western American *T. latifolia* occurs chiefly in woods and sometimes other shaded places from California to British Columbia. Both are 4 to 8 inches high and have four to seven spreading leaves 2 to 4 inches in length, those of *T. borealis* are pointed-lanceolate, those of *T. latifolia* blunter and proportionately broader, ovate to obovate, and abruptly pointed at both ends. Their flowers are about ¾ inch across, those of *T. borealis* white, those of *T. latifolia* white or pink. Native from Oregon to the Aleutians and in Siberia, *T. arctica*, 4 to 8 inches tall, has white flowers. The leaves of its stems below the terminal whorl are several and, although they diminish in size downward, not tiny or scalelike. Native to Europe, *T. europaea* has obovate to obovate-lanceolate, glossy leaves and white flowers ½ to ¾ inch across.

Garden Uses and Cultivation. The prime garden value of these dainty, but certainly not showy plants is as modest embellishments for woodland gardens and shaded rock gardens where they may be grown in woodsy or peaty, moderately to strongly acid soil that does not become dry. Plants may be successfully transplanted from the wild if carefully handled and if a goodly amount of soil is taken with the roots. This should not, of course, be done from places where the species are scarce. Seed sown in porous light soil well fortified with acid leaf mold or peat moss provides a satisfactory means of increase. For established plants, need for attention is minimal and consists chiefly of protecting the site from invasion by weeds or other plants and maintaining a shallow mulch of leaf mold or peat moss. In some locations watering with nonalkaline water may be necessary in dry weather.

TRIFOLIATE-ORANGE is *Poncirus trifoliata*.

TRIFOLIUM (Tri-fòlium) — Clover or Trefoil, Shamrock. Clovers or trefoils constitute the genus *Trifolium*, of which there are about 300 species, of the pea family LEGUMINOSAE. The name is from the Latin *tres*, three, and *folium*, a leaf, and was given in recognition that most species have leaves of three leaflets.

At least some sorts are well known to most people. These plants are more important agriculturally than horticulturally. Because they fix free nitrogen from the air in forms usable by plants, when their roots die they enrich the ground. Because of this, some kinds are grown as green manures. A number of sorts of clovers are grown extensively for nutritious pasture and hay. They are good bee plants. White clover or Dutch clover is frequent in lawns. It, as well as red clover and yellow-flowered *Trifolium procumbens*, it among several plants that have been called "true shamrock." For further discussion see the Encyclopedia entry Shamrock. Clovers are sometimes weeds in gravel paths and untended or waste places, but rarely are they seriously troublesome. A very few are grown as ornamentals.

Clovers or trefoils include annuals, biennials, and herbaceous perennials, both hardy and nonhardy, the majority natives of temperate and subtropical regions north of the equator, but a few occurring in regions further south in Africa and South America. The leaflets, in a few species five or seven, but much more often three, are arranged palmately, spreading in hand-fashion from the tops of the leafstalks. The small, white, red, purple, cream, or occasionally yellow flowers, generally in dense, stalked heads, spikes, or umbels, are more rarely solitary. They resemble tiny pea blooms with blunt keels shorter than the wing petals and an erect standard or banner petal. There are nine stamens joined and one separate.

White clover or Dutch clover (*T. repens*) is a hardy, creeping, hairless perennial with trailing rooting stems and leaves with three reverse heart-shaped leaflets some ½ inch long. The white or pinkish flowers in nearly globular heads ½ inch to 1¼ inches wide are abundantly produced. There are numerous minor variants. One that remains quite constant to type under cultivation and is more abundant in most populations of this species than generally supposed, has leaves with four leaflets and is commonly accepted as a symbol of good luck. Variety *T. r. atropurpureum* has attractive rich bronze-purple leaves narrowly edged with green. One of several plants called Irish shamrock, *T. r. minus*, has leaves smaller than those of the typical species and small heads of pink flowers.

Sometimes grown in rock gardens, *T. alpinum*, of the European Alps, is a creeping, hardy perennial, 3 to 6 inches tall, with short subterranean stems, and long-stalked leaves with three linear-lanceolate, finely-toothed leaflets. Its fragrant flowers, about ¾ inch long and three to twelve together in loose heads, are rosy-purple with the

Trifolium virginicum

Trifolium uniflorum album

Trifolium repens atropurpureum

banner petal pink with purple streaks. They are on stalks, 2 to 6 inches in length, that spring directly from their rootstocks. Variety *T. a. album* has white blooms. Also sometimes grown in rock gardens, but not hardy much north of its native range, *T. virginicum* inhabits shale barrens from Pennsylvania and Maryland to Virginia and West Virginia. It has prostrate stems up to 4 inches long, leaves with linear to oblanceolate leaflets, and slightly creamy-white flowers in heads 1 inch wide.

Probably less hardy than those described above and distinguished by its solitary flowers borne on short stalks from the leaf axils, *T. uniflorum* is a native of Syria and adjacent lands. It is a tufted, creeping

perennial, about 2 inches in height, with leaves of three slender-pointed, ovate leaflets. The flowers have purple keels and wing petals and a blue-purple upper petal. The flowers of *T. u. album* are white.

Garden and Landscape Uses and Cultivation. Except for the purposeful inclusion of white clover in lawns and the occasional use of red clover as a cover crop for green manuring, most other clovers cultivated are plants for rock gardens and similar places. All respond to full sun and, the cultivated ones, to both neutral and alkaline soils. The species are easily raised from seed, but the colored-leaved and the "four-leaved" kinds can only be multiplied reliably by division. To supply the demand for shamrock around St. Patrick's Day, commercial florists grow, from seed sown four to six weeks earlier in small pots in greenhouses, trifoliums, mostly *T. dubium, T. procumbens,* and *T. repens.*

TRIGGER PLANT. See Stylidium.

TRIGONELLA (Trigon-élla) — Fenugreek. Trigonellas are Old World annual or rarely perennial plants of the pea family LEGUMINOSAE. Most are low and their foliage is usually strongly scented. Their name, from the Greek *treis,* three, and *gonia,* an angle, alludes to the triangular appearance of the blooms. A few of the approximately 100 species are grown for forage.

The sorts of *Trigonella* have leaves with three, usually finely-toothed leaflets, and stipules (basal appendages to the leafstalks) joined to the stems. The pea-like, white, yellow, or blue flowers, solitary or in short heads or racemes, come from the leaf axils. They have ten stamens of which nine are joined and one is separate. The fruits are beaked pods containing two rows of seeds.

Fenugreek (*T. foenum-graecum*) is a forage plant used also in veterinary medicine. It has sparsely-hairy, branchless stems, 6 inches to 2 feet tall, and leaves with oblong-lanceolate, finely-toothed leaflets ¾ inch to 2 inches long. The very short-stalked, yellowish-white flowers, tinged lavender at their bases, ½ inch long or slightly longer, are solitary or paired and have hairy calyxes. The slender, curved, flattened, sometimes hairy seed pods, erect or spreading, are 3 to 6 inches long and have beaks about one-third as long. Fenugreek is native to southern Europe and Asia.

With lilac-blue flowers, many together in dense, spherical heads on stalks longer than the leaves, *T. caerulea* is a branchless, erect, almost hairless annual 1 foot to 2 or rarely 3 feet tall. Its leaves have ovate to oblong, finely-toothed leaflets ¾ inch to

Trigonella caerulea

2 inches long and up to ¾ inch wide. The flowers are about ¼ inch long. Longitudinally ribbed, the erect pods, under ¼ inch long, have short beaks. Although occurring spontaneously in many parts of Europe, this plant, which is cultivated for forage, is thought not to represent an original species, but to be derived from *T. procumbens,* a native of Europe that differs in having solid instead of hollow stems and in other minor details.

Garden Uses and Cultivation. As ornamentals, trigonellas have little to recommend them and are rarely grown in gardens. The kinds described are annuals that prosper in sun in ordinary well-drained soil and are raised from seed sown in spring where the plants are to remain.

TRIGONIDIUM (Trigon-ídium). Epiphytic (tree-perching) orchids of ten or more species compose this Mexican, Central American, and tropical South American genus of the orchid family ORCHIDACEAE. The name *Trigonidium* comes from the Greek *trigona,* a triangle, and *eidos,* like. It alludes to the form of parts of the blooms.

Trigonidiums have pseudobulbs with one, two, or sometimes more, fleshy leaves. Fairly big, the flowers, which come from the bases of the pseudobulbs, are not very colorful. Solitary, they terminate longish, usually erect stalks. Their largest and showiest parts are three petal-like, approximately equal sepals, which join at their bases to form a three-angled tube. Above, they are spreading or reflexed. The sepals partly hide the very much smaller petals, lip, and column. The erect side lobes of the lip clasp the column.

Native from Mexico to northern South America, *T. egertonianum* has ovoid to ellipsoid, compressed and clustered pseudobulbs, about 3 inches tall, with two or three linear-lanceolate, long-stalked leaves up to 2 feet long by about 1¼ inches wide. On papery-bracted stalks up to 1½ feet tall, the greenish-yellow to light brownish, pink-flushed flowers, often with darker stripes, are carried. They are up to 1½ inches long.

Very different *T. lankesteri,* of Costa Rica and Panama, has flattened, ovoid pseudobulbs that may exceed 3 inches in length. They are widely spaced along elongate rhizomes clothed with papery bracts. The three to five oblong-lanceolate leaves may be almost 1 foot long by 1½ inches wide. The blooms, cupped in their lower parts, have pale greenish-brown to richer brown sepals with brown or purplish veining. Their upper parts are strongly reflexed. The short-pointed petals are light greenish-tan with purple-brown veins and purple spots. The blooms may be 2 inches long, but often are smaller.

Its pseudobulbs scarcely crowded, about 2 inches tall, and with two leaves up to about 9 inches long by approximately 1 inch

wide, *T. obtusum,* of northern South America, has blooms on papery-bracted stems 3 to 6 inches in length. The sepals are greenish-yellow with flushings of red, the petals yellowish to whitish with brown tips and red veining. The yellow lip is edged with red.

Garden Uses and Cultivation. Trigonidiums are not difficult to grow. They succeed in the warm, humid conditions that suit most tropical orchids and need a little shade from strong sun. They succeed in warm- or intermediate-temperature greenhouses. As a rooting mixture, osmunda or fern fiber or tree barks favored for orchids are suitable. A "totem pole" of tree fern trunk, or some similar support, is needed for the long rhizomes of *T. lankesteri.* Except for a period of three weeks or so of partial rest following blooming, water is given throughout the year to keep the rooting compost always moderately moist without being soggy. For more information see Orchids.

TRILISA (Tríl-isa) — Carolina-Vanilla or Deer's Tongue. This generic name is an anagram of *Liatris,* a group to which the two species of *Trilisa* are closely related. They are herbaceous perennials of the southeastern United States and belong in the daisy family COMPOSITAE, although, like *Liatris,* they are very different in appearance from typical daisies. From *Liatris,* trilisas differ chiefly in their flower heads not being in spikes, in technical characteristics of the involucres (collars of bracts at the backs of the flower heads), and in their roots not being tuberous.

Carolina-vanilla or deer's tongue (*T. odoratissima*) is so called because, if bruised, its foliage emits the odor of vanilla. It has hairless stems 2 to 3 feet tall, branched above, and alternate, toothed or toothless, oblong to spatula-shaped, hairless leaves 4 to 10 inches long by 1 inch to 1½ inches broad. The loosely clustered flower heads, about ¼ inch long, are of rosy-purple disk florets; there are no rays (the petal-like ones in daisies). They develop in fall. The dried leaves of Carolina-vanilla contain coumarin. They are used to flavor cigarettes. The commercial supply is collected from wild populations of this species, which is common in the southeastern United States and along the Gulf Coast to Texas.

From the last, *T. paniculata* differs chiefly in its stems being sticky-hairy and its rosy-purple or white flower heads being in narrower, elongated clusters.

Garden and Landscape Uses and Cultivation. These plants are suited for naturalistic plantings and are hardy as far north as New York. They grow readily in well-drained ordinary soil and are propagated by seed and by division. Seed may be sown as soon as ripe, or in spring, in an outdoor bed or in a cold frame and the seedlings transplanted to nursery beds as soon as they are large enough to handle. Division is best done in early spring.

TRILLIUM (Tríl-lium)—Wake Robin, Toad-shade, Stinking Benjamin. Among the most beautiful and beloved American wild flowers are trilliums. Other species occur in eastern Asia. Trilliums belong to the lily family LILIACEAE and bear a name based on the Latin *tres*, three. The allusion is to the normal numbers of leaves on each stem, to the three sepals, and to the three petals of the flowers.

Comprising about thirty species, *Trillium* consists of low, spring-flowering, deciduous herbaceous perennials. They have short, usually upright, less commonly horizontal, tuber-like rhizomes from which come erect stems, leafless except at their summits where there is a circle of usually three, occasionally fewer or more, leaves that, unlike those of most members of the lily family, are net-veined rather than parallel-veined. The solitary blooms are large and terminal, stalked or stalkless, and erect or nodding. Typically they have three spreading or erect, persistent leafy sepals quite different in appearance from the petals, three petals that wither and remain as they age, six short-stalked stamens, and a stout or slender style. The fruits are berries. In this genus aberrant plants are not uncommon. They occur with leaves in place of petals, with the numbers of the flower parts varying from the normal, and with curiously parti-colored blooms.

The showiest trillium, and one of the easiest to grow, **T. grandiflorum** is wild from Quebec to Minnesota, Pennsylvania, Ohio, and Indiana. From 9 inches high to twice that height, it has ovate to nearly round, stalked or almost stalkless leaves, mostly 3½ to 4½ inches long. The blooms, up to 3 inches or more in diameter, are displayed well above the foliage on stalks 2 to 3 inches in length. At first erect, they nod as they age. They have spreading, lanceolate sepals and arched, spreading, pure white petals that, after a long season of display, gradually fade to pink. This extremely variable species may have its flower parts in fours or more; or it may have pink petals. A beautiful double-flowered variety is prized by gardeners, as are some of the many variants with parti-colored green-and-white flowers. It is believed that this latter phenomenon is associated with a virus infection. Be that as it may, such plants occur in the wild only where a band of particular rock formation cuts across the natural range of the species. From Montana to California and British Columbia, **T. ovatum** takes the place of *T. grandiflorum*. A local portent of spring, it has somewhat smaller, up-facing, shorter-stalked flowers with narrower petals than its Eastern relative. Specimens with four to

A colony of *Trillium grandiflorum*

Trillium grandiflorum (flower)

Trillium grandiflorum with green-and-white flowers

A double-flowered variety of *Trillium grandiflorum*

fifteen or more petals are occasionally found.

The dwarf white or snow trillium (**T. nivale**) resembles a miniature *T. grandiflorum*. From 3 to 6 inches in height and with broad-elliptic to ovate, stalked leaves up to 2 inches in length, this sort grows in rich woodlands and other shaded places from Pennsylvania to Minnesota, Kentucky, and Missouri. It has blunt, broad-elliptic to ovate, stalked leaves up to 2 inches long. Its short-stalked flowers, white, sometimes pink-striped at the bottoms of the petals, come earlier in spring than those of other kinds. Much like the snow trillium, **T. rivale,** of the Siskiyou Mountains of California and Oregon, has smaller, longer-stalked blooms, their ascending petals usually streaked with rose-carmine. From 4 to 10 inches in height, it has ovate, long-stalked leaves.

The painted trillium (**T. undulatum**), one of the latest to bloom, like those discussed above has stalked flowers. They have pointed, wavy-edged petals, ¾ inch to 1½ inches long, white with their bases boldly stenciled with radiating rosy-purple lines. A lover of moist, even wet, acid and sub-acid soils, this is not an easy plant to satisfy in gardens. From 4 inches to nearly 2 feet tall, it has hairless, stalked leaves. The painted trillium not infrequently produces plants with leaves and flower parts in fours or eights, and may vary in other ways. It is the only trillium with brightly colored fruits. When ripe they are scarlet. It ranges in the wild from southern Canada to Michigan, Wisconsin, and Pennsylvania, and in the mountains to Georgia and Tennessee.

Nodding, white to creamy-white or rarely pink, sweetly fragrant, stalked flowers, usually nearly concealed beneath the foliage, are borne by **T. cernuum.** Occurring in the wild from Newfoundland to Pennsylvania and Delaware, and its broader-petaled variety *T. c. macranthum* in the mountains to Georgia and Alabama, this is up to 1½ feet tall or sometimes taller. It has short-stalked leaves. The tips of its ½- to 1-inch-long petals recurve. The stamens have anthers up to one-third longer than their stalks. From the last, **T. flexipes** (syns. *T. gleasonii, T. declinatum*) differs in its stamens having anthers twice as long or even longer than its stalks. This ranges from New York to Minnesota, Maryland, Tennessee, and Missouri. Also with nodding blooms, pretty pink-flowered **T. catesbaei** (syn. *T. stylosum*) is a native of mountains from North Carolina to Georgia and Alabama. Dainty and up to 1½ feet tall, it has usually bronzy, elliptic to ovate leaves. Its flowers, on 2-inch-long stalks, have curved stamens with stalks as long as the yellow anthers. The petals are crisped and recurved. Another with pink flowers, **T. pusillum,** native from Virginia to South Carolina and in the Ozarks, differs from *T. catesbaei* in its blooms being erect and in having straight stamens, the stalks of which are about one-half as long as the anthers. The plants rarely exceed 8 inches in height.

Maroon-red blooms sometimes varying to purple-brown and greenish-purple, their cream-colored stamens with stout stalks much shorter than the anthers, are characteristic of the disagreeably scented stinking Benjamin (**T. erectum**), a kind about 1 foot tall. Long-stalked and nearly erect, its flowers are approximately 2 to 3½ inches across. This species, native from Nova Scotia to North Carolina and Ten-

Trillium viride

nessee, which has broad, lozenge-shaped-ovate leaves up to 6 inches long, tends, more than most kinds, to have clusters of flowering stems from the one tuber. A pure white variety, *T. e. albiflorum* is not ill-scented. One of the largest trilliums, **T. vaseyi** ranges in the wild from Tennessee to South Carolina. Over 2 feet tall, it has pointed-ovate leaves. Its flowers, 4 to 6 inches across, have slightly recurved, purplish-maroon petals. The stamens have slender stalks almost or quite as long as the light brown anthers. A variant with white flowers is reported.

Mottled-variegated or green leaves, broadly-lanceolate to nearly round, are characteristic of **T. viride,** which in its several forms inhabits moist woodlands in the central United States, in the southern Appalachians, and in lowlands from South Carolina to Florida. Typically 9 inches to 1½ feet tall and with the upper parts of the stems, and the veins on the undersides of the leaves, hairy, this has stalkless flowers with spreading sepals, and slim, erect, greenish or brown-purple petals, narrowed toward their bases. The stamens have straight anthers and differ from those of *T. sessile* in being only about one-third as long as the petals. In *T. v. luteum* (syn. *T. luteum*) the stems and leaves are hairless and the petals are yellow or brown-purple. Differing from *T. viride* in its stamens being about one-half as long as its petals, the toadshade (**T. sessile**), up to 1 foot tall, has plain green, not mottled leaves rarely exceeding 4 inches in length. The erect petals, normally brown-purple, but sometimes yellow or green, narrow to their bases. This grows in moist woodlands from

Trillium viride luteum

Trillium sessile

Pennsylvania to Ohio, Tennessee, and Arkansas. Related *T. discolor,* of North Carolina, is sometimes treated as a variety of *T. sessile.* It has yellow petals broadest at their apexes. Unlike the petals of *T. viride* and *T. sessile,* those of *T. recurvatum* are narrowed at their bases into a distinct shaft or claw. This native from Michigan to Nebraska, Tennessee, and Arkansas lives in moist woodlands. It has stalked, elliptic to nearly round, usually purple-mottled leaves, and stalkless blooms with strongly down-turned sepals and erect, normally brown-purple petals. Native from Washington to California, *T. chloropetalum* (syn. *T. sessile californicum*) is akin to *T. sessile.* Up to 1½ feet tall, it has mottled, round-ovate leaves up to 6 inches long, and stalkless, maroon-red, greenish-yellow, or white petals up to 4 inches long.

Garden and Landscape Uses. Trilliums are ideally adapted for woodland and rock gardens and for tucking among deep-rooting shrubs where conditions similar to those the plants know in the wild are approximated. It is expecting too much to plant them close to vigorous surface-rooting shrubs or where they must compete for moisture and nourishment with the roots of such trees as maples. The showier kinds are seen at their magnificent best displayed in generous drifts in open woodlands, but groups of three to twelve in less expansive surroundings can please mightily. All do best in deep, fairly moist soil that contains a truly generous proportion of leaf mold or other organic debris and is acid rather than alkaline.

Cultivation. With few exceptions, trilliums are neither finicky nor fastidious, although western North American species do not adapt to eastern gardens as readily as easterners. In anything approaching ideal conditions of soil, shade, and moisture, most give good accounts of themselves. They are generally a hardy, long-lived lot, blooming faithfully year after year and increasing, although rather slowly, by natural multiplication of the growths and by self-sown seed. Because trilliums begin active root growth early in fall, planting and transplanting should ordinarily be done not later than mid-September. The tubers should be set fairly deep, so that they are covered with soil to a depth of about 4 inches. The only regular attention needed thereafter is the application of a mulch of rich compost, leaf mold, or peat moss early each fall. Because most of the trilliums offered by dealers are collected from the wild, it is good conservation to buy in small quantities only and then to patiently propagate one's own, a somewhat tedious procedure it is true, but a fascinating and rewarding one. Propagation is by seed or vegetatively. Trilliums raised from seed commonly take four or five years from sowing to good bloom. As soon as the

seeds are ripe, remove them from the surrounding pulp and sow immediately or store them in a cool, humid place until fall and then sow. A cold frame or sheltered place outdoors, shaded and where the soil is fat with leaf mold, peat moss, or other agreeable decayed organic matter, yet is sufficiently drained not to become stagnant or waterlogged, suits. Cover the seeds with porous soil to a depth of up to ½ inch. Keep the seed bed moist and shaded from direct sun.

Vegetative propagation can sometimes be achieved by very careful division of the rhizomes at about the time the foliage is dying or by controlled injury to the rhizomes. At the end of the growing season, when the foliage is dying, scrape away the surface soil until the upper part of the rhizome is exposed, then cut off its top at the ring that shows the line of demarcation between the new pointed bud and the older part of the rhizome, and backfill with soil. By the following spring, few to many little rhizomes will have formed, and these can be removed the succeeding fall. If a second decapitation of the original rhizome is done slightly lower down, a second crop of young rhizomes may be obtained the following year. An alternative, less drastic measure is to notch the bulb. To do this expose its top, as in preparation for decapitation, but instead of slicing it off, just remove a narrow, wedge-shaped tongue of tissue from one side or around its circumference at the line separating the new growth, or, if the tuber is horizontal, from along its top, and recover with soil. With reasonable luck almost as many young rhizomes will develop as result from the decapitating procedure, and without missing a season of bloom. Vegetative propagation is the only way of increasing stocks of the double-flowered variety of *T. grandiflorum.*

TRIMEZIA (Tri-mèzia). The name of this genus of the iris family IRIDACEAE has also been spelled *Trimeza.* There are six species, natives of the West Indies and South America. Derived from the Greek *treis,* three, and *megas,* great, the name alludes to the three outer segments of the blooms being much larger than the others.

Trimezias are bulb plants with flat and narrow, or rushlike leaves, and flowers in clusters at the ends of stalks bearing one or no leaves. The six segments (petals) of the flowers are separate to their bases. There are three stamens. The fruits are capsules.

Native to the West Indies and South America, *Trimezia martinicensis* (syn. *Cipura martinicensis*) is sometimes cultivated in greenhouses or outdoors in warm, essentially frost-free climates. Each bulb has about six erect, linear-lanceolate leaves up to about 1 foot long and ¼ to ½ inch wide or a little wider. The yellow flowers, in

clusters of six or fewer and about 1½ inches in diameter, have petals stained at their bases with brown. They are atop stalks up to 2 feet in length that have one stem-clasping leaf. Individual blooms remain open for only a few hours.

Garden Uses and Cultivation. The species described is suitable for outdoor gardens in regions of essentially frost-free winters and for growing in greenhouses. It succeeds in well-drained, sandy, peaty soil. Indoor temperatures at night of about 50°F and five or ten degrees higher by day are satisfactory. Full sun is needed. From spring to fall the soil should be kept evenly moist, drier in winter. Repotting is done in late winter or spring. Propagation is by seed and by offsets.

TRIOLENA (Triolèn-a). This tropical American genus of the melastoma family MELASTOMATACEAE includes twenty to twenty-five species of herbaceous plants similar in appearance and closely related to *Bertolonia.* The name *Triolena* is derived from the Greek *treis,* three, and *olene,* arm, and alludes to three forward-pointing extensions from the base of each anther, which distinguish this genus from *Bertolonia.*

Triolenas inhabit wet rain forests. They have ovate or oblong-ovate leaves and arching racemes of five-petaled flowers, each with ten stamens. The fruits are three-winged capsules.

Best known, *T. hirsuta* (syn. *Bertolonia hirsuta*) is 5 to 8 inches tall. It has pointed-ovate, vivid green, hairy leaves with blades up to 6 inches long by 3½ inches wide, sometimes with a center band of bronzy-red and often with reddish or purplish undersides. The flowers are white, pinkish-white, or sometimes pink. Guatemalan *T. paleolata* has thin, pointed-ovate, hairy leaves, prominently-veined and silvery or pinkish on their undersides. Their blades are up to 6 inches long by 2¼ inches wide. The flowers are pink or white and up to ¾ inch in diameter. Native to Ecuador, *T. pustulata* (in gardens often called *Bertolonia pubescens*) is a low, running plant with pointed-ovate, hairy, quilted leaves, up to 5 inches long, that commonly have a broad center band of red beneath, appearing reddish-green or brown on the upper side. The flowers are white or white tipped with pink.

Garden Uses and Cultivation. These are of especial interest to enthusiastic collectors of rare tropical species. They respond to the same growing conditions and attentions that suit bertolonias.

TRIOSTEUM (Tri-ósteum) — Horse-Gentian, Wild-Coffee or Feverwort. Suitable only for wild flower gardens and similar places, triosteums are too coarse and, in appearance, too weedy to merit appreciable attention from gardeners. They belong in the honeysuckle family CAPRIFOLIACEAE and number five or six species, natives of North America, eastern Asia, and the Himalayan region. The name *Triosteum* stems from the Greek *treis,* three, and *osteon,* bone, refers to the seeds.

These are herbaceous perennials; the Americans, at least, are hardy. Pubescent, they have erect stems and large, opposite, undivided, lobeless or lobed, toothless leaves. Clustered in the leaf axils, the greenish-yellow to dullish-red flowers are funnel- to narrowly-bell-shaped and have asymmetrical faces of five lobes (petals). There are five sepals and five short-stalked stamens. The fruits are dry, yellow, greenish, or red berries with persistent sepals at their apexes.

Wild-coffee or feverwort (*T. perfoliatum*) has obovate or obovate-oblong leaves up to 10 inches long and one-half as broad, softly-hairy on their lower sides and sparsely so above, and with the bases of each pair united so that the stem appears to grow through them. The flowers are solitary or in groups of up to four in the leaf axils. The fruits are greenish-orange to orange-red. This ranges as a wildling in moist or dry woodlands from Massachusetts to Kentucky and Kansas. Also called wild-coffee, *T. aurantiacum* (syn. *T. perfoliatum aurantiacum*) is native in moist and dry woodlands from New Brunswick to North Carolina and Missouri. About as tall as the last, this differs from it in the bases of the pairs of leaves not being united. More slender than the last and rarely over 3 feet tall, *T. angustifolium* is glandular-hairy and has oblanceolate to obovate leaves up to 6 inches in length. Its usually solitary greenish-yellow blooms are succeeded by orange-red fruits. This kind favors moist woodlands from Connecticut to Ohio, Missouri, North Carolina, Alabama, and Louisiana.

Garden Uses and Cultivation. At the beginning of this entry the limited uses of these plants are discussed. Environments similar to those in which they grow naturally are preferred. They are easily raised from seed.

TRIPETALEIA (Tripet-alèia). Confined in the wild to mountains in Japan, *Tripetaleia,* of the heath family ERICACEAE, consists of two species of deciduous shrubs. It is very like *Elliottia,* from which it differs in having fewer petals and stamens. Its name comes from the Greek *tri,* three, and *petalon,* a petal.

Tripetaleias have alternate, short-stalked, undivided, toothless leaves and, in summer, terminal panicles or racemes of small white or pinkish blooms. The calyx is five-lobed or five-parted. The three petals are oblong, reflexed, and longer than the stamens. The fruits are small, many-seeded capsules.

The best known species is *T. paniculata* (syn. *Elliottia paniculata*). About 6 feet tall,

this has three-angled shoots and obovate, pointed or blunt leaves, 1¼ to 3 inches in length, with short hairs on their undersides and above, along the mid-veins. In panicles 3 to 6 inches long, the short-stalked flowers are little more than ½ inch wide. They have toothed calyxes and white to pinkish corollas.

Tripetaleia bracteata

The other species, *T. bracteata* (syns. *Botryostege bracteata, Elliottia bracteata*), is a much-branched shrub 3 to 6 feet tall. It has obovate, nearly round shoots and obovate, very short-stalked, hairless leaves 1 inch to 2 inches long by under ½ to 1 inch wide. The racemes of bloom are erect and 3 to 6 inches long. At the base of each flower is a leafy bract approximately ¼ inch long and ovate or obovate. There are five separate sepals, and three, or rarely four or five, narrowly-oblong, reflexed, pink-tinged, white petals ⅜ inch in length. There are six stamens and a prominently protruding, thick, curved style. The fruits are small capsules.

Garden Uses and Cultivation. These rare shrubs are hardy in southern New England and can be grown without undue difficulty. Of interest to collectors, they associate well with azaleas and other plants of the heath family. They respond to acid soils that, although not constantly wet, are not excessively dry. Light or part-day shade is appreciated. A mulch of peat moss or leaf mold benefits the plants. No pruning is needed. Propagation is by seed sown in sandy, peaty soil and by summer cuttings under mist or in a greenhouse propagating bench. Tripetaleias bloom when quite small.

TRIPHASIA (Tri-phàsia)—Lime-Berry. Three species, close relatives of oranges, grapefruits, lemons, and limes, belong in *Triphasia,* of the rue family RUTACEAE. Native from southeastern Asia and the Philippine Islands to New Guinea, the genus has a name derived from the Greek *triphasios,* triple, in reference to the parts of the flow-

ers being in threes. The plant sometimes called *T. monophylla* is *Severinia buxifolia.*

These are spiny, evergreen shrubs or trees with alternate, glandular-dotted leaves, undivided or of three leaflets. The flowers, solitary or in twos or threes from the leaf axils, have a calyx with three to five teeth, three to five petals, six to ten stamens, and a lobed stigma. The fruits, technically berries, usually contain a single seed, less often two or three.

The lime-berry (*T. trifolia*) is occasionally 15 feet tall, but often less than one-half that height. It has spiny, zigzag branches and dark green, nearly stalkless leaves of three blunt, round-toothed leaflets, the center one 1 inch to 2 inches long and considerably bigger than the others. From the leaf axils originate solitary, very fragrant, white flowers about ½ inch in diameter and with three or sometimes four calyx lobes and petals, six free stamens shorter than the petals, and a stout style exceeding the stamens in length. The fruits, dull red and about ½ inch in diameter, resemble tiny oranges, but usually have only one seed. The native home of the lime-berry, which is naturalized from Florida to Texas, is unknown; it may be Malaya. The fruits contain aromatic, slimy flesh that is edible, but not very palatable. In some countries, however, it is made into marmalade.

Garden and Landscape Uses and Cultivation. This shrub or small tree makes a formidable barrier when used as a hedge. It is also attractive as a lawn specimen and for including in shrub plantings. It grows in sun or part-shade in any ordinary soil and succeeds even in those that are too salty for many plants. It is easily raised from seed and, although it grows rather slowly, plants set 1½ to 2 feet apart and sheared to keep them dense and to a height of at least 3 feet, fairly soon make an impenetrable hedge. The lime-berry stands very little frost. It is only adapted to mild climates.

TRIPLARIS (Tríp-laris) — Ant Tree, Long John Ant Tree. The twenty-five species of this genus are natives of South America. All are said to provide in their hollow stems homes for ferocious, stinging ants, but this is ordinarily true only of specimens in the wild. The group belongs in the knotweed family POLYGONACEAE and is related to the pestiferous, inappropriately named Mexican-bamboo (*Polygonum cuspidatum*). Fortunately, members of this genus are not as aggressive spreaders as that Chinese plant. The name *Triplaris* is from the Latin *triplex,* triple, and refers to the flower parts being in threes.

In *Triplaris* the leaves are alternate and the flowers unisexual on separate plants. The blooms are small and in spikes or racemes. The males have tubular, six-lobed calyxes and nine stamens. The calyxes of the females are three-lobed and there are three petals, a three-angled ovary, and three styles. The calyxes remain as wings with the shuttlecock-like fruits, technically achenes, and act as idling propellers to parachute the seeds slowly to the ground, often some considerable distance away.

The most commonly cultivated species is the ant tree (*T. americana*). An evergreen that attains a maximum height of 70 feet, but often is not over one-half as tall, this native of Central America and northern South America is planted in southern Florida, Puerto Rico, and other tropical and warm-subtropical places. Slender, its shoots are conspicuously swollen at the nodes and terminate in slender buds. The leaves, oblong to oblong-elliptic and pointed, have prominent midribs and numerous parallel lateral veins. They are 9 inches to over 1 foot long and 2½ to 5 inches wide. Their upper sides are almost or quite hairless; there are brownish hairs on the midribs of their lower surfaces. The male blooms are inconspicuous, but the purplish-red females are very showy and so are the fruits, which are reddish with pink wings, the latter 1¼ to 1½ inches in length.

Called Long John ant tree presumably because of its slender outline, *T. surinamensis*, of tropical South America, is sparingly planted in southern Florida and Hawaii. It blooms in fall and has flowers at first ivory or cream-colored, later red. The pointed-ovate leaves are up to 1 foot long. Female specimens make a great show in bloom and fruit and are attractive over a long season. Their rose-pink to purplish flowers, in narrow spikes, are followed by colorful fruits. Male trees in bloom are much less showy than females. From the last species, *T. cumingiana* differs in having blooms that are consistently red and come in winter and spring.

Garden and Landscape Uses and Cultivation. For the warmest parts of Florida and other similar climates, *Triplaris* trees are excellent decoratives well adapted for planting as specimens in gardens and parks. They grow without difficulty in ordinary soil that does not lack moisture, in sunny locations, and are propagated by seed.

TRIPLEUROSPERMUM (Tripleuro-spèr-mum) — Scentless-False-Camomile, Turfing-Daisy. Belonging to the daisy family COMPOSITAE and composed of approximately twenty-five species, *Tripleurospermum* inhabits parts of Europe and Asia Minor. Its name comes from the Greek *tri*, three, *pleuron*, a rib, and *sperma*, a seed, and alludes to the three-ribbed achenes.

Annuals or herbaceous perennials, these plants have finely-pinnately-cleft, alternate leaves and solitary flower heads composed of all disk florets or of disk and ray florets. The fruits are seedlike achenes ribbed on their inner surface and with a pair of oil glands near the tip on their outer surface.

Scentless-false-camomile (*T. maritimum* syn. *Matricaria maritima*) is a native of Europe naturalized in North America. It is a biennial or perennial with procumbent to erect stems, 4 inches to 2 feet long, usually branched near their ends. The somewhat fleshy leaves, up to 3 inches long, are twice-cleft into slender segments. From

Tripleurospermum maritimum

Tripleurospermum maritimum inodorum

1 inch to 2 inches across, the flower heads have a yellow disk or eye and twenty to thirty white ray florets, ½ to ¾ inch long, that spread horizontally. *T. m. inodorum* is erect and has leaves with bristle-tipped or pointed segments. The double-flowered variety 'Bridal Robe' (syn. *Matricaria inodora plenissima*) has flower heads of mostly strap-shaped, petal-like, white florets.

The turfing-daisy (*T. tchihatchewii* syns. *Chrysanthemum tchihatchewii, Matricaria tchihatchewii*) is a hairless, mat-forming, nearly scentless, hardy perennial with spreading, ground-hugging, rooting stems, and leaves once- or twice-finely-divided into short segments. Almost 1 inch in diameter, its short-stalked flower heads have white or pink-tinged ray florets on leafless, usually very short stalks that may, however, become 6 inches tall or taller. This is a native of Asia Minor.

Tripleurospermum tchihatchewii

Garden and Landscape Uses and Cultivation. Scentless-false-camomile is cultivated as an ornamental, chiefly in its double-flowered variety 'Bridal Robe.' This is attractive for the fronts of flower beds and as a cut flower. It is raised as an annual by sowing seed in spring in a sunny place in ordinary garden soil; the seedlings are thinned sufficiently to prevent overcrowding. The turfing-daisy is appropriate for rock gardens and similar places. It thrives in sunny locations in gritty, well-drained soil and is easily propagated by division and from seed.

TRIPLOCHLAMYS (Triplo-chlámys). Half a dozen or more species constitute Brazilian *Triplochlamys*, of the malva family MALVACEAE. The name, derived from the Greek *tri*, three, and *chlamys*, a mantle, is of uncertain application.

The sorts of this genus are shrubs with undivided, lobeless, toothed or toothless leaves that have large stipules (basal appendages) pressed close to the stems. Solitary in the leaf axils, but disposed to give the effect of being in racemes or headlike clusters, the flowers have beneath the calyx an involucre (collar) of often bright red, linear to heart-shaped bracts usually numbering from ten to twenty-four, but sometimes fewer. There is a tubular, five-lobed calyx, a tubular corolla, and a column formed of the united stamens. The style has ten branches each ending in a disklike stigma. The fruits are dry and composed of five one-seeded sections or carpels that eventually break apart.

Apparently the only species in cultivation, *T. multiflora* (syn. *Pavonia multiflora*)

Triplochlamys multiflora

is a shrub up to about 6 feet in height. It has narrowly-oblong to ovate-lanceolate, toothed leaves 6 to 10 inches long by ½ inch to 2 inches wide. The unusual-looking flowers are in the axils of the upper leaves, in short, apparently terminal clusters. Their greatest display is provided by a collar or whorl of richly colored pink or red, hairy bracts. Shorter and broader than the bracts, the calyx segments are purplish. Rolled around each other to form a tube, the 1½-inch-long, dull purple petals surround the protruding column of stamens, which has drooping blue anthers. This species and slight variants of it have been known in gardens as *Pavonia rosea, P. floribunda, P. kerkesina,* and *P. intermedia.* Formerly they were popular greenhouse plants.

Garden Uses and Cultivation. The species described is attractive for shrub beds and borders and other outdoor plantings in the tropics and subtropics and for cultivation in greenhouses and conservatories. In pots it flowers when quite small, within a year or two of being propagated. For its best comfort it needs fertile, well-drained, moderately moist soil and a little shade from strong sun. In greenhouses it thrives where the night temperature in winter is about 60°F and that by day five to fifteen degrees higher. Well-rooted pot specimens benefit from regular applications of dilute, liquid fertilizer. Propagation is easy by cuttings and by seed.

TRIPOGANDRA (Tripo-gándra). The about twenty species of *Tripogandra,* of the spiderwort family COMMELINACEAE, are na-

tives of the warmer parts of the Americas. The generic name, from the Greek *tri,* three, *andros,* male, and *pogon,* a beard, alludes to the number and hairiness of the stamens. The plant formerly named *T. rosea* is *Cuthbertia rosea,* the one previously known as *T. warszewicziana* is *Hadronemas warszewiczianum.*

Nonhardy, evergreen herbaceous perennials of *Tradescantia*-like aspect, tripogandras have pendulous, procumbent, or erect stems and alternate leaves. Their flowers, in pairs of more or less loose, stalkless, coiled sprays, have three green or other colored sepals, three petals, and six stamens, three of which are markedly different from the others. Arranged in two circles, the stamens, or some of them, often have bearded stalks. The fruits are capsules.

Sorts cultivated include these: *T. cumanensis,* native from Mexico to South America, has prostrate stems with erect branches. Its leaves are narrowly-ovate-oblong to lanceolate and up to 3¼ inches long by ¾ inch wide. The stalks of its flower clusters are not longer than the leaves from the axils from which they arise. The small white, pink, or purple flowers have three bearded and three beardless stamens. *T. grandiflora,* of Mexico and Central America, has long, freely-branched stems and lustrous, hairless, elliptic to oblong-lanceolate leaves up to 4 inches long and about 1 inch wide. Borne on short stalks from the leaf axils, the white flowers have an orange-blossom fragrance. Their three longer stamens are bearded. *T. multiflora* has trailing stems with upright

branches. Its ovate to ovate-heart-shaped leaves, sometimes purple beneath, are 1 inch to 2 inches long. The small white, pale lavender-blue, or pink flowers are in rather compact clusters on stalks shorter than the leaves from the axils from which they sprout. The three longer stamens are bearded.

Garden Uses and Cultivation. In warm climates these may be used as groundcovers. They are also useful for growing in pots and hanging baskets. Very easy to grow and propagate, they respond to environments and care that suit zebrinas.

TRIPTERIS. See Osteospermum.

TRIPTEROSPERMUM (Triptero-spérmum) —Climbing-Gentian. A few species native to eastern Asia, India, and Malaysia constitute *Tripterospermum,* of the gentian family GENTIANACEAE. By some botanists they have been named *Crawfurdia,* while by others they are included in *Gentiana.* They are rare in cultivation. The name, from the Greek *tri,* three, *pteron,* a wing, and *sperma,* a seed, alludes to the seeds having three wings.

This genus consists of vining or trailing, hairless herbaceous perennials with opposite, usually three-veined, stalked leaves. Blue-purple or sometimes white, and not erect, the flowers, terminal or axillary, are solitary or in twos or threes. They have a tubular, five-angled or five-winged calyx with five slender lobes and a tubular or bell-shaped corolla with five twisted lobes (petals), often with plaits between each pair of lobes. There are five stamens and a slender style with two stigmas. The fruits are many-seeded berries.

Native to woodlands in Japan, China, and other parts of eastern Asia, *T. japonicum* (syns. *Crawfurdia japonica, C. trinervis, Gentiana trinervis*) has short, creeping rhizomes and slender sparingly-branched or branchless stems 1 foot to 2½ feet in length. The leaves, triangular-ovate to ovate or lanceolate, are up to 3½ inches long by 1¼ inches wide, but often smaller. The light blue-purple flowers are about 1¼ inches long. The fruits, about ⅓ inch in diameter, are reddish-purple.

Garden Uses and Cultivation. This, for the collector of choice and rare plants, may be expected to thrive under conditions that suit gentians. It should be tried in moistish soil rich in organic matter. Seed is probably the most satisfactory means of propagation.

TRIPTERYGIUM (Trip-terýgium). Eastern Asia is home to the four or five species of *Tripterygium,* of the staff tree family CELASTRACEAE. The name, which comes from the Greek *tri,* three, and *pterygion,* a small wing, alludes to the fruits.

Tripterygiums are shrubs or woody vines with alternate, stalked, largish leaves and terminal panicles of small, white flowers with five-lobed calyxes, five petals, five stamens, and a short style. Male, female, and bisexual blooms are on the same plant. The fruits, dry, prominently three-winged, and rather resembling those of some elms, are technically samaras.

Hardy through much of New England, **T. regelii**, of Japan, Korea, and Manchuria, is distinctive, deciduous, and can be grown as a shrub or vine. Of naturally scrambling habit, in cultivation it is 6 to 8 feet tall, but is probably taller in the wild. Its pliable, angled, warty, reddish-brown stems contrast pleasingly with its bright green foliage. The leaves are broad-elliptic to ovate, pointed, coarsely-toothed, 2½ to 6 inches long, and without hairs. In pyramidal panicles 8 to 10 inches long, the flowers are borne in late summer. They are creamy-white, about ⅓ inch in diameter, and sufficiently abundant to make a creditable display. The greenish-white, roundish fruits, approximately ¾ inch in length and found in large clusters, create no particular show.

Garden and Landscape Uses and Cultivation. As a change from more common woody plants, this rather coarse-textured species has merit. By judicious pruning it can be maintained as a shrub or encouraged to cover walls, fences, and other supports. It has no special needs as to soil, it prefers sun, and, apart from pruning to keep it shapely, it needs little care. Pruning is done in late winter or spring. Propagation is by seed and by leafy cuttings, 3 to 5 inches long, made from side growths and planted in summer in a propagating bench under mist, or in a shaded, humid cold frame or greenhouse. Increase can also be had by layering.

TRISETUM (Tri-sètum). The genus *Trisetum* consists of about sixty-five species of the grass family GRAMINEAE, natives of temperate and cold regions of North America and elsewhere. Its name comes from the Latin *tri*, three, and *setum*, a bristle. It alludes to the awns of the flower spikelets of some kinds.

Trisetums are perennial or more rarely annual grasses of tufted growth. Their leaf blades are flat, their flower panicles loose or compact and generally shining. The spikelets are most commonly two-, rarely three- to five-flowered and have conspicuous awns (bristles).

Highly variable, and in the wild distributed throughout northern parts of Europe, Asia, and America, in the mountains to Mexico and South America, and in the Antarctic, **T. spicatum** has slender, erect stems, 4 inches to 1¼ feet tall, and finely-hairy or hairless leaves up to ⅛ inch wide. The panicles of bloom are light to dark purple. They are congested and spikelike, with the lower parts of the spikes sometimes interrupted. They are 1½ to 4 inches long.

Native to Europe and naturalized in North America, **T. flavescens** is perennial. It is 1 foot to 2½ feet tall and has leaves up to ¼ inch broad. Its panicles of bloom, moderately dense, are looser than those of *T. spicatum*. From 3½ to 6 inches long, they have spikelets with usually three or four flowers. At first yellow, they turn brown as they age.

Garden and Landscape Uses and Cultivation. Trisetums are occasionally cultivated for their decorative panicles of flowers, which are sometimes used, fresh or dried, in flower arrangements. These plants are of easy cultivation in ordinary soils and garden locations. They are propagated by seed and by division.

TRISMERIA (Tris-mèria) One species of fern, of the pteris family PTERIDACEAE, closely allied to *Pityrogramma*, constitutes *Trismeria*. Its name, derived from the Greek *treis*, three, alludes to the manner in which the lower primary divisions of its leaves are parted.

A variable native of troical America, including the West Indies, **T. trifoliata** (syn. *Pityrogramma trifoliata*) is a vigorous inhabitant, in sun and part shade, of wet and moist soils. From 2 to 6 feet tall, it forms dense clumps of erect fronds with purplish-black stalks, conspicuously scaly toward their bases. The leaf blades are ovate-

Trismeria trifoliata

Trismeria trifoliata (portion of a frond)

lanceolate, with their primary divisions disposed pinnately. The lowermost primary divisions consist of three leaflets, those above of two or of one. The leaflets are from 2 to 5 inches in length by ⅜ to ⅝ inch in width. The undersides of the fertile fronds are thickly covered with spore capsules and are dusted, usually conspicuously, with bright lemon-yellow to white meal.

Garden Uses and Cultivation. These are as for *Pityrogramma*.

TRISTANIA (Tris-tània) — Brisbane-Box or Vinegar Tree, Water Gum. There are about fifty species of *Tristania*, of the myrtle family MYRTACEAE. Consisting of evergreen trees and shrubs, the genus inhabits Australia, New Caledonia, and the Malay Archipelago. Its name commemorates the French botanist Jules M. C. Tristan, who died in 1861.

Alternate or in whorls (circles of three or more), the leaves of tristanias, at the ends of the branchlets, are undivided. The flowers are in stalked clusters from the leaf axils. Small, white or yellow, they have a five-lobed calyx, five spreading petals, and many stamens united in five groups opposite the petals. The fruits are capsules partially or completely surrounded by persistent calyxes.

The Brisbane-box or vinegar tree (**T. conferta**) has been commonly planted in Hawaii for forestry as well as for ornament and is well adapted for use in parts of California and elsewhere in essentially frost-free climates. Attaining a height of about 150 feet, it has leathery, short-stalked, ovate-lanceolate, hairless leaves 3 to 7 inches in length by up to 2½ inches in width. Borne mostly on the younger shoots immediately below the leaves, the flowers are in clusters of three to seven. They are white and up to ¾ inch across. The cup-shaped, three-parted fruits are ⅓ to ½ inch in diameter. Even quite small specimens bloom.

Native to Australia and ranging from a large shrub up to a tree 70 feet tall, the water gum (**T. laurina**) has alternate leaves up to 4½ inches long by up to 1¼ inches broad. They are lanceolate to obovate-oblong and have undersurfaces glaucous or clothed with silky hairs, and marked with small dots. In short, thick-stalked clusters of up to ten, the disagreeably scented, ½-inch-wide, orange-yellow flowers are succeeded by fruits ¼ inch in diameter.

Garden and Landscape Uses and Cultivation. Tristanias are excellent ornamentals and good shade and street trees. They succeed without special attention in ordinary soils in tropical, subtropical, and warm-temperate climates. They are propagated by seed and by cuttings.

TRITELEIA (Tritel-èia). Sixteen western North American species comprise *Triteleia*, of the lily family LILIACEAE. By some botanists they are included in *Brodiaea*. Critical differences are that its flowers have six fertile stamens, while those of *Brodiaea* have only three, and that the anthers are attached to their stalks by their middles, while those of *Brodiaea* are attached by their bases. Yet another distinction is that the leaves of *Triteleia* are longitudinally keeled on their undersides, those of *Brodiaea* are rounded. The stigmas of *Triteleia* are not cleft, those of *Brodiaea* are. The name comes from the Greek *trias*, of three, in allusion to the arrangement of the parts of the flowers.

Triteleias have underground, fibrous-coated, bulblike organs called corms. These, like those of crocuses and gladioluses, last for only one year and are replaced by new ones that develop in the early fall to late spring growing season. The leaves, usually one or two from each corm, are narrowly-linear and all basal. The slender flower stalks terminate in umbels, each with a collar of papery bracts at their bases, of individually-stalked, blue, purple, yellow, or sometimes white blooms. The flowers have perianths of six segments, their lower parts joined into a tube to above their middles, their upper parts, commonly called petals, separate. There are six nonprotruding stamens and a style with a scarcely lobed stigma. The fruits are capsules.

Pretty face or golden star (*T. ixioides* syns. *Brodiaea ixioides, B. lutea*) is a variable endemic of California. Each corm has two leaves up to 1¼ feet long by up to approximately ½ inch wide. The loose umbels of ten to forty starry blooms, with individual stalks up to 1½ inches long, top stalks 6 inches to 2½ feet in length. The flowers, golden-yellow to buff-yellow with dark mid-veins, have perianth tubes about ¼ inch long and wide-spreading petals that form a face to the bloom 1 inch to 1½ inches across. The stamens are all attached at the same level.

Others with yellow flowers are *T. crocea* (syn. *Brodiaea crocea*), *T. gracilis*, and *T. hendersonii*. Growing wild on dry mountain slopes from Oregon to California, *T. crocea* has leaves up to 1 foot long by up to approximately ⅓ inch wide. Its umbels of bright yellow flowers terminate stalks up to 1 foot tall. The blooms have perianth tubes up to ⅓ inch long and spreading petals nearly ½ inch long. The stamens are alternately attached at two different levels. Variety *T. c. modesta* is smaller and has blue flowers. The blooms of *T. gracilis* (syn. *Brodiaea gracilis*) tend to become purplish with age. A mountain species of California, this has leaves up to 1 foot long by up to ⅕ inch broad. The umbels of flowers, their about ⅓-inch-long petals somewhat spreading, have brief perianth tubes and cream-colored anthers. The blooms are about ½ inch long. From the last, *T. hendersonii* (syn. *Brodiaea hendersonii*), a native of dry slopes in southern Oregon and

perhaps northern California, differs in having its frequently blue-tinged yellow flowers ¾ to 1 inch long and its wide-spreading petals from a little under to a little over ½ inch long.

Blue- to purple-flowered *T. grandiflora* (syn. *Brodiaea douglasii*) is native from Wyoming, Montana, Idaho, and Utah to British Columbia and Oregon. Its leaves are up to approximately 1½ feet long. The flowering stalks, 1 foot to 2 feet tall, bear rather open umbels of more or less bell-shaped blooms with perianth tubes, usually less than ½ inch long, and petals as long or longer, the three inner with wavy margins. The stamens arise at two different levels. Variety *T. g. howellii* (syn. *Brodiaea bicolor*) differs from the species in having more compact umbels. The inner petals of the nearly white to fairly deep blue flowers are not markedly wavy-edged, and the stamens have much flatter, broader stalks than those of the species and arise from nearly one level. Lilac-blue to blue or sometimes pinkish flowers are characteristic of *T. bridgesii* (syn. *Brodiaea bridgesii*). This native of dryish hillsides and woodland fringes in California has leaves up to a little over 1 foot long by less than ½ inch wide. Its umbels of bloom are on stalks 4 inches to 1½ feet tall. They have slender-based perianth tubes, ¾ to 1 inch long and over two-thirds as long as the spreading petals, which are up to ¾ inch long. The stamens, which all attach at the same level, have blue anthers.

Grass-nut, triplet-lily, or Ithuriel's spear (*T. laxa* syn. *Brodiaea laxa*), of California, is variable. In the wild favoring clayey or

Triteleia laxa

adobe soils, it has leaves up to over 1 foot long by sometimes 1 inch broad, but often much narrower. Its violet-blue to white flowers, in umbels of eight to nearly fifty, terminating wiry stalks 6 inches to 2½ feet tall, have perianth tubes ½ to 1 inch long and diverging petals ⅓ to ¾ inch long. The blue-anthered stamens are alternately attached at two levels.

Milky-white, sometimes bluish blooms with green mid-veins, in umbels 3 inches or more in diameter, are borne by *T. hyacinthina* (syn. *Brodiaea hyacinthina*). Ranging in the wild from Idaho to Vancouver Island and California, this attractive spe-

cies has leaves up to a little over 1 foot long by nearly 1 inch wide. Its umbels of ten to forty open-bell-shaped, somewhat papery blooms are on stalks 1 foot to 2 feet tall. The flowers have very short, bowl-shaped perianth tubes and spreading petals ⅓ to ½ inch long. The stamens, their anthers white or blue, are all attached at the same level. With white or lilac-tinged blooms, Californian *T. peduncularis* (syn. *Brodiaea peduncularis*) has leaves up to rather over 1 foot long by about ¼ to ½ inch wide. Its umbels of flowers are on stalks from up to 1 foot to 2½ feet tall. Their flowers have individual stalks two to five times as long as the blooms. Their perianth tubes are approximately ⅓ inch long, the diverging petals up to a little over ½ inch long. The stamens, their anthers white, alternately arise from two different levels. A hybrid between *T. peduncularis* and *T. laxa* that comes true from seed, *T. tubergenii* (syn. *Brodiaea tubergenii*) was raised in Holland. This intermediate, described as man-made, has large umbels of pale blue flowers with slightly deeper blue exteriors. Another hybrid, 'Queen Fabiola' has flowers described as being of a good violet color, with individual stalks 2 to 2½ inches long. They are in umbels at the tops of stalks 2 to 2½ feet tall. This is reported to be a good cut flower.

Garden and Landscape Uses and Cultivation. These are as for *Brodiaea*.

TRITHRINAX (Trithri-nax). Five species of low, fan-leaved palms of the palm family PALMAE constitute *Trithrinax*. All are natives of South America. Some are planted outdoors in southern Florida, southern California, and other warm regions. The name is from the Greek *tri*, three, and *thrinax*, a trident. It refers to the divisions of the leaves.

These palms have solitary or clustered trunks with the persistent sheaths of their leaf bases united at their tips into long, vicious spines. The leaves, more or less circular, are cut deeply into many segments. The branched flower clusters originate from among the foliage and bear their bisexual blooms singly along the branches. The stalks of the six stamens form a tube. The spherical, one-seeded fruits are up to 1 inch in diameter.

A solitary slender trunk up to 12 feet in height is characteristic of *T. brasiliensis*, of Paraguay and southern Brazil. Its stiffish leaves, about 3 feet long, are cleft to their middles into thirty or more spreading segments with deeply-notched apexes. The upper surfaces of the leaves are green, the lower ones glaucous. Similar to *T. brasiliensis*, more rigid-leaved *T. campestris* has leaf segments much more shallowly-notched. Its gray-green leaves, 2 to 3 feet in diameter, are white-hairy above, hairless or nearly hairless beneath. They are cut nearly to their bases into twenty or more spine-tipped segments. This native

Trithrinax acanthocoma

They have slender, sometimes branched stems, and fans of parallel-veined, linear or sword-shaped leaves, which are chiefly basal. The flowers, yellow, coppery-orange, red, pink, or white, are in generally one-sided spikes. Their perianths are tubular, widening above. They have six more or less spreading lobes, commonly called petals, but more correctly, tepals. There are three stamens, and a style with three short, uncleft branches. The fruits are capsules.

From 1 foot to 1¼ feet tall or sometimes taller, **T. crocata** has narrowly-sword-shaped, rigid leaves shorter than the flower stalk and nearly ½ inch broad. The stalk terminates in a loose, one-sided spike of up to twelve blooms displayed in two ranks. They are from a little under to a little over 1 inch long, and across their faces somewhat wider than their lengths. The perianth tube is not more than one-half as long as the spreading petals. Their color is variable, most commonly brilliant orange with some yellow deep in the throat. The stamens are purple. Variants are *T. c. aurantiaca*, with orange-red blooms; *T. c. coccinea*, the flowers of which are scarlet; *T. c. purpurea*, which has purple flowers; *T. c. sanguinea*, with blood red blooms; and comparatively small-bloomed, red-flowered *T. c. miniata*. Much resembling *T. crocata*, but not over 1 foot tall, **T. deusta** has rather smaller, cinnabar-red or yellow blooms that differ from those of *T. crocata*

of Argentina may eventually have a trunk 10 to 12 feet tall, but for a long time it is likely to remain low with the foliage touching the ground. A low, solitary-stemmed palm that resembles *Trachycarpus* in aspect, **T. acanthocoma**, of southern Brazil, has bigger leaves and a trunk conspicuously armed with down-pointing stout spines that terminate the network formed by the bases of the leaf sheaths. The leaves are divided to two-thirds of their depth into many narrow, notched segments.

Garden and Landscape Uses. These are attractive palms for frost-free and nearly frost-free climates and are especially suitable for sites where space is limited. They are effective as solitary specimens and as accents among other plants in borders, groups, foundation plantings, and similar ornamental arrangements. Because of their vicious spines they should not be planted where they are likely to be dangerous to passersby or children. They are attractive for greenhouses and for growing in containers.

Cultivation. Ordinary well-drained, reasonably fertile garden soil and full sun suit members of this easy-to-grow genus. New plants are easily had from fresh seed sown in sandy, peaty soil in a temperature of 75 to 85°F. In greenhouses they respond to planting in ground beds or well-drained pots or tubs in a coarse, fertile, porous soil

kept fairly moist, but not constantly saturated. In winter, less water is required than at other seasons. Specimens that have filled their containers with healthy roots benefit from dilute liquid fertilizer given every two weeks from spring to fall. Shade from strong sun and a reasonably humid atmosphere are requisite. The minimum night temperature in winter should be 55 to 60°F, at other seasons higher. Day temperatures should always be five to fifteen degrees above those maintained at night. For additional information see the Encyclopedia entry Palms.

TRITOMA. See Kniphofia.

TRITONIA (Tri-tònia). Montbretias and some other garden plants previously included here are now classified as *Crocosmia*. Left in *Tritonia* are approximately fifty species. They belong to the iris family IRIDACEAE and are natives of South Africa. The name, from *Triton*, in its significance as a weather vane, alludes to the various directions in which the stamens of some kinds point. Tritonias resemble *Sparaxis*, but differ, as they do from *Crocosmia*, in the spathe valves (bracts at the bases of the flowers) having pointed rather than lacerated or notched tips.

Tritonias have solid bulblike organs called corms and deciduous aboveground parts.

Tritonia deusta

in having an almost black spot on the shafts or claws of the three outer petals. As tall as the last, **T. hyalina** has fairly broad, sword-shaped, pointed leaves, and short-tubed, light orange blooms with spreading petals that are transparent at their sides toward their bases. Similarly with transparent margins to the bottoms of the petals, **T. squalida** has blooms otherwise resembling those of *T. crocata*, but of a beautiful shell-pink hue, with a wine-colored stain in the throat, and pale yellow anthers.

Garden and Landscape Uses and Cultivation. These are as for *Ixia*.

TROCHODENDRACEAE — Trochodendron Family. The characteristics of this family of dicotyledons are those of its only genus, *Trochodendron*.

TROCHODENDRON (Trocho-déndron). One species of evergreen tree of unique appearance, a native of Japan, Korea, and Taiwan, is the only representative of this genus. Hardy in sheltered locations in the vicinity of New York City, it never becomes the large tree there that it does in less severe climates. It belongs in the trochodendron family TROCHODENDRACEAE and is believed to represent a very ancient form of plant life. Its name, from the Greek *trochos*, a wheel, and *dendron*, a tree, refers

Trochodendron aralioides in flower

to the manner in which the stamens are arranged.

A handsome tree, with spreading branches, that in its homelands attains a height of up to 60 feet, *Trochodendron aralioides* has alternate, long-stalked, leathery leaves mostly clustered toward, and spreading in all directions from, the ends of the branches. They are 3 to 6 inches long, lustrous dark green above, somewhat paler on their undersides, and toward their apexes shallowly-toothed. They are lanceolate, ovate, or obovate. Their bisexual, bright green flowers, in erect, loose, terminal, 3-inch-long racemes, are without both sepals and petals, but have many slender-stalked stamens that spread from the margins of a green disk, and an ovary of five to ten carpels (sections) united at their bases. The persistent styles are recurved in the fruiting stage. The individual flowers, on stalks ¾ inch to 1½ inches long, are about ½ inch wide. The fruits consist of five to ten many-seeded brown follicles (podlike structures), about ½ inch in diameter, with their lower ends buried in the receptacle (fleshy end of the stalk). Variety *T. a. longifolium* has narrower, broad-oblanceolate leaves.

Garden and Landscape Uses and Cultivation. As a tree or, toward the northern limits of its hardiness, a broad shrub, *T. aralioides* is distinctive and never fails to attract interest from the botanically curious. It associates well with other evergreens and with deciduous trees and shrubs and prospers in light shade or sun. For its best growth, a fertile, loamy soil, reasonably moist but not wet, is preferred.

Propagation is by seed and by cuttings of firm shoots inserted in late summer or early fall in a greenhouse propagating bench, preferably with mild bottom heat and overhead mist.

TROLLIUS (Tról-lius) — Globe Flower. The genus *Trollius*, of the buttercup family RANUNCULACEAE, comprises twenty-five northern hemisphere species. Its name is derived from the Old German *trol*, round, and alludes to the shape of the blooms of a few kinds. Most trolliuses have flat to slightly cupped flowers, rather than globular flowers.

Natives of damp and wet places, globe flowers have erect, leafy stems and considerable basal foliage. The leaves are palmately- (in hand-fashion) divided or lobed, and generally sharply-toothed. The buttercup-like flowers, yellow, orange, white, or pink, are showy. They have five to fifteen petal-like sepals that are the most conspicuous parts. The true petals, smaller and shorter than the sepals, more or less resemble stamens and number five or more. There are many stamens and five to many pistils. The fruits are tiny podlike follicles. In this feature *Trollius* differs from related *Ranunculus*, which has achenes as fruits.

The European globe flower (**T. europaeus**) is slightly ill-scented and 1 foot to 2½ feet tall. From its base come several hairless, branched or branchless stems. The long-stalked basal leaves are two- to three-times-divided into ovate, toothed leaflets. The stem leaves are smaller, and stalked or stalkless. The blooms, solitary or in pairs, 1 inch to 2 inches in diameter, have ten to

Trochodendron aralioides with young fruits

Trollius europaeus

fifteen pale yellow to greenish-yellow sepals that curve inward. The narrow spatula-shaped petals, never much longer than the stamens, are sometimes shorter. Asian *T. yunnanensis* has up to eight spreading, bright yellow sepals. From 1 foot to 2 feet tall, it has lower leaves markedly cleft into toothed lobes. Mostly in threes, the flat flowers, 2½ to 3 inches wide, look like giant buttercups.

Trollius yunnanensis

Trollius pumilus

Cream-colored to nearly white flowers with five to eight spreading sepals characterize *T. laxus,* which is endemic in swamps from New Hampshire to British Columbia, Delaware, and Utah. This has slender stems up to 1½ feet tall or a little taller, five- to seven-parted, long-obovate basal leaves, and short-stalked stem leaves. From 1 inch to 1½ inches in diameter, its flowers have no more than seven spreading sepals, and petals shorter than the stamens. Himalayan *T. pumilus* has blooms with up to eight spreading sepals, and petals not appreciably longer than the sta-

mens. Up to 1 foot in height, this has basal leaves cleft into five toothed segments, and solitary, yellow, sometimes green-tinged flowers, 1 inch to 1½ inches wide, with five to seven spreading sepals and ten to twelve petals as long as the stamens. Also Himalayan, *T. acaulis,* 3 inches to 1 foot tall, has leaves with five to seven three-parted, toothed leaflets. Its solitary, 1½- to 2-inch-wide, deep yellow blooms overtop the foliage and have five to nine sepals and twelve to sixteen petals shorter than the stamens.

Trollius acaulis

Flowers with petals much longer than the stamens distinguish the species now to be considered. One of the better globe flowers, Siberian *T. ledebourii* is about 2 feet tall. Its basal leaves are cleft to their bases into lobed and toothed divisions. The 2½-inch-wide, yellow flowers have five spreading sepals and ten to twelve narrow petals. From the last, *T. chinensis* differs in its long-stalked, golden-yellow blooms having ten or more spreading sepals and little or no basal foliage. Its stem leaves have blades up to 5 inches in length and more in width. They are kidney-shaped, or the upper ones rounded, and are divided into five broad, oblanceolate segments. The about twenty narrow petals, exceeding 1 inch in length, are a showy feature of the blooms. This is a native of China. From it, *T. asiaticus,* of Siberia, differs in having bronzy-green, finely-divided basal leaves, and orange-colored flowers with ten spreading sepals, and ten petals longer than the stamens, but not protruding or particularly conspicuous. The flowers of *T. a. fortunei* have more sepals.

Hybrid globe flowers of uncertain parentage, but mostly having both European and Asian species as ancestors, are commonly found in gardens. They show characteristics intermediate between those of their parent stocks and are generally superior, usually having larger, finer-colored blooms, good growth habits, and excellent foliage. Here belong such varieties as

Trollius ledebourii

Trollius 'Goldquelle' beside a pool in a rock garden

'Goldquelle', 'Golden Queen', and 'Orange Globe'. This hybrid swarm is variously named **T. hybridus** and **T. cultorum.**

Garden and Landscape Uses. Where conditions are agreeable, globe flowers are among the easier hardy herbaceous perennials to manage. They need moist or even wet, fertile soil, preferably on the heavy rather than sandy side, and full sun or at most a little part-day shade. They are particularly well adapted for waterside planting, but can be made at home in beds with other flowering plants if care is taken that they never lack for moisture.

Cultivation. Established globe flowers need no special care other than thorough and frequent watering in dry weather. A spring application of a complete garden fertilizer makes for vigorous growth, and mulching with organic material is decidedly beneficial. Planting is best done in early fall, but may be done in spring. Propagation is by division in early fall or spring, and by seed. Seeds should be sown as soon as possible after they ripen and before they dry, in soil that can be kept moist, in a cold frame or protected, shaded spot outdoors. Often the seeds do not germinate until the second year, and the young plants, in their early stages, are likely to grow slowly.

TROPAEOLACEAE — Nasturtium Family. Native from southern Mexico to Argentina and Chile, the nasturtium family or TRO-PAEOLACEAE consists of two genera of dicotyledons, *Tropaeolum* and *Magallana*, of which only the first is cultivated. Its members are more or less succulent, sometimes tuberous-rooted, herbaceous plants with stems that are prostrate or climb by means of sensitive leafstalks that wind around convenient supports. The leaves, usually alternate, or the lower sometimes opposite, are lobeless, or palmately-lobed or -divided. The stalks join the blades well in from their margins. Solitary and asymmetrical, the flowers, borne in the axils of the leaves, have a prominently spurred calyx, petal-like in color and texture, five or sometimes fewer petals, eight stamens, one style, and three stigmas. The fruits consist of three loosely-joined, wrinkled, one-seeded compartments. All parts of these plants contain mustard oil.

TROPAEOLUM (Tropaè-olum) — Nasturtium or Indian-Cress, Canary Bird Vine or Canary Bird Flower, Flame Flower. There can be few gardeners unfamiliar with the nasturtiums of seed catalogs and horticultural usage. Most are unaware that the name *Nasturtium*, applied with botanical precision, belongs to an entirely different group of plants, of the mustard family CRUCIFERAE, that includes common watercress, or that the correct name of the garden nasturtiums is *Tropaeolum*. Yet this is so. Other attractive tropaeolums, most familiar of which is the canary bird flower, are cultivated. The flower buds and seeds of the common nasturtium, which is sometimes called Indian-cress, are used to add piquancy to pickles, and the young leaves are sometimes used in salads.

There are ninety species of *Tropaeolum*, a genus that with one other, not in cultivation, composes the nasturtium family TROPAEOLACEAE, and that occurs in the wild from Mexico to Chile. The name is derived from the Greek *tropaion*, or Latin *tropaeum*, a trophy. It alludes to a fanciful resemblance of the shield-shaped leaves of some kinds, and helmet-shaped blooms, to cap-tured shields and helmets displayed in pyramid fashion on battlefields by victorious armies of the ancients.

The genus *Tropaeolum* consists of annuals and nonhardy, sometimes tuberous-rooted, herbaceous perennials, including vines that cling by twisting their leafstalks around suitable supports, and compact, bushy kinds. They have alternate, mostly long-stalked leaves that are shield-shaped, five-angled, or variously lobed and dissected. Solitary from the leaf axils, the usually long-stalked, asymmetrical, generally colorful and showy blooms are yellow, orange, red, varicolored, or less commonly purple or blue. They have five sepals, one of which extends as a nectar-producing spur. Generally there are five petals, although sometimes fewer, that may be smooth-edged, lobed, or fringed. At their bases the petals are contracted into narrow shafts or claws. The two upper ones differ from the others and are commonly smaller. There are eight stamens, and one style ending in three stigmas. The fruits consist of three, more or less loosely united compartments (carpels), each with one seed.

The common garden nasturtium is chiefly derived from South American **T. majus,** but there is little doubt that many varieties reflect hybridity between this and other species. They range from tall vines to dwarf, compact kinds called Tom Thumb nasturtiums, which are grouped as *T. m. nanum,* and include Gleam Hybrids (*T. m. burpeei*), which are low and bushy and have double or semidouble flowers. The first developed of these, 'Golden Gleam', has rich yellow flowers. Varieties with light yellow, scarlet, salmon-cerise, and mahogany-red blooms were developed later. A double-flowered, tall vining kind, *T. m. flore-pleno,* as seen in cultivation, commonly has red flowers, but perhaps also occurs in other colors. Hairless or nearly so, the common nasturtium has round to somewhat kidney-shaped, angled or wavy-

The common garden nasturtium:
(a) Single-flowered

(b) Semidouble-flowered

edged, toothless leaves, the stalks of which are attached to the 2- to 7-inch-wide blades toward their middles. From 1 inch to 2½ inches across, the long-spurred blooms are creamy-white, yellow, red, or varicolored. From the common nasturtium, *T. minus,* of Peru, a nonclimbing kind, differs in being smaller in all its parts, in its leaves having margins with a prominent point projecting from the end of each vein, and in the deep yellow petals of its flowers being bristle-pointed rather than rounded and blunt. The three lower petals are marked with a dark spot.

The canary bird vine or canary bird flower (*T. peregrinum* syn. *T. canariense*), probably native to Peru and Ecuador, is a hairless, annual climber. The long stalks of its leaves are attached near the bases of

Tropaeolum peregrinum

the 1- to 2-inch-wide, circular-in-outline blades, which are deeply-divided into five-cleft, blunt or pointed lobes. From ¾ to 1 inch across, the lemon- to canary-yellow flowers, with a red spot at the bottoms of their petals, have a short, green, hooked spur. Much bigger than the others, the upper two petals are erect, and cleft to form a deep fringe. The lower three petals are edged with hairs. Rather resembling the canary bird vine, *T. seemannii,* of Bolivia and Peru, is an annual climber with long-stalked, deeply-three-lobed leaves with blades 1 inch to 1¾ inches long. The stalks are united to the blades a little distance in from the leaf margin. Yellow to orange-yellow, the flowers are about ¾ inch long by ¾ to 1 inch wide. Their petals are deeply-fringed.

Tropaeolum seemannii

One of the choicest species, the flame flower (*T. speciosum*), of Chile, is magnificent where it thrives, but unfortunately is successful only where winters are mild and summers cool and humid. This tall climber has fleshy, perennial roots, and leaves hairy on their undersides and deeply-divided into usually six, less frequently five or seven, obovate leaflets. The flowers, on stalks much longer than the leaves, are brilliant vermilion and about 1½ inches long. The petals are notched at their apexes.

Other kinds are occasionally cultivated. Annual *T. peltophorum* (syn. *T. lobbianum*) is a taller climber with the stems and the undersides of its leaves hairy. It has round, long-stalked leaves, the blades joined to the leafstalk near their centers and the veins

ending at the leaf margins in projecting points. The orange-red flowers are about 1 inch long, their long-clawed lower petals deeply-toothed. This is a native of Colombia and Ecuador. From Chile and Argentina, *T. polyphyllum* is prostrate or climbing. A fleshy-rooted, hairless perennial, it has long-stalked, roundish leaves very deeply-divided into five to seven ovate, toothed or toothless lobes. The ¾-inch-long blooms, yellow or orange-red, have notched upper petals. Tuberous-

Tropaeolum polyphyllum

Tropaeolum tricolor

rooted *T. pentaphyllum,* of Argentina, is a tall vine with purplish stems and leaf-stalks. Its long-stalked leaves have five elliptic, stalked leaflets. The 1-inch-long flowers are scarlet, with some green on the spurs. Fleshy-rooted *T. tricolor,* of Chile, is a vine with leaves of six usually linear to linear-ovate leaflets, and yellow, red, and purplish flowers 1 inch long. In its native Peru and Bolivia, the large tubers of *T.*

tuberosum are cooked and eaten. A hairless vine, this has nearly round leaves, with usually five lobes extending about one-third of the way to their bases, and flowers, with yellow or red petals and a red spur, that are up to 1 inch long by ½ to ¾ inch wide.

Garden and Landscape Uses. The common nasturtium in its many varieties and the canary bird vine, grown as annuals, are among the most satisfactory and easily managed garden flowers. For their success all that is needed is a very well-drained, moderately moist, but not wet soil, on the lean side rather than overfertile (too much nourishment makes for exuberant production of stems and foliage, but few flowers). Full sun is necessary. Vining varieties of common nasturtium and the canary bird vine require supports around which to twine their leafstalks. Slender stakes, pea brush, strings, or wires suit. The climbers are splendid for growing over tepees of brushwood erected toward the backs of flower borders, for clothing trellises and pergolas, and for training along wires or strings stretched in front of walls. The bushy varieties serve well in flower beds and rocky places where fairly deep soil is available, and they are very suitable for window and porch boxes, hanging baskets, vases, and other types of containers. In greenhouses the common nasturtium and the canary bird vine are excellent as pot plants, and the double-flowered variety of the common nasturtium is grown as a perennial for clothing pillars or for training to wires in front of walls or under the roof glass.

Cultivation. Common nasturtiums and the canary bird vine are raised from seed, ordinarily sown ½ to ¾ inch deep outdoors in spring as soon as it is safe to sow beans and other frost-tender crops. Less commonly, plants are started indoors about five weeks before they are to be planted in the garden or in window boxes or other containers, and are set out from small pots. Spacing for bush kinds may be 6 to 9 inches apart, for climbers 9 inches is appropriate.

For plants in pots for blooming in late winter and spring in greenhouses, the seed is sown in September in a temperature of 55 to 60°F, and the plants are potted successively from small to larger pots as growth makes necessary. A coarse, porous, not overly rich soil suits; watering should be moderate rather than excessive. Full sun and, after germination, a night temperature of 50°F, with an increase, related to light intensity, of five to ten or fifteen degrees by day, are needed. On all favorable occasions the greenhouse must be ventilated freely. Double-flowered *T. m. flore-pleno* produces no seeds. Increase is by cuttings, which root easily. This tropaeolum is usually kept throughout the year in a greenhouse under conditions recommended above for kinds raised as

annuals from seed. Perennial tropaeolums with fleshy and tuberous roots are more difficult to grow. None is hardy. Where mild winters and cool summers occur, *T. speciosum* may be tried. It is often at its best when planted at the foot of a hedge, through which its stems can climb. Other tuberous-rooted kinds are little known in American gardens. They are appropriate only for mild, dryish climates.

TROUT-LILY. See Erythronium.

TROWELS. Basic garden tools, trowels are nearly indispensable for digging up and then planting small plants and also for planting many sorts of bulbs.

The garden trowel has a handle 6 inches long and, extending from one end of it at a slight angle, a round-pointed blade of the same length, about 3 inches wide, and, unlike that of a mason's trowel, curved laterally. Models with narrower blades are convenient for use in rock gardens and similar places.

A narrow-bladed trowel is useful for planting bulbs among low groundcovers

Correct ways of using a trowel are of some importance. To lift (dig up) a plant, it may be necessary to first slice around it by jabbing the blade vertically into the ground at such distance from its center that not too many roots are forfeited. Then insert the blade with its hollow side toward the plant, press backward on the handle to loosen the plant, and lift it out, sitting on the blade.

This procedure comes naturally to most people, but fewer use the trowel properly to make planting holes. Inexperienced gardeners most often stab the blade into the ground with the hollow side facing away from them, and then with a scoop-like action lift the soil upward and forward, depositing it on the far side of the hole. If many holes are to be dug, this is a tiring procedure.

The professional's method is to grasp the handle, with the thumb on top and with

The correct way of using a trowel to make a planting hole

the hollow side of the blade facing the operator, and jab the blade into the ground, pulling the soil forward to make a heap on the near side of the hole. With the other hand, set the plant in place. Then, without putting the trowel down, but only turning the holding hand so that the blade points upward, use both hands to firm the soil about the roots and level its surface. This method employs the muscles of the arm to best advantage, makes for speedy planting, and is very much less tiring.

TRUEHEDGE COLUMNBERRY is *Berberis thunbergii erecta*.

TRUMPET. The word trumpet appears in the common names of these plants: angel's trumpet (*Datura*), herald's trumpet (*Beaumontia grandiflora*), humming bird's trumpet (*Zauschneria*), mangrove trumpet tree (*Dolichandrone spathacea*), orange-trumpet-vine (*Pyrostegia venusta*), trumpet creeper (*Distictis*), trumpet tree (*Cecropia peltata* and *Tabebuia*), and trumpet vine (*Campsis*).

TRUMPET BUSH. See Tecoma.

TRUMPETS is *Sarracenia flava*.

TSUGA (Tsù-ga) — Hemlock. Members of the genus *Tsuga* are called hemlocks in North America and hemlock-spruces in the British Isles. They are not to be confused with the poison-hemlock (*Conium maculatum*) used by the ancient Greeks to poison Socrates and others. This last is a nonwoody member of the carrot family UMBELLIFERAE, whereas hemlocks are trees belonging to the pine family PINACEAE. The genus consists of ten species, natives of North America and Asia. The name *Tsuga* is adopted from the Japanese vernacular name.

Hemlocks are close kin of firs (*Abies*) and spruces (*Picea*). From the former they differ in their cones being pendulous and not disintegrating soon after the seeds ripen, and from spruces in having very brief, slender leafstalks that are pressed against the shoots and in the leaves being glaucous on their undersides or at least paler than above. Hemlocks are pyramidal, evergreen trees (some of their varieties are shrubs), with wide-spreading, horizontal or somewhat drooping branches and numerous slender, pliant branchlets that in most kinds have their ends angled to one side and are usually pendulous toward their extremities. The leaves resemble those of spruces, but are smaller. They are narrowly-linear, flat, close together, usually grooved along the mid-vein on their upper surfaces, and, except in *T. mertensiana* and *T. jeffreyi*, arranged in two ranks. Each leaf sits on a small cushion-like projection from the twig, which remains after the leaf drops. These projections, smaller than those of spruces, are responsible for the roughness of the twigs. Male and female cones are on the same tree, the former in the axils of the leaves of shoots developed the previous year, the latter terminating the last year's lateral shoots. The cones are small and solitary, usually not over 1 inch long and somewhat over one-half as wide, with their scales usually concealing the shorter bracts. They remain hanging on the trees for several months after the seeds have dispersed at the end of the first season. Each cone scale bears two seeds.

Hemlocks are among the most beautiful and graceful of coniferous trees and shrubs. Native kinds lend great charm to the woodlands of North America, as do Oriental species in their homelands. In Japan the wood of *T. diversifolia* is esteemed for construction, especially for important buildings. That of the western American *T. heterophylla* is also useful and is exploited commercially, but the eastern American species, *T. canadensis* and *T. caroliniana*, produce splintery wood of comparatively poor quality, used only for rough carpentry and pulping. The bark of *T. canadensis* and *T. caroliniana* have high tannin contents and are employed for tanning leather.

The native hemlocks of eastern North America are two, one of which has given rise to a great many horticultural varieties. They are the eastern or common hemlock (*T. canadensis*) and the Carolina hemlock (*T. caroliniana*). These differ in their natural ranges, general aspects, and botanical details. Indigenous from southern Canada to Alabama and westward to Ohio and Minnesota, and occasionally 100 feet tall with a trunk up to 4 feet in diameter, but more often not over 70 or 80 feet high, not infrequently with its trunk branched from near its base, *T. canadensis* inhabits moist soils and especially rocky hillsides and ridges. Its bark is brown to purple-brown, its

Tsuga canadensis

Tsuga canadensis (leaves and cones)

A rare, unidentified weeping hemlock in the garden of Harold Epstein, Larchmont, New York

Tsuga canadensis pendula

branches are often rather pendulous, and its twigs are finely-hairy. The leaves, up to about ¾ inch long, have two white lines on their undersides and have very finely-toothed margins (this can be detected by rubbing a finger along them). The short-stalked cones are about ¾ inch long.

Many horticultural varieties of *T. canadensis* have been segregated and cultivated, more than fifty were grown at the Hemlock Arboretum of the late Charles F. Jenkins near Philadelphia, Pennsylvania, and undoubtedly others will appear and be nurtured in the future. They vary from tiny dwarfs to globe types and weeping kinds. Undoubtedly the best known is Sargent's weeping hemlock (*T. c. pendula*

syn. *T. sargentii*), a distinct variety of which four plants were discovered growing in woods near Fishkill, New York, before 1870, by General Joseph Howland, and one recognized early by local inhabitants near Hortontown, New York, but not recorded in botanical literature until 1939. This fine sort is called Sargent's weeping hemlock in honor of Howland's neighbor Henry Winthrop Sargent, brother of Charles Sprague Sargent, director of the Arnold Arboretum, Jamaica Plain, Massachusetts. One of the original trees was moved to the estate of General Howland near Beacon, New York, and another to the estate of Charles Sprague Sargent at Brookline, Massachusetts. These and the one near Hortontown, New York, are still alive al-

Tsuga canadensis pendula, 12 feet tall and 25 feet in diameter, Planting Fields Arboretum, Oyster Bay, New York

Tsuga caroliniana

Tsuga caroliniana (foliage)

most a century after their discovery. Sargent's weeping hemlock becomes an irregular mound, considerably broader than tall, with a flattish top and gracefully arching and drooping branches. It attains an eventual height of 15 feet or more, but grows very slowly, although grafted plants seem to grow more rapidly than the original specimens, which are, of course, on their own roots. Other distinct varieties of *T. canadensis* are *T. c. albospica,* with the tips of its young branchlets white; *T. c. atrovirens,* with exceptionally dark green foliage; *T. c. aurea,* a low plant with foliage tinged yellow; *T. c. 'Cole',* a prostrate kind that has ground-hugging branches and is a good rock garden plant; *T. c. compacta,* a dwarf pyramidal with small leaves; *T. c. fremdii,* a slow-growing, dense, and pyramidal shrub with dark green foliage; *T. c. globosa,* globose and compact; *T. c. gracilis,* with leaves about ¼ inch long and spreading branches with few branchlets that droop at their ends; *T. c. hussii,* very dwarf and with short, twiggy branchlets; *T. c. jenkinsii,* narrowly-pyramidal and with small leaves; *T. c. macrophylla,* distinguished by its large leaves; *T. c. microphylla,* shrubby and with ¼-inch-long leaves; *T. c. minuta,* very dwarf, extremely slow-growing, and with dark green leaves about ¼ inch long; and *T. c. nana,* of dense growth, up to about 7 feet tall, broader than high, and with pendulous branches.

Tsuga canadensis minuta

The Carolina hemlock (*T. caroliniana*) is a native of the Appalachian Mountains from Virginia to Georgia. More compact and, as a landscape subject, even more lovely than the beautiful eastern hemlock, this species, which mostly does not exceed 50 feet in height, occasionally reaches a 70-foot height. Its usually downswept branches are luxuriantly clothed with usually darker green foliage than that of the eastern hemlock. The Carolina hemlock differs from the last in having mostly larger, smooth-edged leaves, and cones, 1 inch to 1½ inches long, on short stalks. A variety, *T. c. compacta* is distinguished as being round-topped, dense, and bushy.

Two species are native to western North America, the mountain hemlock and the western hemlock. The latter inhabits humid coastal regions from California to Alaska, the other has about the same south–north distribution, but is confined to the mountains. From all other hemlocks the mountain hemlock (*T. mertensiana*) is distinguished by its having longitudinal white lines on the upper as well

as the lower surfaces of its leaves, which are usually rounded or slightly keeled above and only rarely have a slight longitudinal groove along the center. Also, its leaves are not in two rows, but radiate around the shoots. They are up to 1 inch long. This species, which attains a maximum height of 150 feet, has slender drooping branches, hairy young shoots, and pale bluish-green foliage. Its cones are 2 to 3 inches in length. Variety *T. m. argentea* has very glaucous, light bluish foliage. The western hemlock (**T. heterophylla**) is one of the giants among conifers. At its best it exceeds 250 feet, but most specimens do not, of course, attain such heights. It differs markedly from the mountain hemlock, generally more closely resembling the eastern *T. canadensis,* but from that it is distinct in having more globose leaf buds and broader, much less well defined white bands on the undersides of its leaves. Also, its trunk does not have a tendency to divide. The leaves of the western hemlock are minutely-toothed and its twigs are pubescent. Its cones, ¾ to 1 inch long, are without stalks. A variety, *T. h. conica* is a broadly-pyramidal, dense, and compact bush.

Native hemlocks of Japan include the one generally called Japanese hemlock (**T. diversifolia**), which chiefly inhabits the northern part of the country, and **T. sieboldii,** which has a more southern range. Both are handsome ornamental trees. The chief difference between them is that the young shoots of the former are hairy, while those of the latter are hairless. Both have smooth-edged leaves notched at their tips and attain maximum heights of about 100 feet, although in cultivation in America and Europe they often are not larger than small trees or even tall shrubs. The trunk of *T. diversifolia* is likely to divide low down into two or more secondary trunks. Its new leaves appear in spring earlier than those of any other hemlock. Both Japanese species are hardy in many parts of New England, but will not live as far north as the eastern American species. Other kinds from Asia include the Chinese hemlock (**T. chinensis**). Widely distributed in China, but little known in cultivation, it is up to 150 feet in height. As it was not introduced to Western gardens until the beginning of the present century, there are no very large specimens in America or Europe. It is a variable species, similar to the Japanese hemlock (*T. diversifolia*), but has less hairy twigs and slightly wider leaves. A variety, *T. c. formosana,* endemic to Taiwan, is said to have hairier twigs. The Himalayan hemlock (**T. dumosa**) is the most tender species; it cannot be expected to survive in the northeastern or northcentral states and is probably only adapted for the Pacific Northwest. It may be identified by its gracefully drooping branches and slender leaves, finely-toothed at their margins and

Tsuga chinensis, Royal Horticultural Society's Garden, Surrey, England

A pair of sheared hemlocks gives height to this foundation planting

Hedges of closely-sheared hemlocks flank the broad driveway to this house

1 inch to 1½ inches long. Its cones are ½ to 1 inch long.

A hybrid hemlock of natural origin, *T. jeffreyi* has as parents *T. mertensiana* and *T. heterophylla*. Apparently it is rather rare, there being only two records of its introduction into cultivation. Its characteristics are intermediate between those of its parents. It has green, not glaucous-green or grayish foliage, and leaves that do not point forward along the shoots, but spread at right angles; they are usually minutely-toothed toward their ends and are about ½ inch long, with white lines beneath and broken white lines toward the tips on the upper sides. The cones are 2 inches long.

Garden and Landscape Uses. Less formal and more graceful than most evergreen conifers, hemlocks are well adapted for landscape embellishment. Versatile and adaptable, they can serve usefully in many ways and are often appropriate where other conifers would be out of place. For example, although they thrive in full sun, they will stand a fair amount of shade and even a certain amount of drip from overhanging trees. When grown in part-shade they are looser, more open, and not as densely-foliaged as they are in sun, but are still charming and elegant in a way that no shade-grown spruce, fir, or pine can possibly be. Grown in shade, the latter look bedraggled, woebegone, and out of place, whereas hemlocks fit such locations congruously, as indeed they should, for they are children of mixed woodlands as well as of pure stands and in the wild are accustomed to have neighboring deciduous forest trees overtop them for the greater part of their lives. Also, hemlocks stand pruning and shearing well and are excellent for formal screens and hedges, as well as for semiformal features of such kinds, and for completely informal plantings. If allowed ample room, they are splendid as single lawn specimens and are also effec-

tive in groups and for use in mixed plantings where their graceful branching and lacy foliage provide welcome contrast and relief from the bolder patterns of branches and leafage of other evergreens. Consider, for example, the delightful possibilities of using rhododendrons and hemlocks together, or of planting hemlocks along the fringes of woodlands to enliven the winter landscape, to give foil for such early-flowering trees and shrubs as dogwoods and forsythias that are leafless when in bloom, and, yet, to lose themselves by melding into the summer foliage of deciduous trees without being, in the slightest, obtrusive. The horticultural varieties of hemlocks are good landscape plants, mostly adapted for smaller scale and more detailed landscape pictures than the more vigorous natural species; the choicest and smallest kinds are best suited for connoisseurs of rock gardens, those taller and bushier as lawn specimens or in shrub borders. The best known, Sargent's weeping hemlock, is extremely handsome when located on a fairly high bank at a waterside where its pendulous branches can cascade to the water. Although not good big city trees, hem-

locks tolerate life in smaller towns and on the outskirts of cities where air pollution is not excessive; for this purpose the Carolina hemlock is probably the best.

So much for the good points of hemlocks as landscape subjects, now their disadvantages. There are none, but only provided that the environment is right; they are rather exacting in this respect. They definitely are not plants for open, wind-swept places or thin, dry soils lacking in humus, nor will they prosper in water-logged or swampy soils or those of an alkaline nature. Hemlocks thrive where the air is fairly still and humid, in moderately deep earth that is fertile, containing an abundance of organic matter, and never excessively dry.

Cultivation. If the site is suitable, no particular difficulties attend the cultivation of hemlocks. They may be transplanted with confidence even when large, and, if the operation is carried out with skill, they will survive. They respond favorably to the ground beneath them being kept under a permanent mulch of compost, peat moss, or other suitable organic material; specimens that lack vigor because of depletion of soil nutrients can be helped by applying a slow-acting complete fertilizer in spring. Should they be located where the soil is dry in summer, periodic deep soaking is essential. Shearing should not, ordinarily, cut into branches more than one year old; if more severe pruning of a branch becomes necessary, care should be taken that some side branches or branchlets bearing foliage remain on the cut-back branch. New shoots rarely grow from stubbed-back branches, but lateral branches that remain on them usually continue to develop and, at first somewhat slowly, eventually provide a new curtain of foliage. The best time for pruning or shearing is in early spring before new growth starts. The propagation of the natural species of hemlocks is best carried out by seed sown in protected beds outdoors, in cold frames, or in a cool greenhouse in a sandy soil that contains a good amount of leaf mold, humus, or peat moss and is kept shaded and evenly moist. Varieties are usually increased by veneer grafting onto seedling understocks in greenhouses in winter or early spring; they can also be propagated by cuttings under mist in summer. For further information see Conifers.

Diseases and Pests. Hemlocks are subject to a not very serious leaf-blight and to cankers and rust diseases. They are also very likely to suffer from scorching of the foliage, especially that of the younger shoots of trees growing in sunny locations when summer temperatures rise above about 95°F. The most common insect pests are scales, red spider mites, leaf miners, leaf borers, and a caterpillar called the hemlock looper.

TSUSIOPHYLLUM (Tsusio-phýllum). The species segregated by some botanists as **Tsusiophyllum tanakae** is treated in this Encyclopedia as *Rhododendron tsusiophyllum* and is described in the Encyclopedia entry Azaleas.

TUART is *Eucalyptus gomphocephala*.

TUBERARIA (Tuber-ària). Closely related to *Helianthemum*, the genus *Tuberaria* differs chiefly in its members producing distinct basal tufts or rosettes of foliage and in the pistils of its flowers being without or nearly without styles. There are a dozen species, annuals and perennials of central Europe and the Mediterranean region. They belong to the rock-rose family CISTACEAE. The name refers to the tuberous character of the roots.

Tuberarias have undivided, three-veined leaves and terminal clusters of yellow flowers with five sepals, five petals that soon fall, and many stamens. The fruits are capsules that split longitudinally in three places to release the seeds.

Sometimes cultivated, **T. lignosa** (syn. *Helianthemum tuberaria*) is a perennial with a woody, branched rootstock and rosettes or tufts of persistent, obovate-lanceolate to elliptic leaves with three or five longitudinal veins. The leaves somewhat resemble those of plantains (*Plantago lanceolata*). This Mediterranean region plant is 8 inches to 1 foot or a little more in height. Its leaves, 1 inch to 3 inches long, narrow gradually into indistinct stalks and are slightly hairy to nearly hairless on their upper surfaces and distinctly pubescent on their undersides. The branchless flowering stems have a few pairs of small, pointed-lanceolate leaves. The blooms, in clusters of three to seven, are about 1¼ inches in diameter. Differing in having leaves that narrow abruptly into their stalks, and flowers, 1¼ to 2 inches wide, with a dark spot at the base of each petal are **T. globularifolia**, of Spain and Portugal, and **T. major**, of Portugal. These are much alike except that the leaves of the latter are thicker than those of the former and their veins do not join each other at the leaf margins. Also, the bracts on the flowering stems of *T. major* are blunt and broadly-ovate, those of *T. globularifolia* are lanceolate and pointed.

Garden Uses and Cultivation. Essentially plants for rock gardens and similar locations, the species described are best adapted for regions of mild winters and dryish summers. They are easily grown in California. At The New York Botanical Garden, *T. lignosa* lived for many years, but the winters are too harsh there for it to really prosper. Tuberarias need full sun and thoroughly well-drained soil. They are easily raised from seed.

TUBEROSE. This is the common name of *Polianthes tuberosa*, the botanical description of which is given under the Encyclopedia entry Polianthes. It is pronounced tuber-ose, not tube-rose. Tuberoses are among the most highly fragrant of garden blooms. So overpowering is their sweet scent that many people find their use as cut flowers objectionable. Yet they are sometimes grown for cutting as well as for embellishing beds and borders. For this last purpose locate them some distance from dwellings or other locations, such as terraces or outdoor living rooms, where much time is spent. Too constant exposure to the cloying perfume is likely to pall, whereas occasional whiffs from distant clumps, especially in the evening, can be delightful.

Tuberoses are not hardy; their bulblike tubers will not stand freezing. Handle them much like gladioluses, planting in spring after the weather warms, digging before fall frost, and storing the bulbs indoors over winter. They bloom in late summer and fall. If a longer season is needed, an early start can be made indoors. Plant the bulbs individually, 5 or 6 weeks before they are to be transplanted outdoors, in 4-inch pots and grow them in a sunny greenhouse where the temperature is about 70°F, until the time it is safe to set out tomatoes. Then harden the tuberoses gradually for a week or ten days and plant them where they are to bloom.

Be sure that the soil is deep, fertile, and aggreeably crumbly. As an aid to this, spread generous amounts of compost or other decayed organic matter and incorporate it thoroughly by deep spading. Also, mix in a fairly liberal dressing of complete fertilizer, one rich in potash is especially favorable. Set the bulbs about 6 inches apart, with their tops 2 to 3 inches below the surface. The site must be warm and sunny.

During dry weather water deeply at intervals of about five days. Keep the surface soil shallowly stirred or lightly mulched. In fall, lift and dry the bulbs and store in a temperature of 65 to 70°F. Increase is by offsets. Remove these in spring and plant them separately, somewhat closer together and not as deep as full-size bulbs, but under similar conditions. The offsets will not bloom the first year, but if well cared for may be expected to the next.

Tuberose: (a) Single-flowered

(b) Double-flowered

Despite apparently good care, in the north, tuberose bulbs are often capricious about blooming after the first year. This may be associated with unsuitable soil, too short a growing season, improper storage conditions, or other imperfectly understood factors. The surest way to circumvent this trouble is to purchase new bulbs each year. The double-flowered variety called 'Double Pearl' is popular, as is single-flowered 'Mexican Everblooming'.

Early bloom in greenhouses is had by starting bulbs in January, singly in 5-inch pots or three together in 6-inch pots, in fertile, well-drained soil. Set the bulbs with their tips just protruding from the soil. After potting put them in a temperature of 50 to 55°F and water discreetly until vigorous root growth has been made. Then remove the pots to a sunny greenhouse where a night temperature of 65 to 70°F is maintained and day temperatures are five to fifteen degrees higher. When flower spikes begin to form, water weekly or semiweekly with dilute liquid fertilizer. Forced bulbs are of no further use after flowering is through.

TUBS. Used as containers for large plants, tubs are generally round or square and ordinarily are approximately as tall as wide. Usually they are made of wood and have sides that slope slightly outward. Drainage holes are provided in their bottoms, which are sometimes raised an inch or two above the surface on which the tub stands by iron feet attached to the lower rim of the tub. Tubs without these may be raised by standing them on three bricks or other convenient supports.

The best tubs are made of such rot-resistant wood as red cedar, cypress, or teak. Additional protection is afforded by coating the inside with asphaltum paint (not tar or creosote) or other wood preservative, or by charring the surface with a plumber's blow torch.

Plant tubs: (a) A square tub, its corners strengthened on their insides by vertical strips of wood

(b) A very strong square tub with metal rods bolted on the outside to pull the sides together; when retubbing is necessary, the old tub can be removed by releasing the bolts

(c) The bottom of the same tub showing cleats that raise it off the ground, and drainage holes

(d) An octagonal tub strengthened by metal bands

Comparatively inexpensive commercial tubs made of pine and strengthened with wire bands

Less expensive tubs made of pine or other woods not especially rot resistant are commonly used by commercial growers of large philodendrons and other, chiefly indoor plants.

TUFA. Tufa is a sedimentary, porous rock, formed by the deposition of calcium carbonate, calcite, or silica under water, that because of the many cavities, voids, and pores it contains is comparatively light in weight. It is used for constructing rock gardens and other plant environments. Typically, tufa is fairly soft, gritty, and white to tannish. It is not to be confused with tuff (Italian, *tufa*), which is a lightweight porous rock resulting from the compressing and cementing together of volcanic ash.

TULBAGHIA (Tul-bághia). This entirely African genus of the lily family LILIACEAE comprises about twenty-five species. It is related to *Agapanthus*, from which it differs in its blooms being urn-shaped or having slender tubes and wide-spreading petals, in having comparatively much longer and usually cylindrical perianth tubes, and in having in their throats a crown or corona consisting of six small scales. The name *Tulbaghia* commemorates Ryk Tulbagh, a Dutch governor of the Cape of Good Hope, who died in 1771.

Tulbaghias are perennial herbaceous plants with rhizomatous or cormlike rootstocks and all-basal, narrowly-strap-shaped, evergreen, rather fleshy leaves. When bruised they emit an onion-like odor. Their flowers are in umbels atop leafless stalks. Each has six spreading perianth lobes (petals) and six stamens. The fruits are capsules.

One of the most robust and decorative species is **T. fragrans,** a native of the Transvaal. This is remarkable for its sweetly-scented blooms, of an attractive mauve color, in umbels of twenty to thirty.

Tulbaghia fragrans

Tulbaghia violacea 'Silver Lace'

They have cuplike coronas. Three of the six stamens are longer than the others. The leaves are 1 foot long or longer and about 1 inch wide. This species is closely similar to and possibly identical to *T. pulchella*. South African *T. violacea* has leaves up to 1 foot long by ¼ inch wide. Its purplish-violet flowers, in umbels of twenty or fewer, terminate stalks 1 foot to 2 feet long. They are up to ¾ inch long and have petals one-half as long as the perianth tubes. The corona consists of small, strap-shaped scales. Variety *T. v.* 'Silver Lace' has leaves attractively longitudinally striped, especially along their margins, with white.

Garden and Landscape Uses. Tulbaghias stand little frost and are useful as permanent outdoor plants only in regions of mild winters. They may be grown in pots indoors. They bloom over a long period, chiefly in spring and summer, and are attractive in flower beds, rock gardens, and other informal areas. Their blooms are useful as cut flowers. For success these plants need well-drained, porous, reasonably fertile soil and full sun. They are easily cultivated.

Cultivation. Propagation is by division and by seed. It is easily effected. The beginning of the growing season is the most appropriate time to start new plants. Outdoors, established plants need little routine care other than removal of spent flower heads. Containers in which tulbaghias are grown must be well drained and the soil porous and fertile. Repotting and needed dividing is done every two or three years. The soil is kept moderately moist throughout the growing season, dry when the plants are leafless and dormant. Occasional applications of dilute liquid fertilizer are beneficial. A sunny greenhouse with a winter night temperature of 45 to 50°F, and day temperatures just a few degrees higher, affords a suitable environment. At other seasons the greenhouse should be ventilated freely or, from late spring to fall, the plants may be put outdoors or in a cold frame with their containers buried to their rims in sand, peat moss, or other material that prevents too rapid drying.

TULIP. See Tulipa. Plants other than those of the genus *Tulipa* that have common names including the word tulip are butterfly-tulip, globe-tulip, and star-tulip (*Calochortus*), Cape-tulip (*Homeria*), Mexican tulip-poppy (*Hunnemannia fumariaefolia*), tulip orchid (*Anguloa*), and tulip poppy (*Papaver glaucum*).

TULIP TREE. See Liriodendron. The African-tulip-tree is *Spathodea campanulata*.

TULIPA (Tù-lipa)—Tulip. The sorts of *Tulipa*, of the lily family LILIACEAE, are among the most familiar garden and florists' flowers. Called tulips, they are natives and horticultural derivitives of natives of temperate parts of the Old World, especially regions of dry summers. The number of species is variously estimated to be from fifty to one hundred and fifty. In addition, there are many hundreds of varieties, mostly hybrids of garden origin. The name, a Latinized derivitive of the Arabic *dulban*, a turban, alludes to the form of the flower.

Tulips were unknown to Europeans until the middle of the sixteenth century. First knowledge of them came from an account of a journey made in 1554 from Adrianople to Constantinople by Ogier Ghiselin de Busbecq, ambassador of the Holy Roman Emperor Ferdinand I, to the court of Suleiman the Magnificent, sultan of the Ottoman Empire. Busbecq reported seeing "an abundance of flowers everywhere—narcissuses, hyacinths, and those the Turks called *tulipam*." He wrote "The Turks pay great attention to the cultivation of flowers, and do not hesitate, although they are far from extravagant, to pay several aspers for one that is beautiful."

Busbecq was surely mistaken when he said the Turks called the flowers tulipam. The Turkish name for the tulip is lale. Undoubtedly the Turks were calling Busbecq's attention to the similarity in shape of the flower to their national headdress, the dulban (turban), when he thought they were telling him its name.

Seeds and probably bulbs were brought to Vienna by Busbecq and planted in gardens there. In 1559, the eminent scholar and naturalist Conrad von Gessner saw a reddish-flowered sort blooming in the garden of "the ingenious and learned Councillor Hertwort." Two years later, in *De Hortis Germaniae Liber*, Gessner published the earliest known illustration of a tulip. By 1561, tulips were being grown by the Fuggers in Augsburg and a year later a consignment of bulbs from Constantinople reached Antwerp. From there, bulbs were sent to Holland, which soon attained and has ever since retained preeminence in the cultivation of tulips.

So popular did tulips become in Holland and later in Turkey that a speculative hysteria known as "tulipomania" developed. In Holland this extraordinary phenomenon reached its height between 1634 and 1637, although as early as 1623 a single bulb of 'Semper Agustus' had changed hands for "thousands of florins." All classes from noblemen to turf diggers, maidservants, chimney sweeps, and beggar women participated in the irrational gambling. Up to 100,000 florins were paid for a single bulb. Houses, coaches and horses, and even artisans' tools were exchanged for tulip bulbs. Speculators, as in present-day commodity futures markets, offered and paid large sums for merchandise they never actually received or even wished to receive, while others sold bulbs they neither possessed nor delivered. For one bulb of 'Viceroy', the seller received two loads of wheat, four fat oxen, eight fat pigs, twelve fat sheep, two hogsheads of wine, four barrels of eight-florin beer, two barrels of butter, 1,000 pounds of cheese, a complete bed, a suit of clothes, and a silver beaker.

The tulipomania madness ended in a shattering crash early in 1637. Then, every owner of bulbs wanted to sell, none to buy. Thousands, including many shrewd businessmen, were bankrupted. Finally the government intervened with controlling legislation, but it was many decades before the country recovered from the effects of its wild spree. But even to this day, although some are produced in North America, England, and elsewhere, Holland is by far the chief source of commercial tulip bulbs. Hollanders have been mainly responsible for breeding the many magnificent varieties now available. The tulip-growing industry in Holland is now strictly controlled by the government; only produce of the highest excellency can be exported.

Tulips are hardy, deciduous, spring-flowering perennials with bulbs clothed in thin, usually brown skins or tunics and generally tapered to a pointed apex. A characteristic of some importance in iden-

Tulips planted informally with peonies and other plants in narrow borders flanking the Long Walk, Van Courtland Manor, Croton-on-Hudson, New York

tifying species is the presence or absence of hairs on the insides of the tunics. The chief leaves are basal, but a few smaller ones, diminishing in size upward, sprout from the usually rather fleshy, erect stems. The latter are commonly branchless and in most sorts terminate in a single, up-facing bloom, but in a few species and varieties the stems branch and bear more than one flower. From broad-lanceolate to strap-shaped to linear, the lobeless, toothless leaves are mainly slightly fleshy and frequently glaucous, but sometimes are mottled, streaked, or otherwise marked with reddish- or chocolate-brown. The flowers typically are cup-, saucer-, or more or less urn-shaped, but some spread their petals widely on sunny days to form a starlike pattern. With the exception of double-flowered varieties in which the number is more than normal for the genus, tulip blooms have six perianth segments, commonly called petals, but more correctly identified as tepals. There are six separate

stamens and sometimes one style, but often the style is wanting and the usually three-lobed stigma sits directly atop the ovary, which occupies the center of the bloom. The fruits are many-seeded capsules.

The tulips that attracted so much attention when first brought from Constantinople to Europe were not wild species, but represented a few of the many hundreds of horticultural varieties developed in Persia and Turkey from the late 1400s on, or at least probably the late 1400s on, since depictions of tulips do not appear in Persian or Turkish art much earlier.

A phenomenon called "breaking" did much to stimulate the tremendous interest in tulips before, during, and following the tulipomania extravagance. Now known to result from a virus infection and to be transmissible by insects and other agents that transfer the sap of an infected plant to an uninfected one, this phenomenon was, until comparatively recent times,

A lavish informal planting of tulips with a foreground of forget-me-nots

An attractive flower border featuring tulips

completely unexplainable. It apparently occured unpredictably as a "sporting," or mutating, sometimes of tulips that had remained plain-colored for many years. Tulips raised from seed nearly always have self-colored flowers, which their offset progeny normally duplicate. But if they become infected with the virus the flowers exhibit various often attractive and sometimes quite startling streaked or flamelike patterns of more than one color. The self-colored varieties were known as "breeder" varieties, the others as "broken" or "rectified" tulips. If their colors were clear and their patterns agreeable, the latter were the more highly prized. Broken tulips were further identified, according to their color patterns, as bizarres, bybloems, and other designations, now outdated, but to which frequent reference is made in old garden books.

Modern garden varieties, like their ancestors brought from Turkey, cannot with certainty be attributed to any wild species, but it is believed that most are derivatives of T. gesnerana, and some others of the early-flowering kinds of T. suaveolens. In addition, there are many modern early-flowering varieties and hybrids of T. fosterana, T. greigii, and T. kaufmanniana.

Classification of tulips for horticultural purposes provides for fifteen divisions, of which the first eleven, arranged in sections as early-flowering, midseason-flowering, and late-flowering, accommodate all varieties not readily identifiable with wild species. The other four divisions comprise wild species and readily recognized hybrids of a few of them. In catalogs and by gardeners, the species are frequently called "botanical tulips." The classification is as follows:

A variety of Single Early tulips

EARLY-FLOWERING SECTION

Division 1: Single Early. Except for a few species the earliest sorts to bloom, Single Early tulips, 10 inches to 1¼ feet tall, have sturdy stems and, in a wide range of self colors, single, cup-shaped, sometimes fragrant flowers.

Division 2: Double Early. Blooming slightly later than most Single Early varieties, Double Early tulips are sturdy-stemmed and 10 inches to 1 foot tall.

Double Early and Single Early tulips in a window box

Their many-petaled flowers, usually 3 to 4 inches across, remain in good condition longer than those of Single Early varieties. These may be had in a wide range of colors and combinations of colors.

MIDSEASON-FLOWERING SECTION

Division 3: Mendel. From 1¼ to 2 feet tall, Mendel tulips have a blooming season that closely follows that of Double Earlies and is about two weeks ahead of that of Darwin varieties. Mendels have large, single, cupped flowers in a wide range of bright colors, solid or with the petals edged with deeper or contrasting hues.

Division 4: Triumph. Sturdier than Mendel varieties, Triumph tulips bloom slightly later. From 1¼ to 2 feet tall, they have large, single, firm-textured flowers of various colors, often striped or edged with contrasting hues.

Division 5: Darwin Hybrids. Notable for their sturdy, tall stems and brilliantly colored flowers prevailingly larger than those of any other division, Darwin Hybrids are 1 foot 10 inches to 2 feet 4 inches high. The color range of the flowers includes various reds, yellows, and combinations, as well as pink. Often the petals have a black basal blotch.

LATE- OR MAY-FLOWERING SECTION

Division 6: Darwin. The superb tulips that belong here are 2 feet to 2 feet 8 inches tall. They have sturdy stems and large satiny, single blooms that in silhouette are decidedly square-based

A Darwin Hybrid tulip variety

and rectangular. They may be had in a very wide range of mostly self colors.

Division 7: Lily-Flowered. Blooming just before Darwin varieties, Lily-Flowered tulips are perhaps the most graceful of all. From 1 foot 8 inches to 2 feet 2 inches tall, they have rather slender stems and single red, reddish-violet, pink, yellow, or white flowers with their pointed, elegantly reflexed petals sometimes edged with a contrasting color.

Division 8: Single Late or Cottage. This group consists of varieties of the May-Flowering section that are inadmissible as Darwins or Lily-Flowered. In height they range from 9 inches to 2 feet 8 inches. Their usually large, single flowers, generally egg-shaped, but sometimes more elongated, mostly have long, pointed petals. A few varieties have stems that branch and carry up to six blooms. Flower colors

cover a wide range of selfs and combinations, in some varieties including green. Light and pastel shades are the most common.

Division 9: Rembrandt. The sorts that belong here include those that Rembrandt and other old Dutch artists loved to paint, the kinds that fueled the seventeenth-century tulipomania speculations. Including varieties previously classified as Bybloems and Bizarres, they are 1½ to 2½ feet in height, but generally are less vigorous than Darwin and Cottage tulips. Characteristically the flowers of Rembrandt tulips have "broken" color patterns with a white, yellow, or red ground, striped or otherwise variegated with black, brown, bronze, purple, red, or pink.

Division 10: Parrot. The extraordinary, sometimes almost freakish flowers that characterize this group have deeply-fringed or otherwise incised, curled,

A variety of Darwin tulips

A group of Cottage tulips

A Cottage tulip variety with green-striped flowers

A variety of Parrot tulips

A Lily-Flowered tulip variety (left foreground) with irises and *Phlox divaricata* (right foreground)

twisted, or waved, sometimes narrow petals. They are available in many colors including pink, red, orange, yellow, violet, and white, with the outsides of the petals often splashed with green. Unfortunately the stems tend to be too weak to adequately support the large blooms. Because of this it is important to plant them only where they are sheltered from wind.

Division 11: Double Late or Peony-Flowered. From 1¼ to 2 feet tall, the vari-

A Double Late or Peony-Flowered tulip

A Greigii tulip variety

These sorts have flowers with hairless stamens: **T. acuminata**, the Turkish tulip, is probably only a variant of *T. gesnerana*. Its large, ovoid bulbs have tunics hairy on their insides near their bases and tops. There are three to five rather narrow, strap-shaped, long-pointed, wavy leaves and a stalk, 1 foot to 1½ feet tall, terminating in a flower, more remarkable for its unusual appearance than its beauty, 3 to 4 inches long and with six usually pale yellow or pink, wavy and more or less spirally twisted petals that taper to long points. **T. batalinii**, of Bokhara, is probably only a variant of *T. linifolia*, from which it differs

Tulipa batalinii

eties of this division have strong stems, and flowers with many more than the normal six petals of single tulips. Ordinarily the blooms, which come in shades of red, violet, and yellow, as well as white, and in combinations of these, remain in good condition longer than those of Single-Flowered tulips.

SPECIES SECTION (The sorts of this section include true wild species, their natural and horticultural varieties, and hybrids that clearly closely resemble wild species.)

Division 12: Kaufmanniana. This division includes very early flowering *T. kaufmanniana* and its varieties and hybrids. Their foliage is sometimes mottled.

Division 13: Fosterana. Very early flowering *T. fosterana* and its varieties and hybrids belong to this group. They have large blooms, and foliage that is sometimes striped or mottled.

Division 14: Greigii. Here belong *T. greigii* and its varieties and hybrids. These always have striped or mottled foliage. They bloom later than tulips of the Kaufmanniana class.

Division 15: Other Species. This is a catch-all class for species and their varieties and obviously distinguishable hybrids that do not fit into any of the other classes.

Horticultural varieties of tulips are adequately described and often illustrated in color in the catalogs of bulb dealers. The descriptions that follow are of wild sorts, mostly species, although some commonly identified as such, especially those spontaneous in southern Europe and closely related to *T. gesnerana*, are strongly suspected of being naturalized descendents of early varieties introduced from Turkey.

Tulips fall readily into two groups, those in which the stamens of the flowers are without hairs and those with stamens hairy at their bases. In the treatment that follows, the sorts of these groups are presented separately. Another feature of diagnostic importance is whether or not the tunics (skins) of the bulbs are hairy on their inner surfaces and, if so, the amount, character, and sometimes the location of the hair.

in having pale yellow flowers with a dark blotch on the inside base of each petal. **T. clusiana**, the lady tulip, is a popular "botanical," indigenous from Iran to Afghanistan and naturalized in southern Europe. It forms stolons. Its nearly spherical bulbs, about ¾ inch in diameter, have tunics densely-woolly near their apexes on their insides. The five or fewer leaves, 8 to 10 inches long by not more than ⅜ inch wide, markedly folded upward along their middles, often have reddish margins. On stems 8 inches to 1 foot tall, the 1½- to 2-inch-long flowers, at first bell-shaped, when mature open in sunny weather and are then starlike. They are white to yellowish with a carmine blotch at the bottom of the inside of each petal. The outsides of the three outer petals are red with white margins. The stamens are dark violet. Variety *T. c. chrysantha* has petals yellow on their insides and without blotches; its stamens are purple. The flowers of *T. c. stellata* have a yellow blotch on their insides; its stamens are yellow. **T. didieri**, of southern Europe, is a close relative of *T. gesnerana*. Up to about 1 foot high, it has ovoid bulbs, about 1 inch in diameter, with tunics that have few hairs on their insides. The more or less glaucous, wavy, hair-fringed, oblong-lanceolate leaves are 4 to 8 inches long. Bright crimson to a reddish-purple, or sometimes yellow margined with red, and with a sweet scent, the about-2-inch-long

A Fosterana tulip variety

Tulipa acuminata

Tulipa clusiana

Tulipa kaufmanniana

flowers have an inside central blotch of yellow-margined grayish-blue. *T. eichleri,* of Turkestan, 6 to 8 inches tall, has 2-inch-thick, ovoid bulbs with tunics slightly hairy at their bases on their insides. The four or five broadly-strap-shaped, slightly glaucous leaves are up to 8 inches long. The handsome, broad-petaled, bell-shaped, glossy flowers, about 4 inches long, have light buff outsides and brilliant scarlet insides with a yellow-bordered black blotch at the base of each petal. Variety *T. e. excelsa* has big scarlet blooms. The crimson-scarlet blooms of *T. e. maxima* are larger than those of the species. *T. elegans,* not known as a wildling, is probably a variant of *T. gesnerana.* From 1 foot to 1½ feet tall, it has fairly large bulbs with tunics hairless on their insides. Its lanceolate-strap-shaped aves are up to 10 inches in length. Bell-shaped and about 3½ inches in length, the flowers have all-similar, acutely-pointed, bright red petals with yellow bases. The stamens are purple. The flowers of *T. e. alba* are white. *T. fosterana,* of Turkestan, 8 to 10 inches tall, has nearly spherical bulbs, 1½ to 2 inches in diameter, with tunics silky-hairy on their insides, and slightly-hairy stems. The three or four leaves, broadly-ovate, are up to 8 inches long. The brilliant scarlet flowers have a yellow-margined, black, basal blotch on the inside of each petal. They are 3½ to 4 inches long when open flat. The stamens are black. Several varieties are cultivated. *T. galatica,* of Asia Minor, 6 to 8 inches in height, has ovoid, 1-inch-thick bulbs densely-hairy on the insides of their tunics. There are four linear-lanceolate, hair-fringed, flat leaves up to 7 inches long. The slender-stalked, bell-shaped flower, nearly 3 inches long, has pointed petals, buff-yellow with a smoke-colored basal blotch inside, and yellow stamens. *T. gesnerana,* of eastern Europe and Asia Minor, is variable. From 1 foot to 2 feet tall, it has medium-sized bulbs with tunics with a few

hairs or none on their insides. The three to five glaucous, lanceolate to ovate-lanceolate, often somewhat wavy leaves are up to 6 inches long. The broad, cup-shaped, dull crimson flowers, 2 to 3 inches long, have on the inside of each petal a yellow-margined, black or nearly black blotch. The stamens are blackish-purple. *T. greigii,* of Turkestan, has broad-ovoid, 1¼-inch-thick bulbs with a few hairs inside the apexes of their tunics. Usually streaked with brownish-purple, the three or four glaucous, wavy-edged, lanceolate leaves are up to 8 inches long by 3 inches wide. The cup-shaped, bright orange-scarlet flowers, up to 3¼ inches long, are carried on downy stems to heights of 6 inches to 1 foot. Their insides have a black or nearly black basal blotch margined with yellow. The stamens are yellow. *T. hoogiana,* of central Asia, appears to be a close relative of *T. oculus-solis,* but is taller. From 9 inches to 1 foot or more in height, it has broad-ovoid bulbs, about 2 inches in diameter, with tunics densely-hairy on their insides. There are four to eight long-pointed, wavy-edged, narrowly-lanceolate, glaucous leaves, up to 10 inches long, folded along their centers. Almost spherical in bud, the cup-shaped flower is brilliant scarlet merging to yellow at its base outside and has a black basal blotch, margined with orange-yellow, inside. The stamens are blackish-violet. *T. ingens,* of central Asia, is almost 1 foot tall. It has long-ovoid bulbs, 1¼ to nearly 2 inches in diameter, with long silky hairs on the insides of their tunics. The three to five glaucous leaves are lanceolate. The stems are slightly hairy. The up-to-4½-inch-long, glossy flowers, downy on their outsides, are brilliant scarlet with some buff on the outsides of the outer petals and a large black center on the inside. *T. kaufmanniana,* the water-lily tulip, is very popular. It has stolons. Native to Turkestan and 5 to 8 inches tall, this sort has ovoid bulbs, about 1½ inches thick, with tunics

sparingly hairy on their insides. Its three to five glaucous leaves are oblongish, up to 10 inches long, and 3½ inches wide. Topping a slightly-hairy stalk, the 3- to 3½-inch-long flower, chalice-shaped at first, expands into a flat, white, creamy-yellow, yellow, pink, or red star, with a yellow base to each petal. The outsides of the petals are flushed and streaked with red. The stamens are yellow. The flowers of *T. k. aurea* are bright yellow with red bands. Those of *T. k. coccinea* are scarlet. Many horticultural selections of this variable species are grown. A close relative of *T. ostrowskiana,* *T. kolpakowskiana,* of Turkestan, 6 to 10 inches tall, has 1-inch-thick

Tulipa kolpakowskiana

bulbs, the tunics of which have some hairs on their insides at their bases and tips. The two to four slightly glaucous, almost flat, linear-lanceolate to lanceolate leaves are 4 to 6 inches long. Solitary or sometimes two on a stalk, the 2- to 2¼-inch-long flowers are bright yellow with reddish or greenish exteriors, or sometimes are coppery-red. At first broadly-bell-shaped, they have petals that later spread widely. The stamens are yellow. *T. kuschkensis,* of Turkestan and Afghanistan, is 9 inches to 1 foot tall or sometimes taller. Its ovoid bulbs, 1½ inches thick, have tunics densely-woolly-hairy on their insides. The usually four leaves, up to 8 inches long, are narrowly-pointed-lanceolate. The 2½- to 3-inch-long, brilliant scarlet, urn- or cup-shaped flowers spread their petals widely in sun. A large black blotch narrowly edged with yellow reaches well up on the inside from the base of each petal. The stamens are black. *T. lanata,* of Iran, Turkestan, and Afghanistan, forms stolons. From 1 foot to 1½ feet tall, it has bulbs with tunics densely-woolly-hairy on their insides. They are about 2 inches thick. The three to five channeled leaves, elliptic to lanceolate, are up to 10 inches long by 2 inches wide. On downy stalks, the 3-inch-long flowers are not glossy; they have scarlet petals with, at their bases on the inside, an olive-green blotch broadly outlined with yellow. The stamens are black with purple anthers. *T. linifolia,* of Bokhara, typically 4 to 6 inches tall but in rich soil sometimes taller, has ovoid bulbs, ½ to ¾ inch thick, with woolly hairs on the insides of their tunics. The leaves form a prostrate basal rosette. They are glaucous, 4 to 6 inches long, very wavy, and usually red-edged. Slender at first, the 1½- to 2-inch-long flower, brilliant scarlet with a black basal blotch inside, eventually spreads its petals widely. The stamens are dark purple to black. *T. marjolettii,* of southern France, is a minor variant of *T. gesnerana.* Up to 2 feet tall, it has glaucous leaves, and yellowish flowers, about 1¾ inches long, that fade to white as they mature; on their outsides they are flushed with purple. *T. mauritiana,* of southern France, is probably a form of *T. gesnerana.* Up to about 1 foot tall, it has largish bulbs, hairless on the insides of their tunics, and about four broad-lanceolate, wavy-edged leaves. Its flowers are red on their insides and

yellow at their centers. The stamens have yellow stalks and purple anthers. *T. maximowiczii,* of Afghanistan and adjacent territory, scarcely differs from *T. linifolia,* except that its leaves do not have wavy margins and are scattered along the stems instead of being in a basal rosette. Also, the dark basal blotches on the insides of petals are edged with white. *T. micheliana,* of Iran and adjacent Russia, 1 foot tall or a little taller, has ovoid bulbs about 1½ inches thick, densely-hairy on the insides of their tunics. Very glaucous, the three or four slightly-wavy-edged leaves, often streaked with brown, have tunics silky-hairy at their bases inside. The 2½-inch-long flowers are scarlet, tinged on their outsides with lilac, and have a large, yellow-edged, black center on their insides. The stamens are black. *T. oculus-solis,* of Asia Minor and naturalized in southern Europe, is 6 to 8 inches tall. This kind forms stolons and has ovoid bulbs, 1¼ inches thick, with tunics densely-hairy on their insides. The three or four leaves, ovate-lanceolate, are up to 10 inches long by 1 inch wide. From 2½ to 3¼ inches long, the flowers have brownish outsides, and scarlet interiors with a basal patch of black margined with yellow. The stamens are blackish. *T. ostrowskiana,* of Turkestan, about 8 inches tall, has ovoid bulbs, 1 inch to 1½ inches in diameter, with tunics hairless on their insides. The two to four leaves are erect and 6 inches to 1 foot long by 1 inch to 1¼ inches wide. The bright scarlet, cup-shaped flowers have reflexing petals about 2 inches long. On their insides at the base is a small, olive-green or yellow blotch. In bud, the flowers nod. They have yellow-stalked stamens and purple anthers. *T. praecox,* of northern Italy, has stolons; up to a little more than 1½ feet tall, it has ovoid bulbs, 1½ inches thick, with tunics felted with hairs on their insides. There are three to five erect, heavily glaucous, oblong-ovate to oblong-lanceolate leaves up to 1 foot long by 3¼ inches wide. The dullish scarlet, wide-opening flowers have, on the inside of each pointed, reflexing, 2½- to 3½-inch-long petal, a dark olive-green basal blotch edged with yellow. *T. praestans* is a variable native of central Asia. From 9 inches to 1½ feet in height, it has ovoid bulbs, about 1¼ inches thick, with a few silky hairs on the insides of their tunics. The five or six, long-pointed, slightly-hairy, narrowly-lanceolate, channeled leaves are up to 10 inches in length. From 2 to 2½ inches long, the cup-shaped, brick-red flowers, without interior basal blotches, have red-stalked stamens with purple anthers. *T. pulchella,* of Asia Minor, is 4 to 5 inches tall. Its bulbs have tough tunics, hairy on their insides at their bases and apexes. There are two or three rather narrow, strap-shaped leaves, up to 6 inches long, and

one to three 1¼-inch-long flowers that have wide-spreading petals. Grey or green on their outsides, the petals are crimson or purple above, with a bluish basal blotch edged with white. The stalks of the stamens are yellow and hairy at their bases. Above they are white or white tipped with blue. The anthers are purple. The flowers of *V. p. humilis* are violet-pink, those of *V. p. pallida* are white with a deep blue blotch at the bottom of each petal. Purple flowers

Tulipa pulchella pallida

are characteristic of *T. p. violacea. T. sharonensis,* of Israel, 3 to 6 inches tall, has bulbs, ½ to 1 inch thick, that are hairy on the insides of their tunics. The three or four erect, narrow-linear to lanceolate leaves, up to 6 inches long, have wavy, hair-fringed edges. About 1¼ inches long, the broad-bell-shaped flowers are deep scarlet with a yellow-margined, dark olive central blotch on the inside. Their petals are pointed and reflexed. The stamens are black. *T. sprengeri,* of Asia Minor, up to 1 foot tall or a little taller, has ovoid bulbs, 1 inch thick or sometimes thicker, with tunics sparsely-hairy on their insides. There are four to six glossy, more or less channeled, pointed-linear leaves 6 to 10 inches long and rather fleshy. The flowers open widely, and have brownish-red petals paler on their outsides than within; they are about 2½ inches long, the outer ones decidedly narrower than the inner, and reflexed. The yellow-stalked stamens have red anthers. This very late-blooming tulip is unusual in that it tolerates considerable shade.

These tulips have flowers with stamens hairy at their bases: *T. australis,* of the Mediterranean region, is a delightful, rather close relative of *T. sylvestris.* From 6 inches to 1 foot tall, it has broadly-ovoid bulbs, about 1¼ inches thick, with tunics hairy on their insides, and two to five channeled, linear to strap-shaped leaves up to 9 inches long and folded along their centers. In bud, urn-shaped and often slightly nodding, the fragrant, 1- to 2-inch-long

Tulipa marjolettii

flowers face upward when fully open. They are clear yellow with greenish and sometimes reddish flushings on their outsides. The stamens are yellow. *T. biflora,* of the Caspian Sea and Caucasus regions, 4 to 5 inches tall, has ovoid bulbs, about ½ inch thick, with tunics silky-hairy on their insides near their apexes. Slightly glaucous, the three or four bronzy-green, linear to strap-shaped leaves are 4 to 5 inches long. Each stalk carries one to five about-¾-inch-long flowers that at full maturity spread their white petals, each with a yellow basal blotch, widely. Their outsides are stained green and red. The yellow stamens are purple-tipped. *T. cretica,* of Crete, 4 to 8 inches tall, forms stolons. Its ovoid bulbs are about 1 inch thick and have a few hairs on the inside of the tunic. There are two or rarely three linear-lanceolate leaves 4 to 5 inches long. The slender-stalked, bell-shaped flowers, occasionally two on a stem, are about 1 inch long. They have white-margined, rose-pink petals, white on their insides. The stamens are yellow. *T. hageri,* native from Greece to Asia Minor, 6 inches tall or sometimes taller, has narrow-ovoid bulbs, up to 1 inch thick, with long, silky hairs on the insides of the tips of their tunics. There are four or five red-edged, strap-shaped leaves up to 8 inches long by about ½ inch wide. On stalks carrying one to four, the 2-inch-long, bell-shaped flowers spread in bright sun like wide stars. They are coppery-buff to greenish on their outsides, to scarlet with a sometimes yellow-margined, olive, basal blotch on their insides. *T. humilis,* of Iran, 4 to 6 inches tall, much resembles *T. pulchella* and *T. violacea;* it has ovoid bulbs, about ½ inch thick, with tunics woolly-hairy on their insides toward their tips. The two to four glaucous, linear, channeled leaves are 3 to 4 inches long. More or less nodding in bud, up-facing and starlike later, and about 2½ inches long, the light purple flowers, reddish to greenish on their outsides, have a yellow blotch at their centers inside. *T. orphanidea,* of Greece, 6 inches to 1 foot tall, has 1-inch-thick, ovoid bulbs with tunics silky-hairy inside at their apexes. The three or four narrow leaves, folded along their centers, are up to 8 inches long. Rarely more than one on a stem, its quaint, dullish, orange to brown flowers have narrow petals that open to form a star 4 inches across. They are stained with green and purple on their outsides. Possibly a natural hybrid between *T. hageri* and *T. australis,* this does not set seeds. *T. polychroma,* of Iran and Afghanistan, 4 to 6 inches tall, has ovoid bulbs, about 1 inch in diameter, with tunics silky-hairy on their insides. The two to four erect, glaucous, linear leaves are up to 6 inches long. From one to five on each stalk, the 1¾-inch-long flowers in bud are nodding, later erect. They have pink- or purple-tinged, white

petals with a yellow basal blotch on their insides. The yellow stamens are tipped with black. *T. sylvestris* (syn. *T. florentina*), of Europe, North Africa, and Iran, is 6 inches to 1 foot tall. Very variable, this forms stolons and has ovoid bulbs, 1¼ inches thick, with tunics with a few hairs on their insides at their bases and apexes. The two or three linear leaves are glaucous and 6 inches to 1 foot long. The one or two fragrant, 2-inch-long flowers, carried on a rather weak stalk, nod in the bud stage and then face upward and, on sunny days, spread their petals widely to display their

Tulipa sylvestris

Tulipa tarda

bright yellow interiors. The outsides of the petals are yellow or greenish often flushed with red. The stamens are yellow to orange. Varieties *T. s. major* and *T. s.* 'Tabriz' are reputed to bloom more reliably than the typical species. The first has two or three golden-yellow flowers on each stalk, the other is taller and has blooms somewhat bigger than those of the species. *T. tarda,* of Turkestan, was for long

misidentified as *T. dasystemon,* which name is properly that of a different species. From 4 to 6 inches high, it produces stolons and has subspherical bulbs, ½ to ¾ inch thick, with tunics with a few hairs on their insides near their bases and apexes. The four to seven linear to lanceolate leaves are up to 6 inches long. The bright yellow star-shaped flowers are more or less suffused with red on their outsides. The apexes of their pointed petals become reflexed with age. *T. turkestanica,* of Turkestan, has bulbs with tunics thickly set with silky hairs toward their apexes. It produces stolons. The flowers, up to seven on each stalk and about 1½ inches long, are ivory-white with an orange blotch at the base of the inside of each petal. The anthers are purple or chocolate-brown.

Tulipa turkestanica

Tulips massed in a curved bed in front of a flowering dogwood

Garden and Landscape Uses. Available in an impressive variety of flower colors and combinations, the taller ones stately in habit, tulips are superb for massing in formal beds alone or with underplantings of such lower spring-blooming plants as English daisies, forget-me-nots, pansies, and polyanthus primroses, as well as for planting in groups of half a dozen to a dozen or more among hardy herbaceous

A tulip bed planted solidly without underplanting

A bed of tulips underplanted with pansies

perennials and other plants in mixed flower beds and borders. Many of the species and their varieties can be displayed to good advantage in rock gardens. Tulips are extensively cultivated outdoors and in greenhouses as cut flowers. They are also grown in greenhouses and sometimes in windows as pot plants. Sunny locations not exposed to strong winds best suit tulips, but they may also be grown in part-day or light shade.

Cultivation. Although splendid displays can be had in all parts of North America that experience sufficient winter

Tulips in a cut flower garden

Parrot tulips as cut flowers

Small groups of tulips planted near dwellings provide cheerful spring color (the above three photographs)

A pot of tulips forced in a greenhouse into early bloom

Part of an Easter display of tulips in a conservatory at The New York Botanical Garden

cold, and from precooled bulbs in some other regions as well, in few places are tulips satisfactory permanent perennials. Ordinarily the best results are had the first season following the planting of newly purchased bulbs. Progressively in succeeding years, the flowers tend to be less uniform in height, size, and number, and after two or three years replacement is likely to be desirable, although this is not always true. Some horticultural varieties and some species will, if conditions are especially favorable, bloom satisfactorily for five or six years or even longer, but this generally cannot be depended upon.

Tulips succeed in a wide variety of well-drained soils, abhorring stagnant moisture. Fertile ground of a somewhat sandy rather than clayey character best suits horticultural varieties, but first- and sometimes second-year displays can usually be had from earths that are less than ideal. Several of the species succeed in less nutritious soil than is desirable for the better known garden varieties and often prefer sites that in summer are hot and dry.

Prepare the ground for planting by spading it deeply and incorporating generous amounts of compost, leaf mold, peat moss, or other decayed organic material. It is unwise to use animal manure unless it is very thoroughly decayed. Even then, employ it sparingly and place it well beneath rather than in contact with the bulbs. Bonemeal, mixed in at the rate of about two ounces to each ten square feet, or superphosphate, at about one-half that rate, is excellent, or a fertilizer prepared especially for bulb plants, in which the nitrogen content is in organic or other slow-release form, may be substituted. It is of great importance that the soil down to several inches below the bulbs is broken up and improved by the suggested additives. To set the bulbs on a base of hardpan or other

compacted, infertile soil, no matter how agreeable the earth above may be, courts failure.

Planting is usually done from mid-October to mid-November, which is convenient if beds first have to be cleared of summer annuals, but earlier and later dates are practicable. The argument often advanced that too early planting encourages premature top growth, especially during late, mild falls, does not seem well founded (if it were, what about tulips left in the ground from year to year?). Certainly, early planting is preferable to storing the bulbs under conditions that differ widely from the ideal. But good results can be had from bulbs planted any time before the soil freezes deeply; if necessary, the planting season can be extended by covering the ground with a heavy mulch of coarse compost, corn stalks, or other material that will delay frost penetration. Although a degree of success has been reported with

To plant tulips: (a) Space the bulbs on the surface of a deeply-spaded, newly-fertilized bed

(b) Set the bulbs, pointed side up, in holes made with a trowel

(c) Next spring the plants are in full bloom

bulbs set out in January and even later, such late planting is not recommended. Store bulbs received prior to planting time in shade in a cellar or room where the temperature is 60 to 70°F, in trays or in bags perforated with holes to permit free circulation of air.

These 1½-foot-tall tulips bloomed, at The New York Botanical Garden in May, from bulbs stored from fall to March in a cool cellar, then planted outdoors

Where rodents are likely to be troublesome: (a) Line the sides of tulip beds with wire mesh (hardware cloth)

(b) Or plant small groups of bulbs in baskets of the same material

similar mesh. An alternative discouragement is, prior to planting the bulbs, to slightly dampen them with kerosene and then dust them lightly with powdered red lead.

In cold climates in which constant winter snow cover cannot be depended upon, it is advantageous to cover the ground, after it has frozen to a depth of 2 to 3 inches, with a mulch of salt hay, branches of evergreens, or other material that permits air to circulate among it and insulates it sufficiently to minimize alternate freezing and thawing. Tulips are not satisfactory in window boxes, porch boxes, and similar planters that remain outdoors all winter in regions where there is likelihood of the soil remaining frozen for long periods. Under such conditions insufficient root growth is made to support satisfactory foliage and flower development.

Where winters are so mild that the ground does not remain at 50°F or lower for a period of several weeks, successful one-season blooming can be achieved by

To make space for summer displays:
(a) Lift (dig up) the tulips

(b) And heel them in (plant them temporarily closely together in a slanted position, to remain until their foliage has completely withered)

Depth to plant, measured to the top, not the bottom of the bulb, should not be less than 4 to 5 inches for most kinds, although species with small bulbs may be set somewhat shallower. For bulbs that are to be left in the ground for more than one year, considerably deeper planting, so long as the earth beneath the bulbs is of good quality and well drained, has much to recommend it. Depths of 8 to 10 inches discourage the bulbs from multiplying and the originals are then likely to bloom satisfactorily for a greater number of years, up to from five to ten perhaps. Also, bulbs set deeply are unlikely to be disturbed or harmed by planting annuals or other shallow-rooted plants above or near them; as

an added dividend, the danger of infection with botrytis disease is reduced. Space bulbs of garden varieties 5 to 6 inches or, if they are to be interplanted with other spring-blooming plants, 9 inches to 1 foot apart. Closer spacing is appropriate for small-flowering species.

Protection from destruction of the bulbs by mice or other rodents is necessary or desirable in some localities. The most effective means is to outline the bed or planting area from the surface to a depth of about 9 inches with a vertical barrier of ½-inch wire mesh and, from time of planting until late winter, to cover the surface with the same material. Small groups of bulbs may be planted in baskets made of

(c) Then remove the dead remains of stems and foliage

(d) Store the bulbs in trays with mesh bottoms until the fall planting season

planting precooled bulbs rather late in the fall. Precooling is done by storing the bulbs at 45 to 50°F for a period of six weeks. Then plant immediately.

When flowering is through it is customary to remove tulips from formal beds to make way for annuals or other plants that are to bloom through the summer. This necessitates digging the bulbs before their season's growth is completed. In order to allow them to mature as fully as possible dig them carefully with a fork, retaining as many roots with soil clinging to them as possible. Then "heel them in," that is, plant them temporarily closely together, slanted at an angle of about forty-five degrees, and 2 to 3 inches deep, in a lightly shaded location. Keep them watered if the weather is dry. When, but not before, the foliage has completely died, take them up, clean off the dead tops, sort to size, and store the bulbs in a cool, dry, airy room until planting time in fall. Because second-year bulbs produce less even displays of blooms than newly purchased ones, it is usual to plant those saved in this way in informal areas or as sources of cut blooms rather than for a second year in formal beds.

Tulips planted in groups among perennials and in rock gardens may be lifted each year and treated as described above for those in formal beds or, if they are at

depths where they can remain without being disturbed by setting other plants above them, they can remain for as long as they continue to bloom satisfactorily.

Spring attentions begin with the removal of any mulch applied in fall. Do this as soon as the young shoots are clearly aboveground and before the leaves begin to unroll. If possible, choose dull, humid weather for the task. Then, too, a fertilizer relatively low in available nitrogen may be applied. If the spring is dry, soaking the ground with water at weekly or ten-day intervals is highly beneficial. As the flowers fade cut them off, preferably immediately below the bloom, but if the stalks left standing are deemed untidy make the cut just above the uppermost leaf. When harvesting tulips for use as cut flowers take no more foliage than a small upper leaf or two on each stem.

When cutting tulip flowers leave as much foliage as possible to "feed" the bulbs for the next year's flowering

Forcing tulips into early bloom indoors is one of the simplest of gardening techniques, easily accomplished in greenhouses and sunny windows. Grown in this way, they are admirable as pot plants and cut flowers. By making suitable selections of varieties and employing the precooling technique for the very earliest to be forced, a succession of blooms can be had from late December until tulips bloom outdoors.

As pot plants and for growing in dwelling houses and similar places, lower sorts such as varieties of the Single Early and Double Early divisions are most satisfactory. Taller growers, often forced in greenhouses to supply cut flowers, are less adaptable for house cultivation because under such conditions they are likely to develop weak stems and flowers of inferior size and substance.

Two conditions are highly desirable and one essential for successful forcing. The first is that top quality bulbs be used and that they be planted early, preferably as

Top quality tulip bulbs suitable for forcing

soon as they are obtainable from the supplier. The essential element is that after planting they be afforded a period of ten to twelve weeks or longer in a cool, damp, dark environment to allow them to develop strong root systems before shoot growth is unduly stimulated. This, of course, simulates the conditions tulips planted outdoors in fall normally experience. The most favorable temperatures for root development are in the 40 to 50°F range. In frozen ground, root growth ceases. At temperatures higher than those suggested, root development is generally unsatisfactory.

Pots or pans (shallow pots) 5 to 8 inches in diameter and flats about 4 inches deep, the latter appropriate for bulbs grown for cut flowers, are suitable containers. It is important that they have holes in their bottoms. To further ensure free drainage, place an inch or so of crocks, coarse cinders, broken clam or oyster shells, or similar material in the bottoms of the containers and over this, to prevent the soil from clogging the drainage, a layer of leaves, straw, hay, or even some old nylon stocking.

To pot tulips for forcing into early bloom: (a) Fill suitable soil into well-drained containers and press it till moderately firm

(b) Space the bulbs

(c) So that they just clear each other

(d) Add more soil and press it with the tips of the fingers till quite firm; then water with a fine spray and put the planted containers in a cool, frost-free root cellar

The soil need not be of the best quality. High fertility is not necessary. What is important is that it be porous enough to allow water to drain through it with fair ease. Almost any ordinary topsoil, if clayey made more permeable by the admixture of coarse

(e) Or bury them outdoors along with other hardy bulbs for forcing beneath a few inches of soil, sand, peat moss, or similar material

To force tulips into early bloom: (a) After the bulbs are well rooted, remove them, along with other hardy bulbs to be forced, from the root cellar or from under the covering of soil or similar material

(b) Stand the containers in a greenhouse; shade them from direct sun

(c) When the shoots become green, remove them from the shade

(d) In a suitable temperature in bright sun, the plants make sturdy growth

(e) In due time they burst into splendid bloom

sand or perlite and perhaps some compost or peat moss, suffices.

Fill enough into each pot or flat so that when lightly compacted with the fingers it will form a base upon which to place the bulbs so that they will be at the right height. This means that when the job is finished their tips will show just above the soil surface, which, to allow for watering, should be ½ inch, or with large pots or pans about 1 inch, below the rim.

The number of bulbs to plant in each pot, pan, or flat depends upon the container's size; five bulbs in a pot or pan 5 inches in diameter, six or seven in a 6-inch pot, and proportionately more in larger containers will prove about right. Space the bulbs so that they nearly, but not quite touch each other, and position them so that their flat rather than their rounded sides are against the walls of the container. This makes best use of the available space and prevents the plants in bloom having a "bunched up" look. After positioning the bulbs, fill soil between them and with the fingers press it quite firmly. Complete the job by watering the soil with a fine spray.

A flat of tulips, forced to supply cut flowers

If very early forcing is to be attempted, bulbs of early varieties may be conditioned by precooling them either in soil or dry storage for a period of six weeks at a temperature of 50°F. Plant such bulbs in pots or flats in a cool place. If the planting is done in a warm room or outdoors on a sunny, warm day, exposure to high temperatures may nullify the effect of the precooling. Precooled bulbs can be brought into bloom up to a month earlier than those of the same varieties not prepared in this way.

Following planting, a suitable environment for root development without undue stimulation of top growth is an immediate requirement. For this, an old-fashioned root cellar or equivalent cool, frost-free place that assures a fairly humid atmosphere and darkness is ideal, but most modern cellars

do not meet these requirements, and garages and similar places are generally unsuitable.

An alternative and eminently practical way of providing suitable conditions for root development is to stand the pots or flats of newly planted bulbs closely together on the ground outdoors, cover them with 7 to 8 inches of soil, sand, peat moss, or sawdust and bank around their sides a similar thickness of the same material. If soil is used for covering, spread sand to a depth of ½ inch or so on top of the containers before shoveling the soil over them. This makes it much easier, when the time comes to remove the bulbs, to separate the covering soil from that in which the bulbs have rooted. In cold climates after the top inch or two of the covering material has frozen, additional protection may be given by spreading over it a layer of salt hay, straw, leaves, branches of evergreens, or some similar material. A modification favored by some gardeners is to bury the pots or flats in a trench excavated in a well-drained location, but this involves more work. Another convenient variation is to bury the pots or flats under sand, peat moss, or sawdust in a cold frame. When the weather becomes consistantly cold, glass sash positioned over them eliminates the need for additional protective covering.

Forcing may begin from mid-January on, or with precooled bulbs about a month earlier. To assure a long succession of bloom, bring successive batches of pots or flats into a greenhouse or other suitable indoor environment at intervals of about two weeks.

Begin with a night temperature of 45 to 50°F and daytime levels about five degrees higher. After ten days to two weeks, raise these by ten degrees. For the first few days, shade the young shoots from direct sun, but after they become green expose them fully. Under this treatment most varieties will flower in five to six weeks. The time can be shortened by employing higher temperatures from when they are first brought indoors, but temperatures above 70°F are inimicable to sturdy development. Give water liberally throughout the forcing period. When the blooms are about half developed a reduction of about five degrees in the temperature results in sturdier, longer-lasting flowers. As full maturity approaches, light shade from strong sun further enhances the lives of the blooms as well as assists in retaining their colors. The bulbs of tulips that have been forced are of no further use. If planted outdoors they rarely recover sufficiently to make the effort worthwhile.

Bulbs to be brought into bloom early may remain buried until it is time to bring them indoors, but any held for late forcing must, if their development makes it necessary, be taken from under the sand, soil, or other

covering and be kept in a cool greenhouse or frost-free cold frame until forcing temperatures are in order. If covered too long, until the shoots are more than about 3 inches high, they are likely to break in the process of uncovering.

For the earliest flowers from bulbs not precooled, depend upon varieties of the Single Early and Double Early divisions that are known to give good results when forced early. Among such Single Earlies are 'Bellona' (golden yellow), 'Couleur Cardinal' (red), 'Christmas Marvel' (bright pink), 'DeWet' (orange veined with scarlet), 'Keizerkroon' (scarlet and yellow), and 'White Hawk' (white). Double Early varieties especially adapted for early forcing include 'Boule de Neige' (white), 'Mr. Van Der Hoeff' (yellow), 'Murillo' (pink), 'Peach Blossom' (pink suffused with white), and 'Schoonoord' (white).

Propagation. The usual method of increasing tulips is by offset bulbs, which most species and varieties under favorable circumstances produce in abundance. They can, however, easily be raised from seed, although horticultural varieties propagated in this way do not breed true to the parental type. Sow the seeds when ripe or store them in a cool, dry place until fall. Sow in well-drained flats in gritty, porous soil. Stand the flats in a shaded cold frame and cover with fine-mesh wire net to prevent disturbance by mice, birds, or other such creatures. Keep the soil evenly damp.

Germination will take place the following spring, but it is advisable to leave the seedlings undisturbed until the autumn of the next year, affording them the protection of a covering of salt hay or branches of evergreens through the winter.

The second fall, transplant the tiny bulbs approximately 3 inches apart and from 3 to 4 inches deep in a bed of fertile, sandy soil in a cold frame and allow them to remain there until they bloom for the first time, which should be at an age of from five to seven years.

Diseases and Pests. The chief diseases of tulips are fire blight, botrytis blight, gray bulb rot, and virus mosaic. Destruction of infected plants and sterilization of infected soil are the only practical remedies. Pests include mice, moles, and gophers, as well as aphids and bulb mites.

TULP. See Homeria.

TUMATU-KURI is *Discaria toumatou*.

TUMERIC. This is an alternate spelling for turmeric (*Curcuma domestica*).

TUNG OIL TREE is *Aleurites fordii*.

TUNIC FLOWER is *Petrorhagia saxifraga*.

TUNICA. See Petrorhagia.

TUPELO is *Nyssa aquatica.*

TUPIDANTHUS (Tupid-ánthus). A one-species genus, this member of the aralia family ARALIACEAE inhabits northern India and Malaya. At first developing as a small evergreen shrub or tree, it later becomes a lofty, woody vine. Its foliage much resembles that of *Brassaia.* The name is from the Greek *typis,* a mallet, and *anthos,* a flower. It alludes to the shape of the flower buds.

The long-stalked leaves of **Tupidanthus calyptratus** have five to nine individually-stalked, leathery, lustrous, elliptic leaflets, 6 inches to 1 foot long, with prominent mid-veins. The leaflets arch downward from the tips of the stalk like the ribs of an umbrella. The green flowers, ¾ inch to 1¼ inches across, are in loose terminal panicles of small, three- to seven-flowered umbels. They have numerous stamens. The fruits are irregular, knoblike, woody, and somewhat over 1 inch across.

Garden and Landscape Uses and Cultivation. In the tropics and frostless or almost frostless subtropics, this species is suitable for outdoor planting in ordinary, well-drained, not excessively dry soil. It grows well with some shade and may be pruned, if necessary, to limit its size. It is also attractive in large pots and tubs to serve the same purposes as *Schefflera.* The containers must be well drained. Coarse, fertile, porous soil is needed. Care must be taken not to keep it constantly saturated, but to allow it to become fairly dry between thorough soakings. Well-rooted specimens benefit from occasional applications of a dilute liquid fertilizer. Repotting of large plants is needed only at intervals of several years. It is best done in late winter or spring. Good light with some shade from bright sun, a moderately humid atmosphere, and a minimum temperature of 55 to 60°F are conducive to satisfactory growth. Propagation is by seed and by air layering.

TUPISTRA (Tu-pístra). Natives of forest regions of the Himalayas and Burma, the about half a dozen species of *Tupistra* belong to the lily family LILIACEAE. The name, from the Greek *typis,* a mallet, alludes to the peculiar stigmas.

Tupistras are herbaceous plants with stout rhizomes from which the all-basal evergreen foliage arises. The leaves are stalked and undivided. On stalks from between the leaves, the flower spikes arise. They have few to several stalkless, dull violet or muddy-purple blooms with bell-shaped corollas that have six or more rarely eight short, spreading lobes (petals), the same number of stamens as petals, and a thick style tipped with a fleshy, six-lobed stigma.

Rare in cultivation, *T. tupistroides* has narrow aspidistra-like leaves up to 2 feet long or longer and 1 inch to 3 inches broad.

The arching or pendulous flower spikes, with stalks 4 to 7 inches long, have several dull-vinous-purple blooms, each about ½ inch in diameter, with their centers paler than their petals.

Garden Uses and Cultivation. A plant for the collector of the rare and unusual, the species described requires essentially the same conditions and care as *Aspidistra,* except that it needs higher temperatures. In the tropics it is a good underplanting for shaded places beneath trees. In greenhouses a winter minimum of 55 to 60°F is suitable. By day this may be increased by five to fifteen degrees. Rich, porous soil kept evenly moist at all times and shade from bright sun are requisite. Vigorous new growth begins in June. Two or three weeks earlier repot, replant, and propagate by division. An alternative method of increase is by seed.

TURBINICARPUS (Turbíni-carpus). Eight species of the cactus family CACTACEAE constitute *Turbinicarpus.* A Mexican genus, its name, alluding to the shape of the fruits, derives from the Latin *turbo,* a top, and *karpos,* fruit. Some sorts are offered by dealers under the name *Strombocactus.*

Turbinicarpuses are small and have more or less spherical stems or plant bodies covered with flat or pointed protrusions (tubercles), all or some crowned with clusters of weak spines. The day-opening, funnel-shaped flowers come from near the apexes of the stems.

Kinds cultivated include *T. klinkerianus,* with plant bodies, 1¼ to 1½ inches high and wide, with pointed tubercles, and ¼-inch-long spines in clusters of three. The white flowers are ½ inch in diameter. *T. krainzianus* (syn. *Toumeya krainzianus*) is very similar to and should probably be considered a variety of *T. pseudomacrochele.* It has somewhat cylindrical plant bodies about 1½ inches tall, slightly less in width. The pointed tubercles have clusters of six to eight spines ½ inch to 1¼ inches long. The ½-inch-wide flowers are creamy-yellow. *T. laui* has solitary, subspherical or flattened plant bodies, about 1½ inches wide by a little more than ½ inch tall, and spines in clusters of six or seven. The white or pink-tinged blooms are approximately 1½ inches across. *T. lophophoroides* has plant bodies, some 1½ inches high by nearly 2 inches in diameter, with mostly ¼-inch-long, thin, rigid, black-tipped gray spines in clusters of two to four. The flowers are pale pink and 1½ inches wide or wider. *T. macrochele* has gray-green plant bodies, about 1¼ inches high by 1½ inches wide, with flat tubercles. The pliable spines are 1 inch to 2 inches long and grayish. About 1 inch across, the flowers are white tinged with pink. *T. polaskii* has plant bodies, 1 inch wide or slightly wider by scarcely one-half as high, with flat, subdued tubercles; only those at the apex have

one or two short, curved, yellowish spines. The flowers, white or slightly tinged with pink, are a little over ½ inch in diameter. *T. pseudomacrochele* (syn. *Toumeya pseudomacrochele*) has plant bodies about 1¼ inches wide and somewhat taller. Its grayish spines, in clusters of eight, are twisted and sometimes interwoven. Approximately 1½ inches across, the blooms are white striped with pink. *T. schmiedickeanus* (syn. *Toumeya schmiedickeanus*) has somewhat egg-shaped plant bodies 2 inches tall by 1¼ inches wide. The spines are in clusters of three or sometimes four on top of pointed tubercles. About ¾ inch wide, the blooms are pink. *T. schwarzii* (syn. *Toumeya schwarzii*) has hemispherical plant bodies about 1¼ inches wide, but scarcely as tall. The whitish or yellow-brown spines, solitary or in pairs, are about ¾ inch in length. The white blooms are 1½ inches in diameter.

Garden Uses and Cultivation. Because of their small sizes and reasonably agreeable dispositions the cactuses of this genus are much esteemed by collectors. Suitable for cultivation outdoors in warm, dry climates and in greenhouses, they succeed in rather loose, porous, sandy soil of reasonable fertility and with a little lime or gypsum included. They are grateful for slight shade from fierce sun. For additional information see the Encyclopedia entry Cactuses.

TURFING-DAISY is *Tripleurospermum tchihatchewii.*

TURKEY BEARD is *Xerophyllum asphodeloides.*

TURK'S. This word forms parts of the common names of these plants: Turk's cap (*Melocactus*), Turk's-cap-hibiscus (*Malvaviscus*), Turk's cap lily (*Lilium superbum, L. chalcedonicum, L. pomponium,* and *L. martagon*), Turk's head or Turk's turban (*Clerodendrum indicum*), and Turk's rug (*Chorizanthe staticoides*).

TURMERIC is *Curcuma domestica.*

TURNERA (Túrn-era)—Sage-Rose. The sixty species of *Turnera,* natives of tropical and subtropical America, belong to the turnera family TURNERACEAE. They include trees, shrubs, and herbaceous plants, most too weedy in appearance to have garden appeal. The name commemorates the English herbalist William Turner, who died in 1568.

Turneras have alternate, undivided, toothed or somewhat pinnately-lobed leaves, often with a pair of glands at their bases and quite commonly with stellate (star-shaped) hairs. Usually solitary, rarely in clusters or racemes, the yellow, mallow-like blooms sometimes appear stalkless or nearly so because their stalks are united with those of the leaves. The flowers have tubular to bell-shaped, five-lobed calyxes, five petals, the same number of stamens, and three styles. The fruits are many-seeded capsules.

Apparently the only species cultivated, and that but rarely, *T. ulmifolia* is a variable native of Mexico, South America, and the West Indies. Sometimes called sagerose, this subshrub, 2 to 4 feet tall, has coarsely, irregularly saw-toothed, oblong-elliptic leaves, up to 6 inches long by 2½

Turnera ulmifolia

inches wide, but often smaller, with a gland on each side at the base of the blade and the veins very distinct. The undersides of the leaves are white- or yellow-hairy, the upper surfaces downy. When crushed, the foliage is rather ill-scented. The flowers have sulfur-yellow petals that deepen to a butter-yellow toward their bases. About 2 inches in diameter and somewhat five-sided in outline, they have petals that meet or slightly overlap throughout their lengths. Because their stalks are united with the leafstalks, the blooms sit at about the base of the leaf blades. They open early in the morning and close by noon, or well before on long, sunny summer days. Each flower opens only once, but a succession is produced over a long period. Variety *T. u. angustifolia* differs from the species in having distinctly narrower leaves, and flowers with narrower petals that are in contact with their neighbor petals only near their bases.

Garden and Landscape Uses and Cultivation. In warm, frost-free and essentially frost-free climates *T. ulmifolia* may be grown permanently outdoors in flower beds and at the fronts of shrub plantings. In colder places it can be planted out in summer after there is no longer danger of frost, and be wintered indoors in a greenhouse or other light place where the temperature ranges from 55 to 65°F. This spe-

Turnera ulmifolia angustifolia

cies grows well in any ordinary soil in full sun. It is easily raised from seed and from cuttings.

TURNERACEAE — Turnera Family. Eight genera of dicotyledons, mostly natives of tropical America and Africa, constitute this family. Their members are trees, shrubs, and herbaceous plants with alternate, undivided leaves sometimes edged with glandular teeth. The symmetrical, usually solitary flowers, which come from the leaf axils, have stalks sometimes joined to those of the leaves. Each has five sepals, the same number of petals and stamens, and three styles. The fruits are capsules. The only genus likely to be cultivated is *Turnera*.

TURNIP. Here we shall consider common turnips, derivatives of *Brassica rapa*, and the seven-top turnip (*B. septiceps*). The latter is grown for its edible foliage. Both are Old World natives of the mustard family CRUCIFERAE. Swede turnips or rutabagas are dealt with under Rutabaga or Swede Turnip. From rutabagas, common and seven-top turnips are easily distinguished by their hairy leaves and the common turnip by its differently shaped swollen roots.

Turnips are esteemed for their usually flattish to globular or sometimes longer, tuberous roots, which are eaten boiled, in soups, and grated in salads, and for their leaves, which are boiled as greens. Decidedly cool weather crops, turnips in most places are sown in spring for harvesting in early summer, in summer for a crop to use in fall and store for winter, and in mild climates to harvest in winter and spring. They are easy to grow. Popular varieties with white flesh are 'Purple-Top White Globe', 'Snowball', 'Tokyo Cross', and 'White Milan'. 'Aberdeen' and 'Golden Ball' have yellow flesh. 'Seven Top' and 'Shogrin' are grown, especially in the south, as greens. The first does not have swollen

roots, whereas the other has small, flavorful ones.

Soil for turnips must be well-drained, reasonably deep, loose, and fertile enough, without being excessively rich in nitrogen, to encourage quick growth. It should not be freshly manured, but residues of manure applied to previous crops are favorable. Its preparation may include incorporating with it, by spading, rotary tilling, or plowing, compost or a green manure crop and a dressing of a complete garden fertilizer. Potash is important. If the ground is deficient in this, mix in unleached wood ashes at the rate of 5 to 10 pounds per 100 square feet or sulfate or muriate of potash at 5 to 10 ounces per 100 square feet. The pH should range from slightly acid to slightly alkaline. Too acid soils are favorable to club root disease.

Sow the seeds in drills, 1 foot to 1¼ feet apart and ½ to ¾ inch deep, at the rate of three or four seeds to 1 inch. Alternatively, the seeds may be broadcast in beds up to 4 feet wide, but unless the ground is very free of weeds, this may present difficulties in controlling them. The drill method is usually preferred. Make the first sowing as early in spring as the ground can be had in a nonsticky, crumbly condition. Where summers are cool, make a second and third sowing at two-week intervals. Sow in July or August for a fall crop, later in regions of mild winters to give roots to be harvested in winter and spring.

Care in the growing season primarily consists of aerating the soil and eliminating weeds by repeated shallow cultivation between the rows and hand-pulling along them, and watering thoroughly at five- to seven-day intervals during dry weather. Thinning to a distance of 3 inches between individuals must be done before the plants crowd. Further thinning is done by pulling the roots for use, in succession, as they attain suitable size.

Harvest turnips while they are yet young, crisp, and succulent. Those between 2 and 3 inches in diameter are best. If they grow too slowly, are left too long, become too large, or develop during hot weather, they become tough, woody, bitter, or pithy. For turnip greens select young, quickly grown leaves. Comparatively hardy, this crop withstands frost and continues to grow much later in the fall than most vegetables. It does not withstand hard freezing. Where winters are severe, pull the roots before freezing weather, trim off their tops, and store them between layers of slightly damp soil, sand, or peat moss in a cool root cellar or covered outdoor pit.

Diseases and pests are those common to cabbage and other brassica crops. The most serious are club root and black rot among diseases, and root maggots, aphids, and flea beetles among pests.

TURNIP, INDIAN. This is *Arisaema triphyllum*.

TURNIP-ROOTED CELERY. See Celeriac, Knob Celery, or Turnip-Rooted Celery.

TURNIP-ROOTED CHERVIL is *Chaerophyllum bulbosum*.

TURPENTINE-BROOM. See Thamnosma.

TURPENTINE TREE is *Syncarpia glomulifera*.

TURQUOISE BERRY is *Drymophila cyanocarpa*.

TURRAEA (Tur-raèa). The tropics and subtropics of the Old World provide native homes for the ninety species of *Turraea*, of the mahogany family MELIACEAE. One South African species is cultivated in California and in the south. The name commemorates the Italian botanist Giorgio della Torre, or Turra, who died in 1688.

This genus comprises trees and shrubs with alternate, undivided, but sometimes obtusely-lobed, stalked leaves, and axillary, generally clustered flowers with four- or five-toothed or -cleft calyxes, the same number of much longer petals, eight or ten stamens united into a tube that is eight- or ten-toothed at its top and has anthers alternating with the teeth, and a solitary style.

Turraea obtusifolia

Sometimes called star-bush, **T. obtusifolia** is a compact, broad shrub about 3 feet tall with beautiful glossy foliage and attractive white, narrow-petaled, starry flowers 1½ to 2½ inches across. These are borne freely in late summer and fall. They are on 1-inch stalks and have protruding stigmas. The leaves, obovate and 1 inch to 2 inches long, are sometimes three-lobed at their apexes. They are hairless and have rolled-under edges.

Garden and Landscape Uses and Cultivation. This is a highly satisfactory plant for borders, rock gardens, and other places that call for a not-too-tall shrub of neat habit and pleasing appearance. It will stand short periods of light frost, but probably will not survive temperatures lower than 18 to 20°F. It succeeds in ordinary garden soil in sun and is increased by cuttings and by seed.

TURRICULA (Tur-rícula). The only species of *Turricula*, of the water leaf family HYDROPHYLLACEAE, is endemic to California and Baja California. Its name, a diminutive of the Latin *turris*, a tower, alludes to its narrow panicles of flowers.

An ill-scented, deep-rooted, sticky-hairy, herbaceous perennial, somewhat woody at its base and branched from there, **T. parryi** (syns. *Eriodictyon parryi*, *Nama parryi*) is 3 to 9 feet tall. It has crowded, stalkless, sinuately-toothed, narrow-lanceolate leaves 4 to 10 inches long. Displayed along the upper sides of the curving branchlets of long, narrow panicles, 6 inches to 1½ feet long, its purplish to blue, pubescent flowers are funnel-shaped, shallowly-five-lobed, and ½ to ¾ inch long. They have a deeply-five-lobed calyx, three long and two short stamens, and two styles. The fruits are capsules.

Garden and Landscape Uses and Cultivation. Occasionally recommended for planting in dry, warm regions, but to be regarded with suspicion because contact with it causes severe dermatitis in many people, this plant may be grown in well-drained soils in sunny locations. Its best uses are in gardens of native plants and in informal areas.

TURTLEHEAD. See Chelone.

TURTLE VINE is *Bauhinia glabra*.

TUSSACIA. See Chrysothemis.

TUSSILAGO (Tussil-àgo) — Coltsfoot. The only species of *Tussilago*, of the daisy family COMPOSITAE, native to northern Europe, North Africa, and Asia, the coltsfoot is naturalized in waste places from Nova Scotia to Quebec, New Jersey, Pennsylvania, and West Virginia and occasionally further inland. Alluding to the following reputed virtues, its name derives from the Latin *tussis*, a cough.

Medicinally *Tussilago* is regarded as a demulcent, expectorant, and tonic. Although not official in the United States, it has been and still is to some extent used in many ways in syrups, decoctions, teas, and candies and is employed in herbal "tobaccos." Pliny suggested drawing smoke from dried roots and leaves burnt on cypress charcoal into the mouth and swallowing it, alternating the swallows with sips of wine. One wonders which phase of the treatment brought the sufferer greater relief.

Tussilago farfara

A deciduous herbaceous perennial, very closely related to *Petasites*, the coltsfoot (*T. farfara*) has creeping underground rhizomes from which arise in late winter or earliest spring, and well before the foliage is evident, erect stalks that terminate in solitary, delicately almond-scented, dandelion-like heads of yellow flowers. These stalks are not smooth like those of dandelions, but have conspicuous up-pointing bracts (small leaflike organs) alternately arranged. At first cylindrical, the heads of flowers expand as they mature until finally they are about 1 inch in diameter. Each consists of a central disk of bisexual, but infertile florets and very numerous slender, fertile ray florets in several rows. A single row of bracts forms the involucre (collar at the base of the flower head). The fruits are seedlike achenes. The leaves of *T. f. variegata* are edged or blotched with creamy-white. The long-stalked leaves, in outline heart-shaped to nearly round, are shallowly-lobed or -angled, and toothed. They are up to 8 inches in diameter, hairless above except when young, and densely-white-felty on their lower surfaces. Their shape, roughly that of a hoof, is responsible for the common name coltsfoot. The leaves begin to sprout before the last flowers fade, but chiefly they succeed the blooms and do not attain full size until well after flowering is through. This led some of the ancients, including Pliny, to believe that the coltsfoot had no leaves, but wise old Dioscorides knew differently. He wrote it "hath leaves like unto Ivy, but greater, 6 or 7 from the root, as concerning ye lower side white, but as concerning ye upper side green, having many corners, a stalk a span long, a pale yellow flower in ye springtime but it doth quickly cast off both ye flower & ye stalk, whence some have thought ye herb to be without stalk & without flower." Not a bad description, even today.

Garden Uses and Cultivation. The horticultural uses of coltsfoot are distinctly limited. It and its variegated variety may sometimes serve to hold stubborn banks, and it can with propriety be included in herb gardens and medicinal gardens. Actually, its dandelion-like flowers and large leaves are not without beauty, but its unseemly habit of spreading so aggressively disenchants gardeners. Were it a rarer species, a denizen of the high Alps, the Himalayas, or western China, or challenging to grow and more willing to expire than to colonize, the coltsfoot would undoubtedly be treasured by rock gardeners and other connoisseurs of the rare and beautiful; but then, the same is true of the dandelion. The cultivation of coltsfoot is simple. It thrives in almost any soil, moist or dry, in full sun or part-day shade. Propagation is easy by division, root-cuttings, and seed.

TUTSAN is *Hypericum androsaemum*.

TWAYBLADE. See Liparis, and Listera.

TWEEDIA. See Oxypetalum.

TWELVE APOSTLES. See Neomarica.

TWIN. This word occurs in the common names of these plants: Mexican twin flower (*Polianthes geminiflora*), twin-berry (*Mitchella*), twin-flower (*Linnaea borealis*), and twin-leaf (*Jeffersonia*).

TWINSPUR is *Diascia barberae*.

TWIST-ARUM is *Helicodiceros muscivorus*.

TWISTED-STALK. See Streptopus.

TYPHA (Tỳ-pha) — Cat-Tail. This, the only genus of the cat-tail family TYPHACEAE, consists of ten species of marsh and shallow-water plants of temperate, subtropical, and tropical regions in many parts of the world. The name *Typha* is a modification of *typhe*, the ancient Greek name for these plants.

Cat-tails have stout, creeping rootstocks and erect, deciduous, long-linear or sword-shaped, mostly basal leaves with sheathing lower parts. Their minute flowers are crowded in dense, erect, terminal, poker-like spikes, the upper portion of which is of all male flowers, the lower part of females intermixed with sterile flowers. The fruits are tiny nutlets containing mealy seeds. Typhas often colonize great areas of marsh land. They provide valuable bird food and stabilize soils and banks. The dried leaves are woven into matting and the hairs of the fruits have been employed for stuffing pillows and mattresses. In Australia, when food is scarce, the roots are eaten by the aborigines. The velvety-brown spikes of fruits are esteemed, both fresh and dried, as floral decorations.

The common cat-tail (*T. latifolia*) is native throughout most of North America as well as Europe and Asia. Up to 6 feet tall or taller, it has stout, reedlike stems, and leaves ½ to 1 inch wide, and the male and female portions of the spike are without a definite space between them. The narrow-leaved cat-tail (*T. angustifolia*), 3 to 4½

Typha latifolia

Typha latifolia (flower spikes)

feet in height, has somewhat convex leaves, up to ½ inch wide, and dark brown flower spikes with a distinct portion of stem separating the male and female parts. It is native to the eastern and southern United States, Europe, Asia, and Africa. Presumed hybrids between *T. latifolia* and *T. angustifolia* that have the general aspect of the last-named, but are taller and more robust, are named **T. glauca**. Distinguished from *T. angustifolia* by its perfectly flat leaves and pale brown flower spikes, **T. domingensis** is indigenous to coastal marshes from Virginia and California to South America. A delightful miniature, **T. minima** has very narrow rushlike leaves and is 1 foot to 2½ feet tall. A native of Europe and Asia, it has the rusty-brown female parts of the spike contiguous with or separated from the male portion.

Garden Uses and Cultivation. Although these are highly decorative plants for boggy ground, watersides, and even areas where their roots are covered with a foot or so of water, due caution should be exercised in introducing them into the landscape for they are great colonizers and aggressive spreaders and may easily take for themselves areas intended for other plants; they do not invade dry ground, however. Deep-rooted, once they are established they are very difficult to eradicate. Often the best way of handling them is to confine them to large tubs or concrete containers and to take them from these and replant them back every two or three years. They prosper in rich, loamy soil and are very easily increased by division, and by seed sown in pots that are immersed almost to their rims in water.

TYPHACEAE — Cat-Tail Family. The characteristic of this family of monocotyledons are those of its only genus, *Typha*.

TYPHONIUM (Ty-phònium). The genus *Typhonium*, of the arum family ARACEAE, comprises about thirty species of tuberous, herbaceous perennials of tropical Asia and Indonesia. Its name, an ancient Greek one for some plant of the arum family, is derived from that of Typhon, a giant of mythology. The tender, young leaves of some species are used in their homelands for food.

Typhoniums are deciduous. They have usually long-stalked, heart-, arrow-, halberd-shaped or three- or five-lobed or deeply-fingered leaves. As is usual in the family, the small, unisexual flowers are clustered along a spikelike spadix (represented in the familiar calla-lily by the central yellow column) at the base of which is a modified leaf called a spathe (in the calla-lily the white, petal-like part). The male and female flowers in *Typhonium* are separated by a section of naked spadix. The spathes are persistent. The entire assemblage of spadix and spathe, known as the inflorescence, terminates a short stalk. The fruits are one- or two-seeded berries.

Native to China, **T. giganteum** has a tuber about ¾ inch in diameter. Its leaves have stalks approximately 2 feet in length, and blades, 1 foot long or longer, with large basal lobes. The ill-scented inflorescences, on 6-inch-long stalks, have spathes with blades up to 6 inches long or longer. Variety *T. g. giraldii* has larger, wider leaves with pale green or ivory-white veins, and stalks spotted with reddish-brown. The spathes are brownish-red. A native of Malaya, **T. filiforme** has heart-shaped leaves, and inflorescences with red-spotted, yellow spathes.

Garden and Landscape Uses and Cultivation. These interesting foliage plants respond to the conditions and general care that suite colocasias, caladiums, and similar tropical plants of the arum family.

TYPHONODORUM (Typhóno-dorum). One remarkable calla-lily relative is the only species of *Typhonodorum*. A native of Malagasy (Madagascar) and Zanzibar, where it grows in fairly shallow water, this imposing evergreen aroid (plant of the aroid family ARACEAE) forms extensive forests of low trees. The import of its name, from the Greek *typhos*, typhoon, and *doron*, a gift, is not apparent.

An evergreen, **T. lindleyanum** has a trunk, up to 1 foot thick and 10 feet tall, crowned with many erect leaves with stalks, 2 to 3 feet long, and ovate blades, deeply-heart- or arrow-shaped at their bases and 1½ to over 3 feet long. The arrangement of the flowers is typical of most aroids. Individual flowers, of insignificant size, are crowded on a spikelike organ called a spadix (the equivalent of the yellow central spike of a calla-lily). From the base of the spadix sprouts a modified leaf called a spathe (represented by the white, trumpet-like part in the calla-lily). In *Typhonodorum*, the spadix is orange-yellow and up to 1¼ feet long. Its lower portion consists of female blooms, its upper part of males, with a band of sterile flowers between. The short-stalked spathe is yellowish, up to 1½ feet long, and at its base is folded around the spadix. The fruits are large berries. In regions where this plant grows plentifully, its seeds are used for food.

Garden and Landscape Uses and Cultivation. For its satisfactory growth this species needs high temperatures and humidity. In the tropics it can be used as a noble ornament of bogs and shallow waters and is sometimes cultivated in large conservatories in botanical gardens, often in association with the giant water-lily (*Victoria amazonica*). It thrives in fertile mud and is easily increased by seeds, which must be sown without allowing them to dry after they ripen, and by offsets.

Typhonodorum lindleyanum

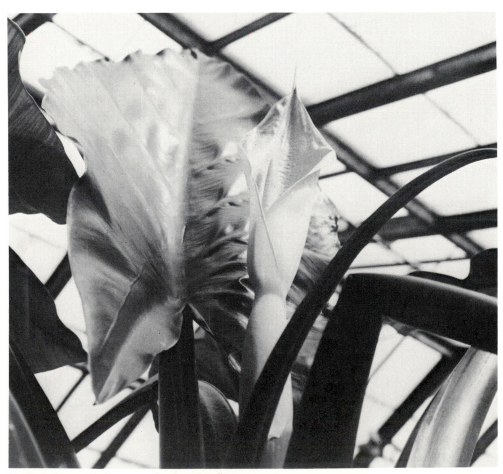

Typhonodorum lindleyanum (leaf and inflorescence)

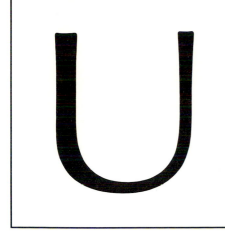

U

UDO is *Aralia cordata*.

UGNI (Úg-ni)—Chilean-Guava or Chilean-Cranberry. To the myrtle family MYRTA-CEAE belong the fifteen species of this genus, a close relative of *Myrtus* from which it differs in the technical details of its floral morphology, especially in the structure of the anthers of its flowers. The name is a modification of a native Chilean one. Like *Myrtus* it has opposite, undivided leaves, and flowers with usually five-lobed calyxes, five petals, and many stamens. The fruits are berries.

The Chilean-guava or Chilean-cranberry (**U. molinae** syns. *Myrtus ugni, Eugenia ugni*) is an evergreen shrub or tree, native to Chile and perhaps beyond the boundaries of that country in South America. It has rich green, elliptic to ovate leaves ½ inch to 1½ inches long by ¼ to slightly over ½ inch wide. Above they are glossy; their undersides are whitish. Profusely borne, the pink-tinged, bell-shaped, solitary flowers are ⅜ inch long and about as wide. Their stalks are approximately 1 inch long. The purplish to deep maroon fruits ripen in fall. They are flattish-spherical, a little over ½ inch in diameter, pleasant to eat, and splendid for making jelly. In cultivation this is commonly a shrub, but it is reported to become a tree of considerable size in its homeland.

Garden and Landscape Uses and Cultivation. In addition to having palatable fruits, the Chilean-guava is a pleasing ornamental for general-purpose planting in mild climates, such as that of California. Once established it needs little care beyond copious watering during dry periods. It flourishes in ordinary garden soil and is not overdemanding in the matter of fertilization. Clothed to the ground with branches and foliage, it lends itself to pruning or shearing to formal shapes, or it may be left uncut so that the natural down-sweeping effect of its branches is displayed to full advantage. This species is singularly free of pests and diseases. It is easily increased by cuttings under mist

or in a greenhouse or cold frame propagating bed. Plants may be raised from seed, but it is a rather slow process.

ULEX (Ù-lex) — Gorse or Furze or Whin. Containing about twenty-five species, *Ulex*, of the pea family LEGUMINOSAE, differs from related *Cytisus* chiefly in the calyxes of its flowers being deeply-lobed. Native to western Europe and North Africa, it is naturalized in parts of North America. Its name is an ancient Latin one for some similar plant.

An old British saying has it that "when gorse is in flower kissing is in season," which is another way of indicating that in the relatively mild climate of Great Britain common gorse is never without blooms. In sheltered locations that is so, although it must be admitted that the few to be found other than in late winter and spring are more likely to provide excuse for osculatory exercise than display.

Ulexes are spiny shrubs with usually alternate leaves that on young seedlings have three leaflets, but on older specimens are scalelike or represented by spines. The pealike, yellow flowers, with persistent calyxes and corollas, are solitary or in small racemes or clusters in the leaf axils. Their calyxes are split to their bases into two lips, the upper one with two teeth, the lower with three. There are ten stamens, nine joined and one separate. The fruits are hairy pods, linear-oblong to broadly-ovate, and contain one to six seeds. Three species, *U. europaeus, U. minor,* and *U. gallii,* cover great areas of heathlands in Europe and provide splendid displays of floral color.

Common gorse, furze, or whin (**U. europaeus**) is erect, densely-branched, and 2 to 7 feet tall. The shoots are more or less hairy, the younger ones and younger spines somewhat glaucous. The stout, straight, terminal spines are ½ to 1 inch or slightly more in length, the others are about ⅓ inch long, stiff, and sharply-pointed. The clear yellow blooms, in lax clusters, are up to ¾ inch long and almond-scented. The

Ulex europaeus

seed pods are about as long as the flowers. The seeds are poisonous. A variety with double flowers is *U. e. plenus.* The species, common throughout western Europe to Italy and naturalized in North America, is in some places cultivated for fodder and animal bedding and, especially its double-flowered variety, as an ornamental. It blooms chiefly in late winter and spring.

Mostly not exceeding 3 feet in height and usually lower, although sometimes one-half again as tall, **U. minor** (syn. *U. nanus*), has often procumbent stems and hairy shoots that, like the foliage, are not glaucous when young. The terminal spines are weaker than those of *U. europaeus* and rarely slightly exceed ½ inch in length; the secondary ones are about ¼ inch long and are usually softer and more bristle-like than spiny. The clear yellow flowers have wing petals and keels about as long as the calyxes, which are under ½ inch in length. This western European native blooms in late summer and fall. Very similar to the last is **U. gallii,** of western Europe. Commonly it is more robust and may have stouter, slightly longer spines. Also its blooms are deeper yellow and the upright, standard petal is proportionately longer than the calyx.

Native to Spain and Portugal, *U. micranthus* (syn. *U. lusitanicus*) is a dark green, rather loose shrub 8 inches to 1½ or, rarely, 2½ feet tall. Its young shoots are clothed with short hairs. The fairly stout, sharply pointed spines are curved, the terminal ones up to nearly ½ inch long, the others smaller. The flowers, about ⅓ inch long, are distributed along the branches. All the petals exceed the calyx in length.

Garden and Landscape Uses. The gorses are not generally hardy in the north, except perhaps in very sheltered locations and in mild areas near the sea, but in warmer climates they flourish with little care. They are well adapted for seaside planting and for poorish sandy and gravelly soils of a rather acid character. In fertile soils they grow too lushly and flower less freely; near their limits of hardiness they are more likely to suffer from winter-killing. They are attractive as informal hedges and for associating with heathers and other plants that prefer nonalkaline soils and full sun. Although their leaves are few and not long-lasting, because of their green stems and abundant green spines they function as evergreens.

Cultivation. These shrubs are difficult to transplant. It is always best to set out young specimens from containers or to sow seeds in spring where the plants are to remain and thin out the seedlings. Container-grown plants are raised from seed sown singly in small pots and the young plants later repotted into larger ones, or, the double variety, by summer cuttings in a greenhouse propagating bed or humid cold frame or under mist. Specimens that have become too large or of untidy appearance may be cut hard back in early spring.

ULLUCO is *Ullucus tuberosus*.

ULLUCUS (Úllu-cus) — Ulluco. The only species of this genus is a sprawling or climbing herbaceous perennial of the basella family BASELLACEAE. Its potato-like tubers are an important food crop in its homelands. Its botanical name is derived from the native one.

Ulluco (*Ullucus tuberosus*) is indigenous to Andean South America. It has somewhat twining, angular stems, 1 foot to 2 feet long, and alternate, long-stalked, fleshy, roundish-heart-shaped leaves up to 8 inches wide, but commonly much smaller. The tiny yellow or greenish-yellow blooms, in slender, loose racemes shorter than the leaves, spring from the leaf axils. They have two sepals, five spreading petals, and five stamens. The fruits are egg-shaped and berry-like. The underground tubers, from pea size to about the size of a pigeon's egg, are usually rose-violet. Those of cultivated varieties are white, yellow, yellowish-red, rose, or red-

dish. In addition to the tubers produced underground, small ones develop in the leaf axils.

Garden Uses and Cultivation. Not hardy in the north, the ulluco is sometimes planted in mild climates for its interest as a plant useful to man. It grows without difficulty in ordinary well-drained soil in sun and is readily raised from tubers in the manner of potatoes.

ULMACEAE — Elm Family. This family of dicotyledons consists of fifteen genera and about 150 species of mostly deciduous trees or more rarely shrubs, natives chiefly of north temperate regions. They have alternate or rarely opposite, undivided, usually toothed leaves usually with asymmetrical bases and arranged in two ranks. The small, bisexual or unisexual, petal-less flowers have a three- to nine-parted or lobed calyx and as many or twice as many stamens as calyx parts. The fruits are small nuts, drupes, or samaras.

Among genera cultivated are *Celtis*, *Hemiptelea*, *Holoptelea*, *Planera*, *Trema*, *Ulmus*, and *Zelkova*.

ULMUS (Úl-mus)—Elm. The sorts of *Ulmus* must be accounted among the handsomest trees native in the northern hemisphere, but despite their fine qualities and due to the spread into many areas of the devastating and presently incurable Dutch elm disease and the at least as serious phloem necrosis disease, they are understandably less frequently planted than formerly. Belonging to the elm family ULMACEAE, this genus has as its botanical name its ancient Latin one. There are forty-five species of elm indigenous to North America, Europe, North Africa, and Asia, as natives extending as far south as Mexico, Indochina, and the Himalayas. In addition to these there are many horticultural varieties. Some sorts are esteemed for their lumber. The water-elm (*Planera aquatica*) is a related tree.

Elms are small to very large, mostly deciduous, rarely evergreen trees with leaf buds clothed with tightly overlapping scales. Their leaves are alternate, undivided, toothed, pinnately-veined, and decidedly asymmetrical, with one side from the midrib outward longer and bigger than the other. The tiny flowers, which are without display value, are bisexual or rarely unisexual. In small tufts or racemes from the leaf axils, they have a four- to nine-lobed calyx and are without petals. There are as many stamens as calyx lobes and two styles. Most species bloom in spring, a few in fall. The fruits are technically samaras with a usually broad, encircling wing. Of the kinds described here only the Chinese elm is under some circumstances evergreen.

The American, white, or water elm (*U. americana*), one of the most magnificent

Ulmus americana in New England

Ulmus americana with young foliage

Ulmus americana (bark)

Ulmus americana (branching habit)

Ulmus americana (leaves)

and beloved native American trees and in the past so widely planted for shade and ornament that it became the outstanding landscape feature of numerous towns and villages, especially in New England, is, alas, because of the inroads made by diseases, rapidly diminishing in numbers. This splendid sort, native from Newfoundland to Florida and westward to the Rocky Mountains, attains a maximum height of 120 feet and a spread of about 75 feet. Its flaky, gray-barked trunk commonly divides into a number of major branches of trunklike size that spread upward and outward to form a lovely vase-shaped head. The twigs are short-hairy or hairless. Ovate-oblong, abruptly-pointed, and double-toothed, the leaves are 3 to 6 inches long and usually not over one-half as broad. Their bases markedly unequal, they are without conspicuous tufts of hair in the vein axils on their somewhat hairy to practically hairless undersides. Their upper surfaces are hairless or have a few short, rough hairs. The flower clusters are pendulous. The wings of the fruits, which otherwise are hairless, are densely hair-fringed. Notable narrow-headed varieties of this species are *U. a. ascendens*, which has a very narrow, columnar head; *U. a. columnaris*, columnar, but much broader than the last; *U. a.* 'Moline', unfortunately reputed to be much subject to storm damage; and *U. a.* 'Princeton'. The graceful weeping American elm (*U. a. pendula*) has long, pendulous branchlets.

The wahoo or winged elm (*U. alata*), native from Virginia to Illinois, Florida, and Texas, rarely exceeds 45 feet in height. It has a rounded-oblong head, gracefully arched branches, and branchlets frequently decorated with a pair of opposite corky wings. Its double-toothed leaves, ovate-oblong to somewhat obovate and 1 inch to 3 inches long by less than one-half as wide, have eight to twelve pairs of veins. Nearly hairless on their upper surfaces, they are hairy beneath. The flowers are in short, pendulous racemes. About ⅓ inch long, the narrowly-winged fruits are hairy. The rock or cork elm (*U. thomasii*), native from Quebec to Nebraska and Tennessee, attains a height of 100 feet. A narrow, round-headed tree, this has thinly-hairy branchlets often with two or more irregular corky wings. Its double-toothed, 3- to 5-inch-long leaves, markedly unequal at their bases and with sixteen to twenty pairs of veins, are essentially hairless above, but have hairy undersurfaces. The flowers are in 1½- to 2-inch-long, pendulous racemes; the ¾-inch-long fruits are hairy.

Slippery or red elm (*U. rubra* syn. *U. fulva*), indigenous from Quebec to North Dakota, Florida, and Texas, up to 60 feet high, has a broad, open head and thick, rigid, double-toothed leaves, 4 to 8 inches long, markedly unequal at their bases. Their upper surfaces are very rough, their undersides hairy. The flowers, in erect clusters, are succeeded by fruits hairless except for a patch at the center of each.

The smooth-leaved elm (*U. carpinifolia*), a variable native of Europe and adjacent Asia, is hardy throughout most of New England. Up to 90 feet tall and with a deeply-fissured, usually single trunk, this characteristically has wide-spreading branches and generally drooping, hairless or nearly hairless branchlets. Its double-toothed, elliptic to obovate, pointed leaves,

Ulmus carpinifolia

2 to 3½ inches long, have smooth, lustrous upper surfaces and tufts of white hairs in the axils of the veins on their undersides. The flowers are crowded in erect clusters. Notable varieties are *U. c.* 'Christine Buisman', reportedly highly disease-resistant; *U. c. koopmanii*, branching from near the ground, with an egg-shaped head, usually corky young branchlets, and small leaves with grayish undersides; *U. c. pendula*, with slender, drooping branches; *U. c. prependens*, with rigid, pendulous, corky branches and small leaves; and the globe elm (*U. c. umbraculifera* syn. *U. procera umbraculifera*), which has a dense, rounded or flat-topped head and elliptic to broad-ovate leaves 2 to 3 inches long. Other sorts ten-

Ulmus carpinifolia umbraculifera

tatively assigned here, although some authorities treat them as varieties of *U. procera*, are *U. c. purpurascens*, with purplish leaves rarely over 1 inch long, and *U. c. purpurea*, with dark purple leaves of normal size for the species.

The wych or Scotch elm (*U. glabra*), of Europe and adjacent Asia, which attains a maximum height of approximately 120 feet, has a round-topped, rather open head. Unlike the English elm, this does not sucker from the lower part of its trunk and, until it attains considerable age, is smooth-barked. Its short-stalked, double-toothed, broadly-obovate, abruptly-pointed leaves have unequal bases; they are 3 to 6 inches long. Their upper surfaces are usually rough, their undersides pubescent. The clusters of flowers are erect. The seeds are at the centers of the 1-inch-wide fruits. Varieties of the wych elm include *U. g. atropurpurea*, with folded, purple leaves; the horned elm (*U. g. cornuta*), its larger leaves with three or five lobes at their apexes; the fern-leaved elm (*U. g. crispa* syn. *U. g. asplenifolia*), often with pendulous branches and with narrow, conspicuously saw-toothed leaves; *U. g. horizontalis* (syn. *U. g. pendula*), which has a wide crown of drooping, rigid, often elbowed branches;

U. g. lutescens, with yellow foliage; and *U. g. variegata*, with leaves variegated with white. The branchlets are pendulous. Another variety is the Exeter elm (*U. g. exoniensis*), of columnar habit.

Ulmus glabra horizontalis

English elm (**U. procera**), of western Europe, at its maximum is 150 feet tall. It has a trunk with deeply-fissured bark and usually a conspicuous growth of sucker shoots around its base. The head, more or less ovoid, is sometimes rather loose and open. Short-stalked, broad-elliptic to ovate, coarsely-double-toothed, and with very unequal bases, the leaves are 2 to 3 inches long or sometimes longer. They have rough-short-hairy upper surfaces, and pubescent undersides with tufts of white hairs in the vein axils. The dense, erect flower clusters are followed by fruits, ¾ to 1 inch across, with the seeds located well out of center and nearly touching their apexes. Variety *U. p. argenteo-variegata* has leaves with white variegation.

The Dutch elm (**U. hollandica**) is a hybrid, its parents *U. carpinifolia*, *U. glabra*, and *U. plotii*, the latter a slender native of Europe. Up to 120 feet tall, it characteris-

Ulmus procera

Ulmus hollandica (trunk)

tically has a comparatively short trunk and a head of wide-spreading to often drooping branches. It has deeply-fissured bark and it usually suckers from the bottom of the trunk. The pointed, broad-elliptic, double-toothed, markedly unequal-based leaves, 3 to 5 inches long and with twelve to fourteen pairs of veins, are nearly hairless and lustrous above and their undersides slightly pubescent. The flowers are erect, in clusters. The Belgian elm (*U. h. belgica*), pyramidal in outline, has a good straight trunk and leaves with fourteen to eighteen pairs of veins. Tall and narrow, *U. h. dampieri* has broadly-ovate, deeply-double-toothed leaves crowded on short branchlets. A wide, pyramidal head, hairy branchlets, and leaves softly-hairy on their undersides, very asymmetrical at their bases, and 4 to 5 inches long are characteristic of *U. h. dauvessei*. Vigorous *U. h. pitteursii* has broadly-ovate to obovate, hairy leaves up to 5 inches long. The Blenford elm (*U. h. superba*), narrowly-pyramidal, has leaves up to 5 inches long and, except for tufts in the vein axils, hairless on their undersides. Other elms that probably belong and are provisionally placed here are *U. h.* 'Klemmer', a fast grower that suckers from its base and forms a tall, dense, narrow-pyramidal head; dwarf *U. h. nana*, at ten years old not over 2 feet tall; and narrow *U. h. webbiana*, which has obovate to ovate leaves up to 3 inches long and folded lon-

Ulmus hollandica wredei

gitudinally. In outline narrowly-pyramidal, *U. h. wredei* has crowded, golden-yellow leaves. The Cornish elm (**U. angustifolia-cornubiensis** syns. *U. carpinifolia cornubiensis*, *U. stricta*), a native of southern England, has a narrow head of ascending or erect branches and elliptic to broadly-elliptic leaves more or less hairy on their undersides. The Wheatley or Guernsey or Jersey elm (**U. sarniensis** syns. *U. campestris wheatleyi*, *U. carpinifolia wheatleyi*), a hybrid between *U. angustifolia* and *U. hollandica*, has much the aspect of the Cornish elm, but is more rigidly erect and has broader leaves less hairy on their undersides.

Ulmus parvifolia (leaves and young fruits)

Chinese elm (**U. parvifolia**) is sometimes called evergreen elm because in climates as mild as that of southern California it retains its foliage throughout the year. Strains that have a most marked tendency to evergreenness are sometimes identified as *U. p. sempervirens*. The Chinese elm grows rapidly to a maximum height of 50 to 70 feet, under favorable conditions attaining one-half this in its first five or six years. Round-headed, densely-foliaged, and of somewhat pendulous growth, this native of China, Korea, and Japan has flaking bark responsible for a mottled effect of the trunk. Its twigs are pubescent into their second year. The single-toothed, elliptic to oblong-lanceolate, short-pointed leaves, slightly unequal at their bases, are ¾ inch to 2½ inches long. They are without hairs, except for sometimes a few in the axils of the veins on their undersides. The flowers come in late summer; the fruits are ⅓ inch long. Variety *U. p.* 'Brea' is more upright and has larger leaves; *U. p.* 'Drake' has somewhat pendulous branches and small leaves.

Ulmus parvifolia

Siberian elm (**U. pumila**), like the last, has single-toothed leaves with only slightly asymmetrical bases. Native from Turkestan to eastern Siberia, this ranges from being a shrubby small tree to a specimen 75 feet in height. Its shoots soon lose any initial hairiness they have. Elliptic to oblongish and ¾ inch to 2½ inches long, the leaves, which terminate in short points, are hairless except sometimes for some pubescence in the vein axils on their undersides. The flowers come in spring before the leaves expand. Varieties are *U. p. arborea*, which has glossy, narrowly-ovate to ovate-lanceolate leaves, and *U. p. pendula*, with pendulous branches and small leaves. Also believed to be a variety of the Siberian elm, although some authorities regard it as a variety of the English elm, *U. p. berardii* is bushy with slender, erect branches.

Garden and Landscape Uses. Elms are predominantly shade trees. They afford no displays of flowers or fruits nor is their fall color at all outstanding. The foliage of most then turns yellow, in regions of cold winters that of the Chinese elm becomes red.

Were it not for the prevalence of Dutch elm and phloem necrosis diseases many elms would be highly recommended, but in view of the deadly nature of these and with the knowledge that they are advancing into previously unaffected areas, prospective planters must be warned to carefully evaluate the risks before proceeding. So far as is known, no kind of elm is completely resistant. For the best chances of survival elms need regular annual care in such procedures as fertilizing, spraying,

and pruning. Elms transplant readily, but have wide-spreading and surface roots that make it difficult or impossible to grow other plants beneath old specimens. They do best in mellow, fertile soil that is well drained, but does not lack for moisture.

Cultivation. Propagation is by seed, which should be sown as soon as ripe, by suckers (some species, notably the English elm), and in the case of varieties by grafting. Weeping elms are often grafted high onto seedlings to permit their pendulous branches to be displayed to advantage. Pruning to establish desirable scaffold branches and staking to support the slender trunks are especially necessary during the first few years with Chinese and Siberian elms. Older specimens are likely to need thinning to prevent their heads from becoming so heavy that they are subject to storm damage. Fertilizing annually and watering deeply in dry weather promotes health. Regular spraying to control the elm bark beetle (which spreads Dutch elm disease) and other insects is important.

UMBELLIFERAE — Carrot Family. This widely dispersed family of dicotyledons includes such well-known vegetables as carrots, celery, parsnips, and, among others, the herbs anise, caraway, chervil, dill, and fennel. Its members are annuals, biennials, herbaceous perennials, and a few more or less shrubby kinds. There are some 250 genera containing approximately 2,800 species. They are mostly inhabitants of temperate, subarctic, arctic, and alpine regions. Most contain aromatic oils. Some, such as the poison-hemlock (*Conium maculatum*), of Socrates, are poisonous. Their stems are hollow and furrowed, their leaves alternate and usually much-divided. The basal parts of their stalks sheathe the stems. Bisexual or rarely unisexual, the small flowers, usually in umbels or compound umbels, less frequently in heads, have a five-lobed calyx, five each petals and stamens, and two styles. The fruits consist of a pair of dry, ribbed or winged achenes.

Among genera cultivated are *Aciphylla*, *Actinothus*, *Aegopodium*, *Ammi*, *Anethum*, *Angelica*, *Anisotome*, *Anthriscus*, *Apium*, *Arracacia*, *Astrantia*, *Athamanta*, *Azorella*, *Bupleurum*, *Carum*, *Chaerophyllum*, *Cicuta*, *Conium*, *Coriandrum*, *Crithmum*, *Cuminum*, *Cymopterus*, *Daucus*, *Erigenia*, *Eryngium*, *Ferula*, *Foeniculum*, *Hacquetia*, *Harbouria*, *Heracleum*, *Hydrocotyle*, *Laserpitium*, *Levisticum*, *Ligusticum*, *Lomatium*, *Meum*, *Molopospermum*, *Musineon*, *Myrrhis*, *Osmorhiza*, *Pastinaca*, *Perideridia*, *Petroselinum*, *Peucedanum*, *Pimpinella*, *Pseudocymopterus*, *Sanicula*, *Scandix*, *Sium*, *Smyrnium*, *Sphenosciadium*, *Taenidia*, *Trachymene*, and *Zizia*.

UMBELLULARIA (Umbel-lulària) — California-Laurel. The one species of *Umbellularia*, of the vast laurel family LAURACEAE, is the only member of the family indigenous to California. It is also a native in southern Oregon. Its name, from the Latin *umbellula*, a little umbel, refers to the arrangement of the flowers.

Like many other members of its family, the California-laurel (**U. californica**) is a handsome, aromatic, broad-headed, densely-foliaged, evergreen tree that in the open may attain a height of 80 feet and under forest conditions much more. It has scaly bark and short-stalked, ovate-oblong to lanceolate, pinnately-veined leaves up to 6 inches long. They are lustrous deep yellow-green above and more or less glaucous on their undersides. When mature, they are hairless. On stalks ½ to 1 inch long the many-flowered umbels of yellowish-green or purplish flowers are borne; in the bud stage they are enclosed by five or

Umbellularia californica

Umbellularia californica, a young specimen

Umbellularia californica (foliage and flowers)

six scales or bracts. Each umbel is ½ inch wide or slightly wider. The individual flowers are ¼ inch in diameter. They have a six-parted, early deciduous calyx, no petals, three rows of stamens, and an inner row of tiny staminodes (sterile stamens). The olive-like, yellowish-green to purplish fruits are about 1 inch long and contain a single seed. Variety *U. c. pendula* has drooping branchlets.

The beautiful wood of the California-laurel, often called Oregon myrtle, is highly esteemed for cabinetwork and interior trim. The bark and leaves contain a volatile oil, which if released by crushing and inhaled through the nostrils induces sneezing and is said to produce violent pain above the eyes. In the wild the California-laurel attains its greatest size in the more humid parts of its range; in drier regions, it is scarcer and less impressive.

Garden and Landscape Uses and Cultivation. Other than in regions of mild winters this tree is not hardy. This is unfortunate, for it is among America's most beautiful and stateliest evergreens. On the West Coast it is favored for planting as a

shade tree in home grounds and parks, and as a street tree. It prospers in an ordinary soil not subject to drought. As a native it sometimes grows, usually in rather stunted form, in apparently dry locations, but then its long roots reach deeply into the ground and tap sources of water that are not obvious from a casual inspection of the terrain. More commonly it occupies locations along watercourses. It thrives near the sea. Seed affords the readiest means of propagation. No special care is needed.

UMBILICUS (Umbíl-icus) — Navelwort or Pennywort. Natives of the Old World with the Mediterranean region their chief center of distribution, the eighteen species of *Umbilicus* belong in the orpine family CRASSULACEAE. Their name, from the Latin *umbilicus*, a navel, alludes to their leaves being depressed at their centers.

These are succulent herbaceous perennials with rhizomatous or tuberous rootstocks, and more or less circular basal leaves, sunken at their centers and often saucer-like, with their stalks attached at or near the middles of their undersides. Sometimes there is an opening between the point of attachment and the leaf margin, often there is not. The stem leaves are much smaller than the basal ones and are alternate. Usually branchless, the stems are erect and terminate in racemes or panicles of bloom. The calyxes are small and five-parted. The tubular or bell-shaped corollas have five more or less upright lobes (petals). There are ten or rarely five short stamens. The pistils have short styles or none. The follicles (seed pods that compose the fruits) are slender. From *Rosularia* this genus differs in not having its basal leaves in dense rosettes.

Navelwort or pennywort, so called from the appearance of its leaves, is **U. rupestris** (syns. *U. pendulinus*, *Cotyledon pendulina*, *C. umbilicus*). It is indigenous from southwest Europe to Scotland and is 8 inches to 1½

Umbilicus rupestris

feet tall. Its basal leaves, long-stalked and in loose, open rosettes, are bowl- or saucer-shaped. They are coarsely-toothed, have wavy margins, and are not cleft from the margins to the tops of the leafstalks. They are ¾ inch or more in diameter. Crowded in spirelike racemes or panicles, the tubular, usually pendent blooms, up to ⅓ inch long, have greenish-white or yellowish flowers that are sometimes tinged with pink or are red-dotted.

Two rather similar kinds sometimes confused with *U. rupestris* are *U. erectus* and *U. horizontalis*. Inhabiting moist rocks in shady places in the Balkans and southern Italy, **U. erectus** differs from the others discussed here in having more or less erect flowers with the lobes of their corollas as long or longer than the corolla tubes. The blooms are in dense racemes. In **U. horizontalis**, as opposed to *U. rupestris*, the portion of the stem that carries blooms does not exceed the lower, flowerless part in length, the slightly shorter and narrower blooms are held horizontally, and their sepals are pointed-lanceolate rather than ovate. Also, the stem leaves of *U. horizontalis* are more numerous and crowded than those of *U. rupestris*, and often many are linear.

Garden Uses and Cultivation. These plants are of more interest to gardeners concerned with variety than to those primarily considering display value or color. They are adapted for rock gardens and similar sites and grow without much care in well-drained soil in sun or part-day shade. They are hardy and are easily increased by seed and by leaf cuttings.

UMBRELLA. This word occurs as parts of the common names of these plants: Queensland umbrella tree (*Brassaia actinophylla*), Texas umbrella tree (*Melia azadirachta umbraculiformis*), umbrella leaf (*Diphylleia cymosa*), umbrella-pine (*Sciadopitys verticillata*), umbrella plant (*Cyperus alternifolius* and *Peltiphyllum peltatum*), and umbrella tree (*Magnolia tripetala*).

UMBRELLA WORT. See Mirabilis.

UMKOKOLA is *Dovyalis caffra*.

UNCARINA (Unca-rìna). Five endemic species of Malagasy (Madagascar) constitute *Uncarina*, of the pedalium family PEDALIACEAE. The name, from the Latin *uncus*, a hook, alludes to the hooked beaks of the seed capsules.

Uncarinas are dry region, deciduous shrubs and small trees, of which only one species appears to be cultivated. The specimen upon which the following description is based has been growing for many years in the succulent greenhouse at the Royal Botanic Gardens, Kew, England. It was raised from seed sent from Malagasy in 1939.

Uncarina grandidieri

Uncarina grandidieri (flowers)

A tree about 15 feet tall, **U. grandidieri** has long-stalked, three- to five-lobed, more or less sticky-hairy leaves with blades, of variable outline, up to 5 inches long by 6 inches broad; those on flowering shoots are smaller than the others. In clusters on young shoots, the flowers have a calyx of five sepals, and a 2½-inch-long corolla with a narrow tube and an oblique face of five wide-spreading, somewhat unequal, about 1-inch-long, rounded, rich yellow lobes (petals). The throat of the flower is stained with purplish-red. There are four fertile stamens, one rudimentary staminode (sterile stamen), and one style. The fruits are capsules.

Garden Uses and Cultivation. Showy in bloom and, because of its rarity, of interest at all times, the species described here may be expected to thrive outdoors in warm desert and semidesert regions such as southern California. At Kew it has prospered planted in a ground bed of well-drained soil in a sunny greenhouse where a minimum winter night temperature of 60°F is maintained. The greenhouse is ventilated freely in summer. Little or no

water is given in winter, but from May until November the soil is kept moderately moist and occasional applications of dilute liquid fertilizer are given. Propagation is by seed and by air layering.

UNDERSHRUB. See Subshrub.

UNDERSTOCK. See Stock.

UNDERWATER-ROSE is *Samolus parviflorus*.

UNGNADIA (Ung-nàdia)—Texas-Buckeye or Mexican-Buckeye or Spanish-Buckeye. The deciduous shrub or small tree that is the only species of *Ungnadia* is endemic to Texas, New Mexico, and adjacent Mexico. It belongs to the soapberry family SAPINDACEAE and has a name commemorating Baron Ungnad, who in 1576 sent the first seeds of common horsechestnut (*Aesculus hippocastanum*) from the Balkans to western Europe.

Texas-, Mexican-, or Spanish-buckeye (**U. speciosa**) is rarely 30 feet tall. Its alternate, pinnate, lustrous leaves are divided into three to seven ovate to ovate-lanceolate, pointed, toothed leaflets up to 4½ inches long by under 1½ inches wide. Hairy on their undersides when young, they soon become hairless. Appearing in spring in lateral clusters, before or with the leaves, the sweet-scented, 1-inch-wide, purplish-pink flowers have deeply-five-lobed calyxes, and four or five obovate petals, hairy and crested toward their bases. There are seven to ten red-anthered stamens. The fruits are leathery, three-lobed, nonprickly capsules, 1½ to 2 inches across, containing several large dark brown to black, poisonous seeds. These are used as marbles by children.

Garden and Landscape Uses and Cultivation. Not hardy in the north, the Texas-buckeye is sometimes planted for ornament in the south and southwest. It succeeds in ordinary, well-drained soils in open locations and is propagated by seed.

UNICORN PLANT. See Proboscidea.

UNIOLA (Unì-ola) — Sea-Oats or Spike Grass. Two species constitute this New World genus of the grass family GRAMINEAE. The name, derived from the Latin *unus*, one, has no obvious application. The plant previously named *Uniola latifolia* is *Chasmanthium latifolium*.

Uniolas are perennials with spreading rhizomes and hairless, erect stems. Their flowers are in panicles of flattened, straw-colored to purplish flower spikelets, reminiscent of those of oats.

Sea-oats or spike grass (**U. paniculata**) inhabits coastal dunes and sands from Virginia to Florida and Texas and in the West Indies. From 2 to 8 feet tall, it has extensively creeping rhizomes. The blades of its leaves are up to 1¼ feet long by under ½ inch wide. The crowded flower panicles have branches at first erect, drooping with age. The numerous 1- to 2-inch-long, pointed-ovate spikelets are straw-colored.

Garden and Landscape Uses. This quite attractive grass is useful for stabilizing dunes. Its flowers are quite charming when cut, and either fresh or dried can be usually employed for indoor decoration. Unfortunately its aggressive, spreading habit of growth renders sea-oats unacceptable for general use in gardens.

Cultivation. Provided the soil is sandy and sufficiently moist this species prospers. It may be propagated by seed and by division.

UPAS TREE is *Antiaris toxicaria*.

URBINIA. See Echeveria.

URCEOCHARIS (Urceo-chàris). This name, its "ch" pronounced as "k," is applied to hybrids between *Urceolina* and *Eucharis*, of the amaryllis family AMARYLLIDACEAE. It is derived from the names of the parent genera.

Rare in cultivation, **U. clibranii** is a man-made hybrid raised in England toward the end of the nineteenth century. Intermediate between its parents, which are *Urceolina urceolata* and *Eucharis grandiflora*, it has broad, pointed-ovate leaves and long-stalked umbels of 2½-inch-long, pure white flowers with slender corolla tubes, and petals that form a cupped face to the bloom. The stamens are almost as long as the petals. The corona or cup between the stamens is toothed. Similar to *U. clibranii*, but without teeth on the corona, **U. edentata** is a natural hybrid that originated in tropical America.

Garden and Landscape Uses and Cultivation. These are as for *Eucharis*.

URCEOLINA (Urceo-lìna). To the amaryllis family AMARYLLIDACEAE belongs *Urceolina*, an Andean genus of about five species. The name comes from the Latin *urceolus*, a small pitcher, and alludes to the form of the flower.

Urceolinas are attractive, deciduous bulb plants with stalked, flat, ovate, oblong, or strap-shaped leaves. Their flowers are in umbels atop leafless, solid stalks. There are two papery bracts at the base of each umbel. At first the blooms are erect, but gradually they become horizontal or pendulous. The perianth tube, narrowly-cylindrical below, expands abruptly into a much broader portion. It has six nearly similar, short, spreading lobes (petals). There are six stamens and a style, all protruding. The fruits are capsules.

Most frequent in cultivation, **U. peruviana** (syn. *U. miniata*) has short-stalked, strap-shaped leaves narrowed toward both ends. They have recurved margins and are 6 inches to 1 foot long by about 1½ inches wide. Usually there are only one or two leaves. The flower stalks, from 8 inches to 1 foot in length or somewhat longer, carry six or fewer scarlet to cinnabar-red blooms approximately 1½ inches in length. A hybrid between *Urceolina* and *Eucharis* is named *Urceocharis*.

Garden Uses and Cultivation. Usually *U. peruviana* is grown in greenhouses, but it succeeds outdoors in regions where no severe freezing occurs. Its cultural needs are very similar to those of amaryllises (*Hippeastrum*), but in greenhouses it grows well where the winter night temperature is 55°F and that by day five to fifteen degrees higher. Full sun, except in the hottest part of summer, is needed. New root growth begins in July, the time to plant or repot. Four to six bulbs can be accommodated in a 5-inch pot. When leaves are present and growth is active, watering should be done freely, but with greater restraint after the foliage matures and the plants begin to rest. During the dormant season the soil is kept dry. Well-rooted bulbs benefit from occasional applications of dilute liquid fertilizer. Propagation is by seed, offsets, and bulb cuttings.

UREA. A highly soluble, slightly acidifying, synthetic fertilizer, urea contains about 42 percent nitrogen. Its chief use, like that of sodium nitrate (nitrate of soda), is for "shot-in-the-arm" treatments rather than as a long-time source of nutrient. It may be used in spring and summer at about ⅓ ounce to 10 square feet or as liquid fertilizer at ⅒ to ⅕ ounce to a gallon of water.

UREA-FORM FERTILIZERS. Sold under various trade names, these are synthetic combinations of urea and formaldehyde. As compared with urea and other man-made nitrogenous fertilizers, they more closely resemble natural manures in that the nitrogen they contain is released slowly over a period of several weeks or months. They are thus well adapted for spring application to lawns and other areas where a continuous supply of nitrogen is desirable over a fairly long period. Follow the manufacturer's recommendations about amounts to use.

URECHITES (Urechìt-es) — Wild-Allamanda. The one, or according to some authorities two, species of *Urechites* belongs to the dogbane family APOCYNACEAE. The genus inhabits southern Florida, the West Indies, and Central America. It is closely related to *Mandevilla*. The name, from the Greek *oura*, a tail, and the name of related *Echites*, alludes to the twisted appendages of the anthers.

A twining, tall-climbing vine, or sometimes prostrate with more or less erect branches, variable **U. lutea** has hairless or pubescent stems, and opposite, very short-stalked, elliptic to ovate, obovate, or nearly round leaves, glossy above and sometimes sparsely to distinctly velvety-hairy on their undersides. They are 1½ to 3 inches long. The bright yellow, allamanda-like blooms have calyxes with five fairly long, narrow, pointed lobes. The corollas have goblet-shaped tubes up to 2 inches in length, which are 1½ to 3 inches across their faces. They have five spreading, usually not overlapping corolla lobes (petals) that curve to give a propeller-like appearance to the faces of the blooms. The fruits are paired, slender, podlike follicles 4 to 7½ inches long.

Garden and Landscape Uses and Cultivation. This is a pretty vine for gardens in the tropics and almost or quite frostless subtropics, and can also be grown in greenhouses. It responds to the same conditions as *Trachelospermum* and *Mandevilla* with the exception that the soil must be decidedly wet for its satisfactory growth.

URERA (Ùr-era) — Cowitch or Chichicaste. Except that they are occasionally grown for educational purposes in botanical collections, the sorts of *Urera*, of the nettle family URTICACEAE, have no attractions for gardeners. They are furnished with viciously-stinging hairs that can make a brush against them painful and even dangerous. Their name, from the Latin *uro*, to burn or sting, is of evident application. The genus occurs in many tropical regions. It comprises thirty-five species.

Ureras are trees and shrubs with alternate leaves and generally unisexual, but sometimes bisexual small flowers in panicles. Male blooms have four- or five-parted perianths and four or five stamens, females have four-lobed perianths that become fleshy and enclose the seedlike achenes (properly the fruits) to form berrylike masses.

Described as one of the most dangerous plants of Central America and common there and in adjacent regions, cowitch or

Urera baccifera

chichicaste (**U. baccifera**) is a shrub or tree up to 20 feet tall. It has rough-hairy, narrow- to broad-ovate leaves, up to 1¼ feet long, with prickly veins and coarsely-toothed margins. Its flowers, with minute white petals, are many together in much-branched, pink to deep red panicles up to 3 inches in length. The waxy-white fruits are about ¹⁄₁₀ inch long.

A shrub or tree up to about 50 feet in height, but often much lower, and armed with slender, stinging hairs, **U. caracasana** is native from Mexico to tropical South America and the West Indies. Of varying shapes, its leaves may be round-ovate to elliptic and are up to 1 foot long by nearly as broad. They are more finely-toothed than those of *U. baccifera*. The tiny greenish flowers are many together in forking clusters up to 5 inches long and broad. When mature the small fleshy fruits are bright red.

Garden and Landscape Uses and Cultivation. In the tropics ureas are used for fencing cattle. Skin contact with them causes extreme pain and inflammation that lasts for several hours. They should not be planted where likely to be brushed by people. In botanical collections they should be isolated and prominently posted with warning signs. Ordinary soil, and sun or part-shade outdoors in warm climates, or in a humid greenhouse with a minimum winter temperature of 60°F, give good results. Propagation is by seed. Stout, protective gloves are needed when handling these plants.

URGINEA (Urgín-ea)—Sea-Onion or Squill. Of the estimated 100 species of this genus of bulb plants native to the Mediterranean region, Canary Islands, Africa, and warmer parts of Asia, only one, the sea-onion, squill, or red squill, seems to have found its way at all into common cultivation. This must not be confused with the other plants called squill (*Scilla*). The group belongs in the lily family LILIACEAE. Its name is derived from that of an Arabian tribe in Algeria named Ben Urgin.

Urgineas are related to *Scilla, Eremurus,* and *Camassia,* but differ in having markedly flattened seeds and in other details. They have all-basal, mostly slender, deciduous leaves. Their flowers are in branchless racemes. They are white and shallowly-bell- to wheel-shaped. There are six perianth segments (usually called petals), six stamens, often with flattened stalks, and a slender style ending in a knoblike stigma. The fruits are three-sided capsules containing blackish or black, disklike, often winged seeds. In some species the bulbs are very large, those of *Urginea altissima,* of South Africa, described as being "as big as a man's head."

Sea-onion bulbs are sources of the once popular medicine syrup of squills, used to relieve croup in babies and children, and

of a very effective rat poison that has the particular virtue of not being harmful to animals other than rodents. It is very effective because rodents are unable to regurgitate, whereas the stomachs of other animals reject the poison. Whether the medicine and rat poison are prepared from slightly different varieties of the same species or whether the result depends upon the method of preparation of the commercial products does not appear to be clearly established.

The sea-onion (**U. maritima** syn. *Scilla maritima*) is native throughout the Mediterranean region. Variable, it has been regarded as representing several distinct species by some botanists, but that is not the common view. Its more or less globose, green- or reddish-skinned bulbs, 4 to 6 inches in diameter, are usually partly aboveground. From their apexes develop many fleshy, glaucous-green, hairless, pointed-lanceolate leaves, 1 foot to 1½ feet long. The purplish, erect flower stalks,

Urginea maritima (flowers)

brittle and naked of foliage, are up to 4 feet tall, the upper foot being a dense raceme of out-facing starry blooms that open in succession from below upward. They are about ¾ inch across and greenish-white, with a greenish-purple to brownish keel down the back of each wide-spreading petal. The stamens, with pale greenish stalks and green anthers, are shorter than the petals. The style is short. The fruits are ¾-inch-long capsules. The flowers come in fall when the bulb is without foliage.

Garden and Landscape Uses. The sea-onion does not survive much frost. Outdoors it is best suited for regions of mild winters and hot, dry summers. It may be used in groups in borders, at the fronts of shrub plantings, in large rock gardens, and for naturalizing. Its tall spires of bloom suggest those of slender foxtail-lilies (*Eremurus*), and it can be used to produce the same interesting vertical accents. A good employment for the sea-onion is in association with yuccas. It blooms at a different season and the yucca foliage complements the tall naked flower stalks of the urgineas.

As a pot plant, the sea-onion is very easy to grow, but because of its size it is more of a curiosity than a generally useful window garden plant. It is often included in greenhouse collections of plants useful to man.

Cultivation. The first essential to the successful cultivation of the sea-onion is that the soil be thoroughly well drained, its chemical characteristics being less important than its physical condition. This plant grows well in slightly acid to slightly alkaline soil, which must be dry during the bulb's dormant season. Full sun is needed. When accommodated in containers, repotting, except with small, young plants, is needed at intervals of a few years only.

Urginea maritima

Watering should be copious when new growth begins until the foliage begins to die naturally, then it should be gradually reduced and finally stopped. When foliage is present, occasional applications of dilute liquid fertilizer may be given. Indoors, from fall to spring, a minimum winter temperature of 45 to 50°F is appropriate, with a daytime increase of a few degrees permitted. Seeds afford a ready means of propagation; bulb cuttings are also satisfactory. Natural offsets also provide increase.

UROPAPPUS. See Microseris.

UROPETALUM. See Dipcadi.

UROSPERMUM (Uro-spérmum). The only two species, one annual and one perennial, of *Urospermum,* of the daisy family COMPOSITAE, are natives of the Mediterranean region. One is occasionally cultivated. The name, from the Greek *oura,* a tail, and *sperma,* a seed, alludes to the seeds being beaked.

Urospermums have lobed or toothed leaves, those on the stems alternate and stalkless, and long-stalked, solitary flower heads. These are of many yellow florets and a bell-shaped involucre (collar of bracts behind the florets). All the florets are strap-shaped and five-toothed at their apexes. The seedlike fruits are achenes.

Perennial in the wild, but sometimes behaving as a biennial in cultivation, softly-hairy **U. dalechampii** forms a wide clump

Urospermum dalechampii

and attains a height of 1 foot to 1½ feet. It has variously-toothed leaves, the lower ones dandelion-like, oblanceolate to obovate, and deeply-pinnately-lobed, those above ovate to lanceolate and often lobeless. The 1½- to 2-inch-wide heads of lemon-yellow flowers, streaked on their outsides with red, terminate leafless stalks that are continuations of the stems.

Garden Uses and Cultivation. The species described here is sometimes grown in borders and for cut flowers. It is easily raised from seed sown outdoors about June and the seedlings transplanted to nursery beds, to be moved to their flow-

ering sites in fall or spring. Where the plants behave as biennials, sowings are made each year. Any ordinary well-drained soil in a sunny location is suitable. The precise hardiness of this species is not determined.

URSINIA (Ursín-ia). The genus *Ursinia,* of the daisy family COMPOSITAE, includes the plants once named *Sphenogyne.* In the wild limited almost entirely to South Africa, but one kind, *U. annua,* occurring also in Ethiopia, it consists of nearly forty species. The name honors the botanical author Johann Ursinus, of Regensburg, who died in 1666.

Annuals, herbaceous perennials, and subshrubs constitute this genus. They have alternate, usually pinnately-lobed or pinnate, toothed leaves; much less often the leaves are undivided, lobeless, and toothless. The long-stalked, solitary or rarely loosely clustered, yellow, orange, or red, daisy-type flower heads have tubular, bisexual disk florets and usually sexually nonfunctional, but sometimes fertile female ray florets. The seedlike fruits are ten-ribbed achenes.

Annual **U. anthemoides** (syn. *U. pulchra*) is a good-looking hairless or slightly hairy species, about 1 foot tall, with leaves deeply-pinnately-dissected into slender flat or threadlike lobes. Its numerous flower heads, on long, erect stalks, nod until nearly fully open and then face upward. From 1 inch to 1½ inches in diameter, they are yellow to orange-yellow with the petal-like ray florets purplish beneath. Variety *U. a. versicolor* differs in having shorter-stalked flower heads about 2 inches in diameter, the ray florets of which have a purple-brown spot at their bases. Its leaves are twice-pinnately-cut into linear lobes. Rather like *U. a. versicolor,* but with less

Ursinia anthemoides

Ursinia anethoides versicolor

Ursinia chrysanthemoides geyeri

Ursinia sericea

Ursinia anethoides

divided, somewhat fleshy leaves is **U. cakilifolia,** an annual with 1½- to 2-inch-wide, deep orange flower heads. Yet another annual, **U. speciosa** is 1 foot to 2 feet tall and hairless. It has leaves pinnately-lobed into linear or oblong-linear, bristle-tipped segments and, on 6-inch-long stalks, flower heads, about 2½ inches across, with purple-black centers and orange rays.

Herbaceous perennial ursinias, generally not long-lived in cultivation and usually propagated anew each year, include **U. anethoides,** a bushy kind 1 foot to 2 feet tall. This has crowded leaves 1 inch to 1½ inches long, thinly-hairy or hairless, and pinnately-cut into linear, subcylindrical segments. The brilliant golden-yellow flower heads are about 1 inch in diameter. A kind with rooting stems, **U. chrysanthemoides** has deeply-lobed leaves, and yellow flower heads, 1 inch to 1½ inches across, that have ray florets usually darker on their undersides than above. Beautiful **U. c. geyeri** (syn. **U. geyeri**) differs from all other ursinias in its flower heads being brilliant red.

Unlike other kinds discussed here in its having finely-cut, wonderfully silvery, silky-hairy foliage, **U. sericea,** 8 inches to about 15 inches tall, has very long-stalked, yellow flower heads approximately 1½ inches in diameter.

Garden and Landscape Uses. Cultivated ursinias are showy outdoor flower garden plants and are very worthwhile for growing in pots for late winter and spring display in cool greenhouses. Like those of so many South African annuals of the daisy family, their flower heads close in darkness and have a tendency to do so on dull days. This limits their usefulness as cut flowers, for which purpose they otherwise are highly acceptable. In climates to their liking, they are splendid for formal beds, grouping in mixed flower borders, and planting in drifts in more informal landscapes. They do best where summers are moderate. Under torrid, humid conditions their flowers are fewer and smaller and the plants tend to peter out. Because of this, where such conditions prevail, it is best to raise young plants indoors, set them out as soon as danger of frost is over, enjoy their flowering early in the season, and then pull them out and replace with more heat-tolerant kinds as soon as they show signs of distress.

Cultivation. Perennial ursinias are hardy only where little or no frost occurs in climates of the Mediterranean or Californian kind. Where harsher winters occur, they may be wintered in pots in a cool, sunny greenhouse or be raised from seed each year and treated as annuals; the latter procedure is usually followed with *U. anethoides.* Ursinias prefer porous, not too fertile soil that is very well drained. They abhor excessive moisture and do not tolerate shade. They may be raised from seed sown in early spring or in very mild climates in fall, where the plants are to remain, and the seedlings thinned out to 6 to 9 inches apart, or in poor soils to perhaps 4 inches apart, depending upon the vigor of the species and the spread the plants are expected to make. An alternative method is to sow seed indoors in a temperature of 55 to 60°F about eight weeks before the expected last frost and to transplant to the garden shortly after the last frost. Summer care consists of little more than staking to prevent storm damage and removing faded flower heads. To have plants in 5- or 6-inch pots for spring blooming in greenhouses, seeds are sown in September or October. Smaller plants can be had from January sowings. As soon as the seedlings are large enough to handle they are transplanted individually to small pots and, as growth makes necessary, to successively larger ones. To promote bushiness, the tips of the stems are pinched out when the seedlings are about 3 inches high. Throughout, the plants are grown in full sun where the temperature at night is 45 to 50°F and that on dull days about five degrees higher. In sunny weather a rise of ten to fifteen degrees is permissible. On all favorable occasions the greenhouse is ventilated freely. The soil is maintained always moderately moist, and when the final pots are filled with roots, a program of weekly applications of dilute liquid fertilizer is initiated. In greenhouses ursinias commonly grow considerably taller than outdoors. Neat staking and tying are generally necessary.

URTICA (Ur-tica)—Nettle. About fifty species of *Urtica*, of the nettle family URTICACEAE, are recognized, members of a genus widely distributed in temperate and subtropical regions. The name, the ancient Latin one of the nettle, is derived from *uro*, to burn, in allusion to the stinging hairs.

This genus includes annual and perennial herbaceous plants with fibrous stems and opposite, variously toothed and sometimes lobed leaves. Stems and foliage are furnished with hairs, usually, to a greater or lesser degree, stinging. The unisexual flowers are in panicles, spikes, or rounded clusters from the leaf axils. The sexes may be on separate or the same plants. The males have four sepals, the same number of slender-stalked stamens, and a vestigial ovary. The two outer sepals of the female blooms are very much smaller than the two inner. There is one style. The small fruits, technically achenes, are enclosed by the persistent pair of larger sepals.

Young shoots of the common nettle and its American variety, cooked like spinach, provide a tasty, healthful food. They may be used as potherbs. In Europe a nearly nonalcoholic, refreshing, fizzing beverage, called nettle beer in Great Britain, is made from more mature shoots. The flaxlike fibers of the stems of this species are of excellent quality and have been used for fabrics described as more beautiful and durable than linen. Nettles have long been used in folk medicines, at one time stinging with nettle foliage was held to be an effective treatment for arthritis.

Urtica dioica

The common nettle (*U. dioica*) is a variable, hardy perennial, widely distributed in both the Old World and the New World. The native American phase, which differs from the typical European species in having less coarsely-toothed, lanceolate to ovate-lanceolate leaves and in being without or nearly without stinging hairs, is *U. d. procera*. Typical *U. dioica*, which occurs as an introduced weed in North America, spreads by underground rhizomes and has erect, usually branchless stems 1 foot to 4 feet tall, or sometimes up to 6 feet tall. The plants are usually single-sexed or predominantly so. Native to Europe, it has slender-stalked, sharply-toothed, pointed-heart-shaped, dull green leaves up to 4½ inches long or sometimes longer. Its slen-

der, greenish, spikelike tassels of blooms are spreading or somewhat pendulous in fruit. This kind has painfully stinging hairs.

The Roman nettle (*U. pilulifera*), of southern Europe, is an annual of some decorative appeal, up to 3 feet tall, with ovate, toothed leaves that have blades 1 inch to 3 inches long. Male and female flowers are on different plants, the former in spikes, the latter, which have an inflated calyx, in long-stalked, spherical, green heads, ⅓ inch or slightly more in diameter, from the leaf axils.

Urtica pilulifera

Garden Uses and Cultivation. The common nettle deserves a place in herb gardens and other collections of plants useful to man. Of little or no ornamental merit, it should be located where people are not likely to brush against it. When working near nettles, cover exposed parts of the body and take care that the face is not brought into contact with the plants. This species and its variety grow best in rich, dampish soil in part-day shade or sun and are very easily increased by seed and by division. The Roman nettle is sometimes grown as a decorative in flower borders and in pots in greenhouses. Sow seed in ordinary soil in spring and thin the seedlings to stand 6 to 8 inches apart. As pot plants, single specimens are satisfactory in 5- or 6-inch containers.

URTICACEAE — Nettle Family. Approximately 500 species distributed among more than forty genera constitute this predominantly tropical family of dicotyledons. Included are herbaceous plants, shrubs, and trees. They have watery sap and sometimes stinging hairs. The leaves are alternate or opposite, and undivided. Gener-

ally unisexual with the sexes on the same or different plants, rarely bisexual, the tiny, often inconspicuous flowers, in clusters from the leaf axils, less often solitary, have a perianth of four or five separate or partially united segments, as many stamens as perianth parts, and one style. The fruits are seedlike achenes or drupes.

Among genera cultivated are *Boehmeria*, *Debregeasia*, *Elatostema*, *Gesnouinia*, *Laportea*, *Myriocarpa*, *Parietaria*, *Pellionia*, *Pilea*, *Soleirolia*, *Urera*, and *Urtica*.

UTAHIA. See Pediocactus.

UTRICULARIA (Utric-ulària) — Bladderwort. Carnivorous plants of more botanical than horticultural interest compose *Utricularia*, of the bladderwort family LENTIBULARIACEAE. They are widely distributed aquatics and wet-soil plants, or in tropical rain forests epiphytes (plants that perch on trees, but take no nourishment from their hosts). The name derives from the Latin *utriculus*, a small bag, and alludes to the tiny animal-trapping bladders of many kinds. In *Utricularia* there is no clear morphological separation between roots, stems, and leaves. Possibly the parts ordinarily and understandably so identified belong to a single system of stems. Botanists are not in agreement as to the number of species. Estimates range from 120 to 300.

Bladderworts include annuals and perennials. Their leaves vary greatly according to species. Those of aquatic sorts, generally finely dissected and frequently not in evidence when the plants are in bloom, like the stems and sometimes the roots, bear tiny bladders. A highly specialized group of floating utricularias lives only in the reservoirs of water that fill the cups formed by the bases of the leaves of certain bromeliads. Terrestrial utricularias have mostly linear to spatula-shaped or sometimes broader leaves, and usually fewer bladders or, in some sorts, only malformed nonfunctional bladders. The aquatic kinds project their flowers on short stems above the surface. Their bladders, often very numerous, are each furnished with an inward-opening trapdoor triggered by bristles that extend outward and that when touched, as by a tiny crustacean, water flea, or other animal, cause the trap to open and the bladder to suddenly expand. The consequent inrush of water is likely to suck the creature into the bladder. Then the trap closes. Following death, the victim's body decays and supplies nutrients to the plant. Not until the creature is digested does the trap open again. The flowers of bladderworts are very asymmetrical. They have two-lipped calyxes, and tubular, spurred, two-lipped corollas with the lips lobed or not. Yellow, violet, or white, they occur in racemes or are solitary at the ends of the stems.

Popular for aquariums, *U. minor,* a native of much of North America, Europe, and temperate Asia and very hardy, has threadlike stems up to about 1 foot long that creep over bottoms under shallow waters. Its leaves, up to ⅓ inch long, are one to three times forked into slender, flat segments; they have few bladders. Yellow flowers, up to ⅓ inch long and with a lower lip twice as long as the upper, are borne two to nine together on stalks up to 8 inches in length. Also grown in aquariums, nonhardy Australian and southern Asian *U. exoleta* (syn. *U. gibba*) has hairlike, floating stems and threadlike, bladder-bearing leaves up to 3 inches long. On stalks 3 to 4 inches long, the yellow flowers, about ¼ inch long, have upper and lower lips of approximately equal length.

Suitable for cultivation in outdoor pools, hardy *U. vulgaris,* of North America, Europe, and Asia, is an aquatic with very leafy stems, up to 6 feet long, that float just beneath the water surface. The leaves, ½ inch to 1½ inches long and repeatedly forked into threadlike segments, have many conspicuous bladders. Rising up to 1 foot above the surface, the flowering stalks carry four to twenty about 1-inch-wide, yellow blooms.

Tropical perennial species include *U. alpina,* of South America and the West Indies, which has little tubers and stalked, elliptic-lanceolate leaves 4 to 6 inches long. From 1½ to 1¾ inches across, its flowers, from one to four on erect, slender stalks longer than the leaves, are white with an orange-yellow blotch on the lower lip and a stout, curved spur. Brazilian *U. longifolia* develops crowded tufts of stalked, bright green, strap-shaped leaves up to 1 foot long. Its slender, up-to-2-foot-long flowering stalks carry up to twelve approximately 1¾-inch-wide rosy-lilac blooms, each with a golden-yellow blotch on the lower lip. Remarkable *U. reniformis,* of Brazil, grows in its homeland in the reservoirs of water contained in the bases of the leaf sheaths of large bromeliads. It propagates by seed and by sending out long, slender runners, which, when they reach water, develop young plantlets from their tips. This species has long-stalked leaves with kidney-shaped to nearly circular blades 2 to 3½ inches wide by nearly as long. The beautiful pale violet to blue flowers have, on their upper lip, two longitudinal yellow ridges. The flowers are few to several toward the apexes of stalks up to 2 feet long. The flowers are ¾ inch to 1½ inches long.

Garden Uses and Cultivation. Occasionally grown as botanical curiosities, bladderworts need various treatments depending upon their habits. Submerged aquatic kinds are best accommodated in aquariums. Those that grow naturally in wet, spongy earth can be kept in deep saucers or shallow pans (shallow pots) containing a little sandy, peaty soil and filled with water in which living sphagnum moss is growing or they can be planted in sandy, peaty soil in containers partly immersed or, for some kinds, submerged an inch or two below the surface. Success has been had with some tropical epiphytic species by growing them in hanging baskets filled with fibrous, peaty compost of a kind that suits many epiphytic orchids. All kinds need high humidity. Temperatures must be approximately those characteristic of the climates to which the species are accustomed to in the wild, which range from tropical to cold-temperate.

UVULARIA (Uvul-ària) — Bellwort or Merrybells. Endemic to eastern North America, the five species of *Uvularia* belong in the lily family LILIACEAE. The name comes from the Latin *uvula,* the soft palate, in fanciful and far-fetched allusion to the pendent blooms.

Bellworts are hardy, deciduous herbaceous perennials with slender rhizomes and clustered, branching, erect stems, leafy mostly in their upper parts. The leaves are alternate and stalkless, in some kinds perfoliate (with the stem apparently passing through the leaf). Usually solitary at the branch ends, the slender, nodding, bell-shaped flowers have six separate petal-like segments and stamens with anthers much longer than their filaments (stalks). The fruits are three-sided capsules. To some extent these plants suggest Solomon's seals (*Polygonatum*), but are of frailer, more delicate aspect and have larger bells.

Having perfoliate leaves and yellow flowers, *U. perfoliata* and *U. grandiflora* are natives of rich woods from Quebec southward and westward. The range of the first extends to Ohio, Tennessee, Florida, and Louisiana. It prefers acid soils. The other, favoring calcareous soils, ranges to Minnesota, Tennessee, and Oklahoma. They can be told apart by their perianth segments; those of *U. perfoliata* have inner surfaces clothed with short, glandular hairs; those of *U. grandiflora* are hairless. When in bloom *U. perfoliata* is 6 inches to 1 foot in height; *U. grandiflora* may be slightly taller. Both increase in height after flowering and may ultimately become 2 to 3 feet tall. The ovate to oblong-lanceolate leaves of *U. perfoliata* are up to 3½ inches long at maturity; those of *U. grandiflora* may attain 4½ inches in length and are similarly shaped. The blooms of *U. perfol-*

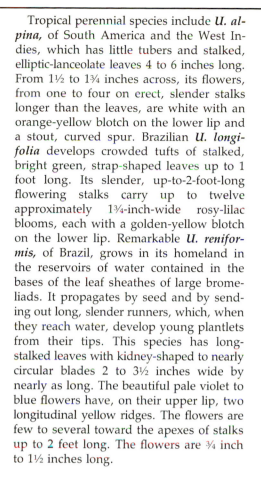

Utricularia alpina

Utricularia longifolia (foliage)

Utricularia longifolia

Utricularia reniformis (foliage)

Uvularia grandiflora

iata are ¾ inch to 1½ inches long; those of *U. grandiflora* 1 inch to 2 inches long.

Similar to each other, but differing from the sorts previously discussed in having leaves that are not perfoliate, are *U. sessilifolia* and *U. pudica*. An inhabitant of moist and dry woods from Quebec to Minnesota, South Dakota, South Carolina, Tennessee, and Arkansas, **U. sessilifolia** (syn. *Oakesiella sessilifolia*) at blooming time is 4 inches to 1 foot tall, but becomes taller later. Its mature leaves are elliptic and up to 3½ inches long. The pale straw-colored flowers are up to 2 inches long, their styles joined for two-thirds or more up from their bases. Indigenous from New Jersey to West Virginia and Georgia, **U. caroliniana** (syn. *U. pudica*) has lustrous leaves, green on their undersides, but otherwise similar to those of *U. sessilifolia*. They often persist through the winter. The flowers are greenish-yellow and 2 inches or rather less long, their styles are separate to well below their middles. Distinguished from *U. sessilifolia* by its narrower, pointed sepals and petals and in having a bract just behind each flower stalk, **U. floridana** occurs in woods of the coastal plain from Georgia to Florida, and in Alabama.

Garden Uses. These are delightful plants of modest mien for woodlands, rock gardens, and informal areas; they can be made equally comfortable in beds and borders of mixed perennials. The bellworts are a tolerant race. Although by nature woodlanders that normally grow in shade and succeed in shaded gardens, they prosper in sunny locations provided they have ample moisture. Because of this, they are well suited for planting at watersides where they can root in ground that is well above the water level, but kept constantly moist by seepage from below. They adjust to any ordinary garden soil, preferring one that is loose and contains an abundance of organic matter. They respond to fertilization, and specimens cultivated in well-nourished flower beds are likely to become much larger and to flower more profusely than those under more natural conditions. The showiest kind is *U. grandiflora*.

Cultivation. Uvularias are easily increased by division in early spring or early fall and by seeds sown, as soon as they are ripe, in a shaded cold frame or outdoor bed where they can remain undisturbed in sandy, peaty soil kept evenly moist, but not saturated. In their permanent locations, a distance of 6 to 8 inches between newly set young plants or divisions is satisfactory. Routine care is minimal. The removal of dead stems and foliage in fall and, if the soil is dryish, watering in times of drought are about all that is necessary. The maintenance of a mulch of peat moss, leaf mold, compost, or similar organic material is helpful and so is an annual application in spring of a complete fertilizer.

V

VACCARIA (Vac-cària) — Cow Herb. Four species closely related to *Saponaria* and belonging to the pink family CARYOPHYLLACEAE comprise *Vaccaria*. One is cultivated. The name is the Latin *vaccaria*, a cow pasture. It alludes to the use of the plants for forage.

Consisting of freely-branching annuals with opposite, undivided leaves, and loose clusters of small pink, red, or occasionally white flowers, *Vaccaria* is native to Europe and temperate Asia. From *Saponaria* it differs in its flowers having much inflated, five-winged calyxes, the wings being especially prominent in the fruiting stage, and in its petals being without scalelike appendages at the bases of their blades. There are five petals, ten stamens, and two or rarely three styles. The fruits are capsules.

Vaccaria pyramidata

Cow herb (*V. pyramidata* syns. *V. segetalis, Saponaria vaccaria*) is 1 foot to 2 feet tall. It has stalkless, lanceolate to ovate, bluish-green leaves 2 to 4 inches long by approximately one-third as broad. The loosely clustered, slender-stalked flowers, ¾ to 1 inch in diameter, have flask-shaped calyxes, ½ to ¾ inch long, and five spreading, pink petals with notched, blunt ends. This species is widely naturalized in North America as far north as Alaska. Variety *V. p. alba* has white flowers.

Garden Uses and Cultivation. Cow herb is useful for the fronts of flower borders and for cutting. It is of the easiest culture and will grow in any ordinary, well-drained soil in sunny locations. Seeds are sown in early spring, or in fall, where the plants are to remain, and the resulting seedlings thinned to 6 to 9 inches apart. For cut flowers, sowing may be in drills 1 foot to 1½ feet apart and the seedlings thinned to 4 to 6 inches apart.

VACCINIUM (Vac-cínium) — Bilberry, Blueberry, Cranberry, Deerberry, Farkleberry, Lingonberry, Whortleberry. Comparatively few of the 150 to 300 species, the number variously established by different authorities, of *Vaccinium*, of the heath family ERICACEAE or, according to those who split that group, of the blueberry family VACCINIACEAE, are commonly cultivated. Several are well known as sources of edible wild berries, some as cultivated blueberries and cranberries. The genus is native throughout much of the northern hemisphere, in mountains in the tropics, except in Africa, and in South Africa, Malagasy (Madagascar), and the Andes. It is abundant in North America as far north as the Arctic Circle. The name is an ancient Latin one of obscure derivation.

Vacciniums are creeping, trailing, or upright, deciduous or evergreen shrubs or rarely small trees with leathery or softer foliage. They have alternate, undivided, toothed or smooth-edged leaves and small flowers, solitary or in racemes or panicles from the leaf axils or ends of shoots. The blooms have four or five sepals, a tubular, ovoid, or bell-shaped, shallowly- to deeply-four- or five-lobed corolla, eight or ten stamens, and a slender style commonly longer than the stamens. The fruits are berries.

Highbush blueberry (*V. corymbosum*) is a variable species thought to have resulted from complex natural hybridization. The source of many horticultural varieties esteemed for their fruits, this is also one of the most ornamental members of the genus. It occurs as a wildling in moist and swampy soils from Maine to Minnesota, Florida, and Louisiana. An intricately branched, deciduous shrub 6 to 12 feet tall, the highbush blueberry has red twigs and rather pointed, ovate to elliptic-lanceolate leaves, 1¼ to about 3 inches long, that are hairy on their undersides, at least along

Vaccinium corymbosum

the veins, or are hairless. In fall, the foliage assumes brilliant tones of orange and scarlet. Expanding when the leaves are half grown, the densely-clustered flowers have cylindrical to narrowly-ovoid or urn-shaped, whitish to pinkish corollas ¼ to ⅓ inch long or a little longer. The bloomy, blue-black fruits, up to a little over ⅓ inch in diameter, are larger in horticultural varieties.

Vaccinium angustifolium

Lowbush blueberry (**V. angustifolium** syn. *V. pensylvanicum*) is endemic from Labrador and Newfoundland to Manitoba, New Jersey, Pennsylvania, Michigan, and Minnesota, and in the mountains to Virginia and West Virginia. The source of much fruit sold commercially, it is cultivated to the extent that natural stands are burned over periodically and fertilized to increase production. Favoring dry, rocky, and sandy soils, this deciduous sort forms large colonies up to 8 inches high. It has lustrous, narrowly-elliptic, sharply-toothed leaves, under 1½ inches long, that are hairless except for occasionally slight pubescence on the veins. In fall they become scarlet. Usually white and in short, crowded clusters, the nearly cylindrical flowers are under ¼ inch long. The berries, typically blue to blue-black, are approximately ¼ inch in diameter.

The dryland blueberry (**V. pallidum**) differs from the lowbush blueberry in being 1 foot to 3 feet tall and having very finely-toothed leaves. The latter are firm-textured, broad-elliptic to ovate, 1¼ to a little over 2 inches long, hairless, dull green above, and glaucous on their undersides. The often reddish-tinged, cylindrical, white flowers, up to ⅓ inch long, are in crowded clusters usually at the branchlet ends. The blue, bloomy, sweet fruits are nearly or quite ⅓ inch in diameter. The dryland blueberry inhabits dry woodlands chiefly in mountain regions from New York to Georgia, Alabama, and Kentucky, and in Missouri, Kansas, and Arkansas. In fall its foliage turns scarlet.

Rabbit-eye blueberry (**V. ashei**) is cultivated in several horticultural varieties for its edible fruits, chiefly in the southeast. Not hardy in the north and rarely exceeding 3 feet in height, it is sometimes evergreen. It has toothless or toothed, broadly-elliptic to broadly-obovate, hairless, glaucous leaves 1½ to 2½ inches long. Usually pink, sometimes white or red, the urn-shaped flowers, nearly ½ inch long, are in leafy racemes or panicles. The fruits are black, covered with copious bloom, and up to ½ inch in diameter. Also called rabbit-eye blueberry, **V. virgatum** (syn. *V. marianum*) occupies swamps and wet woodlands from southern New York to North Carolina. From 3 to 10 feet tall, it has toothless, pointed-elliptic leaves, 2 to 3 inches long by up to 1¼ inches wide, sometimes hairy on their undersides. The cylindrical, dull white flowers are up to ⅓ inch long; the dull black or slightly glaucous fruits are ¼ inch or a little more in diameter.

Deerberry (**V. stamineum**) has foliage that colors well in fall, and flowers among the most attractive of its genus. A loosely branched, deciduous shrub, usually about 2 feet tall, but sometimes twice as high, this inhabits dry woodlands from Maine to Indiana, Georgia, Louisiana, and Missouri. It has thin, elliptic to oblong or obovate, toothless, sparsely-hairy leaves 1¼ to 4 inches long. The bell-shaped flowers, in leafy-bracted racemes or panicles, are greenish sometimes tinged with purple and are up to almost ½ inch wide. The scarcely palatable fruits are yellowish to greenish. Variety *V. s. neglectum* (syn. *V. neglectum*), also called deerberry, differs in its twigs and foliage being completely hairless. This grows in similar habits over approximately the same native range.

Farkleberry (**V. arboreum**) is a spreading, evergreen shrub or small tree up to almost 30 feet tall, native from Virginia to Illinois, Florida, and Texas, and unusual in the genus for being able to prosper in alkaline soil. Not hardy in the north, it is a useful ornamental for southern gardens. This has obovate to oblongish, lustrous leaves ¾ inch to 2 inches long, smooth-edged or obscurely toothed, and sometimes hairy on their undersides. The white flowers, about ¼ inch long, are in racemes up to 2¼ inches long from the leaf axils or ends of branchlets. The fruits are black, ¼ inch in diameter, and unpalatable.

Vaccinium ovatum (foliage)

The evergreen blueberry or evergreen huckleberry (**V. ovatum**), native from California to British Columbia, is a nonhardy, beautifully foliaged shrub that in shade attains heights of 8 to 10 feet, in sun usually not over 2 to 3 feet. Cut branches are shipped for use as greens to florists throughout North America. This has lustrous, leathery, ovate, oblong-ovate, or lanceolate-ovate, pointed, fine-toothed leaves ½ inch to 2 inches long, broadest below their middles, and when young bronzy, but later dark green. Its white to pinkish, small, bell-shaped flowers, with five-lobed corollas, are in short racemes. The ⅓-inch-wide, bloomy, black fruits are used in preserves, jellies, and syrups. Also called evergreen blueberry, **V. myrsinites**, native from Virginia to Florida, is not hardy in the north. An evergreen, prostrate to erect shrub up to 1½ feet tall or a little taller, and almost or quite hairless, this has smooth-edged or toothed, obovate to oblong-lanceolate or spatula-shaped, glossy leaves broadest above their middles and from considerably under to slightly over 1 inch long. The little, cylindrical, white flowers, in short racemes, are followed by blue-black fruits up to ⅓ inch in diameter.

The American cranberry or large cranberry (**V. macrocarpon**) is less familiar as a

Vaccinium macrocarpon

garden plant than are its fruits as the makings for sauce and jelly. This is because of the highly specialized conditions it must have to thrive. For more information about this see the Encyclopedia entry Cranberry. Native from Newfoundland to Saskatchewan, North Carolina, Michigan, and Minnesota, the American cranberry is a slender-stemmed, evergreen creeper or trailer with long shoots upturned at their ends. Its blunt leaves, ¼ to ¾ inch long and elliptic to ovate, have flat or slightly recurved margins and barely glaucous undersides. The little white flowers are in groups of up to ten, beyond which extends a leafy shoot. The red fruits are mostly ½ to ¾ inch in diameter. The small cranberry (**V. oxycoccus**), native across the northern part of the North American continent and in Europe and Asia, differs from the last in being smaller in all its parts and in its oblong to oblong-ovate leaves being pointed, glaucous on their undersides, and usually having strongly-recurved margins. Also, its little flowers, in clusters of four or fewer or solitary, come from the ends of the branchlets and are succeeded by red fruits ⅓ inch or less in diameter. The mountain cranberry is an American variety of the European and Asian lingonberry or cowberry (**V. vitis-idaea**). This sort is an evergreen shrub, about 1 foot tall, that creeps by underground runners. It has

Vaccinium vitis-idaea

leathery, lustrous, broad-elliptic to obovate leaves from under ½ inch to a little over 1 inch long, their undersides pale and with tiny black dots. The white to pinkish, four-lobed, nodding flowers, ¼ inch long and clustered toward the ends of the roots, are bell-shaped. The dark red, acid and rather bitter fruits are esteemed for preserves and syrups. The mountain cranberry or mountain cowberry (**V. v. minus**), native from Labrador to Alaska, Massachusetts, and British Columbia, rarely much exceeds 6 inches in height and is often lower. Because of its dwarf habit and smaller, neater foliage, this is superior to the lingonberry as an ornamental. It forms dense mats and has evergreen leaves, ⅛ to ½ inch long or sometimes slightly longer, and pink to red flowers. Its red fruits are used for preserves and jellies.

Other sorts cultivated include these: **V. alto-montanum** occurs chiefly in mountains from West Virginia to Ohio, Georgia, and Alabama. Forming mats or colonies 1½ to 3 feet tall, it has narrow-elliptic to ellip-

tic-lanceolate, toothless leaves ¾ inch to 2 inches long and hairless on their undersides, and racemes of often pink-tinged, white to greenish-white flowers approximately ¼ inch long. The usually glaucous, spherical fruits are about ⅓ inch in diameter. **V. arctostaphylos**, of the Caucasus and hardy in southern New England, is deciduous and up to 10 feet tall. It has pointed, ovate-oblong leaves, 1¼ to 4 inches long, usually pubescent on their undersides and on the veins above, in fall turning purplish-red. The small, purplish-tinged, greenish-white, bell-shaped flowers, in racemes up to 2 inches long, have ten hairy stamens; they are succeeded by glossy, purple-black fruits ¼ inch or less in diameter. **V. atrococcum**, of Maine to Ontario and North Carolina, much resembles the highbush blueberry (**V. corymbosum**), but

Vaccinium arctostaphylos

has densely-hairy undersides to its leaves and black fruits without a waxy bloom. **V. bracteatum**, of Japan and China and not hardy in the north, is an attractive evergreen, up to 6 feet tall, with elliptic to elliptic-oblong, distantly-toothed, hairless or nearly hairless leaves up to a little over 2 inches long, which are coppery-red when young. In racemes, up to 2 inches long, furnished with persistent, leafy bracts, the cylindrical-ovate, white flowers are succeeded by red fruits. **V. crassifolium**, of North Carolina and Georgia, is a nonhardy, evergreen creeper, about 6 inches high, allied to *V. myrsinites*. It has glossy, elliptic to obovate or nearly round leaves up to ½ inch long, and smooth-edged or slightly toothed. The tiny, rose-red, bell-shaped flowers in terminal racemes are succeeded by red fruits. **V. cylindraceum** is a very fine nonhardy native of the Azores. A medium-sized to large, erect, evergreen or semievergreen shrub, this has finely-

Vaccinium cylindraceum

toothed, elliptic to oblong-elliptic leaves. Its cylindrical, ½-inch-long flowers, red in bud, yellowish-green tinged with red later, are in short racemes strung along shoots of the previous year. The berries, longer than wide, are blue-black with a waxy bloom. **V. delavayi**, of western China, is not hardy in the north. A compact evergreen shrub up to about 5 feet tall, it has boxwood-like, obovate leaves up to ½ inch long, hairless and usually notched at their apexes. The creamy-white, urn-shaped to globular flowers, under ½ inch in length, are in racemes up to 1 inch long. The crimson fruits are up to ¼ inch in diameter. **V. deliciosum**, native from Oregon to British Columbia, forms mats up to 1 foot high or sometimes higher. It has obovate to oblanceolate leaves with glaucous undersides and margins toothed above their middles. Solitary from the leaf axils, the pinkish, globular-urn-shaped flowers are ¼ inch long or a little longer. The very palatable, blue-black, nearly spherical fruits are up to ⅓ inch in diameter. **V. glaucalbum**, of the Himalayas, is a nonhardy evergreen 3 to 5 feet tall. It has firm-textured, bristle-toothed leaves, 1½ to 2 inches long by up to 1¼ inches broad, dark green above and bright bluish-white on their undersides. Bearing showy, bristle-edged, blue-white bracts, the 2- to 3-inch-long racemes of ¼-inch-long, pinkish-white, cylindrical flowers are succeeded by spherical black fruits covered with a blue-white bloom. **V. hirsutum**, the hairy huckleberry, native to North Carolina, Tennessee, and Georgia, is hardy in southern New England. Up to 3 feet tall, it forms thickets of slender, hairy stems and has deciduous, ovate to elliptic-oblong, toothless leaves ¾ inch to a little over 2 inches long. The leaves are hairy on both surfaces. The pink-tinged, white, hairy, ovoid flowers, somewhat under ½ inch long, are crowded in short racemes. The fruits are edible, hairy, purplish-black, and about ¼ inch in diameter. **V. membranaceum**, native from Montana to British Columbia, Idaho, and California, and there called mountain huckleberry, is 6 inches to 1 foot tall or sometimes somewhat taller. It has pointed, ovate to elliptic-lanceolate, finely-round-toothed, conspicuously-veined leaves, ¾ inch to 2 inches long, with slightly paler, sparsely-glandular undersides. The flowers, solitary from the leaf axils and ¼ inch long, are pale yellowish-pink. The purple to reddish-purple or more rarely red fruits, without a glaucous bloom, are about ⅓ inch in diameter. *V. mortinia* (syn. *V. floribundum*), of Ecuador and hardy in mild climates only, is evergreen, 2 to 4 feet tall, and has closely-set, short-stalked, minutely-toothed, ovate leaves, up to ½ inch long, which are slightly downy along their midribs. Coming from the leaf axils, the ¼-inch-long, rose-pink flowers are in racemes along the undersides of the stems. The fruits are small, red, and edible. *V. moupinense*, of the Himalayas, is not hardy in the north. Low, compact, and evergreen, it has obovate to oblong-obovate, ½-inch-long, usually toothless leaves and mahogany-red, urn-shaped, ¼-inch-long flowers in racemes up to 1 inch long. The tiny fruits are purple-black. *V. myrtilloides* is native in dry to moist soils or bogs from Labrador to British Columbia, Virginia, West Virginia, Indiana, and Minnesota. From 9 inches to 1½ feet tall, it forms broad colonies. The soft, thin, toothless leaves, hairy on both surfaces and elliptic-to elliptic-lanceolate, are ¾ inch to 1¼ inches long. The broadly-cylindrical flowers, under ¼ inch long, are white, sometimes tinged with pink. The very glaucous fruits are ¼ inch or less in diameter. *V. myrtillus*, the whortleberry or bilberry of northwestern North America, northern Asia, and Europe, is a hardy, suckering, deciduous sort, 6 inches to 1½ feet tall, that forms considerable patches. It has angular stems and ovate, toothed, very short-stalked leaves ½ to 1 inch long. Mostly solitary, the pale pink, ¼-inch-long, nearly spherical flowers droop from the leaf axils. The bloomy, black, sweet fruits are ⅓ inch in diameter. *V. nummularia* is a nonhardy, evergreen Himalayan of much charm. Its arching, densely-hairy stems are clothed with nearly stalkless, roundish-ovate to broad-elliptic, glossy leaves with recurved, nearly toothless edges. The cylindrical, rose-red to pinkish flowers, in racemes 1 inch to 2 inches long from the shoot ends, are followed by edible black fruits ¼ inch in diameter. Nonhardy *V. padifolium*, of Madeira, is sometimes confused with *V. arctostaphylos*, from which it differs in being more compact, in having smaller foliage, and in the ten stamens of its flowers not being hairy. The Madeiran species is a tall deciduous shrub to small tree with ovate to broad-elliptic leaves 1 inch to 2¼ inches long by up to 1 inch wide. They have finely-toothed margins

and hairy mid-veins. The drooping, bell-shaped, purple-tinged, dull yellow flowers, about ⅓ inch long, are in racemes 1 inch to 2 inches long from shoots of the previous year. The fruits are blue, globose, and ⅓ to ½ inch in diameter. *V. parvifolium*, native from California to Alaska and hardy in southern New England, is a variable deciduous species, 1 foot to 6 feet tall, with sharply-angled shoots. Its broad-elliptic to ovate or nearly round, toothless leaves, ¼ to ½ inch long, become bright red in fall. Solitary and nodding from the leaf axils, the nearly globular flowers are pinkish. The bright red, palatable, acid fruits are ¼ inch in diameter. *V. praestans*, of Japan and northeastern Asia, has creeping rhizomes and erect stems 3 to 6 inches tall. Its leaves, which assume rich red hues in fall, are obovate to broadly-ovate and 1 inch to a little over 2 inches long. Bell-shaped and white to reddish, the flowers are solitary or in twos or threes on stalks with leafy bracts. The sweet, glossy, bright red fruits, nearly or quite ½ inch in diameter, have a fragrance of strawberries. This sort is hardy. *V. smallii* is Japanese and hardy in southern New England. From 3 to 4½ feet tall, it has toothed, elliptic to elliptic-lanceolate, pointed leaves, 1¼ to 2½ inches long, often hairy on the midribs of their undersides. The white to reddish flowers, solitary or two or three together and drooping, are bell-shaped and up to ¼ inch long. The fruits, up to ⅓ inch in diameter, are bluish-black. *V. uliginosum*, the bog bilberry of mountain regions from New York and New Hampshire northward and in northern Europe and Asia, up to 1½ feet tall, has nearly stalkless, broad-elliptic to obovate, toothless leaves, ½ to 1 inch long, glaucous on both surfaces and slightly hairy on their undersides. The pink to white, very short-stalked, ⅙-inch-long blooms are in clusters of two to four or sometimes solitary. Blue-black with a glaucous bloom, the sweet fruits are ¼ inch in diameter. *V. urceolatum* is a Chinese, not hardy in the north. Evergreen and 4 to 6 feet tall, it has hairless, nearly stalkless, long-pointed, elliptic-ovate to oblong-ovate leaves, 2 to 3½ inches in length, and up-to-¼-inch-long, pink, urn-shaped flowers in racemes from the leaf axils.

Garden and Landscape Uses. As ornamentals vacciniums are chiefly esteemed for their generally neat foliage, which in many sorts turns brilliant scarlet in fall, and for their suitability for acid soils. They combine well with such other plants of the heath family as azaleas and other rhododendrons, heaths and heathers, leucothoes, and pierises, as well as with other acid-soil plants. Evergreen sorts of this genus are useful for adding life to winter landscapes; low growers make satisfactory groundcovers.

Some vacciniums, such as cranberries,

are highly selective of the environments in which they will grow and are not widely adaptable as garden plants. With such sorts it is necessary to approximate as closely as possible the conditions of their native habitats. Nearly all abhor alkaline soil. The ground should be wet, moist, or dry according to the preferences of different sorts, all of which prosper in full sun, although some tolerate light shade.

Cultivation. For their satisfactory growth the chief concern with vacciniums planted for ornament is initial selection of locations and soils. If these are favorable, care is minimal. They transplant easily and need no pruning other than any required to keep them tidy and of acceptable size. Those employed as groundcovers benefit from an occasional shearing. Any cutting required is best done just before new growth begins in spring. Like most plants of the heath family, these benefit from having a mulch of organic material, such as peat moss, leaf mold, or wood chips, maintained around them.

Propagation is readily achieved by seed sown as soon as ripe or later, in pots or flats of sandy, peaty soil kept evenly moist. Division in spring is a satisfactory means of increasing many kinds as are leafy summer cuttings and hardwood cuttings taken later.

VAGABOND PLANT. See *Vriesia vagans*.

VAGARIA (Vag-ària). Four species constitute *Vagaria*, of the amaryllis family AMARYLLIDACEAE, of which three are natives of Morocco and the only cultivated one is native to Syria. The name is believed to be derived from the Latin *vagus*, roaming, and to have been applied because the specimen originally described in Paris was at that time of unknown origin. Vagarias are bulb plants similar to *Pancratium* in structure except that the corona, prominent in that genus, is represented by twelve teeth in *Vagaria*.

Syrian *V. parviflora* has an ovoid to spherical, long-necked bulb, 1½ to 2 inches in diameter, and four to six strap-shaped leaves, banded down their middles with white and eventually 2 feet long, but very much shorter at blooming time. The stout flower stalks, appearing in autumn, may be almost 1 foot in length and terminate in umbels of nine or fewer funnel-shaped white blooms up to 1½ inches in length. The narrow corolla-segments, commonly called petals, but more correctly tepals, are separate nearly to their bases; there they are joined into a very short tube. Each has a distinct green keel on its outside. The teeth of the corona are ¼ inch long.

Garden and Landscape Uses and Cultivation. This interesting and quite beautiful plant has the same uses and needs and the same culture as *Pancratium*.

VALERIAN. See Valeriana. African-valerian is *Fedia cornucopiae*; Greek-valerian, *Polemonium caeruleum*; and Red-valerian, *Centranthus ruber*.

VALERIANA (Valer-iàna)—Valerian or Cat's Valerian or Garden-Heliotrope. This, the type genus of the valerian family VALERIANACEAE, contains about 200 species and is represented in the native floras of all continents except Australia. The name *Valeriana* is generally believed to be derived from the Latin *valere*, to be strong, in allusion to the medicinal qualities of *V. officinalis*, but perhaps it honors the Roman emperor Valerianus. In any case, it was used by such ancients as Theophrastus and Dioscorides. Indians used and still use the roots of *V. edulis*, native to western North America, for food. Medicinal valerian is obtained from the roots of *V. officinalis*, a species very attractive to cats. The plant called red-valerian is *Centranthus ruber*.

Valerianas include annuals, herbaceous perennials, subshrubs, and shrubs, commonly with thick taproots or rhizomes. They have opposite, undivided, one- or more-times-pinnately-lobed, or pinnate, toothed or toothless leaves, with the pairs on the stems spreading at right angles to the pairs next below and above them. The little bisexual or single-sexed flowers are in small clusters that are terminal or are in spikes or panicles. They are white, pink, or lavender. Their calyxes have five to fifteen lobes, often divided in feather-like fashion, in-rolled and relatively inconspicuous at blooming time, but later unfurled as crowns or tufts at the apexes of the compressed seedlike fruits (achenes). The tubular corollas have five lobes (petals). There are usually three, rarely fewer or four stamens. The style ends in a three-lobed stigma.

Common valerian, cat's valerian, or garden-heliotrope (*V. officinalis*), of Europe and temperate Asia and naturalized in North America, is most familiar to gardeners. An old-fashioned favorite, it is a robust herbaceous perennial with short rhizomes, some basal foliage, and stems, 2 to 5 feet tall, sometimes branched above. Each stem has four to eight pairs of pinnate or pinnately-lobed leaves, each with a terminal leaflet and seven to ten pairs of lateral segments or leaflets, usually toothed. The leaflets or segments of the lower leaves are ovate-oblong, those of the upper pointed-lanceolate. The leaves may be hairless or somewhat hairy beneath, especially along the veins. The long-stalked, roundish clusters of highly and sweetly fragrant, white, pinkish, or lavender-pink, bisexual flowers are arranged in panicle fashion. The clusters, at first compact and up to 4 inches across, become looser and larger as they age. Variants with white and nearly red flowers are named, respectively, *V. o. alba*

Valeriana officinalis

and *V. o. rubra*. Native to the Caucasus, *V. phu* differs from *V. officinalis* in being about 3 feet tall, in having smooth-edged or only toothed instead of deeply-lobed, long-stalked basal leaves, and in the stem leaves having seven or nine leaflets. Its variety *V. p. aurea* has golden-yellow young shoots and foliage.

North American *V. sitchensis*, a widely distributed and variable species, 1 foot to 3½ feet tall, has stout rhizomes. The leaves are pinnately-lobed or pinnate, and toothed or toothless. There are two to five pairs of stem leaves similar to the basal ones, with one to six pairs of leaflets or lobes shorter than the terminal one. The clusters of generally bisexual, white or pinkish flowers, up to 3 inches wide, become looser as they age. In its typical form, this species is a mountain plant with mostly basal foliage, ranging from Idaho to Alaska and California. Western North American *V. s. scouleri* is slenderer, up to 2½ feet in height, and has hairless stems and foliage, the last mostly basal. Eastern North American *V. s. uliginosa* (syn. *V. uliginosa*) has stem leaves with commonly nine or eleven leaflets or lobes, the terminal one lanceolate to elliptic. It inhabits swamps, bogs, and wet meadows from southern Canada to New York and Michigan.

Low valerianas include *V. arizonica*, of Colorado, New Mexico, and Arizona. From 3 inches to rarely 1 foot tall, this has chiefly

basal foliage. Its lower leaves are mostly undivided and ovate, those on the stems are three- to seven-parted. The bisexual, white or pinkish blooms have protruding stamens. In dense clusters 1 inch wide or a little wider, the blooms later loosen and increase somewhat in diameter. Another interesting American, which differs from the last in its stamens being shorter than the corolla tube, is *V. columbiana*. This endemic of the mountains of Washington is 1 foot or considerably less tall. It has stout rhizomes, basal foliage, and leafy stems. The basal leaves, broadly-ovate to nearly round and up to 6 inches long, are toothed or toothless. The one to four pairs of stem leaves are pinnate or pinnately-lobed. A native of central Europe, *V. supina* is a neat, mat-forming kind 3 or 4 inches in height. It has small, ovate, hair-fringed, glossy leaves and almost stalkless, small, dense clusters of white or pinkish, fragrant flowers.

Other valerians sometimes cultivated include *V. alliariifolia*, a native of woodlands in Greece and the Caucasus. From

Valeriana alliariifolia

1½ to 2½ feet tall, this has undivided, toothed leaves, the basal ones long-stalked and with heart-shaped blades up to 8 inches across. The ovate to lanceolate stem leaves are smaller. The pink flowers are in panicles of rather crowded, rounded heads. Very much like the last, but with the upper stem leaves with one or two pairs of deeply-toothed leaflets and a terminal one, *V. pyrenaica*, of the Pyrenees, inhabits damp woodlands and meadows. Variable *V. montana*, of central and southern Europe, 6 inches to 1½ feet high, has stalked, ovate to elliptic basal leaves, rarely with heart-shaped bases, and smaller, undivided or sometimes three-cleft, toothed or toothless stem leaves. The pink, lilac-colored, or white flowers are in panicles of loose to compact heads.

Garden and Landscape Uses and Cultivation. The taller valerians are suitable for

Valeriana pyrenaica

Valeriana montana

flower borders and naturalizing in informal and semiwild areas; *V. officinalis* is appropriate for herb and medicinal gardens. The lower kinds are best adapted to rock gardens and similar places. All discussed here are hardy, easy-to-grow deciduous perennials. They succeed in ordinary soils in sun or part-day shade, with *V. sitchensis uliginosa* preferring a wet or at least moist location. Routine care is minimal. Increase is easy by seed sown in an outdoor seed bed or cold frame in spring, and by division in early fall or spring.

VALERIANACEAE — Valerian Family. The approximately ten genera and 400 species of dicotyledons that constitute this family are chiefly herbaceous perennials; a few are shrubs. Natives chiefly of the northern hemisphere, they include kinds occasionally cultivated as vegetables and some with medicinal virtues. Characteristic of the plants of this family are opposite or all-basal, undivided, pinnately-lobed, or pinnately-divided leaves. In loose clusters or more or less headlike arrangements, the small, unisexual or bisexual flowers are frequently more or less asymmetrical. The calyx may be lacking or variously lobed, the lobes sometimes plumelike. The corolla, often two-lipped, is five-lobed and, at its base, baggy or spurred. There are one to four stamens and one slender style. The fruits are dry.

Genera cultivated include *Centranthus, Fedia, Nardostachys, Patrinia, Plectritis, Valeriana,* and *Valerianella.*

VALERIANELLA (Valeri-anélla) — Corn-Salad or Lamb's Lettuce. Fifty or more species of the valerian family VALERIANA-CEAE constitute *Valerianella,* a genus native to North America, Europe, and Asia, with the greatest number of kinds in the Mediterranean region. The name is a diminutive of *Valerian,* which is that of another genus of the same family.

Valerianellas are annuals and biennials with repeatedly forked stems. Usually they are hairless or nearly so. The leaves are in basal rosettes and in pairs on the stems. They are not divided into separate leaflets, but those on the stem are sometimes toothed or pinnately-cleft. The flowers are tiny and in crowded globular heads or narrow, branched clusters. They are whitish, pink, or pale lilac and have minute or vestigial calyxes. Their corollas have cylindrical or funnel-shaped tubes, with or without spurs, and five spreading lobes (petals). There are three stamens, less often two. The small fruits (commonly called seeds) have three compartments or cells, one with a single seed. Except for their fruits, the species closely resemble each other. Three salad plants and potherbs of minor importance belong here.

Corn-salad or lamb's-lettuce (*V. locusta* syn. *V. olitoria*), native to Europe, often in grain fields (hence the name corn-salad), is naturalized in North America. It has slender, much-branched, brittle stems, 6

Valerianella locusta

inches to 1 foot tall, and linear-oblong to oblong-lanceolate, or obovate, sometimes toothed leaves 1 inch to 3 inches long. Its tiny pale lilac blooms are in flat or rounded, terminal clusters, about ¾ inch across, and have obscure, one-toothed calyxes. The corolla tubes are without spurs. There are three stamens. The fruits, about 1/10 inch long and nearly spherical, are corky on their backs. From the last, Italian corn-salad (*V. eriocarpa*) differs in having leaves 3 to 5 inches in length, and flattened seeds, hollowed on one side and rounded on the other, topped by the persistent calyx. Spiny lamb's-lettuce (*V. echinata*) has fruits crowned with calyxes with three spiny, conical teeth. Its leaves are lanceolate, the upper ones markedly toothed or lobed.

Garden Uses. These plants are only of use as edibles. For their cultivation see Corn-Salad or Lamb's Lettuce.

VALLARIS (Val-làris). In southern Florida and elsewhere in the humid subtropics and tropics, one of the about six species of this genus of the dogbane family APOCYNA-CEAE is cultivated. The name *Vallaris* perhaps stems from the Latin *vallus,* a palisade, and has reference to the reported use of one or more of its kinds to make fences. The natural range of the genus extends from India to Malaya and the Philippine Islands.

The sorts of this genus are twining, woody, milky-juiced vines with opposite, minutely-dotted leaves, and forked clusters of white or creamy-white flowers with five-lobed calyxes and corollas. The corollas have a short, slender tube, spreading lobes (petals) that in the bud stage overlap each other to the right, five stamens, and two styles, united. The podlike fruits are technically follicles.

Native to Burma, *V. solanacea* (syns. *V. dichotoma, V. heynei*), tall-growing and stout-stemmed, has elliptic to linear-oblong, slender-pointed, prominently-veined leaves 2 to 4 inches long by ¾ inch to 1½ inches broad. Its fragrant, creamy-white, *Vinca*-like flowers, about ⅔ inch in diameter, are succeeded by pointed seed pods about 6 inches long by one-third as wide.

Garden and Landscape Uses and Cultivation. No special care is needed by this strong-growing vine, which is adapted for covering pergolas, arbors, and other supports. It succeeds in ordinary soil and is propagated by seed and by cuttings.

VALLISNERIA (Vallis-nèria) — Tape-Grass, Eel-Grass. The plants called tape-grass and eel-grass are not grasses (members of the family GRAMINEAE). They belong to the frog's bit family HYDROCHARITACEAE and are underwater aquatic perennials with long, thin, ribbon-like leaves that resemble those of grasses. Botanists have not agreed as to the number of species in *Vallisneria.* Some regard it as one variable species, others recognize two, *V. americana,* of North America, and *V. spiralis,* of the Old World, and yet others divide the genus into eight to ten species. The latter view is accepted here. The generic name commemorates the Italian naturalist Antonio Vallisneri, who died in 1730.

Vallisnerias are hardy, tufted plants that root in the mud and send out runners by which they spread. They have ribbon-like leaves, 6 inches to 6 feet long, depending on the depth of the water, and tiny unisexual flowers, the males and females on separate plants. The solitary, white, female blooms float at the surface, attached by a slender, spiraled stalk to the plant below. They have three sepals and three petals and are surrounded by a tubular spathe (bract). After the female blooms are fertilized by pollen from males, their spiral stems contract and pull the fruits, which are cylindrical and few-seeded, under the surface of the water. The minute male flowers are clustered many together in heads enclosed in spathes. They have three sepals, three petals, and one to three, but usually two stamens. At maturity the male flowers separate from the plant, rise to the surface, and float. When they contact female blooms pollen is transferred, resulting in fertilization. This is a very unusual and interesting method of pollination.

Native in still, fresh or brackish waters from Nova Scotia to South Dakota, Florida, and Texas, *V. americana,* sometimes called wild-celery or water-celery, has leaves up to 6 feet long by a little over ½ inch wide. This, even in aquariums, is dormant in winter. Very similar to the last, but less hardy to cold and in aquariums not becoming dormant in winter, *V. spiralis* is a native of southern Europe and adjacent Asia. Known as the Italian type, it has somewhat more slender leaves than *V. americana.* The shorter, wider leaves of *V. s. torta* are closely spiraled throughout their lengths.

Leaves up to ¾ inch wide and 3 feet long, minutely-toothed along their edges, and with lengthways stripes of black and brown distinguish *V. gigantea,* a native from southeast Asia to the Philippine Islands and Australia, from *V. americana* and *V. spiralis.* The plant called *V. rubra,* of which the leaves grown in good light are bronzy-red, may be a variant of *V. gigantea* or perhaps of *V. spiralis.* Linear leaves, ¼ inch wide and slightly-toothed toward their apexes, are typical of *V. asiatica,* of Japan, Taiwan, China, and southeast Asia.

Garden Uses and Cultivation. Vallisnerias are favorite aquarium plants. They are good backgrounds and very decorative, and provide shelter and a consequent sense of security for fish. Tape-grasses grow well in unwashed sand that contains a little mud, in slightly acid water. Temperate or tropical conditions are equally to

Vallisneria spiralis in an aquarium

their liking. They need good light, especially from above, and are readily propagated by division.

VALLOTA (Val-lòta)—Scarborough-Lily. The common name of this South African bulb plant can be traced to a Dutch ship wrecked long ago off the coast of England. Bulbs from it were washed ashore, rescued, and planted in the vicinity of Scarborough. They multiplied, were distributed from near that town, and became known as Scarborough-lilies. An interesting parallel is afforded by the Guernsey-lily (*Nerine serniensis*), also South African, but early distributed from Guernsey in the Channel Islands, where bulbs of it were washed ashore from a shipwreck.

In its homeland, *Vallota,* which belongs in the amaryllis family AMARYLLIDACEAE, is known as the berg-lily, George-lily, and Knysna-lily. Named after Pierre Vallot, a French botanist, who died in 1671, the genus has only one species. It is so closely related to *Cyrtanthus* that some botanists have expressed the opinion that perhaps it should be included there. It is, however, quite different in appearance from cultivated cyrtanthuses, which have slender, curved, pendulous corollas, tubular for most of their length, with comparatively short lobes (petals). Gardeners are generally pleased that it remains *Vallota speciosa* (syn. *V. purpurea*).

The Scarborough-lily (*V. speciosa*) looks rather like a frailer edition of a *Hippeastrum* and may rightly be regarded as an African counterpart of that South American genus. Its broadly-trumpet-shaped flowers have six wide perianth parts (petals) joined at their bases into a funnel-shaped tube at least 2 inches long and with the free parts of the petals flaring and about as long as

Vallota speciosa

the tube. In *Hippeastrum* the petals are usually not joined or are united for a very short distance only from the base. Also, the six stamens of the Scarborough-lily join the corolla near the upper end of the tube, those of *Hippeastrum* arise from the base of the bloom. Another difference is that the flattened seeds of *Vallota* have a wing at their bases. No such appendage is present in *Hippeastrum.* The fruits of *Vallota* are capsules.

The Scarborough-lily has an ovoid bulb, 3 inches or so in diameter, and strap-shaped leaves, 1½ to 2 feet long by 1 inch or more broad. The leaves of cultivated specimens are commonly evergreen, although the plant is usually described in botanical writings as deciduous. The flowers, which come in fall, are in umbel-like clusters of nine or fewer atop leafless, hollow stalks that rise above the arching foliage. In the typical species they are bright red, erect or angled upward, and about 2½ inches long by almost or quite as wide across their mouths. The blooms of *V. s. magnifica* are white-eyed and up to 5 inches across; *V. s. eximia* has 4-inch-wide flowers feathered at their bases with white; and *V. s. alba* has its flowers entirely white. Variety *V. s. minor* is smaller in all of its parts than the species.

Garden and Landscape Uses and Cultivation. The Scarborough-lily is chiefly grown as a pot plant in greenhouses and in sunny windows in cool rooms. Well-drained pots and fertile, loamy, porous soil are needed. Because this plant greatly resents root disturbance, repotting should be delayed as long as growth is satisfactory. Ordinarily it will not be needed more often than every four or five years and may be done in June or July or as soon as flowering is over. Interference with the roots must be minimal. The bulbs are set with their tips showing slightly above the soil surface. Routine care of established plants includes watering them freely from late spring until late fall, considerably less generously for the remainder of the year, but even in winter the soil should never dry completely. Well-rooted specimens respond to weekly applications of dilute liquid fertilizer given from early summer to fall. Exposure to full sun and free ventilation of the greenhouse on all favorable occasions are necessary. During that part of the year when the greenhouse is heated, night temperatures of 40 to 50°F, raised a few degrees during the day, are ample. The Scarborough-lily will even survive a few degrees of frost. In mild climates it may be grown outdoors in sunny locations in fertile soil enriched with generous amounts of peat moss, leaf mold, or compost. It is propagated by seed, offsets, and bulb cuttings.

VAN WYKSHOUT is *Bolusanthus speciosus*.

VANCOUVERIA (Van-couvèria) — Inside-Out Flower or Redwood-Ivy. It is entirely appropriate that a group of plants confined in the wild to the Pacific Northwest should be selected to honor Captain George Vancouver, distinguished explorer of that coast, who died in 1795. The genus *Vancouveria* consists of three species of the barberry family BERBERIDACEAE and is closely related to *Epimedium*.

Vancouverias are herbaceous plants, with foliage of fernlike grace and charm, that spread by slender, creeping, underground rhizomes. Their mostly basal leaves are usually two-times- or three-times-divided into blunt or indented, generally indefinitely three-lobed, often wavy-margined leaflets. Occasionally the flowering stems, which are slender, erect, and have few to

many small, individually long-stalked, nodding blooms, bear a solitary leaf. The flowers differ from those of *Epimedium* in having six to nine quickly deciduous outer sepals, six petal-like inner ones, which, like the six true petals, are reflexed, six stamens, and a single style ending in a cup-shaped stigma. The fruits are follicles (pods).

Deciduous and with thinish leaflets and white flowers, **V. hexandra** is 6 inches to 1½ feet tall. Its flower stems, usually longer than the slightly hairy leaves, are hairy near their bases, smooth above. The blooms, in loose panicles of up to thirty, and approximately ½ inch long, have very short outer

Vancouveria hexandra

sepals of unequal size and inner ones about ⅓ inch long. The petals, narrowed at their bases into slender claws, are shorter than the inner sepals and are folded at their apexes to form a nectar-secreting gland. There are a few red glandular hairs on the sepals and stamens. The leaves, usually twice-, but sometimes thrice-divided, have narrow to broadly-ovate, usually three-lobed leaflets, green above, slightly glaucous on their undersides, and from ¾ inch to 2 inches long.

Evergreen kinds with foliage more leathery than that of *V. hexandra* are *V. planipetala* (syn. *V. parviflora*) and *V. chrysantha*. The blooms of **V. planipetala** are white or slightly lavender. In addition to having persistent foliage, *V. planipetala*, called inside-out flower and redwood-ivy, differs from *V. hexandra* in its ovaries being without hairs instead of being densely-glandular-hairy, and in not having glandular hairs on its sepals and stamens. The leaves are generally two-times-, but sometimes three-times-divided into broadly-ovate leaflets, up to 1½ inches long, and have thickened, usually slightly wavy margins. Dark glossy green on their upper sides and slightly glaucous and with a few hairs beneath, they are three-lobed. The loose, glandular panicle is composed of twenty-five to fifty flowers with unequal-

sized outer sepals, spatula-shaped inner sepals, and flat, oblanceolate petals shorter than the inner sepals and not pouched at their nectar-bearing apexes.

Golden-yellow-flowered **V. chrysantha** has its evergreen leaves from two-times- to as many as five-times-divided. Their stalks are hairy and the leaflets, up to 1½ inches long and wide, are thickened and crisped at their margins. Obscurely three-lobed, they are dark green above and somewhat glaucous and pubescent on their undersides. The flowers, except in color, resemble those of *V. hexandra*. They are up to fifteen together in very glandular, open panicles.

Garden and Landscape Uses. These plants are deserving of more attention from gardeners. Although they make no great displays of bloom, they are attractive because of the delicate appearance of their foliage, which suggests that of large-leafleted maidenhair ferns or of rue. They are splendid groundcovers for partially shaded places at the fringes of shrub borders and for woodland gardens and large rock gardens. They need fertile soil that is not

Vancouveria hexandra as a groundcover

wanting in organic content and that does not dry excessively. In climates as severe as that of southern New York, only *V. hexandra* survives, the others need milder winters.

Cultivation. Vancouverias can be secured from seed or by division in early spring or fall. Established colonies benefit from being lightly mulched with leaf mold, peat moss, or rich compost. Otherwise, no special care is required and the plants, as long as they are doing well, may remain undisturbed for years.

VANDA (Ván-da). The about sixty species of *Vanda*, of the orchid family ORCHIDACEAE, are natives of China, Indo-Malaysia, and the Mariana Islands. In addition there are numerous natural and horticulturally produced hybrids that have resulted from crossing *Vanda* species and from crossing *Vanda* with species of such genera as *Aerides, Arachnis, Ascocentrum, Neofinetia, Renanthera,* and *Vandopsis.* Bigeneric hybrids involving these genera and *Vanda* are named, respectively, *Aeridovanda, Aranda, Ascocenda, Vandofinetia, Renantanda,* and *Opsisanda.* The name *Vanda* is derived from the Hindi name of one sort.

Vandas are chiefly epiphytes, plants that in the wild roost on trees without taking nourishment from them. Some are rock-perchers, still fewer are ground orchids. Without pseudobulbs, they have short to long, sometimes vining, leafy stems. The leaves, in two ranks, are fleshy or stiffish, and often notched at their apexes. Those of the species are generally strap-shaped or slender-cylindrical. Hybrid origin is sometimes indicated by foliage intermediate between these extremes. In racemes from the leaf axils, the short-stalked, often showy flowers have spreading sepals and petals of similar appearance that narrow to their bases and vary considerably in color in different species, often as to shade in the same sort. The short-spurred lip has a pair of small side lobes and a spreading middle one.

Blue or lavender-blue flowers up to 4 inches in diameter, with darker veining on the sepals and petals and a magenta-purple lip, its base whitish and with streaks of red-brown, are usual with splendid **V. coerulea,** a native of Burma, the Himalayan region, and Thailand. On different plants the blooms, which vary quite extraordinarily in form and depth of color, rarely are white or pink. Typically this sort, 1 foot to 4 feet tall, has narrowly-strap-shaped, channeled, leathery leaves, 5 to 10 inches long by up to 1 inch wide, notched at their apexes. The blooms are in erect or gracefully arching, 1- to 2-foot-long racemes of up to fifteen. Their lips are under one-third as long as the sepals. Many horticultural varieties are grown. A natural hybrid of *V. coerulea* and *V. tessellata,* intermediate between its parents, **V. amoena** has 2- to 3-inch-wide flowers with bluish-gray sepals and petals, with violet spots, and a lip with a violet-blue center lobe and whitish side lobes. Variety *V. a. sanderae* has creamy-white sepals and petals with lilac veinings and a violet-purple lip.

Beautiful **V. tricolor,** of Java, has branched stems 3 to 7 feet tall and lemon-yellow flowers with reddish-brown spots on their somewhat wavy sepals and petals. The lip is white with a rosy-purple middle lobe. The tough, strap-shaped leaves, notched at their tips into two unequal lobes, are 1 foot to 1¼ feet long by up to 1½ inches wide. The pleasantly-scented flowers, several together in racemes up to 1 foot long, are 2 to 3 inches wide. As long as the sepals, their lips have small side lobes and a fiddle-shaped middle one indented at its apex. The more nu-

Vanda coerulea

Vanda amoena

merous flowers of *V. t. suavis* have white sepals and petals with fewer red-purple spots, and the basal portion of the chiefly rosy-magenta lip deep purple. Citron-yellow flowers bigger than those of the typical species, heavily spotted with brown and with a large flat rose-pink lip edged with pinkish-mauve and striped at the center with brownish-purple, are characteristic of *V. t. planilabis.* The sepals and petals of *V. t. patersonii* are creamy-white thickly spot-

ted with brown, with the lip a magenta-crimson.

Showy **V. teres** inhabits regions of torrential rains and high humidity in Burma and the Khasi Hills of India. It forms tangles of slender, usually abundantly branched, semivining stems, up to 15 feet long, with cylindrical leaves, 4 to 8 inches long, that look much like short branches. Plentifully produced, the flowers are in more or less erect racemes of six or fewer.

Vanda tricolor

Vanda tricolor suavis

Fragrant and 3 to 4 inches in diameter, they have rose-purple sepals and petals, the latter wavy-edged, and a tawny-yellow to orange-lip often strikingly striped with violet. The flowers of *L. t. alba* are white. Those of *L. t. andersonii* are bigger and more brightly colored than those of the typical species.

One of the most lovely of orchids, *V. sanderana* (syn. *Euanthe sanderana*), of the Philippine Islands, grows natively as an epiphyte on thinly-foliaged trees in coastal areas where there is constant high humidity and high temperatures and where the plants receive but slight shade from intense tropical sun. This splendid orchid, without pseudobulbs, has erect, leafy stems up to 2 feet long. The two-ranked leaves, 10 inches to 1¼ feet long by 1 inch wide, are strap-shaped, often with two or three small teeth at their apexes. From 3½ to 5 inches across, the nearly circular, fragrant, flat flowers, which have overlapping sepals and petals, are in upright, 1-foot-long racemes of six to fifteen. The upper sepal is predominantly lilac-pink suffused with white, the slightly larger lateral ones tawny-yellow netted with brownish-red veins. The petals, smaller than the sepals, colored similarly to the upper sepal, have a red-spotted blotch of tawny-yellow on one side. The small, kidney-shaped, dull red, fleshy lip is much smaller than the sepals. Its side lobes form a cuplike base. Specialists recognize several horticultural varieties.

Native to Burma, *V. parishii* (syn. *Vandopsis parishii*) has thick stems and elliptic-oblong leaves up to 9 inches long. About 2 inches in diameter, the rather fleshy, fragrant flowers have pale yellow sepals and petals, suffused with carmine, and a prominent magenta lip, paler toward its edges. The scentless blooms of *V. p. mar-*

rottiana have magenta-tinged, greenish-buff-yellow sepals and petals, almost white toward their bases. The lip has a magenta center lobe and white side ones.

Vanda parishii marrottiana

Other species favored by collectors are these: *V. alpina,* of the Himalayas, has short, thickish, very leafy stems and leathery, 4- to 5-inch-long leaves, approximately ½ inch wide, ending in a pair of unequal lobes. The short, usually horizontal racemes are of four or fewer nodding, fragrant blooms 1 inch to 1½ inches wide. They have pale to bright green sepals and petals and a greenish-yellow to green lip striped with black-purple. *V. amesiana,* of Indochina and Thailand, has very thick roots and a short, stout stem. Up to nearly 1 foot long, its fleshy, subcylindrical leaves, deeply-grooved along their upper sides, are almost ½ inch wide. The more or less erect racemes of twelve to twenty-five or more fragrant blooms are up to 2½ feet long. In-

dividual flowers are 1½ to 2 inches across. Variable in color, they most commonly have pink-suffused, white sepals and petals and an amethyst-purple to rose-pink, short-spurred lip, sometimes with darker stripes. Somewhat bigger than the sepals, the lip has erect side lobes and a roundish, blunt, wavy-edged middle one. *V. coerulescens* is a native of Burma. It has rather slender stems, up to 2 feet long, and linear, channeled and strongly-keeled leaves, up to 10 inches long by about ¾ inch wide, notched at their apexes into two spiny-tipped lobes. The slender, erect or suberect racemes, up to 2 feet in length, are of nine to fifteen or more 1½-inch-wide, fragrant blooms with similar pale blue to mauve or less commonly white, blunt sepals and petals and a violet-blue lip, as long as the petals, with a notched, obovate center lobe and small, oblong side ones. *V. cristata,* of Nepal, has short stems and recurved, channeled leaves, up to about 7 inches long, three-toothed at their apexes. The 2-inch-wide

Vanda cristata

flowers, in erect racemes of six or fewer, are shorter than the leaves; they have yellowish-green, blunt-oblong sepals and incurved petals and a buff-yellow lip with a short middle lobe and five to seven white ridges with purple between. The side lobes are narrow and spreading. **V. dearei,** of Borneo, may attain a height of 8 feet. It has broad, strap-shaped leaves and short racemes of up to eight lemon-scented blooms 2 to 4 inches wide. They are cream-colored, shading toward the tips of the overlapping sepals and petals to brownish. The lip has a large cream-colored center lobe, which becomes lemon-yellow at its apex. The side lobes are white. **V. denisoniana,** of Burma, has shortish stems, and leaves, up to 1 foot long by about ¾ inch wide, deeply two-lobed at their apexes. Its delightfully fragrant blooms, four to six in arching to horizontal racemes up to 6 inches long, are 2 to 2½ inches across. Somewhat variable in color, their sepals and petals are mostly white to ivory-white or tinged with green. The lip, a little longer than the sepals, is white with a yellow to orange-yellow patch near its base. It has a fiddle-shaped center lobe, forked at its apex, and two small side lobes. **V. hookerana,** of Borneo, Malaya, and Sumatra, has stems many feet long, much-branched from their bases. Its cylindrical leaves, 2 to 4 inches in length, have a noticeable constriction a little distance below their tips. Generally erect, the racemes of up to ten flowers may be nearly 1 foot long. Individual blooms, commonly 2 to 3 inches wide, are sometimes bigger. They are white to delicate mauve with deeper-colored veinings, the lip more intensely colored than the sepals and petals. **V. kimballiana,** of the Himalayan region, 1 foot to 2 feet tall and has nearly cylindrical, bronzy leaves 6 to 9 inches long. Its 1½- to 2-inch-wide flowers, in racemes of up to twenty, have a white or delicately-purple-suffused upper sepal and petals and white, sickle-shaped side sepals. The lip has a pale purple spur, a three-keeled, amethyst-purple middle lobe, and yellowish side lobes spotted with yellowish-brown. **V. lamellata,** of the Philippine Islands, has thick stems up to over 1 foot long, and strap-shaped, overlapped, recurving leaves, folded along their centers, 9 inches to 1¼ feet long by ¾ inch wide. Crowded in erect to horizontal racemes, up to 1 foot long, of six to twenty-five, the strongly fragrant blooms are 1 inch to 1½ inches wide or sometimes wider. Varying in color, they most commonly have yellowish or greenish sepals and petals, striped and blotched irregularly with brown, and a lip, shorter than the sepals, that is whitish or yellowish with its middle lobe streaked with brown. Differing from the species in its more vigorous growth and in having larger leaves and racemes of fifteen to thirty flowers with whitish sepals and petals, with only a few streaks of purple, *V. l. boxallii*

is also a native of the Philippine Islands. **V. limbata,** of Java, resembles *V. lamellata* in habit. Its stems are abundantly foliaged with stiff, leathery leaves 6 to 8 inches long by ¾ inch to 1½ inches wide. Fragrant and about 2 inches in diameter, the flowers, in 10-inch-long racemes of up to twelve, have yellow-edged, cinnamon-brown sepals and petals, with darker reticulations. The pale lilac lip has small side lobes and a short spur. **V. luzonica** (syn. *Euanthe luzonica*), of the Philippine Islands, has much the aspect of *V. tricolor*, but with proportionately longer, narrow, recurved leaves up to 1¼

Vanda luzonica

feet long and more slender aerial roots. In racemes of up to about twenty, the 2-inch-wide blooms have white sepals and petals, with occasional violet-purple or red-purple spots. The lip has a violet-purple to crimson or amethyst-colored middle lobe. In *V. l. dulcis*, the white sepals and petals are margined with rosy-violet. **V. merrillii,** of the Philippine Islands, which has the growth habit of *V. tricolor*, is up to 6 feet tall. The horizontal to nearly erect racemes, up to about 10 inches long, commonly have ten to fifteen 1½- to 2-inch-wide, glossy blooms. Their generally wavy sepals and petals are ordinarily creamy-yellow conspicuously blotched with brown-red or red. The lip is big and flaring and generally yellowish with obscure reddish markings. **V. spathulata,** of Ceylon and southern India, has climbing stems several feet long and rather widely spaced, and often purplish leaves, mostly 4 to 5 inches in length. The erect or arching racemes, up to 1¼ feet long, are of bright yellow blooms, 1¼ to 1½ inches across, usually with brown markings on the side lobes. **V. tessellata,** of Burma, India, and Ceylon, has stems, 1 foot to 2 feet tall, rather crowded with stiff, leathery leaves folded along their centers and 5 to 8 inches long by ½ to ¾ inch wide. Generally somewhat longer than the leaves and spreading to suberect, the racemes are of five to ten

2-inch-wide, fragrant flowers that are variable in color. Most commonly they have wavy-margined, white-backed, pale greenish sepals and petals, reticulated with brown on their faces. The lip has a violet-purple, notched center lobe and a pair of small, white side lobes.

Man-made hybrids of *Vanda*, outcomes of crosses between different species of the genus, and a considerable array that have resulted from crossing species of *Vanda* with those of other genera, are plentiful. Most are beautiful and useful as garden and greenhouse decorations and as cut blooms. In Hawaii, especially, attention has been given to breeding hybrids; a fine range of dwarf varieties with medium-sized flowers of many colors, as well as a group with miniature blooms in drooping, foxtail spikes, have been raised there. All are lovely.

The first *Vanda* hybrid, produced in 1893 by Miss Agnes Joaquim, of Singapore, was named 'Miss Joaquim'. A cross between *V. hookeriana* and *V. teres*, this was brought to Hawaii about 1930. There, it soon attained immense popularity as a garden plant and commercial cut flower, and to a very large extent it was responsible for stimulating the interest that resulted in the multimillion dollar orchid-growing industry now established in Hawaii.

Garden and Landscape Uses. In southern Florida, in Hawaii, and in other parts of the humid tropics and frost-free subtropics, vandas thrive outdoors with minimal care. There, their light requirements are met and, because the plants are not subjected to the short, weakly illuminated days of northern winters, they prosper to the extent that they serve splendidly as outdoor ornaments, as well as providers of a steady supply of cut blooms.

As greenhouse plants these are not difficult, but if starved for light or nourishment or if grown in too low temperatures, they soon decline or persist as only ghosts of what really fine vanda plants should be. Some kinds have flowered well in indoor light gardens. For this purpose short-stemmed sorts are to be preferred.

Cultivation. Vandas are among the most light-hungry of orchids. They will not stand much shade, although the strap-leaved ones need some from the full intensity of summer sun. Those with cylindrical leaves, the teretes as they are called, revel in practically full sun. As is to be expected, the group of hybrid intermediates, the semiteretes, have light requirements midway between those of the two basic groups.

Along with excellent light is a need for warmth and fairly high humidity. Indoors maintain a minimum winter night temperature of 60 to 65°F. By day, allow increases of five to fifteen degrees, depending upon the brightness of the weather.

Summer temperatures of up to 90 to 100°F are favorable. Mist the plants with water freely on all favorable occasions, but not so late in the day that they will not dry before nightfall. Good air circulation, quite essential to success, must be provided to avoid a dank, oppressive atmosphere.

Rooting mediums of various kinds are successfully used for vandas. They should be coarse in texture to allow water to drain through them freely. Chunks of tree fern or osmunda fiber, mixed with some broken crocks or crushed bricks and broken charcoal, give good results; bark chips may be substituted in part or completely for the fiber.

The plants succeed in raised beds, pots, and hanging baskets. Whichever is chosen, excellent drainage is imperative. Set the plants rather high, with only a small part of the lower stem covered by the rooting medium, and allow the aerial roots to hang free. Do not repot or replant more often than necessary, but do so well before the rooting medium becomes stale and sour.

Vandas have no season of complete dormancy, although some slow down considerably in winter. They require watering throughout the year, generously from spring to fall, more circumspectly in winter. Take care when watering and when spraying with water not to allow water to lodge in the leaf axils near the apexes of the stems. From spring to fall, regular applications of dilute liquid fertilizer do much to stimulate satisfactory growth. Propagation is by detaching rooted offshoots (in Hawaii, called keikis) from established plants and potting these separately. Seeds are also much employed as a means of multiplication, but generally produce a variable progeny with a proportion of individuals likely to be inferior to the parent.

VANDOPSIS (Van-dópsis). Twenty-one species of orchids related to *Vanda* comprise the genus *Vandopsis,* of the orchid family ORCHIDACEAE. In the wild the group ranges from China and Taiwan to India and Polynesia. Its name comes from the Sanskrit *vanda,* an orchid, and the Greek *opsis,* resembling.

Vandopsises are epiphytes with stout stems, which may become several feet tall, and two ranks of thick, strap-shaped, leathery, stem-clasping leaves up to 2 feet long by 2 to 3 inches wide. The flower spikes develop from the leaf axils. They are up to 6 feet in length and sometimes carry as many as twenty blooms. Fleshy or somewhat leathery, the flowers resemble those of *Vanda,* but are laterally compressed in front and are without spurs. Their sepals and petals are of the same color and are nearly the same size. The lip is small and three-lobed, the column short and almost as broad as long. The plant sometimes grown as *V. parishii* is *Vanda parishii.*

A beautiful summer-blooming species, native to the Philippine Islands, Bali, and Malacca, *V. lissochiloides* (syns. *Vanda batemannii, Stauropsis lissochiloides*) is up to 6 feet tall. The flower spikes are much longer than the leaves and have twelve to twenty waxy blooms, 2 to 3 inches across, that have yellow sepals and petals, spotted on their insides with crimson and rosy purple on their reverses. Pouched at its base and furrowed and incurved at the front, the lip is purple-red.

Native to Burma, spring-flowering *V. gigantea* (syns. *Vanda gigantea, Stauropsis gigantea*) has spikes of six to twelve 3-inch-wide blooms with deep yellow sepals and petals, with blotches or concentric rings of reddish-brown, and a yellow lip blotched with reddish-brown and with a raised white band down its center. The flower spikes are about one-half as long as the leaves.

Garden and Landscape Uses and Cultivation. Essentially these are as for vandas. Vandopsises grow satisfactorily in osmunda fiber, tree fern fiber, and fir bark and charcoal. Medium humidity and a temperature on winter nights of 60 to 62°F with a five or ten degree increase by day are needed. They may be propagated by cutting off tops below active aerial roots and potting them. For additional information see Orchids.

VANGLOSSUM. This is the name of orchid hybrids the parents of which are *Ascoglossum* and *Vanda.*

VANGUERIA (Van-guèria). Voa-vanguer, the name used in Malagasy (Madagascar) for an edible-fruited native species, is the source of the name of this genus. Consisting of twenty-seven species indigenous to Africa and Malagasy, *Vangueria* belongs in the madder family RUBIACEAE.

Vanguerias are trees and shrubs, sometimes spiny, with undivided leaves that are opposite or may sometimes seem to be in circles of four. The small, white or greenish flowers, in clusters from the leaf axils, have four- to ten-lobed or -toothed calyxes, short-tubed corollas with usually five, rarely four or six lobes (petals) that are spread or sometimes bend backward, five or rarely four stamens, and one style. The fruits, structured like those of plums, are drupes.

A shrub without spines and 8 to 15 feet tall, *V. edulis* (syn. *V. madagascariensis*), a native of Malagasy, called tamarind-of-the-Indies, has hairless, ovate to elliptic, short-stalked leaves 3 to 8 inches long by 1 inch to 4 inches wide. Its ¼-inch-long blooms are in forking clusters. The edible, four- or five-seeded fruits are spherical, green, and ¾ inch to 1½ inches in diameter.

Native to South Africa and northward, *V. infausta* is a symmetrical shrub or sometimes small tree 5 to 20 feet in height,

with ovate to nearly round, strongly-veined, leathery leaves, 2 to 9 inches long, velvety-hairy on both sides and paler beneath than on their upper sides. Its greenish-white flowers, ¼ inch long, are succeeded by smooth, globose, yellowish-brown fruits, about 1 inch in diameter, that have a sour-sweet flavor.

Garden and Landscape Uses and Cultivation. The species described are cultivated in the West Indies, southern Florida, and elsewhere where little or no frost is experienced. It succeeds in sunny, open locations and in well-drained, even dryish soils. Propagation is by seed, and by cuttings of firm, but not hard shoots, under mist or in a greenhouse propagating bench.

VANHEERDIA (Van-heérdia). Among the stone or pebble plants of South Africa, a remarkable group now allotted to several genera, but once all included in *Mesembryanthemum,* is *Vanheerdia.* It belongs to the carpetweed family AIZOACEAE and comprises four species. The name compliments P. van Heerde, a South African who was much interested in the native plants of his country.

Vanheerdias are perennials with much the appearance of succulent gibbaeums and lithops. Their plant bodies are clustered. Each consists of a pair of matching fleshy leaves, usually finely-toothed along their edges and keels. They are united to form a nearly spherical to somewhat elongated, round- to flat-topped or angled unit, cleft across its top, that looks like a pair of pebbles or stone chips. The flowers, which open in the afternoons and are up to three together, are remindful of daisies, but are quite different from those flowers in structure, each being a single bloom, not a head of many florets. Each has a five- to nine-parted calyx, about three rows of yellow to orange-yellow petals, many erect stamens, and seven to fifteen stigmas. The fruits are capsules.

From the other species, *V. primosii* differs in not being covered with almost microscopic hairs and in having, at the tops of its plant bodies, which are about 1½ inches long by nearly 1 inch wide, a pair of translucent areas called windows. The flowers are golden-yellow and 1 inch in diameter. The mature leaves of *V. angusta* are joined for at least two-thirds of their lengths and have rounded apexes. They are three to four times longer than broad and form plant bodies less than one-half as wide as they are long. The rounded leaves of *V. roodiae,* also joined for at least two-thirds of their lengths, are less than twice as long as their breadths and form plant bodies almost as wide as long. Their orange-yellow flowers are 1 inch across. The yellow to golden-yellow flowers of *V. angusta,* mostly in threes, are nearly 1½ inches wide. The mature leaves of *V. divergens,* united for at least one-half their lengths, are compressed at the apex into a sharp rooftop angle. The plant bodies are up to 2¼ inches long by 1 inch wide or somewhat wider. From ½ to ¾ inch across, the blooms are golden-yellow.

Garden Uses and Cultivation. These are collectors' items that need very porous limestone soil and such conditions and care that suit fleshy species of *Gibbaeum* and *Lithops*. Limited experience with the cultivation of vanheerdias indicates that, with the possible exception of *V. angusta*, they are rather difficult to grow.

VANILLA. As well as being the name of the next discussed genus, the word vanilla forms parts of the common names of these plants: Carolina-vanilla (*Trilisia odoratissima*) and vanilla leaf (*Achlys triphylla*).

VANILLA (Van-ílla). The vast orchid family ORCHIDACEAE is more notable for its beautiful and often curiously formed flowers than for its nonaesthetic uses. But one genus, *Vanilla*, is a source of the popular flavoring of that name. "A source" is written instead of "the source" because much vanilla flavoring is synthesized from petroleum and paper mill wastes. As the synthetic product is not equal in quality to natural vanilla extract, the production of the latter continues at favorable places in the tropics. The name *Vanilla* derives from *vainilla*, a diminutive for the Spanish word for a pod.

The genus *Vanilla* comprises about ninety species, vining orchids native to the tropics and subtropics around the world. Their stems climb by attaching aerial roots to tree trunks and other supports. They have alternate, thick, thin, or papery leaves or are essentially leafless, the leaves being represented by small bracts. Usually in stubby racemes or spikes from the leaf axils, the flowers are generally quite large, but usually not especially showy. Their fleshy sepals and petals are spreading and similar. The broad lip narrows to a shaft or claw toward its base and is attached to the bottom of the column, which the lip envelops. The long, fleshy fruits are beanlike capsules.

Knowledge of vanilla as a flavoring agent came to Europeans from the Aztecs, whom, as early as the sixteenth century, they saw mixing an extract of the orchid seed pods with their chocolate beverages. Moreover, the preparation of natural vanilla extract today differs little from that employed by the Aztecs. The beans, as the fruits are called, are picked when fully grown, but still immature. They are spread in the sun for a short time to dry somewhat and then are fermented or "sweated" in barrels or under heavy cloths in the shade. Each night during the sweating period they are protected from chilling and dampness by being put into airtight boxes. This treatment induces the production, as result of the activity of an enzyme, of vanillin, which often shows on the outside of the cured bean as minute, glistening crystals. Commercially, vanilla is cultivated in Mexico, Central America, Malagasy (Madagascar), Java, Tahiti, Réunion, and the Seychelles Islands. Except in Mexico and Central America, where obliging native insects attend to the matter, it is necessary to hand-pollinate the flowers to secure a set of beans.

Common vanilla, the kind most favored for the production of vanilla extract, is *V. planifolia* (syn. *V. fragrans*). This native from southern Florida to Mexico, South America, and the West Indies is a high-climbing, vigorous vine with fleshy, nearly stalkless, pointed-oblong leaves 6 to 9 inches long and 2 to 3 inches wide. Its fragrant, short-lived blooms, in many-flowered racemes, are about 2 inches long, greenish-yellow, and open only partially. Their narrowly-trumpet-shaped lips are shorter than the petals and sepals. The fruits are up to 8 inches long. Variety *V. p. variegata* has leaves striped with creamy-

Vanilla planifolia (flower)

An undetermined species of *Vanilla* ascending the trunk of a royal palm, Hope Botanic Gardens, Kingston, Jamaica

Vanilla planifolia

Vanilla planifolia (young fruits)

Vanilla planifolia variegata

A home vegetable garden: (a) Well planned and carefully tended

white. Other species are used to a lesser extent as sources of vanilla extract, notably **V. pompona,** native from Mexico to Brazil. This is generally similar to *V. planifolia,* but is more robust and has shorter, thicker fruits.

Brazilian **V. chamissonis** has short-stalked, oblong to oblong-lanceolate leaves 7 to 9 inches long by 1½ to 2 inches wide. In racemes of up to twenty, the yellow flowers have oblong sepals and spatula-shaped petals 1¾ to 2¼ inches long, and a wavy-margined lip as long or a little longer. The fruits are about 5 inches long.

The link vine or worm vine (**V. barbellata**) has abortive leaves or bracts in place of leaves. It is a native of southern Florida and the West Indies, where it grows on rocks and river banks. It has short clusters of up to twelve blooms, with green sepals and petals about 1½ inches long. The lip is beautifully marked with red and white. Similar **V. dilloniana,** from the same regions, bears abortive leaves on the lower portions of its stems, scale leaves on the upper parts. Its flowers have green sepals and petals about 2 inches long and a richly colored, red and white lip. Neither of these curious native orchids is much cultivated.

Garden Uses and Cultivation. Vanillas are sometimes included as subjects of interest in orchid collections and are frequently grown in botanic presentations of plants useful to man. They are not difficult to manage, but often do not flower freely and, unless the blooms are hand-pollinated, do not produce fruits. For their best success, they need high temperatures and abundant humidity. Good light, with as much sun as they will stand without the foliage becoming yellow or being scorched, is necessary. A loose, porous rooting medium, such as suits many ter-restrial orchids, is satisfactory. It may be composed of fibrous loam, osmunda or tree fern fiber, coarse sand, coarse leaf mold, pieces of bark, dried manure, and crushed charcoal. The plants may be set in very well-drained pots or beds. Supports for their vining stems must be provided. These may consist of posts or wires. Flowering is more likely if, after growing vertically for a few feet, the stems are trained horizontally. Vanillas have no marked resting season. They must be watered throughout the year, but under no circumstances must the ground be soggy for long periods. Well-rooted specimens benefit from spring-to-fall applications of mild liquid fertilizer. In greenhouses a minimum winter night temperature of 65°F and higher temperatures by day and at other seasons suit. Propagation is extremely easy. The stems are cut into sections each having three to five nodes or joints. These are planted as cuttings in a mixture of sphagnum moss or peat moss and sand in a temperature of 70 to 85°F and kept moderately moist. For more information see Orchids.

VARNISH TREE. See *Rhus verniciflua.* The Japanese varnish tree is *Firmiana simplex.*

VEGETABLE. The word vegetable is used in the common names of these plants: vegetable ivory (*Phytelephas*), vegetable oyster (*Tragopogon porrifolius*), vegetable sheep (*Haastia pulvinaris* and *Raoulia eximia*), and vegetable sponge (*Luffa*). For additional information on the vegetable oyster, see the Encyclopedia entry Salsify, Oyster Plant, or Vegetable Oyster.

VEGETABLE GARDENS. A home vegetable garden can be a source of much pleasure and pride, as well as a supplier of sub-

(b) Provides generous harvests of healthful food

(c) For the kitchen

stantial amounts of healthful food for the family table. Even the most modern production and marketing techniques cannot deliver vegetables, salads, and culinary herbs as delicious and flavorful as those freshly harvested from a home plot, nor can they deliver them in such variety. Other dividends include agreeable exercise and the satisfaction of achievement, as well as, if the labor is not paid for or is not too costly, a reduction in the family food budget. In all likelihood there will be, at times, surplus produce to be shared with friends and neighbors; you may even wish to grow vegetables for freezing, drying, or canning.

All this is not had without some effort and dedication and even occasional frustration. But if the garden is wisely planned and managed, the rewards greatly outweigh any disadvantages. Probably the most common disillusions with home vegetable growing result from beginning with a plot too big for the attentions that must be provided as the season advances, and, as such, neglecting it when other activities make increasing demands upon one's time.

Planning is essential for success. Hit-or-miss procedures fail to take fullest advantage of garden space or of the gardener's time, and neglect the importance of sowing and planting dates. Without planning, it is unlikely that there will be a steady succession of produce; more probably, periods of abundance will alternate with periods of scarcity. Planning, of course, includes selecting a suitable location.

A well-planned demonstration garden at The New York Botanical Garden

A sunny site is necessary for a vegetable garden; all-day sun is desirable and a minimum of seven or eight hours is essential. Be sure the plot is far enough from large trees so that their roots will not invade it. A good rule of thumb is that no boundary of the garden should be nearer a tree than the equivalent of the tree's height. The soil is important. It should be at least 8 inches deep, though deeper is better, and reasonably fertile or capable of being brought into that condition. Do not be dismayed if the topsoil itself is not fully 8 inches deep; so long as the layer beneath it is porous and capable of being loosened by spading, rotary tilling, or plowing, it can be gradually converted into topsoil by those manipulations and by mixing in generous

amounts of such organic materials as compost, green manures (cover crops), and, when available, animal manure.

The plot should be fairly level; a gentle slope is acceptable, however, and if it be to the south, it is an advantage to the extent that it will favor early crops. Severer slopes can often be improved by terracing, but usually not without considerable effort, occasioned in part by the need for having a surface layer of at least 8 inches of acceptable topsoil. Achievement of this may necessitate removing the existing topsoil and regrading the subsoil before replacing the topsoil or, as an alternative, bringing in additional topsoil.

The size of the garden must be decided upon. Beginners are well advised to think small. As experience is gained and competence develops, expansion may be in order, but until then proceed with some caution. The substantial amounts of vegetables that can be harvested from a well-managed plot of even 600 square feet are surprising, and many home gardeners, through necessity or choice, settle for less than that. But where space permits, many enthusiasts prefer larger gardens, say of 1,000 to 3,000 square feet or more. Experiments conducted during World War II proved that abundant vegetable food for one person for an entire year, including produce for canning and winter storage, can be had from an intensively cultivated plot of 750 square feet of soil of good to average fertility. Whatever the size of the

This 150 square feet of vegetable garden:
(a) Keeps a young boy busy

(b) And adds to the family food supply

garden, it is advisable to fence it against rabbits, dogs, and other marauders. The fence need not be elaborate, one of chicken wire will do.

Cold frames and hotbeds are useful adjuncts to vegetable gardens (see the Encyclopedia entries Garden Frames and Hotbeds). They make it possible to steal a start on the season by sowing some crops earlier than would be practicable outdoors, to give plants for setting out later. Both cold frames and hotbeds, but more especially the latter, need practically daily attention during the period they are sheltering young plants; unless you can give this, you may find it better to rely upon commercial sources for early-started plants to set in the garden.

Even a small cold frame is a useful adjunct in a vegetable garden

What to grow depends very largely upon personal and family preferences, but if the garden is small seriously consider passing up sorts that take a great amount of space relative to the quantity or value of their harvests. Applying this yardstick, asparagus and potatoes come first to mind and then such crops grown for storage as onions, winter cabbage, parsnips, and rutabagas. Melons, pumpkins, and squashes occupy considerable space and, most unfortunately, so does sweet corn. With the exception of sweet corn, these can be obtained in nearly as good condition as home grown from retail outlets. Ease of cultivation and certainty of cropping deserves attention. In many regions, cauliflowers and brussels sprouts are not easy to have, and in some areas there are others that are troublesome or too uncertain croppers to be worthwhile where space or labor is decidedly limited. A few crops will be included in almost all vegetable gardens. Tomatoes are the most rewarding for the space and effort they need. Other favorite, generally easy-to-grow kinds are bush snap beans, broccoli, beets, carrots, and lettuce. To these may be added scallions and such leaf crops as spinach, Swiss chard, and

New-Zealand-spinach. Despite the large amount of space it needs relative to its harvest, wherever enough space can be found for even a small planting, sweet corn is a must in almost all American vegetable gardens. Where space permits, such cane and bush fruits as currants, gooseberries, raspberries, blackberries, and loganberries are often planted in vegetable gardens, as are strawberries.

Once the site and size of the garden is settled and the crops to be grown decided upon, make a planting plan. Do this well in advance of the first outdoor work of spring. An important preliminary, it can be an agreeable winter task. Draw the plan to scale. The use of graph paper facilitates this. It is convenient to let the side of each little square on the paper represent 3 inches on the ground, but smaller or bigger scales may be employed. First, mark on the plan the boundaries of the garden, then the paths, if the size of the plot makes one or more necessary or desirable. Be sure the path system is simple and utilitarian; elaborate layouts are out of place. The rows of vegetables will ordinarily be at right angles to the main path. Because soil erosion is less likely to be troublesome on sloping ground if the rows run across the slope rather than up and down, on such sites the chief paths generally will follow the incline. It is sometimes stressed that because north-to-south rows receive equal sun from both sides, whereas those with other orientations do not, vegetable gardens should be planned with this in mind. Any advantage gained in this manner is minor; if other considerations, such as the shape or slope of the garden, make it more realistic to run the rows in another direction have no hesitation in doing so. To avoid shading lower crops it is advantageous to site such tall growers as tomatoes, pole beans, and corn together at the northern side of the area; this is more likely to be of importance in small gardens than big ones.

A number of factors need to be taken in account in positioning the various crops. Unless such cane and bush fruits as raspberries, blackberries, loganberries, currants, gooseberries, and blueberries are to be included, the sorts that will occupy the ground for more than one season are few. Among them are asparagus, rhubarb, strawberries, and a few kinds of herbs, such as horseradish and mint. The herbs can often be accommodated in a separate patch or corner, perhaps along the boundary fence. The other perennial crops should be located in a section at one end or one side of the garden. By leaving the remainder of the area free for crops of annual duration, this facilitates preparing the soil for sowing and planting.

Of the annual crops, some, such as cucumbers, eggplants, New-Zealand-spinach, onions, parsnips, peppers, pole beans, salsify, sweet potatoes, Swiss chard, and tomatoes, occupy the ground for the entire season and should be grouped together, as should those that will be harvested after shorter periods of growth. These last, which include beets, bush beans, carrots, lettuce, and peas, can be succeeded or preceded by other crops or in some instances by second and sometimes even third sowings of the same crop. Thus, peas and spinach can be succeeded by the second sowing of beets, carrots, or leaf lettuce; radishes, and scallions from sets, by beans or carrots; and early beets and carrots by Chinese cabbage or endive. Many other successions can be arranged to keep the ground as fully occupied throughout the season as possible. Much can be gained from judicious intercropping or companion cropping, that is from sowing a row of a rapidly maturing crop between rows of others that are fairly widely spaced and that will occupy the ground for a longer time. It is quite practicable to raise a row of lettuce, radishes, scallions, or spinach between rows of early-sown peas or between rows of sweet corn, celery, eggplants, peppers, or tomatoes to be planted later. Many other combinations can be arranged.

In gardens big enough to make it practicable, rotation of crops is desirable as a means of exploiting the soil nutrients to best advantage and of minimizing dangers from certain diseases and pests. Crop rotation involves siting crops so they do not occupy the same location as the same or a closely related crop did during the previous year or two or three. A good basic annual rotation is to have root crops, such as beets, carrots, and parsnips, succeed leaf crops, such as broccoli, cabbage, celery, and spinach, and the leaf crops, in turn, followed by seed and fruit crops, such as beans, eggplants, peas, peppers, and tomatoes. But even then some accommodation should be made to avoid having a leaf crop succeed a root crop if both are susceptible to the same disease or pest. In small gardens it is rarely practicable to arrange for complete rotation of crops, but it is a matter at least to keep in mind when making the garden plan.

In determining how much space to allow between rows, consider these matters. Related to the size of the garden, maximum yields are had by having the rows as close together as practicable without the quantity or quality of the crops being depressed by crowding. Such spacing also minimizes the amount of surface that must be cultivated or mulched to control weeds. It is ideal for gardens to be worked entirely with hand tools. But where mechanical cultivators are employed, wider spacing is often necessary. Also, the space needed by different vegetables and quite often by varieties of the same kind should be taken into account. Plants of a cabbage variety that matures with a small head should be set considerably closer together than those of a big-headed variety, and rows of 2- to 3-foot-tall peas nearer to one another than those of a variety that attains a height of 4 or 5 feet. Appropriate spacings for the various vegetables are sug-

A center path with rows of vegetables at right angles to it is often a satisfactory layout

gested individually in their respective Encyclopedia entries.

Preparing the soil for planting is one of the first outdoor tasks to need attention. It involves spading, rotary tilling, or plowing. Small plots are commonly manipulated by hand, using a spade or spading fork. If conscientiously done, this indeed

Preparing the soil for planting: (a) With a spade

(b) With a spading fork

(c) With a rotary tiller

is a superior method. But spading is quite hard work (albeit excellent exercise) likely to be beyond the physical capabilities of some who aspire to grow vegetables, and is too time-consuming for some others. Rotary tilling is the most practical alternative and also is the procedure most often employed in vegetable gardens too extensive to be spaded. Be sure the machine is powerful enough to churn the soil to a depth of at least 8 inches. Many lightweight rotary tillers designed for amateurs do not have this capability and, although they have many other uses in gardens, are inadequate for the task we are considering. In many communities suitable rotary tillers and operators can be hired on an hourly or per job basis, and it is often convenient to engage their services. If you do, it is advisable to be on hand at the start of the operation and to keep an eye on it throughout to make sure that maximum depth is reached and an adequate job is done. Plowing, followed by harrowing, is an entirely satisfactory method of soil preparation for a vegetable garden, however, it is only likely to be done in farm communities where the necessary equipment is available.

Opportunity to incorporate with the soil such bulk material as compost, manure, and green manure (a cover crop such as winter rye) is afforded by spading, rotary tilling, and plowing. Such additions are generally highly beneficial; whenever pos-

Manure and other bulk organic materials are excellent soil additives

sible improve your soil in this way as generously as is practicable. Just one caveat, do not add manure where root crops are to be grown. If you do you are likely to stimulate leaf growth at the expense of the below-ground or mostly below-ground parts of such crops as beets, carrots, celariac, rutabagas, and turnips. Contrariwise, such leaf vegetables as broccoli, cabbage, cauliflower, celery, lettuce, and spinach respond favorably indeed to quite heavily manured ground, as do some crops grown for their fruits or seed, among them beans, cucumbers, melons, peas, and squash. Leeks and onions also benefit from generous manuring. More moderate applica-

tions benefit eggplants, peppers, and tomatoes if the soil is low in nitrogen, but excessive amounts stimulate stem and leaf growth and result in poor cropping. None of these strictures applies to compost or green manures, which may be incorporated with the soil to the benefit of all crops.

Liming is only needed if the pH of the soil is below the optimum, which may be taken as pH 6 to 6.5 and is determinable by a soil test, which can be arranged through your Cooperative Extension Agent or which you can do yourself with a simple kit. In many areas an application of lime or ground limestone about every three years works well, but let soil tests determine the frequency. Spread the lime evenly and fork it lightly or harrow it into the top 3 or 4 inches of soil. Whether or not liming is done, do not rake the soil finely; leave it rough-surfaced until immediately before the time you are ready to sow or plant.

Attend to the initial soil preparation as far in advance of sowing and planting as practicable. In regions where the growing

Turning under cover crops, such as buckwheat and winter rye, improves the humus content of the soil

season ends in fall and essentially all sowing and planting are done in spring and summer, fall may be the best season for deep spading, rotary tilling, or plowing, but if a cover crop, such as winter rye, is to be sown in fall for turning under in late winter or spring, delay the deep working of the soil until then, at the first opportunity the weather affords. Fertilizing is ordinarily best done just before sowing or planting. Scatter the fertilizer, which in most cases will be a standard 5-10-5 or other formula favored in the region, at the recommended rate and rake it into the upper 3 to 4 inches of the soil.

Many beginners sow too many feet of row at each sowing and set out too many plants at each planting. As a rough guide to what is likely to prove adequate for a family of two adults, these suggestions are made: bush lima beans and bush snap beans, 50 feet of row; pole beans, four or five hills; broccoli, eight or nine plants; cabbage, ten to twelve plants; carrots, 20 feet of row; corn, 80 to 100 feet of row; cucumbers, three to four hills; eggplants, three or four plants; lettuce, 15 feet of row; muskmelons, three to five hills; New-Zealand-spinach, 10 to 15 feet of row; onions, 20 feet of row; parsley, 10 feet of row; peas, 50 feet of row; peppers, three or four plants; radishes, 10 to 12 feet of row; scallions, 10 to 15 feet of row; spinach, 50 feet of row; summer squash, three to four hills; and tomatoes, six to ten plants.

Most vegetables are raised from seed. A few, such as potatoes, rhubarb, horseradish, and mint, are increased by other means. Methods and times of sowing vary with the crop and with the season of the year (see the Encyclopedia entry Seeds, Propagation By, and those entries of the names of the various vegetables). Outdoors, seeds are usually sown in drills or

Sowing seeds in drills

in hills. Drills are shallow furrows along which the seeds are scattered evenly and then covered shallowly with soil. To sow in hills, scatter a few seeds closely together at rather distant intervals. The hills may be raised, or not, above the ordinary ground level. Crops sown in hills include squash, cucumbers, pole beans, melons, sweet corn, and pumpkins. Other kinds are sown in drills. Tomatoes, peppers, and eggplants are most often sown in a greenhouse, hotbed, or similar convenience, and the plants later set in the garden. The same plan is usual with early crops of lettuce, broccoli, cabbage, and cauliflower. If you are without facilities for raising early plants, they can be purchased. The main crops of

most vegetables are sown directly in the open ground, mostly where they are to mature, although a few, such as broccoli and cabbages, are sown in a seed bed and later transplanted. Successional sowings are made outdoors also.

Seeds started early indoors are sown in pots or flats. These last are shallow, wooden or plastic boxes 3 inches deep, of any convenient size, and with a few cracks or holes in their bottoms for drainage. Be sure the soil is loose and crumbly rather than stiff and clayey. A mixture of equal parts of good garden soil, perlite or coarse sand, and peat moss or leaf mold is suitable.

To ensure harvesting certain crops, such as bush beans, beets, carrots, endive, lettuce, radishes, spinach, and sweet corn, over as long a period as possible, it is necessary to follow the earliest sowing with successional ones, usually at two- to three-week intervals, with the last timed to be ready for harvesting before killing frost, or in some cases before extremely hot weather makes later sowing futile. The latest dates for sowing these crops depend upon geographical location. If you expect the first killing frost in your locality during the first half of October, make your last sowing of sweet corn in mid-July, your last sowings of bush beans, beets, Swiss chard, carrots, endive, and lettuce about the first of August, and your last sowings of radishes and spinach during the first week in September. If the first killing frosts normally come to your garden before or after early October, adjust your last sowing dates accordingly.

Routine care of a vegetable garden calls for frequent attention. Beware of letting weeds grow big—they are much easier to kill with a hoe or cultivator while they are tiny than later, or than to pull by hand. Frequent surface cultivation also checks loss of moisture from the soil. Except for parts that are mulched, cultivate the entire garden often enough to control weeds and keep the surface soil loose, and always as soon as the soil is dry enough after a rain that has caused its surface to cake. Mulching to control weeds, reduce labor, and

Cultivating shallowly to destroy weeds and promote growth is an important summer task

bring other benefits is not practicable between rows planted closely together, but among more widely spaced ones, such as tomatoes, pole beans, and sweet corn, and around hills of such crops as cucumbers, squash, and melons, it is often advantageous. The best mulches are those of a strawy type and black plastic ones. Do not put mulches in place too early in the season; wait until the soil has had a chance to warm.

The secret of having a well-cared-for garden is to attend to tasks when they need doing. Do not let the work get ahead of you. Be a keen observer. Above all, take advantage of the weather and do the work suited to the prevailing conditions. For example, when possible, choose cloudy days for planting, use sunny days for cultivating, and try to avoid dusting or spraying immediately before rain.

Many crops need thinning by removal of surplus young plants. This is because, even though you are economical with seed at sowing time, nearly always more plants

Thinning seedlings early to prevent overcrowding is necessary with some crops

come up than can possibly grow to optimum size. Thin early; do not wait until the plants have been harmed by crowding. It is usually best not to remove all the unwanted plants at one time, but to go over each planting two or three times, always leaving the strongest seedlings and those best spaced. Thinnings of beets, lettuce, onions, and some other crops can be transplanted successfully to other parts of the garden and the later thinnings of some, such as carrots, onions, and turnips, are acceptable for table use.

Some crops need support. Put the supports in place early; for pole beans, before the seeds are sown, and for tomatoes, before the plants are set out. Brushwood or chicken wire to support peas should be put in place when the plants are about 1 inch high. Beans and peas cling to their supports, but tomatoes need tying that must be attended to throughout the summer. If you restrict your tomatoes to one stem you must remove all side shoots while they are still quite small; other methods of training may involve pinching out some side shoots.

Watering will be needed during dry periods. Some crops, such as celery, lettuce, and peas, suffer much more severely from drought than some others, such as onions, peppers, and tomatoes. On sandy soils and on soils that have not been deeply prepared, crops are harmed by drought more quickly than are those grown on heavy soils or on soils that have been spaded, rototilled, or plowed deeply. When you water, give enough to saturate the ground thoroughly to a depth of 8 to 10 inches. Then give no more until the soil is dry again—this may be a week later. Daily sprinklings that merely wet the upper inch or two or three of soil are valueless. It is less wasteful of water to apply it in the early morning or in the evening than in the middle of the day.

Even though the soil is fertile at seeding or planting time, many vegetables benefit from supplemental applications of fertilizer during the summer. Commercial fertilizers applied as side-dressings are good. A complete fertilizer, such as a 5-10-5, may be sprinkled along the rows at 3 to 5 pounds per 100 feet. Never fertilize when the soil is very dry, wait rather until a few hours after rain or watering. Do not let fertilizer come in contact with the foliage. It should be kept about 2 inches away from the base of the plants. Supplementary fertilizing is not usually begun until the crop is at least half-grown. After you have applied the fertilizer, scratch it lightly into the surface with a cultivator and, unless it rains shortly afterward, water with a fine spray.

Harvesting is among the most satisfying chores connected with vegetable gardening. Some experience is needed to know just when a crop is ready for harvesting. Avoid waiting too long before you pick peas, beans, kohlrabi, turnips, radishes, broccoli, sweet corn, and other summer vegetables. If you wait too long, they become tough and lose their delicate flavor. On the other hand it is wasteful to pick very young vegetables, for this greatly reduces the total weight of your crop. Do

Harvesting: (a) Lettuce

(b) Kohlrabi

(c) Potatoes

not pick your vegetables long before they are to be used. Sweet corn cooked within fifteen minutes of being gathered tastes much better than if it has been picked some hours before it is put into the pot. This is true to a lesser extent of most other summer crops. Allow tomatoes to ripen completely on the vines.

In addition to the crops that you pick for summer use, you may raise others for freezing, canning, or winter storage. Vegetables that store well include kohlrabi, parsnips, squash, pumpkins, onions, leeks, rutabagas, carrots, beets, potatoes, celery, and cabbage. Onions, pumpkins, and squash keep best in a dry, cool place—such as a frostproof attic. An unheated, but frostproof cellar provides ideal storage conditions for the others. The air in the cellar must be moist, but not so moist that condensation results and drops of water are deposited on the walls and on the vegetables. If your cellar has an earth floor the air will probably be moist enough, otherwise you will have to wet the floor down occasionally. Keep the temperature as uniform as possible. Never let it go below 34°F and, if possible, prevent it from rising above 40°F. This you can do by careful ventilation. When the outdoor temperature is below 34 or above 40°F, keep the cellar tightly closed. At other times open the windows or doors to admit outside air. If your cellar is heated and the temperature normally rises above 40°F during the win-

Entrance to a root cellar covered with earth (note the ventilator at top left)

ter, it will not be satisfactory for the storage of most vegetables. If you wish, you can set off a portion of it as a storage cellar by insulating the walls. If you do this make sure that the door leading from the heated part of the cellar into the storage room is stout. Arrange also for a window or ventilator opening to the outside.

If you are unable to provide suitable storage in a cellar, you can successfully keep many vegetables over the winter in shallow trenches dug in the open garden. Choose a well-drained spot. Dig an excavation 1 foot deep, 3 to 4 feet wide, and of any desired length. Over the bottom of this trench spread a 6-inch layer of straw. Now pile potatoes, beets, carrots, cabbages, rutabagas, and similar vegetables into a neat pile that comes to a pointed ridge at the top. Separate the different vegetables with boards. Cover the pile with a 1-foot layer of straw and then cover the straw with 8 inches of firmly packed soil. After the soil has frozen, add another 8-inch covering of soil. Dig the soil used for covering from around the heap so that a ditch is made that is deeper than the bottom of the vegetable trench. This ditch must surround the pile and have an outlet so that water will drain away from it. Choose mild periods during the winter for the removal of the vegetables and take out enough on each occasion to last for two or three weeks.

Small quantities of vegetables can be stored in a barrel placed on its side and banked up and covered with 2 or 3 feet of soil. Make sure that the barrel is tilted slightly downward at the front so that water will not collect in it. After you have filled the barrel with vegetables, close the opening with a heavy layer of straw and a well-fitting cover of thick wood.

The vegetables you intend to store must be of prime quality. Do not try to store diseased crops or those injured by insects. Take care not to bruise the vegetables or damage them in any way: handle them with care. Remove the foliage of such root crops as beets, carrots, and turnips before storage. When handling beets do not use a knife (which will make them "bleed"), but take the beet in one hand and the leaves in the other and twist them off. Remove the roots and a few of the outer leaves of cabbages before storage. Onions must be cured by being in the sun for a few days after they are lifted from the soil. Spread them out on a table, in flats, or on boards raised off the ground.

Pest and disease control is important. The number of pests and diseases that are potentially troublesome is legion. Do not let this deter you. Every garden suffers from some insects and some diseases, but no garden is host to all or even most of them. If you take prompt and proper action at the first signs of trouble you will easily control most of the pests that threaten. First, train yourself to be a keen observer. Walk through the garden daily and look carefully at each growing crop. Be inquisitive. Lift up the leaves of your spinach and examine their undersides for aphids; watch for the appearance of the large green tomato worm; look for signs of downy mildew on your lima beans. Notice every change in the appearance of your vegetables. If they are not doing well, find out why and find out why quickly. A correct diagnosis is essential in order for you to begin proper control measures. It is obviously useless to spray with a fungicide if an insect is the cause of the trouble or to dust with rotenone plants that are merely suffering from drought. If you are unable to make a proper diagnosis, seek expert advice. Often other gardeners in the vicinity can help, and your Cooperative Extension Agent and State Experiment Station are always ready to be of service to you.

In small gardens use, when possible, only dusts and sprays that are nonpoisonous to animals and humans. Be careful not to inhale the dust or spray and wear rubber gloves while you are applying it. Discontinue the use of poisonous dusts or sprays at least ten days before harvesting,

Dusting to control pests

and always wash vegetables thoroughly before cooking or eating. In general, dusts are more economical and easier to apply than are liquid sprays. Use dusts whenever practicable and only resort to sprays for pests, such as red spider mites, that are not controlled in other ways.

So far as possible, anticipate weather so that you do not spray or dust just before it rains. Otherwise, your efforts will be wasted and the work will have to be repeated shortly after the rain ceases. It is better to dust and spray in the early morning or in the evening than in the heat of the day. Do a thorough job each time—make sure that both surfaces of the leaves, as well as the stem, are evenly covered.

A few diseases and pests cannot be eradicated by either dusts or sprays. For some, such as the cutworms that attack lettuce, cabbage, and other crops, poison baits are satisfactory; more rarely, diseases will affect your plants for which there are no known remedies, such as the various virus diseases (for example, the mosaic disease of tomatoes) and also several bacterial diseases (including bacterial wilt of corn and bacterial wilt of cucumbers; bacterial wilt-resistant varieties of sweet corn have been developed, however). Destroy at once plants affected by such diseases. As a precaution, plant only resistant varieties if the disease is known to occur in your locality. Above all, practice clean cultivation. Do everything possible to provide good growing conditions. Poorly grown plants are much more susceptible to attack by pests and diseases than are vigorous specimens.

VEITCHIA (Veìtch-ia)—Christmas Palm or Manila Palm or Merrill Palm. This fine genus of the palm family PALMAE consists of eighteen moderately tall to tall species from Fiji, the New Hebrides, New Caledonia, and the Philippine Islands. Its name *Veitchia* honors the English nurseryman James Veitch, who died in 1869.

Veitchias have solitary, rather slender, smooth trunks, often somewhat thickened at their bases, and crowns of spreading or gracefully recurved pinnate leaves with numerous, regularly-spaced leaflets that are very narrow where they join the rachis (central axis of the leaf). The sheathing bases of the leafstalks form a prominent, columnar crownshaft that appears to be an extension of the trunk. From below the crownshaft originate the branched flower clusters, each when young covered with two papery spathes that soon fall. Mostly the flowers are in threes, each group consisting of a female flanked by two males, but sometimes parts of the flower cluster contain only male blooms. The stamens number twenty-four to nearly one hundred and fifty. The red or orange-red fruits sit in little yellow cups in the manner of acorns.

Veitchia merrillii: (a) In Florida

(b) A young seedling

The Christmas, Manila, or Merrill palm (**V. merrillii** syn. *Adonidia merrillii*), a native of the Philippine Islands, has a trunk, 15 to 20 feet tall, ringed with many leaf scars. The short-stalked, dull green leaves, about 6 feet in length and strongly arched, have forty-eight to sixty-three leaflets. One of the showiest palms in fruit, this species has great loose clusters of bright red, egg-shaped fruits 1 inch to 1½ inches long. Up to 100 feet tall in its native Fiji, **V. joannis** has leaves, arched when young, but later nearly horizontal, with seventy to eighty drooping leaflets. The stalks of the flower clusters are covered with yellowish or rust-colored, woolly scales. Normal male flowers have forty-seven to sixty-two stamens. The orange-red fruits, 2 to 2¼ inches long, are bigger than those of any other species of *Veitchia*. Of unknown origin, **V. montgomeryana** is similar to and in gardens is confused with *V. joannis*. It differs in having male flowers with 130 to 140 stamens and in technical botanical details.

Garden and Landscape Uses. In southern Florida, Hawaii, and other parts of the tropics, veitchias are admired for their graceful appearance and colorful fruits. They are not frost-hardy. They are effective as single specimens and for grouping. Veitchias are suitable for cultivating in greenhouses.

Tropaeolum speciosum

Venidium fastuosum

Tulips forced into early bloom indoors

Tropaeolum tricolor

Ursinea hybrid

Tulipa tarda

Verbena hybrida

Verbascum dumulosum

Cultivation. Veitchias succeed in any ordinary garden soil in sun or light shade, preferably the former. The Christmas palm stands seaside conditions well. In greenhouses, these palms need a minimum winter night temperature of 60 to 65°F, with a rise of five to fifteen degrees in the day allowed. At other seasons the minimum night temperature should be 70°F. Well-drained, fertile soil, kept reasonably moist at all times, is needed. So are light shade from strong summer sun and a humid atmosphere. For further information see Palms.

VELLOZIA (Vell-òzia). The horticulturally little known genus *Vellozia,* of the vellozia family VELLOZIACEAE, is native to tropical South America, Africa, Malagasy (Madagascar), and Arabia. It comprises 100 species. The name commemorates the distinguished Brazilian José Mariano Conceicao Vellosa, who died in 1811.

Vellozias are evergreen, more or less shrubby perennials most often native to rocky places and cliffs. They have woody, firm, sharply-keeled, forked stems, the lower parts of which are clothed with roots, the upper parts with persistent old leaf sheaths. The leaves are toothed, undivided, lobeless, and linear to oblong or narrow-elliptic. Purple, yellow, or white, the solitary, often fragrant blooms are tubular or funnel-shaped, with resinous hairs on their outsides. They have six spreading petals (more correctly, tepals), six stamens, and a three-parted style. The fruits are many-seeded, woody capsules.

Sometimes cultivated, *V. elegans* (syn. *Talbotia elegans*), of Africa, has thin, woody stems and glossy, pointed narrow-elliptic, more or less *Dracaena*-like, spreading leaves about 5 inches long by a little over ½ inch wide. Its starry, 1½-inch-wide, slender-stalked flowers, held above the foliage, are creamy-white, sometimes tinged with green. This species is sometimes misnamed *Barbacenia*.

Vellozia elegans

Vellozia elegans (flower)

Garden Uses and Cultivation. Vellozias are for collectors of the rare and unusual. They are adaptable for planting outdoors in the tropics and for growing in pots or hanging baskets of fertile, porous soil in tropical greenhouses. Increase is by seed and by careful division at the beginning of the growing season.

VELLOZIACEAE — Vellozia Family. Restricted in the wild to South America, Africa, Malagasy (Madagascar), and Arabia, this family of monocotyledons comprise two genera totaling 170 species. Shrubby, its members have woody, fibrous, forking stems clothed with the persistent bases of old leaves. The live leaves, in tufts at the branch ends, are narrow and often sharp-pointed. The solitary, long-stalked, white, yellow, or blue, often quite beautiful flowers are bisexual. They have six similar perianth segments or tepals and either six stamens or six bundles of two to six. The slender style terminates in a headlike stigma or has three short branches. The fruits are capsules. The only genus cultivated is *Vellozia*.

VELTHEIMIA (Vel-thèimia). Veltheimias are South African deciduous bulb plants of considerable beauty. They belong to the lily family LILIACEAE. The name commemorates the German patron of botany, Au-gust Ferdinand Graf von Veltheim, who died in 1801. Their charming spikes of soft pink to coral-red flowers suggest, in miniature, those of red hot poker plants (*Kniphofia*), those of certain aloes, or, more precisely, those of their close, but smaller relatives lachenalias. From lachenalias, veltheimias differ in having bigger bulbs with several, instead of usually only two, larger, broader leaves and in having much bigger, sharply three-angled seed capsules. The botanical interpretation of *Veltheimia* has been much confused. As now understood it comprises two species.

Veltheimias have all-basal, slightly fleshy, spreading or recurved leaves. Their pendulous flowers are in dense, cylindrical racemes that terminate leafless stalks. Their long-tubular perianths have six very short teethlike lobes. There are six slender-stalked stamens joined to the perianth tube at about or below its center, and a slender style. After they wither, the flowers hang on instead of falling. The fruits are large top-shaped capsules containing two black seeds in each of three compartments.

Most frequently cultivated, *V. viridifolia* (syn. *V. undulata*), which was for long and still often is wrongly named *V. capensis*, has a bulb about 3 inches long by nearly as broad. From it comes as many as twelve glossy-green leaves that may be over 1 foot long and up to one-third as broad, with undulating margins. The flower spikes and their thick fleshy stalks are 1 foot to 1½ feet tall. They have up to sixty faintly yellow-spotted, light purplish-pink blooms 1¼ to 1½ inches long and under one-fourth as wide. The distinct variety *V. v.* 'Rosalba' has beautiful pink-tinged, white blooms.

The other species, the true *V. capensis* (syns. *V. glauca, V. roodeae*), has a flattish-bottomed, egg-shaped bulb, about as big

Veltheimia viridifolia

Veltheimia viridifolia (flowers)

Veltheimia capensis deasii

as that of the last, and about ten, wavy-margined, glaucous-green, lanceolate leaves up to 1 foot long by 1 inch wide. Its stout, fleshy, glaucous flower stems are mottled with reddish-purple. The blooms, about 1 inch long, are light pink with greenish tips. Variety *V. c. deasii* (syn. *V. deasii*) is distinguished by its stamens being attached well below the middle of the perianth tube. Its foliage is often more glaucous, a bluer green, more wavy-edged, and smaller than that of the typical species.

Garden and Landscape Uses and Cultivation. Easy to grow, especially *V. viridifolia* and its variety, where hardy, veltheimias are suitable for rock gardens and outdoor flower beds. They are splendid pot plants that, with little care, bloom regularly year after year. Well-drained, reasonably fertile soil and a little shade from strong sun are to their liking. So long as they are thriving there is no need to transplant or repot them, but as soon as they begin to give fewer or poorer blooms, or less ample and vigorous foliage, the possible need for these attentions should be reviewed. When needed, replanting and repotting are done in late summer or early fall, just before new foliage growth begins.

Veltheimias are not tropical. When grown indoors they give the best results if the temperature from fall to spring at night is 50 to 55°F and by day does not exceed that by more than five to fifteen degrees, according to the brightness of the weather. During the period of summer dormancy the

soil is kept dry. Watering is resumed at the first signs of new growth and is done to keep the soil moderately and evenly moist until, in late spring, the foliage begins to show signs of yellowing. Then successively longer intervals are allowed between applications until all the leaves have died, at which point water is withheld entirely. During the period of active foliage development, up until the dormant season approaches, well-rooted veltheimias benefit greatly from occasional applications of dilute liquid fertilizer, but care must be taken not to supply so much nitrogen that the leaves become overlarge, soft, and floppy. Veltheimias increase slowly by natural offsets. They are easily raised from seed. Bulb cuttings and leaf cuttings, the latter consisting of entire mature leaves pulled off the bulbs and planted with their bases in sand, vermiculite, or other propagating medium, also give good results.

VELVET. The word velvet forms parts of the common names of these plants: Florida velvet-bean (*Mucuna deeringiana*), velvet-bent (*Agrostis canina*), velvet-geranium (*Senecio petasites*), and velvet plant (*Gynura*).

VENIDIO-ARCTOTIS. This is the name, derived from those of their parent genera, of hybrids between *Venidium fastuosum*, *Arctotis stoechadifolia grandis*, and *A. breviscapa*, of the daisy family COMPOSITAE. Intermediates between the three parents,

the hybrids are herbaceous perennials hardy only in regions where little or no frost occurs. Erect and well-branched, they have oblong-lanceolate, lobed leaves with gray-green upper surfaces and undersides felted with white hairs. From early summer until fall they produce a profusion of daisy-type flowers, 2½ to 3 inches across, in various shades and combinations of ivory-white, yellow, bronze, rose-pink, and purple, often with a zone of crimson or purple. A selection of varieties includes 'Aurora', with chestnut-bronze flowers; 'Bacchus', with wine-purple flowers; 'China Rose', with rose-pink flowers; 'Tangerine', with orange-yellow flowers; and 'Torch', the flowers of which are deep bronze with a crimson center zone.

Garden Uses. These attractive hybrids supply colorful blooms for summer flower beds, porch and window boxes, and other outdoor containers. They do not succeed where summers are hot and humid, but in regions where such cool-climate flowers as sweet peas prosper, they are very satisfactory.

Cultivation. Any ordinary, well-drained soil suits. Propagate by taking cuttings 3 to 4 inches long in late August or September and planting them in a shaded cold frame or greenhouse propagating bench. When well rooted, pot them individually in 3-inch pots and carry them over winter in a frostproof frame or in a greenhouse where the night temperature is 40 to 45°F and that by day five to ten degrees higher. Plant in the garden when it is safe to set out geraniums and tomatoes.

VENIDIUM (Veníd-ium). Two beautiful species of this South African genus of twenty to thirty species, of the daisy family COMPOSITAE, are known to gardeners. The others are mostly not attractive enough to warrant growing. Most are perennial herbaceous plants, but those cultivated are commonly grown as annuals. The name is believed to be derived, in allusion to the fruits of some kinds being ribbed, from the Latin *vena*, a vein.

Venidiums are woolly-haired or pubescent. They have alternate, lobeless and toothless, or sinuously-lobed or -toothed leaves, and long-stalked, daisy-form flower heads with bell-shaped involucres (collars of bracts at the backs of the flower heads). The central eye of the flower head is of bisexual, five-toothed, tubular disk florets. It is encircled by a single row of petal-like ray florets that are female and fertile. The fruits are seedlike achenes that differ from those of nearly related *Arctotis* in having hairs neither on their surfaces nor at their bases. Hybrids between *Venidium fastuosum*, *Arctotis stoechadifolia grandis*, and *A. breviscapa*, named *Venidio-arctotis*, have characteristics intermediate between those of the parents. See Venidio-arctotis.

An erect, strongly-branched, bushy plant, 2 to 3 feet tall, *V. fastuosum* has hollow stems that, like its obovate to fiddle-shaped, deeply-pinnately-lobed leaves, are clothed with shaggy, gray hairs. The leaves are 5 to 6 inches long, the upper ones less incised than those below. The magnificent flower heads, 3 to 4 inches or occasionally more in diameter, have brownish-purple to nearly black centers and rich golden-yellow rays, each ray with a glossy-blackish-purple blotch at its base. Because alternate ray florets stand upward and away from the others, the flower heads appear to have two rows of rays. A variety with white rays blotched at their bases with black is also grown.

Less robust *V. decurrens,* about 1 foot tall, has softly-hairy stems and obovate, lobed, gray-green leaves, 4 to 6 inches long, with the terminal lobe larger than the others and earlike lobes at the base of the leafstalks. The leaves are white-hairy on their undersides, and when young on their upper surfaces. The flower heads are bright yellow and 2 to 2½ inches across. Variety *V. d. calendulaceum* (syn. *V. calendulaceum*), in which the leafstalks are usually without basal ears, has been segregated, but is doubtfully distinct. The plant once named *V. hirsutum* is *Arctotis hirsuta*.

Garden and Landscape Uses. Where summers are not excessively hot and humid, venidiums are magnificent for use as annuals to ornament flower beds and to supply flowers for cutting. For the latter purpose, their effectiveness is limited somewhat by the fact that their flowers, like those of so many South African plants of the daisy family, close or partially close at night and in dim light. Where sultry summers occur, venidiums can be bloomed outdoors early in the season by starting them indoors and planting them outside as soon as there is no longer danger of frost. They are also fine for blooming in greenhouses in late winter and spring. When used in flower gardens, they are viewed to best advantage from the south. Their flowers tend to face the sun.

Cultivation. The prime requisites of venidiums, apart from nonexposure to frost and torrid, humid summers, are thoroughly well-drained soil and exposure to full sun. In greenhouses they grow well and flower freely in spring if afforded winter night temperatures of 45 to 50°F, increased by day by five to fifteen degrees depending upon the brightness of the weather. On all favorable days the greenhouse is ventilated freely. Extra early blooms, available from January onward, can be had from plants from August or early September sowings, grown in temperatures about ten degrees higher than those suggested above, and from early November onward artificially illuminated to increase the day length to sixteen hours.

For outdoor blooming, seeds are sown in early spring where the plants are to remain and the seedlings thinned to 9 inches to 1 foot or a little more apart depending upon the vigor they are expected to display. Where summers are hot it is almost essential, and elsewhere it is usually better, to gain an early start by sowing in a greenhouse six to seven weeks before it is safe to transplant the resulting plants outdoors, which is done as soon as there is no longer danger of frost. Seedlings raised in this way are grown individually in small, well-drained pots of porous soil until planting-out time. In greenhouses, venidiums can be grown in ground beds, benches, or pots. When young, the tips of their shoots are pinched out to encourage branching, and later the plants must be staked. Except for these details, and care in watering, no special attention is needed. Too soggy soil is disastrous, but the plants must not be allowed to suffer for want of water. After the available earth is filled with roots, judicious applications of dilute liquid fertilizer are helpful.

Venidium fastuosum

Venidium decurrens calendulaceum

VENUS. The word Venus forms parts of the names of these plants: Venus' comb (*Scandix pecten-veneris*), Venus' fly trap (*Dionaea muscipula*), Venus' hair (*Adiantum capillus-veneris*), and Venus' looking glass (*Legousia speculum-veneris*).

VEPRIS (Vép-ris). To the rue family RUTACEAE belong the forty species of shrubs and trees of the genus *Vepris*. They are natives of East Africa, South Africa, Malagasy (Madagascar), and the Mascarene Islands. Of no obvious application, the name is derived from the Latin *vepres*, a bramble.

The leaves of *Vepris* are alternate and consist of one to four leaflets, but usually three, arranged digitately like the fingers of a hand. They are dotted with tiny glands. The flowers are unisexual and are in terminal and axillary panicles, clusters, or racemes. The blooms have a cup-shaped, four-lobed or rarely two-lobed calyx, four or rarely two petals much longer than the lobes of the calyx, and, the male blooms, usually eight, four long and four short, or sometimes only four stamens. The females have two or four styles and eight aborted stamens (staminodes). The fruits are drupes (fruits structured like plums).

A shrub or small tree, **V. lanceolata,** of Africa, has firm, long-stalked leaves with three, hairless, dull green, wavy-edged, elliptic to oblong leaflets 2½ to 3½ inches long by up to 1 inch wide. The mid-veins are markedly raised on their undersides. The flowers, in terminal panicles, are tiny, yellowish-green, and aromatic. The two- or three-lobed fruits are as big as large peppercorns.

Garden and Landscape Uses and Cultivation. This little-known species is suitable for cultivation in the tropics, subtropics, and warm-temperate regions where little or no frost is experienced. It grows in ordinary soils in sun or part-day shade, and is increased by seed and by cuttings.

VERATRUM (Ver-àtrum)—False-Hellebore, White-Hellebore. The name of the genus *Veratrum*, of the lily family LILIACEAE, is an ancient one of the not nearly related hellebore (*Helleborus*). Twenty-five or more species are recognized, all natives of temperate parts of the northern hemisphere, and all are believed to contain poisonous principles. From the roots of *V. album*, hellebore powder, employed as an insecticide, is prepared.

Veratrums are strong-growing, bold-foliaged, leafy-stemmed, hardy herbaceous perennials with fleshy rootstocks, stout, erect stems, and broad, conspicuously longitudinally-veined, pleated, stem-clasping leaves. The numerous small, starry, greenish-white, yellowish, or purplish flowers, bisexual or unisexual, with one or both types on the same plant, are displayed in ample, erect panicles. Each has six petals (more correctly, tepals) not joined to the ovary,

and without glands. There are six slender-stalked stamens and three short styles. The fruits are three-lobed capsules.

Native to wet woodlands and swamps from Quebec to Ontario and North Carolina, and from Alaska to Oregon, American white-hellebore (**V. viride**) has stems, 2 to 8 feet tall, that are leafy to their tops. The elliptic leaves are up to 1 foot long by about one-half as broad, the upper ones proportionately nearly as wide as those below. The panicles of downy, yellowish-green flowers may be 1½ feet long or slightly longer. They have drooping lower branches. The blooms, ¾ to 1 inch wide, have plain or toothed margins. Favoring similar woodland habitats, but differing from *V. viride* in having much narrower upper leaves, and flowers that are not downy, are **V. woodii** and **V. parviflorum.** The first, with blunt-petaled, maroon flowers, is native from Ohio to Missouri and Oklahoma. The other, confined in the wild to the southern Appalachian Mountains, has greenish flowers, the males with pointed petals.

Western American **V. californicum** ranges from Montana to Washington, Colorado, New Mexico, and Baja California. Although unrelated to and quite different from the eastern North American plant known by the same colloquial name, it is sometimes called skunk-cabbage. Corn-lily is another name sometimes applied to it. Much like *V. viride*, this species differs in having panicles with erect lower branches and whitish flowers with broader petals.

Veratrum californicum

It is 3 to 7 feet tall and hairy in its upper parts. The fruit capsules are quite decorative. Native to Oregon and California, **V. insolitum,** up to 5 feet tall, differs from *V. californicum* and *V. viride* in the ovaries of its flowers being densely-woolly. This sort has leaves up to 10 inches long, the lower ones pointed-elliptic, those near the tops of the stems smaller and lanceolate. The whitish flowers are in woolly panicles up to 1½ feet long.

European white-hellebore (**V. album**) occurs as a wildling in Europe and northern Asia. From 3 to 5 feet tall, it has leaves up to 1 foot long by nearly one-half as wide, and nearly stalkless flowers, greenish outside and whitish within, the petals with crinkle-toothed margins. Also a native of Europe and Asia, **V. nigrum,** about as tall as the last, has broad-elliptic to linear-lanceolate leaves up to 1 foot in length. Its black-purple flowers in narrow, hairy panicles make a quite striking display.

Japanese **V. stamineum,** up to 3 feet tall and hairless or nearly so, has broad-elliptic leaves, the lower ones up to 8 inches long, those above shorter and oblongish. The whitish flowers are in panicles 6 to 10 inches long. Variety **V. s. lasiophyllum** is hairy on the undersides of its leaves, especially along the veins. Rarely exceeding 2 feet in height and with slender stems leafy only below, **V. maackii** is native to eastern Asia, including Japan. Its broad-linear leaves are 9 inches to 1¼ feet long. The dark purple flowers are in panicles up to 1 foot in length. Variety **V. m. japonicum,** of Japan, has oblong to linear-lanceolate leaves and brown-purple flowers.

Garden and Landscape Uses and Cultivation. Although not among the most showy of hardy herbaceous perennials, veratrums possess a certain stateliness and boldness of aspect that makes them acceptable for naturalizing in dampish woodlands and elsewhere where fertile, moist soil and sufficient shade to protect the foliage from scorching are available. Planted in groups in shaded flower borders, they can be effective. These plants colonize readily and grow vigorously with minimum attention. Established, thriving specimens should not be transplanted unless necessary. Veratrums are easily increased by division in early spring, and by seed sown as soon as ripe or in early spring in a shaded cold frame or in a protected place, where the soil contains considerable organic matter and can be kept evenly moist, outdoors.

VERBASCUM (Verb-áscum)—Mullein. The genus *Verbascum* contains about 250 species of chiefly biennial, less commonly perennial, herbaceous plants and subshrubs, natives of Europe and temperate Asia. A few are widely naturalized in North America. In addition, there are a number of natural hybrids, as well as some sterile garden hybrids, of which some are perennials. Verbascums belong to the figwort family SCROPHULARIACEAE. Their botanical name is their classical Latin one.

Commonly tall, erect, and stately, mulleins have alternate, undivided, but sometimes lobed, toothed leaves, usually diminishing in size from below upward, and flowers in terminal racemes or spikes. The blooms have usually five-parted calyxes, wheel-shaped, nearly tubeless corollas with five broad, spreading lobes (petals) of

Handsome rosettes of foliage of three undetermined species of *Verbascum*

An undetermined species of *Verbascum* in bloom

nearly equal size, and five stamens of which three or all are heavily bearded. The fruits are many-seeded capsules. At least some species are poisonous to and avoided by livestock.

Common mullein (**V. thapsus**) is a frequent inhabitant of dry fields and waste places throughout much of North America, as well as its native Europe and temperate Asia. Strictly upright and 4 to 7 feet tall, it has stems and foliage densely covered with yellowish hairs. Its basal rosettes are of short-stalked, spreading, round-toothed to nearly toothless, oblong-elliptic to elliptic-lanceolate leaves often over 1 foot long. The stem leaves are smaller and have stalks extending as wings down the stems. In clusters of up to seven, or singly, the stalkless or nearly stalkless, yellow, cupped flowers, ½ inch to 1¼ inches wide, are spaced along tall, dense, usually branchless spikes. Two of their stamens are without beards or at most are slightly hairy. Similar to, but more handsome than the last, European **V. thapsiforme** (syn. *V. densiflorum*) has yellow, or rarely white, flat flowers, 1½ to 2 inches wide, in spikes that in their lower parts are often shortly-branched. Also similar to and an improvement on the common mullein is **V. phlomoides**, of Europe. From *V. thapsus* and *V. thapsiforme*, this differs in its leafstalks not being carried down the stems as wings or, at most, in doing this for very short distances. The flowers are 1 inch to 1¼ inches wide.

Flowers with individual stalks at least as long as the calyxes are characteristic of **V. longifolium**, of southern Europe. From 3 to 4 feet tall and yellowish- or whitish-hairy,

Verbascum phlomoides

Verbascum olympicum

this has wavy, narrowly-ovate to oblong-lanceolate leaves, those of the dense basal rosettes 1½ to 2 feet long, the shorter stem leaves with clasping bases. The 1-inch-wide, golden-yellow blooms, in clusters of up to ten, are in densely-branched, 1-foot-long racemes. Two of the stamens are without hairs. Related **V. olympicum** (syn. *V. longifolium olympicum*), of Greece, up to 6 feet tall, branches freely from the base and differs from *V. longifolium* in having its stems, leaves, and calyxes more densely-clothed with white hairs and all of its stamens hairy.

Verbascum bombyciferum: (a) Basal foliage

(b) In bloom

(c) Flowers

One of the most strikingly handsome species, ***V. bombyciferum*** (syn. *V.* 'Broussa'), of Asia Minor, is remarkable for the very dense clothing of silvery-white hairs that covers most of its parts. From 4 to 6 feet tall, this has beautiful basal rosettes of ovate-oblong to obovate leaves up to over 1 foot long by approximately one-half as wide. Its sulfur-yellow blooms, 1 inch to 1½ inches across and with white-hairy stamens, are partly hidden by the abundant white hairs of the spikes. They are in clusters of three to seven.

Moth mullein (***V. blattaria***), a native of Europe and Asia and naturalized in North America, is slender-stemmed, up to 3 feet or so tall, and with or without branches. Its stalkless, hairless leaves, narrowly-triangular to oblong-lanceolate or oblanceolate, are toothed or toothless. The flowers, solitary rather than in groups, are in graceful, loose racemes. About 1 inch across, they are yellow or white. Except for the color of its blooms, and for the undersides of its leaves being sparsely-hairy, ***V. phoeniceum*** closely resembles the moth mullein. Its flowers range from violet to lavender, red, rose-red, pink, and white.

About 3 feet tall, ***V. chaixii***, of southern and central Europe, has whitish-hairy stems and whitish-hairy or green, round-toothed leaves, the lower ones stalked, the upper stalkless. Its round-petaled, yellow flowers, with purple-hairy stamens, are in small clusters along the terminal spike and branches of the panicle. Variety *V. c. album* has white blooms.

Subshrubby and about 1 foot in height, ***V. dumulosum*** is not hardy in the north. Native to Turkey, it has branching, densely-hairy stems, prostrate below, and thickish, slightly wrinkled, hairy-elliptic- to elliptic-oblong, toothed or toothless leaves. The lemon-yellow blooms, in spikes 2 to 4 inches long, are marked with coral-red at their centers and have stamens with pur-

Verbascum spinosum

ple hairs. Closely similar ***V. pestalozzae***, of Asia Minor, is more densely-hairy and not over 8 inches tall. Native to mountains and stony hillsides in Crete, charming and distinctive ***V. spinosum*** is an intricately-branched shrub up to 1 foot tall, with each branch ending in a short spine. Its oblong-lanceolate to oblanceolate, irregularly-toothed or -lobed or sometimes smooth-edged leaves are whitish-hairy and 1¼ to 2 inches long. From rather less than to rather more than ½ inch in diameter, the yellow flowers, each solitary in the axil of a minute bract, are displayed in twiggy panicles.

Hybrid mulleins of garden origin include biennials and usually short-lived perennials. Among the best are 'Harkness Hybrid', 5 to 6 feet tall and with yellow flowers; 'Miss Willmott', about as tall, with

Verbascum dumulosum

Verbascum 'Letitia'

white flowers; 'Cotswold Beauty', 4 feet tall, with bronzy blooms; 'Cotswold Gem', 4 feet tall, with amber-colored flowers with purple centers; 'Cotswold Queen', about 4 feet in height, with bronzy-salmon flowers; 'Pink Domino', which has blooms of mauve-pink and is about 3½ feet tall; and dwarf, attractive 'Letitia', which forms 1-foot-wide plants with grayish leaves and 3-inch-long spikes of primrose-yellow flowers.

Garden and Landscape Uses. Tall mulleins can be used with telling effect in mixed flower borders and are excellent for grouping informally in naturalistic surroundings and at the fronts of shrub beds. Lower kinds, less emphatic in the landscape, can be used similarly and in rock gardens. All succeed in a wide range of soils including limestone ones. They stand dry conditions well, but not wet locations. With the exception of *V. phoeniceum*, which prefers slight shade from strong sun, all stand full exposure.

Cultivation. Mostly of biennial duration and hardy, most mulleins must be raised from seed or be propagated by root cuttings yearly. Because they hybridize readily, seed taken from plants growing in proximity to other kinds is likely to be of mixed parentage. Fortunately, such genetic mixes are usually as satisfactory garden plants as the true species. Frequently, volunteer seedlings spring up near where plants flowered the previous year. Seed may be sown outdoors or in a cold frame in May or June, or root cuttings may be taken at about the same time or earlier. As soon as they are big enough to handle, the young plants are transplanted 6 inches apart in rows 1 foot to 1½ feet apart in nursery beds. In early fall or early spring the plants are transferred to their flowering locations. Because most develop strong taproots, care must be exercised when transplanting not to damage these more than is absolutely necessary.

VERBENA (Verbè-na)—Vervain. The name *Verbena* is the ancient Latin one for *Verbena officinalis*, a native of Europe naturalized in North America. Like the colloquial name vervain, it is derived from the Celtic *fer*, to remove, and *faen*, stone, and alludes to a former use of *V. officinalis* in the treatment of bladder stones. The genus, which consists of 250 species, belongs in the vervain family VERBENACEAE and grows natively chiefly in tropical and subtropical America. A few species occur in temperate North America and South America and two or three in Europe and Asia. Plants that do not belong in the genus *Verbena*, but have common names that include the word verbena are lemon-verbena (*Aloysia triphylla*), sand-verbena (*Abronia*), and sweet-verbena-myrtle (*Backhousia citriodora*).

Verbenas include annuals, herbaceous perennials, and subshrubs. Their leaves are

Tall verbascums in bloom provide strong vertical lines in the landscape

Verbena hybrida varieties in a trial ground

A *Verbena hybrida* variety

opposite or occasionally in threes, more rarely alternate. They are commonly toothed, lobed, or dissected. The small to medium-sized flowers are without individual stalks and are in spikes, usually terminal on the stems, rarely from the leaf axils. In some kinds, the spikes are short, broad, and nearly flat-topped, in others elongated and slender, with only a few flowers open at one time. Sometimes the spikes are on branched flower stalks and form panicles. The corolla tubes are straight or incurved and terminate in five oblongish spreading lobes (petals), uneven in size and disposition to the extent that the face of the flower is somewhat two-lipped. There are four stamens in two pairs. The dry fruits are enclosed in the calyxes and each separates into four nutlets. At one time *V. officinalis* was employed medicinally, but its supposed virtues are not now recognized; particularly it was thought to cure defective vision.

The common garden verbena (*V. hybrida* syn. *V. hortensis*), as its name indicates, is of mixed parentage. In all proba-

bility its lineage includes *V. peruviana* and *V. platensis* as well as other species, but although it was not developed until almost the middle of the nineteenth century, its history is not well recorded. Plants of this handsome hybrid complex have squarish stems, lax or procumbent in their lower parts and often rooting from the nodes (joints). They branch freely and have ovate-oblong to oblong, toothed leaves, sometimes lobed toward their bases and 2 to 4 inches long. Like the stems, they are covered with stiffish hairs. The flowers, sometimes almost 1 inch in diameter, but often smaller, are several together in flattish clusters 2 to 2½ inches across. They come in a wide variety of colors and mixtures, including white, pink, red, lavender, blue, and purple and usually have a white or cream-colored center or "eye." In some varieties the blooms are fragrant. In parts of the United States *V. hybrida* is naturalized.

Another good flower garden sort, like the last commonly cultivated as an annual, *V. rigida* (syn. *V. venosa*) is a native of south-

Verbena rigida

though that is properly a synonym of *V. laciniata*. A native of South America, the moss verbena is naturalized in parts of southern United States. A perennial often cultivated as an annual and not exceeding 1 foot in height, it has procumbent or ascending stems with thrice-pinnately-divided, lacy leaves, up to 1½ inches long, that are only slightly hairy at maturity. The flowers of this attractive species are lilac, lilac-blue, or purple. Their calyxes have white hairs lying flat along their surfaces. Native to Argentina and Chile, *V. laciniata* (syn. *V. erinoides*) is a perennial that can be grown as an annual. It has freely-branched, erect or more or less procumbent stems and deeply-parted or pinnately-cleft, ovate leaves, up to ¾ inch long, smaller and less finely divided than those of *V. tenuisecta*. The blue, reddish-violet, or lavender flowers are in headlike spikes.

South American *V. tenera* has trailing, rooting stems with slender, four-angled

ern Brazil and Argentina. From 1 foot to 2 feet tall, it has tuberous roots and erect, open-branched, four-angled stems. Its very stiff, oblong, pointed leaves, 1½ to 3 inches long and with their bases clasping the stems, are in rather distantly spaced pairs. They are rough-hairy and irregularly-sharply-toothed. Stiff-branched and often in threes, the flower spikes have purple flowers about ¼ inch in diameter. The flowers of *V. r. alba* are white. Those of *V. r. lilacina* are lilac-colored.

Somewhat similar to *V. rigida*, but up to 3 feet tall or taller, *V. bonariensis* is an annual or nonhardy perennial, native to South America, that is naturalized in many parts of the United States. A botanical distinction between it and *V. rigida* is that the floral bracts of the latter are much longer than the calyx, whereas those of *V. bonariensis* equal the calyx in length. The flowers of *V. bonariensis*, less than ¹⁄₁₀ inch across, are lilac-colored. Also resembling *V. rigida*, Chilean *V. corymbosa* is a larger plant most obviously distinguished from *V. rigida* by the presence of two small lobes at the base of each leaf. Its reddish-purple to lavender flowers are in panicles of small, dense spikes.

Completely prostrate, *V. peruviana* (syn. *V. chamaedryfolia*) is remarkable for its heads of intensely scarlet flowers that bespangle the carpeting mass of bright green foliage. The plants are rough-hairy and the leaves oblong-lanceolate to ovate, 1 inch to 2 inches long, and toothed. This native of Argentina and southern Brazil is naturalized in parts of the southern United States.

The moss verbena (*V. tenuisecta*) is sometimes misnamed *V. erinoides*, al-

Verbena peruviana

Verbena tenera

Verbena tenuisecta

Verbena tenera maonettii

branches and short-stalked, three-parted leaves, the divisions of which are pinnately-cut into linear segments; they are rough-hairy. The flowers are strong rose-pink tending toward violet. They have calyxes twice as long as the bracts and furnished with dirty-white hairs that do not lie flat against their surfaces. The Italian verbena (*V. t. maonettii*) is not, as its colloquial name suggests, a native of Europe, but is a variety of *V. tenera*. From the typical species it differs in the color of its blooms. These are candy-striped, the petals carmine-pink margined with white.

Two North American species of garden merit are ***V. bipinnatifida*** and ***V. canadensis.*** The former is indigenous from South

Verbena canadensis

Verbena canadensis (flowers)

Dakota to California and Mexico, the latter from Pennsylvania to Colorado, Florida, and Texas. They are 6 inches to 1½ feet tall and have erect stems from prostrate, rooting bases. In *V. bipinnatifida* the rough-hairy, stalked leaves, 1 inch to 2½ inches long, are twice- or thrice-deeply-lobed or -cleft. Its flowers are up to ½ inch wide and lilac or pink. The leaves of *V. canadensis* are 1 inch to 3 inches long and, like the stems, rough-hairy; they are lobed, but the lobes are only toothed, not lobed again. The flower clusters are comparatively large

with individual blooms ½ to 1 inch wide. Most commonly they are reddish-purple, but variants with lilac, pink, red, and white flowers occur.

Native from Utah to California, Arizona, and Mexico and best suited for cultivation in desert and semidesert regions, ***V. goddingii*** is a perennial up to 1½ feet in height. It has erect or more or less spreading stems, ashy-green, three-cleft and toothed, ovate, hairy leaves up to 2 inches long, and attractive headlike spikes, 1 inch to 1½ inches wide, of pink, blue, or lavender flowers.

Garden Uses. Varieties of *V. hybrida*, among the most satisfactory summer bedding plants, are well suited for window and porch boxes as well as for ground beds, and bloom continuously from the time they are set out in late spring until frost. As cut flowers they are suitable for inclusion in small arrangements, such as table decorations. Also excellent for summer flower beds are *V. rigida* and its varieties, but their flowers are of little use for cutting.

As permanent perennial border plants in regions of fairly mild winters, *V. rigida*, *V. canadensis*, and their respective varieties, as well as *V. bonariensis*, are quite satisfactory. Of these kinds, *V. canadensis* is the hardiest. In sheltered locations it persists through most winters at New York City, but in exceptionally cold ones it may be killed. Other verbenas, such as *V. peruviana*, *V. tenera*, and *V. t. maonettii*, are excellent permanent rock garden subjects in regions where winters are not too severe. Elsewhere they may be employed to brighten rock gardens, dry walls, and crevices between paving stones with summer color by being carried over winter in a cold frame or cool greenhouse and planted outdoors each spring.

Cultivation. Verbenas are sun-loving plants that adapt to ordinary well-drained garden soil of moderate fertility. They will not tolerate constant wetness about their roots, or shade. Although technically tender perennials, the hybrid varieties are usually grown as annuals by raising them from seed each year. Sometimes choice sorts are kept from year to year by taking cuttings in late summer or early fall and carrying the young plants over in greenhouses. At one time this was a common practice, but modern strains of seed produce plants so predominantly true to type that the extra trouble of carrying plants from year to year is rarely warranted. Seeds are sown in February or early March in a temperature of 60 to 65°F, and the young plants are transplanted, as soon as they are big enough to handle easily, 2 inches apart in flats containing porous soil. They are grown in a night temperature of 50 to 55°F in a sunny greenhouse; during the day temperatures of 60 to 65°F are appropriate. When the young plants have developed three or four sets of leaves, their tips are pinched out to encourage branching. A

week or two before they are planted in the open, which may be done about the time it is safe to set out tomatoes, they are hardened by standing the flats in a cold frame or sheltered spot outdoors. In the garden the plants should be spaced about 1 foot apart. The stems may be pegged down with hairpin-like wire pins to encourage them to root and to assure good coverage of the ground. The treatment of *V. rigida* is the same as is detailed above for the common hybrid garden verbena.

Trailing verbenas, such as *V. bipinnatifida*, *V. peruviana*, *V. tenera*, *V. t. maonettii*, and *V. tenuisecta*, thrive without trouble in any reasonably well-drained soil in full sun. They may be planted 1 foot to 1½ feet apart and are very easily increased by division, cuttings, and seed. Where winters are too cold for them to be reliably hardy, young divisions or small plants rooted from cuttings taken in late summer may be accommodated over winter in cool greenhouses or cold frames protected from severe freezing. The taller-growing *V. bonariensis* responds to the same soils and locations, but as it is easily produced from seed, and blooms the first year if sown early indoors as advised for the common garden hybrid verbenas, that is the simplest way of securing and maintaining stock in regions where it does not overwinter.

Diseases and Pests. Diseases to which verbenas are subject are root rots, stem rot, powdery mildew, botrytis blight of the flowers, and bacterial wilt. Pests that infest them are aphids, blister beetles, caterpillars, leaf miners, whiteflies, red spider mites, and nematodes.

VERBENACEAE—Vervain Family. The majority of the 2,600 to 3,000 species of dicotyledons that constitute the seventy-five or more genera of the VERBENACEAE are natives of warm temperate, subtropical, and tropical regions; others inhabit colder parts of the world. Included are herbaceous plants, subshrubs, shrubs, trees, and vines, often with four-angled shoots and frequently thorny. Usually their leaves are opposite or in whorls (circles of more than two). Generally they are undivided, more rarely they are composed of separate leaflets. The usually more or less asymmetrical flowers are in spikes, racemes, or clusters. They have a persistent calyx with four or five lobes or teeth, a tubular corolla with four or five usually spreading lobes (petals), four or less commonly two or six stamens, and one style. The fruits are berry-like, or are dry and usually separated into seedlike nutlets. Genera treated in this Encyclopedia include *Aloysia*, *Amasonia*, *Callicarpa*, *Caryopteris*, *Citharexylum*, *Clerodendrum*, *Congea*, *Cornutia*, *Corokia*, *Diostea*, *Duranta*, *Gmelina*, *Holmskioldia*, *Lantana*, *Nyctanthes*, *Oxera*, *Petrea*, *Phyla*, *Premna*, *Rhaphithamnus*, *Stachytarpheta*, *Tectona*, *Verbena*, and *Vitex*.

VERBESINA (Verb-esìna)—Crown Beard. A temperate to tropical American genus of the daisy family COMPOSITAE, this group of annuals, herbaceous perennials, and shrubs deserves and receives slight attention from gardeners. It comprises over 100 species. Its name is of uncertain origin, but it is thought to be a corruption of *Verbena*, applied because of some fancied resemblance of the foliage.

Verbesinas have opposite or alternate leaves with their stalks often continued down the stems as wings. Sometimes the flower heads are without ray florets (the petal-like ones of daisies) or have few. The florets of the disk are yellow, orange, or white. The fruits are seedlike achenes.

A loosely-branched annual 1 foot to 3 feet tall, *Verbesina encelioides* (syn. *Ximenesia encelioides*) is native from the Mississippi

Verbesina encelioides

Valley to Florida and Mexico. Variety *V. e. exauriculata*, only differing from the typical species in its leaves not having little ear-like flaps at their bases, occurs further west and to California. These plants have erect, wingless stems, and alternate, coarsely-toothed, triangular-ovate, grayish leaves, up to 4 inches long, usually silvery-hairy on their undersides. The bright yellow flower heads are up to 2 inches across. They have many ray as well as disk florets. The ray florets are yellow and toothed at their ends.

Perennial *V. alternifolia* (syn. *Actinomeris alternifolia*) is native to woodlands and moist soils from Ontario to Illinois, Iowa, Florida, Louisiana, and Oklahoma. It blooms in summer and early fall. More or less hairy and 3 to 6 feet tall, it has branched, usually winged stems. Its alternate, or perhaps sometimes opposite, stalked leaves are lanceolate to lanceolate-elliptic to ovate, and are toothed to nearly toothless. They are 4 to 10 inches long by ¾ inch to 3½ inches wide. The flower heads, 1 inch to 2 inches in diameter, are

in loose clusters of ten to a hundred or more. They have two to ten or no sterile yellow ray florets and a loose, rounded, central cluster of disk flowers. Also perennial, *V. helianthoides* ranges as a native from Ohio to Iowa, Georgia, and Texas. Up to 3 feet tall, it has winged stems and alternate, stalkless, ovate-lanceolate, toothed leaves 2 to 6 inches long. In compact clusters of few, the yellow flower heads are 1½ inches wide.

Garden and Landscape Uses and Cultivation. The most appropriate places for these plants are naturalistic areas and wild gardens. They are not sufficiently attractive to ordinarily warrant including in more formal perennial beds. They are easily raised from seed sown in spring in ordinary soil in sunny places and, the perennial, by division.

VERMICULITE. This is a mica-type rock expanded by heating to 1,400°F. Special horticultural grades of smaller particles than the vermiculite sold for insulation and other purposes are used by gardeners in soil mixes and for rooting cuttings. Horticultural grade vermiculites weigh 6 to 8 pounds a cubic foot when dry, about 40 pounds when wet. They are sterile and consist of very porous, spongelike particles that are easily compressed between the thumb and finger. Unlike sponges, after compaction they do not return to their former shapes and sizes when the pressure is removed. Because of this, when added to soil mixes, vermiculite tends to deteriorate in time due to the collapsing of the particles resulting from pressure. Vermiculite differs significantly from most sands and perlite in this and other ways. It contains small amounts of potassium, magnesium, and calcium. Also, because of its ability to exchange cations, it can hold nutrients in reserve and release them slowly. It is a good buffer and thus minimizes rapid changes in pH.

VERNONIA (Vern-ònia) — Ironweed. Although the ironweeds make less appeal as garden plants than some of their kin in the daisy family COMPOSITAE, they are not without their uses, particularly in naturalistic landscapes. The genus *Vernonia* consists of more than 500 (according to some estimates, 1,000) species. It is widely distributed through the tropics and in temperate parts of North America, South America, and Australia. Nineteen species are native to the United States, and these and their hybrids include all those likely to be cultivated. The generic name commemorates William Vernon, an English botanist, who traveled in North America. He died in 1711.

The genus includes tropical trees and shrubs; the sorts native to the United States are all perennial herbaceous plants. Our discussion is limited to these. They have

rather stiff, branchless, erect stems clothed with alternate, toothed or toothless leaves, and flower heads, without ray florets, in large, loose, more or less rounded, terminal clusters. Mostly they are purple or some variant of that color; rarely are they pink or white. The identification of ironweeds is often difficult and is rendered more so by the prevalence of hybrids. Apparently, whenever two species grow together they intercross. Technical differences are chiefly in the pappus (the hairs or bristles attached to the fruits or seeds) and require some botanical knowledge to interpret.

The species discussed here all normally have purple or rosy-purple flowers. One of the most attractive is *V. acaulis,* a native of dry woodlands from North Carolina to Florida. Unlike most, this has its foliage concentrated at or near the bases of its 1- to 4-foot-tall stems. Common from North Carolina to Florida and Mississippi, the quite variable *V. angustifolia* is characterized by narrow leaves, never over ⅖ inch wide. This species favors dryish, sandy soils and is 2 to 4 feet tall. Inhabiting moist soils in Missouri and Arkansas, *V. crinita,* an attractive kind 3 to 9 feet tall, has large flower heads. Another species with large flower heads is *V. glauca.* This is 2½ to 5 feet tall and has pale undersurfaces to its leaves. It inhabits the fringes of woodlands and other lightly shaded places from New Jersey and Pennsylvania to Georgia and Alabama. A native of the Midwest, *V. lettermannii* rarely exceeds 2 feet in height. It has fine grasslike leaves up to 3 inches long. This is a moist soil species. A native of limestone prairies in Texas, *V. lindheimeri,* about 2 feet tall, is one of the more attractive ironweeds. Its stems and foliage are clothed with white hairs. Well adapted to dry soils, *V. marginata,* is a native of the Great Plains, attains a height of about 2 feet. One of the most attractive species is *V. missurica,* a native of low ground and prairies from Ontario to Iowa, Alabama, Mississippi, and Texas. Its stems and the undersides of its leaves are gray-woolly. This plant is 3 to 5 feet tall. A native of moist fields and wet

Vernonia noveboracensis

soils from Massachusetts to Ohio, West Virginia, Georgia, and Mississippi, *V. noveboracensis* resembles *V. glauca,* but does not have pale undersides to its leaves. From 3 to 7 feet tall, it is one of the most ornamental kinds.

Garden and Landscape Uses. In wild gardens and in semiwild and naturalistic areas, ironweeds can be used to good purpose. They are especially effective when planted in association with such late-blooming natives of open pastures and meadows as perennial asters and goldenrods (*Solidago*). To a limited extent they are suitable for grouping in perennial borders; they provide color after many herbaceous perennials have passed the peak of bloom. Unlike perennial asters and chrysanthemums, they are not sufficiently choice to warrant planting in considerable numbers.

Cultivation. Ironweeds are sun-loving plants. They thrive in ordinary soils and some prosper even in wet, ill-drained ground. The best times for planting and transplanting are early fall and early spring, however, these plants are so tenacious to life that, if necessary, as may be the case when specimens are collected from the wild, they may be moved even in full bloom. If this is done, they should be cut down close to the ground before they are dug, be watered very thoroughly, and be kept shaded for a time after they are replanted. Routine care takes little time; about all that is necessary is to keep down competing weeds and cut off and carry away the upper parts of the plants after they have died in fall. For the best results the plants should be lifted, divided, and replanted every two to four years. Propagation is by seed, division, and cuttings. Seed may be sown outdoors or in a cold frame in fall or early spring, or they may be started in a greenhouse.

VERONICA (Verón-ica) — Speedwell. The evergreen shrubs previously known by this name belongs in *Hebe.* The genus *Veronica* consists of about 300 species of mostly deciduous, herbaceous, and subshrubby perennials, widely distributed in the Old World and the New World, chiefly in temperate regions. It belongs in the figwort family SCROPHULARIACEAE. The name honors St. Veronica.

Veronicas usually have opposite leaves. Rarely those on the stems below the flowering parts are alternate or whorled (in circles of more than two). The flowers are sometimes solitary, more often they are in bracted spikes or racemes from the shoot ends or leaf axils. The calyx is four-, five-, or occasionally three-parted. Generally with a short tube, the corolla has four or five spreading lobes (petals). There are two stamens and one style. The fruits are capsules. All dealt with here are perennials.

Kinds with erect stems 1 foot to 2 feet tall or taller, flowers in terminal racemes or

Veronica longifolia

Veronica longifolia (flowers)

Veronica longifolia subsessilis

spikes, and toothed, but not lobed leaves are fairly plentiful. Here belongs slightly hairy or hairless *V. longifolia* (syn. *V. maritima*), of northern Europe and Asia. From 2 to 4 feet high, this has short-stalked, round-based, lanceolate to pointed-ovate, toothed leaves, opposite and in threes, 2½ to 3 inches long, and flowers, with stalks

Veronica longifolia subsessilis (flower)

Veronica 'Icicle'

shorter than the calyx, in long, crowded, spikelike racemes. About ¼ inch in diameter, the blooms are typically lilac-blue. One of the best known of the many variants of this is *V. l. subsessilis,* which has bigger, deep blue blooms and extremely short-stalked leaves. Others are *V. l. alba,* with white blooms; *V. l. rosea,* the flowers of which are pink; and *V. l. glauca,* which has rich purple flowers. Garden varieties referred to as *V. longifolia,* some probably hybrids between it and *V. spicata,* are long-blooming border plants. Here belong appropriately named 'Blue Spires', 'Blue Champion', and white-flowered 'Icicle'. Differing from *V. longifolia* in its leaves having wedge-shaped bases and its looser-flowered racemes being in panicles, bastard speedwell (*V. spuria* syn. *V. amethystina*), of southern Europe, is densely-hairy. Its 1-inch-long, short-stalked, pointed-oblong-lanceolate, toothed leaves are oppo-

Veronica spicata

Veronica incana

Fairly tall, chiefly erect-stemmed veronicas with racemes or spikes of flowers from the leaf axils instead of terminating the stems are now to be considered. Distinguished by its stalkless leaves being deeply-pinnately- or twice-pinnately-lobed, and wedge-shaped at their bases, except those of the terminal portion of the stem above the flowers, which are narrow and nearly lobeless and toothless, downy *V. austriaca* is a very variable native of southeastern Europe and Asia Minor. The long racemes, two to four together from the upper leaf axils, are of ½-inch-wide, rich azure-blue blooms with five-lobed calyxes. This merges into *V. multifida,* of the same general geographical distribution, a usually lower, more sprawling kind with seed capsules wedge-shaped instead of rounded at their bases. Leaves toothed, rather than pinnately-cleft, distinguish those now discussed from *V. austriaca* and *V. multifida.* Very variable *V. latifolia* (syn. *V. teucrium*) ranges from southern Europe to northern Asia. Mostly 1½ to 3 feet tall, erect, and somewhat hairy, it sometimes is shorter and sprawling. Its leaves have rounded bases. Those of the terminal flowerless portion of the shoot are broad and deeply-toothed. The flowers, blue or rarely pink or white in two to four long racemes from the upper leaf axils, are ½ inch in diameter. Germander speedwell (*V. chamaedrys*) is 1 foot to 1½ feet tall. Its stems have two opposite, longitudinal lines of long hairs. Stalkless, round-based, round-toothed, ovate, and hairy, the leaves are ½ inch to 1½ inches long. The ½-inch-wide, blue flowers are on slender stalks as long or considerably longer than the four-lobed calyx. They are in loose racemes 3 to 6 inches long, often displayed in panicles. A native of Europe, this is naturalized in North America. White-flowered *V. c. alba* is cultivated.

Low kinds with flowers in terminal racemes with toothless or toothed, but not pinnately-lobed leaves include several popular kinds. Dainty *V. gentianoides,* native to the Caucasus, makes mats of tufted foliage from which arise, to a height of 6

Veronica spicata (flowers)

Veronica spicata nana

site and in threes on the same plant. The about ½-inch-wide blue flowers have stalks as long as the calyxes. Variety *V. s. elegans* is more hairy and more branched. The kind called 'Royal Blue' is an improved garden variety. Allied to *V. spuria,* but with leaves always in pairs, *V. grandis* (syn. *V. bachofenii*) is up to 2 feet tall. It has rather long-stalked, triangular-ovate leaves, toothed along their margins and up to 2 inches long. Its many terminal, elongated racemes of blue flowers are looser than those of *V. spicata.* This is a native of the Himalayas.

Highly variable *V. spicata,* of Europe and Asia, rarely exceeds 1 foot to 1½ feet in height and in its dwarf varieties *V. s. compacta* and *V. s. nana* is very much shorter. This species is pubescent and has, always

in pairs, ovate to oblong leaves 1 inch to 2 inches long and round-toothed except near their bases and apexes. The blue flowers, in solitary or few dense racemes 1½ to 3 inches long from the shoot ends, and with stalks shorter than the calyxes, are ¼ inch wide. Variety *V. s. alba* has white, variety *V. s. rosea,* lavender-pink flowers. Silvery-white-woolly stems and foliage are characteristic of *V. incana,* native to northern Asia. This forms clumps of low shoots, many with foliage only, above which the spikes of rich blue flowers rise to heights of 1 foot to 2 feet. Oblong to lanceolate, the stalked leaves, 1 inch to 3 inches long, have blunt-toothed edges. Up to 6 inches in length, the solitary or clustered racemes of ¼-inch-wide, short-stalked flowers are 3 to 6 inches long. Variety *V. i. rosea* has pink blooms.

Veronica gentianoides (flowers)

A carpet of Veronica repens in front of a flowering Allium

inches to 1 foot or sometimes more, slender, branchless stems carrying graceful, rather loose, long racemes of delicate lavender-blue blooms with dark margins. The flowers are about ½ inch wide. The thickish leaves, much like those of Gentiana acaulis, are scarcely toothed. The lower ones, obovate to oblong and 1 inch to 3 inches long, are in rosettes. The more distantly spaced stem leaves are oblong to lanceolate. A compact subshrub, 2 to 6 inches tall, with prostrate stems and erect branches, V. fruticans is a native of European mountains. Its hairless, ovate, elliptic, or obovate leaves, up to ½ inch long, are sometimes slightly toothed. Bright blue with red centers, the blooms are ½ inch across and in racemes of six or fewer. They have four-lobed calyxes. A neat creeper somewhat woody at the base, V. nummularia is indigenous to the Pyrenees. It branches freely. Up to 6 inches tall, it has toothless, hairless, short-stalked leaves, ovate to nearly round and under ¼ inch long, mostly near the ends of the stems. In small, downy racemes, the comparatively large, very short-stalked blue or pink flowers have calyxes with four lobes. Differing in its stems not being at all woody, creeping V. repens, of Spain and Corsica, makes a mosslike carpet, scarcely 1 inch high, that at blooming time is smothered beneath sheets of bloom. Its lustrous, slightly round-toothed, hairless leaves have blades under ½ inch long. The blue-tinged, white blooms are in slender, few-flowered racemes or are solitary. The blooms of V. r. macrocarpa are pink.

Veronica repens in bloom

Low veronicas with prostrate or sprawling stems from which erect flowering shoots may arise, and which have deeply-pinnately-lobed or sometimes very deeply-toothed leaves from the axils of which the racemes of flowers come, include V. armena, of Armenia, and V. peduncularis and V. pectinata, of Asia Minor. Pretty V. armena, 2 to 4 inches in height, has many long, trailing stems, and small, stalkless leaves cut into slender, ¼-inch-long lobes. Its vivid blue flowers, ¼ inch wide, with stalks twice or more as long as the five-lobed calyx, are in racemes of few. From 6 inches to 1 foot tall and its stems prostrate to ascending, V. peduncularis has usually bronzy-green, ovate to lanceolate, pinnately-lobed or very deeply-toothed,

Veronica armena

stalkless or short-stalked leaves up to a little over 1 inch long. The pink-veined white flowers, ⅓ inch in diameter, with stalks three times or more as long as the calyxes, are in loose racemes. Densely-white-hairy, evergreen V. pectinata is 3 to 6 inches high. It has rooting stems, and obovate to elliptic-lanceolate leaves, often pinnately-lobed, but sometimes only toothed, up to ¾ inch long. The white-eyed, blue blooms, in many-flowered racemes, singly in the leaf axils, and with stalks about as long as the calyxes, are ¼ inch wide. Variety V. p. rosea has pink blooms.

Low, creeping, prostrate or sprawling kinds with toothless or toothed, but not pinnately-lobed leaves, and flowers in terminal racemes, include several worthies.

Often known in gardens as *V. rupestris*, European *V. prostrata* forms a widespreading mat of slender, prostrate stems from which come many erect flowering shoots 2 to 8 inches tall. The short-stalked or stemless leaves are ovate to linear, toothed, ½ to 1 inch long, and hairy or not. Crowded in short, spikelike racemes, the azure-blue flowers, ⅓ inch wide, have individual stalks about as long as their five-parted calyxes. Variety 'Trehane' has yellow foliage. Another vigorous, slender-stemmed, mat-forming veronica, hairy *V. filiformis* differs from the last in its considerably smaller, ovate to nearly round, slightly-toothed, blunt leaves about ⅓ inch long and in its ⅓-inch-wide flowers being solitary and having stalks several times as long as the calyxes. They are blue with a white lower petal. This native of Asia Minor sometimes invades lawns and, in so doing, although quite pretty in bloom, is considered a weed there. The next two have flowers with four-lobed calyxes. Native to southern Europe, *V. allionii* forms a mat of creeping, rooting stems. Its very short-stalked, hairless or nearly hairless, toothed or toothless, firm leaves are broad-elliptic to obovate-elliptic and under ½ inch long. The sapphire-violet little flowers are in stalked, dense, spikelike racemes, 1 inch to 2 inches long, from the upper leaf axils. Similar in growth habit, prostrate *V. officinalis* is a hairy species, and as a garden plant is inferior to the last. It has erect flowering stems 4 inches to 1 foot tall or sometimes taller, and oblongish, blunt, toothed leaves ¾ inch to 1½ inches long. The blue flowers, with stalks shorter than the calyxes, are about ¼ inch wide. This native of Europe and North America has been used in herbal medicines and is used in making vermouth.

Garden and Landscape Uses. An undemanding race, the speedwells serve usefully in gardens when positioned according to their heights and habits of growth. Low kinds are adaptable for rock gardens, taller ones for flower borders. The blooms of the latter make welcome additions to flower arrangements and bouquets, lending rich blues and purples and spirelike forms that contrast pleasingly with many other summer blooms. Ordinary, reasonably fertile soil that drains freely, but is not dry, suits veronicas. For rock garden kinds, a leaner diet is appropriate and tends to still or at least moderate any tendency to immoderate growth. As a group these are sun-lovers, but most stand at least part-day shade and some of the dwarf kinds may benefit from it.

Cultivation. The kinds described here are hardy and perennial. In general, they benefit from being lifted, divided, and replanted about every third year into earth furbished by deep spading and the addition of such ammendments as compost and fertilizer or manure. Early fall or spring are suitable times to do this. Propagation presents no difficulties. Division and seed are ready means of accomplishing this. Cuttings can also be used.

VERONICASTRUM (Veronic-ástrum)—Culver's Root or Culver's Physic. One of the two species of *Veronicastrum*, of the figwort family SCROPHULARIACEAE, usually recognized is native to North America, the other to eastern Asia. By some authorities they are considered to represent only one species; by certain Japanese botanists the Asian population is splintered into about nine species. Only the American species appears to be cultivated. The name, derived from that of *Veronica*, a closely related genus, and the Latin *astrum*, a star, suggests a resemblance. From *Veronica* the present genus differs in its leaves being in whorls (circles) of three to seven and in its flowers having corollas with tubes markedly longer than the lobes (petals).

Veronicastrums are tall, hardy, herbaceous perennials with pink or white flowers in slender, terminal spikelike racemes that resemble those of some veronicas. The flowers have a deeply-four- or five-parted calyx and a nearly symmetrical tubular corolla with four lobes. The two stamens protrude. The fruits are dry capsules.

Culver's root or Culver's physic (*V. virginicum* syns. *Veronica virginica, Leptandra virginica*) is indigenous from Vermont to Ontario, Manitoba, Georgia, and Louisiana. It inhabits rich woodlands, meadows, and prairies, often favoring limestone soils. From 3 to 7 feet tall, it blooms in summer. Its short-stalked, sharply-toothed leaves, up to 6 inches long, are lanceolate to oblanceolate. The flowers, white or pinkish and ⅓ inch long, are in dense, slender spires up to 9 inches long and usually several together. Sometimes called Culver's

Veronicastrum virginicum

physic (there seems to be no record of whom Culver was), this species has been used medicinally as a purgative and tonic.

Garden and Landscape Uses and Cultivation. Although not one of the showiest of hardy herbaceous perennials, Culver's root is worthy of a place in gardens by way of providing variety and because of its complete hardiness and ease of cultivation. It is, of course, appropriate in native plant gardens and for naturalizing in informal and semiwild areas. It can also be used in clumps toward the rears of perennial borders. It is a vigorous plant that thrives in sun or part-day shade in any ordinary garden soil. Beyond the need for dividing and replanting when the clumps become too large and crowded, say every three or four years, little attention is needed. Propagation is very simple by division in spring or early fall, and by seed. It can also be increased by summer cuttings.

VERSCHAFFELTIA (Verschaffélt-ia). The name of this endemic of the Seychelles Islands commemorates the Belgian horticulturist Ambrose Colletto Alexandre Verschaffelt, who died in 1886. The genus consists of a single species of the palm family PALMAE. Relatively common in its home islands, *Verschaffeltia splendida* plays a part in the local economy. Its trunks are split and used for building huts and rain gutters.

Reported to attain a height of 75 feet, but usually considerably lower, *V. splendida* has a solitary, erect trunk braced at its base with stilt roots that angle outward from the lower part of the trunk and anchor into the ground. They are believed to be devices that aid the plant in retaining its hold on the unstable soils of steep ravines where it frequently grows. The upper part of the trunk, and the lower portion when young, is encircled with rings of down-pointing spines. The handsome crown of foliage consists of leaves with blades 6 to 9 feet long and much shorter, spiny stalks. The oval leaf blades are deeply-notched at their ends, and along their sides are irregularly divided to varying depths, often nearly to the midrib. The divisions are again shallowly-divided or -toothed at their ends and are strongly parallel-ribbed. The branched flower clusters originate among the leaves. The main spathe is about 2½ feet long. Typically the flowers are in groups of three, one female between and below two males. The males have six stamens. The bullet-like fruits, nearly 1 inch in diameter, have hard shells. The seeds are grooved.

Garden and Landscape Uses and Cultivation. This handsome palm is adapted for cultivation only in very humid, tropical conditions and cannot be expected to prosper, except possibly in southern Florida, outdoors in the continental United

States. In greenhouses it requires high humidity, shade from strong sun, and a minimum winter night temperature of 70°F, with a daytime rise of five to ten degrees permitted. At other seasons both day and night temperatures may with advantage be higher. The soil should be porous and fertile and the containers well drained. Watering should be done freely from spring through fall, somewhat less freely in winter. Specimens that have filled their pots or tubs with roots benefit from biweekly applications of dilute liquid fertilizer from spring through fall. Propagation is by fresh seed, which does not retain its ability to germinate for long, sown in sandy, peaty soil in a temperature of 80 to 90°F. For additional information see Palms.

VERTICAL LEAF is *Senecio crassissimus.*

VERTICORDIA (Verti-córdia). Endemic to Australia, most of its forty species in Western Australia, *Verticordia,* of the myrtle family MYRTACEAE, consists of predominately heathlike, evergreen shrubs. The name, from the Latin *verto,* to turn, and *cordis,* a heart, is associated with a title of the goddess Venus, to whom the myrtle (*Myrtus*) was considered sacred.

Verticordias have opposite or rarely alternate, undivided leaves, hairless except for fringes along their margins and about ½ inch long. The whitish, pink, or yellow blooms are in flat-topped clusters, racemes, or spikes. Each bloom has a calyx of five to ten often colored, spreading lobes of feathery appearance because they are deeply-divided into slender or hairlike segments; five-lobed, fringed or smooth-edged petals; and ten stamens. The fruits are capsules.

An inhabitant of Western Australia, *V. densiflora,* 2 to 3 feet in height, is bushy and has very slender, linear, cylindrical or three-angled leaves, mostly in crowded clusters. The ½-inch-wide, pink or white flowers are in dense, long-stalked, leafy groups 2 to 4 inches wide at the branch ends. They have fringed petals, and calyxes bristly in their lower parts. Also Western Australian, *V. nitens* is 2 to 4 feet tall, upright, and freely branched. It has linear leaves ½ to ¾ inch long, and wide, flat-topped clusters of golden-yellow to orange-yellow flowers with obovate petals fringed with short teeth.

Garden and Landscape Uses and Cultivation. Verticordias can be grown outdoors in California and other places with warm, frost-free, dry climates and are beautiful for rock gardens and other locations where they can be displayed to advantage. Also suitable for cool greenhouses, they require the same treatment as leptospermums, acacias, callistemons, and similar plants. They are satisfied with freely drained, sandy, peaty soil of reasonable fertility, kept evenly moist, but not

Vestia lycioides

wet, and are readily propagated by seed and by cuttings of firm, but not hard shoots.

VERVAIN. See Verbena.

VESICARIA. See Alyssoides.

VESTIA (Vés-tia). One species, a native of Chile, is the only member of this genus of the nightshade family SOLANACEAE. Its name commemorates Professor Lorenz Chrysanth von Vest, of Graz, Austria, who died in 1840.

An evergreen, ill-scented shrub, *Vestia lycioides* is closely related to *Cestrum.* It has downy shoots, and alternate, hairless, oblong-elliptic to obovate, toothless leaves up to 2 inches long. Its pendulous flowers come from the leaf axils. They have short, five-toothed calyxes, and pale yellow corollas with slender, cylindrical tubes, 1 inch to 1¼ inches in length, and five spreading lobes (petals). The face of the bloom is about ¾ inch wide. The fruits are small egg-shaped capsules.

Garden and Landscape Uses and Cultivation. Attractive in habit, foliage, and flower, this rather rare plant can be grown outdoors only where there is very little or no frost, as in parts of California. It succeeds in sun or part-day shade in ordinary, well-drained, fertile soil and flowers in spring or early summer. Any pruning needed to keep it shapely is done as soon as blooming is through. Increase is easy by summer cuttings and by seed.

VETCH. See Vicia. Bladder-vetch is *Anthyllis tetraphylla;* crown-vetch, *Coronilla varia;* Hatchet-vetch, *Securigera securidaca;* horseshoe-vetch, *Hippocrepis;* kidney-vetch, *Anthyllis vulneraria;* and milk-vetch, *Astragalus coccineus.*

VETCHLING. See Lathyrus.

VETIVERIA (Vetiv-èria)—Vetiver or Khus-Khus Grass. The chief importance of this genus is that the rhizomes of one of its nine species are the source of vetiver oil used in perfumery. The group belongs in the grass family GRAMINEAE and is native to Africa, Asia, and Australia. Its name is from an ancient Asian one.

Vetiverias are perennials of tufted habit that have slender or stout stems and flat or folded leaf blades. Most commonly their spikelets of flowers are in long, narrow panicles. The spikelets are in pairs with one of each pair with a male and a sterile flower, and the other with a bisexual and a sterile flower. The spikelets drop when mature.

Vetiver or khus-khus grass (*Vetiveria zizanioides*), a native of tropical Asia, is naturalized in southeastern United States. From 6 to 8 feet tall, it has aromatic rhizomes and stout, erect stems. Its pointed-linear, rough-edged leaf blades are 1 foot to 3 feet in length by ⅙ to a little under ½ inch wide. Up to 1½ feet long, the flower panicles, of many slender, erect racemes up to 3 inches long, come in summer.

Garden and Landscape Uses and Cultivation. In addition to its commercial cultivation as a source of oil, vetiver is sometimes planted as a boundary marker and is included, sometimes in greenhouses, in collections of plants useful to man. It grows satisfactorily in sunny locations in ordinary soils. Greenhouse temperatures held at about 50°F on winter nights, with a few degrees rise by day, are suitable. Increase is by division and by seed.

VI is *Spondias cytherea*.

VIBURNUM (Vibúrn-um) — Arrowwood, Cranberry-Bush, Dockmackie, Laurestinus, Snowball Bush, Wayfaring Tree. Popular horticulturally, *Viburnum*, of the honeysuckle family CAPRIFOLIACEAE, comprises about 225 species of mostly rather large deciduous and evergreen shrubs or occasionally small trees, many highly esteemed for their displays of bloom and fruits and attractive habits of growth, and some for the autumn colors of their foliage. The natural geographical range of the genus includes North America, Central America, Europe, and Asia. The name is an ancient Latin one of one of its species.

Viburnums have opposite, undivided, lobed or lobeless, often toothed leaves. Prevailingly white or creamy-white, less often pinkish or pink, the flowers are in flattish, umbel-like, panicle-like, or less often globular, headlike clusters. In some sorts, the outermost blooms that ring the clusters are sterile and much bigger and showier than the more numerous, fertile, inner ones. The calyxes of the flowers have five tiny teeth and the corolla is wheel- or bell-shaped or less often tubular, and five-lobed. Fertile blooms have five stamens and one very short, three-lobed style. The fruits are berry-like drupes, red, yellow, orange, or black when ripe. Those of some kinds exhibit interesting changes of color from green to yellow, orange or red, and often finally black, with more than one color often in evidence in the clusters at the same time. Three horticultural varieties called snowball bushes have showy, globular heads of all-sterile flowers. These, of course, produce no fruits.

Earliest to bloom of deciduous viburnums, *V. farreri* (syn. *V. fragrans*) displays its very fragrant flowers well in advance of its foliage. Although hardy in southern New England, it, unfortunately, may have its flower buds killed or its flowers marred by low temperatures there. This rarely occurs in reasonably sheltered sites in the vicinity of New York City and not at all in milder regions. Native to China, *V. farreri* is up to 10 feet tall. It has elliptic, toothed, reddish-stalked leaves, about 3 inches long, slightly-hairy on their upper surfaces and on the veins of their undersides. The delightfully scented flowers, borne in panicled clusters, about 2 inches long, well in advance of the foliage, have tubular cor-

Viburnum farreri

Viburnum farreri (flowers)

ollas. Pink in the bud stage, when open they are white with a blush of pink. The fruits are red. Flowers, white both in bud and when open, are borne by *V. f. album*. Variety *V. f. nanum*, 1½ to 2 feet tall and up to 5 feet in diameter, has smaller leaves than the typical species. A beautiful hybrid of *V. fragrans* and *V. grandiflorum*, winter- or early-spring-flowering *V. bodnantense* is a deciduous, much-branched shrub about 10 feet tall and intermediate between its parents. In clusters 3 inches wide, its fragrant flowers are about ⅓ inch across. In bud pink, later they become almost white. There are several varieties, the first and one of the best of which is 'Dawn'.

Also early flowering, but with its new foliage well in evidence at blooming time, exquisitely fragrant, Korean *V. carlesii* is hardy throughout most of New England. Because it is difficult to increase from cuttings, this is commonly propagated by grafting, a procedure that has two disadvantages. Sucker shoots from the under-

Viburnum carlesii

stock are likely to sprout abundantly and, unless cut out periodically, to eventually outgrow the bush of *V. carlesii*. More seriously, specimens propagated in this way are subject to an incurable, death-causing graft blight, apparently the result of an incompatibility between stock and scion. An upright, rather rigid, rounded, deciduous shrub 4 to 5 feet tall, *V. carlesii* has deep green, nonlustrous, ovate to elliptic, toothed leaves, 2 to 4 inches long, downy on both surfaces and with the veins on their undersides green. The little flowers have corolla tubes ⅝ inch long. Pink in bud and dazzling white when fully open, they are in clusters 2½ to 3 inches across. The jet-black fruits are without particular decorative appeal. Variety *V. c. compactum* is of more compact habit and blooms more freely.

Hybrids of *V. carlesii*, reliably longer-lived and just as beautiful, afford choice furnishings for home gardens and other landscapes. They bloom just a little later than *V. carlesii* and have fragrant flowers. Here belong *V. burkwoodii*, *V. carlcephalum*, and *V. juddii*. Having as its other parent *V. utile*, **V. burkwoodii** is hardy in southern New England. Deciduous there and in other cold climates, it is semievergreen or evergreen in mild climates. From 5 to 6 feet

Viburnum burkwoodii

Viburnum carlcephalum

Viburnum plicatum (flowers)

Viburnum carlcephalum (flowers)

Viburnum plicatum

tall and of rounded outline, this has ovate, slightly-toothed leaves 3 to 4 inches long, lustrous and nearly hairless above, with undersides felted with brownish-gray hairs, and the veins beneath, brownish. Pinkish at first, changing to white, the flowers, presented when the leaves are well in evidence, are in clusters 3 to 3½ inches across. They have tubular corollas. Variety *V. b.* 'Chenault' blooms a little before the typical kind. Globular heads, up to 5 inches in diameter, of small, white, fragrant flowers with a little pink or red on their outsides are characteristic of **V. carlcephalum,** the parents of which are *V. carlesii* and *V. macrocephalum.* One of the finest of its group, this deciduous sort resembles *V. carlesii,* but has more lustrous foliage and larger heads of less intensely fragrant flowers with

shorter corolla tubes and protruding anthers. The shrub is in leaf at blooming time. The fruits are red to black. Raised at the Arnold Arboretum, Jamaica Plain, Massachusetts in 1920 and named after William Judd, a famous propagator there, **V. juddii** is a hybrid between *V. carlesii* and *V. bitchiuense.* Up to 8 feet tall and of spreading habit, this flowers before its leaves expand and in most respects is intermediate between its parents. Its clusters of pink-changing-to-white flowers, 3 to almost 3½ inches across, are, however, mostly larger than those of either parent and are less intensely perfumed than those of *V. carlesii.* Its shoots are densely-clothed with star-shaped hairs and its ovate to elliptic, 3- to 3½-inch-long, shallowly-toothed leaves have hairy undersides.

The Japanese snowball bush (**V. plica-**

tum syns. *V. tomentosum plicatum, V. t. sterile*) is the finest of the snowball bushes. Because of a nomenclatural technicality, the correct name of this horticultural variety is a binomial (consisting of only two words) as opposed to consisting of the usual three words. Equally as unusual, the botanical name of the species of which the Japanese snowball bush is a variety is a trinomial (of three words). Deciduous and up to 10 feet tall, the Japanese snowball bush has wide-spreading, arching branches, and ovate, toothed leaves 3 to 4 inches long and hairy on their undersides. Borne in late spring, its long-lasting, 2- to 3-inch-wide heads of white flowers are in two rows along the lengths of stems of the previous year's growth. The wild progenitor of the Japanese snowball bush is the double-file viburnum (**V. p. tomentosum** syn. *V. tomentosum*), a native of Japan and China and one of the most beautiful of all viburnums. This species, because of its horizontal branching and its showy displays of flowers, from a little distance away has much the effect of flowering dogwood (*Cornus florida*). From the Japanese snowball bush, the double-file viburnum differs in its flow-

Viburnum plicatum tomentosum

Viburnum plicatum mariesii

Viburnum macrocephalum

Viburnum opulus roseum

Viburnum plicatum mariesii (flowers)

Viburnum opulus

ers being in flat, up-facing clusters, with the many small blooms that form the centers of each ringed with a circle of much larger, showier, sterile blooms. The clusters are displayed in two rows along most of the lengths of the branches. The fruits ripen at first to red, then become black at maturity. Variety *V. p. mariesii*, identical or almost identical with *V. p.* 'Lanarth', is similar to, but lower than *V. p. tomentosum* and has larger sterile flowers.

The Chinese snowball bush (**V. macrocephalum**) affords another instance of a horticultural variety being named as if it were a species and the wild population from which it developed being named as if it were a variety of the species. Deciduous where winters are severe, but partially evergreen or evergreen in mild climates, the Chinese snowball bush is not reliably hardy in climates colder than that of the region of New York City. From 10 to 12 feet high, it has finely-toothed, ovate to elliptic leaves 2½ to 4 inches long and pubescent on both surfaces. Displayed in late spring, its heads of white bloom, reminiscent of those of some varieties of *Hydrangea macrophylla*, are 4 to 6 inches in diameter. Less frequently grown than its sterile-flowered variety, the wild species *V. macrocephalum keteleeri* is a handsome and

slightly hardier shrub. From the Chinese snowball bush this sort differs in its clusters of blooms being of mostly little fertile flowers with an encircling ring of larger sterile ones.

The European snowball bush (**V. opulus roseum** syn. *V. o. sterile*) is a variety of the European cranberry-bush with heads of all sterile flowers. Hardy throughout New England, this deciduous shrub, up to about 12 feet tall, has maple-like, three- to five-lobed leaves up to 4 inches long, hairy on their undersides and with stalks with a narrow groove along their upper sides,

and near their bases large, conspicuous disk-shaped glands. The creamy-white flowers, displayed in late spring, are in stalked, globular heads 3 to 4 inches across.

The European cranberry-bush or guelder-rose (**V. opulus**), a native of Europe, North Africa, and northern Asia and sparingly naturalized in parts of North America, in height and foliage characteristics resembles its variety the European snowball bush. Its mostly coarsely-toothed, three- to five-lobed leaves are 3 to 4 inches long and usually hairy on their under-

Viburnum opulus (fruits)

sides. From those of the American cranberry-bush they differ in their stalks having a narrow, V-shaped groove along their upper sides and distinctly stalked glands near their bases. Its flattish clusters, about 4 inches across, of many small, white, fertile flowers are fringed with a row of much larger, showy sterile blooms. The translucent, shining red fruits, which persist long into the winter, are edible, but are less palatable than those of the American cranberry-bush. Variety *V. o. aureum*, of compact habit, has shoots at first bronze, then changing to bright yellow, and finally to green. Up to about 5 feet tall, *V. o. compactum* flowers and fruits freely. Variety *V. o. nanum*, about 2 feet tall, is usually broader than high and billowy. Its leaves are smaller than those of the typical species. This variety rarely if ever blooms and is not known to fruit. Variety *V. o.* 'Notcutt' is especially vigor-

ous and has larger fruits than the species. Variety *V. o. xanthocarpum* has yellow fruits.

The American cranberry-bush or high-bush-cranberry (**V. trilobum** syn. *V. opulus americanum*), native from New Brunswick to British Columbia, New York, Michigan, South Dakota, and Oregon, and up to 12 feet tall, scarcely differs from the European cranberry-bush and by some authorities is included in that species. The only appreciable differences are that its leaves are usually hairless and have stalks with a broad, shallow groove, instead of a narrow one, along their upper side and small, usually stalked, glands at their base. The long-persistent fruits are much esteemed for jellies and preserves. Variety *V. t. compactum* is lower and more compact.

Viburnum trilobum compactum (fruits)

More or less treelike, deciduous viburnums up to 30 feet tall include *V. sieboldii*, *V. lentago*, and *V. rufidulum*. One of the most handsome viburnums, Japanese **V. sieboldii** is rounded to pyramidal and shapely. It has elliptic to obovate, coarsely-toothed leaves, up to 6 inches long, with glossy upper surfaces and hairy undersides. The numerous small, creamy-white flowers, in panicle-like clusters up to 4 inches long, are succeeded by conspicuously red-stalked fruits that are at first pink, becoming blue-black. A possible slight objection to this species is that if its fallen leaves are allowed to remain on the ground and decay, they give off an unpleasant odor. Native from the Hudson Bay region to Georgia and Mississippi, *V. lentago* is known by the vernacular names sheepberry, nannyberry, nanny-plum, tea-plant, black-haw, and wild-raisin. Nannyberry and black-haw are also common names of *V. prunifolium*. The lower branches of *V. lentago* often arch until they touch the ground. Its leaves are ovate, finely-toothed, and up to 4 inches long. The small, white flowers are in stalkless, flat clusters 4 to 5 inches across. The blue-black fruits have a waxy bloom. The southern black-haw or rusty nannyberry (*V. rufidulum*) is native from Virginia to Illinois, Florida, and Texas and is hardy to about the vicinity of New York City. A handsome sort, it is the southern equivalent of *V. prunifolium*, from which it differs most obviously in its winter buds, young shoots, and leafstalks being clothed with rust-colored hairs. Elliptic to elliptic-

Viburnum opulus nanum

Viburnum opulus xanthocarpum

Viburnum sieboldii

lanceolate and 2 to 4 inches long, the lustrous leaves are rusty-hairy on their undersides. The little, pure white flowers, in clusters up to 4½ inches across, are succeeded by bloomy, dark blue fruits about ⅓ inch long.

Deciduous shrubs up to 15 feet tall or sometimes slightly taller include *V. lantana*, *V. lobophyllum*, *V. prunifolium*, and *V. rhytidophylloides*. The wayfaring tree of Europe, western Asia, and North Africa (the American wayfaring tree is *V. alnifolium*), *V. lantana* has ovate, finely-toothed leaves 4 to 5 inches long and hairy on both surfaces. The small, white flowers, in 4-inch-wide clusters, are succeeded by fruits that change from green to red, then slowly to black. Variety *V. l. rugosum* has bigger, more conspicuously wrinkled leaves and

Viburnum lantana

Viburnum prunifolium

larger clusters of flowers. Variety *V. l.* 'Mohican' has brilliant red-orange fruits that remain colorful for nearly one month. Native to western China, *V. lobophyllum* has leaves of variable shape, but commonly ovate to obovate or rounded, and terminating in short points. They have coarsely-toothed margins and are hairy along the veins. The long-stalked clusters of small, white flowers are up to 4 inches in diam-

eter. The fruits are red. As its other common names, the stagbush (*V. prunifolium*) shares black-haw, sheepberry, and nannyberry with *V. lentago*. Often as broad as tall, and native from Connecticut to Michigan, Florida, and Texas, *V. prunifolium* is hardy throughout New England. An excellent species with somewhat the aspect of a hawthorn, it has finely-toothed ovate to broad-elliptic or obovate, 2- to 3-inch-long, glossy leaves that change to a rich red in fall. The small, creamy-white flowers, in stalkless clusters 2 to 4 inches across, are succeeded by edible, blue-black fruits coated with a waxy bloom and ⅓ to ½ inch long.

Viburnum prunifolium (fruits)

Viburnum acerifolium

Other deciduous viburnums include these: *V. acerifolium*, the arrowwood, dockmackie, or possum-haw, of eastern North America, is hardy throughout New England. Up to 6 feet tall, it has maple-like, three-lobed, coarsely-toothed leaves, 3 to 5 inches long, with hairy stalks, slightly hairy upper surfaces, and densely-hairy undersides sprinkled with tiny black dots. In fall the leaves turn bright crimson. The tiny, creamy-white flowers are in long-stalked clusters up to 3 inches in di-

ameter. The fruits are blackish-purple. *V. alnifolium* (syn. *V. lantanoides*), the hobble bush or American wayfaring tree, native from New Brunswick to Michigan and North Carolina, is up to 10 feet tall and wide-spreading. Also known as moosewood, moose bush, and mooseberry, it has irregularly-toothed, nearly circular leaves, heart-shaped at their bases and 6 to 8 inches long, that in fall become red. The flowers, in flat, stalkless clusters about 5 inches across, are white. The many little fertile ones are margined with fewer, nearly 1-inch-wide sterile blooms. The fruits change from red to purple-black as they ripen. Variety *V. a. praecox* blooms

Viburnum betulifolium

earlier than the typical species. *V. betulifolium*, of China, is hardy in southern New England. Magnificent in fruit, it is 10 to 12 feet tall and of erect habit. Its slender-stalked, ovate leaves are coarsely-toothed except near their bases. Sparingly hairy along the veins beneath, they are elsewhere hairless. The small, white flowers are in short-stalked clusters 2 to 4 inches wide. The fruits are red. *V. bitchiuense*, a native of Japan, differs from closely allied *V. carlesii* in being of looser habit and in having smaller, usually blunt leaves and smaller flower clusters. The stalks of the stamens of the sweetly-scented flowers are about twice as long as the anthers, in contrast to those of *V. carlesii*, which are shorter than the anthers. *V. burejaeticum*, of northern China and Manchuria, is up to 15 feet tall. It has downy shoots and wavy-toothed, ovate to elliptic leaves, downy on their undersides and 3 to 4 inches long. The little white flowers are in dense clusters about 3 inches across. The fruits are bluish-black. *V. cassinoides*, the withe-rod, tea-berry, Appalachian-tea, or wild-raisin, is native from Newfoundland to Minnesota and North

Viburnum burejaeticum

Viburnum dilatatum

flowers, in clusters up to 3½ inches across and with stamens slightly longer than the corolla, and hairless ovaries, are succeeded by spherical-ovoid, red fruits about ¼ inch long. *V. grandiflorum,* native to the Himalayas, is closely allied to *V. farreri.* Hardy in sheltered locations on Long Island, New York, but not where winters are harsher, this attains a height of about 6 feet. Its leaves are elliptic-oblong and 3 to 4 inches long. The pink-tinged white flowers, ½ to ¾ inch wide and in clusters 2 to 3 inches across, are fragrant. *V. ichangense,* a native of China hardy only in climates not harsher than that of Long Island, New York, is loosely-branched and up to 6 feet tall. Its slender-pointed, ovate to ovate-lanceolate leaves, 1½ to 2 inches long, have pubescent undersides. The fragrant, white flowers, profusely borne in spring in clusters 1½ inches across, have stamens shorter than the corolla and densely-hairy ovaries. They are followed by showy displays of bright red fruits. *V. molle,* native from Indiana to Kentucky and Missouri, is up to 12 feet tall. On older stems the bark peels off in thin flakes. Its long-stalked, broad-ovate to nearly circular, short-pointed, coarsely-toothed leaves, more or less hairy on their undersides, are hairless above. The small, white flowers are in long-stalked clusters about 2½ inches across. The fruits are bluish-black. *V. nudum,* native from Connecticut to Florida and Louisiana and up to 15 feet tall,

Viburnum burejaeticum (fruits)

Viburnum erosum

Carolina. From 10 to 12 feet tall and of erect habit, this sort is remarkable for its bright red fall foliage and splendid display of smallish, edible fruits, which change as they ripen from green, to yellowish, to red, and finally to blue-black. The ovate to elliptic, 3- to 4-inch-long, nearly hairless, dull green leaves are obscurely-toothed. The small, white flowers are in short-stalked clusters 4 to 5 inches across. *V. dentatum* shares the common name arrowwood with *V. acerifolium* and is sometimes distinguished as the southern arrowwood. It is a variable native from New Brunswick to Illinois, Florida, and Texas. From 10 to 20 feet tall, this species has ovate to nearly circular, coarsely-toothed, hairless to more or less hairy leaves, 2 to 3 inches long, that in fall become shining red. The little, creamy-white flowers, with long-protruding stamens, are in long-stalked clusters about 3 inches in diameter. The egg-shaped fruits are blue-black. *V. dilatatum,* sometimes called the linden viburnum, is Japanese. An excellent ornamental up to about 10 feet tall, this has ovate to nearly circular, coarsely-toothed leaves up to 5 inches long, hairy on both surfaces, and in fall becoming russet-red. The small, pure white flowers, in clusters 4 to 5 inches across, are suc-

Viburnum erosum (flowers)

ceeded by bright scarlet fruits that remain well into the winter. Variety *V. d. xanthocarpum* has yellow fruits. *V. erosum,* of China and Japan, is akin to *V. ichangense,* but is hardier, surviving outdoors at least as far north as southern New England. Erect and up to 15 feet tall, it has short-stalked, coarsely-toothed, subcircular to ovate leaves 1½ to 3½ inches long and nearly or quite hairless except along the veins on their undersides. The white

Viburnum nudum

shares the common name possum-haw with *V. acerifolium* and is also called smooth withe-rod. Much resembling *V. cassinoides,* but not hardy in climates colder than that of southernmost New England, this sort is distinguished from *V. cassinoides* by its 2- to 4½-inch-long, elliptic-lanceolate to ovate or obovate leaves being toothless or nearly toothless, and lustrous and by the stalks of its flower clusters being at least as long as the clusters. From 2½ to 5 inches across, the clusters of tiny white or creamy-white blooms are suc-

Viburnum sargentii

Viburnum setigerum (fruits)

Viburnum veitchii

ceeded by blue-black fruits. *V. pauciflorum,* like *V. acerifolium* called mooseberry, is an extremely hardy native of northern North America and northern Asia. Of loose, open habit and 3 to 5 feet tall, it has broad-ovate to nearly circular, toothed leaves slightly three-lobed at their apexes. The little white flowers are in clusters about 1 inch wide. The fruits are red. *V. sargentii,* of northeastern Asia, has much the aspect of *V. opulus;* it is up to 12 feet tall and has thick, corky bark. Its 3- to 6-inch-long maple-like leaves have hairless red stalks with conspicuous glands at their tops. Their blades have three toothed lobes or the middle lobe may be toothless and longer than the others. Less often, the leaves are oblong-lanceolate and lobeless. The 3- to 4-inch-wide clusters of white flowers consist of many small, sterile blooms, fringed with a row of 1-inch-wide sterile flowers. The fertile flowers have protruding stamens with purple anthers. The fruits are scarlet. Those of *V. s. flavum* are yellow. *V. setigerum* (syn. *V. theiferum*), of China, is an attractive species of loose habit. Its slender-pointed, ovate-lanceolate to ovate-oblong leaves are slightly-toothed and 3 to 5 inches long by about one-half as wide. The little white flowers, freely borne in stalked clusters some 2 inches across, are succeeded by slightly flattened, ovoid fruits that ripen to orange and finally brilliant red and are so abundant that the branches droop beneath their weight. The fruits of *V. s. aurantiacum* remain orange through full maturity. *V. veitchii,* of China, has much the aspect of *V. lantana.* Hardy in southern New England, this species attains a height of about 6 feet. It has pointed-ovate, distantly-toothed leaves, 3½ to 4½ inches long, with rounded to heart-shaped bases. Their upper surfaces are lightly furnished with star-shaped hairs, their undersides much more densely so. The flowers, small and white, are crowded in short-stalked

clusters from 2 to 4½ inches in diameter. The fruits change as they ripen from green to red and finally black. *V. wrightii,* of Japan, known as leather leaf, is 6 to 10 feet tall. Erect and rather narrow, it has broad-ovate to obovate, coarsely-toothed, strongly-veined leaves 3 to 6 inches long and hairless, except along the veins on their undersides. They become red in fall. The short-stalked clusters of small, white flowers are 2 to 4 inches in diameter. The fruits are sealing-wax-red. Variety *V. w. hessei,* dwarfer and more compact than the typical species, has much merit.

Evergreen viburnums include a number of attractive kinds that, with one notable exception, are not reliably hardy where

winters are colder than those of coastal Virginia. For their best performance, some need even milder climates. Hardiest of the group, *V. rhytidophyllum* is worthy of more

Viburnum wrightii (fruits)

Viburnum rhytidophyllum

Viburnum rhytidophyllum (foliage)

attention from gardeners. It prospers in sheltered locations in the vicinity of New York City and in parts of southern New England. From 6 to 10 feet tall and as broad or broader than high, this Chinese species of somewhat rhododendron-like aspect is plentifully furnished with 4- to 7½-inch-long, lanceolate-oblong leaves with glossy, much-wrinkled, upper surfaces, and undersides heavily clothed with a dense felt of yellowish hairs. Like those of rhododendrons, its leaves droop forlornly in severe cold, but with rising temperatures soon recover. Of little ornamental merit, the ¼-inch-wide, yellowish-white flowers, the buds of which form in fall and remain exposed all winter, are grouped in flattish heads 4 to 8 inches across, and are succeeded by small fruits that change from green to red and finally to black. Variety *V. r. roseum* has pinkish flower buds. Not significantly different from *V. rhytidophyllum*, except that in cold climates it tends to be deciduous, **V. rhytidophylloides** is a hybrid between *V. rhytidophyllum* and *V. lantana*. Its varieties, 'Allegheny' and 'Willowwood', are especially worthwhile.

Laurestinus (**V. tinus**), freely planted in

many southern and West Coast gardens, is also popular in the British Isles and some other parts of Europe. A native of the Mediterranean region introduced to America in colonial times, this attains heights of 6 to 12 feet. Its narrowly-ovate, smooth-edged leaves, 1½ to 4 inches long, are dark glossy-green above, paler on their undersides. Its ¼-inch-wide, white to pinkish flowers, borne from fall to spring in clusters 2 to 4 inches across, are succeeded by ovoid fruits, ¼ inch long, that ripen to a rich indigo-blue before ultimately turning black. Varieties include these: *V. t. lucidum* has larger leaves and

Viburnum tinus

Viburnum tinus (fruits)

is less hardy than the typical species; *V. t. robustum* has coarser, rougher leaves than the typical species; *V. t.* 'Spring Bouquet' is up to about 6 feet tall and has smaller leaves than the typical species; and *V. t. variegatum* has leaves variegated with white and pale yellow.

Other evergreen sorts include these: **V. cinnamomifolium,** of China and the Himalayan region, attains heights of 10 to 20 feet and is approximately as wide as tall. Hardy only in such regions as the Pacific Northwest and California, where winters are decidedly mild, this imposing species was introduced to European and American gardens by the distinguished plant

collector Ernest H. Wilson in 1904. Its handsome, glossy, leathery, toothless or nearly toothless, elliptic to ovate leaves, 3 to 6 inches long by 1 inch to 3 inches wide, have three prominent veins. The slightly honey-scented flowers are small, dull white, and in clusters 4 to 6 inches wide. They are succeeded by little glossy-blue-black fruits. **V. davidii,** a small, compact version of *V. cinnamomifolium*, like that species was introduced to western gardens from China by Ernest H. Wilson in 1904. Although hardier than *V. cinnamomifolium*, it is unlikely to survive in climates harsher than that of Washington, D.C.

Viburnum davidii

From 2 to 3 feet tall, this sort has spreading branches well furnished with glossy, conspicuously three-veined, narrowly-elliptic to obovate leaves 2 to 6 inches long and sometimes slightly-toothed toward their apexes. The tiny whitish flowers, in stiff clusters 2 to 3 inches wide, are without much decorative significance. They are succeeded by turquoise-blue fruits. **V. henryi,** of China, is up to 10 feet tall. It has narrow-elliptic, toothed leaves, 4 to 5 inches long, with glossy upper surfaces, and broad, more or less pyramidal clusters of small white flowers. Its handsome fruits change from green to bright red to black as they ripen. **V. japonicum** (syn. *V. macrophyllum*), of Japan, is somewhat hardier than *V. odoratissimum*, with which it is frequently confused in gardens. A broad shrub or small tree from 10 to 20 feet tall, it is distinguishable from *V. odoratissimum* by its more conspicuously warty young shoots, by the secondary veins of its leaves not extending completely to the leaf margins, and by its flower clusters being somewhat flatter. The glossy, leathery leaves of *V. japonicum*, up to 6 inches long and 4 inches wide, are toothless or are toothed above their middles. Their undersides are paler than their upper surfaces. The small, fragrant, white flowers are borne in spring in dense, rounded clusters. Usually rather sparse, especially

Viburnum suspensum

A screen of Viburnum plicatum

on young specimens, the fruits are red. **V. odoratissimum** differs from closely allied *V. japonicum* in the ways indicated above in the description of that species. Native from Japan to India, near the limits of its hardiness it may lose its foliage for a brief period in winter, but in milder climates it is reliably evergreen. From 10 to 20 feet tall, it has glossy, hairless, elliptic to oblongish leaves 3 to 8 inches long and toothless or sparingly-toothed toward their apexes. The slightly fragrant, small white flowers, in broad-pyramidal clusters 3 to 4 inches long, are succeeded by fruits that change from red to black as they ripen. **V. propinquum,** a bushy native of China, is 3 to 4 feet tall. Among evergreen viburnums, it resembles *V. cinnamomifolium* and *V. davidii* in having leaves with three chief veins, but those of *V. propinquum* are smaller and have veins less conspicuously defined than those of the other two. Ovate-lanceolate to elliptic and sparsely-shallowly-toothed, the glossy, hairless, short-stalked leaves of *V. propinquum* are 2 to 3½ inches long by up to 1¼ inches wide. Tiny and greenish-white, the flowers are in clusters 1½ to 3 inches wide. The fruits are small and blue-black. **V. rigidum,** a native of the Canary Islands, resembles laurestinus (*V. tinus*), but its leaves and clusters of flowers, borne in early spring, are bigger. From 6 to 10 feet tall, this sort is usually as wide or wider than high. Its fruits change from blue-black to black as they ripen. **V. suspensum,** native to the Ryukyu Islands, south of Japan, is reliably hardy only where little or no frost is experienced. From 6 to 10 feet tall and as broad as high, this has elliptic leaves toothed toward their apexes and 3 to 4 inches long. Their upper surfaces are glossy, their undersides duller and paler. In crowded panicles 1½ inches across, the small white to pinkish, somewhat ill-scented flowers are borne in early spring. The fruits change from red to black as they ripen.

An espaliered specimen of *Viburnum plicatum*

Garden and Landscape Uses. Viburnums offer gardeners and landscape designers a truly astonishing variety of useful, easy-to-grow shrubs or occasionally small trees that blend easily and congruously with most other types of vegetation. Practically all sorts are suitable for grouping in shrub beds and borders, and many are appropriate for inclusion in foundation plantings. On lawns, single specimens can often be displayed to advantage, or if the sward is so expansive that a solitary plant may look inadequate or if the viburnum is a kind too narrow to be satisfactory alone, a little corrective "cheating" may be done by planting three young specimens of the same kind 3 to 4 feet apart to form a triangle. They will soon grow together to become what appears to be a bush of more substantial aspect than if only a single plant had been set out.

When making selections for particular sites and purposes, give attention to the characteristics of the various kinds. Tall viburnums are especially useful as informal and semiformal screens, and *V. prunifolium* also for shearing as a formal

hedge. Some sorts are adapted for espaliering against walls; the snowball bush viburnums are appropriate for this purpose. Kinds notable for the fragrance of their blooms are *V. burkwoodii, V. carlcephalum, V. carlesii, V. farreri, V. grandiflorum,* and *V. juddii.* The foliage of evergreen sorts is generally of high quality and that of certain deciduous kinds colors attractively in fall. Among these last are *V. acerifolium* (purplish to crimson), *V. alnifolium* (reddish to deep claret), *V. cassinoides* (red), *V. dentatum* (shining red), *V. dilatatum* (russet), *V. lantana* (red to crimson), *V. lentago* (purplish-red), *V. nudum* (purplish-red), *V. opulus* (glossy red), *V. prunifolium* (bright red), *V. sargentii* (red), *V. sieboldii* (red), *V. trilobum* (glossy-red), and *V. wrightii* (reddish). Showy fruits, red at maturity, are presented by *V. betulifolium, V. dentatum, V. opulus, V. sargentii,* and *V. trilobum.* Fruits yellow when fully ripe are characteristic of *V. dilatatum xanthocarpum, V. opulus xanthocarpum, V. sargentii flavum,* and *V. wrightii.* Orange fruits are borne by *V. setigerum aurantiacum.* Those of *V. davidii* and *V. dentatum* are blue. Sorts with fruits that undergo a series of attractive color changes as they ripen include *V. alnifolium, V. cassinoides, V. lantana, V. prunifolium, V. rufidulum, V. setigerum,* and *V. sieboldii.*

Cultivation. With very few exceptions viburnums are easy to grow. They respond best to deep, reasonably fertile soil that is never excessively dry. Locations in full sun are generally satisfactory, but part-day shade is acceptable to most sorts. Most tolerant of shade are *V. alnifolium,* unfortunately not one of the most decorative species, and *V. cassinoides.* Routine care of viburnums consists chiefly of attending to whatever pruning needs doing to maintain shapeliness and prevent overcrowding and, if the location is at all a dryish one, deep watering at intervals during dry spells. It may also be necessary to spray with an insecticide to control the pesky snowball bush aphid, which stunts and contorts the leaves of some kinds, especially those of *V. opulus roseum*. Spraying should be done before the leaves are much contorted. Viburnums are generally easy to propagate by summer cuttings of firm, but not hard shoots and, the deciduous kinds, by leafless hardwood cuttings taken in fall. Sometimes propagation by division or by layering is appropriate and practicable. Seed sown in fall in a cold frame or outdoor bed protected from disturbance by rodents and other creatures may also be employed as a means of propagation, or the seed may be collected and stratified for five months in a temperature of 60°F or above, followed by three months at 40°F, before sowing in pots or pans in a greenhouse or cold frame.

VICIA (Víc-ia)—Vetch, Broad Bean or Fava Bean or Horse Bean. Except for the broad bean, cultivated as a vegetable, and species sometimes used as green manure crops to improve the texture and fertility of the soil, vetches are of minor horticultural importance. They belong to the pea family LEGUMINOSAE and are natives of north temperate regions and of South America. There are about 150 species. The name *Vicia* is the classical Latin one.

These are annuals and herbaceous perennials, mostly climbing by tendrils and differing from closely related peas (*Pisum*) and sweet-peas (*Lathyrus*) in technical characteristics. Several are important forage crops. They almost always have leaves, those of many kinds ending in a tendril, with an even number of leaflets. The flowers are pea-like and solitary or in clusters or racemes from the leaf axils.

The broad, fava, or horse bean (*V. faba*), probably originally native to North Africa and southwest Asia, is one of man's oldest cultivated crops. It is the bean of history, esteemed as food for man and beast. As a vegetable it is popular in northern Europe, where the lima bean does not

Vicia faba (flowers)

thrive, but is less well known in North America. For its cultivation see Beans. The broad bean is a hardy annual, erect and 1 foot to 5 feet tall. Its somewhat glaucous, slightly bluish-green leaves have one to three pairs of elliptic to ovate leaflets 2 to 4 inches long. There may be a vestigial tendril, though usually not. One to several creamy-white flowers, each with a dull purplish blotch, develop on short stalks in the leaf axils. The thick, soft seed pods may be up to 1 foot long or even longer. They contain several flattish to rounded seeds.

A trailing or vining species, the cow vetch (*V. cracca*), a native of Europe, temperate Asia, and North America, is a hardy perennial with tangled stems 2 to 4 feet long. Its rather pretty, finely-divided foliage is of leaves with mostly ten or fewer pairs of linear leaflets, up to a little over 1 inch long, that terminate in branched tendrils. The bright purplish-blue blooms, ½ inch long, are many together in one-sided racemes at the ends of stalks longer than the leaves.

Attractive *V. canescens*, endemic to Lebanon, is a perennial, 1 foot to 1½ feet tall,

densely clothed with soft, yellowish to gray hairs. Its leaves, the uppermost sometimes with a short tendril, are of eight to ten pairs of leaflets. The rosy-lavender to blue flowers are in racemes about as long as the leaves. An erect hardy perennial without tendrils, *V. oroboides* is a southern European native 1 foot to 2 feet tall. It has usually branchless stems, and leaves with one to four pairs of ovate to oblongish leaflets 1½ to 3 inches long. The short-stalked flowers, in racemes of up to twelve, are yellowish to yellow, sometimes tinged with red, and up to ¾ inch long. The slender pods are 1 inch to 1½ inches long.

Distinctive *V. unijuga*, of northeastern Asia, has erect, slender stems up to about 3 feet tall and leaves, without tendrils, of one pair of broad-pointed-ovate leaflets 1½ to 3 inches long by up to 1½ inches wide. The rich blue to violet-blue flowers are in long-stalked, crowded, one-sided racemes about 3 inches long. In aspect much like the last, but without tendrils, *V. onobrychioides*, of southern Europe, has stems 1 foot to 4 feet long and leaves with four to eleven pairs of linear to oblong leaflets ½ inch to 1½ inches long. From ¾ to 1 inch in length, the purple or sometimes white flowers are in one-sided racemes of four to twelve, with stalks about as long

Vicia onobrychioides

Vicia faba

Vicia canescens

Vicia tenuifolia

as the leaves. A vine up to 5 feet in height, *V. tenuifolia*, of Europe, has leaves, ending in tendrils, of five to thirteen pairs of linear to linear-oblong leaflets ½ inch to 1¼ inches long. Its lavender to bluish-lilac flowers, about ¾ inch long, are in slender racemes of fifteen to thirty.

Garden and Landscape Uses and Cultivation. The cow vetch finds occasional garden use for covering banks and in semiwild areas, but is scarcely suitable for more manicured surroundings. The other sorts with tendrils may be used similarly or allowed to grow as vines up stakes, strings, or other suitable supports. Upright *V. oroboides* may be planted at the fronts of flower borders and in naturalistic areas, as may *V. unijuga* and *V. canescens*. The last is also appropriate in rock gardens. Vicias grow with little difficulty in any ordinary well-drained soil in sun or in slight or part-day shade. They are easy to raise from seed.

VICTORIA (Vic-tòria)—Royal Water-Lily, Santa Cruz Water-Lily. The genus *Victoria*, named in honor of Queen Victoria of England, consists of two truly remarkable species of floating aquatics, natives of quiet backwaters of the Amazon, Orinoco, Essequibo, Parana, and other rivers and some of their tributaries in South America. They belong in the water-lily family NYMPHACEAE.

Victorias, in effect, are immense water-lilies, differing from true water-lilies (*Nymphaea*) only in size and technical details of their flowers. In their native haunts and in gardens in the tropics, they are perennials, but in temperate and subtropical regions, they are generally cultivated as annuals. They have huge leaves that float like enormous platters on the water, and beautiful, very big flowers. The fruits are large, botanically berry-like, prickly structures.

Following the discovery in 1801 of *V. amazonica*, several attempts were made to introduce it to cultivation in European gardens. All failed until 1846, when three of a batch of seeds transported to England in a ball of wet clay germinated at the Royal Botanic Gardens, Kew. These grew vigorously, but died without flowering. In 1849, two English physicians sent home seeds from British Guiana. From these were raised plants, one of which bloomed in November of the year of its introduction in a conservatory in the gardens of Chatsworth House in Derbyshire, the stately home of the Duke of Devonshire. Success with the physician's seeds was made possible because they were shipped in bottles of fresh water and did not, as did most sent earlier, perish as a result of drying in transit. Appropriately, the first flower to open was presented to Queen Victoria. Seeds from the plants that flowered in England were distributed to botanic gar-

Victoria amazonica blooming in a conservatory at The New York Botanical Garden

Victoria amazonica in an outdoor pool, Longwood Gardens, Kennett Square, Pennsylvania

dens and similar establishments in Europe and elsewhere. The first plant to bloom in North America did so in 1851 at Philadelphia, Pennsylvania.

The royal water-lily (*V. amazonica* syn. *V. regia*) has leaves with nearly circular blades, 5 to 6 feet in diameter, with erect, turned-up rims 2 to 4 inches high. The 6- to 17-foot-long leafstalks, which join the blades at their middles, are armed with formidable prickles. The thin tissue of the blades is supported by an intricate and beautiful system of deep, riblike veins and cross-veins of such engineering perfection

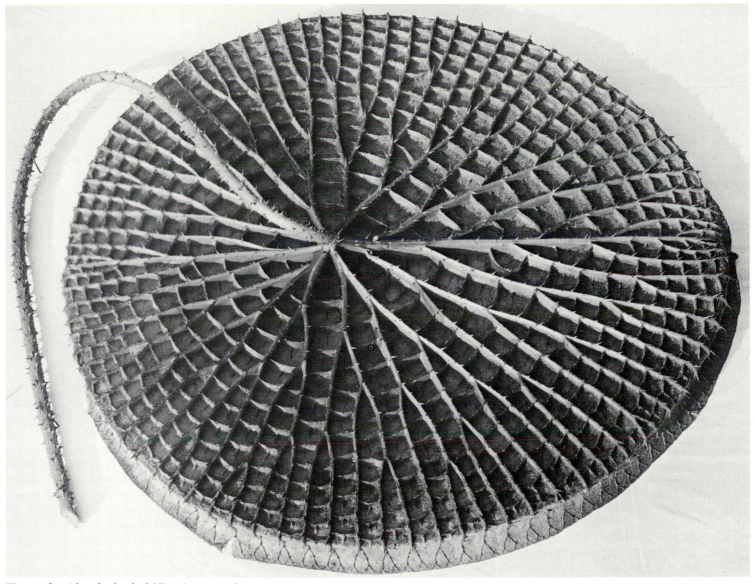

The underside of a leaf of *Victoria amazonica*

that they supplied Sir Joseph Paxton with inspiration for his design of the load-bearing structure of London's famous Crystal Palace. The supporting veins are furnished with stout thorns, which give protection from underwater assault by fish and other animal life. The upper leaf surface is punctured with small holes that allow rainwater that would otherwise collect in the platters to drain away. From 1 foot to 1½ feet in diameter, the many-petaled, fragrant flowers have a calyx very prickly almost throughout its entire length. They open in the evening and remain open for two days. At first ivory-white, on the second day they change to reddish-pink.

The Santa Cruz water-lily (**V. cruziana** syn. *V. trickeri*) differs from the royal water-lily in having leaves rarely exceeding 4½ feet in diameter, densely rather than sparingly pubescent on their under-surfaces, and with rims 6 to 8 inches high. Also, the sepals of its flowers are prickly only toward their bases, not almost or quite to their apexes. A fine intermediate hybrid between *V. amazonica* and *V. cruziana*, developed in the mid-twentieth century at Longwood Gardens, Kennett Square, Pennsylvania, is *V.* 'Longwood Hybrid'.

Garden and Landscape Uses. Most impressive of aquatics, but too big by far for small gardens, even in the tropics and subtropics, victorias are grown as show pieces in botanical gardens and other public horticultural display gardens in many parts of the world, outdoors where long hot summers make that possible (this can be at New York City if strong young plants raised indoors are available for setting out in late June or early July) and in large greenhouses especially constructed for their accommodation.

Cultivation. Victorias are not difficult to grow in quiet waters 3 to 6 feet deep where there is accommodation for their leaves to spread over a circle some 20 feet or more in diameter and where ample root room, warmth, and full sun are assured. They are outstanding, aesthetically satisfying features for water gardens. Except possibly in the tropics, it is best to raise new plants each year from seed. Sow those of *V. amazonica* in January, those of *V. cruziana* and 'Longwood Hybrid', to give plants for setting in outdoor pools, in February or March. Set the seeds 2 inches apart in pans of soil, cover them with 1 inch of sand, and submerge them 2 to 3 inches beneath the water surface. For *V. amazonica* the water must be maintained at a constant 85 to 90°F, for *V. cruziana* and the hybrid, 70 to 75°F. As soon as the seedlings are big enough to handle, pot them in 3-inch pots in fertile soil and, as they increase in size, successively to bigger ones until containers 6 to 8 inches in diameter are attained. Cover the soil with sand and set the 3-inch pots with the sand surface 3 to 4 inches below water level, the bigger containers proportionately deeper. Keep in full sun and maintain water temperatures at levels recommended for starting seed.

Transplant to final containers before the plants become so pot-bound in the 6- to 8-inch pots that their growth is checked. In

Victoria cruziana

Victoria 'Longwood Hybrid'

the tropics and subtropics, planting may be done directly in soil bottoms of quiet pools, but in temperate latitudes and in formal pools elsewhere it is usual to set them in binlike containers (usually of brick or concrete block). For the finest results have these big enough to contain eight to nine cubic yards of earth. Smaller plants can be had with as little as three cubic yards. Use loamy soil enriched with one-fourth part by bulk of rotted cow manure or its equivalent in slow-release fertilizer. There is no need to add sand. In constructing the containers, leave a number of holes in their sides so that water may circulate between the outside and the interior. Have the top of the soil 1½ to 2 feet below water level.

Do not plant outdoors until the weather is warm and settled and the water temperature is expected to remain at or above levels suggested for seed germination. Earlier outdoor planting is practicable if the pool can be heated for a few weeks after setting the plants out. If the plants are shocked by setting them in cold water or if water temperature drops seriously after planting, results will be disappointing.

Summer care consists of prompt removal of any debris that falls on the leaves, occasional cutting off of faded leaves, and, except for possibly two or three retained as seeds, the cutting off of blooms that have faded. To save seeds, pollinate flowers by lightly brushing their stamens and styles with a fine hairbrush. Enclose the ripening pod in cheesecloth secured around the stalk so that the seeds are easily collectable when the pods burst underwater. Store the seeds in bottles of water in a temperature, for *V. amazonica*, of 65°F, for the others some ten degrees lower.

VICTORIAN-BOX is *Pittosporum undulatum.*

VIGNA (Víg-na) — Asparagus-Bean, Cow-Pea or Black-Eyed-Pea, Catjang, Snail Flower or Corkscrew Flower, Mung-Bean. Consisting of more than 200 species, natives of the tropics and subtropics, *Vigna*, of the pea family LEGUMINOSAE, differs from *Phaseolus* in technical details. The name honors Dominicus Vigna, a seventeenth-

century Italian scientist. Most cultivated vignas are agricultural rather than horticultural crops, grown for forage, human foods, and green manures. The cow-pea is used in gardens to some extent for the last purpose and as a cover crop. The asparagus-bean and the corkscrew flower are sometimes planted as novelties. The mung-bean (*V. radiata*), grown in North America mostly for forage, is widely cultivated in the Orient for its edible pods and seeds. The latter are germinated to produce bean sprouts used as food.

Vignas are mostly twining vines, the majority, including those cultivated, annuals. A minority are perennial, a few somewhat woody. They have leaves with three leaflets and, usually at the ends of long stalks, whitish, yellowish, or purplish, pea-shaped blooms, often in alternate pairs. The flowers soon drop and are succeeded by long, slender, nearly cyclindrical seed pods. They have comparatively large, broad upper or standard petals, bigger than the wing or side petals and with earlike lobes at their bases. There are ten stamens, nine of which are joined and one is free, and a style with a line of hairs down one side.

The cow-pea or black-eyed pea (**V. unguiculata** syn. *V. sinensis*), of Africa, has usually nontwining stems, and leaves with ovate to lanceolate leaflets 3 to 5 inches long. The flowers, two to twelve together at the ends of long stalks, are white, pale yellow, or purplish-pink. The seed pods, pendant and up to 1 foot long, are not inflated. Their seeds are of many colors and combinations, often having a dark "eye."

The asparagus-bean or yard-long-bean (*V. u. sesquipedalis*), a native of southern Asia, is a vigorous, rapid-growing twiner with leaves of leaflets 3 to 5 inches in length and sometimes slightly angled. The yellowish or purplish flowers are in twos or threes at the ends of long stalks. They open in the morning and close about midday. Limp and somewhat inflated, the pods are 1 foot to 3 feet long or sometimes longer and are pendent or lie on the ground. The seeds are scarcely flattened and are twice as long as broad.

The catjang (*V. u. cylindrica*) is less commonly grown than those described above. A native of Africa or India, it differs from the cow-pea and asparagus-bean in having erect or spreading, but neither hanging nor limp, pods, 3 to 6 inches in length, with seeds not over ¼ inch long.

The snail flower or corkscrew flower (**V. caracalla** syn. *Phaseolus caracalla*) is a warm-country perennial climber remarkable for its curiously shaped blooms. Attaining a height of 20 to 25 feet, it has leaves with three broad-ovate leaflets 3 to 5 inches long. Its flowers are in erect racemes up to 1 foot long. The blooms, white or yellowish with pink or lilac wing petals, are fragrant and about 2 inches long. Their upper or standard petal is contorted and bent backward, and the keel, instead of being tidily boat-shaped as in most pea-like legumes, is elongated and coiled in four or five spirals that hang to one side of the center. The pods, 6 to 7 inches long by ½ inch wide, contain nearly spherical brown seeds. This species is naturalized in California and there may be something of a weed.

Garden Uses. In warm regions, cowpeas and sometimes the catjang are grown in gardens for their seeds ("peas" or "beans"), which are cooked and eaten as vegetables. The asparagus-bean, because it does not crop heavily, is mostly cultivated as something of a novelty, although its young pods are satisfactory as a vegetable when cooked in the way of snap beans. The snail flower is grown as a curiosity; it may be found outdoors and in pots in greenhouses and even in sunny windows.

Cultivation. Vignas are very susceptible to frost and need a long growing season. Because of this their cultivation is pretty much restricted to the south. The kinds discussed thrive in fertile well-drained soil and, with the exception of the snail flower when it is to be cultivated in pots, are raised from seed sown, as soon as the ground has warmed in spring, outdoors where the plants are to remain. If sowings are to be made in ground where vignas have not previously been grown, it is often helpful or even necessary to inoculate the soil with a culture of a special bacterium. Information about this can be obtained from Cooperative Extension Agents and State Agricultural Experiment Stations.

VILLADIA (Vil-làdia). A *Sedum* relative, *Villadia*, of the orpine family CRASSULACEAE, consists of twenty-five to thirty species of low, mostly herbaceous perennial and some annual succulents of no great ornamental pretensions. Its natural range is from Mexico to Peru. The name honors Dr. Manuel M. Villada, a nineteenth-century Mexican botanist. By some botanists the name *Altamiranoa* is preferred for this genus.

Villadias differ from sedums in having the lower parts of their petals joined to form a tube and from *Echeveria* in not having basal rosettes of leaves and in having the racemes of flowers being terminal. They have erect or creeping, often rooting, more or less branching stems. Their linear to spatula-shaped fleshy leaves are stalkless and sometimes stem-clasping. The white, greenish, yellowish, orange, or reddish flowers are in terminal racemes, panicles, or clusters. They are small and originate singly or in twos, threes, or fours from the axils of leaflike bracts. Each has a five-lobed calyx, five petals separate or slightly united, and ten stamens. The fruits are small fol-

Villadia grandyi

Villadia imbricata

licles. For *V. texana* see *Lenophyllum texanum.*

Peruvian *V. grandyi* (syn. *Altamiranoa grandyi*) is a hairless perennial 4 to 5 inches tall, its erect stems densely clothed with fat, broad-ovate to nearly round, ¼-inch-long leaves. The flowering, branched stalks carry few blooms. Mexican *V. elongata* (syn. *Altamiranoa elongata*) is a minutely-hairy perennial with slender stems, 8 inches to about 1 foot long, at first erect, but later becoming prostrate, and rooting freely. Its ¼-inch-long, pointed, fleshy, linear-ovate leaves, like the stems, have very short hairs. They spread at right angles to the stems along which they are

closely set. The white or pinkish, stalkless flowers, under ¼ inch long, are disposed along one side of the branches of terminal panicles. Sprawling and more or less procumbent, *V. guatemalensis*, of Guatemala, is much branched with its flowering branches erect. Its closely spaced, cylindrical, fleshy leaves, ½ to ¾ inch long, spread at right angles to the stems. The few, small, stalkless, lemon-yellow, short-tubed flowers are terminal from the leaf axils. Mexican *V. imbricata* forms mats of stems, 1 inch to 2 inches long, densely covered with overlapping, ¼-inch-long, fleshy leaves so that they are conelike in appearance. The flowers, under ¼ inch long and white, are in slender spikes about 3 inches tall and do not open widely. Also Mexican, *V. jurgensenii* has trailing or erect stems, up to 1½ feet tall, and pointed-lanceolate, ¼-inch-long leaves that spread horizontally. In clusters of up to twelve, its white or purplish flowers are a little over ¼ inch wide.

Garden and Landscape Uses and Cultivation. Villadias are suitable for collections of succulents in warm, dry regions outdoors and in greenhouses. They grow without difficulty in porous soil, thoroughly well drained and dryish, rather than wet. Sunny locations suit. Indoors winter night temperatures of 40 to 50°F, with slightly more warmth during the day, are satisfactory. Dry, airy conditions such as suit most succulents are appreciated. Propagation is extremely easy by cuttings, single leaves, and seed.

VILLARESIA (Villar-èsia). As now understood, this genus of the icacina family ICACINACEAE consists of one species, a native of Peru; other plants previously so named belong in *Citronella*. The name commemorates Mathiae Villares, an eighteenth-century superintendent of the Monastery Gardens, Santa Espina, Spain.

Holly-like in aspect, *Villaresia mucronata* is a tree up to 60 feet tall. Its young shoots are downy. Its leaves have stalks up to ¼ inch long, and ovate to broad-elliptic blades 1½ to 3½ inches long by ¾ inch to 2 inches wide. On young trees the leaves are spiny, but those of older specimens are mostly spineless. They are dark, glossy-green, and hairless. Borne in summer, the fragrant, yellowish-white flowers, ⅜ inch in diameter, are in clusters 1 inch to 2 inches across. Terminal, they come from the leaf axils near the ends of the shoots. The fruits are egg-shaped and about ⅔ inch long.

Garden and Landscape Uses and Cultivation. Only where little or no frost occurs is this tree hardy. Suitable for California and regions of similar climates, it is a handsome ornamental. It succeeds in ordinary soils and is propagated by seed.

VINCA (Vín-ca) — Periwinkle, Creeping-Myrtle or Running-Myrtle. The genus *Vinca* belongs to the dogbane family APOCYNACEAE. It consists of about ten species. The name, a contraction of the Latin name *vincapervinca*, meaning to wind around or bind, alludes to a one-time use of the flexible stems for making wreaths. The plant called Madagascar-periwinkle and previously named *Vinca rosea* is *Catharanthus roseus*. It is still commonly listed in seed catalogs as *Vinca* and probably will continue to be for a long time because botanical name changes involving well-known plants are often slow to be accepted by gardeners. For information about it see the Encyclopedia entry Catharanthus.

Vincas are evergreen, more or less vining plants with slender, trailing or laxly-erect, persistent stems, woody at least at their bases. The leaves are opposite and undivided, with flowers solitary in the axils of the upper ones. The blooms have deeply-five-parted calyxes, and corollas with slender funnel-shaped tubes and five flat, spreading, blue, purple, or white petals.

The hardiest of the three species cultivated in North America, and in cold regions the best known, the creeping- or running-myrtle (*V. minor*) is grown in a number of varieties and is much esteemed as a groundcover. It is known by its quite prostrate habit, its slender, ground-hugging stems, which often root into the soil, its glossy, dark green, elliptic leaves with

Vinca minor

stalks ¼ to ⅖ inch long, and its decorative flowers, ¾ to under 1 inch in diameter. This is native to Europe and Russia. Several horticultural varieties include *V. m. alba*, with white flowers; *V. m. bowlesii*, free-flowering and with deep blue-violet blooms; *V. m. flore-pleno* (syn. *V. m. multiplex*), with double, plum-purple blooms, or, in a variant, offered in catalogs as *V. m. azurea flore-pleno*, with double, sky-blue blooms; and *V. m. variegata*, with leaves marked with a not-very-pleasing dull yellow.

The giant periwinkle (*V. major*) is larger and more tender. A native of the Mediterranean region, it survives permanently outdoors only in places of mild winters, such as California and the south. This kind has long semi-erect, prostrate, or drooping stems that rarely root along their lengths. Its leaves are broad-ovate and have stalks ⅖ to ½ inch in length. In the typical species they are light green, but the most commonly cultivated kind, *V. m. variegata*, has leaves with whitish-yellow edges.

Despite the implication of its name, *V. herbacea* is not strictly herbaceous, the lower parts of its mostly upright and semi-upright stems are distinctly woody. Its

Vinca major

Vinca major variegata in a tub with blooming petunias

leaves are narrow-elliptic to lanceolate, ordinarily under ½ inch wide and almost or quite stalkless. The flowers are about 1 inch in diameter and blue-purple. This species, native to the Balkans and central Europe, is typically evergreen, but in winters as cold as those of southern New York it becomes deciduous, losing its foliage in winter and renewing it in spring.

Garden and Landscape Uses. The creeping-myrtle and its varieties are highly regarded as beautiful, low, evergreen groundcovers. They carpet the earth effectively with their trailing stems and pretty foliage and are not so strong-rooted that bulbous plants set among them, such as snowdrops, grape-hyacinths, squills, narcissuses, and crocuses, cannot survive. Combinations such as these are practicable and desirable because they assure two seasons of bloom, the bulbs flowering in spring and the groundcover later. The creeping-myrtle is especially esteemed for its ability to stand shade, but is equally as satisfactory in sunny locations if the soil is fairly moist. The giant periwinkle, taller, more billowy, and less neat in appearance, may be employed in mild climates

A groundcover of *Vinca minor*

VINES. The term vines, in the British Isles usually restricted to grapes (*Vitis*), has a much broader application in North America. As used there, it encompasses all climbing and trailing plants with elongated stems that without support are incapable of growing erectly. In the wild, support is commonly provided by trees, shrubs, and other plants, by cliffs and large boulders, or the stems may extend along the ground. There are both annual and perennial vines, the latter including kinds, both deciduous and evergreen, that have permanent, often woody stems, as well as sorts with stems that die to a crown of growth buds and root, or that die to a bulb or bulblike base each year. While most plants known as vines can be clearly designated as such, there are others that are intermediate in habit between evident vines and shrubs or other plants of sprawling growth. With these, the degree of vining may be largely determined by the environment or such cultural practices as pruning.

While there are a fair number of temperate-region vines, the group, as to number of species and frequency of occurrence, is most highly developed and abundant in the humid tropics. There,

as a groundcover for largish areas, but its chief use is for furnishing window boxes, porch boxes, urns, and other containers, in combination with other tender plants, for summer display. It is popular and is grown in considerable quantities by commercial florists for such purposes. The third species, *V. herbacea*, is much less common and is chiefly an item for collectors of unusual plants.

Cultivation. Division, best done at the beginning of the season of new growth, and cuttings afford ready means of increase. Cuttings may be terminal or sectional pieces of stem having three or four nodes (joints) and with their lowermost leaves removed. Those of the hardy kinds are made in summer and are usually inserted in sandy, peaty soil in shaded cold frames where the atmosphere around them can be kept humid until rooting has taken place. The following spring, the rooted cuttings may be planted in shaded nursery beds in rows 1 foot apart with about 6 inches between individuals or they may be set where they are to remain. The former plan is usually preferable because it makes weed control during their early stages easier. The soil should contain an abundance of organic matter and be well drained and fertile. Cuttings of *Vinca major* root readily any time, provided they are not too soft. Common practice is to make them in fall and early winter and insert them in benches in greenhouses. The rooted cuttings are potted individually in

2½-inch pots and grown indoors until the weather is warm and settled. Then they may be set out in nursery beds in rows 1 foot to 1½ feet apart with about 9 inches allowed between individuals. Pinching out the ends of shoots once or twice during their early growth induces bushiness. Water should be applied copiously in dry weather. In September the plants are lifted, cut back to about 4 inches, potted, and transferred to a cool greenhouse. The potting soil should be fertile and porous. From early March on, warmer conditions are in order. Night temperatures of 55 to 60°F, with a daytime rise of five to ten degrees, are not excessive and the atmosphere should be fairly humid. Good light is necessary for strong growth, and generous amounts of water and occasional applications of dilute liquid fertilizer should be supplied. Unless sufficient warmth, moisture, and nourishment are provided during late winter and spring, straggly, poorly foliaged specimens result; few bedding plants are more unsatisfactory than half-starved vincas. Before they are planted outdoors the plants should be hardened for a week or two by keeping the greenhouse well ventilated and the atmosphere somewhat drier than earlier in the season.

VINCETOXICUM. See Cynanchum, and Gonolobus.

VINEGAR TREE is *Tristania conferta*.

Vines climb by various means: (a) English ivy clings by tiny rootlets

(b) Boston-ivy attaches itself by tendrils ending in sucker-like disks

(c) The stems of pole beans twine around appropriate supports

(d) Slender, branched tendrils enable sweet peas to cling to their supports

(e) The leafstalks of clematises serve as tendrils

(f) Climbing roses have scrambling, vinelike stems

some sorts, called lianas, climb to the tops of the tallest trees, seeking the light they need to flower and fruit. Commonly they extend from tree top to tree top, on occasion tying together adjacent trees so securely that if one is felled it may fail to fall to the ground. Because many tropical vines attain great lengths before they bloom, comparatively few are known horticulturally.

As garden and landscape plants, vines have many uses, some of them unique to the group. They climb by various means. Some, such as English ivy, Boston-ivy, and trumpet vine, attach themselves to their supports by tiny rootlets or sucker-like disks and are admirable for clothing surfaces such as walls, for adorning tree trunks, and for similar purposes. Others have twining stems that spiral around stakes, wires, and suchlike supports. Notable among these are akebias, pole beans, and wisterias. The stems of some vines always twine clockwise, those of others always counterclockwise, and a few have stems that twine indiscriminately in both directions. Tendrils that twist around twigs or similar slender supports they encounter are the holdfasts of grapes, peas, sweet peas, and passion flowers; leafstalks function similarly for clematises and some other vines. And some plants without specialized means of attachment, which attain height in the wild simply by scrambling over shrubs or other supports, are often classed with vines. Not infrequently the stems of these sorts are furnished with thorns that help them retain holds on their supports.

When choosing vines for particular uses, one should give consideration to a number of factors. For permanent planting outdoors the local hardiness of the proposed kinds should be known or ascertained. Give thought to whether the choices are to be confined to flowering vines or will include kinds admired only for their foliage. Sunny locations are commonly requisite for the former; the latter are mostly satisfactory in partial or heavier shade. Do not plant vines that cling by

Vines can be grown on pergolas: (a) A light structure supporting grapes

(b) A stone-pillowed pergola planted with a variety of vines

(c) A bamboo pergola supporting wisteria in Japan

rootlets or sucker-like disks against wooden surfaces that must be painted or otherwise treated from time to time. In such places plant only sorts that can be grown on trellises positioned a few inches in front of the wooden surface. It is often a convenience to have such trellises hinged near their bases so that when the time comes to paint or otherwise treat the wood, the supports, with the vines attached, can be temporarily laid along the ground.

Veronica prostrata with a white-flowered *Allium*

Viburnum plicatum

Viburnum lentago (fruits)

Viburnum trilobum (fruits beginning to ripen)

Viburnum rhytidophyllum (flowers)

Veronica longifolia variety

Viburnum rhytidophyllum

Viburnum farreri (fruits)

(d) Clematis on an iron fence

(e) Clematis decorating a post

(f) A handsome openwork trellis planted with vines

Appropriate vines are useful for adorning walls, tree trunks, and other surfaces, and for embellishing fences, arches, arbors, pergolas, and posts. Some kinds that are annuals or are grown as annuals can be displayed to good advantage on "tepees" formed of tall brushwood stakes with their tops leaned inward against each other. Some vines, English ivy for example, serve as excellent groundcovers if they are allowed to trail over the ground without

(g) A strong-growing woody vine supported by a "tepee" of stout poles

support; these are especially useful for clothing banks.

The following lists are of selections of genera that consist of or include vines that climb by the particular means indicated. Where appropriate, common names of one of more species of the genus are given in parentheses. An * following the generic name indicates that one or more kinds are hardy in climates as cold or colder than that of New Jersey. A † following the generic name indicates that one or more sorts are annuals or can be grown as annuals.

Vines with twining stems include *Abrus* (rosary-pea), *Actinidia*, *Akebia*, *Aristolochia*, *Asparagus*, *Basella*, *Beaumontia*, *Bomarea*, *Celastrus* (bittersweet), *Ceropegia*, *Clerodendrum*, *Clytostoma*, *Cocculus*, *Convolvulus*, *Cryptostegia*, *Dioscorea* (cinnamon vine), *Dolichos*† (hyacinth-bean), *Gelsemium* (Carolina yellow-jessamine), *Hardenbergia*, *Hibbertia*, *Hoya*, *Humulus*† (hops), *Ipomoea*† (cypress vine, morning glory, moonflower), *Kadsura*, *Kennedia*, *Lapageria*, *Lonicera* (honeysuckle), *Lygodium*, *Mandevilla* (Chilean-jasmine), *Marsdenia*, *Menispermum* (moonseed), *Mina*†, *Muehlenbeckia* (wire plant), *Periploca* (silk vine), *Petrea*, *Phaseolus*† (scarlet runner bean), *Polygonum* (silver fleece vine), *Porana*, *Pueraria* (kudzu vine), *Schisandra*, *Senecio* (Mexican vine), *Solanum* (potato vine), *Stauntia*, *Stephanotis*, *Thunbergia*, *Trachelospermum*, and *Wisteria*.

Vines with tendrils that do not end in sucker-like disks or, where indicated, leafstalks that serve as tendrils, include *Ampelopsis* (pepper vine), *Anemopaegma*, *Anredera* (Madeira vine, mignonette vine), *Antigonon* (coral vine), *Bauhinia*, *Cardiospermum*† (heartseed), *Cissus* (grape-ivy, kangaroo vine), *Clematis* (by leafstalks), *Cobaea*† (cup-and-saucer vine), *Distictis*, *Eccremocarpus*, *Gloriosa*, *Hidalgoa* (by leafstalks), *Lagenaria* (white-flowered gourd), *Lathyrus*† (pea, everlasting-pea, sweet pea), *Luffa*† (dishcloth gourd), *Mikania* (climbing

hempweed), *Momordica*† (balsam-apple, balsam-pear), *Mutisia*, *Passiflora* (passion flower), *Smilax* (cat brier), *Tropaeolum*† (nasturtium, by leafstalks), and *Vitis* (grape).

Vines that attach themselves by rootlets or aerial roots or by sucker-like disks at the ends of tendrils include *Anthurium*, *Bignonia* (cross vine), *Campsis* (trumpet creeper), *Decumaria*, *Epipremnopsis*, *Epipremnum*, *Euonymus*, *Ficus*, *Hedera* (ivy), *Hydrangea*, *Hylocereus*, *Macfadyena* (cat's claw), *Monstera*, *Nephthytis*, *Parthenocissus* (Boston-ivy, Virginia creeper), *Philodendron*, *Pileostegia*, *Pothos*, *Pyrostegia* (orange-trumpet-vine), *Raphidophora*, *Rhektophyllum*, *Schizophragma* (climbing-hydrangea), *Scindapsus*, *Selenicereus* (moon-cereus, night-blooming-cereus), *Syngonium*, and *Vanilla*.

Vines without twining stems, tendrils, aerial roots, rootlets, or sucker-like disks, that climb by clambering include *Allamanda*, *Camoensia*, *Combretum*, *Congea*, *Harrisia*, *Jasminum*, *Pereskia*, and *Rosa* (climbing roses).

VIOLA (Vi-òla) — Violet, Heartsease, Johnny-Jump-Up. The name genus of the violet family VIOLACEAE, this includes pansies and violets. There are about 500 species of *Viola*, natives of temperate and cold parts of the northern and southern hemispheres. The name comes from the Greek *ion*, earlier *wion*, a violet. Bedding violas and pansies, horticultural derivatives of *V. cornuta* and *V. tricolor*, respectively, are dealt with in this Encyclopedia under the entry Pansies and Garden Violas. Florists' violets are treated under Violets, Sweet or Florists'.

Violas are mostly herbaceous perennials, biennials, or annuals, with or without stolons or runners and stemless or with leafy stems. Very few are subshrubs. When stem leaves are present they are alternate. At the bottoms of the leafstalks are persistent, often leafy appendages called stipules. Two kinds of flowers are produced by most kinds, the showy, familiar ones of spring, which produce few or no seeds, and scarcely noticeable, petal-less summer blooms, near or even under the ground, that are without petals, do not open, are self-fertile, and produce abundant seeds. The showy flowers, usually one, more rarely two, on a stalk, are more or less nodding. They have five sepals and five petals, the lower petal usually larger than the others and with a spur at its base. The other petals form two dissimilar pairs. There are five often dissimilar stamens and one style. The fruits are capsules.

Species of *Viola* are likely to attract gardeners as wildlings worth encouraging or bringing into gardens or as sorts exotic to the region, but deemed worthy of introducing and cultivating. The kinds now to be described are among the best. They are presented in three categories, those native to eastern and central North America, a minority of which are also found in western North America, those native to western North America, but not native in the east, and exotic or foreign kinds not native to the Americas. Where appropriate, the groups are further divided into sorts with only basal foliage and those that have definite leafy stems.

Eastern American violets without leafy stems include these: *V. blanda,* the sweet white violet, native in cool, moist, shady places from Quebec to Minnesota, South Carolina, and Georgia, has long runners, heart-shaped, nearly hairless, toothed leaves, and fragrant white blooms, ¼ to ½ inch wide, with petals beardless or nearly so, the upper ones reflexed or twisted. *V. cucullata,* the blue marsh violet, grows in sun or shade in wet soils from Quebec to Ontario, Georgia, and Missouri. It has thinnish, branched rhizomes that spread to form colonies, and hairless, heart- to kidney-shaped, toothed leaves up to 4 inches wide. The long-stalked, violet-colored blooms, ½ to 1 inch wide and darker-veined at their centers, have heavy beards on the two lateral petals. They are displayed well above the foliage. *V. c. alba* has white flowers, and *V. c. bicolor* has white flowers with violet-colored veins and centers. *V. lanceolata* occurs in bogs and wet soils from Nova Scotia to Minnesota, Florida, and Texas. An attractive sort, it has slender stolons and lanceolate to elliptic, round-toothed leaves, with usually reddish stalks, and blades considerably more than three times as long as wide. The flowers, white with brown-purple lines on the three lower petals, are approximately ½ inch across and without beards. *V. missouriensis,* native from Indiana to South Dakota, Louisiana, and Texas, differs from *V. sororia* in its leaves being longer than broad and in having longer-pointed apexes. *V. palmata,* except for its early spring foliage, has hairy leaves strongly-palmately-cleft or palmately-divided into five to eleven, toothed or cleft lobes or leaflets. From ½ to 1 inch in diameter, the violet-purple blooms have blunt sepals, and lateral petals with beards. This lives in limestone woodlands from Massachusetts to Minnesota and Florida. *V. pedata,* the bird's foot violet, one of the loveliest of the genus, inhabits dry, acid, infertile soils in sunny fields and open woodlands from Maine to Minnesota, Florida, and Texas. A variable, tufted sort without stolons, it has leaves of three leaflets, each three- to five-parted into linear to lanceolate, often toothed segments. The flat, beardless, pansy-like flowers, ¾ inch to 1½ inches wide, have the three lower petals pale lilac with darker veins and the upper two dark violet, or all may be lilac-blue or less often white or pinkish. Some authorities identify plants with uniformly lilac-blue flowers as *V. p. lineariloba* (syn. *V. p. con-*

Viola, undetermined species

Viola pedata lineariloba

color). The name *V. p. alba* has been applied to white-bloomed plants. *V. pedatifida,* the prairie violet, ranges from Ohio to Alberta, Missouri, Texas, and Arizona. Stemless, it has a short rhizome and leaves of three main divisions, each deeply-three-cleft into linear lobes, which may be further incised. From ¾ inch to 1¼ inches wide, the bright violet-colored flowers have beards on the three lower petals. They differ from those of somewhat similar *V. pedata* in not being flat and in having more of the form of pea and sweet-pea flowers. *V. primulifolia* favors wet, somewhat acid soil in full sun. Native from New Brunswick to Minnesota, Florida, and Texas, this is hairless or hairy. It has slender stolons and oblong, ovate, or obovate, finely-toothed leaves with blades not more than three times as long as wide. The flowers, about ¾ inch wide, are white

with brown-purple lines on the three lower petals. *V. septentrionalis* is a showy native of damp, open woodlands from Prince Edward Island to Michigan, Connecticut, and Pennsylvania. It has hairy, heart- to kidney-shaped, toothed leaves and, most commonly, deep to pale violet-colored blooms, ¾ to 1 inch across, with the three lower petals bearded. A variant with white flowers is cultivated. *V. sororia* (syn. *V. papilionacea*), the woolly-blue violet, is a sun-loving sort of dampish meadows and open woodlands from Quebec to Minnesota, North Carolina, and Oklahoma. It is softly-hairy or, in the form by some authorities segregated as *V. papilionacea,* hairless. This sort has round-toothed, heart- to almost kidney-shaped leaves 2 to 4 inches wide and rather less long. On stalks about as tall as the leaves, the ¾-inch-wide flowers, which range from dark blue or dark violet to lavender or white, have densely-bearded side petals. An attractive variant called the Confederate violet, by some botanists named *V. s. priceana* or *V. priceana,* has grayish-white flowers with violet-blue veins. The name *V. s. alba* is sometimes used for white-flowered plants.

Eastern American violets that have definite leafy stems include these: *V. adunca,* native in gravelly and sandy, more or less infertile soils from Quebec to Saskatchewan, Maine, and South Dakota, has tufts of stems that are 2 to 3 inches or so tall and later lengthen considerably and become prostrate. The round-toothed, ovate to nearly circular leaves, clothed with short hairs, are about 1 inch in diameter. Carried well above the foliage, the deep to pale violet- or lilac-colored flowers, white at their

Viola striata

Viola sororia priceana

Viola striata (flowers)

centers, have their lower petals veined with violet. Ranging from Quebec to Alaska, New York, Colorado, and California, *V. a. minor* is hairless and has slightly bigger blooms. **V. canadensis,** the Canada violet, hairless or very minutely-hairy, has a short, thick rootstock, and many stems 6 inches to 1 foot tall or taller. Its pointed-heart-shaped leaves are 2 to 4 inches across. The long-stalked flowers, predominantly white and suffused on the backs of the petals with lilac, have brown-purple veins on the lower petals and a yellow center spot. They are about ¾ inch across. This is a native of woodlands from Newfoundland to Saskatchewan, South Carolina, Alabama, and Arizona. Variety *V. c. rugulosa* (syn. *V. rugulosa*) spreads by branching stolons to form broad patches. Its leaves are clothed with short hairs beneath and with fewer hairs on their upper surfaces. Except in these ways and in being taller and having slightly bigger flowers, this resembles the species. **V. conspersa,** the American dog violet, is native in woodlands and meadows from Nova Scotia to Minnesota, Alabama, and Missouri. Hairless, this has a sometimes branched rhizome and leafy stems eventually up to 8 inches tall. From kidney- to heart-shaped and 1 inch to 1½ inches across, the round-toothed, nearly hairless leaves have conspicuously-fringed stipules. On slender stalks, the flowers, carried well above the foliage and about ¾ inch across, are pale blue-violet with dark violet veins. Variety *V. c. masonii* has white blooms. **V. pubescens,** the downy yellow violet, has softly-hairy stems and foliage. The former, numbering usually not over two and up to about 1 foot tall, have near

their tops two to four round-ovate, round-toothed leaves 1½ to 4 inches across. Sometimes there is also a solitary basal leaf. Just topping the foliage, the clear yellow flowers, brown-veined near the bases of their petals, are on pubescent stalks. This inhabits rich woodlands from Nova Scotia to North Dakota, North Carolina, Georgia, and Oklahoma. Variety *V. p. eriocarpa* (syn. *V. eriocarpa*), the smooth yellow violet, which rarely exceeds 6 inches in height, has finely-hairy or hairless leaves. **V. rostrata,** an attractive native of open woodlands and hillsides from Quebec to Michigan, Wisconsin, Georgia, and Alabama, is a hairless, clumping species with heart-shaped, broad-ovate to nearly round, toothed leaves. The flowers, beardless and with spurs ½ inch long, are lilac-colored with darker spots. **V. rotundifolia,** of wet, acid soils in cool woodlands from Quebec to Ontario, Delaware, Pennsylvania, and in the mountains of South Carolina and Georgia, is small and low. It has stout rhizomes and hairy-stalked, broad-ovate to nearly round, toothed leaves, hairy when young and 1 inch to 4 inches wide. The bright yellow blooms, evident in early spring, their three lower petals brown-veined and the lateral pair bearded, are approximately ½ inch wide. **V. striata,** a free-flowered native in shady places from New York to Illinois, Georgia, and Arkansas, is hairless or nearly so. It forms clumps and has leafy, angular stems that are up to 1 foot tall at flowering time and lengthen later. Its leaves are ovate to subcircular, with round-toothed margins. The long-stalked, ivory- to creamy-white flowers, prominently veined toward their cen-

ters with brown-purple, are displayed well above the foliage. They have a short spur and the fragrance of newly mown grass.

Violets native to western, but not eastern North America, all with leafy stems, include these: **V. cuneata,** an endemic of wet woodland hillsides in Oregon and California, has stems 3 to 8 inches tall with round-ovate to somewhat triangular, round-toothed, purple-veined leaves up to 1 inch or somewhat more across. The flowers, ½ inch wide or a little wider, are white with a dark purple eye spot on each side petal and the upper pair of petals sometimes purplish at their bases. The reverses of all the petals are red-violet. **V. flettii,** one of the choicest American violas, is not very amenable to cultivation. Native to rock crevices and talus slopes high in the Olympic Mountains of Washington, this has a short, thick rootstock, stems 2 to 6 inches long, and thickish, purplish-green, kidney-shaped leaves. Somewhat over ½ inch across, the short-spurred flowers are purplish-violet with the bases of the petals yellow and the lower petals with dark veining. The side petals are bearded. **V. glabella,** a native of moist woodlands and streamsides from Montana to Alaska and California and in northeast Asia, from 3 inches to 1 foot tall, has its foliage concentrated along the upper one-third of its stems. The round-toothed, kidney- to heart-shaped leaves are short-hairy or hairless. Borne chiefly from near the tops of the stems and displayed above the foliage, the pretty, short-spurred flowers, up to ½ inch across, are clear yellow with pencilings of purple on the three lower petals. The side petals are bearded. *V. pedunculata* is outstandingly handsome. Deep-rooted, this Californian endemic has a short, thick rootstock and more or less decumbent stems 1 foot to 2 feet long. The round-ovate, coarsely-toothed leaves have leafy stipules. Pansy-like, its orange-yellow blooms, with brownish reverses to the petals and purple-veined at their centers, are ¾ inch to 1½ inches wide. Their side petals are bearded. *V. sempervirens,* as its name indicates, is more or less evergreen. At least where winters are not too severe, it presents green foliage throughout the year. Native from British Columbia to California, this has long, slender, prostrate, stolon-like stems and usually short-hairy foliage, which typically is marked with purplish spots or blotches. The leathery, toothed leaves, heart- to somewhat kidney-shaped, are up to 1¼ inches across. On stalks mostly longer than the leaves, the short-spurred flowers, up to ½ inch across, are yellow with purplish lines on the lower three petals. The two side petals are bearded. *V. trinervata,* the desert or brush violet, a deep-rooted native of dry, rocky soils and sagebrush flats from Washington to Oregon, has hairless, more or less glaucous foliage. Its stems, naked of foliage in their lower parts, rise from a group of basal leaves. From 3 to 6 inches tall, they have palmately-lobed leaves with the main lobes again irregularly once- or twice-cleft into narrow-elliptic segments. The flowers, a little over ½ inch in diameter, have two reddish-violet upper petals and three pale to medium lilac lower ones with yellow bases lined or blotched with purple.

Exotic species, sorts native to places other than North America, that are without leafy stems include these: *V. alba,* of central and eastern Europe, is a highly variable stemless sort with a close affinity to *V. odorata* and, like it, with stolons and fragrant flowers. From *V. odorata* it differs in the stipules at the bases of its leafstalks being markedly narrower. Slightly over ½ inch across, the flowers are white or sometimes violet and in varieties pink or reddish. *V. dissecta chaerophylloides* (syn. *V. eizanensis*), of Japan, is a decidedly charming miniature that is not very hardy and, where winters are severe, best suited for pans (shallow pots) in alpine greenhouses. About 4 inches tall, it has short rhizomes, and leaves, 1 inch to 2½ inches wide, divided into three segments cleft into lanceolate lobes. The flowers, about

1 inch across, are light rose-pink. *V. hederacea* (syn. *Erpetion reniforme*) is a nonhardy native of Australia that, in cold climates, must be wintered in a greenhouse or well-protected cold frame. Stemless, it has very slender stolons and, spaced along them, tufts of ovate to kidney-shaped, toothed or toothless leaves 1 inch to 1½ inches across. The ½-inch-wide, almost spurless flowers have white-tipped, violet-colored petals. *V. jooi,* a pretty, little, easy-to-grow native of southeast Europe, has creeping rhizomes. About 1 inch in diameter, its long-stalked, hairless, heart-shaped leaves have round-toothed margins, and stipules for much of their lengths united with the leafstalk. From ½ to ¾ inch across, the scented, mauve blooms are streaked with purple. *V. odorata,* the sweet violet of Europe, is the sort from which most fragrant florists' violets have been derived. It forms rosette-like tufts of foliage and sends out slender runners that root from their tips to give rise to new plants. Up to about 2 inches long and toothed, the round to kidney-shaped leaves with heart-shaped bases are up to about 2½ inches wide. Violet, or more rarely purple, pink, or white, the very fragrant blooms are a little over ½ inch wide.

Exotic species native outside of North America that have leafy stems include these: *V. aetolica* (syn. *V. saxatilis aetolica*), endemic to mountains of the Balkan Peninsula, has stems up to 1¼ feet long, and round-toothed, ovate to lanceolate leaves up to ¾ inch long. The short-spurred flowers, with faces ¾ inch long, are yellow or yellow with violet upper petals. *V. arvensis,* the field pansy of Europe, much resembles *V. tricolor,* but has flowers not exceeding ¾ inch in diameter,

often smaller, and chiefly cream-colored stained with violet. Their petals are usually shorter than the sepals. *V. calcarata,* of European subalpine and alpine meadows, resembles *V. lutea,* but differs chiefly in having longer, violet-colored flowers, up to 1½ inches across, with broader petals and a spur as long as the petals. *V. cornuta,* the horned violet, a native of Spain, is a parent species of garden pansies and large-flowered bedding violas (treated in this Encyclopedia under the entry Pansies and Garden Violas). It is a tufted, hairless or nearly hairless, stemmed plant with usually pointed, heart-shaped, round-toothed leaves with large, coarsely-toothed stipules. The flowers, with conspicuous slender spurs shorter than the petals, are prevailingly violet-colored. Those of *V. c. alba* are white. *V. elatior,* wild in marshy soils in Europe and adjacent Asia, has erect, leafy stems 6 inches to over 1 foot in height. The lanceolate to narrowly-ovate, pointed and shallowly-toothed leaves have short hairs, especially on their upper surfaces. About 1 inch across, the flowers are light blue. *V. elegantula* (syn. *V. bosniaca*), of Yugoslavia, is very satisfactory. Individual plants are short-lived, but reproduce freely from self-sown seed. The leafy stems, 4 inches to 1 foot long, are prostrate below, then erect. They have small lower leaves, the upper ones much bigger. Ovate to lanceolate and more or less hairless, they have round-toothed margins and flowers ¾ to 1 inch across, very variable as to color. Variants are *V. e. alba,* with white blooms; *V. e. bicolor,* with violet upper petals and yellow lower ones; *V. e. lutea,* its flowers yellow; and *V. e. rosea,* the blooms of which are pink. *V. gracilis* as known in gardens is frequently a coarser-growing hybrid of the

Viola aetolica

Viola cornuta alba

Viola elatior

Viola tricolor subalpina

Viola tricolor

true species. The latter, native to the Balkan Peninsula and Asia Minor, is 4 to 6 inches tall or sometimes taller. The bases of its stems are prostrate. The blunt, shallowly-round-toothed to nearly toothless leaves are clothed with short hairs. The slender-spurred, rich purple flowers are 1 inch to 1¼ inches across. **V. lutea,** the mountain pansy of western and central Europe, is an attractive, very variable sort

with creeping rhizomes and branchless stems 3 to 10 inches tall. Its lower leaves are elliptic-ovate, those above oblong-lanceolate. All are toothed, hairless or finely-hairy, and have lobed stipules. The flowers, yellow or violet or a combination of the two, are ½ inch to 1¼ inches across and have petals at least twice as long as the spur. **V. tricolor,** the Johnny-jump-up, wild pansy, or heartsease, may be an-

nual, biennial, or perennial. A native of Europe naturalized in North America, this species has erect stems and heart-shaped to lanceolate leaves. At the bottoms of their stalks are conspicuous, usually lobed, leafy stipules. The short-spurred, pansy-like blooms, ¾ inch to 1¼ inches in diameter and with petals generally longer than the sepals, are usually, as the species name implies, of three colors, violet, yellow, and white, although other color forms do occur. Endemic to the mountains of southern and central Europe, *V. t. subalpina* (syn. *V. saxatilis*) is a perennial or sometimes a biennial up to about 1 foot tall. The flowers, which have faces from 1¼ to 1⅜ inches long, are yellow, or have violet upper petals and the other petals yellow, veined with violet.

Garden and Landscape Uses. Many species of *Viola* are charming, unobtrusive plants for wild gardens, rock gardens, and similar naturalistic areas, for use beneath shrubs and trees, and featured as groundcovers in other lightly shaded places. The ubiquitous Johnny-jump-up (*V. tricolor*) enjoys sunnier locations and self-sows with abandon, yet its seedlings threaten none except possibly the most delicate rock garden plants. If in excess, they are very easy to pull out. Some other sorts too are likely to result in violet population explosions. Such sorts, for example, *V. canadensis*, must be located where their prodigality will not cause trouble or will be curbed by virtue of their locations. Lower parts of slopes fetching down to paths or lawns are likely sites.

Cultivation. Except for a few kinds, growing species violets is a simple matter. Most are widely adaptable, and, if due consideration is given to the special conditions under which others more challenging to grow exist in the wild, success is usually fairly easily had with them also. Remember, some kinds have a distinct preference for poor, acid soils, a few for limestone, and yet others for wet soils or bog conditions. Most appreciate some shade, others revel in full sun. Be guided by the notes about these matters that are given along with the descriptions of the various kinds. The woodlanders, for the most part, appreciate a soil of high organic content. They find leaf mold and good compost very agreeable. Propagation is easy by seed, division, and in some cases by cuttings, according to kind. For more information see the Encyclopedia entries titled Pansies and Garden Violas; and Violets, Sweet or Florists'.

VIOLACEAE — Violet Family. From 800 to 900 species apportioned among about twenty genera constitute this family of dicotyledons. The majority are natives of the northern hemisphere or of the Andean region in South America. They include herbaceous plants (mostly perennials), shrubs, and a few trees and vines. The leaves, generally alternate, rarely opposite, are only rarely divided into separate leaflets. The symmetrical or asymmetrical flowers are solitary or in clusters or panicles. Some species produce inconspicuous flowers that never open, but that do produce seed by self-pollination, in addition to the showier flowers that do not develop seed. These flowers are, by definition, cleistogamous. The flowers have five sepals, five petals, the lower one often with a spur, five stamens, and one usually branchless style. The fruits are capsules or berries. Genera treated in this Encyclopedia include *Hybanthus*, *Hymenanthera*, *Melicytus*, and *Viola*.

VIOLET. See Viola. African- or Usambara-violet is *Saintpaulia*, dame's-violet is *Hesperis matronalis*, dog's-tooth-violet is *Erythronium*, flame-violet is *Episcia*, Mexican-violet is *Tetranema*, Philippine-violet is *Barleria cristata*, violet-cress is *Ionopsidium acaule*, and violet-tree is *Securidaca longipedunculata*.

VIOLETS, SWEET OR FLORISTS'. The name violet is correctly employed for any species of the genus *Viola* and under that entry in this Encyclopedia many are de-

scribed and their cultivation discussed. Here we are concerned only with the fragrant sorts called florists' violets, sweet violets, or often simply violets.

These are generally presumed to be derived from European *V. odorata* and this is undoubtedly true of some varieties, but some are certainly hybrids between that and other species and some are probably without any *V. odorata* influence. This seems to be true of the lovely double-flowered sorts called Parma violets, which are believed to be of oriental origin.

The commercial production of florists' violets in the United States is a highly specialized venture conducted in only a few places. Some of the varieties employed are not hardy in cold climates and are generally accommodated in greenhouses, although they may also be grown in cold frames. They bloom in winter and spring.

These plants need well-drained, fertile, mellow soil of a somewhat sandy nature, such as would grow good crops of potatoes or corn, and containing fairly generous, but not extraordinary amounts of organic matter, such as well-rotted manure or rich compost. Good light with shade from strong summer sun is a requirement.

Start new plants each year by division in spring. Plant them in an outdoor bed or cold frame in as cool a spot as possible and where there is a free circulation of air. Either a location on the north or northwest side of a wall or building, or simply one where there is light shade from trees, but not where tree roots will compete strongly with the violets for moisture and nutrients, is appropriate. Space the plants 10 inches to 1 foot apart. Until fall, water as needed to keep the ground moderately moist and cut off all runners that develop. A mulch of peat moss or similar material helps to retain moisture, keep the roots cool, and keep down weeds.

For greenhouses, lift the plants in fall and plant them in beds indoors or individually in 7- or 8-inch pots. Maintain winter night temperatures of 40 to 45°F, daytime ones five to ten degrees higher. Keep the soil moist and the atmosphere humid. Protect violets in cold frames by covering them on cold nights with mats or similar means of protection.

Among the best varieties are 'Double Russian', its flowers double and rich violet; 'Marie Louise', with double mauve-blue flowers; 'Rosina', with smallish flowers of pink to old rose color; 'Royal Robe', with single violet-blue blooms that have a central eye of white; and 'White Czar', with single white blooms.

VIPER'S BUGLOSS. See Echium.

VIPER'S-GRASS is *Scorzonera hispanica*.

VIRGILIA (Vir-gília). Botanists are of different opinions as to whether *Virgilia*, of the pea family LEGUMINOSAE, consists of

one or two species; the latter view prevails, perhaps. In any case it is a genus of limited natural distribution, being confined in the wild to a small, narrow, coastal strip in South Africa. In its homeland it is called keurboom. Its botanical name honors the Roman poet Virgil, who died in 19 B.C. The tree once named *Virgilia lutea* is *Cladrastis lutea*.

Virgilias are trees up to about 30 feet tall with feathery, pinnate, hairy leaves, 3 to 8 inches long by up to 3 inches broad, with six to ten pairs of slender leaflets and a terminal one. Pea-like and with ten separate stamens, the ½-inch-long flowers, in terminal racemes, are succeeded by flat, downy, leathery pods, 2 to 3 inches long, that split to release two to six very hard seeds. If two species are accepted, *V. divaricata* is the more compact and more luxuriant in foliage and bloom. It has deep pink flowers produced chiefly in spring. Said to be somewhat larger, *V. capensis* (syn. *V. oroboides*) is less profuse in its

Virgilia capensis, The Karroo Garden, South Africa

bloom and leafage than *V. divaricata* and bears mauve-pink flowers more or less intermittently from spring through fall. At least that is its behavior as reported from South Africa.

Garden and Landscape Uses and Cultivation. Virgilias, probably *V. capensis*, are sparingly planted in California and succeed in Golden Gate Park, San Francisco, as well as southward. They prosper in mild climates in exposed locations in ordinary well-drained, but not dry soils. They are not hardy in the north. Under favorable conditions, virgilias make rapid growth, but they are short-lived. South African sources estimate their duration to be twelve to twenty years. When young, virgilias are frost-tender, but later can stand a few degrees of frost for short periods. They develop extensive, spreading surface roots, a fact that should be kept in mind when locating them. Propagation is by seed, which retains vitality for many years. To encourage germination they should be abraded, cracked, or soaked in tepid water for twenty-four hours before sowing. A practice recommended by South Africans is to sow them ¾ inch deep, then cover the bed with light brushwood, set it alight, allow it to burn out, and then soak the bed with water. This is also a satisfactory procedure with some western North American dry-country plants.

VIRGINIA-STOCK is *Malcolmia maritima.*

VIRGINIA-WILLOW is *Itea virginica.*

VIRGIN'S BOWER. See Clematis.

VIRUS. Viruses are extremely minute entities, whether or not to be considered as living organisms debatable, capable of reproducing only inside living cells of plants and animals. Most are too small to be seen through even the highest powered conventional light microscope, but they can be detected and photographed with the aid of an electron microscope. The great ma-

Virus infections: (a) Aster yellows

(b) The yellowish-streaked *Veltheimia* infected with a mosaic virus

jority pass through filters that obstruct the passage of bacteria.

The chief horticultural impact of viruses is that they cause a number of serious plant diseases, including aster yellows, cucumber mosaic, lily mosaic, and phloem necrosis of elms. Viruses are also the cause of the variegated foliage of some plants esteemed for this, such as certain abutilons, and of the patterned flowers of some groups of tulips. Viruses are transmitted from plant to plant by insects and other creatures, by tools, by grafting, and in some cases, notably tobacco mosaic virus (which causes disease on tomatoes and some other plants besides tobacco), by the handling of healthy plants after infected ones or even by smoking tobacco prepared from infected plants near healthy plants.

VISCARIA. See Lychnis.

VISCUM (Vís-cum). Here belongs the classical mistletoe of Europe and Asia (*Viscum album*), which is distinct from the American mistletoe (*Phoradendron*), although both belong to the mistletoe family LORANTHA-CEAE.

Confined in the wild to the Old World, including Australia, *Viscum* comprises some sixty species of usually fork-branched, green-leaved or sometimes apparently leafless, parasitic plants. They have inconspicuous, unisexual flowers. The female blooms are succeeded by white, yellow, orange, or red berries. The leaves, or in some species minute scales representing leaves, are opposite. The name, used by Virgil and Pliny, alludes to the sticky pulp of the berries.

Viscums are not ordinarily cultivated in North America. The genus is of interest chiefly because of its habit of growth, because of the use made in the Old World of *V. album* as a popular Christmas decoration, and because of the many legends and superstitions that since ancient times have

Viscum album on *Crataegus*, Chelsea Physic Garden, London, England

been associated with that species. Undoubtedly the chief inspiration for these was the strange appearance of *V. album,* which forms a yellowish-green, more or less globular bush 2 to 3 feet in diameter that hangs from the branches of a wide variety of deciduous and some evergreen trees that serve as its hosts. Its translucent white berries are quite conspicuous. A tiny native of South Africa, *V. minimum* is a minute leafless species that grows as a parasite on succulent species of *Euphorbia.* This curious plant consists of a single internode crowned with three tiny flowers. The spherical berries, up to ¼ inch in diameter, are bigger than the plants upon which they are borne. When ripe they send out a long root that turns around and plants itself in the *Euphorbia* stem.

Viscum minimum on *Euphorbia*, The Karroo Garden, South Africa

VITACEAE — Grape Family. A dozen genera comprising some 700 species of woody, tendril-bearing vines and a few shrubs or small trees constitute this family of dicotyledons. Typically their stems are swollen at the nodes. The leaves, alternate or the lower ones sometimes opposite, are undivided or are composed of separate leaflets. The small, bisexual or unisexual flowers are in panicles or clusters that usually sprout from the stem opposite a leaf. They have four or five each sepals, petals, and stamens and a short style tipped with a headlike or disklike stigma. The fruits are berries. Among cultivated genera of this family are *Ampelopsis, Cissus, Leea, Parthenocissus, Rhoicissus, Tetrastigma,* and *Vitis.*

Vitex agnus-castus

Vitex agnus-castus (flowers)

two-lipped corolla with five lobes (petals), and four stamens in two pairs of unequal lengths. The fruits are small and berry-like.

The chaste tree, hemp tree, or monk's pepper tree (*V. agnus-castus*) inhabits the Mediterranean region. It is a velvety-hairy shrub or small tree, 6 to 25 feet tall, with strongly aromatic shoots and foliage. Tall specimens usually have multiple trunks. Its long-stalked leaves, dark green above and gray-hairy on their undersurfaces, have five or seven short-stalked, lanceolate leaflets, 3 to 4 inches in length, with a few coarse teeth or toothless. The fragrant, 1/3-inch-long, generally pale lilac-blue flowers are in spikes, 5 to 7 inches in length, that are crowded in clusters at the ends of the stems and from the axils of the upper leaves. The stamens and style protrude. Variety *V. a. latifolia* (syn. *V. macrophylla*) is hardier and has mostly broader leaflets, up to 1 inch wide. The flowers of *V. a. alba* are white and those of *V. a. rosea* are pink.

A deciduous shrub or small tree 10 to 15 feet tall, **V. negundo** inhabits much of east-

Vitex negundo

ern Asia, Taiwan, Polynesia, and East Africa. It has long-stalked leaves with usually five, but sometimes three stalked, pointed, elliptic-ovate to lanceolate leaflets 1½ to 4 inches long and with toothed or toothless edges. Their upper surfaces are dark green, beneath they are short-gray-hairy. Barely ¼ inch long, the numerous lilac-blue to lavender flowers are in broad, loose panicles up to 8 inches long. The stamens and style protrude slightly. From the typical species, northern Chinese *V. n. heterophylla* (syns. *V. n. incisa*, *V. laciniata*) is distinguished by its leaflets being deeply-toothed or lobed and its flower panicles being less showy. It is also hardier than the typical species.

Less commonly cultivated, and attaining a height of up to 12 feet or sometimes prostrate, variable *V. trifolia* is indigenous to Asia and Australia. Its leaves are of three, or occasionally one, pointed, ob-

VITEX (Vì-tex)—Chaste Tree or Hemp Tree or Monk's Pepper Tree. The genus *Vitex*, of the vervain family VERBENACEAE, consists of approximately 250 species of deciduous and evergreen trees and shrubs. Chiefly native to the tropics and subtropics of both eastern and western hemispheres, the group bears the ancient Latin name of the chaste tree or some similar shrub.

Vitexes have four-angled, pubescent shoots. Their leaves are opposite and usually of three to seven leaflets that spread from the top of the leafstalk in fanlike fashion (palmately). Rarely they have a single, undivided blade. In many-flowered clusters or panicles of clusters, the little, white, yellowish, blue, or purple-blue flowers have usually five-toothed, bell-shaped calyxes, a tubular to funnel-shaped,

long to oblong-elliptic, stalkless leaflets about 3 inches in length and toothed or toothless. They have hairless upper surfaces and finely-gray-hairy under ones. The ½-inch-wide lavender-blue flowers, their lips with a white spot, are in terminal panicles up to 4 inches long. In *V. t. variegata* the foliage is white-variegated. Interesting *V. t. simplicifolia*, a shrub only a few inches high that inhabits beaches in Hawaii and other Pacific lands, has leaves of usually one obovate leaflet ¾ to 1 inch long. Its blue flowers are in clusters up to 1 inch long.

An evergreen tree up to 65 feet tall, stout-branched *V. lucens* occurs wild only in New Zealand. It has longish-stalked, corrugated, glossy leaves with three to five toothless, elliptic-oblong to ovate leaflets up to 5 inches long by 2 inches broad. In broad panicles about 10 inches long, the hairy, dull red flowers are 1 inch long or longer. The subspherical, bright red fruits are ¾ inch in diameter. Another tree, *V. quinata,* of warm parts of China, Indochina, and Taiwan, is up to 45 feet tall. It has nearly hairless leaves of five ovate-oblong leaflets about 4 inches long and sparsely-toothed or toothless. The yellowish, ¼-inch-long flowers are in crowded, brownish-hairy, terminal panicles.

Others sometimes cultivated include these: *V. altissima,* of India and Ceylon, up to 100 feet high, and esteemed for its lumber, has leaves of three obovate-elliptic, toothless leaflets up to 8 inches long. Its white-lipped, cream flowers are in panicles up to 9 inches long. *V. divaricata*, of Venezuela and the West Indies, is a nearly evergreen shrub or tree up to 60 feet high that produces useful lumber. It has leaves of three, or more rarely one or five, elliptic or oblong-elliptic, toothless leaflets up to 9 inches long. The ¼-inch-wide flowers are blue or violet. *V. parviflora,* of Hawaii, the Philippine Islands, and Malay Archipelago, is up to 50 feet high. Its leaves are of three wavy, toothless, elliptic to oblong-elliptic leaflets 3 to 7 inches long. The blue or purplish flowers are in panicles 6 to 8 inches long. *V. zeyheri,* of South Africa, is up to 10 feet tall. It has finely-hairy, densely-glandular, leathery leaves of three or five nearly stalkless, oblong to oblong-lanceolate, toothless leaflets 1½ to 3 inches long.

Garden and Landscape Uses. The hardiest kind, *V. negundo heterophylla,* succeeds outdoors in southern New England. Nearly as resistant to cold is *V. agnus-castus latifolia.* The others are to a greater or lesser extent more tender. Tall *V. lucens* and *V. quinata* are suitable only for California and similar mild-climate regions. They are attractive as lawn and specimen trees. The first does well near the sea. Lower kinds are excellent for shrub beds either alone or mixed with other shrubs. The hardier ones, even if cut to the ground by frost, send up

new shoots that bloom the first summer if the roots are not killed.

Cultivation. Most vitexes thrive in a wide variety of soils so long as they are not excessively wet, but *V. lucens* prefers a deep, fertile one. All like warm, sunny locations. Although no regular pruning is necessary, some vitexes, including the chaste tree and *V. negundo* and their varieties, can be kept fairly low by severe pruning each spring just before new growth begins. The treatment consists of cutting back last year's branches to within an inch or two of their bases and completely eliminating enough of these to preclude overcrowding of the new shoots. Vitexes have long, stringy roots and therefore do not transplant readily. When they are moved it is important to retain as many roots as possible and to cut the tops back severely. In the north, spring is the best time to transplant. Propagation is easy by summer cuttings under mist or in a greenhouse or cold frame propagating bed, by layering, and by seed. The seed may be sown indoors in winter or in a cold frame in spring.

VITICELLA. See Clematis.

VITIS (Vì-tis) — Grape. This, the name genus of the grape family VITACEAE and the one to which the common grapes of vineyards and orchards belong, consists of between sixty and seventy species. It includes sorts native to many warm and temperate regions of the world, including a few, additional to those grown chiefly for their edible fruits, useful as ornamentals. The name *Vitis* is the ancient Latin one for the wine or vineyard grape of the Old World (*V. vinifera*). The plant cultivated as *V. voinierana* is *Tetrastigma voinieranum.*

Vitises, usually vigorous, woody, perennial vines, some hardy, some not, and often with extensive stems, generally climb by tendrils. They have undivided, more or less palmately-lobed leaves. Tendrils, forked or not, may develop opposite every leaf or all except every third leaf. Panicle-like clusters of flowers occupy some tendril positions. The blooms are small and of no decorative value. Mostly they are, or behave as though they were, unisexual. They have a minute five-parted calyx, five petals that remain joined together and drop as a unit called a cap, five stamens, and one style. A prominent disk surrounds the ovary. The fruits are technically berries.

Grapes cultivated for their edible fruits are dealt with in this Encyclopedia under Grapes. They are too well known for the species involved in their ancestry, not ordinarily grown in their wild forms, to need description. Suffice it to say that the vineyard grapes of California and other parts of western North America are derivatives of the European wine grape (*V. vinifera*), with, in some cases perhaps, infusions by

Vitis girdiana

Vitis vinifera purpurea

Vitis labrusca variety

hybridization of native Californian *V. girdiana.* The European wine grape, probably originally native from southeast Europe to India, is the grape of classical history. A variety of this, the Teinturier grape (*V. v. purpurea*) is sometimes grown as an ornamental. When young its foliage is claret-red, later it is a dull dark red.

Grapes grown for their edible fruits in eastern North America and in the south are derivatives of native species or in some cases represent hybrids between these and the European wine grape. American species chiefly involved are the fox grape (*V. labrusca*), native from New England to Georgia and Indiana; the summer or pigeon grape (*V. aestivalis*), native from New England to Wisconsin, Florida, and Kansas; and the muscadine grape (*V. rotundifolia*), native from Delaware to Kansas, Florida, and Texas.

The finest ornamental grape is Japanese *V. coignetiae.* A very rapid grower, under favorable conditions its stems attain lengths of 50 feet in one season. This has the biggest leaves of cultivated vitises. Roundish in outline and from 6 to 10 inches wide or occasionally wider, they have deeply-heart-shaped bases and are obscurely three- to five-lobed. In fall they assume fiery red and crimson shades. Hardy in southern New England, this has fruits ⅓ inch wide. Also cultivated as an ornamental, Chinese *V. amurensis* has foliage that in fall becomes crimson or purplish. A strong grower, it has broad-ovate leaves with blades 5 to 10 inches long and usually three- to five-lobed. The fruits are black and about ⅓ inch in diameter. This is hardy through most of New England.

Vitis davidii

Other exotic sorts grown for ornament include *V. davidii* and *V. flexuosa*. A robust climber with prickly stems, Chinese *V. davidii* has broad-ovate leaves, dull in their upper surfaces, glaucous beneath, 4 to 8 inches long, and often slightly lobed near their apexes. In clusters longer than the leaves, the edible, black fruits are about ½ inch in diameter. A slender-stemmed vine hardy at least as far north as New York City, *V. flexuosa,* of China, Korea, and Japan, has reddish-hairy young stems and foliage. Its sometimes three-lobed, broad-ovate leaves, 2 to 3 inches across, have glossy upper surfaces and are hairy on the veins on their undersides. The ¼-inch-wide, bluish-black fruits are in clusters up to 3 inches long.

Garden and Landscape Uses and Cultivation. In addition to *V. coignetiae* and other exotics, vineyard varieties and native species are occasionally planted to ornament pergolas, trellises, walls, tree trunks, stumps, or other supports. All prosper in ordinary soils of reasonable fertility and, if production of quality fruit is not an objective, need little care other than pruning to keep them within acceptable limits and tidy. Pruning should be done in fall, winter, or summer, but not in spring, because the vines bleed (lose sap abundantly) from cuts made then. Propagation is by hardwood cuttings and by layering.

VITTADINIA (Vitta-dínia). Belonging in the daisy family COMPOSITAE and native to New Zealand, Australia, New Guinea, New Caledonia, and South America, *Vittadinia* embraces eight or more species. The name commemorates Dr. C. Vittadini, an Italian, who wrote about fungi. He died in 1865. A plant often mistakenly known as *V. triloba* and *V. australis* in gardens is the entirely different, Mexican *Erigeron karvinskianus*. A technical difference between *Vittadinia* and *Erigeron* is that the styles of the flowers of the former have long, awl-shaped branches, while those of the latter are short.

Vittadinias are herbaceous perennials and subshrubs with alternate leaves and daisy-like flower heads, solitary or clustered. The central, disk florets are yellow, the ray florets blue or white. The fruits are seed-like achenes.

Most likely to be cultivated, *V. australis* (syn. *V. triloba*) is a variable native of Australia and Tasmania. Somewhat shrubby at its base and up to 1 foot tall, it is green or minutely-white-woolly, and glandular. Its leaves may be lobeless or have three to seven lobes or are sometimes twice-dissected. The many solitary, terminal flower heads are ¼ to ⅜ inch long. The ray florets, usually in two rows, are lavender, bluish, or less often white.

Garden Uses and Cultivation. Only in climates such as that of California, where there is little or no winter freezing, will *V. triloba* survive outdoors. It is appropriate for rock gardens, the fronts of borders, and similar locations in sun. It prospers in ordinary garden soil and is multiplied by seed and by division.

VOA-VANGUER. See Vangueria.

VOODOO-LILY is *Sauromatum guttatum*.

VRIESIA (Vriè-sia). A rich source of ornamentals, *Vriesia,* of the bromelia family BROMELIACEAE, contains almost 250 species; it is endemic to tropical America including Mexico and the West Indies. The name commemorates the Dutch botanist Willem Hendrik de Vriese, who died in 1862.

Mostly epiphytes (plants that roost on trees or other plants, but take no nourishment from them), but a few sorts terrestrial, vriesias are commonly handsome foliage plants. Their strap-shaped, usually pliable, but sometimes rigid, smooth-edged leaves, in rosettes, are often beautifully colored and sometimes prettily variegated. In spikes with conspicuous, sometimes brightly colored bracts, the prevailingly yellow and green, occasionally white flowers are presented in two or more ranks. They have three sepals, three petals, six stamens, and one style. The fruits are capsules containing seeds that have a tuft of long, straight hairs at their bases.

In the treatment that follows, the species described are grouped, of necessity somewhat arbitrarily, as large, medium-sized, and small, according to the dimensions their rosettes of foliage commonly attain. Besides its species, this genus contains many natural and garden-raised hybrids.

Large vriesias include these: *V. fosterana,* of Brazil, has a vaselike rosette of rigid, blue-green to light green leaves, up to 3 feet long and 2½ inches wide, closely patterned with irregular, crosswise pencilings that on their undersides are maroon and on their upper or inner surfaces dark green. When young, and in some forms of the species persistently, they are flushed with wine-red. From 4 to 7 feet tall, the branchless flowering stalk has scattered, greenish bracts and pale yellow flowers. *V. gigantea* (syn. *V. tessellata*), of Brazil, has a bold rosette of flexible leaves, 2 to 2½ feet long by 2 to 3 inches wide, pointed at their apexes. When young, light green faintly checkered with darker green, as they age they darken and their markings fade. Green bracts, and blooms 1 inch to 1½ inches long, with light yellow sepals and white petals, are borne on up-to-5-foot-tall, branched flowering stalks. *V. gladioliflora,* of Central America, has a rosette of leathery leaves, 1½ to 2 feet long by 2 to 3½ inches broad, with a short, slender point at the apex. At first purplish, they later become green. The branchless flowering stalk, up to 3 feet tall, has two ranks of overlapping bracts and a crowded spike of green bracts and greenish-white flowers up to 2¾ inches long. The fruits are purple. *V. hieroglyphica,* one of the most beautiful of the genus and deservedly frequently called the king of bromeliads, is a native of Brazil. Its rosette of foliage, 3 to 5 feet tall and broad, is of thirty to forty attractively disposed, pliable leaves 1½ to 3 feet long by 2 to 3¼ inches wide. They are glossy-green, strikingly marked with broad, more or less zigzag, interrupted cross-bands of darker green, brown-purple, or purplish-black. The branched flowering stalk is 4 to 6 feet tall. It has small, light green bracts and 1-inch-long blooms of an unappealing yellow. The leaves of *V. h. mar-*

Vriesia hieroglyphica

Vriesia imperialis: (a) In Brazil

(b) In California

ginata are splendidly illuminated with broad bands of ivory-white along their margins. *V. imperialis* justly deserves its name. A ground-growing Brazilian of imposing aspect, it has symmetrical rosettes of leathery leaves, up to 5 feet long and 6 inches wide, that on plants grown in bright light are maroon to wine-red, under more shaded conditions green. Branched and from 5 to 15 feet tall, the flowering stalk has shiny, maroon-red bracts and erect, yellow flowers up to 6 inches long or longer. *V. jonghii,* which in its native Bra-

zil grows both on trees and in the ground, has a crowded rosette of thirty to fifty thin, pliable leaves, 1½ to 2 feet long, by 1½ to 3 inches wide, much recurved at their apexes and sometimes cross-banded with lines of darker green. Their bases are violet. Erect and up to 2½ feet tall, the flowering stalk carries a 1-foot-long, two-ranked spike of yellow flowers and brown-edged, green bracts. *V. longicaulis,* Brazilian, has a rosette of flexible, linear leaves up to 1½ feet long or somewhat longer by 1 inch to 1¼ inches wide and tipped with a short point. The branched flowering stalk, 2½ to 3 feet tall, carries ovate, flat, crowded spikes of bracts and red-spotted flowers. *V. philippocoburgii,* also Brazilian, develops a rosette up to 3 feet across of about twenty thin, pliable, green leaves 1½ to 2½ feet long by 2 to 3¼ inches broad and spotted with red or brown near their apexes. The flowering stalk, up to 3 feet tall, has many rather distantly spaced, ascending, slender branches, up to 1 foot long, with 1½-inch-long, greenish-yellow flowers and bright red bracts. *V. platynema,* of Brazil, Trinidad, Venezuela, and the West Indies, presents a rosette, 2½ to 3 feet across, of leaves up to 2 feet long by 2 to 3 inches wide. They have bluish-green upper surfaces, strikingly blotched with purple at their short-pointed apexes and crossed by indistinct wavy lines, and undersides suffused with violet-purple. The branchless flowering stalk carries a massive, flattened, two-ranked spike of green, greenish-white, or yellowish flowers and purple or reddish-purple bracts. *V. regina* is a giant Brazilian with a foliage rosette up to 7 feet or even more across, and a conspicuously bracted, spirelike panicle of flowers that towers to about the same height. Shallowly-channeled and markedly recurved, the waxy-green leaves, 3½ feet long by 6 to 9 inches wide, are spotted with red-purple at their bases, margins and undersides. The 3- to 4-inch-long, fragrant blooms are two-ranked along the branches of the flowering stalks. *V. schwackeana,* of Brazil, has a rosette of maroon-speckled, dull green leaves up to 2 feet long and 2 inches wide. Its branched flowering stalk, 2 to 3 feet tall, has red or reddish bracts and yellow flowers with protruding stamens.

Medium-sized vriesias in cultivation include these: *V. bituminosa,* of Brazil, which grows natively on trees or in wet soils, has rosettes of maroon-tipped, blue-green leaves up to 2 feet long and 2½ to 3 inches wide and, except for a brief point, blunt-ended. The 2- to 2½-inch-long, yellowish and pinkish-gray blooms are two-ranked on branchless flowering stalks 2 to 3 feet tall. *V. ensiformis* in its native Brazil grows on trees or rocks or in the ground. It has rosettes of about twenty pointed, broad-based, lanceolate, lavender-tinted, green leaves 1½ to 2 feet long by approximately

1½ inches wide. The flowering stalks, branchless or with branches in two ranks, have conspicuous red bracts and yellow blooms. The floral bracts of *V. e. conferta* are orange-red margined with yellow. The leaves of *V. e. striata* are striped lengthwise with creamy-yellow. *V. incurvata,* reported to tolerate light frost in its native Brazil, has a rosette of 1-foot-long, 1¼-inch-wide, light green, pliable leaves. Not or scarcely exceeding the leaves in length, the lower part of the branchless flowering stalk

Vriesia incurvata

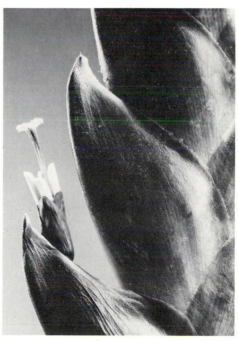

Vriesia incurvata (flower)

leans and then terminates in an erect, showy, two-ranked spike of red-tinged, yellow bracts and yellow blooms. A variant has leaves with ivory-white, or delicate green lengthwise stripes. *V. inflata* (syn. *V. incurvata inflata*) resembles *V. incurvata,* but its bracts of its flower spikes are red, margined with yellow or green. *V.*

ringens, of the West Indies, Central America, and Colombia, varies greatly in size; its leaves, which sometimes reach 3 feet in length by 4 inches in width, are often not over about 1 foot long by about 1½ to 2 inches wide. The branched or branchless flowering stalk, 2 to 3 feet long, carries green, brown, or rusty-red bracts and yellowish-white to yellow blooms, up to about 3 inches long, with stamens protruding beyond the coiled-back petals. *V. splendens,* of northeastern South America and Trinidad, is called flaming sword. Typically it has a rosette of twelve to twenty arching, dull green leaves up to 1 foot to 1½ feet long by 1 inch to 2 inches wide, very boldly cross-banded with dark brown or purplish-black. Erect and from 1½ to 3 feet tall, the flowering stalk, without branches, has a pointed, flat spike of two-ranked, overlapping, brilliant red to orange-red bracts and 2- to 2½-inch-long yellow blooms with protruding stamens. The leaves of *V. s. longibracteata* (syn. *V. s. formosa*) are without cross-bands; *V. s. major* is bigger than the typical species; and *V. s. nigra* has exceptionally dark, cross-banded leaves. Other horticultural varieties are *V. s. 'Flammendes Schwert',* which has intensely brilliant floral bracts, and *V. s. chantrieri,* which has elegantly-recurved, green to blue-green leaves, cross-banded with purple-black, and bright scarlet floral bracts.

Small species of vriesias in cultivation include these: *V. barilletii,* of Brazil, has a rosette of about sixteen flexible, slightly

Vriesia carinata

bronze-tinged, green leaves, up to 1½ feet long and 2 inches wide, tipped with a brief point. Branchless, the flowering stalk, 9 inches to 1 foot tall, has a flat spike of two-ranked, overlapping, purple-based, yellow bracts spotted with purplish-brown and 2-inch-long yellow flowers with protruding stamens. *V. carinata,* often called lobster claws, is a popular and pretty Brazilian. It has a rosette of fifteen to twenty light green leaves, 6 to 8 inches long by ½ to 1 inch wide, tipped with a short point. The branchless flowering stalk, 6 inches to 1 foot long, has a broad, flat, elliptic spike of overlapping bracts, bright crimson at their bases and yellow spotted with green above, and yellow flowers. *V. corcovadensis,* of Brazil, has a rosette of many flexible leaves, 6 inches to 1 foot long, that above their broad, spoon-shaped bases narrow abruptly to a much longer portion, not over ½ inch wide, that tapers to a pointed apex. The usually two- to four-branched flowering stalk, 9 inches to 1 foot tall, has bright red floral bracts and yellow flowers. *V. drepanocarpa,* of Brazil, has a rosette of about twenty flexible, 6- to 8-inch-long leaves with broad bases beyond which they narrow abruptly to not over ½ inch wide and then taper to a pointed apex. About as long as the leaves, the erect flowering stalk has a spike, 5 to 6 inches long, of green bracts and yellowish-white flowers. *V. erythrodactylon,* Brazilian, has a rosette of leaves, 6 inches to 1 foot long by ¾ to 1¼ inches wide, that at their bases are blotched with brownish-purple or violet. Approximately as long as the leaves, the branchless flowering stalk has a broad, flat, two-ranked spike of large, red and green, up-curved bracts and yellow flowers. Leaves banded and striped lengthwise with creamy-white or delicate green distinguish *V. e. striata. V. fenestralis,* of Brazil, has a rosette of twenty to thirty recurved, glossy-green, flexible leaves, up to 1½ feet long and 3 inches wide, decorated with many

Vriesia fenestralis

lengthwise and crosswise dark lines and, on their undersides, with purplish circular spots. The branchless flowering stalk, 1 foot to 2½ feet tall, carries a spike of green bracts and yellowish-white flowers with stamens shorter than the 2- to 2½-inch-long petals. *V. flammea,* of Brazil, spreads by stolons to form clumps. Its compact rosettes are of dark green leaves, 6 inches to 1 foot long, with very broad bases that then narrow abruptly into a much longer and slender part not over ½ inch wide, finally tapering to a pointed apex. The branched or branchless flowering stalk, erect and much longer than the leaves, is clothed with red bracts. The floral bracts are red or red and yellow, the flowers yellow. *V. friburgensis,* of Paraguay, is variable and grows on rocks and in the ground. It has a rosette of lustrous leaves 1½ to 2 inches wide and a loosely-few-branched flowering stalk, 3 to 5 feet tall, with green bracts and loosely-arranged pale yellow flowers. *V. guttata,* of Brazil, has a rosette of leaves 1 foot to 1¼ feet long by 1 inch to 1½ inches wide. Blunt and tipped with a brief point, they are bluish-green haphazardly spotted with claret-purple or maroon. The pendulous, branchless flowering stalk, clothed with a white meal or scurf, terminates in a spike of overlapping, greenish-beige bracts, overlaid with a bloom of silvery-pink or red, and lemon-yellow flowers with protruding stamens. *V. heliconioides* grows natively from Central America to Brazil. It has a rosette of soft, pliable, pointed, green leaves suffused and sometimes spotted with red on their undersides. They are 6 inches to 1¼ feet long by ¾ inch to 1½ inches broad. The flowering stalk, without branches and 8 inches to 1¼ feet tall, has two ranks of large, overlapping, boat-shaped, green-tipped, salmon-red to bright red bracts that almost hide from view the creamy-white to white flowers, *V. malzinei,* of Mexico, has a dense rosette of fifteen to twenty pliable leaves 9 inches to 1 foot long or a little longer by 1½ to 2 inches wide above their dilated bases; they are green sometimes spotted red on their upper surfaces, dark red beneath. Erect, branchless, and up to 2½ feet tall, but generally much lower, the flowering stalk terminates in a spike of greenish-white flowers, in two or more rows, and yellow, brown, or red bracts. *V. psittacina,* of Brazil, has a rosette of pliable, broad-based, pointed, yellowish-green, recurving leaves, 8 inches to 1¼ feet long by ¾ to 1 inch wide, often tinted with violet toward their bases. Its erect or slightly arched, branchless flowering stalk, up to 1½ feet in height, has a loose, showy spike of two-ranked, green-tipped, yellow-edged, red bracts and green-spotted, yellow flowers with protruding stamens. *V. recurvata* is Brazilian. It has a rosette of flexible, spreading or recurved, green leaves 9 inches to 1¼ feet long or sometimes longer by up to 1¼ inches wide.

About as long as the leaves, the erect, branchless flowering stalk has a spike of loosely-arranged, not overlapping, waxy, yellow and red bracts and yellow flowers. *V. rodigasiana*, of Brazil, has a rosette of thirty to forty spreading, pliable, dull green leaves from 9 inches to, in the wild, but not as known in cultivation, 1½ feet in length. They are 1 inch wide and may be spotted with brown on their undersides and suffused with purple near their bases. The flowering stalk, thin, branched, and tending to arch, displays to good advantage a loose panicle of waxy-yellow bracts and light yellow flowers with stamens as long or longer than the petals. *V. saundersii*, of Brazil, has a rosette of about twenty recurved, silvery-gray sometimes pink-tinged leaves, heavily spotted with claret-red on their undersides and to a lesser ex-

Vriesia saundersii

tent above. The arching flowering stalk, 1½ to 2 feet long, branches into a loose panicle with yellow or yellowish-white bracts and yellow blooms. *V. sclaris*, of Brazil, has a rosette of twelve to fifteen light green leaves, 6 inches to 1 foot long by ¾ to 1 inch broad above their broad bases. The slender, up-to-1-foot-long flowering stalk, pendulous and without branches, has distantly spaced, alternately arranged, spreading bracts and flowers. The bracts typically are red with yellow apexes, the petals, yellow or greenish-yellow. The leaves of *V. s. rubra* are flushed with red. The floral bracts of *V. s. viridis* are green. *V. simplex*, of Brazil, Venezuela, Colombia, and Trinidad, has a rosette of flexible, green, green and coppery, or coppery-red, minutely-toothed leaves that taper to a pointed apex; up to 1½ feet long and 1¼ inches wide, they have a short point at the apex. The flowering stalk, slender, pendulous, and without branches, usually

upturned at the apex, and longer than the leaves, has distantly spaced red or red and yellow floral bracts and green-tipped, yellow, 1½-inch-long flowers with protruding stamens. *V. sintenisii*, of Puerto Rico, Cuba, and Jamaica, has a rosette of pointed, erect leaves, 1 foot to 1½ feet long and about 1 inch wide, that usually are flushed with red or purple, especially on their undersides. At flowering time their apexes become red. Erect and with short branches, the flowering stalk, longer than the leaves, has large red floral bracts and light yellow blooms. *V. unilateralis*, Brazilian, has a rosette of twelve to fifteen pliable leaves up to 1 foot long and 1 inch wide. Its erect, branchless flowering stalk, up to 1 foot long, has twelve or fewer creamy-yellow blooms and greenish bracts. *V. vagans* (syn. *V. philippocoburgii vagans*), sometimes called vagabond plant, is Brazilian. It has long stolons. Its clusters of rosettes of pliable green leaves, about 6 inches long and 1 inch wide, are almost black at their bases. The flowering stalk is branched into a loose panicle of greenish-yellow flowers.

Hybrids in cultivation are fairly numerous and undoubtedly others will be bred. Among the best known are these: *V. erecta*, which has *V. poelmanii* and *V. rex* as parents, has a rosette of glossy-green, pointed leaves and a branchless flowering stalk with a flat, elliptic spike of two-ranked, rich-lacquer-red bracts and yellow flowers. *V. 'Favorite'*, one parent of which is *V. ensiformis*, the other unknown, has a bold rosette of spreading, shiny, green leaves and a branched flowering stalk with narrow, flat spikes of red bracts and yellow blooms. *V. 'Gemma'*, a complex hybrid involving several species, has a small rosette of bright green leaves and a flowering stalk with flat spike of red-margined yellow bracts and yellow blooms. *V. 'Marie'*, its parents *V. carinata* and *V. barilletii*, is called painted feather. Larger than its parents, this has a rosette of pink-toned, light green, recurved leaves and a flowering stalk with a flat, elliptic spike, red and chartreuse-yellow bracts, and yellow blooms. *V. poelmanii*, a robust hybrid of more than two species, has a medium-sized rosette and a tall, branched or branchless flowering stalk with a flat spike of yellowish-green-tipped, red bracts and yellow blooms. *V. retroflexa*, a hybrid between *V. psittacina* and *P. scalaris* that occurs natively in Brazil, has a small rosette of pointed, flexible green leaves and a flowering stalk, up to about 1 foot tall, pendent through much of its length and upturned toward the apex, with a loose spike of green-tipped, bright red bracts and yellow blooms. *V. rex* is a variable hybrid involving four species. Characteristically it has a rosette of bright green leaves and a branched or branchless flowering stalk with garnet-red bracts and lemon-yellow flowers.

Garden Uses and Cultivation. Among the most popular bromeliads, vriesias are grown in greenhouses, as houseplants, and, in the tropics and warm subtropics, outdoors. Available in a wide variety of kinds and sizes, they can be accommodated in pots and pans (shallow pots), attached to pieces of tree fern or cork bark, or planted in the crotches of trees or on palm trunks with old leaf bases attached. The terrestrial sorts make good underplantings in ground beds lightly shaded by trees or shrubs. All associate well with warm-climate epiphytes including other bromeliads and orchids. Well chosen, they can be used to create splendid decorative effects and are generally highly attractive in flower as well as foliage.

Cultivation. All vriesias, even those that in the wild root in the ground, prosper potted or planted in a coarse, very porous, slightly acid, soil-less mix suitable for tree-perching kinds and for epiphytic ferns and many orchids. The ingredients should be predominantly organic and may include as the chief component fir bark or redwood bark chips, tree fern fiber, osmunda fiber, redwood fiber, or coarse peat moss. To any of these or a mixture of them add a generous sprinkling of coarse sand or perlite and a dash of bonemeal or slow-release fertilizer pellets. If dried cow manure is available, include some peanut- to walnut-sized nuggets of it. And it is not amiss to add some broken charcoal as an aid to preventing stagnation. For sorts that in their native haunts grow in the ground, one-fourth to one-third part by bulk of the mix may be soil, preferably turf with grass roots still visible through it, but this is not essential. Pack the mix about the roots firmly enough to hold the plants in position, but without impeding drainage.

Indoors, a winter night temperature of 55 to 65°F and an increase of five to fifteen degrees by day are appropriate. At other seasons, higher temperatures are advantageous. A humid atmosphere and a fairly free circulation of air without subjecting the plants to cold drafts are conducive to good growth. Shade from strong sun, sufficient to prevent even slight scorching of the foliage, is needed, but no more. Allow the maximum light the plants can tolerate without any yellowing or scorching of the foliage.

Keep the roots damp, but not constantly saturated, and see that the water-holding bases ("tanks") of the rosettes of kinds that are constructed with these are always filled. Fertilize well-rooted specimens regularly with dilute liquid fertilizer or with pellets of slow-release fertilizer sprinkled on the surface of the rooting medium. Propagation is easy by offsets and by seed. For more information see the Encyclopedia entry Bromeliads or Bromels.

VULPIA. See Festuca.

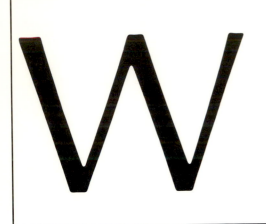

W

WACHENDORFIA (Wachen-dórfia). Known in the wild only in South Africa, *Wachendorfia* is a genus of twenty-five species of evergreen, tuberous-rooted, herbaceous, summer-blooming perennials. It belongs to the bloodwort family HAEMODORACEAE and bears a name honoring E. J. von Wachendorff, professor of botany at Utrecht, Holland, who died in 1758.

Wachendorfias have tubers bright red inside and outside, erect stems, and sword-shaped or rarely linear, mostly basal leaves, in two ranks and more or less corrugated longitudinally. The flowers are in terminal panicles. Individual blooms last one day, but open in succession over a fairly long period. They have perianths with six yellow, narrow to obovate-oblong, spreading, almost similar-sized segments (petals), three slender stamens, two of which are somewhat pendulous and one of which turns sideways, and a slender style, also turned to one side. The fruits are three-seeded capsules. From the tubers of these plants, a red dye was extracted.

Varying in height from 2 to somewhat over 3 feet, **W. thyrsiflora** has erect, sword-shaped, yellow-green, hairless leaves up to 2½ feet long and 3½ inches wide. The flowering stalks are longer and bear their bright yellow blooms with slightly darker markings on their rear petals, in short-branched, cylindrical, almost spikelike panicles. The perianth segments (petals) are up to ¾ inch long by one-half as broad.

Exceedingly variable and at one time including plants now recognized as separate species, **W. paniculata,** typically 8 inches to 2 feet tall, has erect or spreading, linear to lanceolate, dull green, slightly hairy leaves up to 1½ feet long by ¾ to 1½ inches wide. Apricot-yellow with conspicuous dark markings on the rear petals, the flowers are in panicles with the lower branches considerably longer than the upper ones. The petals are up to 1 inch long by about one-half as wide, the stamens are

nearly the same length. Flower panicles with few distantly spaced branches distinguish *W. p. tenella*. Panicles with many branches, and hairy leaves and flower stems, are characteristic of *W. p. hirsuta*.

A dwarf kind that has been misidentified as *W. p. tenella* is **W. parviflora.** Up to 1 foot tall, this has erect or spreading, lanceolate to linear, blue-green, hairy leaves usually somewhat longer than the flower stalks and up to ¾ inch wide. The panicles of dull yellow blooms have many very short branches. The petals, which fade to brownish, are ¾ to 1 inch long and up to ¼ inch wide. The stamens are two-thirds as long as the petals.

Garden and Landscape Uses. Not hardy in the north, wachendorfias are likely to survive in sheltered places outdoors in climates not harsher than that of coastal Virginia and are eminently suitable for outdoor planting in Mediterranean-type climates, such as that of California. They are agreeable in flower beds and rock gardens and at watersides, and associate well with masonry so that they can be used effectively against walls and in similar locations.

Cultivation. Wachendorfias are easy to grow. They appreciate sunny locations and do well in porous, sandy soil that contains some peaty organic matter. In the wild a native of swamps and streamsides, *W. thyrsiflora* needs moister conditions than are necessary for the other species described above, but none should be allowed to suffer for lack of moisture, especially during the spring and summer growing season. Propagation is by division in spring and by seed.

WAFER-ASH is *Ptelea trifoliata*.

WAHANE. See Pritchardia.

WAHLENBERGIA (Wahlen-bérgia). This genus of *Campanula* relatives comprises more than 150 species of annuals and herbaceous perennials widely distributed chiefly in temperate regions, mostly those

Wachendorfia thyrsiflora

Wachendorfia paniculata

in the southern hemisphere. Sometimes *Edraianthus* is included in *Wahlenbergia,* and gardeners are likely to know some of its species as *Wahlenbergia.* Following prevailing botanical thought, in this Encyclopedia the two genera are treated separately. The fairly long-stalked blooms of *Wahlenbergia* are without bracts immediately below them. The short-stalked flowers of *Edraianthus* are in dense terminal clusters, or more rarely are solitary, with bracts just below them. Also, the seed capsules of *Edraianthus* open irregularly, while those of *Wahlenbergia* open regularly by compartments. Differences in the capsules also distinguish *Wahlenbergia* from *Campanula.* Those of the first open at the top between adhering calyx lobes, those of *Campanula* at the sides or base. Wahlenbergias belong in the bellflower family CAMPANULACEAE. Their name commemorates the Swedish botanist Georg Wahlenberg, who died in 1851.

Wahlenbergias have alternate or opposite, undivided leaves. Their blue to white, erect or nodding flowers, solitary or more rarely clustered, have five-lobed calyxes, their tubes joined to the ovaries. The bell-shaped corollas are five-lobed. There are five stamens, and one two- to five-branched style. The fruits are capsules that open at their apexes by valves between the calyx lobes.

Chiefly annual wahlenbergias include *W. capensis* and *W. annularis,* both South Africans. A true annual, **W. capensis** is 1 foot to 1½ feet tall, hairy, and has sometimes branched stems. Its mostly oblong-lanceolate leaves, mostly opposite, are irregularly toothed and up to 2 inches long by ¾ inch wide. The solitary flowers, their calyx tubes clothed with long, white hairs, have saucer-shaped corollas about ¾ inch across, bluish-green outside, blue inside, with violet petals marked with a few black dots. Annual or sometimes perennial **W. annularis,** 6 inches to 2 feet tall, has branched stems, and crowded, mostly basal, hairy, narrow-oblanceolate to nearly linear, toothed leaves up to 2½ inches long by nearly ½ inch broad. The broadly-bell- to saucer-shaped flowers, up to 1 inch wide or wider, are white changing to pale blue or pale violet. Annual or sometimes perennial **W. hederacea** is a low, hairless native of moist soils in Europe. It has very slender, creeping stems, and stalked, nearly round, usually five-angled, ivy-shaped leaves up to ½ inch in diameter. The solitary, narrow-bell-shaped, pale blue flowers, about ⅓ inch long, have long, erect stalks.

The perennial that has been misnamed in gardens *W. gracilis* (syn. *W. vincaeflora*), which name correctly belongs to another species, is **W. trichogyna.** Native to Australia and New Zealand, this has a deep taproot and is 9 inches to 2 feet tall and bristly-hairy. From a thick rootstock it sends

Wahlenbergia hederacea

many usually branchless stems. Its lanceolate to linear-lanceolate, shallowly-toothed, opposite or alternate leaves are up to 2 inches long by ¼ inch wide. The funnel-shaped flowers, ¾ inch long by 1¼ inches across, have short-hairy calyx tubes, blue-violet petals, and yellowish-based, white corolla tubes. Perennial **W. albomarginata,** of New Zealand, is not infrequently misidentified as Tasmanian *W. saxicola.* The New Zealand species has slender, branching rhizomes and rosettes of all basal, ovate-spatula-shaped leaves, up to 1 inch long or a little longer by nearly ¼ inch wide, reddish-brown at their edges and often purplish on their undersides. Except for their stalks, they are without hairs. From ¾ inch to 1¼ inches long and wide, the bell-shaped, white or pale blue, drooping or inclined blooms are on stalks 4 to 10 inches long. Variety *W. a. pygmaea* is a very dwarf alpine.

Garden Uses and Cultivation. Wahlenbergias are best suited for climates without torrid summers or very cold winters. They are appropriate for rock gardens and similar choice sites, as well as for alpine greenhouses. The annuals, and some of the perennials that seem to do best when treated as annuals, can be raised by sowing seed in spring where the plants are to bloom and thinning out the seedlings to circumvent overcrowding. Summer cuttings made from nonflowering shoots can be used to increase the perennials. Most wahlenbergias prefer gritty, well-drained soil of a limestone character, but *W. hederacea* thrives in moist, peaty earth. Sunny locations or those affording slight shade from the full intensity of summer sun give the best results.

WAHOO is *Euonymus atropurpurea.*

WAITZEA (Wàitz-ea). Closely allied to *Helipterum,* the Australian genus *Waitzea,* of the daisy family COMPOSITAE, comprises six species. Its name, first applied in 1808, commemorates F. C. A. Waitz, who traveled in Java and wrote about the plants of that island.

Waitzeas are annuals with everlasting-type flowers, which means that after drying they retain much of the appearance of fresh blooms. As with most members of the daisy family, the so-called flowers are really flower heads, assemblages of many small florets. These plants have alternate, undivided, lobeless and toothless leaves, and clustered or solitary flower heads. Each head has a center of fertile, tubular, yellow florets encircled by several rows of white or colored, petal-like bracts. The fruits are seedlike achenes.

Although not common in gardens, these sorts are sometimes grown: **W. aurea,** 1 foot

Waitzea aurea

Waldsteinia fragarioides

Waldsteinia geoides

to 1½ feet tall, has erect stems, narrow, pointed, hairy leaves, and loose sprays of bright golden-yellow flower heads 1 inch wide or slightly wider. *W. acuminata* (syn. *W. corymbosa*) differs most obviously from the last in its flower heads, up to 1 inch wide, ranging from orange-yellow to red. Its broad-linear leaves are up to 2¾ inches long.

Garden Uses and Cultivation. Waitzeas are attractive for summer flower beds and borders and for pots in greenhouses. Their flowers, after cutting, can be tied in bundles and hung upside down until quite dry; then they are of use in dried arrangements. Waitzeas need well-drained porous soil that is never excessively wet and a sunny location. For garden use sow seed outdoors as soon as the ground has warmed a little in spring and thin the seedlings out to about 6 inches apart, or start the seeds indoors, transplant the seedlings to flats or small pots, and plant them in the garden about the time it is safe to set out tomatoes. For blooming in pots, transplant three seedlings in a 5-inch container filled with porous, fertile soil, and grow them in a sunny greenhouse where the winter night temperature is 50°F and that by day is five to ten degrees higher.

WAKE ROBIN. See Trillium.

WALDMEISTER is *Galium odoratum*.

WALDSTEINIA (Wald-steìnia) — Barren-Strawberry. Charming strawberry-like plants constitute *Waldsteinia*, of the rose family ROSACEAE. There are half a dozen species, natives of the northern hemisphere. From strawberries (*Fragaria*) they are distinguished by their fruits not being juicy and their flowers having ten or fewer pistils. Other close relatives are *Geum* and *Potentilla*, but their flowers have fifteen or more pistils. The name commemorates the German botanist Count von Waldstein-Wartenburg, who died in 1823. The name barren-strawberry is also applied to *Poten-*

tilla simplex, a native of North America not ordinarily cultivated.

Barren-strawberries are low mat-forming plants with rhizomes and long-stalked, chiefly basal leaves, sometimes three- to five-lobed, but more commonly of three broad, separate leaflets. Their flowers, in small clusters atop slender stems, have five sepals, five petals, and numerous stamens. The fruits, technically achenes, are dry and hairy.

The kind most commonly cultivated in American gardens is the native *W. fragarioides*, a delightful occupant of woodlands from New Brunswick to Minnesota and Georgia. It is superior to the much smaller-flowered *W. parviflora*, which occurs in similar habitats from Virginia to Georgia and Alabama. The first is a tufted plant that carpets the ground from spring through fall with beautiful bright glossy-green foliage and, in spring and sporadically afterward, lifts above its greenery few-flowered sprays of upturned golden-yellow, potentilla-like blooms almost or quite ¾ inch in diameter. Its leaves have three leaflets, wedge-shaped toward their bases and toothed above. The petals are broad and rounded. Another American, *W. lobata*, of Georgia, is distinguished by having leaves with three-toothed lobes rather than separate leaflets.

Native to Austria and Yugoslavia and from Siberia to Japan, *W. ternata* (syn. *W. sibirica*) has creeping rhizomes and evergreen leaves of three ½- to 1¼-inch-long, toothed leaflets. Its yellow flowers are ½ to ¾ inch wide. From the last, *W. geoides*, of eastcentral Europe and adjoining Asia, differs in being without extensively creeping rhizomes and in its leaves being broad-kidney-shaped, toothed, and with five or seven lobes. The flowers are ½ to ¾ inch wide.

Garden and Landscape Uses. An admirable carpeting plant, *W. fragarioides* is useful as a groundcover in open wood-

lands and other partly shaded places, in rock gardens, and in native plant gardens. It makes a good edging and may be used to furnish the fringes of shrub borders. For good effect it must be displayed in generous masses. It is 4 to 5 inches in height and forms close, even mats. Although less attractive than the last, the other American species discussed may be used similarly. Old World *W. ternata* is well adapted for rock gardens and other intimate plantings.

Cultivation. Barren-strawberries are accommodating plants for lightly shaded locations. They succeed in garden soils of ordinary quality, but are most luxuriant in those that never lack for moisture. If planted in congenial surroundings in spring or early fall at a spacing of 6 to 8 inches, they soon establish themselves. An annual spring dressing of a complete garden fertilizer helps to promote vigorous growth.

WALKING STICK INSECTS. Rarely major pests, but sometimes destructive of the foliage of trees, shrubs, and other plants to an extent that warrants control measures, walking stick insects, or walking sticks as they are sometimes called, are curious grasshopper relatives. From 2 to 6 inches long, they have long, slender bodies and long, even more slender legs and antennae. Most sorts that occur in North America are wingless. When at rest they closely resemble the twigs among which they live. If control becomes necessary consult a local Cooperative Extension Agent or State Agricultural Experiment Station regarding appropriate measures.

WALL GARDENS. As the designation is understood by sophisticated gardeners, wall gardens have much in common with rock gardens. Both feature rocks as their prominent nonliving element and both are planted in the main with the sorts of low perennials commonly known as rock garden plants or rock plants. But there the visual similarity ends. Rock gardens are most often natural, or are man-made with the rocks disposed in ways calculated to give the impression of naturalness. Or if the rock gardens are more formal and more evidently man-made, the rocky areas will extend for appreciable distances horizontally and will clearly not be walls.

Wall gardens, in addition to being attractive and providing the opportunity to grow many delightful plants in a comparatively small space, can serve usefully in garden design by taking advantage of and emphasizing changing levels and by serving as backgrounds for low plantings. They can be used with great charm to define low center panels in sunken gardens. On occasion, the development of wall gardens will prove the most convenient way of dealing with an abandoned cellar hole of a structure long gone, or perhaps of one never begun beyond the digging of a foundation. Such excavations are not uncommon in country places.

Wall gardens are of two chief types, those in which the walls support banks of soil and are actually retaining walls and those with freestanding walls without such function. These last can serve as backgrounds and as dividers between different parts of the garden. Although it is possible to have a retaining wall constructed of stones cemented together, with holes for plants extending through the wall to agreeable soil behind, by far the most practicable walls, from a plant-growing point of view, are those known as dry walls, that is walls constructed without cement. Freestanding walls should always be of this sort.

Whichever type of wall is employed it is important that it have a firmly packed foundation of crushed rock, brick rubble, coarse cinders, coarse gravel, or other such material deep enough to avoid disturbance by winter freezing and to ensure drainage.

To ensure this, dig a ditch to a minimum depth of 1½ feet, and certainly to below the level of winter freezing, and fill it with drainage material to within about 1 foot of the surface. For best effect, the stones of the wall should be of one sort, not a hodgepodge mixture of different geological types. They may be of irregular shapes and sizes or more formally shaped and evenly sized. Rounded boulders are not suitable.

Construct a dry retaining wall so that its face slopes slightly backward. A batter, as this slope is called, of not less than 1 inch for each 1 foot of height is appropriate. To resist the outward thrust of the soil behind it, the base of the wall should be one-third as wide as it is high; from its bottom up it may narrow gradually. Place the stones so their upper surfaces slope slightly downward from front to back. This ensures that some of the rain or other water that falls on the face of the wall seeps

A retaining-type wall garden with a lavish display of *Aurinia saxatilis* and other spring blooms

A formal wall garden with cemented stones and apertures left for such plants as saxifragas, primulas, androsaces, and other sorts

backward through the soil-filled joints to the roots.

Position the stones in horizontal layers, making sure that the vertical joints between those of each layer are not directly above those of the layer beneath. And at intervals, set a stone, with its length running backward, well into the bank of soil to provide additional stability. As the work proceeds, fill the spaces between the stones with, in place of mortar, sifted, fertile, gritty soil, and pack and tamp some of the same mix firmly behind the stones to form a layer 6 inches thick to serve as a root run for the plants. Initial planting may be done as the wall is built, the easiest and sometimes most effective procedure, or may be delayed until the wall is complete.

Freestanding walls are commonly built so that both sides can be planted. They should not be less than 2 feet wide at the top; wider is better. As with dry retaining walls, the sides should incline backward from bottom to top and the positioning of the stones should follow the recommendations given above for setting the stones

A freestanding wall garden prior to planting

for such retaining walls. A freestanding wall is actually two walls set back to back with a core of soil, averaging at least 1 foot wide, between them. Because the soil of freestanding dry walls dries out more rapidly than that of retaining walls, particular attention must be given to watering in dry weather. To facilitate this, an excellent plan is to install along its top a water pipe with a tiny perforation every few inches along its underside and fitted with a conveniently placed valve that can be opened to allow trickles of water to moisten the central core of soil.

Planting wall gardens calls for some care. If convenient, the initial installation is best done as construction proceeds. This enables the gardener to set his plants most advantageously, with their roots extending backward through the soil, and to water them adequately as soon as they are placed. Avoid overplanting. If the surface of the wall is pleasing to the eye, it is important that some of it shows. And set the plants irregularly rather than in a pattern. In general, have the larger-growing plants toward the bottom of the wall and the less robust kinds above.

If planting is not done as the wall is constructed, it can be done, as later supplementary and replacement plantings must be, after the wall's completion. This involves using a pointed stick or similar instrument to scrape sufficient soil from between the stones, at the spot where the plant is to be inserted, to permit its roots to extend as far to the rear as possible, and, after positioning the plant, packing fresh soil around its roots to hold it securely in place. Complete the job by watering thoroughly with a fine spray. For installation in finished walls, select small specimens of the plants used; success is much more probable with them than with larger specimens. It is quite practicable to start some easy-to-raise sorts from seed sown directly in the chinks between the stones; this is likely to prove less expensive than purchasing plants. Mix the seed with a little

A wall garden in its second season after planting

sifted soil of a slightly clayey character and, following a rainy period or immediately after wetting the face of the wall very thoroughly with a fine spray, push this into the crevices between the stones. Too rapid drying can be diminished by draping burlap or similar material over the area where the seed is planted or by leaning branches of evergreens against the wall at those places. Remove these shading materials as soon as the young seedlings are established and, if too many sprout in one place, pull out the superfluous ones.

A clump of *Dianthus* in full bloom in a wall garden

Plants appropriate for wall gardens include, among many others, aethionemas, androsaces, arabises, aubrietas, *Aurinia saxatilis,* dwarf campanulas, dwarf cytisuses, dianthuses, *Erinus alpinus,* erodiums, dwarf geraniums, *Gypsophila cerastioides, G. repens,* helianthemums, dwarf hypericums, iberises, lavenders, leontopodiums, *Linaria alpina, Linum perenne alpinum, Nepeta faassenii, Oenothera fruticosa, O. missourensis, Petrorhagia rhodopea,* dwarf phloxes, ramondas, santolinas, *Saponaria ocymoides,* saxifrages, sedums, sempervivums, and *Thymus serpyllum* varieties.

WALL-ROCKET. See Diplotaxis.

WALLFLOWER. See Cheiranthus, and Erysimum.

WALLICHIA (Wallích-ia). This genus, native from the eastern Himalayas to southern China, belongs in the palm family PALMAE. It includes six species. The name honors the Danish botanist Nathaniel Wallich, who died in 1854. As with its close relatives *Arenga* and *Caryota,* flowering and fruiting so exhausts *Wallichia* that the plants die after blooming and fruiting once. From arengas and caryotas, wallichias differ in their blooms having united sepals and united petals and in its male flowers usually having only six stamens.

Wallichias are mostly low palms without trunks or stems, or with very short, solitary or clustered ones. Their leaves are pinnate with the leaflets more or less oblanceolate or obovate, narrowing to wedge-shaped bases, and with ragged-toothed, often oblique apexes. The flowers are in much-branched clusters that consist of one sex only or include both male and female flowers. The one- to three-seeded, red or purple fruits are oblong-ovoid and ½ to 1 inch long.

Unusual in the genus because of its height, quite lovely *W. disticha* is an inhabitant of the Himalayan region. It has one or rarely more trunks up to 20 feet tall and arching leaves 8 to 10 feet long and in two distinct ranks. The leaflets, 1 foot to 2 feet long and 2 to 3 inches wide, are green above, slightly glaucous beneath, and their broad ends have a large tooth on either side of the center. The green flowers are in clusters 3 to 6 feet long, those of male flowers usually about twice as long as the clusters of female blooms. A native of India, *W. caryotoides* is a low, clustered plant without an evident trunk or with an extremely short one. Its curving leaves rise to a height of 5 to 9 feet and have leaflets 1 foot to 1¼ feet in length, rich shining-green above and whitish beneath. The flower clusters are about 1½ feet long. The male flowers are yellowish and numerous, the females few and purplish. Very similar to *W. caryotoides,* but with violet flowers and differing in technical botanical details of the ovary, *W. densiflora* is a native of Assam.

Garden and Landscape Uses. Wallichias are attractive ornamentals for landscape use in frost-free, humid, warm climates. They grow in ordinary garden soil in sun or part-shade and are attractive as solitary specimens or grouped with other plants.

Cultivation. These palms may be raised from seed sown in sandy, peaty soil where the temperature is 75 to 85°F. That is the best and simplest means of increase, but the plants can sometimes, with care, be divided. Division is best accomplished by gradually separating the offsets or suckers over a period of weeks so that the parts to be established as new plants have time to form roots before being removed from the parent. After separation, the new plants should be potted in porous, sandy, peaty

Wallichia densiflora, the Botanic Garden, Rio de Janeiro, Brazil

soil and kept in a greenhouse, where high humidity and a temperature of 75 to 90°F are maintained, until new roots are well developed. During this period they must be shaded from sun. When grown in greenhouses, wallichias need the same conditions as *Verschaffeltia.* For additional information see Palms.

WALNUT. Walnuts belong to the genus *Juglans,* of the walnut family JUGLANDACEAE. The genus, its sorts, garden and landscape uses, and cultivation are discussed in the Encyclopedia entry Juglans. Here we are concerned only with kinds ordinarily planted and cultivated for their nuts. These are the Persian or English walnut (*J. regia*), the black walnut (*J. nigra*), their varieties and hybrids, and, to a considerably lesser extent, varieties of two other species of *Juglans,* the heartnut (*J. ailanthifolia cordiformis*) and the butternut (*J. cinerea*).

Walnuts are not satisfactory for nut production where hard freezes occur after their spring growth has begun. Such occurrences destroy the precocious flowers and hence the potential crops of nuts without otherwise damaging the trees. The geographical limits for successfully growing the trees is largely determined by winter cold and are more extensive than for reliable nut

The black walnut (*Juglans nigra*)

The black walnut (fruits)

Persian walnuts (fruits)

production. The black walnut occurs as a native from Massachusetts to Florida and Texas. The Persian walnut, a native of Europe and Asia, is hardy in southern New England, but needs a milder climate to fruit satisfactorily. Varieties of it are much grown in California, parts of the Pacific Northwest, and the south.

Walnut trees succeed best in deep, well-drained, fertile soil that is never excessively dry. Planting may be done in fall or early spring. For the best results allow 60 to 65 feet between trees of Persian walnuts. Closer spacing, from 40 to 50 feet, serves well in early years, but is likely to prove inadequate later. For black walnuts, allow a minimum spacing of 60 feet. Prune the young trees to establish a leader (dominant central axis) and to encourage shapeliness. Little or no subsequent pruning is likely to be needed. Clean cultivation to eliminate weeds is necessary throughout the life of the trees. This may be achieved by maintaining a heavy mulch, extending outward from the trunk to at least as far as the spread of the branches. Commercial growers commonly sow a cover crop in fall and plow it under in spring. An annual application of fertilizer, such as a 10-6-4, made in early spring favors growth and good crops.

Propagation of walnuts for nut production, which usually implies the propagation of selected varieties, is most commonly done by grafting in a greenhouse in winter or outdoors in spring onto seedling understocks of the species to which the variety belongs or, alternatively, with the Persian walnut, onto seedlings of the black walnut or California native walnut *J. hindsii*. Increase may also be had by budding outdoors in summer onto seedling understocks. Propagation by seed is described in the Encyclopedia entry Juglans.

Varieties of Persian walnuts favored in the west include 'Concord', 'Eureka', 'Franquette', 'Placentia', and 'Vina'. For the east 'Broadview', 'Colby', 'Hansen', and 'McKinster' have proved successful. Varieties of black walnuts considered most highly include 'Elmer Meyers', 'Ohio', 'Sparrow', 'Stambaugh', and 'Thomas'.

Selected varieties of the heartnut and the butternut, both of which are hardy in southern Canada with their cultural requirements essentially those of black walnuts, are cultivated to some extent for their nuts. Varieties of the heartnut include 'Bates', 'Fodermaier', 'Lancaster', and 'Ritchie'. Varieties of the butternut include 'Ayers', 'Craxeasy', 'Johnson', and 'Van Syckle'.

Pests of walnuts include aphids, caterpillars, lace bugs, leaf rollers, mites, scale insects, webworms, and weevils. Diseases include anthracnose, canker, leaf blotch, and leaf spot. A witches'-broom condition called bunch disease caused by a virus is occasionally troublesome. For control recommendations, consult the State Agricultural Experiment Station or a Cooperative Extension Agent in the state where the trees are growing.

WALTHERIA (Wal-thèria). The great majority of the fifty species of *Waltheria* are natives of tropical America and the West Indies, with one extending into Florida. One species each occurs in East Africa, Malagasy (Madagascar), Malaya, and Taiwan. The genus belongs in the sterculia family STERCULIACEAE and includes herbaceous plants, shrubs, and trees, some sources of material for cordage and some used in home medicines. It is named for Augustin Friedrich Walther, a German botanist, who died in 1746.

Waltherias have shoots and foliage with stellate (star-shaped) hairs. Their leaves are alternate and toothed. Usually small, the yellow flowers are in clusters in the leaf axils, or are in terminal heads, racemes, or panicles. They have a five-lobed calyx, five each petals and stamens, the latter united at their bases, and a club-shaped or fringed style. The fruits are capsules.

Native from Florida to the West Indies and South America, and naturalized in Hawaii and elsewhere in the tropics, *W. americana* is a velvety, downy shrub 3 to

6 feet tall. Its toothed, ovate, oblong, or lanceolate leaves are prominently veined and 1 inch to 3½ inches long. They are hairy on both sides and usually whitish. The blooms, in crowded, spherical clusters in the leaf axils, have petals about ¼ inch long. The seed capsules are about ¹⁄₁₀ inch long.

Garden and Landscape Uses and Cultivation. The species described above is useful for general landscaping and succeeds in ordinary soils in humid tropical and near tropical climates. It is easily increased by seed and by cuttings.

WAMPI is *Clausena lansium*.

WAND FLOWER. This common name is used for *Dierama* and *Sparaxis*.

WANDERING JEW. This is a common name of *Tradescantia albiflora*, *T. fluminensis*, and *Zebrina pendula*.

WARATAH. This is the common name of *Telopea speciosissima*. The Tasmanian waratah is *T. truncata*. The name waratah-tree is sometimes used for *Oreocallis pinnata*.

WARSCEWICZELLA. See Cochleanthes.

WARSZEWICZIA (Warszew-íczia)—Wild-Poinsettia. Four species of shrubs and trees comprise *Warszewiczia*, an endemic of tropical America and the West Indies. It belongs to the madder family RUBIACEAE and has a name commemorating Josef von Warszewicz, a Polish-Lithuanian, who collected plants in South America and died in 1866.

Warszewiczias have opposite, undivided leaves, and numerous small flowers in raceme-like panicles. The blooms have five-toothed calyxes with, in some of the flowers, one of the teeth enlarged, and leaf- or petal-like. The corolla is funnel-shaped and, in the throat, hairy. It has five lobes (petals). There are five stamens. The fruits are capsules.

The wild-poinsettia (*W. coccinea*), of tropical America and Trinidad, is not related to the true poinsettia (*Euphorbia pulcherrima*) nor, except for the color of the showy parts of its flowers, does it look much like that familiar plant. It is a shrub or tree up to 20 feet in height with obovate leaves 8 inches to 2 feet long or longer. The flowers are many together in panicles that often exceed 1 foot in length. The enlarged bractlike or petal-like lobes of the calyxes are brilliant red and 1 inch to 3½ inches long by one-half as broad. These bracts provide the chief display. The corollas are small, five-toothed, and yellow or orange. The stamens protrude.

Garden and Landscape Uses and Cultivation. Wild-poinsettia is a magnificent ornamental for gardens in the humid tropics. It produces its best display in deep,

Warszewiczia coccinea

A young specimen of *Washingtonia filifera*, Rancho Santa Ana Botanic Garden, California

A young specimen of *Washingtonia robusta*, Baja California

Washingtonia filifera with "skirts" of dead foliage, Southern California

Washingtonia robusta with lower portions of "skirts" removed, Baja California

Washington filifera with "skirts" of dead foliage removed, Pasadena, California

fertile, well-drained soil in part-day shade or full sun. No regular pruning is needed. In greenhouses and conservatories it succeeds in ground beds or in large pots or tubs where the temperature on winter nights does not drop below 60°F, and by day at that season is 65 to 75°F. A humid atmosphere is favorable and the soil must be always moderately moist. Specimens, the roots of which have become crowded, benefit from regular applications of dilute liquid fertilizer from spring through fall. Repotting and any pruning needed to shape the plants is done in late winter or early spring. For best results, forms with the largest and most brightly colored floral bracts should be chosen. These should be propagated by cuttings or by air layering. Seeds give plants of varying display value.

WASHINGTON PLANT is *Cabomba caroliniana*.

WASHINGTONIA (Washingtò-nia). This genus, its name honoring George Washington, first president of the United States, who died in 1799, consists of two species of massive trees of the palm family PALMAE. One is the only palm native to California, the other is restricted as a native to Mexico.

The genus *Washingtonia* is related to *Pritchardia* and was once included in that genus. Its species are fan-leaved and have trunks clothed with long skirts of drooping, persistent remains of dead leaves extending from just beneath the crown of living foliage to, or nearly to, the ground. The orbicular leaves have blades, 3 to 5 feet across, cleft to about their middles into fifty or more segments, which are again split at their ends and often have filamentous margins. The leafstalks, 2 to 5 feet long, are furnished with stout, hooked teeth. The chaffy, bisexual, creamy-white flowers are in branched, corn-tassel-like clusters that originate among the leaves and project beyond them. They have six stamens and are

succeeded by small, berry-like, black fruits. The drooping bracts of the flower clusters are sword-shaped.

Up to 75 feet in height, **W. filifera,** of California, Arizona, and Mexico, has gray-green foliage and massive trunks likely to be 3 feet in diameter at breast height without allowing for the shag of dead leaves. The trunks and shag of Mexican **W. robusta,** which attains 100 feet or more in height, are much more slender and its leaves are brighter green and shorter stalked. The base of the trunk of *W. robusta* flares outward at its base, that of *W. filifera* does not. A specimen of *W. robusta* in the Los Angeles State and County Arboretum is estimated to be 140 feet tall and is quite likely the tallest palm in the United States. Other differences between species of *Washingtonia* are that the leaf margins of *W. filifera* have abundant filaments or threads, whereas those of the other, except in young specimens, have few or

Tall specimens of *Washingtonia robusta* with "skirts" of old foliage removed

none. A brown patch, absent from *W. filifera*, marks the point where the leafstalk joins the leaf blade on the underside of the leaves of *W. robusta*.

Garden and Landscape Uses. These noble palms are magnificent as single specimens and in groups and on avenues. They thrive in full sun in tropical and subtropical climates and in dry atmospheric conditions. This is especially true of *W. filifera*, which has its home in oases in hot dry deserts, but even though its aboveground parts survive the searing conditions prevalent in the hottest, driest parts of North America, these plants grow only where their roots have access to adequate water. In times past, washingtonias led many a knowledgeable, thirsty traveler to the water that likely saved his life. Along the California coast and in Florida, Mexican *W. robusta* thrives better than *W. filifera*. The latter is popular in such drier areas as Palm Springs, California.

Cultivation. No unusual difficulty attends the cultivation of washingtonias. They thrive in any ordinary soil where sufficient moisture is available and are readily propagated from fresh seed sown in sandy, peaty soil at a temperature of 75 to 85°F. Because the skirts of leaf remains are a fire hazard, they are often cut or burned off; this reveals the bare, smooth trunks, but detracts considerably from the ornamental and distinctive appearance of these unique palms. Washingtonias are sometimes planted in large conservatories for ornament and interest. They should be in full sun in a deep bed of fertile, well-drained soil in a greenhouse where the atmosphere is moderately humid and the minimum winter temperature is 50 to 55°F, with a daytime rise of five or ten degrees allowed. From spring through fall the minimum night temperature should be 60°F. For more information see Palms.

WASPS. Few of the nearly 100,000 species of wasps recognized by entomologists pose

problems for gardeners. Many more are beneficial. Allied to ants, bees, and sawflies, wasps are solitary or social insects with a slender waist, and two pairs of thin wings hooked together. Some sorts can inflict painful stings and some authorities apply the name wasp only to these. Wasps sometimes troublesome in gardens include the cicada killer or digger wasp, which is up to 1½ inches long, black with a yellow-banded abdomen, and has an ovipositor (which serves as a stinging instrument) of formidable size. The damage it causes in gardens consists chiefly of disturbing lawns, paths, banks, and similar areas into which it tunnels, leaving at the entrances to the tunnels small mounds of soil. The cicada killer drags cicadas it has captured and paralyzed by stinging into the tunnels. It then lays an egg on the cicada, the body of which provides food for the young wasp that hatches from the egg within two or three days.

With much the aspect of the cicada killer, but stouter, more hairy, and without as large an ovipositor, the giant hornet is reddish brown with orange-yellow markings. This insect damages certain shrubs and trees, especially lilacs, by tearing from the shoots large pieces of bark that it uses in building its nests, which it makes in hollow trees or suspends from eaves of buildings or from ceilings of barns or other buildings to which it has access. Some wasps cause galls on plants. Of such galls,

A wasps' nest

Twigs of lilac girdled by the giant hornet

Mossy rose gall caused by a wasp

those on oaks, including the familiar oak apples, are perhaps best known. The mossy rose gall wasp is responsible for the conspicuous ball-like clusters of greenish, mosslike strands that develop on roses. The rose root gall wasp causes conspicuous swellings on the roots of roses. Other gall wasps affect blackberries and blueberries. There are no practicable control measures for most gall wasps. For suggestions about the best ways of dealing with other sorts consult a local Cooperative Extension Agent or State Agricultural Experiment Station.

WATER. This word appears in the common names of these plants: Chinese water-chestnut (*Eleocharis dulcis*), green water-rose or water-pimpernel (*Samolus parviflorus*), water-aloe or water soldier (*Stratiotes aloides*), water-arum (*Calla palustris*), water avens (*Geum rivale*), water-beech (*Carpinus caroliniana*), water-celery (*Vallisneria americana*), water caltrop or water-chestnut (*Trapa natans*), water-chinquapin (*Nelumbo lutea*), water-clover (*Marsilea*), water-elm (*Planera aquatica*), water gum (*Tristania laurina*), water-hawthorn (*Aponogeton distachyus*), water-hemlock (*Cicuta*), water-hoarhound (*Lycopus*), water-hyacinth (*Eichhornia crassipes*), water-hyssop (*Bacopa*), water leaf (*Hydrophyllum*), water-lemon (*Passiflora lauriflora*), water-lettuce (*Pistia stratiotes*), water-lily (*Nymphaea, Victoria*), water-locust (*Gleditsia aquatica*), water-milfoil (*Myriophyllum*), water nut (*Trapa*), water-parsnip (*Sium suave*), water-plantain (*Alisma*), water-poppy (*Hydrocleys nymphoides*), water-purslane (*Ludwigia palustris*), water shield (*Brasenia schreberi*), water snowflake (*Nymphoides indica*), water-star-grass (*Heteranthera dubia*), water-star-wort (*Callitriche*), water-violet (*Hottonia*), water weed (*Elodea*), and water-willow (*Decodon verticillatus*).

WATER AND WATERSIDE GARDENING. Water features, such as lakes, ponds, pools, brooks, cascades, and fountains, appropriately located and properly maintained, can be charming. Relatively few gardens include natural assets of these sorts; more often, if they are wanted, they must be installed.

In their full glory at The New York Botanical Garden are water-lilies, arrowheads, lotuses, and other aquatics; the tall evergreen in the background is *Magnolia grandiflora*

trate chiefly on ponds and pools devoted to these activities.

A sunny location is a prerequisite for a successful water garden; practically all ornamental aquatics require maximum light. Shelter from sweeping winds, perhaps provided by a belt or hedge of evergreens, is also necessary. Avoid close proximity to trees; fallen leaves float untidily for a time and then sink, decay, and pollute the water. The quality of the water must also be considered. It should be relatively pure, free of industrial wastes and salinity.

Adapting a natural pond, or a fairly calm one that results from the damming of a brook, to the cultivation of aquatics and waterside plants calls for clearing away all unwanted vegetation and sometimes more or less modifying the shoreline to give a more pleasing outline. The banks may benefit from some contouring to provide varying heights so that they slope gently to the water's edge in some places and rise more steeply to 1 foot or more above the water in others. The bottoms of such ponds will, of course, be of mud, the surface of which, where planting is to be done, may be from up to 6 inches to 3 feet (or for a few plants even more) beneath the water.

Artificial ponds and pools are more

Fountains can be attractive, but are likely to disturb pools too much to favor the cultivation of aquatic plants: (a) A small fountain, New Orleans, Louisiana

(b) Longwood Gardens, Kennett Square, Pennsylvania

Formal pools: (a) Flush with surrounding lawn, planted with water-lilies

Of itself, water can be a great asset. Placidly surfaced lakes, ponds, and pools provide reflecting surfaces and tranquility, whereas brooks, cascades, and fountains supply both movement and life. Not always are such features designed as homes for aquatic and waterside plants; a formal pool set in a panel of lawn may be adequate without planting, and water seriously disturbed by fountains, as well as that of fast-flowing brooks and cascades, is not favorable to the growth of aquatics. But here our concern is primarily with growing plants in water and along watersides, with water gardening and waterside gardening, and therefore we shall concen-

(c) Longue Vue Gardens, New Orleans, Louisiana

(b) In a sunken garden, planted with water-lilies and other aquatics; a variety of suitable plants grow in chinks in the surrounding pavement

(c) Edged with irregular stones, planted with hardy water-lilies and other aquatics

(f) At the Royal Botanic Gardens, Kew, England, a large-leaved *Gunnera* backed by tall swamp-cypresses (*Taxodium*) fringe a large pond

(b) On Long Island, New York, a large lake pleasingly planted with hardy water-lilies

(d) With the platter-like leaves of a young plant of the giant water-lily (*Victoria cruziana*), lotuses, and other plants, Wave Hill Garden, the Bronx, New York City

geometrical or curved-free-style in outline and are relatively easy to design and install. Much more skill, or at least sympathetic understanding of natural landscapes, is demanded of the designer of a successful naturalistic lake, pond, or other water feature. Here, true art surely lies in the concealing of art. No landscape feature causes more distress to sensitive viewers than a "natural" pond with concrete showing along unlikely sinuous margins, or a "waterfall" that spouts from the apex of a rocky mound into a more or less chutelike channel. To be satisfactory, naturalistic water features must be convincing, and to achieve that the designer and builder should study natural examples of the sorts he seeks to emulate, and develop an understanding of their reasons for being. Rarely is a natural pond found elsewhere other than in a depression, with the surrounding ground sloping upward from the pond with its outline determined by the contours of the land.

The site for a pool must be well chosen. Usually it should be on level ground or in

(c) A pool backed with tall trees, with appropriate waterside planting, at the Strybing Arboretum and Botanical Gardens, San Francisco

(d) Stepping stones facilitate crossing this pond, surrounded by an area well landscaped with evergreens

(e) With lotuses, colocasias, and water-lilies; at front, in dryish soil, an ornamental grass

common garden accommodations for aquatic and waterside plants than are natural or modified natural ones. They may be formal and frankly artificial in outline or they may cunningly simulate natural lakes or ponds. Those of the first type are

Informal pools: (a) Featuring water-lilies and, at the margin, a tall bamboo

a depression (as in a sunken garden, for instance). Pools located on elevations are likely to look incongruous. This does not mean that the pool itself must necessarily be level with the surrounding ground. Raised pools with masonry sides that ex-

Informal stream gardens: (a) Slowly moving water, its banks planted with a variety of wet-soil plants

(b) A slow-flowing stream with aquatics and bog plants

(c) A small stream, with a cascade, too fast-flowing for aquatics; its banks are decorated with waterside plants

tend to a height of 1 foot to 1½ feet above the ground can be quite effective. Such features have some advantages. They necessitate less excavation than do pools set flush with the ground; the draining off of water, when necessary, is facilitated; less bending over is required to view the plants and fish closely; and there is less danger of the unwary toppling into the water, a

not unlikely possibility, especially at night, and particularly so if the pool is located as a center feature where paths cross.

To accommodate water-lilies, except miniatures that succeed in shallower water, provide a water depth of 2 to 2½ feet. This allows for tubs or other containers, 1 foot to 1½ feet deep, in which the water-lilies are planted, to be positioned so that the soil surface is covered with 1 foot to 1½ feet of water. Many aquatics thrive at lesser depths. Provision for these can be made by having the pool shallower in some parts than in others, or by elevating the containers of these plants by standing them on bricks or concrete blocks.

Provision for filling the pool must be made by running a water line, fitted with a valve or faucet, directly to the pool, or by having a hose, connected with a suitable outlet, available. The need to empty the pool from time to time must be anticipated. If the configuration of the land allows, this can be accomplished by installing a drain with a suitable shut-off device in the lowest part of the bottom of the pool to transport the water by gravity to a place appropriate for its disposal, such as a stream, ditch, sewer, or, if the ground is sufficiently porous, a dry well or sump. A vertical standpipe may screw into the drain to serve as an overflow. Small pools, if the site allows, can be emptied by siphoning the water to a lower level through a hose. If neither gravity flow nor siphoning is practicable, a sump pump may prove to be a suitable alternative.

The soil at the site must be compact. For concrete pools, excavate to a depth that will accommodate a 6-inch layer of well-tamped coarse gravel or cinders beneath the concrete. Construct 6-inch-thick bottom and sides and strengthen them with metal mesh or reinforcing rods positioned approximately through their centers. Place the reinforcement and bend it to the configuration of the pool before any concrete is poured. To facilitate the removal of wooden forms, used to contain wet concrete in the construction of vertical or nearly vertical sides (metal forms may also be used), paint the wooden forms with oil (used motor oil is satisfactory) before pouring in the concrete. A good mix for the concrete consists, by bulk, of three parts ½-inch gravel, two parts sand (the particles of which range in size from the smallest to ⅜ inch in diameter), and one part Portland cement, all thoroughly mixed before water, sufficient to bring the whole to the consistency of a thick mortar, is added. After forty-eight hours remove the forms and rub the concrete vigorously with a piece of Carborundum stone, hard sandstone, or a suitable brick, or, instead, apply and trowel a thin coat of cement to attain a smooth surface. It is important to protect new concrete from the drying effects of sun and wind by keeping it moist for the next ten days or

so. This may be done by covering it with straw, salt hay, or burlap, kept moist, or with sheets of plastic or tarpaulins. Alternatively, after the concrete has set, the pool may be filled with water and allowed to stand undisturbed for the requisite ten days or so of curing. In any case, before plants or fish are introduced, fill and empty the pool three or four times, allowing each filling to remain for two or three days. This rids the concrete of harmful free alkali.

Concrete construction adapts most readily to pools of formal or more or less formal outline, such as rectangular, circular, or elliptical ones, and to those of simple, free-form shapes that are without complicated curves or angles. The margins of such pools are usually rimmed with stone, flagstone, brick, or similar material. Fashioning naturalistic pools of concrete calls for greater skill in shaping them and masking their margins. Success is most likely attained by dispensing with vertical sides and having the concrete simply slope gradually upward from the bottom of the pool to its rim. It is important to conceal all evidence of the concrete. This can be done by the skillful placement of natural rock to slightly overhang the edges of the concrete, by placing bog plants at the pool margins, or by allowing the grass lawn to run down to the water's edge.

As an alternative to concrete, heavy-grade polyethylene plastic film can be used to line pools, especially naturalistic ones for which the excavations have sides that slope gradually and gently from shoreline to center, thus obviating sharp angles. In preparation for laying the plastic, tamp the soil quite firm and rake its surface free of any stones that would be likely to puncture the film. Be sure that all overlapping seams are watertight.

Small pools, preformed of fiberglass or other plastics, are available from nurseries that specialize in aquatics and from some other dealers. Suitable for small gardens, these are installed by sinking them into the ground almost to their rims. It is important to have the excavation at least 3 inches deeper than the pool itself to accommodate a layer of sand that will function as a cushion for the pool to rest upon.

Planting water and waterside plants is commonly done in spring. Plant hardy kinds when their new growth begins, tender, tropical kinds not until settled warm weather arrives and the water temperature is favorable to their growth. The most satisfactory soils and other cultural needs are given in the Encyclopedia entries for the various genera involved. Spring is also the appropriate season to refurbish established plantings. Reduce the size of plants or groups of plants that have become too large and, if extra plants are needed, separate pieces for propagation. Spring fertilizing and top-dressing is of benefit to many plants.

Summer maintenance consists of keeping the water free of dead leaves and other debris, preventing the accumulation of algae, and the prompt removal of old flowers and dead stems. Stock the pool with a reasonable number of fish, which will feed on mosquito larvae so that the pool does not become a source of those troublesome insects, and with scavenger water snails, and clams or freshwater mussels, which will do much to control algae and keep the water clear.

Where winters are severe, it is usual to drain garden pools in fall and store the plants over winter, or to push the containers of hardy kinds together in one corner of the pool and cover them with a layer of straw, leaves, manure, or other insulating mulch thick enough to prevent the water from freezing deeply. Another device sometimes used to relieve pool sides from the possible damaging effects of serious ice pressure is to float a few logs of wood on the water surface in fall and to leave them there until spring.

Aquatic plants suitable for pools are described, and their cultural needs discussed, in the Encyclopedia entries of the appropriate genera. Among the most important of these are those listed below. Plants suitable for planting at watersides may be selected from those listed in the Encyclopedia entry Bog Gardens.

Aquatics, the common names of some in parentheses, that root into soil or mud and have foliage that floats or stands above the water are included within the following genera: *Acorus* (sweet flag), *Aponogeton* (water-hawthorn), *Butomus* (flowering-rush), *Cyperus* (umbrella plant, papyrus), *Euryale*, *Hydrocleys* (water-poppy), *Marsilea* (water-clover), *Myriophyllum* (parrot's feather, water-milfoil), *Nelumbo* (lotus), *Nuphar* (spatterdock, yellow pond-lily), *Nymphoides* (floating heart, water snowflake), *Pontederia* (pickerel weed), *Sagittaria* (arrowhead), *Thalia*, *Typha* (cat-tail), and *Victoria* (royal water-lily).

Free-floating aquatics, the common names of some in parentheses, belong in these genera: *Azolla* (mosquito fern), *Ceratopteris* (water fern), *Eichhornia* (water-hyacinth), *Hydrocharis* (frog's bit), *Pistia* (water-lettuce), *Salvinia* (floating-moss), and *Stratiotes* (water soldier).

Underwater (submersed) aquatics, the common names of some in parentheses, that oxygenate the water and are especially useful in pools that contain fish include species of the following genera: *Aponogeton*, *Cabomba* (fanwort), *Callitriche* (water-starwort), *Ceratophyllum* (hornwort), *Elodea* (water weed), *Hottonia* (water-violet), *Lagarosiphon*, *Myriophyllum*, *Potamogeton* (pondweed), and *Vallisneria* (tapegrass).

WATERCRESS. Native to Europe and temperate Asia and naturalized in North America, watercress (*Nasturtium officinale*), of the mustard family CRUCIFERAE, is entirely different from plants of the genus *Tropaeolum*, commonly known by the colloquial name nasturtium. These latter are members of the nasturtium family TROPAEOLACEAE. The name *Nasturtium* is derived from the Greek *nasus*, nose, and *tortus*, twisted, in an allusion to the pungent flavor of the species *N. officinale*. Besides *N. officinale*, a hybrid between it and closely allied *N. microphyllum* is cultivated as watercress.

Watercress

Esteemed as a salad for its piquant flavor and as a garnish, the best watercress is harvested from plants grown in unpolluted streams or in beds of soil over which 3 to 4 inches of cool, pure water constantly flows, but it can also be cultivated in large tanks or tubs provided with an inflow and outflow of water or, without that, provided that the water is drained and replenished at fairly frequent intervals.

Soil for watercress should be fertile and at least 3 to 4 inches deep. Propagation is usually by cuttings, but watercress is also easily raised from seed sown in spring or summer in pots or pans (shallow pots) kept standing in saucers filled with water so that the soil is constantly wet. Germination occurs in ten to twelve days. When the young plants are approximately 1 inch in height, transplant them to the beds in which they are to grow.

WATERING. The provision of adequate supplies of water is one of the most important routines of plant cultivation. An understanding of watering techniques and mastery of the art of using them are basic to good gardening. Despite the availability of such aids as soil moisture sensors and capillary watering systems sometimes employed, watering in most circumstances remains an art dependent for its successful practice on close observation and human judgment. Plants grown in greenhouses and elsewhere indoors are totally dependent upon the gardener for their water supply; specimens set in containers outdoors are dependent to nearly the same extent. The water needs of plants in the ground outdoors are sometimes wholly satisfied by rainfall, but it is often desirable to supplement this, and in desert and semidesert regions reliance upon watering may be almost as complete as it is for indoor plants.

The equipment available for watering outdoor gardens includes permanently installed irrigation systems, both automatic and hand operated, movable sprinklers of various types, perforated and soil-soaker hoses that leak water throughout their lengths, ordinary hoses, and watering cans. Installed irrigation systems are most frequent in regions of long, dry summers, but

Watering outdoors: (a) With a hose, the stream broken with a sprinkler

(b) With a hose, the stream broken with the thumb

(c) A rotary sprinkler for small areas

(d) A rotary, jet-stream-type sprinkler for large areas

(e) An oscillating sprinkler

(f) A movable, non-oscillating, perforated-pipe-type sprinkler

(g) A young gardener using a watering can

Installed irrigation systems: (a) Making an incision for burying plastic pipe (note the sprinkler head in foreground)

they are by no means unknown elsewhere, especially in vegetable and cut-flower gardens. They may be overhead and highly visible, as is usual in gardens of the last-named types, or underground and largely concealed. Systems of the latter type are generally preferred for lawns and rock gardens. Formerly, underground systems were of metal pipes that required expert installation, particularly in regions where cold winters necessitated draining the pipes in fall. Today, modern plastic pipe is much simpler to employ, and its installation is within the capabilities of most gardeners. Also, plastic pipes do not need to be drained in winter.

Do not water unnecessarily. Make sure that every application counts, that it achieves a desirable objective. The most frequent mistake of inexperienced garden-

(b) A lawn fitted with an underground sprinkler system

(c) The margins of underground sprinkler systems may be of heads that spray in one direction only

ers is too frequent sprinkling with too small amounts of water. Avoid this. As a general rule, established plants, including lawn grasses, benefit much more from the soil being soaked to a depth of 6 inches or more every five to ten days than from more frequent, smaller applications. Newly transplanted trees and shrubs with deep root balls require local soaking, the application of water only to the root balls and their immediate vicinity. Seed beds and recently set plants, the roots of which are confined to the upper 3 to 4 inches of soil, are likely to need more frequent, lighter applications. If the soil between watered plants is not mulched and is bare of vegetation, stir it shallowly the next day, or as soon as it has dried to the extent that it is not sticky, with a cultivator or scuffle hoe.

A common belief of amateurs is that it is harmful to wet plants in sunshine. This is very rarely so. True, it may be slightly more wasteful of water than if done at other times, but it is rarely disadvantageous. In high summer, when light is most intense, bright sunshine frequently follows showers, commonly with advantage to growing plants. An exception sometimes occurs on lawns with compacted, clayey soil. There, water may remain in shallow depressions long enough to heat to such a degree that the grass plants are killed by the high temperatures attained. The same, of course, can happen to tiny seedlings if shallow water remains around them long enough to become excessively hot.

Watering so late in the day that the foliage does not dry within an hour or two and remains wet all night can favor the development of certain disease organisms, such as those that cause black spot of roses and mildews. This is especially true in late summer and fall when warm days are succeeded by cool nights. Interestingly, sprinklers left running all night do not pose this hazard; disease spores that would germinate in a still film of water are washed away by a continuous spray.

Watering with a slow stream from the end of a hose positioned on a piece of canvas

Methods of watering that do not involve the wetting of foliage, such as the use of soil-soaker hoses, the employment of "trickle" systems, and even the simple expedient of placing the end of a hose on a piece of board, slate, tile, or canvas set on the ground, with a slow stream flowing from the hose and spreading over the surrounding surface, do not present the hazard of encouraging disease.

Watering in greenhouses: (a) With a watering can

(b) With a watering can fitted with a sprinkler

(c) With a slow stream from a hose

(d) With a hose fitted with a sprinkler

(e) With a stream broken by the thumb held over the end of the hose

(f) Watering seedlings by the partial immersion of their containers

Watering plants in greenhouses and other indoor locations and in containers placed outdoors profoundly affects their growth and well-being. Many professionals rate the watering technique as the most critical of all greenhouse routines. Quite obviously its successful practice calls for repeated wise judgments, based in large measure on practical experience. One cannot master the art of watering solely by reading about it or from verbal instruction. Surely, an understanding of the underlying principles can be gained in these ways, and that is very necessary, but from then on the gardener must rely on his ability to apply them advantageously and to modify his procedures to best take advantage of a number of variables. There can be no rule of thumb as is presumed by the inexperienced plant grower's frequent question "How often should I water my African-violet (or amaryllis or cactus)?"

Having gained an understanding of underlying principles, which we shall explain later, the next requirement is for the waterer to be observant, to be promptly and fully aware of the responses of his plants to his treatment of them. It is surprising how many people look at plants without really seeing very much or who fail to note adverse changes before they have proceeded too far. Yet plants signal by subtle, and sometimes not so subtle, changes in their appearance whether watering practices are appropriate or not. Quite obviously if the leaves of a cineraria or a chrysanthemum in full growth wilt, need for water is probably indicated. But this is not necessarily so. The wilting may have been caused by exposure to wind or drafts of dry air, forcing the plant to transpire water faster than the roots can possibly replace it, or by the roots having been damaged in recent repotting, by disease, or from some other cause, perhaps even from excessive watering, so that they are rendered incapable of absorbing sufficient water to replace that lost by the leaves. The yellowing of the lower leaves of a Martha Washington geranium, or even an ordinary bedding geranium, at a time when their outer foliage remains green and healthy, may result from fairly recent periods of excessive dryness. Or it may indicate that the plant has been so crowded among others that its bottom leaves have been denied adequate light. And remember, the leaves of deciduous plants, those that lose their foliage before entering a dormant period, usually turn yellow as that time approaches. End-of-the-season yellowing of the foliage of such plants as freesias, hippeastrums, and lachenalias signals that the time has come for gradually reducing watering by lengthening the periods between applications, rather than signaling for more frequent watering. These are examples of several easily observable responses that inexperienced gardeners are likely to misread, signals that may proclaim neglect of watering, but then again, may not. Be cautious about making snap judgments; when possible, take all factors into consideration.

Let it be said at the outset that inexperienced and careless growers kill far more indoor plants by overwatering (that is, excessive watering) than by underwatering. Improperly used watering cans and hoses can be deadly. It is common knowledge that some kinds of plants need more water than others, that ferns, for example, require more water than cactuses. And one does not garden for long before learning that a newly potted tuberous begonia or gloxinia, for example, just starting into growth, needs less water than the same plant later, when it is in full foliage. Awareness comes that not only do some kinds of plants need more water than others, but that the same plant at different periods in its growth cycle or under different environmental conditions may, in common parlance, need a lot of water or comparatively little. But this terminology can be misleading. In all but a few special cases, the words *lot* and *little* used in these contexts do not refer to the amount of water supplied at one time, but rather to the total provided over a considerable period. The usual, sensible practice, whether the plant is one said to need a little water or a lot, is to saturate thoroughly the entire body of soil at each watering, then to withhold water until a degree of dryness deemed to be inimicable to the particular plant is approached. With plants said to need a lot of water this degree of dryness will be reached well before those plants described as requiring moderate amounts or little will reach it.

Besides considering the kind of plant, it is necessary to evaluate its condition. A specimen with comparatively little foliage, such as a dormant one just starting into new growth or one that has had its leafage much reduced in preparation for dormancy, by pruning, or perhaps by pest or disease, needs less frequent watering than does a fuller foliaged plant of the same kind. A newly potted plant requires less frequent applications than one in which the roots have taken comfortable possession of the available soil. And more frequent watering than even the last condition demands is appropriate for pot-bound specimens that have crowded their containers with healthy roots.

Environmental conditions, both below the ground and above, are important determiners of the need for watering. A spongy soil with a high organic content stays moist longer than a porous one that contains a smaller proportion of peat moss, leaf mold, or other organic material, and, other conditions being equal, needs less frequent watering. Similarly, a somewhat clayey soil retains moisture longer than a distinctly sandy one. Because porous clay pots containing damp soil evaporate moisture through their sides, soil contained in them dries more quickly than when in plastic pots; this is especially so when atmospheric humidity is low, as it is likely to be on sunny, breezy days and in freely ventilated greenhouses. Because of this, plants in clay pots usually need more frequent watering than do those in plastic pots.

Other environmental factors that affect the need for watering include temperature and light intensity. As the temperature rises, without a balancing increase in the amount of water in the air, the relative humidity of the atmosphere is lowered and the rate of water loss from foliage and other aboveground plant parts by transpiration, and from the soil by evaporation, increases. Light intensity also affects transpiration. In general, the brighter the illumination, the more rapid the rate of transpiration. And so it is that warm, sunny weather with low humidity necessitates more frequent watering than conditions of the reverse order.

To supplement visual observation, experienced gardeners often employ simple tests to determine whether or not a plant needs water. They may poke a finger an inch or more into the soil to ascertain whether it is sufficiently moist below a shallow, dry surface layer, or they lift the pot or other container and judge from its weight whether the moisture content of the soil is satisfactory. Yet another test is to rap the pot with a small wooden mallet or with the knuckles; a dull, heavy response indicates moist or wet soil, while a ringing or "hollow" sound indicates dryness.

When watering, it is important not to disturb the surface soil. To avoid this, various procedures are employed. An obvious one is not to permit a too vigorous flow from the hose or watering can. Another is to "break" the flow either with a sprinkler head, with a simple "spreader" fashioned from a piece of tin or plastic and fitted into the end of the hose or watering can sprout, or even, as is done by many professional gardeners, by pressing a thumb against the end of the hose. The last method, skillfully employed, is the most versatile because it permits as rapid a change in the direction and fineness of the spray as the judgment of the operator deems expedient.

Watering from above, that is making applications to the soil surface, is the most common procedure, but others are sometimes more appropriate or convenient. With pots or pans containing newly sown seeds or small seedlings, to avoid disturbing the surface soil or wetting the seedlings it may be preferable to stand the containers for

Watering houseplants: (a) Pushing aside the leaves of an African-violet to avoid wetting them

(b) Filling saucers, in which the pots are standing, with water to be absorbed through holes in the bottom of the pot

(c) Immersing well-rooted plants is a very thorough method of watering

(d) After the ball of roots is soaked through, the plant is lifted from the water and allowed to drain

part of their height in water until moisture seeps to the surface. Total immersion or partial immersion (that is, to within a short distance of the rim of the container) until water seeping through the basal drainage hole reaches the soil surface is a very effective way of administering a thorough watering. It is particularly useful with very well-rooted specimens, the balls of which are difficult to saturate from the surface, especially if they have been allowed to dry out to the extent that the center of the root ball is dry. Water poured on the surface then may mostly drain downward between the outside of the root ball and the wall of the container.

WATERMELON. This favorite hot weather fruit is *Citrullus lanatus*, a vining annual of the gourd family CUCURBITACEAE. Native to Africa, it occurs as a naturalized species in many warm parts of the world, including the American tropics and subtropics. A distinct variety, the citron or preserving

Watermelon

melon (*C. l. citroides*) has small, hard-fleshed fruits, unsuitable for eating raw, that are made into preserves. Its cultivation is as for watermelons.

Watermelons are easy to grow where summers are long, warm, and humid. Where the growing season is less than 120 days, reliance should be on selected small-fruited or midget varieties that mature in eighty to eighty-five days and succeed as far north as Long Island, New York, and Cape Cod, Massachusetts.

Cultural requirements of watermelons are essentially those of muskmelons, but most sorts need more space, 10 feet apart each way for typical long-season varieties, 6 feet apart in rows 8 feet asunder for midget sorts. Bush varieties may be planted closer.

Well-drained, sandy or other loose soil, liberally enriched with compost or manure and a dressing of a complete fertilizer, is needed. In home gardens it is practicable and fun to raise a plant or two on an old compost pile by filling a hole scooped in its top with two to three bushels of fertile soil.

Sow the seeds, six to each hill, which may be raised or at ground level, after the weather is stabilized and warm, or steal a start on the season by sowing indoors three weeks earlier and transplanting the young plants outdoors. Before the seedlings crowd, thin them out to two or three to a hill.

Routine care includes keeping weeds under control by shallow surface cultivation or by mulching. Black plastic mulch is very effective and in the north has the additional advantage of absorbing sun heat and, thus, warming the ground at the beginning of the season. Dusting or spraying to check depredations of the striped cucumber beetle is likely to be needed. In dry weather, water regularly and sufficiently to keep the foliage from wilting. Extra large watermelons may be had by choosing large-fruited varieties and limiting the number of fruits each plant is permitted to carry. Select the ones to mature as soon as the first few young fruits are formed, then pinch off all others and continue this at three- to five-day intervals throughout the season.

When to harvest is, for the tyro grower, sometimes a little difficult to determine. It

is important that the fruits be fully mature when taken from the vine. A traditional test is to thump the fruit. A ripe watermelon gives a dull, muffled sound, an immature one a higher, more metallic ring.

Varieties suitable for the north include 'Fordhook Hybrid', 'New Hampshire Midget', and 'Sugar Baby', which require a growing season of eighty-five days. More rampant-growing varieties, such as 'Charleston Gray', 'Congo', 'Dixie Queen', 'Stone Mountain', and 'Klondyke', need a growing season of at least ninety days. The pests and diseases of watermelons are those of muskmelons.

WATERMELON, CHINESE is *Benincasa hispida*.

WATERWORT. See Elatine.

WATSONIA (Wats-ònia). Of the sixty or more species of *Watsonia*, of the iris family IRIDACEAE, all except one native to Malagasy (Madagascar) are endemic to Africa, chiefly South Africa. Their natural distribution is often limited to small areas. One kind, *W. fulgens* (syn. *W. angusta*), is naturalized in California. The generic name commemorates the English botanist Dr. William Watson, who died in 1787. Most watsonias resemble gladioluses, but some are of different aspect. An easy way to distinguish between the two genera is to examine the flowers. Those of *Gladiolus* have a stigma with three short, undivided branches, whereas those of *Watsonia* have branches clearly divided into two or more secondary branches. Also, watsonia blooms are nearly symmetrical and have corolla tubes that have a slender-cylindrical lower part and are much enlarged above instead of being evenly-funnel-shaped.

Watsonias are deciduous or more or less evergreen perennial herbaceous plants with corms (storage organs similar to bulbs and often commonly referred to as such, but

Watsonia, unidentified species

differing in being solid instead of composed of separable scales). They have erect, branchless or branched stems with parallel-veined, swordlike leaves and terminal or lateral spikelike racemes of showy red, pink, or white blooms. The flowers have six perianth lobes (petals, or, more correctly, tepals), three stamens, and one style. The fruits are capsules. The perianth lobes, hereafter referred to as petals, as is commonly done, of some sorts flare widely to produce an open-faced flower, in others the blooms are narrowly-tubular and suggest those of lachenalias. The former are more commonly cultivated. For convenience, cultivated watsonias may be grouped as those that bloom in spring or early summer and those that bloom later.

Early-bloomers include popular **W. pyramidata** (syn. *W. rosea*), which attains a height of 4 or 5 feet and has leaves up to 2½ feet long and 1 inch broad. Its many rose-red blooms are on branched stems. Their perianth tubes, conspicuously expanded in their upper parts, are about 1¼ inches long. The flaring petals are 1½ inches long or slightly longer. Closely akin to, and perhaps only a variety of this, **W.**

Watsonia ardernei (flowers)

ardernei (syns. *W. rosea ardernei, W. iridifolia o'brienii*) is a lovely sort not found in the wild since a single clump was discovered in South Africa in 1886. From *W. pyramidata* it differs in having larger, pure white flowers with perianth tubes 2 inches long or longer. Beautiful early-blooming **W. versfeldii** differs from *W. pyramidata* in the upper parts of the perianth tubes of its flowers being narrow- rather than broad-funnel-shaped. Its leaves are up to 3 feet long by 2 inches wide. The bright rose-pink blooms, 3 inches or more across, are on branched stems.

Other early bloomers include rather variable **W. meriana.** From 2 to 3 feet tall, this has leaves 1 foot to 2 feet long and up to ½ inch wide. Its usually branchless stems display pinkish to rose-red flowers about 2 inches long and as much or more across their faces. Also early-flowering, **W. marginata,** up to 5 feet tall, has rose-pink flowers with perianth tubes ¾ inch long and spreading petals almost 1 inch long. Its leaves are up to 2½ feet long by 1½ inches wide.

Rarely exceeding 1 foot in height, early-flowering **W. coccinea** has leaves up to about 9 inches long by ½ inch wide and bright red blooms in branchless, few-flowered spikes. They have curved, cylindrical perianth tubes 2 inches long or a little longer and spreading petals about 1 inch long. From 1 foot to 1½ feet tall, **W. brevifolia** has leaves 9 inches long and under ½ inch wide. Its branchless stems have well-spaced, orange-red flowers with perianth tubes up to 1 inch long and spreading petals up to ¾ inch long. From 9 inches to 1½ feet tall, **W. humilis** has narrow leaves 6 to 9 inches long. Its bright pink flowers have a perianth with a curved tube 1¼ to 1¾ inches long and lobes (petals) about ¾ inch long. From closely similar **W. maculata,** this species differs in its slightly smaller flowers being without purple blotches between the bases of each pair of perianth lobes and in the branches of the stigma overtopping the anthers instead of,

Watsonia meriana

Watsonia aletroides

as in *W. maculata,* being shorter than the anthers.

Very different from the kinds described so far, early blooming **W. aletroides,** up to 2 feet tall, has leaves about 1 foot long by ½ inch wide. Its mostly branchless stems carry up to twelve nodding, slender, cylindrical flowers, about 2 inches long, with petals only about ¼ inch long and not spreading.

Late-blooming **W. beatricis** is especially handsome. Its lovely orange-red flowers are borne on stems that rarely branch. Up to

Watsonia pyramidata

Watsonia ardernei in South Africa

3 feet in height, this has leaves that may be 2½ feet long by 1¼ inches broad. The narrowly-funnel-shaped corolla tube is about 2 inches long, the spreading or slightly recurved petals approximately 1 inch long. Another late bloomer, *W. densiflora* attains a height of 2 to 3 feet and has many rose-red or sometimes white flowers in crowded spikes. Its blooms have perianth tubes 1¼ inches long and spreading petals about ¾ inch long. The leaves are 2 to 3 feet long by ½ to ¾ inch wide. Differing in its flower spikes being looser, *W. longiflora*, 4 to 5 feet tall, has leaves up to 3 feet long by ½ inch wide. On usually branchless stems, its pink to almost white flowers have perianth tubes 2¼ inches long and spreading petals about ¾ inch long. With leaves up to 2 feet long by up to 1½ inches wide and branched stems, *W. wordsworthiana* grows to a height of 4 to 5 feet or more. Its many flowers, in loose spikes, are purplish-lilac and have dark purple anthers. The upper portions of their 2-inch-long perianth tubes are broadly-funnel-shaped. The petals are semispreading and 1¼ inches long.

Garden and Landscape Uses. As garden plants watsonias have the same uses as gladioluses. They are stately and are decorative in groups in flower beds and borders; they provide excellent flowers for cutting. They are also very satisfactory for cultivation in cool greenhouses. Watsonias are sun-lovers that revel in fertile, porous soil that, when their foliage is in evidence, never is excessively dry. They are about as hardy as gladioluses, which means that they can be grown permanently outdoors only where the ground does not freeze deeply enough to injure the corms (bulbs). Elsewhere, the late summer-blooming kinds can be handled like gladioluses and stored over winter.

Cultivation. Outdoors, the corms are planted 3 to 4 inches deep and 4 or 6 inches apart in fall in mild climates, elsewhere in spring. Subsequent care consists of controlling weeds and watering adequately during dry weather. Light staking may be required. Where the plants remain permanently outdoors, they should be fertilized at the beginning of each growing season and be lifted, separated, and replanted every second or third year. A summer mulch helps conserve ground moisture. Where harsh winters prevail, the bulbs must be taken up before frost and stored over winter in a temperature of 40 to 50°F. Those sorts of an evergreen nature that tend to retain their foliage are best packed in very slightly moist peat moss or sand; deciduous kinds may be stored dry like gladioluses.

For early blooming in greenhouses, corms are planted in well-drained pots 6 to 9 inches in diameter in early fall. Fertile, porous soil is used and the corms are set 1 inch to 2 inches beneath the surface

with about as much space between individuals as the diameter of the corms. Water sparingly at first, with increasing frequency as the roots occupy the soil. At all times the greenhouse must be cool and, on favorable occasions, freely ventilated. A night temperature of 45 to 50°F is adequate. Day temperatures should not be more than five to ten degrees higher. Full sun is necessary. As the stems develop, support may be needed; this may be provided by slender bamboo stakes or wires carefully placed so that the corms are not injured. In spring, when the flower stems begin to push up, weekly applications of dilute fertilizers are appropriate. After blooming, water to keep the foliage alive as long as possible, but withhold water from the deciduous kinds after the leaves have died and reduce water for the evergreen kinds during their season of partial rest that follows blooming. Repotting is done in early fall. Propagation is easy by natural multiplication of the corms and by seed.

WATTAKAKA. See Dregea.

WATTLE. See Acacia.

WAX. This word appears in the common names of these plants: Geraldton wax flower (*Chamelaucium uncinatum*), wax flower (*Crowea saligna*, *Eriostemon*), wax gourd (*Benincasa hispida*), wax-mallow (*Malvaviscus arboreus drummondii*), wax-myrtle (*Myrica cerifera*), wax plant (*Hoya*), and wax vine (*Senecio macroglossus*).

WAXBERRY is *Symphoricarpos albus*.

WAXWORK is *Celastrus scandens*.

WAYFARING TREE is *Viburnum lantana*. The American wayfaring tree is *V. alnifolium*.

WEAVERS'-BROOM is *Spartium junceum*.

WEBEROCEREUS (Webero-cèreus). Related to *Selenicereus*, the infrequently cultivated genus *Weberocereus*, of the cactus family CACTACEAE, comprises four more or less vining species, natives of Costa Rica and Panama. The name is derived from that of a Dr. Albert Weber, of France, a student of the cactus family, who died in 1903, and the name of the related genus *Cereus*.

Weberocereuses are epiphytes (plants that perch on trees without taking nourishment from them, sometimes on rocks). They have clambering or pendent, usually three-angled or cylindrical stems, sometimes flattened or three-winged when young, that develop aerial roots. The spines are short. Opening only at night, the short-funnel- to somewhat bell-shaped flowers are pink. The fruits are tubercled and hairy.

The first species described, *W. tunilla* (syn. *Cereus tunilla*) has trailing or hang-

ing, sharply two- to six-, usually four-angled stems, ¼ to 1 inch thick, with clusters of six to twenty short spines commonly at intervals of 1¼ to 2 inches. The solitary, funnel-shaped, pungently scented blooms, up to 3 inches long by 1 inch to 1½ inches wide, have nearly thirty petals (more correctly, tepals), the inner ones pink, the outer pinkish-amber and smaller. The stamens are cream-colored. The pinkish-cream style ends in an eight- to ten-lobed stigma. The fruits are oblongish and about 1¾ inches long by 1¼ inches wide. From the last, *W. trichophorus* differs in having round to blunt-angled stems and clusters, each of thirty to forty hairlike spines and ten ½-inch-long, rigid ones. Intermediate hybrids between the species described above have been raised in California. Other species are *W. biolleyi*, which has stems with four blunt angles that usually lack spines, and *W. panamensis*, the stems of which have usually three or four, but sometimes two or three sharp angles and few spines.

Garden Uses and Cultivation. Weberocereuses are worth growing for their freely produced, fragrant blooms and are very amenable to cultivation. They form tangled masses of stems. In southern California they have survived for several years outdoors. In greenhouses they prosper under conditions that suit many thin-stemmed cactuses. Increase is easy by seed and by cuttings. For further information see Cactuses.

WEBWORMS. The larvae (caterpillars) of certain moths that feed while protected by fine silky webs are called webworms. Many plants, including *Ailanthus*, *Albizia*, *Berberis*, beets, cabbages and cabbage relatives, oaks, pines, and lawn grasses, are the foods of specific kinds. The fall webworm and the garden webworm both feed on many different kinds of plants. For methods of control best suited to particular kinds and regions consult a Cooperative Extension Agent or other local authority.

WEDELIA (Wed-èlia). This is a genus of seventy annuals, herbaceous perennials, subshrubs, and shrubs of the daisy family COMPOSITAE, natives of the tropics and subtropics. They are prostrate or erect and sometimes vining. They have opposite, lobed or lobeless leaves, or the upper ones sometimes alternate, and daisy-like yellow flower heads, occurring either singly or in few-headed clusters. The name of the genus commemorates George Wolfgang Wedel, a German botanist, who died in 1721.

One species, *Wedelia trilobata*, native from southern Florida to South America, is cultivated. It is a trailing, evergreen perennial with rooting stems, and solitary "suns" of flowers about ½ inch in diame-

Wedelia trilobata

ter. Bright green and 2 to 4 inches long, its leaves are shallowly-lobed and coarsely-toothed. It forms a dense carpet 6 to 8 inches tall.

Garden and Landscape Uses and Cultivation. In frost-free climates this is a very good groundcover. It spreads vigorously, endures sun or shade, and thrives in almost any soil. It is suitable for banks and seaside plantings and for use beneath trees. It needs no mowing, but will tolerate it and even stands a certain amount of walking upon. In addition to its value as an outdoor plant in the tropics and warm subtropics, this is a charming plant for hanging baskets in greenhouses. Wherever it is grown, its cultural requirements are of the simplest and it is readily and rapidly multiplied by cuttings and by transplanted rooted pieces. For its best development plenty of moisture and fertilizer should be supplied. Under greenhouse cultivation minimum temperatures of 50 to 60°F are appropriate.

WEDGE-PEA. See Gompholobium.

WEEDS AND THEIR CONTROL. In a broad sense any plant growing where it is not wanted is a weed, however, the designation is most often limited to kinds that not only satisfy that requirement but that also proliferate and colonize new territories where they are equally unwelcome. Some plants, such as crab grass, Canada thistle, mugwort, dodder, and poison-ivy, are regarded as weeds whenever they invade gardens; they are without redeeming horticultural features. Certain other sorts, of which Japanese honeysuckle, bouncing Bet, and water-hyacinths are examples, can serve usefully in appropriate places if kept under control, but may be considered troublesome weeds if they are allowed to run rampant. For instance, the last named can be exquisite in a garden pool, but in

the southern United States and some other warm regions the water-hyacinth can be a very-difficult-to-control weed. It clogs lakes, streams, and other bodies of water, sometimes to the extent of hampering navigation. Because of the large amounts of money that have been spent in attempting to eliminate it, this plant has been called the "million-dollar weed."

Often, location determines whether or not an individual plant is a weed. Dandelions in a lawn are generally so considered, but dandelions cultivated in a vegetable garden are welcome sources of salad greens. The kinds of grass carefully tended as components of lawns may be pestiferous weeds in gravel paths.

Apart from aesthetic considerations, weeds frequently seriously interfere with the well-being of crops and other desirable plants by competing with them for water, nutrients, and light. Also, they may harbor pests and diseases likely to transfer to the more desirable plants. And some, poison-ivy and ragweed, for example, bring discomfort to humans by causing dermatitis, hay fever, and some other ills. Added to all this is the additional cost in labor or money or both, of eliminating or controlling weeds. From the gardeners' point of view weeds are decidedly "bad actors."

Weeds include annuals, biennials, and perennials, the individual plants of which live, respectively, for one year, two years, or three or more years. Methods of control are often related to these life durations. Quite clearly, with annual and biennial weeds measures that prevent them from maturing seeds, and thus providing for a succeeding season's crop, are important and effective. To a greater or lesser extent, as with dandelions, for example, this is also true of perennial weeds. But there are other perennials whose extension and multiplication are achieved by other means as well as, in most cases, by seed. Many, mugwort and some buttercups are examples, spread vigorously by surface stolons or by underground runners. Others, including species of onions (*Allium*) and star-of-Bethlehem (*Ornithogalum*), proliferate by underground bulblets or by aerial bulbils. All of these and many others are frequently multiplied and dispersed, in many cases after being chopped into small pieces, during such common cultural practices as spading, forking, hoeing, raking, and mowing.

Methods of controlling weeds fall into a few patterns. In areas such as vegetable gardens and flower beds devoted to annuals, yearly or more frequent disturbance of the soil by spading, rotary tilling, or plowing eliminates perennial weeds, and annual sorts are relatively easily controlled by hoeing, cultivating, and mulching, supplemented by a certain amount of hand weeding. An unusual method that has been employed by nurseries where large

Geese weeding small evergreens in a nursery in Virginia

A scuffle hoe in use

Using a wheel cultivator in a vegetable garden

Hand weeding may be necessary in flower beds

Digging dandelions from lawns with an asparagus knife, which cuts the roots well below the surface

A teaspoonful of nitrate of soda placed in the center of a dandelion plant will kill it completely

acreages of evergreens are grown, is to turn geese loose among them. The geese devour grasses and many other weeds.

In areas devoted to desirable trees, shrubs, and herbaceous perennials, including lawn grasses, annual deep turning-over of the soil is impracticable. Therefore, perennial weeds can become established more easily and are more difficult to eliminate. The first defense against such colonizers is to avoid inadvertently introducing them to the garden, which is often done by bringing in soil containing seeds or live pieces of them or, not infrequently, by transferring plants with similarly contaminated root balls to clean soil.

To control perennial weeds already present in the garden, constant vigilance and positive action are required. Of primary importance is the need to act promptly. If the infestation is a small one, do not allow it to spread. There are several ways of doing this. One is to dig out the offenders, a procedure effective, for instance, with dandelions and wild onions in lawns. Remove every possible scrap of the plants, even small pieces of their roots and other underground parts, which, if left in the soil, are likely to grow into new individuals. As an alternative to digging out perennial weeds that develop deep taproots, such as dandelions, slice their tops off at surface level and heap about a teaspoonful of nitrate of soda or sulfate of ammonia on the decapitated root. In strong concentrations these nitrogen-rich fertilizers kill the roots and, in lawns, a small circle of grass around them. But as the fertilizer becomes diluted by rain or irrigation, it stimulates the surrounding grass into more vigorous growth, and fertilizes the spots where the weeds and surrounding grass have been killed and thus prepares them for reseeding.

Hoeing is effective against all but the deepest-rooted weeds, and even they are destroyed if the operation is repeated at such short intervals that the weeds have no opportunity to develop any substantial growth of leaves. Any green-leaved plant, including the most persistent weed, will die if denied opportunity to develop foliage. To assure this, one may have to hoe more than once, because parts left in the ground after the first hoeing, and sometimes after the second and third, are likely to contain enough stored food to engender new growth. And in the leaves of this new growth more food is elaborated, which in turn, supports further growth. Of the various types of hoes, none is as generally useful for the destruction of small or smallish weeds as is the scuffle hoe. For bigger weeds, the pull hoe or chop hoe is often more suitable. For additional information about these see the Encyclopedia entry Hoes and Hoeing. The effort needed to hoe is greatly lightened if the weeds are attacked while quite small, which also minimizes the harm they are

likely to do to desirable neighbor plants and maximizes the speed with which ground will be freed of weeds. Cultivators, both hand-operated and powered, serve much the same purpose as hoes, but are less efficient in the destruction of well-established weeds. They disturb the upper 1 inch to 2 inches of soil and the weeds growing therein, but they do not necessarily slice the tops off the weeds, as do hoes. They are most effective when used at fairly frequent intervals, as is commonly done in vegetable gardens.

Mulching to smother weeds by denying them light can give good results. Some strong-growing weeds may push a few shoots up through loose organic mulches, but those are much easier to hand pull than shoots that sprout directly from hard ground; weaker-growing weeds are likely to be completely smothered. Sheets of black plastic mulch, spread over the ground and held in place by a little soil heaped along their edges or by stones, are very effective. Between crops in rows, plastic mulch can be laid in continuous strips; around individual hills of crops, such as cucumbers and squashes, and newly-planted small trees, small squares of plastic mulch can be used to good purpose.

A cleaning procedure that in some cases can produce good results with weed-infested land is to plant the land with a crop of potatoes. This crop will develop heavy growths of foliage that deny light to competing weeds. And their proper care necessitates the fairly frequent disturbance of the soil in the process of hilling them up, with the consequent destruction of young weeds. Other "smother crops" that can be used similarly, but because they do not require hilling up may be less effective than potatoes, are soy beans and buckwheat.

Altering the character of the soil to favor desirable plants is likely to discourage weeds that find existing conditions agreeable. Draining ground that is too wet for the plants one wishes to grow is one example of this technique. Another, more commonly practiced, is changing the pH of the soil, by applying lime or ground limestone to raise it, or sulfur, iron sulfate, or aluminum sulfate to lower it. Soils that lack sufficient nutrients to promote the vigorous growth of desirable plants may be capable of supporting generous populations of weeds that prosper in less fertile ground. In such instances fertilizing to increase the available plant nutrients in the soil brings improvement.

Herbicides, chemicals that kill weeds or adversely affect their growth, have been used for a long time; since World War II their number has increased dramatically. Some are employed extensively and effectively in agriculture, forestry, nursery practice, roadside maintenance, and other large-scale operations concerned with crop production and land management. The use of most kinds by amateur gardeners, except in the care of lawns, is less likely to prove practical and is largely unnecessary. There are several reasons for this. For one, many herbicides are selective as to the kinds of plants they harm. This characteristic can be turned to good use where single crops occupy large areas and their tolerance to particular herbicides is known. However, in gardens, where many kinds of plants are likely to be present in limited areas and their tolerances to herbicides may not be known, the use of such materials is apt to damage desirable plants as well as weeds. Desirable plants, too, are as easily killed by the improper or careless use of nonselective herbicides, those that destroy all vegetation with which they come in contact. A frequent cause of damage comes from the drifting of the mist in which many herbicides are applied. So fine are many of the droplets of this mist that the slightest breeze or movement of the air may carry them considerable distances to settle where they may seriously damage plants they are not intended to harm, some perhaps on neighboring property. Trouble may also come from using sprayers or other equipment that has contained herbicides for other purposes, such as applying insecticides or fungicides. Some herbicides are so persistent and potent that traces of them, even after a thorough rinsing of the equipment, may be enough to do serious damage later. It is always wise to keep equipment used for herbicides quite separate from that used for other purposes. And be sure to always read and follow the manufacturer's directions.

Herbicides are grouped according to the manner in which they are used and in the way in which they kill. Preemergent weed-killers, usually in granular or powder form, are applied to fairly moist soil before the weed seeds germinate. An often practical alternative to the employment of pre-emergent herbicides when making the ground ready for seed sowing is to complete the preparation of the soil two or three weeks ahead of the sowing date, then to keep its surface moist enough to encourage the germination of weed seeds, and finally, when the young plants appear, to eradicate them by shallowly cultivating with a scuffle hoe. Postemergent weed killers, usually sprayed on in liquid form, are applied after the plants are in evidence.

Some herbicides kill plant tissues by direct contact, others are hormone-type preparations that, after being absorbed, destroy by disrupting the metabolism of the plant, often to the extent that the foliage and other aboveground parts become distorted and crippled as a prelude to death. Yet other herbicides are absorbed by the foliage and are translocated through the plant tissues to the roots, which they kill. With herbicides of this type, which are generally used on such woody plants as brush and poison-ivy, it is important that the weeds are in full foliage at the time of application so that as much leaf surface as possible is present to absorb the spray.

The sorts of weeds likely to be most troublesome vary somewhat in different parts of North America, and most State Agricultural Experiment Stations issue pamphlets describing and often illustrating the worst offenders and recommending methods of control. These are usually available from the local Cooperative Extension Agent.

Kinds that are best kept in check by hoeing or cultivating, or, if they invade lawns, by digging out, hand pulling, or using a selective herbicide include the following: beggar ticks (*Bidens frondosa*), flowers yellow, fruits barbed, and capable of sticking to clothing; bird's-foot trefoil (*Lotus corniculatus*), resembling a miniature clover with yellow flower heads; black bindweed or wild-buckwheat (*Polygonum convolvulus*), a vigorous, twining vine with more or less heart-shaped leaves and little, white to pink, morning-glory-like flowers; black nightshade (*Solanum nigrum*), erect and bushy, with elliptic to ovate leaves, drooping clusters of starry, white flowers, and black, berry-like fruits; burdock (*Arctium lappa*), erect, with large, coarse, nonprickly leaves and somewhat thistle-like flower heads succeeded by burlike fruits; cat's ear or California-dandelion (*Hypochoeris radicata* and *H. glabra*), with basal rosettes of coarsely-toothed to deeply-lobed, lanceolate to oblanceolate leaves, and erect, leafless stalks topped by yellow, dandelion-like flower heads; chickory (*Cichorium intybus*), erect, with milky juice, oblanceolate, lobed or toothed leaves, and on slender branches rather distantly-spaced, rather dandelion-like, beautiful blue to purplish flower heads with many strap-shaped petals; chickweed (*Stellaria media*) and mouse-ear chickweed (*Cerastium vulgatum*), low creepers with small, elliptic to ovate leaves and little, starry, white flowers; crab grass (*Digitaria sanguinalis*), with spreading, rooting stems and erect stalks with flower spikes displayed in finger-like fashion; dayflower (*Commelina* species), erect to sprawling annuals and perennials, with ovate to elliptic leaves and blue to purple flowers with two large petals and one smaller one; gallant soldier (*Galinsoga* species), freely-branching, erect annuals with more or less ovate leaves and small, yellow-centered flower heads with a few white, toothed, petal-like ray florets; ground-ivy (*Glechoma hederacea*), a trailer with small, roundish, round-toothed leaves and, from the leaf axils, small blue flowers; horsetail (*Equisetum arvense*), with erect, branched, leafless, green stems of feathery aspect that terminate in conelike reproductive organs; knawel (*Scleranthus annuus*), a prostrate carpeter with forked stems, tiny, slender leaves, and tiny, greenish flowers; knotweed (*Polygonum aviculare*), a spreader with slender, prostrate stems, small, bluish-green leaves, and tiny, green flowers; lady's thumb (*Polygonum persicaria*), branched, erect to sprawling, and with lanceolate leaves, each with a dark spot, and tiny, pinkish flowers; mallow or cheeses (*Malva rotundifolia*), a low, spreading biennial with shallowly-

The narrow-leaved plantain (*Plantago lanceolata*)

Crab grass

Purslane or pussley

lobed, toothed, roundish leaves and white flowers from their axils; May-weed or dog fennel (*Anthemis* species), erect plants with a strong odor, finely-dissected leaves, and yellow-centered, white, daisy-like flowers; Mexican-tea or wormseed (*Chenopodium ambrosioides*), vigorous, erect, with an unpleasant odor, and almost stalkless, with lanceolate to ovate, lobed or toothed leaves and, from the upper leaf axils, spikes of tiny, greenish flowers; mouse-ear hawkweed (*Hieraceum pilosella*) and orange hawkweed or devil's paintbrush (*H. aurantiacum*), spreading by prostrate runners and having oblanceolate or elliptic, hairy leaves, and erect, nearly leafless stems carrying small, dandelion-like flower heads, those of the mouse-ear hawkweed yellow, those of the orange hawkweed red-orange; pigweed or lamb's quarters (*Chenopodium album*), erect, usually much-branched, with ovate to lanceolate leaves, the young ones, especially, of white-mealy appearance, the older ones often reddish, and, from the leaf axils, clusters of tiny, greenish-white flowers; plantain (*Plantago* species), with basal rosettes of spreading or erect, ribbed leaves, and slender, crowded spikes, atop erect stalks, of tiny flowers; prickly-lettuce (*Lactuca serriola*), tall, erect, with elliptic, deeply-lobed to sometimes lobeless, prickly-edged and -margined, bluish-green leaves and, in loose clusters, pale yellow flowers; prostrate pigweed (*Amaranthus graecizans*), spreading, mat-forming, with usually crowded, oblong to obovate leaves and, clustered in their axils, tiny, greenish flowers; purslane or pussley (*Portulaca oleracea*), low, with prostrate stems, flat, more or less spatula-shaped, succulent leaves, and tiny, stalkless, yellowish flowers; ragweed (*Ambrosia artemisiifolia*), tall, coarse, usually branched, with large, deeply-lobed and toothed, ovate to elliptic leaves and, in slender spikes, clusters of small, greenish flowers; sandbur (*Cenchrus pauciflorus*), shallow-rooted, upright or spreading grass, with terminal spikes of prickly burs that contain the inconspicuous flowers; scarlet pimpernel or poor man's weatherglass (*Anagallis arvensis*), low, more or less prostrate, with little, ovate, stalkless leaves, and small, bell-shaped, red, blue, or white flowers from the leaf axils; self-heal (*Prunella vulgaris*), low and spreading, with lanceolate to ovate leaves and mostly terminal, cylindrical spikes of small, violet-blue, pinkish, or white flowers; sheep's sorrel (*Rumex acetosella*), low, acid-flavored, with variable, usually three-lobed leaves and slender spikes of tiny clusters of minute flowers; shepherd's purse (*Capsella bursa-pastoris*), erect, with clustered, oblong, lobed, basal leaves, and erect stems with tiny, four-petaled, white flowers followed by little, purse-shaped, stalked seed pods; sow-thistle (*Sonchus* species), erect, with milky sap, lobed or lobeless, toothed, elliptic to

ovate leaves, and loose clusters of yellow, dandelion-like flowers; spearscale or orach (*Atriplex patula*), erect to prostrate, with linear to lanceolate or triangular, often toothed leaves and, from the leaf axils, slender spikes of minute flowers; speedwell (*Veronica arvensis*), low to prostrate, with small, ovate leaves and erect spikes of little, blue flowers; spotted spurge (*Euphorbia maculata*), with spreading, prostrate stems, little, ovate leaves, each with a red spot, minute flowers, and milky sap; spurrey (*Spergula arvensis*), low, spreading, with threadlike leaves in whorls, and minute flowers; strawberry blite (*Chenopodium capitatum*), erect, branched from the base, with more or less triangular, coarsely-toothed leaves and globular clusters of tiny flowers, followed by red fruits; wild mustard (*Brassica* species), erect, often branched, with leaves and many bright yellow, four-petaled flowers; and yarrow (*Achillea millefolium*), erect, strong-smelling, with fine, ferny leaves and flat clusters of small, white flowers.

Deep-rooted weeds that, except when small, usually should be dug out, but that may be eradicated by repeated hoeing at frequent intervals, include the following: Canada thistle (*Cirsium arvense*), tall, erect,

with coarsely-toothed, spiny, lanceolate leaves and showy, thistle heads of pinkish-purple or sometimes white flowers; dock (*Rumex* species), erect, with coarse, broad to narrower, sometimes wavy-margined leaves and terminal, crowded clusters of greenish to brownish flowers and fruits; dandelion (*Taraxacum officinale*), with basal rosettes of jagged-toothed leaves, and erect, hollow stalks terminating in large, showy, golden-yellow flower heads, succeeded by globular, fluffy heads of white seeds; poison-ivy (*Rhus radicans* and related species), woody-stemmed, vining or shrubby, with leaves of three large, broad leaflets, and tiny, greenish flowers, all parts of the entire plant causing severe dermatitis if they come in contact with the skin; quack grass or witch grass (*Agropyron repens*), with long, prostrate rhizomes, more or less erect stems with flat leaves, and slender, terminal spikes of inconspicuous flowers; and Russian-thistle (*Salsola kali tenuifolia*), tall, erect, freely-branched, with red stems, more or less prickly, slender leaves, and little, inconspicuous flowers.

WEEVILS. Weevils, which include sorts called curculios and snout beetles, form a

Dandelions develop long, deep taproots

suborder of beetles characterized by heads that extend into long or short snouts from which a pair of club-ended, elbowed antennae protrude. Like all beetles, they have four distinct life phases: the egg, the grub or larva, the pupa, and the adult insect. As larvae and adults, many sorts feed on roots, stems, fruits, seeds, or other plant parts.

Probably unique among insects in having a monument erected to it, the cotton boll weevil (still a serious pest), following its introduction to the United States from Mexico in 1892, caused such devastation in the cotton belt that farmers were obliged to institute sanitary measures, abandon one-crop agriculture in favor of diversification, and institute crop rotations, all to the benefit of their region. In recognition of this, at Enterprise, Alabama, a fountain was installed inscribed as follows:

IN PROFOUND APPRECIATION
OF THE BOLL WEEVIL
AND WHAT IT HAS DONE
AS THE HERALD OF PROSPERITY
THIS MONUMENT IS ERECTED
BY THE CITIZENS OF
ENTERPRISE, COFFEE COUNTY,
ALABAMA

The cotton boll weevil is of little direct concern to gardeners, but a number of other weevils are, some of these are highly destructive. They include the black orchid weevil, black vine or taxus weevil, cattleya weevil, hollyhock weevil, strawberry root weevil, and white pine weevil. Control measures must be tailored to the particular sort of weevil. For up-to-date information on control, consult County Cooperative Agents or State Agricultural Experiment Stations.

WEIGELA (Wei-gèla). Quite distinct from the strictly American, closely related genus *Diervilla*, in which they were formerly included, the dozen species of eastern Asian *Weigela* (sometimes spelled *Weigelia*), together with horticultural selections and hybrids, compose a group of mostly hardy deciduous shrubs, the chief attraction of which is their usually profuse displays of showy blooms. Belonging to the honeysuckle family CAPRIFOLIACEAE, these bear a name commemorating the German professor Christian Ehrenfried Weigel, who died in 1831.

Unlike diervillas, weigelas do not spread by underground stolons and almost always have white, pink, or red flowers, very rarely yellow or greenish-yellow ones. Their leaves are opposite, undivided, and toothed. The blooms, on short, leafy shoots of the current season's growth that come from stems of the previous year, are tubular, but not two-lipped as are those of diervillas. They have a five-parted or five-

Weigela florida

cleft calyx and a corolla funnel-shaped in its lower half, bell-shaped above. The five spreading lobes (petals) of the corolla are usually of unequal size. There are five stamens and one style. The fruits are many-seeded capsules.

Two species that have played important parts in the parentage of hybrid weigelas are *W. florida* (syn. *W. rosea*), of China and Korea, and *W. floribunda*, of Japan. The earliest weigela to be brought to European and American gardens, **W. florida,** was introduced in 1845. A spreading shrub about 6 feet tall with young shoots with two longitudinal lines of hairs or hairless, it has short-stalked to nearly stalkless, elliptic to obovate, long-pointed leaves, 2 to 4 inches long, hairy on the veins of their undersides and on the midribs above. The 1¼-inch-long flowers, mostly in groups of three or four, have narrow calyx lobes and roundish petals. The stigma is two-lobed. The seed capsules are hairless. Varieties are *W. f. foliis-purpureis*, not over 4 feet tall, with dark purplish-green foliage and pink blooms; *W. f. variegata*, compact and with leaves margined with light yellow; and *W. f. v. nana*, even smaller than the last and with similarly variegated foliage. One of the most attractive *W. florida* varieties and one of the hardiest weigelas, *W. f. venusta* has light purplish-pink blooms. The variant generally grown as *W. candida*, especially noteworthy because its flowers do not

Weigela florida variegata

become pinkish as they age, appears to be a white-flowered variety of *W. florida*.

About 10 feet tall, **W. floribunda** has slender, softly-hairy branches and short-stalked, ovate to broad-elliptic leaves 2 to 4 inches in length, hairy on both surfaces and more conspicuously so beneath than above. Usually in clusters and commonly stalkless, the 1-inch-long, funnel-shaped blooms have calyxes divided to their bases.

Weigela floribunda versicolor

The blood-red corollas, hairy on their outsides, have spreading lobes. The style protrudes and is tipped with a headlike stigma. The seed capsules are hairy. Variety *W. f. grandiflora* has large brownish-red flowers, those of *W. f. versicolor* open greenish-white and change to red or crimson.

Other species occasionally cultivated, some of which have entered into the parentage of hybrids, are these: *W. coraeensis,* of Japan, up to 15 feet tall, has hairless stems and broad-elliptic to elliptic or obovate, abruptly-pointed leaves 3 to 4½ inches long, hairless above except on the veins, beneath hairless or sparsely hairy. In clusters of several, the flowers are stalkless. Their calyxes are divided to their bases. Whitish or pale pink when they first open, they become deeper pink as they age. *W. hortensis* is Japanese. Up to 10 feet tall, this has hairy young shoots and ovate to obovate leaves, 2 to 4 inches in length, their upper surfaces slightly hairy at first, later hairless or practically so. Beneath, they are heavily clothed with grayish hairs. In threes on long stalks, the carmine-red flowers are about 1¼ inches long. Their styles protrude. *W. japonica,* a native of Japan and attaining 10 feet in height, has

Weigela coraeensis

young shoots with or without two longitudinal lines of hairs. Its 2- to 4-inch-long, elliptic to elliptic-oblong leaves, slightly hairy above, are hairy along the veins on their undersides. Three on each stalk, the flowers, whitish at first, become carmine-red as they age. Their calyxes are cleft to their bases. *W. middendorffiana,* of Japan, China, and Manchuria, 4 to 5 feet tall, has two longitudinal rows of hairs on its young shoots. Its leaves are oblong to narrowly-ovate, pointed, and 2 to 3½ inches long. The veins on the upper surfaces are short-hairy. The undersides are coarsely-hairy, especially on the veins. Terminal on the shoots and in the axils of the upper leaves, the nearly stalkless flowers are solitary or paired. They have a deeply-cleft, two-lipped calyx. The flowers, approximately 1½ inches long, are sulfur-yellow spotted with orange. *W. praecox,* of Japan, Korea, and Manchuria, is the earliest species in bloom. Up to 6 feet tall, it has young shoots

Weigela praecox

with two longitudinal lines of hairs and nearly stalkless, ovate to ovate-oblong leaves, 1½ to 3 inches long, that are hairy on their upper surfaces, softly so below. The stalkless blooms, solitary or in pairs and approximately 1¼ inches long, have calyxes cleft to about their middles. They are pink to purplish-pink, purple-throated, and hairy on the outsides of the calyxes.

Garden varieties and hybrids are numerous and more commonly planted than the species. Many are too similar to warrant having more than a few in any one garden. Here are some of the best. Of erect growth, vigorous 'Bristol Ruby' has bright ruby-red blooms. Largest-flowered, 'Conquerant' has rose-pink blooms about 2 inches wide. Because its flowers open white and then change to pink, 'Dame Blanche' is bicolored when in bloom. An old favorite and still very worthwhile, 'Eva Rathke' is compact and has bright crimson flowers. Vigorous 'Mont Blanc' has fragrant,

A hybrid Weigela

white blooms. The flowers of 'Perle' are large, white with a yellow throat, and pink-edged on the petals. The darkest red-flowered weigela, 'Seduction' blooms early and very freely. Of purplish-pink-flowered sorts, 'Styriaca' is outstanding. An excellent, very hardy kind most correctly identified as 'Vanicekii' is grown under several names including 'Cardinal Red', 'Newport Red', and 'Rhode Island Red'. Hardier than similar and popular 'Bristol Ruby', it has bright red blooms.

Garden and Landscape Uses. Formerly more popular, weigelas must in the main be accounted among flowering shrubs highly attractive for the short time they are in bloom, but are of little interest at other seasons. The only exceptions are variegated-leaved varieties, and these, like most shrubs with variegated foliage, must be used sparingly and with some caution if incongruous effects are to be avoided. These sorts are usually at their best where they receive just a little shade.

Weigelas possess the virtues of being remarkably free of pests and diseases and of withstanding city conditions well. They have the disadvantage, in the north at least, of their many twiggy shoots dying back from the tips in winter, necessitating minor early spring pruning to maintain a tidy appearance. They can be employed in shrub borders, foundation plantings, and at the fringes of woodlands. They look particularly well at watersides, where they must be on ground at least a foot or two above water level.

Cultivation. Best results are had with weigelas in fertile soils not excessively dry. They succeed in sun or part-day shade. Given conditions approximating these, they need no special care. Prune annually as soon as flowering is through by removing branches beginning to crowd and weak ones that cannot be expected to bloom well the next year. Some of the strongest branches may need to be shortened, but pruning is chiefly a thinning-out process whose purpose is to admit light and air and encourage the development of strong new shoots. A secondary pruning in late winter or early spring to snip off shoots that may have died back or have been killed back in winter is frequently needed. Propagation is very easily achieved by summer cuttings of fairly firm shoots planted in a greenhouse or cold frame propagating bed or under mist, and by hardwood cuttings taken after the leaves drop in fall. Species are also easily had from seed, but hybrids and varieties do not reproduce true to type from this method of reproduction.

WEINGARTIA (Wein-gàrtia). Some students of the cactus family CACTACEAE include *Weingartia* in *Gymnocalycium*. Those who consider it separately recognize five species, all South American. The name is commemorative of Wilhelm Weingart, a nineteenth-century German botanist.

Weingartias are small, often having big taproots and usually solitary, spherical to cylindrical stems (plant bodies) with conspicuous ribs deeply notched into tubercles, each tipped with an areole sprouting a cluster of strong spines. The funnel-shaped blooms remain open by day.

Native to Bolivia and Peru, *W. neocumingii* (syn. *Gymnocalycium neocumingii*) has a flattened-spherical to flat-topped cylindrical stem, up to 8 inches tall by one-half as wide, with sixteen to eighteen or more spiraled ribs. The starlike clusters of spines have generally twenty or more needlelike, white-tipped radials ¼ to ⅜ inch long and up to ten similar, scarcely longer centrals. The flowers, from the sides of the plant bodies near their tops, are orange-yellow to yellow and 1 inch long or a little longer. From the last, *W. neumanniana* (syn. *Gymnocalycium neumannianum*), of Argentina, differs in its stems being up to 3 inches high by two-thirds as wide and in having about fourteen ribs. Also, its considerably longer spines are in clusters of six radials and one central. The radials are ¾ inch long, the central nearly twice as long. The yellow to reddish-orange flowers are 1 inch in length. Deep yellow blooms, about 1 inch wide, are borne by Bolivian *W. fidaiana* (syn. *Gymnocalycium fidaianum*). This has formidably-spined, gray-green plant bodies, sometimes exceeding 8 inches in height and 4½ inches in width, with usually thirteen to fifteen ribs of rounded tubercles and spine clusters of about nine pale yellow to blackish radials, some 1¼ inches long, and three or four 2-inch-long centrals. The fruits are small.

Garden Uses and Cultivation. Not much trouble is likely to accompany the cultivation of these cacti. They are adaptable for rock gardens in mild desert regions and for greenhouse cactus collections. They respond to treatment that suits most small desert cacti and are easily raised from seed and cuttings or offsets. They succeed in well-drained gritty soil and need moderate watering and a sunny location. Indoors a winter night temperature of 50°F is adequate, with a rise of a few degrees by day allowed. For more information see Cactuses.

WEINMANNIA (Wein-mánnia). The genus *Weinmannia*, of the cunonia family CUNONIACEAE, consists of 100 or more species mostly of the southern hemisphere and widely distributed there except in Africa. The only two native to New Zealand are occasionally cultivated in mild parts of the United States. The name honors Johann Wilhelm Weinmann, an early eighteenth-century German apothecary.

Weinmannias are evergreen trees and shrubs, with opposite, pinnately-divided or undivided leaves, and flowers with four- or five-cleft calyxes, four or five petals, eight or ten stamens, and two persistent styles. The fruits are leathery capsules.

A tree 70 to 90 feet tall, *W. racemosa* has stalked, leathery, mostly undivided, toothed, ovate-elliptic to elliptic or ovate leaves 1¼ to 4 inches long by up to 1½ inches wide. Those of young seedlings and juvenile specimens are thinner than the leaves of older specimens and have three leaflets or are three-lobed. The white, cream, or pink flowers are in hairless or nearly hairless, erect racemes up to 4 or 5 inches in length. Their petals are up to ⅛ inch long. The stamens protrude.

From 40 to 50 feet tall, *W. sylvicola* has its younger shoots, leafstalks, and branches of the flower clusters densely-hairy. As a seedling, its leaves typically are of five leaflets, some of which may be divided again. Juvenile specimens commonly have leaves of up to ten leaflets. Adult foliage is variable in form and size. Its leaves have three to five leaflets or rarely are undivided. The leaflets are leathery-obovate to broadly-elliptic, toothed, and 1½ to 2½ inches in length. White to pale pink, the flowers, about 1/12 inch in diameter, are in racemes 2 to 6 inches in length. The leaves of variety *W. s. betulina* have three obovate leaflets, smaller than those of the species.

Garden and Landscape Uses and Cultivation. In New Zealand the foliage of *W. racemosa*, there called red-birch, is esteemed for cutting for decorative purposes. Weinmannias are interesting trees for California and regions with similarly mild climates. They are propagated by seed, and by cuttings in a greenhouse propagating bench or under mist.

WELDENIA (Wel-dènia). Named in honor of Ludwig von Weldon, an officer in the Austrian army and a naturalist, who died in 1853, *Weldenia* is a charming member of the spiderwort family COMMELINACEAE.

The only species of the genus, *W. candida* is a tuberous herbaceous plant not hardy in the north. A native of mountain-

Weldenia candida (flowers partly open)

Weldenia candida (flowers wide open)

ous parts of Mexico and Guatemala, it has a short, branchless stem and a rosette of usually six to eight strap-shaped to triangular-lanceolate, wavy-edged leaves, 2 to 6 inches long, folded inward toward their bases. The 1-inch-wide, pure white blooms come in clusters from near the centers of the rosettes. They have a three-cleft, loosely tubular calyx, a corolla with a long, slender tube and three broad, spreading lobes (petals), six stamens, and one style. The fruits are capsules.

Garden Uses and Cultivation. This is choice for growing in pots in alpine greenhouses, and in regions of mild winters and cool summers for rock gardens outdoors. For its successful cultivation it needs extremely well-drained soil, which should be kept dryish during the plant's season of dormancy. Propagation is easy by root cuttings and by seed.

WELSH-POPPY is *Meconopsis cambrica*.

WELWITSCHIA (Welwítsch-ia). The only representative of this genus is one of the most extraordinary of the world's plants. It has no close relatives, living or fossil. It neither looks nor behaves like any other species. It is a unique relic of a flora of long bygone ages. Because of this, botanists regard **Welwitschia mirabilis** (syn. *W. bainesii*) as constituting the distinct welwitschia family WELWITSCHIACEAE. Distantly related to it are *Gnetum* and *Ephedra*. No flowers, in the ordinary sense of the word, are produced by *Welwitschia*. Its reproductive organs are conelike. Because its ovules are naked, *Welwitschia* is included in the gymnosperms. It inhabits deserts in southwest Africa, regions so dry that the rainfall averages only about 2 inches a year and in some years is nil. The name commemorates Dr. Friedrich Welwitsch, a botanical explorer, who died in 1872.

Welwitschia mirabilis, the botanic garden, Stellenbosch, South Africa

Welwitschia mirabilis in fruit, the botanic garden, Stellenbosch, South Africa

To gain a clear picture of this species, it is necessary to understand something of its development and structure. Each plant has a short, nearly circular stem or trunk that in large specimens may be 4 feet in diameter and up to 1 foot long. Below, it tapers into a very long taproot. Except for a short portion of its two-lobed top, the trunk is buried in the ground. From a groove in each of its terminal lobes arises a broad, flat, tough, leathery, strap-shaped leaf. These begin to develop when the plant is about one year old and at the time the cotyledons of the young seedling shrivel. No other leaves are produced throughout

the plant's life, even though this may be one century or more. Unlike the leaves of other plants, those of welwitschias retain the power to grow throughout their lives. Cells at their bases continue to divide and increase in number. As they do, the leaves lengthen and at the same time widen at their bottoms, so that no matter how large the circumference of the trunk becomes the bases of the pair of leaves completely encircle it. The leaves of sizable specimens arch upward for a foot or two and outward from the trunk and then bend downward until they are in contact with the ground, perhaps six feet from the center of the plant. As a result of this contact and of being whipped about by wind, the ends of the leaves fray and subsequently die. This splitting often extends back into living parts and gives the effect of an octopus-like specimen with several radiating leaves. Male cones are described as being "as big as the last two joints of most little fingers" and female cones "red and about the size of turkey eggs." The sexes are on different plants. Under favorable circumstances female cones produce many winged seeds.

Garden Uses and Cultivation. Only in botanical gardens and similar places is the cultivation of this very interesting species ordinarily attempted, and then rarely with success. Fresh seeds germinate without difficulty, but in the majority of cases the plants perish in early life. At botanical gardens in Berlin, Germany, and Montreal, Canada, as well as in its native South Africa and some other places, specimens raised from seed have flourished for one or two decades or more and have produced cones. Here is the method that proved satisfactory at Montreal. Seeds were sown in very well-drained pans (shallow pots) containing, according to a horticulturist there, "a very lean mixture of granitic sand and crushed brick with a trace of very old leaf mold." Immediately after sowing, the pan was well watered; later

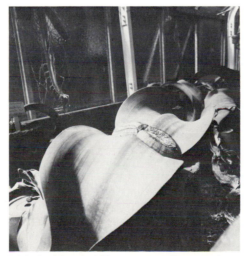

Welwitschia mirabilis in a greenhouse, the botanic gardens, Berlin, Germany

applications, however, were very sparingly made by immersing the pan partway and permitting moisture to seep from below. At the end of about five months the pan was emptied and the seedlings separated, with care taken not to break their brittle roots. Then a 1½-inch layer of pieces of broken pot was placed into the bottom of a 12-inch pot. These were moistened, and a drain tile 1 foot long and 3 inches wide was stood vertically in the center of the pot. A seedling was then carefully taken and held in the center of the drain tile with its roots dangling straight down. With a long-handled spoon, soil of the kind used in the seed pan was added at the bottom of the tile to a depth of about 3 inches. The rest of the tile, with the exception of the top 2 inches, was filled around the roots with a mixture of equal parts of limestone crushed to about ¼ inch size and granitic sand, and this was topped off with crushed limestone. Into the bottom of the space between the outside of the drain tile and the pot was put a 2- or 3-inch layer of good topsoil mixed with sand and a small amount each of bonemeal and dried sheep manure; the remainder was filled with crushed limestone and sand topped with a layer of limestone.

The newly transplanted seedlings were watered sparingly at first, later about once a week. No water was ever applied to the interior of the drain tile, only to the area between the tile and the pot. After the plants had become well established, water given from April to September was enriched by the addition of a very little highly soluble complete liquid fertilizer. No fertilizer was added to the water given from fall to spring. The plants were kept in a sunny greenhouse along with cactuses and other succulents. A winter night temperature of 50°F was maintained. Temperatures by day in winter were only a few degrees higher. Summer temperatures often exceeded 90°F. Every third year the layers of stone, sand, and soil within and without the drain tile were carefully removed, until the roots were reached, and were replaced with fresh supplies of the same mixtures. Because of the serious hazard of damaging the root system, repotting was never attempted.

A slightly different procedure proved successful in Arizona. A red clay agricultural drain tile 2 feet, or better 4 feet, long and 6 inches wide was chosen as a container in which to sow the seed. A clay flower pot that just fitted inside the tile was inserted at one end and cemented to form the bottom of the container. Crocks, or similar coarse material, were placed in the bottom of the pot to a depth of 2 to 3 inches; the tile was then filled to within 2 inches of its brim with a mixture of two-thirds ⅛- to ¼-inch pumice and one-third commercial potting soil and its surface covered with a thin layer of pumice. Next, the membranous wings were removed from the seeds, which were then dusted with a fungicide, sown on the surface of the pumice, covered with a ½-inch layer of pumice, and lightly misted with water. The top of the tile was then covered with a sheet of glass or polyethylene plastic film. The seeds germinated in about one week. As soon as the seedlings were well up, the cover was removed and the seedlings exposed to bright light. More pumice was added around seedlings that tended to push themselves out of the soil. Watering was done sparingly and, from the end of the fourth month on, a houseplant fertilizer, used at one-quarter the recommended strength, was applied once a month from spring to fall. The plants were grown in full sun.

WELWITSCHIACEAE — Welwitschia Family. The characteristics of this family of gymnosperms are those of its only genus *Welwitschia*.

WERCKLEA (Wèrck-lea). Two Costa Rican trees of the mallow family MALVACEAE are the only representatives of *Wercklea*, named in honor of Carlo Werckle, a nineteenth-century Costa Rican botanical collector. One is planted for ornament in Florida, southern California, Hawaii, and other warm-climate regions.

Closely related to *Hibiscus*, the genus *Wercklea* differs in that the bracts beneath its blooms form a three-lobed cup instead of being several and separate. The fruits are capsules.

From 20 to 35 feet in height, **W. insignis** is an evergreen with round to kidney-shaped, bright green leaves, 8 inches to 1¼ feet in diameter, that have green or reddish stalks, and veins that extend from the leaf bases like the fingers of an outspread hand. The solitary flowers, much like those of single hibiscuses or hollyhocks, are borne in winter or spring. They have stalks 6 inches long and blades about 5 inches wide. Rosy-lilac with paler or yellow bases to their corollas, they are succeeded by bristly, 2-inch-long seed capsules. Equally attractive, but with yellow blooms, **W. lutea**, is not known to be cultivated.

Garden and Landscape Uses and Cultivation. In ordinary garden soil in sun, *W. insignis* grows without appreciable trouble. Its hardiness is not definitely known, but it is unlikely that it will survive more than light frosts and undoubtedly it is at its best where not subjected even to those. It is easily propagated by seed.

WERCKLEOCEREUS (Werckleo-cèreus). Two species of climbing cactuses that, except for their flowers, much resemble *Hylocereus* constitute *Werckleocereus*. The genus belongs in the cactus family CACTACEAE and is native to Central America. Its name honors C. Werckle, a Costa Rican collector of the late nineteenth century.

These cactuses are epiphytes, they perch on trees without taking nourishment from them. Their usually three-angled stems develop aerial roots and have areoles (areas from which the spines of cactuses arise) bearing a tuft of wool and bristles or soft spines. The flowers are short-funnel-shaped with the outsides of the perianth tubes and ovaries with almost black spines sprouting from black woolly areoles. The fruits are spherical and spiny. The ovaries and fruits are without leafy scales.

Native to Guatemala, **W. glaber** differs from *W. tonduzii*, of Costa Rica, in having more slender stems, and weak spines instead of only bristles. Its slightly glaucous stems are lumpy at their angles and have areoles with one to four spines. The flowers are at least 4 inches long, their ovaries and perianth tubes furnished with clusters of eight short, yellow to brown spines. The outer perianth segments (petals) are greenish or brownish, the inner white. The style is pale yellow, the stigma white. The stems of **W. tonduzii** are not glaucous and have almost straight edges with usually three, but occasionally four angles. The flowers are not over 3¼ inches long and have clusters of black wool and black spines on their ovaries and the outsides of the perianth tubes. The outer perianth segments are brownish-pink, the inner pink to creamy-yellow. The stigma is green, the fruit yellow and spiny.

Garden and Landscape Uses and Cultivation. These forest cactuses need warm conditions and some shade. Their requirements and uses are those of *Hylocereus*. For a general discussion of their needs see Cactuses.

WEST INDIAN. This forms parts of the common names of these plants: West Indian arrowroot (*Maranta arundinacea*), West-Indian-birch (*Bursera simaruba*), West-Indian-cedar (*Cedrela odorata*), West-Indian-Ebony (*Brya ebenus*), West Indian gherkin (*Cucumis anguria*), and West-Indian-locust (*Hymenaea courbaril*).

WESTRINGIA (West-ríngia) — Australian-Rosemary. Native only in Australia and Tasmania, *Westringia*, of the mint family LABIATAE, comprises about twenty species of bushy shrubs. Its name commemorates Dr. Johan Peter Westring, a Swedish physician, who died in 1833.

Westringias have undivided, generally rigid leaves in whorls (circles) of three to six and, from the leaf axils or rarely in terminal clusters, stalkless or nearly stalkless, asymmetrical, two-lipped, white to mauve flowers. The blooms have a five-toothed calyx and a tubular corolla generally hairy on its inside, with the upper lip two- and the lower lip three-lobed. There are two fertile and two sterile stamens and one style. The fruits consist of four little nutlets (commonly called seeds).

Because of its similarity in aspect to true rosemary (*Rosmarinus*), **W. rosmariniformis** (syn. *W. fruticosa*) is called Australian-rosemary and coast-rosemary in its homeland. Bushy and 3 to 5 feet tall, it has gray-green, leathery, lanceolate to linear leaves, up to 1 inch long, in circles of four. They have recurved margins, glossy upper surfaces, and white undersides. The flowers, ½ inch long and hairy on their outsides, are white to pale blue and in circles of four. It is planted to some extent in gardens in southern California.

Westringia rosmariniformis

Westringia rosmariniformis (flowers)

Garden and Landscape Uses and Cultivation. Australian-rosemary is suited for outdoor cultivation in sunny, dryish climates with little or no frost. It withstands exposure to sun, wind, and salt spray. Because of this and its liking for rather sandy, well-drained soil, it is useful for seaside gardens. It can be employed effectively in many places where a low dense shrub is needed, and can be sheared or pruned to become a low hedge. This species comes readily from seed and is easily propagated by cuttings.

WHAU is *Entelea arborescens*.

WHIN is *Ulex europaeus*. Petty whin is *Genista anglica*.

WHIPPLEA (Whíp-plea)—Modesty or Yerba-de-Selva. Related to currants and gooseberries, although not closely resembling them, and to *Jamesia*, modesty or yerba-de-selva is a deciduous subshrub abundant on shaded slopes from Oregon to California. It belongs in the saxifrage family SAXIFRAGACEAE and bears a name commemorating the commander of a mid-nineteenth-century surveying expedition to the Pacific Coast, Lieutenant A. W. Whipple.

There is only one species, **Whipplea modesta.** This has slender, trailing, somewhat woody, rooting stems, 1 foot to 2 feet in length, and opposite, scarcely-stalked, slightly-toothed, ovate leaves, ⅓ inch to 1¼ inches long, clothed with stiff hairs. The fragrant flowers, ⅕ inch across, are crowded in clusters about ¾ inch in diameter atop stalks ⅓ inch to 2½ inches long. They have five or six sepals, the same number of spreading, white petals, and twice as many stamens, one-half of which are longer than the others. There are four or five styles. The fruits are spherical, leathery capsules about 1 inch across. Unlike those of *Jamesia*, they do not have beaks formed of persistent styles.

Garden Uses and Cultivation. This shrub is not hardy in the north. In woodland gardens and rockeries in mild climates, places may be found for this horticulturally not very effective shrub. It is a collector's plant rather than one to excite the interest of those primarily concerned with display. Dryish conditions and well-drained soil suit it. Propagation is by division, cuttings, and seed.

WHISPERING BELLS is *Emmenanthe penduliflora*.

WHITE. The word white occurs as parts of the common names of these plants: white-alder (*Clethra*), white beam tree (*Sorbus aria*), white brush (*Aloysia gratissima*), white-camas (*Zigadenus elegans* and *Z. glaucus*), white-cedar (*Chamaecyparis thyoides*), white-corallita (*Porana paniculata*), white cup (*Nierembergia repens*), white featherling (*Tofieldia glabra*), white-forsythia (*Abeliophyllum distichum*), white heads (*Sphenosciadium capitellatum*), white-heather (*Cassiope mertensiana*), white-hellebore (*Veratrum album*), white-popinac (*Leucaena glauca*), white quebracho (*Aspidosperma quebracho-blanco*), white-sage (*Eurotia lanata*), white sapote (*Casimiroa edulis*), and white visnagita (*Echinomastus intertextus*).

WHITEFLIES. A considerable number of species of whiteflies are garden pests. The most common and widespread, the green-

Whiteflies on the underside of a *Pelargonium* leaf

house whitefly, infests a wide variety of plants outdoors and in greenhouses, as well as some houseplants.

Whiteflies are not true flies, from which they differ in having four, instead of two, equal wings, but are more closely related to aphids, mealybugs, and scale insects. Minute creatures, they commonly congregate in great numbers on the undersides of leaves, where they may remain undetected unless the plant is disturbed. Then, the adults, which have much the aspect of tiny moths, those of most kinds chalky-white, fly off in clouds, only to return when the disturbance ceases. The eggs, attached to the undersides of the leaves, hatch into minute, pale yellow crawlers which soon insert their beaks into the plant tissues and begin sucking sap. After a first molt they resemble flat scales, usually fringed with waxy threads, and after a second molt they change to pupae from which adult insects eventually emerge. The adults also feed by sucking sap from the undersides of the foliage.

Heavy infestations of whiteflies seriously debiliate plants and exude copious honeydew (a sweet, sticky substance), which attracts ants and is particularly disfiguring when a black, sooty mold grows on it. Control of whiteflies is usually effected by repeated spraying with a contact insecticide or by the use of aerosol bombs. A method that some houseplant enthusiasts have used successfully is to shake the plants slightly to cause the adults to fly, at which point sucking the airborne adults into a vacuum cleaner. If repeated at intervals of a few days, over a period of three or four weeks the entire population will be collected and destroyed.

WHITEHEADIA (White-héadia). Rare in cultivation and consisting of one South African species, *Whiteheadia* belongs in the lily family LILIACEAE. Its name honors the Reverend Henry Whitehead, discoverer of many interesting South African plants.

From a roundish bulb about 2 inches in diameter, **W. nana** develops a pair of opposite, broad-elliptic, parallel-veined, spreading leaves 6 to 8 inches long or longer. Between these is produced a thick, short, erect stalk that carries a crowded, spikelike raceme, 3 to 6 inches in length, of greenish-white, nearly stalkless flowers that come from the axils of bracts two or three times as long as the blooms. The fruits are capsules containing flat, flask-shaped, shining black seeds.

Garden Uses and Cultivation. This interesting species is suitable for rock gardens in warm, dry, Mediterranean climates, such as that of southern California, and for growing in sunny greenhouses where the winter night temperature is 50°F, that by day five to ten degrees higher. On all favorable occasions the greenhouse must be ventilated freely. Fertile, porous soil is needed. Water is withheld when the bulb is leafless, applied freely during the season of active growth. Propagation is by seed and by offsets.

WHITETOP is *Agrostis gigantea*.

WHITEWOOD. This common name is applied to *Drypetes diversifolia*, *Lagunaria patersonii*, and *Tilia*.

WHITEY WOOD is *Melicytus ramiflorus*.

WHITFIELDIA (Whit-fièldia). Natives of tropical Africa, the about ten species of *Whitfieldia*, which name commemorates Thomas Whitfield, a botanist who collected plants in Africa, belong to the acanthus family ACANTHACEAE. Thomas Whitfield "flourished in the nineteenth century." The date of his death does not seem to be recorded.

Whitfieldias have opposite, undivided, toothless leaves. Their flowers are in terminal racemes, each bloom in the axil of a sometimes colored bract. They have a five-lobed calyx, and a slightly two-lipped corolla with a trumpet- or bell-shaped tube and five twisted lobes (petals). There are four stamens and one style. The fruits are capsules.

A showy, evergreen shrub 3 to 4 feet tall, **W. lateritia,** of West Africa, has four-angled shoots and short-stalked, leathery, broad-lanceolate to pointed-ovate leaves, 3 to 6 inches long, that have a few teeth toward their apexes. The veins on their undersides are red and short-hairy. The flowers, about 1 inch long, have brick-red calyxes and corollas, the latter twice as long as the former.

Garden and Landscape Uses and Cultivation. In the humid tropics and warm subtropics this is a useful decorative for outdoor beds and the fronts of shrub borders. It is also beautiful in tropical greenhouses. It grows with minimum attention in fertile soil, sufficiently drained to prevent it from staying wet for long periods, yet not excessively dry, and prospers in sun or part-day shade. In greenhouses light shade from strong summer sun and a minimum winter night temperature of 60°F, rising by day five to fifteen degrees according to the brightness of the weather, are needed. The atmosphere must be humid. New plants are easily raised from cuttings and seed. In greenhouses the cuttings are usually taken in late winter or spring. The tips of the resulting young plants are pinched out to encourage branching, and this may be repeated later. When in active growth, specimens that have filled their pots with roots benefit from regular applications of dilute liquid fertilizer. Indoors, and in warm climates outdoors, old plants are pruned to shape when new growth starts, normally in late winter. Then, too, pot specimens are repotted.

WHITLAVIA. See Phacelia.

WHITLOW-WORT. See Paronychia.

WHORL. Whorl is a botanical term for a circle of three or more organs of the same sort, such as branches, leaves, or flowers, that arise from the same node.

WHORL FLOWER is *Morina longifolia.*

WHORLED-POGONIA. See Isotria.

WHORTLEBERRY. This name is applied to *Vaccinium myrtillus* and sometimes other species of *Vaccinium.*

WIDDRINGTONIA (Widdringtò-nia). Five species of evergreen trees or occasionally shrubs of tropical Africa, South Africa, and Malagasy (Madagascar) constitute *Widdringtonia,* of the cypress family CUPRESSACEAE. They are closely allied to and at one time were combined with the Australian genus *Callitris.* From their Australian cousins they differ in having the overlapping, scalelike leaves of mature plants in pairs rather than in whorls of three and in normally having cones with four scales of approximately equal size. Those of *Callitris* have six or eight usually unequal scales. In South Africa, widdringtonias are commonly called cedars. The generic name commemorates Edward Widdrington, an early nineteenth-century student of the CONIFERAE.

A native of Table Mountain and regions to the east and north of that landmark, **W. cupressoides** rarely attains a height of 30 feet, usually remaining a shrub up to 12 feet tall. It differs from the Clanwilliam-cedar in being smaller and in having cones

Widdringtonia, undetermined species in South Africa

Widdringtonia juniperoides in South Africa

with smooth scales. The Clanwilliam-cedar (**W. juniperoides**) has a limited natural distribution in the Cedarberg, a mountainous locality about 150 miles north of Cape Town. Its habitat is now protected by the South African government. When young, pyramidal and shapely, this species develops an irregular crown later. It attains a height of 60 to 70 feet. The leaves on juvenile specimens are arranged spirally instead of in pairs. The cones, solitary or clustered, are spherical, warty, and ½ to ¾ inch in diameter. The Clanwilliam-cedar inhabits a region of hot, dry summers and wet winters, where snow is not unknown.

Widdringtonia juniperoides (foliage and fruits)

Widdringtonia schwarzii, Kirstenbosch, South Africa

The Willowmore-cedar (**W. schwarzii**) is a native of almost inaccessible mountains some 350 miles east of the home of the Clanwilliam-cedar. It closely resembles the latter, differing chiefly in its thicker, blunter leaves and smaller cones. It attains a maximum height of 100 feet. East Africa is the home of the Mlanje-cedar (**W. whytei**), a magnificent tree that may attain a height of 140 feet and a trunk diameter of 5 feet. When young it is symmetrical, but with age it develops a wide-spreading, irregular crown. Its juvenile leaves are arranged spirally and are up to 1 inch long. Adult leaves are scalelike and smaller. The ovoid cones are ½ to 1 inch long. This species grows outdoors, but not to a large size, in southern England.

Garden and Landscape Uses and Cultivation. These plants are practically unknown in North America and must be regarded as subjects for outdoor trial only in mild climate regions. Experience elsewhere indicates that they grow well in light loamy soil enriched with peat moss, compost, or humus and that they require full sun. Any pruning needed to shape them should be done just before new growth begins in spring. They are quite attractive as decorative pot plants. For this purpose they need the same culture as *Callitris* and may be propagated in the same ways as members of that genus.

WIDOW'S TEARS is *Commelinantia anomala*.

WIGANDIA (Wigánd-ia). Visitors to Mexico and parts of Central America and South America may see along roadsides and in other places erect shrubby plants with very large, ovate to more or less paddle-shaped leaves covered with irritating or stinging hairs. These are likely to be members of the genus *Wigandia*, the five species of which inhabit warmer parts of the Americas. The name commemorates Johannes Wigand, a Prussian bishop interested in botany, who died in 1587. These plants belong in the water leaf family HYDRO-PHYLLACEAE and so are related to the more familiar nemophilas and phacelias of western North America, although they do not much resemble them.

Wigandias are coarse herbaceous perennials, subshrubs, shrubs, or sometimes small trees, with alternate, toothed leaves. Their stalkless flowers, in curving spikes, have a deeply-five-lobed calyx and a broadly-bell-shaped corolla with five spreading lobes (petals). There are five stamens and two threadlike styles ending in club-shaped stigmas. The fruits are capsules containing tiny winged seeds.

The most commonly cultivated kinds are *W. caracasana, W. macrophylla*, and *W. urens*. A vigorous subshrub up to about 10 feet in height, **W. caracasana** is covered with yellowish or whitish pubescence. It is native from southern Mexico to Venezuela and Colombia. Its long-stalked, ovate, blunt-ended, rough-surfaced leaves are up to 1½ feet long by two-thirds as broad. Their edges are doubly crenated with coarse teeth. The flowers, about 1 inch across and

Wigandia caracasana

Wigandia caracasana (flowers)

Wigandia macrophylla

½ to ¾ inch long, have corollas with a white tubular part and violet petals. From the last, **W. macrophylla** (syn. *W. caracasana macrophylla*), of Mexico, is distinguishable by its larger leaves and white-hairy flower spikes. Native from Mexico to Peru, *W.*

Wigandia urens

urens, a subshrub or shrub 6 to 18 feet tall, has persistently-hairy stems and broad-elliptic to ovate or ovate-oblong, irregularly-toothed, hairy leaves 9 inches to 1¼ feet long. In large, hairy-stalked clusters, its lilac to purple flowers are 1½ to 2 inches across.

Garden and Landscape Uses. The chief importance of wigandias as garden plants depends upon the bold appearance of their foliage. In warm climates, such as those of the deep south and parts of California, they can be grown permanently outdoors; where colder winters make this impracticable they are sometimes raised as annuals for use in subtropical bedding displays.

Cultivation. Wigandias need rich, porous soil kept constantly moist, and full sun. Where they will not live through the winters outdoors, the usual procedure is to raise new plants from seed each year. This can be done by treating them in much the same way as tomatoes, but sowing the seed earlier, say, in January or February. Better results are had by growing the young plants individually in pots than by transplanting them several together in flats. They make rapid growth in a greenhouse where the night temperature is about 60°F and day temperatures are five to fifteen degrees higher depending upon the outside weather (when sunny, higher temperatures are appropriate). By the time they are ready for planting in the garden they may occupy 6- or 7-inch pots. For a week or two before they are set out they should be hardened by taking them from the greenhouse and standing them in their pots in a cold frame or a sheltered sunny place outdoors. Wigandias need plenty of room, 5 to 6 feet or more between individuals is not too much. An alternative method to raising them from seed each year is to winter stock plants in the greenhouse, prune them back somewhat in January, and take the shoots that develop as cuttings to be inserted in a propagating bed in a warm humid greenhouse in February or March.

WIGGINSIA (Wiggín-sia). Thirteen species of the cactus family CACTACEAE constitute *Wigginsia*, a genus endemic to South America formerly named *Malacocarpus* and by some botanists included in *Notocactus*. The name honors the American twentieth-century botanist Dr. Ira L. Wiggins.

These plants are smallish, spherical to short-cylindrical, and have strong-spined, notched or notchless, straight or wavy ribs. Their tops are heavily felted with woolly hairs from among which the flowers come. Open by day and yellow with a red-lobed stigma, the blooms have scaly or hairy perianth tubes and ovaries. The fruits are soft, scaly, and partially buried in the wool at the tops of the stems.

Wigginsia tephracantha

Variable **W. tephracantha** (syns. *Malacocarpus tephranthus, Echinocactus tephracanthus*) is grayish-green, flattish, and up to 5½ inches tall by 1 inch wider. It has sixteen to eighteen or perhaps sometimes more ribs, and spine clusters of five to seven outward-curved radials and one or no centrals. All spines are yellowish and ½ to 1 inch long. The flowers, 1½ to 2 inches wide, are canary-yellow. Spherical to cylindrical and up to 8 inches tall or sometimes taller by one-half as thick, **W. corynodes** (syns. *Malacocarpus corynodes, Echinocactus corynodes*) has thirteen to sixteen ribs and clusters of seven to twelve dark-zoned, yellow spines. There may be one central ¾ inch long or the clusters may be without centrals. The 2-inch-wide flowers are golden-yellow, the oblongish fruits sooty-red. Not over 6 inches tall and broad, and with fifteen to twenty spiraling ribs,

Wigginsia erinacea

W. erinacea (syn. *Malacocarpus erinaceus*) has clusters of dark brown spines consisting of five to seven radials nearly ½ inch long and one somewhat longer. The canary-yellow flowers are about 2½ inches in diameter.

Garden Uses and Cultivation. These are desirable plants for cactus collections and are not difficult to manage. With age they have a distinct and natural tendency to become unattractively corky and brown upward from their bases. This can be delayed to some extent by not denying the plants adequate moisture and by fertilizing occasionally. For more information see Cactuses.

WILCOXIA (Wil-cóxia) — Pencil Cactus or Dahlia Cactus or Sacasil. Eight species constitute *Wilcoxia*, of the cactus family CACTACEAE, an endemic genus of south-western United States and Mexico. Its name commemorates the American Brigadier-General Timothy E. Wilcox, an enthusiastic student of plants, who died in 1932.

Wilcoxias have tuberous roots and few-ribbed, slender, cylindrical stems of mostly not more than pencil thickness and with fine, often hairlike spines. Comparatively large, the funnel- to bell-shaped blooms have densely-bristly-hairy perianth tubes. Their stigmas are green. The spiny fruits contain black seeds.

The pencil cactus, dahlia cactus, or sacasil (**W. poselgeri** syns. *Echinocereus poselgeri, Cereus poselgeri*) is a native of a narrow strip in Texas along the Mexican border and of Mexico. Called pencil cactus in reference to its stems, and dahlia cactus because of its cluster of spindle-shaped, dahlia-like roots, in the wild this grows in thickets that support its sparingly-branched stems and provide desirable shade. Under favorable conditions it may be 2 to 3 feet tall or sometimes taller. Except for the stems of *Opuntia leptocaulis*, those of this species are slenderer than those of any cactus native to the United States. Never exceeding the thickness of an ordinary lead pencil, they are branched, having eight indefinite ribs and clusters of nine to twelve very slender radial spines, up to ⅜ inch long, that lie flat against the stems and a solitary ¼-inch-long central. Arising from the sides of the stems near their ends, the deep pink flowers are 1½ to 2 inches wide and slightly longer than wide. Inhabiting thickets in deserts in Arizona and Mexico, **W. striata**

Wilcoxia striata

(syn. *Cereus striatus*) has long, parsnip-like roots, and stems some 3 feet in length by under ¼ inch in diameter. They have eight or nine ribs with, between them, slender, straight furrows that are responsible for their striated (streaked) appearance. The purplish-red flowers from the sides of the stems are 3 to 4 inches long. They are followed by red-pulped, red fruits up to 1½ inches in length.

Other wilcoxias are these: *W. albiflora,* up to 8 inches long, has ¼-inch-thick, gray-green stems with clusters of nine to twelve very short, whitish spines that spread parallel with the surfaces of the

Wilcoxia albiflora

stems. The off-white flowers are 1½ to 2½ inches wide. The fruits are not known. *W. papillosa* has minutely-pimpled stems, 1 foot to 2 feet long by up to ¼ inch wide. They are three- to five-ribbed and have minute spines in groups of six to eight. The scarlet flowers are 1½ to 2 inches wide. The fruits are unknown. *W. schmollii* becomes

2 feet tall. Its soft, 1-inch-thick stems have eight to ten distinct ribs and closely-spaced areoles with minute spines and many long whitish to grayish hairs that conceal the stems. The purplish-pink to violet-red flowers, about 1¼ inches in diameter, have perianth tubes clothed with scales, bristles, and hairs. *W. tamaulipensis,* about 1 foot high, has stems with about ten shallow ribs. The spines, in clusters of fifteen to twenty, are white tipped with brown. About 2 inches long and 1½ inches wide, the flowers are pale pink with darker stripes. *W. tomentosa* has seven-ribbed stems up to ½ inch thick. The spine clusters are of eight to ten short radials and one central. About 1¼ inches in diameter, the flowers are rose-pink with a purplish overtone. They have downy sepals. The fruits are red and 1¼ inches wide. *W. viperina,* up to 7 feet high, has stems ¼ to ¾ inch in diameter with about eight indistinct ribs and, unusual for cactuses, minutely-hairy. They have clusters of eight to nine short, thin, radial spines and three or four centrals. The red flowers are about 2 inches in diameter. The fruits, under ½ inch in diameter, are approximately spherical.

Garden Uses and Cultivation. Wilcoxias are interesting and generally easy to grow, attractive to beginners as well as to more sophisticated cactus collectors. They prosper in very well-drained, moderately fertile, sandy soil and generally bloom freely. Because they are sensitive to excessive wetness about the roots, water them cautiously. Allow the soil to become dry between applications, but not to remain parched for extended periods. Except that they need partial shade from the strong sun

of summer, wilcoxias respond to conditions agreeable to most desert cactuses. Success in propagation and more rapid growth is often had by grafting them onto hylocereuses, opuntias, selenicereuses, or other strong-growing cactuses. They may also be raised from cuttings and from seed. For more information see Cactuses.

WILD. This word occurs as parts of the common names of these plants: wild-allamanda (*Urechites lutea*), wild-basil (*Clinopodium vulgare*), wild-Canterbury-bell (*Phacelia minor*), wild-celery (*Vallisneria americana*), wild-honeysuckle (*Rhododendron periclymenoides*), wild Irishman (*Discaria toumatou*), wild-lily-of-the-valley (*Maianthemum*), wild-pink (*Silene caroliniana*), wild-plantain (*Heliconia bihai*), wild-poinsettia (*Warszewiczia coccinea*), wild-raisin (*Viburnum lentago* and *V. cassinoides*), wild-sarsaparilla (*Aralia nudicaulis* and *Schisandra coccinea*), and wild-tamarind (*Lysiloma bahamensis*).

WILD GARDENS. As used in North America, the term wild garden usually refers to a portion of a natural landscape or to an area of land developed to resemble a natural landscape that is devoted exclusively or nearly exclusively to the cultivation and preservation of plants native to a selected region, which may be local or of wider geographical significance. Informality should characterize the design of such gardens, which may represent or include meadow, prairie, waterside, hillside, woodland, desert, and seaside floras. Horticultural varieties, such as those of *Aster, Helianthus,* and *Phlox,* should not be admitted.

A portion of a wild garden in California

A portion of a wild garden in New York

The British conception of a wild garden differs from the American in that the plants employed are not restricted to native ones, but may include exotic (foreign) species not too gardenesque in appearance, provided they blend satisfactorily with informal landscape and require a minimum of cultural care. Plants with variegated foliage, double flowers, or other characteristics that too blatantly advertise the art of the horticulturist or plant breeder are generally omitted from such gardens.

WILIWILI is *Erythrina tahitensis*.

WILLARDIA (Will-àrdia). Six species of nonhardy small trees or shrubs constitute Mexican and Central American *Willardia*, of the pea family LEGUMINOSAE. The name honors Alexander Willard, a nineteenth-century United States consul to Mexico.

Willardias have pinnate leaves and, in racemes from the leaf axils, bluish-lilac or lilac-colored, pea-like flowers. Each bloom has a calyx with five tiny teeth, a spreading, round standard or banner petal, somewhat sickle-shaped wing petals, and a slightly incurved keel. The ten stamens are united except for one that is free in its upper part. The style is incurved. The fruits are much flattened, linear-oblong pods.

A shrub or tree 10 to 40 feet tall, Mexican **W. mexicana** has leaves with nine to fifteen blunt, oblong-elliptic leaflets up to 1¼ inches long and, especially on their undersides, hairy. The plentiful, about ½-inch-long, lilac-colored flowers are in racemes 4 to 5 inches long. The fruits are up to 5 inches in length. The roots of this species have been used as a fish poison. Honey derived from its flowers is reported to be poisonous.

Planted at Fort Lauderdale, Florida, **W. schiedeana,** of Panama, has proved to be a satisfactory and attractive ornamental. It has pendulous branches and small, twice-pinnate leaves. The purplish-blue flowers make a good show in fall.

Garden and Landscape Uses and Cultivation. The species described here thrive in ordinary soil, in full sun, and without special care. Propagation is by seed, possibly by cuttings.

WILLOW. See Salix. Australian-willow is *Geijera parviflora*. Desert- or flowering-willow is *Chilopsis linearis*. Primrose-willow is *Ludwigia*. Virginia-willow is *Itea virginica*. Water-willow is *Decodon verticillatus*. Willow herb is *Epilobium*.

WILLOWMORE-CEDAR is *Widdringtonia schwarzii*.

WILMATTEA (Wil-máttea). The name *Wilmattea* honors Mrs. T. D. A. (Wilmatte P.) Cockerell, a naturalist interested in the plants and animals of Central America. The only species, a native of Guatemala and Honduras, belongs in the cactus family

African-violet: (a) Wilting

(b) In normal condition

Cineraria: (a) Wilting

(b) In normal condition

CACTACEAE. By some authorities it is included in *Hylocereus*.

Night-blooming **W. minutiflora** (syn. *Hylocereus minutiflorus*) in aspect resembles *Hylocereus*, but has much smaller blooms with extremely short perianth tubes. It is a high-climbing, slender vine with jointed, three-angled, dark green, aerial-rooting stems. As in all cactuses, the stems have specialized areas called areoles (points of origin of spines, bristles, branches, and flowers). In *Wilmattea* these are felty, each bearing one to three short spines. The flowers are solitary and fragrant. Their ovaries are covered with short scales with felty hairs and occasionally one or more bristles in their axils. The bloom is about 1 inch in diameter. Its inner perianth segments (petals) are pointed and white, the outer reddish and broader.

Garden and Landscape Uses and Cultivation. This is a forest cactus. It has the same uses and requires the same treatment, including warm conditions and part shade, as *Hylocereus*. For general information consult Cactuses.

WILT. As a verb, wilt refers to the loss of normal turgidity of plants or parts of plants and cut flowers, the leaves, flowers, or comparatively soft stems of which ultimately become flaccid. Wilting, or flagging as gardeners sometimes call it, re-sults from a lack of sufficient water in the tissues; the plant cells are dehydrated to the extent that they are not fully distended.

Wilting is likely to occur whenever loss of water by transpiration exceeds the amount that can be replaced by the roots or by the stems of cut flowers. Wilting, then, is promoted by high temperatures, low humidity, wind and drafts, and bright sun, all of which increase the rate of transpiration. Factors that reduce water intake, such as too dry or excessively cold soil and damage to roots during transplanting or as the result of other disturbances, of pests or diseases, or of excessively wet soil that rots them, may also result in wilting.

Measures to check wilting include keeping the soil adequately, but not excessively wet, promoting high humidity (in greenhouses, for example, by wetting down paths and other surfaces), spraying or misting plants with water, shading from strong sun, and sheltering from wind and drafts. Under some circumstances, wilting of newly transplanted plants may be minimized by using antidesiccant (antitranspirent) sprays or by reducing the amount of foliage by pruning or by cutting back or picking off some or all of the leaves. Wilting as a consequence of repotting or other disturbance of the roots of houseplants that cannot be

Tetranema: (a) Wilting

(b) In normal condition

moved to a more humid environment can often be checked by covering the plants with a polyethylene plastic bag for a few to several days.

WILTS or WILT DISEASES. Plant diseases caused by pathogenic organisms, such as funguses, the most obvious symptom of which is the wilting (loss of turgidity) of leaves and other parts, are called wilt diseases or wilts. The flaccid condition of the tissues is caused by the disease organism interfering with the normal conduction of water through the plant tissues. Often, the infection is localized at some considerable distance from the wilting leaves, for example, at the base of a tree whose leaves exhibit the most characteristic symptoms. Among the more common wilt diseases are aster wilt, Dutch elm disease, oak wilt, fusarium wilt of tomatoes, verticillium wilt

(which attacks a wide variety of plants), and watermelon wilt. Wilt diseases are notoriously difficult to control. In a few cases the use of seeds of wilt-resistant varieties brings some measure of success, but with many sorts of plants this is not practicable. In all cases consult local authorities such as Cooperative Extension Agents and State Agricultural Experiment Stations for the latest recommendations.

WIND-POPPY is *Stylomecon heterophylla.*

WINDFLOWER is *Anemone.*

WINDOW BOXES. See Container Gardening.

WINDOWED PLANTS. This is a group name for a few remarkable South African succulent plants of the *Mesembryanthemum*

relationship in the family AIZOACEAE. They are characterized by having an ingenious means of reducing the intensity of light before it reaches their chlorophyll-containing tissues, where photosynthesis takes place.

Inhabitants of semideserts or deserts lit by brilliant sun, in their native homes these plants grow with their major portions, which are modified leaves, more or less buried in stony ground with only their tips exposed. Located on the tips are the so-called windows, considerable areas of translucent tissue without chlorophyll, but containing an abundance of calcium oxalate crystals. Filtered through the windows, the sunlight is greatly reduced in intensity before it reaches the chlorophyll-containing tissues deep within the leaf.

Intriguing and, in the main, easy to grow, windowed plants are part of the group commonly called stone or pebble plants. For more information about them see the Encyclopedia entries Fenestraria, Frithia, Lithops, and Ophthalmophyllum, as well as Stone or Pebble Plants.

WINE CUPS. This name is used for *Babiana rubrocyanea* and *Geissorhiza rochensis.*

WINE FLOWER is *Boerhavia coccinea.*

WINEBERRY is *Rubus phoenicolasius.* The New Zealand wineberry is *Aristotelia racemosa.*

WINGED. This word forms parts of the common names of these plants: winged-bean (*Psophocarpus tetragonolobus*), winged everlasting (*Ammobium alatum*), and winged-pea (*Lotus tetragonolobus*).

WINGNUT. See Pterocarya.

WINTER. This word appears in the common names of these plants: winter-aconite (*Eranthis*), winter-cress (*Barbarea*), winter fat (*Eurotia lanata*), winter-hazel (*Corylopsis*), winter-heliotrope (*Petasites fragrans*), winter-purslane (*Montia perfoliata*), winter snowflake (*Leucojum nicaeense*), and winter sweet (*Acokanthera oblongifolia, Chimonanthus praecox*).

WINTER PROTECTION. See Protection For Plants.

WINTER RYE. See Rye, Winter.

WINTERBERRY is *Ilex verticillata.*

WINTERGREEN. See *Gaultheria procumbens* and Pyrola. For chickweed-wintergreen, see Trientalis. Flowering-wintergreen is *Polygala paucifolia.* Spotted-wintergreen is *Chimaphila maculata.*

WINTERIA. See Hildewintera.

WINTEROCEREUS. See Hildewintera.

A typical windowed plant, *Lithops olivacea*

WINTER'S BARK is *Drimys winteri.*

WIRE PLANT is *Muehlenbeckia complexa.*

WISHBONE BUSH is *Mirabilis laevis.*

WISHBONE FLOWER is *Torenia fournieri.*

WISTERIA (Wis-tèria). Few hardy, perennial vines are better known or more admired than wisterias. That they sometimes are agonizingly perverse with regard to blooming is regrettable and will be discussed under Cultivation. There are ten species, two natives of the southern United States, the others of eastern Asia.

The genus *Wisteria* belongs in the pea family LEGUMINOSAE. Its name commemorates Caspar Wistar, professor of anatomy at the University of Pennsylvania, who died in 1818. Because the botanist who first described the genus intentionally spelled *Wisteria* with an *e* in place of the *a* in Wistar's name, his spelling is retained. The plant known as South-African-wisteria and Rhodesian-wisteria is *Bolusanthus speciosus.*

Wisterias climb trees or other supports to great heights and develop, for vines, quite massive woody trunks. They attain great ages and have twining stems and alternate, pinnate leaves with alternate, lateral leaflets and a terminal one. The pealike flowers, in pendulous racemes, are purple, blue-purple, lilac-blue, pink, or white. They have five-toothed calyxes, the two upper teeth often more or less united and shorter than the others. The standard or banner petal is large and reflexed, the wing petals, like the keel, are sickle-shaped. There are ten stamens, one of which is free and the others united. The fruits are long,

Wisteria floribunda

The stout trunk of a *Wisteria* embracing the trunk of an elm tree

flattened pods, more or less constricted between the seeds.

Japanese wisteria (**W. floribunda**) is a favorite that comes in several beautiful varieties. A vigorous, high climber, it has stems that twine clockwise, except those of *W. f. praecox,* some of which twine in one direction and some in the other. The leaves have thirteen to nineteen ovate-elliptic leaflets, 1½ to 2½ inches long, that in fall turn yellow. In racemes 1 foot to 1½ feet in length, the ¾-inch-long, distinctly fragrant, violet to violet-blue blooms are borne about the same time as the leaves. The upper blooms of the racemes are the earliest to open, the others follow in succession downward. The seed pods are 2 to 6 inches long and velvety-hairy. In *W. f. alba* the blooms are white. Variety *W. f. macrobotrys* (syn. *W. multijuga*) is remarkable for its extraordinary racemes of bloom, which are 2 to 3 feet long or even longer. Pale pink flowers tinged with purple are borne by *W. f. rosea,* paler pink ones by *W. f. carnea.* Double, dark violet flowers in racemes of moderate length are characteristic of *W. f. violacea-plena.* Other varieties include *W. f. longissima* (syn. *W. multijuga longissima*), with extremely long racemes of light purple blooms; *W. f. longissima-alba,* with similar racemes of white flowers; *W. f. praecox* (syn. *W. f.* 'Issai'), a kind with deep violet flowers that blooms when

young; and *W. f.* 'Royal Purple', with long racemes of violet-purple blooms.

Chinese wisteria (**W. sinensis**) differs from the Japanese wisteria in its shoots twining counterclockwise (from left to right) and in having somewhat larger leaves with usually eleven, sometimes fewer, occasionally thirteen, longer-pointed, ovate to ovate-lanceolate leaflets that assume no bright fall color. The leaflets, 2 to 3½ inches long, are downy when young, nearly hairless later. The 1-inch-long, faintly fragrant

Wisteria floribunda alba

Victoria 'Longwood Hybrid'

Vinca major

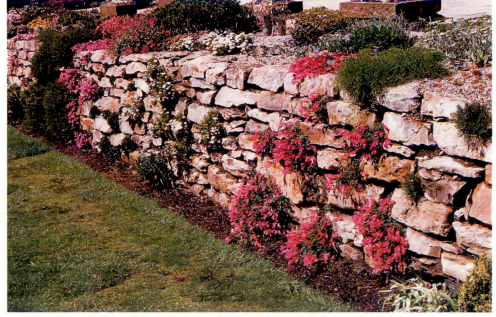

A wall garden with red-flowered *Penstemon* and white-flowered *Iberis*

Viola lutea

Viola sororia

Watsonia 'Adelaide'

Wittia panamensis

Wigandia urens

Wisteria floribunda macrobotrys

Wisteria frutescens

Wisteria frutescens (flowers)

flowers, in racemes up to 1 foot long, but often shorter, expand before the foliage. The velvety-hairy seed pods are 4 to 6 inches long. Variety *W. s. alba* has white flowers, as does an especially fragrant-flowered variety named *W. s.* 'Jako.'

Another native of China, the silky wisteria (*W. venusta*) differs from those described above in that its mature leaves are hairy on both surfaces. They have nine to thirteen short-pointed, oblong-lanceolate to ovate-oblong leaflets 2 to 4 inches in length. The shoots of this species twine from right to left. The racemes of white, 1-inch-long flowers are up to 6 inches long. The velvety seed pods are 6 to 8 inches long. Variety *W. v. violacea* has purple blooms. Double white flowers are borne by *W. v. plena.*

A popular American-raised hybrid between *W. floribunda* and *W. sinensis* is *W. formosa.* Intermediate between its parents in most characteristics, it follows its Japanese progenitor in having shoots twining clockwise and in the strong fragrance of its blooms; it follows its Chinese forebear in its leaves having seven to thirteen leaflets and in the flowers of its racemes opening simultaneously. It is not improbable that many of the plants grown as *W. sinensis* represent this hybrid.

The two American species, *W. frutescens* and *W. macrostachya*, are less commonly cultivated than the Orientals previously discussed. Both naturally inhabit moist soils or swamps and have shoots that twine in a counterclockwise direction. The first is native from Virginia to Florida and Texas, the second from Tennessee to Texas. These are vigorous, tall vines that differ from others dealt with here in their seed pods being hairless. Leaves with nine to fifteen ovate to ovate-lanceolate, somewhat hairy leaflets 1 inch to 2 inches long are characteristic of *W. frutescens.* The crowded racemes, not longer than 4½ inches, are of lilac-purple flowers ½ to ¾ inch long. The calyx lobes are much shorter than the calyx tube. The seed pods are 2 to 4

inches long. Slenderer-stemmed *W. macrostachya* has leaves, hairy when young, but later nearly hairless, with commonly nine pointed-ovate leaflets 1 inch to 3 inches long. The ¾-inch-long light blue to lilac-purple blooms are in racemes 8 inches to 1 foot long or sometimes longer. The lobes of the calyx are nearly as long as its tube.

Garden and Landscape Uses. Wisterias are among the most splendid vines. All are hardy in southern New England, the common Japanese wisteria even further north. Nearly all bloom in spring and many provide less abundant display of flowers later.

They are admirably suited for clothing pillars and posts, for covering arbors and pergolas, for draping terrace walls and masonry balustrades, and for training along wires to decorate walls. Care should be taken not to locate them where their strong, twining stems are likely to invade gutters or become entangled with leaders from gutters. These vines sometimes climb to great heights up tall trees, but then are usually seen to best advantage only after the supporting tree has passed maturity and is in a state of reduced vigor, so that the wisteria receives more sun than it

Landscape uses of wisterias: (a) On a pergola in California

(b) Clothing a wall, Hever Castle Gardens, England

(c) Covering an arbor, Villa D'Este, Como, Italy

(d) As a free-standing specimen, the Royal Botanic Gardens, Kew, England

would if its host were heavily foliaged. Standard (free-standing, tree-form) wisterias are highly ornamental and are admirable for formal and semiformal locations, such as beside pools. They also make very fine container-grown ornamentals for terraces and similar places, and for forcing gently into early bloom in large greenhouses and conservatories. These vines do well in a variety of soils, preferring those of medium fertility that are deep and moderately moist. They need full sun. Because they do not transplant readily it is best to keep wisterias in containers until they are planted permanently.

Cultivation. The most commonly asked question about wisterias is why some individuals do not bloom satisfactorily. There is more than one possible cause. In very cold climates the flower buds, which form in fall, may be winter-killed. Plants raised from seeds do not flower for many years, often twenty or more. Because of this, seedlings should not ordinarily be planted. They are not sold by reputable nurseries. To bloom well, wisterias must not be shaded for more than a minor part of each day. They grow, but do not flower in shade. A common cause of nonflowering is the production of excessively exuberant vegetative growth induced by faulty pruning or fertilizing. It is too much to expect the vines to make a rambunctious growth of stems and foliage, as well as an abundant bloom. To flower freely, vegetative growth must not be more than moderate. Unfortunately, the usual means tried to curb exuberance, heavy pruning in winter or spring, is self-defeating. Such treatment merely encourages vigorous shoot growth, as does fertilizing and watering.

If you have a young vine that has not yet filled its allotted space, by all means fertilize and water generously to encourage growth, but do not expect bloom. Train selected shoots along wires or other supports in directions you wish them to assume as part of a framework of permanent branches, so spaced that they adequately furnish the area you wish to cover, but do not excessively crowd it. From 1½ to 2 feet between major branches is about right. Prune in summer and in winter. Summer pruning consists of cutting off the ends of all side shoots just beyond the sixth or seventh leaf as soon as that leaf develops and of cutting the ends off shoots that develop from the cut-back side shoots, immediately after they have developed their first or second leaves. Allow one strong leader shoot to grow from the end, or from near the end, of each main framework branch without cutting it. Stretch it tautly along the wire or other support in the position you wish the branch to be. In late winter cut the leader shoots back to two-thirds or one-half of their lengths (the more drastic treatment is for weak shoots) and cut the side shoots that were pruned the previous summer back to within an inch or two of their bases. In this way the permanent branches will be extended each year by one-half or more the length of the annual growth of the leader shoots, and

side shoots will be converted into short flowering spurs instead of developing into hopeless tangles. Once the vine has occupied its allotted space, follow the same pruning practices, except in winter prune the leader shoots in the same way as the side shoots, by cutting them back to within an inch or two of their bases. Also, after the vine has covered the area you wish, do not use fertilizer unless shoot and foliage growth is definitely scanty, and water only if there is danger of the foliage wilting, which will only happen under drought conditions.

Old, neglected wisterias that fail to bloom present a different problem. Often they are tangled masses of intertwined stems, branches, and dense foliage. If faced with taming one of these, take drastic action. In winter prune away all except a framework of the most advantageously placed stems and branches. Not all will be exactly where you would like them to be, but choose those that best fill, but do not crowd, the area you have in mind. Shorten the other branches drastically, being quite ruthless

Pruning wisterias: (a) In winter (note plump flower buds below where cut is being made)

(b) New shoots, in summer

in removing any that are truly ill-placed or obviously crowded. When you have finished, your vine should look like a skeleton of its former self. It should consist of a gaunt framework of fairly well-spaced branches. Do not fertilize, and do not water unless at a later date the foliage begins to wilt. If the soil is acid, an application of lime, at the rate of ½ to 1 pound per 10 square feet, lightly forked into the surface, will be of benefit. The drastic pruning will stimulate vigorous growth. Treat this growth in the manner described above for younger wisteria vines that have not been neglected. If there are too large gaps between the old framework branches, train into them shoots selected as leaders, treating them in the manner described above for young, newly planted vines. Prune side shoots in summer and in winter. Under this treatment the vine is likely to flower within two or three years. Root-pruning is sometimes advocated as a means of bringing nonflowering wisterias into bloom, but unless combined with summer pruning of the shoots, as described above, it is unlikely to be effective. If done in addition to summer pruning it can be helpful, especially if the roots have access to large bodies of fertile soil. To root-prune, dig a ditch 2 to 3 feet deep around the trunk of the vine at a distance outward of 4 to 8 feet. The distance should relate to the size of the vine. Severing the roots checks top growth and favors flower production. Mix superphosphate with the excavated soil at the rate of approximately 1 pound per 10 feet of ditch and back fill it into the trench.

Tree (standard) wisterias are developed by planting young vines, well-spaced so that they do not grow into each other, in not over-fertile soil in open sunny locations. A main shoot is tied to a stout stake and when it has reached the height the trunk is to be, usually 4 or 5 feet, its top is cut off. Side shoots are allowed to develop from the upper part, but not lower down. The side shoots are pruned in winter to a length of 6 inches to a foot; this is done each succeeding winter until the head is as big as required. Thin, spindling, and any obviously crowded shoots are cut out completely. After the heads are large enough, pruning consists of shortening all summer shoots at the sixth or seventh leaf as soon as that leaf expands and of cutting off all secondary shoots that develop just beyond their first or second leaves. In winter these same shoots are cut back to within an inch of their bases. As a variation from single-trunk standards, the vines may be allowed to form several erect trunks from the base, each treated in the same manner as the single trunk of a standard. In this way, broad, bushy, upright-stemmed specimens are developed. Propagation of wisterias is accomplished by layering, by grafting scions of flowering specimens onto pieces of root, and by

To layer a wisteria: (a) Select a pliable young stem that can be bent to the ground, and make on its underside, 1 foot to 2 feet from its apex, a slantwise cut about halfway through it

(b) Peg the wounded portion securely into a shallow hole made in the ground, leaving the remainder of the stem, on both sides of the wound, exposed; cover the wounded part with a mound of a mixture of sand and peat moss and keep this moist

(c) After a few months, roots will have developed from the wound; sever the rooted upper portion of the stem and plant it as a separate individual

summer cuttings under mist or in a greenhouse propagating bench.

Container-grown tree wisterias are pruned in the same way as standards grown in the open ground. Keep the soil evenly moist, and from spring to fall give

regular applications of dilute liquid fertilizer. If the plants are to be forced into early bloom, bring them into a greenhouse in late winter where the night temperature is about 50°F, that by day five to ten degrees higher. Spray the tops with water two or three times a day to encourage the buds to grow. After flowering is through and danger of frost is over, put the plants in a sunny place outdoors.

WITCH-HAZEL. See Hamamelis.

WITCHES'-BROOMS. Witches'-brooms are abnormal much-branched, bushlike growths that develop chiefly on some kinds of trees and shrubs. Among sorts especially likely to develop witches'-brooms are various conifers, notably Norway spruce (*Picea abies*) and junipers (*Juniperus*), as well as cherries (*Prunus*), hackberries (*Celtis*), and blueberries (*Vaccinium*). Viruses and funguses are common causes of these abnormal growths, which usually do no serious harm and are best controlled by being cut out. A goodly number of dwarf horticultural varieties of conifers were origi-

Witches'-brooms on: (a) *Celtis occidentalis*

(b) *Prunus mahaleb*

nated by propagating from witches'-brooms.

WITHE-ROD is *Viburnum cassinoides.* Smooth withe-rod is *V. nudum.*

WITHNERARA. This is the name of orchid hybrids the parents of which include *Aspasia, Miltonia, Odontoglossum,* and *Oncidium.*

WITTIA (Wít-tia). The genus *Wittia,* of the cactus family CACTACEAE, has only two species and is native to Panama and northern South America. Some authorities include it in closely related *Disocactus,* from which it differs in its flowers being smaller and in having erect instead of wide-spreading perianth segments. The name commemorates N. H. Witt, a nineteenth-century merchant of Manáos, Brazil, who collected plants.

Wittias are tree-perchers that, like many orchids and other epiphytes, live on trees without abstracting nourishment from them. They have flat, spineless, leaflike stems similar to those of *Epiphyllum* and notched at their edges. Their small, cylindrical to narrowly-trumpet-shaped flowers develop from areoles along the edges of the stems. The blooms open chiefly at night, but sometimes remain expanded on dull days. The fruits are small and berry-like.

A native of Panama, Colombia, and Venezuela, ***W. panamensis*** has shallowly-lobed, branched stems up to 3 feet long and 3 inches wide. Solitary from areoles in the upper halves of the leaf segments, the violet-purple blooms, 1 inch to 1¼ inches long, have perianth segments arched slightly outward. The top of the four-lobed white stigma protrudes from the mouth of the flower. The fruits are smooth.

Garden Uses and Cultivation. These are as for *Epiphyllum, Rhipsalis,* and most other epiphytic cactuses. For more information see Cactuses.

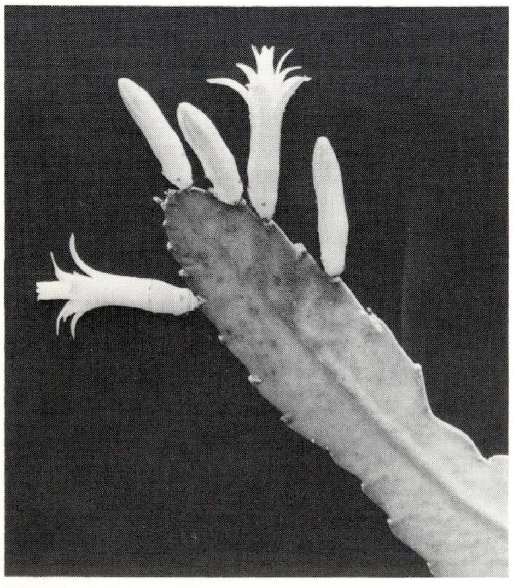

Wittia panamensis

WITTROCKIA (Witt-róckia). Endemic to mountains in southern Brazil, *Wittrockia,* of the pineapple family BROMELIACEAE, comprises seven species of epiphytes (plants that grow on trees without taking nourishment from their hosts). Its name commemorates the Swedish botanist Veit Brecher Wittrock. He died in 1914.

Wittrockias are nonhardy herbaceous perennials with toothed leaves forming rosettes from the centers of which the headlike inflorescences (flower clusters) develop. The inflorescences terminate very brief to longer stalks. They have very short branches, an involucre (basal collar) of well-developed bracts, and many nearly stalkless flowers. The blooms have three separate sepals, three petals united at their tips, but not at their bases, so that there are three peep holes into the inside of the corolla, six nonprotruding stamens, and a three-parted style. The fruits are small and berry-like. The united tips of the petals distinguish this genus from *Canistrum,* which has petals separate at their extremities. From *Neoregelia* and *Nidularium,* which it much resembles, *Wittrockia* is also distinguished by its petals not being free at their extremities and by having a pair of scales at the base of each petal.

Most frequent in cultivation and the finest of the genus, robust ***W. superba*** has many firm, glossy, spreading, somewhat channeled leaves in a crowded rosette. They are 1½ to 3 feet long and have broad-ovate, sheathing bases, and pointed, strap-shaped blades that widen somewhat from their middles outward and are 1 inch to 3 inches wide. Their margins are furnished with coarse, red-tipped, sharp spines. The apexes of some of the leaves are blood-red. The showy, broadly-hemispherical flower head has numerous lanceolate-ovate, bright red, spine-tipped bracts. The blue petals, shorter than the sepals, have fringed scales at their bases. Quite different ***W. smithii*** has rosettes of thin, almost papery, broad, olive-green leaves, up to 2¼ inches wide, with rich deep red undersides, and purplish spines much smaller than those of *W. superba* along the margins. The head of white and green flowers nestles in the heart of the rosette. Unlike those of *W. superba,* which are pointed, the petals of *W. smithii* are blunt.

Garden and Landscape Uses and Cultivation. These are attractive additions to collections of bromeliads. They respond to conditions and care suitable for *Aechmea.* For more information see Bromeliads or Bromels.

WOAD. See Isatis.

WOLFBERRY is *Symphoricarpos occidentalis.*

WOLFFIA (Wólff-ia). The smallest flowering plant is one of the about ten species of *Wolffia,* of the duckweed family LEMNACEAE. Widely distributed in temperate and tropical regions, the genus name commemorates J. H. Wolff, who died in 1806.

Wolffias are floating aquatics frequently so numerous that they completely cover considerable expanses of water and so tiny that in the aggregate they resemble coarse green meal. Individuals are 1/50 to 1/16 inch in diameter. From duckweeds (*Lemna*) and *Spirodela* they differ in having no roots. As with those genera, the plant body is a thallus, not differentiated into stems and leaves. In *Wolffia* it is plump, egg- or foot-ball-shaped and sometimes flattened on the top, rather than thin and flat. A lens must be used to see the flowers. The males consist of a single stamen, the females of one pistil. They develop infrequently, one of each sex in a bowl-like depression on the upper side of the plant body.

The smallest flowering plant, ***W. microscopica,*** of India, has plant bodies no more than 1/32 of an inch long. Those of ***W. arrhiza,*** a native of Europe, Asia, Africa, and Australia, and of ***W. punctata,*** of North America and the West Indies, may attain twice that size as may the plant bodies of North American and South American ***W. columbiana.***

Garden Uses and Cultivation. Wolffias are grown for biological studies in schools and other institutions of learning and to some extent in aquariums. Their cultural needs are the same as those of *Lemna.*

WOLFFIELLA (Wolff-iélla). Differing from *Wolffia* in its thalluses (plant bodies undifferentiated into stems and leaves) being thin and flat, the genus *Wolffiella,* of the duckweed family LEMNACEAE, consists of eight mostly tropical species in America and Africa. Its name is a diminutive of *Wolffia.*

Wolffiellas are tiny, floating, rootless aquatics that inhabit stagnant waters. Individuals are rarely more than ¼ inch long and are sickle-, strap-, or tongue-shaped. They grow in colonies, with the younger plants, developed as offsets, remaining attached to their parents. At the basal end of the thallus is a single reproductive pouch, but neither flowers nor fruits have been observed.

Native from Massachusetts to Wisconsin, Florida, Texas, and Mexico, ***W. floridana*** has sickle-shaped or double-curved thalluses, ⅙ to ½ inch long, rounded at their bases and tapering to a long, slender apex. Californian and Mexican ***W. lingulata*** has solitary or in pairs, ovate to ovate-oblong thalluses mostly up to ¼ inch long. Native to California, Mexico, and South America, ***W. oblonga*** has thalluses, solitary or in twos or sometimes threes, about ⅙ inch long and usually slightly sickle-shaped.

Garden Uses and Cultivation. These are as for *Lemna.*

WOLFSBANE. See Aconitum.

WOMAN'S TONGUE TREE is *Albizia lebbek*.

WOMBAT BERRY is *Eustrephus latifolius*.

WONDERBERRY is *Solanum burbankii*.

WONGA-WONGA VINE is *Pandorea pandorana*.

WOOD. The word wood forms parts of the colloquial names of these plants: China wood oil tree (*Aleurites fordii*), Japan wood oil tree (*Aleurites cordata*), small-wood-rose (*Argyreia nervosa*), wood-apple (*Feronia limonia*), wood-betony (*Pedicularis*), wood-rose (*Merremia tuberosa*), wood-rush (*Luzula*), and wood-sorrel (*Oxalis acetosella*).

WOOD ASHES. Unleached wood ash, particularly that resulting from burning hardwoods, is a valuable fertilizer. The chief nutritive element it supplies is potassium in the form of potash. The amount of potash wood ash contains varies from 5 to 25 percent. It also contains about 2 percent phosphoric acid and 30 to 35 percent lime. Strongly alkaline, wood ashes should not be used for acid-soil plants. For others it may be applied at any time of the year, except when the soil is frozen, at rates of 4 to 5 ounces per 10 square feet or may be mixed with potting soil at the rate of about a quart per bushel. To preserve its fertilizer value prior to usage, wood ashes must be stored dry.

WOOD OIL TREE, CHINA, or TUNG OIL TREE is *Aleurites fordii*.

WOOD OIL TREE, JAPAN is *Aleurites cordata*.

WOOD, TALLOW is *Ximenia americana*.

WOODBINE is a common name of *Lonicera periclymenum* and of some species of *Parthenocissus*.

WOODCHUCKS. Woodchucks are large rodents capable of causing much damage in gardens, especially to vegetables. They construct burrows, usually with two entrances, in which they hibernate in winter. In early spring the females bear litters of four or five, which live with the mothers in the burrows until early summer and then leave. They feed on grasses, clovers, and a variety of other succulent vegetation. The most effective methods of eliminating garden-oriented woodchucks are by shooting and gassing. The latter can be done once the entrances to the burrows, usually easily identified by the mound of soil outside, are located. Use, according to directions, one of the commercially available gas bombs, or attach a hose to the exhaust pipe of an automobile, lead the other end into the burrow, and run the engine for fifteen or twenty minutes.

WOODFORDIA (Wood-fórdia). One of the two species of this genus of the loosestrife family LYTHRACEAE is sparingly cultivated in Florida, Hawaii, and other warm regions. Named to honor John Alexander Woodford, an early nineteenth-century fancier of rare plants in London, England, *Woodfordia* is indigenous to Asia, Africa, and Malagasy (Madagascar).

Woodfordias are shrubs with opposite, two-ranked, undivided leaves, and flowers, usually in clustered panicles, with tubular, generally six-, but sometimes five-lobed red calyxes and five or rarely six persistent petals. There are twelve long-protruding stamens and a long-protruding style. The fruits are capsules.

Up to 12 feet tall and with long, spreading branches, *W. fruticosa* has shoots downy when young, hairless later. From older stems, the bark flakes or peels. The stalkless, lanceolate or curved, ovate-lanceolate leaves, in twos or threes along the stems, are 2 to 4 inches long and pale and more or less distinctly minutely-black-dotted on their undersides. The abundant flowers, in dense clusters from the leaf axils or leafless parts of the stems, come chiefly in spring, sporadically later. They have orange-red to coral-red or brick-red blooms slightly over ½ inch long and a little over ⅓ inch wide. Their often brightly colored calyx tubes (hypanthiums) persist with the seed capsules.

Garden and Landscape Uses and Cultivation. The species described is an attractive ornamental for areas of warm, essentially frost-free climates. It thrives in ordinary soils and situations without special care, withstands exposure to wind well, and is little affected by pests or disease. Propagation is by seed and by cuttings.

An inviting entrance to a woodland garden

WOODLAND GARDENS. A wooded area is likely to afford opportunity for developing one of the most charming and distinctive of horticultural achievements—a woodland garden. It does not need to be a large area, an acre or less will suffice, however, more acreage can always be used to good advantage. The terrain can be level or hilly, rocky or rockless; it can include dry, moist, and wet areas, even a stream, rill, or pond.

Begin by surveying the area. If it is new to you, allow one full growing season before beginning operations. This gives you time to become familiar with the existing vegetation growing on the site. Without a knowledge of this, it is impossible to make wise decisions as to which plants to retain and which to eliminate. After you complete your survey, the next step is to decide what needs to be done. There may be need for judicious thinning by cutting out some unduly crowded trees as well as, perhaps, some that are decrepit or seriously diseased. It may be advantageous to "raise the heads" of some trees by pruning off some lower branches to admit more light to the underplanting. All this must be done with great discretion; there can be no putting back trees or limbs that have been removed.

Some clearing of underbrush may also be in order, most especially along the fringes of the woodland and in open areas within it. This is likely to entail digging out tangles of such plants as brambles, catbriers, and poison-ivy. Even if the last is first killed by a selective herbicide (weed killer), it is still necessary to remove the dead, aboveground parts, which are as toxic to human skin as are living stems and foliage. It is best to wear gloves when doing this.

The herbaceous (non-woody-stemmed) flora, which will consist chiefly of perennials, since few annuals or biennials occur in the woodlands, should also be evaluated with the objective of retaining desirable plants that are favorably located. Some woodland perennials, such as the Christmas fern (*Polygonum acrostichoides*) and some other ferns, galax, and Oconee bells (*Shortia galacifolia*), are evergreens. Others, examples of which are the native American bleeding hearts (*Dicentra eximea* and *D. formosa*), cimicifugas, and Solomon's seals (*Polygonatum*), have foliage in evidence from spring to fall but are dormant in winter. Yet others, which include Dutchman's breeches (*Dicentra cucullaria*), spring beauties (*Claytonia virginica*), and trilliums, have bulbs, tubers, or other underground food storage organs and are evident above the ground for only a short period each year, usually in spring.

An essential task is to plan for the viewing and servicing of the garden-to-be by establishing at least one path or trail. If practicable, this should be wide enough for

Woodland gardens: (a) Featuring azaleas

(b) With rhododendrons blooming

(c) With outcropping rocks, a curving path, and irises in the foreground

at least two people to walk side by side, but in small areas a somewhat narrower one may be more appropriate. Have the path lead to or past the most interesting and beautiful parts of the area. Make sure that it is easy to traverse; gentle curves, easy grades, and, if needed, steps that pose no hazards are advantageous. Its surface should be rustic, composed of gravel, cinders, tanbark, sawdust, or some similar material. If the terrain permits, it is often desirable to have the path follow a course that ultimately leads back to its beginning.

(d) With hostas as a groundcover

Next, one must decide on the kinds of plants to be introduced and make stations ready for them. The latter is done by clearing away any existing vegetation and forking into the soil generous amounts of leaf mold, compost, peat moss, or other organic amendment, and usually little else. In the main, it is better to suit the kinds of plants to the terrain rather than attempt the reverse. Even small patches of woodland are likely to encompass a variety of microenvironments, and in larger ones changes from place to place are often dramatic. The soil in some areas may be deep and remarkably free of tree roots, in other areas it may be much shallower, with root competition more severe. There may be moist spots and dry ones, and density of shade is likely to vary from one place to another. Consider these and other local variations when deciding what to plant and where.

Distribute the plants to achieve as natural an effect as possible; formality is out of place in woodland gardens. Give particular thought to this if young trees or shrubs are to be added. Improper location, possibly making transplanting necessary at some future date, is more serious with them than with herbaceous plants, which are more easily moved. Where space permits, generous irregulr drifts of such showy plants as astilbes, bloodroots (*Sanguinaria canadensis*), English and Spanish bluebells (*Endymion non-scriptus* and *E. hispanicus*), hostas, primulas, trilliums, and Virginia bluebells (*Mertensia virginica*) can be impressive. However, lesser groupings and even occasional solitary specimens of these and of kinds less showy in bloom should also be part of the woodland garden. If rocks are prominent in the landscape, use chinks between them and locations at their bases as places to display appropriate choice plants. Patches of low groundcovers, such as bugle weed (*Ajuga*), heucheras, lily-of-the-valley (*Convallaria majalis*), Partridge-berry (*Mitchella repens*), *Phlox divaricata*, pick-a-back plant (*Tolmiea menziesii*), violets, wild-gingers (*Asarum*), and wintergreen (*Gaultheria procumbens*), look well near paths and as contrast between taller growers.

The care of woodland gardens, compared to that required by sunny gardens of equivalent size, is minimal. Besides any thinning out needed to curb rambunctious growers that threaten weaker neighbors, and occasional replanting or planting to restore or replenish areas from which plants have been lost by death or other causes, the chief needs are to keep the ground covered with a layer of leaf mold, rich compost, or equivalent mulch and to maintain a tidy appearance by removing, as becomes necessary, the tops of plants that have died down. Another necessity is to make sure that the natural leaf fall from the trees does not accumulate in some places to such depths that the well-being of the herbaceous plants it covers is threatened. In times of drought, selective watering of plants likely to benefit from this attention is in order.

Plants suitable for woodland gardens include most sufficiently attractive kinds that inhabit the forests and woods of the region. In addition, sorts native to similar environments in other parts of North America, Europe, Asia, and elsewhere are appropriate. It is well to avoid highly developed, gardenesque horticultural varieties (including practically all annuals) that too clearly be-

(c) *Pieris japonica*

(c) *Cypripedium calceolus*

(d) *Viburnum acerifolium*

(d) *Gentiana asclepiadea*

Shrubs for woodland gardens include:
(a) *Camellia japonica* varieties

Herbaceous perennials for woodland gardens: (a) *Anemone canadensis*

(e) *Mertensia virginica*

(b) *Leucothoe axillaris*

(b) *Endymion hispanicus*

(f) *Polystichum munitum*

(g) *Primula pulverulenta*

(h) *Trillium grandiflorum*

speak the art of the hybridizer, but hybrids and horticultural varieties that are not too blatant, such as most of those of azaleas, camellias, and rhododendrons, can, with propriety, be introduced. The selection is largely a matter of taste; it is important that the plants "look right" in the environment, that they belong under trees and meld with the undergrowth. For lists of evergreens, deciduous shrubs, vines, and herbaceous perennials (including bulb plants) from which selections for inclusion in woodland gardens can be made, see the Encyclopedia entry Shady Gardens, as well as the entry Groundcovers.

WOODLAND STAR. See Lithophragma.

WOODRUFF. See Asperula. Sweet woodruff is *Galium odoratum.*

WOODSIA (Woóds-ia). Named to honor the English botanist Joseph Woods, who died in 1864, *Woodsia* is a genus of about forty species of deciduous or, in mild climates, evergreen small ferns that inhabit rocky places in temperate and cold regions of the northern hemisphere and in South America and South Africa. It belongs in the aspidium family ASPIDIACEAE or, if the division of the polypody family POLYPODIACEAE into smaller families is not accepted, to the polypody family itself.

Woodsias have erect, clustered rhi-

zomes and pinnate or twice-pinnate fronds (leaves) with usually thick stalks shorter than the blades. Their clusters of round spore capsules are on the veins on the undersides of the fronds. They have indusia (covers) that at an early stage become cleft or frayed to form a starlike pattern of slender divisions.

Species with more or less glandular leaves that have stalks without joints include the blunt-lobed, mountain, and Oregon woodsias. The first of these, *W. obtusa,* native from Maine to Alaska, Florida, and Texas, generally occurs in approximately neutral, often dryish soils. It has sparsely-scaly rhizomes and clusters of gray-green fronds, up to 1¼ feet long, their stalks and midribs furnished with distant scales. The lanceolate blades are twice-pinnate with the eight to twenty pairs of approximately opposite primary leaflets rather distantly spaced and the final segments deeply-pinnately-lobed. From the last, mountain woodsia (*W. scopulina*) differs in the midribs and veins of its narrower, linear-lanceolate, sticky, aromatic fronds having long hairs and in the midribs being without scales. This is native, most usually in limestone soils, throughout much of North America, chiefly in mountain regions. Variety *W. s. appalachia* (syn. *W. appalachia*), which occurs in Virginia, West Virginia, and the Ozark Mountains, has narrower rhizome scales. Oregon woodsia (*W. oregana*) ranges from Quebec to British Columbia, South Dakota, and New Mexico in limestone or sandstone soils. It has stout rhizomes. Its fronds, up to 1 foot long, have lanceolate blades, ¾ inch to 2 inches wide, sparingly-glandular, but without hairs on the scaleless midribs or on the veins. The indusium lobes are slender and often hairlike. The variety *W. o. cathcartiana* (syn. *W. cathcartiana*) has leaf blades conspicuously glandular beneath.

Differing from the sorts described above in having nonglandular leaves with stalks jointed below their middles are the alpine, smooth, and rusty woodsias. The first, *W. alpina,* is wild from Greenland to Labrador, Vermont, and Michigan in both limestone and nonlimestone regions. This has fronds, 3 to 6 inches long, with thin, linear blades, up to ¾ inch wide, with slightly scaly and hairy midribs and eight to fifteen pairs of distantly spaced, pinnately-lobed leaflets, sparingly-hairy on their undersides. The smooth woodsia (*W. glabella*) grows natively on limestone rocks from Newfoundland to Alaska, New York, and British Columbia, and in northern Europe and Asia. This has very slender rhizomes and pointed-linear, once-pinnate fronds 2 to 6 inches long by up to ½ inch wide. The triangular to nearly round leaflets, without scales or hairs, are three-lobed or round-toothed at their margins. Favoring usually acid, frequently sterile soils and

Woodsia ilvensis

often exposed sites from Greenland to Alaska, Michigan, and Minnesota and in the mountains south to North Carolina, as well as in northern Europe and Asia, the rusty woodsia (*W. ilvensis*) has rhizomes thickly clothed with scales. Its gray-green fronds are 3 to 9 inches long and have glossy stalks, and oblong-lanceolate blades, ¾ inch to 1½ inches wide, of ten to sixteen pairs of deeply-pinnately-cleft leaflets fringed with a few hairs.

Garden Uses and Cultivation. Woodsias are choice for inclusion in fern collections and for rock gardens. Their cultural needs make no very special demands of the gardener. They grow best in loose rocky soil of an acid, neutral, or limy character in accordance with the preferences of individual species. Increase is by careful division and by spores. For more information see Ferns.

WOODWARDIA (Wood-wàrdia) — Chain Fern. Natives of North America, Europe, and Asia, the possibly dozen species of the genus *Woodwardia* belong in the blechnum family BLECHNACEAE. The name commemorates the English botanist Thomas J. Woodward, who died in 1820.

Woodwardias are large, rather coarse ferns with erect, ascending, or creeping rhizomes. Their firm leaves are in clusters or are scattered along creeping rhizomes. Usually twice-pinnate or -pinnately-lobed, they may be toothed at their margins or not. The groups of spore capsules are in rows or chains parallel with the mid-veins.

Native from Nova Scotia to Michigan, Florida, Louisiana, and Bermuda, the Virginia chain fern (*W. virginica*) has stout, widely spreading rhizomes with, scattered along their lengths, firm, once-pinnate, deciduous leaves with blades about as long as their stalks. There are about ten pinnately-lobed, alternately arranged leaflets on each side of the midrib. The leaves somewhat resemble those of the cinnamon fern (*Osmunda cinnamomea*). From 2 to 4 feet long by 9 inches to 1¼ feet wide, arching or erect, the fertile and sterile fronds are similar. This species inhabits bogs, swamps, and shallow ponds in soils ranging from extremely acid to mildly alkaline. It is too invasive and weedy to be admitted to landscapes other than wet-soil ones where little or nothing else can be expected to grow.

Netted chain fern (**W. areolata**) is by some authorities given separate generic rank as *Lorinseria areolata* on the basis that it produces two distinct kinds of leaves. It occupies wet, acid swamps and woods from Nova Scotia to Missouri, Florida, and

Woodwardia areolata

Texas, and in Michigan. Unlike the last, its scattered, 1- to 3-foot-long leaves, from widely spreading and branching rhizomes, are of two kinds. The sterile ones come in spring and have pale yellow to lustrous-brown stalks as long as the ovate blades, which are 6 inches to 1 foot long by two-thirds as broad, and are very deeply-pinnately-cleft into alternate, finely-toothed lobes. It is fall before the fertile leaves appear; sometimes they overtop the others. They have nearly black stalks, about as long as the blades and two-thirds as wide, and are cut into narrower, more widely spaced lobes and segments than the sterile leaves. This species has attractive, lustrous, bronzy-green foliage.

A native of moist and boggy soils from California to Arizona and British Columbia, **W. fimbriata** (syns. *W. chamissoi, W. radicans americana*) is much like *W. radicans*, but differs in not developing propagating buds on its leaves. It has woody rhizomes, and round clusters of firm, erect, short-stalked, typically twice-pinnately-lobed, more or less oblong fronds 3 to 6 feet high and 8 inches to 1½ feet wide or slightly wider. Their principal divisions are 4 to 10 inches long and are deeply-lobed into toothed, lanceolate segments.

Native to Europe and Asia, **W. radicans** has fertile and barren fronds similar to each other. They arch or rise erectly from stout rhizomes and are 3 or 4 feet long and pinnately-divided into numerous lanceolate-ovate, pinnately-lobed leaflets 6 inches to 1½ feet in length. The ultimate segments are pointed-lanceolate or linear-lanceolate,

Woodwardia radicans

and up to 3 inches long. Characteristically the leaves bear toward their ends large scaly buds, which develop into new plants.

Asian woodwardias include **W. japonica** (syn. *W. radicans japonica*), of Japan, Korea, China, Indochina, and Taiwan. This has oblong-ovate, deeply-lobed leaves, 1½ to 2½ feet tall and 9 inches to a little over 1 foot wide, with stalks with prominent brown scales, and ten to fifteen pairs of lanceolate-linear primary divisions. Differing in that the stalks of their leaves soon lose their scales are *W. unigemmata* (syn. *W. radicans unigemmata*) and *W. orientalis* (syn. *W. radicans orientalis*). Ranging from southeast Asia to the Himalayas, China, Japan, Taiwan, and the Philippine Islands, **W. unigemmata** has broadly-ovate leaves, 1 foot to 3½ feet long, twice-pinnately-divided with the divisions pinnately-divided or -lobed. There are large, scaly propagating buds in the axils of the upper primary leaf divisions. In **W. orientalis**, a native of Japan and China, the leaves often produce propagating buds and plantlets over the entire upper sides of the leaves, which are 1 foot to 3½ feet long by 8 inches to 1 foot wide, ovate-lanceolate, and pinnately-divided with the division pinnately-lobed.

Garden and Landscape Uses and Cultivation. Woodwardias are vigorous ferns of often aggressive, spreading habits. Generally they should be confined to places where they are unlikely to smother weaker-growing species. In masses they are attractive. Easy to grow, they are plants for wet and moist soils and generally partly shaded locations, but the Virginia chain fern grows satisfactorily in full sun. The hardiness of the various kinds can be judged from the regions to which they are native. Those from warm countries are sometimes cultivated in greenhouses. They grow readily in porous, fertile soil, fairly well supplied with peat or other organic material, and need a humid atmosphere and shade from bright sun. A winter night temperature of from 45 to 55°F suits, by day at that season it may be ten to fifteen degrees higher. These ferns respond gen-

erously to regular applications of dilute liquid fertilizers. They are propagated by spores, division, and some kinds by reproductive buds that develop on the fronds. See the entry Ferns for additional information.

WOODY NIGHTSHADE is *Solanum dulcamara*.

WOOLLY-MORNING-GLORY is *Argyreia nervosa*.

WOOLLYBUTT is *Eucalyptus longifolia*.

WORM. This word forms parts of the common names of these plants: worm-grass (*Spigelia marilandica*), worm plant (*Scorpiurus*), and worm vine (*Vanilla barbellata*).

WORMS. See Earthworms. The caterpillars or larvae of some insects are often colloquially called worms. Among such are the cabbage worm, the corn earworm, the currant worm, and the railroad worm.

WORMSEED. See Chenopodium.

WORMWOOD. See Artemisia.

WORSLEYA (Wòrs-leya)—Blue-Amaryllis. Some botanists retain *Worsleya* in *Hippeastrum*, but there seems to be sufficient botanical differences to warrant separating it as a genus of its own. The chief distinction is that *Worsleya* has four spathe valves, *Hippeastrum* two. Certainly the blue-amaryllis is quite distinct in appearance from the more familiar cultivated hippeastrums. There is only one species, a native of the Organ Mountains of Brazil. A member of the amaryllis family AMARYLLIDACEAE, this genus has a name that commemorates Arthington Worsley, an English student of the amaryllis family, who died in 1943.

The blue-amaryllis (**W. rayneri** syn. *Hippeastrum procerum*) scarcely meets the expectations likely to be conjured up by its colloquial name. Its blooms are not blue, but lavender to heliotrope, paling toward their bases to almost white and bespeckled with mauve spots; the coloring varies

Worsleya rayneri

Worsleya rayneri (base of bulb)

Worsleya rayneri in bloom at The New York Botanical Garden

somewhat between individuals. Nor do the flowers resemble those of the popular cultivated plants called amaryllis (*Hippeastrum*). They are more like those of *Amaryllis belladonna*, the South African belladonna-lily. The bulbs of the blue-amaryllis are quite astonishing. Very large, they have thick, tapering necks up to more than 1½ feet long, and form false stems. The glaucous, blue-gray, markedly sickle-shaped leaves spread outward from the summit of the false stem, and, from among them, in summer, is produced the leafless flower stalk. The leaves are up to 3 feet long by about 2 inches wide. The flower stalk is topped by an umbel of up to about half a dozen flowers. Trumpet-shaped and 5 or 6 inches long, they have very short tubes and six curving petals (more correctly, tepals) about 1 inch wide. There are six stamens and one style. The fruits are capsules.

Garden Uses and Cultivation. The blue-amaryllis is a choice item for collectors of rare plants and a very real challenge to even experienced gardeners. Only rarely has it bloomed in cultivation. Bulbs that have done so have mostly been fresh imports that presumably contained sufficient stores of food to ensure flowering, and perhaps even flower buds, at the time they were acquired. In the 1940s, the flowering in successive years of the same bulbs was achieved at The New York Botanical Garden and in Santa Barbara, California. These experiences strongly suggest that for its successful cultivation the blue-amaryllis needs cooler conditions than was generally supposed. At The New York Botanical Garden, slow but persisting deterioration occurred in specimens grown under the tropical, humid conditions that suit hybrid amaryllises (*Hippeastrum*), and such plants appeared particularly distressed during the

heat of summer. Only plants accommodated in a sunny greenhouse in which the winter night temperature was 45 to 50°F and by day not more than five to fifteen degrees higher, and which at all seasons was ventilated as freely as outdoor conditions permitted, prospered and bloomed more than once. These plants were grown in large, exceptionally well-drained containers that comfortably accommodated the wide-spreading roots. The soil was a very porous mixture of osmunda fiber, granite chips, coarse sand, and crushed charcoal, to which was added a small proportion of partially rotted, fibrous grass turf from which the finer soil had been shaken, a little dried cow manure, and a generous dash of bonemeal. Watering was moderate from spring to fall, more sparing in winter. After the containers were well filled with roots, regular spring-to-fall applications of very dilute liquid fertilizer were given. It probably would have been advantageous to have put the plants in a sunny place outdoors during the summer with their containers buried nearly to their rims in a bed of sand, peat moss, or similar material. The specimens cultivated successfully in Santa Barbara were accommodated in beds of decomposed granite raised 5 inches above the ground, where they received full sun except for a little shade in the afternoon. Such conditions approximate those under which the blue-amaryllis grows in its natural habitat, on ledges

of precipitous cliffs of soft, porous granite at altitudes of about 4,000 feet in mountains not far from Rio de Janeiro. Propagation is by seed and by offsets.

WOUNDWORT. See Stachys.

WREFORDARA. This is the name of orchid hybrids the parents of which include *Aerides*, *Arachnis*, *Euanthe*, and *Vanda*.

WRIGHTIA (Wright-ia). Named in honor of William Wright, a Scottish physician and botanist, who died in 1827, the genus *Wrightia*, of the dogbane family APOCYNACEAE, is native to tropical Africa, tropical Asia, and Australia. It comprises twenty-three species.

Wrightias are small trees and shrubs with often slender branches. They have opposite, undivided leaves. The flowers, in stalkless, branched clusters, are red, yellow, or white. They have a five-toothed calyx, a corolla with a slender tube, five spreading petals, and, in the throat, a corona of fringed, overlapping scales. There are five stamens with anthers adhering to the stigma. The fruits are paired, erect, slender, podlike follicles.

A native of India, **W. coccinea** is a tree with very short-stalked, elliptic-lanceolate leaves up to 5 inches long. In clusters of three or four, the rather fleshy, about 1-inch-wide flowers are dark red. Their stamens are conspicuously hairy. A small tree,

Wrightia antidysenterica

Wulfenia carinthiaca

native from India to Burma and Timor, **W. tinctoria** has variable, mostly elliptic-ovate to obovate-oblong leaves up to 5 inches long. Its white flowers, about ¾ inch in diameter, are in clusters up to 5 inches across. The species often cultivated as **W. antidysenterica** is by some botanists identified as *Holarrhena antidysenterica* of the same family. Native to tropical Asia, this species is a small deciduous tree with short-stalked, elliptic-oblong leaves 5 inches to 1 foot long. In clusters 3 to 6 inches wide, the attractive, scentless, pure white flowers, 1 inch to 2 inches across, are produced over a long period. In the Orient, the seeds, as well as other parts, of this species are reputed to have tonic and aphrodisiac properties and are used medicinally.

Garden and Landscape Uses and Cultivation. Wrightias are attractive for landscape plantings in the humid tropics and warm subtropics and for cultivation in tropical greenhouses. They succeed in any reasonably fertile, well-drained soil in sun or light shade and are easily propagated by seed and by cuttings.

WULFENIA (Wulf-ènia). The name of *Wulfenia*, of the figwort family SCROPHULARIACEAE, commemorates the Austrian botanist Franz Xavier Freiherr von Wulfen, who died in 1805. About five species constitute the genus, native to southeastern Europe, western Asia, and the Himalayas.

Wulfenias are tufted, hardy herbaceous perennials with mostly basal foliage. Their leaves are stalked and round-toothed to nearly lobed. The blue-violet or less often white, nodding flowers are in spikelike racemes terminating erect stalks. They have a five-lobed calyx, a tubular, four-lobed corolla, two stamens, and one style. The fruits are capsules.

Most commonly cultivated, **W. carinthiaca,** of the Balkans and the eastern European Alps, has erect, oblong to oblan-

ceolate leaves 3 to 9 inches long and hairless except along their winged stalks and midribs. The flower stalks, 1 foot to 2 feet tall, carry dense, many-flowered racemes, 1½ to 4 inches long, of round-petaled, blue-violet blooms about ½ inch long. The flowers of *W. c. alba* are white. Inhabiting shaded cliffs and rocks in mountains of Albania, **W. baldaccii** differs from *W. carinthiaca* in not exceeding 9 inches in height and in having hairy leaves and looser racemes of ⅓-inch-long, glandular-hairy flowers. Himalayan **W. amherstiana** has coarsely-toothed, obovate-oblong leaves, up to 1 foot long, and one-sided racemes, up to 1 foot tall, of ⅓-inch-long, blue-purple flowers.

Garden Uses and Cultivation. Although not rankable with the finest herbaceous perennials, wulfenias are deserving of garden space. Appropriate for flower beds and rock gardens, they are not difficult to satisfy. Best results are had in fertile soil, moist rather than dry, but certainly not excessively wet, especially in winter. New plants are easily had from seed and divisions.

WYETHIA (Wyèth-ia)—Compass Plant. The daisy family COMPOSITAE is particularly well represented in the flora of North America, notably by such vigorous, yellow-flowered herbaceous plants as sunflowers, heleniums, and goldenrods, to mention but a representative few. Here belongs *Wyethia*, a genus of fourteen species confined in the wild to the western part of the continent. The name commemorates Captain Nathaniel Wyeth, a botanical collector, who discovered its first species in 1833. Not

important horticulturally, these plants are occasionally introduced into gardens.

Wyethias usually have thick taproots, erect, branchless stems, and basal and stem leaves, the basal leaves more or less in rosettes. The leaves are linear, lanceolate, or triangular-ovate, with smooth or toothed margins. Commonly the flower heads are daisy-like and fairly large. They are solitary or are few in the leaf axils and at the end of the main stem. They have bisexual disk florets and female ray florets; both are fertile. In appearance the flower heads are much like those of balsam root (*Balsamorhiza*), but the leaves of the two genera are distinct. Incidentally, those of *Wyethia* are believed by some people to point only north and south. Because of this unfounded belief, they are sometimes called compass plants, a name equally as mistakenly applied to *Silphium*.

The commonest species, a native of moist meadows in California, **W. angustifolia** has branchless stems 8 inches to 2 feet tall. Its long-stalked basal leaves, about as long as the stems, are pointed-linear-lanceolate and without teeth. The stem leaves are stalkless, smaller, and often ovate-lanceolate; sometimes their margins are wavy or toothed. The flower heads have long stalks and are 1¼ to 1¾ inches wide. The seeds and leaves of this species, and probably others, were used by the Indians as food; its roots were employed medicinally. Favoring drier slopes and rocky places, **W. mollis** inhabits parts of California and Oregon and attains a height of up to 3 feet. When young its resin-dotted foliage is densely-tomentose, but most of the hairiness disappears with age. The lanceolate to oblong-ovate basal leaves are 8 inches to 1¼ feet long and have broad stalks. The stem leaves are similar, but smaller. The one to four flower heads are from ¾ inch to 1¼ inches in diameter.

Other sorts occasionally cultivated include **W. amplexicaulis,** native from Montana to Washington, Nevada, and Colorado. Up to about 3 feet high and hairless, this has short-stalked, oblong-lanceolate basal leaves, 8 inches to 1½ feet long, and smaller, stalkless stem leaves. Solitary or in clusters of few, the flower heads are 3 to 4 inches in diameter. With younger parts white-hairy, but becoming almost hairless later, **W. helenioides,** of California, has short-stalked, lanceolate to elliptic-ovate basal leaves up to 1 foot in length, and similar, but smaller stem leaves. Its mostly solitary flower heads are 4 to 5 inches wide.

Garden and Landscape Uses and Cultivation. Wyethias are hardy and have some horticultural uses in semiwild areas and occasionally, chiefly for variety, in flower borders. In their home territories they are appropriate in native plant gardens. They grow in ordinary garden soil in sunny locations and are increased by seed and by division.

X

XANTHERANTHEMUM (Xanth-eránthemum). The only species of *Xantheranthemum*, of the acanthus family ACANTHACEAE, is a native of the Andean region of Peru. Its name derives from the Greek *xanthos*, yellow, and *Eranthemum*, the name of a related genus.

A low, ornamental-leaved perennial, *X. igneum* (syn. *Chamaeranthemum igneum*) has prostrate stems and opposite leaves, their dark green upper surfaces embellished with yellow veins. The small, somewhat asymmetrical flowers, in terminal spikes with toothed green bracts, have a deeply-five-

Xantheranthemum igneum

Xantheranthemum igneum in bloom

parted calyx, a tubular, five-lobed, yellow corolla, four stamens, and one style. The fruits are capsules.

Garden Uses and Cultivation. Attractive for rock gardens and similar intimate outdoor plantings in the humid tropics, this species is useful also as an ornamental in tropical greenhouses and terrariums. It needs a minimum temperature of 60°F, high humidity, and shade. A well-drained soil rich with organic matter and kept evenly moist is best to its liking. Propagation is easy by cuttings, division, and seed.

XANTHISMA (Xan-thísma) — Star-of-Texas or Sleepy-Daisy. One showy annual or biennial, native to Texas and adjacent Louisiana, is the only member of this genus of the daisy family COMPOSITAE. Its name, derived from the Greek *xanthos*, yellow, alludes to the color of the blooms.

The star-of-Texas or sleepy-daisy (*Xanthisma texanum* syn. *Centauridium drummondii*) is an erect, branching, nearly hairless plant, 2 to 3 feet tall, with alternate, linear to narrowly-lanceolate leaves, the upper ones smooth-edged, the lower ones toothed or sometimes pinnately-lobed. The citron-yellow, daisy-like flower heads, sol-

Xanthisma texanum

itary at the ends of the branches, are about 2 inches wide. Their involucres (collars of leafy bracts at the backs of the flower heads) consist of several rows of green bracts with whitish margins. The fruits are seedlike achenes. The name sleepy-daisy refers to the flower heads being closed for part of the day.

Garden Uses. The star-of-Texas is decidedly worthwhile for inclusion in flower beds and borders and for cutting for indoor decoration. It makes a pleasing combination with blue-flowered ageratum. In its home territory it is appropriate in gardens of native plants. It stands hot weather well and blooms for a long period in summer and fall. From seed sown in early fall it can be flowered in sunny greenhouses in late winter and spring. When so grown, a night temperature of about 50°F, with a daytime increase of five to ten degrees, suits.

Cultivation. A sunny location and dryish, moderately fertile, well-drained soil suits this plant. Seeds are sown in spring where the plants are to bloom and the seedlings thinned to 6 to 8 inches apart, or they are started earlier in a greenhouse (temperature 60°F) and the young plants transplanted 2 to 2½ inches apart in flats or individually in small pots to be set in the garden when they are eight to ten weeks old and danger of frost has passed. While in the greenhouse, a night temperature of 50°F, with an increase of five to fifteen degrees by day, the smaller rise on dull days and the larger on bright sunny days, is adequate. Subsequent care chiefly consists of weeding and removing faded blooms. Staking is usually necessary. To have plants blooming in greenhouses from late winter onward, seeds are sown in September and the plants potted, in fertile well-drained soil, successively from small containers to larger ones until they are in receptacles about 6 inches in diameter. Watering is done to keep the soil always moderately moist, not constantly saturated. After the final pots are filled with roots, weekly applications of dilute liquid fertilizer do much to maintain vigor. Staking is needed. Temperatures of 50°F at night and 55 to 60°F by day are generally adequate; on bright sunny days an increase to 65°F is acceptable.

XANTHOCERAS (Xanthócer-as). Only one of the two species of the Chinese genus *Xanthoceras,* of the soapberry family SAP-INDACEAE, is cultivated. The name is from the Greek *xanthos,* yellow, and *keros,* a horn. It alludes to the yellow hornlike processes on the disks of the flowers.

Xanthocerases are shrubs or small trees with alternate, pinnate leaves. The flowers, in racemes from the ends of the branches and leaf axils, have five each sepals and petals, eight stamens, and a disk with five horns. There is one pistil. The fruits are horse-chestnut-like capsules.

A beautiful deciduous shrub or small tree up to about 25 feet tall, **X. sorbifolium** was introduced to cultivation in France in 1866 by the Abbé David. It has rather stout and stiff, erect branches, the younger ones with a thick core or pith. Its hairless, pinnate leaves of nine to seventeen leaflets have

Xanthoceras sorbifolium

lustrous dark green upper surfaces and are paler beneath. The flowers, which appear with the leaves in spring, are in erect panicles at the shoot ends and from side buds. They somewhat resemble the blooms of the horse-chestnut. The terminal panicles are 6 to 8 inches long, about twice the size of the lateral ones. Individual flowers, ¾ inch to 1¼ inches across, have white petals with a golden blotch at the base of each that changes to carmine as the bloom ages. Only the upper flowers of the terminal panicle are fertile; those toward its base and the flowers of the lateral panicles do not produce fruits. Smooth and top-shaped, the fruits are about 2 inches wide and contain black-brown seeds up to ½ inch in diameter.

Garden and Landscape Uses and Cultivation. This neat species, in cultivation

rarely more than of shrub dimensions, should be more commonly planted. It is well adapted to small properties and grows without special care in ordinary garden soils. Hardy as far north as Boston, Massachusetts, it can be relied upon to survive temperatures of −10°F, perhaps lower. It withstands heat and drought well. To flower profusely it needs a sunny location. No regular pruning is needed. Unfortunately this species does not transplant easily, especially when old. For the best results, set small plants out in spring.

Besides being excellent outdoors, *X. sorbifolium* forces well, and potted and tubbed specimens can be used to good effect for the winter decoration of large conservatories and other indoor areas. Propagation is easily effected by seed, as well as by root cuttings taken in January or February and planted indoors in a temperature of about 60°F. The young plants will be ready for planting in an outdoor nursery bed in about three months from the time the cuttings were taken. This species can also be increased by layering.

XANTHORHIZA (Xantho-rhìza) — Shrub Yellow-Root. One deciduous species of the buttercup family RANUNCULACEAE is the only representative of *Xanthorhiza.* The name, in allusion to the roots, derives from the Greek *xanthos,* yellow, and *rhiza,* a root. A native of damp woods from New York to Florida and Kentucky, this species earns its colloquial name by reason of the color beneath the bark of its roots. Like the below-bark color of the stems, this is bright yellow. The roots contain a bitter principle formerly used medicinally and are the source of a yellow dye.

The shrub yellow-root (**X. simplicissima** syns. *X. apiifolia, Zanthorhiza apiifolia*) is a suckering plant, 1 foot to 2 feet in height, with pinnate leaves of about five leaflets that are sharply-lobed and -toothed or often are again pinnately-divided. The leaves spread from the upper parts of the stems, forming more or less terminal clusters. From below the foliage, slender, pendu-

Xanthorhiza simplicissima

lous flower clusters, branched or branchless and up to 4 inches long, are borne in spring. They are without ornamental qualities and are practically hidden by the foliage. The brownish, purple, starry flowers, up to ¼ inch across, have five petal-like sepals and five smaller, two-lobed petals. There are five to ten stamens and five or more pistils. The fruits are one-seeded follicles.

Garden and Landscape Uses. Although without showy flowers or fruits or autumn color, the shrub yellow-root commends itself by its neat habit of growth and ornamental foliage. It is very satisfactory as a large-scale groundcover, either in sun or partial shade, and is also useful in clumps or patches at the fronts of shrub

Xanthorhiza simplicissima as a groundcover, the Arnold Arboretum, Jamaica Plain, Massachusetts

borders. Because its stems are many and of surprisingly uniform height and because its foliage is ample and well disposed, it always presents a neat, tailored appearance. It is hardy through most of New England. It prefers a reasonably moist, fertile soil.

Cultivation. This species is easily increased by division in early spring or early fall and by seed sown in a shaded cold frame in fall or spring in soil kept evenly moist, but not wet. Plant in early spring or fall, spacing rooted suckers or young plants 1½ to 2 feet apart. Mulching new plantings minimizes trouble with weeds. Established plantings need practically no care. If they become overgrown or ragged, the plants, if cut back close to the ground in spring, soon renew themselves by developing new shoots from the stumps of the old stems and the roots.

XANTHORRHOEA (Xantho-rrhoèa) — Grass Tree or Blackboy. The about fifteen species of curious and picturesque plants that constitute *Xanthorrhoea,* of the lily family LILIACEAE, are natives of desert and semidesert regions in Australia. Rather rare in cultivation, in aspect they suggest dasylirions, a circumstance undoubtedly related to the similar environments under which these plants grow. The name is from the Greek *xanthos*, yellow, and *rheo*, to flow. It alludes to the exudation of resin from the trunks of several kinds. This resin is used commercially for making varnishes, glazes, and sealing wax.

Grass trees or blackboys have woody, palmlike trunks largely concealed by the bases of old leaves and up to 10 feet tall or, in some kinds, so short that the plants appear to be stemless. They are topped by huge mops of narrow-linear leaves up to 3 feet long or longer. Blooming is often irregular and frequently follows exposure to brush fires.

The flowering spikes are extraordinary. They stretch upward from the foliage like huge pokers or candles, often to a great height. Fancifully, specimens in bloom observed from a distance have been likened to natives carrying spears. This is the reason for the name blackboys. The flowering spikes are straight, rigid, 1 inch to 2 inches in diameter, and, according to species, 3 to 10 feet long. Their upper halves bear numerous, small, fragrant, yellow or cream-colored, stalkless, starry flowers tucked among an abundance of small bracts. The blooms have six petals (correctly, tepals) and six stamens. The fruits are triangular, sharp-pointed capsules.

Kinds cultivated include **X. arborea**, which has a trunk up to 10 feet tall and flower spikes that may extend up to 10 feet higher. Its leaves are flat and up to 4 feet long. From this kind, **X. quadrangulata** differs in having four-angled leaves 1½ to 3 feet in length. At maturity its trunk is 4 to 9 feet high. Flower spikes, up to 3 feet long, are held aloft on stalks as long as the spikes or, more rarely, on much shorter stalks.

Garden and Landscape Uses and Cultivation. Only in such warm, dry climates that characterize parts of the southwest, and in full sun where the soil is well drained, are these unusual plants likely to succeed. They are propagated by seed.

XANTHOSOMA (Xantho-sòma)—Yautia or Malanga or Tanier. A few species of this genus are the source of one of the most ancient food crops of the Americas, yautia, malanga, or tanier, which is much like taro (*Colocasia esculenta*) and is cooked and eaten in tropical countries. Belonging to the arum family ARACEAE, and usually having tuberous rhizomes, the approximately forty species of *Xanthosoma* are milky-juiced, herbaceous perennials of tropical America. They closely resemble the Old World genera *Alocasia* and *Colocasia*, but differ in technical details of the attachment of the ovaries. From nearly related *Caladium* they are differentiated by their flowers having projecting, shield-shaped styles. The name, alluding to the color of the disk of the flowers, comes from the Greek *xanthos*, yellow, and *soma*, a body.

Xanthosomas have usually large, arrow- or spear-shaped or sometimes pedately-divided (like a spreading foot), long-stalked leaves, with the stalks attached at, not in from, the edge of the blade. Their flowers, as is usual with the arum family, are crowded in spikes called spadices, from the base of each of which comes a leaf- or petal-like bract called a spathe. In *Xanthosoma*, the spadix is shorter than the spathe and is crowded with little unisexual flowers, the female ones on its lower part separated from the pollen-bearing males by a short, constricted section bearing imperfect, sterile male flowers. The lower part of the persistent spathe is narrowed below its middle into a tube that encloses the spadix. Above, it flares into a boat-shaped blade. Kinds known variously as yautia, malanga, tanier, badu, and oto include *X. violaceum*, *X. atrovirens*, *X. sagittaefolium*, and perhaps other species. Their tubers are cooked and eaten like taro or potatoes. The leaves of some kinds, especially those of *X. brasiliense*, are cooked and eaten. No parts are edible without cooking.

Native to the West Indies and South America, and cultivated there and in many tropical places for its edible tubers, **X. violaceum** is a handsome, stemless species. Its leaves are dusted with waxy, white powder that gives it something of a plum-like appearance. They have brownish to violet stalks up to 3 feet long, about twice the length of the blades. The latter are ar-

Xanthorrhoea arborea

Xanthorrhoea quadrangulata

row-shaped, with slightly spreading basal lobes very much shorter than the middle one. Their upper sides are dull green with purplish veins, their undersides green and purplish. The inflorescences have yellowish-white spathes, purplish in their lower parts and about 1 foot long. The sterile portion of the spadix is violet.

Also with edible tubers, **X. atrovirens** is a South American native up to 3 feet tall. Stemless, it has leaves similar in shape to those of the last and with a dusting of fine waxy particles. The sterile part of the spadix is pale rose-pink. The leaves are dark green above, with lighter veins, and are paler on their undersides. They have green stalks. The spathes are green. Very ornamental and compact, **X. a. albo-marginatum** has gray-veined, bluish-green leaves edged with white. A curious variant, **X. a. albo-marginatum monstrosum** has smaller, partly-lobed, white-edged leaves, with some of the lobes with their edges rolled to form shallow cups. Another curious variety, and something of a monstrosity, **X. a. appendiculatum** has on the undersides of its small leaves a leafy, cup-shaped attachment.

Differing from the kinds discussed above in having a stout stem or trunk 3 to 4 feet tall, **X. sagittaefolium** has green, pale-veined, arrow-shaped leaves without a white powdery coating; the stalks are winged at their bases, but not channeled. Its greenish-white spathes are 6 to 9 inches long.

In Hawaii called Tahitian-spinach, **X. brasiliense,** a native of the West Indies, is cultivated there and elsewhere for its leaves, which are cooked as greens. From 1 foot to 3 feet tall, this has thin tubers. Its spear-shaped leaves have blades, up to 1¼ feet long, with basal lobes prominently notched near their apexes. The green spathes are about 6 inches long.

A handsome ornamental, **X. lindenii,** a native of Colombia, has leathery, arrow-shaped, pale green leaves clearly veined in zebra pattern with white, and with the center lobe about twice as long as the

Xanthosoma lindenii

Xanthosoma lindenii magnificum

spreading basal ones. The spathes are white. Two variants, *X. l. magnificum* and *X. l. albescens*, are cultivated. The first has leaves, larger than those of *X. lindenii*, that are yellowish to darker green and broadly-veined with white or creamy-white, and have a pale line paralleling the leaf edge. Wider white featherings extending from the midrib and white margins are characteristic of *X. l. albescens*.

Other kinds occasionally cultivated as ornamentals are **X. jacquinii lineatum,** of Brazil, which has large, white-veined, green leaves; **X. roseum variegatum,** a Mexican kind with parti-colored leaves of green and white; and **X. wendlandii** (syn. *X. hoffmannii*). The last differs markedly from other kinds discussed here in that its leaves are divided into separate leaflets. Oblanceolate, they spread from a curved base. Their upper sides are dull green with the veins depressed. Beneath they are lustrous.

Garden and Landscape Uses and Cultivation. In addition to some kinds being cultivated in the tropics as food crops, xanthosomas are grown outdoors in the humid tropics and warm subtropics, and in tropical greenhouses, as ornamental foliage plants. They prosper under conditions that suit alocasias, anthuriums, and many other tropical aroids, reveling in deep, rich, moist soil where there is some shade from the full intensity of the sun. They are commonly propagated by division, but in some cases they can be raised from seed sown while fresh in sandy, peaty soil at a temperature of 70 to 80°F.

XANTHOXYLUM. See Zanthoxylum.

XENOPHYA (Xenó-phya). Differing technically from *Alocasia* in details of its ovules, *Xenophya*, of the arum family ARACEAE, comprises two species of the Old World tropics. The name comes, perhaps, from the Greek *xenos*, strange, and *phyas*, a shoot or sucker.

Xenophyas are erect, evergreen, herbaceous perennials with long-stalked, lanceolate, lobeless or pinnately-lobed leaves. As is common in the arum family, the inflorescences, commonly referred to as "flowers," consist of a spadix (spike) crowded with the tiny blooms and, from its base, a spathe (petal-like or leaflike bract). In *Xenophya* the spathe is rolled for its entire length into a persistent tube that encloses the spadix. It does not have, as do the inflorescences of *Alocasia*, a spreading blade. When the flowers are ripe for pollination a short opening develops on one side of the tube opposite the male flowers. This presumably serves to admit pollinating insects. The individual flowers are unisexual, the males on the upper part of the spadix, the females below. The latter have pistils consisting of an ovary and a stigma without an intervening style.

Native from New Guinea to New Ireland, **X. lauterbachiana** (syns. *Schizocasia lauterbachiana, Alocasia wavriniana*) has rigid, metallic-bronzy-green, lanceolate, lobeless leaves, arrow-shaped at their bases and with veins paler than the body of the leaf. Not known to be in cultivation, **X. acuta,** of New Guinea, differs in having deeply-pinnately-lobed leaves.

Garden and Landscape Uses and Cultivation. The uses and cultivation of xenophyas are those of *Alocasia* as grown for ornament.

XERANTHEMUM (Xerán-themum) — Immortelle, Everlasting Flower. The genus *Xeranthemum* consists of half a dozen species of the Mediterranean region that belong to the daisy family COMPOSITAE. The name, from the Greek *xeros*, dry, and *anthos*, a flower, alludes to the flower heads being membranous or papery and, after cutting and drying, capable of retaining their form and color for months or years.

Xeranthemums are erect, pubescent annuals. They have alternate, undivided leaves and long-stalked, compact heads of small florets with associated spreading, papery, white, pink, lavender, or purple, petal-like bracts. The fruits are seedlike achenes.

The common immortelle (**X. annuum**), one of the best everlasting flowers, is from 2 to 3 feet tall and freely-branched. It has white-hairy, oblong-lanceolate leaves up to 2 inches long. The flower heads are showy, white, pink, or purple, and about 1½ inches in diameter. Double or semidouble blooms are borne by *X. a. ligulosum*. Seedsmen's varieties of *X. annuum*, named *compactum, multiflorum, album,* and *roseum,* are selected strains with characteristics as indicated by their names. Occasionally cultivated, **X. cylindraceum,** up to 2 feet high, has linear to elliptic-oblong leaves densely-white-hairy on their undersides, less thickly so on their upper surfaces. The flower heads are ovoid and pink.

Garden Uses. In addition to their usefulness as dried "everlastings," xeranthemums are attractive as freshly cut flowers and as showy plants to ornament garden beds and borders. They are easy to grow and remain in good condition in the garden for a long period. To prepare them for use as "everlastings," cut them with long stems just before they attain maturity, tie them in small, loose bundles, and hang them upside down in a dry, airy place, shaded from direct sun, until quite dry.

Cultivation. For best results, xeranthemums should be grown on rather poor, well-drained, porous soil. They then flower more freely than in very fertile soil. The seed is sown in spring directly where the plants are to bloom and is covered to a depth of not over ¼ inch. Before the young plants crowd each other they are thinned to about 6 inches apart. Alternatively, seed can be sown indoors, some six to eight weeks before the plants are to be set in the garden and the young plants grown in flats, until planting out time; ordinarily there is no advantage in this procedure. Summer care involves keeping the plants free of weeds and removing spent flowers. Staking is usually needed and this can be provided by inserting light brushwood stakes between the plants or by other suitable means. The plants bloom ten or eleven weeks from seed sowing.

XEROMPHIS (Xeróm-phis). The about seven species of *Xeromphis*, of the madder family RUBIACEAE, are by some authorities included in *Randia*. They are natives of tropical Africa and Asia. The name, alluding to the habitats of some kinds, comes from the Greek *xeros*, dry. In East Africa the fruits of *X. nilotica* are employed as an aphrodisiac and its roots in the treatment of syphilis.

The sorts of this genus, relatives of gardenias, are generally spiny shrubs and small trees. They have opposite leaves, those of each pair often of different sizes. Solitary or in twos or threes at the ends of leafy side shoots, the flowers have a lobeless, toothless calyx, a tubular, five-lobed corolla, five stamens, and one style. The fruits are berries.

Cultivated in the warm subtropics and tropics, *X. spinosa* (syn. *Randia dumetorum*), of tropical Asia, is a rigidly-branched, deciduous shrub or less often tree up to about 25 feet tall, viciously armed with long, stout spines. Its obovate leaves are 1 inch to 2 inches long. Mostly solitary, the white to greenish-yellow flowers are downy on the outside of the corolla. The spherical to egg-shaped fruits are 1 inch to 1½ inches long.

Garden and Landscape Uses and Cultivation. The species described is suitable for planting outdoors in warm, essentially frost-free climates. It succeeds in ordinary, well-drained soil and may be increased by seed and by cuttings.

XEROPHYLLUM (Xero-phýllum) — Turkey Beard, Bear-Grass or Squaw-Grass. Two or, according to some botanists, three species constitute *Xerophyllum*, of the lily family LILIACEAE. The eastern American turkey beard inhabits the pine barrens of New Jersey, the dry mountain woods from Virginia to Tennessee, and North Carolina. The bear-grass, native to dry slopes in western North America, is also called squaw-grass; this because Indian women used the tough leaves for basket making and similar work. The name of the genus, derived from the Greek *xeros*, dry, and *phyllon*, a leaf, alludes to the foliage.

Xerophyllums are deciduous, hardy, perennial herbaceous plants with stout, stemlike rhizomes from which arise dense clusters of numerous slender, rigid, rough-edged, grasslike leaves and erect annual branchless stems, furnished with similar, but smaller leaves. The creamy-white flowers are in showy, dense, terminal racemes. Each has six separate spreading petals (more correctly, tepals) that do not fall, but wither and remain surrounding the fruits, six flat-stalked stamens, and three slender styles. The fruits are oblong, three-compartmented capsules with two to four seeds in each compartment.

The eastern American turkey beard (**X. asphodeloides**) attains a height up to 5 feet and has basal leaves up to 1½ feet in length, but usually shorter. The stem leaves gradually become shorter from the base upward. The flower cluster, 2 to 2½ inches in diameter, gradually elongates up to 6 inches or even 1 foot in length. The ¼-inch-wide blooms are delicately fragrant. Their stamens are shorter than the petals.

The bear-grass or squaw-grass (**X. tenax**) is astonishingly beautiful in its native range and no less attractive when thriving under cultivation. In the wild it sometimes forms nearly pure stands, often many acres in extent, and presents an unforgettable sight when in bloom. It is native from California to British Columbia and the Rocky Mountains. This kind forms hummocks of slender basal leaves up to 1 foot in length and has stems clothed with leaves that gradually diminish in size from the base upward. The flower stems, up to 5 feet tall, terminate in plumy racemes 4 inches to 2 feet in length. The blooms, about ¼ inch in diameter, have stamens as long as or longer than the petals. A third species, **X. douglasii,** is distinguished by some botanists as distinct from *X. tenax* on the basis that it has a six-valved rather than a three-valved seed capsule. It occurs rarely as a native from Montana to Oregon and is reported to be inferior to *X. tenax* as a decorative.

Garden and Landscape Uses. These plants are less frequently cultivated than their merits deserve. They are admirable for wild gardens and medium-sized to large rock gardens and for featuring on gentle slopes or elsewhere where their beauty can

be displayed without the plants being crowded among others. They are agreeable in lawn beds, if well spaced and underplanted with a low groundcover. Their summer season of bloom is an extended one. In general, the eastern species is best adapted to eastern American gardens and the western ones to gardens in the west.

Cultivation. Once established, no special treatment is needed and xerophyllums may remain undisturbed for many years. It is better not to transplant them unless absolutely necessary. A spring application of a complete garden fertilizer is helpful. Propagation is by seed.

XEROSICYOS (Xero-sícyos). That these desert inhabitants belong to the gourd family CUCURBITACEAE comes as a surprise to almost all who learn of it. It is difficult to imagine plants less similar in appearance to cucumbers, squashes, gourds, pumpkins, melons, and others of that relationship. Only an examination of the botanical details of their blooms and fruits places them. Their name comes from the Greek *xeros*, dry, and the name of the genus *Sicyos* of the same family.

There are two species of *Xerosicyos*. They are shrubs endemic to Malagasy (Madagascar). They have slender, erect or more or less trailing stems and attain heights of about 1½ feet. Their thick leaves are alternate and have short stalks. Tendrils, shortly-forked at their tips, are borne opposite some of the leaves. The flowers, whitish and tiny, are in clusters in the leaf axils.

In **X. danguyi** the leaves are obovate and about 1¼ inches wide. They have flat or slightly hollowed upper surfaces and rounded lower ones. Similar **X. perrieri** has leaves that are obovate and terminate in a distinct, abrupt, short point.

Garden and Landscape Uses and Cultivation. These shrubs were not brought into cultivation until the 1940s and have not been planted extensively. They grow readily under conditions that suit the majority of succulent plants and propagate easily by cuttings and layers. They must have well-drained soil maintained on the

Xerosicyos perrieri

Xerosicyos perrieri (flowers)

dryish rather than the wet side, and do best in full sun. They are appropriate for inclusion in collections of succulents and as interesting shrubs for outdoor landscaping in warm, dry climates. For general information see Succulents.

XIMENESIA ENCELIOIDES is *Verbesina encelioides.*

XIMENIA (Xim-ènia)—Tallow Nut or Tallow Wood or Hog-Plum. This genus belongs in the olax family OLACACEAE. It comprises ten or more species of the Americas from Florida southward, and of Africa. Its name commemorates the Spanish monk Francis Ximenes, who early in the seventeenth century wrote about Mexican plants. The name hog-plum is also applied to *Spondias mombin.*

Ximenias are usually thorny, hairy or hairless shrubs and trees with alternate or clustered, more or less leathery, undivided leaves. The flowers are in short axillary clusters or more rarely are solitary. They have calyxes with four or five teeth or lobes, and four or five narrow petals hairy on their insides. There are twice as many stamens as petals. The fruits are one-seeded, fleshy, plumlike drupes.

The tallow wood, tallow nut, or hog-plum (*Ximenia americana*) is a semiparasitic, spiny shrub or tree sometimes 30 feet in height. A native of tropical and subtropical regions in many parts of the world, in the United States it is indigenous to Florida. Its fragrant fruits are edible. Their seeds contain abundant oil. The bark has been used locally for tanning, the wood as a substitute for sandalwood. The leaves of tallow wood are in twos or threes. Short-stalked, oblong, and blunt, they are 1½ to 3 inches long. Shorter than the leaves, the flower clusters are of two to four, yellow or yellowish-white, thick-petaled blooms, about ¾ inch wide, with brownish hairs on their insides. The yellow, plum-shaped fruits are about 1 inch long. Each contains a large stone.

Garden and Landscape Uses and Cultivation. Rarely cultivated, tallow wood is

sometimes incorporated into developed landscapes by allowing natural stands to remain. Under such conditions it requires no particular care other than any trimming needed to keep it shapely. It is propagated by seed.

XYLOBIUM (Xy-lòbium). Orchids native from Mexico to the West Indies, Brazil, and Peru, akin to *Lycaste* and *Bifrenaria,* constitute *Xylobium.* They number thirty-three species of the orchid family ORCHIDACEAE. The name, from the Greek *xylon,* wood, and *bios,* life, alludes to their living on trees.

Usually epiphytes (tree-perchers), xylobiums take no nourishment from their hosts. Rarely they grow on rocks or in the ground. Xylobiums have thick, fleshy pseudobulbs, each with one or two or occasionally three large leaves pleated lengthwise and narrowed to their stalks. Rising from the bases of the pseudobulbs, the erect flower stalks carry, in short, dense racemes, medium-sized to fairly large, short-stalked blooms in the axils of linear bracts. Each flower has three sepals, at first pointing forward, later spreading, the upper one narrower than the others; two petals similar to or smaller than the upper sepal; and a lip with a short, broad middle

Xylobium bractescens

Xylobium squalens

lobe and a pair of side lobes that embrace the column.

Native to Peru, *X. bractescens* has pointed-ovate pseudobulbs about 2½ inches tall and a pair of leaves from 1 foot to 1½ feet long. Its greenish-yellow blooms, with sepals and petals about 1 inch long, have several fleshy, brown ridges on the obscurely-three-lobed lip. The bracts are 1½ to 2 inches long. The five- or six-ribbed, ovoid-oblong pseudobulbs of *X. squalens,* of Central America, are 1½ to 2¾ inches tall. Each carries two leaves 1 foot to 2 feet in length. The dingy, pink-tinged, yellowish-white flowers, densely packed in racemes 4 to 8 inches long, have purple-streaked sepals and petals ¾ inch long. The lip has purple side lobes. Somewhat similar *X. foveatum* has smooth or ridged, more or less pointed, ovoid pseudobulbs up to 4 inches in length. They have two or sometimes three lanceolate leaves up to 1¼ feet long. Up to 1 foot in length, the crowded racemes have broad bracts and many straw-colored blooms. The sepals and petals are about ¾ inch long. This is native from Mexico to northern South America and Jamaica.

Pseudobulbs up to nearly 1 foot long by ½ inch wide are characteristic of *X. elon-*

Xylobium elongatum

gatum. Each has two linear-lanceolate to broad-elliptic leaves up to 1½ feet long. From 3 inches to 1 foot in length, the racemes are of five to fifteen flowers, prevailingly white to pale yellow with purple or maroon stripes on their conspicuously warty lips. The sepals and petals are ¾ inch long. The bracts are brownish-red. A single leaf, broadly-lanceolate and up to 1½ feet long, comes from each ovoid to broad-cylindrical, 2- to 3-inch-tall pseudobulb of *X. palmifolium,* a native of Central America. The racemes, not over 4 inches long, are of loosely arranged, yellowish-white blooms with sepals and petals ¾ inch long and a lip with a warty middle lobe. This is endemic to the West Indies. Another with usually one, rarely two leaves from each

Xylobium powellii

pseudobulb is **X. powellii,** of Central America. The pseudobulbs are up to 3 inches long by ½ inch wide, the leaves up to 2 feet long by 2 inches wide. The racemes, with several papery bracts below the flowering part, are of sometimes green-tinged, yellow to tan blooms, with ½-inch-long sepals and petals. The lips are frequently without lateral lobes. Nearly spherical pseudobulbs up to 1 inch long and crowned with a single leaf up to 1¼ feet long are typical of **X. colleyi,** of tropical South America and Trinidad. Its drooping racemes are of four or five fleshy, maroon-spotted, pinkish-light-brown blooms with ¾-inch-long sepals and shorter petals. As long as the sepals, the lip is pinkish-maroon with a dark red, sticky apex.

Garden Uses and Cultivation. By no means among the most spectacular of orchids, xylobiums are unlikely to make much appeal except to collectors. They need the same conditions and care as lycastes. For more information see Lycaste, and Orchids.

XYLOCOCCUS (Xylo-cóccus). Formerly known as *Arctostaphylos bicolor*, the only species of *Xylococcus* may be distinguished from *Arctostaphylos* by its fruits containing a solid smooth stone not separable into a few nutlets as those of *Arctostaphylos* usually can be and by the stamen filaments not being dilated at their bases. The name of this genus of the heath family ERICA-CEAE is derived from the Greek *xylon*, wood, and *kokkos*, a berry, and alludes to the fruits.

A densely-branched shrub, up to 10 feet tall, with shedding bark, grayish branches, and evergreen, alternate or opposite leaves, **X. bicolor** is a native of dry soils in southern California and Baja California. Its short-stalked, ovate to oblong leaves, pointed at both ends, are 1¼ to 2 inches long, dark green and hairless above, and grayish-pubescent beneath; their margins are strongly rolled under. The white or pink, shortly-five-lobed blooms are few together in dense, branched or branchless, terminal

clusters. Urn-shaped and about ⅓ inch long, they have ten, or rarely fewer, stamens. The fruits are red to almost black and about ¼ inch in diameter.

Garden Uses and Cultivation. These are similar to those of the manzanita kinds of *Arctostaphylos*. The plant is hardy only in mild climates.

XYLOPHYLLA. See Phyllanthus.

XYLOSMA (Xy-lósma). Widely distributed in the tropics and subtropics, except Africa, *Xylosma*, of the flacourtia family FLA-COURTIACEAE, consists of 100 species of spiny evergreen trees and shrubs. Its name derives from the Greek *xylon*, wood, and *osme*, fragrance. It alludes to the scented wood of some kinds.

Xylosmas have alternate, undivided, toothed or less often toothless leaves, and small, usually unisexual flowers in clusters or in racemes from the leaf axils. Each bloom has four or five sepals, usually united at their bases, numerous stamens, and a single, sometimes more or less divided style. There are no petals. The fruits are small, two- to eight-seeded berries.

Cultivated in California and other mild climate regions, **X. congestum** (syns. *X. senticosum, Myroxylon senticosum*) is an attractive low shrub with rusty-hairy shoots and sharp, slender spines. Its pointed-ovate, glandular-toothed leaves, about ¾ inch long, have revolute margins. The unisexual, yellow flowers, few together in racemes, are fringed with hairs. The berries are greenish-red. This is native to China.

A native of the Bahamas, **X. bahamensis** is an upright, intricately-branched, neat-foliaged shrub usually not over 12 feet, but occasionally up to 20 feet tall. The branches are plentifully furnished with needle-like, often branched spines. The nearly stalkless, leathery leaves, ⅓ to 1 inch long or a little longer, are elliptic to ovate and are toothless or have one to four small, blunt teeth along their margins. The fruits, which ripen in summer, are red and about ¼ inch long.

Others cultivated include *X. flexuosum,* of Mexico and Central America, and *X. heterophyllum*, of Colombia. A spiny shrub or tree up to 20 feet tall, **X. flexuosum** has leathery, elliptic-oblong to obovate, toothed leaves up to 2½ inches long. Its fruits are red, subspherical, and about ¼ inch in diameter. Spineless and shrubby **X. heterophyllum** has short-stalked, pointed-ovate, toothed, leathery leaves up to 2½ inches long. Its fruits are spherical, red, and ¼ inch in diameter.

Garden and Landscape Uses and Cultivation. Xylosmas are useful for mild-climate planting. They have neat foliage and can be used as barrier plantings and in other ways. They stand shearing well and so lend themselves for use as formal hedges. Full sun or part-shade is satisfac-

tory, and they accommodate to poor, rocky soils. Propagation is by seed and by cuttings.

XYLOTHECA. See Oncoba.

XYRIDACEAE—Yellow-Eyed-Grass Family. The about fifty species of this family of monocotyledons are accommodated in two genera, one of which, *Xyris*, is cultivated. Most abundant in the tropics, the yellow-eyed-grass family is represented in the native floras of most parts of the world except Europe. Of rushlike aspect, its members are herbaceous perennials or annuals with mostly basal, sheathing leaves arranged in two ranks. In crowded, bracted heads topping leafless stalks, the flowers have three or less often two unequal sepals, three petals, three stamens, three staminodes (nonfunctional stamens), and one branchless or three-branched style. The fruits are capsules.

XYRIS (Xỳ-ris) — Yellow-Eyed-Grass. Despite the common name, these plants are not grasses. They belong to the yellow-eyed-grass family XYRIDACEAE, a group that comprises only two genera and is chiefly tropical. There are about 100 species of *Xyris*, mostly natives of South America, but some inhabit North America and some the Old World. Their name is one applied by Dioscorides to *Iris foetidissima*.

Rushlike perennials, members of this genus have erect stems with the foliage mostly at or close to their bases. The bottoms of the linear or lanceolate leaves sheath the stems. The flower stalks are crowned with a solitary, rounded, ovate, or more or less cylindrical head of several flowers and many overlapping bracts. There are three sepals, three yellow, or rarely white, petals, three stamens, and three staminodes (nonfunctional stamens) to each flower.

In bloom 1¼ to 2½ feet tall, and with a bulbous base, **X. flexuosa** inhabits moist and dry, acid soils from New Jersey to Florida, Texas, and Arkansas. Its leaves, 8 inches to 1½ feet long, are very slender and conspicuously twisted. The flower heads, narrowly-egg-shaped and approximately ½ inch long, have straw-colored or tan bracts. Not bulbous-based, but forming dense mats, **X. montana** inhabits peat bogs from Newfoundland to Ontario, New Jersey, and Michigan. From 1 foot to 1½ feet tall, it has very slender, straight leaves up to 6 inches long, and egg-shaped to narrowly-egg-shaped flower heads ¼ to ½ inch long.

Garden Uses and Cultivation. This genus is of slight horticultural importance. Native species may occasionally be grown in wild gardens, bog gardens, and similar areas. They succeed under conditions similar to those under which they occur naturally, and are increased by seed and by division.

YAM. See Dioscorea. The cockscomb-yam is *Rajania pleioneura*. The yam-bean is *Pachyrhizus erosa*. In North America, some varieties of sweet-potatoes are called yams.

YAMPEE or YAMPI is *Dioscorea trifida*.

YANG-TAO is *Actinidia chinensis*.

YAPARA. This is the name of orchid hybrids the parents of which include *Phalaenopsis, Rhynchostylis,* and *Vanda*.

YARD-LONG-BEAN is *Vigna unguiculata sesquipedalis*.

YARROW. See Achillea.

YATE TREE is *Eucalyptus cornuta*.

YAUPON is *Ilex vomitoria*.

YAUTIA. See Xanthosoma.

YEDDO-HAWTHORN is *Raphiolepis umbellata*.

YELLOW. The word yellow forms parts of the common names of these plants: Australian-yellow-wood (*Rhodosphaera rhodanthema*), Carolina yellow-jessamine (*Gelseminum sempervirens*), double yellow-rocket (*Barbarea vulgaris flore-pleno*), golden yellow hawkweed (*Tolpis barbata*), scrub-yellow-wood (*Acronychia baueri*), shrub yellow-root (*Xanthorhiza simplicissima*), upright-yellow-wood (*Podocarpus latifolius*), yellow archangel (*Lamiastrum galeobdolon*), yellow bachelor's button (*Ranunculus repens pleniflorus*), yellow bells (*Emmenanthe penduliflora* and *Tecoma stans*), yellow-box (*Eucalyptus melliodora*), yellow-caesalpinia (*Peltophorum*), yellow Chinese-poppy (*Meconopsis integrifolia*), yellow colic root (*Aletris aurea*), yellow-elder (*Tecoma stans*), yellow-eyed-grass (*Xyris*), yellow flag (*Iris pseudacorus*), yellow-flamboyant (*Peltophorum pterocarpum*), yellow-flax (*Reinwardtia indica*), yellow kowhai (*Sophora tetraptera*), yellow latan (*Latania verschaffeltii*), yellow mombin (*Spondias mombin*), yellow-olean-

der (*Thevetia peruviana*), yellow-poinciana (*Peltophorum pterocarpum*), yellow rattle (*Rhinanthus*), yellow-skunk-cabbage (*Lysichiton americanum*), yellow snake tree (*Stereospermum chelonoides*), yellow tulip wood (*Drypetes australasica*), and yellow-wood (*Cladrastis*).

YERBA. This word, the Spanish word for plant, forms parts of the common names of these plants: yerba buena (*Satureja douglasii*), yerba-de-selva (*Whipplea modesta*), yerba mansa (*Anemopsis californica*), yerba maté (*Ilex paraguariensis*), and yerba santa (*Eriodictyon californicum*).

YESTERDAY-TODAY-AND-TOMORROW. See Brunfelsia.

YEW. See Taxus. The plum-yew is *Cephalotaxus*. The Prince-Albert-yew is *Saxegothaea conspicua*.

YLANG-YLANG is *Cananga odorata*. For climbing-ylang-ylang, see Artabotrys.

YOKEWOOD is *Catalpa longissima*.

YOKOHAMA-BEAN is *Mucuna hassjoo*.

YOUNGBERRY. See Blackberry.

YOUTH-AND-OLD-AGE is *Zinnia elegans*.

YUCA is *Manihot esculenta*.

YUCCA (Yúc-ca)—Adam's Needle, Joshua Tree, Our Lord's Candle, Spanish Bayonet, Spanish Dagger. Belonging to the lily family LILIACEAE or, according to an alternative classification, to the agave family AGAVACEAE, the genus *Yucca*, a native of warm parts of North America, comprises some forty species. Its name is derived from the Carib Indian name for the entirely different *Manihot esculenta*, the cassava or manioc, of the spurge family EUPHORBIACEAE.

Prevailingly, but not exclusively denizens of semidesert and desert regions, yuccas are showy-flowered evergreens of

impressive decorative merit. Trunkless and with the rosettes of foliage at ground level, or with definite trunks and of shrub or tree dimensions, they have abundant tough, frequently rigid, broad-based, long-pointed, sword-shaped or linear, parallel-veined leaves with margins often toothed or more or less furnished with loose, threadlike fibers. The white, creamy-white, or violet, saucer- to cup-shaped flowers, commonly fragrant at night, are in generally erect panicles. An exception is *Y. filifera*, of Mexico, the panicles of which are pendulous. The blooms have perianths with six fleshy segments, commonly called petals (more accurately, tepals), that are completely separate or united only near their bases, six stamens, and one short style. The fruits are dry capsules that, when mature, either split and release their seeds or are fleshy and do not break open.

The flowers of yuccas are pollinated (essential to the production of seeds) in an unusual and intriguing way. Female yucca moths (*Pronuba yuccasella*) collect the grains of pollen and form them into little balls that they stuff into the cup-shaped ends of the stigmas of the flowers. Then they lay one or two eggs on the ovary of the bloom. The transfer of pollen assures fertilization, which stimulates the ovaries to develop into seeds. The caterpillars that hatch from the eggs feed on some of the developing ovaries, but many ovaries are not so destroyed and develop to maturity. Thus, both plant and insect benefit from this nearly unique symbiotic relationship. Yuccas cultivated in regions where yucca moths are absent, as in the Old World, do not set seeds unless they are hand-pollinated.

Yuccas have several economic uses. The leaves of some sorts are employed as sources of fibers for cordage and ropes and at times have been used to make paper. Grazing animals, wild and domestic, relish the leaves of many kinds; in some regions the leaves are of very considerable significance as stock feed. In addition to accepted species, many hybrids and apparent hybrids occur in the wild, while others have been raised under cultivation.

Yucca filamentosa

Yucca aloifolia marginata

bracts on the flowering stalk. The flowers of *Y. s. rosea* are flushed with pink on their outsides. The foliage of *Y. s. variegata* is variegated. The leaves of **Y. flaccida,** which otherwise closely resembles *Y. filamentosa,* are more pliable and are edged with straight threadlike fibers, the outer ones recurving. Also, the branches of the flower panicles are pubescent. Variety *Y. f. variegata* has most of its leaves banded with creamy-white along their margins.

Yucca flaccida variegata

Yucca aloifolia tricolor

Adam's needle is a popular name applied to *Y. filamentosa, Y. smalliana,* and sometimes *Y. flaccida.* These closely related trunkless or practically trunkless species are natives of the southeastern United States. Frequently confused with the others, **Y. filamentosa** has 1-inch-wide, narrow-spatula-shaped leaves 1 foot to 2½ feet long. Their toothless margins are furnished with long, curly threads and their apexes narrow abruptly and end in a stout spine. From 6 to 15 feet tall, the flowering stalk, which has nonpubescent branches, carries a handsome panicle of 1½- to 2-inch-long, almost white blooms. The fruits are dry and split open when fully ripe. The leaves of **Y. smalliana,** which is sometimes known as bear-grass, as well as Adam's needle, are erect or spreading, taper to their bases and their apexes, and are up to 2 feet in length. Their margins, without teeth, are furnished with curly threads. The panicles of white blooms, carried to heights of up to 15 feet, are of 1½- to 2-inch-long flowers. The fruits split open at maturity. Variety *Y. s. maxima* is larger and has leafy

Spanish bayonet is the colloquial name of *Y. aloifolia* and *Y. baccata.* Native to the West Indies, the southern United States, and Mexico, **Y. aloifolia,** called dagger plant as well as Spanish bayonet, has a branched or branchless trunk, 2 to 3 to up to 25 feet high, with at its termination or the end of each branch a rosette of very sharp-pointed, rigid leaves 1 foot to 2½ feet long by 1½ to 2½ inches wide, their margins finely-toothed, but without loose filaments. In panicles 1½ to 2 feet long, the white flowers, often flushed with purple, are 3 to 4 inches across. The fleshy fruits do not open at maturity. Variety *Y. a. draconis* has a branched trunk, and pliable, recurved leaves about 2 inches wide. Leaves edged with creamy-yellow are typical of *Y. a. marginata;* those of *Y. a. tricolor* (syn. *Y. a. quadricolor*) have a yellow or whitish stripe along the center, when young they are suffused with pink. Called datil, banana yucca, and blue yucca, as well as Spanish bayonet, **Y. baccata,** of the southwestern United States, is stemless or has only short, prostrate stems. It forms clumps of rosettes of erect, sword-shaped leaves, 2 to 3 feet long by 1 inch to 2¼ inches broad, with long, thickish, curly fibers shredding from their margins. The bell-shaped,

Yucca baccata

Yucca flaccida

sometimes red- or purple-tinged, white to creamy-white flowers, 2½ to 4 inches long and with the petals united briefly at their bases, are in panicles 2 to 2½ feet long. The fruits do not split at maturity. Variety *Y. b. vespertina* forms larger colonies of stemless rosettes of blue-green leaves.

Spanish dagger as a common name is applied to *Y. gloriosa, Y. treculeana,* and *Y. carnerosana.* Native from North Carolina to Florida, **Y. gloriosa** is also known as the Lord's candlestick, Roman candle, and

Yucca gloriosa

Yucca treculeana

Yucca treculeana in a conservatory of The New York Botanical Garden

Yucca gloriosa (flowers)

palm-lily. It has a trunk up to 9 feet tall. Up to 2½ feet long and about 2 inches wide, the glaucous-green leaves terminate in a stiff point; when young they have a few teeth that soon drop, when old a few marginal threads. The 2- to 2½-inch-long, greenish-white to reddish flowers are 3 to 4 inches in diameter. The fruits are barely-fleshy, six-ribbed capsules that do not split at maturity. The leaves of Y. g. medio-striata have a center band of white. Known as palma pita as well as Spanish dagger, **Y. treculeana,** of Texas and adjacent Mexico, attains heights of up to 10 feet. Its leaves are up to 3 feet long and ¾ inch wide, with no or few straight and very slender marginal threads. Longer than the leaves, the hairless panicles of bloom are of white or purple-tinted, white flowers about 1½ inches in length. The fruits do not break open at maturity. Also Texan and Mexican, **Y. carnerosana,** up to 18 feet tall, has stiff, sword-shaped leaves, up to about 3 feet long by 3 inches wide, without teeth or loose fibers along the margins. Towering well above the foliage, the rather short-stalked, densely-crowded, erect-branched

panicles of bloom have persistent bracts and white flowers up to 3¼ inches in length. The fleshy fruits do not split open at maturity.

Soapwell, soapweed, and bear-grass are colloquial names applied to **Y. glauca,** a native of prairies and open woodlands from South Dakota to Montana, Missouri, Texas, and Arizona, mostly east of the Rocky

Yucca treculeana (flowers)

Yucca glauca

Mountains. It forms clumps and has short, usually prostrate stems and rigid, white- or greenish-white-edged leaves, 9 inches to 2¼ feet long, ending in sharp points. Their toothless margins are furnished with stiff, fibrous threads. In racemes or few-branched panicles up to 3 feet long, the 2- to 2½-inch-long, fragrant flowers, greenish-cream frequently tinged with pinkish-brown, have petals separate or slightly united at their bases. The style is green. The fruits, 2 inches long or a little longer, split open when fully mature. The flowers of *Y. g. rosea* are flushed pink on their outsides. Also known as soapweed, as well as soap tree and palmella, branched or branchless **Y. elata** (syn. *Y. radiosa*), of Texas, Arizona, and Mexico, is up to 15 or

Yucca elata, the Royal Botanic Gardens, Kew, England

20 feet tall. Its pliable, linear leaves, up to 3 feet long and ½ to 1 inch wide, have narrow, white or greenish margins with threads shredding from them. Lifted well above the foliage, the up-to-10-foot-long flowering stalks carry panicles of white to green, often pink-tinged flowers 2 inches long or a little longer. The petals are united for a short way from their bases. The fruits split at maturity.

Yucca whipplei, Rancho Santa Ana Botanic Garden, California

Our Lord's candle (**Y. whipplei** syn. *Hesperoyucca whipplei*) is a magnificent native of California and Baja California. Trunkless or almost so, this forms a usually solitary rosette of spine-tipped, rigid, often glaucous, yellow- or brown-margined, finely-toothed leaves up to 1¾ feet long by ¾ inch broad that dies after flowering and fruiting. Carried to heights of up to 12 feet, the huge candle-flame-shaped panicles are of creamy-white, sometimes purple-tinted, fragrant blooms about 2½ inches long. The fruits split when they are mature. From the typical species, *Y. w. caespitosa* differs in developing clumps of rosettes of foliage that at blooming time produce several flowering stalks. Secondary rosettes are also characteristic of *Y. w. intermedia*, but this sort usually has only one flowering stalk each season. Larger, less compact clumps of rosettes developed chiefly from the rhizomes are typical of *Y. w. percursa*.

The Mojave yucca (**Y. schidigera** syn. *Y. mohavensis*), a native of Nevada to California, Arizona, and Baja California, is 3 to 12 feet tall and has a branched or branchless trunk. Sword-shaped and broadest at their middles, yellow-green, and spine-tipped, the leaf blades are up to 2½ feet long by 1 inch to 2 inches wide and have a few coarse fibers along their thick margins. The nearly globular, lavender- or purple-tinted, white or cream-colored blooms, about 1¾ inches long, are in panicles up to 1 foot long. The fruits do not split at maturity.

Yucca schidigera

Yucca elephantipes, Huntington Botanical Gardens, San Marino, California

The giant or spineless yucca (**Y. elephantipes** syn. *Y. guatemalensis*), of Mexico, one of the most imposing of the clan and up to 30 feet tall, has a stout, branched trunk swollen at its base. Its rough-edged leaves, up to 4 feet long by 3 inches broad, are not spine-tipped. *Y. e. variegata* has leaves margined with creamy-white. The fleshy fruits do not split at maturity.

The Joshua tree (**Y. brevifolia**), up to 40 or exceptionally 65 feet high, branches mostly at from 2 to 6 feet above the ground and spreads up to 20 feet or more. Clustered at the branch ends, the toothed, spine-tipped, rigid leaves, without loose fibers along their edges, have blades 9 inches to 1¼ feet long by ½ inch wide or slightly wider. The greenish-yellow to green or less commonly cream-colored flowers, on panicles 1 foot to 1½ feet long, are about 2¾ inches long; their petals are united for about one-half their lengths. The fruits, which do not split at maturity, become dry as they age. Not exceeding about 10 feet in height and branched or branchless, *Y. b. jaegerana* has leaves 4 to 8 inches long and panicles of bloom only about 1 foot in length. Clump-forming *Y. b. herbertii*, 3 to

Yucca filifera, the botanic garden, Mexico City

Yucca brevifolia in the Mohave Desert

Yucca brevifolia jaegerana in California

15 feet tall, has many trunks that sprout from underground rootstocks.

Other species include these: **Y. angustissima,** of Arizona, New Mexico, and Utah, much resembles Y. glauca. It has a short, prostrate trunk or none, and forms clumps of rosettes of about ¼-inch-wide, linear leaves with white or greenish-white margins, the bases of which are furnished with loosely-curled fibers. Rarely branched, the racemes of bloom, up to 7 feet tall, are of rose-purple-tinted, pale green flowers up to 2¼ inches long. The fruits split at maturity. **Y. filifera** (syn. Y. australis), of Mexico, is a tree 20 to 50 feet tall, with a trunk up to 5 feet in diameter. From 1 foot to 1½ feet long and 1 inch to 1½ inches wide, its spine-tipped leaves have margins shredded into coarse threads. In pendent panicles 3 to 6 feet long, the creamy-white flowers are about 2 inches long. **Y. gilbertiana,** endemic to Utah, forms small, crowded clumps of usually asymmetrical rosettes of lanceolate to lanceolate-spatula-shaped leaves, up to about 1½ feet long and 1¾ inches broad, with white or brown margins that eventually fray into curly hairs. The flowering stalk carries a dense raceme, up to 2½ feet long, of purple-tinged, yellow or greenish-yellow blooms up to 2¼ inches long. The fruits split at maturity. **Y. neomexicana,** native from Colorado to Oklahoma and New Mexico, resembles the last, but forms larger, looser clumps of rosettes of linear to lanceolate leaves with slender, straight fibers at their margins. Also, the racemes of bloom of Y.

neomexicana are more sparsely flowered. **Y. reverchonii,** the San Angelo yucca of Texas, has dense clumps of yellow-, brown-, or red-edged, straight, linear, minutely-toothed leaves 1 foot to 2 feet long by ½ to ¾ inch wide. The white to greenish-white flowers, up to 2¼ inches long, are in panicles up to 3 feet long. The fruits split when mature. **Y. rigida,** of Mexico, has a branchless or sparingly-branched trunk up to about 15 feet tall. Mostly with concave upper surfaces, its rigid leaves, up to 2 feet long and 1¼ inches wide, spread widely. The flowers are in panicles of moderate size. **Y. rupicola,** of Texas, resembles the last, but has less densely-clumped rosettes of distinctly twisted, sword-shaped leaves, broadest at their middles, where they are

Yucca rigida, the botanic garden, Mexico City

Yucca valida in Baja California

¾ inch to 1½ inches wide. Its fruits split at maturity. **Y. schottii,** of New Mexico, Arizona, and adjacent Mexico, attains heights up to 15 feet; it has rosettes of thin, pliable, blue-green leaves up to 3 feet long and 2¼ inches wide, their margins without fibers or at most with very fine ones. From ¾ inch to 1¼ inches long, the white flowers are in short-stalked panicles, the lower parts of which are concealed by the foliage. The fruits do not split at maturity. Endemic to Baja California, **Y. valida** somewhat resembles *Y. brevifolia,* but its branches are more slender and its leaves, 6 inches to 1 foot long, are not toothed. Unlike those of *Y. brevifolia,* their margins are plentifully furnished with loose fibers. The flowers have a faint odor of dill. The fruits do not split at maturity.

Garden and Landscape Uses. Of bold and even noble aspect, yuccas lend themselves to exciting employments by skillful landscape architects and gardeners. In the ground or in containers, they associate splendidly with such architectural features as buildings, walls, and steps and can be used to create quite dramatic effects. As is true of most desert, semidesert, and other dry-soil plants, crowding detracts from their

effectiveness. Allow them adequate space to display their lines and masses unimpinged by neighbors. Particularly, desert and semidesert sorts should not be crowded by lusher vegetation that does not belong in arid regions or dry soils. Such incongruity detracts from the simple, even severe beauty of yuccas and destroys the all-important feeling of rightness that all satisfying gardenscapes inspire. Although not succulents, yuccas show to best advantage when associated with cactuses and other succulents and with plants that, in the wild, grow with them. The few species native to the southeastern United States are not as much out of place when planted in association with moist region plants as are those that hail from the southwest and west, but even they are at their best in dryish environments. All yuccas do well exposed to sun and wind and stand seaside environments well.

Cultivation. As long as soil drainage is so sharp that there is no danger of the plants suffering from "wet feet," and excessive irrigation is avoided, the cultivation of yuccas presents few problems. They thrive in a wide variety of soils, in the wild most often favoring sandy and gravelly

ones, often of limestone derivation. Although too much irrigation can cause the plants to rot, in dry regions yuccas that receive some supplemental water commonly retain individual leaves longer and so develop bigger rosettes than plants neglected of this attention. Also, the leaves of irrigated specimens are usually larger. Yuccas, especially those with fibrous root systems, are easy to transplant and, if reasonable care is taken, soon become reestablished or, as gardeners say, "take hold." Propagation is by seed, offsets, and division, and by cuttings made of stem, rhizomes, or roots.

YULAN is *Magnolia denudata.*

YUSHANIA (Yushán-ia). Native at high altitudes in Taiwan and the Philippine Islands, the only species of *Yushania,* of the grass family GRAMINEAE, is a bamboo not hardy where winters are severe, but sufficiently hardy to live outdoors in the south of England. Its name commemorates the Japanese botanist Dr. Yushan Kudo, who died in 1934.

As it occurs in the wild, the height of **Y. niitakayamensis** (syn. *Arundinaria niitakayamensis*) varies very considerably, perhaps in response to altitude or other environmental conditions. Reports of plants not over a few inches tall and of others several feet high are recorded. As known in England, *Y. niitakayamensis* produces slender canes over 30 feet tall, the upper parts of which cascade over, during their second year, under the weight of the numerous branches and foliage. At first the canes are glossy-dark-green, but with age become yellowish-green and finally dull brown. The leaf sheaths of canes formed late in the season are retained until spring, those that develop earlier are quickly deciduous. The leaves are mostly 3 inches long by ½ inch wide, rarely larger, and taper to long points. They are medium green above, grayish-green beneath, and moderately tessellated. One leaf margin is fringed with bristly hairs. The flowers have two stigmas.

Some botanists consider the plant native to Taiwan to be a variety of the Philippine Island plant and name it *Y. n. microcarpa,* but even though the variety is said to have smaller flowers, no obvious difference is apparent under casual inspection. This bamboo is a running kind that has the curious habit of forming a compact clump of canes around which scattered clusters of younger canes develop.

Garden and Landscape Uses and Cultivation. For information on these see the entry Bamboos.

Z

ZALUZIANSKYA (Zaluz-iánskya) — Night-Phlox. Thirty-five species of annuals, herbaceous perennials, and subshrubs of the figwort family SCROPHULARIACEAE compose *Zaluzianskya*. Its members are natives of South Africa. The name commemorates Adam Zaluziansky von Zaluzian, a physician of Prague, who died in 1613.

Clammy, with opposite lower leaves and alternate upper ones, zaluzianskyas have stalkless blooms in crowded or interrupted terminal spikes. Most commonly the leaves have a few teeth. The blooms have calyxes with five short teeth. The corollas are persistent. They have slender tubes that eventually split to their bases and five spreading or cupped lobes (petals) that may or may not be cleft at their apexes. There are usually four stamens. The fruits are capsules.

Night-phlox (**Z. capensis** syn. *Nycterinia capensis*) is an erect, bushy annual, 9 inches to 1½ feet tall, with few-toothed or toothless linear leaves up to 2 inches long. Usually their margins and midribs are fringed with hairs. The phloxlike flowers are few together in short spikes. They are about ½ inch in diameter and have a slender, purple-black corolla tube, pubescent on its outside, and cupped petals, white on their insides, purple-black on their undersides, and deeply-notched at their apexes.

Another annual, **Z. villosa** (syns. *Z. selaginoides*, *Nycterinia selaginoides*) is 6 inches to 1 foot tall and softly-pubescent. Its leaves are spatula-shaped to obovate and approximately 1 inch long. The blooms are white or lilac with orange centers; the outsides of the nearly hairless corolla tubes, ¾ to 1 inch long, are purple. The petals have notched apexes.

Garden Uses. The species discussed are especially appreciated for their heavily scented blooms, open in the evening and at night, but closed by day. These are pretty plants for the fronts of beds, rock gardens, and groups near paths and beneath windows where their fragrance can be easily enjoyed. They grow satisfactorily in sunny places in ordinary well-drained, reasonably fertile soil.

Cultivation. Seed may be sown outdoors in spring and the young plants thinned to about 6 inches apart, or they may be sown indoors some ten weeks before it is safe to set the young plants in the garden, which must not be done until after the last frost. In the interim the seedlings are transplanted individually to small pots, or 2 inches apart in flats, and grown in a greenhouse where the temperature at night is 50°F and by day five to fifteen degrees higher.

ZAMIA (Zà-mia)—Coontie, Seminole Bread. Of the ten genera of the ancient cycad family CYCADACEAE, only *Zamia* is native to the United States. Three of its thirty to forty species occur there. They are almost entirely restricted to Florida. The other species are endemic to other warm parts of the Americas and West Indies. From the stems of the Florida species the Seminole Indians obtained sago starch, which, after washing to remove a poison, they used as food. The starch has been called Florida arrowroot. The name is from *zamiae*, a mistaken spelling in some texts of Pliny for *azaniae*, pine cones, and alludes to the appearance of the reproductive parts.

Zamias are mostly low, evergreen, palmlike shrubs with partly or entirely subterranean, thick stems or trunks. Their leathery, parallel-veined, toothed or toothless, pinnate leaves have an almost fernlike aspect. The unisexual reproductive bodies, not true flowers, are in separate cones, the female cones usually larger than the male cones. The fruits are berry-like drupes.

Coontie and seminole bread are colloquial names applied to three species, now to be discussed, that are native to Florida. Endemic to that state, **Z. floridana** has a short portion of its stem above ground level. Its ovate to ovate-lanceolate leaves have fourteen to twenty pairs of somewhat twisted, sickle-shaped

Zamia floridana

leaflets up to 6 inches long by ¼ inch wide. They have rolled-under, few-toothed margins. The densely-downy female cones are 5 to 6 inches long. Variety *Z. f. portoricensis*, of Puerto Rico, differs from the species in being of a looser growth habit. From its usually subterranean stem sprout wiry-stalked leaves with rather distantly spaced, narrow-lanceolate, bright green leaflets. An intermediate hybrid between *Z. floridana* and this variety is sometimes

A hybrid between *Zamia floridana* and *Z. f. portoricensis*

cultivated. Occurring natively in the West Indies as well as Florida, *Z. integrifolia* has a trunk up to 1½ feet tall and leaves with angled stalks and six to eighteen pairs of toothless or, near their apexes, slightly-toothed leaflets. A native of Mexico as well as of the West Indies and Florida, *Z. pumila* (syns. *Z. furfuracea*, *Z. umbrosa*) has a stem below ground or exposed for not more than about 6 inches. From 2 to 4 feet long, its prickly-stalked leaves have two to thirteen pairs of linear, lanceolate, or oblong-ovate leaflets, with rolled-under margins, toothed above their middles. Female cones, narrowly-egg-shaped, are up to 5 inches in length. Often in clusters, male cones are somewhat shorter and cylindrical.

Zamia ottonis

Zamia latifolia

Zamia pumila

Zamia ottonis (cones)

Zamia fischeri

Zamia angustifolia

West Indian *Z. debilis* (syn. *Z. media*) has leaves, up to 2½ feet long, with non-prickly stalks and six to about twenty-four linear-lanceolate to oblong-wedge-shaped leaflets, up to 8 inches long, notched at their blunt apexes and toothless or irregularly toothed. Female cones are up to 4 inches long and 2 inches wide. Male cones are up to about 3 inches long. Also West Indian, *Z. angustifolia* has an ovoid stem, and leaves with comparatively long, slender stalks and four to twenty pairs of narrow leaflets 4 to 8 inches long. The reddish-hairy cones are up to 3 inches long. Native to Cuba, *Z. ottonis* has a short,

thick, aboveground stem and leaves 1 foot to 1½ feet long with nine to fifteen pairs of obovate, 2- to 4-inch-long leaflets, brownish-hairy on their undersides and toothed at their apexes. The cones are brown-hairy.

Native to Mexico and Guatemala, *Z. loddigesii* has a trunk up to 8 inches tall, and leaves up to 3 feet long that have prickly stalks and three to twenty-seven pairs of linear-lanceolate leaflets up to 8 inches long and spiny-toothed along the margins of their upper halves. The female cones are about 2 inches long. By some botanists accepted as a variety of the last, *Z. latifolia*, of Mexico, has a stem up to 8 inches tall and leaves with usually prickly stalks and lanceolate to obovate leaflets, 4 to 10 inches long, with teeth or spines on the margins above their middles. Wild from Guatemala to Panama, *Z. skinneri* has a trunk up to 4 feet high and leaves with cylindrical stalks and two to eleven pairs of oblong-lanceolate to broad-ovate leaflets 8 inches to 1 foot long. In clusters of up to four, the male cones are cylindrical. Mexican *Z. fischeri*, an elegant species with a thick trunk, has leaves of somewhat fernlike aspect, up to 1½ feet long and with narrowly-lanceolate leaflets, toothed above

their middles. The cylindrical cones are 1 inch to 2¾ inches long.

Garden and Landscape Uses and Cultivation. In Florida and places with approximately similar climates, zamias do well in ordinary soils outdoors. They prefer just a little shade, but will grow where it is sunny if the soil does not become excessively dry. They may be used at the fronts of shrub beds, for edging paths, among rocks, as groundcovers, and as underplantings beneath palms and other trees. They do well in pots and other containers, outdoors in warm climates, and in greenhouses. They are propagated by seed. For more information see Cycads.

ZAMIOCULCAS (Zamio-cúlcas). The great primary class of flowering and seed-bearing plants called monocotyledons contains few with pinnate leaves, among them *Zamioculcas*. From its foliage one would scarcely guess that the only representative of this genus is a calla-lily relative, a member of the arum family ARACEAE, but a glance at its flowering parts reveals this to be so. Native to tropical East Africa, *Zamioculcas* has intrigued students of plant life for long and is fairly frequently represented in botanical garden collections. Its name is derived from that of the unrelated genus *Zamia*, and *culcas*, the Arabic name for the elephant's ear (*Colocasia antiquorum*), which also belongs in the arum family.

As is typical in the arum family, the apparent blooms are assemblages, technically called inflorescences, of many tiny flowers crowded along a spikelike organ called a spadix (in the calla-lily, the central yellow column), with a modified leaf called a spathe (in the calla-lily the part that forms the white trumpet) arising from its base. The spathe in *Zamioculcas*, at first erect, does not remain so and envelops the spadix as completely as in the calla-lily. At maturity only its base does this, its upper part reflexes and hangs downward. The inflorescence stalk is up to 6 inches long. The persistent spathe, eventually up to 4½ inches long by nearly 2 inches wide, is yellowish with pink or red overtones. The approximately upper two-thirds of the cylindrical to club-shaped spadix has only male blooms, the lower one-third only female. Between are a few sterile flowers. Each little flower has four perianth segments (petals). The males have four stamens and a nonfunctional ovary, the females are without stamens, but have a functional pistil with a short, knob-ended style. Berry-like, the fruits, nearly ½ inch in diameter, are white with a central dark spot. They contain one or two seeds.

In the wild, curious, handsome *Z. zamiifolia* usually loses its leaf blades at the end of the growing season, and the leaf-

Zamioculcas zamiifolia

stalks die back to within about 3 inches of the ground, leaving their swollen, bulblike bases. However, in cultivation it is generally evergreen, forming an attractive bushy specimen, 2 to 3 feet tall and wide, of coarse-patterned, lustrous foliage. From short, gnarled, woody, horizontal rhizomes are developed upright leaves with fleshy stalks 10 inches to 1½ feet long and green with transverse bands of mottled darker green. There are six to eight pairs of somewhat asymmetrical, elliptic to obovate-lanceolate leaflets, 2½ to 4½ inches long and 1½ to 2½ inches broad, their greatest widths above their middles.

Garden and Landscape Uses. Easily grown, this is an ornamental of considerable merit for the tropics and the frost-free subtropics. It may be displayed in beds, at the fronts of shrubberies, in informal landscapes, and in rock gardens. It is also a satisfactory greenhouse ornamental for growing in ground beds and large containers.

Cultivation. Well-drained, nourishing soil and fairly open locations shaded from the strongest sun suit *Zamioculcas*. The soil should be moderately moist without holding stagnant water, but this species successfully survives considerable periods of dryness. As a greenhouse inhabitant it prefers a minimum winter night temperature of 60 to 65°F and a daytime increase, at that season, of five to fifteen degrees; in summer considerably higher temperatures are appropriate. High humidity is beneficial. Propagation is very easily achieved by removing mature leaflets and laying them in moist soil, peat moss, sand, or similar material in a humid atmosphere where the temperature is 70 to 80°F. Each leaflet develops a little tuber and then should be planted or potted with that just beneath the surface. Division and seed afford alternative means of multiplication.

ZANTEDESCHIA (Zanted-éschia) — Calla-Lily or Calla. Probably few people unversed in plant geography connect the calla or calla-lily, that popular and immensely useful florists' flower, with Africa. Yet it and the about eight other species of *Zantedeschia* are natives to the southern end of that continent and nowhere else. It may come as an additional surprise to learn that in South Africa the white calla-lily is a common wayside weed, there called pig-lily. A story, possibly apocryphal, is told of a wealthy South African who commissioned a leading florist of London, England, to make the bouquets for his daughter's wedding. At great expense this was done and the creations shipped by air to Cape Town. When the floral art arrived and the boxes were opened they were—you've guessed it—bouquets of pig-lilies!

Calla-lilies are not lilies, nor are they related to lilies (*Lilium*). They belong with jack-in-the-pulpits, caladiums, and so-different-looking philodendrons in the arum family ARACEAE. Their botanical name commemorates the Italian botanist Francesco Zantedeschi, who died in 1873. In using the name calla as a common one for *Zantedeschia*, care must be taken not to confuse that genus with the quite different botanical genus *Calla*.

Zantedeschias are nonhardy herbaceous perennials with short, tuber-like rhizomes and all-basal, long-stalked, ovate-heart- or arrow-shaped or lanceolate leaves. As is commonly true of members of the arum family, the floral parts generally referred to as flowers are not individual blooms, but are inflorescences (aggregations of many blooms with attendant parts). Each inflorescence of *Zantedeschia* consists of a spike, called a spadix, crowded with tiny, insig-

nificant true flowers, those toward its top, male, the lower ones, female. From the bottom of the spadix is developed a large, petal-like bract called a spathe. This is wrapped to form a corolla-like broad trumpet around the spadix. The fruits are berries.

The common white calla-lily (**Z. aethiopica**) is so abundant in parts of South Africa that from May until Christmas "every furrow, gulley, and marshy spot is filled with its ivory-white spathes—in places even defying the ever encroaching plough." Robust, this attains heights of 2½ feet or more. Its lush, glossy-green leaves

Zantedeschia aethiopica in South Africa

Zantedeschia aethiopica

are ovate-heart- to arrow-shaped. Carried well above the foliage and solitary on thick stalks, the slightly fragrant "flowers," 5 to 10 inches long, have white or creamy-white spathes and yellow spadixes. Occasionally, inflorescences with two or three spathes nested one within the other develop. Variety *Z. a. minor* (syn. 'Little Gem'), only about 1½ feet tall, is smaller in all its parts than the typical species. Another dwarf variety, *Z. a. childsiana*, which may be identical with the one grown as *Z. a. godfreyana*, is an exceptionally free bloomer. Variety *Z. a.* 'Crowborough', 1½ to 2 feet tall, is hardier than other kinds; in the south of England it survives outdoors in very sheltered places.

The black-throated calla-lily (*Z. albo-maculata* syn. *Z. melanoleuca*) has leaves with stalks 1 foot to 1½ feet long. They have triangular to arrow-shaped, lustrous green blades from 5 to 10 inches long and slightly broader across their bases. Nearly always they are freely and conspicuously sprinkled with translucent white spots. The spathes, 2 to 4½ inches long, are pale greenish-yellow with, on their insides, a very dark purple-maroon blotch. Variety *Z. a.* 'Helen O'Connor' has the spathes of its

Zantedeschia aethiopica childsiana (7 inches tall)

Zantedeschia aethiopica 'Crowborough' outdoors in England

Zantedeschia elliottiana

Zantedeschia rehmannii

Zantedeschia aethiopica outdoors in California

Zantedeschia aethiopica as a pot plant

inflorescences flushed with shades of peach and apricot. Except for the larger size and more exciting color of its spathes and the absence of white spots on its foliage, *Z. pentlandii* (syn. *Z. angustiloba*) is much like *Z. albomaculata*. Its spathes are 4 to 5 inches long and brilliant golden-yellow with a dark purple blotch at the base inside. Similar, but with white-spotted foliage and lacking the dark blotch at the bottom of the spathe, *Z. elliottiana* is not recorded as having been found in the wild; it, apparently, is of garden origin.

The red or pink calla-lily (*Z. rehmannii*) has prevailingly dark wine-red to deep purple spathes, but there is much variation, ranging from these more somber hues through pink to nearly white. The spathes are 4 to 6 inches long. The leaves, the lowest of which are reduced to mere sheaths, have stalks 6 inches to 1 foot long and

pointed-lanceolate blades, 1 foot to 2 feet in length by 4 inches wide, that narrow gradually to the stalk.

Garden and Landscape Uses. In California and other warm regions calla-lilies are grown permanently outdoors. They are especially well suited for planting near watersides and look well in narrow borders, along fences, and as dividers between properties and parts of gardens. They are also grown in greenhouses for cut flowers. Although sometimes recommended as houseplants, they rarely prove

satisfactory when so grown. As greenhouse plants, they are chiefly raised for their cut blooms, and the pink calla-lily as a decorative pot plant. They are also grown in greenhouses for cut flowers.

Cultivation. In regions where they can be grown permanently outdoors calla-lilies luxuriate with minimum care. They do best in deep, moist, rich soil, the white calla-lily not objecting to boggy locations or soils of a decided alkaline character. Except in dry climates, where a little part-day shade is helpful, full exposure to sun gives the best results. An annual application of a complete fertilizer at the beginning of each new growing season enhances vigor. The maintenance of an organic mulch about the plants is helpful.

In greenhouses it is usual to grow white calla-lilies as deciduous perennials, drying the soil so that the foliage dies, and storing them in a dormant condition for a couple of months in the summer. This is not absolutely necessary. If the soil is kept moist, the plants will be evergreen. The usual procedure with the white calla-lily is to pot the tubers, setting them vertically with the bud end up, in late August or September. They need comparatively large pots and coarse, fertile, loamy soil. One tuber can be accommodated in a 6- or 7-inch pot, three in a container 9 inches in diameter. Set the tubers with their tips just level with the soil surface, which should be sufficiently below the rim of the pot to allow for a 2-inch top dressing later. Alternatively, for cut flowers, the tubers may be planted in deep benches or ground beds. Until good root growth is made, water must be given in moderation; however, after the earth is well filled with roots, watering should be much more generous. When that is achieved weekly applications of dilute liquid fertilizer are highly benefi-

Potting a white calla-lily: (a) The pot, soil, and tuber

(b) Setting the tuber vertically in the pot

(c) As the roots penetrate the soil, a vigorous new shoot develops

cial. White calla-lilies are most satisfactory where the night temperature is 50 to 55°F and day temperatures are five to ten degrees higher. Unless the plants are being grown in the summer, no shade is required. Usually, in May, white calla-lilies are forced into dormancy by drying them off, by gradually increasing the length of time between successive applications of water, and finally by withholding it. Then the pots are laid on their sides beneath a greenhouse bench, in a covered cold frame, or in some other airy place where there is no danger of them being wetted. There they remain until repotting time.

(d) Well on its way to flowering, the plant spreads its new leaves

The cultivation of other kinds of calla-lilies is very similar, although in their being smaller, the containers need not be so big. Single rhizomes of Z. elliottiana, for example, do well in 5-inch pots, and those of Z. rehmanii in that size or one size smaller. In greenhouses, Z. elliottiana and Z. pentlandii succeed better if temperatures are about five degrees higher than those recommended for the white calla-lily. These two, unlike the white calla-lily, pink calla-lily, and other kinds, cannot be increased by division, but are easily grown from seed. Those calla-lilies with yellow, pink, or red inflorescences (flowers) seem to do best when they are kept growing throughout the year without a period of summer dormancy.

ZANTHORHIZA. See Xanthorhiza.

ZANTHOXYLUM (Zanth-óxylum)—Toothache Tree, Prickly-Ash or Hercules' Club. Mostly inhabitants of the tropics and subtropics, but with a few native to temperate regions, the about 200, or fewer according to some authorities, species of Zanthoxylum are indigenous to North America and the Old World. They belong in the rue family RUTACEAE. The name, of obvious application to some species, comes from the Greek xanthos, yellow, and xylon, wood. The name has been spelled Xanthoxylum.

These are evergreen and deciduous, aromatic trees and shrubs, sometimes sprawling, usually prickly, with the prickles generally in pairs. They have alternate leaves, rarely of three leaflets, more often of four or more, opposite, lateral leaflets and a terminal one. Toothed or toothless, they are sprinkled with tiny translucent dots, which are easily seen when the leaf is held up against the light. The little flowers, in panicles or clusters, are unisexual with the sexes on separate plants or have unisexual and bisexual ones on the same

plant. They have three to five sepals and four, five, or no petals. The fruits are capsules that split to reveal the seeds attached by short threads, these often hang for some time after the capsules open.

The barks of some species have been employed medicinally, those of Z. americanum and Z. clava-herculis in North America, that of Z. alatum in India. Especially in the southern states, the bark of Z. clava-herculis, which produces a stinging sensation when chewed, was a popular home remedy for the relief of toothache pain. In Japan the seeds of Z. piperitum are used like pepper and its leaves and inner bark to flavor foods. Some West Indian kinds and Australian Z. brachyacanthum are sources of useful lumber.

Prickly-ash (Z. americanum), much the hardiest, is indigenous from Quebec to Minnesota, South Dakota, Florida, Alabama, and Oklahoma. Sometimes a small tree, but more commonly a tall, round-headed shrub, it attains a maximum height of 25 feet and is deciduous. Its leaves, which attain a maximum length of 1¼ feet, but are usually considerably smaller, have an odd number, from five to eleven or occasionally thirteen, of round-toothed or toothless, elliptic, ovate, or oblongish leaflets, with often a few prickles on their stalks and midribs. At least when young, the leaflets are pubescent on their undersides, especially along their mid-veins. In lateral, short-stalked clusters, the flowers are borne shortly before the leaves on last year's branches. They are without sepals and have little yellowish-green petals fringed at their ends. The fruits are blackish, the seeds black. The common name toothache tree is sometimes applied to this species.

Hercules' club or southern prickly-ash (Z. clava-herculis) is indigenous to moist woods chiefly in the coastal plain from Virginia to Oklahoma, Florida, and Texas. Sometimes a tree 30 to 50 feet in height, more often it is a tall shrub. Its peculiar bluish-gray trunks and branches are formidably armed with stout prickles, each set at the tip of a large corky protrusion that remains after the prickle falls. The hairless leaves have an odd number, from five to nineteen, of shallowly-toothed, lanceolate to ovate leaflets, with often prickly stalks and midribs. The tiny flowers, in large, terminal panicles, come after the leaves. They have minute sepals and tiny, greenish petals. The fruits are pitted or wrinkled and contain one seed.

The wild-lime (Z. fagara), native from Florida to Texas, the West Indies, and South America, and not hardy in the north, is an evergreen shrub or tree up to 30 feet in height. It has 4-inch-long leaves of five to thirteen obovate to nearly circular, round-toothed leaflets up to 1 inch long. The leafstalks and midribs of the leaves are winged. The four-petaled flowers are in cylindrical clusters from the leaf axils.

Zanthoxylum simulans (foliage and fruits)

Zanthoxylum simulans (fruits)

Asian species of interest include handsome **Z. simulans** (syn. *Z. bungei*), a broad deciduous shrub up to 10 feet in height, or sometimes a small tree as high as 25 feet. Its hairless or slightly pubescent branches have many stout prickles with very broad, flat bases. The glossy leaves, 3 to 9 inches long, have an odd number, seven to eleven, of ovate to ovate-oblong, toothed leaflets, and often prickly stalks and midribs. The flowers, in stalkless clusters or short panicles up to 2½ inches wide and without sepals, are at the ends of short lateral branchlets. They come after the foliage. The fruits are reddish with darker dots. This Chinese species is hardy in southern New England. About as hardy, graceful **Z. schinifolium,** a native of China, Korea, and Japan, is a deciduous shrub or small tree up to 25 feet tall. Its prickles are solitary at the joints of the stems. In odd numbers, the elliptic-ovate to lanceolate leaflets number thirteen to twenty-one to each leaf. The leaves, 3 to 7 inches long, are notched at their ends and have round-toothed edges. They are hairless and have prickly midribs. The greenish flowers, in short-stalked, flattish, terminal clusters 2 to 4 inches wide, are succeeded by con-

spicuous, brownish or greenish fruits with blue-black seeds.

Native to China, Korea, and Japan, **Z. piperitum** is an ornamental shrub or tree much like the last, but with prickles in pairs and more elongated flower clusters. Its branches are pubescent when young. When crushed, the foliage and other parts are rather lemon-scented. The leaves, 2 to 6 inches long, have, in odd numbers, eleven to nineteen hairless, ovate to oblong-ovate leaflets, up to 1½ inches in length, with distantly spaced teeth with a conspicuous gland at the bottom of each tooth. The leafstalks and midribs often have a few prickles and are pubescent above. The tiny greenish blooms are in clusters up to 2 inches wide. They are succeeded by reddish fruits dotted with glands and containing black seeds. This kind is hardy to about Philadelphia or somewhat further north.

Native to China, Korea, and the Ryukyu Islands, **Z. planispinum** (syn. *Z. alatum planispinum*), in the wild, is an evergreen shrub up to 12 feet tall. However, when it is cultivated in cold climates it is deciduous. It has hairless branches furnished with pairs of prickles that have broadly flattened bases. The leaves, 1½ to 4½ inches long, have usually three or five, but sometimes seven leaflets. They are finely-toothed. Their midribs, like the stalks of the leaflets, are broadly-winged. The flowers are yellowish and in nearly stalkless, axillary panicles about 1½ inches long. The reddish fruits are warty and have black seeds. This species is hardy about as far north as New York City.

A climbing shrub, up to 10 feet tall, native to China, **Z. stenophyllum** has hairless stems with small prickles, and leaves with an uneven number, from seven to thirteen, of ovate-oblong to lanceolate, pointed, slightly-toothed leaflets up to 3 inches long. The flowers, with protruding stamens, are in loose, terminal clusters 2 to 4 inches wide. The reddish fruits have black seeds. This species is probably not hardy in the north.

Garden and Landscape Uses. Although not among the most important shrubs and trees employed in landscaping, zanthoxylums should not be disregarded by planters. Their chief merit lies in their forms and attractive foliage, with additional interest provided by the fruits of at least some. They are useful for adding variety to mixed plantings and succeed without special attention. They are at their best in deep, well-drained, fertile soil in sun or part-day shade.

Cultivation. The only attention ordinarily needed is an occasional little pruning, best done in late winter or spring, to shape or thin the bushes. Propagation is usually by seed sown indoors in spring. It can also be by root cuttings 2 to 3 inches long and by leafy stem cuttings of firm, but not hard

shoots, 3 to 4 inches long, planted under mist or in a greenhouse or cold frame propagating bed in summer.

ZAUSCHNERIA (Zausch-nèria) — California-Fuchsia or Humming Bird's Trumpet. The genus *Zauschneria*, named to commemorate Dr. M. Zauschner, professor of natural history at University of Prague, who died in 1799, belongs in the evening-primrose family ONAGRACEAE. Consisting of four species, natives of North America, it is related to *Fuchsia*, but differs in its fruits being dry, slender, angled capsules containing seeds with a tuft of hairs at their apex, rather than juicy berries with nonhairy seeds. In this respect the fruits resemble those of willow herb (*Epilobium*).

Zauschnerias are erect or procumbent, mostly nonhardy, herbaceous perennials with stems sometimes woody at their bases and with shredding bark. They have stalkless or nearly stalkless, mostly alternate leaves, but the lower ones are often opposite. The handsome, brilliant red, fuchsia-like flowers, in loose spikes or racemes, have long tubes, spherical at their bases and funnel-shaped above. In the throat of the bloom are eight small scale-like appendages. There are four sepals, four petals, and eight protruding stamens, one-half of which are shorter than and alternate with the others. The stigma is four-lobed. The species rather closely resemble each other in many respects and often are rather difficult to tell apart.

The most important kind horticulturally is the California-fuchsia or humming bird's trumpet (*Z. californica*). It inhabits dry, gravelly or stony soils in California and Baja California. At its base subshrubby, this rather variable species branches freely, the branches being 1 foot to 3 feet long. The green to grayish, more or less glandular and pubescent leaves are lanceolate to oblong and up to 1½ inches in length. The flowers are 1 inch to 2 inches long or

Zauschneria californica

Zauschneria californica (flowers)

slightly longer. They are borne in late summer and early fall. In *Z. c. angustifolia*, the leaves are densely-gray-hairy and more slender than those of the typical species. The stems of *Z. c. latifolia*, which ranges in the wild from Oregon to California, do not become woody toward their bases and its leaves are broader than those of *Z. californica*. From *Z. californica* and its varieties, *Z. cana* (syn. *Z. c. microphylla* differs in its gray-hairy leaves being less than 1/10 inch wide and crowded. Its stems, 1 foot to 2 feet long, become woody at their bases. This species is native to California.

Garden and Landscape Uses and Cultivation. As garden plants zauschnerias are generally more appreciated in the British Isles than in America. Except for *Z. californica latifolia*, which survives in some parts of the north, they are hardy only where winters are decidedly mild. They are appropriate for steep rocky slopes and suchlike places where their more or less lax stems display their colorful flowers to advantage. A sunny location and thoroughly well-drained, moderately fertile soil are requisite. Propagation is by seed, division, and cuttings. These plants are resistant to drought and need little routine care. As a measure of tidiness it is well to remove spent blooms to prevent the formation of seed pods.

ZEA (Zé-a)—Corn or Indian Corn or Maize. The genus *Zea*, of the grass family GRAMINEAE, is of primary importance because it includes corn, one of the world's three most important grain crops, the others being wheat and rice. As now understood, there are four recognizable species of *Zea*, natives of warm parts of the Americas. The name is derived from the Greek name for some other cereal grain.

Zeas are vigorous annuals or, as with two species, nonhardy herbaceous perennial grasses with female flowers in pairs of generally one fertile and one sterile flower arranged in two to many rows to form a usually lateral ear (spike) surrounded by one or more bracts called husks. Male flowers are in spikelets arranged in twos or threes to form one-sided racemes, which are usually aggregated in a terminal panicle called a tassel. Each spikelet contains one stalked and one stalkless flower.

Corn, Indian corn, or maize (**Z. mays**), unknown in the wild and incapable of maintaining itself out of cultivation, is be-

Zea mays

lieved to have been developed in South America many centuries ago from one or more species long extinct. It is probable that these early corns were later hybridized with Mexican teosinte to produce most of the sorts we now grow. Modern varieties are vigorous annuals, 3 to 15 feet tall, that sucker from the base and have two-ranked leaves up to 3 feet long.

Europeans' first acquaintance with *Z. mays* occurred on November 5, 1492. On that day two Spaniards sent by Columbus to explore the interior of Cuba returned to report, in English translation, that they had discovered natives using "a sort of graine they call maize which was well tasted, bak'd, dry'd and made into flour." At the time of this discovery this grain was in cultivation from Chile to Canada. Within approximately the half-century, following its introduction to Europe by Columbus and contemporary Spanish explorers, it was being grown as a food crop throughout most parts of Europe, Africa, and Asia that were suitable for its cultivation. American corn is the New World's most important contribution among food plants to the Old World.

The varieties of *Z. mays* fall into several groups. Dent corn (*Z. m. indentata*), char-acterized by the dried grains having a dent or dimple at one end, is, in its yellow and to a lesser degree white varieties, the principal field corn of the North American corn belt, most of South America, and much of Africa. Sweet corn (*Z. m. rugosa*) nearly attains maturity before the sugars contained in its grains are transformed into starches. This is the corn grown in gardens as a vegetable. Upon drying, its grains shrink and become wrinkled. Flint corn (*Z. m. indurata*), cultivated as a field crop in North America chiefly in the northern United States and Canada, has grains that because of the very hard starch they contain do not shrink or wrinkle when dried. Popcorn (*Z. m. praecox*) has grains in which the starch and some water is enclosed in a tough skin, which ruptures explosively when applied heat converts the water into steam. Pod corn or husk corn (*Z. m. tunicata*), grown chiefly by Andean Indians, and in North America sometimes as a novelty, has each individual kernel as well as the entire cob or ear enclosed in a membranous bract.

Ornamental corns include, with variegated foliage, very dwarf *Z. m. gracillima variegata*, which has narrow leaves longitudinally variegated with white, and taller, broader-leaved *Z. m. japonica variegata* and *Z. m. japonica quadricolor*, which have leaves with lengthwise stripes of yellow, creamy-

Zea mays japonica variegata

white, and sometimes pink. Varieties with ornamental cobs are 'Rainbow', the ears of which are composed of grains of various hues, including dark red, yellow, orange, and blue, and which are used only as decorations, and 'Strawberry', which has tiny mahogany-red ears and which is useful for popping and eating as well as decoration.

Teosinte (**Z. luxurians** syn. *Euchlaena mexicana*), of Mexico, a vigorous annual occasionally 15 feet tall, more often not exceeding 10 feet, has sword-shaped leaves with prominent mid-veins. The spikelets of female flowers are arranged in two opposite rows on a jointed rachis (slender stalk). There are two perennial species of teosinte, both endemic to Mexico. *Z. diploperennis* is a robust plant tht forms many-stemmed clumps. *Z. perennis* is similar, but more slender. Plant breeders are experimenting with hybridizing *Z. mays* with these perennial species with the objective of developing perennial corn.

Garden and Landscape Uses and Cultivation. The cultivation of sweet corn, popular as a vegetable garden crop, is discussed in the Encyclopedia entry Corn. Other sorts respond to the same procedures. Popcorn is occasionally grown in home gardens as a novelty, teosinte to some extent as a forage crop and also for its scientific interest. Ornamental-leaved varieties of corn can be employed effectively in groups in flower beds and borders. Those with ornamental ears can be used as Thanksgiving and other holiday decorations.

ZEBRA PLANT. This is a common name of *Aphelandra squarrosa* and *Calathea zebrina*.

ZEBRA-RUSH is *Scirpus tabernaemontani*.

ZEBRINA (Ze-brìna)—Wandering Jew. Belonging in the spiderwort family COMMELINACEAE, this genus consists of two or more species from Texas, New Mexico, and Mexico. From nearly related *Tradescantia* it differs in the lower parts of the petals being fused into a tube. The name *Zebrina* comes from the Amharic *zebra*, the name of the well-known animal, and alludes to the striped foliage. The common name is also applied to *Tradescantia fluminensis*.

Zebrinas are evergreen, trailing, herbaceous plants, sparingly-hairy, with alternate, ovate to oblongish, undivided, toothless leaves that at their bases enfold the stems. The nearly stalkless flower clusters sit between a pair of leaflike bracts. There are three sepals, three blue-purple, ovate or lanceolate petals, six short stamens, and one style. The fruits are capsules.

Wandering jew (**Z. pendula**), native to Mexico, is a favorite window garden and greenhouse plant that lives with minimum

Zebrina pendula

care. Not uncommonly, it decorates the windows of barber's shops and other stores with little merchandise to display, that are operated by plant lovers. Of a somewhat fleshy nature, it has branching, juicy stems, swollen at the joints, that, if in contact with the earth, root as they travel. Its ovate-oblong, toothless leaves, 1 inch to 3 inches long, are rich purple beneath, a feature that, along with others, serves to distinguish it from the other wandering jew (*Tradescantia fluminensis*). The upper sides of the leaves are longitudinally striped with green and glistening silvery-white. The undersides may be somewhat hairy, and the edges of the parts that sheathe the stem are hairy at their tops and bottoms. A pair of very uneven-sized, stalkless bracts backs each cluster of blooms, which have whitish calyxes, white corolla tubes, and tiny red-purple petals. The slender style is capped with a three-lobed stigma. Variety *Z. p. quadricolor* has metallic-purplish-green leaves beautifully variegated lengthwise with glistening bands and stripes of white, pink, carmine-red, and green. Other varieties are *Z. p. discolor*, with large coppery and nile-green leaves margined and suffused with metallic-purple, blotched with rusty-red, and decorated with two longitudinal, narrow bands of silvery-white; *Z. p. d. multicolor*, which is a vigorous grower with large green leaves striped with cream, tinged with pink, and touched with silvery-white; and *Z. p. minima*, which differs from more typical *Z. pendula* in being smaller in its parts and having narrower leaves that display two silvery longitudinal bands. *Z. p. purpusii* (syn. *Z. purpusii*), of robust growth, has dark-green to red-green or purplish-brown, stripeless or very indistinctly-striped, hairy leaves with bright purple undersides. The flowers are lavender.

Garden and Landscape Uses. These most easy-to-grow trailers are ideal for those who like to dabble with growing a few window plants, but whose thumbs are not especially green. Shut-ins and children get great pleasure from them. Besides being fast growers and easy to cultivate, their rapid propagation from cuttings is about as foolproof as any horticultural venture can be. It is simple to plant a few cuttings in a pot and, within six weeks or two months, have a nice decorative specimen suitable for house embellishment or as a gift. Besides being excellent houseplants, zebrinas thrive in greenhouses. Often they are grown there under the benches, as groundcovers, and as edgings. They are attractive in pots and hanging baskets. They are also often used for surfacing the soil of palms and other tall plants in large pots and tubs. In warm, frost-free or nearly frost-free climates they are useful as outdoor groundcovers.

Cultivation. Little needs to be said about this, it is so extraordinarily simple. Cuttings root within two or three weeks,

planted in sandy soil, sand, sand and peat moss, or any other common rooting medium in a temperature of about 70°F. At lower temperatures they take a little longer. Cuttings also root readily if stood with their stems in water. Any porous soil kept moderately moist suits these adaptable plants, and temperatures from 50 or 55°F upward are satisfactory. For *Z. p. purpusii*, moderate temperatures are better than high ones. Some shade from strong summer sun is advisable.

Nice 4- or 5-inch-pot specimens are had by placing drainage in the bottoms of containers, filling them partway with porous, fertile soil, topped off about ¾ inch below the rim with ½ inch of sand, and planting cuttings (five in a 4-inch pot, seven in a 5-inch pot) evenly over the surface. The newly planted pots are watered thoroughly and put in a greenhouse, terrarium, or under a glass jar or a cover of transparent polyethylene plastic, in a temperature of 60°F or higher. When rooting has taken place, any covering is removed; soon after the cuttings begin to lengthen, their tips are pinched out to encourage branching. This is repeated when the branches are 3 or 4 inches long.

ZEHNTNERELLA (Zehnt-nerélla). One shrub or treelike species of the cactus family CACTACEAE is the only representative of *Zehntnerella*. A native of Brazil, it was named to honor Dr. Leo Zehntner, an early twentieth-century botanist of that country.

From a much-branched base, **Z. squamulosa** produces numerous very spiny, branching stems, up to 25 feet tall and 2 to 3 inches in diameter, with seventeen to twenty low, longitudinal ribs. From each circular areole (spine-producing area) sprout ten to fifteen needle-like spines, the longest about 1¼ inches in length. The flowers are white, tubular, and about 1¼ inches long. The fruits are spherical and ¾ inch in diameter.

Garden and Landscape Uses and Cultivation. Of interest to cactus hobbyists, *Zehntnerella* requires conditions and care appropriate for other tree cacti. For more information see Cactuses.

ZELKOVA (Zel-kòva). Belonging to the elm family ULMACEAE and resembling elms in aspect, the six or seven species of *Zelkova* are deciduous trees or shrubs of Asia. From related hackberries (*Celtis*) they differ in having pinnately-veined leaves with seven or more pairs of lateral veins, instead of leaves with three main veins spreading from the base, and also in the sepals of their flowers being united instead of separate. The name is derived from the Caucasian name for these plants, *tselkva*.

Zelkovas have short-stalked, toothed, alternate leaves and insignificant greenish flowers. The blooms clustered in the axils of the lower leaves of the current season's

Zinnia elegans with pompon-type flowers

Xerophyllum tenax

Woodwardia radicans

A large-flowered variety of *Zinnia elegans* with dwarf yellow marigolds in front

Yucca whipplei

ZEPHYRANTHES (Zephyr-ánthes)—Zephyr-Lily, Rain-Lily, Atamasco-Lily, Fairy-Lily. Flower of the west wind is the literal meaning of *Zephyranthes*. It derives from the Greek *zephyros*, the west wind, and *anthos*, a flower, fancifully emphasizing that these natives of the western hemisphere were brought to Europe from the west. There are thirty-five to forty species, members of the amaryllis family AMARYLLIDACEAE. Related to *Habranthus* and *Hippeastrum*, they inhabit warm-temperate, subtropical, and tropical parts of the Americas. The Rio de la Plata (river of silver) in South America is said to have been named because of the abundant white blooms of *Z. candida* along its banks.

Zephyranthes are bulb plants with deciduous or evergreen, narrowly-strap-shaped, linear, grassy leaves. Their up-facing, white, yellow, pink, or red, scent-less blooms, solitary atop leafless, hollow stalks, are of two types, funnel-shaped and lily-like, the upper parts of the petals flaring outward, or egg-shaped and crocus-like. The lower portions of the six perianth segments (petals or, more properly, tepals) form a tube. There are three long and three shorter stamens, and a long or short style ending in a three-branched or three-lobed stigma. The fruits are nearly spherical capsules. The plant previously known as *Z. robusta* is *Habranthus tubispathus*.

The atamasco-lilies of the southeastern United States, formerly all included in *Z. atamasco*, constitute three distinct, but similar species. In early spring vast numbers of their delightful blooms stud the meadows and moist, open woodlands throughout the coastal and piedmont regions. Most northerly of the three, **Z. atamasco** is found from southern Virginia to Alabama. This has leaves up to 1 foot long or slightly longer by 1¼ to 2 inches wide. Its flower stalks are about as long as the foliage. The funnel-shaped, purplish-tinged, white blooms are 3 to 4 inches long and approximately as wide. In the wild restricted to Florida and Georgia, **Z. treatiae** is distinguished from the last by its leaves being half-cylindrical and having blunt apexes. The other southern species, **Z. simpsonii** differs from *Z. atamasco* in its blooms having narrower perianths with upright rather than wide-spreading, often red-edged petals.

Other northern hemisphere white-flowered zephyr-lilies include West Indian **Z. tubispatha** (syn. *Z. insularum*), which has spreading leaves, present at blooming time, up to 1 foot long by about ¼ inch wide. On stalks 4 to 8 inches long, the green-based flowers are 1½ to 2¼ inches long. Their petals are up to ⅔ inch wide. Longer than the stamens, the style ends in a three-cleft stigma. Its foliage appearing during or after flowering time, **Z. verecunda**, of Mexico, has leaves up to 1 foot long and not over ¼ inch wide. The blooms, 1½ to 2 inches or rarely slightly less or more in length, have green bases and are more or less suffused with red on their outsides. Their stigmas are three-branched.

Night-blooming, white-flowered species of the northern hemisphere, sorts that close their blooms during the day, include **Z. brazosensis**, of Texas, New Mexico, and Mexico. This has large, nearly spherical bulbs and erect or down-curved, gray-green, linear leaves. The fragrant blooms, tinged red on their outsides, have a perianth tube up to 5 inches long and petals up to 1 inch long. Also a night-bloomer, variable **Z. drummondii** (syn. *Cooperia pedunculata*), of Texas and adjacent Mexico, has spherical, long-necked bulbs and two to five, narrowly-linear, gray-green, rather glaucous leaves up to 1 foot long and not over ¼ inch wide. Its fragrant flowers, 2½ to 3 inches long, are tinged pink on their outsides. They come chiefly in fall, on stalks 4 to 9 inches tall. The blooms open on about four successive evenings. Similar, but more slender, more delicate in appearance, and with smaller bulbs, night-blooming **Z. traubii** (syn. *Cooperia traubii*) in the wild is limited to Texas.

A South American with white blooms, **Z. candida** is one of the most attractive and highly esteemed kinds. It is naturalized in the southern United States. Its beautifully starry flowers, sometimes tinged pink on their outsides, and greenish at their bases,

Zephyranthes candida

are 1¼ to 2 inches long. This endemic of moist soils near the mouth of the Rio de la Plata in Argentina and Uruguay blooms in fall. Its slightly fleshy, evergreen leaves are 8 inches to 1 foot in length by up to ⅛ inch in width. Approximating the stamens in length, the style is tipped with an obscurely-three-lobed stigma. Variety *Z. c. major* is larger in all its parts. Also native to Argentina and Uruguay, and extending into Paraguay, spring- or early-summer-blooming **Z. mesochloa** is easily distinguishable from the last by its 1½- to 2-inch-long flowers, which are green in their lower parts and white blushed with pink above. They have styles, longer than the stamens, tipped with deeply-three-cleft stigmas.

Pink to rosy-red blooms of impressive size are raised to heights of 4 to 8 inches on the tubelike flower stalks of **Z. grandiflora** (syn. *Z. carinata*). This, one of the most commonly cultivated zephyr-lilies, is a native of Mexico, Guatemala, and the West Indies. It has narrowly-linear leaves

Zephyranthes grandiflora

up to 1 foot long, which appear with the lily-shaped flowers. The latter have corollas, 2½ to 4 inches long, with rounded-obovate petals up to ¾ inch wide. The style is markedly three-cleft. Similar to the last and sometimes confused with it, but its pink flowers not over 1½ inches in length, **Z. rosea** is indigenous to the West Indies and Guatemala.

Yellow flowers are characteristic of some cultivated zephyr flowers, among North American natives are *Z. longifolia* and *Z. pulchella*. An inhabitant of alkaline soils in Arizona, Texas, New Mexico, and Mexico, **Z. longifolia** has slender leaves from 6 inches to nearly 1 foot long, and bright yellow flowers almost or quite 1 inch long, often coppery on their outsides. The stigma is three-cleft. Much like the last, **Z. pulchella**, known as a wildling only from Texas, differs most markedly in its flowers having a headlike, three-lobed stigma instead of one with three distinct branches.

Yellow-flowered natives of South America include **Z. citrina**. This has channeled, blunt-linear leaves ⅛ to ¼ inch wide by 8 inches to 1 foot long or somewhat longer. Shorter than the leaves, the flower stalks end in a green-based, golden-yellow bloom, 1½ to 2 inches long, with petals up to ½ inch wide. The three-lobed, headlike stigma tops a style shorter than the stamens. Sometimes called the fire-lily, Peruvian **Z. tubiflora** (syns. *Z. aurea*, *Pyrolirion aureum*) has about five slender, somewhat sickle-shaped, green leaves up to 1 foot in length. Its tapering flower stalks are shorter than or as long as the leaves. The bright golden-yellow or orange-yellow blooms have 2-inch-long perianth tubes abruptly expanded near their centers, and lanceolate, suberect petals nearly as long. The stamens are shorter. The style is as long as the petals. The stigma is three-lobed.

Hybrid zephyranthes include pretty Z. 'Ajax', which has primrose-yellow "crocuses," green at their bases and 2 inches long or a bit longer, on tubelike stalks to a height of 6 to 8 inches. This result of mating Z. candida with Z. citrina has the ever-

Zephyranthes 'Ajax'

green foliage of the first and blooms clearly influenced by the flower color of the second. A hybrid between Mexican Z. lindleyana and Z. citrina named 'Stanley Kiem' has evergreen leaves, up to about 1¼ feet long by ¼ inch wide, and nearly cylindrical flower stalks. Probably hybrids between Z. drummondii and Z. pulchella, plants named Z. jonesii (syn. Cooperia jonesii) and Z. smallii (syn. Cooperia smallii), both known only from Texas and intermediate between their presumptive parents, have yellow flowers that open in the afternoon or evening. In those of the first the perianth tube is usually considerably longer than the spathe, whereas in Z. smallii the spathe is generally longer than the perianth tube.

Garden and Landscape Uses. North of Washington, D.C., zephyr-lilies, with the exception of Z. candida, cannot be relied upon to winter outdoors, although they may do so if set in very sheltered places and protected by a loose covering of leaves, salt hay, or similar material. Under such conditions, at the base of a warm, south-facing wall, Z. candida, which is the hardiest kind, Z. atamasco, and Z. grandiflora have survived at The New York Botanical Garden. Fortunately, most kinds may be handled satisfactorily by planting them outdoors in spring, lifting them before

Zephyranthes smallii

heavy fall frosts, and storing them over winter in dryish soil at a temperature of 40 to 50°F.

As garden adornments, zephyr-lilies are delightful for grouping at the fronts of flower beds, for planting as ribbon edgings, for colonizing informally in naturalistic areas, and for placement in rock gardens. For the last use, selected kinds bring welcome color in summer and fall.

Cultivation. Zephyranthes prosper in a wide variety of soils so long as they are reasonably fertile, drain freely, and do not lack for moisture at times when the plants are in foliage. They need sunny locations and, toward the northern limits of their endurance, warm and sheltered ones. In mild climates, early fall planting is satisfactory, elsewhere spring is preferred. The bulbs should be at depths of three to four times their own height and 2 to 3 inches apart.

For indoor cultivation, zephyranthes do very well in window gardens and greenhouses. The bulbs are planted fairly close together in well-drained pots or pans (shallow pots) in fall. If given fair treatment they bloom year after year, needing repotting only every third or fourth one. Their simple care includes ample watering from the time the foliage appears until the time it dies down naturally, or in the case of evergreen kinds, throughout the year. No watering, or perhaps just an occasional soaking to prevent the earth from becoming so parched that the bulbs shrivel, should be given during the dormant seasons of deciduous kinds. No fertilization is needed the year following repotting, but subsequently, semimonthly applications of dilute liquid fertilizer from spring to fall are beneficial. Indoors, night temperatures of 45 to 50°F in winter, and

five to fifteen degrees warmer by day, suit; at other seasons normal outdoor temperatures are satisfactory. Propagation is easy by seed, and by offsets, which should not be taken from the mother bulbs prematurely, but allowed to separate naturally before they are removed. Bulb cuttings also afford a satisfactory means of increase.

ZEXMENIA (Zex-mènia). The New World genus Zexmenia, of the daisy family COMPOSITAE, in the wild is confined to warm-temperate, subtropical, and tropical areas. It consists of about eighty species of shrubs. Its name is from an anagram of the surname of the Spanish monk Francisco Ximenez, who in 1615 wrote about Mexican plants.

Zexmenias are annuals, subshrubs, and shrubs. They have mostly opposite, short-stalked or stalkless, frequently rough-hairy, generally lobeless leaves, and flower heads, each with usually eight ray florets (comparable to the petal-like ones of daisies) that like the disk florets (those that form the centers of daisy-type flowers) are yellow or orange. The fruits, produced by both ray and disk florets, and technically achenes, are seedlike.

Occasionally cultivated, **Z. hispida,** of Texas and Mexico, is 1½ to 3 feet tall and rough-hairy. Its lanceolate to ovate-lanceolate leaves are sparingly-toothed, and sometimes two-lobed at their bases. Generally they are 2 inches long or longer. The yellow-orange flower heads terminate long stalks. They are somewhat less than ½ inch long by 1 inch wide or wider and have conspicuous, broad ray florets.

Garden and Landscape Uses and Cultivation. Not hardy in the north, this species is sometimes planted in the southwest and elsewhere in areas with approximately similar climates. It succeeds in very well-drained, fertile soil in sunny locations and is chiefly of use in wild gardens and other informal areas. It is propagated by seed and by cuttings.

ZIGADENE. See Zigadenus.

ZIGADENUS (Ziga-dènus) — Zigadene, Death-Camas, Poison-Camas, White-Camas, Sand-Corn, Star-Lily. Its name often incorrectly spelled Zygadenus, the genus Zigadenus, of the lily family LILIACEAE, except for one of its fifteen species, is endemic to North America. The exception Z. sibiricus inhabits eastern Asia. The name comes from the Greek zygon, a yoke, and aden, a gland. It alludes to the paired glands on the petals of the first species described.

These are Camassia-like deciduous, herbaceous perennials with thick rhizomes or bulbs and erect, leaf-bearing stems. Chiefly basal, the many leaves are linear. In terminal racemes or panicles, the bisexual or unisexual flowers have nearly flat to shallow-bell-shaped perianths of six greenish-white to yellowish-white or purplish petals (more properly, tepals) often united at their bases and frequently with one or two glands there. When the flowers fade, the petals wither and remain attached. There are six slender-stalked stamens, about equal in length to the petals, and three styles. The fruits are three-lobed capsules. Some species are poisonous to livestock and to humans.

Most attractive horticulturally, the star-lily (*Z. fremontii*), native from Oregon to Baja California, is bulbous and 1 foot to 3 feet tall. Its many basal leaves are up to 2 feet long by 1 inch wide. In racemes or panicles, the ½-inch-long, creamy-white, starry flowers, sometimes with a greenish cast, have long individual stalks. The petals, narrowed to a claw at their bases, have a greenish-yellow gland.

White-camas is the name of both *Z. elegans* and *Z. glaucus*. Native from Minnesota to Missouri, Arizona, Saskatchewan, and Alaska, *Z. elegans* is bulbous and from 1½ to 3 feet tall. It makes an ample clump of spreading and recurved, sharp-pointed, keeled, glaucous basal leaves up to about

Zigadenus elegans

1 foot long by ¼ to ½ inch wide. The stem leaves are shorter, bractlike, and purplish. Usually in racemes, rarely panicles, the ½-inch-long, cup-shaped flowers have petals with one two-lobed gland. Also bulbous, *Z. glaucus*, native from eastern Canada to Minnesota, North Carolina, and Illinois, is 1½ to 3 feet tall. Its leaves, glaucous and keeled, are up to 1¼ feet long by ½ inch wide. White to greenish with purplish or brownish shadings, the ½-inch-long flowers are in panicles. Each petal has one two-lobed gland.

Death-camas is a name applied to *Z. nuttallii* and *Z. venenosus*, both of which have very poisonous bulbs. Also called poison-camas and merry hearts, *Z. nuttallii* ranges as a wildling from Tennessee to Kansas and Texas. From 1 foot to 2½ feet tall, this has sickle-shaped basal leaves up

to 1½ feet long by ½ inch wide. Usually in racemes, rarely panicled, the ½-inch-wide, yellowish-green flowers have petals with one gland at the base. Native from Montana to British Columbia and California, bulbous *Z. venenosus* is variable. It has slender stems 1 foot to 2 feet tall and basal leaves up to 1 foot long by ⅜ inch wide. The whitish flowers, all usually bisexual and ⅛ inch long, are generally in slender racemes. They have white anthers and at the bottom of each petal a solitary gland. Variety *Z. v. gramineus* (syn. *Z. gramineus*), native from Alberta and Saskatchewan to Utah and New Mexico, has larger flowers with inconspicuous glands.

Sand-corn (*Z. paniculatus*), native from Montana to Washington, New Mexico, Arizona, and California, is 1 foot to 2 feet high. It has rough-edged, mostly basal leaves that are folded along their centers and up to 1½ feet long by ¾ inch wide. The flowers, nearly always in panicles that include both bisexual and male blooms, and ⅛ inch long, have white to yellowish-white petals with a yellowish-green gland, and yellow anthers.

Endemic to California, attractive *Z. exaltatus* is 2 to 3 feet tall. Bulbous, it has basal leaves 1¼ to 2¼ feet long by ½ to 1 inch wide. The yellowish-white flowers, about ½ inch long, are usually in panicles, the lower branches of which carry only male blooms; sometimes they are in racemes. They have petals narrowed at their bases into claws.

Garden and Landscape Uses. So little known horticulturally that most books devoted to bulb plants and their cultivation

Zigadenus exaltatus

pass them by, zigadenuses are yet worthy of modest recognition by gardeners. Most, perhaps all, are hardy in the north. They lend themselves to growing in native plant gardens and other naturalistic areas.

Cultivation. Most zigadenuses prosper in deep, fairly moist soil that contains generous amounts of peat moss, leaf mold, or good compost, and most do well in light shade. But *Z. exaltatus*, *Z. freemontii*, and *Z. paniculatus* thrive in drier locations and in full sun. Plant the bulbs 4 to 8 inches apart and 3 to 4 inches deep. They may need lifting and replanting every three or four years, but as long as they are doing well it is best not to disturb them. Propagation is by seed and by offsets, also by bulb cuttings.

ZINGIBER (Zíng-iber) — Ginger. The aromatic rhizomes, commonly called roots, of *Zingiber officinale* are the ginger of commerce. The plant that supplies them and the eighty to ninety other species of *Zingiber* belong in the same family, but not to the same genera as ginger-lilies and other plants commonly called gingers that are popular as garden and floral decoratives in Hawaii and other tropical places belong chiefly in *Alpinia*, *Hedychium*, and *Nicolaia*. These, as well as the true gingers (*Zingiber*), belong in the ginger family ZINGIBER-ACEAE. The name *Zingiber* is corrupted from a Sanskrit word meaning horn-shaped, in allusion, presumably, to the rhizomes. It is considered an equivalent of the Malayan *inchiver* from *inchi*, a root.

Zingibers are perennial herbaceous plants, of Indo-Malaysia, Indonesia, eastern Asia, and Australia, with reedlike leafy stems arising from stout, branching rhizomes. Usually the flowering stems are distinct from the leafy ones. Generally the stalkless or very short-stalked leaves are oblong-lanceolate, in two ranks, and clasp the stems with their bases. The flowers, individuals of which last for only one day, are in more or less spikelike or conelike clusters and arise, usually singly, from beneath persistent, often colored bracts. Each bloom has a shortly-three-lobed calyx, usually split down one side, and a tubular, unequally-three-lobed corolla. The deflexed lip is a petaloid staminode (infertile stamen expanded to look like a petal) that may be notched or briefly three-lobed; the lateral lobes morphologically represent other staminodes. There is one short-stalked, fertile stamen. There is a slender style tipped with a solitary stigma. The fruits are capsules containing relatively large seeds. In addition to the well-known uses of common ginger, other kinds, including *Z. zerumbet*, are used medicinally where they are native.

Common ginger (*Z. officinale*) is probably a native of tropical Asia, but its exact place of origin is unknown. It has been cultivated for untold centuries and is now

Rhizomes of *Zingiber officinale*

widely distributed through the tropics and subtropics. From 2 to 4 feet tall, it has scattered, pointed, narrowly-lanceolate or linear-lanceolate, almost grasslike leaves 6 inches to 1 foot long and not over ¾ inch wide. The flowering stems, rarely produced by cultivated plants, are considerably shorter than the leafy ones and terminate in dense, spindle-shaped spikes of bloom up to 3 inches long and about 1 inch wide. The 1-inch-long, ovate, green bracts are paler or yellow at their edges. The corolla has an oblong-ovate, dark purple lip spotted and striped with yellow, and shorter than the other two yellow-green, ¾-inch-long, pointed segments. Fruits are seemingly not produced.

Zingiber zerumbet

Wild ginger (**Z. zerumbet**) must not be confused with totally different *Asarum*, members of which in temperate regions are called wild-ginger. The wild ginger of the tropics, native to India, is commonly naturalized in damp, open forests in Hawaii, where it covers the ground quite densely over large areas, and in other parts of the tropics. From 1 foot to 2 feet tall, it has much broader leaves than common ginger, up to 1 foot long by 3 inches wide, pointed, lanceolate to oblong-lanceolate, and crowded on the stems. On stalks separate from the leafy ones, and shorter, the dense, almost spherical flower heads, up

to about 3 inches long, are borne in late summer. They have overlapping bracts, pale green when young, but becoming red later, and inconspicuous, whitish to yellowish flowers with orange bands on the lip. The thick, forked, aromatic rhizomes have a bitter aftertaste; because of this this species is sometimes called bitter ginger. The Hawaiians used the slimy mature flower heads for making a beverage and for shampooing their hair.

Native to woodlands in Japan, **Z. mioga** is cultivated there, in Hawaii, and elsewhere for the edible bracts of its flowers and shoots that are used to flavor soup and employed as a relish. About 3 feet tall, this sort has long-pointed, lanceolate to linear-lanceolate leaves up to about 1 foot long. The spindle-shaped flower spikes, on very short stalks, up to 3 inches in length, have white bracts and flowers, the latter with a yellow lip.

Beautifully variegated with creamy-white to pinkish bands along the margins, and to a lesser extent the interiors, of the leaves, **Z. darceyi** is unknown in the wild. Distributed from the botanical garden, Sydney, Australia, in about 1890, it is much like and perhaps a variety of *Z. zerumbet*. From that species, in addition to its color-

Zingiber darceyi

ing, it differs in having leaves 2 to 2½ inches in width by 6 to 8 inches in length. Another kind with much the aspect of *Z. zerumbet* is **Z. fairchildii.** Its conelike flower heads have red overlapping bracts and cream flowers.

More robust than any described above, **Z. spectabile** is the largest Malaysian species. It has somewhat flattened stems, 6 feet tall or taller, and deep green, slender-pointed, oblong-lanceolate leaves up to 1 foot long. Their undersides, paler than the upper, are downy. On 1-foot-long stems, the rather loose, conelike flower spikes, 8 inches to 1 foot long, have yellow to scarlet bracts and yellowish flowers with black-tipped, lemon-yellow, obovate lips.

Zingiber fairchildii

Zingiber spectabile

Garden and Landscape Uses. In addition to its commercial cultivation, common ginger is grown to some extent in Hawaii, Florida, and other warm regions for its edible rhizomes, which are candied, preserved, and used in other ways. Variegated-leaved *Z. darceyi* and occasionally other kinds are planted as ornamentals in shade in fairly moist soils. Zingibers are sometimes grown in greenhouses, the variegated one especially, for their decorative foliage; common ginger is often grown in collections of plants useful to man.

Cultivation. Zingibers grow satisfactorily with little care. They revel in deep, fertile soil, not lacking for moisture, but not saturated, and need partial shade. They are planted with their rhizomes just beneath the surface. For the best results they need a long growing season, but where winters are too cold for them to remain outdoors they may be stored in a temperature of about 50°F in a dry condition. As greenhouse plants they are started into growth in spring by potting divisions of the rhizomes in well-drained pots of rich, porous soil and watering them moderately at first and freely after they are well rooted. They are grown in a minimum temperature of 60°F with considerably higher temperatures in sunny weather and as the season advances. A humid atmosphere and shaded location are favorable. Applications of dilute liquid fertilizer benefit well-rooted, actively growing specimens. In fall, watering is gradually reduced until after the foliage has died, when it is stopped until the following spring. Propagation is almost entirely by division. Seed, not available in the case of common ginger, may also be used.

ZINGIBERACEAE—Ginger Family. Forty or more genera totaling perhaps more than 1,000 species constitute this tropical and subtropical family of monocotyledons. Included are the common ginger (*Zingiber officinale*) and a number of other plants employed as sources of condiments, spices, medicines, and dyes, as well as several fine ornamentals. Members of the ginger family are mostly herbaceous perennials, usually aromatic and mostly with horizontal rhizomes or subterranean tubers. Their stems, short or long and canelike, bear, in two ranks, alternate, undivided, smooth-edged, linear or elliptic leaves with pinnately-arranged or longitudinally-parallel veins. The flowers, solitary, in heads, or in panicles that terminate the leafy stems or separate leafless stems, are usually associated with conspicuous bracts. Asymmetrical, they have a tubular, three-toothed or spathelike calyx, a tubular, three-lobed corolla with one lobe (petal) usually bigger than the others, one fertile stamen, one large staminode (nonfunctional stamen) and sometimes one smaller one, and one branchless style. The fruits are capsules or are berry-like. Cultivated genera include *Alpinia*, *Amomum*, *Brachychilum*, *Cautleya*, *Costus*, *Curcuma*, *Elettaria*, *Globba*, *Hedychium*, *Kaempferia*, *Nicolaia*, *Renealmia*, *Roscoea*, *Tapeinocheilos*, and *Zingiber*.

ZINNIA (Zín-nia) — Youth-and-Old-Age. Zinnias are among the best known and highly regarded of the many annuals cultivated in American gardens. Because they are easy to grow, stand heat and humidity well, and bloom abundantly and in an extravagant range of colors, they are great favorites for summer display in most parts of North America. In addition to annuals, the genus *Zinnia*, of the daisy family COMPOSITAE, includes herbaceous perennials and subshrubs, but these are little known to gardeners. The generic name commem-

Horticultural varieties of *Zinnia*

orates Johann Gottfried Zinn, professor of medicine at Göttingen, Germany, who died in 1759.

Zinnias have opposite, undivided, almost or quite stalkless leaves and, at the shoot ends, solitary, showy flower heads. In the wild species the flower heads are daisy-like, each with a center of disk florets encircled by petal-like ray florets, but in cultivated varieties the disk florets are often replaced by ray florets to produce double flower heads. All the ray florets are females, those of the disk are bisexual. A characteristic of zinnias is that the ray florets do not drop, but gradually fade, wither, and remain attached to the fruits, which are seedlike achenes.

Zinnias are all natives of the Americas and those ordinarily cultivated are derived from species native to Mexico. The most important of these is the one called youth-and-old-age (**Z. elegans**), an erect plant, 1 foot to 3 feet in height, with more or less clasping, heart-shaped-ovate to elliptic, stalkless leaves, 1½ to 4 inches long and about one-half as wide, and flower heads 2 to 4½ inches wide. In this species the scalelike bracts that form the involucre (collar of bracts behind the flower heads) are fringed at their ends. Both stems and foliage are rough-hairy. In the wild species the disk florets that form the centers of the flower heads are yellow to orange

Horticultural varieties of *Zinnia*

and the rays lavender to purple, but modern garden varieties come in a wide range of colors including almost every hue except true blue. There are even varieties with chartreuse-green flower heads. In height, cultivated varieties range from 6 inches to 3 feet or more, and in diameter of flower head, from 1½ to 6 inches. In form, the flower heads vary from strictly formal to informal. Descriptions and, in many cases, pictures of varieties available are found in seedsmen's catalogs.

Also fairly common in cultivation, **Z. haageana** (syn. *Z. mexicana*), a native of Mexico, is quite often misidentified as *Z. angustifolia*. It is a bushy annual, up to about 2 feet tall, with stalkless, lanceolate leaves 2 to 3 inches long. Its orange flower heads, 1½ to 2 inches wide, have eight or nine ray florets. Garden varieties such as 'Old Mexico' and 'Persian Carpet' have more ray florets, and these are often red and yellow or red and orange.

A few other kinds are grown, but to a lesser extent than the magnificent varieties of *Z. elegans* and *Z. haageana*. A much-branched Mexican species, 1 foot to 1¼ feet tall and with linear-lanceolate leaves up to 3 inches long and up to ¼ inch wide, **Z. angustifolia** (syn. *Z. linearis*) has orange flower heads, 1½ to 2 inches in diameter, with the ray florets more brightly colored along their margins than at their centers. The bracts of the involucres are not divided or fringed at their ends.

Zinnia angustifolia

An attractive planting of zinnias, with dwarf lobelias in front

Garden Uses. Zinnias are among the most satisfactory annuals for summer beds and borders and for supplying cut blooms. Their stiff-stemmed flowers last well in water and have a quality that allows them to be arranged with minimum effort to achieve really charming effects. They associate well with many other kinds of

Rows of zinnias in a cutting garden bloom profusely

summer flowers and are especially lovely when finer-textured kinds, such as baby's breath (*Gypsophila*), are mixed with them. Because the flower parts do not wilt or drop as the blooms age and fade, they are clean in use. Zinnias are also attractive in porch boxes and window boxes and for planting in urns, tubs, and other decorative containers. The dwarfer kinds are useful for edging paths.

Cultivation. Annual zinnias are raised from seed sown outdoors, usually where the plants are to bloom, or indoors earlier to produce plants to be set out later. If sown outdoors, seedings may be done where the plants are to remain or in a seed bed from which the seedlings will be transplanted to the places where they are to bloom. Outdoor sowings may be made as soon as the ground has dried and warmed a little in spring. Later sowings may be made at about three-week intervals up to the end of June to provide successional bloom; this is especially worthwhile if a continuous supply of cut flowers is to be maintained. Young plants raised in greenhouses may be transplanted to the garden after the weather is warm and settled, about the time it is appropriate to plant tomatoes. To secure such plants, seeds are sown in a greenhouse in a temperature of 60°F about eight weeks prior to the expected planting out date, and the seedlings are transplanted, as soon as they have formed their second pair of leaves, about 2 to 3 inches apart in flats. They are kept in a sunny greenhouse in a night temperature of 50°F and a day temperature five to ten degrees higher until a week or two before they are to be transferred to their flowering locations; then the flats are stood in a cold frame or sheltered place outdoors to harden the plants before transplanting. Pinching the tips out of the young plants when they have developed three or four pairs of leaves encourages branching, but is unnecessary when large blooms for cutting are desired.

It must be borne in mind that zinnias are sun-lovers and need an open location

where good air circulation is assured; plants set in stuffy, stagnant corners or pockets where high humidity prevails are likely to suffer unduly from mildew and other troubles. Spacing in the garden will vary according to the size and vigor of the variety and whether the plants are to be massed in flower beds or in patches in borders or to be grown in rows for cut flowers. In the latter case the rows may be 1½ to 2 feet apart and the plants in the rows 9 inches to 1 foot between individuals. For mass effects 1 foot to 2 feet is appropriate spacing. Zinnias need deep, porous, fertile soil. To secure the finest blooms for cutting, the large-flowered kinds should be restricted in the number of flowers they are permitted to develop by removing many of the side shoots, especially those high on the branches. This is done while the shoots are small and results in long-stemmed flowers of superior quality. In dry weather, periodic soaking of the soil with water should receive routine attention. The amount of water required may be reduced by keeping the ground around the plants mulched. If this is not done, the surface one-half inch should be stirred frequently enough with a cultivator to prevent caking. Tall varieties are likely to need staking.

ZINNIA, CREEPING- is *Sanvitalia procumbens*.

ZIZANIA (Ziz-ània) — Wild-Rice. Two or three species of aquatic and marsh grasses of the grass family GRAMINEAE are the only members of *Zizania*. One is a native of eastern Asia, and one or possibly two, of North America. The name is a modification of *zizanion*, an ancient Greek one for some kind of grass. Zizanias provide extremely valuable feed for water birds, and their seeds are prized as human food, for which purpose American Indians made much use of them. The Asian perennial *Z. latifolia* is cultivated in the Orient where its young shoots are eaten as a vegetable and its leaves used for mat-making.

Zizania aquatica

The common wild-rice of North America (**Z. aquatica**) is a variable annual divided by botanists into four intergrading varieties. It is indigenous from Nova Scotia and Quebec to Manitoba, Florida, and Louisiana and attains a height up to 10 feet or more. It has stout, sometimes branched stems and soft leaves, 1 foot long or longer and 2 inches wide. The panicles of flower, up to 2 feet long, have female flowers in their upper parts, males below, with the former on erect branches and the latter on spreading branches. The spikelets of male flowers are pendulous. The grains (seeds) are as big or bigger than those of rice. Commercial supplies are gathered from wild stands and, in recent years, from cultivated crops.

Garden Uses and Cultivation. Horticulturally, wild-rice is one of the most decorative grasses and is very appropriate for planting by watersides in relatively shallow water where there is a mud bottom. If the seeds have been dried before sowing they should be placed in cheesecloth bags and steeped in water for twenty-four hours. A better plan is to store the seeds from the time they ripen until sowing time in water, or mixed with moist peat moss contained in polyethylene plastic bags, in a temperature of 35 to 40°F. Sow by scattering the seeds where the water is 6 inches to 5 feet deep, but not where there is any very appreciable current. This plant may also be grown in pools or in large tubs or other containers of fertile, loamy soil submerged so that the soil surface is a few inches below water level. Sowing should be done in spring and the young plants thinned to stand 6 to 8 inches apart.

ZIZIA (Zíz-ia)—Golden Alexanders. There are three species of *Zizia*, all North American. They belong in the carrot family UMBELLIFERAE. The name commemorates the German botanist Johann Baptist Ziz, who died in 1829.

These are deciduous, branched, hairless or nearly hairless, herbaceous perennials with thickened roots and once- to thrice-divided leaves. Their tiny, bright yellow flowers are in flattish, compound umbels. Of no considerable horticultural importance, they are occasionally transplanted into gardens and are appropriate in those devoted to native plants.

Occurring in moist fields and meadows from Quebec to Saskatchewan, Florida, and Texas, **Z. aurea** is 1 foot to 1½ feet in height. Its lower leaves are two- or three-times-divided, its upper ones usually once-divided. The leaflets are ovate to lanceolate, finely-toothed, and usually pointed.

Garden and Landscape Uses and Cultivation. These plants are most suitable for informal areas. They are easily grown from seed and succeed in moist soil in sun.

ZIZIPHUS (Zízi-phus)—Jujube. This name has been spelled *Zizyphus*. It is that of

possibly 100 species of the buckthorn family RHAMNACEAE, widely distributed in warm parts of America, Africa, Europe, Indo-Malaysia, and Australia. The name is derived from the Arabian one, *zizouf*, of *Z. lotus*.

Deciduous and evergreen, mostly spiny shrubs and trees compose *Ziziphus*. They have alternate, undivided, toothed or toothless leaves, usually with three, or sometimes five, chief veins spreading from their bases. The flowers are without ornamental significance. They are small, yellow, and in clusters from the leaf axils. Each has five sepals, the same number of petals and stamens, and a two-parted style. The fruits are fleshy drupes (fruits plumlike in structure); those of some species are edible. Some tropical kinds furnish useful lumber. Here belong the mistol (*Z. mistol*), of Argentina, and the cogwood or greenheart (*Z. chloroxylon*), of Jamaica.

Common or Chinese jujube (*Z. jujuba*) has been cultivated in its native Orient for thousands of years for its edible fruits, and there are a number of improved large-fruited varieties. Of upright habit, especially in its early years, the common jujube is an attractive, usually prickly, deciduous ornamental, as well as, in warm, dry climates, a good fruit producer. In humid regions it does not fruit satisfactorily. The glossy leaves are ovate-lanceolate, 1 inch to 3 inches long, and have three prominent veins. The whitish-fleshed fruits are oblongish to somewhat pear-shaped, and up to 1¼ inches long or longer, or in selected varieties even longer. Glossy-green before maturity, when ripe they turn dark brown. They may be eaten out of hand, but generally are preferred after they have been candied, preserved, or dried. When dried they become prunelike and are sometimes known as Chinese dates. This tree is naturalized in parts of the southern United States.

Indian jujube (**Z. mauritiana**) is a small, nonhardy evergreen tree that grows vigorously and has wide-spreading, pendulous, spiny branches. From those of common jujube, the leaves of the Indian jujube differ in being finely-hairy on their undersurfaces. Similar to those of the common jujube, the fruits of its Indian relative are spherical to ovoid and greenish-yellow to reddish-brown. Their eating quality varies considerably among seedling trees. They are used in jellies and preserves. This species is much better suited to humid climates than is the common jujube.

The Texan jujube, buckthorn, or lote bush (**Z. obtusifolia**) is a rigid, much-branched, spiny shrub with whitish branches, and elliptic, toothed or toothless leaves ¾ inch to 1¼ inches long. The black fruits are about ⅓ inch long. Although edible, they are of inferior quality. This species is a native of the southwestern United States and Mexico. Its variety, *Z. o. canescens*, differs in its flowers being in

clusters of up to fifty instead of not more than the six typical of the species.

Native to southern California and Baja California, **Z. parryi** is a deciduous, flexuous-branched shrub up to 12 feet tall. It has spine-tipped secondary branches, and elliptic to obovate leaves ¾ to 1 inch long. The fruits are ovoid, brownish to purplish-brown, and up to 1 inch long.

Garden and Landscape Uses and Cultivation. In addition to their value as producers of edible fruits, jujubes are useful as general-purpose ornamentals. The common kind is hardy as far north as southern New England, but is best suited for regions of long, hot, dry summers. It does well even in decidedly alkaline soil. The Texas jujube requires similar climatic conditions. The Indian jujube thrives in Florida and elsewhere in a variety of soils. Other than pruning to keep them shapely, no special care is needed. Propagation is by seed, which should be removed from the stones before sowing, or superior varieties of common jujube by grafting onto seedling understocks.

ZOISIA. See Zoysia.

ZOMBIA (Zòm-bia)—Zombi Palm. The only species of *Zombia* is a curious fan-leaved cluster palm, a native of Haiti. It belongs in the palm family PALMAE. Its name is derived from a native one for the species.

Attaining a height of about 10 feet, **Z. antillarum** has slender, erect stems completely enclosed in sleeves composed of persisting sheathing parts of old leafstalks. The upper edge of each segment is fringed with a row of formidable, spreading or down-pointing spines and the body of the sheath has the appearance of a loose, open, handwoven textile. Dull green above and silvery on their undersides, the leaves have long stalks, and hand-shaped blades with many fingers one-half to two-thirds as long as the diameter of the leaf. The leaves soon fall and expose the interestingly clothed trunks. The bisexual flowers, in short, rather erect clusters, develop in summer and are succeeded by somewhat two-lobed fruits, ½ to ¾ inch in diameter, white at maturity and heavy enough to cause their stalks to arch outward.

Garden and Landscape Uses. This is an attractive palm for collectors. It is suitable for planting even where space is limited. It thrives in sun, but stands some shade. In sun it tends to develop more stems and grow more quickly, but even under optimum conditions its growth is slow in its young stages. This is hardy in southern Florida.

Cultivation. Any ordinary, well-drained garden soil is suitable for this palm. In greenhouses it should have a minimum winter temperature of 60°F, a humid atmosphere, coarse, porous, fertile soil, and shade from strong, summer sun. It is propagated by fresh seed, which germinates in about six weeks if sown in sandy, peaty soil in a temperature of 75 to 80°F. For additional information see Palms.

ZOSTERELLA. See Heteranthera.

ZOYSIA (Zoý-sia). Its name sometimes spelled *Zoisia*, this genus of eight or fewer species of the grass family GRAMINEAE contains some esteemed as lawn grasses, chiefly in mild climates. It is native to eastern Asia, Australia, New Zealand, and islands of Polynesia and the Indian Ocean. The name commemorates Karl von Zois, an Austrian botanist, who died about 1800.

Zoysias are perennials with long, creeping stolons and rhizomes, and upright, short, slender stems with short, stiff-pointed, flat or rolled leaves. The one-flowered, very short spikelets of the racemes of flowers press closely against the stems that bear them in spikelike fashion.

Japanese or Korean lawn grass (*Zoysia japonica*), believed to be the hardiest species, is coarser than the others here described and less admired for lawns. Native to Japan, Korea, and China, it has stems 4 to 8 inches long, and in bloom is about 1½ feet tall. The flat or nearly flat, linear-lanceolate leaf blades are 2 to 4 inches long by ⅛ inch broad or broader. The racemes of light purplish-brown spikelets are about 1 inch in length.

Of much finer texture, Manila grass (*Z. matrella*), in bloom 1 foot to 1½ feet tall, has flat leaf blades 2 to 3 or sometimes up to 4 inches long by about ⅟₁₆ inch broad.

Its racemes of usually greenish spikelets are about 1½ inches long. This forms beautiful, dense turf. Korean velvet grass or Mascarene grass (*Z. tenuifolia*) differs from the others described in having its leaf blades rolled lengthwise, and wiry or threadlike. They are 1 inch to 2 inches long. The spikelets are slender and compressed. This native of Japan, China, southeast Asia, and Taiwan forms a fine-textured turf.

Garden and Landscape Uses and Cultivation. The only horticultural use of these grasses is for lawns. For further information see the entry Lawns, Their Making and Renovation.

ZYGOCACTUS. See Schlumbergera.

ZYGOCOLAX (Zygo-còlax). Hybrids between *Zygopetalum* and *Colax*, of the orchid family ORCHIDACEAE, are named *Zygocolax*. Occurring naturally in Brazil and bred artificially, handsome *Zygocolax veitchii* is intermediate in its characteristics and appearance between its parents *Zygopetalum crinitum* and *Colax jugosus* and responds to the same care. For more information see Orchids.

ZYGOMENA. This is the name of hybrid orchids the parents of which are *Zygopetalum* and *Zygosepalum*.

ZYGOPETALUM (Zygo-pétalum). The very beautiful orchids that compose *Zygopetalum*, of the orchid family ORCHIDACEAE, number twenty species native to Central

America, South America, and Trinidad. The name, from the Greek *zygos*, a yoke, and *petalon*, a petal, alludes to a swelling at the bottom of the lip that appears to join together the lateral segments of the blooms.

Zygopetalums are mostly ground orchids, more rarely tree-perchers or cliff-dwellers, with conspicuous pseudobulbs and fans of deciduous, lustrous, thinnish leaves. The arching to erect racemes are of big, showy, usually long-lasting blooms. Each has three sepals and two petals nearly similar in shape, size, and color, and often joined at their bases, and a large, spreading or somewhat recurved lip with a prominent crest. The column curves inward. There are hybrids between species of *Zygopetalum* and between *Zygopetalum* and other genera. Some plants previously included in *Zygopetalum* now belong in *Bollea* and *Neogardneria*.

Two sorts often confused in cultivation, *Z. intermedium* and *Z. mackayi* are natives of Brazil. The commoner, *Z. intermedium*, has tightly crowded, slightly flattened pseudobulbs, 3 to 3½ inches long, clothed with leafy sheaths. From their tops come five or fewer thickish, leathery, lanceolate-elliptic to somewhat strap-shaped, glossy leaves approximately 1½ feet long and up to 2 inches wide or a little wider. The flowering stalks, from the bases of the pseudobulbs, carry three to five or sometimes more, strongly fragrant blooms 2¾ to 3½ inches in diameter. They have pointed-strap-shaped sepals and petals, green or yellowish-green blotched with

Zygopetalum mackayi

Zygopetalum brachypetalum

A hybrid between *Zygopetalum blackii* and *Z. maxillare*

ally two linear-lanceolate leaves up to 1¼ feet long. The flowers are fragrant. Up to four or five on erect stalks 1 foot to 1½ feet long, they have sepals and petals 1 inch to 1¼ inches long and green to light brown with lengthwise bands of chestnut-brown more or less spotted or blotched. The three-lobed, obovate lip is white with two ribs of pink-veined teeth. The column is yellow. A native of Brazil and Paraguay, *Z. maxillare* has creeping rhizomes with, spaced, often rather distantly, along them, ovoid-oblong, usually compressed and angular pseudobulbs 1½ to 3 inches long. Each has two or three lanceolate leaves 8 inches to 1¼ feet long and 1 inch wide or slightly wider. The arching to erect flower stalks bear up to eight about-2½-inch-long, fragrant blooms with an up-pointing dorsal (upper) sepal, up-pointing petals, and down-pointing lateral sepals. The pale green ground color of the sepals and petals is to a large extent obscured by cross-bands of bronze-purple to chocolate-brown. The bluish-purple lip has a large, rounded center lobe and two small, erect side lobes.

There are a fair number of hybrid zygopetalums, many made during the late nineteenth and early twentieth centuries and others since. One of the older sorts, *Z. blackii* (its parents *Z. crinitum* and *Z. perrinoudii*) is known in several varieties, mostly remarkable for the rich, dark colors of their sepals and petals, and their lighter, variously variegated lips. Crossed with other zygopetalums, *Z. blackii* has produced other interesting hybrids.

Garden Uses and Cultivation. The very useful, easily grown orchids described here are admirable for outdoor or lath house cultivation in the humid tropics and in greenhouses. Their blooms last well as cut flowers. In general, zygopetalums respond to conditions and care that suit cattleyas. They abhor a dank atmosphere and revel in airy conditions with only minimum shade essential to prevent the foliage from being scorched. Potting mixes appropriate for cymbidiums and calanthes, left fairly loose instead of being packed firmly, suit zygopetalums. When required, repot just as new root growth begins. Keep the rooting medium pleasantly moist at all times, but never for long periods saturated. Increase is by division. After potting keep the divisions at a higher temperature for a month or so to encourage root action. For more information see the Encyclopedia entry Orchids.

reddish-brown, and a white, wavy, spreading lip, 2 inches across, with purple, branched, veinlike lines spreading outward from the hairy crest at its base. From the last, *Z. mackayi* differs in its petals being slightly shorter than the uppermost or dorsal sepal, rather than being about equal to it, and in the disk and inner surface of the column being hairless instead of having a fuzz of hairs. Brazilian *Z. brachypetalum* in aspect resembles *Z. intermedium*, differing most noticeably in having longer, less rigid leaves and taller, slenderer flower stalks with blooms more widely spaced. The stalks are up to 3 feet long and carry up to ten fragrant blooms. The flowers have spreading sepals and petals of a nondescript green on their outsides, on their face sides deep purplish- or wine-red, and with pale green margins and bases. The lip is white, veined with purplish-red.

From the kinds described above, somewhat similar, but less robust *Z. crinitum* differs in its flowering stalks usually spreading horizontally instead of being strictly erect and in having its flowers, more sparingly blotched with brown than those of *Z. intermedium*, in one-sided racemes. A native of Brazil, this has somewhat flattened pseudobulbs 3 to 4 inches tall, each with from their apexes two or three thickish, leathery, lanceolate, glossy leaves up to 1½ feet long by 2 inches wide. Fragrant and long-lasting, the blooms, in racemes of few to ten, are 3 to 3½ inches across. Their green to grayish-green sepals and petals are streaked and blotched with reddish-brown. The lip, white with red to pinkish-red or blue lines radiating from its hairy base, has a frilled margin.

Native to Guayana, Venezuela, and Peru, *Z. burkei* has clustered pseudobulbs, 2 to 3½ inches long, each crowned with usu-

Index to Color Plates

Unlike the black-and-white pictures in this Encyclopedia, which are positioned close to the text they illustrate, the color pictures are on full-page plates interspersed at regular intervals throughout each Volume and are not always close to the appropriate text. Here, the color picture captions, listed alphabetically, are followed by the number of the Volume in which they appear, in **bold** type, and the text page opposite which they appear.